Lecture Notes in Computer Science   2287
Edited by G. Goos, J. Hartmanis, and J. van Leeuwen

Springer
*Berlin
Heidelberg
New York
Barcelona
Hong Kong
London
Milan
Paris
Tokyo*

Christian S. Jensen   Keith G. Jeffery
Jaroslav Pokorny   Simonas Šaltenis   Elisa Bertino
Klemens Böhm   Matthias Jarke (Eds.)

Advances in Database Technology – EDBT 2002

8th International Conference
on Extending Database Technology
Prague, Czech Republic, March 25-27, 2002
Proceedings

 Springer

Volume Editors

Christian S. Jensen
Simonas Šaltenis
Aalborg University, Department of Computer Science
E-mail: {csj/simas}@cs.auc.dk

Keith G. Jeffery
CLRC Rutherford Appleton Laboratory, Business and Information Technology Dept.
E-mail: keith.g.jeffery@rl.ac.uk

Jaroslav Pokorny
Charles University, Faculty of Mathematics and Physics
E-mail: pokorny@ksi.ms.mff.cuni.cz

Elisa Bertino
University of Milan, Department of Information Science
E-mail: bertino@dsi.unimi.it

Klemens Böhn
ETH Zurich, Institute of Information Systems
E-mail: boehm@inf.ethz.ch

Matthias Jarke
RWTH Aachen, Informatik V
E-mail: jarke@informatik.rwth-aachen.de

Cataloging-in-Publication Data applied for

Die Deutsche Bibliothek - CIP-Einheitsaufnahme

Advances in database technology : proceedings / EDBT 2002, 8th International Conference on Extending Database Technology, Prague, Czech Republic, March 25 - 27, 2002. Christian S. Jensen ... (ed.). - Berlin ; Heidelberg ; New York ; Barcelona ; Hong Kong ; London ; Milan ; Paris ; Tokyo : Springer, 2002
  (Lecture notes in computer science ; Vol. 2287)
  ISBN 3-540-43324-4

CR Subject Classification (1998): H.2, H.4, H.3, C.2.4, K.4.4

ISSN 0302-9743
ISBN 3-540-43324-4 Springer-Verlag Berlin Heidelberg New York

This work is subject to copyright. All rights are reserved, whether the whole or part of the material is concerned, specifically the rights of translation, reprinting, re-use of illustrations, recitation, broadcasting, reproduction on microfilms or in any other way, and storage in data banks. Duplication of this publication or parts thereof is permitted only under the provisions of the German Copyright Law of September 9, 1965, in its current version, and permission for use must always be obtained from Springer-Verlag. Violations are liable for prosecution under the German Copyright Law.

Springer-Verlag Berlin Heidelberg New York
a member of BertelsmannSpringer Science+Business Media GmbH

http://www.springer.de

© Springer-Verlag Berlin Heidelberg 2002
Printed in Germany

Typesetting: Camera-ready by author, data conversion by Steingräber Satztechnik GmbH, Heidelberg
Printed on acid-free paper   SPIN: 10846335   06/3142   5 4 3 2 1 0

Preface

The Eighth International Conference on Extending Database Technology, EDBT 2002, was held in Prague, Czech Republic, March 25–27, 2002. It marks the 50th anniversary of Charles University's Faculty of Mathematics and Physics and is the most recent in a series of conferences dedicated to the dissemination and exchange of the latest advances in data management. Previous conferences occurred in Konstanz, Valencia, Avignon, Cambridge, Vienna, and Venice.

The topical theme of this year's conference is *Data Management in the New Millennium*, which encourages the community to see beyond the management of massive databases by conventional database management systems and to extend database technology to support new services and application areas. The intention is to spur greater interest in more integrated solutions to user problems, which often implies the consideration of data management issues in entire information systems infrastructures. There is data (almost) everywhere, and data access is needed (almost) always and everywhere. New technologies, services, and applications that involve the broader notion of data management are emerging more rapidly than ever, and the database community has much to offer.

The call for papers attracted numerous submissions, including 207 research papers, which is a new record for EDBT. The program committee selected 36 research papers, 6 industrial and applications papers, 13 software demos, and 6 tutorials for presentation at the conference. In addition, the conference program includes three keynote speeches, by Jari Ahola, Ian Horrocks, and Hans-Jörg Schek, and a panel.

This volume presents all research papers, industrial and applications papers, and software demos presented at the conference, in addition to an invited paper. Many of the papers pursue the general direction indicated by the conference theme, and together, the papers cover a range of active areas of data management research. These areas include XML and Internet data management and the management of distributed data, sensor data, and moving-object data, as well as data mining and more traditional, advanced query processing. We hope that these proceedings will serve as a valuable reference to data management researchers and developers.

Putting together EDBT 2002 was a team effort. Special thanks go to the members of the program committee, and the external reviewers they enlisted, for their hard and diligent work. We would also like to thank the local organizers at Charles University and Action M Agency, in particular Martin Beran, Julius Stuller, Lucie Vachova, and Milena Zeithamlova. Finally, Alfred Hofmann, Antje Endemann, and Karin Henzold at Springer-Verlag offered invaluable help during the preparation of these proceedings.

January 2002

Christian S. Jensen, Keith G. Jeffery
Jaroslav Pokorny, Simonas Šaltenis
Elisa Bertino, Klemens Böhm, Matthias Jarke

Sponsorship

Promoted by the EDBT Endowment.
In cooperation with the VLDB Endowment.

Sponsored by: Hewlet Packard, s.r.o.
INTAX s.r.o.
KOMIX, s.r.o.
ORACLE Czech, s.r.o.

Conference Organization

General Chair:	Keith G. Jeffery
	CLRC Rutherford Appleton Lab (UK)
Program Chair:	Christian S. Jensen
	Aalborg University (Denmark)
Executive Chair:	Jaroslav Pokorny
	Charles University (Czech Republic)
Proceedings Chair:	Simonas Šaltenis
	Aalborg University (Denmark)
Panel & Tutorial Chair:	Elisa Bertino
	University of Milan (Italy)
Software Demonstrations Chair:	Klemens Böhm
	ETH Zurich (Switzerland)
Industrial & Applications Chair:	Matthias Jarke
	RWTH Aachen (Germany)

Local Organization Team

Martin Beran	Charles University (Czech Republic)
Julius Stuller	Charles University (Czech Republic)
Lucie Vachova	Action M Agency (Czech Republic)
Milena Zeithamlova	Action M Agency (Czech Republic)

Program Committee

Bernd Amann	(France)	Leo Mark	(USA)
Paolo Atzeni	(Italy)	Bernhard Mitschang	(Germany)
Karen Becker	(Brazil)	Bongki Moon	(USA)
Claudio Bettini	(Italy)	Pavol Navrat	(Slovakia)
Peter A. Boncz	(The Netherlands)	Beng Chin Ooi	(Singapore)
Silvana Castano	(Italy)	Dimitris Papadias	(Hong Kong)
Barbara Catania	(Italy)	Stefano Paraboschi	(Italy)
Wojciech Cellary	(Poland)	Jignesh M. Patel	(USA)
Christine Collet	(France)	Norman Paton	(UK)
Alex Delis	(USA)	Torben B. Pedersen	(Denmark)
Johannes Gehrke	(USA)	Alexandra Poulovassilis	(UK)
Andreas Geppert	(Switzerland)	Louiqa Raschid	(USA)
Fosca Giannotti	(Italy)	Karel Richta	(Czech Republic)
Ralf H. Güting	(Germany)	Tore Risch	(Sweden)
Mohand-Said Hacid	(France)	Nick Roussopoulos	(USA)
Manfred A. Jeusfeld	(The Netherlands)	Heiko Schuldt	(Switzerland)
Leonid Kalinichenko	(Russia)	Bernhard Seeger	(Germany)
Daniel A. Keim	(Germany)	Thomas Seidl	(Germany)
Alfons Kemper	(Germany)	Dennis Shasha	(USA)
Myoung-Ho Kim	(Korea)	Kyuseok Shim	(Korea)
Masaru Kitsuregawa	(Japan)	Bernhard Thalheim	(Germany)
Hank Korth	(USA)	Riccardo Torlone	(Italy)
Nick Koudas	(USA)	Agma Traina	(Brazil)
Wolfgang Lehner	(Germany)	Vassilis Tsotras	(USA)
Hongjun Lu	(PR China)	Sean Wang	(USA)
Bertram Ludäscher	(USA)	Gerhard Weikum	(Germany)
Yannis Manolopoulos	(Greece)	Peter Wood	(UK)
		Pavel Zezula	(Czech Republic)

Additional Referees

Ilkay Altintas
Alex van Ballegooij
Andrey Balmin
Udit Batra
Andreas Bauer
Khalid Belhajjame
Alberto Belussi
Edgard Benitez-Guerrero
Alex Biliris
Björn Blohsfeld
Stephen Blott
Francesco Bonchi
Daniele M. Braga
Reinhard Braumandl
Laura Bright
Thomas Brinkhoff
Josiane M. Bueno
Luca Cabibbo
Chee Yong Chan
Shu-Yao Chien
Vassilis Christophides
Panos K. Chrysanthis
Yon Dohn Chung
Brian Cochran
Sam Collins
Valter Crescenzi
Daniela Damm
Thierry Delot
Katsaros Dimitrios
Jens-Peter Dittrich
Peter Dolog
Ruxandra Domenig
Martin Erwig
Mohammad Fakhar
Weiguo Fan
Alvaro A.A. Fernandes
Elena Ferrari
Thomas Feyer
Béatrice Finance
Enrico Franconi
Irini Fundulaki
Renata Galante
Minos N. Garofalakis
Cristian Gozzi

Jens Graupmann
Tony Griffiths
Amarnath Gupta
Marios Hadjieleftheriou
Richard Hankins
Sven Helmer
Alexander Hinneburg
Naureen Hooda
Wolfgang Huemmer
Dongjoon Hyun
Yannis Ioannidis
Yoshiharu Ishikawa
Viviane Jensen
Caetano Traina Jr.
Steffen Jurk
Panos Kalnis
Martin Kersten
Meike Klettke
Arnd Christian Koenig
George Kollios
Manolis Koubarakis
Mojmir Kretinsky
Cyril Labbé
Hans J. Lenz
Sebastian Link
Paola Magillo
Nikos Mamoulis
Stefan Manegold
Karol Matiasko
Gianni Mecca
Michele Molohiori
Kazuhiko Mogi
Ana M. De Carvalho Moura
Miyuki Nakano
Mirco Nanni
Alex Nanopoulos
Benjamin Nguyen
Masato Oguchi
Christian Panse
Dimitris Papadopoulos
Chang-Won Park
Chang Sup Park
Peter Peinl
Marco Pötke

Gabriela Polcicova
Iko Pramudiono
Alessandro Provetti
Alessandra Raffaeta
Manish Rana
Ralf Rantzau
Krishina Reddy
Chiara Renso
Solange Oliveira Rezende
Webb Roberts
Claudia Roncancio
Jarogniew Rykowski
Sandra Sampaio
Klaus-Dieter Schewe
Lutz Schlesinger
Albrecht Schmidt
Markus Schneider
Martin Schoenhoff
Takahiko Shintani
Antonis Sidiropoulos
Giuseppe Sindoni
Mike Sips
Sergej Sizov
Spiros Skiadopoulos
Maria Smolarova
Genoveva Vargas Solar
Jin Hyun Son
Bernhard Stegmaier
Torsten Suel
Katsumi Takahashi
Kian-Lee Tan
Yufei Tao
Anja Theobald
Yannis Theodoridis
Leonardo Tininini
Farouk Toumani
Masashi Toyoda
Michael Vassilakopoulos
Athanasios Vavouras
Maurizio Vincini
Michalis Vlachos
Peter Vojtas
Vladimir Vojtek
Valentino Vranic

Arjen de Vries
Tuyet-Trinh Vu
Changzhou Wang
Min Wang

Markus Wawryniuk
Christian Wiesner
Hua Yang
Jeffrey Xu Yu

Ilya Zaslavsky
Donghui Zhang
Jun Zhang
Xiaofang Zhou

Table of Contents

Invited Papers

Hyperdatabases: Infrastructure for the Information Space 1
  Hans-Jörg Schek (ETH Zürich)

DAML+OIL: A Reason-able Web Ontology Language 2
  Ian Horrocks (Univ. of Manchester)

Ambient Intelligence: Plenty of Challenges by 2010 14
  Jari Ahola (VTT Information Technology)

Query Transformation

An Approach to Integrating Query Refinement in SQL 15
  Michael Ortega-Binderberger, Kaushik Chakrabarti (Univ. of Illinois, Urbana-Champaign) Sharad Mehrotra (Univ. of California, Irvine)

Querying with Intrinsic Preferences 34
  Jan Chomicki (Univ. at Buffalo)

Rewriting Unions of General Conjunctive Queries Using Views........... 52
  Junhu Wang, Michael Maher, Rodney Topor (Griffith Univ.)

Data Mining

Profit Mining: From Patterns to Actions 70
  Ke Wang, Senqiang Zhou (Simon Fraser Univ.), Jiawei Han (Univ. of Illinois at Urbana-Champaign)

Cut-and-Pick Transactions for Proxy Log Mining 88
  Wenwu Lou, Guimei Liu, Hongjun Lu, Qiang Yang (Hong Kong Univ. of Science and Technology)

Composition of Mining Contexts
for Efficient Extraction of Association Rules 106
  Cheikh Talibouya Diop, Arnaud Giacometti, Dominique Laurent (Univ. de Tours), Nicolas Spyratos (Univ. Paris 11)

XML

Designing Functional Dependencies for XML 124
  Mong Li Lee, Tok Wang Ling (National Univ. of Singapore), Wai Lup Low (DSO National Laboratories)

On Efficient Matching of Streaming XML Documents and Queries 142
  Laks V.S. Lakshmanan (Univ. of British Columbia), Sailaja Parthasarathy (Sun Microsystems)

Efficient Complex Query Support for Multiversion XML Documents 161
  Shu-Yao Chien (UC Los Angeles), Vassilis J. Tsotras (UC Riverside), Carlo Zaniolo (UC Los Angeles), Donghui Zhang (UC Riverside)

Advanced Query Processing

Approximate Processing of Multiway Spatial Joins
in Very Large Databases 179
  Dimitris Papadias (Hong Kong Univ. of Science and Technology), Dinos Arkoumanis (National Technical Univ. of Athens)

Indexing Values in Continuous Field Databases 197
  Myoung-Ah Kang (Lyon Scientific and Technical Univ.), Christos Faloutsos (CMU), Robert Laurini, Sylvie Servigne (Lyon Scientific and Technical Univ.)

Efficient and Adaptive Processing Of Multiple Continuous Queries 215
  Wee Hyong Tok, Stéphane Bressan (National Univ. of Singapore)

Moving Objects

The Geometry of Uncertainty in Moving Objects Databases 233
  Goce Trajcevski, Ouri Wolfson, Fengli Zhang (Univ. of Illinois at Chicago), Sam Chamberlain (Army Research Lab, Aberdeen)

Efficient Indexing of Spatiotemporal Objects 251
  Marios Hadjieleftheriou (UC Riverside), George Kollios (Boston Univ.), Vassilis J. Tsotras, Dimitrios Gunopulos (UC Riverside)

Dynamic Queries over Mobile Objects 269
  Iosif Lazaridis (UC Irvine), Kriengkrai Porkaew (King Mongkut's Univ. of Technology Thonburi), Sharad Mehrotra (UC Irvine)

Industrial and Applications Track—I

Semantic Analysis of Business Process Executions 287
  Fabio Casati, Ming-Chien Shan (Hewlett-Packard Labs)

An Introduction to the e-XML Data Integration Suite 297
  Georges Gardarin, Antoine Mensch, Anthony Tomasic (e-XMLMedia)

Spatio-temporal Information Systems in a Statistical Context 307
  Leonardo Tininini, Mario Paolucci, Giuseppe Sindoni, Stefano De Francisci (ISTAT)

Distributed Data

A Systematic Approach to Selecting Maintenance Policies
in a Data Warehouse Environment 317
 Henrik Engström (Univ. of Skövde), Sharma Chakravarthy (Univ.
 of Texas at Arlington), Brian Lings (Univ. of Exeter)

Efficient OLAP Query Processing in Distributed Data Warehouses 336
 Michael O. Akinde, Michael H. Böhlen (Aalborg Univ.),
 Theodore Johnson (AT&T Labs–Research), Laks V.S. Lakshmanan
 (Univ. of British Columbia), Divesh Srivastava (AT&T Labs–Research)

Incremental Maintenance of Schema-Restructuring Views 354
 Andreas Koeller, Elke A. Rundensteiner (Worcester Polytechnic
 Institute)

Distributed Processing

Coupling of FDBS and WfMS for Integrating Database
and Application Systems: Architecture, Complexity, Performance 372
 Klaudia Hergula (DaimlerChrysler AG), Theo Härder (Univ.
 of Kaiserslautern)

Optimizing Scientific Databases for Client Side Data Processing 390
 Etzard Stolte, Gustavo Alonso (ETH Zürich)

Supporting Efficient Parametric Search of E-Commerce Data:
A Loosely-Coupled Solution 409
 Min Wang, Yuan-Chi Chang, Sriram Padmanabhan (IBM Watson)

Advanced Querying

Divide-and-Conquer Algorithm for Computing Set Containment Joins 427
 Sergey Melnik, Hector Garcia-Molina (Stanford Univ.)

Universal Quantification in Relational Databases:
A Classification of Data and Algorithms 445
 Ralf Rantzau (Univ. of Stuttgart), Leonard Shapiro (Portland State
 Univ.), Bernhard Mitschang (Univ. of Stuttgart), Quan Wang (Oracle)

Efficient Algorithms for Mining Inclusion Dependencies 464
 Fabien De Marchi (Univ. Blaise Pascal), Stéphane Lopes (Laboratoire
 PRISM), Jean-Marc Petit (Univ. Blaise Pascal)

XML—Advanced Querying

The Index-Based XXL Search Engine for Querying XML Data
with Relevance Ranking 477
   Anja Theobald, Gerhard Weikum (Univ. of the Saarland)

Tree Pattern Relaxation 496
   *Sihem Amer-Yahia (AT&T Labs–Research), SungRan Cho (Stevens
Institute of Technology), Divesh Srivastava (AT&T Labs–Research)*

Schema-Driven Evaluation of Approximate Tree-Pattern Queries 514
   Torsten Schlieder (Freie Univ. Berlin)

Fundamental Query Services

A Robust and Self-Tuning Page-Replacement Strategy
for Spatial Database Systems 533
   Thomas Brinkhoff (Fachhochschule Oldenburg)

Broadcast-Based Data Access in Wireless Environments 553
   Xu Yang, Athman Bouguettaya (Virginia Tech)

Bridging the Gap between Response Time and Energy-Efficiency
in Broadcast Schedule Design... 572
   *Wai Gen Yee, Shamkant B. Navathe, Edward Omiecinski, Christopher
Jermaine (Georgia Tech)*

Estimation/Histograms

Estimating Answer Sizes for XML Queries 590
   Yuqing Wu, Jignesh M. Patel, H.V. Jagadish (Univ. of Michigan)

Selectivity Estimation for Spatial Joins with Geometric Selections 609
   Chengyu Sun, Divyakant Agrawal, Amr El Abbadi (UC Santa Barbara)

A Framework for the Physical Design Problem for Data Synopses 627
   Arnd Christian König, Gerhard Weikum (Univ. of the Saarland)

Aggregation

Temporal Aggregation over Data Streams Using Multiple Granularities ... 646
   *Donghui Zhang, Dimitrios Gunopulos, Vassilis J. Tsotras
(UC Riverside), Bernhard Seeger (Philipps Univ.)*

ProPolyne: A Fast Wavelet-Based Algorithm for Progressive Evaluation
of Polynomial Range-Sum Queries 664
   Rolfe R. Schmidt, Cyrus Shahabi (Univ. of Southern California)

Aggregate Processing of Planar Points 682
 Yufei Tao, Dimitris Papadias, Jun Zhang (Hong Kong Univ. of Science
 and Technology)

Industrial and Applications Track—II

TDB: A Database System for Digital Rights Management 701
 Radek Vingralek, Umesh Maheshwari, William Shapiro (STAR Lab,
 InterTrust)

Content Schema Evolution
in the CoreMedia Content Application Platform CAP 712
 Axel Wienberg, Matthias Ernst, Andreas Gawecki, Olaf Kummer,
 Frank Wienberg (CoreMedia AG), Joachim W. Schmidt (TU Hamburg)

Gene Expression Data Management: A Case Study 722
 Victor M. Markowitz, I-Min A. Chen, Anthony Kosky (Gene Logic)

Demo Paper Track

With HEART towards Response Time Guarantees
for Message-Based e-Services 732
 Achim Kraiss (SAP AG), Frank Schoen (Dresdner Bank),
 Gerhard Weikum (Univ. of the Saarland), Uwe Deppisch (Dresdner
 Bank)

Cobra: A Content-Based Video Retrieval System 736
 Milan Petković, Willem Jonker (Univ. of Twente)

Navigating Virtual Information Sources with Know-ME 739
 Xufei Qian, Bertram Ludäscher (San Diego Supercomputer Center),
 Maryann E. Martone (UC San Diego), Amarnath Gupta (San Diego
 Supercomputer Center)

XQuery by the Book: The IPSI XQuery Demonstrator 742
 Peter Fankhauser (Fraunhofer IPSI), Tobias Groh, Sven Overhage (TU
 Darmstadt)

The ORDB-Based SFB-501-Reuse-Repository 745
 Wolfgang Mahnke, Norbert Ritter (Univ. of Kaiserslautern)

Building Dynamic Market Places Using HyperQueries 749
 Christian Wiesner, Peter Winklhofer, Alfons Kemper (Univ. Passau)

The APPROXML Tool Demonstration 753
 Ernesto Damiani (Univ. di Milano), Nico Lavarini, Stefania Marrara,
 Barbara Oliboni (Politecnico di Milano), Daniele Pasini (Univ. di Milano), Letizia Tanca (Politecnico di Milano), Giuseppe Viviani (Univ.
 di Milano)

A Database-Supported Workbench for Information Fusion: INFUSE 756
    Oliver Dunemann, Ingolf Geist, Roland Jesse, Kai-Uwe Sattler,
    Andreas Stephanik (Univ. of Magdeburg)

ST_YX : Connecting the XML Web to the World of Semantics 759
    Irini Fundulaki, Bernd Amann (Cedric-CNAM Paris), Catriel Beeri
    (Hebrew Univ.), Michel Scholl (Cedric-CNAM Paris),
    Anne-Marie Vercoustre (INRIA Rocquencourt)

UMiner: A Data mining system handling uncertainty and quality 762
    Christos Amanatidis, Maria Halkidi, Michalis Vazirgiannis
    (Athens Univ. of Economics and Business)

Managing Web Sites with OntoWebber 766
    Yuhui Jin, Sichun Xu, Stefan Decker, Gio Wiederhold (Stanford Univ.)

Management of Dynamic Location Information in DOMINO............. 769
    Ouri Wolfson, Hu Cao, Hai Lin, Goce Trajcevski, Fengli Zhang (Univ.
    of Illinois at Chicago), N. Rishe (Florida International Univ.)

Situation Aware Mobile Access to Digital Libraries 772
    Peter Haase (Univ. of Rostock)

Author Index 775

Hyperdatabases:
Infrastructure for the Information Space

Hans-Jörg Schek

Institute of Information Systems, Database Research Group,
Swiss Federal Institute of Technology, Zurich, Switzerland
schek@inf.ethz.ch

Abstract. The amount of stored information is exploding as a consequence of the immense progress in computer and communication technology during the last decades. However tools for accessing relevant information and processing globally distributed information in a convenient manner are under-developed. In short, the infrastructure for the "Information Space" needs much higher attention. In order to improve this situation, we envision the concept of a hyperdatabase that provides database functionality at a much higher level of abstraction, i.e., at the level of complete information components in an n-tier architecture. In analogy to traditional database systems that manage shared data and transactions, a hyperdatabase manages shared information components and transactional processes. It provides "higher-order data independence" by guaranteeing the immunity of applications not only against changes in the data storage and access structures but also against changes in the application components and services, e.g., with respect to the location, implementation, workload, and number of replica of components. In our vision, a hyperdatabase will be the key infrastructure for developing and managing the information space.

DAML+OIL:
A Reason-able Web Ontology Language

Ian Horrocks

Department of Computer Science, University of Manchester
Oxford Road, Manchester M13 9PL, UK
horrocks@cs.man.ac.uk

Abstract. Ontologies are set to play a key role in the "Semantic Web", extending syntactic interoperability to semantic interoperability by providing a source of shared and precisely defined terms. DAML+OIL is an ontology language specifically designed for use on the Web; it exploits existing Web standards (XML and RDF), adding the familiar ontological primitives of object oriented and frame based systems, and the formal rigor of a very expressive description logic. The logical basis of the language means that reasoning services can be provided, both to support ontology design and to make DAML+OIL described Web resources more accessible to automated processes.

1 Introduction

The World Wide Web has been made possible through a set of widely established standards which guarantee interoperability at various levels: the TCP/IP protocol has ensured that nobody has to worry about transporting bits over the wire anymore; similarly, HTTP and HTML have provided a standard way of retrieving and presenting hyperlinked text documents. Applications were able to use this common infrastructure and this has led to the WWW as we know it now.

The current Web can be characterised as the second generation Web: the first generation Web was characterised by handwritten HTML pages; the second generation made the step to machine generated and often active HTML pages. These generations of the Web were meant for direct human processing (reading, browsing, form-filling, etc.). The third generation Web aims to make Web resources more readily accessible to automated processes by adding meta-data annotations that describe their content—this coincides with the vision that Tim Berners-Lee calls the Semantic Web in his recent book "Weaving the Web" [5].

1.1 Ontologies

If meta-data annotations are to make resources more accessible to automated agents, it is essential that their meaning can be understood by such agents. Ontologies will play a pivotal role here by providing a source of shared and precisely defined terms that can be used in such meta-data. An ontology typically consists of a hierarchical description of important concepts in a domain, along with descriptions of the properties of each concept. The degree of formality employed in capturing these descriptions can be quite variable, ranging from natural language to logical formalisms, but increased formality and regularity clearly facilitates machine understanding.

Examples of the use of ontologies could include:

- in e-commerce sites [25], where ontologies can facilitate machine-based communication between buyer and seller, enable vertical integration of markets (see, e.g., http://www.verticalnet.com/), and allow descriptions to be reused in different marketplaces;
- in search engines [26], where ontologies can help searching to go beyond the current keyword-based approach, and allow pages to be found that contain syntactically different, but semantically similar words/phrases (see, e.g., http://www.hotbot.com/);
- in Web services [28], where ontologies can provide semantically richer service descriptions that can be more flexibly interpreted by intelligent agents.

2 Ontology Languages

The recognition of the key role that ontologies are likely to play in the future of the Web has led to the extension of Web markup languages in order to facilitate content description and the development of Web based ontologies, e.g., XML Schema,[1] RDF[2] (Resource Description Framework), and RDF Schema [9]. RDF Schema (RDFS) in particular is recognisable as an ontology/knowledge representation language: it talks about classes and properties (binary relations), range and domain constraints (on properties), and subclass and subproperty (subsumption) relations.

RDFS is, however, a very primitive language (the above is an almost complete description of its functionality), and more expressive power would clearly be necessary/desirable in order to describe resources in sufficient detail. Moreover, such descriptions should be amenable to *automated reasoning* if they are to be used effectively by automated processes, e.g., to determine the semantic relationship between syntactically different terms.

2.1 DAML and OIL

In 1999 the DARPA Agent Markup Language (DAML) program[3] was initiated with the aim of providing the foundations of a next generation "semantic" Web [17]. As a first step, it was decided that the adoption of a common ontology language would facilitate semantic interoperability across the various projects

---

[1] http://www.w3.org/XML/Schema/
[2] http://www.w3c.org/RDF/
[3] http://www.daml.org/

making up the program. RDFS was seen as a good starting point, and was already a proposed World Wide Web Consortium (W3C) standard, but it was not expressive enough to meet DAML's requirements. A new language called DAML-ONT was therefore developed that extended RDF with language constructors from object-oriented and frame-based knowledge representation languages. Like RDFS, DAML-ONT suffered from a rather weak semantic specification, and it was soon realised that this could lead to disagreements, both amongst humans and machines, as to the precise meaning of terms in a DAML-ONT ontology.

At around the same time, a group of (largely European) researchers with aims similar to those of the DAML researchers (i.e., to provide a foundation for the next generation Web) had designed another Web oriented ontology language called OIL (the Ontology Inference Layer) [11, 12]. Like DAML-ONT, OIL had an RDFS based syntax (as well as an alternative XML syntax) and a set of language constructors based on frame-based languages. The developers of OIL, however, placed a stronger emphasis on formal rigor, and the language was explicitly designed so that its semantics could be specified via a mapping to a very expressive description logic, $\mathcal{SHIQ}$ [22].

It became obvious to both groups that their objectives could best be served by combining their efforts, the result being the merging of DAML-ONT and OIL to produce DAML+OIL. The merged language has a formal (model theoretic) semantics that provides machine and human understandability (as well as an axiomatization [13]), and a reconciliation of the language constructors from the two languages.

Until recently, the development of DAML+OIL has been undertaken by a committee largely made up of members of the two language design teams (and rather grandly titled the Joint EU/US Committee on Agent Markup Languages). More recently, DAML+OIL has been submitted to W3C[4] and is to form the basis for the W3C's Web ontology language which the Web-Ontology Working Group has been mandated to deliver.[5]

2.2 DAML+OIL

DAML+OIL is an ontology language, and as such is designed to describe the *structure* of a domain. DAML+OIL takes an object oriented approach, with the structure of the domain being described in terms of *classes* and *properties*. An ontology consists of a set of *axioms* that assert, e.g., subsumption relationships between classes or properties. Asserting that resources[6] (pairs of resources) are instances of DAML+OIL classes (properties) is left to RDF, a task for which it

---

[4] http://www.w3.org/Submission/2001/12/
[5] http://www.w3c.org/2001/sw/WebOnt/
[6] Everything describable by RDF is called a resource. A resource could be Web accessible, e.g., a Web page or part of a Web page, but it could also be an object that is not directly accessible via the Web, e.g., a person. Resources are named by URIs plus optional anchor ids. See http://www.w3.org/TR/1999/REC-rdf-syntax-19990222/ for more details.

is well suited. When a resource r is an instance of a class C we say that r has type C.

From a formal point of view, DAML+OIL can be seen to be equivalent to a very expressive description logic, with a DAML+OIL ontology corresponding to a DL terminology (Tbox). As in a DL, DAML+OIL classes can be names (URIs) or *expressions*, and a variety of *constructors* are provided for building class expressions. The expressive power of the language is determined by the class (and property) constructors supported, and by the kinds of axiom supported.

Constructor	DL Syntax	Example
intersectionOf	$C_1 \sqcap \ldots \sqcap C_n$	Human $\sqcap$ Male
unionOf	$C_1 \sqcup \ldots \sqcup C_n$	Doctor $\sqcup$ Lawyer
complementOf	$\neg C$	$\neg$Male
oneOf	$\{x_1 \ldots x_n\}$	{john, mary}
toClass	$\forall P.C$	$\forall$hasChild.Doctor
hasClass	$\exists P.C$	$\exists$hasChild.Lawyer
hasValue	$\exists P.\{x\}$	$\exists$citizenOf.{USA}
minCardinalityQ	$\geqslant n P.C$	$\geqslant$2hasChild.Lawyer
maxCardinalityQ	$\leqslant n P.C$	$\leqslant$1hasChild.Male
cardinalityQ	$=n\ P.C$	=1 hasParent.Female

Fig. 1. DAML+OIL class constructors

Figure 1 summarises the constructors supported by DAML+OIL. The standard DL syntax is used for compactness as the RDF syntax is rather verbose. In the RDF syntax, for example, Human $\sqcap$ Male would be written as

```
<daml:Class>
  <daml:intersectionOf rdf:parseType="daml:collection">
    <daml:Class rdf:about="#Human"/>
    <daml:Class rdf:about="#Male"/>
  </daml:intersectionOf>
</daml:Class>
```

while $\geqslant$2hasChild.Lawyer would be written as

```
<daml:Restriction daml:minCardinalityQ="2">
  <daml:onProperty rdf:resource="#hasChild"/>
  <daml:hasClassQ rdf:resource="#Lawyer"/>
</daml:Restriction>
```

The meaning of the first three constructors (intersectionOf, unionOf and complementOf) is relatively self-explanatory: they are just the standard boolean operators that allow classes to be formed from the intersection, union and negation of other classes. The oneOf constructor allows classes to be defined existentially, i.e., by enumerating their members.

The toClass and hasClass constructors correspond to slot constraints in a frame-based language. The class $\forall P.C$ is the class all of whose instances are related via the property P only to resources of type C, while the class $\exists P.C$ is the class all of whose instances are related via the property P to at least one resource of type C. The hasValue constructor is just shorthand for a combination of hasValue and oneOf.

The minCardinalityQ, maxCardinalityQ and cardinalityQ constructors (known in DLs as qualified number restrictions) are generalisations of the hasClass and hasValue constructors. The class $\geqslant nP.C$ ($\leqslant nP.C$, $=n\,P.C$) is the class all of whose instances are related via the property P to at least (at most, exactly) n *different* resources of type C. The emphasis on different is because there is no unique name assumption with respect to resource names (URIs): it is possible that many URIs could name the same resource.

Note that arbitrarily complex nesting of constructors is possible. Moreover, XML Schema *datatypes* (e.g., so called primitive datatypes such as strings, decimal or float, as well as more complex derived datatypes such as integer subranges) can be used anywhere that a class name might appear.

The formal semantics of the class constructors is given by DAML+OIL's model-theoretic semantics[7] or can be derived from the specification of a suitably expressive DL (e.g., see [21]).

Axiom	DL Syntax	Example
subClassOf	$C_1 \sqsubseteq C_2$	Human $\sqsubseteq$ Animal $\sqcap$ Biped
sameClassAs	$C_1 \equiv C_2$	Man $\equiv$ Human $\sqcap$ Male
subPropertyOf	$P_1 \sqsubseteq P_2$	hasDaughter $\sqsubseteq$ hasChild
samePropertyAs	$P_1 \equiv P_2$	cost $\equiv$ price
disjointWith	$C_1 \sqsubseteq \neg C_2$	Male $\sqsubseteq \neg$Female
sameIndividualAs	$\{x_1\} \equiv \{x_2\}$	{President_Bush} $\equiv$ {G_W_Bush}
differentIndividualFrom	$\{x_1\} \sqsubseteq \neg\{x_2\}$	{john} $\sqsubseteq \neg$\{peter\}
inverseOf	$P_1 \equiv P_2^-$	hasChild $\equiv$ hasParent$^-$
transitiveProperty	$P^+ \sqsubseteq P$	ancestor$^+$ $\sqsubseteq$ ancestor
uniqueProperty	$\top \sqsubseteq \leqslant 1P$	$\top \sqsubseteq \leqslant 1$hasMother
unambiguousProperty	$\top \sqsubseteq \leqslant 1P^-$	$\top \sqsubseteq \leqslant 1$isMotherOf$^-$

Fig. 2. DAML+OIL axioms

As already mentioned, besides the set of constructors supported, the other aspect of a language that determines its expressive power is the kinds of axiom supported. Figure 2 summarises the axioms supported by DAML+OIL. These axioms make it possible to assert subsumption or equivalence with respect to classes or properties, the disjointness of classes, the equivalence or non-equivalence of individuals (resources), and various properties of properties.

A crucial feature of DAML+OIL is that subClassOf and sameClassAs axioms can be applied to arbitrary class expressions. This provides greatly increased

---

[7] http://www.w3.org/TR/daml+oil-model

expressive power with respect to standard frame-based languages where such axioms are invariably restricted to the form where the left hand side is an atomic name, there is only one such axiom per name, and there are no cycles (the class on the right hand side of an axiom cannot refer, either directly or indirectly, to the class name on the left hand side).

A consequence of this expressive power is that all of the class and individual axioms, as well as the uniqueProperty and unambiguousProperty axioms, can be reduced to subClassOf and sameClassAs axioms (as can be seen from the DL syntax). In fact sameClassAs could also be reduced to subClassOf as a sameClassAs axiom $C \equiv D$ is equivalent to a pair of subClassOf axioms, $C \sqsubseteq D$ and $D \sqsubseteq C$.

As we have seen, DAML+OIL allows properties of properties to be asserted. It is possible to assert that a property is unique (i.e., functional) and unambiguous (i.e., its inverse is functional). It is also possible to use inverse properties and to assert that a property is transitive.

3 Reasoning Services

As we have seen, DAML+OIL is equivalent to a very expressive description logic. More precisely, DAML+OIL is equivalent to the $\mathcal{SHIQ}$ DL [22] with the addition of existentially defined classes (i.e., the oneOf constructor) and *datatypes* (often called concrete domains in DLs [1]). This equivalence allows DAML+OIL to exploit the considerable existing body of description logic research, e.g.:

- to define the semantics of the language and to understand its formal properties, in particular the decidability and complexity of key inference problems [10];
- as a source of sound and complete algorithms and optimised implementation techniques for deciding key inference problems [22, 21];
- to use implemented DL systems in order to provide (partial) reasoning support [19, 29, 16].

A important consideration in the design of DAML+OIL was that key inference problems in the language, in particular class consistency/subsumption,[8] should be decidable, as this facilitates the provision of reasoning services. Moreover, the correspondence with DLs facilitates the use of DL algorithms that are known to be amenable to optimised implementation and to behave well in realistic applications in spite of their high worst case complexity [20, 15].

Maintaining the decidability of the language requires certain constraints on its expressive power that may not be acceptable to all applications. However, the designers of the language decided that reasoning would be important if the full

---

[8] In propositionally closed languages like DAML+OIL, class consistency and subsumption are mutually reducible. Moreover, in DAML+OIL the consistency of an entire "knowledge base" (an ontology plus a set of class and property membership assertions) can be reduced to class consistency.

power of ontologies was to be realised, and that a powerful but still decidable ontology language would be a good starting point.

Reasoning can be useful at many stages during the design, maintenance and deployment of ontologies.

- Reasoning can be used to support ontology design and to improve the quality of the resulting ontology. For example, class consistency and subsumption reasoning can be used to check for logically inconsistent classes and (possibly unexpected) implicit subsumption relationships [4]. This kind of support has been shown to be particularly important with large ontologies, which are often built and maintained over a long period by multiple authors. Other reasoning tasks, such as "matching" [3] and/or computing least common subsumers [2] could also be used to support "bottom up" ontology design, i.e., the identification and description of relevant classes from sets of example instances.
- Like information integration [8], ontology integration can also be supported by reasoning. For example, integration can be performed using inter-ontology assertions specifying relationships between classes and properties, with reasoning being used to compute the integrated hierarchy and to highlight any problems/inconsistencies. Unlike some other integration techniques (e.g., name reconciliation [27]), this method has the advantage of being non-intrusive with respect to the original ontologies.
- Reasoning with respect to deployed ontologies will enhance the power of "intelligent agents", allowing them to determine if a set of facts is consistent w.r.t. an ontology, to identify individuals that are implicitly members of a given class etc. A suitable service ontology could, for example, allow an agent seeking secure services to identify a service requiring a userid and password as a possible candidate.

4 Datatypes

DAML+OIL supports the full range of XML Schema datatypes. This is facilitated by maintaining a clean separation between instances of "object" classes (defined using the ontology language) and instances of datatypes (defined using the XML Schema type system). In particular, it is assumed that that the domain of interpretation of object classes is disjoint from the domain of interpretation of datatypes, so that an instance of an object class (e.g., the individual "Italy") can never have the same interpretation as a value of a datatype (e.g., the integer 5), and that the set of object properties (which map individuals to individuals) is disjoint from the set of datatype properties (which map individuals to datatype values).

The disjointness of object and datatype domains was motivated by both philosophical and pragmatic considerations:

- Datatypes are considered to be already sufficiently structured by the built-in predicates, and it is, therefore, not appropriate to form new classes of datatype values using the ontology language [18].

- The simplicity and compactness of the ontology language are not compromised: even enumerating all the XML Schema datatypes would add greatly to its complexity, while adding a logical theory for each datatype, even if it were possible, would lead to a language of monumental proportions.
- The semantic integrity of the language is not compromised—defining theories for all the XML Schema datatypes would be difficult or impossible without extending the language in directions whose semantics may be difficult to capture within the existing framework.
- The "implementability" of the language is not compromised—a hybrid reasoner can easily be implemented by combining a reasoner for the "object" language with one capable of deciding satisfiability questions with respect to conjunctions of (possibly negated) datatypes [21].

From a theoretical point of view, this design means that the ontology language can specify constraints on data values, but as data values can never be instances of object classes they cannot apply additional constraints to elements of the object domain. This allows the type system to be extended without having any impact on the ontology language, and vice versa. Similarly, the formal properties of hybrid reasoners are determined by those of the two components; in particular, the combined reasoner will be sound and complete if both components are sound and complete.

From a practical point of view, DAML+OIL implementations can choose to support some or all of the XML Schema datatypes. For supported data types, they can either implement their own type checker/validater or rely on some external component. The job of a type checker/validater is simply to take zero or more data values and one or more datatypes, and determine if there exists any data value that is equal to every one of the specified data values and is an instance of every one of the specified data types.

5 Research Challenges for DAML+OIL

Class consistency/subsumption reasoning in DAML+OIL is know to be decidable (as it is contained in the C2 fragment of first order logic [14]), but many challenges remain for implementors of "practical" reasoning systems, i.e., systems that perform well with the kinds of reasoning problem generated by realistic applications.

5.1 Individuals

The OIL language was designed so that it could be mapped to the $\mathcal{SHIQ}$ DL, thereby providing a implementation path for reasoning services. This mapping is made possible by a very weak treatment of individuals occurring in existentially defined classes, which are treated not as single elements but as the extensions of corresponding primitive classes. This is a well known technique for avoiding the reasoning problems that arise with existentially defined classes (such as classes defined using DAML+OIL's oneOf constructor) and is also used, e.g., in the CLASSIC knowledge representation system [6].

In contrast, DAML+OIL gives a standard semantics to such individuals, i.e., they are interpreted as single elements in the domain of discourse. This treatment of individuals is very powerful, and justifies intuitive inferences that would not be valid for OIL, e.g., that persons all of whose countries of residence are (oneOf) Italy are kinds of person that have at most one country of residence:

$$\text{Person} \sqcap \forall \text{residence}.\{\text{Italy}\} \sqsubseteq \leqslant 1\text{residence}$$

Unfortunately, the combination of such individuals with inverse properties is so powerful that it pushes the worst case complexity of the class consistency problem from ExpTime (for $\mathcal{SHIQ}$/OIL) to NExpTime. No "practical" decision procedure is currently known for this logic, and there is no implemented system that can provide sound and complete reasoning for the whole DAML+OIL language. In the absence of inverse properties, however, a tableaux algorithm has been devised [21], and in the absence of individuals (in existentially defined classes), DAML+OIL can exploit implemented DL systems via a translation into $\mathcal{SHIQ}$ (extended with datatypes) similar to the one used by OIL. It would, of course, also be possible to translate DAML+OIL ontologies into $\mathcal{SHIQ}$ using OIL's weak treatment of individuals,[9] but in this case reasoning with individuals would not be sound and complete with respect to the semantics of the language.

5.2 Scalability

Even without the oneOf constructor, class consistency reasoning is still a hard problem. Moreover, Web ontologies can be expected to grow very large, and with deployed ontologies it may also be desirable to reason w.r.t. a large numbers of class/property instances.

There is good evidence of empirical tractability and scalability for implemented DL systems [20, 15], but this is mostly w.r.t. logics that do not include inverse properties (e.g., $\mathcal{SHF}$ [10]). Adding inverse properties makes practical implementations more problematical as several important optimisation techniques become much less effective. Work is required in order to develop more highly optimised implementations supporting inverse properties, and to demonstrate that they can scale as well as $\mathcal{SHF}$ implementations. It is also unclear if existing techniques will be able to cope with large numbers of class/property instances [23].

Finally, it is an inevitable consequence of the high worst case complexity that some problems will be intractable, even for highly optimised implementations. It is conjectured that such problems rarely arise in practice, but the evidence for this conjecture is drawn from a relatively small number of applications, and it remains to be seen if a much wider range of Web application domains will demonstrate similar characteristics.

---

[9] This approach is taken by some existing applications, e.g., OilEd [4].
[10] $\mathcal{SHF}$ is equivalent to $\mathcal{SHIQ}$ without inverse properties and with only functional properties instead of qualified number restrictions [22].

5.3 New Reasoning Tasks

So far we have mainly discussed class consistency/subsumption reasoning, but this may not be the only reasoning problem that is of interest. Other tasks could include querying, explanation, matching, computing least common subsumers, etc. Querying in particular may be important in Semantic Web applications. Some work on query languages for description logics has already been done [30, 7, 24], and work is underway on the design of a DAML+OIL query language, but the computational properties of such a language, either theoretical or empirical, have yet to be determined.

Explanation may also be an important problem, e.g., to help an ontology designer to rectify problems identified by reasoning support, or to explain to a user why an application behaved in an unexpected manner. As discussed in Section 3, reasoning problems such as matching and computing least common subsumers could also be important in ontology design.

6 Summary

DAML+OIL is an ontology language specifically designed for use on the Web; it exploits existing Web standards (XML and RDF), adding the formal rigor of a description logic and the ontological primitives of object oriented and frame based systems.

This combination of features has proved very attractive and DAML+OIL has already been widely adopted, with some major efforts already committed to encoding their ontologies in DAML+OIL. This has been particularly evident in the bio-ontology domain, where the Bio-Ontology Consortium has specified DAML+OIL as their ontology exchange language, and the Gene Ontology [31] is being migrated to DAML+OIL in a project partially funded by GlaxoSmithKline Pharmaceuticals in cooperation with the Gene Ontology Consortium.[11]

What of the future? The development of the semantic Web, and of Web ontology languages, presents many opportunities and challenges. A "practical" (satisfiability/subsumption) algorithm for the full DAML+OIL language has yet to be developed, and it is not yet clear that sound and complete reasoners can provide adequate performance for typical Web applications.

Acknowledgements

I would like to acknowledge the contribution of all those involved in the development of DAML-ONT, OIL and DAML+OIL, amongst whom Dieter Fensel, Frank van Harmelen, Deborah McGuinness and Peter F. Patel-Schneider deserve particular mention.

---

[11] http://www.geneontology.org/.

References

1. F. Baader and P. Hanschke. A schema for integrating concrete domains into concept languages. In *Proc. of the 12th Int. Joint Conf. on Artificial Intelligence (IJCAI'91)*, pages 452–457, 1991.
2. F. Baader and R. Küsters. Computing the least common subsumer and the most specific concept in the presence of cyclic $\mathcal{ALN}$-concept descriptions. In *Proc. of the 22nd German Annual Conf. on Artificial Intelligence (KI'98)*, volume 1504 of *Lecture Notes in Computer Science*, pages 129–140. Springer-Verlag, 1998.
3. F. Baader, R. Küsters, A. Borgida, and D. L. McGuinness. Matching in description logics. *J. of Logic and Computation*, 9(3):411–447, 1999.
4. S. Bechhofer, I. Horrocks, C. Goble, and R. Stevens. OilEd: a reason-able ontology editor for the semantic web. In *Proc. of the Joint German/Austrian Conf. on Artificial Intelligence (KI 2001)*, number 2174 in Lecture Notes in Artificial Intelligence, pages 396–408. Springer-Verlag, 2001.
5. T. Berners-Lee. *Weaving the Web*. Harpur, San Francisco, 1999.
6. A. Borgida and P. F. Patel-Schneider. A semantics and complete algorithm for subsumption in the CLASSIC description logic. *J. of Artificial Intelligence Research*, 1:277–308, 1994.
7. D. Calvanese, G. De Giacomo, and M. Lenzerini. Answering queries using views in description logics. In *Proc. of the 1999 Description Logic Workshop (DL'99)*, pages 9–13. CEUR Electronic Workshop Proceedings, http://ceur-ws.org/Vol-22/, 1999.
8. D. Calvanese, G. De Giacomo, M. Lenzerini, D. Nardi, and R. Rosati. Information integration: Conceptual modeling and reasoning support. In *Proc. of the 6th Int. Conf. on Cooperative Information Systems (CoopIS'98)*, pages 280–291, 1998.
9. S. Decker, F. van Harmelen, J. Broekstra, M. Erdmann, D. Fensel, I. Horrocks, M. Klein, and S. Melnik. The semantic web: The roles of XML and RDF. *IEEE Internet Computing*, 4(5), 2000.
10. F. M. Donini, M. Lenzerini, D. Nardi, and W. Nutt. The complexity of concept languages. *Information and Computation*, 134:1–58, 1997.
11. D. Fensel, I. Horrocks, F. van Harmelen, S. Decker, M. Erdmann, and M. Klein. OIL in a nutshell. In R. Dieng, editor, *Proc. of the 12th European Workshop on Knowledge Acquisition, Modeling, and Management (EKAW'00)*, number 1937 in Lecture Notes in Artificial Intelligence, pages 1–16. Springer-Verlag, 2000.
12. D. Fensel, F. van Harmelen, I. Horrocks, D. L. McGuinness, and P. F. Patel-Schneider. OIL: An ontology infrastructure for the semantic web. *IEEE Intelligent Systems*, 16(2):38–45, 2001.
13. R. Fikes and D. L. McGuinness. An axiomatic semantics for rdf, rdf schema, and daml+oil. In *Stanford University KSL Technical Report KSL-01-01*. http://www.ksl.stanford.edu/people/dlm/daml-semantics/abstract-axiomatic-semantics.html, 2001.
14. E. Grädel, M. Otto, and E. Rosen. Two-variable logic with counting is decidable. In *Proc. of the 12th IEEE Symp. on Logic in Computer Science (LICS'97)*, pages 306–317. IEEE Computer Society Press, 1997.
15. V. Haarslev and R. Möller. High performance reasoning with very large knowledge bases: A practical case study. In *Proc. of the 17th Int. Joint Conf. on Artificial Intelligence (IJCAI 2001)*, 2001.
16. V. Haarslev and R. Möller. RACER system description. In *Proc. of the Int. Joint Conf. on Automated Reasoning (IJCAR 2001)*, 2001.

17. J. Hendler and D. L. McGuinness. The darpa agent markup language". *IEEE Intelligent Systems*, 15(6):67–73, 2000.
18. B. Hollunder and F. Baader. Qualifying number restrictions in concept languages. In *Proc. of the 2nd Int. Conf. on the Principles of Knowledge Representation and Reasoning (KR'91)*, pages 335–346, 1991.
19. I. Horrocks. The FaCT system. In H. de Swart, editor, *Proc. of the 2nd Int. Conf. on Analytic Tableaux and Related Methods (TABLEAUX'98)*, volume 1397 of *Lecture Notes in Artificial Intelligence*, pages 307–312. Springer-Verlag, 1998.
20. I. Horrocks. Using an expressive description logic: FaCT or fiction? In *Proc. of the 6th Int. Conf. on Principles of Knowledge Representation and Reasoning (KR'98)*, pages 636–647, 1998.
21. I. Horrocks and U. Sattler. Ontology reasoning in the $\mathcal{SHOQ}$(D) description logic. In *Proc. of the 17th Int. Joint Conf. on Artificial Intelligence (IJCAI 2001)*. Morgan Kaufmann, Los Altos, 2001.
22. I. Horrocks, U. Sattler, and S. Tobies. Practical reasoning for expressive description logics. In H. Ganzinger, D. McAllester, and A. Voronkov, editors, *Proc. of the 6th Int. Conf. on Logic for Programming and Automated Reasoning (LPAR'99)*, number 1705 in Lecture Notes in Artificial Intelligence, pages 161–180. Springer-Verlag, 1999.
23. I. Horrocks, U. Sattler, and S. Tobies. Reasoning with individuals for the description logic $\mathcal{SHIQ}$. In *Proc. of the 17th Int. Conf. on Automated Deduction (CADE 2000)*, number 1831 in Lecture Notes in Artificial Intelligence, pages 482–496. Springer-Verlag, 2000.
24. I. Horrocks and S. Tessaris. A conjunctive query language for description logic aboxes. In *Proc. of the 17th Nat. Conf. on Artificial Intelligence (AAAI 2000)*, pages 399–404, 2000.
25. D. L. McGuinness. Ontological issues for knowledge-enhanced search. In *Proc. of FOIS*, Frontiers in Artificial Intelligence and Applications. IOS-press, 1998.
26. D. L. McGuinness. Ontologies for electronic commerce. In *Proc. of the AAAI '99 Artificial Intelligence for Electronic Commerce Workshop*, 1999.
27. D. L. McGuinness, R. Fikes, J. Rice, and S. Wilder. The Chimaera ontology environment. In *Proc. of the 17th Nat. Conf. on Artificial Intelligence (AAAI 2000)*, 2000.
28. S. McIlraith, T. Son, and H. Zeng. Semantic web services. *IEEE Intelligent Systems*, 16(2):46–53, March/April 2001.
29. P. F. Patel-Schneider. DLP system description. In *Proc. of the 1998 Description Logic Workshop (DL'98)*, pages 87–89. CEUR Electronic Workshop Proceedings, http://ceur-ws.org/Vol-11/, 1998.
30. M.-C. Rousset. Backward reasoning in ABoxes for query answering. In *Proc. of the 1999 Description Logic Workshop (DL'99)*, pages 18–22. CEUR Electronic Workshop Proceedings, http://ceur-ws.org/Vol-22/, 1999.
31. The Gene Ontology Consortium. Gene ontolgy: tool for the unification of biology. *Nature Genetics*, 25(1):25–29, 2000.

Ambient Intelligence: Plenty of Challenges by 2010

Jari Ahola

VTT Information Technology, Finland
jari.ahola@vtt.fi

Abstract. Ambient Intelligence refers to an environment that is sensitive, adaptive, and responsive to the presence of people. It builds on three recent key technologies: Ubiquitous Computing, Ubiquitous Communication, and Intelligent User Interfaces. To add intelligence to our environment places many challenges also for the databases essential for the implementation of intelligent environments, for instance in homes and workplaces. Such an environment relies heavily on constant information flows from the numerous sensors monitoring not only the environment, but also the occupants. Solving the problem of how to intelligently translate this data to correct behaviors of the environment is the key to be found.

An Approach to Integrating Query Refinement in SQL*

Michael Ortega-Binderberger[1], Kaushik Chakrabarti[1], and Sharad Mehrotra[2]

[1] University of Illinois, Urbana-Champaign, Urbana, IL, 61801, USA
miki@acm.org, kaushikc@uiuc.edu
[2] University of California, Irvine, Irvine, CA, 92697-3425, USA
sharad@ics.uci.edu

Abstract. With the emergence of applications that require content-based similarity retrieval, techniques to support such a retrieval paradigm over database systems have emerged as a critical area of research. User subjectivity is an important aspect of such queries, i.e., which objects are relevant to the user and which are not depends on the perception of the user. Query refinement is used to handle user subjectivity in similarity search systems. This paper explores how to enhance database systems with query refinement for content-based (similarity) searches in object-relational databases. Query refinement is achieved through relevance feedback where the user judges individual result tuples and the system adapts and restructures the query to better reflect the users information need. We present a query refinement framework and an array of strategies for refinement that address different aspects of the problem. Our experiments demonstrate the effectiveness of the query refinement techniques proposed in this paper.

1 Introduction

Similarity retrieval has been recently explored for multimedia retrieval, especially in the context of image databases. Multimedia objects are typically represented using a collection of features such as color, texture, shape, etc. that partially capture the content of the multimedia object. Since features imperfectly represent the content of the multimedia object, when searching for a multimedia object, it is infeasible to insist on retrieving only those objects that exactly match the query features. Instead, a similarity feature matching approach to retrieving multimedia objects makes much more sense. Accordingly, users expect to see the results of their query in ranked order, starting with the results most similar to the query first. Multimedia similarity retrieval has been studied extensively by several researchers and projects including QBIC [10], MARS [16], WebSeek[7], DELOS [13] and HERMES [3] among others. Another field where similarity retrieval has been explored extensively is in Text Information Retrieval [4].

---

* This work was supported by NSF CAREER award IIS-9734300, and in part by the Army Research Laboratory under Cooperative Agreement No. DAAL01-96-2-0003. Michael Ortega-Binderberger is supported in part by CONACYT award 89061.

The initial result ranking computed in response to a query may not adequately capture the users preconceived notion of similarity or *information need* [4], prompting the user to refine the query. The gap between the actual and desired rankings is due to the subjective perception of similarity by users on one hand, and the difficulty to express similarity queries that accurately capture the users information need on the other. This gap may arise due to many reasons, including the users unfamiliarity with the database, difficulty in assigning weights to different similarity predicates, differing priorities, etc. Therefore, in an effort to close this gap, users initiate an information discovery cycleby iteratively posing a query, examining the answers, and re-formulating the query to improve the quality (ranking) of the answers they receive. Research in multimedia [19, 12, 21, 5] and text retrieval [18, 4, 6] has therefore also focused on refining a query with the help of the users feedback.

This paper advances the notion that similarity retrieval and query refinement are critical not just in the context of multimedia and/or text retrieval, but in general in the context of structured and semi-structured data. Some example applications where such a need arises are:

Example 1 (Job Openings). In a job marketplace application, a listing of job openings (description, salary offered, job location, etc.) and job applications (name, age, resume, home location, etc.) are matched to each other. Resume and job description are text descriptions, location is a two dimensional (latitude, longitude) position, and desired and offered salary are numeric. Applicants and job listings are *joined* with a (similarity) condition to obtain the best matches. Unstated preferences in the initial condition may produce an undesirable ranking. A user then points out to the system a few desirable and/or undesirable examples where job location and the applicants home are close (short commute times desired); the system then modifies the condition and produces a new ranking that emphasizes geographic proximity. ∎

Example 2 (Multimedia E-catalog search). Consider an online garment retailer. The store has an online catalog with many attributes for each garment: the manufacturer, price, item description, and garment picture. We can define similarity functions for each of these attributes, e.g., we can define how similar two given prices are and can extract visual features from the garment image [10]. Through a *query by example* (QBE) user interface, users select or enter a desired price, description, and/or select pictures of attractive garments. Users then request the "most similar" garments in terms of those attributes. The initial result ranking may not be satisfactory. The user then expresses her preferences by marking the attributes appropriately, and re-submits the query. The system computes a new set of answers ranked closer to the users desire. ∎

We propose to shift as much as possible the burden of refinement from the user to the database management system (DBMS). When users examine answers, they naturally know which ones fit the desired results, instead of initiating the mental process of refinement, users off-load the task to the DBMS by merely judging some of the answers. Judging takes the form of a user interaction with the system where *relevance judgments* about results – which results the user thinks are good examples, and which ones are bad examples – are *fed back* to the DBMS. The DBMS uses these *relevance feedback judgments* to refine the query

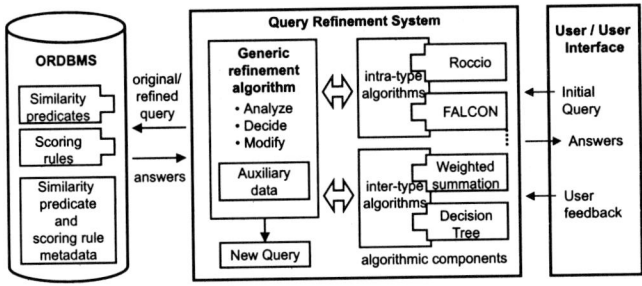

Fig. 1. Query Refinement System Architecture

and re-evaluates[1] it to produce a new ranked answer set which may be subject to more iterations of *query refinement*. The burden on the user is thus reduced to selecting a subset of results as good or bad and informing the DBMS. This interaction can be done directly through SQL, or through a context specific user interface reducing the users burden. This approach mirrors Information Retrieval and Cooperative Databases that involve the user in the query answering loop.

We integrate data-type specific refinement algorithms into a framework that combines multiple such algorithms and provides refinement across them. This two-level approach to query refinement is also shown in figure 1, as intra-, and inter- type refinement modules with specific algorithm plug-ins. Refinement algorithms for specific data-types have been explored in the past, such as Rocchios [18] algorithm for text vector models, MARS and Mindreader algorithms for image retrieval [19, 17, 12], and FALCON [21] for metric spaces, among others. Our framework uses these and other algorithms as building blocks of a complete system with query refinement support.

The main contribution of this paper is a proposal on how to support query refinement through user relevance feedback in an object-relational DBMS (ORDBMS). Specifically, our contributions are:

- a generic refinement framework, or *meta model*, which accepts specific algorithm "plug-ins"
- DBMS support interfaces and data structures to enable query refinement
- review several domain specific and domain independent query refinement techniques

We implemented our proposed framework as a wrapper on top of the Informix Object Relational DBMS. Figure 1 shows the system architecture. A user interface client connects to our wrapper, sends queries and feedback and gets answers incrementally in order of their relevance to the query. We implemented the similarity and refinement functionality described in this paper and also developed a sample application to validate our approach in addition to our experiments.

---

[1] Re-evaluation of a refined query may benefit from re-using the work done to answer the original (or previous) query, but is not strictly part of the query refinement process, therefore we do not discuss this topic in this paper. We assume a naive re-evaluation that treats the refined query as an original query.

The rest of this paper is developed as follows. Section 2 presents some background. Section 3 presents our query refinement framework, and section 4 presents some specific refinement algorithms. Section 5 presents some experiments and an example query refinement application. Section 6 presents related work. Section 7 offers some conclusions.

2 Preliminaries — Similarity Retrieval Model

Before we embark on an explanation of query refinement, we first discuss the similarity retrieval model on which we build our query refinement work. Let us consider an example query:

Example 3 (Similarity Query). The following query joins a table of houses with a table of schools. The house table has price and availability attributes, and both tables share a location attribute:
    select $wsum(p_s, 0.3, l_s, 0.7)$ as S, a, d
       from Houses H, Schools S
       where $H.available$ **and** similar_price(H.price, 100000, "30000", 0.4, p_s)
              and close_to(H.loc, S.loc, "1, 1" , 0.5, l_s)
    order by S **desc**
This query finds homes that are close to schools, are priced around \$100,000, and are available. The query has two similarity predicates: *similar_price*, and *close_to*. Both predicates return similarity scores (p_s, l_s) that are combined into a single score S for the whole tuple, here we use the *wsum scoring rule* to combine them. Note that a similarity query contains both precise predicates and similarity predicates. ∎

In the context of a similarity query, the following concepts are important: *similarity score, similarity predicate, scoring rule, and ranked retrieval*. Ranked retrieval stems from the intuitive desire of users of similarity based searching systems to see the best answers first [15, 4], therefore the answers are sorted, or *ranked* on their overall score S. We now cover the remaining concepts in detail.

A similarity based search in a database is an SQL query with both precise and *similarity predicates*. Precise predicates return only those data objects that exactly satisfy them, i.e., traditional Boolean predicates. Similarity predicates instead specify target values and do not produce exact matches, they return a similarity *score S* for objects that approximately match the predicate. To be compatible with SQL, similarity predicates return Boolean values if the similarity score is higher than a threshold. Data is represented in the object-relational model which supports user-defined types and functions. In this work we focus on select-project-join queries.

A similarity score provides a fine grained differentiation for a comparison between values or objects, i.e., how good or bad they match. This is in contrast to the prevalent precise comparisons that yield Boolean values, i.e., complete match or not. We define a similarity score as follows:

Definition 1 (Similarity score S). *S is a value in the range $[0,1]$. Higher values indicate higher similarity.* ∎

Similarity predicates compare values and compute a similarity score S for the degree to which the values match. For example, a similarity predicate for 2 dimensional geographic locations may say that identical locations are 100% close ($S = 1$), 5 kilometers distance is 50% close ($S = 0.5$) and 10 kilometers and beyond is 0% close ($S = 0$), etc. We define similarity predicates as follows:

Definition 2 (Similarity predicate). *A similarity predicate is a function with four inputs: (1) a value to be compared, (2) a set of query values, (3) a parameter string to configure the similarity predicate, and (4) a similarity cutoff value α in the range [0,1] (also called* alpha cut *or* threshold*), and returns two values: (1) a Boolean value (true, false), and (2) a similarity score S (as a side effect). The function returns true if $S > \alpha$, else it returns false. The function has the form:*
   Similarity Predicate(input value, set of query values, parameters, α, S) $\rightarrow$ \{true, false\} ∎

This function compares an input value to one or more values of the same or a compatible type. We support a set of values since in a Query-by-Example paradigm it often makes sense to compute the similarity of an object with respect to multiple examples rather than just one [17, 21]. To offer flexibility to the user, similarity predicates may take additional parameters to configure the predicate and adapt it to a specific situation, for example parameters may include weights that indicate a preferred matching direction between geographic locations, or select between Manhattan and Euclidean distance models. We use a string to pass the parameters as it can easily capture a variable number of numeric and textual values. The similarity score S output parameter is set during the matching. Similarity predicates of this form were used in other similarity searching systems such as VAGUE [15] and others [1].

We further designate some similarity predicates as *joinable*:

Definition 3 (Joinable similarity predicate). *A similarity predicate is joinable iff it is not dependent on the set of query values remaining the same during a query execution, and can accept a query values set with exactly one value which may change from call to call.* ∎

Joinable similarity predicates can be used for both join and selection predicates, while non-joinable predicates can only be used as selection predicates.

Our system stores the meta-data related to similarity predicates in the table *SIM_PREDICATES(predicate_name, applicable_data_type, is_joinable).*

In queries with multiple similarity predicates, a *scoring rule* combines the individual scores of predicate matches, weighted by their relative importance, into a single score [16, 9]. We store the meta-data related to scoring rules in the table *SCORING_RULES(rule_name).*

Definition 4 (Scoring rule). *Given a list of scores $s_1, s_2, ..., s_n$, $s_i \in [0, 1]$, and a weight for each score $w_1, w_2, ..., w_n$ with $w_i \in [0, 1]$ and $\sum_i w_i = 1$, the* scoring rule function returns an overall score in the range $[0, 1]$. A scoring rule function has the form: scoring rule$(s_1, w_1, s_2, w_2, ..., s_n, w_n) \rightarrow [0, 1]^2$ ∎

In addition to the scoring rule and similarity predicate meta-data, we maintain several tables that keep operational data for the similarity predicates and scoring functions. For each similarity predicate (SP) in the query, we store the user supplied parameters, cutoff, score variable, and the attribute(s) and query values involved. The schema for this table is *QUERY_SP(predicate name, parameters, α, input attribute, query attribute, list of query values, score variable)*. For the scoring rule, we store the scoring rule (SR) used, and a list of output score variables and their corresponding weights. The schema for this table is *QUERY_SR(rule name, list of attribute scores, list of weights)*.

3 Query Refinement System

In this section, we describe our query refinement system. We built our system as a wrapper on top of a commercial database and support refinement over SQL queries. We support a minimally modified SQL syntax to express refinement. Figure 1 shows our system architecture, it shows a generic refinement algorithm which accepts specific similarity predicates, scoring rules and refinement algorithms as plug-ins. We now discuss this generic refinement algorithm and in section 4 present some specific refinement algorithms we use.

The users querying process starts with several tables, user-defined data-types, similarity predicates, and scoring rules, and proceeds as follows:

1. The user expresses her abstract *information need* as an SQL statement with a scoring rule and one or more similarity predicates over some tables. Figure 2 shows a query with two similarity predicates on table T.
2. The system executes the query and populates a temporary *answer* table with the results. Figure 2 shows this *answer* table.
3. The user incrementally browses the answers in rank order, i.e., the best results first. As the user sees the results, she can mark *entire tuples* or *individual attributes*[3] as good, bad, or neutral examples, this is recorded in a *feedback* table (figure 2). It is not necessary for the user to see all answers or to provide feedback for all answer tuples or attributes.
4. With the users feedback, the system generates a new query by modifying the scoring rule and similarity predicates and goes back to step 2, executes the new query and populates the *answer* table with the new results.
5. This process is repeated as desired.

To support query refinement the DBMS must maintain sufficient state information and provide supporting interfaces to query refinement functions, we now discuss these tables and functions.

---

[2] *In the implementation, we used arrays for the similarity scores and weights to accommodate the variable number of parameters to scoring rule functions.*

[3] When submitting feedback, our system offers two granularities: tuple and attribute (or column). In tuple level feedback the user selects entire tuples for feedback. In attribute level feedback, the user provides finer grained information, judging individual attributes.

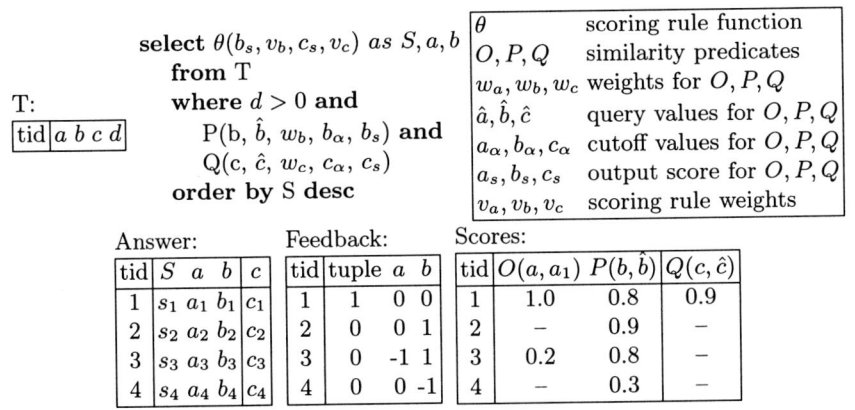

Fig. 2. Data Structure Example for Query Refinement – Single Table

Support Tables. To refine a query, all values of tuples where the user gave feedback judgments must be available, they are needed since refinement is guided by the values of relevant and non-relevant tuples. In some queries, maintaining this information may be complicated due to loss of source attributes in projections or joins where attributes may be eliminated. To enable query refinement, we must include sufficient information in the answer to recompute similarity scores. Therefore, we construct an *Answer* table as follows:

Algorithm 1 (Construction of temporary *Answer* table for a query) The *answer* table has the following attributes: (1) a tuple id (*tid*), (2) a similarity score S that is the result of evaluating the scoring rule, (3) all attributes requested in the select clause, and (4) a set H of hidden attributes. The set of hidden attributes is constructed as follows: for each similarity predicate (from the *SIM_PREDICATES* table) in the query, add to H all fully qualified[4] attribute(s) that appear and are not already in H or the attribute was requested in the query select clause. All attributes retain their original data-type. ∎

Results for the hidden attributes are not returned to the calling user or application. We also construct a *Feedback* table for the query as follows:

Algorithm 2 (Construction of temporary *Feedback* table for a query) The attributes for the *Feedback* table are: (1) the tuple id (tid), (2) a *tuple* attribute for overall tuple relevance, and (3) all attributes in the select clause of the query. All attributes are of type integer (except the tid). ∎

Example 4 (Answer and Feedback table construction). Figure 2 shows a table T, and a query that requests only the score S, and the attributes a and b. The query has similarity predicates P on b, and Q on c, so attributes b and c must be in H. But b is in the select clause, so only c is in H and becomes the only hidden attribute. The feedback table is constructed as described and contains the *tid*, *tuple*, *a*, and *b*

---
[4] Same attributes from different tables are listed individually.

Fig. 3. Data Structure Example for Query Refinement – Similarity Join

R:
tid	a	b	c

S:
tid	b	c	d

select $\theta(a_s, v_a, b_s, v_b)$ as S, a, d
from R, S
where $d > 0$ and
$\quad O(a, \hat{a}, w_a, a_\alpha, a_s)$ and
$\quad P(R.b, S.b, w_b, b_\alpha, b_s)$
order by S desc

θ	scoring rule function
O, P, U	similarity predicates
w_a, w_b	weights for O, P
$\hat{a}, \hat{b}$	query values for O, P
a_α, b_α	cutoff values for O, P
a_s, b_s	output score for O, P
v_a, v_b	scoring rule weights

Answer:
tid	S	a	d	⟨b⟩
1	s_1	a_1	d_1	$R.b_1, S.b_1$
2	s_2	a_2	d_2	$R.b_2, S.b_2$
3	s_3	a_3	d_3	$R.b_3, S.b_3$
4	s_4	a_4	d_4	$R.b_4, S.b_4$

Feedback:
tid	tuple	a	d
1	1	0	0
2	-1	0	0
3	1	0	0
4	0	-1	0

Scores:
tid	$O(a, \hat{a})$	$U(d, d_1)$	$P(R.b, S.b)$
1	0.7	0.9	0.8
2	0.8	0.5	0.7
3	0.3	0.4	0.6
4	0.6	--	--

attributes. A sample Feedback table[5] is shown with both tuple and attribute level feedback. Figure 3 shows Answer and Feedback tables when a join involves a similarity predicate. When constructing the Answer table, we do not include attribute a in H since it is listed in the select clause. We include two copies of attribute b in the set H since it comes from two different tables. The figure lists them together. The Feedback table is constructed as above and populated with sample data. The headings a_1 and d_1 will be explained later. ∎

We build an auxiliary *Scores* table that combines the user supplied feedback and the values from the answer table, and then populate the table:

Algorithm 3 (Construction of *Scores* table) The Scores table has the following attributes: (1) a tuple id (tid), (2) all attributes in the select clause, (3) all attributes in the hidden set H. If two attributes appear in a similarity join predicate, they are fused into a single attribute. All attributes except the tid are real valued in the range [0,1] or are undefined. The table is populated with the scores of values for which the user specifies feedback and whose attributes are involved in some similarity predicate in the query. For a pair of values such as in a join predicate, a single score results. Figure 4 shows the algorithm to populate the *Scores* table. ∎

Example 5 (Scores table). Figs. 2 and 3 show corresponding *Scores* tables. ∎

4 Query Refinement Strategies

Our query refinement system supports an interface for refinement algorithms paired to their corresponding similarity predicates, here we present several specific strategies for query refinement we have implemented. Query refinement is

---
[5] It is not necessary for the user to give feedback for all tuples in the answer set despite what is shown here.

```
——for-all tuples t in Feedback table
— —for-all attributes x in t
— —if ((t.x ≠ 0) ∨ (t.tuple ≠ 0) ∧ ∃ predicate Z on x
— —// there is non-neutral feedback on attribute x
— —Scores table [tid = t.tid, attribute = x] =
— —Z(Answer table [tid = t.tid, attribute = x]) —
—// recreate detailed scores
```

Fig. 4. *Scores* Table Computation

achieved by modifying queries in three ways: (1) changing the interpretation and weights of scoring rules that connect predicates together (inter-predicate refinement), (2) adding or removing predicates to the scoring rule (inter-predicate refinement), and (3) changing the interpretation of the user-defined domain-specific similarity predicate functions (intra-predicate refinement). Many different refinement implementations are possible, here we only present some of those that we implemented.

The scores of the several predicates in the query condition are combined via weights and a scoring rule function denoted by θ in figures 2 and 3. The techniques discussed here are possible implementations for the scoring rule refinement function discussed in section 3.

The goal of inter-predicate refinement via query re-weighting is to find the optimal relative weights among different predicates used in the scoring rule. Let $p_1, p_2, ..., p_n$ be similarity predicates, $s_1, s_2, ..., s_n$ their similarity scores, and $v_1^{opt}, v_2^{opt}, ..., v_n^{opt}$ the weights used in the scoring rule θ of a query, such that $\theta(s_1, v_1^{opt}, s_2, v_2^{opt}, ..., s_n, v_n^{opt})$ captures the user's notion of similarity of a tuple to the users query. Let $v_1^0, v_2^0, ..., v_n^0$ be the initial weights associated with the scoring rule (for simplicity start with equal weights for all predicates). Reweighting modifies these weights based on the user's feedback to converge them to the optimal weights: $\lim_{k \rightarrow \infty} v_i^k = v_i^{opt}$. For each predicate, the new weight is computed based on the similarity score of all attribute values for which relevance judgments exist. In section 3 we described how a *Scores* table is derived from the answer table and the feedback values. Using this information we develop two strategies:

- *Minimum Weight:* use the minimum relevant similarity score for the predicate as the new weight. When the new weight is high, all relevant values are scored high, and the predicate is a good predictor of the users need. A low weight indicates the low predictive importance of the predicate. Following figure 2, the new weight for $P(b)$ is: $v_b = \min_{i \in relevant(b)}(P(b_i)) = \min(0.8, 0.9, 0.8) = 0.8$, similarly, $v_c = 0.9$. Non-relevant judgments are ignored.
- *Average Weight:* use the average of relevant minus non-relevant scores as the new weight. Here, the score of all relevant and non-relevant values is considered, therefore this strategy is more sensitive to the distribution of scores among relevant and non-relevant values. Generically, for attribute x and predicate X, we use $v_x = \max(0, \frac{\sum_{x_i \in relevant(x)} X(x_i) - \sum_{x_j \in non-relevant(x)} X(x_j)}{|relevant(x)| + |non-relevant(x)|})$.

We use max to ensure that $v_x \geq 0$. Following figure 2, the new weight for $P(b)$ is: $v_b = \frac{\sum_{b_i \in relevant(b)} P(b_i) - \sum_{b_j \in non-relevant(b)} P(b_j)}{|relevant(b)| + |non-relevant(b)|} = \frac{0.8+0.9+0.8-0.3}{3+1} = 0.55$, similarly, $v_c = 0.9$.

In both strategies, if there are no relevance judgments for any objects involving a predicate, then the original weight is preserved as the new weight. These strategies also apply to predicates used as a join condition.

Once the new weights are computed, they are normalized, and their values updated in the QUERY_SR table.

The inter-predicate selection policy adds predicates to or removes them from the query and scoring rule. Users may submit coarse initial queries with only a few predicates, therefore supporting the addition of predicates to a query is important. In figure 2, attribute a was ranked relevant for tuple 1 (since the tuple is relevant overall), and non-relevant for tuple 3. This suggests there might be merit in adding a predicate on attribute a to the query and adding it to the scoring rule. We now discuss if and how this can be achieved.

Intuitively, we must be conservative when adding a new predicate to the query as it may significantly increase the cost of computing the answers, and may not reflect the users intentions. For these reasons, when adding a predicate, it must be (1) added with a small initial weight in the scoring rule to keep the addition from significantly disrupting the ranking of tuples, and (2) have a very low cutoff since before the addition the effective predicate on the attribute was *true* thus returning all values and therefore equivalent to a cutoff of 0.

To add a predicate on an attribute to the query, a suitable predicate must be found that applies to the given data-type, fits good the given feedback, and has sufficient support. Our algorithm for predicate addition is as follows: Based on the SIM_PREDICATES table, a list of similarity predicates that apply to the data-type of attribute a is constructed, this list is denoted by $applies(a)$. The *Answer* table is explored to find the highest ranked tuple that contains positive feedback on attribute a and take a's value. In figure 2, this value is a_1. This value (a_1) becomes the plausible query point for the new predicate. Next, we iterate through all predicates in the list $applies(a)$, and for each value of attribute a in the *Answer* table that has non-neutral feedback, we evaluate its score using a_1 as the query value, and set the score in the *Scores* table. The weights for the predicate are the default weights, and the cutoff value is 0. Say predicate $O(a, a_1, ...) \in applies(a)$ is under test. Under the *Scores* table in figure 2, $O(a_1) = 1.0$ and $O(a_3) = 0.2$ where a_1 is relevant and a_3 is not relevant. A predicate has a good fit if the average of the relevant scores is higher than the average of the non-relevant scores. In this case, this is true. In addition to this good fit, to justify the added cost of a predicate, we require that there be sufficient support. Sufficient support is present if there is significant difference between the average of relevant and non-relevant scores; this difference should be at least as large as the sum of one standard deviation among relevant scores and one standard deviation among non-relevant scores. If there are not enough scores to meaningfully compute such standard deviation, we empirically choose a default value of one standard deviation of 0.2. In this example thus, the default standard deviations for relevant and non-relevant scores add up to $0.2+0.2 = 0.4$ and since $average(relevant) - average(non-relevant) = 1.0 - 0.2 = 0.8 > 0.4$ then we decide that predicate $O(a)$ is a good fit and has sufficient support (i.e., separation) and is therefore a candidate to being added to the query. We choose $O(a, a_1, ...)$ over other predicates in $applies(a)$ if the separation among the averages is the largest among all predicates in $applies(a)$.

The new predicate $O(a, a_1, ...)$ is added to the query tree and to the scoring rule with a weight equal to one half of its fair share, i.e., $1/(2 \times |$ *predicates in scoring rule* $|)$. We do this to compensate for the fact that we are introducing a predicate not initially specified and do not want to greatly disrupt the ranking. If there were four predicates before adding O, then O is the fifth predicate and its fair share would be 0.2, we set a weight of $0.2/2 = 0.1$, and re-normalize all the weights in the scoring rule so that they add up to 1 as described above, and update the QUERY_SR table appropriately.

Predicate Deletion. A predicate is eliminated from the query and scoring rule function if its weight in the scoring rule falls below a threshold during re-weighting since its contribution becomes negligible, the remaining weights are re-normalized to add up to 1. For example, if we use *average weight* re-weighting in figure 3, then the new weight for attribute a is: $\max(0, \frac{(0.7+0.3)-(0.8+0.6)}{2+2}) = \max(0, -0.1) = 0$. Therefore, predicate $O(a, \hat{a})$ is removed.

In intra-predicate refinement, the similarity predicates are modified in several ways. Predicates, in addition to a single query point (value), may use a number of points as a query region, possibly with its own private, attribute-specific scoring rule function [17]. The refinement task is to use the provided feedback to update the query points, parameters, and cutoff values in the QUERY_SP table, to better reflect the users intentions.

Intra-predicate refinement is by its very nature *domain dependent*, hence each user-defined type specifies its own *scoring* and *refinement* functions to operate on objects of that type. We present some strategies in the context of a 2D geographic *location* data-type (cf. *close-to* in example 3). In the context of figure 2, let attribute b be of type *location*, and P be the *close_to* function, then we invoke the corresponding refinement function $close\_to\_refine(\{b_1, b_2, b_3, b_4\}, \{1, 1, 1, -1\})$, with the list of b values for which the user gave feedback and the corresponding feedback. The following approaches are used for this type:[6]

- **Query Weight Re-balancing** adjusts the weights for individual dimensions to better fit the users feedback. The new weight for each dimension of the query vector is proportional to the importance of the dimension, i.e., low variance among relevant values indicates the dimension is important [12, 19]. If $b_1.x$, $b_2.x$, and $b_3.x$ are similar (i.e., small variance), and $b_1.y$, $b_2.y$, and $b_3.y$ are different (i.e., larger variance), we infer that the x dimension captures the users intention better, and set $w_x = \frac{1}{std\ dev(b_x)}$ and $w_y = \frac{1}{std\ dev(b_y)}$, and then re-normalize the weights such that $w_x + w_y = 1$.

---

[6] Note that this discussion uses distance functions rather than similarity functions since it is more natural to visualize the distance between points than their similarity; distance can easily be converted to a similarity value.

- **Cutoff Value Determination**, since this setting does not affect the result ranking, we leave this at 0 for our experiments, but one useful strategy is to set it to the lowest relevant score.
- **Query Point Selection** computes a new point or set of points as query values that is/are closer to relevant and away from non-relevant objects. Notice that query point selection relies on the query values remaining stable during an iteration and is therefore suited only for predicates that are not involved in a join, or predicates that are not joinable (cf. definition 3). Two ways to compute new query points are:
  - *Query Point Movement* uses a single value or point per predicate as the query, and we use Rocchios method for vector space models [18, 19] for refinement. The query value $\hat{b}$ migrates to $\hat{b}'$ by the formula (Rocchio) $\hat{b}' = \alpha \times \hat{b} + \beta \times \frac{\sum(b_1,b_2,b_3)}{3} - \gamma \times \frac{\sum(b_4)}{1}$, $\alpha+\beta+\gamma = 1$ where α, β, and γ are constants that regulate the speed at which the query point moves towards relevant values and away from non-relevant values.
  - *Query Expansion* uses multiple values per attribute as a *multi-point query* [17, 21], multiple points are combined with a scoring rule λ. Good representative points are constructed by clustering the relevant points and choosing the cluster centroids as the new set of query points, this can increase or decrease the number of points over the previous iteration. Any clustering method may be used such as the *k-means* algorithm, as well as the technique presented in FALCON [21] which we also implemented in our system.

This set of intra-predicate refinement techniques provides for rich flexibility in adapting predicates to the users intentions. These techniques may be used individually, or combined to effect single-attribute predicate changes. Specific datatypes may have specially designed similarity predicates and refinement functions that achieve refinement in a different way, but as long as they follow the established interface, they can be seamlessly incorporated into our system.

5 Experiments

Similarity retrieval and query refinement represent a significant departure from the existing access paradigm (based on precise SQL semantics) supported by current databases. Our purpose in this section is to show some experimental results, and illustrate that the proposed access mechanism can benefit realistic database application domains.

We built our prototype system as a wrapper on top of the Informix Universal Server ORDBMS. We place our system in-between the user and the DBMS as shown in figure 1. We handle user queries, analyze and rework them, and forward relevant queries and data to the DBMS for query execution. The client application navigates through the results, starting with the best ranked ones, and submits feedback for some or all tuples seen so far. The client can stop at any time, refine and re-execute the updated query.

We study our systems various components, and present a realistic sample e-commerce catalog search application to validate the approach.

5.1 Evaluation Methodology

To evaluate the quality of retrieval we establish a baseline ground truth set of relevant tuples. This ground truth can be defined objectively, or subjectively by a human users perception. When defined subjectively, the ground truth captures the users information need and links the human perception into the query answering loop. In our experiments we establish a ground truth and then measure the retrieval quality with precision and recall [4]. Precision is the ratio of the number of relevant tuples retrieved to the total number of retrieved tuples: $precision = \frac{|relevant \cap retrieved|}{|retrieved|}$, while recall is the ratio of the number of relevant tuples retrieved to the total number of relevant tuples: $recall = \frac{|relevant \cap retrieved|}{|relevant|}$. We compute precision and recall after each tuple is returned by our system in rank order.

The effectiveness of refinement is tied to the convergence of the results to the users information need. Careful studies of convergence have been done in the past in restricted domains, e.g., Rocchio [18] for text retrieval, MARS [19, 17], Mindreader [12], and FeedbackBypass [5] for image retrieval, and FALCON [21] for metric functions. We believe (and our experiments will show) that these convergence experiments carry over to the more general SQL context in which we are exploring refinement.

5.2 Experimental Results

For these experiments, we used two datasets. One is the fixed source air pollution dataset from the AIRS[7] system of the EPA and contains 51,801 tuples with geographic location and emissions of 7 pollutants (carbon monoxide, nitrogen oxide, particulate less than 2.5 and 10 micrometers, sulfur dioxide, ammonia, and volatile organic compounds). The second dataset is the US census data with geographic location at the granularity of one zip code, population, average and median household income, and contains 29470 tuples. We used several similarity predicates and refinement algorithms.

For the first experiment we implemented a similarity predicate and refinement algorithm based on FALCON [21] for geographic locations, and a query point movement and dimension re-weighting for the pollution vector of the EPA dataset. We started with a conceptual query looking for a specific pollution profile in the state of Florida. We executed the desired query and noted the first 50 tuple as the ground truth. Next, we formulated this query in 5 different ways, similar to what a user would do, retrieved only the top 100 tuples, and submitted tuple level feedback for those retrieved tuples that are also in the ground truth. Here we performed 5 iterations of refinement. Figure 5a) shows the results of using only the location based predicate, without allowing predicate addition. Similarly figure 5b) shows the result of using only the pollution profile, without allowing predicate addition. Note that in these queries feedback was of little use in spite of several feedback iterations. In figure 5c) we instead used both

---

[7] http://www.epa.gov/airs

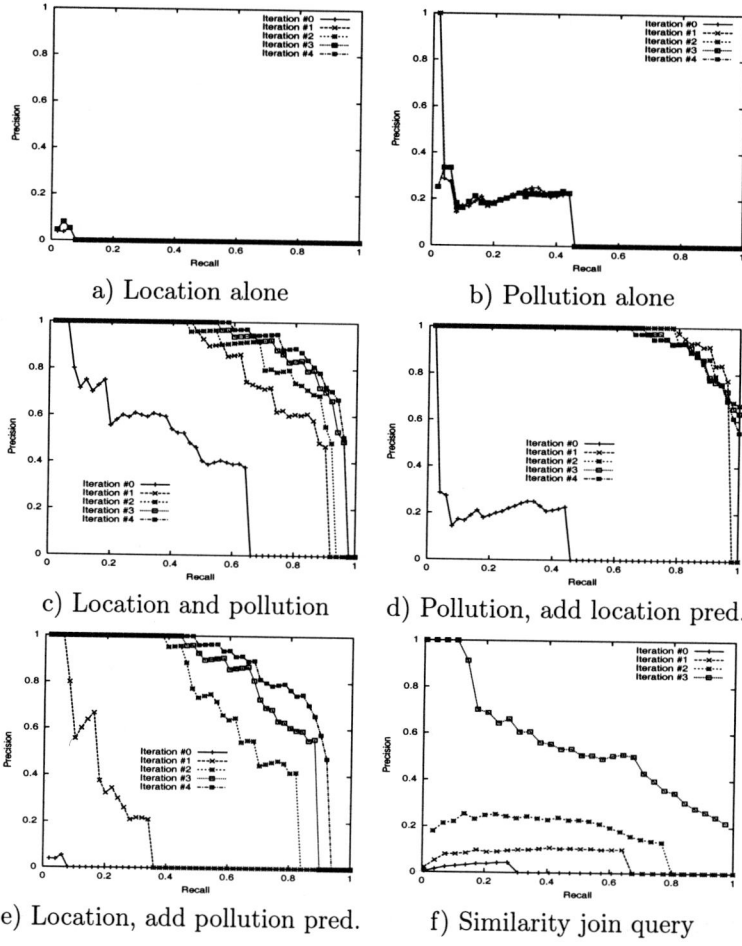

Fig. 5. Precision–recall graphs for several iterations, and refinement strategies

predicates but with the default weights and parameters, notice how the query slowly improves. Figure 5d) starts the query with the pollution profile only, but allowing predicate addition. The predicate on location is added after the first iteration resulting in much better results. Similarly figure 5e) starts only with the location predicate. The initial query execution yields very low results, but the pollution predicate is added after the initial query resulting in a marked improvement. In the next iteration, the scoring rule better adapts to the intended query which results in another high jump in retrieval quality. It is sufficient to provide feedback on only a few tuples, e.g., in this query, only 3 tuples were submitted for feedback after the initial query, and 14 after the first iteration. The number of tuples with feedback was similarly low (5%-20%) in the other queries.

In the second experiment, we use a join query over the EPA and census datasets. Notice that we cannot use the location similarity predicate from the first experiment since the FALCON [21] based similarity predicate is not joinable. This is because it relies on a set of "good points" which must remain the same over the execution of a query iteration. If we change the set of good points to a single point from the joining table in each call, then this measure degenerates to simple Euclidean distance and the refinement algorithm does not work. Figure 5f) shows the results of a query where the census and EPA datasets are joined by location, and we're interested in a pollution level of 500 tons per year of particles 10 micrometers or smaller in areas with average household income of around $50,000. We constructed the ground truth with a query that expressed this desire and then started from default parameters and query values.

5.3 Sample E-Commerce Application

To illustrate a realistic application, we built a sample E-commerce application on top of our query refinement system. We felt that the flexibility and power offered by similarity retrieval and refinement is naturally more useful in tasks involving exploratory data analysis in which users are not initially sure of their exact information need. One such application domain is searching product catalogs over the Internet. We develop a sample catalog search application in the context of garment searching. We explore how the granularity (i.e., tuple vs. column level feedback) and the amount of feedback affect the quality of results. We emphasize that searching e-tailer catalogs represents only a single point in a wide array of application domains which can benefit from similarity retrieval and refinement. Other natural application domains include bioinformatics and geographic information systems.

E-Commerce Prototype Implementation. To build our sample garment catalog search application, we collected from various apparel web sites[8] 1747 garment item descriptions of a variety of garment types including pants, shirts, jackets, and dresses. For each item, we collected its manufacturer, type (e.g., shirt, jacket, etc.), a short and long description, price, gender (male, female, unisex), colors and sizes available, and a picture of the garment itself. We also built a Java based front end user interface for the garment search application that lets users browse, construct queries and refine answers.

Each data-type has its own similarity function implemented as a user-defined function (UDF). The similarity for textual data is implemented by a text vector model [4] and is used for the manufacturer, type, and short and long description attributes. The similarity function for the price attribute is: $sim_{price}(p_1, p_2) = 1 - \frac{|p_1 - p_2|}{6 \times \sigma(p)}$.[9] The Image is represented through multiple attributes: the image is stored as a blob itself, a small thumbnail image is also stored as a blob, and two image derived features that are used for content-based image retrieval [16, 19].

---

[8] Sources: JCrew, Eddie Bauer, Landsend, Polo, Altrec, Bluefly, and REI.
[9] This assumes that prices are distributed as a Gaussian sequence, and suitably normalized.

The features used are for color the color histogram [16] feature with a histogram intersection similarity function, and for texture the coocurrence matrix texture feature with an Euclidean distance based similarity function [16]. The remaining attributes of the garment data set were not used for search. The similarity values of the data-type specific similarity functions are combined with a weighted linear combination (weighted summation) scoring rule function.

To complement the similarity and scoring functions for retrieval, we implemented refinement algorithms for each similarity predicate, and across predicates. We used Rocchios text vector model relevance feedback algorithm [18] for the textual data. For the price, color histogram and coocurrence texture attributes we use re-weighting, and query point movement and expansion as described in section 4 [19, 17].

Example Query. We explore our system through the following conceptual query: "men's red jacket at around $150.00". We browsed the entire collection and constructed a set of relevant results (ground truth) for the query, we found 10 items out of 1747 to be relevant and included them in the ground truth. Several ways exist to express this query, we try the following:

1. Free text search of *type, short* and *long description* for "men's red jacket at around $150.00".
2. Free text search of *type* with "red jacket at around $150.00" and *gender* as male.
3. Free text search of *type* with "red jacket", *gender* as male, and *price* around $150.00.
4. Free text search of *type* with "red jacket", *gender* as male, *price* around $150.00, and pick a picture of a red jacket which will include the image features for search.

We ran all four queries with feedback and evaluate the effectiveness of refinement comparing tuple versus column level feedback using precision and recall.

Effect of Feedback Granularity on Refinement Quality. Our framework provides for two granularities of feedback: tuple and column level. In tuple level feedback the user judges the tuple as a whole, while in column level she judges individual attributes of a tuple. Column level feedback presents a higher burden on the user, but can result in better refinement quality. This is shown in figures 6a) which shows tuple level feedback and 6b) which shows column level feedback. For these figures we used 4 different queries with their ground truth, gave feedback on exactly 2 tuples and averaged the results. For tuple level feedback, 2 entire tuples were selected, for column level feedback, we chose only the relevant attributes within the tuples and judged those. As expected, column level feedback produces better results.

Effect of Amount of Feedback Judgments on Refinement Quality. While in general the refinement system adapts better to the users information need when it receives more relevance judgments, in practice this is burdensome to users. The amount of feedback may vary from user to user; here we explore how the amount of feedback affects the retrieval quality. Empirically, even a few feedback judgments can improve query results substantially. We explore the same 4 queries from above and give tuple level feedback for 2, 4 and 8 tuples. The results are shown in figures 6a,c,d) respectively. More feedback improves the results, but with diminishing returns, in fact column level feedback for 2 tuples

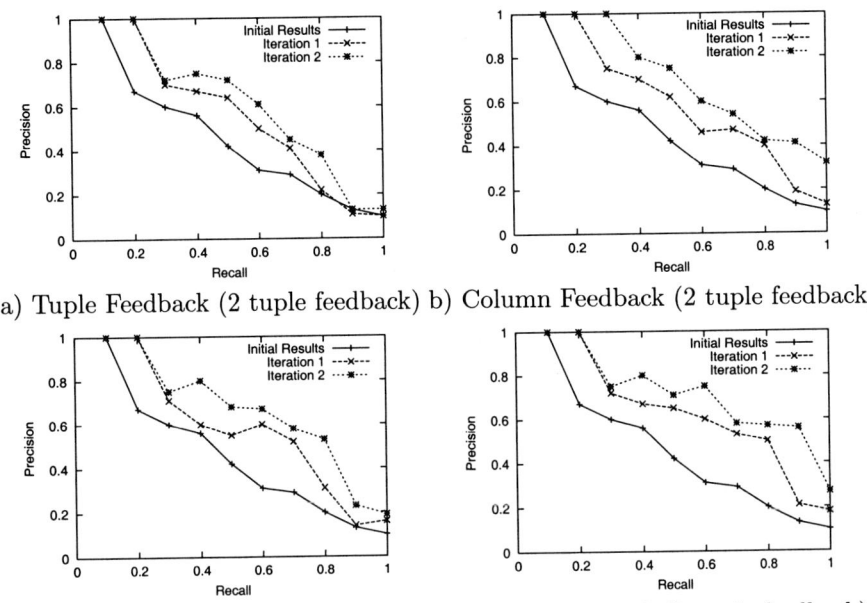

Fig. 6. Precision–recall graphs averaged for 5 queries for different amount and granularity of feedback

is competitive with tuple level feedback for 8 tuples. Based on this, we conclude that users need not expend a huge effort in feedback to improve their answers.

6 Related Work

While there is much research on improving the effectiveness of queries in specific applications, we are not aware of work that addresses generalized query refinement in general purpose SQL databases.

Traditionally, similarity retrieval and relevance feedback have been studied for textual data in the IR [4] community and have recently been generalized to other domains. IR models have been generalized to multimedia documents, e.g., image retrieval [19, 16, 10] uses image features to capture aspects of the image content, and provide searching. Techniques to incorporate similarity retrieval in databases have also been considered for text and multimedia [11, 1], but generally do not consider query refinement.

Query refinement through relevance feedback has been studied extensively in the IR literature [4, 18] and has recently been explored in multimedia domains, e.g., for image retrieval by Mindreader [12], MARS [19, 17], and Photobook [14], among others. FALCON [21] uses a multi-point example approach similar to MARS [17] and generalizes it to any suitably defined metric distance function, regardless of the native space. FALCON assumes that all examples are drawn from the same domain and does not handle multiple independent attributes. Under our framework, we consider FALCON as a non-joinable algorithm since it is dependent on the good set of points remaining constant during a query iteration. FALCON however fits perfectly in our framework as an intra-predicate algorithm for selection queries as we discussed in section 4 and showed in our experiments. Given the applicability of refinement to textual and multimedia data, our paper takes the next step, extending refinement to general SQL queries.

Cooperative databases seek to assist the user to find the desired information through interaction. VAGUE [15], in addition to adding distance functions to relational queries, helps the user pose imprecise queries. The Eureka [20] browser is a user interface that lets users interactively manipulate the conditions of a query with instantly update the results. The goal of the CoBase [8] cooperative database system is to avoid empty answers to queries through condition relaxation. Agrawal [2] proposes a framework where users submit preferences (feedback) and explains how they may be composed into compound preferences.

7 Conclusions

In this paper, we concentrated on developing a data access model based on similarity retrieval and query refinement. We presented a framework to integrate similarity functions and query refinement in SQL databases, and presented several specific refinement strategies along with experiments to validate our approach.

References

1. S. Adali, P. Bonatti, M. L. Sapino, and V. S. Subrahmanian. A multi-similarity algebra. In *Proc. ACM SIGMOD98*, pages 402–413, 1998.
2. Rakesh Agrawal and Edward L. Wimmers. A framework for expressing and combining preferences. In *ACM SIGMOD*, 2000.
3. G. Amato, F. Rabitti, and P.Savino. Multimedia document search on the web. In *7th Int. World Wide Web Conference (WWW7)*.
4. Ricardo Baeza-Yates and Ribeiro-Neto. *Modern Information Retrieval*. ACM Press Series/Addison Wesley, New York, May 1999.
5. Ilaria Bartolini, Paolo Ciaccia, and Florian Waas. Feedback bypass: A new approach to interactive similarity query processing. In *27th Very Large Databases (VLDB)*, Rome, Italy, September 2001.
6. J. P. Callan, W. B. Croft, and S. M. Harding. The inquery retrieval system. In *In Proceedings of the Third International Conference on Database and Expert Systems Applications*, Valencia, Spain, 1992.
7. Shih-Fu Chang and john R. Smith. Finding images/video in large archives. *D-Lib Magazine*, 1997.
8. Wesley W. Chu et al. CoBase: A Scalable and Extensible Cooperative Information System. *Journal of Intelligent Information Systems*, 6, 1996.
9. Ronald Fagin and Edward L. Wimmers. Incorporating user preferences in multimedia queries. In *Proc of Int. Conf. on Database Theory*, 1997.

10. M. Flickner, Harpreet Sawhney, Wayne Niblack, and Jonathan Ashley. Query by Image and Video Content: The QBIC System. *IEEE Computer*, 28(9):23–32, September 1995.
11. Norbert Fuhr. Logical and conceptual models for the integration of information retrieval and database systems. 1996.
12. Yoshiharu Ishikawa, Ravishankar Subramanya, and Christos Faloutsos. Mindreader: Querying databases through multiple examples. In *Int'l Conf. on Very Large Data Bases*, 1998.
13. Carlo Meghini. *Fourth DELOS Workshop – Image Indexing and Retrieval*. ERCIM Report, San Miniato, Pisa, Italy, August 1997.
14. T. P. Minka and R. W. Picard. Interactive learning using a "society of models". Technical Report 349, MIT Media Lab, 1996.
15. Amihai Motro. VAGUE: A user interface to relational databases that permits vague queries. *ACM TOIS*, 6(3):187–214, July 1988.
16. Michael Ortega, Yong Rui, Kaushik Chakrabarti, Kriengkrai Porkaew, Sharad Mehrotra, , and Thomas S. Huang. Supporting ranked boolean similarity queries in mars. *IEEE Trans. on Data Engineering*, 10(6), December 1998.
17. Kriengkrai Porkaew, Sharad Mehrotra, Michael Ortega, and Kaushik Chakrabarti. Similarity search using multiple examples in mars. In *Proc. Visual'99*, June 1999.
18. J.J. Rocchio. Relevance feedback in information retrieval. In Gerard Salton, editor, *The SMART Retrieval System*, pages 313–323. Prentice–Hall, Englewood NJ, 1971.
19. Yong Rui, Thomas S. Huang, Michael Ortega, and Sharad Mehrotra. Relevance feedback: A power tool for interactive content-based image retrieval. *IEEE CSVT*, September 1998.
20. John C. Shafer and Rakesh Agrawal. Continuous querying in database-centric web applications. In *WWW9 conference*, Amsterdam, Netherlands, May 2000.
21. L. Wu, C. Faloutsos, K. Sycara, and T. Payne. FALCON: Feedback adaptive loop for content-based retrieval. *Proceedings of VLDB Conference*, 2000.

Querying with Intrinsic Preferences

Jan Chomicki

Dept. of Computer Science and Engineering, University at Buffalo, Buffalo, NY
14260-2000, chomicki@cse.buffalo.edu

Abstract. The handling of user preferences is becoming an increasingly important issue in present-day information systems. Among others, preferences are used for *information filtering and extraction* to reduce the volume of data presented to the user. They are also used to keep track of *user profiles* and formulate *policies* to improve and automate decision making. We propose a logical framework for formulating preferences and its embedding into relational query languages. The framework is simple, and entirely neutral with respect to the properties of preferences. It makes it possible to formulate different kinds of preferences and to use preferences in querying databases. We demonstrate the usefulness of the framework through numerous examples.

1 Introduction

The handling of user preferences is becoming an increasingly important issue in present-day information systems. Among others, preferences are used for *information filtering and extraction* to reduce the volume of data presented to the user. They are also used to keep track of *user profiles* and formulate *policies* to improve and automate decision making.

The research literature on preferences is extensive. It encompasses preference logics [23, 19, 13], preference reasoning [24, 22, 4], prioritized nonmonotonic reasoning and logic programming [5, 6, 21] and decision theory [7, 8] (the list is by no means exhaustive). However, only a few papers [18, 3, 11, 2, 14, 17] address the issue of user preferences in the context of database queries. Two different approaches are pursued: qualitative and quantitative. In the *qualitative* approach [18, 3, 11, 17], the preferences between tuples in the answer to a query are specified directly, typically using binary *preference relations*.

Example 1. We introduce here one of the examples used throughout the paper. Consider the relation $Book(ISBN, Vendor, Price)$ and the following preference relation $\succ_1$ between $Book$ tuples:

> if two tuples have the same ISBN and different Price, prefer the one with the lower Price.

Consider the following instance r_1 of *Book*

ISBN	Vendor	Price
0679726691	BooksForLess	$14.75
0679726691	LowestPrices	$13.50
0679726691	QualityBooks	$18.80
0062059041	BooksForLess	$7.30
0374164770	LowestPrices	$21.88

Then clearly the second tuple is preferred to the first one which in turn is preferred to the third one. There is no preference defined between any of those three tuples and the remaining tuples.

In the *quantitative* approach [2, 14], preferences are specified indirectly using *scoring functions* that associate a numeric score with every tuple of the query answer. Then a tuple $\bar{t}_1$ is preferred to a tuple $\bar{t}_2$ iff the score of $\bar{t}_1$ is higher than the score of $\bar{t}_2$. The qualitative approach is strictly more general than the quantitative one, since one can define preference relations in terms of scoring functions (if the latter are explicitly given), while not every intuitively plausible preference relation can be captured by scoring functions.

Example 2. There is no scoring function that captures the preference relation described in Example 1. Since there is no preference defined between any of the first three tuples and the fourth one, the score of the fourth tuple should be equal to all of the scores of the first three tuples. But this implies that the scores of the first three tuples are the same, which is not possible since the second tuple is preferred to the first one which in turn is preferred to the third one.

This lack of expressiveness of the quantitative approach is well known in utility theory [7, 8].

In the present paper, we contribute to the qualitative approach by defining a logical framework for formulating preferences and its embedding into relational query languages.

We believe that combining preferences with queries is very natural and useful. The applications in which user preferences are prominent will benefit from applying the modern database technology. For example, in decision-making applications databases may be used to store the space of possible configurations. Also, the use of a full-fledged query language makes it possible to formulate complex decision problems, a feature missing from most previous, non-database, approaches to preferences. For example, the formulation of the problem may now involve quantifiers, grouping, or aggregation. At the same time by explicitly addressing the technical issues involved in querying with preferences present-day DBMS may expand their scope.

The framework presented in this paper consists of two parts: a formal first-order logic notation for specifying preferences and an embedding of preferences into relational query languages. In this way both abstract properties of preferences (like asymmetry or transitivity) and evaluation of preference queries can be studied to a large degree separately.

Preferences are defined using binary *preference relations* between tuples. Preference relations are specified using first-order formulas. We focus mostly on *intrinsic* preference formulas. Such formulas can refer only to built-in predicates. In that way we capture preferences that are based only on the values occuring in tuples, not on other properties like membership of tuples in database relations. We show how the latter kind of preferences, called *extrinsic*, can also be simulated in our framework in some cases.

We propose a new relational algebra operator called *winnow* that selects from its argument relation the *most preferred tuples* according to the given preference relation. Although the winnow operator can be expressed using other operators of relational algebra, by considering it on its own we can on one hand focus on the abstract properties of preference relations (e.g., transitivity) and on the other, study special evaluation and optimization techniques for the winnow operator itself. The winnow operator can also be expressed in SQL.

We want to capture many different varieties of preference and related notions: *unconditional* vs. *conditional* preferences, *nested* and *hierarchical* preferences, *groupwise* preferences, *indifference*, *iterated* preferences and *ranking*, and *integrity constraints* and *vetoes*.

In Section 2, we define the basic concepts of preference relation, preference formula, and the winnow operator. In Section 3, we study the basic properties of the above concepts. In Section 4, we explore the composition of preferences. In Section 5, we show how the winnow operator together with other operators of relational algebra makes it possible to express integrity constraints and extrinsic preferences. In Section 6, we show how iterating the winnow operator provides a ranking of tuples and introduce a weak version of the winnow operator that is helpful for non-asymmetric preference relations. We discuss related work in Section 7 and conclude with a brief discussion of further work in Section 8.

2   Basic Notions

We are working in the context of the relational model of data. We assume two infinite domains: D (uninterpreted constants) and N (numbers). We do not distinguish between different numeric domains, since it is not necessary for the present paper. We assume that database instances are finite (this is important). Additionally, we have the standard built-in predicates. In the paper, we will move freely between relational algebra and SQL.

2.1   Basic Definitions

Preference formulas are used to define binary preference relations.

Definition 1. *Given $U = (U_1, \ldots, U_k)$ such that U_i, $1 \leq i \leq k$, is either D or N, a relation $\succ$ is a preference relation over U if it is a subset of $(U_1 \times \cdots \times U_k) \times (U_1 \times \cdots \times U_k)$.*

Intuitively, $\succ$ will be a binary relation between pairs of tuples from the same (database) relation. We say that a tuple $\bar{t}_1$ *dominates* a tuple $\bar{t}_2$ in $\succ$ if $\bar{t}_1 \succ \bar{t}_2$.

Typical properties of the relation $\succ$ include:

- *irreflexivity:* $\forall x. x \not\succ x$,
- *asymmetry:* $\forall x, y. x \succ y \Rightarrow y \not\succ x$,
- *transitivity:* $\forall x, y, z. (x \succ y \land y \succ z) \Rightarrow x \succ z$.

The relation $\succ$ is a *strict partial order* if it is irreflexive, asymmetric and transitive. At this point, we do not assume any properties of $\succ$, although in most applications it will be at least a strict partial order.

Definition 2. *A* preference formula (pf) $C(\bar{t}_1, \bar{t}_2)$ *is a first-order formula defining a preference relation $\succ$ in the standard sense, namely*

$$\bar{t}_1 \succ \bar{t}_2 \text{ iff } C(\bar{t}_1, \bar{t}_2).$$

An intrinsic preference formula (ipf) *is a preference formula that uses only built-in predicates.*

Ipfs can refer to equality ($=$) and inequality ($\neq$) when comparing values that are uninterpreted constants, and to the standard set of built-in arithmetic comparison operators when referring to numeric values (there no function symbols). We will call an ipf that references only arithmetic comparisons ($=, \neq, <, >, \leq, \geq$) *arithmetical*. Without loss of generality, we will assume that ipfs are in DNF (Disjunctive Normal Form) and quantifier-free (the theories involving the above predicates admit quantifier elimination).

In this paper, we mostly restrict ourselves to ipfs and preference relations defined by such formulas. The main reason is that ipfs define *fixed*, although possibly, infinite relations. As a result, they are computationally easier and more amenable to syntactic manipulation that general pfs. For instance, transitively closing an ipf results in a finite formula (Theorem 4), which is typically not the case for pfs. However, we formulate in full generality the results that hold for arbitrary pfs.

We define now an algebraic operator that picks from a given relation the set of the *most preferred tuples*, according to a given preference formula.

Definition 3. *If R is a relation schema and C a preference formula defining a preference relation $\succ$ over R, then the* winnow operator *is written as $\omega_C(R)$, and for every instance r of R:*

$$\omega_C(r) = \{\bar{t} \in r \mid \neg \exists \bar{t}' \in r.\ \bar{t}' \succ \bar{t}\}.$$

A preference query is a relational algebra query containing at least one occurrence of the winnow operator.

2.2 Examples

The first example illustrates how preference queries are applied to *information extraction*: here obtaining the best price of a given book.

Example 3. Consider the relation $Book(ISBN, Vendor, Price)$ from Example 1. The preference relation $\succ_1$ from this example can be defined using the formula C_1:

$$(i, v, p) \succ_1 (i', v', p') \equiv i = i' \wedge p < p'.$$

The answer to the preference query $\omega_{C_1}(Book)$ provides for every book the information about the vendors offering the lowest price for that book. For the given instance r_1 of $Book$, applying the winnow operator ω_{C_1} returns the tuples

ISBN	Vendor	Price
0679726691	LowestPrices	$13.50
0062059041	BooksForLess	$7.30
0374164770	LowestPrices	$21.88

Note that in the above example, the preferences are applied *groupwise*: separately for each book. Note also that due to the properties of $<$, the preference relation $\succ_1$ is irreflexive, asymmetric and transitive.

The second example illustrates how preference queries are used in *automated decision making* to obtain the most desirable solution to a (very simple) configuration problem.

Example 4. Consider two relations $Wine(Name, Type)$ and $Dish(Name, Type)$ and a view $Meal$ that contains possible meal configurations

CREATE VIEW Meal(Dish,DishType,Wine,WineType) AS
  SELECT * FROM Wine, Dish;

Now the preference for white wine in the presence of fish and for red wine in the presence of meat can be expressed as the following preference formula C_2 over $Meal$:

$$\begin{aligned}(d, dt, w, wt) \succ_2 (d', dt', w', wt') \equiv &\; (d = d' \wedge dt = \text{'fish'} \wedge wt = \text{'white'} \\ &\wedge dt' = \text{'fish'} \wedge wt' = \text{'red'}) \\ \vee &\; (d = d' \wedge dt = \text{'meat'} \wedge wt = \text{'red'} \\ &\wedge dt' = \text{'meat'} \wedge wt' = \text{'white'})\end{aligned}$$

Notice that this will force any white wine to be preferred over any red wine for fish, and just the opposite for meat. For other kinds of dishes, no preference is indicated. Consider now the preference query $\omega_{C_2}(Meal)$. It will pick the most preferred meals, according to the above-stated preferences. Notice that in the absence of any white wine, red wine (or some other kind of wine, e.g., rosé) can be selected for fish.

The above preferences are conditional, since they depend on the type of the dish being considered. Note that the relation $\succ_2$ in this example is irreflexive and asymmetric. Transitivity is obtained trivially because the chains of $\succ_2$ are of length at most 2. Note also that the preference relation is defined without referring to any domain order.

The unconditional preference for red wine for any kind of meal can also be defined as a first-order formula C_3:

$$(d, dt, w, wt) \succ_3 (d', dt', w', wt') \equiv d = d' \wedge wt = \text{'red'} \wedge wt' \neq \text{'red'}.$$

3 Properties of Preference Queries

3.1 Preference Relations

Since pfs can be essentially arbitrary formulas, no properties of preference relations can be assumed. So our framework is entirely neutral in this respect.

In the examples above, the preference relations were strict partial orders. This is likely to be the case for most applications of preference queries. However, there are cases where such relations fail to satisfy one of the properties of partial orders. We will see in Section 5 when irreflexivity fails. For asymmetry: We may have two tuples $\bar{t}_1$ and $\bar{t}_2$ such that $\bar{t}_1 \succ \bar{t}_2$ and $\bar{t}_2 \succ \bar{t}_1$ simply because we may have one reason to prefer $\bar{t}_1$ over $\bar{t}_2$ and another reason to prefer $\bar{t}_2$ over $\bar{t}_1$. Similarly, transitivity is not always guaranteed [15, 19, 7, 13]. For example, $\bar{t}_1$ may be preferred over $\bar{t}_2$ and $\bar{t}_2$ over $\bar{t}_3$, but the gap between $\bar{t}_1$ and $\bar{t}_3$ with respect to some heretofore ignored property may be so large as to prevent preferring $\bar{t}_1$ over $\bar{t}_3$. Or, transitivity may have to be abandoned to prevent cycles in preferences.

However, it is not difficult to check the properties of a preference relation defined using an ipf.

Theorem 1. *If a preference relation is defined using an arithmetical ipf, it can be checked for irreflexivity, asymmetry and transitivity in PTIME.*

Proof: We discuss asymmetry, the remaining properties can be handled in a similar way. If $\bar{t}_1 \succ \bar{t}_2$ is defined as $D_1 \vee \ldots \vee D_m$ and $\bar{t}_2 \succ \bar{t}_1$ as $D'_1 \vee \ldots \vee D'_m$, we can write down the negation of asymmetry as $(D_1 \vee \ldots \vee D_m) \wedge (D'_1 \vee \ldots \vee D'_m)$. The satisfiability of this formula can be checked in PTIME using the methods of [12]. □

Theorem 2. *If a preference relation over R defined using a pf C is a strict partial order, then for every finite, nonempty instance r of R, $\omega_C(r)$ is nonempty.*

If the properties of strict partial orders are not satisfied, then Theorem 2 may fail to hold and the winnow operator may return an empty set, even though the relation to which it is applied is nonempty. For instance, if $r_0 = \{\bar{t}_0\}$ and $\bar{t}_0 \succ \bar{t}_0$ (violation of irreflexivity), then the winnow operator applied to r_0 returns an empty set. Similarly, if two tuples are involved in a violation of asymmetry, they may block each other from appearing in the result of the winnow operator. Also, if the relation r is infinite, it may happen that $\omega_C(r) = \emptyset$, for example if r contains all natural numbers and the preference relation is the standard ordering $>$.

We conclude this subsection by noting that there is a natural notion of *indifference* associated with our approach: two tuples $\bar{t}_1$ and $\bar{t}_2$ are *indifferent* ($\bar{t}_1 \sim \bar{t}_2$) if neither is preferred to the other one, i.e., $\bar{t}_1 \not\succ \bar{t}_2$ and $\bar{t}_2 \not\succ \bar{t}_1$.

Proposition 1. *For every pf C, every relation r and every tuple $\bar{t}_1, \bar{t}_2 \in \omega_C(r)$, we have $\bar{t}_1 = \bar{t}_2$ or $\bar{t}_1 \sim \bar{t}_2$.*

It is a well-known result in decision theory [7, 8] that in order for a preference relation to be representable using scoring functions the corresponding indifference relation (defined as above) has to be *transitive*. This is not the case for the preference relation $\succ_1$ defined in Example 1.

3.2 The Winnow Operator

The winnow operator $\omega_C(R)$ such that $C = D_1 \vee \ldots \vee D_k$ is an ipf can be expressed in relational algebra, and thus does not add any expressive power to it. To see that notice that each D_i, $i = 1, \ldots, k$, is a formula over free variables $\bar{t}_1$ and $\bar{t}_2$. It can be viewed as a conjunction $D_i \equiv \phi_i \wedge \psi_i \wedge \gamma_i$ where ϕ_i refers only to the variables of $\bar{t}_1$, ψ_i to the variables of $\bar{t}_2$, and γ_i to the variables of both $\bar{t}_1$ and $\bar{t}_2$. The formula ϕ_i has an obvious translation to a selection condition Φ_i over R, and the formula ψ_i a similar translation to a selection condition Ψ_i over $\varrho(R)$, where ϱ is a renaming of R. The formula γ_i can similarly be translated to a join condition Γ_i over R and $\varrho(R)$. Then

$$\omega_C(R) = \varrho^{-1}(\varrho(R) - \pi_{\varrho(R)}(\bigcup_{i=1}^{k}(\sigma_{\Phi_i}(R) \underset{\Gamma_i}{\bowtie} \sigma_{\Psi_i}(\varrho(R)))))$$

where ϱ^{-1} is the inverse of the renaming ϱ.

However, the use of the winnow operator makes possible a clean separation of preference formulas from other aspects of the query. This has several advantages. First, the properties of preference relations can be studied in an abstract way, as demonstrated in this section and the next. Second, specialized query evaluation methods for the winnow operator can be developed. Third, algebraic properties of that operator can be formulated, in order to be used in query optimization.

To see the importance of the second point, note that a simple nested loops strategy is sufficient for evaluating the winnow operator. This is not at all obvious from considering the equivalent relational algebra expression. For restricted cases of the winnow operator, e.g., skylines [3], even more efficient evaluation strategies may be available. For the third point, we identify in Theorem 3 below a condition under which the winnow operator and a relational algebra selection commute. This is helpful for pushing selections past winnow operators in preference queries.

Theorem 3. *If the formula* $\forall (C_1(\bar{t}_2) \wedge C_2(\bar{t}_1, \bar{t}_2)) \Rightarrow C_1(\bar{t}_1)$ *(where C_1 is a selection condition and C_2 is a preference formula) is valid, then*

$$\sigma_{C_1}(\omega_{C_2}(R)) = \omega_{C_2}(\sigma_{C_1}(R)).$$

If the preference formula C_2 in the above theorem is an arithmetical ipf and the selection condition C_1 refers only to the arithmetic comparison predicates, then checking the validity of the formula

$$\forall (C_1(\bar{t}_2) \wedge C_2(\bar{t}_1, \bar{t}_2)) \Rightarrow C_1(\bar{t}_1)$$

can be done in PTIME.

Finally, we note that the winnow operator $\omega_C(R)$ such that C is an arbitrary preference formula (not necessarily an ipf) is still first-order definable. However, since the preference formula can now reference database relations, the relational algebra formulation may be considerably more complicated.

4 Composition of Preferences

In this section, we study several ways of composing preference relations. Since in our approach such relations are defined using preference formulas, composing them will amount to generating a formula defining the result of the composition. We will consider Boolean composition, transitive closure and prioritized composition.

4.1 Boolean Composition

Union, intersection and difference of preference relations are obviously captured by the Boolean operations on the corresponding preference formulas. The following table summarizes the preservation of properties of relations by the appropriate boolean composition operator.

	Union	Intersection	Difference
Irreflexivity	Yes	Yes	Yes
Asymmetry	No	Yes	Yes
Transitivity	No	Yes	No

4.2 Transitive Closure

We have seen an example (Example 1) of a preference relation that is already transitive. However, there are cases when we expect the preference relation to be the *transitive closure* of another preference relation which is not transitive.

Example 5. Consider the following relation:

$$x \succ y \equiv x = a \land y = b \lor x = b \land y = c.$$

In this relation, a and c are not related though there are contexts in which this might be natural. (Assume I prefer to walk than to drive, and to drive than to ride a bus. Thus, I also prefer to walk than to ride a bus.)

In our framework, we can specify the preference relation $\succ^*$ to be the *transitive closure* of another preference relation $\succ$ defined using a first-order formula. This is similar to transitive closure queries in relational databases. However, there is an important difference. In databases, we are computing the transitive closure of a *finite* relation, while here we are transitively closing an infinite relation defined using a first-order formula.

Formally, assuming that the underlying preference relation is $\succ$, the preference relation $\succ^*$ is now defined as

$$\bar{t}_1 \succ^* \bar{t}_2 \text{ iff } \bar{t}_1 \succ^n \bar{t}_2 \text{ for some } n \geq 0,$$

where:

$$\bar{t}_1 \succ^1 \bar{t}_2 \equiv \bar{t}_1 \succ \bar{t}_2$$
$$\bar{t}_1 \succ^{n+1} \bar{t}_2 \equiv \exists \bar{t}_3. \, \bar{t}_1 \succ \bar{t}_3 \land \bar{t}_3 \succ^n \bar{t}_2.$$

Clearly, in general such an approach leads to infinite formulas. However, in many important cases this does not happen.

Theorem 4. *If a preference relation $\succ$ is defined using an arithmetical ipf, the transitive closure $\succ^*$ of $\succ$ is also defined using an arithmetical ipf and that definition can be effectively obtained.*

Proof: The computation of the transitive closure can in this case be formulated as the evaluation of Datalog with order or gap-order (for integers) constraints. Such an evaluation terminates [16, 20] and its result represents the desired formula. □

An analogous result holds if instead of arithmetic comparisons we consider equality constraints over an infinite domain [16].

Example 6. Continuing Example 5, we obtain the following preference relation $\succ^*$ by transitively closing $\succ$:

$$x \succ^* y \equiv x = a \wedge y = b \vee x = b \wedge y = c \vee x = a \wedge y = c.$$

Theorem 4 is not in conflict with the well-known non-first order definability of transitive closure on finite structures. In the latter case it is shown that there is no finite first-order formula expressing transitive closure for arbitrary (finite) binary relations. In Theorem 4 the relation to be closed, although possibly infinite, is fixed (since it is defined using the given ipf). In particular, given an encoding of a fixed finite binary relation using an ipf, the transitive closure of this relation is defined using another ipf.

The transitive closure of a irreflexive (resp. asymmetric) preference relation may fail to be irreflexive (resp. asymmetric).

4.3 Preference Hierarchies

It is often the case that preferences form hierarchies. For instance, I may have a general preference for red wine but in specific cases, e.g., when eating fish, this preference is overridden by the one for white wine. Also a preference for less expensive books (Example 1) can be overridden by a preference for certain vendors.

Definition 4. *Consider two preference relations $\succ_1$ and $\succ_2$ defined over the same schema U. The prioritized composition $\succ_{1,2} = \succ_1 \triangleright \succ_2$ of $\succ_1$ and $\succ_2$ is defined as:*

$$\bar{t}_1 \succ_{1,2} \bar{t}_2 \equiv \bar{t}_1 \succ_1 \bar{t}_2 \vee (\bar{t}_2 \not\succ_1 \bar{t}_1 \wedge \bar{t}_1 \succ_2 \bar{t}_2).$$

Example 7. Continuing Example 1, instead of the preference relation $\succ_1$ defined there we consider the relation $\succ_0 \triangleright \succ_1$ where $\succ_0$ is defined by the following formula C_0:

$$(i, v, p) \succ_0 (i', v', p') \equiv i = i' \wedge v = \text{'BooksForLess'} \wedge v' = \text{'LowestPrices'}.$$

Assume the relation $\succ_{0,1} = \succ_0 \triangleright \succ_1$ is defined by a formula $C_{0,1}$ (this formula is easily obtained from the formulas C_0 and C_1 by substitution). Then $\omega_{C_{0,1}}(r_1)$ returns the following tuples

ISBN	Vendor	Price
0679726691	BooksForLess	$14.75
0062059041	BooksForLess	$7.30
0374164770	LowestPrices	$21.88

Note that now a more expensive copy of the first book is preferred, due to the preference for 'BooksForLess' over 'LowestPrices'. However, 'BooksForLess' does not offer the last book, and that's why the copy offered by 'LowestPrices' is preferred.

Theorem 5. *If $\succ_1$ and $\succ_2$ are defined using intrinsic preference formulas, so is $\succ_{1,2}$. If $\succ_1$ and $\succ_2$ are both irreflexive or asymmetric, so is $\succ_{1,2}$.*

However, a relation defined as the prioritized composition of two transitive preference relations does not have to be transitive.

Example 8. Consider the following preference relations:

$$a \succ_1 b, b \succ_2 c.$$

Both $\succ_1$ and $\succ_2$ are trivially transitive. However, $\succ_1 \triangleright \succ_2$ is not.

Theorem 6. *Prioritized composition is associative:*

$$(\succ_1 \triangleright \succ_2) \triangleright \succ_3 \equiv \succ_1 \triangleright (\succ_2 \triangleright \succ_3).$$

Thanks to the associativity of $\triangleright$, the above construction can be generalized to an arbitrary finite partial order between preference relations. Such an order can be viewed as a graph in which the nodes consist of preference relations and the edges represent relative priorities (there would be an edge $(\succ_1, \succ_2)$ in the situation described above). To encode this graph as a single preference relation, one would construct first the definitions corresponding to individual paths from roots to leaves, and then take a disjunction of all such definitions.

There may be other ways of combining preferences. For instance, preference relations defined on individual database relations may induce other preferences defined on the Cartesian product of the database relations. In general, any first-order definable way of composing preference relations leads to first-order preference formulas, which in turn can be used as parameters of the winnow operator. The composition does not even have to be first-order definable, as long as it produces a (first-order) preference formula.

5 More Expressive Preferences

We show here that the winnow operator when used together with other operators of the relational algebra can express more complex decision problems involving preferences. We consider the following: integrity constraints, extrinsic preferences, and aggregation.

5.1 Integrity Constraints

There are cases when we wish to impose a constraint on the result of the winnow operator. In Example 1, we may say that we are interested only in the books under $20. In Example 4, we may restrict our attention only to the meat or fish dishes (note that currently the dishes that are not meat or fish do not have a preferred kind of wine). In the same example, we may ask for a specific number of meal recommendations.

In general, we need to distinguish between *local* and *global* constraints. A local constraint imposes a condition on the components of a single tuple, for instance Book.Price<$20. A global constraint imposes a condition on a set of tuples. The first two examples above are local constraints; the third is global. To satisfy a global constraint on the result of the winnow operator, one would have to construct a maximal subset of this answer that satisfies the constraint. Since in general there may be more than one such subset, the required construction cannot be described using a single relational algebra query. On the other hand, local constraints are easily handled, since they can be expressed using selection.

Example 9. Consider Example 1. The preference formula C_1 captures the preference for getting the same book cheaper. If we want to limit ourselves to books that cost less than $20, we can use the following relational algebra query:

$$\sigma_{Price<\$20}(\omega_{C_1}(Book)).$$

According to Theorem 3, this query is equivalent to the query

$$\omega_{C_1}(\sigma_{Price<\$20}(Book))$$

which may be easier to evaluate, since the selection is applied directly to a database table. On the other hand, if we ask for books that cost at least $20, the corresponding selection will not commute with the winnow operator. Intuitively, such a selection can eliminate some of the best deals on books. So in general it matters whether the integrity constraints are imposed before or after applying the winnow operator.

A *veto* expresses a prohibition on the presence of a specific set of values in the elements of the answer to a preference query and thus can be viewed as a local constraint. To veto a specific tuple $w = (a_1, \ldots, a_n)$ in a relation S (which can be defined by a preference query) of arity n, we write the selection:

$$\sigma_{A_1 \neq a_1 \vee \cdots \vee A_n \neq a_n}(S).$$

5.2 Intrinsic vs. Extrinsic Preferences

So far we have talked only about *intrinsic* preference formulas. Such formulas establish the preference relation between two tuples purely on the basis of the values occurring in those tuples. *Extrinsic* preference formulas may refer not only to built-in predicates but also to other constructs, e.g., database relations.

In general, extrinsic preferences can use a variety of criteria: properties of the relations from which the tuples were selected, properties of other relations, or comparisons of aggregate values, and do not even have to be defined using first-order formulas.

It is possible to express some extrinsic preferences using the winnow operator together with other relational algebra operators using the following multi-step strategy:

1. using a relational query, combine all the information relevant for the preference in a single relation,
2. apply the appropriate winnow operator to this relation,
3. project out the extra columns introduced in the first step.

The following example demonstrates the above strategy, as well as the use of aggregation for the formulation of preferences.

Example 10. Consider again the relation $Book(ISBN, Vendor, Price)$. Suppose for each part a preferred vendor (there may be more than one) is a vendor that sells the *maximum total* number of books. Clearly, this is an extrinsic preference since it cannot be established solely by comparing pairs of tuples from this relation. However, we can provide the required aggregate values and connect them with individual parts through new, separate views:

```
CREATE VIEW BookNum(Vendor,Num) AS
    SELECT B1.Vendor, COUNT(DISTINCT B1.ISBN)
    FROM Book B1
    GROUP BY B1.Vendor;

CREATE VIEW ExtBook(ISBN,Vendor,Num) AS
    SELECT B1.ISBN, B1.Vendor, BN.Num
    FROM Book B1, BookNum BN
    WHERE B1.Vendor=BN.Vendor;
```

Now the extrinsic preference is captured by the query

$$\pi_{ISBN,Vendor}(\omega_{C_5}(ExtBook))$$

where the preference formula C_5 is defined as follows:

$$(i, v, n) \succ_5 (i', v', n') \equiv i = i' \land n > n'.$$

Example 11. To see another example of extrinsic preference, consider the situation in which we prefer any tuple from a relation R over any tuple from a relation S. Notice that this is truly an extrinsic preference, since it is based on where the tuples come from and not on their values. It can be handled in our approach by *tagging* the tuples with the appropriate relation names (easily done in relational algebra or SQL) and then defining the preference relation using the tags. If there is a tuple which belongs both to R and S, then the above preference relation will fail to be irreflexive. Note also that an approach similar to tagging was used in Example 4.

6 Iterated Preferences and Ranking

A natural notion of *ranking* is implicit in our approach. A ranking is defined using *iterated preference*.

Definition 5. *Given a preference relation $\succ$ defined by a pf C, the n-th iteration of the winnow operator ω_C in r is defined as:*

$$\omega_C^1(r) = \omega_C(r)$$
$$\omega_C^{n+1}(r) = \omega_C(r - \bigcup_{1 \leq i \leq n} \omega_C^i(r))$$

For example, the query $\omega_C^2(r)$ computes the set of "second-best" tuples.

Example 12. Continuing Example 1, the query $\omega_{C_1}^2(r_1)$ returns

ISBN	Vendor	Price
0679726691	BooksForLess	$14.75

and the query $\omega_{C_1}^3(r_1)$ returns

ISBN	Vendor	Price
0679726691	QualityBooks	$18.80

Therefore, by iterating the winnow operator one can *rank* the tuples in the given relation instance.

Theorem 7. *If a preference relation $\succ$ defined by a first-order formula C over R is a strict partial order, then for every finite instance r of R and every tuple $\bar{t} \in r$, there exists an i, $i \geq 1$, such that $\bar{t} \in \omega_C^i(r)$.*

If a preference relation is not a strict partial order, then Theorem 7 may fail to hold. A number of tuples can block one another from appearing in the result of any iteration of the winnow operator. However, even in this case there may be a weaker form of ranking available.

Example 13. Consider Examples 1 and 7. If the preference formula C' is defined as $C_0 \vee C_1$, then the first two tuples of the instance r_1 block each other from appearing in the result of $\omega_{C'}(r_1)$, since according to C_0 the first tuple is preferred to the second but just the opposite is true according to C_1. Intuitively, both those tuples should be preferred to (and ranked higher) than the third tuple. But since neither the first not the second tuple is a member of $\omega_{C'}(r_1)$, none of the first three tuples can be ranked.

We define now a weaker form of the winnow operator that will return all the tuples that are dominated only by the tuples that they dominate themselves. We relax the asymmetry requirement but preserve transitivity.

Definition 6. *If R is a relation schema and C a pf defining a transitive preference relation $\succ$ over R, then the* weak winnow operator *is written as $\psi_C(R)$ and for every instance r of R*

$$\psi_C(r) = \{\bar{t} \in r | \forall \bar{t}' \in r. \bar{t} \succ \bar{t}' \vee \bar{t}' \not\succ \bar{t}\}.$$

Example 14. Considering Example 13, we see that the query $\psi_{C'}(r_1)$ returns now

ISBN	Vendor	Price
0679726691	BooksForLess	$14.75
0679726691	LowestPrices	$13.50
0062059041	BooksForLess	$7.30
0374164770	LowestPrices	$21.88

Below we formulate a few properties of the weak winnow operator.

Theorem 8. *If R is a relation schema and C a preference formula defining a transitive preference relation $\succ$ over R, then for every instance r of R, $\psi_C(r)$ is uniquely defined and $\omega_C(r) \subseteq \psi_C(r)$.*

Theorem 9. *For every finite, nonempty relation instance r of R, and a transitive preference relation $\succ$ over R defined by a preference formula C, $\psi_C(r)$ is nonempty.*

One can define the iteration of the weak winnow operator similarly to that of the winnow operator (Definition 5).

Theorem 10. *If a preference relation $\succ$ over R defined by a first-order formula C is transitive, then for every finite instance r of R and for every tuple $\bar{t} \in r$, there exists an i, $i \geq 1$, such that $\bar{t} \in \psi_C^i(r)$.*

7 Related Work

7.1 Preference Queries

[18] originated the study of *preference queries*. It proposed an extension of the relational calculus in which preferences for tuples satisfying given logical conditions can be expressed. For instance, one could say: *Among the tuples of R satisfying Q, I prefer those satisfying P_1; among the latter I prefer those satisfying P_2*. Such a specification was to mean the following: Pick the tuples satisfying $Q \wedge P_1 \wedge P_2$; if the result is empty, pick the tuples satisfying $Q \wedge P_1 \wedge \neg P_2$; if the result is empty, pick the remaining tuples of R satisfying Q. This can be simulated in our framework as the relational algebra expression $\omega_{C^*}(\sigma_Q(R))$ where C^* is an ipf defined in the following way:

1. obtain the formula C defining a preference relation $\succ$

$$\bar{t}_1 \succ \bar{t}_2 \equiv P_1(\bar{t}_1) \wedge P_2(\bar{t}_1) \wedge P_1(\bar{t}_2) \wedge \neg P_2(\bar{t}_2) \vee P_1(\bar{t}_1) \wedge \neg P_1(\bar{t}_2) \wedge \neg P_1(\bar{t}_2),$$

2. transform C into DNF to obtain an ipf C', and
3. close the result transitively to obtain an ipf C^* defining a transitive preference relation $\succ^*$ (as described in Section 4).

Other kinds of logical conditions from [18] can be similarly expressed in our framework. Maximum/minimum value preferences (as in Example 1) are handled in [18] through the explicit use of aggregate functions. The use of such functions is implicit in the definition of our winnow operator.

Unfortunately, [18] does not contain a formal definition of the proposed language, so a complete comparison with our approach is not possible. It should be noted, however, that the framework of [18] seems unable to capture very simple conditional preferences like the ones in Examples 4 and 5. Also, it can only handle strict partial orders of bounded depth (except in the case where aggregate functions can be used, as in Example 1). Hierarchical or iterated preferences are not considered.

[11] was one of the sources of inspiration for the present paper. It defines *Preference Datalog*: a combination of Datalog and clausally-defined preference relations. Preference Datalog captures, among others, the class of preference queries discussed in [18]. The declarative semantics of Preference Datalog is based on the notion of *preferential consequence*, introduced earlier by the authors in [10]. This semantics requires preferences to be reflexive and transitive. Also, the operational semantics of Preference Datalog uses specialized versions of the standard logic program evaluation methods: bottom-up [11] or top-down [10]. In the context of database queries, the approach proposed in the present paper achieves similar goals to that of [10] and [11], remaining, however, entirely within the relational data model and classical first-order logic. Finally, [10, 11] do not address some of the issues we deal with in the present paper like transitive closure of preferences, prioritized composition or iterated preferences (a similar concept to the last one is presented under the name of "relaxation").

[17] discusses Preference SQL, a query language in which preferences between atomic conditions can be stated. For example, I can say that I prefer the book "ABC" with price under $20 over the same book with price over $20. However, saying simply that I prefer a lower price on a book (as we do in Example 1) does not seems possible in Preference SQL. The description of Preference SQL in [17] is so brief that a detailed comparison with our proposal is not possible at this point. [3] introduces the *skyline* operator and describes several evaluation methods for this operator. The skyline is a special case of our winnow operator. It is restricted to use an arithmetical ipf which is a conjunction of pairwise comparisons of corresponding tuple components. So in particular Example 4 does not fit in that framework.

[2] uses quantitative preferences in queries and focuses on the issues arising in combining such preferences. [14] explores in this context the problems of efficient query processing. Since the preferences in this approach are based on comparing the scores of individual tuples under given scoring functions, they have to be intrinsic. However, the simulation of extrinsic preferences using intrinsic ones (Section 5) is not readily available in this approach because the scoring functions are not integrated with the query language. So, for instance, Example 10 cannot be handled. In fact, even for preference relations that satisfy the property of transitivity of the corresponding indifference relation, it is not

clear whether the scoring function capturing the preference relation can be defined intrinsically (i.e., the function value be determined solely by the the values of the tuple components). The general construction of a scoring function on the basis of a preference relation [7, 8] does not provide such a definition. So the exact expressive power of the quantitative approach to preference queries remains unclear.

7.2 Preferences in Logic and Artificial Intelligence

The papers on *preference logics* [23, 19, 13] address the issue of capturing the common-sense meaning of preference through appropriate axiomatizations. Preferences are defined on formulas, not tuples, and with the exception of [19] limited to the propositional case. The application of the results obtained in this area to database queries is unclear.

The papers on *preference reasoning* [24, 22, 4] attempt to develop practical mechanisms for making inferences about preferences and solving decision or configuration problems similar to the one described in Example 4. A central notion there is that of *ceteris paribus* preference: preferring one outcome to another, all else being equal. Typically, the problems addressed in this work are propositional (or finite-domain). Such problems can be encoded in the relational data model and the inferences obtained by evaluating preference queries. A detailed study of such an approach remains still to be done. We note that the use of a full-fledged query language in this context makes it possible to formulate considerably more complex decision and configuration problems than before.

The work on *prioritized logic programming and nonmonotonic reasoning* [5, 6, 21] has potential applications to databases. However, like [11] it relies on specialized evaluation mechanisms.

8 Conclusions and Future Work

We have presented a framework for specifying preferences using logical formulas and its embedding into relational algebra. As the result, preference queries and complex decision problems involving preferences can be formulated in a simple and clean way.

Clearly, our framework is limited to applications that can be entirely modeled within the relational model of data. Here are several examples that do not quite fit in this paradigm:

- preferences defined between *sets* of elements;
- *heterogenous* preferences between tuples of different arity or type (how to say I prefer a meal without a wine to a meal with one in Example 4?);
- preferences requiring nondeterministic choice. We believe this is properly handled using a nondeterministic choice [9] or witness [1] operator.

In addition to addressing the above limitations, future work directions include:

- evaluation and optimization of preference queries;
- merging and propagation of preference relations;
- extrinsic preferences;
- defeasible and default preferences;
- preference elicitation.

Acknowledgments

This paper is dedicated to the memory of Javier Pinto whose premature death prevented him from participating in this research. The conversations with Svet Braynov, Jarek Gryz, Bharat Jayaraman, and Jorge Lobo, and the comments by the anonymous referees are gratefully acknowledged. Special thanks go to Agnieszka Grabska for her skeptical enthusiasm and timely feedback.

References

1. S. Abiteboul, R. Hull, and V. Vianu. *Foundations of Databases.* Addison-Wesley, 1995.
2. R. Agrawal and E.L. Wimmers. A Framework for Expressing and Combining Preferences. In *ACM SIGMOD International Conference on Management of Data,* pages 297-306, 2000.
3. S. Börzsönyi, D. Kossmann, and K. Stocker. The Skyline Operator. In *IEEE International Conference on Data Engineering,* pages 421-430, 2001.
4. C. Boutilier, R. I. Brafman, H. H. Hoos, and D. Poole. Reasoning with Conditional Ceteris Paribus Preference Statements. In *Symposium on Uncertainty in Artificial Intelligence,* 1999.
5. G. Brewka and T. Eiter. Preferred Answer Sets for Extended Logic Programs. *Artificial Intelligence,* 109(1-2):297-356, 1999.
6. J. P. Delgrande, T. Schaub, and H. Tompits. Logic Programs with Compiled Preferences. In *European Conference on Artificial Intelligence,* 2000.
7. P. Fishburn. Preference Structures and their Numerical Representations. *Theoretical Computer Science,* 217:359-383, 1999.
8. P.C. Fishburn. *Utility Theory for Decision Making.* Wiley & Sons, 1970.
9. F. Giannotti, S. Greco, D. Sacca, and C. Zaniolo. Programming with Nondeterminism in Deductive Databases. *Annals of Mathematics and Artificial Intelligence,* 19(3-4), 1997.
10. K. Govindarajan, B. Jayaraman, and S. Mantha. Preference Logic Programming. In *International Conference on Logic Programming,* pages 731-745, 1995.
11. K. Govindarajan, B. Jayaraman, and S. Mantha. Preference Queries in Deductive Databases. *New Generation Computing,* pages 57-86, 2001.
12. S. Guo, W. Sun, and M.A. Weiss. Solving Satisfiability and Implication Problems in Database Systems. *ACM Transactions on Database Systems,* 21(2):270-293, 1996.
13. S. O. Hansson. Preference Logic. In D. Gabbay, editor, *Handbook of Philosophical Logic,* volume 8. 2001.
14. V. Hristidis, N. Koudas, and Y. Papakonstantinou. PREFER: A System for the Efficient Execution of Multiparametric Ranked Queries. In *ACM SIGMOD International Conference on Management of Data,* pages 259-270, 2001.
15. R.G. Hughes. Rationality and Intransitive Preferences. *Analysis,* 40:132-134, 1980.

16. P. C. Kanellakis, G. M. Kuper, and P. Z. Revesz. Constraint Query Languages. *Journal of Computer and System Sciences*, 51(1):26-52, August 1995.
17. W. Kiessling, S. Fischer, S. Holland, and T. Ehm. Design and Implementation of COSIMA – A Smart and Speaking E-sales Assistant. In *International Workshop on Advanced Issues of E-Commerce and Web-Based Information Systems*, 2001.
18. M. Lacroix and P. Lavency. Preferences: Putting More Knowledge Into Queries. In *International Conference on Very Large Data Bases*, pages 217-225, 1987.
19. S. M. Mantha. *First-Order Preference Theories and their Applications*. PhD thesis, University of Utah, 1991.
20. P. Z. Revesz. A Closed-Form Evaluation for Datalog Queries with Integer (Gap)-Order Constraints. *Theoretical Computer Science*, 116:117-149, 1993.
21. C. Sakama and K. Inoue. Prioritized Logic Programming and its Application to Commonsense Reasoning. *Artificial Intelligence*, 123:185-222, 2000.
22. S-W. Tan and J. Pearl. Specification and Evaluation of Preferences under Uncertainty. In *International Conference on Principles of Knowledge Representation and Reasoning*, 1994.
23. G. H. von Wright. *The Logic of Preference*. Edinburgh University Press, 1963.
24. M. P. Wellman and J. Doyle. Preferential Semantics for Goals. In *National Conference on Artificial Intelligence*, pages 698-703, 1991.

Rewriting Unions
of General Conjunctive Queries Using Views*

Junhu Wang[1,2], Michael Maher[1,3], and Rodney Topor[1]

[1] CIT, Griffith University, Brisbane, Australia 4111
{jwang, rwt, mjm}@cit.gu.edu.au
[2] GSCIT, Monash University, Churchill, Australia 3842
John.Wang@infotech.monash.edu.au
[3] DMCS, Loyola University, Chicago, USA
mjm@math.luc.edu

Abstract. The problem of finding contained rewritings of queries using views is of great importance in mediated data integration systems. In this paper, we first present a general approach for finding contained rewritings of unions of conjunctive queries with arbitrary built-in predicates. Our approach is based on an improved method for testing conjunctive query containment in this context. Although conceptually simple, our approach generalizes previous methods for finding contained rewritings of conjunctive queries and is more powerful in the sense that many rewritings that can not be found using existing methods can be found by our approach. Furthermore, nullity-generating dependencies over the base relations can be easily handled. We then present a simplified approach which is less complete, but is much faster than the general approach, and it still finds maximum rewritings in several special cases. Our approaches compare favorably with existing methods.

1 Introduction

The problem of rewriting queries using views (aka query folding [1]) is of key importance in mediated data integration systems. In such systems, users are usually presented with a uniform interface through which queries are submitted. The uniform interface, also called the *global schema*, consists of a set of *virtual relations* (aka *base relations*) which may not be physically stored. The actual data sources (i.e, the stored data) are regarded as logical views defined on the virtual relations [2]. Thus in order to answer a user query, the system must first rewrite the query into one that is defined on the views only. In other words, given a query Q defined on the base relations we need to find a query Q_r defined on the view relations such that Q_r gives correct answers to Q. If so, Q_r is called a rewriting of Q. Usually two types of rewritings are sought: equivalent rewritings and contained rewritings. Equivalent rewritings are those that give exactly the same set of answers to the original query. Contained rewritings are those that

---
* This work is partially supported by the Australian Research Council.

give possibly only part of the answers to the original query. In this paper, we will focus on the latter. More specifically, we will study the problem of finding contained rewritings using views when the views are conjunctive queries with arbitrary built-in predicates (which we call *general conjunctive queries (GCQs)*) and the user query is a union of general conjunctive queries (referred to as a *union query*). The rewritings we obtain are union queries. Our attention is focused on how to quickly find rewritings that give as many correct answers as possible, rather than on how efficiently the rewritings can be evaluated.

1.1 Previous Work

Apparently the first papers dealing with query rewriting using views are [3] and [4], in which equivalent rewritings of conjunctive queries are discussed. Over the past few years, the problem has received intensive attention mainly because of its relevance to data integration and query optimization. For a comprehensive survey, see [5]. Here we only mention a few papers that are closely related to our work. Among the early algorithms, the *U-join* algorithm [1] and the *Bucket* algorithm [6] are used to find rewritings of conjunctive queries using conjunctive views (in the Bucket algorithm, the views and the query may contain comparison predicates such as $x < a, y \neq x$), and the *Inverse-rule* algorithm [7] was proposed for rewriting Datalog programs using Datalog views. More recently, the *MiniCon* algorithm [8] and the *Shared-Variable-Bucket* (hereafter abbreviated as *SVB*) algorithm [9] have been developed as faster (but less powerful) versions of the Bucket algorithm. Algorithms for finding contained rewritings in the presence of functional dependencies, inclusion dependencies, and full dependencies are studied in [10, 11].

1.2 The Problem and Our Contribution

The problem we study is the rewriting of unions of general conjunctive queries. We also consider the case where *nullity-generating dependencies (NGDs)* (see the next section for definition) over the base relations are present. As mentioned above, several previous algorithms consider rewritings of conjunctive queries with or without built-in predicates. However, for a union query such as $Q_u = Q_1 \cup Q_2$, it is not enough to find the rewritings for each of the conjunctive queries and then union them. It is possible that a conjunctive query defined on the views is not a rewriting of any of the conjunctive queries in the union, but it is a rewriting of the union. For instance, the rewriting of Q_u in the next example is not a rewriting of either Q_1 or Q_2.

Example 1. Let $Q_u = Q_1 \cup Q_2$, where Q_1 and Q_2 are
$q(y) :- p(x, y), p'(x', y), x > y$ and
$q(y) :- p(x, y), r(y, z), x \leq y$ respectively.
Let the views be
$v_1(y) :- p(x, y),$
$v_2(y) :- r(y, x),$ and

$v_3(y) := p'(x, y)$.

Then $q(y) := v_1(y), v_2(y), v_3(y)$ is a contained rewriting of Q_u, but not of Q_1, nor Q_2. The rewriting is not a union of the rewritings of Q_1 and Q_2.

Existing algorithms may fail to find all contained rewritings even if the query is a conjunctive query, as shown in the next example.

Example 2. Suppose all relation attributes in this example are from the integers. Let the query Q be $q(x) := p_1(x, y), p_2(x, y)$.
Let the views be

$v_1(x) := p_1(x, y), y > 0, y < 3$,
$v_2(x) := p_2(x, 1)$, and
$v_3(x) := p_2(x, 2)$.

It can be verified that $q(x) := v_1(x), v_2(x), v_3(x)$ is a contained rewriting of Q, but this rewriting can not be found by existing algorithms.

Although the Inverse-rule algorithm in [7] considers rewritings of Datalog queries, it does not consider the case where built-in predicates are present. The presence of general-form NGDs are not considered by previous work.

In this paper, we first revise a previous result on query containment to one that does not require the queries to be in any normal form. This revised result is used extensively in the analysis of our rewritings. We then present a general approach for rewriting union queries using views which, for instance, can find the rewritings in Examples 1 and 2. Furthermore, NGDs can be handled easily. We then present a simplified version of the general approach (referred to as the *simplified approach*) which is less complete but significantly more efficient. When used in rewriting GCQs, our simplified approach finds strictly more rewritings than the MiniCon and the SVB algorithms when built-in predicates exists in the query, and it finds maximum rewritings (see the next section for definition) in several special cases. Also in these special cases, the simplified approach compares favorably with the MiniCon and the SVB algorithms in terms of efficiency. When there are no built-in predicates in the query and the views, the simplified approach finds the same rewritings as the U-join algorithm with similar costs.

The rest of the paper is organized as follows. Section 2 provides the technical background. In Section 3 we introduce the concept of *relevance mappings* and present the improved method for testing query containment. In Section 4 we present our general approach on rewriting union queries. The simplified approach is described in Section 5. Section 6 compares our approaches with the Bucket, the U-Join, the MiniCon and the SVB algorithms. Section 7 concludes the paper with a summary and a discussion about further research.

2 Preliminaries

2.1 General Conjunctive Queries and Union Queries

A *general conjunctive query (GCQ)* is of the form

$$q(X) := p_1(X_1), ..., p_n(X_n), C \qquad (1)$$

where $q, p_1, \ldots, p_n$ are relation names (q is distinct from $p_1, \ldots, p_n$), $X, X_1, \ldots, X_n$ are tuples of variables and constants, C is a conjunction of atomic constraints over the variables in $X \cup X_1 \cup \cdots \cup X_n$. We call $q(X)$ the *head*, $p_1(X_1), \ldots, p_n(X_n), C$ the *body*, and C the *constraint*[1] of the query. Each atom $p_i(X_i)$ ($i = 1, \ldots, n$) is called a *subgoal*, and each atomic constraint in C is called a *built-in predicate*. The tuple X is called the *output* of the query. The variables in the head and those that are equated, by C, to some head variables or constants are called *distinguished variables*.

We make the following safety assumptions about the GCQs

1. There is at least one atom in the body.
2. Every variable in X either appears explicitly as an argument in a subgoal, or is (implicitly or explicitly) equated, by C, to a variable in at least one of the subgoals or to a constant.

Two GCQs are said to be *comparable* if they have the same number of output arguments and the corresponding output arguments are from the same domains. A *union query* is a finite union of comparable GCQs. Clearly, a GCQ can be regarded as a union query. In what follows, when we say a *query*, we mean a GCQ or a union query.

Query containment and equivalence are defined in the usual way. We will use $Q_1 \sqsubseteq Q_2$ and $Q_1 = Q_2$ to denote Q_1 is contained in Q_2 and Q_1 is equivalent to Q_2 respectively. We will use *empty query* to refer to any query whose answer set is empty for any database instance. Clearly, a GCQ is empty if and only if its constraint is unsatisfiable.

A GCQ is said to be in *normal form*, if the arguments in every atom (head or subgoal) are distinct variables only, and the sets of variables in different atoms are pairwise disjoint. A GCQ is said to be in *compact form* if there are no explicit or implicit *basic equalities* (i.e, non-tautological equalities between two variables or between a variable and a constant, e.g, $x \geq y \wedge x \leq y$, where $x = y$ is not a tautology) in the constraint. Clearly, every GCQ can be put into normal form. It can be put into compact form provided we can find all the implicit equalities in the constraint.

2.2 Nullity-Generating Dependencies

A *nullity-generating dependency (NGD)* is a formula of the form

$$r_1(X_1), \ldots, r_m(X_m), D \rightarrow FALSE \qquad (2)$$

where $r_1, \ldots, r_m$ are relation names, $X_1, \ldots, X_m$ are tuples of variables and constants, and D is a constraint over the variables in $X_1 \cup \cdots \cup X_m$.

Functional dependencies and equality-generating dependencies are special cases of NGDs.

---
[1] Note that the constraint of a GCQ refers to built-in predicates, rather than integrity constraints.

Let $\triangle$ be a set of NGDs. If for any database instance $\mathcal{I}$ which satisfies the NGDs in $\triangle$, the answer set of Q_1 is a subset of that of Q_2, then we say Q_1 is *contained in Q_2 under $\triangle$*, denoted $Q_1 \sqsubseteq_\triangle Q_2$.

2.3 Rewritings and Maximum Rewritings

We assume the existence of a set of base relations and a set W of *views*. A *view* is a GCQ defined on the base relations. Without loss of generality, we assume the arguments in the head of a view are *distinct variables* only. We refer to the relation in the head of the view as the *view relation*.

There are two world assumptions [12]: under the *closed world assumption*, the view relation stores all of the answers to the view; under the *open world assumption*, the view relation stores possibly only part of the answers to the view. The open world assumption is usually used in data integration [5] because it is usually not known that all answers of the views are actually stored. In this paper, we will use the open world assumption.

For any *base instance* $\mathcal{D}$ consisting of instances of the base relations, we use $W(\mathcal{D})$ to denote a *view instance* (with respect to $\mathcal{D}$) consisting of instances of the view relations. Since the open world assumption is used, each relation instance in $W(\mathcal{D})$ may contain only part of the answers computed to the corresponding view using $\mathcal{D}$.

Given a union query Q_u defined on the base relations, our task is to find a query Q_r defined solely on the view relations such that, for any base instance $\mathcal{D}$, all of the answers to Q_r computed using any view instance $W(\mathcal{D})$ are correct answers to Q_u. We call such a query Q_r a *contained rewriting* or simply a *rewriting* of Q_u. If Q_r does not always give the empty answer set, we call it a *non-empty* rewriting.

To check whether a query Q_r is a rewriting of Q, we need the *expansion* of Q_r, as defined below.

Definition 1. *If Q_r is a GCQ defined on the view relations, then the* expansion *Q_r^{exp} of Q_r is the GCQ obtained as follows: For each subgoal $v(x_1, \ldots, x_k)$ of Q_r, suppose $v(y_1, \ldots, y_k)$ is the head of the corresponding view V, and σ is a mapping that maps the variable y_i to the argument x_i for $i = 1, \ldots, k$, and maps every non-head variable in V to a distinct new variable, then*

(1) replace $v(x_1, \ldots, x_k)$ with the body of $\sigma(V)$,

(2) now if a variable x_i ($1 \leq i \leq k$) appears only in the constraint, then replace x_i with the variable in the subgoals of $\sigma(V)$ (or the constant) to which x_i is equated by the constraint of $\sigma(V)$.

The expansion Q_u^{exp} of a union query Q_u is the union of the expansions of the GCQs in Q_u.

For example, if Q_r is $q(x) :- v(y), x = y$, and V is $v(y) :- p(z), y = z$, then Q_r^{exp} is $q(x) :- p(z), x = z$.

There may be many different rewritings of a query. To compare them, we define maximum rewritings.

Definition 2. A rewriting Q_1 of Q is said to be a maximum rewriting *with respect to a query language $\mathcal{L}$* if for any rewriting Q_2 of Q in $\mathcal{L}$, every answer to Q_2 is an answer to Q_1 for any view instance $W(\mathcal{D})$ with respect to any base instance $\mathcal{D}$.

Note that for a rewriting Q_1 to be maximum under the open world assumption, it is not enough that $Q_2^{exp} \sqsubseteq Q_1^{exp}$ holds for any other rewriting Q_2. Note also that the condition for a maximum rewriting is slightly stronger than that for a *maximally contained rewriting* in [8, 9], and that for a *maximally contained retrievable program* in [7], and that for a *maximally contained query plan* in [11].

The above definition of rewritings extends straightforwardly to the case where NGDs on the base relations exist. In this case, the rewriting is called a *semantic rewriting*.

Definition 3. Let $\triangle$ be a set of NGDs on the base relations, Q be a query defined on the base relations, and W be a set of views. If Q_r is a query defined on the view relations in W such that $Q_r^{exp} \sqsubseteq_\triangle Q$, then we say Q_r is a semantic rewriting of Q wrt W and $\triangle$.

2.4 Inverse Rules and Inferred Constraints

Given a view V:
$$v(X) :\!\!- p_1(X_1), \ldots, p_n(X_n), C$$
we can compute a set of *inverse rules* [7]: First, replace each non-distinguished variable in the body with a distinct Skolem function. The resulting view is said to be *Skolemized*. Suppose ρ is the mapping that maps the non-distinguished variables to the corresponding Skolem functions, then the inverse rules are
$$\rho(p_i(X_i)) \leftarrow v(X) \text{ (for } i = 1, \ldots, n).$$
The left side of an inverse rule is called the *head*, and the right side is called the *body*. A variable in an inverse rule is said to be *free* if it appears as an independent argument of the head, that is, it appears in the head, and appears not only inside the Skolem functions. In addition, we will call $\rho(C)$ the *inferred constraint* of the atom $v(X)$.

Example 3. For the view
$\quad v(x,z) :\!\!- p_1(x,y), p_2(y,z), x > y,$
there are two inverse rules:
$\quad p_1(x, f(x,z)) \leftarrow v(x,z)$ and
$\quad p_2(f(x,z), z) \leftarrow v(x,z).$
In the first inverse rule x is a free variable, but z is not. In the second one, z is a free variable, but x is not. The inferred constraint of $v(x,z)$ is $x > f(x,z)$.

If we have more than one view, we can generate a set of inverse rules from each of them. In this case, the inverse rules generated from different views must use different Skolem functions.

In the sequel, when we say a *rule*, we mean an inverse rule. For simplicity, we also assume the rules are compact as defined below.

Definition 4. *The set of rules generated from a view is said to be compact, if the inferred constraint does not imply a non-tautological equality between a constant and a Skolem function, or between a constant and a variable, or between a variable and a Skolem function, or between two Skolem functions, or between two variables.*

Clearly, if the views are in compact form, then the rules generated will be compact.

3 An Improved Method for Testing Query Containment

Let us use $Var(Q)$ (resp. $Arg(Q)$) to denote the set of variables (resp. the set of variables and constants) in a GCQ Q. A *containment mapping* from a GCQ Q_2 to another GCQ Q_1 is a mapping from $Var(Q_2)$ to $Arg(Q_1)$ such that it maps the output of Q_2 to the output of Q_1, and maps each subgoal of Q_2 to a subgoal of Q_1.

The following lemma relates query containment to the existence of some particular containment mappings [13].

Lemma 1. *Let Q_i ($i=0,\ldots,s$) be GCQs. Let C_i be the constraints in Q_i.*
(1) If there are containment mappings $\delta_{i,1},\ldots,\delta_{i,k_i}$ from Q_i to Q_0 such that $C_0 \to \vee_{i=1}^{s} \vee_{j=1}^{k_i} \delta_{i,j}(C_i)$, then $Q_0 \sqsubseteq \cup_{i=1}^{s} Q_i$.
(2) If $Q_1,\ldots,Q_s$ are in normal form, C_0 is satisfiable, and $Q_0 \sqsubseteq \cup_{i=1}^{s} Q_i$, then there must be containment mappings $\delta_{i,1},\ldots,\delta_{i,k_i}$ from Q_i to Q_0 such that $C_0 \to \vee_{i=1}^{s} \vee_{j=1}^{k_i} \delta_{i,j}(C_i)$.

The condition that Q_i ($i=1,\ldots,s$) are in normal form in (2) of Lemma 1 is necessary even if C_0 is a tautology. This is demonstrated in the next example.

Example 4. Let Q_1 and Q_2 be
$h(w) :\!-\ q(w), p(x,y,2,1,u,u), p(1,2,x,y,u,u), p(1,2,2,1,x,y)$ and
$h(w) :\!-\ q(w), p(x,y,z,z',u,u), x<y, z>z'$, respectively. Suppose all relation attributes are from the reals. There are only two containment mappings from Q_2 to Q_1:
$\delta_1 : w \to w, x \to x, y \to y, z \to 2, z' \to 1, u \to u$ and
$\delta_2 : w \to w, x \to 1, y \to 2, z \to x, z' \to y, u \to u$
Clearly $TRUE \not\to \delta_1(x<y, z>z') \vee \delta_2(x<y, z>z')$, but $Q_1 \sqsubseteq Q_2$.

Thus in order to use Lemma 1, we need to put all of the queries $Q_1,\ldots,Q_s$ into normal form. This sometimes makes the application of Lemma 1 inconvenient. Next, we present a revised method for testing query containment using *relevance mappings*.

Before introducing relevance mappings, we need the concept of *targets*.

Definition 5. *Let Q_2 be the GCQ $q(X) :\!-\ p_1(X_1),\ldots,p_n(X_n), C$, and Q_1 be a GCQ comparable to Q_2.*
A target T of Q_2 in Q_1 is a formula $q'(Y) :\!-\ p'_1(Y_1),\ldots,p'_n(Y_n)$ such that

1. $q'(Y)$ is the head of Q_1, and for each $i \in \{1, \ldots, n\}$, $p'_i(Y_i)$ is a subgoal of Q_1 with the same relation name as that of $p_i(X_i)$.
2. If we denote the sequence of all arguments in Q_2 by $S_2 = (x_1, x_2, \ldots, x_m)$ and denote the sequence of all arguments in T by $S_1 = (y_1, y_2, \ldots, y_m)$, then none of the following holds:
    (a) There is a position i such that x_i and y_i are two different constants.
    (b) There are two positions i and j such that x_i and x_j are two different constants, but y_i and y_j are the same variable.
    (c) There are two positions i and j such that y_i and y_j are two different constants, but x_i and x_j are the same variable.

We now give a constructive definition of relevance mappings and their associated equalities.

Definition 6. Let T be a target of Q_2 in Q_1. Let $S_2 = (x_1, x_2, \ldots, x_m)$ and $S_1 = (y_1, y_2, \ldots, y_m)$ be the sequences of arguments in Q_2 and T respectively. The relevance mapping δ from Q_2 to Q_1 wrt T and its associated equality E_δ are constructed as follows: Initially, $E_\delta = TRUE$. For $i = 1$ to m

1. If x_i is a constant α, but y_i is a variable y, then let $E_\delta = E_\delta \wedge (y = \alpha)$.
2. If x_i is a variable x, and x appears the first time in position i, then let δ map x to y_i. If x appears again in a later position j ($> i$) of S_2, and $y_j \neq y_i$, then let $E_\delta = E_\delta \wedge (y_j = y_i)$.

Relevance mappings are closely related to containment mappings. Any containment mapping is a relevance mapping with the associated equality being a tautology, and a relevance mapping is a containment mapping iff its associated equality is a tautology.

If δ is a relevance mapping from Q_2 to Q_1 wrt T, then we will use $\delta(Q_2)$ to denote the query obtained by applying δ to Q_2, and use $T \wedge E_\delta \wedge \delta(C_2)$ to denote the query $q'(Y) :- p'_1(Y_1), \ldots, p'_n(Y_n), E_\delta \wedge \delta(C_2)$, where C_2 is the constraint of Q_2. Clearly $\delta(Q_2)$ is equivalent to $T \wedge E_\delta \wedge \delta(C_2)$, and it is contained in Q_2. Let us call $\delta(Q_2)$ an *image* of Q_2 in Q_1. The next lemma implies that Q_1 is contained in Q_2 if and only if Q_1 is contained in the union of all of the images of Q_2 in Q_1.

Lemma 2. Let C_i be the constraint in the GCQ Q_i ($i = 0, 1, \ldots, s$). Suppose C_0 is satisfiable. Then $Q_0 \sqsubseteq \cup_{i=1}^s Q_i$ iff there are relevance mappings $\delta_{i,1}, \ldots, \delta_{i,k_i}$ from Q_i to Q_0 such that $C_0 \rightarrow \vee_{i=1}^s \vee_{j=1}^{k_i} (\delta_{i,j}(C_i) \wedge E_{\delta_{i,j}})$, where $E_{\delta_{i,j}}$ is the associated equality of $\delta_{i,j}$.

Note there is no need to put $Q_1, \ldots, Q_s$ in any normal form. The next example demonstrates the application of Lemma 2.

Example 5. For the queries in Example 4, there is a third relevance mapping δ_3 from Q_2 to Q_1 in addition to δ_1 and δ_2:

$\delta_3 : w \rightarrow w, x \rightarrow 1, y \rightarrow 2, z \rightarrow 2, z' \rightarrow 1, u \rightarrow x$, with $E_{\delta_3} = (x = y)$.
Since $\delta_1(x < y, z > z') = x < y$, $\delta_2(x < y, z > z') = x > y$ and $\delta_3(x < y, z > z') = TRUE$, and $x < y \vee x > y \vee x = y$ is always true, we know $Q_1 \sqsubseteq Q_2$.

Lemma 2 has an additional advantage over Lemma 1: the number of mappings we have to consider can be drastically reduced in some cases. The next example shows one of such cases.

Example 6. Let Q_2 and Q_1 be
$$q(x,y) :\!- \ p(x,y,0), p(x,y,z), p(x,y',z), x \leq y, z < 10 \text{ and}$$
$$q(x,y) :\!- \ p(x,y,1), p(x,y,2), \ldots, p(x,y,N), x < y, z < 1 \text{ respectively.}$$
If we use Lemma 1 to test whether $Q_1 \sqsubseteq Q_2$, then we need to put Q_2 into normal form, and consider 3^N containment mappings from Q_2 to Q_1. If we use Lemma 2, we can see $Q_1 \not\sqsubseteq Q_2$ immediately because there are obviously no relevance mappings from Q_2 to Q_1.

Similarly, query containment under NGDs can be characterized by relevance mappings. Given a NGD ic as in (2) and a GCQ Q as in (1), we can construct *relevance mappings* and the *associated equalities* from ic to Q in a way similar to what we use in constructing relevance mappings from one GCQ to another. The only difference is that a target of ic in Q is defined to be a sequence of m subgoals $p'_1, \ldots, p'_m$ in Q such that (1) p'_i and $r_i(X_i)$ ($i = 1, \ldots, m$) have the same relation name, (2) a constant in $r_i(X_i)$ corresponds either to a variable or the same constant in p'_i, (3) no two occurrences of the same variable in $p'_1, \ldots, p'_m$ correspond to two different constants in $r_1(X_1), \ldots, r_m(X_m)$ and vice versa.

The next lemma is revised from a result in [14].

Lemma 3. *Let $\Delta = \{ic_i \equiv P_i, D_i \rightarrow FALSE | i = 1, \ldots, t\}$ be a set of NGDs, and $Q_1, \ldots, Q_s$ be GCQs. Suppose the constraint of Q_i is C_i, and C_0 is satisfiable. Then $Q_0 \sqsubseteq_\Delta \cup_{i=1}^s Q_i$ iff there are relevance mappings $\delta_{i,1}, \ldots, \delta_{i,m_i}$ from Q_i to Q_0 ($i = 1, \ldots, s$) and relevance mappings $\rho_{i,1}, \ldots, \rho_{i,k_i}$ from ic_i to Q_0 ($i = 1, \ldots, t$, $m_1 + \cdots + m_s + k_1 + \cdots + k_t > 0$) such that*
$$C_0 \rightarrow \bigvee_{i=1}^s \bigvee_{j=1}^{m_i} (\delta_{i,j}(C_i) \wedge E_{\delta_{i,j}}) \bigvee \bigvee_{i=1}^t \bigvee_{j=1}^{k_i} (\rho_{i,j}(D_i) \wedge E_{\rho_{i,j}}).$$

4 The General Approach for Rewriting Union Queries

Let Q_u be the union query to be rewritten. Without loss of generality, we assume all the GCQs in Q_u have the same head. Our method for rewriting Q_u consists of two major steps. In the first step, we generate a set of *potential formulas* (or *p-formulas* for short) which may or may not be rewritings; these p-formulas are generated separately for every GCQ in Q_u. In the second step, we combine all these p-formulas to see whether we can obtain correct rewritings.

4.1 Generating p-formulas

We assume the compact set IR of inverse rules has been computed in advance. To generate a p-formula for a GCQ, we need to find a *destination* first.

Definition 7. *Given the GCQ Q as in (1) and a set IR of compact inverse rules, a destination of Q wrt to IR is a sequence DS of n atoms $DS = p_1(Y_1), \ldots, p_n(Y_n)$ such that*

1. Each atom $p_i(Y_i)$ is the head of some rule, and it has the same relation name as that of $p_i(X_i)$, the ith subgoal of Q.
2. There is no i such that a constant in $p_i(X_i)$ corresponds to a different constant in $p_i(Y_i)$.
3. No two occurrences of the same variable in Q correspond to two different constants in DS, and no two occurrences of the same variable or Skolem function in the same rule head correspond to two different constants in Q.

Intuitively, a destination "connects" the subgoals of the query to the view atoms in a rewriting. Once a destination DS of Q is found, we can use it to (try to) construct a p-formula as follows:

1. For each atom $p_i(Y_i)$ in DS, do the following:
   Suppose the arguments in $p_i(Y_i)$ are $y_1, y_2, \ldots, y_l$, and the corresponding arguments in $p_i(X_i)$ are $x_1, x_2, \ldots, x_l$. Suppose $p_i(Y_i)$ is the head of the rule $p_i(Y_i) \leftarrow v_i(Z_i)$ (If there are rules that have the same head but different bodies, then choose one of them in turn to generate different p-formulas). Define a variable mapping ϕ_i as follows: For each free variable $z \in Y_i$, if z first appears (checking the argument positions from left to right) at position i, then map z to x_i. For each variable z in $v(Z_i)$ which does not appear in $p_i(Y_i)$ as a free variable, let ϕ_i map z to a distinct new variable not occurring in Q or any other view atom $\phi_j(v_j(Z_j))$ $(j \neq i)$.
2. Construct a formula T: $q(X) \coloneq \phi_1(p_1(Y_1)), \ldots, \phi_n(p_n(Y_n))$.
   Regard T as a target of Q and construct the relevance mapping δ from Q wrt to T (Skolem functions in the target are treated in the same way other arguments in the target are treated). We will get a GCQ

   $$q(X) \coloneq \phi_1(p_1(Y_1)), \ldots, \phi_n(p_n(Y_n)) \wedge \delta(C) \wedge E_\delta \qquad (F)$$

3. Replace $\phi_i(p_i(Y_i))$ with $\phi_i(v_i(Z_i))$ (for $i = 1, \ldots, n$), in the above GCQ to get the formula

   $$q(X) \coloneq \phi_1(v_1(Z_1)), \ldots, \phi_n(v_n(Z_n)), \delta(C) \wedge E_\delta \qquad (PF)$$

4. Suppose the inferred constraints of $v_1(Z_1), \ldots, v_n(Z_n)$ are $C_1, \ldots, C_n$ respectively. If the constraint $\delta(C) \wedge E_\delta \wedge \phi_1(C_1) \wedge \cdots \wedge \phi_n(C_n)$ is satisfiable, then output the formula (PF) (remove duplicate atoms if possible).

The formula (PF) is the *p-formula* of Q we get. Any p-formula of a GCQ in the union Q_u is called a *p-formula* of Q_u. The p-formula (PF) has the following property: If we replace each view atom with the corresponding Skolemized view body and treat the Skolem functions as variables, then we will get a safe GCQ Q'' (hereafter referred to as the *expansion* of (PF), denoted $(PF)^{exp}$) which is contained in Q. This is because (F) is a safe GCQ which is equivalent to $\delta(Q)$, and all subgoals and built-in predicates of (F) are in the body of Q''.

Lemma 4. *The expansion of a p-formula of Q is a safe GCQ contained in Q.*

Thus if there happen to be no Skolem functions in the p-formula, then the formula is a rewriting of Q.

Theorem 1. *For any query Q, if there are no Skolem functions in a p-formula of Q, then the p-formula is a rewriting of Q.*

However, if there are Skolem functions in $E_\delta \wedge \delta(C)$, then the formula (PF) is not a correct GCQ because the Skolem functions appear only in the constraint part $\delta(C) \wedge E_\delta$, and their values can not be determined. So (PF) is not a rewriting if it contains Skolem functions.

Example 7. Let the query be
$$q(u) :- p'(u), p(x,y), r(y,v), x<y, y<v+1.$$
Let the views be
$v_1(u) :- p'(u),$
$v_2(y,z) :- p(x,y), p(y,z), x<z,$ and
$v_3(y,z) :- r(x,y), r(y,z), x<z.$
The compact inverse rules are:
R1: $p'(u) \leftarrow v_1(u)$
R2: $p(f(y,z), y) \leftarrow v_2(y,z)$
R3: $p(y,z) \leftarrow v_2(y,z)$
R4: $r(g(y,z), y) \leftarrow v_3(y,z)$
R5: $r(y,z) \leftarrow v_3(y,z)$
There are four destinations:
 (1) $p'(u), p(f(y,z), y), r(y,z)$
 (2) $p'(u), p(y,z), r(y,z)$
 (3) $p'(u), p(f(y,z), y), r(g(y,z), y)$
 (4) $p'(u), p(y,z), r(g(y,z), y)$
For the first destination, we first define the mappings
$\phi_1 : u \to u$; $\phi_2 : y \to y$; and $\phi_3 : y \to y, z \to v$.
and construct the target
$$q(u) :- p'(u), p(f(y,z), y), r(y,v).$$
Then we obtain the image of Q wrt the above target
$$q(u) :- p'(u), p(f(y,z), y), r(y,v), f(y,z) < y, y < v+1.$$
Finally we replace $p'(u), p(f(y,z), y), r(y,v)$ with $v_1(u), v_2(y,z), v_3(y,v)$ to get the p-formula
$$q(u) :- v_1(u), v_2(y,z), v_3(y,v), f(y,z) < y, y < v+1.$$
Similarly, for the second destination (2), we can get the p-formula
$$q(u) :- v_1(u), v_2(x,y), v_3(y,v), x<y, y<v+1.$$
The second p-formula is a rewriting because it involves no Skolem functions.

4.2 Obtaining Rewritings from the p-formulas

As noted earlier, when there are Skolem functions in a p-formula, the p-formula is not a rewriting. However, it is possible that such p-formulas can be combined to obtain correct rewritings. Generally, the following two steps are needed.

First, we choose some p-formulas and combine them into a single formula. Suppose we have chosen k p-formulas $PF_1, \ldots, PF_k$, where PF_i is of the form

$$q(X) :\!\!- v_{i,1}(Z_{i,1}), \ldots, v_{i,n_i}(Z_{i,n_i}), C_i.$$

Then the combined formula (CF) is

$$q(X) :\!\!- v_{1,1}(Z_{1,1}), \ldots, v_{1,n_1}(Z_{1,n_1}), \ldots, v_{k,1}(Z_{k,1}), \ldots, v_{k,n_k}(Z_{k,n_k}), C_1 \vee \cdots \vee C_k$$

where the variables which appear only in the view atoms (not in $q(X)$) of different p-formulas should be renamed to different variables.

Second, for the above combined formula (CF), we try to remove those constraints that involve Skolem functions, or to replace them with another constraint (over the variables in the ordinary atoms of the formula) that does not involve Skolem functions. Generally, we need to utilize the inferred constraints of view atoms as follows.

Let D be the conjunction of the inferred constraints of the view atoms in (CF). Write the constraint $C_1 \vee \cdots \vee C_k$ into conjunctive normal form, and divide it into the conjunction of C' and C'', where C' involves Skolem functions, but C'' does not. If there exists a constraint D' over the variables in $X, Z_{1,1}, \ldots, Z_{k,n_k}$ such that $D \wedge D' \wedge C''$ is satisfiable and $D \wedge D' \wedge C'' \rightarrow C'$, then output the following query (CR):

$$q(X) :\!\!- v_{1,1}(Z_{1,1}), \ldots, v_{1,n_1}(Z_{1,n_1}), \ldots, v_{k,1}(Z_{k,1}), \ldots, V_{k,n_k}(Z_{k,n_k}), C'' \wedge D'$$

The following theorem is straightforward.

Theorem 2. *The query* (CR) *computed above, if safe, is a rewriting of* Q_u.

In order to get more rewritings, we should check all possible combinations of the p-formulas. In particular, we should check whether it is possible to get a rewriting from a single p-formula. In addition, the constraint D' should be as weak as possible (for example, when it is possible, choose D' to be $TRUE$), so that the rewriting we obtain is as general as possible.

Let us look at some examples. In Example 8, we get a rewriting from a single p-formula.

Example 8. For the first p-formula in Example 7, the conjunction of the inferred constraints of the view atoms is $f(y,z) < z \wedge g(y,v) < v$. Since $(z \leq y) \wedge (f(y,z) < z) \rightarrow f(y,z) < y$, we can replace $f(y,z) < y$ with $z \leq y$ and get the rewriting

$$q(u) :\!\!- v_1(u), v_2(y,z), v_3(y,v), z \leq y, y < v+1.$$

In the next example, we combine two p-formulas by conjoining their view atoms and "disjuncting" their constraints.

Example 9. For the views in Example 1, the inverse rules are
$p(f_1(y), y) \leftarrow v_1(y)$,
$r(y, f_2(y)) \leftarrow v_2(y)$, and
$p'(f_3(y), y) \leftarrow v_3(y)$.

For Q_1, we find the destination $p(f_1(y), y), p'(f_3(y), y)$ and then the p-formula
$q(y) :- v_1(y), v_3(y), f_1(y) > y$.
For Q_2, we find the destination $p(f_1(y), y), r(y, f_2(y))$ and then the p-formula
$q(y) :- v_1(y), v_2(y), f_1(y) \leq y$.
Combining the above two p-formulas, we will get the rewriting
$q(y) :- v_1(y), v_2(y), v_3(y)$.

The rewriting in Example 2 can be found similarly.

There are two remarks about the above general approach.

First, about the completeness of the rewritings. Due to the inherent complexity of the problem (see [12]), we do not expect to find a rewriting which can produce all possible correct answers to the original query using the views. However, we do have the following theorem, which shows that p-formulas are an appropriate basis for performing rewritings.

Theorem 3. *For any non-empty union rewriting Q_r of Q_u, there are p-formulas $PF_1, \ldots, PF_s$ of Q_u such that $Q_r^{exp} \sqsubseteq \cup_{i=1}^{s} PF_i^{exp}$.*

Second, about the complexity of the general approach. The above approach is exponential in the number of views. The step of combining the p-formulas is particularly expensive because the number of possible combinations may grow explosively and the constraint implication problem is intractable in general.

In practice, one can use various simplified versions of the general approach. For example, we may choose to consider some, rather than all of the p-formulas. In Section 5, we focus on such a version which is practically much more efficient, yet it still produces maximum rewritings in some special cases. We can also consider only some, rather than all of combinations (e.g., only combinations of p-formulas which involve common Skolem functions). We can also use a more systematic way for combining the p-formulas. For example, as a rule of thumb, we should check each single p-formula first to see whether we can get rewritings; then combine p-formulas with the same non-constraint part (modulo variable renaming); and finally conjoin the view atoms of chosen p-formulas as stated before.

4.3 Handling Nullity-Generating Dependencies

Suppose there is a set $\Delta = \{ic_i \equiv P_i, D_i \rightarrow FALSE \mid i = 1, \ldots, s\}$ of NGDs. Our general method for handling these CGDs is as follows: First, regard every CGD ic_i as an empty query $\emptyset :- P_i, D_1$ (let us call it the *induced query* of ic_i), and find the p-formulas of this query. Second, combine the p-formulas of these induced queries and the p-formulas of Q_u in the same way as before, except that the p-formulas of the induced queries should be combined with at least one p-formula of Q_u and the resulting query should use the head $q(X)$, to find semantic rewritings of Q_u under Δ.

The correctness of the above method is clear from Lemma 3.

The next example is modified from Example 1.

Example 10. Let $Q_u = Q_1 \cup Q_2$, where Q_1 and Q_2 are
$q(y) :- p(x,y), p_1(x_1, y), x > y$ and
$q(y) :- p(x,y), r(y,z), x < y$ respectively.
Let $\triangle$ contain $p(x,y), p_2(y), x = y \to FALSE$ only.
The induced query is $\emptyset :- p(x,y), p_2(y), x = y$.
Let the views be
$v_1(y) :- p(x,y),$
$v_2(y) :- r(y,x),$
$v_3(y) :- p'(x,y),$ and
$v_4(y) :- p_2(y).$
For Q_1, we find the p-formula $q(y) :- v_1(y), v_3(y), f_1(y) > y$.
For Q_2, we find the p-formula $q(y) :- v_1(y), v_2(y), f_1(y) < y$.
For the induced query, we find the p-formula $\emptyset :- v_1(y), v_4(y), f_1(y) = y$.
Combine the three p-formulas, we get a combined formula
$q(y) :- v_1(y), v_2(y), v_3(y), v_1(z), v_4(z), f_1(y) > y \vee f_1(y) < y \vee f_1(z) = z$.
Clearly $z = y \to f_1(y) > y \vee f_1(y) < y \vee f_1(z) = z$, therefore, we can get the semantic rewriting $q(y) :- v_1(y), v_2(y), v_3(y), v_4(y)$.

5 A Simplified Approach

As mentioned earlier, the most difficult part of the general approach is in the p-formula combination step. The simplified approach imposes extra conditions on p-formulas, so that the combination step is simplified.

Naturally, we would like to get as many rewritings as possible from the single p-formulas. We start with the simple case where there are no built-in predicates in the query or the views. In this case, the p-formula (PF) becomes

$$q(X) :- \phi_1(v_1(Z_1)), \ldots, \phi_n(v_n(Z_n)), E_\delta.$$

That is, the constraint in the p-formula is E_δ. To make sure that there are no Skolem functions in E_δ, we first require that every distinguished variable x or constant α in the GCQ does not correspond to a Skolem function in the destination DS, otherwise there will be the equality $x = \phi_i(f(Z))$ or $\alpha = \phi_i(f(Z))$ (where $f(Z)$ is the Skolem function in $p_i(Y_i)$ corresponding to x or α) because the GCQ and the target have the same head; we then require that no variable in the GCQ corresponds to two different Skolem functions, otherwise there will be an equality between two different Skolem functions. Even when the query and views do have built-in predicates, we may still want the above requirements for DS in order to reduce the number of p-formulas.

Based on the above analysis, we can define *valid destinations* and *valid p-formulas*. We assume Q is in compact form so that we know all of the distinguished variables and non-distinguished variables.

Definition 8. *Given the GCQ Q as in (1) and a set IR of compact rules, a destination DS of Q wrt to IR is said to be a* valid destination *if*

1. *Each distinguished variable or constant in $p_i(X_i)$ corresponds to a free variable or to a constant.*

2. *All occurrences of the same non-distinguished variable in Q correspond either all to free variables and constants, or all to the same Skolem function.*

For instance, among the four destinations in Example 7, only the first two are valid destinations.

Once we have found a valid destination DS of Q, we can generate a p-formula as before. Note that even with a valid destination, there may still be equalities of the form $f(Z_1) \equiv \phi_i(f(Z)) = \phi_j(f(Z)) \equiv f(Z_2)$ in the E_δ part of the p-formula. In this case, we can remove the equality $f(Z_1) = f(Z_2)$ by replacing it with $Z_1 = Z_2$. The resulting formula is called a *valid p-formula*.

Example 11. Let the query Q be $q(x, x') := p(x, y), p(x', y)$.
Let the view V be $v(x) := p(x, y)$.
The inverse rule is $p(x, f(x)) \leftarrow v(x)$, and $p(x, f(x)), p(x, f(x))$ is a valid destination of Q. Therefore, we can construct a target
$q(x, x') := p(x, f(x)), p(x', f(x'))$ and then get the p-formula
$q(x, x') := v(x), v(x'), f(x') = f(x)$.
Replacing $f(x') = f(x)$ with $x = x'$, we get a valid p-formula
$q(x, x') := v(x), v(x'), x' = x$
which is equivalent to $q(x, x') := v(x), x' = x$. This is a rewriting of Q.

Note the valid p-formula may still have Skolem functions if Q has a constraint involving non-distinguished variables. However, if Q does not have constraints, or if the constraint of the GCQ involves distinguished variables only, then it is impossible for any valid p-formula to have Skolem functions. Thus every valid p-formula will be a rewriting.

Theorem 4. *If Q is a GCQ without constraint, or the constraint of Q involves only distinguished variables, then every valid p-formula of Q is a rewriting of Q.*

Obviously, if we limit the destinations to valid destinations, and p-formulas to valid p-formulas in the destination-based approach, then we will achieve a simplification of the rewriting process. We call this simplified version of our approach the *simplified approach*. This approach is less powerful than the general approach in the sense that it finds less rewritings. However, the simplified approach still finds maximum rewritings in some special cases. Before summarizing these cases in Theorem 5, we need to define *linear arithmetic constraints* and *basic comparisons*. A linear arithmetic constraint is a constraint of the form

$$a_1 x_1 + a_2 x_2 + \cdots + a_l x_l \; op \; b,$$

where $a_1, \ldots, a_l$ and b are constants, $x_1, \ldots, x_l$ are variables, op is one of $<, \leq, >, \geq, =, \neq$. A basic comparison is a constraint of the form $x \; op \; y$, where x, y are variables or constants, op is one of $<, \leq, >, \geq, =, \neq$.

Theorem 5. *1. Suppose the relation attributes are all from infinite domains. If the GCQs in the union query Q_u and views do not have constraints, then the* union of all valid p-formulas is a maximum rewriting wrt to the language of union queries.

2. Suppose the relation attributes are all from the reals, and the GCQs in the union query Q_u do not have constraints. If the constraints of the views are conjunctions of basic comparisons (resp. linear arithmetic constraints involving only distinguished variables), then the union of all valid p-formulas of Q_u is a maximum rewriting with respect to the language of unions of conjunctive queries with conjunctions of basic comparisons (resp. linear arithmetic constraints).

Note the assumption that the attributes are from infinite domains (resp. the reals) is necessary in 1 (resp. 2) of the theorem. For instance, the rewriting in Example 2 can not be found by the simplified approach.

6 Comparison with Related Work

In this section, we compare our approaches with some most related work, namely the Bucket, U-join, MiniCon and SVB algorithms. The Bucket algorithm is the most powerful (albeit the slowest) among these previous algorithms.

6.1 The Bucket Algorithm and the General Approach

The Bucket algorithm [6] is as follows: For each subgoal p_i of the query Q, a bucket B_i is created. If a view V has a subgoal p'_i which is unifiable with p_i, then let ϕ map every distinguished variable in p'_i to the corresponding argument in p_i. If $C \wedge \phi(C_V)$ is satisfiable (where C and C_V are the constraints of Q and V respectively), then put the view atom $\phi(v)$ in B_i. Then one view atom is taken from each of the buckets to form the body of a query Q' which has the head identical to that of Q. Then the algorithm tries to find a constraint C' such that $Q'^{exp} \wedge C' \sqsubseteq Q$. If C' can be found, then return $Q' \wedge C'$ as a rewriting.

As seen earlier, our general approach can find rewritings that can not be found by the Bucket algorithm, e.g., the rewritings in Examples 1 and 2. It is not difficult to see that any rewriting found by the Bucket algorithm can also be found by our general approach. In terms of efficiency, the Bucket algorithm does not need to combine p-formulas as in our general approach. However, for each query Q' resulting from a combination of the atoms in the buckets, it needs to do a containment test and find the constraint C', which is expensive.

6.2 The U-join Algorithm and the Simplified Approach

The U-join algorithm [1] can be used to find contained rewritings of conjunctive queries using conjunctive views when neither the query nor the views have constraints. It proceeds as follows. First a set of inverse rules is obtained in the same way as in this paper. Then for each subgoal p_i in the user query, a "label" L_i is created. Define $attr(L_i) = Arg(p_i)$. If $r := v$ is an inverse rule, and r and p_i are unifiable, then the pair $(\sigma(Arg(p_i)), \sigma(v))$ is inserted into L_i provided that

$\sigma(q)$ does not contain any Skolem functions. Here, σ is the most general unifier of p_i and r, and q is the head of the user query. The U-join of two labels L_1 and L_2, denoted $L_1 \stackrel{u}{\bowtie} L_2$, is defined as follows. Let $Y = attr(L_1) \cap attr(L_2)$, and $Z = attr(L_2) - attr(L_1)$. Define $attr(L_1 \stackrel{u}{\bowtie} L_2) = attr(L_1) \cup Z$. If L_1 contains a pair (t_1, u_1) and L_2 contains a pair (t_2, u_2), then $L_1 \stackrel{u}{\bowtie} L_2$ contains the pair $(\sigma(t_1, t_2[Z]), \sigma(u_1 \wedge u_2))$ where σ is a most general unifier of $t_1[Y]$ and $t_2[Y]$ such that $\sigma(u_1 \wedge u_2)$ does not contain Skolem functions, provided such σ exists. If $(\sigma, v_{i_1} \wedge \cdots \wedge v_{i_n})$ is in the U-join of all labels corresponding to the subgoals of the query, and the head of the query is q, then $q\sigma := v_{i_1}, \ldots, v_{i_n}$ is a conjunctive rewriting of Q. The union of all such conjunctive rewritings is returned by the U-join algorithm.

It is not difficult to see that the U-join algorithm and our simplified approach generate the same rewritings. This is because the condition in generating the label L_i "$\sigma(q)$ does not contain any Skolem functions" has the same effect as requiring that no distinguished variables of the query corresponds to a Skolem function in the valid destination, and the condition in U-joining L_1 and L_2 "σ is a most general unifier of $t_1[Y]$ and $t_2[Y]$ such that $\sigma(u_1 \wedge u_2)$ does not contain Skolem functions" has the same effect as requiring that no argument in the query corresponds to two different Skolem functions or to both a free variable (constant) and a Skolem function in the valid destination. The efficiency of the two are similar because both need to do similar variable substitutions. One can use the simplified approach to the examples in [1] to get better understanding of our claim.

6.3 MiniCon, SVB and the Simplified Approach

We claim (for proof and more detailed comparisons, see [15]) that our simplified approach finds strictly more rewritings than the MiniCon and the SVB algorithms. For instance, the rewriting in Example 8 can not be found by MiniCon or SVB but it can be found by our simplified approach. Furthermore, if the query has many subgoals, our simplified approach tends to be faster. In addition, MiniCon and SVB do not handle constants properly. The authors do not say whether a constant should be treated like a distinguished variable or not. If not, the algorithm may fail to find a rewriting even for conjunctive queries without built-in predicates. For example, if $Q(x, y) := p(x, y)$ is the query, and $V(x) := p(x, 1)$ is the view, then no MCDs can be generated for Q and V, and no rewriting can be generated, but clearly $Q(x, 1) := V(x)$ is a rewriting. On the other hand, if constants are treated like distinguished variables, the MiniCon algorithm may generate incorrect rewritings. For example, if the query is $q(u) := p_1(x, u), p_2(u, x)$, and the views are $v_1(y) := p_1(1, y)$ and $v_2(z) := p_2(z, 2)$, then MiniCon will produce an incorrect "rewriting" $q(u) := p_1(x, u), p_2(u, x)$.

7 Conclusion and Further Research

We presented a destination-based general approach for rewriting union queries using views. When used to rewrite GCQs, our approach is more powerful than existing algorithms. Furthermore, it can exploit NGDs to find semantic rewritings. A simplified version of the approach is less complete, but is faster and can still find maximum rewritings in some special cases. Our approaches generalize existing algorithms for rewriting GCQs using general conjunctive views.

Currently we are trying to identify more classes of built-in predicates with which there is a more efficient way of combining the p-formulas and with which we can obtain the maximum rewritings. We plan to investigate the effect of more complex integrity constraints on the rewriting. We also plan to implement our approaches so as to get empirical evaluation of their performance.

References

[1] X. Qian. Query folding. In *Proc. of 12th ICDE*, pages 48–55, 1996.
[2] J.D. Ullman. Information integration using logical views. *TCS: Theoretical Computer Science*, 239(2):189–210, 2000.
[3] P.-A. Larson and H. Z. Yang. Computing queries from derived relations. In *Proc. of VLDB*, pages 259–269, 1985.
[4] H. Z. Yang and P.-A. Larson. Query transformation for PSJ-queries. In *VLDB*, pages 245–254, 1987.
[5] A. Levy. Answering queries using views: a survey. Technical report, Computer Science Dept, Washington Univ., 2000.
[6] A. Levy, A. Rajaraman, and J. J. Ordille. Querying heterogeneous information sources using source descriptions. In *Proc. of VLDB*, pages 251–262, 1996.
[7] O. M. Duschka and M. R. Genesereth. Answering recursive queries using views. In *Proc. 16th PODS*, pages 109–116, 1997.
[8] R. Pottinger and A. Levy. A scalable algorithm for answering queries using views. In *Proc. of VLDB*, pages 484–495, 2000.
[9] P. Mitra. An algorithm for answering queries efficiently using views. In *Proc. of the 12th Australasian database conference*, 2001.
[10] J. Gryz. Query rewriting using views in the presence of functional and inclusion dependencies. *Information Systems*, 24(7):597–612, 1999.
[11] O. Duschka, M. Genesereth, and A. Levy. Recursive query plans for data integration. *Journal of Logic Programming, special issue on Logic Based Heterogeneous Information Systems*, pages 778–784, 2000.
[12] S. Abiteboul and O. Duschka. Complexity of answering queries using materialized views. In *Proc. of PODS*, pages 254–263, 1998.
[13] M. J. Maher. A logic programming view of CLP. In *Proc. 10th International Conference on Logic Programming*, pages 737–753, 1993.
[14] M. Maher and J. Wang. Optimizing queries in extended relational databases. In *Proc. of the 11th DEXA conference, LNCS 1873*, pages 386–396, 2000.
[15] J. Wang, M. Maher, and R. Topor. Rewriting general conjunctive queries using views. In *Proc. of the 13th Australasian Database Conference*, Australia, 28 January–1 February 2002.

Profit Mining: From Patterns to Actions*

Ke Wang[1], Senqiang Zhou[1], and Jiawei Han[2]

[1] Simon Fraser University
{wangk,szhou}@cs.sfu.ca
[2] University of Illinois at Urbana-Champaign
hanj@cs.uiuc.edu

Abstract. A major obstacle in data mining applications is the gap between the statistic-based pattern extraction and the value-based decision making. We present a *profit mining* approach to reduce this gap. In profit mining, we are given a set of past transactions and pre-selected target items, and we like to build a model for recommending target items and promotion strategies to new customers, with the goal of maximizing the net profit. We identify several issues in profit mining and propose solutions. We evaluate the effectiveness of this approach using data sets of a wide range of characteristics.

1 Introduction

Data management today is required of the ability to extract interesting patterns from large and raw data to help decision making, i.e., *data mining*. Often, patterns are deemed "interesting" on the basis of passing certain statistical tests such as support/confidence [AIS93,AMSTV96,AS94]. To an enterprise, however, it remains unclear how such patterns can be used to maximize a business objective. For example, knowing association rules {*Perfume*} → *Lipstick*, {*Perfume*} → *Diamond*, ... that are related to *Perfume*, a store manager wishing to maximize the profit margin still cannot tell which of *Lipstick*, *Diamond*, ..., and what price, should be recommended to a customer buying *Perfume*. Simply recommending all items will overwhelm the customer and defeat the purpose of recommendation. Simply recommending the most profitable item, say *Diamond*, or the most likely item, say *Lipstick*, does not maximize the profit because there is often an inverse correlation between the likelihood to buy and the dollar amount to spend. The major obstacle lies at the gap between *individual, statistic-based summaries* extracted by traditional rule mining and a *global, profit-driven action* required by business decision making.

1.1 The Profit Mining Problem

We propose the *profit mining* approach to address this issue. In profit mining, we are given a collection of past transactions, target items and non-target items,

---

* Research was supported in part by research grants from the Natural Science and Engineering Research Council of Canada.

and promotion codes containing the pricing and cost information of items. A transaction contains one target sale of the form $\langle I, P, Q\rangle$, for some target item I, and several non-target sales of the form $\langle I', P, Q\rangle$, for non-target items I'. The presence of $\langle I, P, Q\rangle$ (or $\langle I', P, Q\rangle$) in a transaction conveys that I (or I') was sold in the quantity of Q under the promotion code P. *Profit mining* is to build a model, called the *recommender*, that recommends a pair of target item I and promotion code P to future customers whenever they buy non-target items. A successful recommendation generates $(Price(P) - Cost(P)) \times Q$ profit, where $Price(P)$ and $Cost(P)$ are the price and cost represented by P, and Q is the quantity sold because of the recommendation. The goal is to maximize the total profit of target items on future customers.

Unlike a basic prediction model that "repeats the past", profit mining is expected to "get smarter from the past". An example illustrates the point. Suppose that 100 customers each bought 1 pack of Egg at the pack price of $1/pack, and another 100 customers each bought one package of 4-pack at the package price of $3.2/4-pack. Assume that each pack costs $0.5 in both cases. The first 100 customers generate the profit of $100 \times (1 - 0.5) = \$50$, and the second 100 customers generate the profit of $100 \times (3.2 - 2) = \$120$. The total profit is $170. With no inherent difference between the two groups of customers, to the next 200 new customers a basic prediction model will recommend the pack price in one half case and the package price in the other half case. This will repeat the profit of $170. In contrast, profit mining is expected to reveal that the profit has increased at the package price and recommend this price to all the next 200 customers. This will generate the profit of $240.

A "quick solution" to profit mining is to find several most probable recommendations using a basic prediction model, and re-rank them by taking into account both probability and profit. In this solution, the profit is considered as an afterthought. For example, for the decision tree [Q93] (as the basic predication model), whether a rule is extracted as a pattern or is pruned as a noise is solely based on the frequency information. The study in [MS96] shows that pushing the profit objective into model building is a significant win over the afterthought strategy.

1.2 The Issues

The key to profit mining is to recommend "right" items and "right" prices. If the price is too high, the customer will go away without generating any profit; if the price is too low or if the item is not profitable, the profit will not be maximized. Our approach is to exploit data mining to extract the patterns for right items and right prices. Let us examine the issues/requirements in this context.

1. **Profit-based patterns**. A pure statistic-based approach will favor the rule $\{Perfume\} \rightarrow Lipstick$ because of higher confidence, and a pure profit-based approach will favor rule $\{Perfume\} \rightarrow Diamond$ because of higher profit. Neither necessarily maximizes the profit. Indeed, items of high profit are often statistically insignificant because fewer people buy expensive stuffs.

To maximize profit, the rule extraction needs to take into account both statistical significance and profit significance.
2. **Shopping on unavailability**. To maximize profit, it is important to recognize that paying a higher price does not imply that the customer will not pay a lower price; rather, it is because no lower price was available at the transaction time. This behavior is called *shopping on unavailability*. Taking into account this behavior in rule extraction will bring new opportunities for increasing the profit.
3. **Explosive search space**. A typical application has thousands of items and much more sales, any combination of which could be a trigger of recommendation. Any table-based representation such as decision tree and neural network require thousands of columns or input nodes to encode items and sales. To make matters worse, patterns are often searched at alternative concepts (e.g., food, meat, etc.) and prices of items.
4. **Optimality of recommendation**. Given the large search space, finding the exact optimal recommender is infeasible. Still, it is important, both theoretically and practically, to obtain some optimality guarantee within some important classes of recommenders.
5. **Interpretability of recommendation**. It is highly desirable or even necessary to have a recommender that is able to explain the rationale of recommendation in a human understandable way. For example, knowing what triggers the recommendation of certain target items could be useful for setting up a cross-selling plan.

1.3 Our Approaches

To address the scalability and interpretability in Requirements 3 and 5, we exploit association rules [AIS93,AS94] for constructing the recommender. By some extension of association rules, we are able to incorporate the customer preference into the mining. This addresses Requirement 2. However, association rules alone do not maximize the profit because they are not profit sensitive and do not optimize a global objective. One technical contribution of this work is to combine individually extracted association rules into a single model that maximizes the projected profit on future customers. The novelty of this approach is the selection of association rules based on both statistical significance and profit significance. We show that the recommender constructed is optimal within an important class of recommenders. Experiments show encouraging results.

In Section 2, we define the profit mining problem. In Section 3, we construct a recommender using extended association rules. In Section 4, we simplify the recommender to increase the projected profit on future transactions. In Section 5, we study the effectiveness of the approach. We review related work in Section 6. Finally, we conclude the paper.

2 Problem Definition

In profit mining, we like to promote the sales of *target items* based on the sales of *non-target items*. Every item has one or more *promotion codes*. A promotion codes contain the price and cost information for a promotion package. A *target sale* (resp. *non-target sale*) has the form $\langle I, P, Q \rangle$, representing a sale of quantity Q of item I under promotion code P. A *transaction*, written as $\{s_1, \ldots, s_k, s\}$, consists of one target sale s and several non-target sales $s_1, \ldots, s_k$. A *recommender* recommends a target item I and a promotion code P (of I) to future customers whenever they buy some non-target items. If the recommendation is successful, i.e., the customer actually buys some quantity Q of item I under P, it generates $(Price(P) - Cost(P)) \times Q$ profit, where $Price(P)$ and $Cost(P)$ are the price and cost represented by P.

Example 1. Suppose that an item 2%_Milk has four promotion codes (not necessarily offered at the same time): ($3.2/4-pack,$2), ($3.0/4-pack,$1.8), ($1.2/pack, $0.5), and ($1/pack, $0.5), where the first element denotes the price and the second element denotes the cost. Let P denote ($3.2/4-pack,$2). A sale $\langle Egg, P, 5 \rangle$ generates of $5 \times (3.2 - 2) = \$6$ profit. Note that the price, cost and quantity in a sale refer to the same packing (e.g., 4-pack).

Some (descriptive) items, such as $Gender = Male$, do not have a natural notion of promotion code. For such items, we set $Price(P)$ and Q to 1 and $Cost(P)$ to 0, and the notion of profit becomes the notion of support. In this paper, we assume that all target items have a natural notion of promotion code.

Definition 1 (Profit mining). Given a collection of past transactions (over some specified target and non-target items), the problem of *profit mining* is to find a recommender that generates as much profit as possible on target items over future transactions. ▽

This problem implicitly assumes that the given transactions are representative in recommendation structure of the entire population. To define the profit mining problem precisely, we need to specify the representation of recommenders. Our first consideration is that recommendation often depends on some categories (or concepts) of items. The categorization of items can be specified by a concept hierarchy [HF95,SA95].

A *concept hierarchy*, denoted H, is a rooted, directed acyclic graph, with each leaf node representing an item and a non-leaf node representing a concept. For example, assume that an item *Flake_Chicken* belongs to categories *Chicken*, *Meat*, *Food*, *ANY*. If a customer bought *Flake_Chicken*, obviously the customer also "bought" *Chicken*, *Meat*, *Food*, *Any*. For non-target items, such generalization allows us to search for the best category that capture certain recommendations. We do not consider categories for target items because it does not make sense to recommend a concept and a price (such as *Applicance* for$100) unless the concept refers to a specific item known to the customer. Therefore, in the concept hierarchy, target items are (immediate) children of the root ANY.

Our second consideration has to do with the *shopping on unavailability* mentioned in Introduction. Consider a customer who has bought one 2-pack of Egg for 3.80\$. If the lower price 3.50\$/2-pack has been offered (for the same item) before his/her purchase, clearly the customer would have taken the offer, even though there is a mismatch in the two prices. This suggests that the acceptance of recommendation should be based on the "intention" of customers, rather than on the exact match of price. We say that a promotion code P is *more favorable than* a promotion code P', denoted $P \prec P'$, if P offers more value (to the customer) for the same or lower price, or offers a lower price for the same or more value, than P' does.

For example, \$3.50/2-pack offers a lower price than \$3.80/2-pack for the same value, and \$3.50/2-pack offers more value than \$3.50/1-pack for the same price. In both cases, the former is more favorable than the latter. However, \$3.80/2-pack is not (always) more favorable than \$3.50/pack because it is not favorable to pay more for unwanted quantity.

Mining on availability - MOA. If a customer is willing to buy an item under some promotion code, we assume that the customer will buy the item under a more favorable promotion code. This assumption is called the *mining on availability*, or simply *MOA*. To incorporate the knowledge of MOA into search, we treat a more favorable promotion code P as a "concept" of a less favorable one P'. The effect is that a sale under P' implies a sale under P. This can be done by extending the concept hierarchy H as follows.

Definition 2 (MOA(H)). For each item I, let $(\prec, I)$ denote the hierarchy of pairs $\langle I, P \rangle$ induced by $\prec$ on the promotion codes P for I, with I being added as the root. $MOA(H)$ is the hierarchy obtained by making each leaf node I in H as the root of the hierarchy $(\prec, I)$. ▽

A transaction is generalized by generalizing its sales using $MOA(H)$ as described below.

Definition 3 (Generalized sales). In $MOA(H)$, (i) every parent node is a *generalized sale* of every child node; (ii) every node of the form $\langle I, P \rangle$ is a *generalized sale* of a sale of the form $\langle I, P, Q \rangle$; (iii) "is a generalized sale of" is transitive. A set of generalized sales $G = \{g_1, \ldots, g_k\}$ *matches* a set of sales $S = \{s_1, \ldots, s_p\}$ if each g_i is a generalized sale of some s_j. ▽

(i) generalizes a sale using concepts and favorable promotion codes. (ii) generalizes a sale by ignoring the quantity of the sale. A generalized sale has one of the forms $\langle I, P \rangle$, or I, or C, where P is a promotion code, I is an item, C is a concept. For a target item I, we consider only generalized sales of the form $\langle I, P \rangle$ because only this form represents our recommendation of a pair of target item and promotion code. Note that a generalized sale of the form $\langle I, P \rangle$ contains the packing quantity defined by the promotion code P. The quantity of individual sales will be factored in the profit of rules.

Example 2. Consider a non-target item *Flaked_Chicken*, abbreviated as *FC*, and a target item *Sunchip*. Figure 1(a) shows the concept hierarchy H. Suppose that *FC* has three promotion codes: \$3, \$3.5, and \$3.8, and *Sunchip* has three promotion codes: $3.8, $4.5,$ and $5. For simplicity, we omit the cost and assume that the packing quantity for all promotion codes is 1. Figure 1(b) shows $MOA(H)$. $\langle FC, \$3.8 \rangle$ and its ancestors are generalized sales of sales $\langle FC, \$3.8, Q \rangle$. $\langle FC, \$3.5 \rangle$ and its ancestors are generalized sales of sales $\langle FC, \$3.5, Q \rangle$ or $\langle FC, \$3.8, Q \rangle$. $\langle FC, \$3 \rangle$ and its ancestors are generalized sales of sales $\langle FC, \$3, Q \rangle$, or $\langle FC, \$3.5, Q \rangle$, or $\langle FC, \$3.8, Q \rangle$. Similar generalization exists for target item Sunchip.

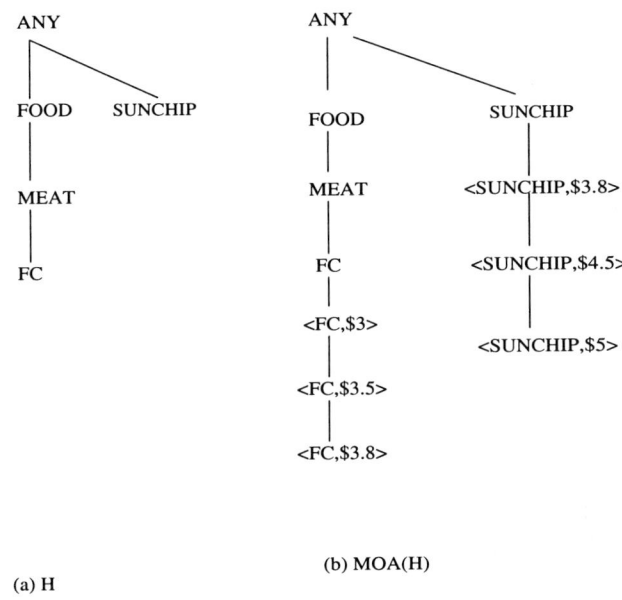

Fig. 1. H and $MOA(H)$

Definition 4 (Recommenders). A *rule* has the form $\{g_1, \ldots, g_k\} \rightarrow \langle I, P \rangle$, where $g_1, \ldots, g_k$ are generalized non-target sales such that no g_i is a generalized sale of other g_j, and $\langle I, P \rangle$ is a generalized target sale. Consider a customer represented by a set of non-target sales $\{s_1, \ldots, s_p\}$. A rule $\{g_1, \ldots, g_k\} \rightarrow \langle I, P \rangle$ *matches* the customer if $\{g_1, \ldots, g_k\}$ generalizes $\{s_1, \ldots, s_p\}$. If a matching rule $\{g_1, \ldots, g_k\} \rightarrow \langle I, P \rangle$ is selected to make recommendation and if the customer buys some quantity Q of I under the recommended promotion code, the profit generated is $(Price(P) - Cost(P)) \times Q$. A *recommender* is a set of rules plus a method for selecting rules to make recommendation to future customers. ▽

Note that the condition that no g_i is a generalized sale of other g_j implies that $k \leq p$. In the above framework, each transaction contains one target sale and each rule recommends one pair of target item and promotion code. To apply to transactions containing several target sales and recommendation of several pairs of target item and promotion code, we can generate the same type of rules but we select several rules for each recommendation. The number of rules selected per recommendation can be specified by the user. Therefore, our framework is not a restriction.

3 Constructing the Initial Recommender

We construct a recommender in two steps. In the first step, we generate association rules and specify the method for selecting recommendation rules. This recommender does not necessarily produce a high profit on future transactions because many rules are too specific. In the second step, we remove such rules on a basis of increasing the projected profit on future customers. This section focuses on the first step.

3.1 Generating Rules

Since the space of candidate rules is extremely large, we must focus on rules of some minimum "worth". The worth is a measure of how well a rule captures the "customer intention". Suppose that a rule $r : \{g_1, \ldots, g_k\} \to \langle I, P \rangle$ matches a given transaction $t : \{s_1, \ldots, s_p, \langle I_t, P_t, Q_t \rangle\}$, where $\langle I_t, P_t, Q_t \rangle$ is the target sale. If $\langle I, P \rangle$ generalizes $\langle I_t, P_t, Q_t \rangle$, that is, $I = I_t$ and $P \prec P_t$, then r has captured the intention of t. In this case, we credit the worth of r by the profit of r generated on t. To estimate this profit, we regard t as a future customer and determine the quantity Q the customer will buy under the more favorable promotion code P. The *generated profit* of r on t is defined as

- $p(r,t) = (Price(P) - Cost(P)) \times Q$, if $\langle I, P \rangle$ generalizes $\langle I_t, P_t, Q_t \rangle$, or
- $p(r,t) = 0$, otherwise.

We consider two methods of estimating the actual purchase quantity Q for the more favorable promotion code P under MOA. **Saving MOA** assumes that the customer keeps the original quantity Q_t unchanged, thus, saving money. **Buying MOA** assumes that the customer keeps the original spending $P_t \times Q_t$ unchanged, thus, increasing the quantity to $Q = P_t \times Q_t / P$. Both assumptions are conservative by not increasing the spending at a favorable promotion. These assumptions are favorable to the customer in that the customer either spends less for the same quantity or spends the same for more quantity. A more greedy estimation could associate the increase of spending with the relative favorability of P over P_t and the uncertainty of customer behaviors. We will consider such estimation in our experiments.

Definition 5 (Worth of a rule). For any set of generalized sales X, let $Supp(X)$ denote the percentage of the transactions matched by X. Consider a rule $G \to g$.

- $Supp(G \to g)$: The *support* of $G \to g$, defined as $Supp(G \cup \{g\})$.

- $Conf(G \to g)$: The *confidence* of $G \to g$, defined as $Supp(G \cup \{g\})/Supp(G)$.
- $Prof_{ru}(G \to g)$: The *rule profit* of $G \to g$, defined as $\Sigma_t p(G \to g, t)$, where t is a transaction matched by $G \to g$.
- $Prof_{re}(G \to g)$: The *recommendation profit* of $G \to g$, defined as $Prof_{ru}(G \to g)/N$, where N is the number of transactions matched by $G \to g$. ▽

The recommendation profit is on a per-recommendation basis and factors in both the hit rate (i.e., confidence) and the profit of the recommended item. It is possible that a rule of high recommendation profit matches only a small number of transactions that have large profit. Determining whether such rules should be used is a tricky issue and will be examined in Section 4.

To find rules of minimum worth, the user can specify minimum thresholds on these measures. The minimum support must be specified to take advantage of the support-based pruning [AS94]. If all target items have non-negative profit, a similar pruning is possible for rule profit and the minimum support can be replaced with the minimum rule profit. We follow [SA95,HF95] to find association rules, with $MOA(H)$ being the input concept hierarchy.

In the rest of discussion, let $\mathcal{R}$ denotes the set of rules generated as above, plus the *default rule* $\emptyset \to g$, where g is the generalized target sale that maximizes $Prof_{re}(\emptyset \to g)$. Adding the default rule ensures that any set of non-target sales has at least one matching rule in $\mathcal{R}$.

3.2 Specifying Recommendation Rules

A key for making recommendation is to select a recommendation rule from $\mathcal{R}$ for a given customer. Our selection criterion is maximizing the recommendation profit of the selected rule, as stated below.

Definition 6 (Coverage of rules). Let $body(r)$ denote the set of generalized sales in the body of r, and let $|body(r)|$ denote the number of such generalized sales. For any two rules r and r', we say that r is *ranked higher than* r'

- (Profit per recommendation) if $Prof_{re}(r) > Prof_{re}(r')$, or
- (Generality) if $Prof_{re}(r) = Prof_{re}(r')$, but $Supp(r) > Supp(r')$, or
- (Simplicity) if $Supp(r) = Supp(r')$, but $|body(r)| < |body(r')|$, or
- (Totality of order) if $|body(r)| = |body(r')|$, but r is generated before r',

in that order. Given a set B of non-target sales, a rule r in $\mathcal{R}$ is the *recommendation rule* for B if r matches B and has highest possible rank. This is called the *most-profitable-first* selection, or *MPF*. We also say that recommendation rule r covers B. ▽

Confidence is not mentioned here because it is indirectly factored in the recommendation profit.

Definition 7 (MPF recommender). The *MPF recommender* is the set of rules $\mathcal{R}$ plus the MPF for recommendation rules. ▽

4 Optimizing the MPF Recommender

However, the MPF does not deal with the overfitting of rules because a high recommendation profit does not imply a high support. It does not work to simply remove rules of low support by a high minimum support because high-profit items typically have a low support. Our approach is to prune rules on the basis of increasing the *projected profit* on future customers: Suppose that we know how to estimate the projected profit of a rule r using the given transactions covered by r, denoted by $Cover(r)$. We can prune one rule at a time if doing so increases the projected profit of the recommender, defined as the sum of the projected profit of all rules in the recommender. This approach must answer the following questions:

- Question 1: If some rule is pruned, which remaining rules will cover those transactions that were previously covered by the pruned rule? This information is necessary for subsequent prunings.
- Question 2: How do we select the rule for pruning at each step? Does the pruning order matter? Does such pruning produce an "optimal" recommender?
- Question 3: How do we estimate the projected profit of a rule?

We answer these questions in the rest of this section.

4.1 The Covering Relationship

If a rule is pruned, we choose the "next best" rule to take over the coverage of its transactions. To define this notion of "next best", we say that r is *more general than* r', or r' is *more special than* r, if $body(r)$ generalizes $body(r')$. r and r' do not necessarily have the same head. If a rule is more special and ranked lower than some other rule in $\mathcal{R}$, this rule will never be used as a recommendation rule because some general rule of a higher rank will cover whatever it matches. From now on, we assume that all such rules are removed from $\mathcal{R}$.

Definition 8. In the *covering tree* of $\mathcal{R}$, denoted $\mathcal{CT}$, a rule r is the *parent* of a rule r' if r is more general than r' and has the highest possible rank. If a rule r is pruned, the parent of r will cover the transactions covered by r ▽

In $\mathcal{CT}$, rules are increasingly more specific and ranked higher walking down the tree. Therefore, it makes sense to prune specific rules in the bottom-up order. The effect is to "cut off" some subtrees to maximize the projected profit.

4.2 The Cut-Optimal Recommender

By "cutting off" the subtree at a rule r, r becomes a leaf node and covers all the transactions previously covered by (the rules in) the subtree, according to the covering tree. The "best cut" should yield the maximum projected profit, defined below.

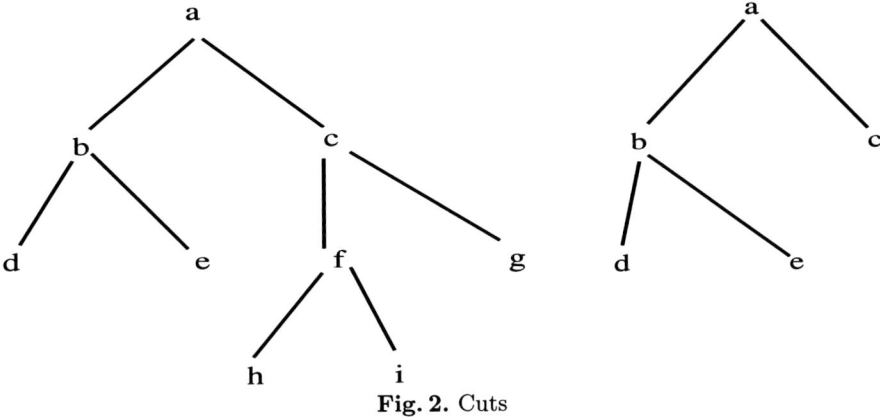
Fig. 2. Cuts

Definition 9. A *cut* of CT contains exactly one node on each root-to-leaf path in CT. For a cut C, CT_C denotes the tree obtained from CT by pruning all subtrees at the nodes in C. A cut C is *optimal* if CT_C has the maximum (estimated) projected profit and C is as small as possible. CT_C is the *cut-optimal recommender* if C is an optimal cut. ▽

The essence of cuts is that either all children are pruned or none is pruned. By cutting the tree this way, we avoid the sensitivity caused by different orders of pruning child nodes. Consider the covering tree CT on the left in Figure 2. Examples of cuts are $\{a\}$, $\{b,c\}$, $\{d,e,c\}$, $\{b,f,g\}$, $\{b,h,i,g\}$, $\{d,e,f,g\}$, $\{d,e,h,i,g\}$. $\{a,b\}$ and $\{d,e,f\}$ are not a cut because they contain two nodes or no node on some root-to-leaf path. On the right in Figure 2 is CT_C for $C = \{d,e,c\}$.

We can show that the optimal cut is unique.

Theorem 1. A covering tree has exactly one optimal cut (therefore, exactly one cut-optimal recommender). ▽

Proof: If there are two optimal cuts C_1 and C_2, they must cross over in the sense that some portion of C_1, say $\overline{C_1}$, is above C_2, and some portion of C_2, say $\overline{C_2}$, is above C_2. Then it can be shown that the smaller cut formed by $\overline{C_1}$ and $\overline{C_2}$ yields a recommender that has no less projected profit than CT_{C_1} or CT_{C_2}, contradicting that C_i's are optimal cuts. ▽

To find the optimal cut of CT, one can start with the root of CT and consider every possible subset of child nodes for expanding the current node, and for each subset considered, recursively repeat this expansion for each node in the subset. This method examines an exponential number of subsets of child nodes and is not scalable for large recommenders. We present a linear time algorithm for finding the optimal cut of a given covering tree.

Finding the cut-optimal recommender. The algorithm finds the optimal cut of CT in a bottom-up traversal of the tree. Consider the current non-leaf node r. Let $Tree\_Prof(r)$ denote the projected profit of the subtree at r. Let $Leaf\_Prof(r)$ denote the projected profit of r as a leaf node. The estimation of of these profits will be explained shortly. Intuitively, $Tree\_Prof(r)$ and

$Leaf\_Prof(r)$ are the projected profit before and after pruning the subtree at r. If $Leaf\_Prof(r) \leq Tree\_Prof(r)$, we prune the subtree at r immediately; otherwise, we do nothing at r. "Pruning the subtree at r" means deleting the nodes and edges below r and modifying the coverage $Cover(r)$ to contain all transactions previously covered by the nodes in the subtree. After all nodes are traversed, the unpruned top portion of $\mathcal{CT}$ is the cut-optimal recommender, as stated in Theorem 2 below.

Theorem 2. The recommender $\mathcal{CT}$ at the end of the above bottom-up traversal is cut-optimal. ▽

Proof: Note that the pruning at each node does not affect the pruning at other nodes. Therefore, if the test at a node is in favor of pruning the subtree at the node to increase the projected profit of the recommender, an optimal cut will never contain this subtree. ▽

Now we sketch the idea of estimating the projected profit of a rule r, denoted $Prof_{pr}(r)$. We estimate $Prof_{pr}(r)$ by $X \times Y$. X is the (estimated) # of "hits" of r, i.e., # of acceptances of the recommendation, in a random population of $N = |Cover(r)|$ customers that are covered by r. Y is the observed average profit per hit. We compute X using the *pessimistic estimation* borrowed from [CP34,Q93]: Suppose that E of the N transactions covered by r are not hit by the recommendation of r, i.e., do not match the righ-hand side of r. If this is regarded as a sample of a binomial distribution over the entire population of transactions, for a given confidence level CF the upper limit of the probability of non-hit in the entire population is estimated by $U_{CF}(N, E)$ as computed in [CP34,Q93]. Then, $X = N \times (1 - U_{CF}(N, E))$. Y is estimated by

$$\frac{\Sigma_{t \in Cover(r)} p(r,t)}{\# \text{ of hits in } Cover(r)}. \quad (1)$$

Recall that $p(r,t)$ is the generated profit of r on transaction t (defined in Section 2). $Tree\_Prof(r)$ is computed as the sum of $Prof_{pr}(u)$ over all nodes u in the subtree at r. This sum can be computed incrementally in the bottom-up traversal of the tree. $Leaf\_Prof(r)$ is computed as $Prof_{pr}(r)$ by assuming that r covers all the transactions covered by the subtree at r.

5 Evaluation

We like to validate two claims: the cut-optimal recommender is profitable, and incorporating profit and MOA into model building is essential for achieving this profitability.

5.1 The Methodology

We perform 5 runs on each dataset using the 5-fold cross-validation. In particular, the dataset is divided into 5 partitions of equal size, and each run holds back one (distinct) partition for validating the model and uses the other 4 partitions for building the model. The average result of the 5 runs is reported. We define the *gain* of a recommender as the ratio of generated profit over the recorded profit in the validating transactions in the held-back partition:

$$\Sigma_t p(r,t)/\Sigma_t \text{ the recorded profit in } t$$

where $p(r,t)$ (defined in Section 2) is the generated profit of the recommendation rule r on a validating transaction t. The higher the gain, the more profitable the recommender. For saving MOA and buying MOA, the maximum gain is 1 because the spending is never increased under a favorable promotion code. Unless otherwise stated, saving MOA is the default. (The gain for buying MOA will be higher if all target items have non-negative profit.)

PROF+MOA represents the cut-optimal recommender, emphasizing that both profit and MOA are used in building the recommender. We compare PROF+MOA with:

- PROF–MOA: the cut-optimal recommender without MOA. This comparison will reveal the effectiveness of MOA.
- CONF+MOA: the cut-optimal recommender using the binary profit: $p(r,t) = 1$ if the recommendation is a hit; otherwise, $p(r,t) = 0$. Thus, the model building ignores the profit and relies on the hit rate (i.e., confidence) for ranking and pruning rules. This comparison will reveal the effectiveness of profit-based model building.
- CONF–MOA: CONF+MOA without MOA.
- kNN: the *k-nearest neighbor* classifier [YP97]. Given a set of non-target sales, kNN selects k transactions (the k nearest neighbors), for some fixed integer k, that are most similar to the given non-target sales and recommends the pair of target item and promotion code most "voted" by these transactions. We used the kNN that is tailored to sparse data, as in [YP97] for classifying text documents, and we applied MOA to tell whether a recommendation is a hit. These modifications substantially increase the hit rate and profit.
- MPI: the *most profitable item* approach, which simply recommends the pair of target item and promotion code that has generated most profit in past transactions.

5.2 Datasets

The synthetic datasets were generated by the IBM synthetic data generator [1], but modified to have price and cost for each item in a transaction. First, we apply the IBM generator to generate a set of transactions, with the number of transactions $|T| = 100K$ and the number of items $|I| = 1000$, and default settings for other parameters. Items are numbered from 1 to $|I|$. For simplicity, each item has a single cost and a single packing for all promotion codes. In this case, we use "price" for "promotion code". The cost of item i is denoted by $Cost(i)$. For

---
[1] http://www.almaden.ibm.com/cs/quest/syndata.html#assocSynData

item i, we generate the cost $Cost(i) = c/i$, where c is the maximum cost of a single item, and m prices $P_j = (1 + j \times \delta)Cost(i)$, $j = 1, \ldots, m$. We use $m = 4$ and $\delta = 10\%$. Thus, the profit of item i at its price P_j is $j \times \delta \times Cost(i)$. Each item in a transaction is mapped to a non-target sale by randomly selecting one price from the m prices of the item. For simplicity, all sales have unit quantity.

We consider two distributions for generating the target sale in each transaction. In dataset I, we consider two target items with cost of \$2 and \$10 respectively. Many important decision makings such as *direct marketing* [MS96] are in the form of two-target recommendation. We model the sales distribution of the two target items using the Zipf law [2]: the target item of cost \$2 occurs five times as frequently in the dataset as the target item of cost \$10. Therefore, the higher the cost, the fewer the sales. The price generation and selection for target items are similar to those for non-target items. In dataset II, there are 10 target items, numbered from 1 to 10. The cost of target item i is $Cost(i) = 10 \times i$. Unlike dataset I, the frequency of target items follows the normal distribution [3]: most customers buy target items with the cost around the mean. Figure 3(e) and Figure 4(e) show the profit distribution of target sales in dataset I and dataset II.

5.3 Results

Figure 3 shows that the result on dataset I. Figure 3(a) shows the gain of the six recommenders (for kNN, $k = 5$ gives the best result) with two obvious trends: PROF+MOA performs significantly better than other recommenders, and the recommenders with MOA perform significantly better than their counterparts without MOA. This clearly demonstrates the effectiveness of incorporating profit and MOA into the search of recommenders. PROF+MOA achieves 76% gain at minimum support 0.1%. This gain is encouraging because the saving MOA adopted is conservative in profit estimation. Interestingly, the curve for PROF−MOA shows that profit-based mining is not effective without MOA, and the curves for CONF+MOA shows that MOA is not effective either without profit-based mining.

To model that a customer buys and spends more at a more favorable price, for each validating transaction, we compare the recommended price P_p with the recorded price P_q of the target item. Recall that $P_j = (1 + j \times \delta)Cost(i)$, $j = 1, \ldots, 4$, for item i. If $q - p = 1$ or $q - p = 2$, that is, the recommended price P_p is 1 or 2 step lower than the recorded price P_q, we assume that the customer doubles the purchase quantity in the transaction with the probability of 30%. We denote this setting by $(x = 2, y = 30\%)$. If $q - p = 3$ or $q - p = 4$, we assume that the customer triples the purchase quantity in the transaction with the probability of 40%. We denote this setting by $(x = 3, y = 40\%)$. Figure 3(b) shows the gain of all recommenders using MOA with the purchase quantity determined

---
[2] http://alexia.lis.uiuc.edu/ standrfr/zipf.html
[3] see http://www.itl.nist.gov/div898/handbook/eda/section3/eda3661.htm, for example

by ($x = 2, y = 30\%$) and ($x = 3, y = 40\%$). With this more realistic shopping behavior, the gain for all recommenders increases. PROF+MOA with the setting ($x = 3, y = 40\%$), denoted PROF(x=3,y=40%), achieves the encouraging gain of 2.23 (at minimum support of 0.1%)!

Figure 3(c), which uses the legend in Figure 3(a), shows the hit rate of recommenders. PROF+MOA and CONF+MOA achieve the hit rate of 95%. For minimum support of 0.08%, Figure 3(d) shows the hit rate at different profit ranges. "Low", "Medium", and "High" represent the lower, middle, and higher 1/3 of the maximum profit of a single recommendation. The legend from top to bottom corresponds to left to right in the bar chart. For example, kNN has nearly 100% hit rate at the "Low" range, but less than 10% at the "High" range. CONF+MOA and CONF−MOA also have a similar trend. In contrast, PROF+MOA is "profit smart" in maintaining a high hit rate in a high profit range. Though MPI picks up the hit rate in a high profit range, the hit rate is still too low compared to PROF+MOA. PROF−MOA is unstable for this dataset.

Figure 3(f), which uses the legend in Figure 3(a), shows the number of rules in recommenders. kNN and MPI have no model, so no curve is shown. The number of rules prior to the cut-optimal phase (not shown here) is typically several hundreds times the final number. This shows that the pruning method proposed effectively improves the interpretability of recommenders. MOA generally increases the size due to additional rules for alternative prices. Not surprisingly, the minimum support has a major impact of the size. The execution time is dominated by the step of generating association rules. In our experiments, we adopted the multi-level association rules mining whose performance has been studied elsewhere [SA95,HF95]. The time for constructing the covering tree from generated association rules and for the bottom-up traversal is insignificant.

Figure 4 shows the result on dataset II. This dataset has 40 item/price pairs for recommendation because each target item has 4 prices. Therefore, the random hit rate is 1/40, which is more challenging than dataset I. Despite the difference in cost distribution and a lower hit rate, the result is consistent with that of dataset I, that is, supports the effectiveness of profit-based mining and MOA.

We also modified kNN to recommend the item/price of the most profit in the k nearest neighbors. This is a post-processing approach because the profit is considered only after the k nearest neighbors are determined. For dataset I, the gain increases by about 2%, and for dataset II, the gain decreases by about 5% (not shown in the figure). Thus, the post-processing does not improve much.

In summary, the experiments confirm our goals set at the beginning of the section.

6 Related Work

[MS96] considers the customer value while training a neural network. As discussed in Introduction, neural network does not scale up for sparse data and large databases, does not easily incorporate domain knowledge, and does not produce an understandable model. [BSVW99] considered the problem of stock-

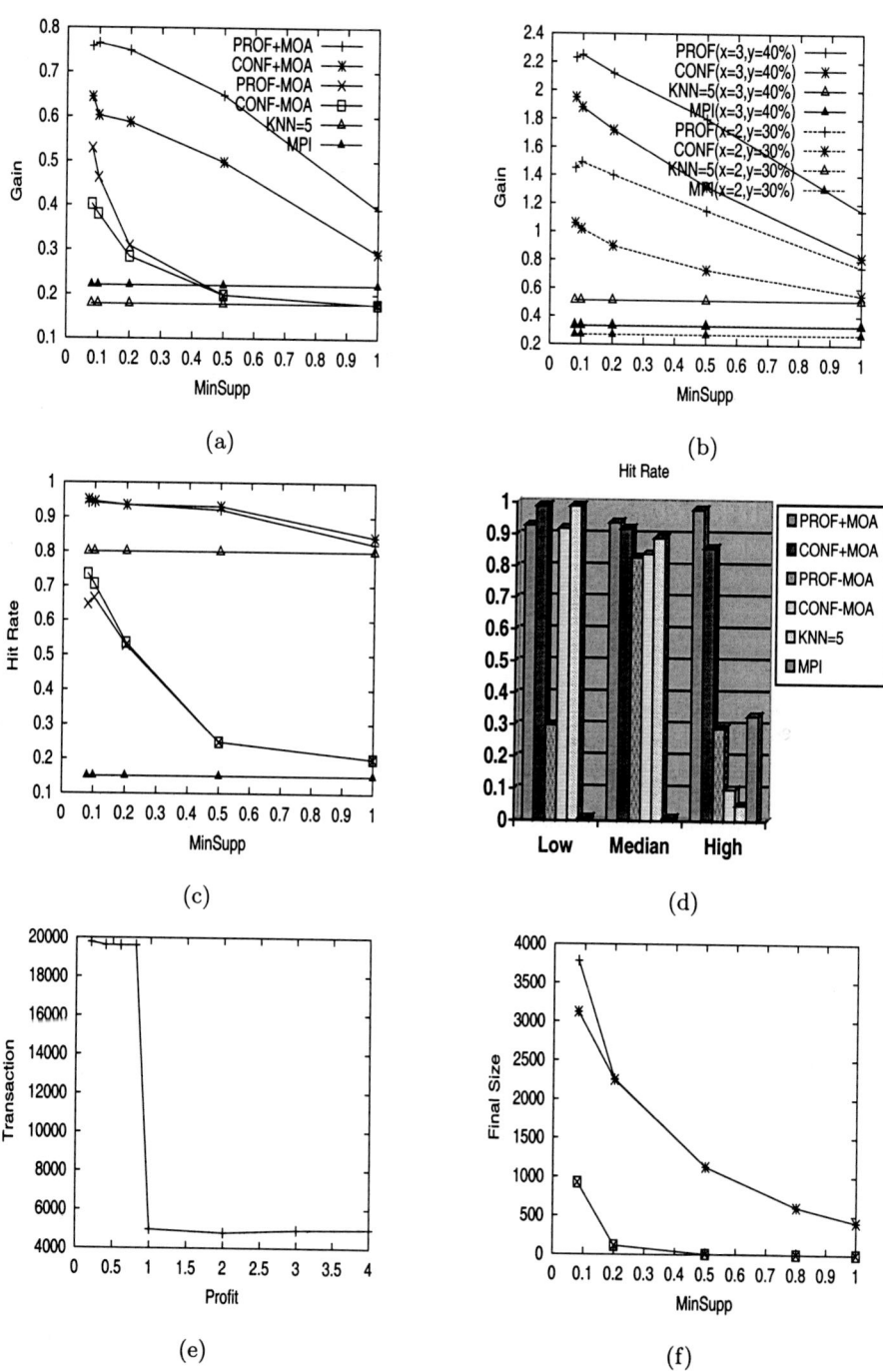

Fig. 3. The result for dataset I

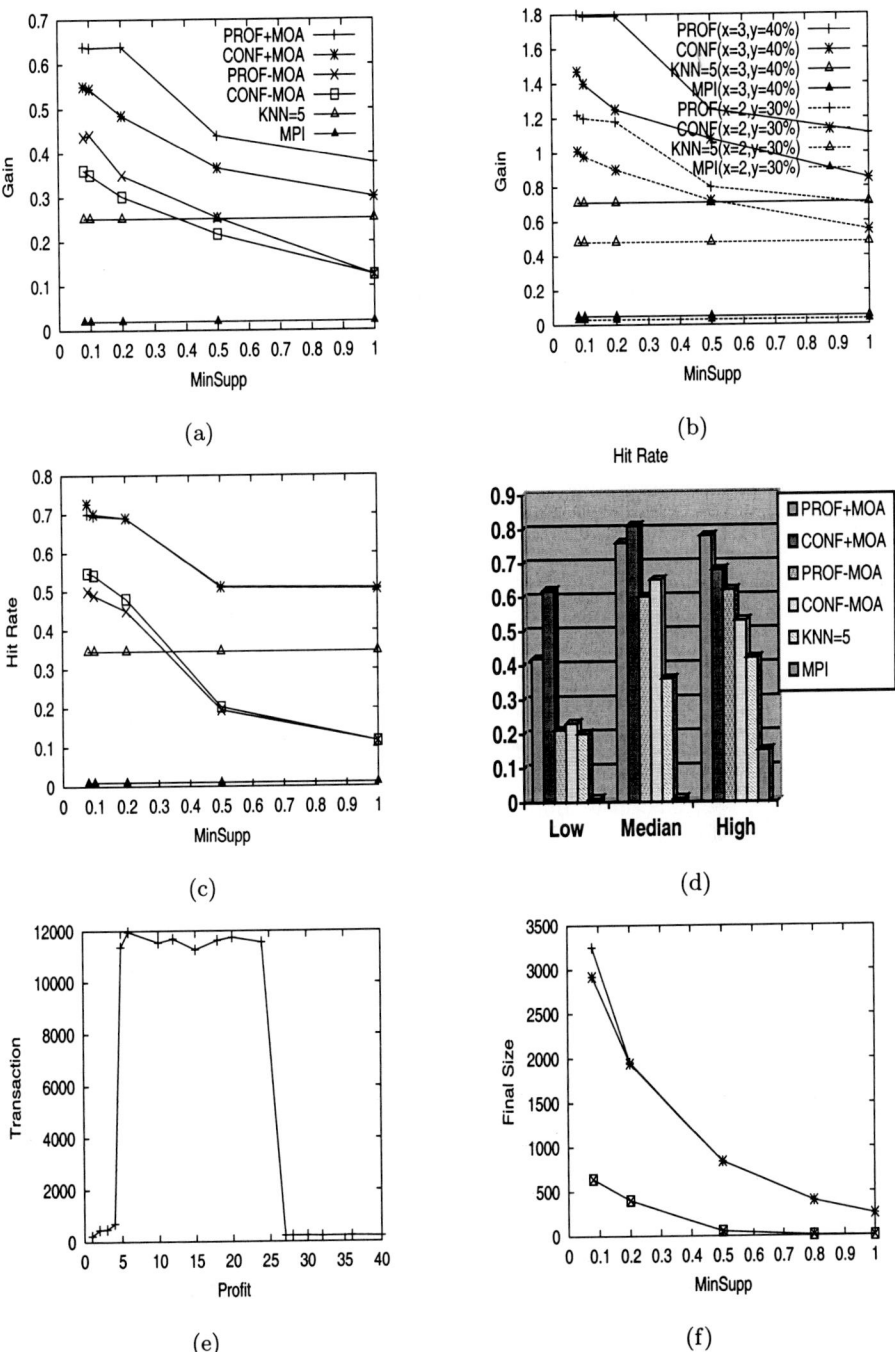

Fig. 4. The result for dataset II

ing a profitable set of items in supermarket environments. In profit mining, we recommend items and promotion codes on a per-customer basis, not on a per-problem basis like in the stocking problem. Indeed, a solution to the stocking problem does not give a clue on how to make such recommendations.

Our work is similar in motivation to the *actionability* of patterns [ST96] - the ability of the pattern to suggest concrete and profitable action by the decision-makers. Recently, Kleinberg el at presented the *microeconomic view* of data mining [KPR98]. The microeconomic view approach is to $max_{x \in D} \Sigma_{i \in C} g(x, y_i)$, where $g(x, y_i)$ is the "utility" of a decision x on a given customer i. In profit mining, we are to $max_{x \in D} g(x, C)$, where g is the total profit (a kind of utility) of a recommender x on *future* customers, given the data about *current* customers C which is a sample of the entire population. In the latter case, the model building has to tell whether a pattern is too specific for the entire population.

Our work benefits from the scalability of mining *(generalized) association rules* for large databases [AIS93,AS94,SA95,HF95]. However, association rules neither address the economic value of transactions nor produce a global action plan for decision making.

The *cost-sensitive classification* [P99] assumes an error metric of misclassification and minimizes the error on new cases. No such error metric is given in profit mining. Rather, we assume that customers spend some money on recommended items at recommended prices, and we maximize the profit by recommending right items and prices. It does not work to map each item/price recommendation to a class because the sales quantity, which obviously affects the profit, is not factored. More fundamentally, the cost-sensitive classification follows the trend of the (historical) data as correctly as possible (with respect to the given error metric), whereas profit mining may depart from the trend, if necessary, to increase the profit, as explained in Introduction.

Collaborative filtering [RV97] makes recommendation to a customer by aggregating the "opinions" (such as rating about movies) of a few "advisors" who share the same taste with the customer. The goal is to maximize the hit rate of recommendation. For items of varied profit, maximizing profit is quite different from maximizing hit rate. Collaborative filtering relies on carefully selected "item endorsements" for similarity computation, and a good set of "advisors" to offer opinions. Such data are not easy to obtain. The ability of recommending prices, in addition to items, is another major difference between profit mining and other recommender systems.

7 Conclusion

We presented a profit-based data mining called *profit mining*. The goal of profit mining is to construct a recommender that recommends target items and promotion codes on the basis of maximizing the profit of target sales on future customers. We presented a scalable construction of recommenders to address several important requirements in profit mining: pruning specific rules on a profit-sensitive basis, dealing with the behavior of shopping on unavailability, dealing with sparse and explosive search space, ensuring optimality and interpretability of recommenders. Experiments on a wide range of data characteristics show very encouraging results. The novelty of this research is extracting patterns on a profit-sensitive basis and combining them into a global actionable plan for decision making. This economic orientation and actionability will contribute to wider and faster deployment of data mining technologies in real life applications.

References

[AIS93] R. Agrawal, T. Imilienski, and A. Swami. Mining association rules between sets of items in large datasets. SIGMOD 1993, 207-216

[AMSTV96] R. Agrawal, H. Mannila, R. Srikant, H. Toivonen, A.I. Verkamo. Fast discovery of association rules. Advances in knowledge discovery and data mining, 307-328, AAAI/MIT Press, 1996

[AS94] R. Agrawal and R. Srikant. Fast algorithm for mining association rules. VLDB 1994, 487-499

[BSVW99] T. Brijs, G. Swinnen, K. Vanhoof, and G. Wets. Using association rules for product assortment decisions: a case study. KDD 1999, 254-260

[CP34] C.J. Clopper and E.S. Pearson. The use of confidence or Fiducial limits illustrated in the case of the binomial. Biometrika, 26:4, Dec. 1934, 404-413. Also available from http://www.jstor.org/journals/bio.html

[HF95] J. Han and Y. Fu. Discovery of multiple-level association rules from large databases. VLDB 1995, 420-431

[KPR98] J. Kleinberg, C. Papadimitriou, and P. Raghavan. A microeconomic view of data mining. Journal of Knowledge Discovery and Data Mining, 1998, vol.2, 311-324 (also http://www.cs.berkeley.edu/ christos/dm1.ps)

[MS96] B. Masand and G. P. Shapiro. A comparison of approaches for maximizing business payoff of prediction models. KDD 1996, 195-201

[P99] P. Domingos. MetaCost: a general method for making classifiers cost-sensitive. KDD 1999, 155-164

[Q93] J.R. Quinlan, C4.5: programs for machine learning, Morgan Kaufmann, 1993

[RV97] P. Resnick and H.R. Varian, Eds. CACM special issue on recommender systems. *Communications of the ACM*, Vol. 40, No. 3, 56-58, 1997

[SA95] R. Srikant and R. Agrawal. Mining generalized association rules. VLDB 1995, 407- 419

[ST96] A. Silberschatz and A. Tuzhilin. What makes patterns interresting in knowledge discovery systems. IEEE Transactions on Knowledge and Data Engineering, Vol. 8, No. 6, 1996

[YP97] Y. Yang and J.O. Pederson. A comparative study on feature selection in text categorization. International Conference on Machine Learning 1997

Cut-and-Pick Transactions for Proxy Log Mining

Wenwu Lou, Guimei Liu, Hongjun Lu, and Qiang Yang

Department of Computer Science
Hong Kong University of Science and Technology
Clear Water Bay, Hong Kong
{wwlou,cslgm,luhj,qyang}@cs.ust.hk

Abstract. Web logs collected by proxy servers, referred to as *proxy logs* or *proxy traces*, contain information about Web document accesses by many users against many Web sites. This *"many-to-many"* characteristic poses a challenge to Web log mining techniques due to the difficulty in identifying individual access transactions. This is because in a proxy log, user transactions are not clearly bounded and are sometimes interleaved with each other as well as with noise. Most previous work has used simplistic measures such as a fixed time interval as a determination method for the transaction boundaries, and has not addressed the problem of interleaving and noisy transactions. In this paper, we show that this simplistic view can lead to poor performance in building models to predict future access patterns. We present a more advanced *cut-and-pick* method for determining the access transactions from proxy logs, by deciding on more reasonable transaction boundaries and by removing noisy accesses. Our method takes advantage of the user behavior that in most transactions, the same user typically visits multiple, related Web sites that form clusters. These clusters can be discovered by our algorithm based on the connectivity among Web sites. By using real-world proxy logs, we experimentally show that this *cut-and-pick* method can produce more accurate transactions that result in Web-access prediction models with higher accuracy.

1 Introduction

Web logs collected by Web servers or by proxy servers contain information about user accesses to Web documents. Web logs are usually very large in size, and the analysis of these logs calls for more advanced methods such as data mining techniques. Recently, the application of data mining techniques to the Web logs, referred to as *Web Log Mining*, has draw extensively attention from researchers from various disciplines [CSM97]. From Web logs, one can identify user access patterns which can be used for various purposes such as Web site design [SPF99], page recommendation [PPR96,DH99], Web caching and prefetching [PM96,PM98,SKS98,PP99,YZL01].

A key problem for Web log mining, e.g., association rule mining, is to identify individual user transactions in a Web log [CMS99]. When correctly extracted, a user transaction can be regarded as a semantically meaningful representation of a sequence of page references corresponding to a single search task of the user. Previous work [BL99,BL00,NM00] of Web log mining has been conducted on Web server logs, and typically used simplistic measures such as a fixed time window or a pre-defined time interval as a determination method for the transaction boundaries. These simple measures, however, may lead to poor performance in the context of proxy Web log mining. This is because in proxy logs, page accesses made by Web users against different servers are often interleaved with each other. This makes it more difficult to identify user transaction due to two reasons. The first reason is that in a proxy log, user transactions are often interleaved with each other. This is because a) there is no easy way to identify a real-world user in proxy logs, b) the same user may concurrently perform multiple search tasks. The second reason is that unlike the case of user transactions in server logs, user transactions in proxy logs often involve page accesses to multiple Web sites. In both cases, the simplistic approaches, such as a fixed time interval based method, may not perform well on proxy logs.

In this paper, we will explore a more advanced approach for transaction identification in Web proxy logs, by deciding on more reasonable boundaries between transactions and by selecting the right reference sequence in each transaction. We assume that in one transaction, the same user usually focus on one subject and they often visits one or multiple Web sites that are related to the subject. They focus on different subjects in different transactions. Web users' online browsing and search behavior is often threaded by the linkage information among the Web sites. A group of Web sites that users often visit together forms a cluster of sites, which can serve as a representative of a particular subject. These clusters can be discovered by our Web site clustering algorithm based on site traversal graphs constructed from the proxy logs. Our approach is to apply this common user behavior in transaction identification by identifying the subject of each transaction, so that its boundary and content can be determined more accurately. The idea is as the following: if two consecutive page references in a proxy log visit two Web sites that fall in two clusters, the two visits are regarded as irrelevant and are therefore classified into two user transactions. Our experiment results showed that, by also taking into account the client-side information and the time stamp of a page references, our *cut-and-pick* method can produce more realistic transactions that lead to better Web-access prediction models with higher accuracy.

Our study distinguishes from previous work in mainly two aspects. First, previous work has discussed the issue of identifying transaction boundaries, but no one has addressed the problem of content selection of transactions. Since in a proxy log, multiple transactions are interleaved with each other as well as with noise, even when it is filtered into independent sequences by IP addresses. Picking out the right sequence for each transaction becomes a tough task. Taking advantage of the common user behavior, our approach not only addresses the problem of transaction boundary identification, but also provides a solution to select page reference sequence for each user transaction. Second, most of the previous studies have been analyzing of the *server logs*, but not the proxy logs. A server log only contains information of pages accesses on a single Web server. Consequently, the problem of transaction identification is relatively simple as there's no need to identify transactions that involve multiple Web sites.

The remaining of this paper is organized as follows. Section 2 reviews related work. This is followed by a brief discussion of three transaction identification approaches we compared to in this study in Section 3. Section 4 describes the procedure of identifying Web site clusters from proxy logs. Our *cut-and-pick* approach for identification of user transactions is presented in Section 5. The effectiveness of our algorithm is evaluated in this paper by comparing the quality of derived prediction models trained on the user transactions identified by our algorithm and other approaches. The experimental results are reported in Section 6. We conclude our paper in Section 7 with a brief discussion of the future work.

2 Related Work

The Web log data records information of the Web users' visits to Web sites. Researchers have been trying to discover significant user patterns from the logs, and to build prediction models to make predictions on users' future access needs. These prediction models can be used to reduce the network traffic [SKS98,YZL01], to judge the quality of Web sites [SP01] and to automatically customize the user interface [ADW01,PE00].

Various data preparation techniques have be described in [CMS99]. Three transaction identification approaches are compared in this study. The reference length transaction identification approach is based on the assumption that the amount of time that a user spends on a page depends on how well this page is related to the user's search task. The second approach called maximal forwarding transaction identification, which was originally proposed by [CPY96]. It defines each transaction as a maximal set of page references in a path that contains no backward reference. While this approach is reasonable in dealing with server Web logs, it is not applicable for the transaction identification in proxy logs. This is because in a proxy log, there's no single "first" pages to start with. In addition, user sessions are normally much longer in a proxy log than on a server log. For example, it is often the case that a user visits several pages located at some related Web sites in a row, but stays on each site only over a limited number of pages. The third approach is the time window transaction identification approach. It assumes that meaningful transactions have an overall average length associated with them. It simply partitions a user session into time intervals no larger than a specified parameter.

A significant amount of work has been done in the sequential data mining area. Agrawal et al. [AMS+96,AS95] discovered frequent items that are bought together in certain sequential order using intra-transaction and inter-transaction patterns. The general idea of sequential mining is an extension of the original Apriori algorithm, where k-large itemsets, with k denoting the size of itemsets, are recognized from k-candidates and are used to generate (k+1)-candidates. The resultant association rules correspond to sequences of Web accesses that comprise the LHS of a prediction rule.

Another line of work is to discover frequent patterns on users' browsing path that are longest in length; these are called the longest repeating subsequences. When the users are observed to make a sequence of Web page visits, these path patterns are consulted to determine the next page that the user might access. In fact, researchers have studied algorithms that discover longest paths [PP99] or a hybrid of N-gram models [SYZ00,PP99,BL99].

A unifying theme of the above work is that they all build their models based on Web server logs. These are the log files accumulated on the server side, rather than on the client or proxy side. When we deal with Web logs that come from the proxy side, new problems arise. For example, instead of accessing the Web pages on one server in each user session, a user may access multiple servers in one session. This many to many relationship provides both a challenge and a new opportunity for data mining researchers. In this paper, we address the new problems from the Web proxy-server logs.

3 Framework

In this section, we present the framework of our approach for identifying user transactions in proxy logs. For clarity of presentation, we first define some terminologies which we use frequently throughout this paper.

3.1 Definitions

In this paper, a *proxy log* L is viewed as a sequence of page references. Each reference R is defined as a quintuplet $R :< R_{id}, IP, S_{id}, P_{id}, t >$, where R_{id} represents for a unique identifier of a page reference within a Web log, IP for the requesting IP, S_{id} for the server, and P_{id} for the page being requested respectively. The t value indicates the time of the request. While the actual representation of a page reference may contain additional information, it is irrelevant to this paper and is excluded from the analysis.

We first define IP sequence. Intuitively, an IP sequence is the lifetime sequence of Web accesses originating from the same IP address in an entire Web log.

Definition 1 (IP sequence). *An IP sequence, denoted by L_{IP}, is an order-preserving subsequence of page references in a proxy log L, such that: a). $\forall R \in L_{IP}, R.IP = IP$; and b). $\forall R \in L, and R.IP = IP, R \in L_{IP}$;*

In other words, a page in a Web log belongs to an IP sequence if and only if it shares the same IP address. In related literature, an IP sequence is often referred to as a *user sessions* as they assume that each IP address represents an individual Web user. However, we note this is misleading in a proxy log, as it is often the case that multiple users may share the same IP address on a proxy, either due to multiple accesses of the same computer by a group of users or by dynamic allocation of an IP address to a set of client terminals. Moreover, in some cases such as a public computer in a shopping mall or library, the same computer is shared among multiple users. Thus, a single IP sequence can actually contain requests from multiple users. Deriving IP sequences from a proxy log is the first step that most Web log mining algorithms perform. This can be done by partitioning the Web log L according to U_{ip}.

An IP sequence is divided into segments of subsequences by time windows. The time windows represent significant "idle" periods. Each IP subsequence is called an IP transaction.

Definition 2 (IP transaction). *An IP transaction, denoted by T_{IP}, is an order-preserving subsequence of page references of an IP sequence L_{IP}, such that: a) if $R_i \to R_j$ are two consecutive references in T_{IP}, $R_i \to R_j$ are also two consecutive references in L_{IP}; b) Let $T_{IP}^1, T_{IP}^2, \ldots, T_{IP}^n$ be all IP transactions that derived from one IP sequence L_{IP}, then there exist a permutation $i_1, i_2, \ldots, i_n$ of $1, 2, \ldots, n$, such that $L_{IP} = T_{IP}^{i_1} + T_{IP}^{i_2} + + T_{IP}^{i_n}$.*

"+" above means string concatenation. Note that our notion of *IP transaction* is often referred to as *user transaction* in previous literature (e.g., [CMS99]). However, as we have shown that an IP sequence can actually contain requests from *multiple users*, an IP transaction may also be composed of page references from *multiple users*. Thus, to be more precise, we call it an *IP transaction*, and reserve the term *user transaction* to the following. The purpose of this study is to identify these *real* user transactions.

Definition 3 (user transaction). *A user transaction, denoted by UT_{IP}, is any order-preserving subsequence of page references of an IP sequence L_{IP}. Each user transaction only contains the page references that semantically correspond to an individual search task conducted from an IP address IP.*

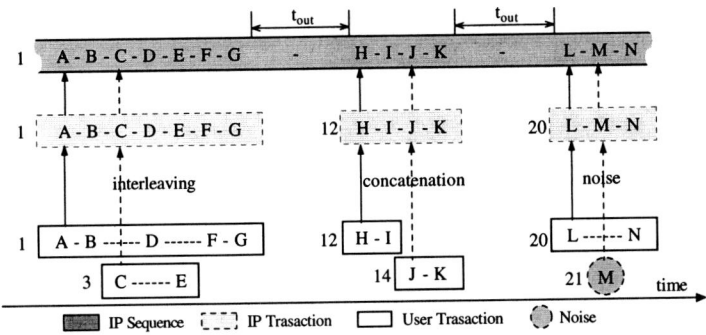

Fig. 1. IP Sequence, IP Transaction and User Transaction

Note that the definition is intentionally left vague because there is difficulty in identifying the semantically identical search tasks. However, our work reported in this paper will attempt to approximate this note empirically.

Page references in a *user transaction* are not necessarily consecutive in an IP sequence, but they must come from the same user's single search task. The relationship among IP sequences, IP transactions and user transactions is illustrated using an example in Figure 1. In this example, an IP client runs multiple user transactions in parallel. The final ordering of page references depends on the ordering of their arrival at the proxy. Three IP transactions can be identified by the t_{out} value. The first IP transaction is composed of two user transactions that are interleaved with each other. The second one is a concatenation of two consecutive user transactions. In the third IP transaction, it is a noisy access. Thus, in order to identify the *user transactions* correctly from proxy logs, not only the transaction boundaries need to be identified, but also the transaction contents, i.e., the sequence of pages references, need to be correctly selected.

3.2 Transaction Identification in Proxy Logs

The problem of transaction identification can be described as follows: given a proxy log L, derive a set of user transactions from the logs. Basically, there are two tasks. One is to find the "start" and "end" for each transaction, i.e. the transaction boundaries. In fact, we only need to find out the "ends" of transactions because the reference following the "end" of a transaction will be the "start" of the next transaction. The second task is to select the right subsequence of references for each transaction, by decomposing interleaved transactions and removing noisy accesses in the original sequence.

In the remaining of this section, we briefly describe the three transaction identification approaches that we studied in this paper, including a simplistic approach through fixed time interval, a new proposed server-based approach to identify transactions within individual Web sites, and an overview of our *cut-and-pick* approach.

Fixed Time Interval Approach. A popular solution applied in previous work has been a fixed time interval t_{out} approach, where users are assumed to start a new transaction when the time interval between two page references exceeds the specified t_{out} threshold. The rational behind this simplistic approach is that users typically make longer pauses between transactions than within a transaction. Hence, if we can derive a reasonable cutoff time value t_{out} from the data, we can identify transactions based on the time value.

Our procedure in implementing this approach is as the following: Scan the proxy log from the beginning, on encountering a page reference R from an new IP address, we always start a new transaction of this new IP address, taking R as its first page reference. If R is from an existing IP address with its last page reference being R_{last}, we check whether the time interval between R_{last} and R has exceeded a given threshold t_{out}. If $R.t - R_{last}.t < t_{out}$, we add the R to the end of its current transaction. Otherwise, we start a new transaction of this IP starting with R.

In essence, the transactions that are identified by this simplistic approach are IP transactions, but not user transactions. While it is easy to implement, this approach has a number of major drawbacks. First, it is not appropriate to assume that a user makes longer pauses between transactions than within a transaction. Secondly, selecting an appropriate t_{out} is critical to its performance and has to be determined on a case by case basis. Generally, it is determined by analyzing the density distribution of time interval between pages reference. Thirdly, it cannot identify transactions that are interleaved with each other and it can not remove noisy pages from the log. Here, a noisy page refers to a page that does not belong to any user transactions.

Server Based Approach. The server based approach is to first partition a proxy log into many server logs by server id S_{id}, then apply the similar idea of time interval approaches for processing each individual server log. In adopting this method, a basic assumption is that a user typically visits a single Web site within one transaction. While this approach is effective in identifying transactions that only involve one Web site, it fails to identify transactions that involve multiple Web sites.

Overview of *Cut-and-Pick*. As illustrated in Figure 1, the presence of interleaved transactions and noisy accesses calls for more sophisticated approaches for user transactions identification in Web logs. When dealing with proxy logs, an effective transaction identifier is one that is able to identify interleaved transactions and transactions with noise, and can capture both the intra-site transactions and the inter-site transactions. The *cut-and-pick* approach that we proposed in this paper tries to exploit available information to identify user transactions besides simple indicators like transaction length and time interval between page references. Note that each semantically meaningful user transaction has to be associated with a search task that has a unique purpose or subject. Thus, by identifying the subject of a current transaction, one can distinguish multiple interleaved transactions in a proxy log. We notice that most users browse the Web by following the links and typically visit one site or multiple, related Web sites within one transaction. These sites form clusters of related information. Thus, by grouping Web sites into clusters that users often visit together, the subject of a transaction can be roughly identified by the cluster information of Web sites visited within a transaction. This enables us to cut on the right boundaries among user transactions as well as to pick the right "content" for individual transactions.

In *cut-and-pick* approach, the Web site clusters are first identified offline in a data preprocess phase. We first extract site inter-referencing information from the proxy logs, then identify Web site clusters using our connectivity-based clustering algorithm. The *cut-and-pick* algorithm then combines the IP address, time stamp and the identified clusters for deciding on whether a current checked reference in a proxy log needs be treated as a subsequent reference of a current transactions or a starting page reference of a new transaction. The details of our clustering method is presented in the next two sections.

4   Identify Web Site Clusters

In this section, we describe how to identify Web site clusters without looking at the Web site contents. Web pages on one Web site often contain linkage information to multiple related information sources for facilitating Web users' locating process of interesting information. Typically, Web users visit multiple, related Web sites by following the links. This confines Web users' browse activities to a small portion of the Web and to certain patterns, which also makes it possible for us to discover the connection among Web site based on user access patterns, without looking at contents of Web sites.

4.1   Extract Inter-site Referencing Information

In the data preprocessing phase, a set of IP transactions are first derived from the log. As we are only interested in looking at the relationship between servers, the page information in the IP transaction can be excluded from the analysis. Therefore, when deriving the IP transactions, we omit the page information and only keep the sever sequences. We use an example to illustrate this process. Suppose an IP transaction contains the following page references, $(S_1.A, S_2.B, S_2.C, S_1.D, S_1.E, S_2.C)$, where S_i is a server I and A, B, C etc. are the pages located on these servers. By removing the page information, the resulting site access sequence looks like $(S_1, S_2, S_2, S_1, S_1, S_2)$. We than further abbreviate it to (S_1, S_2, S_1, S_2). The resulting transactions with only site information will be referred to as *site traversal paths*.

By doing so, some of the adjacent references in IP transaction will collapse into single references if multiple Web pages are from the same server. This helps reduce the average length of each IP transaction. In the extreme case, when all the references in an IP transaction collapse into one reference, this transaction will be removed from further analysis as it provides no information about links between Web sites. As such extreme cases are often observed for Web transactions, analyzing the references at server level can also greatly reduce the total number of transactions.

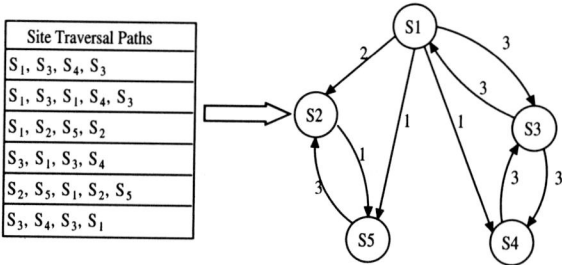

Fig. 2. Constructing STG from Site Traversal Pathes

Once we generate the site traversal path set, a *Site Traversal Graph* is then constructed, where each node in the graph represents a Web site and each direct edge represents a connection from its origin site to its end site. An illustration example for constructing STG is shown in Figure 2.

4.2 Measuring *Distance* between Web Sites

Based on the site traversal graph, we identify Web clusters by the strength of the connections among sites, i.e., whether two sites will be classified into one cluster depends on how strong the connection is between them. In our approach, the connectivity between two sites is measured by two parameters: support and confidence. Let $E :< S_i, S_j >$ be an edge from Web site S_i to S_j, the support of E, denoted by $freq(S_i, S_j)$, is defined as the frequency of inter-references between S_i to S_j. The confidence of E is defined as $\frac{freq(S_i, S_j)}{freq(S_i)}$.

The reason that we include confidence as an indicator of the connectivity among two sites is that the distribution of page references on the Web is highly skewed in the site dimension and using support as the single metric will result in a large number of sites to be glued together by some hot site erroneously. For example, in our data sets, while the average number of accesses to one site is as few as 4 times per day, a hot site can actually have as many as 20,000 accesses, which provides enough "support" for most sites to be linked to the hot site.

4.3 The Clustering Algorithm

Our clustering algorithm takes a traversal graph, a support threshold and confidence threshold as inputs. All edges with support or confidence value less than the corresponding threshold values will be removed from the graph. Then nodes in each connected sub-graph in the remaining site traversal graph constitute a site cluster. The detailed algorithm is described in figure 3.

```
ALGORITHM: ClusterSite(STG, minSup, minConf)
01) S ← {all sites};
02) cluster ← 0;
03) WHILE (∃ edge ε ∈ STG and ε.sup < minSup and ε < minConf)
04)     Remove ε from STG;
05) WHILE (S is not empty) {
06)     H ← the 1st site in S;
07)     STG_H ← BFS(STG, H);      /* STG_H is a subgraph of STG */
08)                                /* that is reachable from site H */
09)     ∀ s ∈ STG_H) {
10)         s.cluster ← cluster;
11)         Remove site s from S;
12)     }
12)     cluster ← cluster + 1;
13) }
```

Fig. 3. The Clustering Algorithm

5 Cut-and-Pick

Assuming that the site clustering information has been obtained by applying our clustering algorithm, we now describe how to use this information to obtain more accurate boundaries of user transactions.

Recall that the simplistic time interval approaches has assumed that an IP address uniquely identifies a user, and that a user always makes a longer pause between transactions than within a transaction. We have identified two exceptions to the simplistic case.

- First, in proxy logs, the real-world individual users cannot be uniquely identified. The only information about user identification in a proxy log is the information about client machines, e.g., IP addresses. Thus, while multiple users are mapped into one IP addresses, the transactions conducted by different users are mixed up together.
- Second, although one can assume that a long pause indicates a gap between two user transactions, the opposite is not always true. In other words, user may often start a new transaction immediately after one transaction. For example, a sport fan may too impatient to finish his current browsing but quickly change to view a football match on live at FOXSPORTS.COM. Moreover, it is also quite common for a user to conduct multiple transactions at the same time in parallel in a multi-task system.

We notice that Web site cluster information can be used for managing the above-mentioned difficult cases effectively. First, for the case that multiple users are mapped into the same IP addresses, Web site cluster information can helps to identify these different individuals in proxy logs, as different users have different interests and will presumably visit different cluster of Web sites. In fact, the probability is very low that two users visit the same cluster Web site simultaneously. Second, for the case that multiple transactions are interleaved or concatenate with each other, Web cluster information can help to decompose them into individual transactions, while the simple time interval based approach can not. This is because that different transactions have different focuses, and in one transaction, a user typically visit multiple, related Web sites that fall into one cluster.

Basically, the *cut-and-pick* approach integrates the three indicators for user transaction identification, including IP address, time interval, and Web cluster information. In outmost loop, page references are filtered into individual *IP sequences* according to the requesting IP addresses. Then, for each IP sequences, there are three cases to determine. Let R be a current page reference, P be the previous page reference in the same IP sequences of R. If $R.time - P.time > t_{out}$, i.e., the time interval between the current page reference and a previous one exceeds the time interval threshold t_{out}, it is considered that R starts a new transaction. Otherwise, we check for the site information of R and P. If they fall into one cluster, R is regarded as a subsequent visit of P in the same transaction; otherwise, R and P are considered to be irrelevant, but happen to arrive at the proxy one after another.

The detailed *cut-and-pick* procedure is provided in Figure 4. For each IP, we maintain an index on its current active user transactions. Active user transactions refer to those transactions that haven't been completely identified when we scan the IP sequence. A subtle problem is that we need to check the time interval again in line 10. This is because a previous page reference related to current page

ALGORITHM: Cut&Pick(L_{IP}) ——— L_{IP} is an IP sequence of a proxy log;
01) $UT_{active} \leftarrow$ empty set;
02) $P \leftarrow$ the header of L_{IP}; Remove P from L_{IP};
03) WHILE (L_{IP} is not empty) {
04) $R \leftarrow$ the current page reference in L_{IP}; Remove P from L_{IP};
05)   IF ($R.time - P.time > t_{out}$) {
06)   WHILE ($\exists\ UT \in UT_{active}$ and $UT.length > 1$) Output UT;
07) $UT_{active} \leftarrow$ empty set;
08)   }ELSE IF ($\exists\ UT \in UT_{active}$ and $UT.cluster = R.cluster$){
09) $P \leftarrow$ the tail of UT;
10)   IF ($R.time - P.time <= t_{out}$) Attach R to the tail of UT; CONTINUE;
11)   }
12)   Start a new user transaction $UT_{new} \leftarrow \{R\}$;
13)   Add UT_{new} to UT_{active};
14) $P \leftarrow R$;
15) }
16) WHILE ($\exists\ UT \in UT_{active}$ and $UT.length > 1$) Output UT;

Fig. 4. Cut-and-Pick

reference may actually be far apart, even when the time interval between current two consecutive pages references in the IP sequence satisfies the interval criteria. On the contrary, when the current two consecutive references do not satisfy the interval criteria, no subsequent reference will satisfies the interval criteria with previous references that has already been checked. Thus our algorithm deactivates all the current active transaction for output (line 07). Noise removal is done on output by checking every transaction's length. If a transaction contains only one page reference, it is regarded as noise and can thus be excluded from the final transaction set.

6 Experiments

Our method for evaluating the effectiveness of our approach in transaction identification is through trace-driven simulation using a set of real-world proxy trace data from Digital Equipment Corporation [Coo96]. We first apply the approach presented by Yang et al. [YZL01] to establish an association-based prediction models from the user transaction set that we identified. Then, based on the prediction models, we experimentally assess the prediction accuracy. The evaluation compares the prediction-model accuracy using transactions derived by time-outs only approach, server-based approach and cut-and-pick approach.

We first perform some pre-processing over the traces. In particular, we removed those requests that are obviously generated by programs running on a

Table 1. Data Sets

Data Set	♯Requests	♯IPs	♯Servers	Size(KB)	Testing Size
1	110,019	302	4,295	4,960	85,963
2	231,116	1,003	7,838	10,356	192,909
3	162,204	2,425	1,003	7,303	256,083
4	379,224	3,517	11,317	16,866	740,832

client. In addition, we do not include those requests are queries with "?" in the URLs and "CGI-BIN" requests. Table 1 gives an overview of four data sets for presenting our results. Specifically, Data set 1 and Data set 2 contain sequences of references by relatively small number of clients (w.r.t different IP addresses) against a relatively lager Web site community. Data Set 3 is a sequence of references where the number of Web sites is relatively small. Data Set 4 is full day logs. In all experiments, we use one day's data set for training the prediction model, and use the next day's logs for prediction.

6.1 Experimental Results

Three transaction identification approaches are examined in this experiment. One is the simplistic approaches using a fixed time interval, denoted by "client" in the figures. For this experiment, the associated time interval threshold is set to 30 minutes for all of the four data sets. The other two are server-based approach and cut-and-pick approach. "server" denotes the approach that each single Web server picks transactions from IP sequences. "cluster" denotes the approach that exploits Web site cluster information. In both of these two approaches, the associated time interval threshold is also 30 mins to be consistent. We compare these three approaches by constructing corresponding prediction models from the transaction sets that they identified. For presentation convenience, we refer to the three models as the *client model*, the *server model* and the *cluster model* respectively in the follow context.

In the first experiment, we quantitatively examined the effect of the three approaches on transaction identification, through constructing association rules from each transaction sets identified. We conduct experiments on all of the four data sets with various settings of maximum rule length (Figure 5(a)), minimum support (Figure 5(b)) and minimum confidence (Figure 5(c,d)). We found that, for all settings, the *cluster model* allow a larger number of rules to be discovered by our association rule mining algorithm. All the four data sets exhibit consistent results in increasing the rule-size.

In addition, we made three observations. First, *Cut-and-pick* approach is effective in identifying long transactions. As we can see in Figure 5(a), when the

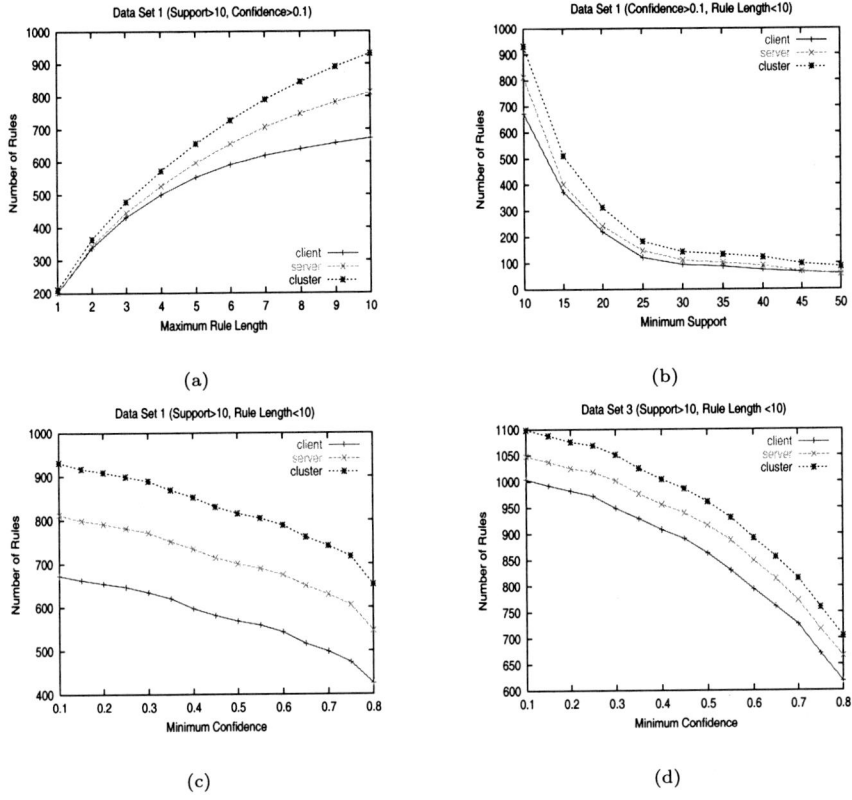

Fig. 5. Number of Rules w.r.t Rule Length/Support/Confidence

rule length increases, the increase in the number of rules become more obvious. This means that there are more longer rules than without using the cut-and-pick method. Second, in Figure 5(a), when the minimum support increases, the curve gets flatter. This is because in proxy logs, there are many low support rules which are typically more vulnerable to noise in the sequence. Third, the mean confidence of all effecting rules in predicting future accesses is also slightly higher in the cut-and-pick approach than in the other two approaches, as illustrated in Figure 8(a). This suggests that exploiting Web site information can be beneficial in extracting appropriate user transactions. Figure 5 also showed that *Cut-and-Pick(server)* can discover more rules than the simplistic methods, suggesting that considerable improvement in association rule discovery can be achieved by separating page references on different sites in the process of identifying user transactions.

The second experiment examines the effectiveness of resulting prediction model in terms of number of hits and prediction accuracy. First, we consider

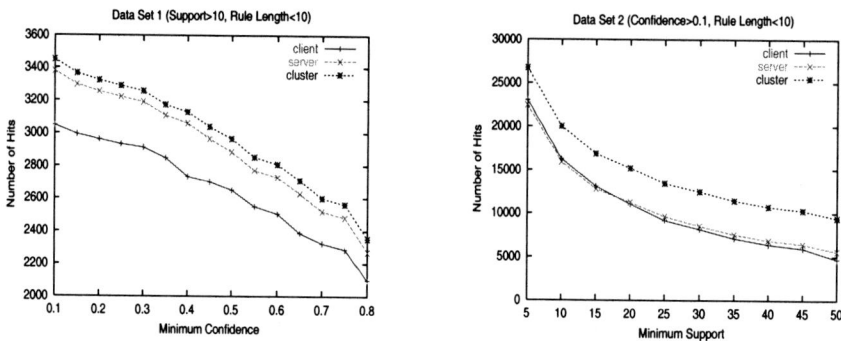

Fig. 6. Number of Hits w.r.t Minimum Confidence/Support

there is a **match** when the current references sequence matches the left hand side of any rule in the model. When there are multiple matches found for one sequence, principle of *longest-match* will be applied [LYW01]. Furthermore, if the next reference in the sequence also matches the right hand side of that particular rule, we count it as a **hit**, i.e., a correct prediction. **Accuracy** of prediction is calculated by dividing the total number of hits by the total number of matches. While the number of hits is used as a quantitative measurement, accuracy is used for qualitatively assessment of a prediction model.

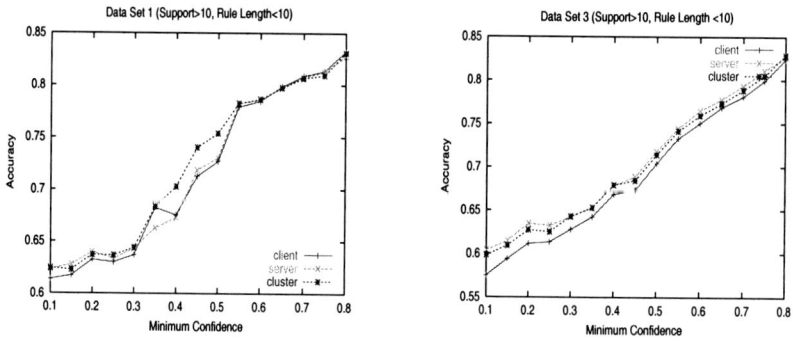

Fig. 7. Accuracy w.r.t Minimum Confidence/Support

As it can be noticed from Figure 6, significant improvement in the total number of hits was found when *cut-and-pick* approaches are used. With minimum confidence varying from 0.1 to 0.8, the number of hits increased by an average of 11.3% for data set 1. Similarly, we also observe increasing improvement up to 35.2% in the number of hits with minimum support ranging from 5 to 50.

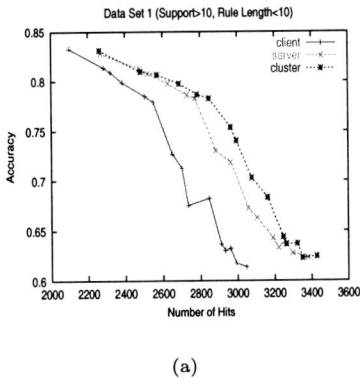 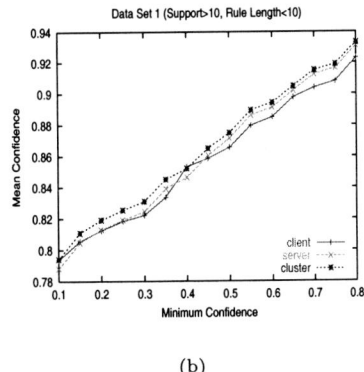

Fig. 8. (a). Accuracy w.r.t Number of Hits; (b). Mean Confidence of Effecting Rules in Prediction

With increased number of hits, the accuracy of our predictions remains similar to that of the simplistic method. Slight improvement of about 2-5 percentage in accuracy was also found when the confidence is between 0.3 and 0.5 for data set 1, and for the whole range of data set 2. Figure 7 illustrates the accuracy results. In Figure 8(a), we exhibit the plot of both accuracy and number of hits with respect to minimum confidence raging from 0.1 to 0.8. The curve of $Cut\&Pick(cluster)$ is clearly located above other two curves, indicating that $Cut\&Pick(cluster)$ lead to a prediction model that is not only quantitatively better but also qualitatively more accurate.

7 Conclusions

In this paper, we investigate the problem of user transaction identification in proxy logs. In a proxy logs, a single user transaction may include pages references from one site as well as from multiple sites. Moreover, different types of transactions are not clearly bounded and are sometimes interleaved with each other as well as with noise. Thus an effective transaction identifier has to identify interleaved transactions and transactions with noise, and capture both the intra-site transactions and the inter-site transactions. We presented a *cut-and-pick* method for extracting all these transactions, by *cutting* on more reasonable transaction boundaries and by *picking* the right page sequences in each transaction. Our method takes advantages of user behavior that in most transactions, the same user typically visits multiple, related Web sites that form clusters.

We experimentally examine the effectiveness of our approach by using the real-world proxy log data. The results show that our *cut-and-pick* approach can produce more accurate transactions that result in higher accuracy of Web-access prediction models, indicating that relationships among Web sites provide critical information for transaction identification. In the future, we would like to incorporate our approach into proxy caching and prefetching algorithms to improve their performance.

References

[ADW01] C. Anderson, P. Domingos, and D. Weld. Personalizing web sites for mobile users. In *Proceedings of the 10th World Wide Web Conference (WWW10)*, Hong Kong, China, May 2-4 2001.

[AMS+96] Rakesh Agrawal, Heikki Mannila, Ramakrishnan Srikant, Hannu Toivonen, and A. Inkeri Verkamo. Fast discovery of association rules. In *Advances in Knowledge Discovery and Data Mining.*, pages 307–328. AAAI/MIT Press, 1996.

[AS95] Rakesh Agrawal and Ramakrishnan Srikant. Mining sequential patterns. In Philip S. Yu and Arbee L. P. Chen, editors, *Proc. 11th Int. Conf. Data Engineering, ICDE*, pages 3–14, Taipei, Taiwan, March 6–10 1995. IEEE Press.

[BL99] Jose Borges and Mark Levene. Data mining of user navigation patterns. In *Proc. of the Web Usage Analysis and User Profiling Workshop*, pages 31–36, San Diego, California, 1999.

[BL00] J. Borges and M. Levene. A heuristic to capture longer user web navigation patterns. In *Proc. of the first International Conference on Electronic Commerce and Web Technologies*, Greenwich, U.K., September 2000.

[CMS99] Robert Cooley, Bamshad Mobasher, and Jaideep Srivastava. Data preparation for mining world wide web browsing patterns. *Knowledge and Information Systems*, 1(1):5–32, 1999.

[Coo96] Digitial Equipment Cooperation. Digital's web proxy traces. Available at ftp://ftp.digital.com/pub/DEC/traces/proxy/webtraces.html, 1996.

[CPY96] M.-S. Chen, J. S. Park, and P. S. Yu. Data mining for path traversal patterns in a web environment. In *Proceedings of the 16th International Conference on Distributed Computing Systems (ICDCS)*, pages 385–393, Hong Kong, May 27-30 1996.

[CSM97] R. Cooley, J. Srivastava, and B. Mobasher. Web mining: Information and pattern discovery on the world wide web. In *Proceedings of the 9th IEEE International Conference on Tools with Artificial Intelligence (ICTAI'97)*, Newport Beach, CA, November 1997.

[DH99] J. Dean and M. Henzinger. Finding related pages in the world wide web. In *Proceedings of the 8th International World Wide Web Conference*, pages 1467–1479, Toronto, Canada, 1999.

[LYW01] Tianyi Li, Qiang Yang, and Ke Wang. Classification pruning for web-request prediction. In *Proceedings of the 10th World Wide Web Conference (WWW10)*, Hong Kong, China, May 2-4 2001.

[NM00] Alexandros Nanopoulos and Yannis Manolopoulos. Finding generalized path patterns for web log data mining. In *Proceedings of East-European Conference on Advances in Databases and Information Systems*, pages 215–228, 2000.

[PE00] Mike Perkowitz and Oren Etzioni. Towards adaptive web sites: Conceptual framework and case study. *Artificial Intelligence*, 118(1–2):245–275, 2000.

[PM96] Venkata N. Padmanabhan and Jeffrey C. Mogul. Using predictive prefetching to improve World-Wide Web latency. In *Proceedings of the SIGCOMM '96 conference*, 1996.

[PM98] T. Palpanas and A. Mendelzon. Web prefetching using partial match prediction. Technical Report CSRG-376, Departement of Computer Science, University of Toronto, 1998.

[PP99] James E. Pitkow and Peter Pirolli. Mining longest repeating subsequences to predict world wide web surfing. In *USENIX Symposium on Internet Technologies and Systems*, 1999.

[PPR96] Peter Pirolli, James Pitkow, and Ramana Rao. Silk from a sow's ear: Extracting usable structures from the web. In *Proc. ACM Conf. Human Factors in Computing Systems, CHI*. ACM Press, 1996.

[SKS98] S. Schechter, M. Krishnan, and M. Smith. Using path profiles to predict HTTP request. In *Proceedings of 7th International World Wide Web Conference*, Brisbane, Australia, April 14-18 1998.

[SP01] M. Spiliopoulou and C. Pohle. Data mining for measuring and improving the success of web sites. *Data Mining and Knowledge Discovery*, 5(1/2), 2001.

[SPF99] Myra Spiliopoulou, Carsten Pohle, and Lukas Faulstich. Improving the effectiveness of a web site with web usage mining. In *Proc. of the Web Usage Analysis and User Profiling Workshop*, pages 51–56, San Diego, California, 1999.

[SYZ00] Z. Su, Q. Yang, and H. Zhang. A prediction system for multimedia prefetching on the internet. In *Proceedings of the ACM Multimedia Conference*, October 2000.

[YZL01] Qiang Yang, Haining Henry Zhang, and Tianyi Li. Mining web logs for prediction models in www caching and prefetching. In *Proc. of the 7th ACM SIGKDD'01*, San Francisco, California, USA, August 2001.

Composition of Mining Contexts for Efficient Extraction of Association Rules

Cheikh Talibouya Diop[1,3], Arnaud Giacometti[1],
Dominique Laurent[1], and Nicolas Spyratos[2]

[1] LI, Université de Tours, 41000 Blois, France
{giaco,laurent}@univ-tours.fr
[2] LRI, Université Paris 11, 91405 Orsay Cedex, France
spyratos@lri.fr [†]
[3] Université Gaston Berger, Saint-Louis, Senegal
cdiop@ugb.sn

Abstract. Association rule mining often requires the repeated execution of some extraction algorithm for different values of the support and confidence thresholds, as well as for different source datasets. This is an expensive process, even if we use the best existing algorithms. Hence the need for *incremental* mining, whereby mining results already obtained can be used to accelerate subsequent steps in the mining process.

In this paper, we present an approach for the incremental mining of *multidimensional* association rules. In our approach, association rule mining takes place in a *mining context* which specifies the form of rules to be mined. Incremental mining is obtained by combining mining contexts using relational algebra operations.

1 Introduction

Association rule mining often requires the repeated execution of some extraction algorithm for different values of the support and confidence thresholds, as well as for different source datasets. This is an expensive process, even if we use the best existing algorithms. Hence the need for *incremental* mining, whereby mining results already obtained can be used to accelerate subsequent steps in the mining process.

In this paper, we present an approach for the incremental mining of *multidimensional* association rules, i.e., association rules that involve one or more tables from a given relational database [11]. In our approach, association rule mining takes place in a *mining context* which specifies the form of rules to be mined. Incremental mining is obtained by combining mining contexts using relational algebra operations.

[†] Work by this author was conducted, in part, while visiting at the National Technical University of Athens, Greece, under a Pened/Geget project.

1.1 Association Rules and Mining Contexts

Whereas most formalisms to represent multi-dimensional association rules are based on Dalalog and first-order logic ([6, 11, 19]), we shall use relational algebra to define association rules and mining tasks.

In our approach, a mining context, or simply a context, specifies the form of rules to be mined for a data mining task. More precisely, a context specifies the objects of interest, as well as attributes of these objects and conditions on those attributes. Let us explain these concepts through an example that will serve as a running example throughout the paper.

Example 1. Consider a database *DBSales* containing the following tables:

- $Cust(Cid, Cjob, Caddr)$, where Cid, $Cjob$ and $Caddr$ are the ids, jobs and home addresses of customers, respectively,
- $Prod(Pid, Ptype)$, where Pid and $Ptype$ are the ids and the types of products, respectively,
- $Store(Sid, Sname, Saddr)$, where Sid, $Sname$ et $Saddr$ are the ids, names and addresses of stores, respectively,
- $Sales(Cid, Pid, Sid, Date)$, where a tuple $\langle c, p, s, d \rangle$ in the *Sales* table means that customer c issued a transaction concerning product p in the store s on date d.

Assuming that the objects of interest are all customers whose *ids* are stored in the *Cust* table, we consider the relational expression $AllCust = \pi_{Cid}(Cust)$. Suppose now that the attributes of interest for customers are their jobs, addresses and the types of products they buy. We can specify this by the following relational expression, $B_1 = Cust \bowtie Sales \bowtie Prod$.

Moreover, if we are only interested in association rules dealing with customers whose job is professor or lawyer, and who buy tea or milk, then we can consider the set of selection conditions Σ_1 defined by $\Sigma_1 = \{Cjob = Professor, Cjob = Lawyer, Ptype = Tea, Ptype = Milk\}$.

The triple $\mathcal{C}_1 = \langle AllCust, B_1, \Sigma_1 \rangle$ is an example of what we call a *mining context*, or simply a *context*. Moreover, $AllCust$, B_1 and Σ_1 are called the *reference*, the *basis* and the *domain* of $\mathcal{C}_1$, respectively. Given the context $\mathcal{C}_1 = \langle AllCust, B_1, \Sigma_1 \rangle$, the following rule is an example of association rule that can be considered:

$$AllCust \bowtie \sigma_{Cjob=Lawyer}(B_1) \Rightarrow AllCust \bowtie \sigma_{Cjob=Lawyer \wedge Ptype=Tea}(B_1)$$

This rule means intuitively that if a customer is a lawyer, then he buys tea.

More generally, a context is a triple $\mathcal{C} = \langle R, B, \Sigma \rangle$ where R and B are two relational expressions and Σ is a set of selection conditions. Given a context $\mathcal{C} = \langle R, B, \Sigma \rangle$, we consider two types of patterns:

1. A *query of* $\mathcal{C}$ is a query of the form $R \bowtie \sigma_S(B)$ where S is a conjunction of selection conditions in Σ.

2. An *association rule of* $\mathcal{C}$ is an expression of the form $q_1 \Rightarrow q_2$ where q_1 and q_2 are queries of $\mathcal{C}$, and q_2 is contained in q_1 (in the sense of query containment [20]).

Let $\mathcal{C} = \langle R, B, \Sigma \rangle$ be a context and let I be an instance of the database. Denoting by K the set of attributes of the reference R, the interestingness in I of association rules of $\mathcal{C}$ is defined as follows:

1. Let q be a query of $\mathcal{C}$. The *support* of q in I is the ratio $|(\pi_K(q))(I)|/|R(I)|$. If this ratio is greater than a given support threshold, then we say that q is *frequent* in I.
2. Let $q_1 \Rightarrow q_2$ be a rule of $\mathcal{C}$. The *confidence* of $q_1 \Rightarrow q_2$ in I is the ratio $|(\pi_K(q_2))(I)|/|(\pi_K(q_1))(I)|$. If this ratio is greater than a given confidence threshold, and if q_1 and q_2 are frequent in I, then we say that $q_1 \Rightarrow q_2$ is *interesting* in I.

As in other approaches, given a context $\mathcal{C}$, a minimum support threshold and a minimum confidence threshold, the problem is to find all interesting association rules of $\mathcal{C}$. This problem can be solved in a two-steps process: (1) Find all frequent queries of $\mathcal{C}$, and (2) Generate all interesting rules of $\mathcal{C}$ from the frequent queries in $\mathcal{C}$.

The overall performance of the mining task is determined by the first step. Clearly, in implementing our approach, we can use any of the existing level-wise algorithms [1, 3, 16] to compute the frequent queries of a context. In the following, we show how the computation of the frequent queries of a context using these algorithms can be accelerated, assuming that the results of previously computed tasks are stored.

1.2 Composition of Mining Contexts

The main contribution of this paper is to show the following: Suppose that a number of tasks have already been performed and that their frequent queries have been stored. Then any new mining task, whose context is defined by composition of the contexts of old tasks, can be performed more efficiently than if this new mining task had been defined without reference to the old tasks. To this end, we define operations over contexts similar to those of the relational algebra, and we study their properties. The following example shows how contexts are composed.

Example 2. In the database *DBSales* of Example 1, assume that we want to discover the relationships between the jobs of customers living in *Paris* and the types of products they buy. Using the context $\mathcal{C}_1$ given previously, a context $\mathcal{C}_1^*$, denoted by $\sigma^b_{Caddr=Paris}(\mathcal{C}_1)$, can be defined by applying the selection condition $(Caddr = Paris)$ on the basis of $\mathcal{C}_1$. That is, $\mathcal{C}_1^* = \langle AllCust, \sigma_{Caddr=Paris}(B_1), \Sigma_1 \rangle$.

Given the new context $\mathcal{C}_1^*$, let $q_1^* = AllCust \bowtie \sigma_S(\sigma_{Caddr=Paris}(B_1))$ be a query of $\mathcal{C}_1^*$. We can see easily that the answer to q_1^* is always included in the answer to the query $q_1 = AllCust \bowtie \sigma_S(B_1)$ of $\mathcal{C}_1$. More generally, it can be seen that every query q_1^* of $\mathcal{C}_1^*$ is contained (in the sense of query containment [20]) in a query q_1 of $\mathcal{C}_1$.

Therefore, the support of every query q_1^* of $\mathcal{C}_1^*$ is less than or equal to the support of a query q_1 of $\mathcal{C}_1$. It follows that if a query q_1^* of $\mathcal{C}_1^*$ is frequent, then it is contained in a frequent query q_1 of $\mathcal{C}_1$. Conversely, if a query q_1^* of $\mathcal{C}_1^*$ is not contained in a frequent query q_1 of $\mathcal{C}_1$, then it can not be frequent.

As a consequence, if we assume that the frequent queries of $\mathcal{C}_1$ are stored, this property can be used to prune some of the candidate queries of $\mathcal{C}_1^*$ when computing its frequent queries. Moreover, this new pruning step can be done without any access to the database, implying that the computation of the frequent queries of $\mathcal{C}_1^*$ can be accelerated.

In the remaining of this paper, we show how the example above can be generalized and how the computation of frequent queries in composed contexts can be optimized.

1.3 Related Works

So far, many SQL based query languages have been proposed in order to facilitate the specification of mining tasks [9, 10, 19], but to our knowledge, none of these languages allows to combine such tasks based on properties of the relational algebra. We can also note that our notion of context is closed to the notion of query flock introduced in [19]. However, the objective of the approach presented in [19] is not to store and use the results of mining tasks in order to optimize new mining tasks, but rather to optimize the computation of one mining task using query containment.

On the other hand, storing and using the results of mining tasks in order to optimize new mining tasks has been studied in [13–15]. However, these approaches compare only mining tasks defined over a single reference and a single basis (using our terminology), and they do not propose any composition operations as we do.

In [13, 14], the authors consider the traditional case where the source database contains only one table (the basis in our terminology), whose rows contain sets of items. In [13], mining tasks are compared with respect to three criterions: the support thresholds, the selection conditions on the source dataset and the constraints on the patterns. Moreover, the authors use materialized views to store the results of mining tasks already computed.

In [14], mining tasks are mainly compared with respect to their support thresholds, and the authors propose different caching strategies aiming at storing only the most useful frequent itemsets that can be used to answer new mining tasks. In [15], the same authors present an extension of their approach, whereby the source database is not the traditional table, but a data cube.

In this paper, we dot not compare mining tasks with different support thresholds, although our formalism allows for such comparisons. Instead, we focus on the case where the source database contains *multiple tables*. It follows that we can specify and compare mining tasks with *different basis* or with *different references*. Finally, in our storage technique, only the positive boundaries of the results of mining tasks are stored.

The rest of the paper is organized as follows: In Section 2, we formally define the notion of mining context, and we provide definitions and properties for the measures of support and confidence. The operations for combining mining contexts are studied in Section 3, and in Section 4, we show how to improve the efficiency of association rule discovery. Section 5 concludes the paper and outlines further research based on this work. Proofs are omitted due to a lack of space; the interested reader is referred to [8] for more details.

2 Mining Contexts and Mining Tasks

2.1 Definitions and Notations

The formalism used in this paper is based on the relational model of databases ([20]). We recall that a relational database schema is a set of relation names, each of which is associated with a set of attributes. We call schema of a relation R the set of attributes associated with R and we denote it by $sch(R)$. For each attribute A, the possible values for A belong to a specific set of values, called the domain of A and denoted by $dom(A)$.

In the remainder of this paper, we assume a fixed database schema, $DB = \{R_1, R_2, \ldots, R_n\}$, and we call instance of DB any set of relations $I = \{r_1, r_2, \ldots, r_n\}$, where r_i is a relation over $sch(R_i)$, for every $i = 1, 2, \ldots, n$. Given a relational expression, or a query q, over DB, we call schema of q the set of attributes over which q is defined, and we denote it by $sch(q)$. Moreover, we denote by $q(I)$ the answer to q in I.

As in [4], if q_1 and q_2 are two queries such that $sch(q_1) = sch(q_2)$, we say that q_1 is *contained* in q_2, or that q_1 is *more specific* than q_2, denoted by $q_1 \sqsubseteq q_2$, if for every instance I we have $q_1(I) \subseteq q_2(I)$. Queries q_1 and q_2 are said *equivalent*, denoted by $q_1 \equiv q_2$, if both $q_1 \sqsubseteq q_2$ and $q_2 \sqsubseteq q_1$ hold.

2.2 Mining Contexts

In our approach, the form of rules to be mined for a data mining task is specified by a *mining context*.

Definition 1. - Mining Context. *A mining context $\mathcal{C}$, or simply a context, is a triple $\mathcal{C} = \langle R, B, \Sigma \rangle$ where:*

- *R is a relational expression, called the reference of $\mathcal{C}$.*
- *B is a relational expression such that $sch(R) \subseteq sch(B)$, called the basis of $\mathcal{C}$.*
- *Σ is a set of atomic selection conditions, called the domain of $\mathcal{C}$. These selection conditions are of the form $(A = a)$ where A is an attribute of B not present among the attributes of R, and a is a constant in $dom(A)$.*

We note that the reference of a context specifies the values that are subject to counting when searching for frequent queries. Hence, our notion of reference is similar to that of *key atom* introduced in [6].

Definition 2. - Search Space. *Given a context $C = \langle R, B, \Sigma \rangle$*

1. *Σ^* denotes the set of all selection conditions of the form $(A_1 = a_1) \wedge \ldots \wedge (A_n = a_n)$, where $(A_i = a_i)$ is in Σ $(i = 1 \ldots n)$.*
2. *$\mathcal{Q}(C)$ denotes the set of all queries of the form $R \bowtie \sigma_S(B)$ where $S \in \Sigma^*$. Queries in $\mathcal{Q}(C)$ are called* candidate queries of C, *or simply* queries of C.
3. *$\mathcal{R}(C)$ denotes the set of all rules of the form $q_1 \Rightarrow q_2$ where $q_1 = R \bowtie \sigma_{S_1}(B)$ and $q_2 = R \bowtie \sigma_{S_1 \wedge S_2}(B)$ are queries of C. Rules of $\mathcal{R}(C)$ are called* candidate rules of C, *or simply* rules of C. *Moreover, we say that a rule $q_1 \Rightarrow q_2$ is* satisfied *in an instance I if $(\pi_K(q_1))(I) \subseteq (\pi_K(q_2))(I)$, where $K = sch(R)$.*

2.3 Support and Confidence

We now define the support of a query and the confidence of a rule.

Definition 3. - Support of a Query. *Let $C = \langle R, B, \Sigma \rangle$ be a context and q be a query such that $sch(R) \subseteq sch(q)$. For every instance I, the support of q relatively to C and I, denoted by $Sup(q \mid C, I)$, is the following ratio:*

$$Sup(q \mid C, I) = \frac{|(\pi_K(q))(I)|}{|R(I)|}, \text{ where } K = sch(R).$$

Given a support threshold α, we denote by $freq_\alpha(C, I)$ the set of all queries in $\mathcal{Q}(C)$ whose support relatively to C and I is greater than or equal to α. Queries in $freq_\alpha(C, I)$ are called α-frequent in I, or simply frequent if α and I are understood.

The following proposition generalizes the basic property of monotonicity used for standard association rules in [1].

Proposition 1. *Let $C_1 = \langle R_1, B_1, \Sigma_1 \rangle$ and $C_2 = \langle R_2, B_2, \Sigma_2 \rangle$ be two contexts such that $K = sch(R_1) = sch(R_2)$, let q_1 and q_2 be queries of C_1 and C_2 respectively. If $R_1 \sqsubseteq R_2$ and $\pi_K(q_2) \sqsubseteq \pi_K(q_1)$, then for every instance I, we have:*

$$Sup(q_2 \mid C_2, I) \leq Sup(q_1 \mid C_1, I).$$

Based on this proposition and using properties of the relational algebra, we can easily show the following facts.

Corollary 1. *Let $C_1 = \langle R_1, B_1, \Sigma_1 \rangle$ and $C_2 = \langle R_2, B_2, \Sigma_2 \rangle$ be two contexts such that $K = sch(R_1) = sch(R_2)$, let q_1 and q_2 be two queries of C_1 and C_2 respectively, and let S be a selection condition in Σ_1^*. Then for every instance I, we have:*
1. *$Sup(\sigma_S(q_1) \mid C_1, I) \leq Sup(q_1 \mid C_1, I)$,*
2. *$Sup(q_1 \bowtie q_2 \mid C_i, I) \leq Sup(q_i \mid C_i, I)$ for $i = 1, 2$.*

Given a context $\mathcal{C} = \langle R, B, \Sigma \rangle$, the confidence of an association rule of $\mathcal{C}$ is defined as follows.

Definition 4. - Confidence of a Rule. *Let $\mathcal{C} = \langle R, B, \Sigma \rangle$ be a context and let q_1 and q_2 be two queries of $\mathcal{C}$. For every instance I, the confidence of the rule $\mathcal{R} : q_1 \Rightarrow q_2$ relatively to $\mathcal{C}$ and I, denoted by $Conf(\mathcal{R} \mid \mathcal{C}, I)$, is the ratio:*

$$Conf(\mathcal{R} \mid \mathcal{C}, I) = \frac{|(\pi_K(q_2))(I)|}{|(\pi_K(q_1))(I)|}, \text{ where } K = sch(R).$$

Given a support threshold α and a confidence threshold β, we denote by $int_{\alpha,\beta}(\mathcal{C}, I)$ the set of all rules $q_1 \Rightarrow q_2$ in $\mathcal{R}(\mathcal{C})$ such that q_1 and q_2 are frequent queries in $freq_\alpha(\mathcal{C}, I)$, and $Conf(q_1 \Rightarrow q_2 \mid \mathcal{C}, I) \geq \beta$.
Rules in $int_{\alpha,\beta}(\mathcal{C}, I)$ are called (α, β)-interesting *in I, or simply* interesting *if α, β and I are understood*.

Let $\mathcal{C}$ be a context and let I be an instance of the database. We can note that the confidence of a rule $\mathcal{R} : q_1 \Rightarrow q_2$ of $\mathcal{C}$ is equal to 1 in I iff this rule is satisfied in I. Moreover, we have: $Conf(\mathcal{R} \mid \mathcal{C}, I) = Sup(q_2 \mid \mathcal{C}, I)/Sup(q_1 \mid \mathcal{C}, I)$. It follows that the confidence of a rule can be computed without accessing the database (assuming that the supports of all frequent queries are available). Therefore, when we extract interesting association rules, the most important task is to compute the set of all frequent queries. In the following section, we shall see how context composition can optimize the computation of frequent queries.

3 Composition of Contexts

The operations defined in this section are based on those of the relational algebra ([20]) and allow for the definition of new tasks from "old".

3.1 Manipulation and Comparison of Sets of Queries

First, we extend the usual operators of the relational algebra to sets of queries over the same schema, and we define a new operator that we call *reduction*.

Definition 5. - Operations on Sets of Queries. *Let $\mathcal{Q}$, $\mathcal{Q}_1$ and $\mathcal{Q}_2$ be sets of queries, and let us assume that all queries in $\mathcal{Q}$, $\mathcal{Q}_1$ and $\mathcal{Q}_2$ are over schemas Sch, Sch_1 and Sch_2, respectively.*

1. *Let X be a subset of Sch, the* projection *of $\mathcal{Q}$ over X, denoted by $\pi_X(\mathcal{Q})$, is defined by: $\pi_X(\mathcal{Q}) = \{\pi_X(q) \mid q \in \mathcal{Q}\}$.*
2. *Given a selection condition S containing only attributes from Sch, the* selection *of $\mathcal{Q}$ with respect to S, denoted by $\sigma_S(\mathcal{Q})$, is defined by:*
   $\sigma_S(\mathcal{Q}) = \{\sigma_S(q) \mid q \in \mathcal{Q}\}$.
3. *Given a selection condition S containing only attributes from Sch, the* reduction *of $\mathcal{Q}$ with respect to S, denoted by $\tau_S(\mathcal{Q})$, is defined by:*
   $\tau_S(\mathcal{Q}) = \{q \in \mathcal{Q} \mid \sigma_S(q) \equiv q\}$.

4. The join of $\mathcal{Q}_1$ and $\mathcal{Q}_2$, denoted by $\mathcal{Q}_1 \bowtie \mathcal{Q}_2$, is defined by:
$\mathcal{Q}_1 \bowtie \mathcal{Q}_2 = \{q_1 \bowtie q_2 \mid q_1 \in \mathcal{Q}_1 \text{ and } q_2 \in \mathcal{Q}_2\}$.

Example 3. We illustrate the difference between selection and reduction using Example 1. Consider the selection condition $S = (Caddr = Paris)$ and the set of queries $\mathcal{Q} = \{q_1, q_2\}$ where $q_1 = \sigma_{(Cjob=Lawyer \wedge Caddr=Paris)}(Cust)$ and $q_2 = \sigma_{Cjob=Professor}(Cust)$.
Since selection over $\mathcal{Q}$ operates on every query, $\sigma_S(\mathcal{Q}) = \{\sigma_S(q_1), \sigma_S(q_2)\}$, and replacing S, q_1 and q_2 by their respective definitions, we obtain: $\sigma_S(\mathcal{Q}) = \{\sigma_{(Cjob=Lawyer \wedge Caddr=Paris)}(Cust), \sigma_{(Cjob=Professor \wedge Caddr=Paris)}(Cust)\}$.
On the other hand, the reduction of $\mathcal{Q}$ results in keeping q_1 and removing q_2 from $\mathcal{Q}$, because $\sigma_S(q_1) \equiv q_1$ and $\sigma_S(q_2) \not\equiv q_2$. Therefore we have: $\tau_S(\mathcal{Q}) = \{q_1\}$, i.e. $\tau_S(\mathcal{Q}) = \{\sigma_{(Cjob=Lawyer \wedge Caddr=Paris)}(Cust)\}$.

We now define two different ways for comparing sets of queries. The first uses the standard query containment ([20]), whereas the second uses equivalence.

Definition 6. - Comparison of Sets of Queries. *Let $\mathcal{Q}_1$ and $\mathcal{Q}_2$ be two sets of queries over the same schema.*

- *$\mathcal{Q}_1$ is included in $\mathcal{Q}_2$, denoted by $\mathcal{Q}_1 \sqsubseteq \mathcal{Q}_2$, if for every q_1 in $\mathcal{Q}_1$, there exists q_2 in $\mathcal{Q}_2$ such that $q_1 \sqsubseteq q_2$.*
- *$\mathcal{Q}_1$ is strongly included in $\mathcal{Q}_2$, denoted by $\mathcal{Q}_1 \widetilde{\subseteq} \mathcal{Q}_2$, if for every q_1 in $\mathcal{Q}_1$, there exists q_2 in $\mathcal{Q}_2$ such that $q_1 \equiv q_2$.*
  Moreover, $\mathcal{Q}_1$ is strongly equivalent to $\mathcal{Q}_2$, denoted by $\mathcal{Q}_1 \sim \mathcal{Q}_2$, if $\mathcal{Q}_1 \widetilde{\subseteq} \mathcal{Q}_2$ and $\mathcal{Q}_2 \widetilde{\subseteq} \mathcal{Q}_1$.

Clearly, if $\mathcal{Q}_1$ and $\mathcal{Q}_2$ are two sets of queries over the same schema such that $\mathcal{Q}_1 \widetilde{\subseteq} \mathcal{Q}_2$, then we have $\mathcal{Q}_1 \sqsubseteq \mathcal{Q}_2$, whereas the converse does not hold. Moreover, the following proposition holds.

Proposition 2. *Let $\mathcal{C}_1 = \langle R_1, B_1, \Sigma_1 \rangle$ and $\mathcal{C}_2 = \langle R_2, B_2, \Sigma_2 \rangle$ be two contexts such that $K = sch(R_1) = sch(R_2)$ and $sch(R_1 \bowtie B_1) = sch(R_2 \bowtie B_2)$. Then for every instance I, we have:*

1. *If $\mathcal{Q}(\mathcal{C}_1) \sqsubseteq \mathcal{Q}(\mathcal{C}_2)$ and $R_2 \sqsubseteq R_1$, then for every $q_1 \in \mathcal{Q}(\mathcal{C}_1)$, there exists $q_2 \in \mathcal{Q}(\mathcal{C}_2)$ such that $Sup(q_1 \mid \mathcal{C}, I) \leq Sup(q_2 \mid \mathcal{C}, I)$.*
2. *If $\mathcal{Q}(\mathcal{C}_1) \widetilde{\subseteq} \mathcal{Q}(\mathcal{C}_2)$, then for every $q_1 \in \mathcal{Q}(\mathcal{C}_1)$, there exists $q_2 \in \mathcal{Q}(\mathcal{C}_2)$ such that $Sup(q_1 \mid \mathcal{C}_1, I) / Sup(q_2 \mid \mathcal{C}_2, I) = |R_1(I)| / |R_2(I)|$.*

We note that when $R_1 = R_2 = R$, case 2 above reduces to $Sup(q_1 \mid \mathcal{C}_1, I) = Sup(q_2 \mid \mathcal{C}_2, I)$. This proposition will be used in Section 4 to decide whether a query is frequent without having to access the database.

3.2 Projection over the Basis of a Context

In the following definition and proposition, given a domain Σ of a context, we denote by $att(\Sigma)$ the set of all attributes occurring in Σ.

Definition 7. - Projection of a Context. Let $\mathcal{C} = \langle R, B, \Sigma \rangle$ be a context, and let X be a set of attributes. If $att(\Sigma) \subseteq X \subseteq sch(B)$, then the b-projection of $\mathcal{C}$ over X, denoted by $\pi^b_X(\mathcal{C})$, is defined by: $\pi^b_X(\mathcal{C}) = \langle R, \pi_X(B), \Sigma \rangle$.

Proposition 3. Let $\mathcal{C} = \langle R, B, \Sigma \rangle$ be a context, and let X be a set of attributes. If $sch(R) \subseteq X$ and $att(\Sigma) \subseteq X \subseteq sch(B)$, then for every support threshold α and every instance I, we have:

$$freq_\alpha(\pi^b_X(\mathcal{C}), I) \sim \pi_X(freq_\alpha(\mathcal{C}, I)).$$

Intuitively, given a context $\mathcal{C} = \langle R, B, \Sigma \rangle$, Proposition 3 above implies that all attributes that do not occur in R or in Σ can be discarded.

3.3 Selection over the Basis of a Context

In the following definition and propositions, given a selection condition S, we denote by $att(S)$ the set of all attributes occurring in S.

Definition 8. - Selection over a Context. Let $\mathcal{C} = \langle R, B, \Sigma \rangle$ be a context, and let S be a selection condition. If $att(S) \subseteq sch(B)$, then the b-selection of $\mathcal{C}$ according to S, denoted by $\sigma^b_S(\mathcal{C})$, is defined by: $\sigma^b_S(\mathcal{C}) = \langle R, \sigma_S(B), \Sigma \rangle$.

Proposition 4. Let $\mathcal{C} = \langle R, B, \Sigma \rangle$ be a context. If S is a selection condition in Σ^*, then for every support threshold α and every instance I, we have:

$$freq_\alpha(\sigma^b_S(\mathcal{C}), I) \sim \tau_S(freq_\alpha(\mathcal{C}, I)).$$

In what follows, we say that a conjunction of atomic selection conditions $S = (A_1 = a_1) \wedge \ldots \wedge (A_n = a_n)$ is *independent* from a domain Σ if for every $i = 1 \ldots n$, the atomic selection condition $(A_i = a_i)$ is not in Σ.

Proposition 5. Let $\mathcal{C} = \langle R, B, \Sigma \rangle$ be a context. If S is a selection condition independent from Σ such that $att(S) \subseteq sch(B)$, then for every support threshold α and every instance I, we have:

$$freq_\alpha(\sigma^b_S(\mathcal{C}), I) \overset{\sim}{\subseteq} \sigma_S(freq_\alpha(\mathcal{C}, I)).$$

The following corollary is an immediate consequence of Propositions 4 and 5.

Corollary 2. Let $\mathcal{C} = \langle R, B, \Sigma \rangle$ be a context, and $S = S_1 \wedge S_2$ be a selection condition such that $att(S) \subseteq sch(B)$, $S_1 \in \Sigma^*$, and S_2 is independent from Σ. For every support threshold α and every instance I, we have:

$$freq_\alpha(\sigma^b_S(\mathcal{C}), I) \overset{\sim}{\subseteq} \tau_{S_1}(\sigma_{S_2}(freq_\alpha(\mathcal{C}, I))).$$

It is easy to see that $\tau_{S_1}(\sigma_{S_2}(freq_\alpha(\mathcal{C}, I))) \sim \sigma_{S_2}(\tau_{S_1}(freq_\alpha(\mathcal{C}, I)))$. Thus, Corollary 2 implies that: $freq_\alpha(\sigma^b_S(\mathcal{C}), I) \overset{\sim}{\subseteq} \sigma_{S_2}(\tau_{S_1}(freq_\alpha(\mathcal{C}, I)))$.

Example 4. Consider again the database *DBSales* of Example 1 and the query *AllCust* defined by: $AllCust = \pi_{Cid}(Cust)$.

Assume first that we are interested in the relationships between the jobs of customers and the types of products they buy. Then we consider the context $C_1 = \langle AllCust, Cust \bowtie Sales \bowtie Prod, \Sigma \rangle$ where Σ is the set of all selection conditions of the form $(Cjob = job)$ or $(Ptype = type)$ where job and $type$ are constants in $dom(Cjob)$ and $dom(Ptype)$ respectively. In the following examples, we denote such a domain by: $\Sigma = \{Cjob = *, Ptype = *\}$.

Assume now that we are interested only in the rules concerning lawyers. If we consider the context $C_2 = \sigma^b_{Cjob=Lawyer}(C_1)$, then, according to Proposition 4, for every support threshold α and every instance I of $DBSales$, we have: $freq_\alpha(C_2, I) \sim \tau_{Cjob=Lawyer}(freq_\alpha(C_1, I))$.
Thus, applying Proposition 2, it turns out that the frequent queries of C_1 that deal with lawyers are exactly the frequent queries of C_2.

Finally, assume that we are interested in the rules involving only customers living in Paris. The corresponding context C_3 is defined by $C_3 = \sigma^b_{Caddr=Paris}(C_1)$, and, according to Proposition 5, for every instance I of $DBSales$, we have: $freq_\alpha(C_3, I) \widetilde{\subseteq} \sigma_{Caddr=Paris}(freq_\alpha(C_1, I))$. In this case, applying Proposition 2, if a query q_1 of C_1 is not frequent, the corresponding query $q_3 = \sigma_{Caddr=Paris}(Q_1)$ of C_3 is not frequent either, and this conclusion is reached without any access to the database.

3.4 Join of Contexts

Definition 9. - Joining Contexts. Let $C_1 = \langle R, B_1, \Sigma_1 \rangle$ and $C_2 = \langle R, B_2, \Sigma_2 \rangle$ be two contexts having the same reference R. The join of C_1 and C_2, denoted by $C_1 \bowtie_b C_2$, is defined by: $C_1 \bowtie_b C_2 = \langle R, B_1 \bowtie B_2, \Sigma_1 \cup \Sigma_2 \rangle$.

Proposition 6. Let $C_1 = \langle R, B_1, \Sigma_1 \rangle$ and $C_2 = \langle R, B_2, \Sigma_2 \rangle$ be two contexts having the same reference R. For every support threshold α and every instance I, we have:

$$freq_\alpha(C_1 \bowtie_b C_2, I) \widetilde{\subseteq} freq_\alpha(C_1, I) \bowtie freq_\alpha(C_2, I).$$

Example 5. Consider again the database *DBSales* of Example 1 and the query $AllCust = \pi_{Cid}(Cust)$.

Assume first that we are interested in the relationships between the jobs of customers and the types of products they buy. Then, as already mentioned, we specify the context $C_1 = \langle AllCust, Cust \bowtie Sales \bowtie Prod, \Sigma_1 \rangle$ where $\Sigma_1 = \{Cjob = *, Ptype = *\}$.

Then assume that we are interested in the relationships between the names of stores where customers issue their transactions and the types of products they buy. The corresponding context C_2 is defined by $C_2 = \langle AllCust, Store \bowtie Sales \bowtie Prod, \Sigma_2 \rangle$ where $\Sigma_2 = \{Sname = *, Ptype = *\}$.

Now, if we consider the relationships between the jobs of customers, the names of stores where they issue their transactions and the types of products they buy, then the corresponding context C_{12} can be defined by: $C_{12} = C_1 \bowtie_b C_2$.

According to Proposition 6, for every support threshold α and every instance I of $DBSales$, we have: $freq_\alpha(\mathcal{C}_{12}, I) \sqsubseteq freq_\alpha(\mathcal{C}_1, I) \bowtie freq_\alpha(\mathcal{C}_2, I)$. Thus, by Definition 6, for any query q_{12} in $\mathcal{Q}(\mathcal{C}_{12})$, there exist two queries q_1 and q_2 of $\mathcal{C}_1$ and $\mathcal{C}_2$ respectively, such that $q_{12} \equiv q_1 \bowtie q_2$. Moreover, by Corollary 1, $Sup(q_1 \bowtie q_2 \mid \mathcal{C}_{12}, I) \leq Sup(q_i \mid \mathcal{C}_i, I)$, for $i = 1, 2$. Therefore, if q_{12} is frequent, then so are q_1 and q_2.

Note that we can also define new contexts from two contexts $\mathcal{C}_1 = \langle R, B_1, \Sigma \rangle$ and $\mathcal{C}_2 = \langle R, B_2, \Sigma \rangle$ by applying set theoretical operations to their basis B_1 and B_2 (if $sch(B_1) = sch(B_2)$). For example, the difference of $\mathcal{C}_2$ and $\mathcal{C}_1$, denoted by $\mathcal{C}_2 \setminus_b \mathcal{C}_2$, is defined by: $\mathcal{C}_2 \setminus_b \mathcal{C}_1 = \langle R, B_2 - B_1, \Sigma \rangle$. Moreover, it is easy to see that we have: $freq_\alpha(\mathcal{C}_2 \setminus_b \mathcal{C}_1, I) \sqsubseteq freq_\alpha(\mathcal{C}_2, I)$. More generally, set theoretical operations for contexts are studied in [8].

3.5 Restriction of a Context

In this section, we consider an operation that restricts the reference of a context.

Definition 10. *Let $\mathcal{C} = \langle R, B, \Sigma \rangle$ be a context with $K = sch(R)$, and let S be a selection condition in Σ^*. The restriction of $\mathcal{C}$ over S is defined by: $\rho_S(\mathcal{C}) = \langle \pi_K(R \bowtie \sigma_S(B)), \sigma_S(B), \Sigma \rangle$.*

Proposition 7. *Let $\mathcal{C} = \langle R, B, \Sigma \rangle$ be a context, and let S be a selection condition in Σ^*. Then, for every threshold α and every instance I, we have:*

$$\tau_S(freq_\alpha(\mathcal{C})) \widetilde{\sqsubseteq} freq_\alpha(\rho_S(\mathcal{C})).$$

Example 6. Consider again the database $DBSales$ of Example 1 and assume now that we are interested in the relationships between the jobs of customers, the town where they live and the types of products they buy. Then we specify the context $\mathcal{C}_1 = \langle AllCust, Cust \bowtie Sales \bowtie Prod, \Sigma \rangle$ where $\Sigma = \{Cjob = *, Caddr = *, Ptype = *\}$.

Suppose that we are interested in focussing on customers living in $Paris$. The corresponding context $\mathcal{C}_2$ can be defined by $\mathcal{C}_2 = \rho_{Caddr=Paris}(\mathcal{C}_1)$. Note that the reference of $\mathcal{C}_2$ is defined by the query $\pi_{Cid}(AllCust \bowtie \sigma_{Caddr=Paris}(Cust \bowtie Sales \bowtie Prod))$, meaning that the support of queries is computed with respect to the number of customers living in $Paris$ (and not with respect to the total number of customers). Moreover, by Proposition 7, for every support threshold α and every instance I of $DBSales$, we have: $\tau_{Caddr=Paris}(freq_\alpha(\mathcal{C}_1, I)) \widetilde{\sqsubseteq} freq_\alpha(\mathcal{C}_2, I)$.

As a consequence, if q_1 is a frequent query in $\tau_{Caddr=Paris}(freq_\alpha(\mathcal{C}_1, I))$, then there exists a query in $freq_\alpha(\mathcal{C}_2, I)$ which is equivalent to q_1, and this conclusion can be reached without any access to the database.

4 Implementation Issues

We have seen so far operations for combining contexts in order to define new contexts. We have also given properties that show how the set of frequent queries of a context changes when we apply operations over its reference or basis. In this section, we review all cases where these properties allow for optimization in the computation of frequent queries of combined contexts.

Of course, in order to be able to use the frequent queries of the component contexts, we must store them. In our approach, we propose to store only the positive boundaries of sets of frequent queries already computed ([12]).

4.1 Possible Optimizations

Let $\mathcal{C}_{new}$ be a new context defined by combining other contexts. Given a support threshold α and an instance I of DB, we consider all cases where the computation of $freq_\alpha(\mathcal{C}_{new}, I)$ can be optimized using the sets of frequent queries in I that have already been computed. We distinguish three such cases:

1. $freq_\alpha(\mathcal{C}_{new}, I)$ is strongly equivalent to a set of frequent queries already computed;
2. $freq_\alpha(\mathcal{C}_{new}, I)$ is included or strongly included in a set of frequent queries already computed;
3. $freq_\alpha(\mathcal{C}_{new}, I)$ contains, strongly or not, a set of frequent queries already computed.

Strongly Equivalent Sets of Frequent Queries. Such case occurs when $\mathcal{C}_{new}$ is defined from $\mathcal{C}_{old}$ in one of the following ways:

- by projection of $\mathcal{C}_{old}$ (see Corollary 3),
- by selection of $\mathcal{C}_{old}$, with a selection condition involving only conditions in the domain of $\mathcal{C}_{old}$ (see Proposition 4).

In both cases, no access to data is needed to obtain $freq_\alpha(\mathcal{C}_{new}, I)$. One has just to apply the corresponding operation to the queries of $freq_\alpha(\mathcal{C}_{old}, I)$ to get the set $freq_\alpha(\mathcal{C}_{new}, I)$. Moreover, the supports of the queries in $freq_\alpha(\mathcal{C}_{new}, I)$ can be computed through one pass over the data, only.

Subset of a Set of Frequent Queries. This case occurs when $\mathcal{C}_{new}$ is defined in one of the following ways:

- by selection of $\mathcal{C}_{old}$ with a selection condition involving conditions not in the domain of $\mathcal{C}_{old}$ (see Proposition 5 and Corollary 2),
- by join of two contexts $\mathcal{C}_{old_1}$ and $\mathcal{C}_{old_2}$ (see Proposition 6).

In both cases, we only know an upper bound of the supports of the candidate queries in $\mathcal{C}_{new}$. Thus, these supports have to be computed. On the other hand, it is important to note that considering the positive boundaries of the sets of frequent queries already computed, allows for some additional pruning (with respect to standard levelwise algorithms) when generating the candidate queries of level $k+1$ from the frequent queries of level k.

To see this, consider the case of a b-selection with selection condition S independent from the domain of $\mathcal{C}_{old}$. If a candidate query q_{new} belongs to $freq_\alpha(\mathcal{C}_{new}, I)$, then by Proposition 5, there exists q_{old} in $freq_\alpha(\mathcal{C}_{old}, I)$ such that $q_{new} \equiv \sigma_S(q_{old})$. Moreover, since q_{old} is in $freq_\alpha(\mathcal{C}_{old}, I)$, there exists a query q_{old}^+ in the positive boundary of $freq_\alpha(\mathcal{C}_{old}, I)$ such that $q_{old}^+ \sqsubseteq q_{old}$. By monotonicity of the selection operation, we have that $\sigma_S(q_{old}^+) \sqsubseteq \sigma_S(q_{old})$. Thus we obtain $\sigma_S(q_{old}^+) \sqsubseteq q_{new}$.

Therefore, if there is no query q_{old}^+ as above, then q_{new} can be removed from the set of candidate queries of $\mathcal{C}_{new}$. We show in Section 4.3 how to efficiently test the existence of q_{old}^+.

Similarly, in the case of a join, if a candidate query q_{new} belongs to $freq_\alpha(\mathcal{C}_{new}, I)$, then by Proposition 6, there exist two frequent queries q_{old_1} and q_{old_2} such that $q_{new} \equiv q_{old_1} \bowtie q_{old_2}$. Thus, there exist $q_{old_1}^+$ and $q_{old_2}^+$ in the positive boundaries of $freq_\alpha(\mathcal{C}_1, I)$ and $freq_\alpha(\mathcal{C}_2, I)$ such that $q_{old_1}^+ \bowtie q_{old_2}^+ \sqsubseteq q_{new}$. Thus, we have the same case as above, and we show in Section 4.3 how to efficiently test the existence of $q_{old_1}^+$ and $q_{old_2}^+$.

Superset of a Set of Frequent Queries. This case occur when $\mathcal{C}_{new}$ is defined by restriction of $\mathcal{C}_{old}$ (see Proposition 7). We note that a subset $\mathcal{F}$ of $freq_\alpha(\mathcal{C}_{new}, I)$ is known without any further computation. Indeed, by Proposition 2, for every query q_{old} in $freq_\alpha(\mathcal{C}_{old}, I)$, there exists a query q_{new} in $freq_\alpha(\mathcal{C}_{new}, I)$ whose support is greater than or equal to that of q_{old}. Thus $\mathcal{F}$ is precisely the reduction of $freq_\alpha(\mathcal{C}_{old}, I)$ with respect to the corresponding selection condition. Moreover, the supports of the queries in $\mathcal{F}$ can be easily obtained, since only the support denominator of the corresponding queries in $freq_\alpha(\mathcal{C}_{old}, I)$ is changed.

Finally, for queries that are not in $\mathcal{F}$, no further optimization is possible. For such queries one will have to use the standard approach [1].

4.2 Storage of the Sets of Frequent Queries

In this section, we outline how the sets of frequent queries can be stored in a database that we call $DMining$. This database contains the following four tables:

- $Freq(CId, RQuery, BQuery, DId, Minsup)$, where CId stores the context identifier, $RQuery$ and $BQuery$ store expressions defining respectively the reference and the basis of the context, DId stores the identifier of the domain and $Minsup$ stores the support threshold.
- $Dom(DId, Name)$, where DId is as above and $Name$ stores the attribute occurring in the domain. We implicitly assume here that if attribute A is in the domain of a context, then the corresponding selection conditions are of the form $A = a$, for $a \in dom(A)$.
- $Query(CId, QId, Sup)$, where CId stores a context identifier, QId stores a query identifier, Sup stores the support of this query.

– $Cond(CId, QId, Name, Const)$, where CId and QId are as above and where $Name$ stores an attribute name and $Const$ stores a constant of the domain of that attribute.

Example 7. Figure 1 shows how the positive boundaries of two contexts are stored. In our example, the query identified by 3 is a frequent query of the context identified by 1. This query is defined by the following expression: $q_3 = AllCust \bowtie \sigma_{Cjob=Lawyer \wedge Ptype=Bread}(Cust \bowtie Sales \bowtie Prod)$.

Freq

CId	RQuery	BQuery	DId	Minsup
1	AllCust	Join(Cust,Sales,Prod)	1	0,1
2	AllCust	Join(Cust,Sales,Store)	2	0,1

Query

CId	QId	Sup
1	1	0,3
1	2	0,2
1	3	0,4
1	4	0,2
2	5	0,3
2	6	0,2
2	7	0,3

Dom

DId	Name
1	Cjob
1	Caddr
1	Ptype
2	Cjob
2	Caddr
2	Sname

Cond

CId	QId	Name	Const
1	1	Cjob	Professor
1	1	Caddr	Blois
1	2	Cjob	Lawyer
1	2	Caddr	Paris
1	2	Ptype	Milk
1	3	Cjob	Lawyer
1	3	Ptype	Bread
1	4	Cjob	Professor
1	4	Ptype	Bread
2	5	Sname	Carrefour
2	5	Caddr	Paris
2	5	Cjob	Lawyer
2	6	Sname	Ikea
2	6	Caddr	Paris
2	6	Cjob	Lawyer
2	7	Caddr	Paris
2	7	Sname	Fnac

Fig. 1. Storage of the frequent queries of two contexts with identifiers 1 and 2

4.3 Effective Use of the Stored Frequent Queries

In Subsection 4.1, we have seen that the positive boundary of sets of frequent queries can be used in order to optimize the computation of sets of frequent queries when new contexts are defined from old using b-selection or join. However, as mentioned above, this optimization is based on the comparison of a candidate query with all queries of the positive boundary.

We propose an efficient way to process this test, using an *inverse representation* of the positive boundary. Roughly speaking, the inverse representation of a given boundary consists in considering separately, for each atomic selection condition S, the set of identifiers of the queries involving S. Then, given a conjunction S' of atomic selection conditions, the set of queries involving S' is simply the intersection of the sets associated with each atomic selection condition of S'. We illustrate our method next.

Let $C_1 = \langle R, B_1, \Sigma_1 \rangle$ and $C_2 = \langle R, B_2, \Sigma_2 \rangle$ be two contexts, and let C_{new} be the context defined by $C_{new} = C_1 \bowtie_b C_2$. Given a support threshold α and an instance I, let Bd_1^+ and Bd_2^+ be the positive boundaries of $freq_\alpha(C_1, I)$ and $freq_\alpha(C_2, I)$, respectively.

For $i = 1, 2$, let $QId(i, A = a)$ be the set of identifiers of all queries in Bd_i^+ whose selection condition involves $A = a$. As seen in Subsection 4.1, a candidate query $q_{new} = R \bowtie \sigma_S(B_1 \bowtie B_2)$ of C_{new} is frequent if and only if there exist q_1^+ in Bd_1^+ and q_2^+ in Bd_2^+ such that $q_1^+ \bowtie q_2^+ \sqsubseteq q_{new}$.

On the other hand, the selection condition $S = (A_1 = a_1) \wedge \ldots \wedge (A_n = a_n)$ of q_{new} can be written as $S = S_1 \wedge S_2$ where $S_1 = (A_{11} = a_{11}) \wedge \ldots \wedge (A_{1p} = a_{1p})$ is in Σ_1^* and $S_2 = (A_{21} = a_{21}) \wedge \ldots \wedge (A_{2q} = a_{2q})$ is in Σ_2^*.

Then, it can easily be seen that there exist q_1^+ in Bd_1^+ and q_2^+ in Bd_2^+ such that $q_1^+ \bowtie q_2^+ \sqsubseteq q_{new}$ if and only if:

$$QId(1, A_{11} = a_{11}) \cap \ldots \cap QId(1, A_{1p} = a_{1p}) \neq \emptyset \text{ and}$$
$$QId(2, A_{21} = a_{21}) \cap \ldots \cap QId(2, A_{2q} = a_{2q}) \neq \emptyset.$$

As shown in the following example, the two statements above can be tested efficiently.

Example 8. In the database of Example 1, consider the positive boundaries Bd_1^+ and Bd_2^+ as shown in Figure 1. Let $C_{new} = C_1 \bowtie_b C_2$, and let $q_{new} = AllCust \bowtie \sigma_S(Cust \bowtie Sales \bowtie Prod \bowtie Store)$ with $S = (Cjob = Lawyer) \wedge (Caddr = Paris)$.

With the notation just introduced, we have $S = S_1 = S_2$, and since:

$$QId(1, Cjob = Lawyer) \cap QId(1, Caddr = Paris) = \{2, 3\} \cap \{1\} = \emptyset,$$

it turns out that q_{new} is *not* frequent. Therefore, this query is removed from the set of candidates of level 2.

Consider now $q_{new} = AllCust \bowtie \sigma_S(Cust \bowtie Sales \bowtie Prod \bowtie Store)$ with $S = (Cjob = Lawyer) \wedge (Ptype = Milk) \wedge (Sname = Ikea)$ as a candidate query of C_{new}. We have: $S_1 = (Cjob = Lawyer) \wedge (Ptype = Milk)$ and $S_2 = (Cjob = Lawyer) \wedge (Sname = Ikea)$, and thus:

$$QId(1, Cjob = Lawyer) \cap QId(1, Ptype = Milk) = \{2, 3\} \cap \{2\} \neq \emptyset \text{ and}$$
$$QId(2, Cjob = Lawyer) \cap QId(2, Sname = Ikea) = \{5, 6\} \cap \{6\} \neq \emptyset.$$

As a consequence, q_{new} can be frequent and must be kept among the candidate queries of level 3.

4.4 First Experiments

In this section, we present the results of our first experiments using synthetic data that have been generated in a similar way as in [1]. However, the generator used in [1] has been modified so as to comply with the case where the data is stored in more than one table.

More precisely, the tests have been conducted on a database, called $DBTest$ and containing three tables over the schemas $Cust(X1, X2, \ldots, X10)$, $Sales(X1, Y1, Z1, D1)$ and $Prod(Y1, Y2, \ldots, Y10)$, as in our running example (but with additional attributes).

Two instances of this database, called $I10$ and $I40$, have been considered, with respective cardinalities of 2.000, 6.000 and 54.000 for the tables $Cust$, $Sales$ and $Prod$. In instance $I10$ (respectively $I40$), all domains of attributes A in the domains of contexts are such that $|dom(A)| = 10$ (respectively $|dom(A)| = 40$). Moreover, the data are such that when the size of the domain increases, then the ratios of frequent queries in positive boundaries decrease.

For example, let $\alpha = 0.5\%$ and $\mathcal{C} = \langle AllCust, Cust \bowtie Sales \bowtie Prod, \Sigma \rangle$ where $AllCust = \pi_{X1}(Cust)$ and $\Sigma = \{X_i = *, Y_i = * \mid i = 2, \ldots, 6\}$. In instance $I10$, 45% out of the 10.086 frequent queries in $\mathcal{Q}(\mathcal{C})$ belong to the positive boundary of $freq_\alpha(\mathcal{C}, I10)$, whereas, in instance $I40$, 18% out of the 2.678 frequent queries in $\mathcal{Q}(\mathcal{C})$ belong to the positive boundary of $freq_\alpha(\mathcal{C}, I40)$.

We consider now the case of a b-selection with an empty selection condition S, and the context $\mathcal{C}$ given just above. In each of the instances $I10$ and $I40$, we compare:

- the time for the computation of the frequent queries of $\mathcal{C}$, without any optimization, and
- the time for the incremental computation of the frequent queries in $\sigma_S^b(\mathcal{C})$, assuming that *the positive boundaries* of $freq_\alpha(\mathcal{C}, I10)$ and $freq_\alpha(\mathcal{C}, I40)$ are stored.

In this case, for every candidate query of $\sigma_S^b(\mathcal{C})$, we search for the corresponding query in the positive boundary, as explained in the previous subsection. Since S is always satisfied, this search is performed with respect to *every* query in the positive boundary. This shows that considering an empty selection condition is the worst case in the number of searches. Moreover, since only the positive boundaries are stored, we have to recompute the supports of *all* queries in $freq_\alpha(\mathcal{C}, I10)$ and $freq_\alpha(\mathcal{C}, I40)$, which is also the worst case in this respect.

The results of this comparison are shown in Figure 2. We observe that the gain is generally more important for the instance $I40$ than for the instance $I10$. This is due to the fact that the relative size of the positive boundary is smaller for $I40$ than for $I10$ (18% and 45%, respectively). Indeed, the smaller the size of the boundary, the more efficient the pruning phase in the incremental approach.

These tests clearly show that our approach is more efficient than a non incremental approach. Moreover, it is important to note that the sizes of the positive boundaries that are stored have a significant impact on the gain in computation time obtained by our approach. We are currently running tests using all operations introduced in this paper. The corresponding results are reported in the full paper [8].

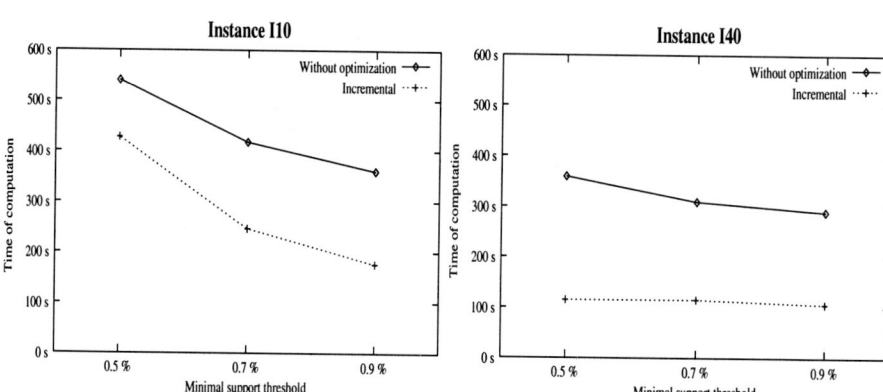

Fig. 2. Time of computation without optimization and using our incremental approach

5 Conclusion and Further Work

We have introduced a new formalism for the incremental learning of association rules through composition of mining contexts. Assuming that the frequent queries of the component contexts are stored, we have shown that our incremental approach results in a significant reduction of computation time for the computation of frequent queries of composed contexts.

Based on this work, we are considering the following lines for further research:

- More experimental results have to be considered in order to better quantify the gain that our approach provide. We are currently working on this issue.
- Our incremental approach can be generalized as follows: even if the new context is not expressed as the composition of other contexts, find a relationship between this new context and the contexts that are currently stored. Preliminary results have been obtained in the case of conjunctive queries [7].
- The influence of redundancies in the storage of frequent queries of the component contexts is crucial in our model. The approach of [14, 15] provides interesting issues in this respect.
- Given a set of contexts, determine a subset such that the storage of their frequent queries can optimize the computation time of the frequent queries for the whole set.
- So far, in this work, we assume that the database is static, which is not the case in practice. Therefore, an important issue is to consider updates. This problem is clearly similar to the problem of maintenance of association rules, already considered in [5, 18].

References

1. R. Agrawal, H. Mannila, R. Srikant, H. Toivonen, A.I. Verkamo (1996). *Fast Discovery of Association Rules*. In Advances in Knowledge Discovery and Data Mining, pp 309-328, AAAI-MIT Press.

2. E. Baralis and G. Psaila (1999). *Incremental Refinement of Mining Queries.* In Proc. of DAWAK'99, pp. 173-182, Florence.
3. S. Brin, R. Motwani, J.D. Ullman and S. Tsur (1997), *Dynamic Itemset Counting and Implication Rules for Market Basket Data.* In Proc. of SIGMOD Conference, pp. 255-264.
4. A. K. Chandra and P. M. Merlin (1977). *Optimal implementation of conjunctive queries in relational databases.* In Proc. of the Ninth ACM Symposium on Theory of Computing, pp. 77-90.
5. D. Cheung, J. Han, V. Ng, and C.Y. Wong (1996) *Maintenance of Discovered Association Rules in Large Databases: An Incremental Updating Technique.* In Proc. of ICDE'96, pp. 106-114, New Orleans, USA.
6. L. Dehaspe and H. Toivonen (1999). *Discovery of Frequent Datalog Patterns.* Data Mining and Knowledge Discovery, 3, pp. 7-36, Kluwer Academic Publishers.
7. C.T. Diop, A. Giacometti, D. Laurent and N. Spyratos (2000). *Extraction de règles d'association entre vues : vers une approche incrémentale* (French). In Proc. of BDA'2000, pp. 323-344, Blois, France. English version available as Tech. Rep. LI/E3I No. 241, University of Tours, France.
8. C.T. Diop, A. Giacometti, D. Laurent and N. Spyratos (2001). *Combining Mining Tasks through Relational Algebra.* Techn. Rep. LI/E3I, Tours, France (full paper, to appear).
9. J. Han, Y. Fu, K. Kopersky and O. Zaiane (1996). *DMQL: A Data Mining Query Language for Relational Databases.* In Proc. of DMKD'96 (SIGMOD'96 Workshop on KDD), Montreal, Canada.
10. T. Imielinski and A. Virmani (1999). *MSQL: A Query Language for Database Mining.* Data Mining and Knowledge Discovery, Vol. 3, No. 4, pp. 373-408, Kluwer Academic Publishers.
11. M. Kamber, J. Han, J. Chiang (1997). *Metarule-Guided Mining of Multi-Dimensional Association Rules Using Data Cubes.* In Proc. of KDD'97, pp. 207-210, Newport Beach, USA.
12. H. Mannila, H. Toivonen (1997). *Levelwise Search and Borders of Theories in Knowledge Discovery.* Techn. Rep. C-1997-8, University of Helsinki.
13. T.Morzy, M. Wojciechowski and M. Zakrzewicz (2000). *Materialized Data Mining Views.* In Proc. of PKDD'2000, Springer Verlag, pp. 65-74, France.
14. B. Nag, P. Deshpande and D.J. DeWitt (1999). *Using a Knowledge Cache for Interactive Discovery of Association Rules.* In Proc. of KDD'99, pp. 244-253, San Diego, USA.
15. B. Nag, P. Deshpande and D.J. DeWitt (2001). *Caching for Multi-dimensional Data Mining Queries.* In Proc. of SCI'2001, Orlando, Florida.
16. J.S. Park, M. Chen, P.S. Yu (1995). *An Effective Hash Based Algorithm for Mining Association Rules.* SIGMOD Conference, pp. 175-186.
17. A. Savasere, E. Omiecinski and S.B. Navathe (1995). *An Efficient Algorithm for Mining Association Rules in Large Databases.* VLDB Conference, pp. 432-444.
18. S. Thomas, S. Bodagala, K. Alsabti and Sanjay Ranka (1997). *An Efficient Algorithm for the Incremental Updation of Association Rules in Large Databases.* In Proc. of KDD'97, pp. 263-266, Newport Beach, USA.
19. S. Tsur and al. (1998), *Query Flocks: A Generalization of Association-Rule Mining.* SIGMOD Conference, pp. 1-12.
20. J.D. Ullman (1989). *Principles of Databases and Knowledge-Base Systems.* Vol. 1-2, Computer Science Press.

Designing Functional Dependencies for XML

Mong Li Lee[1], Tok Wang Ling[1], and Wai Lup Low[2],*

[1] School of Computing, National University of Singapore
{leeml,lingtw}@comp.nus.edu.sg
[2] DSO National Laboratories, Singapore
lwailup@dso.org.sg

Abstract. Functional dependencies are an integral part of database theory and they form the basis for normalizing relational tables up to BCNF. With the increasing relevance of the data-centric aspects of XML, it is pertinent to study functional dependencies in the context of XML, which will form the basis for further studies into XML keys and normalization. In this work, we investigate the design of functional dependencies in XML databases. We propose FD_{XML}, a notation and DTD for representing functional dependencies in XML. We observe that many databases are hierarchical in nature and the corresponding nested XML data[1] may inevitably contain redundancy. We develop a model based on FD_{XML} to estimate the amount of data replication in XML data. We show how functional dependencies in XML can be verified with a single pass through the XML data, and present supporting experimental results. A platform-independent framework is also drawn up to demonstrate how the techniques proposed in this work can enrich the semantics of XML.

1 Introduction

Functional dependencies [Cod70] are an integral part of database theory, and they have been well studied for the past thirty years in the context of the relational data model. The concept of a *key* in databases is derived from functional dependencies. They also form the basis for the normalization process up to Boyce-Codd Normal Form (BCNF) [Cod72]. Studies on functional dependencies have also resulted in inference rules [Arm74], semantic data models [Wed92] and dependency-preserving decomposition techniques [Ber76,TF82].

The emergence of XML [BPSMM00] as a standard for data representation on the Web is fueling semistructured data models as strong contenders to the traditional relational data model. Although an XML document is not a database in the strictest sense, there is much work done in the research community to move XML towards a real data model (e.g., Lore [MAG+97], XML Schema [Fal00], XML data query model [FR01] etc.). These works deal with query languages,

---
* This work was done while the author was on a research scholarship from the National University of Singapore.
[1] For this paper, *XML data* refers to data represented in XML. It is not to be confused with the W3C Note XML-Data.

structural constraints, path consistency, and issues concerning the modeling of key and foreign key relationships. While it is equally important to see how the concept of functional dependencies can be applied to XML databases, there has been little work on functional dependencies representation and modeling in semistructured data models.

Figure 1 shows a typical Project-Supplier-Part semistructured database together with its DTD. In the instance diagram shown in Figure 1b, an entity (in the Entity-Relationship terminology) is denoted by a rectangle. Dark circles represent the identifier attributes of the entity, and hollow circles represent properties. The '@' symbols preceding the name of labeled edges indicate that the data is modeled as XML attributes. Unlabeled edges indicate that the data is modeled as XML elements. Entity types **Project**, **Supplier** and **Part** have the keys **PName**, **SName** and **PartNo** respectively. Suppose we have a constraint that a supplier must supply a part at the same price regardless of projects. Unfortunately, this information **cannot** be deduced from the DTD nor the database instance. This information is useful to anyone using this XML data as it can alert them to violations of this integrity constraint. For instance, knowledge of this constraint can help users to identify semantically incorrect transformations (e.g. transformations that result in a supplier supplying a part at different prices to different projects). How can we embed this knowledge into the XML data? Is this information best treated as meta-data or should it be embedded into the data itself? How should it be represented? And how can we efficiently check if the constraints are violated? We need a way to express functional dependency constraints in XML databases. These constraints will be part of the XML data interchange which governs the semantics of the data.

The contributions of this work are :

1. We propose FD_{XML}, a notation and DTD, for representing functional dependencies in XML. This notation takes into consideration the hierarchical nature of XML databases.
2. We formulate a replication cost model based on XML functional dependencies to measure the data replication factor of XML database designs.
3. We develop a scalable technique for verifying XML functional dependencies with a single pass through the XML database. This technique can be easily extended for efficient incremental verification.
4. We present a platform-independent framework to illustrate how functional dependencies can enhance semantics in the use of XML.

The rest of the paper is organized as follows. Related works are discussed in Section 2. In Section 3, we propose a notation for functional dependencies in XML. In Section 4, a model is developed to estimate the replication factor for different designs of XML functional dependencies. We develop in Section 5 a technique that verifies the functional dependencies on an XML database with a single pass through the data and present the experimental results. We conclude in Section 6.

```
<!ELEMENT PSJ (Project)*>
<!ELEMENT Project (Supplier*)>
<!ELEMENT Supplier (Part*)>
<!ELEMENT Part (Price?,Quantity?)>
<!ATTLIST Project PName IDREF #REQUIRED>
<!ATTLIST Supplier SName IDREF #REQUIRED>
<!ATTLIST Part PartNo IDREF #REQUIRED>
<!ELEMENT Price (#PCDATA)>
<!ELEMENT Quantity (#PCDATA)>
```

(a) DTD

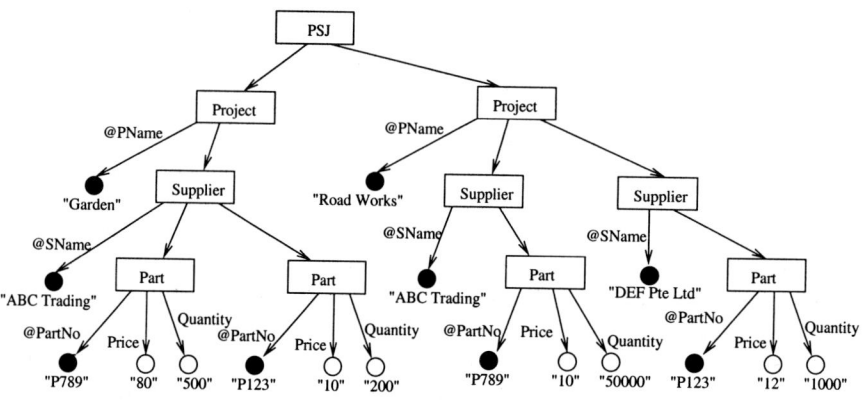

(b) Sample data instance

```
1   <PSJ>                                      16    <Project PName="Road Works">
2     <Project PName="Garden">                 17      <Supplier SName="ABC Trading">
3       <Supplier SName="ABC Trading">         18        <Part PartNo="P789">
4         <Part PartNo="P789">                 19          <Price>10</Price>
5           <Price>80</Price>                  20          <Quantity>50000</Quantity>
6           <Quantity>500</Quantity>           21        </Part>
7         </Part>                              22      </Supplier>
8         <Part PartNo="P123">                 23      <Supplier SName="DEF Pte Ltd">
9           <Price>10</Price>                  24        <Part PartNo="P123">
10          <Quantity>200</Quantity>           25          <Price>12</Price>
11        </Price>                             26          <Quantity>1000</Quantity>
12      </Supplier>                            27        </Part>
13    </Project>                               28      </Supplier>
14                                             29    </Project>
15                                             30  </PSJ>
```

(c) XML instance

Fig. 1. A Project-Supplier-Part XML Database

2 Related Works

XML is now the de-facto standard for information representation and interchange over the Internet. The basic idea behind XML is surprisingly simple. Instead of storing semantics-related information in data dictionaries as in the relational data model, XML embeds tags within the data to give meaning to the associated data fragments. Although verbose, XML has the advantage of being simple, interoperable and extensible. However, XML is not a data model, and there are currently no notions in XML corresponding to functional dependencies in the relational data model [Wid99].

Schema languages for XML have been heavily researched [Don00], with the Document Type Definition (DTD) [BPSMM00] and XML Schema [Fal00] being the most popular currently. DTD has been the de-facto schema language for XML for the past couple of years. DTD's support for key and foreign key concepts come in the form of ID and IDREF(s). However, there are many problems in using them as (database) key constructs. In this work, we use the ID/IDREF(s) mechanisms as "internal pointers" rather than key constructs. XML Schema is an effort by W3C to overcome some shortfalls of the DTD and is touted to eventually replace DTD. XML Schema's improvements over DTD include the ability to specify type constraints and more complex cardinality constraints. However, current XML schema languages do not offer mechanisms to specify functional dependency constraints (which are different from key constraints).

In a survey which takes a database-centric view of XML, [Wid99] noted that the concept of functional dependencies in the context of XML has not been explored. However, *keys*, which is a special case of functional dependencies, is studied in the context of XML by [BDF+01]. It offers two basic definitions for keys in XML : strong keys and weak keys. At one end of the spectrum, strong keys constrain that all key paths must exist and be unique. For weak keys, no structural constraint is imposed on key paths. Weak key paths can be missing, which makes weak keys similar to null-valued keys in the relational context. [BDF+01] also noted that there is a spectrum of other possibilities in between their strong and weak definitions. [BDF+01] also introduced the concept of *relative keys*. Noting that keys in many data formats (e.g. scientific databases) have a hierarchical structure, relative keys provide hierarchical key structures to accommodate such databases. Such structures are similar to the notion of ID dependent relationships in Entity Relationship diagrams. [FS00] proposed constraints languages to capture semantics of XML documents using simply key, foreign key and inverse constraints. However, functional dependencies, which form the theoretic foundation for keys, were not addressed in these works.

The concept of allowing controlled data redundancy in exchange for faster processing was introduced in [LGL96]. In this work, we present analogous arguments in the XML context for allowing controlled data redundancy. Preliminary work has also been done on semantics preservation when translating data between the relational tables and XML [LC00].

3 Functional Dependencies in XML

The well-known definition of functional dependencies for the relational data model is :

> Let r be a relation on scheme R, with X and Y being subsets of attributes in R. Relation r *satisfies* the *functional dependency* (FD) $X \rightarrow Y$ if for every X-value x, $\pi_Y(\sigma_{X=x}(r))$ has at most one tuple, with π and σ being the projection and selection operators respectively. □

This notation is designed for use with flat and tabular relational data, and cannot be directly applied to XML data. We need another notation that takes into consideration XML's hierarchical characteristics.

Definition 1. *An **XML functional dependency**, FD_{XML}, is an expression of the form :*

$$(Q, [P_{x_1}, \ldots, P_{x_n} \rightarrow P_y]) \tag{1}$$

where

1. Q is the FD_{XML} header path and is a fully qualified path expression (i.e. a path starting from the XML document root). It defines the scope in which the constraint holds.
2. Each P_{x_i} is a LHS (Left-Hand-Side) entity type. A LHS entity type consists of an element name in the XML document, and the optional key attribute(s). Instances of LHS entity types are called LHS entities and they can be uniquely identified by the key attribute(s).
3. P_y is a RHS (Right-Hand-Side) entity type. A RHS entity type consists of an element name in the XML document, and an optional attribute name. Instances of the RHS entity type is called a RHS entity.

For any two instance subtrees identified by the FD_{XML} header, Q, if all LHS entities agree on their values, then they must also agree on the value of the RHS entity, if it exists. □

Our notation makes use of XPath [CD99] expressions. Informally, the FD_{XML} header, Q, restricts the scope and defines the *node set* in which the functional dependency holds. The node set can be seen as a collection of "records" over which the FD_{XML} holds. P_{x_i}, $1 \leq i \leq n$, identify the LHS entity types of the functional dependency, and P_y identifies the RHS entity type. They are synonymous with the LHS and RHS expressions of the conventional functional dependency expressions respectively.

Figure 2 shows two FD_{XML}s defined on the DTD shown in Figure 1a. The FD_{XML} header path of the first FD_{XML} (Figure 2a) asserts that this functional dependency holds over the subtrees rooted at /PSJ/Project. This FD_{XML} states that a supplier must supply a part at the same price regardless of projects. In the relational form, this will be $SName, PartNo \rightarrow Price$. This FD_{XML} is violated in the instance in Figure 1b. Supplier "ABC Trading" sells

(/PSJ/Project , [Supplier.SName,
               Part.PartNo
               → Price])

(/PSJ , [Project.PName,
           Supplier.SName,
           Part.PartNo
           → Quantity])

(a) (b)

Fig. 2. Examples of FD_{XML} from Figure 1a

part "P789" at price "80" to project "Garden", but sells the same part to project "Road Works" at price "10". The second FD_{XML} (Figure 2b) states that the quantity of parts is determined by the project, supplier and part concerned. This FD_{XML} holds over the subtree(s) rooted at /PSJ.

The attributes PName, SName and PartNo are the key attributes of the elements Project, Supplier and Part respectively. If we assume that these key attributes are known, then the notation in Figure 2 can be simplified to that shown in Figure 3.

(/PSJ/Project , [Supplier,
                   Part
                   → Price])

(/PSJ , [Project,
           Supplier,
           Part
           → Quantity])

(a) (b)

Fig. 3. A simplified notation for FD_{XML}

Figure 4 shows another XML database instance conforming to the same DTD in Figure 1a. Suppose the FD_{XML} in Figure 2a holds on this database. In order not to violate the functional dependency, C_1 has to be of the same value as C_2 since they have the same values for the LHS entities of the FD_{XML}. Note that the absence of a Price element in the rightmost subtree does not violate the FD_{XML}.

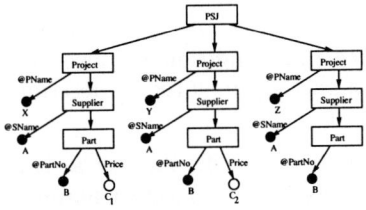

Fig. 4. Illustrating FD_{XML}

3.1 Well-Structured FD_{XML}s

XML models hierarchical data naturally and such models are especially useful for modeling attributes of relationships (although such "attributes" may be modeled as elements in XML). As a result, many FD_{XML}s are also hierarchically structured. In this section, we define what it means to be *well-structured* for the hierarchically structured FD_{XML}s. We first introduce the concept of a lineage. A set of nodes, L, in a tree is a lineage if:

1. There is a node N in L such that all the nodes in the set are ancestors of N, and
2. For every node M in L, if the set contains an ancestor of M, it also contains the parent of M.

We use the DTD in Figure 1a to illustrate the concept of lineages. {PSJ , Project, Supplier , Part} is a lineage. Part satisfies condition 1 as all the other nodes are its ancestors. It can be verified that condition 2 for a lineage is satisfied by the nodes in this set. However, {PSJ , Project , Part} is not a lineage as condition 2 is not satisfied. Ancestors of Part (i.e. PSJ and Project) are in the set, but its parent (i.e. Supplier) is not[2].

Definition 2. *Consider the DTD :*

<!ELEMENT H_1 (H_2)*>
...
<!ELEMENT H_m (P_1)*>
<!ELEMENT P_1 (P_2)*>
...
<!ELEMENT P_{x-1} (P_x)*>

*The FD_{XML}, $\mathcal{F}=(Q,[P_1,\ldots,P_{x-1} \to P_x])$, where $Q = /H_1/\ldots/H_m$, holds on this DTD. $\mathcal{F}$ is **well-structured** if :*

1. *there is a single RHS entity type.*
2. *the ordered XML elements in Q, LHS entity types and RHS entity type, in that order, form a lineage.*
3. *the LHS entity types are minimal (i.e. no redundant LHS entity types).* □

The FD_{XML} in Figure 2a is well-structured because:

1. There is a single RHS entity type (i.e. Price)
2. The XML elements in Q, LHS entity types, and RHS entity type (in that order) form a lineage. The RHS entity type satisfies condition 1 for a lineage. It can be easily verified that condition 2 is also satisfied.
3. Both the supplier and part are required to determine the price (i.e. there is no redundant LHS entity types).

Well-structured FD_{XML}s are of specific interest as it presents the semantics of functional dependencies in a clear and succinct manner.

---
[2] For the purpose of a lineage, the path needs not start from the document root, but can begin from any position in the XML document. This example can also be read as : "Since //PSJ/Project/Part (in XPath notation) is not a valid path in the DTD, it is not a lineage".

3.2 Non Well-Structured FD_{XML}s

The semantics for non well-structured FD_{XML}s cannot be generalised in a clear and consistent manner. For instance, the meaning of FD_{XML}s whose LHS entity types and RHS entity type do not form a lineage is ambiguous. Another case in point, the meaning of FD_{XML}s with LHS entities not sub-rooted under Q is unclear. Thus, as far as possible, functional dependencies in XML databases should be modeled as well-structured FD_{XML}s.

However, there is one special class of non well-structured FD_{XML}s, defined in *flat XML data*, that is meaningful. A characteristic of flat XML data is little or no nesting of elements and such databases model their data mainly as attributes. XML data with one level of element nesting is also known as *record-oriented* XML. Flat XML data is common because it is the simplest way to publish relational data as XML. In this section, we show how FD_{XML}s on them can be represented. Figure 5 shows a relational schema, its corresponding form in XML and the FD_{XML} representation for the functional dependency $city, state \rightarrow zipcode$ in the relation.

```
                                <student_table>
                                  <student>
Student ( matric, name,             <matric>...</matric> <name>...</name>
          street, city,              <street>...</street> <city>...</city>
          state, zipcode)            <state>...</state> <zipcode>...</zipcode>
FD : city, state → zipcode        </student>
                                  .......
                                </student_table>
```

   (a) Relational schema   (b) Data in XML

```
( /student_table/student, [ city,
                            state
                            → zipcode] )
```

(c) FD_{XML}

Fig. 5. Example of flat XML data : A student database

The FD_{XML} header path states that this constraint holds for the node set identified by the path `/student_table/student` (i.e. all student records). For every (student) node, if they agree on the values of `city` and `state`, they must also agree on the value of `zipcode`. The *well-structured* concept described previously does not apply to FD_{XML}s defined on flat XML data because all the LHS entity types are on the same level with no notion of a lineage. Thus, FD_{XML}s on flat XML data is a special case of non well-structured FD_{XML}s having clear semantics.

3.3 DTD for FD_{XML}

To facilitate interchange of the functional dependency constraints over the web, we propose a DTD for FD_{XML} (Figure 6a). We can easily to translate this DTD to other schema languages. The Constraints tag (line 1) will nest the functional dependencies, and can be extended to include other types of integrity constraints. The Fid (line 3) is the identifier of the functional dependency. Each FD will have a HeaderPath (line 6), at least one LHS (line 4) and one RHS (line 5), corresponding to Q, P_{x_i} and P_y respectively in FD_{XML}. The ElementName (line 7) child of both LHS and RHS elements contain element names in the XML database. The Attribute children of the LHS elements are the names of key attribute(s) of ElementName. Each LHS element can have multiple Attribute children to allow for multiple attributes from the same LHS element. The ElementName and Attribute children of RHS elements hold the name of the element/location which stores the value determined by the functional dependency. Each RHS element can have multiple Attribute children whose values are determined by the same LHS elements. Figure 6b shows how the FD_{XML} shown in Figure 2a is represented using our proposed DTD.

4 A Model for Measuring Replication in Well-Structured FD_{XML}s

Many databases are hierarchical in nature and nested XML data is well-suited for them. In contrast to the relational model, redundancy and replication are natural in hierarchical models (of which XML is one). In Figure 1, the price of each part is repeated each time the supplier supplies the part to a project. Although the schema can be carefully designed to remove redundancy and replication, this may destroy the natural structure and result in less efficient access. A possible "normalized" version of the database instance in Figure 1b is shown in Figure 7. This design does not replicate the price, but the database structure becomes less obvious since it makes extensive use of pointing relationships/references whose access are slower than containment/parent-child relationships [W+00]. If re-ordering of the Project-Supplier-Part hierarchy is allowed, a better "normalized" version can be obtained by following the design rules in [WLLD01]. This design is not shown here due to lack of space, but the hierarchy in our running example becomes Supplier-Part-Project.

In the previous section, we have shown how FD_{XML}s can be modeled. In many cases, there will be replication of the same FD_{XML} instances due to the natural redundancy in XML data models. The degree of replication is of concern as it affects the effort needed to keep the database consistent. For example, an update to the value of a RHS entity must result in updating all RHS entities of the FD_{XML} instances to keep the data consistent. In this section, we present a model for estimating the degree of FD_{XML} replication. For simplicity, we limit our discussion of the model to **well-structured** FD_{XML}s. First, we introduce the concept of "*context cardinality*" of an element.

```
1  <!ELEMENT Constraints (Fd*)>
2  <!ELEMENT Fd (HeaderPath,LHS+,RHS)>
3  <!ATTLIST Fd Fid ID #REQUIRED>
4  <!ELEMENT LHS (ElementName,Attribute*)>
5  <!ELEMENT RHS (ElementName,Attribute*)>
6  <!ELEMENT HeaderPath (#PCDATA)>
7  <!ELEMENT ElementName (#PCDATA)>
8  <!ELEMENT Attribute (#PCDATA)>
```

(a) DTD

```
<Constraints>
  <Fd Fid="SP_Price_FD">
    <HeaderPath>/PSJ/Project</HeaderPath>
    <LHS>
      <ElementName>Supplier</ElementName>
      <Attribute>SName</Attribute>
    </LHS>
    <LHS>
      <ElementName>Part</ElementName>
      <Attribute>PartNo</Attribute>
    </LHS>
    <RHS>
      <ElementName>Price</ElementName>
    </RHS>
  </Fd>
</Constraints>
```

(b) A FD_{XML} for the Project-Supplier-Part Database conforming to the DTD

Fig. 6. DTD for FD_{XML}

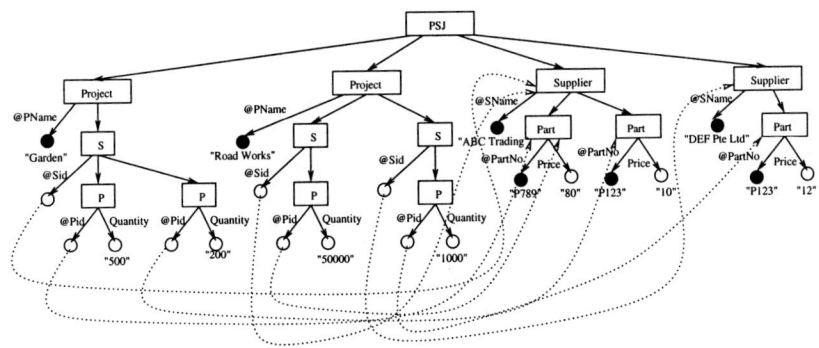

Fig. 7. A possible "normalized" instance of the Project-Supplier-Part database

Definition 3. *The **context cardinality** of element X to element Y, denoted as $Card_Y^X(\mathcal{D})$ is the number of times Y can participate in a relationship with X in the context of X's entire ancestry in an XML document (denoted $\mathcal{D}$).* □

We can use various derivatives such as *maximum* or *average* context cardinalities. Suppose we have the following constraints for Figure 1: (1) Each supplier can supply at most 500 different parts. (2) Each supplier can supply at most 10 different parts to the same project. Then the maximum context cardinality of Supplier to Part is 10 since this cardinality is in the context of Supplier's ancestry (i.e. PSJ and Project). We have $Card_{Part}^{Supplier}(\mathcal{D}) = 10$, where $\mathcal{D}$ is the context of our PSJ DTD. We use the Entity Relationship Diagram (ERD) in Figure 8 to illustrate the difference between traditional cardinality and the proposed context cardinality for XML. For simplicity, we omit the context parameter (i.e $\mathcal{D}$) in the notation when the context is obvious.

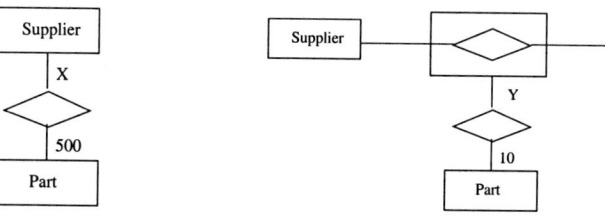

(a) ERD showing cardinalities of the relationship between Supplier and Part. (Each supplier can supply at most 500 different parts)

(b) ERD showing **context cardinalities** of the relationship between Supplier and Part. (Each supplier can supply at most 10 different parts to the same project)

Fig. 8. Context cardinality represented in ERD

Suppose we have the following **well-structured** FD_{XML}, $\mathcal{F}$:

$$\mathcal{F} = (Q, [P_1, \ldots, P_{x-1} \to P_x]), \text{ where } Q = /H_1/H_2/\ldots/H_m \quad (2)$$

The header path of $\mathcal{F}$ consists of the absolute path $/H_1/H_2/\ldots/H_m$. P_1 to P_{x-1} are LHS entity types and P_x is the RHS entity type. $\mathcal{F}$ is depicted graphically in Figure 9. Suppose this $\mathcal{F}$ holds on a DTD. Then the model for the replication factor, RF, for $\mathcal{F}$ is :

$$RF(\mathcal{F}) = min\left((\prod_{R=1}^{m-1} Card_{H_{R+1}}^{H_R}), Card_{H_m}^{P_1} \right) \quad (3)$$

This model obtains the frequency of repetition based on the context cardinalities of the elements. The frequency of repetition is determined by the smaller of two parameters. The first parameter is the product sum of the branching

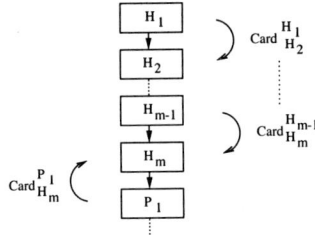

Fig. 9. Graphical depiction of $\mathcal{F}$

out factors of the header path elements (i.e. $(\prod_{R=1}^{m-1} Card_{H_{R+1}}^{H_R}))$. Intuitively, the number of times the data is replicated will be determined by how much "branching out" is caused by the elements in Q. In fact, if there are no other constraints, then this will be the replication factor. But the second parameter presents a constraint. This parameter $Card_{H_m}^{P_1}$ represents the number of times an element P_1 can be related to H_m in the context of P_1's ancestry. The final repetition factor of the FD_{XML} is constrained to be the smaller of the two parameters. Note that as $\mathcal{F}$ is well-formed, the entity types $P_2, P_3, \ldots, P_{x-1}, P_x$ are not involved in the model.

We illustrate the model using the DTD in Figure 1a. This example shows the process of estimating the number of times the price is replicated. Let the FD_{XML} in Figure 2a be $\mathcal{F}$ and assume it holds on the DTD in Figure 1a. Suppose we have at most 100 projects under the element (/PSJ) and each supplier can supply parts to at most 5 projects. Thus, we have :

$$\text{Constraint 1}: Card_{Project}^{PSJ} = 100$$
$$\text{Constraint 2}: Card_{Project}^{Supplier} = 5$$

$$\text{RF}(\mathcal{F}) = min\left((\prod_{R=1}^{m-1} Card_{H_{R+1}}^{H_R}), Card_{H_m}^{P_1}\right)$$
$$= min(100, 5) = 5$$

If we ignore constraint 2, then the repetition factor will be 100. Since a supplier supplies a part at the same price regardless of projects, the price will be repeated for every project the supplier supplies the part to. If this supplier supplies this part to all projects (i.e. 100), this price value will be repeated 100 times. However, constraint 2 states that a supplier can supply to a maximum of only 5 projects. Hence, this constraint limits the price value to repeat at most 5 times.

The replication factor can be used to gauge if the extra maintenance costs and increased effort to ensure data consistency is worth the faster response time for queries by replicating data. This factor obtained is the *maximum* replication factor as we used the maximum context cardinalities in the calculation. The *average* replication factor would have been computed if we have used the average context cardinalities. Numerical maximum (and minimum) context cardinalities can be obtained from some schema languages (e.g. XML Schema), but average context cardinalities may have to be estimated. As usual, the better the estimates are, the more accurate the model will be.

There are several design insights we can obtain from this model. One is that the FD_{XML} header path, Q, should be as short as possible (i.e. it should contain as few XML elements as possible). Each element in Q will increase the "branching out" and increase replication. Another insight is that by reducing the value of the second parameter in the model through careful design of the schema, the "branching out" of Q can be neutralized. For example, if the second parameter (i.e. $Card_{H_m}^{P_i}$) has the value 1, then we can ignore other constraints and be certain that there will not be any replication of FD_{XML} instances.

5 Verification of FD_{XML}s

We have presented FD_{XML} representations and redundancy considerations when designing XML databases with functional dependencies. In this section, we describe how FD_{XML}s can fit into a platform-independent framework that enriches the semantics of XML data. We also develop a scalable technique to verify FD_{XML}s with a single pass through the XML database.

In the framework, FD_{XML}s are first specified for an XML database. The XML database may then be distributed together with the FD_{XML} specification. The FD_{XML} specification is used to check if the distributed or updated XML data instances violate the specified constraints. If violations are detected, it may mean that the semantics of the data have changed, or that the data has undergone invalid transformations. The FD_{XML} specification is separate from the data, and it will not pose any overheads. It is introduced only to check the data for violations. Since the specification is also in XML, any existing XML tools or parsers can be used to process the specification.

Figure 10 gives the details of the verification process. The database and the FD_{XML} specification are parsed using an XML parser. The context information required is stored in state variables during parsing. The state variables provide context for the elements encountered during the parsing by retaining information such as the tag names and attribute values of their ancestors. The context information that needs to be stored is derived from the FD_{XML} specification.

When the parser encounters an element of the RHS entity type, we check the state variables to see if it occurs in the context as specified in the FD_{XML}.

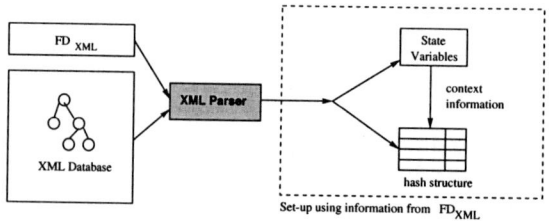

Fig. 10. Architecture for FD_{XML} verification

If the context is correct, the values of the LHS entities and the RHS entity are stored into a hash structure. The hash structure maintains the values of the LHS entities, their RHS entities and the associated counts.

After the XML database is parsed, the entries in the hash structure which have more than one distinct RHS values are retrieved. These entries consist of those LHS entities who have different distinct RHS entity values, and hence, violate the FD_{XML}. The associated counts will be useful in determining the erroneous values. We use the XML database shown in Figure 1c to illustrate the approach. The hash structure after parsing this database is depicted in Figure 11. The first entry in the hash structure violates the FD_{XML} and subsequent differing RHS entity values and their counts are stored in a linked list.

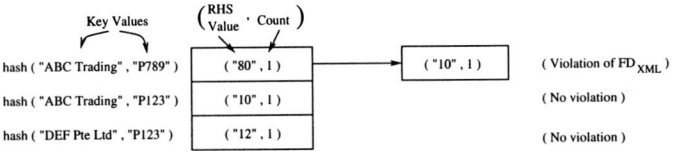

Fig. 11. State of hash structure after parsing the XML database in Figure 1c

Note that only a single pass through the data is required for verification. If the hash structure is stored, future updates to the data will only require checking of possible violations against the data in the hash structure, and no file scan is necessary. This is an efficient way of performing **incremental** verification.

5.1 Experimental Results

We conducted experiments to evaluate our technique for FD_{XML} verification using two popular interfaces for XML parsing. We also test the scalability of the technique by measuring the response times and the size of the hash structure as we increase the size of the XML database. The journal article entries (about 80000) in the DBLP database [Ley01], an example of flat XML data, are used for the experiments. The experiments are performed on a Pentium III 850 MHz machine with 128MB of RAM running Windows NT 4.0. The verification program is implemented using Java and makes use of the Xerces parser [Pro01].

A sample article entry is shown in Figure 12. To illustrate how our technique works when violations occur, we assume that *"all articles in the same volume of the same journal should be published in the same year"*[3]. This FD_{XML} is denoted as :

$$(\text{/dblp/article}, [\text{ journal}, \\ \text{volume} \\ \rightarrow \text{year}])$$

---

[3] This is typically not true as not all issues of the volume may be published in the same year. But this FD_{XML} is assumed so as to generate "errors".

```
<article key="journals/cacm/Mayer79">
  <author>Richard E. Mayer</author>
  <title>A Psychology of Learning BASIC.</title>
  <journal>CACM</journal> <volume>22</volume> <number>11</number>
  <pages>589-593</pages> <year>1979</year>
  <url>db/journals/cacm/cacm22.html#Mayer79</url>
</article>
```

Fig. 12. A sample journal article entry in the DBLP database

Note that in this flat XML database, the order of occurrence of the `journal`, `volume` and `year` elements is not important. However, they have to be children of the path `/dblp/article`.

Experiment 1. We evaluate the performance and scalability of two popular interfaces for XML parsing : Simple API for XML (SAX) [Meg01] and the Document Object Model (DOM) [W3C01]. SAX uses event-driven parsing and DOM is a tree-based API. Figure 13 shows the runtime of the experiments using SAX and DOM parsers. Using a DOM parser, which builds an in-memory DOM tree of the articles, an out-of-memory error was encountered at about 18000 articles. Using a SAX parser, we are able to verify the FD_{XML} across all 80000 articles successfully. The runtime using SAX increases linearly with the number of articles, which is expected since the data needs to be parsed only once. Due to space constraints, we do not compare SAX and DOM further. But clearly, SAX is the more scalable interface for XML parsing.

Experiment 2. We measure the size of the hash structure as we increase the number of articles. The results are shown in Figure 14. Although there is a linear increase, the absolute numbers of hashed keys (i.e. {journal,volume}) is very much smaller than the number of articles. This is attributed to the fact that there are many journal articles with the same `journal` and `volume` values. In fact, for the worst case, the hash structure will only get as large as the number of articles. Only a small number of the hashed keys have "errors" or "violations" (i.e. a volume of a journal contains articles published in different years). Such "violations" will result in a linked-list containing the different RHS entity values and their counts. Further analysis shows that the average length of the linked lists of such "violations" is only about 2-3.

Figure 15 shows sample output after verification of our assumed FD_{XML} (i.e. the journal name and volume number uniquely determines the year of publications). For Volume 32 of the journal "Communications of the ACM", 100 articles have the year "1989", while a single article has the year "1988". This seems to be an error, and a good guess for the correct year value will be "1989". However, if this FD_{XML} is to hold, the correct value for Volume 11 of the "AI Magazine" will not be so clear, as the counts of the different year values are not as indicative[4].

---

[4] This is not an error. Issues 1-4 of AI Magazine Volume 11 were published in 1990. Issue 5 of Volume 11 was published in 1991.

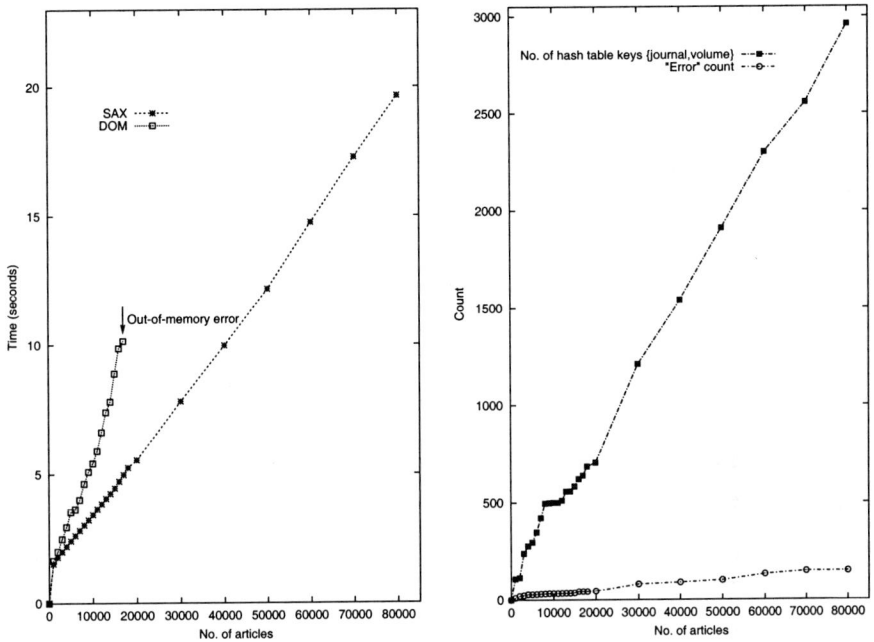

Fig. 13. Runtime vs. number of articles using SAX and DOM

Fig. 14. Size of hash structure and number of key entries with linked-list

```
Journal : CACM              Volume : 32
    Year : 1989    ( Count = 100 )
    Year : 1988    ( Count = 1 )
Journal : AI Magazine       Volume : 11
    Year : 1990    ( Count = 38 )
    Year : 1991    ( Count = 14 )
```

Fig. 15. Sample output of verification process

The experimental results show that functional dependency constraints in XML databases can be efficiently verified in a single pass through the database. Our technique of FD_{XML} verification does not take up much memory and scales up well, especially with the use of the SAX API for parsing the XML database. We have also shown how violations of a known FD_{XML} constraint are detected.

6 Conclusion

Functional dependency constraints have been an integral part of traditional database theory and it is important to see how this concept can be applied to XML. Existing works on XML keys define key dependencies within XML structures, but not relationships between these XML structures. This work fills this gap by proposing a representation and semantics for functional dependencies in XML databases to complement the work on XML keys. FD_{XML} is a schema language-independent representation for XML functional dependencies and is expressed in XML. Redundancy is natural in XML and we have developed a replication cost model to give a measure of data replication with well-structured FD_{XML}s. This model also provides insights into the design of FD_{XML}s to minimize redundancy. We also present a platform-independent framework for FD_{XML}'s use and deployment. We show how FD_{XML}s semantically enrich XML through the specification of functional dependencies on XML data. The specified constraints can be used for the verification of data consistency and to prevent illegal insert and update operations. We also present a technique for verifying FD_{XML}s which requires only a single pass through the XML database. Experimental results show that this technique is scalable with large real life XML databases. Our technique can be easily extended for efficient incremental verification.

There is much future work in this area. It is worthwhile to investigate if there exists other classes of non well-structured FD_{XML}s (besides those defined in flat XML data) which are meaningful. The cost model can then be extended to include such classes. In the relational data model, reasoning about functional dependencies have led to useful implication rules. It is interesting to see if such implication rules can be extended for FD_{XML}.

References

[Arm74]   W. W. Armstrong. Dependency Structures of Database Relationships. In *Proceedings of the tri-annual IFIP Conf 74, N-H (Amsterdam)*, 1974.

[BDF+01]   Peter Bunemana, Susan Davidson, Wenfei Fan, Carmem Hara, and Wang-Chiew Tan. Keys for XML. In *Proceedings of the WWW'10, Hong Kong, China*, 2001.

[Ber76]   P. A. Bernstein. Synthesizing Third Normal Form Relations from Functional Dependencies. *ACM Transactions on Database Systems*, 1(4):277–298, Dec 1976.

[BPSMM00]   Tim Bray, Jean Paoli, C. M. Sperberg-McQueen, and Eve Maler. Extensible Markup Language (XML) 1.0 (Second Edition). http://www.w3.org/TR/2000/REC-xml-20001006, 2000.

[CD99]   James Clark and Steve DeRose. XML Path Language (XPath) Version 1.0. Available at http://www.w3.org/TR/xpath, 1999.

[Cod70]   E. F. Codd. A Relational Model of Data for Large Shared Data Banks. *j-CACM*, 13(6):377–387, June 1970.

[Cod72]   E. F. Codd. *Further Normalization of the Database Relational Model*. R. Rustin, Ed. Prentice-Hall, Englewood Cliffs, NJ, 1972.

[Don00]   Dongwon Lee and Wesley W. Chu. Comparative Analysis of Six XML Schema Languages. *SIGMOD Record*, 29(3):76–87, 2000.

[Fal00]   D. Fallside. XML Schema Part 0: Primer. Available at http://www.w3.org/TR/xmlschema-0/, 2000.

[FR01]   Mary Fernandez and Jonathan Robie. XML Query Data Model. W3C Working Draft. Available at http://www.w3.org/TR/query-datamodel/, 2001.

[FS00]   W Fan and J Siméon. Integrity Constraints for XML. In *Proceedings of the Nineteenth ACM SIGMOD-SIGACT-SIGART Symposium on Principles of Database Systems, Dallas, Texas, USA*, pages 23–34. ACM, 2000.

[LC00]   Dongwon Lee and Wesley W. Chu. Constraints-Preserving Transformation from XML Document Type Definition to Relational Schema. In *Proceedings of the 19th International Conference on Conceptual Modeling*, pages 323–338, 2000.

[Ley01]   Michael Ley. DBLP Bibliography. Available at http://www.informatik.uni-trier.de/ ley/db/, 2001.

[LGL96]   Tok Wang Ling, Cheng Hian Goh, and Mong Li Lee. Extending classical functional dependencies for physical database design. *Information and Software Technology*, 9(38):601–608, 1996.

[MAG+97]   J. McHugh, S. Abiteboul, R. Goldman, D. Quass, and J. Widom. Lore: A Database Management System for Semistructured Data. *SIGMOD Record*, 26(3), 1997.

[Meg01]   David Megginson. SAX: The Simple API for XML. Available at http://www.megginson.com/SAX/, 2001.

[Pro01]   The Apache XML Project. Xerces Java Parser. Available at http://xml.apache.org/xerces-j/index.html, 2001.

[TF82]   Tsou and Fischer. Decomposition of a Relation Scheme into Boyce-Codd Normal Form. *SIGACTN: SIGACT News*, 14, 1982.

[W+00]   Kevin Williams et al. *Professional XML Databases*. Wrox Press Inc, 2000.

[W3C01]   W3C DOM Working Group. Document Object Model (DOM). Available at http://www.w3.org/DOM/, 2001.

[Wed92]   Grant E. Weddell. Reasoning About Functional Dependencies Generalized for Semantic Data Models. *ACM Transactions on Database Systems*, 17(1):32–64, Mar 1992.

[Wid99]   Jennifer Widom. Data Management for XML: Research Directions. *IEEE Data Engineering Bulletin*, 22(3):44–52, 1999.

[WLLD01]   Xiaoying Wu, Tok Wang Ling, Mong Li Lee, and Gillian Dobbie. Designing Semistructured Databases Using the ORA-SS Model. In *Proceedings of the 2nd International Conference on Web Information Systems Engineering (WISE)*. IEEE Computer Society, 2001.

On Efficient Matching of Streaming XML Documents and Queries

Laks V.S. Lakshmanan[1] and Sailaja Parthasarathy[2]

[1] Univ. of British Columbia, Vancouver, BC V6T 1Z4, Canada
laks@cs.ubc.ca
[2] Sun Microsystems, Bangalore, India
Sailaja.Parthasarathy@sun.com

Abstract. Applications such as online shopping, e-commerce, and supply-chain management require the ability to manage large sets of specifications of products and/or services as well as of consumer requirements, and call for efficient matching of requirements to specifications.

Requirements are best viewed as "queries" and specifications as data, often represented in XML. We present a framework where requirements and specifications are both registered with and are maintained by a registry. On a periodical basis, the registry matches new incoming specifications, e.g., of products and services, against requirements, and notifies the owners of the requirements of matches found. This problem is dual to the conventional problem of database query processing in that the size of data (e.g., a document that is streaming by) is quite small compared to the number of registered queries (which can be very large). For performing matches efficiently, we propose the notion of a "requirements index", a notion that is dual to a traditional index. We provide efficient matching algorithms that use the proposed indexes. Our prototype MatchMaker system implementation uses our requirements index-based matching algorithms as a core and provides timely notification service to registered users. We illustrate the effectiveness and scalability of the techniques developed with a detailed set of experiments.

1 Introduction

There are several applications where entities (e.g., records, objects, or trees) stream through and it is required to quickly determine which users have potential interest in them based on their known set of requirements. Applications such as online shopping, e-commerce, and supply chain management involve a large number of users, products, and services. Establishment of links between them cannot just rely on the consumer browsing the online database of products and services available, because (i) the number of items can be large, (ii) the consumers can be processes as well, e.g., as in a supply chain, and (iii) a setting where products and services are "matched" to the interested consumers out of many, based on the consumer requirements, as the products arrive, will be more effective than a static model which assumes a fixed database of available items, from which consumers pick out what they want. As another example, the huge volume of information flowing through the internet has spurred the so-called *publish-and-subscribe* applications (e.g., see [6]) where data items are conveyed to users selectively based on their "subscriptions", or expressions of interest, stated as queries. At the heart of these applications is a system that we call a *registry* which records and maintains the requirements of all registered consumers. The registry should manage large sets of specifications of products and/or services (which may stream through it) as well as of consumer requirements. It monitors incoming data, efficiently detects the portions of the data that are relevant to various consumers, and dispatches the appropriate information to them.

Requirements are best viewed as "queries" and specifications as "data". On a periodical basis (which can be controlled), the registry matches new incoming specifications (e.g., of products and services) against registered requirements and notifies the owners of the requirements of matches found. In this paper, we assume all specifications are represented in XML. We adopt the now popular view that XML documents can be regarded as node-labeled trees.[1] For clarity and brevity, we depict XML documents in the form of such trees rather than use XML syntax. Figure 1(a) shows an example of a tree representing an XML document, where we have deliberately chosen a document with a DTD (not shown) permitting considerable flexibility. In the sequel, we call such trees *data trees*. We associate a number with each node of a data tree. Following a commonly used convention (e.g., see [4, 13]), we assume that node numbers are assigned by a preorder enumeration of nodes. Popular XML query languages such as XQL, Quilt, and XQuery employ a paradigm where information in an XML document is extracted by specifying patterns which are themselves trees. E.g., the XQuery query[2]

```
         <Result>
FOR      $p IN sourceDB//part,
         $b IN $p/brand,
         $q IN $p//part
WHERE    A2D IN $q/name AND
         AMD IN $q/brand
RETURN   $p
         </Result>
```

which asks for parts which have an associated brand and a subpart with name 'A2D' and brand 'AMD', corresponds to the tree pattern Figure 1(b), "**P**". In that figure, each node is labeled by a constant representing either the tag associated with an XML element (e.g., part) or a domain value (e.g., 'AMD') that is supposed to be found in the document queried. A unique node (root in the case of **P**) marked with a '*', identifies the "distinguished node", which corresponds to the element returned by the query. Solid edges represent direct element-subelement (i.e. parent-child) relationship and dotted edges represent transitive (i.e. ancestor-descendant) relationship. As another example, the XQL query `part/subpart[//'speakers']`, which finds all subparts of parts at any level of the document which have a subelement occurrence of 'speakers' at any level, corresponds to the tree pattern Figure 1(b), "**T**".

---

[1] Cross-links corresponding to IDREFS are distinguished from edges corresponding to subelements for this purpose.

[2] The requirement/query is directed against a conceptual "sourceDB" that various specifications (documents) stream through.

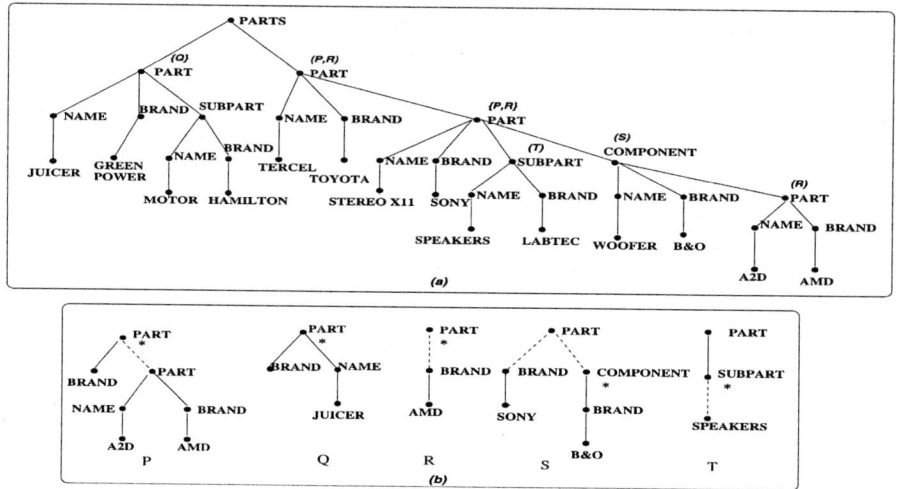

Fig. 1. The Labeling Problem Illustrated: (a)A data tree showing query labeling (node numbers omitted to avoid clutter); (b) A collection of queries (distinguished nodes marked '*').

We call trees such as in Figure 1(b) *query trees*. Query trees are trees whose nodes are labeled by constants, and edges can be either of ancestor-descendant (ad) type or of parent-child (pc) type. There is a unique node (marked '*') in a query tree called the *distinguished node*.

We have implemented a MatchMaker system for matching XML documents to queries and for providing notification service. As an overview, XML data streams through the MatchMaker, with which users have registered their requirements in the form of queries, in a requirements registry. The MatchMaker consults the registry in determining which users a given data element is relevant to. It then dispatches the data elements relevant to different users. The architecture of MatchMaker as well as implementation details are discussed in the full version of this paper [14]. A prototype demo of MatchMaker is described in [15].

One of the key problems in realizing a MatchMaker is the *query labeling problem* (formally defined in Section 2 and illustrated below). Intuitively, given an XML document, for each element, we need to determine efficiently those queries that are answered by this element.

Example 11 [Query Labeling Problem Illustrated]
Suppose the user requirements correspond to the queries in Figure 1(b). Each user (i.e. query) is identified with a name. What we would like to do is identify for each element of the document of Figure 1(a), those users whose query is answered by it. For example, the right child of the root is associated with the set $\{P, R\}$, since precisely queries P, R in Figure 1(b) are answered by the subelement rooted at this node. Since a query may have multiple answers from one document, we need to determine not just whether a given document is relevant to a user/query, but also which part of the document a user is

interested in. In Figure 1(a), each node is labeled with the set of queries that are answered by the element represented by the node.

A naive way to obtain these labels is to process the user queries, one at a time, finding all its matchings, and compile the answers into appropriate label sets for the document nodes. This strategy is very inefficient as it makes a number of passes over the given document, proportional to the number of queries. A more clever approach is to devise algorithms that make a constant number of passes over the document and determine the queries answered by each of its elements. This will permit set-oriented processing whereby multiple queries are processed together. Such an algorithm is non-trivial since: (i) queries may have repeating tags and (ii) the same query may have mutiple matchings into a given document. Both these features are illustrated in Figure 1. A main contribution of the paper is the development of algorithms which make a bounded number (usually two) of passes over documents to obtain a correct query labeling. ∎

It is worth noting that the problem of determining the set of queries answered by (the subtree rooted at) a given data tree node is *dual* to the usual problem of finding answers to a given query. The reason is that in the latter case, we consider answering one query against a large collection of data objects. By contrast, our problem is one of determining the set of queries (out of many) that are answered by one specific data object. Thus, whereas scalability w.r.t. the database size is an important concern for the usual query answering problem, for the query labeling problem, it is scalability w.r.t. the number of queries that is the major concern. Besides, given the streaming nature of our data objects, it is crucial that whatever algorithms we develop for query labeling make a small number of passes over the incoming data tree and efficiently determine all relevant queries.

We make the following specific contributions in this paper.

- We propose the notion of a "requirements index" for solving the query labeling problem efficiently. A requirements index is *dual* to the usual notion of index. We propose two different dual indexes (Section 3).
- Using the application of matching product requirements to product specifications as an example, we illustrate how our dual indexes work and provide efficient algorithms for query labeling (Sections 4 and 5). Our algorithms make no more than two passes over an input XML document.
- To evaluate our ideas and the labeling algorithms, we ran a detailed set of experiments (Section 6). Our results establish the effectiveness and scalability of our algorithms as well illustrate the tradeoffs involved.

Section 2 formalizes the problem studied. Section 7 presents related work, while 8 summarizes the paper and discusses future research. Proofs are suppressed for lack of space and can be found in [14].

2 The Problem

In this section, we describe the class of queries considered, formalize the notion of query answers, and give a precise statement of the problem addressed in the paper.

The Class of Queries Considered : As mentioned in the introduction, almost all known languages for querying XML data employ a basic paradigm of specifying a tree pattern and extracting all instances (matchings) of such a pattern in the XML database. In some cases, the pattern might simply be a chain, in others a general tree. The edges in the pattern may specify a simple parent-child (direct element-subelement) relationship or an ancestor-descendant (transitive element-subelement) relationship (see Section 1 for examples). Rather than consider arbitrary queries expressible in XML query languages, we consider the class of queries captured by query trees (formally defined in Section 1). We note that query trees abstract a large fragment of XPath expressions.

The semistructured nature of the data contributes to an inherent complexity. In addition, the query pattern specification allows ancestor-descendant edges. Efficiently matching a large collection of patterns containing such edges against a data tree is non-trivial.

Matchings and Answers : Answers to queries are found by matchings. Given a query tree Q and a data tree T, a *matching* of Q into T is a mapping h from the nodes of Q to those of T such that: (i) for every non-leaf node x in Q, the tag that labels x in Q is identical to the tag of $h(x)$ in T; (ii) for every leaf x in Q, either the label of x is identical to the tag of $h(x)$ or the label of x is identical to the domain value at the node $h(x)$ in T;[3] (iii) whenever (x, y) is a pc (resp., ad) edge in Q, $h(y)$ is a child (resp., (proper) descendant) of $h(x)$ in T. For a given matching h of Q into T, the corresponding answer is the subtree of T rooted at $h(x_d)$, where x_d is the distinguished node of the query tree Q. In this case, we call $h(x_d)$ the *answer node* associated with the matching h. A query may have more than one matching into a data tree and corresponding answers.

User queries are specified using query trees, optionally with additional order predicates. An order predicate is of the form $u \prec v$, where u, v are node labels in a query tree, and $\prec$ says u must precede v in any matching. As an example, in Figure 1(b), query Q, we might wish to state that the element BRAND appears before the NAME element. This may be accomplished by adding in the predicate BRAND $\prec$ NAME.[4] The notion of matching extends in a straightforward way to handle such order predicates. Specifically, a predicate $x \prec y$ is satisfied by a matching h provided the node number associated with $h(x)$ is less than that associated with $h(y)$. Decoupling query trees from order is valuable and affords flexibility in imposing order in a selective way, based on user requirements. For example, a user may not care about the relative order between author list and publisher, but may consider the order of authors important.

Problem Statement : The problem is to label each node of the document tree with the list of queries that are answered by the subtree rooted at the node. We formalize this notion as follows. We begin with query trees which are chains. We call them chain queries.
1. **The Chain Labeling Problem:** Let T be a data tree and let $Q_1, ..., Q_n$ be chain queries. Then label each node of T with the list of queries such that query Q_i belongs to the label of node u if and only if there is a matching h of Q_i into T such that h maps the distinguished node of Q_i to u.

---

[3] Instead of exact identity, we could have similarity or substring occurrence.
[4] A more rigorous way is to associate a unique number with each query tree node and use these numbers in place of node labels, as in $x \prec y$.

The importance of considering chain queries is two-fold: firstly, they frequently arise in practice and as such, represent a basic class of queries; secondly, we will derive one of our algorithms for the tree labeling problem below by building on the algorithm for chain labeling.

2. **The Tree Labeling Problem**: The problem is the same as the chain labeling problem, except the queries $Q_1, ..., Q_n$ are arbitrary query trees.

3 Dual Index

The "requirements index" is dual to the conventional index, so we call it the *dual index*: given an XML document in which a certain tag, a domain value, or a parent-child pair, ancestor-descendant pair, or some such "pattern" appears, it helps quickly determine the queries to which this pattern is relevant. Depending on the labeling algorithm adopted, the nature of the dual index may vary.

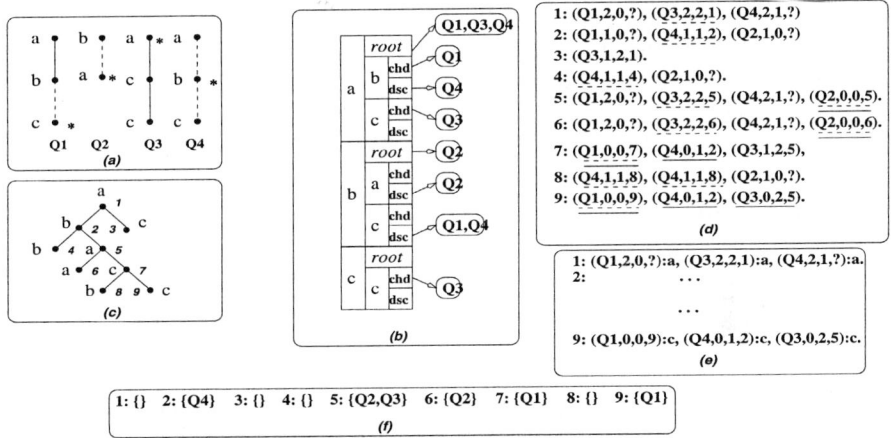

Fig. 2. Chain Dual Index: (a) queries; (b) dual index (lists not shown are empty; *chd* = *child*, *dsc* = *desc*); (c) a sample document; (d) CML lists; (e) PL lists: for brevity, only shown nodes 1 and 9; besides, only those entries of $PL(9)$ not "inherited" from anestors of 9 are shown; (f) QL lists.

For chain labeling, the basic questions that need to be answered quickly are: (i) given a constant t, which queries contain an occurrence of t as a root?[5] (ii) given a pair of constants t_i, t_j, in which queries do they appear as a parent-child pair, and in which queries as an ancestor-descendant pair?[6] Notice that an ancestor-descendant pair (t_i, t_j) in a query Q means that t_j is an ad-child of t_i in Q. We call an access structure that supports efficient lookups of this form *chain dual index*. In our chain labeling algorithm, we denote lookup operations as DualIndex$[t](root)$, DualIndex$[t_i][t_j](child)$,

---

[5] So, t must be a tag.
[6] Here, t_i must be a tag, while t_j may be a tag or a domain value.

or DualIndex$[t_i][t_j](desc)$, which respectively return the list of queries where t appears as the root tag, (t_i, t_j) appears as the tags/constants of a parent-child pair, and of an ancestor-descendant pair. E.g., Figure 2 (a)-(b) shows a sample chain dual index: e.g., DualIndex$[a](root) = \{Q1, Q3, Q4\}$, DualIndex$[a][b](child) = \{Q1\}$, and DualIndex$[a][b](desc) = \{Q4\}$.

For tree labeling, the questions that need to be answered quickly are: (i) given a constant, which are the queries in which it occurs as a leaf and the node numbers of the occurrences, and what are the node numbers of the distinguished node of these queries, and (ii) given a tag, for each query in which it has a non-leaf occurrence, what are the node numbers of its pc-children and the node numbers of its ad-children? We call an access structure that supports efficient lookups of this form *tree dual index*. Figure 3(a)-(b) shows some queries and their associated tree dual index. In our tree labeling algorithm, we denote the above lookups as DualIndex$[t](L)$ and DualIndex$[t](N)$ respectively. Each entry in DualIndex$[t](L)$ is of the form (P, l, S), where P is a query, l is the number of its distinguished node, and S is the set of numbers of leaves of P with constant t. Each entry in DualIndex$[t](N)$ is of the form (P, i, B, S, S'), where P is a query, i is the number a node in P with constant t, and S, S' are respectively the sets of numbers of i's pc-children and ad-children; finally, B is a boolean which says whether node i has an ad-parent in P (True) or not (False). The motivation for this additional bit will be clear in Section 5. Figure 3(b) illustrates the tree dual index for the sample set of queries in Figure 3(a). E.g., DualIndex$[a](N)$ contains the entries $(P, 1, F, \{2, 3\}, \{\})$ and $(P, 4, T, \{6\}, \{5\})$. This is because a occurs at nodes 1 and 4 in query P. Of these, the first occurrence has nodes 2, 3 as its pc-children and no ad-children, while the second has pc-child 6 and ad-child 5.

4 Chain Queries

In this section, we present an algorithm called Algorithm Node-Centric-Chain for chain labeling. Given a data tree, we seek to label each of its nodes with the list of chain queries that are answered by it. The main challenge is to do this with a small number of passes over the data tree, regardless of the number of queries, processing many queries at once. Figure 4 gives an algorithm for chain labeling. For expository reasons, in our presentation of query labeling algorithms in this and the next section, we associate several lists with each data tree node. We stress that in our implementation we compress these lists into a single one for reasons of efficiency [14].

With each data tree node, we associate three lists: the QL (for query labeling) list, which will eventually contain those queries answered by the (subtree rooted at the) node, a list called CML (for chain matching list) that tracks which queries have so far been matched and how far, and an auxiliary list called PL (for push list) that is necessary to manage CML. Each entry in the CML of a node u will be of the form (P, i, j, x), where P is a query, and i, j are non-negative integers, and x is either '?' or is an integer. Such an entry signifies that there is a partial matching of the part of the chain P from its root down to the node whose distance from leaf is i, and j is the distance between the distinguished node and the leaf. In addition, when x is an integer, it says the data tree node with number x is the answer node corresponding to this matching. E.g., in Figure 2(d), for node 1 of

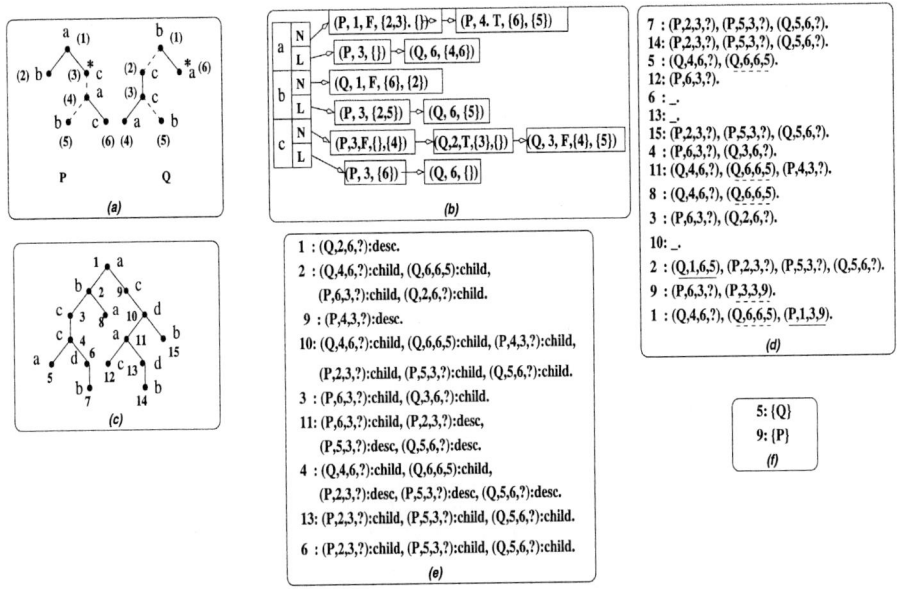

Fig. 3. Tree Dual Index: (a) queries; (b) dual index; (c) sample document; (d)TML; (e)PL; (f) QL.

the document, one of the CML entries is $(Q1, 2, 0, ?)$, signifying that in query $Q1$, the part that includes only the query root (tag a) can be partially matched into node 1. The number 2 says the matched query node is at a distance[7] 2 from the query leaf, and the number 0 says the distinguished node is at distance 0 from the query leaf, i.e. it *is* the leaf. The '?' says the location of the answer node for this matching is unknown at this point. Note that the CML associated with a data tree node may have multiple entries corresponding to the same query, signifying multiple matchings. Entries in PL are of the form $(P, l, m, x) : t$, where P, l, m, x are as above and t is a constant (tag). Such an entry belongs to the PL of a node u exactly when some ancestor of u in the document has tag t and the part of P from root down to the node with distance l to the leaf has been matched to this ancestor, and x has the same interpretation as above, i.e. the ancestor's CML contains (P, l, m, x).

An entry (P, l, m, x) can get into the CML of a data tree node u in one of two ways: (1) The root of P has tag identical to $tag(u)$. In this case, l must be the height of P and m the distance from leaf to distinguished node. If $l = m$, we know the location of the answer node, viz., node u. (2) The CML of u's parent in the document, say v, contains the entry $(P, l+1, m, x)$ and $(tag(v), tag(u))$ appears either as a pc-edge or as an ad-edge in query P. Note that the latter check can be performed by looking up the chain dual index via DualIndex$[tag(v)][tag(u)](rel)$, where rel is either *child* or *desc*. It is possible that an ancestor (which is not the parent) v of u contains the entry $(P, l+1, m, x)$ instead. This should cause (P, l, m, x) to be added to the CML of u, where x should be set to the number of node u if $l = m$, and left as '?' otherwise. Instead

---

[7] Solid and dotted edges are counted alike for this purpose.

```
Algorithm Node-Centric-Chain
Input: User queries Q₁,...,Qₙ;
Node labeled data tree T;
For simplicity, we use u also as the preorder rank associated with node u;
Output: A query labeling of T;
1.      Initialize the lists CML, PL, and QL of every node to empty lists;
2.      Traverse nodes of T in preorder;
        for each node u {
2.1.        for every (Q ∈ DualIndex[tag(u)](root)) {
                add (Q, h, d, ?) to CML(u), where h is the height of Q and
                d is the distance of distinguished node from leaf;
                add (Q, h, d, ?) : tag(u) to PL(u);
                if (h = d) replace '?' by u;
                //u is then a node to which the distinguished node of Q is matched. }
2.2.        if (u has parent) {
                let v be the parent;
2.2.1.          for every (Q ∈ DualIndex[tag(v)][tag(u)](desc) ∪
                    DualIndex[tag(v)][tag(u)](child)) {
                        if (∃i, j, x : (Q, i+1, j, x) ∈ CML(v)) {
                            add (Q, i, j, x) to CML(u) and tag(u) : (Q, i, j, x) to PL(u);
                            if (x = '?') { if (i = j) replace x by u; } } }
2.2.2.          for every ((Q, i+1, j, x) : t ∈ PL(v)) {
                    if (Q ∈ DualIndex[t][tag(u)](desc)) {
                        add (Q, i, j, x) to CML(u) and tag(u) : (Q, i, j, x) to PL(u);
                        if (x = '?') { if (i = j) replace x by u; } } }
2.2.3.          for every ((P, m, n, x) : t ∈ PL(v)) add (P, m, n, x) : t to PL(u); } }
3.      Traverse T postorder;
        for each node u {
3.1.        for (every (P, 0, j, x) ∈ CML(u)) {
                add P to QL(x); } }
```

Fig. 4. Labeling Chain Queries: The Node-Centric Way

of searching ancestors of u (which will make the number of passes large), we look for an entry of the form $(P, l+1, m, x) : t$ in the PL of u, such that $(t, tag(u))$ appears as an ad-edge in query P. Here, t denotes the ancestor's tag. This keeps the number of passes constant.

Next, the PL is maintained as follows. Whenever an entry (P, l, m, x) is added to the CML of a node u, the entry $(P, l, m, x) : tag(u)$ is added to the PL of u. Whenever x is set to a node number in a CML entry, the component x in the corresponding PL entry is also replaced. The contents of the PL of a node are propagated to its children. The following theorem shows there is an algorithm for chain labeling that makes two passes over the data tree. It assumes the existence of a chain dual index. Construction of dual indexes is discussed in [14].

As an example, in Figure 2(c), the CML of node 1 will initially get the entries $(Q1, 2, 0, ?), (Q3, 2, 2, 1), (Q4, 2, 1, ?)$. In the second entry, the last component 1 says node 1 in the document is the answer node (corresponding to that matching). Figure 2(d)-

(e) shows the CML and PL lists computed at the end of step 2 of the algorithm. Figure 2(f) shows the QL lists computed at the end of step 3. Note that the entry $(Q4, 1, 1, 8)$ appears twice in $CML(8)$. They are inserted by two different matchings, one that involves node 1 and another that involves node 5. In the figure, entries underlined by a dotted line indicate the first time (in step 2) when the component is replaced from a '?' to a node number for those entries. Entries underlined by a solid line indicate successful completion of matchings (as indicated by the third component being zero).

Theorem 1. (Chain Labeling) : Let T be a data tree and $Q_1, ..., Q_n$ any set of chain queries. There is an algorithm that correctly obtains the query labeling of every node of T. The algorithm makes no more than two passes over T. Furthermore, the number of I/O invocations of the algorithm is no more than $n * (2 + p)$, where n is the number of nodes in the document tree and p is the average size of the node PL lists associated with data tree nodes. ∎

5 Tree Queries

In this section, we first discuss a direct bottom-up algorithm called Algorithm Node-Centric-Trees for tree labeling. As will be shown later, this algorithm makes just two passes over the data tree T and correctly obtains its query labeling w.r.t. a given set of queries which are general trees.

5.1 A Direct Algorithm

Figure 5 shows Algorithm Algorithm Node-Centric-Trees. As with the chain labeling algorithm, we associate several lists with each node u in T. (1) The Tree Matching List (TML) contains entries of the form (P, l, m, x) where P is a query, l the number of a node in P, m the number of the distinguished node of P, and x is either '?' or the number of the node in T to which the distinguished node of P has been matched. (2) The push list (PL) contains entries of the form $(P, l, m, x) : rel$ where P, l, m, x are as above and rel is either $child$ or $desc$. It says there is a child or descendant (depending on rel) of the current node u whose TML contains the entry (P, l, m, x). (3) The query labeling list (QL) contains the list of queries for which u is an answer node.

These lists are managed as follows. Leaf entries in the tree dual index cause entries to be inserted into the TML lists of nodes. More precisely, let the current node u have tag t, and let DualIndex$[t](L)$ contain the entry (P, m, S). In this case, for every node $l \in S$, we insert the entry $(P, l, m, ?)$ into $TML(u)$; in case $l = m$, we replace '?' by the node number u. This signifies that the distinguished node of P has been matched into node u of T. Inductively, let (P, l, B, C, D) be an entry in DualIndex$[tag(u)](N)$. If according to $PL(u)$, for every $c \in C$, there is a child of u into which the subtree of P rooted at c can be successfully matched, and for every $d \in D$, there is a descendant of u into which the subtree of P rooted at d can be matched, then we add the entry (P, l, m, x) to $TML(u)$. Here, the value of m is obtained from the entries in $PL(u)$ that were used to make this decision. If at least one of the relevant $PL(u)$ entries contains a value for x other than '?', we use that value in the newly added entry in $TML(u)$; otherwise, we set x to '?' in $TML(u)$.

The PL list is first fed by entries added to TML: for every entry (P, l, m, x) added to $TML(u)$, we add the entry $(P, l, m, x) : child$ to $PL(parent(u))$. Secondly, whenever $PL(u)$ contains the entry $(P, l, m, x) : rel$, we add the entry $(P, l, m, x) : desc$ to $PL(parent(u))$. This latter step can result in an explosion in the size of the PL lists as every entry added to the PL of a node contributes entries to all its ancestors' PL lists. This can be pruned as follows. Suppose $PL(u)$ contains (P, l, m, x) and suppose node l of query P has no ad-parent, i.e. either it has no parent or it has a pc-parent. In the former case, there is no need to "propagate" the PL entry from u to its parent. In the latter case, since the propagated entry would be $(P, l, m, x) : desc$, it cannot contribute to the addition of any entry to $PL(parent(u))$.

Algorithm Node-Centric-Trees
Input: User queries $Q_1, ..., Q_n$; Node labeled data tree T;
Output: A query labeling of T;
1.   let h = height of T;
2.   for $(i = h; i \geq 0; i--)$ {
2.1   for (each node u at level i) {
2.1.1.   for (each (P, m, S) in DualIndex$[tag(u)](L)$) {
                for (each l in S) {
                  add $(P, l, m, ?)$ to $TML(u)$; //base case entries
                  if $(l = m)$ replace '?' by u; } }
2.1.2.   for (each entry e in DualIndex$[tag(u)](N)$) {
2.1.2.1.   let e be (P, l, B, C, D);
2.1.2.2.   if (not B) $mask(P, l) = true$;
                //if u has no ad-parent, mask propagation of PL entries.
2.1.2.3.   let $R = \{(m, x) \mid [\forall ci \in C : (P, ci, m, y) : child \in PL(u) \& ((y = x) \vee (y = `?'))]\ \&\ [\forall di \in D : ((P, ci, m, y) : child \in PL(u) \vee (P, ci, m, y) : desc \in PL(u)) \& ((y = x) \vee (y = `?'))]\}$;
2.1.2.4.   if $(R \neq \emptyset)$ {
                for (each (m, x) in R) {
                  add (P, l, m, x) to $TML(u)$;
                  if $(l = m)$ replace x by u; } }
2.1.3   for (each entry (P, l, m, x) in $TML(u)$) {
2.1.3.1.   add $(P, l, m, x) : child$ to $PL(parent(u))$;
                //Push that entry to the parent's pushlist
                //indicating that this corresp. to a child edge. }
2.1.4.   for (each entry $(P, l, m, x) : rel$ in $PL(u)$) {
                if (not $mask(P, l)$)
                add $(P, l, m, x) : desc$ to $PL(parent(u))$; } }
3.   Traverse T preorder;
        for each node u of T {
        if $((P, l, l, x)$ is in $TML(u))$ add P to $QL(u)$; }

Fig. 5. Labeling Tree Queries: The Node-Centric Way

As an example, in Figure 3(c), there is a sample document. The figure illustrates how its query labeling is constructed by Algorithm Node-Centric-Trees w.r.t. the queries of Figure 3(a), including the details of the TML, PL, and QL lists. For instance, $(P, 2, 3, ?)$ is added to $TML(7)$ since $tag(7) = b$ and $(P, 3, \{2, 5\})$ belongs to DualIndex$[b](L)$. As an example of the inductive case for adding entries into TML, consider the addition of $(Q, 3, 6, ?)$ into $TML(4)$. This is justified by the presence of $(Q, 4, 6, ?)$: *child* and $(Q, 5, 6, ?)$: *desc* in $PL(4)$. The PL entries can be similarly explained. In the figure, those TML entries where the last component x gets defined for the first time are underlined in dotted line, whereas those entries which signify a complete matching (as indicated by $l = 1$) are underlined in solid line.

Theorem 2. (Tree Labeling) : Let T be a data tree and $Q_1, ..., Q_n$ any set of query trees. There is an algorithm that correctly obtains the query labeling of every node of T. The algorithm makes no more than two passes over T. Furthermore, the number of I/O invocations of the algorithm is at most $2 * n$, where n is the number of nodes of the document tree. ∎

5.2 The Chain-Split Algorithm

In this section, we develop an approach for tree labeling that builds on the previously developed approach for chain labeling. The main motivation of this approach is based on the assumption that matching chains is easier than matching arbitrary trees, so if a query contains many chains, it makes sense to exploit them. A *chain* in a query tree P is any path $(x_1, ..., x_k)$ such that every node $x_i, 1 < i < k$, has outdegree 1 in P.[8] Such a chain is maximal provided: (i) either x_k is a leaf of P, or it has outdegree > 1 and (ii) either x_1 is the root of P, or it has outdegree > 1. In the sequel, by chains we mean maximal chains. For example, consider Figure 6(a). It shows four chains in query P – $P1 = (1, 2), P2 = (1, 3, 4), P3 = (4, 5), P4 = (4, 6)$; similarly, there are four chains in query Q – $Q1, Q2, Q3, Q4$. Suppose we split given queries into chains and match them into the data tree. Then, we should be able to make use of the information collected about the various matchings of chains in matching the original queries themselves efficiently.

For brevity, we only outline the main steps of the Chain-Split algorithm for tree labeling (instead of a formal description). We will need the following notions. A node of a query tree P is a *junction node* if it is either the root, or a leaf, or has outdegree > 1. In the chain split algorithm, we first match all the chains obtained from query trees using a chain dual index. In addition, we use an auxiliary data structure called *junction index*. The junction index is indexed by constants, just like the dual index. The index for any tag consists of entries of the form $(P, n) : (Pi, l_i), ..., (Pj, l_j)$, where P is a query, $Pi, ..., Pj$ are its chains, and $n, l_i, ..., l_j$ are node numbers in P. It says *if* a node u in a data tree satisfies the following conditions: (i) the chains $Pi, ..., Pj$ are matched into the data tree and u is the match of all their roots; (ii) $v_i, ..., v_j$ are the corresponding matches of their leaves[9]; (iii) the subtree of P rooted at l_i (resp., ..., l_j) is matched into the subtree of the data tree rooted at v_i (resp., ..., v_j); *then* one can conclude that the subtree of P rooted at n is matched into the subtree rooted at u. In this sense, a junction

---

[8] Note that all paths in our trees are downward.
[9] They need *not* be P's leaves.

index entry is like a rule with a consequent (P, n) and an antecedent $(Pi, l_i), ..., (Pj, l_j)$. Entries may have an empty antecedent. Note that the junction index may contain more than one entry for a given tag and a given query.

Figure 6 illustrates how this algorithm works. A detailed exposition is suppressed for lack of space and can be found in [14].

A formal presentation of the chain split algorithm, omitted here for brevity, can be easily formulated from this exposition. A theorem similar to Theorem 2 can be proved for this algorithm as well.

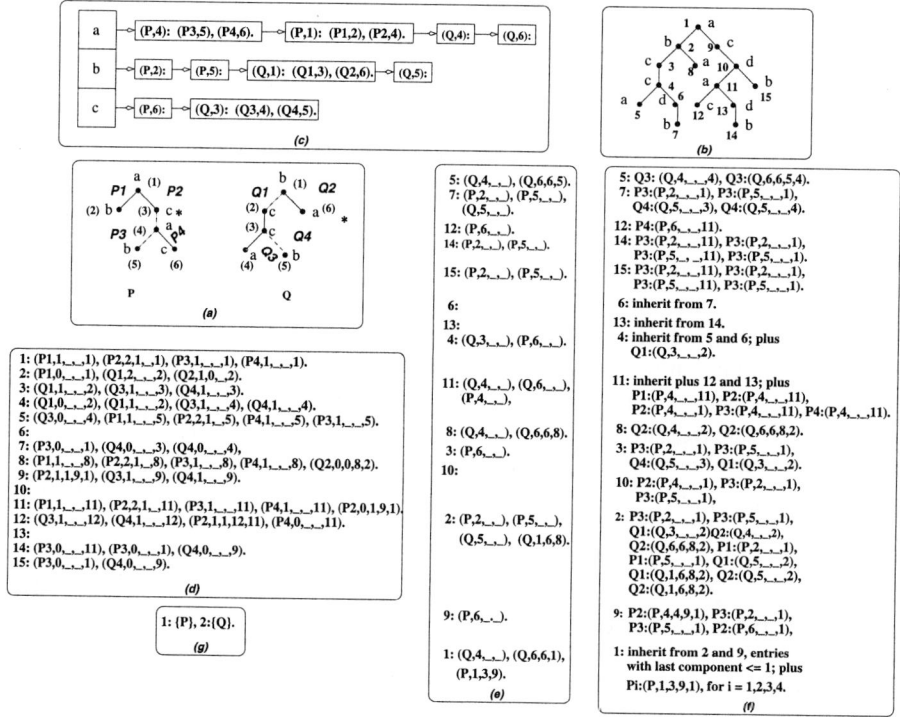

Fig. 6. Chain Split Algorithm Illustrated: (a) Queries; (b) Document; (c) Junction Index; (d) CML lists for the split chains; (e) TML lists corresponding to the queries; (f) PropList; (g) QL lists.

6 Experiments

We conducted a series of experiments to evaluate the effectiveness of the labeling algorithms developed. The algorithms presented were rigorously tested under different workloads.

Experimental setup: Our MatchMaker system is implemented using JDK1.3, GnuC++2.96, and BerkeleyDB3.17 [2]. The requirements indexes, that we proposed are all disk resident and all other data structures are memory resident. The experiments were conducted on a Intel Pentium III, dual processor with 1GB RAM, and 512KB cache operating on RedHat Linux 7.0. We ran our bunch of experiments using the GedML DTD. It is a DTD for encoding genealogical datasets in XML, based on GEDCOM which is a widely used data format for genealogical data [9]. This DTD has about 120 elements. For analyzing our algorithms, we generated both queries and documents. For generating documents, we made use of IBM's XML Generator tool [5], that generates random instances of valid XML documents from a DTD and a set of constraints. We analyzed the algorithms for various kinds of workloads.

Results: The results that we describe in this section pertain to documents with 120 nodes. We conducted an extensive set of experiments by varying the length of chain queries (or depth for tree queries), the distance of distinguished node from the leaf node, and the results we furnish here are averaged over 3 runs. The document depth was set to 10 while the average fanout (for non-leaves) was randomly chosen between 2 and 5. The results are summarized in Figures 7**A-H**. For the sake of comparison, we implemented the query-at-a-time approach for query labeling. However, we found that for tree queries, this approach took too much time and hence we only show its performance for chain queries.

Chain Queries: For chain queries, we determined the time needed to label the document by varying the number of queries. We compared the time taken with a query-at-a-time approach for query labeling. The number of queries was varied from 10,000 to 100,000 and the time taken for labeling the document was measured. The queries were generated with uniform distribution as well as with skewed distribution. In both cases, the chain length was randomly chosen in the range 2 to 9 and the chain tags were chosen from a uniform distribution over the DTD tags. For the skew distribution, tags were chosen using a Zipf distribution. The queries generated may have multiple matchings as well. Figure 7:A depicts the results of this experiment. For the skew distribution, we chose a case where there was a 100% hit ratio (= 1 in the graph), meaning every query had one or more matchings into the document. The figure shows a speedup of about 5 for the chain labeling algorithm compared with the query-at-a-time approach. Figure 7:B shows the memory usage of the chain labeling algorithm under both distributions. Both figures show that the algorithm scales gracefully. For 100,000 queries time is about 100 sec and memory consumed is about 300MB.

Effect of Skewness: For analyzing the effect of skewness of the queries on the total time taken for labeling the document, we ran a set of experiments by fixing the number of queries to 20,000 and controlling the skew using Zipf distribution. In interpreting the results, we found it more informative to use the hit ratio defined above than to use the actual value of the skewness factor. As can be seen from Figure 7:C, as the ratio increases from 0 (no queries have a matching) to 1 (all of them have at least one matching), the chain labeling algorithm has a performance that scales gracefully, whereas the query-at-a-time approach degrades quickly. The reason is that as more queries start to have (matchings) answeres, the amount of work done by this approach increases dramatically. On the other hand, for the chain labeling algorithm, the amount of work is only indirectly influenced by the hit ratio, since this is determined by the number of document nodes and the length of the associated lists.

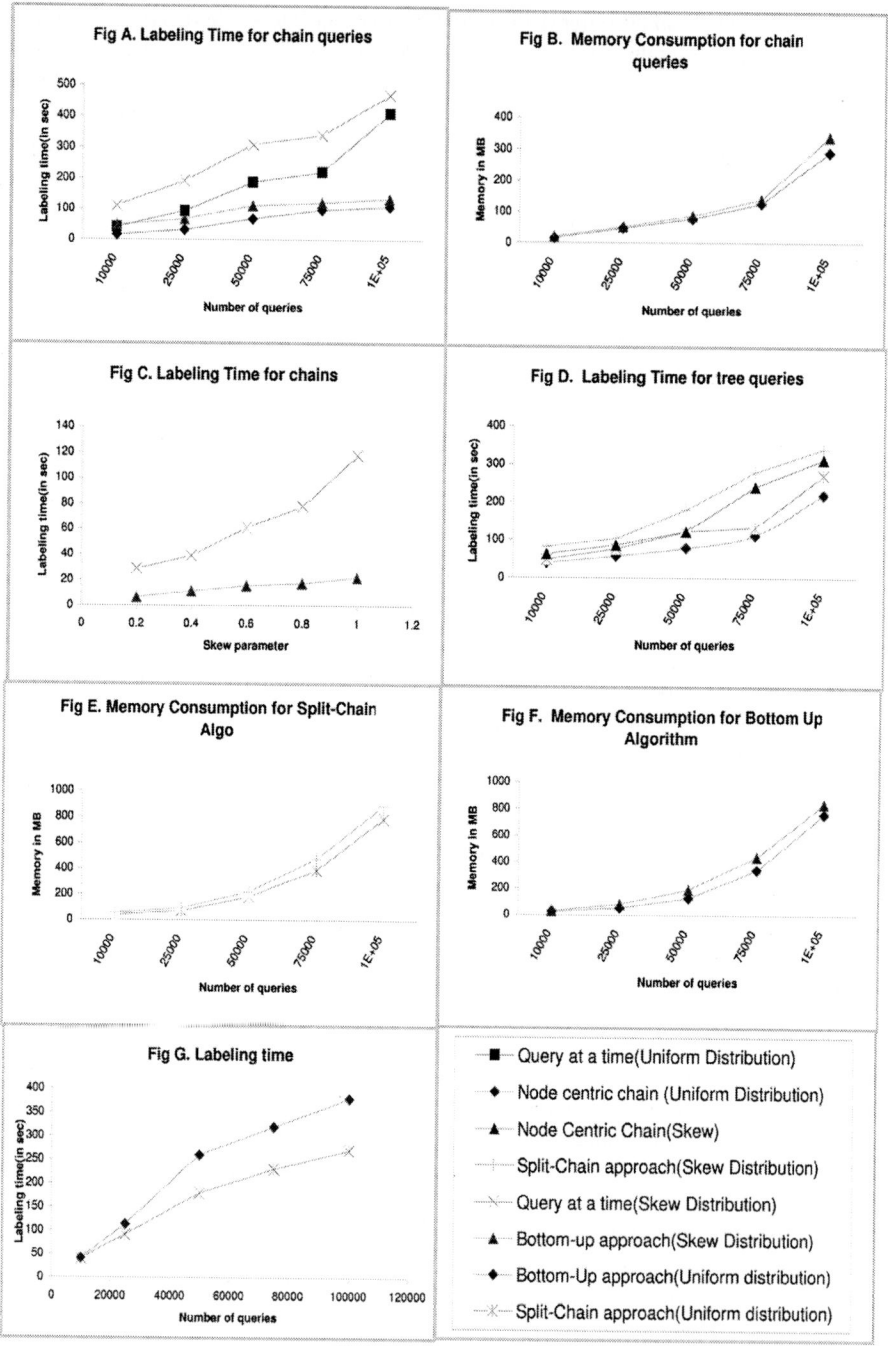

Fig. 7. Experimental Results

Tree Queries: As mentioned in the beginning of this section, we were unable to obtain the performance results for the query-at-a-time approach for tree queries in a reasonable amount of time. Consequently, our goal here was to compare the relative performance of the direct (bottom-up) tree labeling algorithm and the chain split algorithm and understand the tradeoffs. First, we focused on a realm where the number of junction nodes is a large proportion of the total number of nodes, for queries in the distribution. As expected, the direct algorithm performs better than chain split for this case. Figures 7:D, E, F show this. The memory usage for the algorithms is comparable. The figures show the performance for both uniform distribution and skewed distribution. As for chain queries, for skew, we used the Zipf distribution. The hit ratio used for the skew distribution case is 1. With respect to labeling time, the bottom-up algorithm is about 1.25-1.5 times better than the split chain algorithm.

Bottom-up vs. Split Chain Tradeoff: When the junction nodes form a small proportion of the total number of nodes, we expect that the split chain algorithm would take advantage of the ease of labeling chains. The additional overhead of matching the tree (using junction index) may well be offset by the speedup gained because of chain decomposition. To test this conjecture, we ran a set of experiments. By fixing the ratio of the number of junction nodes and the total number of nodes in a query to 0.125, we generated tree queries. Once again, we generated both uniform and Zipf distribution (with hit ratio 1) for queries. As shown by Figure 7:G, split chain can be about 1.4 faster than the bottom-up algorithm under these circumstances.

Summary: In sum, the experiments reveal that query labeling algorithms easily outperform query-at-a-time approach. In many cases (especially for tree labeling), query-at-a-time does not even finish in a reasonable amount of time, whereas the labeling algorithms show a performance that scales well with number of queries and skew factor. In the realm of tree labeling, the experiments show that direct bottom-up and chain split algorithms may be preferable under different conditions. The tradeoff is mainly driven by the ratio of junction nodes to the total number of nodes.

7 Related Work

The Tapestry mail management system [18], developed at Xerox Park, supports "continuous queries" against append-only databases, and provides perodical notification. Gupta and Srivastava [10] study the problem of view maintenance for a warehouse of newsgroups. The TriggerMan [11] system at the University of Florida is a scalable system for supporting millions of triggers in a DBMS context, using the notion of "expression signature", a common structure shared by many triggers. The NiagaraCQ system at Wisconsin [4] extends continuous queries to XML, and adapts the notion of expression signature for grouping XML-QL queries.

More recently, Fabret et al. [6, 7] describe a publish-and-subscribe system that maintains long-term subscription queries and notifies their owners whenever an incoming event matches the subscription, using a main memory algorithm with sophisticated caching policies. Subscription predicates are restricted to conjunctions of attribute relOp value. A direct adaptation of this approach for XML would not take advantage of the tree structure of documents and queries. The query subscription [8] project at Stanford has focused on merging overlapping queries to save on query compute time as well as broadcast time. The MatchMaker approach presented in this paper is fundamentally different from all the above in that it can be regarded as the dual of conventional query processing.

The XFilter project at Berkeley [1] is perhaps the closest to our work and is perhaps the first paper to adopt a dual approach to matching of XML documents to queries. There are important differences with our work. Firstly, they merely determine whether a document is relevant to a query (i.e. *contains* an answer to a query) as opposed to locating the answer element(s). Besides, they do not address multiple answers to a query within one document. As pointed out earlier, these two issues alone raise a major challenge for efficient matching, and we deal with both. Our formulation of the matching problem in terms of query labeling, as well as our matching algorithms, to the best of our knowledge, are novel. Also, we can formally show the correctness of our algorithms [14]. The problem of matching documents to queries (sometimes called user profiles) has been studied in the IR community. A critique of their approaches and a comparison with the database approach to matching appears in [1]. Intel's XML Accelerator [12] is an industry product providing XML document filtering.

Finally, in very recent work, Chan et al. at Bell Labs [3] develop a trie-based index, called XTrie, for indexing a large collection of subscription queries, stated as XPath expressions. The intuitive idea is to split an XPath tree into maximal paths free of ad edges, called substrings, and index them using a trie. The resulting XTrie index, together with their matching algorithm, makes it possible to reduce unnecessary index probes and avoid redundant matchings. Just like the XFilter work, the authors are mainly interested in finding queries which have at least one matching (anywhere) in a given document, which distinguishes our work. The notion of substring decomposition of [3] is similar in spirit to, but is technically different from, our chain decomposition of tree queries. Since these two ideas are orthogonal, it suggests they can be combined to take advantage of the best of both worlds. In particular, this makes it possible to extend the XTrie approach not only for determining existence of matchings, but to actually extract the answers and do so efficiently. Nguyen et al. [17] describe a system for efficient monitoring of changes to XML documents flowing through a warehouse, and as such the concerns are somewhat different.

8 Summary and Future Work

Motivated by applications requiring efficient matching of specifications to requirements, both in XML, we proposed the problem of query labeling. We presented efficient algorithms for query labeling for chain as well as tree queries. The algorithms can be formally shown to be correct. Our experimental results show the effectiveness of our labeling algorithms. As discussed earlier, the algorithms, by virtue of handling streaming XML documents, are also applicable for publish-and-subscribe applications on the internet, involving XML documents and queries.

Like the XFilter and XTrie papers, this paper addresses the first steps in developing large scale publish-and-subscribe systems involving streaming XML data. Specifically, our goal is to extend MatchMaker so as to cater to subscriptions covering larger fragments of XML query languages. The recently proposed TAX algebra for XML [13] offers a convenient framework with which to proceed.

We plan to do detailed experiments comparing the performance of our labeling algorithms and index structures with the XTrie approach. In addition, it would also be fruitful to determine how ideas from the two works can be combined to lead to even more powerful algorithms.

Maintaining dual indexes in an incremental fashion is an important issue. Integration of database style matching of documents to queries with keyword search and handling of the concomitant uncertainty is another interesting direction. Our ongoing work addresses some of these issues.

Acknowledgements

Lakshmanan's work was supported in part by grants from NSERC, NCE/IRIS/NSERC, and by a seed grant from IIT-Bombay. Sailaja's research was done while she was at IIT-Bombay and was supported by a Ramarao V. Nilekani Fellowship.

References

1. Mehmet Altinel, Michael J.Franklin. Efficient Filtering of XML Documents for Selective Dissemination of Information. In *Proc. VLDB*, 2000.
2. Berkeley DB Database System. Downloadable from http://www.sleepycat.com/.
3. Chee-Yong Chan, Pascal Felber, Minos Garofalakis, and Rajeev Rastogi. Efficient Filtering of XML Documents with XPath Expressions. *Proc. ICDE*, San Jose, CA, Feb. 2002. To appear.
4. J.Chen, D.DeWitt, F.Tian, and Y.Wang. NiagaraCQ: A scalable continuous query System for Internet Dtatabases. In *ACM SIGMOD*, May 2000.
5. A.L. Diaz and D. Lovell. XML Generator. http://www.alphaworks/ibm.com/tech/ xmlgnerator, Sept. 1999.
6. Françoise Fabret, Hans-Arno Jacobsen, François LLirbat, João Pereira, Kenneth A. Ross, and Dennis Shasha. Filtering Algorithms and Implementation for Very Fast Publish/Subscribe. In *ACM SIGMOD*, May 2001.
7. F.B Fabret et al. Efficient matching for content-based publish/subscribe systems. In *Proc. CoopIS*, 2000.
8. Hector Garcia-Molina A.Crespo, and O.Buyukkokten. Efficient Query subscription Processing in a Multicast Environment. In *Proc. ICDE*, 2000.
9. GedML: Genealogical Data in XML. http://users.iclway.co.uk/mhkay/gedml/.
10. Himanshu Gupta and Divesh Srivastava. Data Warehouse of Newsgroups. In *Proc. ICDT*, 1999.
11. Eric N. Hanson Chris Carnes, Lan Huang, Mohan Konyala, Lloyd Noronha, Sashi Parthasarathy, J. B. Park, and Albert Vernon. Scalable Trigger Processing. In *Proc. ICDE*, pages 266–275, April 1999.
12. The Intel Corporation. Intel Netstructure XML Accelerators. http://www.intel.com/netstructure/products/xml_accelerators.htm, 2000.
13. H.V. Jagadish, Laks V.S. Lakshmanan, Divesh Srivastava, and Keith Thompson. TAX: A Tree Algebra for XML. *Proc. DBPL*, Roma, Italy, September 2001.

14. Laks V.S. Lakshmanan and P. Sailaja. On Efficient Matching of Streaming XML Documents and Queries. Tech. Report, Univ. Of British Columbia, December 2001. http://www.cs.ubc.ca/ laks/matchmaker-edbt02-full.ps.gz.
15. Laks V.S. Lakshmanan and P. Sailaja. MatchMaker: A system for matching XML documents and queries. Demo paper, *Proc. ICDE*, San Jose, CA, Feb. 2002. To appear.
16. L. Liu C. Pu, and W. Tang. Continual queries for internet-scale event-driven information delivery. *IEEE Trans. on Knowledge and Data Eng.* 11(4): 610-628 (1999).
17. Benjamin Nguyen, Serge Abiteboul, Gregory Cobena, and Mihai Preda. Monitoring XML Data on the Web. *ACM SIGMOD*, 2001.
18. Douglas Terry David Goldberg, David Nichols, and Brian Oke. Continuous queries over Append-only databases. In *ACM SIGMOD*, June 1992.

Efficient Complex Query Support for Multiversion XML Documents[*]

Shu-Yao Chien[1], Vassilis J. Tsotras[2], Carlo Zaniolo[1], and Donghui Zhang[2]

[1] Department of Computer Science, University of California, Los Angeles, CA 90095
{csy,zaniolo}@cs.ucla.edu
[2] Computer Science Department, University of California, Riverside, CA 92521
{tsotras,donghui}@cs.ucr.edu

Abstract. Managing multiple versions of XML documents represents a critical requirement for many applications. Also, there has been much recent interest in supporting complex queries on XML data (e.g., regular path expressions, structural projections, DIFF queries). In this paper, we examine the problem of supporting efficiently complex queries on multiversioned XML documents. Our approach relies on a scheme based on durable node numbers (DNNs) that preserve the order among the XML tree nodes and are invariant with respect to updates. Using the document's DNNs various complex queries are reduced to combinations of *partial version retrieval* queries. We examine three indexing schemes to efficiently evaluate partial version retrieval queries in this environment. A thorough performance analysis is then presented to reveal the advantages of each scheme.

1 Introduction

The management of multiple versions of XML documents finds important applications [28] and poses interesting technical challenges. Indeed, the problem is important for application domains, such as software configuration and cooperative work, that have traditionally relied on version management. As these applications migrate to a web-based environment, they are increasingly using XML for representing and exchanging information—often seeking standard vendor-supported tools and environments for processing and exchanging their XML documents.

Many new applications of versioning are also emerging because of the web; a particularly important and pervasive one is assuring link permanence for web documents. Any URL becoming invalid causes serious problems for all documents referring to it—a problem that is particularly severe for search engines that risk directing millions of users to pages that no longer exist. Replacing the old version with a new one, at the same location, does not cure the problem completely, since the new version might no longer contain the keywords used in the search. The

---

[*] This work was partially supported by NSF grants IIS-0070135, IIS-9907477, EIA-9983445, and the Department of Defense.

ideal solution is a version management system supporting multiple versions of the same document, while avoiding duplicate storage of their shared segments. For this reason, professionally managed sites and content providers will have to use document versioning systems; frequently, web service providers will also support searches and queries on their repositories of multiversion documents. Specialty warehouses and archives that monitor and collect content from web sites of interest will also rely on versioning to preserve information, track the history of downloaded documents, and support queries on these documents and their history [18].

Various techniques for versioning have also been proposed by database researchers who have focused on problems such as transaction-time management of temporal databases [19], support for versions of CAD artifacts in O-O databases [12] and, more recently, change management for semistructured information [7].

In the past, the approaches to versioning taken by database systems and document management systems have often been different, because of the different requirements facing the two application areas. In fact:

– Database systems are designed to support complex queries, while document management systems are not, and
– Databases assume that the order of the objects is not significant—but the lexicographical order of the objects in a document is essential to its reconstruction.

This state of affairs has been changed dramatically by XML that merges applications, requirements and enabling technology from the two areas. Indeed the differences mentioned above are fast disappearing since support for complex queries on XML documents is critical. This is demonstrated by the amount of current research on this topic [22, 24] and the emergence of powerful XML query languages [2, 11, 5, 29, 6, 30]. A particularly challenging problem is that of supporting efficiently path expression queries such as:

$$doc/chapter/*/figure.$$

This query specifies figures that are immediate elements of chapters or their transitive sub-elements (e.g., figures in sub-sections). Various techniques have been proposed to support regular path expressions [14–16] in the literature. These techniques use durable numbering schemes to preserve the logical document structure in the presence of updates.

For multiversion documents, we have to support such complex queries on any user-selected version. Furthermore, we need to support difference queries between two versions, and queries on the evolution of documents or selected parts of it, such as for lineage queries.

In [8] and [9] we proposed schemes for the efficient storage and retrieval of multiversion documents and showed that these provide significant improvements with respect to traditional schemes such as RCS [23] and SCCS [20]. To enhance the version retrieval efficiency, [8] places document elements in disk pages using a clustering mechanism called UBCC (for Usefulness Based Copy Control).

The UBCC mechanism achieves better version clustering by copying elements that live through many versions. A variation of UBCC was used in [9], where a reference-based versioning scheme was presented.

While the versioning schemes proposed in [8,9] are effective at supporting simple queries, they cannot handle complex queries such as the path-expression queries. For complex queries, we have recently outlined [10] the *SPaR* scheme that adapts the *durable node numbers* [16] to a multiversion environment. Furthermore, SPaR uses *timestamping* to preserve the logical structure of the document and represent the history of its evolution. In this paper, we expand the properties of the *SPaR* scheme and investigate efficient physical realizations for it. Different storage and indexing strategies are examined so as to optimize SPaR's implementation. Our study builds on the observation that evaluating complex version queries mainly depends on the efficiency of evaluating one basic type of query: the *partial version retrieval* query. Such query retrieves a specific segment of an individual version instead of the whole version. Retrieving a segment for a single-versioned XML document is efficient since the target elements are clustered on secondary store by their logical order, but this might not be the case for a multiversion document. For a multiversion document, a segment of a later version may have its elements physically scattered in different pages due to version updates. Therefore, retrieving a small segment could require reading a lot of unnecessary data.

While UBCC is very effective at supporting full version retrieval queries, complex queries on content and history combined call for indexing techniques such are the Multiversion B-Tree [17,3,27] and the Multiversion R-Tree [13]. We investigate the following three approaches:

Scheme 1: single Multiversion B-Tree,
Scheme 2: UBCC with a Multiversion B-Tree, and
Scheme 3: UBCC with a Multiversion R-Tree.

The last two approaches still use the UBCC mechanism as the main storage scheme for the document elements. The additional indices are used as secondary indices so that partial version retrievals are efficiently supported. The first approach lets the Multiversion B-Tree organize the document elements in disk pages and at the same time uses the index for partial retrievals. The Multiversion B-Tree also uses a clustering technique. However, this technique is more elaborate and uses more disk space, since it clusters by versions and (durable) element numbers. A performance evaluation is presented to compare the the different schemes.

The rest of this paper is organized as follows. Section 2 provides background, while section 3 presents the SPaR scheme. In section 4, the three storage and indexing combinations are described. Their performance is presented in section 5 while conclusions appear in section 6.

2 Background

A new document version (V_{j+1}) is established by applying a number of changes (object insertions, deletions or updates) to the current version (V_j). In a typical

RCS scheme, these changes are stored in a (forward) edit script. Such script could be generated directly from the edit commands of a structured editor, if one was used to revise the XML document. In most situations, however, the script is obtained by applying, to the pair (V_j, V_{j+1}), a structured DIFF package [4].

For forward editing scripts, the RCS scheme stores the script and the data together is successive pages. Thus, to reconstruct version (V_j) all pages stored by successive versions up to version (V_j) must be retrieved. The SCCS tries to improve the situation by keeping an index that identifies the pages used by each version. However, as the document evolves, document objects valid for a given version can be dispersed in various disk pages. Since a given page may contain very few of the document objects for the requested version, many more pages must be accessed to reconstruct a version.

To solve these problems, in [8] we introduced an edit-based versioning scheme that (i) separates the actual document data from the edit script, and (ii) uses the usefulness-based clustering scheme (UBCC) for page management. Because of (i) the script is rather small and can be easily accessed. The usefulness-based clustering is similar to a technique used in transaction-time databases [17, 25, 3] to cluster temporal data and is outlined below.

2.1 Usefulness-Based Clustering

Consider the actual document objects and their organization in disk pages. For simplicity, assume the only changes between document versions are object additions and deletions. As objects are added in the document, they are stored sequentially in pages. Object deletions are not physical but logical; the objects remain in the pages where they were recorded, but are marked as deleted. As the document evolution proceeds, various pages will contain many "deleted" objects and few, if any, valid objects for the current version. Such pages, will provide few objects for reconstructing the current version. As a result, a version retrieval algorithm will have to access many pages. Ideally we would like to cluster the objects valid at a given version in few, *useful* pages. We define the *usefulness* of a full page P, for a given version V, as the percentage of the page that corresponds to valid objects for V.

For example, assume that at version V_1, a document consists of five objects O_1, O_2, O_3, O_4 and O_5 whose records are stored in data page P. Let the size of these objects be 30%, 10%, 20%, 25% and 15% of the page size, respectively. Consider the following evolving history for this document: At version V_2, O_2 is deleted; at version V_3, O_3 is deleted, and at version V_4, object O_5 is deleted. Hence page P is 100% useful for version V_1. Its usefulness falls to 90% for version V_2, since object O_2 is deleted at V_2. Similarly, P is 70% useful for version V_3. For version V_4, P is only 55% useful.

Clearly, as new versions are created, the usefulness of existing pages *for the current version* diminish. We would like to maintain a minimum page usefulness, U_{min}, over all versions. When a page's usefulness falls below U_{min}, for the current version, all the records that are still valid in this page are copied (i.e., salvaged) to another page (hence the name UBCC). When copied records are stored in new disk pages they preserve their relative document order. For instance, if $U_{min} = 60\%$, then page P falls below this threshold of usefulness at Version 4; at this point objects O_1, and O_4 are copied to a new page. The value of U_{min} is set between 0 and 1 and represents a performance tuning parameter.

We note that the above page usefulness definition holds for full pages. A page is called an *acceptor* for as long as document objects are stored in this page. While being the acceptor (and thus not yet full), a page is by definition useful. This is needed since an acceptor page may not be full but can still contain elements alive for the current version. Note that there is always only one acceptor page. After a page becomes full (and stops being the acceptor) it remains useful only as long as it contains enough alive elements (the U_{min} parameter).

The advantage of UBCC is that the records valid for a given version are clustered into the disk pages that are useful for that version. Reconstructing the full document at version V_i is then reduced to retrieving only the pages that were useful at V_i. Various schemes can be used to assure that only useful pages are accessed for full version retrieval. For example [8] uses the edit script to determine the useful pages for each version, while [9] facilitates the object references.

While the UBCC clustering is very effective for full version retrieval queries, it is not efficient with complex queries like path-expression queries. Path-expression queries need to maintain the logical document order and UBCC does not.

2.2 Path-Expression Queries

A path-expression query is described by a regular expression on the document tree. For example, the query "find all the figures in chapter 10 of the document" is supported in XML query languages [6] by a special path-expression notation: `chapter[10]/*/figure`. Figures may be anywhere in the subtree rooted in the `chapter[10]` node of the document. To answer such queries efficiently (in a single-version environment) without fully traversing document subtrees, a method is needed to quickly identify ancestor-descendant relationships between document elements. [16] proposes a numbering scheme for the document elements, whereby the numbers assigned to elements remain unchanged even if elements are added/deleted from the document. This is achieved by sorting the nodes as in the pre-order traversal, but leaving space between them to make room for future insertions.

Such a durable numbering scheme is advantageous since it automatically maintains the logical document tree structure. An ordered list with the node durable numbers is enough to reconstruct the document in logical order. Moreover since the numbering scheme does not change, it allows indexing various document elements in a persistent way. In [10] we outlined SPaR, a new versioning scheme that adapts the durable numbers of [16] as well as timestamps in order to efficiently support complex queries on multiversion XML documents. Below we expand the SPaR scheme properties and justify the reduction on various complex multiversion queries to partial version retrieval queries.

3 The SPaR Versioning Scheme

The new versioning scheme assigns durable structure-encoding ID numbers and timestamps to the elements of the document. SPaR stands for Sparse Preorder and Range, i.e., the numbering consists of two numbers: a Durable Node Number (DNN) and a Range, discussed next.

3.1 The Numbering Scheme

An XML document is viewed as an ordered tree, where the tree nodes corresponds to document elements (and the two terms will be used as synonyms). A pre-order traversal number can then to identify uniquely the elements of the XML tree. While this easy to compute, it does not provide a *durable reference* for external indexes and other objects that need to point to the document element, since insertions and deletions normally change the pre-order numbers of the document elements which follow. Instead, we need durable node IDs that can be used as stable references in indexing the elements and will also allow the decomposition of the documents in several linked files [16]. Furthermore, these durable IDs must also describe the position of the element in the original document— a requirement not typically found for IDs in O-O databases. The DNN establishes the same total order on the elements of the document as the pre-order traversal, but, rather than using consecutive integers, leaves as much an interval between nodes as possible; thus DNN is a sparse numbering scheme that preserves the lexicographical order of the document elements.

The second element in the SPaR scheme is the Range. This was proposed in [16] as a mechanism for supporting efficiently *path expression queries*. For instance, a document might have chapter elements and figure elements contained in such chapters. A typical query is: *"Retrieve all titles under chapter elements"*. Using recently proposed XML query languages ([6], etc.) this query is described as a path expression, as follows:

$$doc/chapter/*/figure$$

In the XML document tree, figure elements could be children of chapter elements, or they might be descendants of chapter elements (e.g., contained in sections or subsections). To support the efficient execution of such path expression queries we need the ability of finding all the sub-elements of a given elements provided by the SPaR scheme. Let $dnn(E)$ and $range(E)$ denote the DNN and the range of a given element E; then a node B is descendant of a node A [1] iff:

$$dnn(A) \leq dnn(B) \leq dnn(A) + range(A).$$

Therefore, the interval $[dnn(X), dnn(X) + range(X)]$ is associated with element X. When the elements in the document are updated, their SPaR numbers

---
[1] If the pre-order traversal number is used as DNN, $range(A)$ is equal to the number of descendants of A.

remain unchanged. When new elements are inserted, they are assigned a DNN and a range that do not interfere with the SPaR of their neighbors—actually, we want to maintain sparsity by keeping the intervals of nearby nodes as far apart as possible.

Consider two consecutive document elements X and Z where $dnn(X) < dnn(Z)$. Then, element Z can either be (i) the first child of X, (ii) the next sibling of X, or (iii) the next sibling of an element K who is an ancestor of X. If a new element Y is inserted between elements X and Z, it can similarly be the first child of X, the next sibling of X or the next sibling of one of X's ancestors. For each of these three cases, the location of Z creates three subcases, for a total of nine possibilities. For simplicity, we discuss the insertion of Y as the first child of X and consider the possible locations for element Z (the other cases are treated similarly). Then we have that:

1. Z becomes the first child of Y. In this case the following conditions should hold: $dnn(X) < dnn(Y) < dnn(Z)$ and $dnn(Z) + range(Z) \leq dnn(Y) + range(Y) \leq dnn(X) + range(X)$.
2. Z becomes the next sibling of Y under X. The interval of new element Y is inserted in the middle of the empty interval between $dnn(X)$ and $dnn(Z)$ (thus, the conditions $dnn(X) < dnn(Y)$ and $dnn(Y) + range(Y) \leq dnn(Z)$ must hold).
3. Z becomes the next sibling of an ancestor of Y. Then element Y is "covered" by element X which implies that: $dnn(X) < dnn(Y)$ and $dnn(Y) + range(Y) \leq dnn(X) + range(X)$.

Thus, our insertion scheme assumes that an empty interval is at hand for every new element being inserted. When integers are used, occasional SPaR reassignments might be needed to assure this property. A better solution is to use floating point numbers, where additional decimal digits can be added as needed for new insertions. Nevertheless, for simplicity of exposition, in the following examples we will use integers.

Figure 1 shows a sample XML document with $SPaR$ values. The root element is assigned range [1,2100]. That range is split into five sub-ranges — [1,199], [200,1200], [1201,1299], [1300,2000], and [2001,2100] for its two direct child elements, CH 1 and CH 2, and three insertion points, before CH 1, after CH 1 and after CH 2. The range assigned to each of these chapter element continues to be split and assigned to their direct child elements until leaf elements are met.

3.2 The Version Model

Since the SPaR numbering scheme maintains the logical document order and supplies durable node IDs, it makes it possible to use timestamps to manage changes in both the content and the structure of documents. Hence the record of each XML document element contains the element's SPaR and the element's version lifespan. The lifespan is described by two timestamps (V_{start}, V_{end})— where V_{start} is the version where the element is created and V_{end} is the version where the element is deleted (if ever). An element is called "alive" for all versions

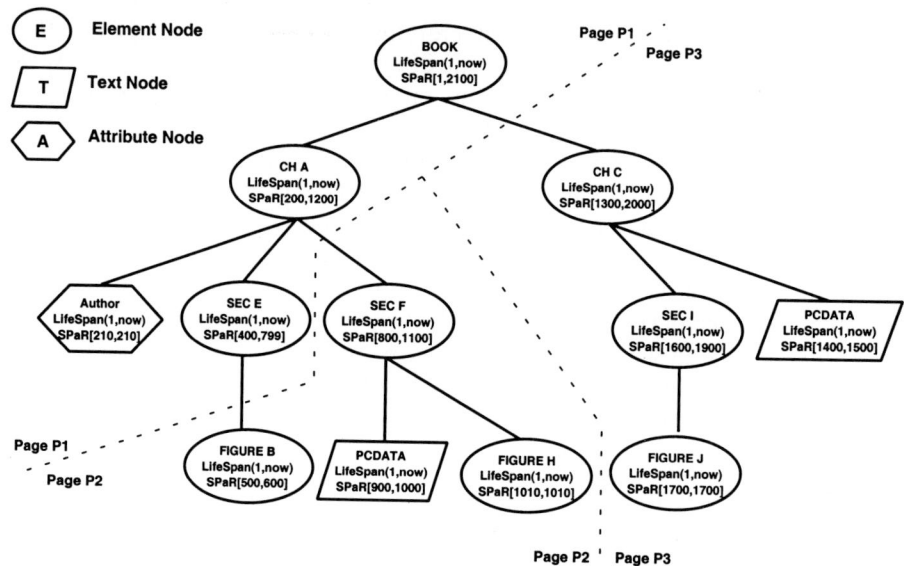

Fig. 1. An XML document version represented in the SPaR model.

in its lifespan. If an element is alive in the current version, its V_{end} value is *now* which is a variable representing the ever increasing current version number. A lifespan interval is left-closed and right-open; moreover, the lifespan of an element contains the lifespans of its descendants (much in the same way in which its SPaR interval contains those of its descendants). An example is shown in Figure 1.

The elements of the initial version, are stored as records in disk pages, ordered by their document order. In Figure 1 it was assumed that a page can hold four records (for simplicity all document elements have same size); the elements of the first version are stored in pages P1, P2 and P3, based on their SPaR order.

Successive versions are described as changes with respect to the previous version. Such changes are contained in an edit script generated from the structured XML editor, or otherwise by a package that computes the structured DIFF between the two documents. For simplicity we consider the following basic change operations: DELETE, INSERT and UPDATE. (Additional operations, such as MOVE or COPY elements can be reduced to these.) A new version is created by applying the basic operations on elements of the previous version. Below we discuss the effect of performing each basic operation, to create version V_N:

- *DELETE* — This operation updates the V_{end} timestamp of the deleted element and all its descendants from *now* to Version V_N. The *SPaR* range of the deleted elements is freed for reuse.
- *INSERT* — An INSERT operation creates a record for the newly inserted element and initializes its lifespan to (V_N, now). An unused range is assigned to the new element based on the weighted range allocation algorithm. The new record is stored in the acceptor page.

- $UPDATE$ — The V_{end} timestamp of the updated element is changed to Version V_N. Subsequently, a new record is created with lifespan initialized to (V_N, now). This new record keeps the same $SPaR$ values as the original record (since the position of the updated element in the document did not change).

UBCC and Full Version Retrieval. Consider a SPaR scheme that adopts the UBCC clustering strategy (section 2.1) as its physical storage management. In addition to the above updates, records are copied due to the UBCC page usefulness threshold. We will now discuss how UBCC leads to fast full version reconstruction.

The first step of reconstructing a complete version is to identify the useful pages for the specified version. The notion of usefulness associates with each page a *usefulness interval*. This interval has also the form of (V_{start}, V_{end}), where V_{start} is the version when the page became acceptor and V_{end} is the version when the page became non-useful. As with the document element records, a page usefulness interval is initiated as (V_{start}, now) and later updated at V_{end}. Identifying the data pages that were useful at V_i is then equivalent to finding which pages have intervals that contain V_i. This problem has been solved in temporal databases [19] with an access method called the Snapshot Index [25, 21]. If there were k useful pages at V_i, they are located with $O(k)$ effort.

These useful pages contain all document elements at V_i, however, the elements may be stored out of their logical document order. Therefore, the second step is to sort the elements by their SPaR number. (It should be noted that versioning schemes not based on durable numbers [8, 9] use the edit script or object references to reconstruct the document order). A straightforward sort over all useful pages is not as efficient as it may require reading various useful pages many times. A better solution takes advantage of the partial order existing among the elements stored in a useful page and uses a one-pass sort-merge approach. Finally, using the SPaR numbers and a stack mechanism, the document tree structure is reconstructed.

In the next subsection we reduce various complex versioning queries to partial version retrievals. Since the UBCC does not maintain the SPaR order additional indexing schemes will be needed.

3.3 Complex Queries

While full version retrieval is important, many other versioning queries are of interest. For example, we might want to find only the abstract (or the conclusions section) that the document had at version V_i, or the part of the document from the fifth until the tenth chapter in version V_i. Similarly, we may need subsections two through six in the fourth section of chapter ten in version V_i. A common characteristic of the above queries is that a path in the document tree is provided. Yet, other interesting queries are those that instead of providing an exact path, they use a regular expression to specify a pattern for the path. For example, an expression such as `version[i]/chapter[10]/*/figure` might be used to find all figures in chapter 10 of version V_i (or, symmetrically, the chapter that contains a given figure in version V_i).

To address these queries efficiently, additional indices are needed. Consider the set of all element DNNs (and their SPaR ranges) in the first document version. As the document evolves to a new version, this set evolves by adding/deleting DNNs to/from the set. Assume that an index is available which (i) indexes this version-evolving set and (ii) can answer retrieval queries of the form: "given a DNN range (x, y) and a version V_i, find which DNNs were in this range during version V_i". Since this index indexes all document elements, we will refer to it as the *full-index*.

The full-index assumes that the document SPaR DNNs are available. However, SPaR numbers are invisible to the user who expresses queries in terms of document *tag* names (abstract, chapter, etc.). Therefore, given a tag and a version number, the DNN of this tag in the given version must be identified.

Document tags are typically of two types. First, there are *individual* tags that only occur a small number of times in the document. Most of these tags, such as *example, abstract, references* and *conclusions* might occur only once in the document, although some individual tags can occur a few times (e.g., we might have an address tag for both sender and receiver). Then, there are *list* tags, such as: *chapters, sections*, and all the tags under them. Such tags can occur an unlimited number of times in a document. For simplicity assume that individual tags have a SPaR DNN and range that remain unchanged over versions. This information can be stored and accessed on request.

Consider for example a query requesting the *abstract* in version 10. Assume that under the *abstract* tag, the document contains a subtree that maintains the abstract text, and a list of *index terms*. While the abstract SPaRs remained unchanged, the subtree under the abstract tag may have changed. That is, the abstract text and the index terms could have changed between versions. To answer the above query we simply perform a range search (using the abstract's SPaR range) on the full-index for version 10. Determining the SPaR numbers of list tags is more complex. This is because a new tag added in the list affects the position of all tags that follow it. For example, adding a new chapter after the first chapter in a document, makes the previously second, third,..., chapters to become third, fourth etc. Hence to identify the DNN of the tenth chapter in version 20, we need to maintain the ordered list of chapter DNNs. Such a list can also been maintained by using an index on the SPaR DNNs (and SPaR ranges) of *chapter* tags (the *ch_index*). Similarly with the full-index the ch-index can answer partial version retrieval queries specified by a version number and a range of chapter DNNs. We also maintain one index per list tag in the document (for example, *sec_index* indexes the DNNs of all document sections while *fig_index* indexes all figure DNNs.)

The overall index architecture is illustrated in Figure 2. This figure assumes that at the bottom level, the disk pages are organized by UBCC. Each UBCC page has a usefulness interval and contains three element records. Each UBCC record has its tag, SPaR range, lifespan and data (not shown). The records in the

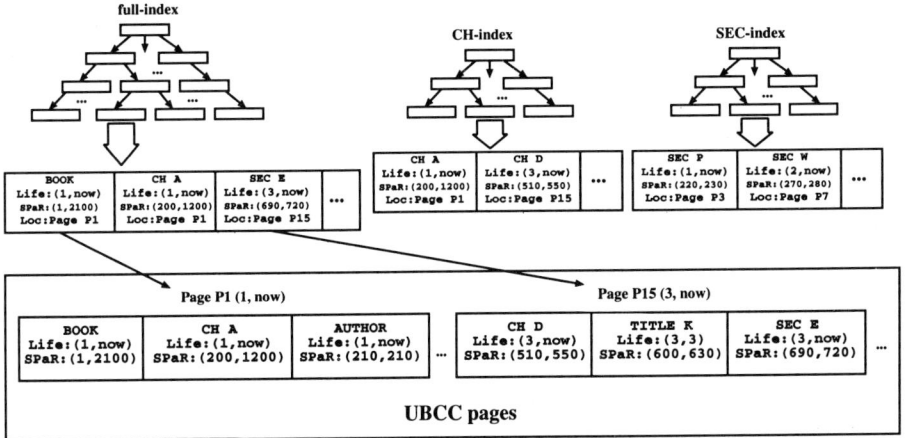

Fig. 2. The overall index architecture.

leaf pages of the full- and tag- indices contain pointers to the UBCC pages that contain these records. An index leaf page contains more records than a UBCC page since the latter stores the element data as well.

Using the above index combination various complex queries can be answered efficiently. These queries are first translated into partial version retrieval queries as the following examples indicate.

Structural Projection — *Project the part of the document between the second and the fifth chapters in version 20.* To answer this query we first access the *ch_index* and retrieve the ordered list of chapter DNNs as it was in version 20. From this list we identify the SPaR range between chapters 2 and 5. With this SPaR range we perform a range search for version 20 in the *full_index*. This search will identify all elements with DNNs inside this range. From the SPaR properties, all such elements are between chapters 2 and 5.

Regular Path Expression— *Find all sections under the third chapter in version 10.* We first identify the SPaR range of the third chapter in version 10 from *ch_index*. With this SPaR range we perform a range search in the *sec_index* for version 10. Only the sections under the third chapter will have SPaR numbers in the given range.

As another example, consider the query: *find the chapter that contains figure 10 in version 5.* To answer this query we first identify the DNN of the tenth figure in version 5 from *fig_index*. Using this SPaR we perform a search in *ch_index* for version 5. According to the properties of the SPaR numbering scheme, we find the chapter with the largest SPaR that is less than the figure SPaR.

Parent-Child Expression— *For version 10, retrieve all titles directly under chapter elements.* Using the *ch_index* we identify the *chapter* elements alive in version 10. For each *chapter*, its SPaR range value is used to locate all *title* elements under it in version 10 through the *title_index*. Then, the level number of located titles are compared with that of the chapter element to determine their parent-child relationship.

4 Indexing Schemes

In this section we elaborate on the various data storage organization and indexing possibilities.

Data Storage Organization. We have already discussed one approach for the data storage organization, namely, UBCC. Another approach is to cluster the document element records using a multiversion B+-tree instead. Consider a B+-tree indexing the element DNNs in the first version of a document. Each element is stored in this B+-tree as a record that contains the element id, tag, SPaR DNN (and range) as well as the actual data (text, image, etc) of this element. This B+-tree facilitates interesting queries on the document's first version. For example, if we know the SPaR range of chapter10 we can find all document elements in this chapter (a range search). Furthermore, the full document can be reconstructed by simply following the leaf pages of this tree. As the document evolves through versions, new elements are added, updated or deleted. These changes can update the above B+-tree using the element DNNs. In order to answer queries over a multiversion document we need to maintain the multiple versions of this B+-tree.

Various multiversion B+-tree structures have been proposed [17, 3, 27]; here we consider the Multiversion B-tree (MVBT) [3] which has optimal asymptotic behavior for partial version retrievals and its code is readily available. The MVBT has the form of a directed graph with multiple roots. Associated with each root is a consecutive version interval. A root provides access to the portion of the structure valid for the root's version interval. While conceptually the MVBT maintains all versions of a given B+-tree, it does not store snapshots of these versions, since this would require large space. Instead, portions of the tree that remain unchanged through versions are shared between many versions. The MVBT uses space that is proportional to the number of version changes. A query requesting the elements in range R from version V_i is answered with effort proportional to r, the number of elements version V_i had in range R.

Below we compare the choice of MVBT against UBCC for the data storage organization. An advantage of the MVBT is that it offers partial version retrievals, too. The MVBT also uses a notion of page usefulness. However, the page copies are more elaborate than in UBCC, since the MVBT maintains also the total order among all elements valid for a given version. As a result, each new page in the MVBT needs to preallocate some free space for future elements that may be added in this page. This implies that the space utilization of the MVBT is higher than UBCC. Moreover, the MVBT copies a page easier than the UBCC. This becomes important since the document element records are usually large (since they contain the element's data as well).

Full-index Implementation. The choice of the access method needed to implement the *full-index* is affected by the choice of the storage organization. If the

MVBT is used as the main storage organization, it serves as the full-index as well. Since the actual data records are stored at the leaves of this MVBT, it corresponds to a "primary" index. If the UBCC data organization is chosen, an additional index is needed so as to provide partial version retrievals. The leaf pages of this additional index will store element DNNs (and ranges) and pointers to the actual document element records in the UBCC pages. Hence it corresponds to a "secondary" index structure; furthermore, it is a dense index since all the element DNNs that exist in UBCC records appear also at the leaves of this index. As a result, a MVBT secondary dense index can be used to implement the full-index. Various optimizations on this combination of UBCC and MVBT can be applied as discussed in subsection 4.1.

We also propose an alternative that combines UBCC with a sparse secondary index, that indexes the range of element DNNs in each UBCC page. These ranges correspond to intervals and they may be updated as elements are added/updated in the page. To answer a range retrieval query, the index should identify the UBCC pages with range intervals that intersect the query range at the given version. Hence, this index must support multiversion interval intersection queries. The *Multiversion R-tree (MVRT)* [13, 26] is such an index. Like the MVBT, the MVRT conceptually maintains many versions of an ephemeral R-tree. We note that this MVRT is a sparse index: it does not store the element DNNs; rather, the ranges of page DNNs are stored. As a result, using the MVRT to implement the full-index will result in a much smaller structure.

Tag-index Implementation. A tag-index is used for each list tag, indexing the DNNs of all document elements using this tag. Since the actual element records are physically stored using the UBCC or the MVBT, each tag-index is a secondary dense index. To support partial version retrievals a MVBT or its variants can be used to implement a tag-index.

4.1 UBCC with Dense Secondary MVBT

Structures. When a new version is created, its updates are first applied on the document element records. Using these updates, the UBCC strategy may result into page copying. The alive records from the copied pages as well as the newly inserted document element records are first ordered by DNN. The ordered records are then placed in UBCC pages. Each update is also applied to the dense MVBT index. (A record copy is managed as the logical deletion of the previous record followed by a newly inserted record pointing to the record's new position in UBCC).

A partial version retrieval is accomplished by searching the MVBT using the given DNN range and version number. For all MVBT records found their pointers to the UBCC pages are followed to access the actual document element.

An interesting optimization is possible. First, note that in the above scheme, the version lifespan for a document element is kept in both the UBCC file and in the MVBT records. Second, when an element is updated as deleted the UBCC page that contains it is brought into main memory so as to change the record's lifespan. In the proposed optimization the version lifespans are kept in the MVBT index only. This saves space in the UBCC, and, saves I/O during element updates since the UBCC pages do not need to be accessed.

Nevertheless, when a UBCC page becomes useless in the optimized scheme, we need to know which of its records are still alive. This is implemented by a (main-memory) hashing scheme that stores the UBCC pages that are currently useful. The scheme is implemented on the page ids. For each useful page, the hashing scheme stores a record that contains: (UBCC page-id, current page usefulness, list of alive DNNs). The "current page usefulness" is a counter that maintains the number of alive records in the page. The "list of alive DNNs" lists the DNNs of these alive records. This hashing scheme is easily maintainable as records are updated/inserted.

4.2 UBCC with Sparse Secondary MVRT

A difference from the previous approach is that the MVRT is used as a sparse index. Hence, the element lifespans are kept in the UBCC records. Moreover, to facilitate fast updates a hashing scheme that stores the currently alive document elements is implemented. For each alive element, the hashing scheme stores a record: (DNN, UBCC page-id), where the page-id corresponds to the UBCC page that stores this element. Element updates are then processed by first consulting this hashing scheme.

When a UBCC page becomes full, its DNN range is computed and inserted in the MVRT. In particular, the MVRT record contains: (DNN range, lifespan, UBCC page-id). This range is the largest DNN range this page will ever have since no new records can be added in it. While records are logically deleted from this page its DNN range may decrease. However, to save update processing, the MVRT stores the largest DNN range for every page. When a UBCC page becomes useless, the MVRT updates the lifespan of this page's record. This update process may result in accessing a page which intersects the query DNN range but contains no alive element for the query version. However, in our experimental performance the savings in update were very drastic to justify few irrelevant page accesses at query time.

Special attention is needed when reporting the answer to a partial version retrieval. In particular, elements in the query range must be reported in DNN order. One straightforward approach is to find all elements in the query answer and sort them. A better approach is to utilize the fact that data pages created in the same version have their elements in relative DNN order (since new elements and coped elements are first sorted before stored in UBCC pages). Hence the following sort-merge approach is possible: (1) use the records retrieved from the MVRT to group the UBCC page references by the V_{start} version in their lifespan, then (2) treat each group of data pages as a sorted list of objects and merge them using a standard sort-merge algorithm. With enough memory buffer a single scan of the data pages is sufficient.

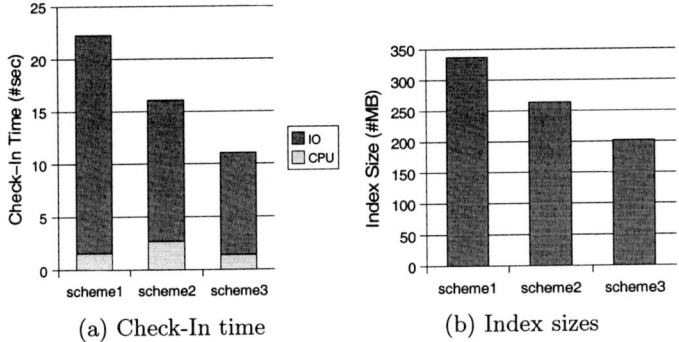

Fig. 3. Comparing the check-in time and the index sizes

5 Performance

We present results comparing the performance of the three choices for data organization and full-index implementation. Scheme 1 uses a single dense primary MVBT, scheme 2 uses UBCC plus a dense secondary MVBT (section 4.1), while scheme 3 uses UBCC plus a sparse MVRT index (section 4.2). The usefulness in both UBCC based schemes was set to 0.5.

The schemes were implemented in C++ using GNU compilers. The programs were run on a Sun Enterprise 250 Server machine with two 300MHz UltraSPARC-II processors using Solaris 2.8. We used a 20GB Seagate disk. To compare the performance of the various algorithms we used the estimated running time. This estimate is commonly obtained by multiplying the number of I/Os by the average disk page read access time, and then adding the measured CPU time. The CPU cost was measured by adding the amounts of time spent in *user* and *system* mode as returned by the *getrusage* system call. We assume all disk I/Os are random which was counted as 10ms. We used a 16KB page size. For all the three schemes we used the LRU buffering where the buffer size was 100 pages.

We present results using a representative dataset. The representative dataset contains 1000 versions. The initial version has 10,000 objects, and an object occupies on average 200 bytes. Each later version was generated by performing 10% changes to the previous version, where about half of the changes were deletions and the other half were insertions. Following the *80/20 rule*, we assume that 80% of the changes took place in 20% of the document.

For the scheme that uses UBCC and the dense MVBT index, we implemented the optimized approach which keeps the element lifespans in the MVBT and utilizes the alive-page hashing (see section 4.1). This optimization led to a drastic 35% improvement in version check-in time when compared to the original approach. (The space improvement was less, around 1%, while the query times of both approaches were equivalent.)

Figure 3a compares the check-in time per version of the three schemes, while figure 3b compares the index sizes. The version check-in time measures the total

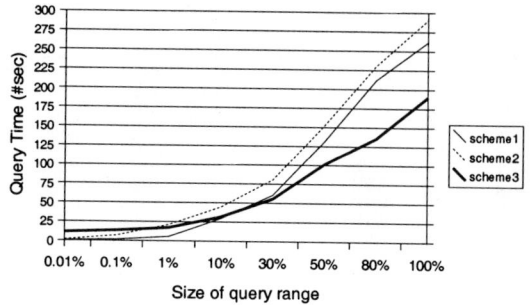

Fig. 4. Query performance varying length of DNN range.

time to finish all the updates within a given version. Scheme 3 has the fastest check-in time and uses the least index size. For the version check-in time, scheme 2 spent less I/O, but more CPU time than scheme 1. The MVBT used in scheme 1 stores the actual document elements in its leaf pages. Its update algorithms can trigger a copy more often than the UBCC. As a result, scheme 1 uses more update time and index space than scheme 2. Even though scheme 2 has also a secondary MVBT, this index is much smaller (since it does not contain the actual objects) and does not affect the relative performance. Scheme 3 is better than scheme 2 both in check-in time and in index size, since scheme 3 uses the sparse index (MVRT) which is much smaller than the dense index (MVBT) used in scheme 2.

To evaluate the performance of various queries, we measured the total execution time of 10 randomly generated queries with fixed-length DNN ranges. The performance is shown in figure 4. When the query DNN range is large, scheme 3 is the best. The reason is that a large query DNN range is like a full version retrieval, where all the UBCC pages that are useful at the query version need to be examined. In this case, scheme 3 is the most efficient since it spends the least time in finding these UBCC pages (as it uses a smaller sparse index). For small query DNN ranges, however, the other schemes are faster. The reason is that scheme 3 may check some UBCC pages which do not contain any qualifying object, while this is not the case for schemes 1 and 2. Scheme 1 is the best for small DNN ranges since it directly finds the qualifying objects. Scheme 2 has a little worse query time than scheme 1, since the actual objects and the references to these objects are maintained in two different structures and thus they have different clustering.

Overall, when considering both the check-in time, space as well as query time, the UBCC plus sparse MVRT (scheme 3) showed the most robust performance.

6 Conclusions and Future Work

As many applications make use of multiversion XML documents, the problem of managing repositories of such documents and supporting efficient queries on such repositories poses interesting challenges for database researchers. Foremost among these, is the efficient execution of complex queries, such as the path expression queries which are now part of the XML query languages being proposed as standards [29, 30]. In this paper, we investigated the problem of supporting these complex queries on multiversion documents. To solve this problem, we proposed solutions based on three main ideas:

- a durable numbering scheme for the document elements to capture their position and parent/child relations in a version-independent fashion,
- a version storage and clustering scheme based on the notion of page usefulness, and
- various multidimensional indexing schemes such multiversion B-trees and R-trees.

We first showed that, using this approach, complex path expression queries can be reduced to partial version retrieval queries; then, we evaluated alternative indexing and clustering schemes for the efficient execution of partial version retrieval queries. In addition to full version reconstruction, the proposed solution supports efficiently complex queries on version content, and queries involving the structure of the XML document (e.g., path expression queries).

Note that this paper assumes that there are no tag repetitions in the document tree paths. In that case, path queries involve join operations [16, 1]. We are currently investigating efficient ways to address multiversion path queries under tag repetitions. Other interesting problems, such as the generalization of XML query languages to determine document evolution and the optimization of such queries, will also be the topic of future investigations.

Acknowledgments

The authors would like to thank Bongki Moon for many useful discussions.

References

1. S. Al-Khalifa, H. V. Jagadish, N. Koudas, J. M. Patel, D. Srivastava and Y. Wu, "Structural Joins: A Primitive for Efficient XML Query Pattern Matching", *Proc. of ICDE*, 2002.
2. S. Abiteboul, D. Quass, J. McHugh, J. Widom and J. L. Wiener, "The Lorel Query Language for Semistructured Data", *Journal on Digital Libraries* 1(1), pp. 68-88, Apr 1997.
3. B. Becker, S. Gschwind, T. Ohler, B. Seeger and P. Widmayer, "An Asymptotically Optimal Multiversion B-Tree", *VLDB Journal* 5(4), pp. 264-275, 1996.
4. G. Cobena, S. Abiteboul and A. Marian, "XyDiff Tools Detecting changes in XML Documents", http://www-rocq.inria.fr/~cobena
5. S. Ceri, S. Comai, E. Damiani, P. Fraternali, S. Paraboschi and L. Tanca, "XML-GL: A Graphical Language for Querying and Restructuring XML", *Proc. of WWW Conf.*, pp. 93-109, 1999.
6. D. Chamberlin, J. Robie, D. Florescu, "Quilt: An XML Query Language for Heterogeneous Data Sources", *Proc. of WebDB*, 2000.

7. S. Chawathe, A. Rajaraman, H. Garcia-Molina and J. Widom, "Change Detection in Hierarchically Structured Information", *Proc. of SIGMOD*, 1996.
8. S.-Y. Chien, V.J. Tsotras and C. Zaniolo, "Version Management of XML Documents", *WebDB Workshop*, 2000.
9. S.-Y. Chien, V.J. Tsotras and C. Zaniolo, "Efficient Management of Multiversion Documents by Object Referencing", *Proc. of VLDB*, 2001.
10. S.-Y. Chien, V.J. Tsotras, C. Zaniolo, and D. Zhang, "Storing and Querying Multiversion XML Documents using Durable Node Numbers", *Proc. of WISE*, 2001.
11. A. Deutsch, M. Fernandez, D. Florescu, A. Levy and D. Suciu, "A Query Language for XML", *Proc. of WWW Conf.*, pp. 77-91, 1999.
12. R. H. Katz and E. Change, "Managing Change in Computer-Aided Design Databases", *Proc. of VLDB*, 1987.
13. A. Kumar, V. J. Tsotras and C. Faloutsos, "Designing Access Methods for bitemporal Databases", *IEEE TKDE* 10(1), pp. 1-20, 1998.
14. M. Fernandez and D. Suciu, "Optimizing Regular Path Expressions Using Graph Schemas", *Proc. of ICDE*, 1998.
15. J. McHugh and J. Widom, "Query optimization for XML", *Proc. of VLDB*, 1999.
16. Q. Li and B. Moon, "Indexing and Querying XML Data for Regular Path Expressions", *Proc. of VLDB*, 2001.
17. D. Lomet and B. Salzberg, "Access Methods for Multiversion Data", *Proc. of SIGMOD*, pp. 315-324, 1989.
18. A. Marian, S. Abiteboul, G. Cobena and L. Mignet, "Change-Centric Management of Versions in An XML Warehouse", *Proc. of VLDB*, 2001.
19. G. Ozsoyoglu and R. Snodgrass, "Temporal and Real-Time Databases: A Survey", *IEEE TKDE* 7(4), pp. 513-532, 1995.
20. M. J. Rochkind, "The Source Code Control System", *IEEE Tran. on Software Engineering* SE-1(4), pp. 364-370, Dec 1975.
21. B. Salzberg and V. J. Tsotras, "Comparison of Access Methods for Time-Evolving Data", *ACM Computing Surveys* 31(2), pp. 158-221, 1999.
22. J. Shanmugasundaram, K. Tufte, G. He, C. Zhang, D. J. DeWitt and J. F. Naughton, "Relational Databases for Querying XML Documents: Limitations and Opportunities" *Proc. of VLDB*, pp. 302-314, 1999.
23. W. F. Tichy, "RCS–A System for Version Control", *Software–Practice&Experience* 15(7), pp. 637-654, July 1985.
24. F. Tian, D. J. DeWitt, J. Chen and C. Zhang, "The Design and Performance Evaluation of Various XML Storage Strategies", http://www.cs.wisc.edu/niagara/Publications.html
25. V.J. Tsotras and N. Kangelaris, "The Snapshot Index: An I/O-Optimal Access Method for Timeslice Queries", *Information Systems* 20(3), pp. 237-260, 1995.
26. Y. Tao and D. Papadias, "MV3R-Tree: A Spatio-Temporal Access Method for Timestamp and Interval Queries", *Proc. of VLDB*, pp. 431-440, 2001.
27. P. Varman and R. Verma, "An Efficient Multiversion Access Structure", *IEEE TKDE* 9(3), pp. 391-409, 1997.
28. webdav, WWW Distributed Authoring and Versioning, last modified: Jul 31, 2001. http://www.ietf.org/ html.charters/webdav-charter.html
29. World Wide Web Consortium, "XML Path Language (XPath)", version 1.0, Nov 16, 1999. http:// www.w3.org/TR/xpath.html
30. World Wide Web Consortium, "XQuery 1.0: An XML Query Language", W3C Working Draft Jun 7, 2001 (work in progress). http://www.w3.org/TR/xquery/

Approximate Processing
of Multiway Spatial Joins in Very Large Databases

Dimitris Papadias[1] and Dinos Arkoumanis[2]

[1] Department of Computer Science
Hong Kong University of Science and Technology
Clear Water Bay, Hong Kong
dimitris@cs.ust.hk

[2] Dept of Electrical and Computer Engineering
National Technical University of Athens
Greece, 15773
dinosar@dbnet.ece.ntua.gr

Abstract. Existing work on multiway spatial joins focuses on the retrieval of all exact solutions with no time limit for query processing. Depending on the query and data properties, however, exhaustive processing of multiway spatial joins can be prohibitively expensive due to the exponential nature of the problem. Furthermore, if there do not exist any exact solutions, the result will be empty even though there may exist solutions that match the query very closely. These shortcomings motivate the current work, which aims at the retrieval of the best possible (exact or approximate) solutions within a time threshold, since fast retrieval of approximate matches is the only way to deal with the ever increasing amounts of multimedia information in several real time systems. We propose various techniques that combine local and evolutionary search with underlying indexes to prune the search space. In addition to their usefulness as standalone methods for approximate query processing, the techniques can be combined with systematic search to enhance performance when the goal is retrieval of the best solutions.

1. Introduction

Several specialized access methods have been proposed for the efficient manipulation of multi-dimensional data. Among the most popular methods, are the R-tree [G84] and its variations, currently used in several commercial products (e.g., Oracle, Informix). R-trees are extensions of B-trees in two or more dimensions. Figure 1 shows an image containing objects $r_1,..., r_8$, and the corresponding R-tree assuming capacity of three entries per node. Leaf entries store the minimum bounding rectangles (MBRs) of the actual objects, and nodes are created by grouping entries in a way that preserves proximity, and avoids excessive overlap between nodes. In Figure 1, objects r_1, r_2, and r_3, are grouped together in node e_1, objects r_4, r_5, and r_6 in node e_2, etc.

In this work we consider multimedia databases involving maps/images containing a large number (in the order of 10^5-10^6) of objects with well-defined semantics (e.g., maps created through topographic surveys, VLSI designs, CAD diagrams). Each map/image is not stored as a single entity, but information about objects is kept in relational tables with a spatial index for each type of objects covering the same area (e.g., an R-tree for the roads of California, another for residential areas etc). This facilitates the processing of traditional spatial selections (e.g., find all roads inside a query window) and spatial joins [BKS93] (e.g., find all pairs of intersecting roads and railroad lines in California).

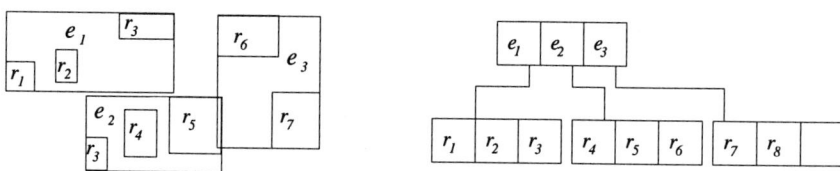

Fig. 1. R-tree example

A multiway spatial join is the natural extension of pairwise joins, combining more than two inputs (e.g., find all triplets <c,r,a> of cities c, rivers r and industrial areas a such that c is *crossed by* r which also *crosses a*). Multiway spatial joins constitute a special form of content based retrieval, which focuses on spatial relations rather than visual characteristics such as color, shape or texture. In accordance with related work on content based retrieval, query processing mechanisms should be able to handle approximate retrieval using some measure of similarity. Unfortunately existing techniques (presented in the next section) only deal with exact retrieval, i.e., if there does not exist some stored configuration matching exactly the query constraints, the result will be empty (even if there exist very close matches). Furthermore, these techniques assume that there is unlimited time for query processing. This assumption may not always be valid, given the exponential nature of the problem and the huge amounts of multimedia information in several applications.

This paper deals with these problems by proposing methods that can handle approximate retrieval of multiway spatial joins under limited time. The methods combine well known search heuristics, such as local and evolutionary search, with spatial indexing (R-trees) in order to quickly locate good, but not necessarily optimal, solutions. In addition to their usefulness as standalone methods, they can be employed in conjunction with systematic search to speed up retrieval of the optimal solutions by orders of magnitude. The rest of the paper is structured as follows: section 2 overviews related work in the context of multiway spatial joins and content-based retrieval; sections 3, 4 and 5, present algorithms that combine R-trees with local search, guided local search and genetic algorithms, respectively. Section 6 contains the experimental evaluation and section 7 concludes with a discussion about future work.

2. Definitions and Related Work

Formally, a multiway spatial join can be expressed as follows: Given n multi-dimensional datasets $D_1, D_2, ... D_n$ and a *query* Q, where Q_{ij} is the spatial predicate that should hold between D_i and D_j, retrieve all n-tuples $\{(r_{1,w},..,r_{i,x},..,r_{j,y},..,r_{n,z}) \mid \forall\ i,j:$

$r_{i,x} \in D_i$, $r_{j,y} \in D_j$ and $r_{i,x} Q_{ij} r_{j,y}$}. Such a query can be represented by a graph where nodes correspond to datasets and edges to join predicates. Equivalently, the graph can be viewed as a *constraint network* [DM94] where the nodes are problem variables, and edges are binary spatial constraints. In the sequel we use the terms variable/dataset and constraint/join condition interchangeably. Following the common methodology in the spatial database literature we assume that the standard join condition is *overlap* (*intersect, non-disjoint*). Figure 2 illustrates two query graphs joining three datasets and two solution tuples $(r_{1,1}, r_{2,1}, r_{3,1})$ such that $r_{i,1}$ is an object in D_i. Figure 2a corresponds to a chain query (e.g., "find all cities *crossed by* a river which *crosses* an industrial area"), while 2b to a clique ("the industrial area should also intersect the city").

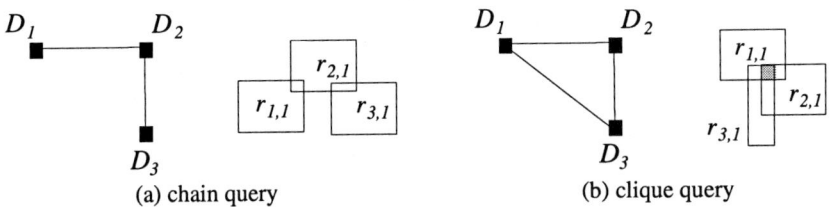

Fig. 2. Examples of multiway spatial joins

We use the notation $v_i \leftarrow r_{i,x}$ to express that variable v_i is instantiated to rectangle $r_{i,x}$ (which belongs to domain D_i). A *binary instantiation* $\{v_i \leftarrow r_{i,x}, v_j \leftarrow r_{j,y}\}$ is *inconsistent* if there is a join condition Q_{ij}, but $r_{i,x}$ and $r_{j,y}$ do not *overlap*. A solution is a set of n instantiations $\{v_1 \leftarrow r_{1,w}, .., v_i \leftarrow r_{i,x}, .., v_j \leftarrow r_{j,y}, .., v_n \leftarrow r_{n,z}\}$ which, for simplicity, can be described as a tuple of values $(r_{1,w}, .., r_{i,x}, .., r_{j,y}, .., r_{n,z})$ since the order of variables is implied. The *inconsistency degree* of a solution is equal to the total number of inconsistent binary instantiations, i.e., the number of join conditions violated. A solution with zero inconsistency degree is *exact*; otherwise it is *approximate*. The lower the inconsistency degree, the higher the *similarity* of the solution.

Approximate retrieval of the solutions with the highest similarity (i.e., solutions with the minimum number of inconsistencies / join condition violations) is desirable in several applications (e.g., architectural and VLSI design), where queries often involve numerous variables and the database may not contain configurations that match all the query constraints. Furthermore, since the problem is in general exponential, even if there exist exact solutions, there may not be enough processing time or computational resources to find them.

As in the case of relational joins, multiway spatial joins can be processed by combining pairwise join algorithms. The *pairwise join method (PJM)* [MP99] considers a join order that is expected to result in the minimum cost (in terms of page accesses). However, PJM (and any method based on pairwise algorithms) cannot be extended for approximate retrieval since if no exact solution exists, the results of some joins should contain non-intersecting pairs of objects. Two alternative methodologies for multiway spatial joins, motivated by algorithms for constraint satisfaction problems (CSPs), were proposed in [PMT99]. *Synchronous traversal (ST)* starts from the roots of the R-trees and finds combinations of entries that satisfy the query constraints. For each such combination the algorithm is recursively called, taking the references to the underlying nodes as parameters, until the leaf level is reached. The calculation of combinations of the qualifying nodes for each level is expensive, as their number can be as high as C^n (where C is the node capacity, and n the number of query variables). In order to avoid exhaustive search of all combinations, the authors use search algorithms and optimization techniques.

The second methodology, called *window reduction* (*WR*) integrates the ideas of backtracking and index nested loop algorithms. When the first variable gets a value $v_1 \leftarrow r_{1,w}$, this rectangle ($r_{1,w}$) is used as a query window to find qualifying entries in the second dataset. If such entries are found, the second variable is instantiated to one of them, i.e., $v_2 \leftarrow r_{2,w}$. The algorithm proceeds forward using the values of instantiated variables as query windows. When a window query yields no results, the algorithm backtracks to the previous variable and tries another value for it. Although *ST* and *WR* can be applied for retrieval of approximate solutions, they are not suitable for query processing within a time limit (see experimental evaluation), since they may initially spend a lot of time in regions with low quality solutions, failing to quickly find some good ones.

Also related to this paper, is previous work on spatial (or configuration) similarity retrieval. The corresponding queries describe some prototype configuration and the goal is to retrieve arrangements of objects matching the input exactly or approximately. Thus, these queries can be thought of as approximate multiway spatial joins with arbitrary predicates. Petrakis and Faloutsos [PF97] solve such problems by mapping images (datasets) and queries into high-dimensional points, which are then indexed by R-trees. Similarity retrieval is processed by nearest neighbor search. The method, however, assumes medical images with about 10 objects and cannot be employed for even the smallest datasets normally found in spatial databases. In general, techniques based on high-dimensional indexing and nearest neighbor search are not applicable due to the huge number of dimensions required to represent the problem.

A number of techniques are based on several variations of 2D strings [LYC92, LH92], which encode the arrangement of objects on each dimension into sequential structures. Every database image is indexed by a 2D string; queries are also transformed to 2D strings, and similarity retrieval is performed by applying appropriate string matching algorithms [CSY87]. Although this methodology can handle larger datasets (experimental evaluations usually include images with about 100 objects) it is still not adequate for real-life spatial datasets.

In order to deal with similarity retrieval under limited time, Papadias et al., [PMK+99] use heuristics based on local search, simulated annealing and genetic algorithms. Unlike *ST* and *WR*, which search systematically, guaranteeing to find the best solutions, these heuristics are non-systematic (i.e., random). The evaluation of [PMK+99] suggests that local search, the most efficient algorithm, can retrieve good solutions even for large problems (images with about 10^5 objects). In the next section we propose heuristics based on similar principles, for inexact retrieval of multiway spatial joins. However, unlike [PMK+99] where the algorithms were a straightforward adaptation of local and evolutionary search for similarity retrieval, the proposed methods take advantage of the spatial structure of the problem and existing indexes to achieve high performance.

For the rest of the paper we consider that all datasets are indexed by R*-trees [BKSS90] on minimum bounding rectangles, and we deal with intersection joins. We start with indexed local search in the next section, followed by guided indexed local search and a spatial evolutionary algorithm.

3. Indexed Local Search

The search space of multiway spatial joins can be considered as a graph, where each solution corresponds to a node having some inconsistency degree. If all n datasets have the same cardinality N, the graph has N^n nodes. Two nodes/solutions are connected through an edge if one can be derived from the other by changing the instantiation of a single variable. Excluding its current assignment, a variable can take $N-1$ values; thus, each solution has $n \cdot (N-1)$ neighbors. A node that has lower inconsistency degree than all its neighbors, is a *local maximum*. Notice that a local maximum is not necessarily a global maximum since there may exist solutions with higher similarity in other regions of the graph.

Local search methods start with a random solution called *seed*, and then try to reach a local maximum by performing uphill moves, i.e., by visiting neighbors with higher similarity. When they reach a local maximum (from where uphill moves are not possible) they restart the same process from a different seed until the time limit is exhausted. Throughout this process the best solutions are kept. Algorithms based on this general concept have been successfully employed for a variety of problems. *Indexed local search (ILS)* also applies this idea, but uses R*-trees to improve the solutions. The pseudocode of the algorithm is illustrated in Figure 3.

```
Indexed Local Search
WHILE NOT (Time limit) {
  S := random seed
  WHILE NOT(Local_Maximum) {
        determine worst variable vᵢ
        value := find best value (Root of tree Rᵢ, vᵢ)
        IF better value THEN S = S ∧ { vᵢ ← value }
        IF S is the best solution found so far THEN bestSolution=S
  } /* END WHILE NOT Local_Maximum */
} /* END WHILE NOT Time Limit */
```

Fig. 3. Indexed local search

Motivated by conflict minimization algorithms [MJP+92], we choose to re-instantiate the "worst" variable, i.e., the one whose current instantiation violates the most join conditions. In case of a tie we select the one that participates in the smallest number of satisfied constraints. If the worst variable cannot be improved, the algorithm considers the second worst; if it cannot be improved either, the third worst, and so on. If one variable can be improved, the next step will consider again the new worst one; otherwise, if all variables are exhausted with no improvement, the current solution is considered a local maximum.

Consider, for example the query of Figure 4a and the approximate solution of Figure 4b. The inconsistency degree of the solution is 3 since the conditions $Q_{1,4}$, $Q_{2,3}$, and $Q_{3,4}$ are violated (in Figure 4b satisfied conditions are denoted with bold lines and violated ones with thin lines). Variables v_3 and v_4 participate in two violations each; v_3, however, participates in one satisfied condition, so v_4 is chosen for re-assignment. *Find best value* will find the best possible value for the variable to be re-instantiated, i.e., the rectangle that satisfies the maximum number of join conditions given the assignments of the other variables. In the example of Figure 4b, the best value for v_4 should overlap both $r_{1,1}$ and $r_{3,1}$. If such a rectangle does not exist, the next better choice should intersect either $r_{1,1}$, or $r_{3,1}$.

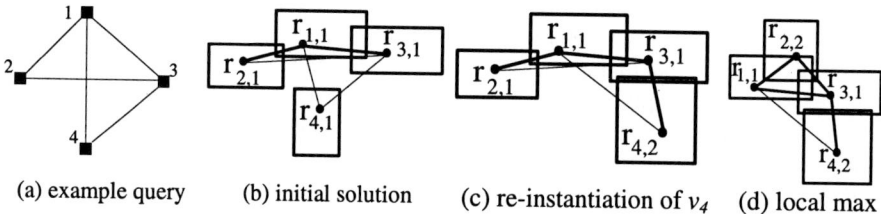

(a) example query (b) initial solution (c) re-instantiation of v_4 (d) local max

Fig. 4. Example of ILS

The pseudo-code for *find best value* is illustrated in Figure 5; the variable to be re-instantiated is v_i. Essentially this is like a *branch-and-bound window query*, where there exist multiple windows and the goal is to retrieve the rectangle that intersects most of them. The windows are the assignments of all variables v_j such that Q_{ij}=True (for the current example there exist two windows $w_1=r_{1,1}$ and $w_3=r_{3,1}$).

```
maxConditions=0
bestValue=∅

Find best value (Node N, integer i)
FOR EACH entry eₓ of N
   FOR EACH Qᵢⱼ such that Qᵢⱼ = True
      IF eₓ intersects wⱼ THEN conditionsₓ=conditionsₓ+1
Sort all entries eₓ such that conditionsₓ>0 with respect to conditionsₓ
IF N intermediate node
   FOR each eₓ in the sorted list
      IF conditionsₓ > maxConditions THEN
             Find best value (eₓ, i)
ELSE //leaf node
   FOR each eₓ in the sorted list
             IF conditionsₓ > maxConditions THEN
                   maxConditions=conditionsₓ
                   bestValue=eₓ
```

Fig. 5. *Find best value* algorithm

The algorithm starts from the root of the corresponding tree and sorts the entries according to the conditions they satisfy (i.e., how many windows they overlap). The entries with the maximum number are visited first because their descendants are more likely to intersect more windows. At the leaf level, an entry is compared with the maximum number of conditions found so far (*maxConditions*). If it is better, then this is kept as *bestValue*, and *maxConditions* is updated accordingly. Notice that if an intermediate node satisfies the same or a smaller number of conditions than *maxConditions*, it cannot contain any better solution and is not visited.

Figure 6 illustrates this process for the example of Figures 4a and b. *Find best value* will retrieve the rectangle (in the dataset corresponding to v_4) that intersects the maximum number of windows, in this case $w_1=r_{1,1}$ and $w_3=r_{3,1}$. Suppose that the node (of R-tree R_4) considered has three entries e_1, e_2 and e_3; e_1 is visited first because it overlaps both query windows. However, no good values are found inside it so *maxConditions* remains zero. The next entry to be visited is e_2 which contains a rectangle ($r_{4,2}$) that intersects w_3. *MaxConditions* is updated to 1 and e_3 will not be visited since it may not contain values better than $r_{4,2}$ (it only satisfies one condition). $r_{4,2}$ becomes the new value of v_4 and the inconsistency degree of the new solution (Figure 4c) is 2 ($Q_{3,4}$ is now satisfied). At the next step (Figure 4d), a better value (let $r_{2,2}$) is found for v_2 using *find best value* (R_2,2). At this point, the algorithm reaches a local maximum. The violation of $Q_{1,4}$ cannot be avoided since, according to Figure 6, there is no object in the fourth dataset that intersects both $r_{1,1}$ and $r_{3,1}$.

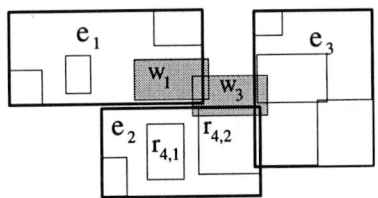

Fig. 6. Example of *find best value*

4. Guided Indexed Local Search

There have been many attempts to include some deterministic features in local search and achieve a more systematic exploration of the problem space. "Memory" mechanisms guarantee that the algorithm will not find the same nodes repeatedly by keeping a list of visited nodes [GL97]. These nodes become forbidden (*tabu*) in the graph, forcing the algorithms to move to new neighborhoods. A limitation of this approach for the current problem is the huge number of nodes, since there exist N^n solutions a significant percentage of which may be visited. Other approaches [DTW+94] try to avoid revisiting the same maxima by storing their features (e.g., the route length in traveling salesman problem). Solutions matching these features, are not rejected, but "punished". As a result, the probability of finding the same maximum multiple times is decreased. The trade-off is that unrelated nodes that share features with visited local maxima are avoided too, and good solutions may be missed.

Guided indexed local search (*GILS*) combines the above ideas by keeping a memory, not of all solutions visited, but of the variable assignments at local maxima. When a local maximum $(r_{1,w},...,r_{i,x},...,r_{j,y},..., r_{n,z})$ is found, some of the assignments $v_1 \leftarrow r_{1,w}, ..., v_i \leftarrow r_{i,x}, .., v_j \leftarrow r_{j,y}, .., v_n \leftarrow r_{n,z}$ get a penalty. In particular, *GILS* penalizes the assignments with the minimum penalties so far; e.g., if $v_1 \leftarrow r_{1,w}$ already has a punishment from a previous maximum (while the others do not), only the other assignments are penalized in order to avoid over-punishing $v_1 \leftarrow r_{1,w}$.

The code for *GILS* (Figure 7) is similar to *ILS* since both algorithms re-instantiate the worst variable for improving the current solution. Their difference is that *GILS* only generates one random seed during its execution and has some additional code for penalty assignment. The penalty is used to increase the inconsistency degree of the current local maximum, and to a lesser to degree of solutions that include a subset of the assignments. In particular, for its similarity computations *GILS* applies the *effective inconsistency degree* which is computed by adding the penalties

$$\lambda \cdot \sum_{i=1}^{n} \text{penalty}(v_i \leftarrow r_{i,x})$$

to the actual inconsistency degree (i.e., the number of condition violations) of a solution. The *penalty weight parameter* λ is a constant that tunes the relative importance of penalties and controls the effect of memory in search. A large value of λ will punish significantly local maxima and their neighbors causing the algorithm to quickly visit other areas of the graph. A small value will achieve better (local) exploration of the neighborhoods around maxima at the expense of global graph exploration.

```
Guided Indexed Local Search
S := random seed
WHILE NOT (Time limit) {
    WHILE NOT(Local_Maximum) {
        determine worst variable vᵢ
        value := find best value (Root of tree Rᵢ, vᵢ)
        IF better value THEN S = S ∧ {vᵢ ← value}
        IF S is the best solution found so far THEN bestSolution=S
    /* END WHILE NOT Local_Maximum */
    P = among the assignments of the current local maximum, select the
    ones with the minimum penalty
    FOR EACH assignment  vᵢ ← rᵢ,ₓ in  P
        penalty(vᵢ ← rᵢ,ₓ)= penalty(vᵢ ← rᵢ,ₓ) + 1
/* END WHILE NOT Time limit */
```

Fig. 7. Guided indexed local search

The results of this punishment process are:
- search does not restart from various random seeds but continues from local maxima. This is because the penalty increases the effective inconsistency degree of the current local maximum (sometimes repeatedly) and eventually worse neighbors appear to be better and are followed by *GILS*. The intuition

behind this is to perform some downhill moves, expecting better local maxima in subsequent steps.
- solutions that share many common assignments with one or more local maxima have high effective inconsistency degrees and usually are not chosen during search. Thus, possible visits to the same regions of the search space are avoided.

Like *ILS*, *GILS* uses *find best value*, to select the new object for the variable to be re-instantiated. The process is modified in order to deal with penalties as follows: after the calculation of the inconsistency degree of a leaf object, the penalty value of this assignment is added, and compared with the best found so far. *Find best value* is identical with the one for *ILS* when it operates at intermediate nodes.

For small problems, the penalties are kept in a two dimensional ($n \cdot N$) array where the cell (i,j) stores the penalty of assigning the ith variable with the jth value in its domain ($v_i \leftarrow r_{i,j}$). This array is, in general, very sparse since only a small subset of the possible assignments are penalized (most of the cells contain zeros). For large problems, where there is not enough main memory to keep such an array, a hash table (which only stores the assignments with positive penalties) can be built in-memory.

5. Spatial Evolutionary Algorithm

Evolutionary algorithms are search methods based on the concepts of natural mutation and the survival of the fittest individuals. Before the search process starts, a set of *p* solutions (called initial population *P*) is initialized to form the first generation. Then, three genetic operations, *selection, crossover* and *mutation*, are repeatedly applied in order to obtain a population (i.e., a new set of solutions) with better characteristics. This set will constitute the next generation, at which the algorithm will perform the same actions and so on, until a stopping criterion is met. In this section we propose a *spatial evolutionary algorithm* (*SEA*) that takes advantage of spatial indexes and the problem structure to improve solutions.

Selection mechanism: This operation consists of two parts: *evaluation* and *offspring allocation*. Evaluation is performed by measuring the similarity of every solution; offspring generation then allocates to each solution, a number of offspring proportional to its similarity. Techniques for offspring allocation include *ranking, proportional selection, stochastic remainder* etc. The comparison of [BT96] suggests that the *tournament* method gives the best results for a variety of problems and we adopt it in our implementation. According to this technique, each solution S_i competes with a set of *T* random solutions in the generation. Among the *T*+1 solutions, the one with the highest similarity replaces S_i. After offspring allocation, the population contains multiple copies of the best solutions, while the worst ones are likely to disappear.

Crossover mechanism is the driving force of *exploration* in evolutionary algorithms. In the simplest approach [H75], pairs of solutions are selected randomly from the population. For each pair a *crossover point* is defined randomly, and the solutions beyond it are mutually exchanged with probability μ_c (*crossover rate*), producing two new solutions. The rationale is that after the exchange of genetic materials, the two newly generated solutions are likely to possess the good characteristics of their parents (*building-block hypothesis* [G89]). In our case randomly swapping assignments will most probably generate multiple condition violations. Especially for latter generations, where solutions may have reached high similarities, random crossover may lead to the removal of good solutions.

In order to limit the number of violations, we propose a variable crossover point c ($1 \leq c < n$) which is initially 1 and increases every g_c generations. When a solution S is chosen for crossover, c variables will retain their current assignments, while the remaining $n-c$ will get the assignments of another solution. A small value of c means that S will change dramatically after crossover, while a value close to n implies that only a small part will be affected (e.g., if $c=n-1$ only one variable will change its assignment). This leads to the desired result that during the early generations, crossover has a significant effect in generating variety in the population, but this effect diminishes with time in order to preserve good solutions.

Given the value of c, a greedy crossover mechanism uses a set X to store the c best variables in S, i.e., the ones that have relatively low inconsistency degrees and should not change their assignment during crossover. Initially variables are sorted according to the number of satisfied join conditions in S. In case of ties the variable with the smallest number of violations has higher priority. The first variable in the ordered list is inserted into X. From this point on, the variable inserted, is the one that satisfies the largest number of conditions with respect to variables already in X. Ties are resolved using the initial order. The process stops when c variables are in X. The rest of the variables are re-instantiated using the corresponding values of a another solution.

Figure 8 illustrates a solution where satisfied (violated) conditions are denoted with bold (thin) lines. Assume that $c=3$, meaning that three variables will keep their current assignments. The initial sorting will produce the order ($v_6, v_4, v_2, v_1, v_3, v_5$). The insertion order in X is v_6, then v_4 (because of $Q_{4,6}$) and finally v_1 (because of $Q_{1,6}$ and $Q_{1,4}$). Intuitively this is a very good splitting because the sub-graph involving v_1, v_4 and v_6 is already solved. Now another solution is chosen at random and v_2, v_3 and v_5 obtain the instantiations of this solution.

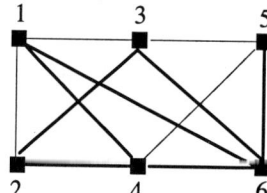

Variable	Conditions Satisfied	Conditions Violated
v_6	4	0
v_4	3	1
v_2	2	1
v_1	2	2
v_3	2	2
v_5	1	2

Fig. 8. Example of solution splitting during crossover

Mutation mechanism: Although it is not the primary search operation and sometimes is omitted, mutation is very important for *SEA* and the only operation that uses the index. At each generation, mutation is applied to every solution in the population with probability μ_m, called the *mutation rate*. The process is similar to *ILS*; the worst variable is chosen and it gets a new value using *find best value*. Thus, in our case mutation can only have positive results.

Figure 9 illustrates the pseudo-code for *SEA*. The algorithm first computes the similarity of the solutions, and then performs offspring allocation (using the tournament approach), crossover and mutation (following the methods described above) in this order. During the initial generations crossover plays an important role in the formation of new solutions. As time passes its role gradually diminishes and the algorithm behaves increasingly like *ILS*, since mutation becomes the main operation that alters solutions.

```
Spatial Evolutionary Algorithm
P := generate initial set of solutions {S₁,..,Sp}
WHILE NOT (Time limit) {
  compute crossover point c /* increase c every gc generations */
  FOR EACH Si in P /*evaluation */
    evaluate Si
    IF Si is the best solution found so far THEN keep Si
  FOR EACH Si in P /* offspring allocation */
    compare Si with T other random solutions in P
    replace Si with the best among the T+1 solutions
  FOR EACH Si in P /*crossover*/
    with probability μc change Si as follows
    determine set of c variables to keep their current values
    re-instantiate the remaining variables using their values in an-
    other solution Sj (Sj ∈ P)
  FOR EACH Si in P  /* mutation */
    with probability μm change  Si as follows
    determine worst variable vk
    vk ← find best value (Root of tree Rk, vk)
}/* END WHILE NOT Time limit */
```

Fig. 9. Spatial evolutionary algorithm

Unlike *ILS* (which does not include any problem specific parameters), and *GILS* (which only contains λ), *SEA* involves numerous parameters, namely, the number T of solutions participating in the tournament, the crossover (μ_c) and mutation (μ_m) rates, the number of generations g_c during which the crossover point remains constant, and the number p of solutions in each population. Furthermore, these parameters are interrelated in the sense that the optimal value for one depends on the rest. Careful tuning of the parameters is essential for the good performance of *SEA*, and evolutionary algorithms in general [G86].

Based on extensive experiments (described in the long version of this paper [PA]) we chose the following set of parameters to be used in the subsequent experimental comparison: $\lambda=10^{-10} \cdot s$, $T=0.05 \cdot s$, $\mu_c= 0.6$, $g_c=10 \cdot s$, $\mu_m=1$, and $p=100 \cdot s$, where s is the size of a problem and corresponds to the number of bits required to represent the search space [CFG+98], i.e., the number of bits needed to express all possible solutions:

$$s = \log_2 \cdot \prod_{i=1}^{n} N_i$$

The tuning of parameters as a function of s, provides good performance independently of the problem size. Although even better parameter values could be obtained for specific problem instances, the above set achieves good overall performance for a variety of query graphs and datasets.

6. Experimental Evaluation

In this section we compare the proposed techniques, according to the common CSP and optimization methodology, using problem instances in the, so-called, *hard region*. It is a well known fact, that over-constrained problems do not have exact solutions and it is usually easy to determine this. On the other hand, under-constrained problems have numerous solutions which can be easily found. Between these types occurs a *phase transition*. Several studies on systematic [CA93] and non-systematic search [CFG+98] in a variety of combinatorial problems, experimentally demonstrate that the most difficult problems to solve are in the (hard) region defined by the phase transition. This hard region occurs when the expected number of exact solutions is small, i.e., in the range [1,10].

In order to generate such problem instances we need analytical formulae for the number of exact solutions. The general formula for the expected output size of multiway spatial joins is: $Sol = \#(\text{possible tuples}) \cdot Prob(\text{a tuple is a solution})$, where the first part of the product equals the cardinality of the Cartesian product of the n domains, while the second part corresponds to multiway join selectivity. According to [TSS98] the selectivity of a pairwise join over two uniform datasets D_i and D_j that cover a unit workspace is $(|r_i|+|r_j|)^2$, where $|r_i|$ is the average MBR extent in each dimension for D_i. For acyclic graphs, the pairwise probabilities of the join edges are independent and selectivity is the product of pairwise join selectivities. Thus, in this case the number of exact solutions is:

$$Sol = \prod_{i=1}^{n}|N_i| \cdot \prod_{\forall i,j: Q(i,j)=TRUE}(|r_i|+|r_j|)^2$$

When the query graph contains cycles, the pairwise selectivities are not independent anymore and the above equation is not accurate. Based on the fact that if a set of rectangles mutually overlap, then they must share a common area, [PMT99] propose the following estimation for *Sol*, in case of clique joins:

$$Sol = \prod_{i=1}^{n}|N_i| \cdot \left(\sum_{i=1}^{n}\prod_{\substack{j=1 \\ j \neq i}}^{n}|r_j|\right)^2$$

The above formulae are applicable for queries that can be decomposed to acyclic and clique graphs. For simplicity, in the rest of the paper we assume that all (uniform) datasets have the same cardinality N and MBR extents $|r|$. Under these assumptions, and by substituting average extents with density[1] values, the formulae can be trans-

---

[1] The density d of a dataset is the average number of rectangles that contain a point in the workspace. Equivalently, d can be expressed as the ratio of the sum of the areas of all rectangles over the area of the workspace. Density is related with the average rectangle extent $|r|$ by the equation $d = N \cdot |r|^2$ [TSS98]. Obviously the number of solutions increases with density

formed as follows. For acyclic queries, there are $n-1$ join conditions. Thus, the number of solutions is: $Sol = N^n \cdot (2 \cdot |r|)^{2 \cdot (n-1)} = N \cdot 2^{2 \cdot (n-1)} \cdot d^{n-1}$. Similarly, for cliques the number of solutions is: $Sol = N^n \cdot n^2 \cdot |r|^{2 \cdot (n-1)} = N \cdot n^2 \cdot d^{n-1}$. The importance of these equations is that by varying the density of the datasets we can create synthetic domains such that the number of solutions can be controlled. In case of acyclic graphs, for instance, the value of density that produces problems with one expected solution is $d = 1/4 \cdot \sqrt[n-1]{N}$, while for cliques this value is $d = 1/\sqrt[n-1]{N \cdot n^2}$.

The following experiments were executed by Pentium III PCs at 500 MHz with 512MB Ram. For each experimental result we measure the average of 100 executions for each query (since the heuristics are non-deterministic the same query/data combination usually gives different results in different executions). In order to have a uniform treatment of similarity, independent of the number of the constraints, similarity is computed as 1-(#violated constraints/#total constraints).

The first experiment measures the quality of the solutions retrieved by the algorithms as a function of the number of query variables. In particular we constructed uniform datasets of 100,000 objects and executed acyclic and clique queries involving 5, 10, 15, 20 and 25 variables[2]. Depending on the number of variables/datasets involved and the query type, we adjusted the density of the datasets so that the expected number of solutions is 1. The time of every execution is proportional to the query size and set to $10 \cdot n$ seconds. Figure 10a illustrates the similarity of the best solution retrieved by the algorithms as a function of n, for chain and clique queries (average of 100 executions). The numbers in italics (top row) show the corresponding density values.

The second experiment studies the quality of the solutions retrieved over time. Since all algorithms start with random solutions which probably have very low similarities, during the initial steps of their execution there is significant improvement. As time passes the algorithms reach a *convergence point* where further improvement is very slow because a good solution has already been found and it is difficult for the algorithms to locate a better one. In order to measure how quickly this point is reached, we used the data sets produced for the 15-variable case and allowed the algorithms to run for 40 (chains) and 120 (cliques) seconds. Since chain queries are under-constrained, it is easier for the algorithms to quickly find good solutions. On the other hand, the large number of constraints in cliques necessitates more processing time. Figure 10b illustrates the (average) best similarity retrieved by each algorithm as a function of time.

The third experiment studies the behavior of algorithms as a function of the expected number of solutions. In particular, we use datasets of 15 variables and gradually increase the density so that the expected number of solutions grows from 1, to 10,

---

(since larger MBRs have a higher chance to overlap) and decreases with the number of join conditions in the query.

[2] We used synthetic datasets because, to the best of our knowledge, there do not exist 5 or more real datasets covering the same area publicly available. The query types were chosen so that they represent two extreme cases of constrainedness: acyclic queries are the most under-constrained, while cliques the most over-constrained.

100 and so on until 10^5. Each algorithm is executed for 150 seconds (i.e., $10 \cdot n$). Figure 10c shows the best similarity as a function of *Sol*.

The ubiquitous winner of the experiments is *SEA* which significantly outperforms *ILS* and *GILS* in most cases. *The solutions retrieved by the algorithm are often perfect matches.* This is very important since as we will see shortly, systematic search for exact solutions may require several hours for some problem instances. According to Figure 10c the performance gap does not decrease considerably as the number of solutions increases, meaning that the structure of the search space does not have a serious effect on the relative effectiveness of the algorithms.

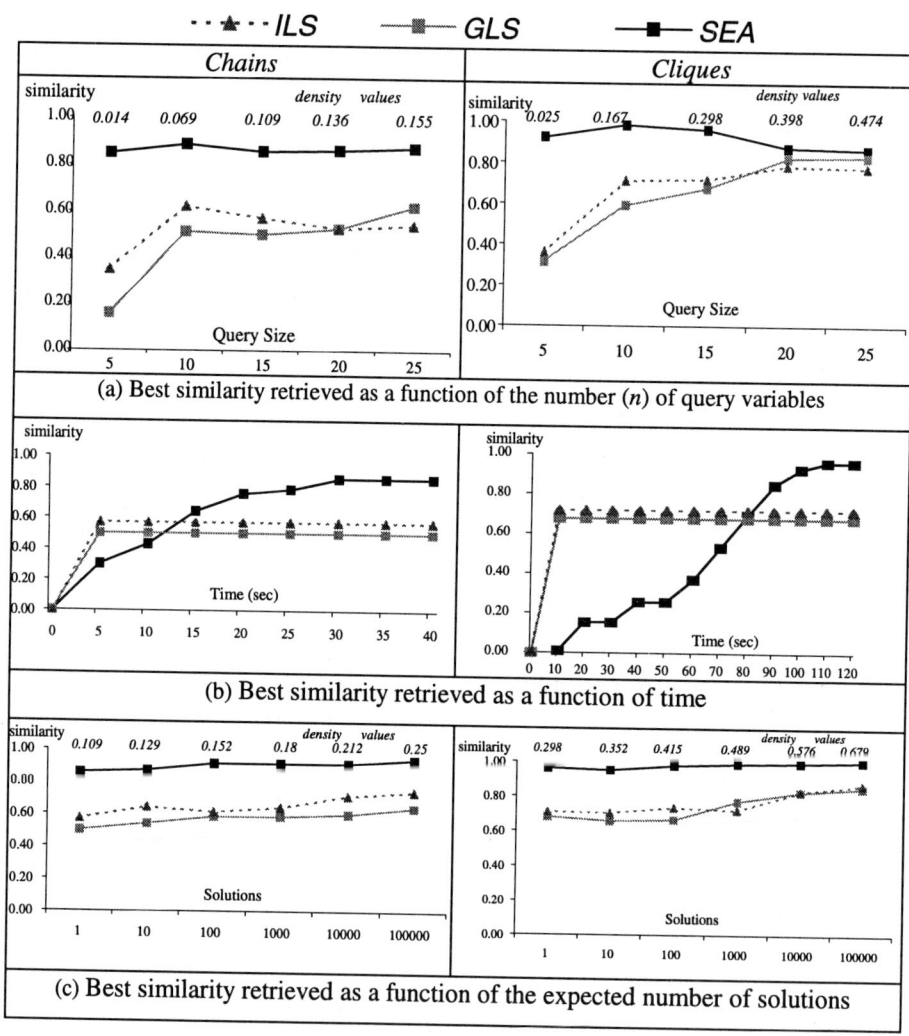

Fig. 10. Comparison of algorithms

The poor performance of *ILS* (and *GILS*) is rather surprising considering that local search significantly outperformed a genetic algorithm in the experimental evaluation of [PMK+99] for configuration similarity. This can be partially caused by the different images sizes (on the average, about an order of magnitude smaller than the datasets used in our experiments), version of the problem (soft spatial constraints that can be partially violated), implementation and parameter choices. The main reason, however, is that the current approach has some substantial improvements that affect relative performance: (i) we use indexes to re-assign the worst variable with the best value in its domain, while in [PMK+99] variables were re-assigned with random values, and (ii) we apply a sophisticated crossover mechanism that takes into account the quality of assignments in order to split solutions, while the genetic algorithm of [PMK+99] involves a random crossover mechanism. The first improvement enhances the performance of both local and evolutionary search, since indexes are used by *SEA*, for mutation, and by *ILS* (and *GILS*) for variable re-instantiation. Therefore, the main difference in relative efficiency is generated by the crossover mechanism. The careful swapping of assignments between solutions produces some better solutions which in subsequent generations will multiply through offspring allocation and mutate to better solutions.

ILS and *GILS* are still useful in cases where there is very limited time for processing since, as shown in Figure 10b, they reach their convergence point before 5 and 10 seconds for chains and cliques respectively (for chains, within 5 seconds *ILS* visits about 60,000 local maxima!). Although *SEA* will eventually outperform them, it requires longer time to reach high quality solutions due to the application of the genetic operations on a large population of solutions. Especially in the case of cliques, the crossover mechanism is not as efficient as for chains, because the constraints between all pairs of variables are very likely to generate large numbers of inconsistencies during the early steps where solutions have low similarities. *ILS*, in general, performs better than *GILS*, except for queries involving 20 and 25 variables. For large queries the similarity difference between a local maximum and its best neighbors is relatively small (due to the large number of constraints, each violation contributes little to the inconsistency degree of the solution), and good solutions are often found in the same neighborhood. So while *ILS* will retrieve one of them and then restart from a completely different point, the punishment process of *GILS* leads to a more systematic search by achieving gradual transitions between maxima and their neighbors.

In addition to their usefulness as standalone retrieval techniques, the above heuristics can be applied as a preliminary step to speed up systematic algorithms. In order to demonstrate this, we implemented a variation of the *WR* technique [PMT99], that finds the best approximate solutions, if no exact solutions exist. The resulting algorithm, *Indexed Branch and Bound* (*IBB*), instantiates variables by applying window queries in the corresponding tree. If there does not exist an object satisfying all join conditions with respect to already instantiated variables, the algorithm does not backtrack, but continues searching if the existing partial solution can potentially lead to a higher similarity than the best solution found so far. As in the case of *find best value* (Figure 5), objects that satisfy the largest number of join conditions are tried first (for details see [PA]).

IBB, and similar systematic search algorithms, can quickly discover the best solutions, if they have some "target" similarity to prune the search space. Otherwise, they may initially spend a lot of time exhaustively exploring areas of the search space with low quality solutions. A good value for this target similarity is very difficult to estimate because it depends on the dataset and the query characteristics. The proposed heuristics can be applied as a pre-processing step to provide such a value. In the next experiment we test the effectiveness of methods that first apply some search heuristic (*ILS* and *SEA*) to find a solution with high similarity, which is then input to *IBB*.

Figure 11 compares these two-step methods with the direct application of *IBB*. In particular we use "clique" queries over the datasets presented in Figure 10a. The datasets are such that the actual number of exact solutions is 1, and we measure the time (in seconds) that it takes for each method to retrieve the exact solution. The results are averaged over 10 executions because the target similarity returned by the heuristics differs each time due to their non-deterministic nature. Notice that often, especially for small queries, the exact solution is found by the non-systematic heuristics (usually *SEA*) in which case systematic search is not performed at all. The threshold for *SEA* is again $10 \cdot n$ (i.e., 150) seconds which are sufficient for its convergence (see Figure 10b), while *ILS* is executed for 1 second (during this time it visits about 12,000 maxima and returns the best).

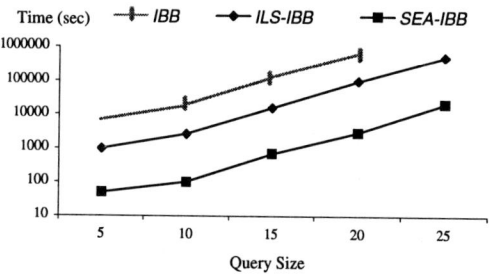

Fig. 11. Combinations of systematic with heuristic search

An important observation about Figure 11, refers to the processing time required for systematic search. *IBB* needs more than 100 minutes to process the smallest query (5 datasets). Cliques involving 25 variables take several days to terminate! This motivates the need for efficient retrieval of sub-optimal solutions through heuristic search. But, even when the optimal solutions are required, the incorporation of *SEA* speeds up *IBB* 1-2 orders of magnitude with respect to simple systematic search. This improvement is not so significant for *ILS* due to the lower similarity of the solutions retrieved.

7. Discussion

In this paper we propose several heuristics for multiway spatial join processing when the goal is retrieval of the most similar solutions within limited time. The best algorithm, *SEA*, can usually find optimal solutions even for difficult problems. In addition, we integrate systematic and non systematic search in a two-step processing method that boosts performance up to two orders of magnitude. To the best of our knowledge, our techniques are the only ones applicable for inexact retrieval of very large problems without any restrictions on the type of datasets, query topologies, output similarities etc. As such, they are useful in a variety of domains involving multiway spatial join processing and spatial similarity retrieval, including VLSI design, GIS and satellite imagery etc. Another potential application is the WWW, where the ever increasing availability of multimedia information will also require efficient mechanisms for multi-dimensional information retrieval. The methods are easily extensible to other spatial predicates, such as *northeast, inside*, near etc. Furthermore, they can be applied for cases where the image contains several types of objects and the query asks for configurations of objects within the same image (i.e., self-joins).

Regarding future directions, first we believe that the excellent performance of *SEA*, could be further improved in many aspects. An idea is to apply variable parameter values depending on the time available for query processing. For instance, the number of solutions p in the initial population may be reduced for very-limited-time cases, in order achieve fast convergence of the algorithm within the limit. Other non-systematic heuristics can also be developed. Given that using the indexes, local search can find local maxima extremely fast, we expect its efficiency to increase by including appropriate deterministic mechanisms that lead search to areas with high similarity solutions. Furthermore, several heuristics could be combined; for instance instead of generating the initial population of *SEA* randomly, we could apply *ILS* and use the first p local maxima visited as the p solutions of the first generation. Although we have not experimented with this approach, we expect it to augment the quality of the solutions and reduce the convergence time. For systematic search, we believe that the focus should be on two-step methods, like *SEA-IBB*, that utilize sub-optimal solutions to guide search for optimal ones. Finally another interesting direction is the application of our techniques to other (e.g., direction, distance) spatial predicates [ZSI01], as well as the incorporation of optimization heuristics similar to the ones that have been proposed for exhaustive processing of multiway spatial joins [PLC00].

Acknowledgments

This work was supported by grants HKUST 6081/01E and HKUST 6070/00E from Hong Kong RGC.

References

[BKS93]	Brinkhoff, T., Kriegel, H., Seeger B. Efficient Processing of Spatial Joins Using R-trees. *ACM SIGMOD*, 1993.
[BKSS90]	Beckmann, N., Kriegel, H. Schneider, R., Seeger, B. The R*-tree: an Efficient and Robust Access Method for Points and Rectangles. *ACM SIGMOD*, 1990.
[BT96]	Blickle, T., Thiele, L. *A Comparison of Selection Schemes used in Genetic Algorithms*. TIK-Report No. 11, ETH, Zurich, 1996.
[CA93]	Crawford, J., Auton, L. Experimental Results on the Crossover Point in Satisfiability Problems. *AAAI*, 1993.

[CFG+98]   Clark, D., Frank, J., Gent, I., MacIntyre, E., Tomov, N., Walsh, T. Local Search and the Number of Solutions. *Constraint Programming*, 1998.
[CSY87]   Chang, S, Shi, Q., Yan C. Iconic Indexing by 2-D String. *IEEE PAMI* 9(3), 413-428, 1987.
[DM94]   Dechter R., Meiri I. Experimental Evaluation of preprocessing algorithms for constraint satisfaction problems. *Artificial Intelligence*, 68: 211-241, 1994.
[DTW+94]   Davenport, A., Tsang, E., Wang, C., Zhu, K. GENET: A Connectionist Architecture for Solving Constraint Satisfaction Problems by Iterative Improvement. *AAAI*, 1994.
[G84]   Guttman, A. R-trees: A Dynamic Index Structure for Spatial Searching. *ACM SIGMOD*, 1984.
[G86]   Grefenstette, J. Optimization of Control Parameters for Genetic Algorithms. *IEEE Trans. on Systems, Man and Cybernetics*, 16 (1), 1986.
[G89]   Goldberg, D. *Genetic Algorithms in Search, Optimization and Machine Learning*. Addison-Wesley, Reading, Mass., 1989.
[GL97]   Glover F., Laguna, M. *Tabu Search*. Kluwer, London, 1997.
[H75]   Holland, J. *Adaptation in Natural and Artificial Systems*. University of Michigan Press, Ann Arbor, Michigan, 1975.
[LH92]   Lee, S, Hsu, F. Spatial Reasoning and Similarity Retrieval of Images using 2D C-Strings Knowledge Representation. *Pattern Recognition*, 25(3), 305-318, 1992.
[LYC92]   Lee, S, Yang, M, Chen, J. Signature File as a Spatial Filter for Iconic Image Database. *Journal of Visual Languages and Computing*, 3, 373-397, 1992.
[MJP+92]   Minton, S. Johnston, M., Philips, A., Laird P. Minimizing Conflicts: A Heuristic Repair Method for Constraint Satisfaction and Scheduling Problems. *Artificial Intelligence* 58(1-3), 161-205, 1992.
[MP99]   Mamoulis, N, Papadias, D., Integration of Spatial Join Algorithms for Processing Multiple Inputs. *ACM SIGMOD*, 1999.
[PA]   Papadias, D., Arkoumanis D. Search Algorithms for Multiway Spatial Joins. To appear in the *International Journal of Geographic Information Science (IJGIS)*. Available at: http://www.cs.ust.hk/~dimitris/
[PF97]   Petrakis, E., Faloutsos, C. Similarity Searching in Medical Image Databases. *IEEE TKDE*, 9 (3) 435-447, 1997.
[PLC00]   Park, H-H., Lee, J-Y., Chung, C-W. Spatial Query Optimization Utilizing Early Separated Filter and Refinement Strategy. *Information Systems* 25(1): 1-22, 2000.
[PMK+99]   Papadias, D., Mantzourogiannis, M., Kalnis, P., Mamoulis, N., Ahmad, I. Content-Based Retrieval Using Heuristic Search. *ACM SIGIR*, 1999.
[PMT99]   Papadias, D., Mamoulis, N., Theodoridis, Y. Processing and Optimization of Multiway Spatial Joins Using R-trees. *ACM PODS*, 1999.
[TSS98]   Theodoridis, Y., Stefanakis, E., Sellis, T., Cost Models for Join Queries in Spatial Databases, *ICDE*, 1998.
[ZSI01]   Zhu, H, Su, J, Ibarra, O. On Multi-way Spatial Joins with Direction Predicates. *SSTD*, 2001.

Indexing Values in Continuous Field Databases

Myoung-Ah Kang[1], Christos Faloutsos[2], Robert Laurini[1], and Sylvie Servigne[1]

[1] LISI, INSA de Lyon-Lyon Scientific and Technical University
20 Av.Einstein 69621 Villeurbanne, France
{makang, laurini, servigne}@lisi.insa-lyon.fr
[2] Dept. of Computer Science, Carnegie Mellon University
Wean Hall, 5000 Forbes Avenue, Pittsburgh, PA 15213-3891
christos@cs.cmu.edu

Abstract. With the extension of spatial database applications, during the last years continuous field databases emerge as an important research issue in order to deal with continuous natural phenomena during the last years. A field can be represented by a set of cells containing some explicit measured sample points and by arbitrary interpolation methods used to derive implicit values on non-sampled positions. The form of cells depends on the specific data model in an application. In this paper, we present an efficient indexing method on the value domain in a large field database for field value queries (e.g. finding regions where the temperature is between 20 degrees and 30 degrees). The main idea is to divide a field into *subfields* [15] in order that all of explicit and implicit values inside a subfield are similar each other on the value domain. Then the intervals of the value domain of subfields can be indexed using traditional spatial access methods, like R*-tree [1]. We propose an efficient and effective algorithm for constructing subfields. This is done by using the field property that values close spatially in a field are likely to be closer together. In more details, we linearize cells in order of the Hilbert value of the center position of cells. Then we form subfields by grouping sequentially cells by means of the cost function proposed in this paper, which tries to minimize the probability that subfields will be accessed by a value query. We implemented our method and carried out experiments on real and synthetic data. The results of experiments show that our method dramatically improves query processing time of field value queries compared to linear scanning.

1 Introduction

The concept of field has been widely discussed for dealing with natural and environmental continuous phenomena. Field data have a great impact in GIS to describe the distribution of some physical property that varies continuously over a domain. A typical example is altitude over a two-dimensional domain to describe a terrain. Other examples of two-dimensional fields are distributions of temperature, pressure, pollution agents, etc., over the surface of a territory. Three-dimensional fields can model geological structures and, in general, physical properties distributed in space. These involve large data set and their analysis. The technology of field databases serves as an important bridge for extending spatial database to scientific databases.

A field can be defined as a function over space and time from a mathematical point of view. Field data are either scalar or vectorial depending on the result of the corresponding function. When the result is of single value, such as the temperature at a point, the field becomes scalar. On the other hand, the field is vectorial, when the result is of multiple values (for instance wind). And the most common queries for analyzing field data can be divided into two categories as follows :
1. Queries based on a given position: e.g. *what is the value at a given point p* ?
2. Queries based on a given field value: e.g. *what are the regions where the rainfall is more than 2000 mm per year* ?

The first type of queries is to find the field values at a given position. On the other hand, the second type, which is more difficult than the first type, inquires the regions, where the field has a given value. We term the second type of queries as *field value queries* in contrast to conventional queries of first type of queries. Although the two types of queries are related with field, their processing methods are different and the processing cost is expensive due to the large volume of data. The processing of the field value queries are more difficult and expensive with comparison to the conventional queries. There is no proposed indexing method for field value queries to our knowledge even though the conventional queries can be supported by a existing spatial indexing method. By contrast, in many applications, field value queries are important for the analysis. Specific applications include the following :

– In ocean environmental databases with ocean temperature and salinity field data, suppose that salmons can be found in the part of sea under a certain condition of temperature and salinity. The queries we can ask for fishing salmons would be *"Find regions where the temperature is between 20° and 25° and the salinity is between 12% and 13%"*.
– In the urban noise system, a typical query to know the noisy regions would be *"Find regions where the noise level is higher than 80 dB "*, where *dB* is an unit of noise level.

Despite the importance, no significant attention has been paid and no remarkable work has been done on the indexing and query processing for field data. Although a certain amount of researches are found, they still focus on the representation or modeling issues for field. Most of the researches deal with the issues of the representation of continuous fields and appropriate data models [16, 20, 25]. In [10] an object oriented model to implement a new estimation method for field data has been specified and the refined object oriented model which permit to change dynamically the estimation method has been studied.

The goal of this paper is to design of indexing methods for efficient field value queries processing in large field databases. The proposed indexing methods exploit the continuity of field, which is an important property of field. And our methods are based on the division of a field into several *subfields* in the context of the homogeneity of field values. The notion of subfield allows an approximate search in the level of subfields instead of the exhaustive search on the entire field, by discarding non-qualified subfields for a given search condition.

The organization of this paper is as follows. In section 2, we will introduce the field representation, the overall procedures of query processing in field databases. In particular, the difficulties of query processing of field value queries will be presented in that section. In section 3, the concept *subfield* [15] will be introduced and we will show how to use it for indexing field values. Then, we will define two aspects to consider in order to determine subfields in the given field. We will propose a new indexing method defined by these two aspects so that the indexing method could be adaptable to the distribution of data and could try to minimize the number of disk accesses. We present results of some experiments not only on real data but also on synthetic data generated by a fractal method, which show the improvement of the performance by using our indexing methods in section 4. And we conclude our paper in section 5.

2 Field Databases and Related Work

2.1 Field Representation

In many cases, the phenomenon under consideration can not be sampled in every point belonging to the study area: for example groundwater, temperature. Instead, the sample dataset is measured or generated at some points or in some zones and the spatial interpolation methods are used in order to estimate the field value at not sampled locations. A field based on a sample point dataset can be formally modeled as follows :

A sample dataset in a field of *d*-dimension is a pair of (V,W), where $V = \{v_i \in R^d, i=1,\ldots, n\}$ is a finite set of points in a domain R^d, in which integer *d* represents the dimension of the domain, i.e., R^3 for a 3-d dataset V which is a set of points with a coordinate (x, y, z) or R^4 for 3-D spatial and 1-D temporal domain with coordinate (x, y, z, t). And $W = \{w_i \in R^k, i=1, \ldots, n\}$ is a corresponding set of field values obtained by $w_i = F(v_i)$, in which F is the interpolation function and the integer *k* decides if the field is scalar or vector, thus if $k = 1$ then scalar field, or if $k >= 2$ then vector field respectively. A continuous field with a dataset (V, W) is by a pair (C, F), where C is a subdivision of the domain R^d into cells c_i $(c_1, c_2, \ldots, c_n)$ containing some points of V, and F is a set of corresponding interpolation functions $f_i(f_1, f_2, \ldots, f_n)$ of cells; f_i represents the corresponding cell c_i, which means that it is possible to define some different interpolation methods to represent a field, if necessary.

A scalar field has a single value at every point, i.e., temperature, land surface elevation or noise level. By contrast, a vector field has a vector rather than a single value, i.e., the gradient of the land surface (aspect and slope) or wind (direction and magnitude). In this paper, we only consider scalar fields.

Cells can be of regular or irregular form and the number of sample points contained by a cell can vary even in a field space, i.e., regular square in DEM (grids, Digital Elevation Model) or irregular triangle in TIN (Triangulated Irregular Networks), or hybrid model of hexahedra or tetrahedra in a 3-D volume field. In most cases, the sample points contained by a cell (we term these points as *sample points of cell*) are vertices of the cell like the models DEM, TIN, etc.. However we do not exclude the possibility to have sample points inside a cell for a certain interpolation method in the case of necessity such as the *Voronoi* interpolation.

The function f_i is used to interpolate field values of all the points inside cell c_i by applying f_i to the sample points of cell c_i. The reason is that the sample points of a cell are generally the nearest neighbor points of the given query point and the field value on a point is influenced principally by the nearest sample points by the field continuity property. For example, in the 2-D TIN with a 'linear interpolation', we take three vertices of the triangle containing the given point to apply the function.

A conventional raster-based DEM for imagery is not suitable to represent a continuous field. Because it defines just one value (i.e., the terrain elevation measured in the center of cell) for all points inside a cell, which means the lost of the all within-cell variation [20] and the discontinuity between adjacent cells. In order that a DEM can be considered as a continuous field, interpolation methods need to be specified [26]. To meet this condition, we can generate (measure) sample points at each vertex of grid and specify an interpolation function, i.e., a linear interpolation. Thus all the points inside a cell can be interpolated by their nearest neighbor sample points, so that their vertices of the cell. Figure 1 illustrates an example of the transformation of a conventional DEM to the DEM for a continuous field such as a terrain.

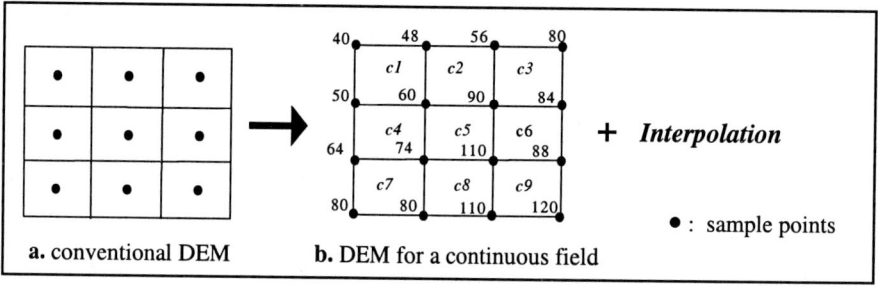

Fig. 1. Example of a DEM for continuous fields

2.2 Queries on Field Databases

For simplicity we assume the interpolation function f as a linear interpolation in all the illustrating examples in this paper. Note that the approaches in this section can be applied to other interpolation methods as well. Depending on different query conditions we can classify the type of queries in field databases as follows :
- Q1 : Queries based on a spatial condition, i.e., *Find field value on a given point v'*.
- Q2 : Queries based on a field value condition, i.e., *Find regions with a given field value w'*.

Complex queries can be composed by combining these basic queries.

2.2.1 Conventional Queries. The type Q1 is the conventional query type in field databases, denoted as $F(v')$. It returns the field value on a given point v', i.e., *"what is the temperature on a given point v'?"*. To process this type of queries, we find firstly the cell c' containing the query point v' and we apply the corresponding interpolation function on the neighbor sample points of the query point v', namely samples points of the c' retrieved in the previous step ; $w' = f(v', sample\_points(c'))$. Therefore the problem in a large field database is to efficiently find the qualified cell c'. This is one of the traditional spatial operations in spatial databases. Thus these queries can be easily supported by an conventional spatial indexing method, such as R-tree or its variants [1, 12, 23].

2.2.2 Field Value Queries. The type Q2 is to find the regions with a given field value w'. The query condition value w' involves not only exact match conditions but also range conditions. For example, a range query such as *"Find the regions where temperature is between [20°C, 25°C]"* or *"Find the regions where temperature is more than 25°C"* belongs to this query type. Most applications of field databases do not really care about "where are the value *exactly* equal to w' ?", instead they are interested in the queries such as "where are the value *approximately* equal to w' ?", since errors and uncertainty exist in the measurements. These queries can be denoted as $F^{-1}(w'-e < w < w'+e)$ where e is an error limit. More generally, they can be denoted as $F^{-1}(w' < w < w'')$, which is a range query.

Compared with the type Q1 queries, value queries are more difficult to support since there can be more than one cell where the field value is equal to (larger than, smaller than) w'. Figure 2 illustrates an example of a value query in a 2-D continuous field. Note that the spatial XY plan is simplified to the axis 'Space v' in this figure to show intuitively the value queries processing procedure. The field is viewed as continuous from their sample points and interpolation functions. The cell c_1 contains sample points $<v_1, v_2, v_3>$ and it is represented by an interpolation function f_1. The cell c_2 contains $<v_3, v_4, v_5>$ and it is represented by f_2, respectively, etc. We can remark that the sample points of each cell support implicitly the interval of all possible values inside a cell ; not only explicit sample values and also implicit values to be interpolated. These intervals are represented by I_i for the cell c_i in Figure 2.

In Figure 2, the answer points where the field value is equal to the query value w' are v' and v''. These answer points can be calculated by interpolation if we can retrieve all cells $<c_1, c_3>$ whose intervals intersect the query value w'. In detail, v' can be calculated by applying the inverse interpolation function on the sample points of c_1, namely $<v_1, v_2, v_3>$; $f_1^{-1}(w', sample\_points(c_1))$. And v'' can be done by the function f_3^{-1} on the sample points of c_3 $<v_5, v_6, v_7>$; $f_3^{-1}(w', sample\_points(c_3))$. In the same way, in Figure 1, for a given query such as *"Find the regions where the value is between 55 and 59"*, firstly we need to retrieve the cells $<c_1, c_2, c_3, c_4>$, whose intervals intersect the range query value [55, 59]. Then, the final exact answer regions can be retrieved by applying the inverse function on the vertices of each cell retrieved in previous step.

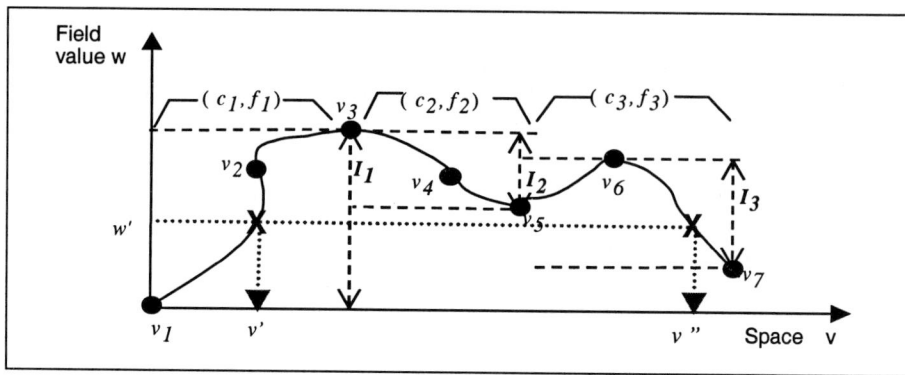

Fig. 2. Example of a continuous field and a value query

Thus, the problem of value queries in a continuous field database is transformed into the problem of *"finding all the cells whose value intervals intersect the given query value condition"*. Without indexing, we should scan all cells of the database, which will degrade dramatically the system performance. We term this method as *'LinearScan'* method. Thus in this paper, we propose an efficient indexing method to support value queries in large continuous databases by accelerating the retrieval of all the cells intersecting a query value condition w'. We should point out that if the interpolation function introduces new extreme points having values outside the original interval of cells, these points must be considered when deciding intervals of cells.

2.3 Related Work

The similar approaches of the value query processing have been proposed for isosurface extraction from volumetric scalar dataset [4] and for the extraction of isolines from TIN [24]. Thus each volume or triangle is associated with an interval bounded by the elevation of the vertices of the cell (volume or triangle) with lowest and highest elevation. For any query elevation w' between this interval (the lowest and the highest elevation), the cell contributes to the isosurface or isoline map. An Interval tree [5] was used in order to index intervals of cells for intersection query. However, the Interval tree data structure is a main-memory based indexing method thus it is not suitable for a large field database.

In [19], IP-index [18] for indexing values of time sequences was used for the terrain-added navigation application. The IP-index was applied to the terrain elevation map of DEM to find area whose the elevations are inside the given query interval. Since the IP-index is designed for 1-D sequences, an IP-index was used for each row of the map by considering it as a time sequence. This approach could not handle the continuity of terrain by considering only the continuity of one dimension (the axis X).

2.4 Motivation

As we saw before, without indexing value query processing requires to scan the entire field database. Despite the importance of the efficient value query processing, no significant attention has been paid and no remarkable work has been done on the indexing methods. In this paper, we would like to build new indexing schemes which can improve the value query processing with in large field databases. This is the motivation of this paper.

3 Proposed Method

As mentioned above, the problem of answering value queries translates to finding a way to index cells intersecting the query value. Given a field database, we can associate with each cell c_i an interval, whose extremes are the minimum and maximum value among all possible values inside c_i, respectively. One straightforward way is therefore to index all these intervals associated with the cells. An interval of values represents the one dimensional minimum bounding rectangle (MBR) of values that it includes. Thus we can use 1-D R*-tree to index intervals. We term this method as '*I-All*' method, where *I* represents 'Indexing'. Given a query value *w'*, we can search the 1-D R*-tree in order to find intervals intersecting *w'*. Then we retrieve the cells associated with found intervals and we calculate the final exact answer regions by the interpolation method with sample points of retrieved cells. Because these cells correspond to cells containing a part of answer regions. We term these cells as candidate cells. However storing all these individual intervals in an R*-tree has the problems as follows:

The R*-tree will become tall and slow due to a large number of intervals in a large field database. This is not efficient both in terms of space as well as search speed. Moreover the search speed will also suffer because of the overlapping of so many similar intervals. Sometime they lead to more poor performance than the 'Linear-Scan' method as we can see in Figure 11.a in Section 4.

Thus we propose an another efficient method based on the continuity of field, which is an important property of field concept. By the continuity property, the values close spatially in a continuous field are likely to be closer together. It means that the adjacent cells probably become the candidate cells together for a given query.

Therefore we propose to group these (connected) adjacent cells having similar values into *subfields*. Since a field is entirely covered by a set of cells, subfields mean also a division of a entire field space into some subspaces. Thus a subfield can be defined as a subspace where field values are close together. Then we can get the intervals of all possible values inside subfields instead of individual intervals of all cells, and we can index only these a few intervals of subfields by using 1-D R*-tree. It means that a value query firstly retrieves the subfields whose intervals intersect the query value by R*-tree. It is evident that if a value query intersects some intervals of cells inside a subfield then it has to intersect also the interval of subfield itself. The

final exact answer regions need to be calculated by interpolating the cells inside retrieved subfields. The i-th subfield can be defined by its interval as follows :
$$SF_i = (W_{min,i}, W_{max,i}),$$
where $W_{min,i}$ and $W_{max,i}$ mean the minimum and maximum value of values inside SF_i, respectively.

We may append other kinds of values to $V_{min,i}$ and $V_{max,i}$, if necessary, for example, the average of field values of subfield. Figure 3 shows an example of the division of a continuous field into some subfields. The spatial XY plan is simplified on the axis 'Space (x,y)'. In this figure, subfields are represented by rectangles. It means that each rectangle contains (or intersect) some adjacent cells that are not drawn in this figure for the simplicity. The width of rectangle implies the area of subfield covering some cells. The height of rectangle does the interval of subfield. Note that these heights are not very large since the values inside subfields are similar each other. In other words, the similarity of values inside a subfield can be represented by the *interval size of the subfield*, which means the difference between maximum and minimum value inside.

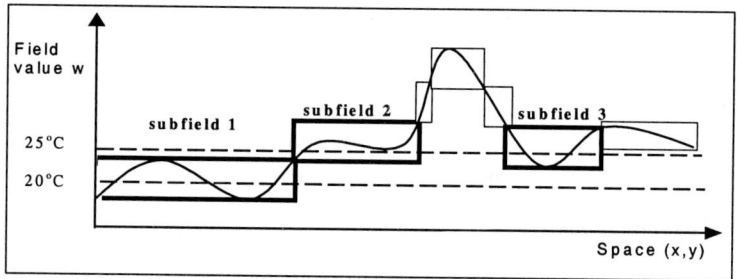

Fig. 3. Indexing for field value queries with subfields

Since we use 1-D R*-tree with these intervals of subfields, the procedure of value query processing can be defined as follows :
- Step 1 (filtering step) : find all subfields whose intervals intersect the query value by the R*-tree.
- Step 2 (estimation step) : retrieve all cells inside the selected subfields by step 1, and estimate the exact answer regions where the value is equal to (more than or less than) the query value.

Suppose that a TIN is used to represent the field in Figure 3 and that a query such as *"Find the zone where temperature is more than 20°C and less than 25°C"* is given. For the filtering step, we select three subfields 1, 2, and 3, which intersect query interval. And we retrieve the triangles contained or intersected by the selected subfields and compute the regions where the temperature is between [20°C, 25°C] with the sample points of retrieved triangles.

3.1 Insertion

Before insertion of intervals of subfield in 1-D R*-Tree, we have to define how to get these subfields for indexing for value queries. How can we divide a field space into some subfields so that these subfields could have the similar values ?

3.1.1 Subfields. In order to get subfields, we must consider two aspects so that the number of disk accesses can be minimized.
1. The manner to divide the field space : It means also how to group some (connected) adjacent cells into subfields, since a field space is totally covered by cells.
2. The criterion of similarity of values inside a subfield : As we saw before, we can use the *interval size of subfield* as a criterion of measurement of similarity of values inside a subfield.

In the paper [15], Interval Quadtrees have been proposed. The division of space is based on that of Quadtree [22]. And they used a pre-determined, fixed threshold for *the interval size of subfield*. It means that the interval size of a subfield must be less than the given fixed threshold in order that values inside are similar. In detail, the field space is recursively divided into four subspaces in the manner of Quadtree until each subspace satisfies the condition that interval size of the subspace must be less than the given threshold. Then the final subspaces of this division procedure become subfields. However, there is no justifiable way to decide the optimal threshold that can give the best performance. And the quadratic division is not very suitable to a field represented by non quadratic forms of cells such as TIN. Thus we would like to find a method that will group cells in order that subfields could have more natural and realistic forms by trying maximum of adjacent cells. It means no limitation of forms quadratic or triangular, etc., like in the case of *Interval Quadtree*. We propose to use a space filling curve to impose a linear ordering on the cells covering a field space. We term this method as '*I-Hilbert*'.

3.1.2 The Manner to Divide the Field Space Using Hilbert Value Order. A space filling curve visits all the points in a k-dimensional grid exactly once and never crosses itself. The Z-order (or Peano curve, or bit-interleaving), the Hilbert curve, and the Gray-code curve [6] are the examples of space filling curves. In [7, 13], it was shown experimentally that the Hilbert curve achieves the best clustering among the three above methods. Thus we choose the Hilbert curve. Indeed, the fact that all successive cells in a linear order are the adjacent cells each other in k-dimension; there is no "jumps" in the linear traversal, allows to examine sequentially all cells when generating subfields.

The Hilbert curve can be generalized for higher dimensionalities. Algorithms to generate two-dimensional curve for a given order can be found in [11, 13]. An algorithm for higher dimensionalities is in [2]. Figure 4 shows examples of the Hilbert curve ordering.

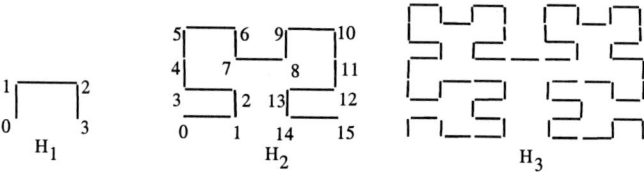

Fig. 4. Example of Hilbert curves

The cells will be linealized in order of the Hilbert value of their spatial position, specifically the Hilbert value of the center of cells (from now, in this paper the Hilbert value of a cell means that of the center of the cell). Then we check sequentially intervals of linealized cells if their values are similar or not in order to generate subfields. Therefore, each cell can be represented only by its interval in the procedure of subfields generation like in the Figure 5.b. Figure 5.a presents an example of a continuous field represented by a regular DEM and Figure 5.b shows some subfields generated according to the intervals of cells.

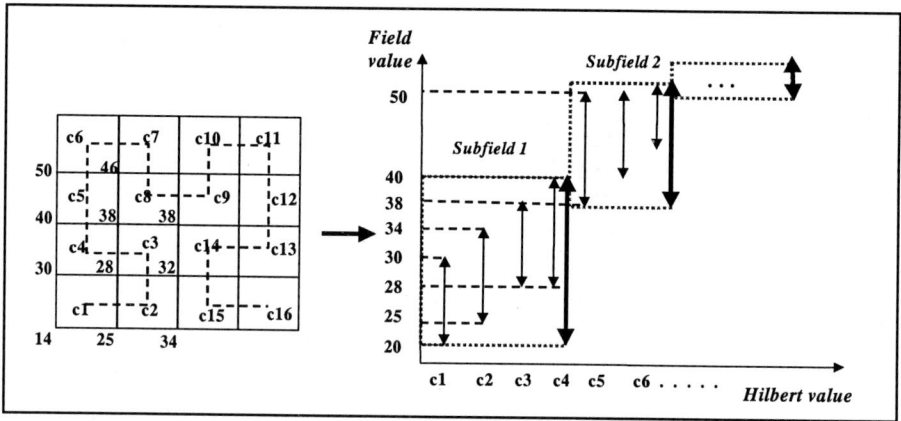

Fig. 5. : a. Example of continuous DEM, b. Generated subfields and their intervals

Data Structure of subfields As mentioned above, each interval of subfields shown in Figure 5.b can be indexed by 1-D R*-tree storing it in a 1-D MBR. We should point out that at the leaf nodes of the R*-tree, we need to store disk addresses where cells within the corresponding subfield are stored. The adjacent cells in subfields are already clustered by linealiring them physically in order of Hilbert value of cells. Therefore it is sufficient to store the pointers of starting and ending cells of the subfield in the linear Hilbert value order. Figure 6 shows the structure of a leaf node and a non-leaf node of 1-D R*-tree for intervals of subfields.

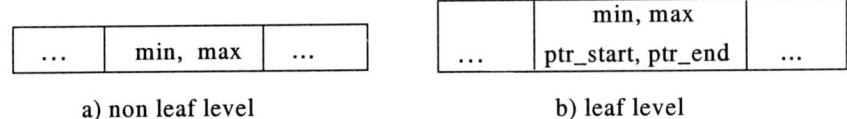

a) non leaf level   b) leaf level

Fig. 6. Data structure of nodes of 1-D R*-tree for intervals of subfields

Before describing the cost function, we define an interval size of a cell or that of a subfield having minimum and maximum values as,

interval size *I = maximum-minimum + 1.*

In the special case that the minimum and maximum value are the same, for example when a interpolation function returns a constant value for all points in a cell, the interval size is 1. According to [14], the probability P that a subfield of interval size L, that is, an 1-D MBR of length L will be accessed by the average range query is :

P = L + 0.5

It assumes that the data space is normalized to the range [0,1] and that average range query is of length 0.5. Then we define the cost C of the subfield as followings :

C = P / SI,

where *SI* is the sum of interval sizes of all cells inside the subfield. Namely, the probability of accessing a subfield is divided by the sum of interval sizes of cells included by the subfield.

The strategy is that the insertion of the interval of a new adjacent cell into a subfield containing already some cells must not increase the cost *C* of the subfield before the insertion. Suppose that C_a be the cost of a subfield before the insertion of a new cell and C_b after the insertion, respectively. This insertion can be executed only if $C_a > C_b$. Thus at first, we start with the interval of first cell of the whole linearized cells. Then we form a subfield by including all the successive cells until the cost of subfield before insertion of a cell C_a is more than that of the subfield after intersection C_b. In the case of $C_a <= C_b$, we start a new subfield. In this way, subfields are generated by including sequentially cells in a field. For example, in Figure 5.b the cost of *Subfield 1* before the insertion of cell c_5 into *Subfield 1* was about 0.466; 21/(11+10+11+13). The cost of *Subfield 1* after this insertion will be about 0.534; 31/(11+10+11+13+13). This insertion increased the cost of *Subfield 1* before insertion, thus a new *Subfield 2* was started with c_5.

Figure 7 shows an example of the subfields generated by the proposed method above with real terrain data of a part of ROSEBURG city in USA obtained at http://edcwww.cr.usgs.gov. The areas of subfields are represented by polygon on the map where the terrain elevations are represented by different colors.

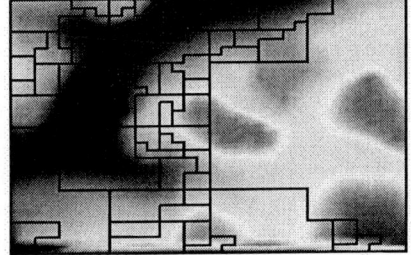

Fig. 7. Examples of generated subfields of a terrain data

3.2 Search

In the previous subsection, we showed how to construct '*I-Hilbert*' indexing method. Here we examine how to search the index for value queries. The searching algorithm starts to perform a intersect query within the 1-D R*-tree constructed by intervals of subfields. It retrieves all leaf MBRs intersecting the given query field value then estimate the exact answer regions by retrieving cells located between the pointers of starting and ending cell.

```
Algorithm Search(node Root, query value w) :

    S1. Search non-leaf nodes : invoke Search for every
    entry whose MBR intersects the query value w.

    S2. Search leaf nodes : invoke Estimate(ptr_start,
    ptr_end, w) of every entry whose MBR intersects the
    query value w.

Algorithm Estimate(pointer ptr_str, pointer ptr_end,
query value w) :

    E1. Retrieve sample points of cells at the disk ad-
    dress between ptr_str and ptr_end.

    E2. Estimate the exact answer regions corresponding
    to w with retrieved sample points.
```

4 Experiments

We implemented the our method 'I-Hilbert' and we carried out experiments on two spatial dimensional field data. The method was implemented in C, under Unix. We compared our method against the 'LinearScan' and 'I-All' methods. For each experiment, we used interval field value queries with variable query intervals :

Qinterval : ranged from 0-0.1 relatively to the normalized interval range of the total field value space to [0, 1]. For example, interval value queries ranged 0 mean exact field value queries such that "*Find all regions where the value is equal to 30*".

We generated randomly 200 interval field value queries for each query interval *Qinterval*. We measured the execution time of field value queries by calculating the average of total query processing time of these 200 queries. The page size used is 4KB. Both real and synthetic data were used in the measurement. The reason for using real data was to evaluate how the our method behaves in reality. We used synthetic data by controlling several parameters of field data in order to test our method on larger and various types of data. A simple linear interpolation was used for interpolating all the points inside a cell for every kind of data.

4.1 Real Data

Two kinds of real field data were used as followings :
1. Real terrain data : The USGS DEM elevation data of a region in USA was obtained from http://edcwww.cr.usgs.gov. Their resolution was 512*512, so 266,144 rectangular cells having four vertexis in the field space. Figure 8.a shows the results of performance comparison of 'I-Hilbert' against the 'LinearScan' and 'I-All' methods.
2. Real urban noise data : A real urban noise data measured in a region of Lyon, France were used. The noise data were represented by TIN with about 9000 triangles. Figure 8.b shows the results of performance according to varied field value query interval.

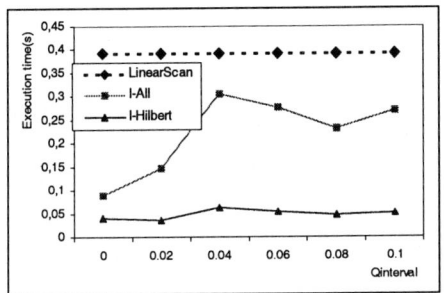 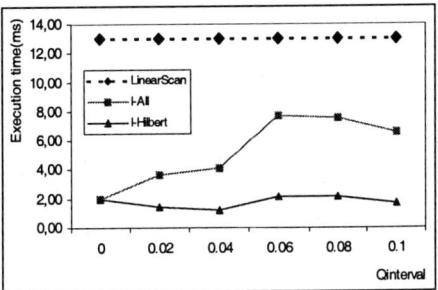

a. real terrain data   b. real urban nose data

Fig. 8. Execution time of field value queries with the real data

Our method 'I-Hilbert' outperforms 'LinearScan' and 'I-All' methods with the terrain data and also urban noise data. Our method achieves from 6 up to 12 times better query processing time than 'LinearScan' method in Figure 8.a.

4.2 Synthetic Data by Fractal

We used synthetic data of various characteristics. As synthetic field data, we generated 2-D random fractal terrain of DEM by the diamond-square algorithm using the midpoint displacement algorithm as random displacements [21]. Thus an height of terrain at each vertex is generated. In the diamond-square algorithm, we start out with a big square and initial heights chosen at random at the four vertices. The square grid is subdivided recursively into the next with half grid size by one pass consisting of two steps, see Figure 9 :
- The diamond step : The midpoints of all squares are computed by interpolation from their four neighbor points (average of four neighbor points) plus an offset by the random displacement.
- The square step : The remaining intermediate points are computed by interpolation from their four neighbor points plus an offset by the random displacement.

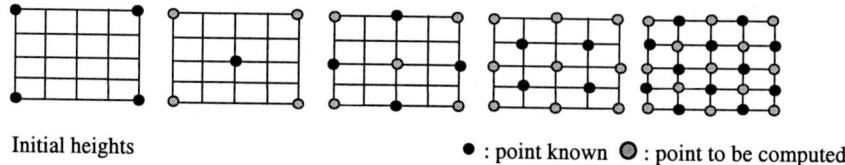

Initial heights　　　　　　　　　　● : point known　◎ : point to be computed

Fig. 9. Two passes of subdivision for generation fractal surfaces by diamond-square algorithm on a square of 4 x 4

The midpoint displacement algorithm is used as random displacement for generating an offset. Therefore when we assumes that value space (heights of terrain) is normalized to [-1.0, 1.0], the initial random value range from [-1.0, 1.0]. In each pass, an offset is randomly generated in the random value range in each of two steps and then the random value range is reduced by the scaling factor of $2^{(-H)}$.

The H is a parameter for the roughness constant of terrain. This is the value which will determine how much the random number range is reduced each time through the loop (pass) and, therefore, will determine the roughness of the resulting fractal :

H : ranged from 0.0 to 1.0, thus the $2^{(-H)}$ is ranged from 1.0 (for small H) to 0.05 (for large H).

The random value range is reduced by $2^{(-H)}$ each time through the pass. With H set to 1.0, the random value range will be halved each time, resulting in a very smooth fractal. With H set to 0.0, the range will not be reduced at all, resulting in something quite jagged.

Figure 10 shows examples of the produced synthetic terrain data with 32*32 cells. The roughness H of the terrain data of Figure 10.a and Figure 10.b is equal to 0.2 and 0.8 respectively. We used the same initial values randomly generated at four vertices in the two cases in order to show the effect of the different H values in the same condition.

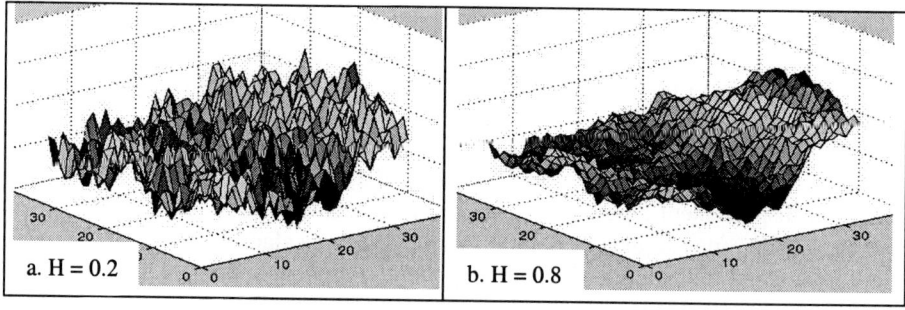

a. H = 0.2　　　　　　　　　　　b. H = 0.8

Fig. 10. Examples of synthetic terrain data

We generated the fractal terrain with 1,048,576 rectangular cells with variable H from 0.1 to 0.9 in order to measure the performance of our method 'I-Hilbert' with various type of field dataset. Figure 11 gives the results of experiments according to the value of H. The horizontal axis is the variable query interval and the vertical axis is the average of total query processing time of 200 randomly generated for each query interval.

We see that our method is more efficient than the others in all the cases of H, achieving up to more than 50 times better query processing time than 'LinearScan' method for the *Qinterval* from 0 to 0.01 in the case of H = 0.9. The results also show that the 'I-All' method gives the performance with big differences according to the value of H and *Qinterval*. The 'I-All' method was slower than 'LinearScan' method in the case that H is small or *Qinterval* is large, that results in the high query selectivity; the query selectivity is defined as the rate of the number of answer data over the total number of data. The small H leads to the high query selectivity due to many overlapped values in the field space as shown in Figure 10.a. We remark that our method outperforms consistently the other methods by giving stable results in all the cases.

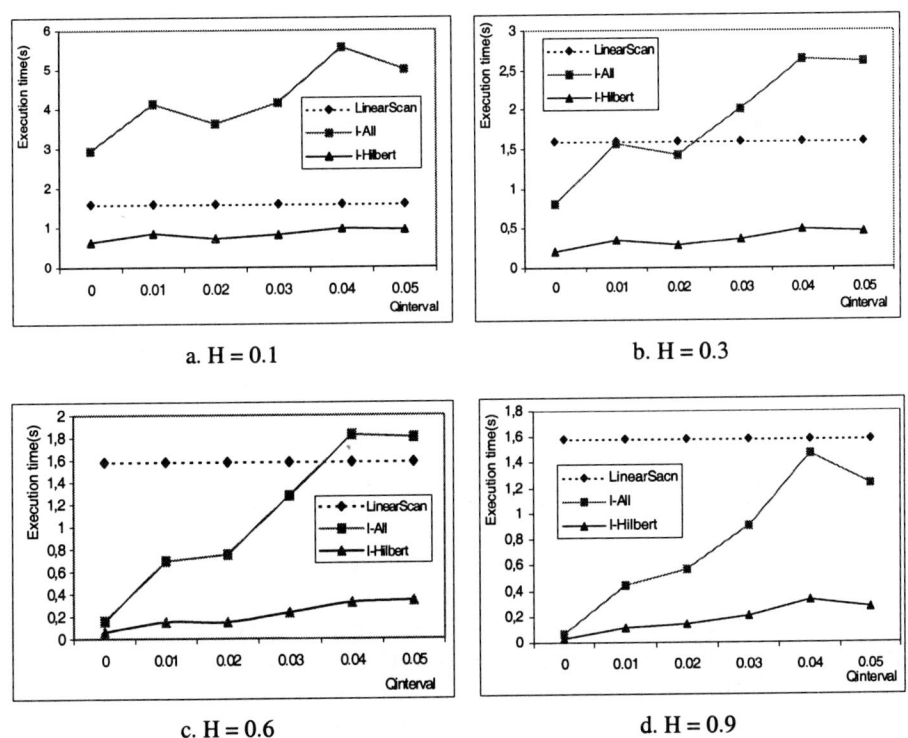

a. H = 0.1   b. H = 0.3

c. H = 0.6   d. H = 0.9

Fig. 11. Execution times of field values queries with synthetic fractal data

4.3 Synthetic Monotonic Data

We generated a synthetic monotonic DEM field data with 512* 512 rectangular cells modeled by:

$$w(x, y) = x + y,$$

where $w(P)$ is the elevation of the terrain at the point P.

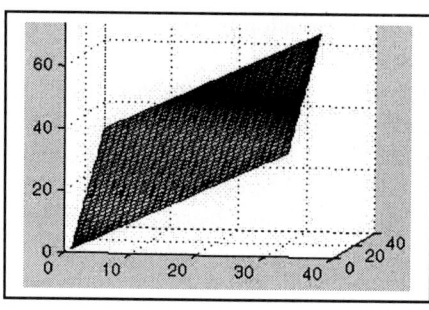
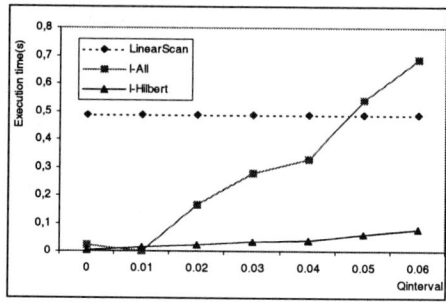

a. Example of monotonic terrain data   b. Execution times of field value queries

Fig. 12. Test on monotonic field data

Figure 12.a shows an example of this monotonic data of 32 * 32 rectangular cells. Figure 12.b shows that our method outperforms the other methods also for this kind of monotonic field data.

5 Conclusion

A field can be represented by a large number of cells containing some explicit sample points and by arbitrary interpolation methods used to calculate the implicit field values on non-sample positions. To process the value queries in these continuous field databases is very expensive due to the large volume of data. In this paper, we have proposed new indexing structures which index on the value domain in continuous field databases.

One straightforward way is to index the interval of the possible values of each cell, termed 'I-All' method in this paper. However storing all these individual intervals in an index structure (ex. 1-D R*-tree) gives poor performances due to the large and slow index structure. Thus we proposed to adopt the concept *subfields* [15]. The main idea is to divide the field space into several subfields in which the field values (not only explicit but also implicite) are similar, each other on the value domain. By indexing the intervals of subfields instead of each individual cell, we can execute an approximate search at the level of subfields instead of the exhaustive search on the entire cells in the field. In order to get subfields, we proposed to linearize cells in order of the Hilbert value of the centre position of cells. Then we form subfields by grouping sequentially cells accroding to *the cost of a subfield* proposed in this paper. The cost of a subfield is based on the probability of a MBR to be accessed for a given query [14]. We extended this probability for subfields. The strategy of forming subfields based on this cost model was proposed. We used 1-D R*-tree in order to index the intervals of subfields and we termed this proposed method *'I-Hilbert'*. Notice that the proposed method can be used with any indexing method that can handle interval data.

We evaluated the proposed method 'I-Hilbert', 'I-All' and the linear scan method. The 'I-Hilbert' method is more efficient than the others. The performance measurements shows that the proposed method outperformes consistently the others for all of the different data types used for the test.

In fact, in this paper we were interested in scalar field databases. In future work we would like to extend our method to process value queries in vector field databases such as wind.

References

1. BECKMANN N., KRIEGEL R., SCHNEIDER R. and SEEGER B., "*The R*-tree: An efficient and Robust Access Method for Points and Rectangles*", Proceedings of SIGMOD, pp. 322-331, 1990.
2. BIALLY T., "*Space-filling Curves : Their generation and their application to bandwidth reduction*", IEEE Trans. on Information Theory, IT-15(6) : 658-664, Nov. 1969.
3. BURROUGH PA. and FRANK AU., *Geographic Objects with Indeterminate Boundaries*, Taylor and Francis. 345 p., 1996.
4. CIGNONI P., MONTANI C., PUPPO E., and SCOPIGNO R., "*Optimal isosurface extraction from irregular volume data*", Proc., of Symposium on Volume Visualization, pp. 31-38, San Francisco, Oct. 1996.
5. EDELSBRUNNER H. *Dynamic data structures for orthogonal intersection queries*, Technical Report. F59. Inst. Informationsverarb., Technical University of Graz, Austria, 1980.
6. FALOUTSOS C., *Gray Codes for Partial Match and Range Queries*, IEEE Transactions on Software Engineering (TSE), Volume 14, pp. 1381-1393, 1989.
7. FALOUTSOS C. and ROSEMAN S., *Fractals for Secondary Key Retrieval*, Proceedings of the 18th ACM SIGACT-SIGMOD-SIGART Symposium on PODS, Philadelphia, Pennsylvania, pp. 247-252, 1989.
8. FALOUTSOS C., *Searching Multimedia Databases by Contents*, Kluwer Academic Press. 155p, 1996.
9. GOODCHILD M.F , *Unit 054-Representing Fields*, The NCGIA Core Curriculum in GIScience, http://www.ncgia.ucsb.edu/education/curricula/giscc/units/u054.
10. GORDILLO S. and BALAGUER F., "*Refining an Object-oriented GIS design Model: Topologies and Field Data*". Proceedings of the 6th Int. Symposium on Advances in Geographic Information Systems, pp.76-81, Washington, D.C., USA, 1998.
11. GRIFFITHS J.G., "*An algorithm for displaying a class of space-filling curves*", Software-Practice and Experience, 16(5):403-411, May 1986.
12. GUTTMAN A., "*R-trees – a Dynamic Index Structure for Spatial Searching*", Proceedings of the ACM SIGMOD Conf., pp.47-57, Boston MA, 1994.
13. JAGADISH H.V., "*Linear clustering of objects with multiple attributes*", ACM SIGMOD Conf., pp.332-342, May 1990.
14. KAMEL I. and FALOUTSOS C., "*On packing r-trees*", Second Int. Conf. on Information and Knowledge Management (CIKM), Nov. 1993.
15. KANG M-A., SERVIGNE S., LI K.J., LAURINI R., "*Indexing Field Values in Field Oriented Systems: Interval Quadtree*", 8th Int. CIKM, pp. 335-342, Kansas City, USA, Nov. 1999.
16. KEMP K., "*Environmental Modelling with GIS: A Strategy for Dealing with Spatial Continuity*", Technical Report No. 93-3, National Center for Geographical Information and Analysis, University of California, Santa Barbara, 1993.

17. LAURINI R. and THOMPSON D., *Fundamentals of Spatial Information Systems*, Academic Press, 1992.
18. LIN L., RISCH T., SKOLD M. and BADAL D.Z. *Indexing Values of Time Sequences*. Proceedings of the 5th Int. CIKM. Rockville, Maryland, USA., November 12-16, 1996. p. 223-232.
19. LIN L. and RISCH T. "*Using a Sequential Index in Terrain-aided Navigation*", Proceedings of 6th Int. CIKM, Las Vegas, Nevada, Nov. 1997.
20. PARIENTE D., "*Estimation, Modélisation et Langage de Déclaration et de Manipulation de Champs Spatiaux Continus*". PhD, Institut National des Sciences Appliquées de Lyon, 6 December, 192p, 1994.
21. PEITGEN H.O., *Fractals for the classroom*, New York : Springer-Verlag, 1992.
22. SAMET H., *The Design and Analysis of Spatial Data Structures*, Addison-Wesley, 1990.
23. SELLIS T., ROUSSOPOULOS N. and FALOUTSOS C., *"The R+-tree: A Dynamic Index for Multidimensional Objects"*, Proceedings of VLDB, pp. 507-518, 1987.
24. VAN KREVELD M., *"Efficient Methods for Isoline Extraction from a Digital Elevation Model based on Triangulated Irregular Networks"*, Proceedings of 6th Int. Symposium on Spatial Data Handling, pp. 835-847, 1994.
25. VCKOVSKI A., *"Representation of Continuous Fields"*, Proceedings of 12th Auto Carto, Vol.4, pp.127-136, 1995.
26. YU S., VAN KREVELD M., *"Drainage Queries in TIN"*, 7th Int. Symposium on Spatial Data Handling(SDH), Delft, Netherlands, Aug. 1996.

Efficient and Adaptive Processing of Multiple Continuous Queries

Wee Hyong Tok and Stéphane Bressan

School of Computing,
National University of Singapore
{tokweehy,steph}@comp.nus.edu.sg

Abstract. Continuous queries are queries executed on data streams within a potentially open-ended time interval specified by the user and are usually long running. The data streams are likely to exhibit fluctuating characteristics such as varying inter-arrival times, as well as varying data characteristics during the query execution. In the presence of such unpredictable factors, continuous query systems must still be able to efficiently handle large number of queries, as well as to offer acceptable individual query performance.

In this paper, we propose and discuss a novel framework, called AdaptiveCQ, for the efficient processing of multiple continuous queries. In our framework, multiple queries share intermediate results at a fine level of granularity. Unlike previous approaches to sharing or reusing that relied on materialization to disk, AdaptiveCQ allows on-the-fly sharing of results. We show that this feature improves both the initial query response time, and the overall response time. Finally, AdaptiveCQ, which extrapolates the idea proposed by the eddy query-processing model, adapts well to fluctuations of the data streams characteristics by this combination of fine grain and on-the-fly sharing. We implemented AdaptiveCQ from scratch in Java and made use of it to conduct the experiments. We present experimental results that substantiate our claim that AdaptiveCQ can provide substantial performance improvements over existing methods of reusing intermediate results that relied on materialization to disk. In addition, we also show that AdaptiveCQ can adapt well to fluctuations in the query environment.

1 Introduction

Continuous queries are queries that are executed on data streams within a time interval (potentially open-ended and long running) specified by the user. These data streams could come from the Internet, or data servers deployed in a distributed wide-area environment. In [1, 16], continuous queries were used to perform content-based filtering of data from local data sources such as a database management system (DBMS) or XML documents. In addition, with the emergence of sensors database system [5], where sensors are deployed for data collection and measurement, continuous queries would be useful in the monitoring of the incoming data.

In continuous query systems [8, 11], multiple continuous queries could be running simultaneously. The queries posed could usually be over shared data streams, and is likely to share common sub-expressions with other running queries. If each of these queries is handled separately, requiring individual memory and CPU resources being allocated, scalability issues arise when the number of queries increases. There are two issues that need to be tackled when designing continuous quer y systems. The first issue is on the scalability of continuous query systems, when a large number of queries are running simultaneously. The second issue is how a continuous query system can adapt to fluctuating data characteristic of the data streams, as well as the unpredictable inter-arrival times in a wide-area environment.

In order to handle scalability issues, multi-query optimization techniques [12, 13] might be useful in optimizing the queries collectively in order to find an efficient execution strategy. However, it was noted in [15] that if the queries are evaluated as they arrive, and are not batch-processed, multi-query optimization techniques cannot be directly applied in this context. The observations made by [15] apply to continuous queries system too, as c ontinuous queries are not batched processed, but evaluated and added to the system as the queries arrive.

In the literature, OpenCQ [11] handles scalability issues by using a query-processing algorithm based on incremental view maintenance. NiagaraCQ [8] addresses the problem of scalability by proposing the sharing of computation by an incremental group optimization method based on expression signatures [9]. The basic idea of sharing computation among queries is intuitive. If we can reduce the total computations that a continuous query systems need to proc ess, then it is likely we will improve the overall query performance. Besides sharing of computation, if we can also share intermediate results, such as that from a join between two data streams, we can possibly reap substantial performance improvement.

In [6, 7, 10, 14, 15], caching techniques were used for storing intermediate results from earlier queries. However, most of the existing caching strategies cannot be readily applied in the context of continuous queries. This is because most of these caching technique are not fully pipelined, and incoming queries would block if it was waiting for an earlier query to finish processing in order to make use of the cached results. In addition, an incoming query can re-use the cache results from an earlier query only when at least one of the CSE in a query plan has been completely processed. However, in continuous que ries systems where data streams can be possibly unbounded, it is difficult to establish when a CSE has been completely processed.

The second issue of adapting to fluctuations in the query environment is well studied in the context of one-time queries in traditional database management systems [2, 3, 17, 18]. Recently, the eddy mechanism was introduced in [4], which adapts to fluctuations by run-time re-ordering of the order in which tuples are passed to the respective operators. Our work on introducing adaptivity to continuous query systems is based on an extension to the eddy mechanism. The eddy mechanism was designed for handling one-time queries, and does not cater to the handling of multiple continuous queries.

In this paper, we identify and address the issues in the efficient processing of multiple queries in a continuous query system. As join processing is one of the most expensive operations both in traditional database management systems, as well as continuous query systems, we will focus on the efficient processing of multi-join queries in our work. We show how our propose framework, AdaptiveCQ, can handle both issues of efficient processing of multiple continuous queries and adapting to fluctuations at the s ame time. In addition, we propose a novel method for sharing of results amongst multiple queries on-the-fly as well as introduces a garbage collection mechanism to remove data that are no longer required by any of the running queries. Lastly, we show how the eddy can handle both multi-join queries, and adapt at run-time to fluctuations at the same time. We conducted an extensive study to evaluate the performance of the proposed techniques. Our results show that AdaptiveCQ can provide substantial performance improvements when compared to existing multi-query processing techniques that relied on sharing results between queries by reusing materialized intermediate results.

2 AdaptiveCQ

In this section, we will present the AdaptiveCQ framework and show how it can be used to handle multiple continuous queries. In addition, we will introduce the use of the State and Query Vector to allow a tuple to be shared amongst multiple queries. In the first sub-section, we will provide a quick overview of the eddy mechanism. In the next few sections, we will present the various mechanisms in AdaptiveCQ that allows it to handle multiple continuous queries and allowing on-the-fly reuse of intermediate re sult between queries.

2.1 Eddies Revisited

Let us first recall the eddy [4] query-processing model. An eddy routes tuples from its inputs to the various operators, specified in a query plan, for processing before sending a tuple, which has completed processing to the output.

Each tuple entering the eddy is associated with a Ready Vector and Done Vector. The bits in the Ready vector is used to indicate whether the tuple is ready to be processed by an operator, and the bits in the Done vector is used to indicate whether a tuple been processed by the corresponding operator. When all the bits in the Done Vector are set, the tuple is sent to output.

ision on which operator the eddy should give a tuple to is dependent on the tuple routing policy used. The tuple routing policy determines amongst several eligible operators for a tuple, which operator is assigned to process a tuple. In [4], a lottery-based policy is used. When an operator has processed a tuple, the corresponding bit in the Ready Vector would be set to false, and the corresponding bit in the Done Vector would be set to true.

We note that the Done and Ready Vector are applied in the context of a one-time query. Now, let us suppose we wish to extend the use of the Done and Ready Vector to multiple queries. Naively, we could associate a pair of Ready and Done vectors for each query that is introduces into the system. However, when the number of queries increases, the number of Ready and Done vectors would increase proportionally to the number of queries. In a continuous query system with a large number of queries, the memory resources needed for the vectors would be significantly large. Clearly, this method is not feasible. We propose a new data structure to replace the Done and Ready vector to handle multiple queries.

2.2 Multiple Continuous Queries Dynamics

Each tuple entering the AdaptiveCQ system is associated with a State vector and a Query vector. The bits in the State vector indicate the state of a tuple for each operator, and the bits in the Query vector indicate whether the tuple has completed all the processing for a specific query.

State Vector. Since there are several operators running in AdaptiveCQ, it is likely that a tuple might only be required to be processed by some of these operators. For each operator, each tuple can be in four possible states, which can be encoded using two bits. The four possible states and their description are presented in Figure 1. For example, let us consider the queries given in Figure 2.

State	Description
ELIGIBLE(1)	Eligible for processing by the operator
NOT ELIGIBLE(2)	Not eligible for processing by the operator
PROCESSED AND SUCCESSFUL(3)	Processed by the operator and it has been marked as successful
PROCESSED AND FAILED(4)	Processed by the operator and the operator has marked it as not meeting the filter criteria

Fig. 1. Possible tuple states

```
Query 1:  Select * from R,S where (R.a = S.a)
Query 2:  Select * from R,S,T where (R.a = S.a) and (S.b = T.b)
```

Fig. 2. Sample join queries

In Figure 2, query 1 performs a 2-way join between R and S and query 2 performs a 3-way join between R, S and T. Let us denote the join between R and

S as J1 and join between S and T as J2 respectively. Figure 3a, 3b and 3c shows the possible state vector for a new tuple from relation R, S and T respectively. Henceforth, we will denote a tuple from relation R, S and T as R-tuple, S-tuple and T-tuple respectively.

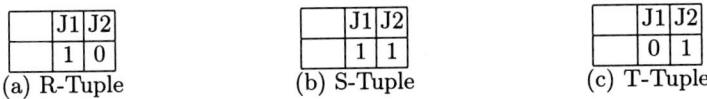

Fig. 3. Possible state vector for a tuple from relation R, S and T

In Figure 3a, we restrict an R-tuple from be given to J2 since J2 is a join between S and T, and that a new R-tuple would not be able to participate in the join unless it has already been joined with an S-tuple. Similarly, in figure 3c, we restrict the T-tuple from given to J1 until it has been joined with an S-tuple. However, we note that a S-tuple can either participates in the join between R and S, as well as S and T. Therefore, both bits in the State Vector ar e set in Figure 3b.

When a new query is added to AdaptiveCQ, the corresponding numbers of bits are added to the front of the State vector depending on the number of existing operators that can be shared. If no existing running operators can be shared, then new operators are added to the AdaptiveCQ system, and new bits corresponding to the newly introduced operators are added to the front of the State vector.

Query Vector. Each bit in the query vector denotes a query that is running in the AdaptiveCQ system. Suppose there are n queries, n bits will be needed. However, since it is likely that the query vector consists of a long series of 1s and 0s, the query vector is compressed on-the-fly with run-length encoding to reduce the size of the query vector. This makes the solution scalable to a large number of queries in a continuous query system. A new tuple entering the system would have all the bits in the Query Vector set to f alse. If a new tuple entering the system is needed by only some of the queries. We turn on (i.e. set to 1) the bits in the Query vector for the queries that do not require the tuple to indicate that it is by default done for queries that do not require it.

For example, let us consider the 2 queries given in Figure 2. A new R-tuple, S-tuple, T-tuple entering the system would have the bits set as in Figure 4a, 4b and 4c respectively. In the figures, we note that the first bit of the T-tuple is set to indicate that it is not required by query 1. This allows the T-tuple to be discarded from the system once it is processed by Q2.

When a new query is added to the AdaptiveCQ system, a new bit is added to the front of the Query Vector. Here, it is important to note that we do not add to the back of the Query Vector. This ensures that the newly added bits

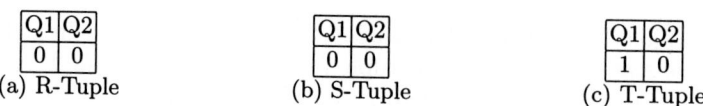

	Q1	Q2
	0	0

(a) R-Tuple

	Q1	Q2
	0	0

(b) S-Tuple

	Q1	Q2
	1	0

(c) T-Tuple

Fig. 4. Query Vectors for new tuples

do not interfere with the already defined query vector of existing tuples in the system.

The main difference between the eddy Ready and Done vector and AdaptiveCQ State and Query vector is that the length of the eddy's Ready and Done vector is equal to the number of operators required for a one-time query. In contrast, the length of AdaptiveCQ's State Vector is equal to the total number of operators required by all queries in the continuous query system, and the length of AdaptiveCQ's Query Vector is equal to the number of queries in the system. This allows a tuple to be shared across all queries, instead of limiting it to a single one-time query. Consider the join queries, Q1 and Q2, given in Figure 2. Even though Query 1 only requires a single join operator to handle the join between R and S, the length of the State Vector associated with the R-tuple and the S-tuple is 2, instead of 1.

Query footprint. Let us assume a continuous query system with several continuous queries running. For an incoming query, we can perform fast identification of the operators that could be shared by the incoming query using the techniques described in [8, 9, 15].

A query footprint is a small in-memory data structure that describes the operators that the query will use in order to process the query. When the eddy needs to determine whether a tuple should be output for a particular query, the tuple's state vector is compared against the query footprints. A copy of the tuple is sent to output for the queries that have completed processing. If the tuple is still required by other queries, it is put back into the eddy for further processing. When there are no more queries that require the tuples (which can be checked from the query footprint), the tuple is discarded from the system.

Figure 5a and 5b shows how the query footprints for the queries in Figure 2. Since query 1 only require the use of J1, the corresponding bit is turned on (i.e. set to 1), and the bit for J2 is turned off (i.e. set to 0). In query 2, both bits are turned on as it requires both J1 and J2.

	J1	J2
States	1	0

(a) Query 1 footprint

	J1	J2
States	1	1

(b) Query 2 footprint

Fig. 5. Query footprints

2.3 AdaptiveCQ Dynamics

When a query is added to AdaptiveCQ, it first transforms the query into an equivalent query footprint. The algorithm for transforming the query to the footprint is given in Figure 6. The transformation process will first check whether there are any common sub expressions that the query can share with other queries. This can be achieved using the techniques described in [9]. New operators that cannot be shared are introduced on the fly to the continuous query system . Each new tuple entering AdaptiveCQ is associated with a pair of State and Query vectors. The bits in the Query Vector are all set to false to indicate that the tuple has not completed processing for all the queries. The bits in the State vector are set corresponding to the operators that are required to process the tuple.

AdaptiveCQ relies on the query footprints of the running queries as well as the state and query vector to determine whether a processed tuple should be sent to the output or be sent to another eligible operator for processing. Each operator in AdaptiveCQ, including the AdaptiveCQ itself, is implemented as a separate thread. The algorithm for AdaptiveCQ is presented in Figure 7.

3 Multi-query Join Processing

In this section, we shall present our approach to handling joins in continuous query systems, that performs on the fly re-use of results. In addition, we introduce the notion of data span and show how 'old data' can be removed from the system using garbage collection techniques.

3.1 Join Processing in Continuous Query Systems

Joins constitute the most expensive operation both in a traditional database management system as well as in a continuous query system. Most join operators need to maintain state information. Examples of such state information include: (1) tuples joined so far (2) in the context of partitioned based hash joins [17], information for determining partitions that has not been joined yet. In the context of a continuous query system where the data streams are possibly unbounded, maintaining the sta te information for join processing is a challenge. We present our study in the context of partitioned-based symmetric hash joins [17].

 partition of the other relation involved in the join. We refer to this as the insert-probe operation. If a match occurs, a joined tuple is produced and sent to output. When a partition is full, it is flushed to disk. In a partition-based symmetric hash join, such as XJoin [17], join processing usually consists of 3 stages. In the first stage, usually referred to as the regular stage, tuples arrive from the inputs from the join operator, and join processing proceeds in an insert-probe manner. The second stage, referred to as the reactive stage, is usually invoked when the inputs to the join operators blocks. A disk-resident partition is selected

```
/**
 * Q denotes the query to be transformed
 * opList denotes the list of all operators in AdaptiveCQ
 */
queryFootPrint transformQueryToFootprint(Q, opList) {
    Create new query footprint, qfp, whose length is equal to the
    length of opList

    Let O[n] denote the set of n operators identified in Q

    The difference between opList and O[n] is that opList contains
    all operators used by all the queries in AdaptiveCQ whereas
    O[n] contains only the set of operators identified in Q.

    for(int i=0; i < n; i++) {
      if ( O[i] can be shared with an operator in opList ) {
          Let j denote the jth operator in opList that can be shared
          Set the jth bit in qfp
      }
      else {
          /* no operator can be shared */
          Create new operator newop, and add it to opList

          Set the corresponding bit of qfp that denotes the
          newly created operator to be true
      }
    } /* for i */
    /* return the newly created footprint */
    return qfp;
}
```

Fig. 6. Algorithm to transforming a query to a query footprint

and used to probe with the memory-resident portion of the cor responding partition. The third stage, referred to as the cleanup stage, performs the join of tuples that has not been joined in the earlier two stages. A duplicate elimination strategy such as that proposed in [17] is used to ensure that no duplicate tuples are produced.

3.2 CQ-Join

As the data streams in a continuous query system could possibly be unbounded or long running, two practical issues arise. The first issue that arises is that the size of the disk-resident partitions maintained by the partitioned hash-based would increase with time, and would use up the available disk space quickly. The second issue is that if the data streams are unbounded or long running, it is difficult to determine when the cleanup stage should be invoked. In order to

```
while ( AdaptiveCQ is active ) {
 /**
    Note: When a tuple is given to an operator, the tuple's priority
    is incremented by the operator when the operator next put it
    back into AdaptiveCQ
 */
 t = Get a tuple from AdaptiveCQ's priority queue
 if ( t != null ) {
  /**
     In eligibleForOutput(..), we check whether the tuple is eligible for
     output by comapring the tuple's state vector against all the query
     footprints of the running query.

     If the bits in the state vector indicates that it is has been
     processed successfully by the respective operator (i.e. state
     TUPLE_PROCESSED_PASSED ), it is marked as eligible for output for
     the query in which the query footprint matches
  */
  if ( eligibleForOutput(t) ) {
     Send tuple t to output for the queries which has completed processing
     /* Tuple that has completed processing are marked as done */
     Update the query vector of t
  }

  /**
     We check whether the bits in the tuple Query Vector is all set.
     If it is all set, then the tuple is no longer needed in the system
     and we can discard it. If there are still queries that require the
     tuple, then the tuple cannot be discarded from the system, and should
     be given to a selected eligible operator
  */
  if ( !discardFromSystem(t) ) {
    /**
       Get the id of the operator that we need to give the tuple to
       In assignTupleToOperator(..), we first check t's state vector
       to see which are the eligible operators.
       Note: The tuple routing policies (e.g. lottery, randomized
             static) are implemented in assignTupleTOperator(..)
    */
    int op_id = assignTupleToOperator(t);
    Give tuple to operator[op_id];
  }
 } /* t is not null */
} // while AdaptiveCQ is active
```

Fig. 7. Algorithm for AdaptiveCQ

tackle these issues, we propose a novel partitioned-based symmetric hash join technique, called CQ-Join. The algorithm for CQ-Join is presented in Figure 9.

We chose to base our implementation of CQ-Join on XJoin for two reasons. One, the X-Join operator has frequent moments of symmetry [4], and is suitable for use in the eddy. Second, the X-Join operator is able to react to fluctuations in the query environment by switching to a reactive stage. Even though in an eddy query-processing model, the eddy would adaptively adapt to fluctuations in the query environment, it is also necessary for each operator that is operating in tandem with the eddy to have a high overall throughput (i.e. produces tuples quickly and putting it back to the eddy), which would indirectly influence the eddy's choice in which operator the eddy should give a tuple to. Thus, we observe that besides introducing join operators that exhibit frequent moments of symmetry, we need to introduce join operators that have a high throughput.

The two main differences between CQ-Join and X-Join are: (1) CQ-Join performs garbage collection when a user-defined disk threshold is reached. (2) CQ-Join's cleanup stage is well defined, even in the presence of long running queries and unbounded data streams. We achieve this by using the notion of data span. By associating a data span to queries and the partitions used in CQ-Join, we are able to selectively remove partitions that are no longer needed. This prevents continuous queries that operate on an unbounded data stream from using all available disk resources.

3.3 Tuple Data Span

The data span of a tuple is a 2-tuple {span_start, span_end} that defines the time interval in which the data is valid and used for join processing of a query. When data is not within the data span, then it should be discarded from the system. Let us illustrate the notion of data span with an example. Consider the queries given in Figure 8. In the queries, we introduce the a new function into SQL, called time_interval(start,end). The time_interval() semantics defines how long the query would be processed by the continuous query system. If it is not specified, it is treated as a one-time query on the data stream, and would terminate when the subsequent garbage collection is invoked. Both query 1 and 2 define a bounded time interval of which the query is executed. In query 3, the continuous query is unbounded, and would require the continuous query system to process the query as long as the continuous query system is running. For the purpose of illustration, we will assume that the default time unit used is in minutes. Thus, the data span for the tuples from data sources R, S, T and U are $\{0, 100\}$, $\{0, \infty\}$, $\{10, \infty\}$ and $\{0, \infty\}$ respectively.

In addition, it can be noted that the data span of a partition is the same as the tuple data span, since all tuples found in a partition are essentially from the same data stream.

Let us consider the case of a binary join. Suppose we have two tuples A and B from two different data sources. The tuple data span are $\{span\_start_A, span\_end_A\}$ and $\{span\_start_B, span\_end_B\}$ respectively. Then, the data span of the joined tuple can be derived as follows:

$$min(span\_start_A, span\_start_B), max(span\_end_A, span\_end_B)$$

```
Query 1:   Select * from R,S where (R.a = S.a)
           and time_interval(0,10)

Query 2:   Select * from R,S,T where R.a = S.a and S.b = T.b
           and time_interval(10,100)

Query 3:   Select * from S,T,U where S.a = T.a and T.b = U.b
           and time_interval(0, ∞)
```

Fig. 8. Sample join queries with time interval

3.4 Garbage Collection/Cleanup Stage

We define the process of removing partitions that consists of tuples that are no longer required by any of the running queries as garbage collection. Garbage collection is invoked under two scenarios: (1) When the size of the disk resident partitions exceeds the disk threshold defined by the user (2) When the query terminates, and that the data streams used by the query is not shared with other running queries.

This can be determined by checking the data span of the partitions. Partitions that have data span less than or equal to the current timestamp are removed after the cleanup stage.

In Figure 9, prior to garbage collection, we invoke the cleanup stage, which performs memory-disk partitions joins as well as disk-disk partition joins. Once the cleanup stage completes, garbage collection removes all partitions that are older than the current timestamp.

4 Performance Study

The AdaptiveCQ system is implemented from scratch in Java, and consists of an eddy-variant, which uses a randomized routing policy if there is more than one operator eligible to process a tuple. Though the performance of Java is comparatively slower than C++ (which is noted by the longer execution time in all our experiments), we chose Java for its portability and compatibility with the other Java-based relational operators that we have developed prior. The experiments are conducted on a Pentium III 550Mhz machine with 128MB of RAM, and running Windows NT.

In order to determine whether the incoming queries are similar with existing queries, we define a parameter call degree of overlap, denoted by α, which is the probability of a new incoming query being similar to an existing query. When α is 0, there is no overlap between the incoming query and existing running queries,

```
while( continuous query system is active ) {
  /**
    Note: CQ-Join's input buffer consists of tuples from
    both input source
  */
  Get tuple t from CQ-Join's input buffer
  if ( input source blocks ) {
    /**
      input source blocks, we switch to the reactiveStage
      which joins a in-memory partition with a disk partition
    */
    Switch to ReactiveStage();
  }
  else {
    Let partition R be the partition to insert t
    Let partition S be the corresponding partition which we use
    t to probe

    for each tuple s in partition S {
      if ( joinable(s,t) ) {
        new_tuple = join(s,t);

        Set the corresponding bit in new_tuple's state vector
        to indicate that it has been processed by this join

        Put new_tuple back to AdaptiveCQ for further processing
      }
  } /* else */

  /**
    This is used by the cleanupStage to perform duplicate
    elimination
  */
  Mark partition S as joined with the last tuple
  of partition R

  Mark partition R as joined with the last
  tuple of partition S

  /* check whether disk threshold is reached */
  if ( partitions_disk_size >= disk_threshold ) {
    /* perform join of memory-disk, and disk-disk
       partitions*/
    Switch to cleanupStage();
    garbageCollectOldPartition();
  }
} /* while active */
```

Fig. 9. Algorithm for CQ-Join

and all queries are different. When α is 1, each incoming query is similar to one of the running queries.

4.1 Effect of Sharing Computation

In this experiment, we wish to study the effect of sharing computation amongst the multiple continuous queries. Each continuous query is a one-to-one (i..e. each tuple in one relation finds a corresponding tuple in the other relation) binary join. Each dataset consists of 1000 tuples, and the data values are uniformly distributed. The continuous query system consists of 10 basic queries, and 50 queries are introduced into the system at runtime. A new incoming query is checked whether it can be shared with one of the basic queries. If the incoming query cannot be shared, it is processed separately from the existing queries. This is controlled by the parameter α, which denotes the degree of overlap. The results are presented in Figure 10. In this experiment, we vary α from 0.0 to 1.0.

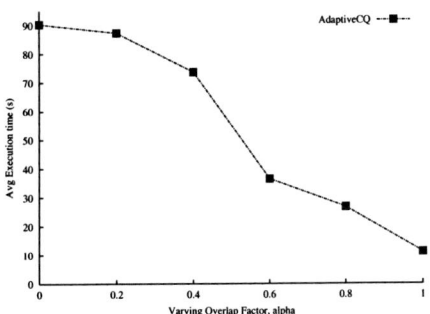

Fig. 10. Effect of sharing computation

From the results, we can observe that through sharing computation for join queries, there is significant performance improvement. In Figure 10, when we compare the case when there is no sharing ($\alpha = 0.0$) and that where all incoming queries can be shared with one of the existing running basic query ($\alpha = 1.0$), the performance improvement is by a factor of 9!

The performance improvement is more significant for join queries than selection queries because join queries are computationally more expensive than selection queries, which merely filters values based on some user-defined predicates. In addition, when sharing computation amongst the queries, we can reduce the overheads of handling the query separately.

4.2 Comparing Sharing of Results (Materializing Intermediate Results vs On-the-fly Sharing)

In this experiment, we wish to study the effect of how AdaptiveCQ, which allows on-the-fly sharing of results, compares to existing multi-query join processing techniques which materialize intermediate results so that it can be reused by other queries. Datasets consisting of 100, 1000 and 10000 tuples each are used.

The setup of the experiments is as follows: The experiment consists of two equi-join queries as follows: Query 1: R ⋈ S and Query 2: R ⋈ S ⋈ T respectively. For simplicity, each join is a one-to-one join. In addition, we assume that the data streams are bounded and that query processing terminates once the data streams feeding the join produces no more tuples. We compare our technique (i.e. AdaptiveCQ) and the existing multi-query join processing technique of reusing which materializes intermediate results of running queries (i.e. which we will refer to as the reuse method), so that it can be used by other new incoming queries.

In the reuse method, intermediate results are materialized. Thus, Query 2 blocks until query 1 completes. Query 1 performs the join and writes the result of the join to disk so that Query 2 can re-use the results and avoid performing joining R and S again. Note: Both query 1 and 2 uses only 1 join operator at one time. Query 1 performs the join between R and S, Query 2 performs the join between I and T, where I is the materialized intermediate result from Query 1.

In the AdaptiveCQ approach, 2 join operators are executed, one performing R ⋈ S, and the other performing S ⋈ T. There is no need to materialize intermediate results, since a tuple that has completed processing for R ⋈ S is fed back into the eddy and given to the other unprocessed operators.

The results of the experiments on measuring the total execution time of the queries for both methods are shown in Figure 11. From Figure 11, we can see that as the dataset size increases, AdaptiveCQ performs much better than the reuse method. This /nfiis due to AdaptiveCQ ability to adapt and reuse intermediate results on-the-fly. In contrast, the reuse method need to materialize the intermediate results of Query 1 to disk before it can be used by Query 2, thus incurring expensive I/O overheads.

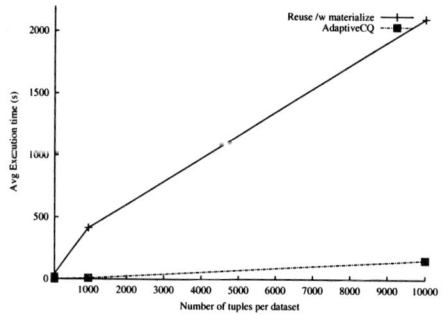

Fig. 11. Comparison between reuse with materialized results vs AdaptiveCQ

In addition, we also conducted experiments to study AdaptiveCQ performance in producing the initial N tuples for multiple continuous join queries. The results of the experiments are shown in Figure 12a and 12b. From the graph, we can observe that AdaptiveCQ's method of on-the-fly sharing of results amongst

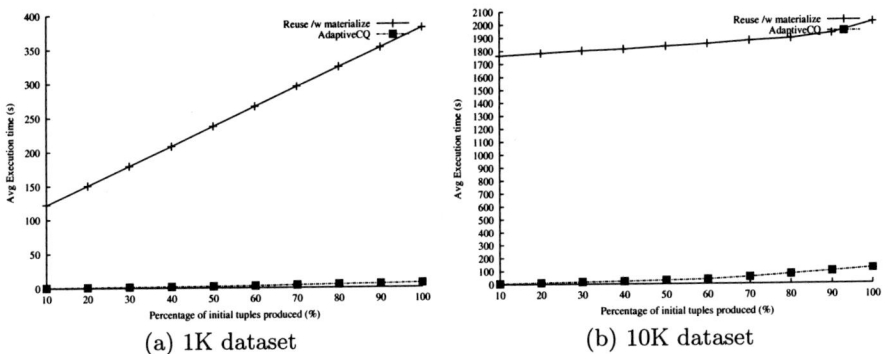

Fig. 12. Comparison between reuse with materialized results vs AdaptiveCQ (Time taken to produce the initial N% tuples)

queries improves the timing taken to produce the initial N tuples significantly. This is because by allowing on-the-fly sharing of intermediate results, we eliminate the expensive I/O overheads that is incurred during materialization of intermediate results. In addition, by allowing on-the-fly sharing of results, a tuple from data stream S entering AdaptiveCQ can be given either to the join operator performing R ⋈ S or the join operator performing S ⋈ T. This contributes to the significant performance improvement.

4.3 Varying Data Distribution

As continuous queries are long running, the data streams would exhibit varying characteristics. In this experiment, we wish to study the effect of varying the skewness of the distribution of values in the datasets on query performance. In addition, we wish to study AdaptiveCQ ability to adapt to varying data characteristics, which are common in long running queries

By controlling the value of a parameter θ, the skewness of the distribution of values is varied. When $\theta=0$, the dataset is uniformly distributed, and when $\theta=1.0$, the dataset follows a Zipfian distribution. The size of the datasets used are 1k, and 10k. The results of the experiments are presented in Figure 13a and Figure 13b. In Figure 13a and Figure 13b, we see that AdaptiveCQ adapts well to data distr ibution with varying degree of skewness.

4.4 Varying Burst Rate and Tuple Inter-arrival Rate

In a wide-area environment, data streams are susceptible to fluctuations such as different data transfer rates. In addition, it is likely that the data are likely to arrive in short bursts of varying intensity (i.e the amount of tuples arriving varies.). In this experiment, we wish to study how the effects of such fluctuations affect AdaptiveCQ's performance. In addition, we wish to compare AdaptiveCQ's against techniques, which reuse intermediate results via materialization.

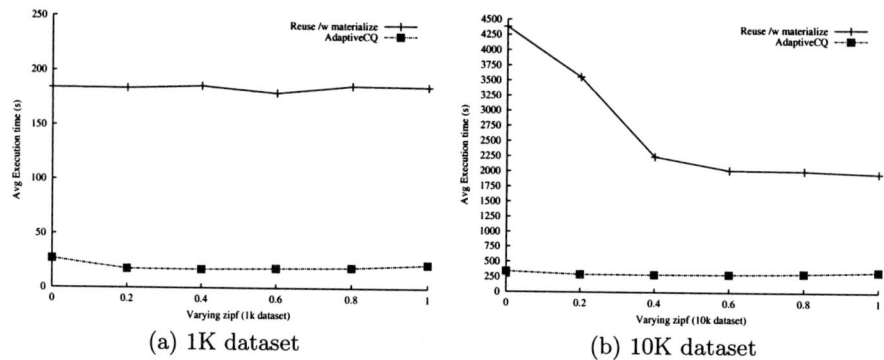

Fig. 13. Comparison between reuse with materialized results vs AdaptiveCQ with varying zipfian distribution

In these experiments, a data stream generator generates the tuples arriving in a data stream. The tuples is then 'fed' into AdaptiveCQ, to be sent to the eligible operators for processing. We define two parameters - (1) Data Stream Burst Rate, β and (2) Data Inter-arrival rate, η. β controls the number of tuples that arrive within a burst. This is implemented within the data stream generator as a loop which determines the amount of tuples to generate before the data stream generator r elinquish control to other running threads. η controls the rate in which tuples arrive. This is implemented within the data stream generator as a sleep(l), which means to ask the data stream generator thread to sleep for l seconds, prior to generating the next set of tuples. We vary β and η in order to study the effects on AdaptiveCQ.

The setup of the experiments is as follows: The experiment consists of two equi-join queries as follows: Query 1: R ⋈ S and Query 2: R ⋈ S ⋈ T respectively. Two joins operators are identified. The first join operator (J1) performs R ⋈ S and the second join operator (J2) performs the join of (R ⋈ S) T For simplicity, each join is a one-to-one join. The dataset used for R, S, and T consists of 5000 tuples each. In the experiment, we fix the data generation rate for data stream R and T. We vary the inter-arrival times and burst rate of data stream S. In addition, we assume that the data streams are bounded. The results of the experiments are presented in Figure 14. In Figure 14, the value in parentheses indicates the burst rate (i.e. the number of tuples that are generated in a burst).

From Figure 14, we can observe that AdaptiveCQ consistently outperforms the reuse method. This is due to the following: (1) Since a S-tuple in AdaptiveCQ can be given to either J1 or J2, it has better chance of being processed and matched with either a tuple from R or a tuple from T, thus improving the overall performance. (2) When the data stream producing S tuples blocks, the tuples produced by the reactive stage of either CQ-Join (i.e. either J1 or J2) could be 'fed' into the other join operator for processing. In comparison, using the reuse method, a S-tuple can only be given to J1, and the intermediate results materialized to disk before the results can be used by J2. In addition, the tuples

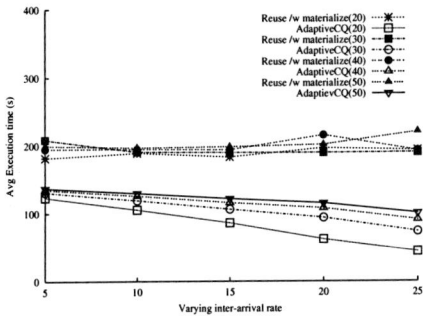

Fig. 14. Effect of varying burst rate and inter-arrival times

produced by the reactive stage of J1 would have to be materialized to disk, and only when J1 completes, then J2 can start processing the join. This gives little opportunities for 'hiding' the delays experienced by the data stream producing tuples.

5 Conclusion and Future Work

In this paper, we propose a novel approach for adaptive multi-query processing, based on an extension of the Eddies model. In addition, we demonstrate the use of the approach in join processing, and showed how multiple join operators can be shared amongst several queries, thus improving query performance. We also propose a novel join technique, CQ-Join, which is suitable for use in a continuous query system. Lastly, we perform extensive performance analysis, which shows promising results.

In our current work, we have considered only join queries and selection. We are currently exploring the application of the AdaptiveCQ framework in handling aggregation and sub queries. If computation for aggregation could also be shared amongst queries, we believe it would have a significant impact on system performance.

Acknowledgments

We thank Philippe Bonnet, Kian-Lee Tan and Ullas Nambiar for their generous suggestions and comments on the initial drafts of the paper. The work was supported by the academic research grant SINGA, R-252-000-064-107, of National University of Singapore.

References

1. Mehmet Altinel and Michael J. Franklin. Efficient filtering of XML documents for selective dissemination of information. In *The VLDB Journal*, pages 53–64, 2000.
2. Laurent Amsaleg, Michael J. Franklin, and Anthony Tomasic. Dynamic query operator scheduling for wide-area remote access. *Distributed and Parallel Databases*, 6(3):217–246, 1998.
3. Laurent Amsaleg, Michael J. Franklin, Anthony Tomasic, and Tolga Urhan. Scrambling query plans to cope with unexpected delays. In *PDIS*, pages 208–219, 1996.
4. Ron Avnur and Joseph M. Hellerstein. Eddies: Continuously adaptive query processing. In *Proceedings of the ACM SIGMOD International Conference on Management of Data*, pages 261–272, May 2000.
5. Philippe Bonnet, Johannes Gehrke, and Praveen Seshadri. Towards sensor database systems. In *Proceedings of Mobile Data Management, Second International Conference, MDM 2001, Hong Kong, China*, January 2001.
6. Surajit Chaudhuri, Ravi Krishnamurthy, Spyros Potamianos, and Kyuseak Shim. Optimizing queries with materialized views. In *11th Int. Conference on Data Engineering*, pages 190–200, Los Alamitos, CA, 1995. IEEE Computer Soc. Press.
7. C. Chen and N. Roussopoulos. The implementation and performance evaluation of the adms query optimizer: Integrating query result caching and matching, 1994.
8. Jianjun Chen, David J. DeWitt, Feng Tian, and Yuan Wang. NiagaraCQ: a scalable continuous query system for Internet databases. In *Proceedings of the ACM SIGMOD International Conference on Management of Data*, pages 379–390, 2000.
9. E. N. Hanson, C. Carnes, L. Huang, M. Konyala, L. Noronha, S. Parthasarathy, J. B. Park, and A. Vernon. Scalable Trigger Processing. In *Proceedings of the 15th International Conference on Data Engineering*, pages 266–275. IEEE Computer Society Press, 1999.
10. Donald Kossmann, Michael J. Franklin, Gerhard Drasch, and Wig Ag. Cache investment: Integrating query optimization and distributed data placement. *ACM Transactions on Database Systems (TODS)*, 25(4), December 2000.
11. Ling Liu, Calton Pu, and Wei Tang. Continual queries for internet scale event-driven information delivery. *Knowledge and Data Engineering*, 11(4):610–628, 1999.
12. Prasan Roy, S. Seshadri, S. Sudarshan, and Siddhesh Bhobe. Efficient and extensible algorithms for multi query optimization. In *Proceedings of the ACM SIGMOD International Conference on Management of Data*, pages 249–260, 2000.
13. Timos K. Sellis. Multiple query optimization. *ACM Transactions on Database Systems (TODS)*, 13(1):23–52, March 1988.
14. J. Shim, P. Scheuermann, and R. Vingralek. Dynamic caching of query results for decision support systems, 1999.
15. Kian Lee Tan, Shen Tat Goh, and Beng Chin Ooi. Cache-on-demand: Recycling with certainty. In *International Conference on Data Engineering*, April 2001.
16. Douglas Terry, David Goldberg, David Nichols, and Brian Oki. Continuous queries over append-only databases. In *Proceedings of the ACM SIGMOD International Conference on Management of Data*, pages 321–330, June 1992.
17. Tolga Urhan and Michael J. Franklin. XJoin: Getting fast answers from slow and bursty networks. Technical Report CS-TR-3994, University of Maryland, February 1999, 1999.
18. Tolga Urhan, Michael J. Franklin, and Laurent Amsaleg. Cost-based query scrambling for initial delays. In *Proceedings of the ACM SIGMOD International Conference on Management of Data*, pages 130–141, 1998.

The Geometry of Uncertainty
in Moving Objects Databases

Goce Trajcevski[1], Ouri Wolfson[1,2,*], Fengli Zhang[1], and Sam Chamberlain[3]

[1] University of Illinois at Chicago, Dept. of CS
{gtrajcev,wolfson,fzhang}@cs.uic.edu
[2] Mobitrac, Inc., Chicago
[3] Army Research Laboratory, Aberdeen Proving Ground, MD wildman@arl.mil

Abstract. This work addresses the problem of querying moving objects databases. which capture the inherent uncertainty associated with the location of moving point objects. We address the issue of modeling, constructing, and querying a trajectories database. We propose to model a trajectory as a 3D cylindrical body. The model incorporates uncertainty in a manner that enables efficient querying. Thus our model strikes a balance between modeling power, and computational efficiency. To demonstrate efficiency, we report on experimental results that relate the length of a trajectory to its size in bytes. The experiments were conducted using a real map of the Chicago Metropolitan area.
We introduce a set of novel but natural spatio-temporal operators which capture uncertainty, and are used to express spatio-temporal range queries. We also devise and analyze algorithms to process the operators. The operators have been implemented as a part of our DOMINO project.

1 Introduction and Motivation

Miniaturization of computing devices, and advances in wireless communication and sensor technology are some of the forces that are propagating computing from the stationary desktop to the mobile outdoors. Important classes of new applications that will be enabled by this revolutionary development include location based services, tourist services, mobile electronic commerce, and digital battlefield. Many existing applications will also benefit from this development: transportation and air traffic control, weather forecasting, emergency response, mobile resource management, and mobile workforce. Location management, i.e. the management of transient location information, is an enabling technology for all these applications. It is also a fundamental component of other technologies such as fly-through visualization, context awareness, augmented reality, cellular communication, and dynamic resource discovery.

Database researchers have addressed some aspects of the problem of modeling and querying the location of moving objects. Largest efforts were made in the

---

* Research supported by ARL Grant DAAL01-96-2-0003, NSF Grants ITR-0086144, CCR-9816633, CCR-9803974, IRI-9712967, EIA-0000516, INT-9812325

area of access methods. Aside from a purely spatial ([8] surveys 50+ structures) and temporal databases [27], there are several recent results which tackle various problems of indexing *spatio-temporal* objects and dynamic attributes [1, 12, 13, 17, 22, 28, 30, 31]. Representing and querying the location of moving objects as a function of time is introduced in [24], and the works in [36, 37] address policies for updating and modeling imprecision and communication costs. Modeling and querying location uncertainties due to sampling and GPS imprecision is presented in [16]. Algebraic specifications of a system of abstract data types, their constructors and a set of operations are given in [4, 6, 9].

In this paper we deal in a systematic way with the issue of *uncertainty* of the *trajectory* of a moving object. Uncertainty is an inherent aspect in databases which store information about the location of moving objects. Due to continuous motion and network delays, the database location of a moving object will not always precisely represent its real location. Unless uncertainty is captured in the model and query language, the burden of factoring uncertainty into answers to queries is left to the user.

Traditionally, the trajectory of a moving object was modeled as a polyline in three dimensional space (two dimensions for geography, and one for time). In this paper, in order to capture uncertainty we model the trajectory as a cylindrical volume in 3D. Traditionally, spatio-temporal range queries ask for the objects that are inside a particular region, during a particular time interval. However, for the moving objects one may query the objects that are inside the region *sometime* during the time interval, or for the ones that are *always* inside during the time interval. Similarly, one may query the objects that are *possibly* inside the region or for the ones that are *definitely* there. For example, one may ask queries such as:

Q1: *"Retrieve the current location of the delivery trucks that will possibly be inside a region R, sometime between 3:00PM and 3:15PM"*.

Q2: *"Retrieve the number of tanks which will definitely be inside the region R sometime between 1:30PM and 1:45PM."*.

Q3: *"Retrieve the police cars which will possibly be inside the region R, always between 2:30AM and 2:40AM"*.

We provide the syntax of the operators for spatio-temporal range queries, and their processing algorithms. It turns out that these algorithms have a strong geometric flavor. We also wanted to determine whether for realistic applications the trajectories database can be stored in main memory. We generated over 1000 trajectories using a map of Chicagoland and analyzed their average size – approximately 7.25 line segments per mile. Thus, for fleets of thousands of vehicles the trajectories database can indeed be stored in main memory.

The model and the operators that we introduce in this paper have been implemented in our DOMINO system. The operators are built as User Defined Functions (UDF) in Informix IDS2000. A demo version of the DOMINO system is available at `http://131.193.39.205/mapcafe/mypage.html`. The operators are built as User Defined Functions (UDF) in Informix IDS2000. Our main contributions can be summarized as follows:

1. – We introduce a trajectory model with uncertainty, and its construction based on electronic maps;
2. – We experimentally evaluate the average length of a trajectory and determine that it is about 7.25 line segments per mile;
3. – We introduce a set of operators for querying trajectories with uncertainty. We provide both linguistic constructs and processing algorithms, and show that the complexity of the algorithms is either linear or quadratic.

The rest of the article is structured as follows. In section 2 we define the model of a trajectory and show how it can be constructed based on electronic maps. Section 3 discusses the experiments to determine the average size of a trajectory. Section 4. defines the uncertainty concepts for a trajectory. In Section 5. we present the *syntax* and the *semantics* of the new operators for querying trajectories with uncertainty. Section 6. provides the processing algorithms and their analysis. Section 7 concludes the paper, positions it in the context of related work, and outlines the future work.

2 Representing and Constructing the Trajectories

In this section we define our model of a *trajectory*, and we describe how to construct it from the data available in electronic maps. In order to capture the spatio-temporal nature of a moving object we use the following:

Definition 1. *A* trajectory *of a moving object is a polyline in three-dimensional space (two-dimensional geography, plus time), represented as a sequence of points* (x_1, y_1, t_1), (x_2, y_2, t_2), ..., (x_n, y_n, t_n) $(t_1 < t_2 < ... < t_n)$. *For a given a trajectory* Tr, *its projection on the X-Y plane is called the* route *of* Tr.

A trajectory defines the location of a moving object as an implicit function of time. The object is at (x_i, y_i) at time t_i, and during each segment $[t_i, t_{i+1}]$, the object moves along a straight line from (x_i, y_i) to (x_{i+1}, y_{i+1}), and at a constant speed.

Definition 2. *Given a trajectory* Tr, *the* expected location *of the object at a point in time* t *between* t_i *and* t_{i+1} $(1 \leq i < n)$ *is obtained by a linear interpolation between* (x_i, y_i) *and* (x_{i+1}, y_{i+1}).

Note that a trajectory can represent both the past and future motion of objects. As far as future time is concerned, one can think of the trajectory as a set of points describing the *motion plan* of the object. Namely, we have a set of points that the object is going to visit, and we assume that in between the points the object is moving along the shortest path. Given an electronic map, along with the beginning time of the object's motion, we construct a trajectory as a superset of the set of the given – "to-be-visited" – points. In order to explain how we do so, we need to define an electronic map (or a map, for brevity).

Definition 3. *A* map *is a graph, represented as a relation where each tuple corresponds to a block with the following attributes:*
– Polyline: *Each block is a polygonal line segment. Polyline gives the sequence of the endpoints:* $(x_1, y_1), (x_2, y_2), \ldots (x_n, y_n)$.

- Length: *Length of the block.*
- Fid: *The block id number.*
- Drive_Time: *Typical drive time from one end of the block to the other, in minutes.*

Plus, among others, a set of geo-coding attributes which enable translating between an (x,y) *coordinate and an address, such as* "1030 North State St.".:
(e.g. – L_f_add: *Left side from street number.)*

Such maps are provided by, among the others, Geographic Data Technology[1] Co. An intersection of two streets is the endpoint of the four block – polylines. Thus, each map is an undirected graph, with the tuples representing edges of the graph.

The route of a moving object O is specified by giving the starting address or (x, y) coordinate, namely the *start_point*; the starting time; and the destination address or (x, y) coordinate, namely the *(end_point)*. An external routine, available in most Geographic Information Systems, which we assume is given a priori, computes the shortest cost (distance or travel – time) path in the map graph. This path, denoted $P(O)$, is a sequence of blocks (edges), i.e. tuples of the map. Since $P(O)$ is a path in the map graph, the endpoint of one block polyline is the beginning point of the next block polyline. Thus, the route represented by $P(O)$ is a polyline denoted by $L(O)$. Given that the trip has a starting time, we compute the trajectory by computing for each straight line segment on $L(O)$, the time at which the object O will arrive to the point at the end of the segment. For this purpose, the only relevant attributes of the tuples in $P(O)$ are *Polyline* and *Drive_Time*.

Finally, let us observe that a trajectory can be constructed based on past motion. Specifically, consider a set of 3D points $(x_1, y_1, t_1), (x_2, y_2, t_2), \ldots, (x_n, y_n, t_n)$ which were transmitted by a moving object periodically, during its past motion. One can construct a trajectory by first "snapping" the points on the road network, then simply connecting the snapped points with the shortest path on the map.

3 Experimental Evaluation of Trajectory Sizes

In this section we describe our experiments designed to evaluate the number of line segments per trajectory.

As a part of out DOMINO project we have constructed 1141 trajectories based on the electronic map of 18 counties around Chicagoland. The map size is 154.8MB, and has 497,735 records representing this many city-blocks.

The trajectories were constructed by randomly choosing a pair of end points, and connecting them by the shortest path in the map (shortest in terms of the *Drive_Time*) Our results are depicted on Figure 1. The length of the routes was between 1 and 289 miles, as shown on the left graph.

The right graph represents the number of segments per trajectory, as a function of the length of the route. We observed a linear dependency between the "storage requirements" (number of segments) and the length of a route.

---
[1] *(www.geographic.com)*

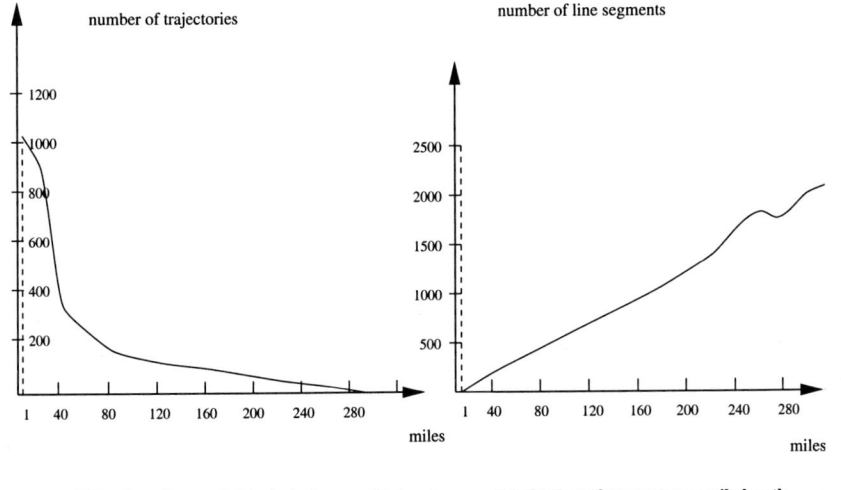

Fig. 1. Number of segments in real - map trajectories

The average number of segments per mile turned out to be 7.2561. Assuming that a trajectory point (x, y, t) uses 12 bytes and that each vehicle from a given fleet (e.g. a metropolitan delivery company), drives a route of approximately 100 miles, we need $\approx$ 10K bytes for a trajectory. Then the storage requirements for all the trajectories of a fleet of 1000 vehicles is $\approx$ 10 MB. This means that the trajectories of the entire fleet can be kept in the main memory.

4 Uncertainty Concepts for Trajectories

An uncertain trajectory is obtained by associating an uncertainty threshold r with each line segment of the trajectory. For a given motion plan, the line segment together with the uncertainty threshold constitute an "agreement" between the moving object and the server. The agreement specifies the following: the moving object will update the server if and only if it deviates from its expected location (according to the trajectory) by r of more. How does the moving object compute the deviation at any point in time? Its on-board computer receives a GPS update every two seconds, so it knows its actual location. Also, it has the trajectory, so by interpolation it can compute its expected location at any point in time. The deviation is simply the distance between the actual and the expected location.

Definition 4. *Let r denote a positive real number and Tr denote a trajectory. An uncertain trajectory is the pair (Tr, r). r is called the uncertainty threshold.*

Definition 5. *Let $Tr \equiv (x_1, y_1, t_1), (x_2, y_2, t_2), ..., (x_n, y_n, t_n)$ denote a trajectory and let r be the uncertainty threshold. For each point (x, y, t) along T, its r-uncertainty area* (or the uncertainty area for short) is a horizontal circle with radius r centered at (x, y, t), where (x,y) is the expected location at time $t \in [t_1, t_n]$.

Note that our model of uncertainty is a little simpler than the one proposed in [16]. There, the uncertainty associated with the location of an object traveling between two endpoints of a line segment is an ellipse with foci at the endpoints.

Definition 6. *Let $Tr \equiv (x_1, y_1, t_1), (x_2, y_2, t_2), ..., (x_n, y_n, t_n)$, be a trajectory, and let r be an uncertainty threshold. A* Possible Motion Curve *$PMC^T r$ is any continuous function $f_{PMC^T r} : Time \to R^2$ defined on the interval $[t_1, t_n]$ such that for any $t \in [t_1, t_n]$, $f_{PMC^T r}(t)$ is inside the uncertainty area of the expected location at time t.*

Intuitively, a possible motion curve describes a route with its associated times, which a moving object may take, without generating an update. An object does not update the database as long as it is on some possible motion curve of its uncertain trajectory (see Figure 2). We will refer to a 2D projection of a possible motion curve as a *possible route*.

Definition 7. *Given an uncertain trajectory (Tr, r) and two end-points $(x_i, y_i, t_i), (x_{i+1}, y_{i+1}, t_{i+1}) \in Tr$, the* trajectory volume *of Tr* between *t_i and t_{i+1} is the set of all the points (x, y, t) such that (x, y, t) belongs to a possible motion curve of Tr and $t_i \leq t \leq t_{i+1}$. The 2D projection of the trajectory volume is called an* uncertainty zone.

Definition 8. *Given a trajectory $Tr \equiv (x_1, y_1, t_1), (x_2, y_2, t_2), ..., (x_n, y_n, t_n)$ and an uncertainty threshold r, the* trajectory volume *of (Tr, r) is the set of all the trajectory volumes between t_i and t_{i+1} $(i = 1, ..., (n-1))$.*

Definitions 6, 7 and 8, are illustrated in Figure 2. Viewed in 3D, a trajectory volume between t_1 and t_n is sequence of volumes, each bounded by a cylindrical body. The axis of each is the vector which specifies the 3D trajectory segment, and the bases are the circles with radius r in the planes $t = t\_begin$ and $t = t\_end$. Observe that the cylindrical body is different from a tilted cylinder. The intersection with of a tilted cylinder with a horizontal plane (parallel to the (X,Y) plane) yields an ellipse, whereas the intersection of our cylindrical body with such a plane yields a circle. Thus, the trajectory volume between two points resembles a set of circles of the uncertainty areas, stacked on top of each other. Let v_{xi} and v_{yi} denote the x and y components of the velocity of a moving object along the i-th segment of the route (i.e. between (x_i, y_i) and (x_{i+1}, y_{i+1})). It can be shown [32] that the trajectory volume between t_i and t_{i+1} is the set of all the points which satisfy: $t_i \leq t \leq t_{i+1}$ and $(x - (x_i + v_{xi} \cdot t))^2 + (y - (y_i + v_{yi} \cdot t))^2 \leq r^2$

5 Querying Moving Objects with Uncertainty

In this section we introduce two categories of operators for querying moving objects with uncertainty. The first category, discussed in section 5.1, deals with *point* queries and it consists of two operators which pertain to a single trajectory. The second category, discussed in section 5.2, is a set of six (boolean) predicates which give a qualitative description of a relative position of a moving object with respect to a region, within a given time interval. Thus, each one of these operators corresponds to a spatio-temporal *range* query.

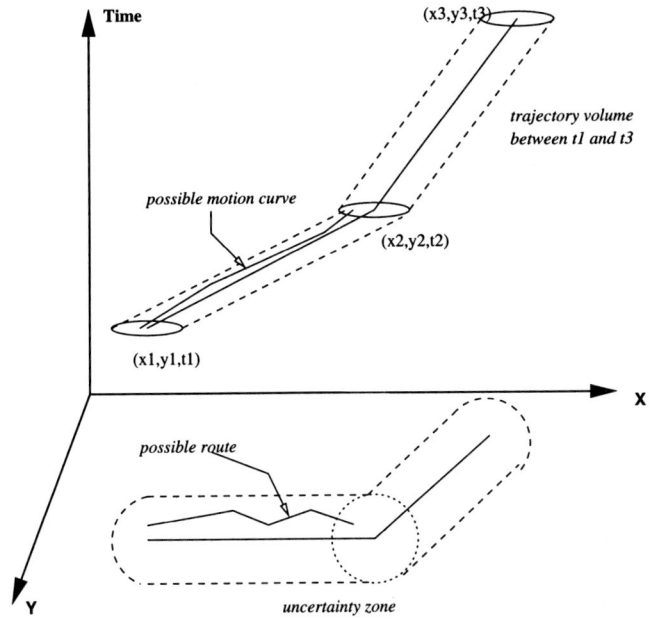

Fig. 2. Possible motion curve and trajectory volume

5.1 Point Queries

The two operators for point queries are defined as follows:
- *Where_At(trajectory Tr, time t)* – returns the expected location *on the route or Tr at time t.*
- *When_At(trajectory Tr, location l)*– returns the times *at which the object on Tr is at expected location l.* The answer may be a set of times, in case the moving object passes through a certain point more than once. If the location l is not on the route of the trajectory Tr, we find the set of all the points C on this route which are <u>closest</u> to l. The function then returns the set of times at which the object is expected to be at each point in C.

The algorithms which implement the point query operators are straightforward. The *Where_at* operator is implemented in $O(\log n)$ by a simple binary search, where n is the number of line segments of the trajectory. The *When_at* operator is implemented in linear time by examining each line segment of a trajectory. As we demonstrated in Section 3, any reasonable trajectory has no more than several thousand line segments. It can be stored in the main memory and the processing time of each one of the above operators is acceptable.

5.2 Operators for Spatio-temporal Range Queries

The second category of operators is a set of conditions (i.e. boolean predicates). Each condition is satisfied if a moving object is inside a given region R, during a given time interval $[t_1, t_2]$. Clearly, this corresponds to a spatio-temporal range query. But then, why more than one operator? The answer is threefold: 1. – The location of the object changes continuously, hence one may ask if the condition is satisfied *sometime* or *always* within $[t_1, t_2]$; 2. – The object may satisfy the condition *everywhere* or *somewhere* within the region R; 3. – Due to the uncertainty, the object may *possibly* satisfy the condition or it may *definitely* do so.

Thus, we have three domains of quantification, with two quantifiers in each. Combining all of them would yield $2^3 \cdot 3! = 48$ operators. However, some of them are meaningless in our case. In particular, it makes no sense to ask if a point object is *everywhere* within a 2D region R (we do not consider "everywhere in all the route segments within a region" in this paper). Hence we have only $2^2 \cdot 2! = 8$ operators.

A region is a polygon[2]. In what follows, we let PMC^T denote a possible motion curve of a given uncertain trajectory $T = (Tr, r)$:

- *Possibly_Sometime_Inside(T,R,t_1,t_2)* – is *true* iff there exist a possible motion curve PMC^T and there exists a time $t \in [t_1, t_2]$ such that PMC^T at the time t, is inside the region R. Intuitively, the truth of the predicate means that the moving object may take a possible route, within its uncertainty zone, such that the particular route will intersect the query polygon R between t_1 and t_2.
- *Sometime_Possibly_Inside(T,R,t_1,t_2)* – is *true* iff there exist a time $t \in [t_1, t_2]$ and a possible motion curve PMC^T of the trajectory T, which at the time t is inside the region R. Observe that this operator is semantically equivalent to *Possibly_Sometime_Inside*. Similarly, it will be clear that *Definitely_Always_Inside* is equivalent to *Always_Definitely_Inside*. Therefore, in effect, we have a total of 6 operators for spatio-temporal range queries.
- *Possibly_Always_Inside(T,R,t_1,t_2)* – is *true* iff there exists a possible motion curve PMC^T of the trajectory T which is inside the region R for every t in $[t_1, t_2]$. In other words, the motion of the object is such that it may take (at least one) specific 2D possible route, which is entirely contained within the polygon R, during the whole query time interval.
- *Always_Possibly_Inside(T,R,t_1,t_2)* – is *true* iff for every time point $t \in [t_1, t_2]$, there exists a PMC^T which will intersect the region R at t.

Figure 3 illustrates (a 2D projection of) a plausible scenario for each of the three predicates above (dashed lines indicate the possible motion curve(s) due to which the predicates are satisfied; solid lines indicate the routes and the boundaries of the uncertainty zone).

The next theorem indicates that one of the last two predicates is stronger than the other:

Theorem 9. *Let $Tr = (T, r)$ denote an uncertain trajectory; R denote a polygon; and t_1 and t_2 denote two time points. If Possibly_Always_Inside(T,R,t_1,t_2) is true, then Always_Possibly_Inside(T,R,t_1,t_2) is also true*[3].

---

[2] We will consider *simple* polygons (c.f. [18, 19]) and without any holes.
[3] Due to lack of space, we omit the proofs of the Theorems and the Claims in this paper (see [32]).

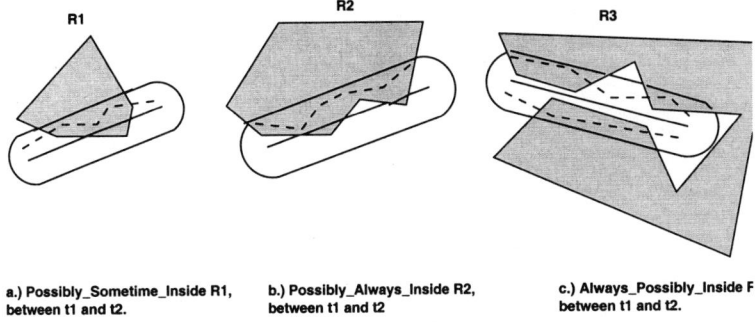

a.) Possibly_Sometime_Inside R1, between t1 and t2.
b.) Possibly_Always_Inside R2, between t1 and t2
c.) Always_Possibly_Inside F between t1 and t2.

Fig. 3. *Possible* positions of a moving point with respect to region R_i

Note that the converse of Theorem 9 is not true. As illustrated on Figure 3, the predicate Always_Possibly_Inside maybe satisfied due to two or more possible motion curves, none of which satisfies Possibly_Always_Inside by itself. However, as the next theorem indicates, this situation cannot occur for a convex polygon:

Theorem 10. *Let $Tr = (T,r)$ denote an uncertain trajectory; R denote a convex polygon; and t_1 and t_2 denote two time points. Possibly_Always_Inside(T,R,t1,t2) is true, iff Always_Possibly_Inside(T,R,t1,t2) is true.*

The other three predicates are defined as follows:
- *Always_Definitely_Inside(T,R,t1,t2)* – is *true* iff at every time $t \in [t_1, t_2]$, every possible motion curve PMC^T of the trajectory T, is in the region R. In other words, no matter which possible motion curve the object takes, it is guaranteed to be within the query polygon R throughout the entire interval $[t_1, t_2]$. Note that this predicate is semantically equivalent to *Definitely_Always_Inside*.
- *Definitely_Sometime_Inside(T,R,t1,t2)* – is *true* iff for every possible motion curve PMC^T of the trajectory T, there exists some time $t \in [t_1, t_2]$ in which the particular motion curve is inside the region R. Intuitively, no matter which possible motion curve within the uncertainty zone is taken by the moving object, it will intersect the polygon at some time between t_1 and t_2. However, the time of the intersection may be different for different possible motion curves.
- *Sometime_Definitely_Inside(T,R,t1,t2)* – is *true* iff there exists a time point $t \in [t_1, t_2]$ at which every possible route PMC^T of the trajectory T is inside the region R. Satisfaction of this predicate means that no matter which possible motion curve is taken by the moving object, at the specific time t the object will be inside query polygon.

The intuition behind the last three predicates is depicted on Figure 4.

Again we observe that *Sometime_Definitely_Inside* is stronger than *Definitely_Sometime_Inside*:

Theorem 11. *Let $Tr = (T,r)$ denote an uncertain trajectory; R denote a polygon; and t_1 and t_2 denote two time points. If Sometime_Definitely_Inside(T,R,t1,t2) is true, then Definitely_Sometime_Inside(T,R,t1,t2) is also true.*

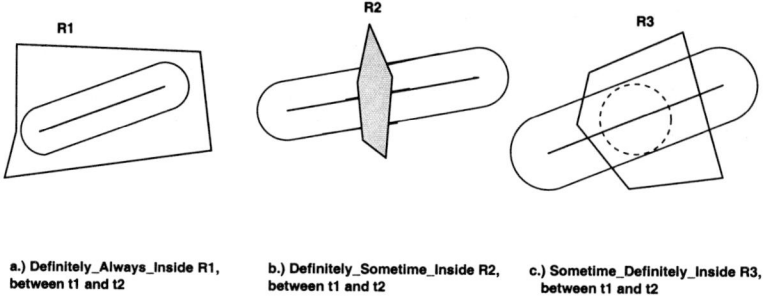

a.) Definitely_Always_Inside R1, between t1 and t2

b.) Definitely_Sometime_Inside R2, between t1 and t2

c.) Sometime_Definitely_Inside R3, between t1 and t2

Fig. 4. *Definite* positions of a moving point with respect to region R_i

However, the above two predicates are not equivalent even if the polygon R is convex. An example demonstrating this is given in of Figure 4(b). The polygon R_2 satisfies *Definitely_Sometime_Inside*, but since it does not contain the uncertainty area for any time point, it does not satisfy *Sometime_Definitely_Inside*.

Note that the proofs of Theorems 9 and 11 are straightforward consequence of $\exists x \forall y P(x,y) \rightarrow \forall y \exists x P(x,y)$ (where P denotes "the property"). However, Theorem 10 is specific to the problem domain.

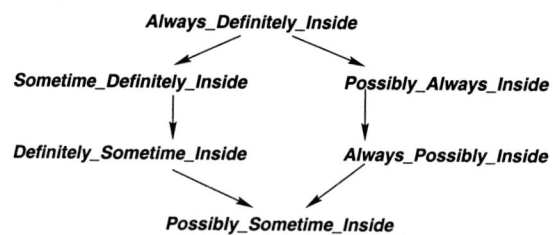

Fig. 5. Relationships among the spatiotemporal predicates

The relationships among our predicates is depicted on Figure 5, where the arrow denotes an implication. More complex query conditions can be expressed by composition of the operators. Consider, for example, *"Retrieve all the objects which are possibly within a region R, always between the times the object A arrives at locations L_1 and L_2"*. This query can be expressed as:

$Possibly\_Always\_Inside(T, R, When\_At(T_A, L_1), When\_At(T_A, L_2))$.

We have implemented the six spatio-temporal range query operators in our DOMINO project. The implementation algorithms are described in the next section, but we conclude this section with a discussion of the user interface.

Figure 6 illustrates the GUI part of the DOMINO project which implements our operators. It represents a visual tool which, in this particular example, shows the answer to the query: "Retrieve the trajectories which <u>possibly</u> intersect the region <u>sometime</u> between 12:15 and 12:30". The figure shows three trajectories

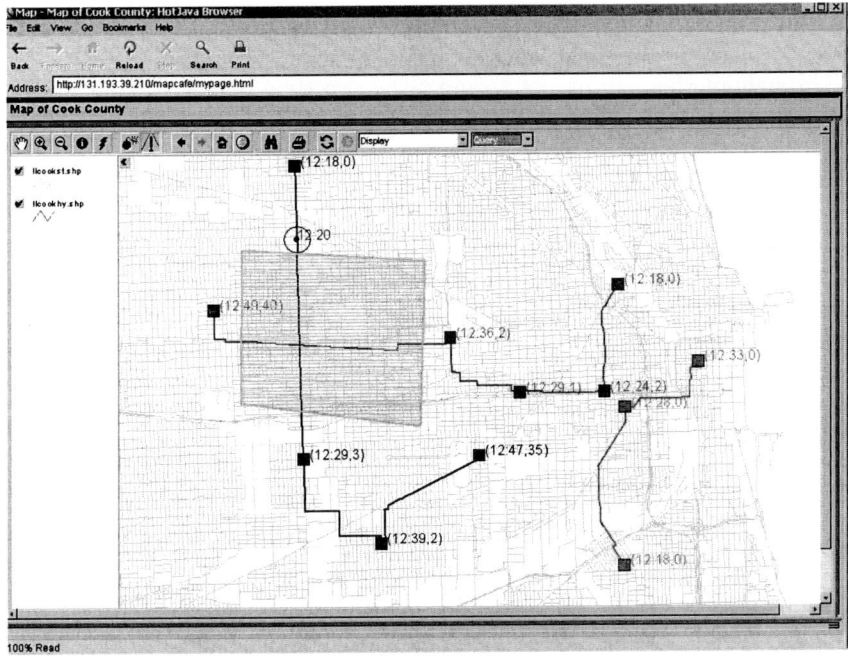

Fig. 6. Visualization of Possibly_Sometime_Inside

in the Cook County, Illinois, and the query region (polygon) represented by the shaded area. The region was drawn by the user on the screen when entering the query. Each trajectory shows the route with planned stops along it (indicated by dark squares). It also shows the expected time of arrival and the duration of the job (i.e. the stay) at each stop. Observe that only one of the trajectories satisfies the predicate *Possibly_Sometime_Inside* with respect to the polygon. It is the one with the circle labeled *12:20*, the earliest time at which the object could enter the query polygon. The other two trajectories fail to satisfy the predicate, each for a separate reason. One of them will not intersect the polygon ever (i.e. the polygon is not on the route). Although the other trajectory's route intersects the polygon, the intersection will occur at a time which is not within the query time - interval $[12:15, 12:30]$.

6 Processing the Range Operators

In this section, for each of the operators we identify the topological properties which are necessary and sufficient conditions for their truth, and we present the algorithms which implement them. The complexities of the algorithms we provide assume relatively straightforward computational geometry techniques. Some of them may be improved using more sophisticated techniques (c.f. [18,

19]), which we omit for space consideration. We only consider query regions that are represented by convex polygons[4].

Throughout this section, let t_1 and t_2 be two time-points. Taking time as a third dimension, the region R along with the query time-interval $[t_1, t_2]$ can be represented as a prism P_R in 3D space: $P_R = \{(x, y, t) \mid (x, y) \in R \wedge t_1 \leq t \leq t_2\}$. P_R is the *query-prism*.

For the purpose of query processing, we assume an available 3D indexing scheme in the underlying DBMS, similar to the ones proposed in [17, 28, 34]. The insertion of a trajectory is done by enclosing, for each trajectory, each trajectory volume between t_i and t_{i+1} in a Minimum Bounding Box (MBB). During the *filtering* stage we retrieve the trajectories which have a MBB that intersect with P_R. Throughout the rest of this work we focus on the *refinement* stage of the processing. Let VTr denote the trajectory volume of a given uncertain trajectory $T = (Tr, r)$ between t_1 and t_2. Also, let $VT' = VTr \cap P_R$.

Theorem 12. *The predicate Possibly_Sometime_Inside is true iff* $VT' \neq \emptyset$

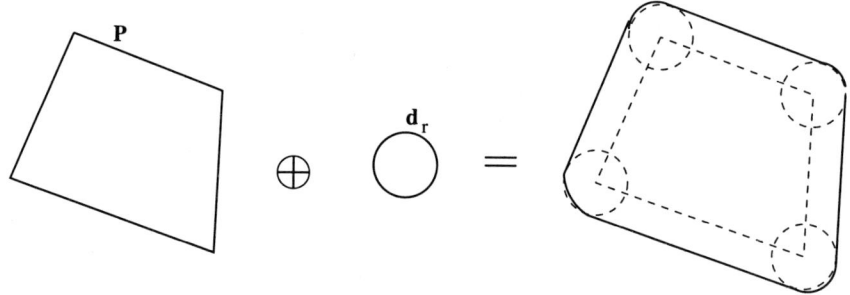

Fig. 7. Minkowski sum of a polygon with a disk

To present the processing algorithm, we need the following concept used in Motion Planning (c.f. [19, 23, ?]). The operation of *Minkowski sum* – denoted as $\oplus$ is described as follows: Let P denote a polygon and d_r denote a disk with radius r. $P \oplus d_r$ is the set of all the points in plane which are elements of $\{P \cup$ *interior of P* $\cup$ *the points which are in the "sweep" of d_r when its center moves along the edges of P* $\}$. Visually, the outer boundary of $P \oplus d_r$, for a convex polygon P, will consist of line segments and circle segments by the vertices of P, as illustrated on Figure 7. If P has n edges, then the complexity of constructing the Minkowski sum $P \oplus d_r$ is $O(n)$) (c.f. [19]).

In what follows, let $Tr_{X,Y}$ denote the projection of the trajectory Tr between t_1 and t_2, on the $X - Y$ plane (i.e. its route).

---

[4] Due to lack of space, we do not present the formal treatment of the concave query polygons. Detailed description is presented in [32].

Algorithm 1. (Possibly_Sometime_Inside(R, T, t_1, t_2))
1. Construct the Minkowski sum of R and the disk d_r with radius r, where r is the uncertainty of T.
Denote it $R \oplus d_r$;
2. If $Tr_{X,Y} \cap (R \oplus r) = \emptyset$
3.   return **false**;
4. else
5.   return **true**;

In other words, VT' is nonempty if and only if $Tr_{X,Y}$ intersects the expanded polygon. The complexity of the Algorithm 1 is $O(kn)$ where k is the number of segments of the trajectory between t_1 and t_2, and n is the number of edges of R.

The next Theorem gives the necessary and sufficient condition for satisfaction of the *Possibly_Always_Inside* predicate:

Theorem 13. *Possibly_Always_Inside(T, R, t1, t2) is true if and only if VT' contains a possible motion curve between t_1 and t_2.*

The implementation is given by the following:

Algorithm 2. (Possibly_Always_Inside(R, T, t_1, t_2))
1. Construct the Minkowski sum of R and the disk d_r with radius r, where r is the uncertainty of T.
      Denote it $R \oplus d_r$;
2. If $Tr_{X,Y}$ lies completely inside $R \oplus d_r$
3.   return **true**;
4. else
5.   return **false**;

The complexity of Algorithm 2 is, again, $O(kn)$.

Recall that we are dealing with convex polygonal regions. As a consequence of the Theorem 10, we can also use the last algorithm to process the predicate *Always_Possibly_Inside*.

Now we proceed with the algorithms that implement the predicates which have the *Definitely* quantifier in their spatial domain.

Theorem 14. *The predicate Definitely_Always_Inside(Tr,R,t_1,t_2) is true if an only if $VTr \cap P_R = VTr$*

As for the implementation of the predicate, we have the following:

Algorithm 3. Definitely_Always_Inside(Tr, R, t_1, t_2)
1. For each straight line segment of Tr
2.   If the uncertainty zone of the segment is <u>not</u> entirely contained in R;
3.   return **false** and exit;
4. return **true**.

Step 2 above can be processed by checking if the route segment has a distance from some edge of R which is less than r, which implies a complexity of $O(kn)$ again.

Theorem 15. *Sometime_Definitely_Inside(T, R, t_1, t_2) is true if and only if $VTr \cap P_R$ contains an entire horizontal disk (i.e. a circle along with its interior)*

Let us point out that Theorem 15 holds for concave polygon as well [32].
The implementation of the predicate *Sometime_Definitely_Inside* is specified by the following:

Algorithm 4. Sometime_Definitely_Inside(Tr, R, t_1, t_2)
1. For each segment of Tr such that $Tr_{X,Y} \cap R \neq \emptyset$
2.   If R contains a circle with radius r centered at some point on $Tr_{X,Y}$;
3.   return **true** and exit
4. return **false**

The complexity of Algorithm 4 is again $O(kn)$.

Now we discuss the last predicate. The property of connectivity is commonly viewed as an existence of some *path* between two points in a given set. Clearly, in our setting we are dealing with subsets of $\mathcal{R}^3$. Given any two points a and b in $\mathcal{R}^3$, a *path* from a to b is any continuous function[5] $f : [0,1] \to \mathcal{R}^3$ such that $f(a) = 0$ and $f(1) = b$. Given two time – points t_1 and t_2, we say that a set $\mathcal{S} \subseteq \mathcal{R}^3$ is <u>connected between</u> t_1 and t_2 if there exist two points (x_1, y_1, t_1) and $(x_2, y_2, t_2) \in \mathcal{S}$ which are connected by a path in $\mathcal{S}$. Thus, we have the following Theorem for the predicate *Definitely_Sometime_Inside* (a consequence of Claim 6 below):

Theorem 16. *Definitely_Sometime_Inside(T, R, t_1, t_2) is true if and only if $VT'' = VTr \setminus P_R$ is not connected between t_1 and t_2.*

Claim. If $VT'' = VTr \setminus P_R$ is connected between t_1 and t_2, then there exists a possible motion curve PMC^T between t_1 and t_2 which is entirely in VT''.

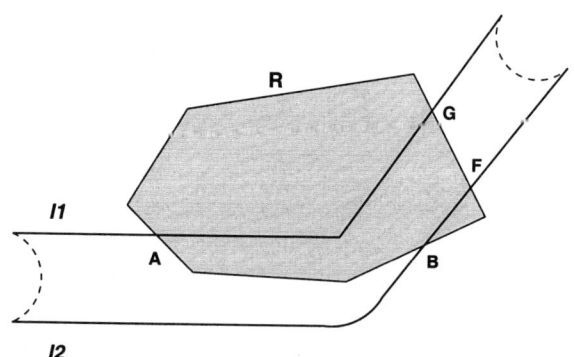

Fig. 8. Processing of *Definitely_Sometime_Inside* predicate

---

[5] There are propositions (c.f. [26]) about the equivalence of the connectedness of a topological space with the path – connectedness.

Now we present the algorithm that processes the *Definitely_Sometime_Inside* predicate. Let PT_r be the uncertainty zone of the trajectory (equivalently, the 2D projection of VT_r, the trajectory volume). Let PT'_r be PT_r with the uncertainty areas at t_1 and t_2 eliminated. Let L be the boundary of PT'_r. L will consists of (at most) $2k$ line segments and $k+1$ circular segments (at most one around the endpoints of each segment). Let $L' = L \setminus D$, where D denotes the two half-circles which bound the uncertainty areas at t_1 and t_2. Clearly, L' consists of two disjoint "lines" l_1 and l_2 which are left from the initial boundaries of the uncertainty zone. Figure 8 illustrates the concepts that we introduced. Note that the boundary l_2 has a circular segment at the end of the first route-segment. Dashed semi-circles correspond to the boundaries of the uncertainty areas at t_1 and t_2, which are removed when evaluating the predicate. For the query region R, we have the path between A on l_1 and B on l_2 (also the path between F and G) which makes the predicate true.

Algorithm 5. Definitely_Sometime_Inside(T, R, t_1, t_2)
1. If there exists a path P between a point on l_1 and one on l_2 which consists entirely of edges of R (or parts thereof) AND P is entirely in PT_r.'
2.   return **true** and exit
3. return **false**

It is not hard to see that the complexity of Algorithm 5 is $O(kn^2)$.

7 Conclusion, Related Work and Future Directions

We have proposed a model for representing moving objects under realistic assumptions of location uncertainty. We also gave a set of operators which can be used to pose queries in that context. The model and the operators combine spatial, temporal, and uncertainty constructs, and can be fully implemented on top of "off the shelf" existing ORDBMS's.

Linguistic issues in moving objects databases have been addressed before. Modeling and querying issues have been addressed from several perspectives. Sistla et al. [24] introduce the MOST model for representing moving objects (similar to [22]) as a function of (location, velocity_vector). The underlying query language is nonstandard, and is based on the Future Temporal Logic (FTL). Similar issues are addressed in [34]. A trajectory model similar to ours is given in [35] where the authors extend range queries with new operators for special cases of spatio-temporal range queries. The series of works [4, 6, 9] addresses the issue of modeling and querying moving objects by presenting a rich algebra of operators and a very comprehensive framework of abstract data types. However, in all the above works there is no treatment of the uncertainty of the moving object's location.

As for uncertainty issues, Wolfson et al. [36, 37] introduce a cost based approach to determine the size of the uncertainty area (r in this paper). However, linguistic and querying aspects are not addressed in these papers. A formal quantitative approach to the aspect of uncertainty in modeling moving objects is presented in [16]. The authors limit the uncertainty to the past of the moving objects and the error may become very large as time approaches *now*. It is a less "collaborative" approach than ours – there is no clear notion of the motion *plan* given by the trajectory. Uncertainty of moving objects is also treated in [25] in the framework of modal temporal logic. The difference from the present work is that here we treat the uncertainty in traditional range queries.

A large body of work in moving objects databases has been concentrated on indexing in primal [17, 22, 20, 21, 28] or dual space [1, 12, 13]. [30, 31] present specifications of *what* an indexing of moving objects needs to consider, and generation of spatial datasets for benchmarking data. These works will be useful in studying the most appropriate access method for processing the operators introduced in this paper.

On the commercial side, there is a plethora of related GIS products [33, 5, 7]; maps with real – time traffic information [11] and GPS devices and management software. IBM's DB2 Spatial Extender [3], Oracle's Spatial Cartridge [15] and Informix Spatial DataBlade [29] provide several 2D – spatial types (e.g. line, polyline, polygon, ...); and include a set of predicates (e.g. *intersects, contains*) and functions for spatial calculations (e.g. *distance*). However, the existing commercial products still lack the ability to model and query spatio-temporal contexts for moving objects.

In terms of future work, a particularly challenging problem is the one of query optimization for spatio-temporal databases. We will investigate how to incorporate an indexing schema within the existing ORDBMS (c.f. [2, 14]), and develop and experimentally test a hybrid indexing schema which would pick an appropriate access method for a particular environment.

Acknowledgement

We wish to thank Pankaj Agrawal for pointing to us a way to significantly simplify the algorithms for processing the Possibly-Sometime and Always-Possibly operators. We are grateful to Prof. Eleni Kostis from Truman College, and we also thank the anonymous referees for their valuable comments.

References

1. A. K. Agarwal, L. Arge, and J. Erickson. Indexing moving points. In *19th ACM PODS Conference*, 2000.
2. W. Chen, J. Chow, Y. Fuh, J. grandbois, M. Jou, N. Mattos, B. Tran, and Y. Wang. High level indexing of user – defined types. In *25th VLDB Conference*, 1999.
3. J. R. Davis. *Managing geo – spatial information within the DBMS*, 1998. IBM DB2 Spatial Extender.
4. M. Erwig, M. Schneider, and R. H. G üting. Temporal and spatio – temporal datasets and their expressive power. Technical Report 225-12/1997, Informatik berichte, 1997.

5. ESRI. *ArcView GIS:The Geographic Information System for Everyone*. Environmental Systems Research Institute Inc., 1996.
6. L. Forlizzi, R. H. G üting, E. Nardelli, and M. Schneider. A data model and data structures for moving objects databases. In *ACM SIGMOD*, 2000.
7. Geographic Data Technology Co. *GDT Maps*, 2000. http://www.geographic.com.
8. V. Graede and O. G ünther. Multidimensional access methods. *ACM Computing Surveys*, 11(4), 1998.
9. R. H. G üting, M. H. B öhlen, M. Erwig, C. Jensen, N. Lorentzos, M. Schneider, and M. Vazirgiannis. A foundation for representing and queirying moving objects. *ACM TODS*, 2000.
10. C. M. Hoffman. Solid modeling. In J. E. Goodman and J. O'Rourke, editors, *Handbook of Discrete and Computational Geometry*. CRC Press, 1997.
11. Intelligent Transportation Systems. *ITS maps*, 2000. http://www.itsonline.com.
12. D. Kollios, D. Gunopulos, and V. J. Tsotras. On indexing mobile objects. In *18th ACM PODS Conference*, 1999.
13. G. Kollios, D. Gunopulos, and V. J. Tsotras. Nearest neighbour queries in a mobile environment. In *STDBM*, 1999.
14. M. Kornacker. High - performance extensible indexing. In *25th VLDB Conference*, 1999.
15. Oracle Corporation. *Oracle8: Spatial Cartridge User's Guide and Reference, Release 8.0.4*, 2000. http://technet.oracle.com/docs/products/oracle8/doc-index.htm.
16. D. Pfoser and C. Jensen. Capturing the uncertainty of moving objects representation. In *SSDB*, 1999.
17. D. Pfoser, Y. Theodoridis, and C. Jensen. Indexing trajectories of moving point objects. Technical Report 99/07/03, Dept. of Computer Science, University of Aalborg, 1999.
18. F. P. Preparata and M. I. Shamos. *Computational Geometry: an introduction*. Springer Verlag, 1985.
19. J. O' Rourke. *Computational Geometry in C*. Cambridge University Press, 2000.
20. S. Saltenis and C. Jensen. R-tree based indexing of general spatio-temporal data. Technical Report TR-45, TimeCenter, 1999.
21. S. Saltenis and C. Jensen. Indexing of moving objects for location-based services. Technical Report TR-63, TimeCenter, 2001.
22. S. Saltenis, C. S. Jensen, S. T. Leutenegger, and M. A. Lopez. Indexing the positions of continuously moving objects. Technical Report TR - 44, TimeCenter, 1999.
23. M. Sharir. Algorithmic motion planning. In J. E. Goodman and J. O'Rourke, editors, *Handbook of Discrete and Computational Geometry*. CRC Press, 1997.
24. A. P. Sistla, O. Wolfson, S. Chamberlain, and S. Dao. Modeling and querying moving objects. In *13th Int'l Conf. on Data Engineering (ICDE)*, 1997.
25. A.P. Sistla, P. Wolfson, S. Chamberlain, and S. Dao. Querying the uncertain positions of moving objects. In O. Etzion, S. Jajodia, and S. Sripada, editors, *Temporal Databases: Research and Practice*. 1999.
26. W. A. Sutherland. *Introduction to Metric and Topological Spaces*. Oxford University Press, 1998.
27. A. Tansel, J. Clifford, S. Jajodia, A. Segev, and R. Snodgrass. *Temporal Databases: Theory and Implementation*. Benjamin/ Cummings Publishing Co., 1993.
28. J. Tayeb, O. Ulusoy, and O. Wolfson. A quadtree – based dynamic attribute indexing method. *The Computer Journal*, 41(3), 1998.

29. Informix Documentation Team. Informix datablade technology: Transforming data into smart data. Informix Press, 1999.
30. Y. Theodoridis, T. Sellis, A. N. Papadopoulos, and Y. Manolopoulos. Specifications for efficient indexing in spatiotemporal databases. In *IEEE SSDBM*, 1999.
31. Y. Theodoridis, J. R. O. Silva, and M. A. Nascimento. On the generation of spatiotemporal datasets. In *6th Int'l symposium on Large Spatial Databases*, 1999.
32. G. Trajcevski, O. Wolfson, and B. Xu. Modeling and querying trajectories of moving objects with uncertainty. Technical Report UIC - EECS - 01 - 2, May 2001.
33. U S Dept. of Commerce. *Tiger/Line Census Files: Technical Documentation*, 1991.
34. M. Vazirgiannis, Y. Theodoridis, and T. Sellis. Spatiotemporal composition and indexing for large multimedia applications. *Multimedia systems*, 6(4), 1998.
35. M. Vazirgiannis and O. Wolfson. A spatiotemporal model and language for movign objects on road networks. In *SSTD*, 2001.
36. O. Wolfson, S. Chamberlain, S. Dao, L. Jiang, and G. Mendez. Cost and imprecision in modeling the position of moving objects. In *14 -th ICDE*, 1998.
37. O. Wolfson, A. P. Sistla, S. Chamberlain, and Y. Yesha. Updating and querying databases that track mobile units. *Distributed and Parallel Databases*, 7, 1999.

Efficient Indexing of Spatiotemporal Objects*

Marios Hadjieleftheriou[1], George Kollios[2],
Vassilis J. Tsotras[1], and Dimitrios Gunopulos[1]

[1] University of California, Riverside
[2] Boston University

Abstract. Spatiotemporal objects i.e., objects which change their position and/or extent over time, appear in many applications. This paper addresses the problem of indexing large volumes of such data. We consider general object movements and extent changes. We further concentrate on "snapshot" as well as small "interval" historical queries on the gathered data. The obvious approach that approximates spatiotemporal objects with MBRs and uses a traditional multidimensional access method to index them is inefficient. Objects that "live" for long time intervals have large MBRs which introduce a lot of empty space. Clustering long intervals has been dealt in temporal databases by the use of partially persistent indices. What differentiates this problem from traditional temporal indexing is that objects are allowed to move/change during their lifetime. Better methods are thus needed to approximate general spatiotemporal objects. One obvious solution is to introduce artificial splits: the lifetime of a long-lived object is split into smaller consecutive pieces. This decreases the empty space but increases the number of indexed MBRs. We first introduce two algorithms for splitting a given spatiotemporal object. Then, given an upper bound on the total number of possible splits, we present three algorithms that decide how the splits should be distributed among the objects so that the total empty space is minimized.

1 Introduction

There are many applications that create spatiotemporal data. Examples include transportation (cars moving in the highway system), satellite and earth change data (evolution of forest boundaries), planetary movements, etc. The common characteristic is that spatiotemporal objects move and/or change their extent over time.

Recent works that address indexing problems in a spatiotemporal environment include [28, 11, 10, 23, 29, 1, 20, 21, 12, 25, 28]. Two variations of the problem are examined: approaches that optimize queries about the future positions of spatiotemporal objects [11, 23, 1, 21, 22] and those that optimize historical queries [28, 29, 10, 17, 20, 21, 12, 25] (i.e., queries about past states of the spatiotemporal evolution). Here we concentrate on historical queries, so for brevity the term "historical" is omitted. Furthermore, we assume the "off-line" version of the problem, that is, all data from the spatiotemporal evolution has already been gathered and the purpose is to index it efficiently.

For simplicity we assume that objects move/change on a 2-dimensional space that evolves over time; the extension to a 3-dimensional space is straightforward. An example

---

* This work was partially supported by NSF grants IIS-9907477, EIA-9983445, and the Department of Defense.

of such a spatiotemporal evolution appears in figure 1. The x and y axes represent the 2-dimensional space while the t axis corresponds to the time dimension. For the rest of this discussion *time is assumed to be discrete*, described by a succession of increasing integers. At time t_1 objects o_1 (which is a point) and o_2 (which is a 2D region) are inserted. At time t_2, object o_3 is inserted while o_1 moves to a new position and o_2 shrinks. Object o_1 moves again at time t_5; o_2 continues to shrink and disappears at time t_5. Based on its behavior in the spatiotemporal evolution, each object is assigned a record with a "lifetime" interval $[t_i, t_j)$ created by the time instants when the object was inserted and deleted (if ever). For example, the lifetime of o_2 is $[t_1, t_5)$. During its lifetime, an object is termed *alive*.

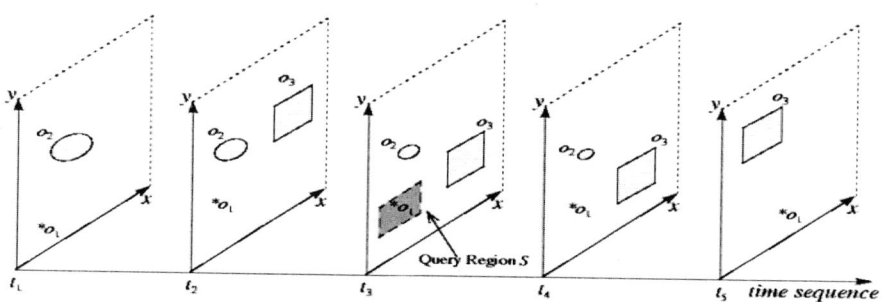

Fig. 1. An example of spatiotemporal object evolution.

An important decision for the index design is the class of queries that the index optimizes. In this paper we are interested in optimizing topological snapshot queries of the form: "find all objects that appear in area S during time t". That is, the user is typically interested on what happened at a given time instant (or even for small time periods around it). An example snapshot query is illustrated in figure 1: "find all objects inside area S at time t_3"; only object o_1 satisfies this query.

One approach for indexing spatiotemporal objects is to consider time as another (spatial) dimension and use a 3-dimensional spatial access method (like an R-Tree [8]oritsvariants[3]). Each object is represented as a 3-dimensional rectangle whose "height" corresponds to the object's lifetime interval, while the rectangle "base" corresponds to the largest 2-dimensional minimum bounding region (MBR) that the object obtained during its lifetime. While simple to implement, this approach does not take advantage of the specific properties of the time dimension. First, it introduces a lot of empty space. Second, objects that remain unchanged for many time instants will have long lifetimes and thus, they will be stored as long rectangles. A long-lived rectangle determines the length of the time range associated with the index node (page) in which it resides. This creates node overlapping and leads to decreased query performance [13, 14, 24, 25, 28, 12]. Better interval clustering can be achieved by using "packed" R-Trees (like the Hilbert R-Tree [9]ortheSTR-Tree[15]); another idea is to perform interval fragmentation using the Segment R-Tree [13].However,thequeryperformanceisnotgreatlyimproved[12].

Another approach is to exploit the monotonicity of the temporal dimension, and transform a 2-dimensional spatial access method to become partially persistent [29, 17, 10, 12, 25]. A partially persistent structure "logically" stores all its past states and allows updates only to its most current state [6, 16, 2, 30, 14, 24]. A historical query about time t is directed to the state the structure had at time t. Hence, answering such a query is proportional to the number of alive objects the structure contains at time t. That is, it behaves as if an "ephemeral" structure was present for time t, indexing the alive objects at t. Two ways have been proposed to achieve partial persistence: the overlapping [4] and multi-version approaches [6]. In the overlapping approach [17, 29], a 2-dimensional index is conceptually maintained for each time instant. Since consecutive trees do not differ much, common (overlapping) branches are shared between the trees. While easy to implement, overlapping creates a logarithmic overhead on the index storage requirements [24]. Conceptually, the multi-version approach [16, 2, 30, 14, 25] also maintains a 2-dimensional index per time instant, but the overall storage used is linear to the number of changes in the evolution. In the rest we use a partially persistent R-Tree (PPR-Tree) [14, 25]. A short description of a PPR-Tree appears in section 2.2.

Our approach for improving query performance is to reduce the empty space introduced by approximating spatiotemporal objects by their MBRs. This can be accomplished by introducing artificial object updates. Such an update issued at time t, artificially "deletes" an alive object at t and reinserts it at the same time. The net effect is that the original object is represented by two records, one with lifetime that ends at t and one with lifetime that starts at t. Consider for example a spatiotemporal object created by the linear movement shown in figure 2. Here, the 2-dimensional rectangle moved linearly, starting at t_1 from the lower left part of the (x, y) plane and reaching the upper right part at t_2. The original MBR is shown, as well. However, if this object is split (say, at the middle of its lifetime) the empty space is reduced since two smaller MBRs are now used (see figure 3 where the (x, t) plane is represented).

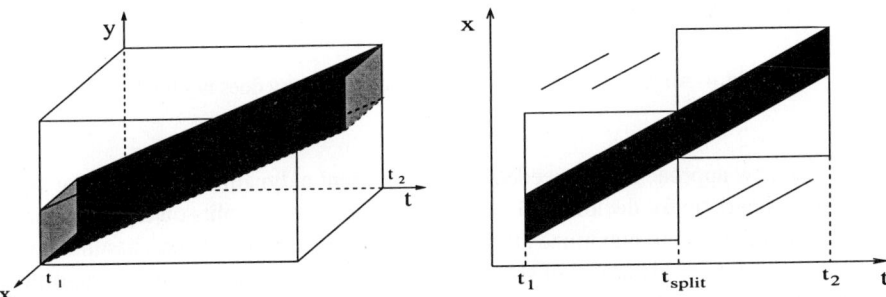

Fig. 2. A spatiotemporal object in linear motion.

Fig. 3. An example of splitting an object once.

Clearly an artificial split reduces empty space and thus we would expect that query performance improves. However, it is not clear if the 3D R-Tree query performance will improve by these splits. An intuitive explanation is based on Pagel's query cost formula [19]. This formula states that the query performance of any bounding box-based index structure depends on the total (spatial) volume, the total surface and the total number of data nodes. Using the artificial splits, we try to decrease the total volume of the data nodes (by decreasing the size of the objects themselves). On the other hand, the total number of indexed objects increases. In contrast, for the PPR-Tree the number of alive records (i.e., the number of indexed records) at any time instant remains the same while the empty space and the total volume is reduced. Therefore, it is expected that the PPR-Tree performance for snapshot and small interval queries will be improved.

In [12] we addressed the problem of indexing spatiotemporal objects that move or change extent using *linear* functions of time. Assuming we are given a number of possible splits that are proportional to the number of spatiotemporal objects (i.e., the overall storage used remains linear) a greedy algorithm was presented that minimizes the overall empty space. In particular, the algorithm decides (i) which objects to split and (ii) how the splits are distributed among objects. The algorithm's optimality is based on a special *monotonicity* property which holds for linearly moving/changing objects: *given a spatiotemporal object and a number of splits, the gain in empty space decreases as the number of splits applied to the object increases*. Equivalently, the first few splits will yield big gain in empty space, while the more we split the less gain is obtained.

In this paper we address the more difficult problem where objects are allowed to move/change with general motions over time. Unfortunately, in this case the monotonicity property does not always hold. An example is shown in figure 4. One split will give much less gain in empty space than two.

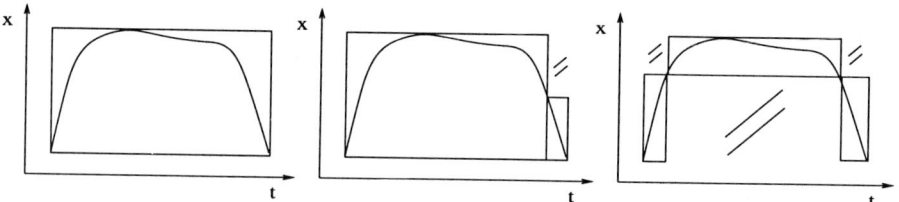

Fig. 4. An example where the monotonicity property does not hold.

Hence, new approaches are needed. We first present a dynamic programming algorithm and a heuristic for deciding how to apply any number of splits on a given general spatiotemporal object to maximize the gain in empty space. Furthermore, assuming that there is a predetermined number of splits, we provide a dynamic programming algorithm for optimally distributing the splits among a collection of general spatiotemporal objects. The difficulty lies in the fact that the number of splits might not be enough to split every object in the collection, so an optimization criterion has to be considered. Finally, we implement two greedy algorithms that give results close to the optimal algorithm but with huge gain in terms of running time. While by using more splits the gain is increased, after a while the increase will be minimal. A related problem is how to decide on the number of artificial splits. Assuming that a model is available for predicting the query cost of the index method used [27, 26], the number of splits can be easily decided.

To show the merits of our approach the collection of objects (including objects created by the artificial splits) are indexed using a PPR-Tree and a 3D R*-Tree [3]. Our experimental results show that the PPR-Tree consistently outperforms the R*-Tree for snapshot as well as small interval queries.

We note that some special cases of indexing general spatiotemporal objects have also been considered in the literature: (i) when the objects have no spatial extents (moving points) [20, 21], and (ii) when the motion of each object can be represented as a set of linear functions (piecewise linear trajectories) [7, 12]. For the case that points move with linear functions of time, extensions to the R-Tree have been proposed (Parametric R-Tree [5] and the PSI approach in [21]). The problem examined here is however more complex as objects are allowed to move/change with a general motion over time.

The rest of the paper is organized as follows. Section 2 formalizes the notion of general movements/changes and provides background on the PPR-Tree. Section 3 presents the proposed algorithms. Section 4 discusses how to use analytical models to find a good number of splits for a given dataset. Section 5 contains experimental results. Related work is given in section 6. Finally, section 7 concludes the paper.

2 Preliminaries

2.1 Formal Notion of General Movements

Consider a set of N spatiotemporal objects that move independently on a plane. Suppose that the objects move/change with linear functions of time: $x = F_x(t)$, $y = F_y(t)$, $t \in [t_i, t_j)$. Then the representation of a spatiotemporal object O can be defined as a set of tuples:

$$O = \{([t_s, t_j), F_{x_1}(t), F_{y_1}(t)), \ldots, ([t_k, t_e), F_{x_n}(t), F_{y_n}(t))\}$$

where t_s is the object creation time, t_e is the object deletion time, $t_j, \ldots, t_k$ are the intermediate time instants when the movement of the object changes characteristics and $F_{x_1}, \ldots, F_{x_n}, F_{y_1}, \ldots, F_{y_n}$ are the corresponding functions.

In the general case, objects can move arbitrarily towards any direction. Representing an object's movement by the collection of locations for every time instant is not efficient in terms of space. It cannot be approximated very well with combinations of linear functions either, since the number of segments required cannot be bounded. A better approach is to use combinations of polynomial functions. An example of a point moving on the (x, t) plane with the corresponding functions describing its movement is shown in figure 5. For two dimensional movements every tuple would contain two functions, the first giving a movement on the x-axis and the second on the y-axis. This results to an object following a trajectory which is a combination of both functions. An alteration in the object's shape could be described in the same way. An example is shown in figure 6 where the object follows a general movement, keeps constant extent along the x-axis and changes extent along the y-axis.

By restricting the degree of the polynomials up to a maximal value, most common movements can be approximated or even represented exactly by using only a few tuples. As the number of tuples increases, more complicated movements may be represented and

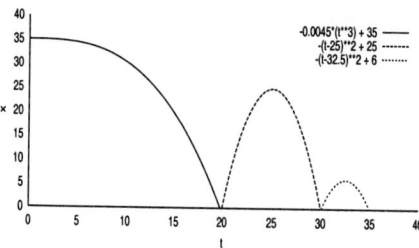 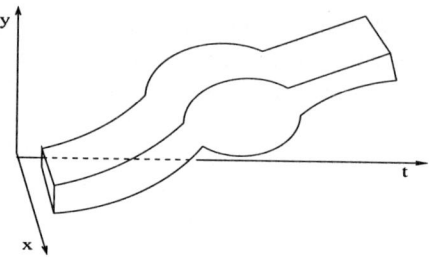

Fig. 5. A moving point and a corresponding set of polynomial functions representing the movement.

Fig. 6. A moving object that follows a general trajectory while changing shape.

better approximations can be obtained. This approach is storage efficient, since few tuples are required for the representation of general movements/changes. It further guarantees that the MBR of any movement can be found easily by computing the minimum and maximum of the appropriate functions for all instants in a time interval. In this paper we focus in general movements/changes of objects and our algorithms are designed accordingly. We use, though, polynomial functions for generating moving objects for our experiments, due to the arguments given above.

2.2 The Partially Persistent R-Tree

Consider a spatiotemporal evolution that starts at time t_1 and assume that a 2-dimensional R-Tree indexes the objects as they are at time t_1. As the evolution advances, the 2D R-Tree evolves too, by applying the evolution updates (object additions/deletions) as they occur. Storing this 2D R-Tree evolution corresponds to making a 2D R-Tree partially persistent. The following discussion is based on [14]. While conceptually the partially persistent R-Tree (PPR-Tree) records the evolution of an ephemeral R-Tree, it does not physically store snapshots of all the states in the ephemeral R-Tree evolution. Instead, it records the evolution updates efficiently so that the storage remains linear, while still providing fast query time.

The PPR-Tree is actually a directed acyclic graph of nodes (a node corresponds to a disk page). Moreover, it has a number of root nodes, each of which is responsible for recording a consecutive part of the ephemeral R-Tree evolution. Data records in the leaf nodes of a PPR-Tree maintain the temporal evolution of the ephemeral R-Tree data objects. Each data record is thus extended to include the two lifetime fields: *insertion-time* and *deletion-time*. Similarly, index records in the directory nodes of a PPR-Tree maintain the evolution of the corresponding index records of the ephemeral R-Tree and are also augmented with *insertion-time* and *deletion-time* fields.

An index or data record is *alive* for all time instants during its lifetime interval. With the exception of root nodes, a leaf or a directory node is called *alive* for all time instants that it contains at least D alive records ($D < B$, where B is the maximum node capacity). When the number of alive records falls below D the node is split and its remaining alive records are copied to another node. This requirement enables clustering the objects that are alive at a given time instant in a small number of nodes (pages), which in turn will minimize the query I/O. Searching the PPR-Tree takes into account the lifetime intervals of the index and the data records visited. Consider answering a query about region S and time t. First, the root which is alive at t is found. This is equivalent to accessing the ephemeral R-Tree which indexes time t. Second, the objects intersecting S are found by searching this tree in a top-down fashion as in a regular R-Tree. The lifetime interval of every record traversed should contain time t, and its MBR should intersect region S.

3 Representation of Spatiotemporal Objects

Consider a spatiotemporal object O that moved from its initial position at time instant t_0 to a final position at time t_n with a general movement pattern. We can represent this object using its bounding box in space and time. However, this creates large empty space and overlap among the index nodes (we assume that an index like the 3D R-Tree or the PPR-Tree is used). A better approach is to represent the object using multiple boxes. That way a better approximation is obtained and the empty space is reduced. The object is split into smaller consecutive objects and each one is approximated with a smaller bounding box (see figure 7). Note that we consider splitting along *the time axis only*, since the time dimension is the main reason of the increased empty space and overlap.

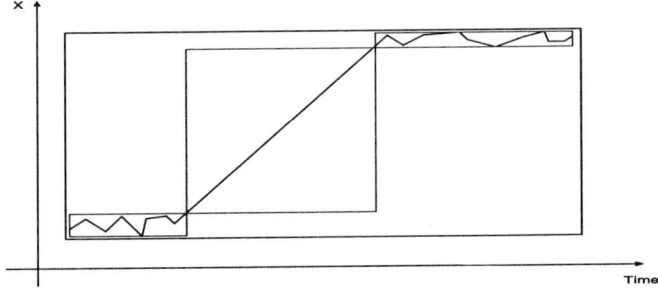

Fig. 7. An 1-dimensional example of representing an object with one and three MBRs.

Next, we present methods for splitting objects in spatiotemporal datasets in order to decrease the overall empty space and increase the query performance. We break the problem into two sub-problems:

1. Given an object and an upper limit in the number of splits we have to find how to split the object such that the maximum possible gain in empty space is obtained.
2. Given a collection of objects and a predetermined number of splits we try to distribute the splits among all objects in order to optimize the query performance of the index.

3.1 Splitting One Object

Consider a spatiotemporal object O with lifetime $[t_0, t_n)$. Assume that we want to split the object into k consecutive objects in a way that minimizes the total volume of its representation. As we discussed above, we use splits in the form of artificial updates. It would be logical to assume that we only need to consider splitting an object at the points where the movement changes its characteristics (in case that the movement is represented by a combination of functions for example). This approach does not give optimal gain results in most cases, as could be shown with a counter example (see figure 7 for an intuition behind the problem).

An Optimal Algorithm (DPSplit). Let $V_l[0, i]$ be the volume of the MBRs corresponding to the part of the spatiotemporal object between t_0 and t_i after using l optimal splits. Then, the following holds:

$$V_l[0, i] = \min_{0 \le j < i} \{V_{l-1}[0, j] + V[j, i]\}$$

where $V[j, i]$ is the volume of the MBR that contains the part of the spatiotemporal object between t_j and t_i, without any splits. The formula states that in order to find the optimal solution for splitting the object between t_0 and t_i, we have to consider all intermediate time instants and combine the previous solutions. Using the above formula we obtain a dynamic programming algorithm that computes the optimal positions for the k splits and the total volume after these splits. This is achieved by computing the value $V_k[0, n]$.

Theorem 1. *Splitting one object optimally using k splits can be done in $O(n^2 k)$, where the lifetime of the object is $[t_0, t_n]$.*

Proof. We have to compute the nk values of the array $V_l[0, i]$, $0 \le l < k, 0 \le i < n$. Each value in the array can be found by computing the minimum of n values using the formula above. The volume $V[j, i]$ of the object between positions j and i can be precomputed for every run i, for all values of j, using $O(n)$ space and $O(n)$ time and thus does not affect the time complexity of the algorithm.

An Approximate Algorithm (MergeSplit). The dynamic programming algorithm is quadratic to the lifetime of the object. For objects that live for long time periods the above algorithm is not very efficient. A faster algorithm is based on a greedy approach. The idea is to start with n different boxes, one for each time instant and merge the boxes in a greedy way (figure 8). The running time of the algorithm is $O(n \log n)$. To improve the running time we can merge all consecutive boxes that give a small increase in volume. Then, we can run the greedy algorithm starting with fewer boxes. This greedy algorithm gives in general sub-optimal solutions.

3.2 Splitting a Collection of Objects

In this subsection we discuss methods for distributing a number of splits K among a collection of N spatiotemporal objects. While using more splits to approximate the objects improves query performance by reducing the empty space, every split corresponds to a new record (the new MBR) and thus increases the storage requirements. Hence, if we are given a total number of splits K (which may correspond to an upper limit on the disk space) and a set of spatiotemporal objects, we want to decide which objects to split and how many splits each object is allocated.

> **Input:** A spatiotemporal object O as a sequence of n spatial objects, one at each time instant.
> **Output:** A set of MBRs that cover O.
>
> 1. For $0 \leq i < n$ compute the volume of the MBR for merging O_i with O_{i+1}. Store the results in a priority queue.
> 2. Repeat n times: Use the priority queue to merge the pair of consecutive MBRs that give the smallest increase in volume. Update the priority queue with the new MBR.

Fig. 8. The greedy heuristic (MergeSplit).

An Optimal Algorithm. Assuming an ordering on the spatiotemporal objects (each object gets a number between 1 and N), let $TV_l[i]$ be the minimum total volume occupied by the first i objects with optimal l splits, and $V_j[i]$ be the total volume for approximating the ith object using j splits (e.g. with $j+1$ boxes.) we observe that:

$$TV_l[i] = \min_{0 \leq j \leq l} \{TV_{l-j}[i-1] + V_j[i]\}$$

We use the above formula to find the total volume for each number of splits. A dynamic programming algorithm can be used with running time $O(NK^2)$. To compute the optimal solution first we need the optimal splits for each object, which can be found by using the dynamic programming algorithm presented in section 3.1. Hence, the following theorem holds:

Theorem 2. *Optimally distributing K splits among N objects can be done in $O(NK^2)$.*

The Greedy Algorithm. The dynamic programming algorithm described above is quadratic to the number of splits. That makes the algorithm impractical for many real life applications. Therefore, it is intuitive to look for an approximate solution. The simplest form of such a solution would be to use a greedy strategy: Given the split distribution so far, find the object that if split one more time (or for the first time) it will yield the maximum possible volume reduction, and assign the split to that object. Continue in the same way until there are no more available splits. The algorithm is shown in figure 9. The complexity of the main loop is $O(K)$ and the complexity of the algorithm is $O(K + N \log N)$.

The Look-Ahead Greedy Algorithm (LAGreedy). The result of the previous algorithm will not be optimal in the general case. One reason is the following. Consider an object that if split once gives a very small improvement in empty space but if split twice most of its empty space is removed (see figure 4 for an example). Using the greedy algorithm it is probable that this object will not be given the chance to be allocated any splits, because the first split is poor and other objects with better initial splits, will be chosen before it. However, if we allow the algorithm to consider more than one splits for every object at each step, the possibility for this object to be chosen for splitting is much higher. This observation gives an intuition about how the greedy strategy could be

> **Input**: A set of spatiotemporal objects with cardinality N.
> **Output**: A near optimal minimum volume required to approximate all objects with K splits.
>
> 1. Find volume change for every object using one split. Store in a max priority queue.
> 2. For K iterations: Remove the top element of the queue. Assign the split to the corresponding object. Calculate the volume change if one more split was used on the same object. Reinsert the object in the queue.

Fig. 9. Greedy Algorithm.

improved to give a better result, closer to the optimal. At every step, instead of finding the object that yields the largest gain by performing one more split, we could look ahead and find objects that result in even larger gain if two, three or more splits are assigned all at once.

For example, the look-ahead-2 algorithm works as follows (figure 10). First, all splits are allocated one by one in a greedy fashion, as before. When the greedy assignment is complete, one new priority queue PQ_{la1} is created, which sorts the objects by the gain offered by the last split allocated to them (if an object is split k times, sort the object according to the volume gain yielded by the kth split). The top of the queue is the minimum. A second priority queue PQ_{la2} is also needed, which sorts the objects by the volume that would be gained if two more splits were allocated to each one (if an object is split k times, sort the object according to what the volume gain would be if it was split $k+2$ times). The top of the queue is the maximum. If the gain of the top element of PQ_{la2} is bigger than the sum of the gains of the two top elements of PQ_{la1} the splits are reassigned accordingly, the queues are updated and the same procedure continues until there is no more change in the distribution of splits. In essence, the algorithm tries to find two objects for which the combined gain from their last splits is less than the gain obtained if a different, third object, is split two times extra (obviously an object not conforming to the monotonicity property).

The algorithm has the same worst case complexity as the greedy approach. However, experimental results show that it achieves much better results for the small time penalty it entails.

The real objective of a split distribution algorithm is not to minimize the total volume itself, but to reduce the cost of answering a query if a predefined query distribution model is given. The objective function that should be optimized must represent this cost. Therefore, we need to define a function that is evaluated after each split and gives the average number of I/Os for answering a query. This function will help us find the number of splits that gives the best query results. We discuss possible ways to express this function and choose a good value for the total number of splits in the next section.

> **Input**: A set of spatiotemporal objects with cardinality N.
> **Output**: A near optimal minimum volume required to approximate all objects with K splits.
>
> 1. Allocate splits by calling the *Greedy Algorithm*.
> PQ_{la1} is a min priority queue that sorts objects according to the gain given by their last split.
> PQ_{la2} is a max priority queue that sorts objects according to the gain given if two extra splits are used per object.
> 2. Remove top two elements from PQ_{la1}, let O_1, O_2. Remove top element from PQ_{la2}, let O_3. Make sure that $O_1 \neq O_2 \neq O_3$. If the gain for O_3 is larger than the combined gain for O_1 and O_2, redistribute the splits and update the priority queues.
> 3. Repeat last step until there is no change in the distribution of splits.

Fig. 10. LAGreedy Algorithm.

4 Finding the Number of Splits

The splitting algorithms discussed in the previous section take as input the total number of splits and generate a new dataset with smaller total volume. However, it is important to choose a number of splits that gives a good trade-off between query time and space overhead. The choice of a good value for this parameter affects the performance of the index structure. In this section, we present two methods for automatically computing a good value for this parameter.

The first method is based on using analytical models to predict the performance of the index. For a given number of splits, compute a distribution of splits and estimate some statistics about the generated dataset after splitting. Use the statistics as an input to the analytical model of the index that will be used and get a prediction on the number of disk accesses required to answer a random query from a query distribution. Repeat for a different split distribution. Thus, instead of trying to minimize the total volume, try to minimize the average query cost which is the ultimate goal!

Another way to find the best number of splits among a set of possible values is by using sampling. For each number of splits, an index is created and a set of representatives queries are evaluated on each index. The number that gives the best query performance is then chosen. However, instead of using the full dataset, it is possible to use a small sample and create the indices over this sample. The number of splits should be normalized to the full dataset.

5 Experimental Results

To test our algorithms we created four random datasets (uniform) of various sizes with moving rectangles in 2D space, and another four datasets with trains moving on a railway system (skewed). All object trajectories were approximated with MBRs. First, each object is split with the optimal (DPSplit) algorithm and the merge heuristic (MergeSplit) and the results are stored. Then, the optimal (Optimal), greedy (Greedy) and look-ahead-2 greedy (LAGreedy) algorithms are used to distribute various numbers of splits (from 1% to 150% of the total number of objects) among the objects; again the splitting results are stored. In the rest of the section, $a\%$ splits means that we use $\frac{a}{100}N$ total number of splits on a dataset with N spatiotemporal objects. For comparison purposes we also generated datasets using the simpler approach of splitting the objects in a piecewise manner, i.e., at the points in time where the polynomial representing the movement changes characteristics, which is the same as representing the movements with linear functions as in [21]. This method resulted in a number of splits about 400% of the total number of objects. Finally, we used the 3D R*-Tree and the PPR-Tree to index the resulting data. We decided not to use any packing algorithms for the R*-Tree, since from our previous experience, packing does not help substantially with datasets of moving objects. Packing algorithms tend to cluster together objects that might be consecutive in order even though they may correspond to large and small intervals. This leads to more overlapping and empty space [12]. Details about all datasets are presented in Table 1.

Table 1. Random and Railway datasets.

Random	10k	30k	50k	80k
Total Objects	10000	30000	50000	80000
Objects Per Instant (Avg.)	545.873	642.25	2749.97	4390.54
Total Segments	37179	111774	186539	297413
Object Lifetime (Avg.)	50	50	50	50
Object Extent (%)	0.1%-1%	0.1%-1%	0.1%-1%	0.1%-1%
Railway	10k	30k	50k	80k
Total Objects	10000	30000	50000	80000
Objects Per Instant (Avg.)	190.605	570.7	948.026	1522.78
Total Segments	27678	82792	137011	220996
Object Lifetime (Avg.)	18	18	18	18

For the moving rectangles time extents from 0 to 999 time instants. The lifetime of each object is randomly selected between 1 and 100 time instants. The object movement is approximated with a random number of polynomials between 1 and 10. The polynomials have randomly generated coefficients but are either of first or second degree (of course any type of polynomials could easily be generated). All movements are normalized in the unit square $[0,1]^2$. The extents of the rectangles are randomly selected between 1/1000 and 1/100 of the total space.

For the railway datasets we generated a map containing 22 cities and 51 railways. The map approximates the states of California and New York with most of the tracks connecting intra state cities with each other. Few cities belong to different states in-between and there is a number of tracks connecting all the states across country. The distances of the cities were approximated to match reality. The trains are allowed to make up to 10 stops and travel for as long as 36 hours with a speed that is randomly selected between 60 and 75 miles per hour. No train is allowed to go back to the city were it originated without stopping somewhere else in-between. After all the parameters of the route have been calculated, a series of linear functions is generated, describing the trajectories in time. The railway tracks are considered to be straight lines. For these datasets also, time extents from 0 to 999 time instants.

For both index structures page capacity was set to 50 entries and we used a 10 page LRU buffer. In addition, for the PPR-Tree we set the minimum alive records per node parameter to $P_{version} = 0.22$, the strong version overflow parameter to $P_{svo} = 0.8$ and the strong version underflow to $P_{svu} = 0.4$. Also, the objects were first sorted by insertion time. For the R*-Tree objects were inserted in random order, but the time dimension was scaled down to the unit range first [25]. For the PPR-Tree the time dimension extent does not matter. To test the resulting structures we randomly generated four snapshot and two range query sets with 1000 queries each. Details about these sets are summarized in Table 2. For all experiments the buffer was reset before the execution of any query. All experiments where run on an Intel Pentium III 1GHz personal computer, with 1GB of main memory.

Table 2. Snapshot and Range query sets.

Snapshot	Cardinality	Extents (%)	Duration
Tiny	1000	0.01-0.1	1
Small	1000	0.1-1	1
Mixed	1000	0.1-5	1
Large	1000	1-5	1
Range	Cardinality	Extents (%)	Duration
Small	1000	0.1-1	1 - 10
Medium	1000	0.1-1	10 - 50

5.1 Comparison of Single-Object Splitting Algorithms

First, we compare the dynamic programming (DPSplit) and the greedy (MergeSplit) algorithms for splitting a single object. In order to test their efficiency, we calculated the best splits of all objects contained in the random datasets, using as many splits as necessary and computed the CPU time needed. In figure 11, time is represented in a logarithmic scale, since for the large datasets the DPSplit algorithm needed almost one day to finish splitting the objects. On the other hand, the MergeSplit algorithm was very fast, requiring from a few minutes to a few hours. In order to show that the MergeSplit algorithm produces good splits, we optimally distributed 50% splits on all random datasets, and calculated the total volume of the resulting MBRs. The results are shown in figure 12. Clearly, MergeSplit behaves very closely to DPSplit.

5.2 Comparison of Split Distribution Algorithms

Next, we evaluate the performance of the Greedy and LAGreedy algorithms, in comparison with the optimal dynamic programming approach. We distributed 50% splits on the random datasets using all three algorithms and calculated the CPU cost of each

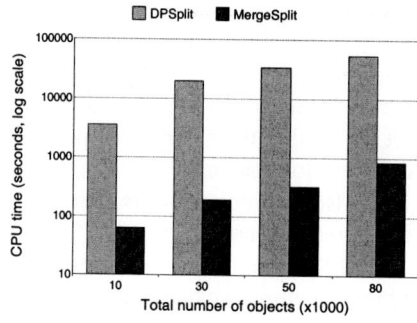

Fig. 11. CPU time for object split algorithms using random datasets.

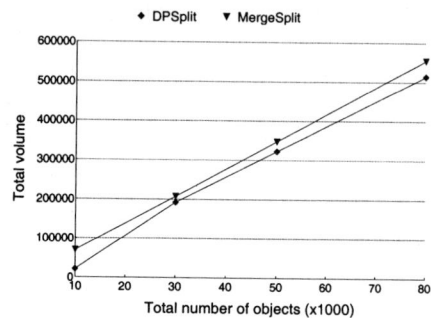

Fig. 12. Total volume for object split algorithms using random datasets.

approach. The results are shown in figure 13. Time is represented again in a logarithmic scale, since the optimal algorithm requires up to a few hours to distribute the splits for the bigger datasets. On the other hand, the two greedy approaches are much faster with the LAGreedy algorithm performing about only 10% slower than the Greedy algorithm, both requiring from a few seconds to a few minutes. To test the efficiency of our algorithms we distributed 150% splits using the LAGreedy algorithm on the random datasets and indexed the resulting MBRs using the PPR-Tree. Finally, we queried the resulting structures with the mixed snapshot query set, recording the average number of disk accesses needed. The results are shown in figure 14. For all the datasets that we tried, the LAGreedy algorithm performed as well as the optimal algorithm, while the Greedy approach was always inferior.

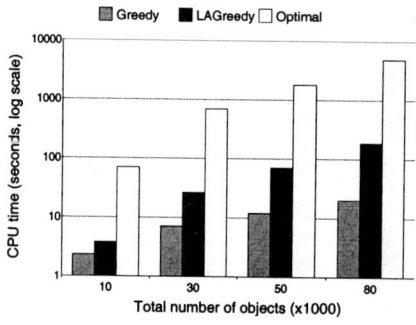

Fig. 13. CPU time for split distribution algorithms using random datasets.

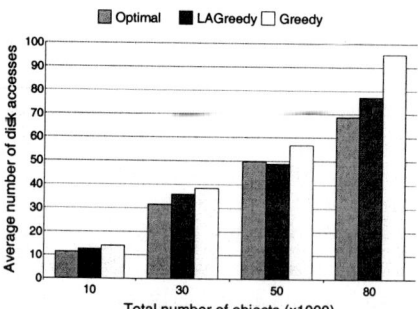

Fig. 14. Mixed snapshot queries using random datasets.

5.3 Benefits and Drawbacks of Splitting

In order to show that splitting a dataset is beneficial only for the partial persistence indexing approach, we distributed a series of different numbers of splits on all datasets using the LAGreedy algorithm. Then, we indexed the resulting MBRs using the 3D R*-Tree and the PPR-Tree. We queried the resulting structures using the small range queries and recorded the average number of disk accesses needed. The results for the 50k random dataset are shown in figure 15. Observe that as the number of splits increases the average number of disk accesses needed decreases substantially for the PPR-Tree, while there is a negative effect for the 3D R*-Tree. For completeness, in figure 16 we present the disk space required by the two structures, for an increasing number of splits. We can see that the PPR-Tree requires almost twice as much space as the 3D R*-Tree, which is a reasonable tradeoff considering the gain in query performance. The LAGreedy combined with the PPR-Tree achieves an improvement of 30% in query performance over the best alternative (75 vs 110 I/Os).

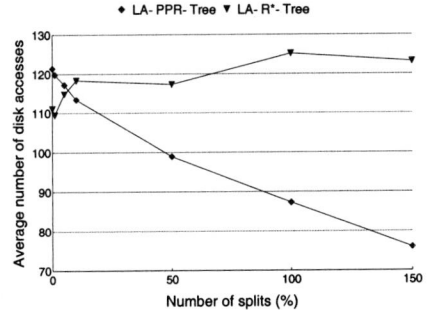
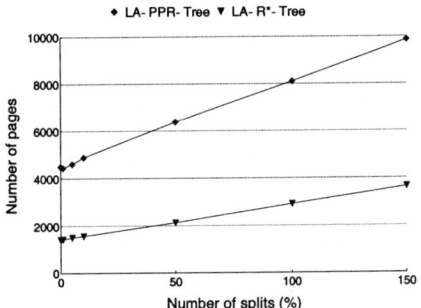

Fig. 15. Small range queries using the 50k random dataset.

Fig. 16. Total space needed using the 50k random dataset.

5.4 Comparing Partially Persistent and Straightforward Approaches

Finally, we performed a number of snapshot and range queries in order to test how the partially persistent and the normal R-Tree structures react when increasing the number and type of objects. For the small range queries the 3D R*-Tree is somewhat better for unsegmented data and 1% up to 5% splits, while the PPR-Tree becomes much better when the number of splits increases. In figure 17 we plot the average number of disk accesses for small range queries and 150% splits for the PPR-Tree and 1% splits for the 3D R*-Tree, distributed with the LAGreedy algorithm. We also plot the performance of the 3D R*-Tree with the piecewise data. It is obvious that the partial persistence approach is by far superior after splitting. For all datasets and any number of splits we observed that the PPR-Tree is consistently better than the 3D R*-Tree approaches for small, large and mixed snapshot queries. An example is shown in figure 18 for the mixed

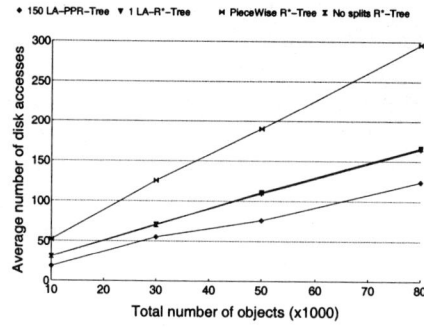 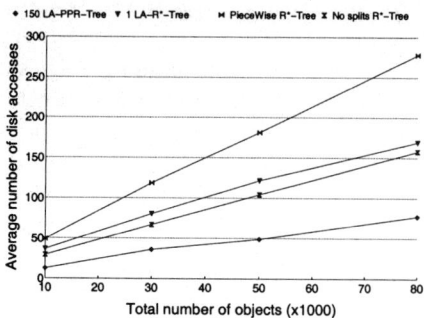

Fig. 17. Small range queries using random datasets.

Fig. 18. Mixed snapshot queries using random datasets.

snapshot queries. We used the 150% PPR-Tree, the 1% 3D R*-Tree and the piecewise 3D R*-Tree. The interesting result here is that the piecewise approach [21] is much worse than the no splits approach. The benefit from splitting the spatiotemporal objects ranges from 20% for small interval queries to more than 50% for snapshot queries. For the railway datasets we observe that the PPR-Tree is again superior for all the cases. Due to lack of space the figures have been omitted.

6 Related Work

Spatiotemporal data management has received increased interest in the last few years and a number of interesting articles appeared in this area. As a result, a number of new index methods for spatiotemporal data have been developed.

In [12] we discuss methods for indexing the history of spatial objects that move with a linear function of time. [21] examines indexing moving points that have piecewise linear trajectories. Two approaches are used, the Native Space Indexing where a 3D R-tree is used to index the line segments of object's trajectories and the Parametric Space Indexing, where a parametric approach to store the moving points is used. A similar idea is used in [5].[20] presents methods to answer efficiently navigation and trajectory historical queries. This type of queries, though, are different than the topological queries examined in this paper. [18] addresses the problem of approximating spatial objects with small number of z-values, trying to balance the number of z-values with the extra space of the approximation.

Methods that can be used to index static spatiotemporal objects include [25, 17, 29, 5, 28]. These approaches are based either on the overlapping or on the multi-version approach for transforming a spatial structure into a partially persistent one. Another related paper is [7] where general structures to index spatiotemporal objects are discussed.

7 Conclusions

In this paper we investigated the problem of indexing spatiotemporal data. We assume that objects move with general motion patterns and we are interested in answering snapshot and small range queries. The obvious approach for indexing spatiotemporal objects is to approximate each object with an MBR and use a spatial access method. However this approach is problematic due to extensive empty space and overlap. In this paper we show how to use artificial splits on a set of spatiotemporal objects in order to reduce overlap and empty space and improve query performance. We present algorithms to find good split positions for a single spatiotemporal object and methods to distribute a given number of splits between a collection of objects. Also, we discuss how to find a value for the number of splits that achieves a good trade-off between query time and space overhead. Experimental results validate the efficiency of the proposed methods. The combination of splitting algorithms and the PPR-Tree can achieve up to 50% better query time than the best previous alternative. An interesting avenue for future work is addressing the on-line version of the problem.

References

[1] P. K. Agarwal, L. Arge, and J. Erickson. Indexing moving points. *In Proc. of the 19th ACM Symp. on Principles of Database Systems (PODS)*, pages 175–186, 2000.
[2] B. Becker, T. Ohler S. Gschwind, B. Seeger, and P. Widmayer. An Asymptotically Optimal Multiversion B-Tree. *VLDB Journal 5(4)*, pages 264–275, 1996.
[3] N. Beckmann, Hans-Peter Kriegel, Ralf Schneider, and Bernhard Seeger. The R* - tree: An Efficient and Robust Access Method for Points and Rectangles. *Proceedings of ACM SIGMOD*, pages 220–231, June 1990.
[4] F. Burton, J. Kollias, V. Kollias, and D. Matsakis. Implementation of overlapping btrees for time and space efficient representation of collection of similar files. *The Computer Journal, Vol.33, No.3*, pages 279–280, 1990.
[5] M. Cai and P. Revesz. Parametric r-tree: An index structure for moving objects. In *Proc. of the COMAD*, 2000.
[6] J. Driscoll, N. Sarnak, D. Sleator, and R.E. Tarjan. Making Data Structures Persistent. *Journal of Computer and System Sciences, Vol. 38, No. 1*, pages 86–124, 1989.
[7] R. Guting, M. Bohlen, M. Erwig, C. Jensen, N. Lorentzos, M. Schneider, and M. Vazirgiannis. A Foundation for Representing and Querying Moving Objects. *In ACM TODS, Vol. 25, No 1*, pages 1–42, 2000.
[8] A. Guttman. R-trees: A dynamic index structure for spatial searching. In *Proc. of ACM SIGMOD*, pages 47–57, 1984.
[9] I. Kamel and C. Faloutsos. Hilbert R-tree: An Improved R-tree Using Fractals. *Proceedings of VLDB*, pages 500–510, September 1994.
[10] G. Kollios, D. Gunopulos, and V. Tsotras. Indexing Animated Objects. *In Proc. 5th Int. MIS Workshop, Palm Springs Desert, CA*, 1999.
[11] G. Kollios, D. Gunopulos, and V. Tsotras. On Indexing Mobile Objects. *In Proc. of the 18th ACM Symp. on Principles of Database Systems (PODS)*, pages 261–272, June 1999.
[12] G. Kollios, D. Gunopulos, V. Tsotras, A. Delis, and M. Hadjieleftheriou. Indexing Animated Objects Using Spatio-Temporal Access Methods. *IEEE Trans. Knowledge and Data Engineering*, pages 742–777, September 2001.

[13] C. Kolovson and M. Stonebraker. Segment Indexes: Dynamic indexing techniques for multi-dimensional interval data. In *Proc. of ACM SIGMOD*, pages 138–147, 1991.
[14] A. Kumar, V.J. Tsotras, and C. Faloutsos. Designing access methods for bitemporal databases. *IEEE Trans. Knowledge and Data Engineering*, 10(1):1–20, 1998.
[15] S.T. Leutenegger, M.A. Lopez, and J.M. Edgington. STR: A simple and efficient algorithm for r-tree packing. In *Proc. of IEEE ICDE*, 1997.
[16] D. Lomet and B. Salzberg. Access Methods for Multiversion Data. *In Proceedings of ACM SIGMOD Conf., Portland, Oregon*, pages 315–324, 1989.
[17] M. Nascimento and J. Silva. Towards historical r-trees. *Proc. of SAC*, 1998.
[18] J. A. Orenstein. Redundancy in spatial databases. In *Proceedings of the 1989 ACM SIGMOD International Conference on Management of Data*, pages 294–305, Portland, Oregon, 31 May–2 June 1989.
[19] B.-U. Pagel, H.-W. Six, H. Toben, and P. Widmayer. Towards an analysis of range query performance in spatial data structures. In *Proc. of ACM PODS*, pages 214–221, 1993.
[20] D. Pfoser, C. Jensen, and Y. Theodoridis. Novel Approaches in Query Processing for Moving Objects. *In Proceedings of VLDB, Cairo Egypt*, September 2000.
[21] K. Porkaew, I. Lazaridis, and S. Mehrotra. Querying mobile objects in spatio-temporal databases. In *Proc. of 7th SSTD*, July 2001.
[22] S. Saltenis and C. Jensen. Indexing of Moving Objects for Location-Based Services. *To Appear in Proc. of IEEE ICDE*, 2002.
[23] S. Saltenis, C. Jensen, S. Leutenegger, and Mario A. Lopez. Indexing the Positions of Continuously Moving Objects. *In Proceedings of the ACM SIGMOD*, pages 331–342, May 2000.
[24] B. Salzberg and V. Tsotras. Comparison of access methods for time-evolving data. *ACM Computing Surveys*, 31(2):158–221, 1999.
[25] Y. Tao and D. Papadias. Mv3r-tree: a spatio-temporal access method for timestamp and interval queries. In *Proc. of the VLDB*, 2001.
[26] Y. Tao and D. Papadias. Cost models for overlapping and multi-version structures. In *Proc. of IEEE ICDE*, 2002.
[27] Y. Theodoridis and T. Sellis. A model for the prediction of R-tree performance. In *Proc. of ACM PODS*, pages 161–171, 1996.
[28] Y. Theodoridis, T. Sellis, A. Papadopoulos, and Y. Manolopoulos. Specifications for efficient indexing in spatiotemporal databases. *In Proc. of 11th Int. Conf. on SSDBMs*, pages 123–132, 1998.
[29] T. Tzouramanis, M. Vassilakopoulos, and Y. Manolopoulos. Overlapping linear quadtrees and spatio-temporal query processing. *The Computer Journal 43(3)*, pages 325–343, 2000.
[30] P.J. Varman and R.M. Verma. An Efficient Multiversion Access Structure. *IEEE Transactions on Knowledge and Data Engineering, Vol. 9, No 3.*, pages 391–409, 1997.

Dynamic Queries over Mobile Objects*

Iosif Lazaridis[1], Kriengkrai Porkaew[2], and Sharad Mehrotra[1]

[1] University of California, Irvine, USA
[2] King Mongkut's University of Technology Thonburi, Bangkok, Thailand

Abstract. Increasingly applications require the storage and retrieval of spatio-temporal information in a database management system. A type of such information is *mobile objects*, i.e., objects whose location changes continuously with time. Various techniques have been proposed to address problems of incorporating such objects in databases. In this paper, we introduce new query processing techniques for *dynamic queries* over mobile objects, i.e., queries that are themselves continuously changing with time. Dynamic queries are natural in situational awareness systems when an observer is navigating through space. All objects visible by the observer must be retrieved and presented to her at very high rates, to ensure a high-quality visualization. We show how our proposed techniques offer a great performance improvement over a traditional approach of multiple instantaneous queries.

1 Introduction

Many new applications require storage and retrieval of spatio-temporal data. A class of such data is *mobile objects*, i.e., objects whose location changes continuously with time. Mobile objects require special handling from the database system, since unlike most other item types, their attributes change continuously. Thus, using traditional approaches, very high update rates must be sustained by the DBMS for complete accuracy of the objects' representation.

Our motivating application is that of a large scale situational awareness system in which a large volume of spatio-temporal information must be accessed and presented to the user at interactive rates as she navigates through virtual space: all objects within her view frustum must be retrieved and presented. A reasonable approach is to use a database system for storage and a spatial index for data access. The rate at which queries are posed is very high. If retrieval performance is weak then either (i) the frame rate will drop ("choppy" motion), or (ii) geometry will be omitted, (inaccurate presentation).

In this paper we explore a special kind of query, *Dynamic Query* (DQ) arising in spatial databases. A DQ, associated with a mobile observer, is evaluated

---

* This work was supported in part by the National Science Foundation under Grant No. IIS-0086124, in part by the Army Research Laboratory under Cooperative Agreements No. DAAL-01-96-2-0003 and No. DAAD-19-00-1-0188, and in part by Air Force Grant F33615-01-C-1902. We thank the anonymous reviewers for their detailed and helpful comments.

continuously as the observer moves in space. In nearby locations many of the objects retrieved by the query will tend to be the same. It makes sense to conserve disk I/O by retrieving them only once, reusing them for as long as they are visible. This paper provides techniques to achieve this for both *Non-Predictive Dynamic Query* (NPDQ) where the observer's motion is not a priori known and in *Predictive Dynamic Query* (PDQ) where it is known.

The notion of a Dynamic Query applies equally well to static objects co-existing in an application with mobile ones. Consider a query being generated by a vehicle during a military exercise. This may involve friendly and enemy vehicles, also landmarks (e.g., natural obstructions), temperature readings from field sensors, mine fields, etc., which are static. Our query evaluation algorithms can be used for static objects as well, since these are a special case of mobile ones.

The rest of the paper is organized as follows: in Sect. 2 we review related work for indexing and retrieving mobile objects. In Sect. 3 we describe how we can represent and index motion. In Sect. 4 we deal with dynamic queries and their implementation. Specifically, in Sect. 4.1 we deal with PDQ, in which the trajectory of the observer is known beforehand while Sect. 4.2 with the general case (NPDQ, unknown trajectory). In Sect. 5 we present some results from the experimental evaluation of our techniques, supporting their effectiveness. In Sect. 6 we conclude, presenting directions of future research.

2 Related Work

The problem of indexing and querying mobile objects in database systems has been studied in the literature [25, 8, 19, 14, 15, 18, 24]. Most of this work uses a multidimensional index structure (R-Tree and its family [5, 2, 22], Quadtree [21], or hB-tree [10]). For temporal objects special indexing techniques have been proposed such as multi-version index structures, e.g., Time-Split B-tree (TSB-tree) [11], multi-version B-tree [1], and others, summarized in [20]. Proposals for spatio-temporal index structures have been summarized in [27].

All these data structures focus on static objects whose value changes explicitly with an update. Recent work has explored indexing for dynamic properties (which may change without explicit update). Research has focused on indexing and query processing over mobile data [25, 8, 19, 14, 15]. Most of this work deals with spatio-temporal range queries. [24] deals with nearest-neighbor queries.

Our work in [14, 15] classifies selection queries, including spatio-temporal range and nearest neighbor queries on both temporal and spatial dimensions. Algorithms for these types of queries are presented using Native Space Indexing (NSI) in which indexing is performed in the original space where motion occurs and Parametric Space Indexing (PSI) where a space defined by motion parameters is used. A comparative study between the two indicates that NSI outperforms PSI, because of the loss of locality associated with PSI. In the present, we use NSI exclusively; dynamic queries can be applied to PSI as well.

3 Motion Representation and Indexing

We now describe how we represent and index the motion of objects. The following forms a background for the query processing schemes to be discussed in Sect. 4.

3.1 Motion Representation

Objects are translating continuously in a d-dimensional space. In most spatial applications, d is 2 or 3. We ignore other motion types (e.g., rotation), since an object's visibility is dictated by its position. The location vector $\bar{x} = (x_1, ..., x_d)$ of object O changes with time, so we write $O.\bar{x} = f(t, \bar{\theta})$, where t is time and $\bar{\theta}$ is a parameter vector (e.g., initial location, speed, etc.).

We observe that the object's motion changes continuously making it impossible to maintain its precise location at every instance of time. This would entail a very high number of updates being generated. Instead, we use the following model. The object (or sensors tracking it), sends at time $O.t_l$ an update of its motion information. This consists of a time interval $O.\bar{t} = [O.t_l, O.t_h]$ in which this update is valid and a vector of *motion parameters* $O.\bar{\theta}$. The database can then, for all queries involving time $t \in O.\bar{t}$ deduce the object's location as $O.\bar{x} = f(t, \bar{\theta})$, using *location function* f which returns the location of an object at time t given its parameters $\bar{\theta}$ stored in the database.

Consider an object translating linearly with constant velocity. At each update the parameter vector is $\bar{\theta} = (O.\bar{x}_{t_l}, O.\bar{v})$, i.e., the object's initial location $O.\bar{x}_{t_l}$ at time $O.t_l$ and its constant vector velocity $O.\bar{v}$. Subsequently, we can easily write the object's location function as:

$$O.\bar{x} = f(t, O.\bar{x}_{t_l}, O.\bar{v}) = O.\bar{x}_{t_l} + O.\bar{v} \cdot (t - O.t_l), \forall t \in O.\bar{t} = [O.t_l, O.t_h] \quad (1)$$

If at some time t' velocity $O.\bar{v}$ changes, then the information stored in the database becomes imprecise ($f(t', \bar{\theta}) \neq O.\bar{x}$) unless an update is issued immediately. Such a change is expected to occur frequently (even continuously); it is thus unreasonable to issue an update whenever needed. Instead, we only issue an update if the object's location (as deduced by the database, by applying f, given $\bar{\theta}$) differs from its current one by more than a threshold value. Thus, the error in the database representation of each object is bounded.

There is a natural tradeoff between the cost of an update (which depends on the update frequency) and the precision of information captured by the database. The issues involved in update management (including this tradeoff) were dealt with in [28]. If we take into account the uncertainty about the location of an object, then its position at any instance of time will no longer be a point (as per the above given location function) but rather it will be a bounded region that captures the *potential* location of the object. More generally, we can think of a distribution $f(\bar{x}, t, \bar{\theta})$ capturing the probability that an object will be in some location $\bar{x}$ at time t, given its last update $\bar{\theta}$. A thorough treatment of the subject of managing the uncertainty of object locations can be found in [12].

For simplicity of exposition, we will assume that the object's location can be precisely determined via f. We can easily generalize to the imprecise case. As we will see, a motion segment's bounding rectangle (minimal rectangle containing its trajectory between updates) is used for indexing. If the object's location is imprecise, then a larger bounding rectangle for the motion will be used, resulting in some false admissions. This is to be expected: allowing for imprecision entails retrieving objects that in reality do not fall within the query region. However, no objects will be missed, as the larger "imprecise" bounding box always contains the smaller "true" bounding box of the motion.

We will be using the following notation for the rest of the paper:

Definition 1 (Interval). $\bar{I} = [l, h]$ *is a range of values from l to h. If $l > h$, I is an empty interval ($\varnothing$). A single value v is equivalent to $[v, v]$. Operations on intervals that we will use are intersection ($\cap$), coverage ($\uplus$), overlap ($\Diamond$) and precedes ($\preceq$). Let $\bar{J} = [J_l, J_h]$ and $\bar{K} = [K_l, K_h]$.*

$$\bar{J} \cap \bar{K} = [\max(J_l, K_l), \min(J_h, K_h)] \qquad \bar{J} \Diamond \bar{K} \Leftrightarrow \bar{J} \cap \bar{K} \neq \varnothing$$
$$\bar{J} \uplus \bar{K} = [\min(J_l, K_l), \max(J_h, K_h)] \qquad \bar{I} \preceq \bar{J} \Leftrightarrow \forall P \in \bar{I} : P \leq J_l$$

Definition 2 (Box). $\Box B = \langle \bar{I}_1, \bar{I}_2, \ldots, \bar{I}_n \rangle = \langle \bar{I}_{1\ldots n} \rangle$ *is an n-dimensional box covering the region of space $\bar{I}_1 \times \bar{I}_2 \times \ldots \times \bar{I}_n \subset \Re^n$. A box $\Box B$ may be empty ($\Box B = \varnothing$) iff $\exists i : \bar{I}_i = \varnothing$). An n-dimensional point $p = \langle v_{1\ldots n} \rangle$ is equivalent to box $\langle [v_1, v_1], [v_2, v_2], \ldots, [v_n, v_n] \rangle$. By $\Box B.\bar{I}_i$ we note a box's extent along the ith dimension. Operations on boxes are the same as those on intervals.*

3.2 Motion Indexing

We summarized motion indexing work in Sect. 2. Here, we describe the Native Space Indexing (NSI) technique of [14, 15], following the framework proposed in [27]. This was shown [15] to be effective for indexing mobile objects and is thus used in this paper, in conjunction with the new Dynamic Query algorithms.

Consider an object O translating in space. Its motion is captured by a location function $O.\bar{x}(t)$ [1]. Let the valid time for the motion be $O.\bar{t}$. The motion is represented as a bounding rectangle with extents $[min_{t \in O.\bar{t}} x_i(t), max_{t \in O.\bar{t}} x_i(t)]$ along each spatial dimension i, and an extent $O.\bar{t}$ along the temporal dimension. A multi-dimensional data structure (e.g., R-Tree) is then used to index this Bounding Box (BB) representation of the motion. The index will contain multiple (non-overlapping) BBs per object, one per each of its motion updates.

We will now show how spatio-temporal selection range queries can be answered using this index. The query is given as a rectangle Q with extents along the spatial and temporal dimensions. Intuitively, this means: "retrieve all objects that were in a rectangle of space, within an interval of time". Evaluating the query is straightforward using the normal index range search algorithm. As an example, for an R-Tree, all children nodes of the root whose BBs intersect

---

[1] Since we will be assuming precision of information, we can assume that the object's location $O.\bar{x}$ is precisely given by the location function f. If we omit the parameter vector $\bar{\theta}$ this assumes that it is understood that the location function is applied with the appropriate $\bar{\theta}$ for the time on which the query is issued.

with Q will be retrieved, and subsequently all children of these with the same property, and so on, all the way to the leaf level in which the actual motion segment BBs are stored. More formally, an R-Tree node with bounding rectangle R will be visited, given a query Q iff $R \lozenge Q$.

An optimization introduced in [13] and [14, 15] follows from the observation that a motion's BB may intersect with Q, while the motion may not. Since the motion is represented as a simple line segment, it is simple to test its intersection with Q directly. Thus, at the leaf level of the index structure, actual motion segments are represented via their end points, not their BBs. This saves a great deal of I/O as we no longer have to retrieve motion segments that don't intersect with the query, even though their BBs do. The precise way of checking the intersection of a query rectangle with a line segment is given in [14, 15].

Spatio-temporal range queries are only one of the possible types of interesting queries in an application with mobile objects. Other types of selection queries, e.g., nearest neighbor search in either the temporal or spatial dimensions were studied in [14, 15]. Other query types, e.g., distance joins [6] are also possible. In the present we will deal with spatio-temporal range queries.

4 Dynamic Queries and Associated Algorithms

The notion of a *Dynamic Query* over mobile objects was introduced in the classification of [23] where it was named Continuous Query. Such a query changes continuously with time, as contrasted with a a *Snapshot Query* [14] which is posed to the system once, is evaluated and then ceases to exist (and can thus be thought of as taking a snapshot over the database at some particular time). A Dynamic Query has a different meaning from continuous queries discussed in [4, 26], and from triggers (also evaluated continuously), in that the condition ("query window") changes with time.

Definition 3 (Snaphost Query). *A Snapshot Query Q is a selection query for all motion segments intersecting box $\langle \bar{t}, \bar{x}_1, \ldots, \bar{x}_d, \rangle$ in space-time. d is the space dimensionality (usually 2 or 3).*

Note that we define a snapshot as having temporal extent. In visualization we need the special case in which this is reduced to a single time instance.

Definition 4 (Dynamic Query). *A Dynamic Query DQ is a series of snapshot queries $Q_1, Q_2, \ldots, Q_n$ such that $Q_i.\bar{t} \preceq Q_{i+1}.\bar{t}, i = 1, \ldots, n-1$.*

Dynamic queries arise naturally in spatio-temporal environments where the observer and/or the objects are in continuous motion. For example, a mobile object may wish to continuously monitor other objects in its vicinity – for instance, within a distance δ of its location at each instance of time. Similarly, in a virtual environment, in order to support a fly-through navigation over a terrain, objects in the observer's view frustum along her trajectory need to be continuously retrieved. A fly-through over the terrain can be thought of as a dynamic query for which each frame rendered corresponds to a snapshot range query for objects in the observer's view at that time. For smooth motion perception, the renderer may pose to the database 15-30 snapshot queries/sec.

A naive approach to handling dynamic queries is to evaluate each snapshot query in the sequence independently of all others. Doing so is far from optimal since the spatial overlap between consecutive snapshot queries can be very high. Imagine a user moving in a virtual environment at a speed of 500 km/hour and her view at each instance of time is a 10 km by 10 km window in the terrain. Given that 20-30 snapshot queries/sec are fired at the database (one per frame of the visualization), the spatial overlap between consecutive snapshots comes out to be approximately 99.9%. Even if the objects being visualized are themselves mobile, a great deal of overlap is expected in the results of successive queries. It makes sense to exploit this overlap, avoiding multiple retrievals of objects that are relevant for more than one snapshot queries. A natural question is to ask whether or not handling this overlap explicitly is beneficial or not, since objects retrieved in the previous query will already be buffered in main memory, e.g., if we use an LRU buffer. Unfortunately, this is not the case, since buffering takes place at the client (where the results are rendered), and not at the server (where retrieval is done). If each session (e.g., a fly-through by some user) used a buffer on the server, then the server's ability to handle multiple sessions would be diminished. More importantly, there would be significant communication overhead in transmitting large volumes of geometrical data from the server to the client.

Recall that we classify dynamic queries as predictive (PDQ) and non-predictive (NPDQ). In the first case, the sequence Q_i is known a priori and can be used to create an I/O optimal algorithm for them. In the non-predictive (more general) case, knowledge of Q_i allows us to make no inferences about Q_{i+1}, i.e., the query changes arbitrarily.

Both types of queries occur frequently in large-scale visualization. PDQ corresponds to "tour mode" in which the user follows a pre-specified trajectory in the virtual world. It is also useful in situations where the user's trajectory changes infrequently; this is common, since usually the user changes her motion parameters in the virtual world every few seconds by appropriate interaction. In the interim – corresponding to hundreds of frames – her motion is predictable based on her last motion parameters. Algorithms for NPDQ are also very useful, because it is precisely at the times of maximum user interaction, when the user's view frustum changes abruptly that the database subsystem is pushed to its limit, trying to load up new data from disk for the changing query parameters. Our algorithms for NPDQ help alleviate this problem.

A system using the concept of Dynamic Queries would operate in three modes:
- **Snapshot.**— The query changes so fast that there is little overlap between Q_i and Q_{i+1}. Thus, multiple snapshot queries are used. This case is very rare in visualization, in which motion is smooth. In this context it would correspond to Q_i and Q_{i+1} being completely different; this might happen e.g., if the user is "teleported" from one part of the virtual world to another.

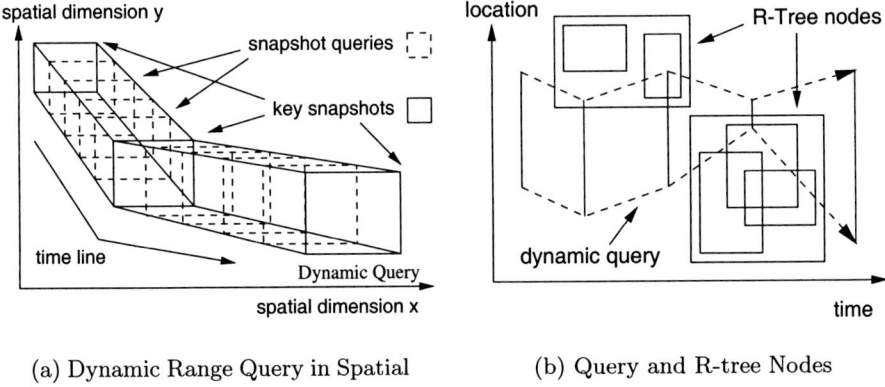

Fig. 1. Dynamic range query

- **Predictive.**— The system uses the user's motion parameters to predict his path (Q_i sequence) and uses the PDQ algorithm. Also used in "tour mode" in which the user's path is known a priori.
- **Non-Predictive.**— As the user's motion parameters change, the system uses the NPDQ algorithm until she settles down to a new direction/speed of motion; then PDQ takes over.

It must be noted that whether PDQ/NPDQ mode is used depends largely on the type of interaction in the system. A good direction of future research is to find automated ways to handle the PDQ ↔ NPDQ hand-off. A third type of algorithm is also possible, that of *Semi-Predictive Dynamic Query* (SPDQ). In SPDQ, the trajectory of the user is allowed to deviate from the predicted trajectory by some $\delta(t)$, i.e., if the location of the observer at time t is $\bar{x}(t)$ and her predicted location is $\bar{x}_p(t)$, then SPDQ can be employed if $\parallel \bar{x}_p(t) - \bar{x}(t) \parallel \leq \delta(t)$. SPDQ can be easily implemented using the PDQ algorithms, but it will result in each snapshot query Q_i being "larger" than the corresponding simple PDQ one, allowing for the uncertainty of the observer's position.

4.1 Predictive Dynamic Queries

A predictive dynamic query (PDQ) is a dynamic query for which the database knows the trajectory of the observer and its associated range before executing it. In such cases, the query processor can partially precompute the answers for each snapshot of the dynamic query to optimize the cost. A predictive dynamic query is thus associated with a trajectory corresponding to that of the observer.

The trajectory of a PDQ query is captured by a sequence of key snapshot queries (as shown in Fig. 1) where a key snapshot query (K) is a spatial range window at a given time. That is, a trajectory of a PDQ query is identified with key snapshot queries $K^1, \ldots, K^n$ where

$$K^j = \langle K^j.t, K^j.\bar{x}_1, \ldots, K^j.\bar{x}_d \rangle \wedge K^j.t < K^{j+1}.t \wedge j = 1, \ldots, n \quad (2)$$

A PDQ query corresponds to the spatio-temporal region covered by joining all the key snapshot queries as illustrated in Fig. 1 (a). Two spatial dimensions are shown; you may visualize the observer moving from left to right in space as time (perpendicular to paper surface) progresses. Notice that, as shown in Fig. 1 (a), the application may ask numerous snapshot queries to the database in the context of a dynamic query in between two key snapshot queries. For example, in the visualization domain, the key snapshots correspond to the points of the fly-through defining the observer's trajectory. During the fly-through, numerous snapshot queries will be posed to the database, (one per each rendered frame). Our PDQ is different from the Type 3 (Moving Query) of [19] chiefly in that in [19] only a single segment of the trajectory is known (i.e., two key snapshots).

In Fig. 1 (b) a dynamic query is seen over the space indexed by an R-Tree. The query evolves with time from left to right. The vertical axis corresponds to the location of the observer; one spatial dimension is shown for simplicity. The query moves up or down along this vertical axis, as the observer moves in space. The query also becomes narrower, or broader, e.g., as the result of viewing the ground from different altitudes.

A simple approach to evaluating a PDQ query is to evaluate the set of answers for the entire duration of the query and return all these answers to the rendering system before they are needed. There are many problems with this approach:

- Since a PDQ query may cover a large spatial and temporal region with many objects in its path, the observer (rendering system in case of visualization example) must maintain a large buffer. In our approach, only currently visible objects need to be in the buffer.
- Even though the trajectory is considered predictive, an observer may deviate from the prescribed path of the trajectory. Such a deviation will result in wasted disk access since answers beyond the point of deviation may no longer be useful. If pre-computation of answers takes place and the observer deviates from her trajectory halfway through, then 50% of the expended effort was wasted. In our case, we can restart the PDQ algorithm if the trajectory changes; we don't retrieve objects before they are needed.
- Since objects being visualized are mobile and send location updates when they deviate from their motion information stored in the database, the location of those objects based on information at query evaluation time will not be valid. In our case, we retrieve objects when they are needed (late retrieval), giving them ample time to update their motion information, never reading the same object twice.

We propose an incremental approach to retrieve non-overlapping answers for evaluating dynamic queries. For each snapshot query asked, the database will only retrieve objects that have not been retrieved in previous snapshot queries. Along with each object returned, the database will inform the application about how long that object will stay in the view so that it will know how long the object should be kept in the application's cache. For lack of space, we refer the reader to [14] for a more thorough study of caching issues. We only mention

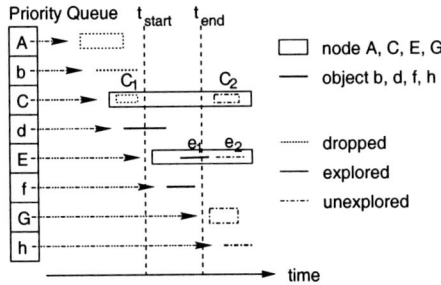

Fig. 2. Priority queue for dynamic query

that it is easy (at the client) to maintain objects keyed on their "disappearance time", discarding them from the cache at that time.

The approach works as follows. Once the application has given the database all of the key snapshots, the database starts executing the PDQ by traversing the underlying multidimensional data structure. In describing the algorithm, we will assume that this structure is an R-tree though our technique works generally. We use a priority-based approach, similar to those of [17, 7] for kNN searches. Starting from the root node, the query processor computes the time interval that the root overlaps with the dynamic query and inserts it along with this interval in a priority queue, ordered by the start time of such time intervals. Note that if the time interval is empty, nothing is inserted in the queue. Next, for objects that will appear in view (i.e., be inside the query trajectory of Fig. 1) at time $t \in [t_{start}, t_{end}]$, repeated calls are made to $getNext(t_{start}, t_{end})$ (in Algorithm 4.1) until no object is returned or the priority queue is empty. Note that the function allows the application to query for objects that will appear in the view during time interval $[t_{start}, t_{end}]$. The time interval corresponds to the period between two key queries. By increasing t_{end} we would increase pre-fetching. We have already enumerated the reasons making this problematic without providing a benefit over our I/O optimal algorithm.

First, the query processor retrieves the top element in the priority queue. or ∅ if it is empty. Otherwise, it keeps reading items from the queue and examining their children by computing the time interval that each child will overlap with the query. Then, each child will be inserted along with its time interval in the queue. This step goes on until an object is found at the top of the queue with an associated time interval overlapping with t. If such an object is found, it is returned. If the time interval of the item at the head of the queue is greater than t (future with respect to t) or the queue is empty, ∅ is returned. Fig. 2 illustrates how the algorithm works. Node A and object b are at the head of the queue and will be dropped off the queue. Node C will be explored and C_1 will be dropped while C_2 will be inserted to the queue. Object d is the first object that will be returned. Subsequent calls to $getNext()$ (with the same arguments) will explore node E, insert e_1 and e_2 to the queue, and return f and e_1 eventually. Node G,

Pseudo-code 4.1 getNext() function

```
1   item function getNext(t_start, t_end)
2   {
3       item = PriorityQueue.peek();
4       if (item == ∅) return ∅;
5       while (t_end ≥ item.time_start) {
6           item = PriorityQueue.pop();
7           if (t_start ≤ item.time_end) {
8               if (item.isObject()) return item;
9               RTree.loadNode(item); // disk access
10              for each (i ∈ item.children) {
11                  i.time = Query.computeOverlappingTime(i);
12                  if (t_start ≤ i.time_end) PriorityQueue.push(i);
13              }
14          }
15          item = PriorityQueue.peek();
16          if (item == ∅) return ∅;
17      }
18      return ∅;
19  }
```

node C_2, object e_2, and object h will remain in the queue until the application calls the function with different argument values.

This algorithm guarantees that the first object appearing during $[t_{start}, t_{end}]$ will be returned. In Fig. 2, objects d, f, and e_1 will be returned in that order.

We compute the time interval that a bounding box R will overlap with the dynamic query by identifying the subsequence of key snapshots (K) that temporally overlap with the bounding box. For each pair of consecutive key snapshots in the subsequence, we compute the time interval T^j that the trajectory between K^j and K^{j+1} overlaps with R. We call the trajectory between K^j and K^{j+1} a segment S^j. Each segment has a trapezoid shape as shown in Fig. 3 where a single spatial dimension (vertical axis) and the temporal dimension (horizontal) is shown. Let R be $\langle \bar{t}, \bar{x}_1, \ldots, \bar{x}_d \rangle$. We compute T^j as follows:

$$T^j = \bigcap_{i=1}^{d} T_i^{j,u} \cap T_i^{j,l} \cap [K^j.t, K^{j+1}.t] \cap R.\bar{t} \tag{3}$$

where $T_i^{j,u} = [t_{i,s}^{j,u}, t_{i,e}^{j,u}]$ is the time interval that the upper border of S^j overlaps with R along the ith dimension and $T_i^{j,l} = [t_{i,s}^{j,l}, t_{i,e}^{j,l}]$ is the time interval that the lower border of S^j overlaps with R along the ith dimension (see Fig. 3 (a)).

We compute $T_i^{j,u}$ and $T_i^{j,l}$ by checking four cases as shown in Fig. 3 (b). For example, in Case 1, where the upper border of the segment moves upward in

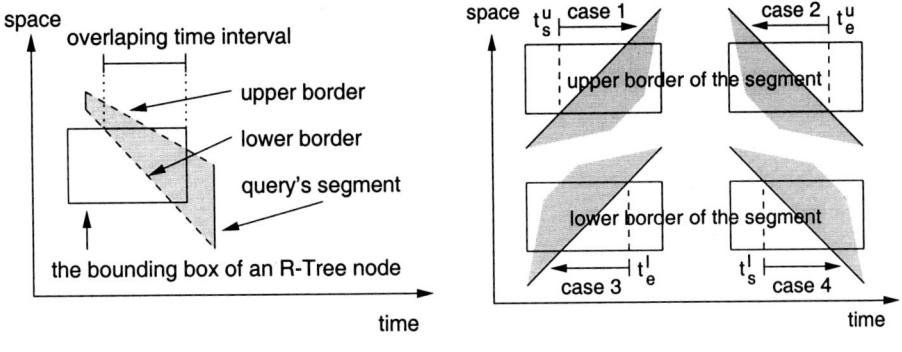

Fig. 3. Overlapping time interval

(a) Overlapping Time Interval

(b) Intersection of a Bounding Box and a Segment

time, t_s^u is the intersection of the upper border of the segment and the lower border of the bounding box and t_e^u is the ending time of the bounding box.

For each S^j with $j = 1, \ldots, n-1$, we compute T^j. Next, we compute the overlapping time interval of the dynamic query and a bounding box $T_{Q,R}$ as $\uplus_{j=1}^{n-1} T^j$. We insert $T_{Q,R}$ along with the node corresponding to R in the queue.

For the leaf node where motions are stored, similar to the bounding boxes in internal nodes, we can compute $T_i^{j,u}$ and $T_i^{j,l}$ by checking the four cases. The geometric intuition for computing the intersection of both motion segments and bounding boxes with the query trajectory is fairly simple. To conserve space, we give the precise formulae in [9].

The benefit of this over the naive approach (in which each snapshot query is independently evaluated) is that we access each R-tree node at most once irrespective of the frame rate (snapshot rate) that the application attempts to render. In the naive approach, each frame corresponds to a snapshot query and thus the disk access cost is proportional to the frame rate.

Update Management: The described mechanism works in a situation where there are no motion updates submitted to the R-Tree while the query is running. Such a situation is common in historical databases. If updates occur concurrently with dynamic queries, a special mechanism is needed to handle them. Each such update is in fact an insertion operation, resulting in the insertion of a new line-segment object into the R-tree. All ongoing dynamic queries must be aware of newly inserted objects. For each inserted object, the query processor checks whether it will appear in any dynamic queries, and inserts it in the queues of such queries. Similarly, if a node overflows, a new node is created to share the overflow node's load. We check whether this new node overlaps with any current dynamic queries. If so, then we insert it in the queue of that query. This ensures that dynamic queries are aware of new branches in the R-tree.

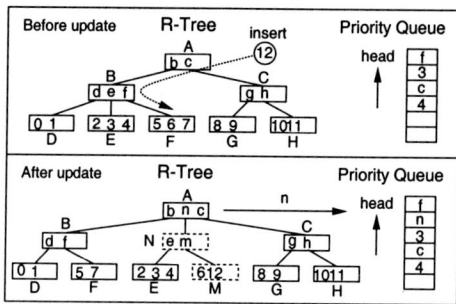

Fig. 4. Update management for PDQ

Note that when a leaf node overflows, a sequence of overflows and splits all the way to the root node may occur. The original R-tree insertion algorithm [5] did not guarantee that all newly created nodes will be in the same path. However, it is possible to force them to be on the same path as the data causing the overflow. Doing so incurs no extra cost nor conflict with the original splitting policy. The benefit of this is that only the lowest-common ancestor of the newly created nodes needs to be inserted into the priority queue; this covers all the new nodes (including the inserted data). Figure 4 demonstrates such a scenario. When the object with ID 12 is inserted in node F, node F overflows and splits to node M. Node M is then inserted into node B, which causes node B to overflow and split to node N. Node N is then inserted to node A. Since node A is not split further, N is the highest node of the sequence (12, M, N), n is sent to all dynamic queries for consideration to be inserted into their priority queues.

Notice that, before an update occurs, for each node in the priority queue, it is impossible for its ancestors to be in the same queue. This is because a node cannot be in the queue unless its parent has been explored. A node that has been explored won't be put back in the queue. In other words, the priority queue will never explore any node more than once. However, unfortunately, this is not true when the update mechanism is involved. For example, in Fig. 4, node N is an ancestor of object ID 3 and 4 which are also in the queue. When node N is explored, node E and M will be inserted into the queue and eventually object ID 3 and 4 will be inserted into the queue again. Although, we cannot prevent duplicate insertions into the queue, we can eliminate the duplication when popping nodes from the queue. Although duplicate items are inserted in the queue at different times, they are popped out of the queue consecutively since they have the same priority. Thus, each time that we pop an item from the queue, we check if it is the same as the previous one[2]. If yes, we just ignore that item since it has just been taken care of.

If the lowest common ancestor of newly created nodes is close to the root node, it is better to empty the priority queues of the current dynamic queries and

---

[2] More generally, we check a few objects with the same priority, since two objects may appear concurrently

rebuild the queue from the root node since there is a high possibility of duplicate insertion. Similar to the growth rate of the height of the R-tree, the rate that such a node will become close to the root node is exponentially decreasing.

4.2 Non-predictive Dynamic Queries

Predictive dynamic queries described in the previous section take advantage of the known trajectory of the query and precompute the search path. In some cases, it is not possible to know the trajectory beforehand. The techniques to evaluate non-predictive dynamic queries are designed for this purpose.

A non-predictive dynamic query is a dynamic query for which the database does not know the trajectory nor the range of the query beforehand. As a result, the query processor cannot precompute the answers or the search path prior to receiving each snapshot query. However, the query processor remembers the previously executed query, and thus can still avoid repeating *some* of the work previously done. Similar to PDQ, NPDQ returns only additional answers that have not been returned in the previous query. Like PDQ, since the query rate is high, there may be significant overlap between consecutive queries. The naive approach (independent evaluation of snapshot queries) will visit nodes of the data structure multiple times retrieving the same objects repeatedly. The approach described below overcomes this problem.

Formally, we define a non-predictive query (NPDQ) as a pair of snapshot queries P and Q where $P.t < Q.t$ and the objective is to retrieve all objects that satisfy Q and have not been retrieved by P. The first snapshot query of NPDQ is evaluated as a normal snapshot query. For subsequent queries, the query processor will check each bounding box (starting from that of the root node) if it is **discardable**. A bounding box R is discardable iff the overlapping part of R and Q is covered by P. Otherwise, the node corresponding to the box R needs to be explored. The following lemma (proven in [9]) formalizes the condition when a given node R of a data structure is discardable.

Lemma 1 (Discardable). *Let Q be the current query box and P be the previous one. Let R be a bounding box corresponding to an R-tree node. R is* **discardable** *iff $(Q \cap R) \subset P$.*

The search algorithm for NPDQ works as follows. The algorithm starts by visiting the root node of the R-tree. For each child R of the currently visited node, R is visited if $discardable(P, Q, R)$ is false where $discardable(P, Q, R)$ has the truth value of $(Q \cap R) \subset P$. In dynamic queries, notice that P and Q never overlap along the temporal axis since P extends from time t_i to t_j and Q extends from t_j to t_k where $t_i < t_j < t_k$. This implies that if $(Q \cap R)$ is not empty, $(Q \cap R) \subset P$ is always false. That is, *discardability* is useless since the previous query does not reduce the number of nodes that need to be visited in the current one. To overcome this problem we can: (i) use an open-ended temporal range query (Fig. 5(a)), or (ii) use double-temporal axes (Fig. 5(b)).

Using an open-ended temporal range query can overcome the problem since the previous query retrieves all objects which satisfy the spatial range of the

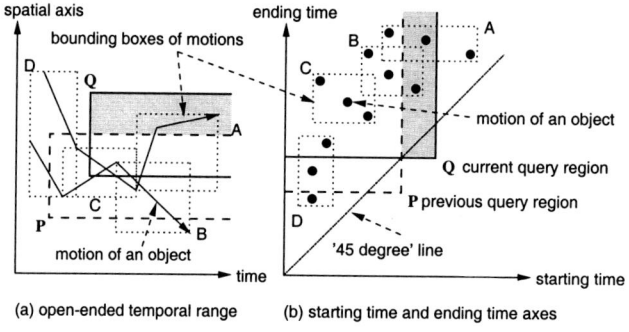

Fig. 5. Discardability

query either now or in the future. This is suitable for querying future or recent past motions only. See Fig. 5(a): B and C do not need to be visited by the current query Q since they have already been visited by the previous query P. D corresponds to a node that Q does not need to visit since it does not overlap with Q. However, Q needs to visit A because A may contain an object which does not overlap with P, and was thus not retrieved in the previous query.

Another approach to overcome the same problem is to separate the starting time and the ending time of motions into independent axes. See Fig. 5(b): all objects reside on one side of the 45 degree line since all motions start before they end. A and B are BBs that Q needs to visit while C and D are BBs that P has visited and Q does not need to visit. This approach is suitable for both historical and future queries. We choose this approach in our implementation of NPDQ. We give a formal definition of the *discardable*(P, Q, R) condition in [9].

Update Management: We use a timestamp mechanism to handle updates (i.e., insertions of new motions). For each insertion, all nodes along the insertion path will update their timestamp to the current time. This lets the search algorithm know if the discardability condition is to be employed. When a BB is checked during the search algorithm, initially its timestamp is read; if it is newer than that of the previous query P then R has been modified since the last visit and P cannot be used to eliminate R for Q. Thus, the normal condition ($R \lozenge Q$) is employed. If $P.t$ is not older than the timestamp of R, then R has not changed since the last visit; P can be used to check if R is discardable for query Q.

5 Empirical Evaluation

We studied the performance of our DQ algorithms (for both PDQs and NPDQs), comparing them to the naive approach of multiple instantaneous queries. Our performance measures are I/O cost measured in number of disk accesses/query and CPU utilization in terms of number of distance computations.

Data and Index Buildup: We generate data as follows: 5000 objects are created, moving randomly in a 2-d space of size 100-by-100 length units, updating

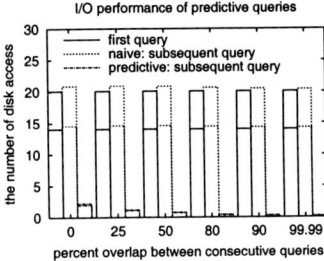
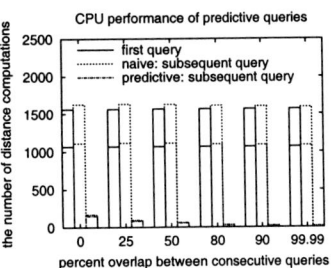

Fig. 6. I/O performance of PDQ

Fig. 7. CPU performance of PDQ

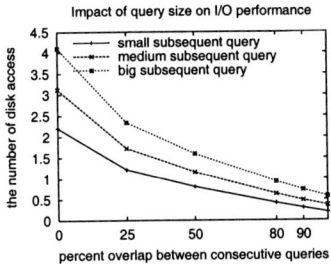
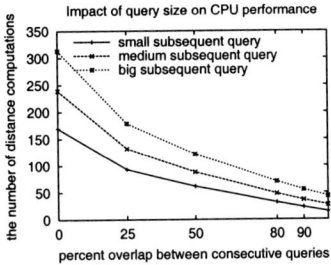

Fig. 8. Impact of Query Size on I/O Performance of Subsequent Queries (PDQ)

Fig. 9. Impact of Query Size on CPU Performance of Subsequent Queries (PDQ)

their motion approximately (random variable, normally distributed) every 1 time unit over a time period of 100 time units. This results in 502,504 linear motion segments being generated. Each object moves in various directions with a speed of approximately 1 length unit/1 time unit. Experiments at higher speeds were also run with similar results. Plotted figures correspond to the first case. An R-tree, NSI index is used to store this motion data as discussed in Section 3.

Page size is 4KB with a 0.5 fill factor for both internal and leaf nodes. Fanout is 145 and 127 for internal– and leaf-level nodes respectively; tree height is 3.

Queries: To compare performance of our approach with the naive one, 1000 query trajectories of each speed of the query trajectory are generated and results are averaged. Query performance is measured at various speeds of the query trajectory. For each DQ, a snapshot query is generated every 0.1 time unit. For a high speed query, the overlap between consecutive snapshot queries is low; this increases as speed decreases. We measure the query performance at overlap levels of 0, 25, 50, 80, 90, and 99.99%. We also measure the impact of the spatial range of the query on the performance of the dynamic query. We use the spatial range of 8x8 (small range), 14x14 (medium range), and 20x20 (big range). Unless otherwise stated, the experiments reported are based on the small range query.

Experiments for PDQ: Figure 6 plots the total number of disk accesses (including the fraction of them at the leaf level) for different percent overlap between consecutive snapshot queries. For each histogram bar, the lower part of the bar shows the number of disk accesses at the leaf level while the upper part of the bar shows the number of disk accesses at higher levels of the R-tree. The figure shows the I/O performance of the first query and subsequent queries. The results of subsequent queries are averaged over 50 consecutive queries of each dynamic query. The figure shows that, in the naive approach, the query performance of subsequent queries is the same as that of the first snapshot query and independent of the percent overlap between the consecutive snapshot queries. This is because the naive approach re-executes each snapshot query from scratch. The proposed approach to predictive query significantly improves the query performance for subsequent queries. The more the percent overlap is, the better I/O performance is. Even in the case of no overlap between subsequent queries, the predictive approach still improves the query performance significantly. This is because the predictive approach benefits from spatio-temporal proximity between consecutive queries. Similar to Fig. 6, Fig. 7 shows the CPU performance of predictive queries in term of the number of distance computation. The number of distance computations is proportional to the number of disk accesses since, for each node loaded, all its children are examined. So, Fig. 7 is similar to Fig. 6.

Figures 8, 9 show the impact of spatial range of the dynamic query on the I/O and CPU performance respectively. The figures show the performance of the subsequent queries of the dynamic query. The results are intuitive in that a big query range requires a higher number of disk accesses and a higher number of distance computations as compared as opposed to a smaller one.

Experiments for NPDQ: Similar to the results for PDQ, Fig. 10 plots the total number of disk accesses (including the fraction of them at the leaf level) for varying degree of overlap between consecutive snapshot queries. Here as well, NPDQ improves performance significantly for subsequent queries. As overlap increases, I/O performance improves. If there is no overlap between two consecutive queries, the NPDQ algorithm does not cause improvement; neither does it cause harm. Fig. 11 shows the CPU performance of NPDQ, similar to the result for I/O shown in Fig. 10. Similarly to PDQ, Figures 12, Fig. 13 indicate that the size of the spatial range of the query impacts its I/O and CPU performance. That is, increase in size results in more disk I/O and a higher number of distance computations. Comparison of PDQ versus NPDQ performance favors the former; this is expected due to the extra knowledge being used.

6 Conclusion

In this paper, we presented efficient algorithms to evaluate *Dynamic Queries* in database systems. We have dealt with two types of such queries: *predictive* and *non-predictive* ones (PDQ/NPDQ). In PDQ we utilize knowledge of the query's trajectory and precompute answers as needed. NPDQ is the general case in which the query trajectory is not known beforehand and thus answers can't be precomputed. However, since some of the query results from previous snapshot queries can be re-used, the algorithm for NPDQ avoids performing multiple disk accesses. An intermediate case, Semi-Predictive Dynamic Query (SPDQ) in

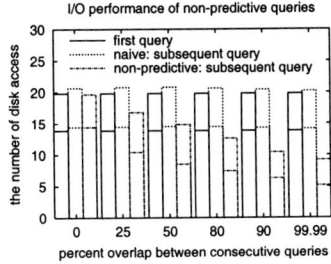

Fig. 10. I/O performance of non-predictive dynamic query

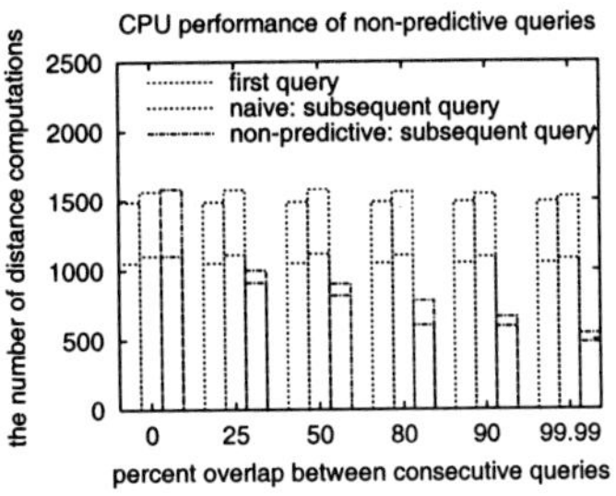

Fig. 11. CPU performance of non-predictive dynamic query

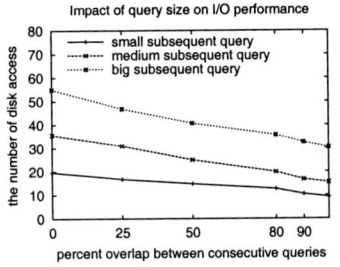
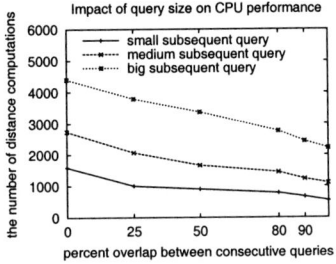

Fig. 12. Impact of query size on I/O performance of subsequent queries (NPDQ)

Fig. 13. Impact of query range on CPU performance of subsequent queries (NPDQ)

which the query trajectory is known approximately within an error bound, was also explored. Our experimental study indicates that both predictive and non-predictive queries resulted in significant improvement of retrieval performance.

There are many directions of future research: (i) generalizing the concept of dynamic queries to nearest neighbor searches as well, similar to moving-query point of [24], (ii) generalizing dynamic queries to include more complex queries involving simple or distance-joins and aggregation, (iii) adapting dynamic queries to a specialized index for mobile objects such as TPR-tree, [19] (iv) investigating the spectrum of possibilities between complete unpredictability and complete predictability of query motion and automating this in the query processor.

References

1. B. Becker, S. Gschwind, T. Ohler, B. Seeger, and P. Widmayer. An asymptotically optimal multiversion B-tree. *VLDB Journal*, 5(4):264–275, 1996.
2. N. Beckmann, H.-P. Kriegel, R. Schneider, and B.Seeger. The R*-tree: an efficient and robust access method for points and rectangles. In *ACM SIGMOD*, 1990.
3. K. Chakrabarti, K. Porkaew, and S. Mehrotra. Efficient query refinement in multimedia databases. In *IEEE ICDE 2000*.

4. J. Chen, D. J. DeWitt, F. Tian, and Y. Wang. NiagaraCQ: A scalable continuous query system for internet databa ses. In *ACM SIGMOD*, 2000.
5. A. Guttman. R-tree: a dynamic index structure for spatial searching. In *ACM SIGMOD*, 1984.
6. G. Hjaltason and H. Samet. Incremental distance join algorithms for spatial databases. In *ACM SIGMOD*, 1998.
7. G. R. Hjaltason and H. Samet. Ranking in spatial databases. In *Int'l Symposium on Large Spatial Databases*, 1995.
8. G. Kollios, D. Gunopulos, and V. J. Tsotras. On indexing mobile objects. In *Symposium on Principles of Database Systems*, 1999.
9. I. Lazaridis, K. Porkaew, and S. Mehrotra. Dynamic queries over mobile objects. (full version) Technical Report TR-DB-01-07, UC Irvine, 2001.
10. D. Lomet and B. Salzberg. The hB-Tree: A multiattribute indexing method with good guaranteed performance. *ACM TODS*, 15(4):625–658, 1990.
11. D. Lomet and B. Salzberg. The performance of a multiversion access method. In *ACM SIGMOD*, 1990.
12. D. Pfoser and C. Jensen. Capturing the uncertainty of moving-object representations. In *SSD*, 1999.
13. D. Pfoser, C. Jensen, and Y. Theodoridis. Novel approaches to the indexing of moving object trajectories. In *VLDB*, 2000.
14. K. Porkaew. Database support for similarity retrieval and querying mobile objects. Technical report, PhD thesis, University of Illinois at Urbana-Champaign, 2000.
15. K. Porkaew, I. Lazaridis, and S. Mehrotra. Querying mobile objects in spatiotemporal databases. In *SSTD 2001, Redondo Beach, CA, USA*.
16. J. T. Robinson. The k-d-b-tree: A search structure for large multidimensional dynamic indexes. In *ACM SIGMOD*, 1981.
17. N. Roussopoulos, S. Kelley, and F. Vincent. Nearest neighbor queries. In *ACM SIGMOD*, 1995.
18. S. Saltenis and C. Jensen. Indexing of moving objects for location-based services. In *ICDE (to appear)*, 2002.
19. S. Saltenis, C. Jensen, S. Leutenegger, and M. Lopez. Indexing the positions of continuously moving objects. In *ACM SIGMOD*, 2000.
20. B. Salzberg and V. Tsotras. Comparison of access methods for time-evolving data. *ACM Computing Surveys*, 31(2):158–221, 1999.
21. H. Samet. The quadtree and related hierarchial data structures. *ACM Computing Surveys*, 16(2):187–260, 1984.
22. T. Sellis, N. Roussopoulos, and C. Faloutsos. The R+ tree: A dynamic index for multi-dimensional objects. In *VLDB*, 1987.
23. A. P. Sistla, O. Wolfson, S. Chamberlain, and S. Dao. Modeling and querying moving objects. In *IEEE ICDE 1997*.
24. Z. Song and N. Roussopoulos. K-nearest neighbor search for moving query point. In *SSTD*, 2001.
25. J. Tayeb, O. Ulusoy, and O. Wolfson. A quadtree based dynamic attribute indexing method. *Computer Journal*, 41(3):185–200, 1998.
26. D. B. Terry, D. Goldberg, D. Nichols, and B. M. Oki. Continuous queries over append-only databases. In *ACM SIGMOD*, 1992.
27. Y. Theodoridis, T. Sellis, A. N. Papadopoulos, and Y. Manolopoulos. Specifications for efficient indexing in spatiotemporal databases. In *SSDBM*, 1998.
28. O. Wolfson, S. Chamberlain, S. Dao, L. Jiang, and G. Mendez. Cost and imprecision in modeling the position of moving objects. In *IEEE ICDE*, 1998.

Semantic Analysis of Business Process Executions

Fabio Casati and Ming-Chien Shan

Hewlett-Packard Laboratories
1501 Page Mill Road, 1U-4
Palo Alto, CA, 94304 USA
{casati,shan}@hpl.hp.com

Abstract. Business Process Management Systems log a large amount of operational data about processes and about the (human and automated) resources involved in their executions. This information can be analyzed for assessing the quality of business operations, identify problems, and suggest solutions. However, current process analysis systems lack the functionalities required to provide information that can be immediately digested and used by business analysts to take decisions. In this paper we discuss the limitations of existing approaches and we present a system and a set of techniques, developed at Hewlett-Packard, that overcome this limitations, enabling the use of log data for efficient business-level analysis of business processes.

1. Introduction

Business Process Management Systems (BPMS) are tools that support the definition, execution, and management of business processes [4]. BPMSs have been traditionally used to enact administrative processes, such as travel expense reimbursement or employee relocations. More recently, they have been also used to automate the supply chain and to implement services offered via the web.

The benefits of using a BPMS, as opposed to hardcoding the business logic or executing the flow manually, include faster process executions, lower operating costs, automated exception handling, shorter time to market, and more flexibility. However, until recently, these advantages have not proven convincing enough for many companies to adopt a process management solutions. Indeed, IT architects often decide for approaches that involve hardcoding the flow, or adopting the simple process automation functionalities offered by EAI tools, application servers, or other e-business applications already in use in the organization.

Another (potential) benefit of BPMSs is that they provide functionalities for logging and subsequently analyzing process executions, in order to track operations, detect inefficiencies, and identify solutions. Indeed, this capability is often highlighted by BPMSs vendors (sometimes successfully [3]) as a key advantage with respect to both competing vendors and competing technologies.

However, BPMS analysis and monitoring capabilities are still primitive, and are by no means sufficient to enable the monitoring, understanding, and improvement of business operations. There are indeed a variety of problems in current process analysis technologies and in the reporting tools that are provided with the BPMS, ranging from performance (speed) of the tools to the quality of the operational data logged by the system, often characterized by errors and inconsistencies. However, besides these "technical" limitations, a key problem is that it is very difficult to gain *business* insights from the reports, that are at a very low level of abstraction and do not support any kind of business-level analysis. Therefore, they do not support business manager in identifying and addressing problems.

This paper discusses the main limitations of current process analysis technologies and presents a system, recently developed at Hewlett-Packard, that overcomes many of these limitations. The system, called *HPPM intelligent Process Data Warehouse*, or PDW for short, is based on warehousing process execution data, and then on adding semantics to it, in order to provide a comprehensive view of the business operations, assess their quality, and quickly identify the critical issues that need to be addressed. While our purpose is to support both technical and business users (and we believe that the system improves the state of the art for both kinds of analysis), in this paper we particularly emphasize the PDW techniques that provide support for business users, since it involves more innovative techniques, and is therefore more suited to an industrial track of a research conference. The interested reader is referred to [5] for a detailed description of the functionalities and technical details of PDW.

2. Semantics, Semantics, Semantics[1]

This section discusses the main limitations of current process reporting techniques. BPMSs today enable execution data analysis by logging process execution data into a database, that is then typically queried with either built-in or third party reporting tools such as Crystal Reports, Oracle Discoverer, or Microsoft Excel.

Fig. 1 shows a typical report provided by built-in BPMS analysis tools: It provides information on the average execution time of each node in a process. Obtaining and using these kinds of report with current BPMSs presents three major limitations:
- *Performance:* process logs are typically designed to ease (i.e, do not delay) the job of the process engine, but they are not structured for data analysis. This is reflected by the lack of indexes, partitions, and by the structure of the database schema. Due to these limitations, it may literally take days to generate even simple reports if the volume of process instances is high.
- *Data quality:* even assuming that data are retrieved in an acceptable time, it is very likely that the information shown is incorrect. In fact, very often the data logged by the operational systems include inconsistencies, and even special "codes" written in activity completion timestamps (the typical one is Jan 1, 1970) to denote failures or other events. The presence of even a single "code" like this, if not properly handled, can invalid the statistics returned by the reporting tool.
- *Semantics:* even assuming that data are retrieved with acceptable performance and that they accurately reflect the process executions, they are still useless for many analysis purposes, because they lack the abstraction level required from (business) analysts in order to understand business operations, as detailed in the following.

---

[1] "Borrowed" from an expression used by Stefano Ceri at the Asilomar Workshop on the database challenges for the XXI century [1].

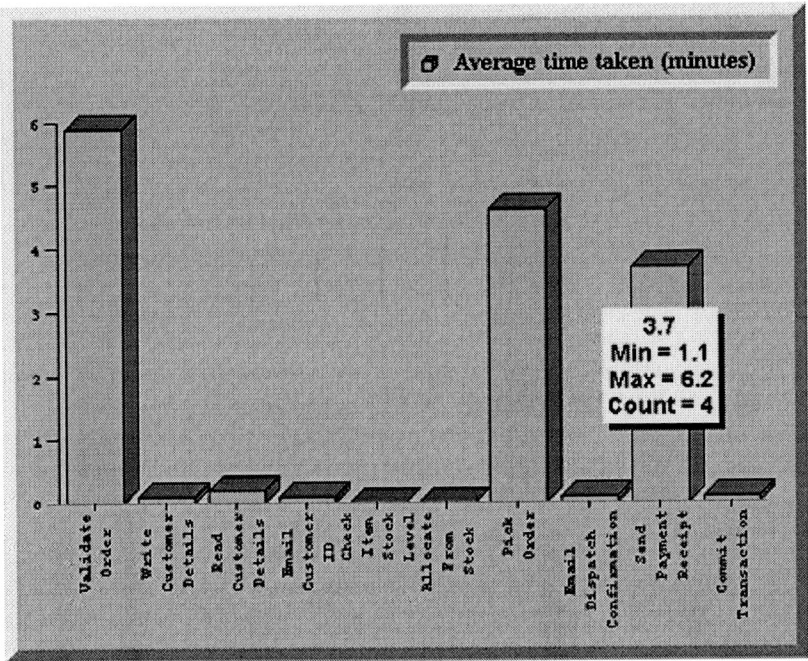

Fig. 1. A typical report than can be obtained by using BPMS reporting tools

The first two issues are "classic" log analysis problem, typically solved by using a data warehousing approach to data analysis. Indeed, PDW is also based on warehousing process execution data. While building a data warehouse for business processes does present some interesting data warehousing problems, in this paper we focus on the "semantic" aspect of the problem and of the solution we propose.

Consider the diagram of Fig. 2, representing a process executed by a supply chain hub to support negotiations of purchase order requests between buyers and sellers (this example has been taken from one of our customers). The figure shows the "business-level" view of the process. Indeed, a business analyst would benefit from statistics on this process, such as how long it takes to execute each step in average, how many orders are accepted for each week, and the like. Therefore, a report such as the one shown in Fig. 1 would indeed be helpful if it could be applied to this process.

However, when the process is implemented, additions and modifications are needed, to take care of many detailed issues that must be considered in real-life operations, such as getting information from the database, checking permissions, or managing deadlines. In the case at hand, the process that was actually implemented is shown in Fig. 3[2]. The reporting tools will provide statistics based on the actual process of Fig. 3, that include cryptic node names and no apparent relation to the conceptual process. Therefore, the report is virtually useless (or at least very hard to interpret) for a business user.

---

[2] The figure is small both because of space constraints but also because we were not allowed to show the details of the process.

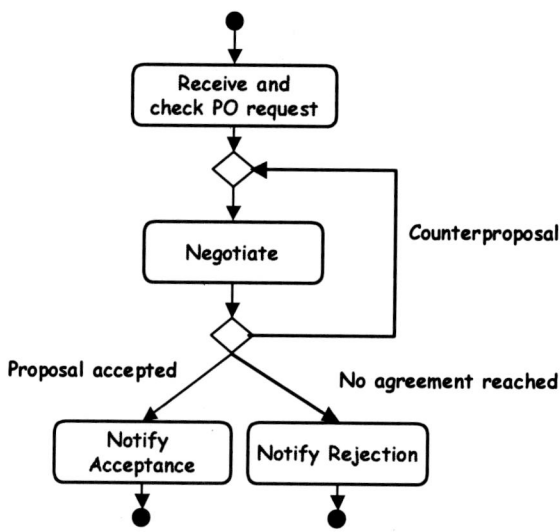

Fig. 2. Supply Chain Hub process (conceptual view)

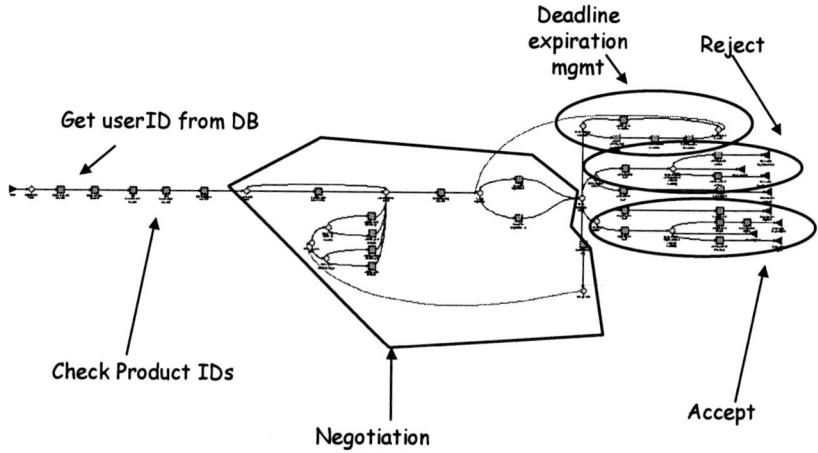

Fig. 3. Supply Chain Hub process (actual implementation)

Typically, the relation between the conceptual and the actual process is only known to the IT personnel who implemented the process, and this knowledge is often spread among different persons. In principle, the use of *subprocesses* in the implementation could help preserve the structure of the conceptual process. However, this does not happen in practice for a variety of reasons, ranging from detailed operational issues that require a deviation from the clean and simple conceptual structure, to the technical characteristics (limitations) of the process model provided by the BPMS, and to the fact that implementers are very focused on the challenging task of making things work correctly and with the required performance, leaving little room for a "design for analysis".

Besides the problem of mapping between the conceptual and actual process, existing approaches have many other limitations. For example, analysts typically want to classify processes according to taxonomies of their choice (such as "Fast/Slow", or "Accepted/AcceptedWithNegotiation/Rejected", etc.) and examine data and trends depending on the classes to which processes belong (e.g., see the number of accepted purchase orders by week). Current BPMSs cannot offer these kinds of high-level reports, since they do not provide mechanisms to associate semantic information to process executions in order to facilitate their analysis.

3. PDW Concepts

This section describes the support that PDW provides for adding semantics to process execution data, in order to overcome the limitations of existing approaches and enable business-level analysis.

3.1 PDW Data Structure

This section briefly introduces the PDW warehouse structure, as a background for the description of the following subsections. The PDW database is structured according to a star schema design, where data are described in terms of *"facts"*, i.e., happenings of interest to be analyzed, and *"dimensions"*, i.e. perspectives under which the facts are analyzed. A design based on a star schema enables the analysis of facts seen from different perspectives and allows the use of many query optimization techniques. The PDW includes the following facts: *Process instance executions*, *Node instance executions*, and *Behaviors*. These facts can be analyzed based on the following dimensions:
- *Processes and process groups*, to focus on facts related to a specific process definition, or to processes within a process group.
- *Nodes*, to focus on facts related to a specific process node or set of nodes.
- *Resources*, to focus on processes started by, nodes assigned to, or node executed by a specific human or automated resource or group of resources.
- *Time,* to focus on facts occurred in a certain (fiscal or calendar) time window, or on specific days, weekdays, or hours of the day.
- *Behaviors*, to focus on instances that exhibited a user-defined behavior of interest (details on behaviors are provided below).

In addition, PDW includes a large set of views on top of facts and dimension that make it easy for users to retrieve key statistics and performance metrics, without having to write complex queries. PDW also includes pre-packaged configuration files for many commercial reporting tools, so that users can access business reports without writing any code. Details are provided in [5].

3.2 Behaviors

One of the most significant and innovative feature of PDW is *behavior analysis*. In fact, a frequent analysis need is that of identifying process instances that exhibit specific behaviors, and to understand the *causes* of such behaviors. Examples of behaviors of interest are *Supply Chain* process instances that last more than 20 days or include more than 3 negotiation cycles, *Claim Management* instances in which node "Examine expenses" was executed by a manager, or processes instances related to order for goods over 20,000$.

The PDW approach is agnostic about the behaviors that users may be interested in analyzing. Indeed, it allows users to define the behaviors to be monitored. PDW will then take care of identifying which processes instances exhibit a specific behavior and of analyzing them. As shown throughout this paper, we use the behavior concept for a variety of purposes. This approach allows us to simplify the user interaction with the system since, by getting familiar with the notion of behaviors, users can configure a variety of different analysis and monitoring functionalities.

Behaviors are defined by instantiating *behavior templates*. A template is a parametric definition of a behavior, such as *"Instances of process P that takes more than N days to complete"*. In order to define a behavior of interest for a specific process definition, users simply need to instantiate the template, i.e., provide values for the parameters. No coding is needed. Multiple specific behaviors to be monitored (on the same or different processes) can be defined for each behavior type, and a process can be analyzed for multiple behaviors.

Behavior templates are (conceptually) defined by Boolean conditions over process and node execution data available in the warehouse. Templates are implemented by means of SQL statements, that detect behaviors of interest when data are loaded into the warehouse. PDW includes a large set of predefined behavior templates, to account for the most common monitoring and analysis needs. Users can add new behavior templates by downloading them from template libraries, made available on the web[3]. If users need to monitor a kind of behavior that is neither among the predefined ones nor downloadable from web template libraries, they can still specify the behavior template they need, although in this case they would need to define the corresponding condition (and consequently the SQL statement that detects whether an instance has a behavior of a given type). The occurrence of a behavior is stored as a fact in the warehouse, so that processes can be also analyzed from the behavior perspective.

By detecting behaviors of interest, analysts can perform multidimensional analysis to understand the causes of "good" and "bad" process executions. In particular, a very useful analysis consists in examining *correlations* among behaviors, i.e., in examining which other behaviors occur when a process instance has a behavior B. In this way, the effects of B on the process can be analyzed. For example, the analyst can define B as processes being "started by John Smith" and B2 as processes being "too slow". Behavior analysis can be used to first examine how many processes are "too slow" (say, 15%), and then to examine how many processes among those "started by John Smith" are "too slow" (say, 55%), thereby indicating a cause-effect relationship between John Smith and the process being slow.

---

[3] The PDW web site is currently available only on the HP internal web site.

PDW analysts can also associate a *value* (or *cost*) to behaviors, to denote the associated benefit or cost. For example, it is possible to say that the fact that when a certain node in a process execution is performed by a unit manager, then a value (cost) of –3 is assigned to the process instance. When the same node is performed by a department manager, then a value (cost) of –2 is assigned, and so on. In this way it is possible to get reports about the combined value (cost) of a set of process executions. Fig. 4 shows a chart, obtained by accessing a PDW view with Oracle Discoverer, that shows the total process value (i.e, the sum of the values or costs of the individual process instances). Data are aggregated based on the week in which the process instances started.

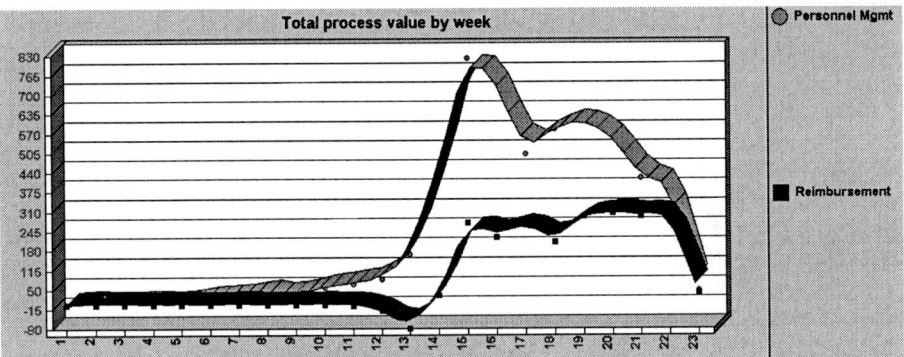

Fig. 4. A chart depicting the total process value, shown by week of the year

3.3 Taxonomies

Another concept that allows PDW users to add semantics to process execution data is that of process *taxonomies*. A taxonomy is a user-defined criterion to classify instances of a process depending on their characteristics. Many taxonomies can be defined for the same process. Each taxonomy can have several *categories*, and for each taxonomy a process instance can be in one and only one category. For example, a taxonomy *outcome* may include the categories *accepted* and *rejected*, while the taxonomy *duration* may include the categories *fast, acceptable, slow,* and *very slow*.

Taxonomies can be defined by specifying the categories that compose the taxonomy. Each category is then associated to a behavior, with the meaning that the process instance is classified in a given taxonomy if the process instance has the corresponding behavior. Taxonomies are flat, that is, there is no hierarchy among categories. Two categories, *Other* and *Error*, are automatically defined by PDW for each taxonomy. *Other* contains instances that do not fall in any other category within the taxonomy, while *Error* includes instances belonging to more than one category.

Once taxonomies have been defined, then business analysts can access reports that can immediately provide information which is easy to consume. For example, Fig. 5. shows, for each week, the distribution of process instances within the categories of the user-defined "duration" taxonomy, described above.

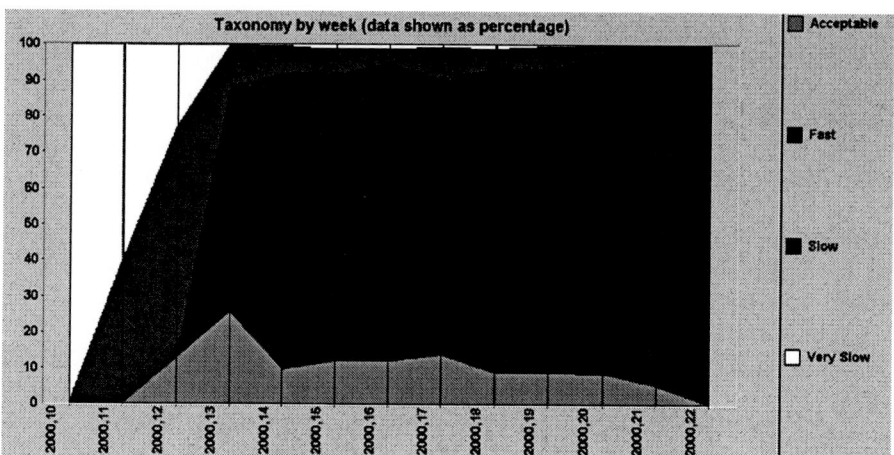

Fig. 5. Distribution of process instances within the categories of the "duration" taxonomy. For each week, the areas describe the percentage of instances started in the specified week that fall in each category of the taxonomy

Analogously to behaviors, PDW users can also examine correlations among categories of different taxonomies. This kind of analysis is very powerful, since it allows users to easily understand the cause-effect relationships among the categories of the two taxonomies. For example, Fig. 6 shows the correlation between the categories of taxonomies *duration* and *deadline* (that describes whether the deadline for node "approve" within process "reimbursement" has expired at least once in process instance execution). Users can examine the process performance distribution, depending on whether the deadline for the "approve" node has expired or not[4]. The two bars in the Figure correspond to instances that are in the categories "expired" (left) and "not expired" (right) of the *deadline* taxonomy. Each bar is then divided according to the percentage distribution of instances within the categories of the *duration* taxonomy. The figure shows for instance that less then half of the instances in which the node deadline expired are "very slow", while no instance is "very slow" if the deadline is "not expired".

Note that, while taxonomy correlations can typically produce reports that are at a higher level of abstraction with respect to behavior correlations (and therefore easier to interpret), they do not replace it. Indeed, users often need to define behaviors that do not belong to specific taxonomies (possibly because they do not generate a partition in the process instance space), and to analyze correlation among these behaviors. Hence, both taxonomy and correlation analysis are useful and needed.

3.4 Process Regions

Another PDW concept that supports semantic analysis is the *process region*. A process region is a subgraph of a process that can be treated as a unit from a business analysis perspective. The purpose of process regions is to bridge the gap between the

---

[4] Note therefore that we are comparing the duration of the *process* with the deadline expriation of a given *node* in the process.

conceptual process and the actual (implemented) process, which typically include many nodes to implement a single conceptual step. A region R is defined by selecting two nodes *s* and *e* in an underlying process *P*, such that:
1. *s* has only one input arc, and this arc comes from a node outside R;
2. *e* has only one output arc *a*, that connects *e* to a node that does not belong to R;
3. Every other arc in R must only connect nodes in R.

All the nodes between *s* and *e* (included) belong to the region. Once a region has been defined, PDW can provide reports that include region-level statistics. For example, with respect to the example of Figures 2 and 3, it is possible to define process regions to analyze steps "Notify Acceptance" and "Notify Rejection" and obtain reports about these regions. However, the nodes that implement steps "Check PO" and "Negotiation" are intermingled, so that a clear division into process region was not possible for those steps.

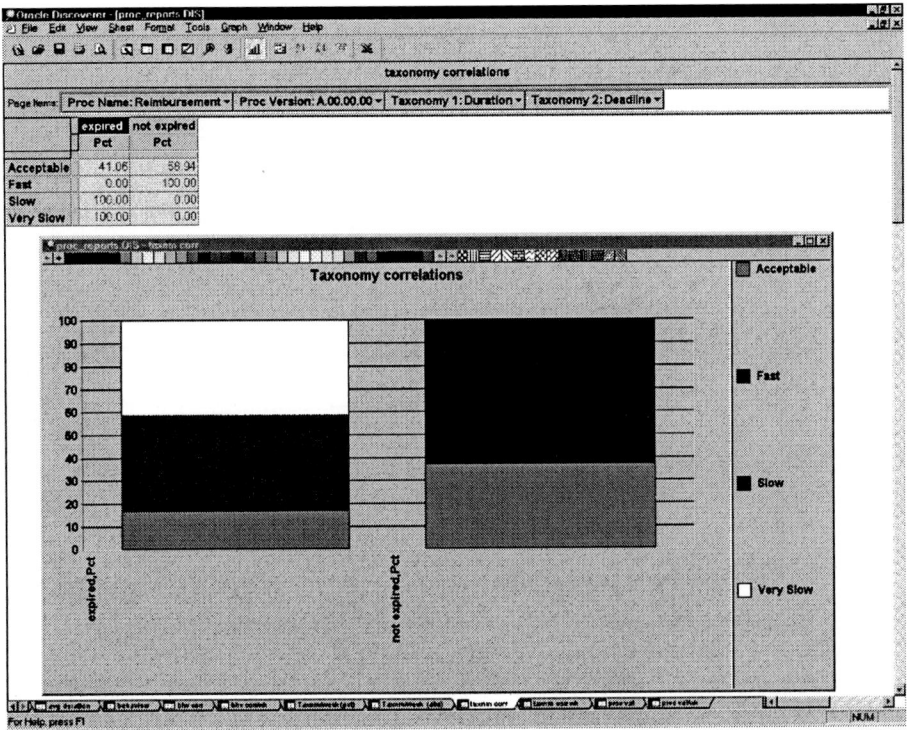

Fig. 6. Correlations among categories of different taxonomies

3.5 Alerts

Besides providing data and statistics on completed processes, PDW can also provide information on active processes, to enable process monitoring and management, and to provide high (business) level as well as detailed information about the health not only of the operational system, but also of the overall business. In addition, PDW allows users to define *alerts*. An alert is a condition on active process data that is of particular interest to the analyst, possibly because it corresponds to an undesired situation that needs to be addressed. Like behaviors and taxonomies, alerts allow users to add semantics to information stored in the warehouse, to allow higher-level business process analysis (or monitoring, in this case).

In order to keep the PDW configuration and usage simple, alerts (like taxonomies) are defined by reusing the notion of behaviors: in fact, an alert is characterized by a name and by an associated behavior. When data on active processes are refreshed, PDW detects behaviors (alerts) of interest and stores them into tables that can be queried to get the number and kind of alert. Value information in behavior definition can be used to indicate the perceived importance of the alert.

4. Concluding Remarks

This paper has discussed the limitations of existing process analysis systems, and has described the approach that we took in order to address them. In particular, we have emphasized that a major challenge consists in adding semantics to process execution data, in order to make the monitoring and analysis meaningful for business managers. The system described in this paper has been fully implemented at HP. It is intended to augment the capabilities of HP Process Manager, the BPMS provided by HP. We are currently working to add more capabilities to the PDW. In particular, we plan to add a prediction module, that derives prediction models and applies them on running processes, in order to make predictions on behaviors of interest (such as the probability of deadline expirations or of a purchase order being accepted). In particular, we plan to extend initial studies, described in [2], with the goal of designing a fully automated approach that does not require human input in building prediction models and that automatically understands if that data allows building a "reasonably" accurate prediction model (consistently with the idea of keeping the system easy to use for non-technical people).

References

[1] P. Bernstein et al. The Asilomar Report on Database Research. *Sigmod Record 27(4),* Dec 1998.
[2] F. Casati, U. Dayal, D. Grigori, M.C. Shan. Improving Business Process Quality through Exception Understanding, Prediction, and Prevention. *Procs. of VLDB'01*, Rome, Italy. Sept. 2001
[3] Hewlett-Packard. Let'sBuyIt.com Case Study. Aug. 2000. Available from www.hp.com/go/e-process
[4] F. Leymann, D. Roller: *Production Workflow*. Prentice-Hall, 2000.
[5] F. Casati. Intelligent Process Data Warehouse for HPPM 5.0. HP Labs Technical Report. Available from www.hpl.hp.com. Nov. 2001.

An Introduction to the e-XML Data Integration Suite

Georges Gardarin, Antoine Mensch, and Anthony Tomasic

e-XMLMedia, 29 Avenue du Général Leclerc, 92340 Bourg La Reine, France
georges.gardarin@e-xmlmedia.fr

Abstract. This paper describes the e-XML component suite, a modular product for integrating heterogeneous data sources under an XML schema and querying in real-time the integrated information using XQuery, the emerging W3C standard for XML query. We describe the two main components of the suite, i.e., the repository for warehousing XML and the mediator for distributed query processing. We also discuss some typical applications.

1 Introduction

In the past few years, XML has become the standard for exchanging data on the Internet and on intranets in the enterprise. Different approaches have been proposed for efficiently managing, storing, querying and presenting XML data from diverse sources [1,2,3]. e-XMLMedia believes that building on strong foundations is the best approach for developing efficient and powerful web-enabled information systems. Thus, as relational and object-relational database systems are providing successful solutions for handling data, the e-XML suite of e-XMLMedia is a collection of components built to work and cooperate with relational DBMSs, such as Oracle, DB2, SQL Server, TimesTen and Postgres. More precisely, the suite is composed of Java components able to work with any database supporting a JDBC 2.0 driver. In addition, extensive attention has been given to the incorporation of legacy data sources.

The e-XML suite provides an efficient way to integrate access to multiple data sources on the Internet or on intranets through XML queries. The suite components can be assembled together or used separately in different application contexts. Possible applications include the constitution of electronic libraries from existing sources, the collect of information for trading systems, the assembling of fragments of data for automatic report generation, and more generally knowledge management and information diffusion in the enterprise. Used together, the components form a unique solution to support iterative definition and manipulation of virtual semi-structured databases derived from existing data sources or loosely structured files in Internet/Intranet environments.

This paper is an overview of the e-XML component suite. It presents information that will help you understanding the suite main objectives, functionalities and architectures. The topics in this paper include:
1. A summary of the functional objectives and architecture of the e-XML suite.
2. A description of the main e-XML components: Repository and Mediator.
3. A presentation of typical applications in which e-XML components are currently being integrated

2 Principles of the e-XML Suite

This section summarizes the objectives, presents the architecture, and discusses the functionality of the e-XML component suite.

2.1 Objectives

Many research projects have focused on logical data integration using the relational model or the object model as integration model [4,5,6]. Most of them have difficulties in integrating a large number of data sources with very heterogeneous data including documents, as they exist in many enterprises and on the Web. In addition, performance is a real issue for distributed query processing on multiple sources. The main objective of the e-XML suite is to address these diversity and scalability problems through the use of XML as an exchange format associated with an efficient XQuery processing technology.

More precisely, the objectives of our component suite can be formulated as follows:

- **Use XML as integration model.** By using XML and its derivatives (XQuery, XSchema, DOM, SAX, SOAP, XForms, XSL), a wide range of data sources with different data formats can be integrated and multiple client tools can be interfaced.
- **Process queries in real-time.** Queries are as much as possible distributed to local sources and processed against the current data, thus delivering up to date information. However, components in the suite are able to warehouse XML data, which can be included in the query process somehow as a cache.
- **Optimize query performance.** Maximum delegation of sub-queries, minimum network traffic, event driven approach to XML processing, are key features in query processing performance. A simple but efficient capability-based distributed query-processing algorithm should minimize response time.
- **Facilitate user acceptance.** The e-XML Data Integration Suite can be used incrementally, first to solve simple problems (e.g., XML-ize your relational database), then to query uniformly heterogeneous sources, finally to set a global e-business infrastructure in your enterprise.

2.2 Architecture

The overall global functional architecture is shown in Figure 1.

The top layer consists of four client interfaces: a Java-based client interface, an XForms client interface for forms processing, a SOAP/WSDL client interface for binding RPC calls to arbitrary client programming languages (for example to .NET clients), and the XML/DBC interface consisting of a JDBC style client interface supporting XQuery and XML. The first three interfaces are standardized. The last interface is an adaptation of the JDBC interface for XML document repositories. This interface is uniformly used to access wrappers, mediators and repositories.

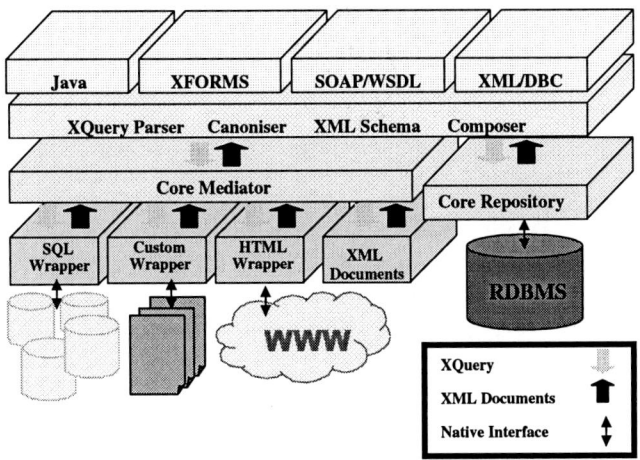

Fig. 1. The e-XML Data Integration Suite Global Architecture

The second layer consists of the functionality shared by the Mediator and the Repository products. An XQuery Parser generates parse trees of queries. These are handed to Canoniser that generates a canonical form for the query. Since both the Mediator and Repository understand XML Schemas, a common library of Schema management routines is used, insuring identical semantics for all products. Finally, when multiple answers are returned from the Mediator or Repository, the Composer combines them into a single answer.

The next layer consists of the core functionality. The Repository functionality is described in Section 3. The Mediator functionality is described in Section 4.

The final layer consists of the collection of wrappers – SQL wrappers access RDBMS, Custom wrappers access arbitrary applications, and a specially designed HTML wrapper access the WWW. In addition the core Repository manages XML documents in an object/relational DBMS.

2.3 The XML/DBC Uniform Interface

All components that process queries in the toolkit architecture are accessible through XML/DBC. Thus, XQuery queries can be submitted through a uniform interface to a mediator, a repository or an SQL Wrapper. Thus, XML/DBC is both the input interface and the wrapper interface of a mediator. As a consequence, a mediator can call another mediator or itself as a wrapper. This is quite powerful. However, wrappers are generally not able to support fully XQuery. For example, a file wrapper cannot process joins. Thus, a capability interface is included in XML/DBC, to be able to get the supported functionalities of a wrapper.

The basic functionalities of XML/DBC are the following:
– Management of connections to an XQuery data source (repository, mediator and wrappers),
– Submission of XML queries and updates;

- Fetch of XML fragments as answers to queries;
- Retrieval of the XML schema describing the data source.

A SOAP version of XML/DBC is available, i.e., the API functions can be invoked through SOAP, making the tools ideal components for developing Web Services.

3 The e-XML Repository

In this section, we describe the e-XML Repository, which is able to store XML documents in any object-relational DBMS and which provides XQuery access to retrieve XML document fragments and assemble them. The XML Repository component manages persistent collections of XML documents in a relational database and provides query access to them. A name and an owner identify an XML collection. By default this owner is the same as the database user. Each collection is backed by a set of relational tables. In a generic mapping, the tables are fixed by the Repository implementation. In the case of a schema mapping, the tables consist of a combination of implementation dependent tables and user tables defined in the mapping.

3.1 Storage Module

The Repository storage module performs the mapping of XML documents either into generic tables or into existing relational tables when the schema mapping option has been selected. The storage module, when storing XML documents without schema, builds metadata information under the form of a dataguide. The dataguide is constructed dynamically for repositories without associated schemas. The Repository provides several functions to retrieve metadata.

The storage module is natively designed to use the SAX 2.0 standard as an external interface with applications. Helpers are provided with the product in order to supply conversion between SAX 2.0 and DOM Level 2. As a consequence, the storage module relies on an external SAX parser, which is responsible for XML parsing and validation. The Apache Xerces parser by default is used as a parsing device.

Note that order information is maintained, even for attributes, so that the original document can be accurately reconstructed.

3.2 Query Module

The query language supported is XQuery, as described in [7]. Document insert and deletion is supported, however, no sophisticated updates are allowed in the current version. The Query object gives a read-only access to data stored in the Repository. Queries can perform joins over several XML collections. Query results are XML document fragments.

Query processing is efficient due to some sophisticated optimization features. Generally, relational systems are considered inefficient for processing queries containing path traversals. However, in the context of XML documents, some characteristics of relational systems can compensate for this handicap. In particular, the XML document graph is encoded in an efficient manner that translates path traversal operations into index driven selection on tables. Thus, inefficient solutions such as complex join queries or recursive query processing are avoided.

In XML databases, regular path expressions with Kleene star operators have special importance. XML data have irregular and changing structures. By means of regular path expressions, users can query the database without the full knowledge on data structures. Although convenient to use, regular path expressions in general cannot be evaluated directly due to their prohibitive cost. To avoid this cost, the Repository query processor expands regular path expressions using metadata.

3.3 Mapping XML Objects to Tables

Current applications are often built on object-relational DBMS. Databases are composed of tables with columns of various types, including numeric and string, but also full text, images, and geometry. Thus, there is a strong demand in mapping XML documents to tables and vice-versa.

As explained above, an XML object is a tree with leaves bearing data. Trees can be mapped into tables in many ways. Hence, several mapping schemes are possible for storing XML objects in an object-relational DBMS. Our experience confirms that mapping schemes offer a wide range of performance for a given query workload according to very specific detailed choices, such as OIDs assignment, clustering and indexing schemes, etc. In addition, applications differ in mapping requirements; some may require specific table schemas to process data through standard tools, while others have no such requirement. However, mappings require administrative effort.

To comply with these different requirements, the e-XML Repository provides two types of mappings: generic and schema-based. With the generic mapping, application tables are automatically created and mapping directives are implicitly given. With the schema-based mapping, the documents have a schema, mapping directives are given, and an administrator creates application tables. Generic mappings are convenient and schema-based mappings offer maximum flexibility and performance.

This sophisticated mapping method provides capabilities to map part of XML documents to existing relational tables. Unmapped elements are stored in internal generated tables (as with the generic method), allowing the complete restoration of original documents. To make it possible, documents must be validated against an XML Schema. This XML Schema is unique for a Repository. The validation is performed by an external validating parser. Mapping directives are defined through an XML document with a specific grammar. A specific namespace (represented by the xrm prefix) has been defined for XML relational mapping directives.

4 The e-XML Mediator

In this section, we describe the e-XML Mediator, which provides a uniform view of multiple heterogeneous data sources and query access with the XQuery language. To accomplish this task, the Mediator manages data sources and processes queries The Mediator is composed of several packages, among them:
- The administration console is a simple interface to administrate the Mediator and register wrapped data sources.

- The evaluator is responsible for query processing, including parsing, decomposition, optimization, and composition of results.
- The exchanger provides the communication interface between Mediators and Wrappers based on XML/DBC, and manages the metadata cache including wrapper capabilities.
- A Wrapper is able to execute a query sent by the Mediator on a specific data source and to give back the results as a compressed DOM tree of objects.

4.1 Wrapping Data Sources

Data sources are managed through an XML based configuration file. Data sources are wrapped with a standard interface. This interface uses dynamic attachment of wrappers to the mediator. Metadata from the source is loaded at attachment time. In particular, configuration of the Mediator is entirely dynamic; no static "compile time" configuration is required. Data sources are distinguished as pure relational data sources accessible through JDBC, wrapped data sources translated in XML and often not supporting complex queries, and XML Repositories supporting XQuery via the XML/DBC interface. Wrappers are available for SQL (object-relational DBMS accessed through JDBC), XQuery (Repository and Mediator), and HTML pages. Specific wrappers can be added; they have to comply with the XML/DBC interface.

4.2 Query Processing

The query processing component is composed of several packages in charge of decomposing XQuery queries into mono-source sub-queries, efficiently shipping local queries to data sources, gathering results, processing and assembling them. In particular this component chooses an execution strategy for the query.

The Mediator makes three key decisions during query processing. First the Mediator determines the localization of the relevant sources to process a query among those accessible by the Mediator. Using the metadata information on each data source, the location of data that appears in a query is determined. Second the Mediator determines the amount of sequential or parallel execution that occurs during execution. The mix between parallel and sequential is determined by the binding relationship between different data sources as expressed by join predicates. Independent data sources are contacted in parallel. Dependent data sources are accessed in a pipelined fashion. Third, the Mediator determines the amount of query processing that can be offloaded onto the data source. This determination is the result of a comparison of the requirements of a particular query and the query processing power available to a data source.

The Mediator also provides a way to structure the result in an integrated XML document, according to the RETURN clause of the query. The three main facilities provided at this level are the following:
- Renaming Tags.
- Changing the initial data structure.
- Composing results when coming from multiple data sources.

5 Examples of Applications

In this section, we present an overview of several applications that have been or are prototyped with the e-XML component suite.

5.1 Semi-structured Document Manager

This scenario is derived from a major legislation assembly system in Europe that plans to manage textual law amendments (with structured descriptions) in a central Repository. In this case, semi-structured XML documents include a mix of free text and tabular data, to be stored in a relational database. Such an application requires a flexible mapping capability between the XML documents and the underlying database. Transactions are developed on an application server to query and update the database. To publish in HTML, PDF, RTF, etc., the XML results of queries are fed to an XSL transformer. XSL style-sheets guide the transformation process. This architecture has three advantages – flexible representation of documents that permit easy future extension, independence from the document presentation format, and independence from the on-line interaction process of document management.

5.2 XML Web Cache

This scenario is derived from a major financial institution that plans to introduce a new product: a WWW based information delivery system for its clients. The institution's goal is to improve the information delivered to its clients with minimal programming expenditures. The institution currently has a large legacy infrastructure. Clients are given Internet access to the information in the legacy infrastructure through a WWW server that operates through multiple firewalls – first through the security server, then through the client server, and finally through the legacy infrastructure. The use of a Repository for XML data transmitted throughout the system speeds up performance by storing copies of XML data in a central location managed through a main memory database. In addition to a Repository facility, the use of XQuery query access affects the implementation cost of the application logic by saving months of application development time. With the addition of a Mediator to the architecture, the system has the ability to dynamically fetch data from the legacy infrastructure. Thus, the ``cache'' is effectively a mini-database with integration capabilities.

5.3 XML Meta-directory Manager

This scenario is derived from an Internet provider willing to establish a unique identification point for all its clients and applications. The institution already uses some LDAP directories with specific queries. Fast and interoperable identification is required. There exists an XML standard (DTD and schema) for LDAP entries, called DSML. XQuery queries are appropriate for querying, in an interoperable way, LDAP directories. Thus, the XML Repository will be used to identify new customers in a central identification point. Wrappers for existing directories make them XML capable. As a result, identification in the new system will first be evaluated on the XML Repository, and then if an entry is not found, it will be evaluated on the pre-existing directories through the Mediator. If the result of the identification is positive, the central Repository will be updated by inserting the XML retrieved entry. Duplicates can be eliminated. This architecture requires a very fast query engine. To satisfy the engine requirements, a main memory relational database with the Repository running on top is used.

5.4 Source Specific Search Engine

Search engines are in general based on robots that crawl the WWW and build intelligent indexes of URLs. Currently, as the WWW is HTML-based, search engines are based on information retrieval technology that provides a fairly "flat" interpretation of the WWW. That is, the documents contain little structure. However, when data sources are well defined and structured WWW sites (financial WWW sites, electronic libraries, business sites using XML based document exchange), documents can be translated into XML on the fly (with the aid of the appropriate extraction language or tool). In this case, the e-XML components are an ideal platform to develop a search engine dealing with multiple (possibly heterogeneous) sources. The mediator acts as a search engine dealing with multiple HTML sites and associated extractors. The Repository is used for storing the results of robot crawling. The query manager manages search requests by issuing queries to the Mediator – note that these requests reference both the HTML sites and the Repository. The robot manager handles both periodic robot crawling and the administration console for the robot. Results of crawling are stored in the Repository.

6 Comparison with Other Approaches

DBMS supporting XML can be classified in four categories:
1. XOR-DBMS (XML Object relational DBMS). This approach consists in extending object-relational DBMSs to support storage of XML documents in tables and publication of SQL query results in XML. Most RDBMSs suppliers are proposing simple solutions to map flat XML to tables and tables to XML. Non-flat XML can be flattened using XSL or specific nesting of tables, and vice-versa.
2. XML-DBMS (XML DBMS). Pure XML DBMSs are brand new systems developing specific storage and access methods for XML. In general, XML is stored in files and specific indexing techniques are used for improving query performance. These systems claim to be efficient in query processing, but this is not proved yet and even difficult to prove as XML queries can be very diverse.
3. XOO-DBMS (XML Object-Oriented DBMS). This class corresponds to the enhancement of previously existing Object-Oriented DBMSs to support XML. Generally, XML is transformed in DOM objects that are made persistent in the object database. Query languages can be extensions of OQL.
4. XML-DOCM (XML DOcument Manager). This class corresponds to document management systems that have been extended to handle XML. Previous versions

where often based on SGML. Queries are based on keywords. They generally return a list of qualifying documents with ranking. Their interfaces have some similarities with that of search engines.

The e-XML-SUITE does not belong to any of these categories, but rather take advantages of several of them. The first advantage of the e-XML-SUITE is that it is a middleware product, which does not require a new DBMS: you can built and query XML views on top of your favorite RDBMS. Second, it is a suite of Java components that integrate several tools accessible through APIs. The suite includes the Repository and the Mediator, as described below, but also other tools such as the XMLizer to extract or map XML from/to relational databases and the XForms component to enter data in XML through forms from Web clients. Table 1 summarizes some determinant advantages of the e-XMLMEDIA approach.

Table 1. Functionality Comparison Between Classes of XML Database Software

	XOR-DBMS	XML-DBMS	XOO-DBMS	XML-DOCM	e-XMLSuite
Standards Compliant	No	Possible	Possible	No	Yes
Query Language	SQL+	XQuery	OQL+	Doc+	XQuery
Application compatible	Possible	No	No	No	Yes
Order Preserving	No	Yes	Yes	Yes	Yes
Distributed Queries	No	Possible	Possible	No	Yes
Heterogeneous Data	No	No	No	No	Yes
Adaptable	No	No	No	No	Yes

7 Conclusion

In this paper, we have presented the e-XML component suite, a suite of components based on XML. The e-XML Mediator federates XML documents, HTML pages, and SQL tables; it unifies them in a virtual XML digital library. It offers the XQuery query language to query the virtual libraries of XML documents. The e-XML Repository provides the necessary functionalities to store and manipulate XML documents on top of an object-relational DBMS. Coupling the capabilities of the Repository with multimedia features now available in most object-relational DBMS gives powerful functions to retrieve documents by contents, e.g., using similarity search on keywords or image features.

The suite can be used to built various architectures for:
– Developing modern web sites;
– Federating heterogeneous data sources;
– Building XML datawebhouse for decision support, data presentation or publication;
– Caching Web data in main memory databases;
– And much more.

In addition, the suite pushes the development of software towards component-ware, thus making possible the cross-fertilization with external components, including EJB libraries.

References

1. M. Fernandez, A. Morishima, D. Suciu : Efficient Evaluation of XML Middleware Queries. In: Proc. of ACM SIGMOD Conf. On Management of data, Santa Barbara, CA (2001) 103-114
2. V. Christophides, S. Cluet, J. Simeon : On Wrapping Query Language and Efficient XML Integration. In: Proc. of ACM SIGMOD Conf. On Management of data, Dallas, TX (2000) 141-152
3. I. Manolescu, D. Florescu, D. Kossman : Answering XML Queries over Heterogeneous Data Sources. In : Proc. of VLDB 27th Conf. On Very Large Data Bases, ROMA, IT (2001) 241-250
4. H. Naacke, G. Gardarin, A. Tomasic : Leveraging Mediator Cost Models with Heterogeneous Data Sources. ICDE Conf. On data Engineering, Orlando, FL (1998) 351-360
5. O. Bukhres and A. Elmagarmid Editors : Object Oriented Multidatabases Systems : A Solution for Advanced Applications, Book, Prentice Hall (1996).
6. M. Carey, L. Haas, et. al. : Towards Heterogeneous Multimedia Information Systems – The Garlic Approach. In: Proc of International Workshop on Research Issues in Data Engineering - Distributed Object Management, Taipei, Taiwan (1995).
7. World Wide Web Consortium (W3C) : XQuery 1.0 – An XML Query Language, W3C Working Draft (2001).

Spatio-temporal Information Systems in a Statistical Context

Leonardo Tininini*, Mario Paolucci,
Giuseppe Sindoni, and Stefano De Francisci

ISTAT, via Adolfo Ravà, 150, I-00184 – Roma, Italy
{paolucci, sindoni, tininini, defranci}@istat.it

Abstract. The Italian National Statistics Institute is currently integrating its various spatio-temporal data collections. It has been developed an integrated system, whose implementation relied on Web and relational technologies to cope with data heterogeneity. The system provides users with many different classes of functions with which to analyse and visualise territorial data. It can be viewed as a spatio-temporal data warehouse, where space and time are the main access dimensions to statistical data, but also where space can be analysed according to its temporal mutations as a preliminary step in the design activity of a statistical survey. The system overcomes a drawback of current commercial data warehouse systems, which are not able to cope with the dynamic behaviour of a dimension - that is, its temporal evolution.

1 Introduction

Space and time are the most important dimensional aspects to be taken into account during all phases of statistical data production. Data are in fact collected with specific reference to a given set of territorial entities, and aggregated and disseminated according to a given territorial hierarchy. This hierarchy is normally not static. In particular, a territorial entity (such as a town) may change its name, its boundaries, or its membership to a "higher" territorial entity (e.g. the province, in the case of a town). Such changes must be taken into account when we refer data to territorial entities and perform time series analysis, as an incomplete understanding of territory evolution may lead to an incorrect interpretation of the figures obtained.

For these reasons, many large organisations normally give a lot of attention to the management of spatio-temporal data and this normally generates several different information systems. For example at ISTAT (the Italian National Statistics Institute) there are four systems dealing with the territory and its history alone:

- SISTAT, the territorial history database system, which provides information about the temporal evolution of territorial administrative partitions. The system records the administrative provisions, the date when they become

---

* Partly supported by CNR-IASI, viale Manzoni 30, 00185 ROMA (ITALY)

effective and the involved territorial entities (towns, provinces, etc.). Spatial data, however, are not explicitly included;
- CENSUS, the Institute GIS, providing the cartography of the Italian territory, down to the census tract level. The "layers" describing the entities of the Italian territorial hierarchy have been "time-stamped" to provide a cartographic description of the territory evolution. The system is very dynamic both technologically and in its degree of detail. For example, all layers are currently being updated from a collection of fine-grained orthographic photos of the Italian territory in scale 1:10,000;
- BDT, a territorial statistical data warehouse, which was originally designed in the 80's for mainframe technology, and is based on a non-relational information system for data dissemination purposes. During the integration process, the information system has been migrated to a relational (Oracle) database and a completely new navigational interface has been developed, based on the data warehouse paradigm. Aggregate data coming mainly from the 1971, 1981 and 1991 censuses are available down to the town level of detail;
- SISTER, an address normalizing-geomatching system, providing information about the limits of census tracts (e.g. portions of streets or the sides of town squares). The system contains the limits of the 1991 and 2001 census tracts.

In such a heterogeneous scenario there is the need to provide corporate users with many different classes of functions by means of which is possible to analyse, visualise and use territorial data in a unified way. This implies the development of integrated systems which are not only the result of a classical system integration activity, but which may also become a reference integration framework for any other corporate system with spatio-temporal references.

This paper presents, as an application of the above principles, the SIT-IN [9] spatio-temporal information system, which is based on Web technologies, a unified spatio-temporal conceptual model and an extensive use of metadata [1] and meta-queries [8, 13] to "wrap" the component sub-systems and "mediate" [14] the extracted information to realise a federated database system.

The resulting system can be viewed as a spatio-temporal data warehouse, i.e. where space and time are the main access dimensions to statistical data, but also where space can be analysed according to its temporal mutations as a preliminary step in the design activity of a statistical survey.

The system hence manages the Italian territorial hierarchy and its temporal dynamic behaviour as well as the statistical aggregate data referring to the territory itself. The spatio-temporal database has been designed according to a generalised model which allows the representation of:

- territorial objects (e.g. regions, towns, census tracts, ecc.);
- the temporal spatial representation of a territorial object (e.g. the polygons representing each temporal version of a territorial object);
- temporal attributes of a territorial object (e.g. name, code or any statistical value which is temporally associated with the object);
- the territorial hierarchy and its temporal evolution.

This high level of flexibility in the management of the space dimension allows the SIT-IN system to overcome a drawback of current commercial data warehouse systems. In fact, those systems are not able to cope with the dynamic behaviour of a dimension, that is, its slow temporal evolution. With SIT-IN, it is possible to query the statistical data warehouse for a given space-time plane or produce a time series of data for a given area of interest, without the need to consider the temporal evolution of the territorial hierarchy. The system manages the spatio-temporal relationships in such a way as to present the user with the correct territorial and statistical object sets for a given time stamp or interval.

The paper is organised as follows: Section 2 briefly outlines the principles underlying the integration process and the overall architecture of the system. Section 3 demonstrates the main functions of the system and how it addresses some important features lacking in commercial products.

2 Integration Principles and Architecture

One of the main goals of the SIT-IN project has been to define guidelines for database integration activities involving coexistence with and migration of legacy applications. Our approach to the problem is based on a loosely coupled association of databases [6, 7, 11]: the integrated systems continue to exist individually, but are connected through a dynamic data linking mechanism (similar to the lightweight alliances approach in [4]). The main principles followed in the implementation [12] of database federation are:

1. *legacy systems are kept independent of the association*; they are fully responsible for creation and maintenance of an *export scheme*, comprising all components accessible from the other systems [1]. The concept separation is made possible by an accurate definition of the areas of competence of each component, restricting to small, clearly identifiable parts only the areas of interrelation and/or overlapping [2];
2. *time and space are the main access dimensions* for each integrated database. For example the territorial data warehouse system is accessed through a set of *navigational metadata*, which allow the user to dynamically define the structure of statistical tables. At run time, the visualised report table refers to the temporally correct set of territorial entities (i.e. those in existence at the time selected).
3. *data coming from different physical representations are integrated using relational technologies*. For example, the geographical legacy database is run by ESRI Arc/Info, but has been migrated into SDE (Spatial Data Engine),

---

[1] For each overlapping concept, only one of the component systems is chosen as the "owner". For example, the system responsible for the data about the administrative history of the Italian territory exports a snapshot to the federation. The snapshot contains data elaborated from official provisions, is authoritative on dates and names, but has no geographical information. For an extensive description of these concepts, see for example [10].

the ESRI spatial indexing system that makes use of a relational database (Oracle).

The database schema has been designed in order to accommodate enough semantic power to completely describe all possible mutations in time of the objects of interest, i.e. object birth, destruction, modification (in borders, name, and ISTAT territorial codes) and inclusion in a container object.

The complexity of the application context described above has required the use of a three-layer architecture in the system's development. The tiers, shown in Fig.1, will be described briefly.

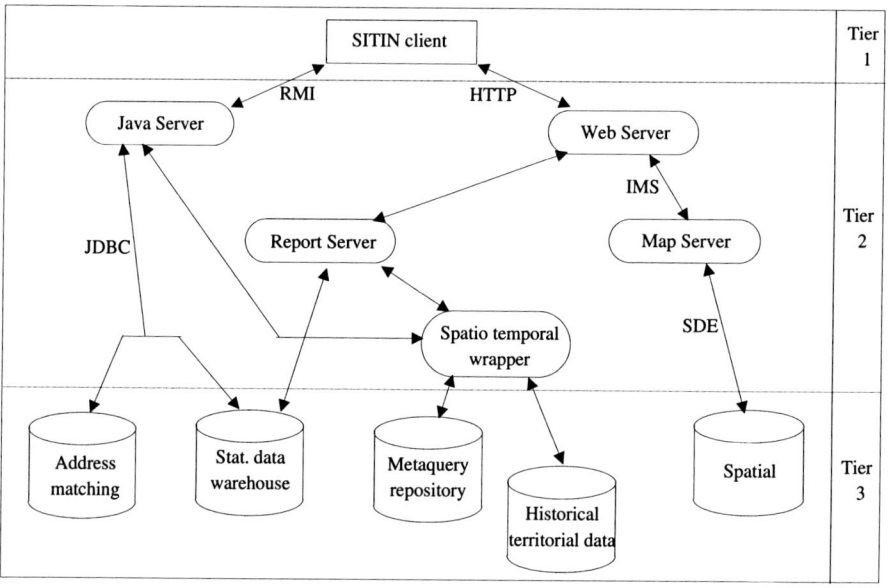

Fig. 1. The application deployment architecture.

Tier 3. The data level is composed of a few relational (Oracle) DB instances, containing data from all the integrated legacy applications. In addition, as a set of mediators [1, 14] is needed to wrap and interconnect the different system areas, a collection of *metadata* and *metaqueries* is memorized on this tier for use by the application servers.

Tier 2. The application layer consists of several application servers, comprising: (i) a home-made Java server handling communications to and from the databases, so separating the user interface from data access; (ii) an *Internet Map Server* extending the GIS capabilities and allowing cartography serving on the Web; (iii) a Report Server based on ad-hoc scripts encapsulating a proprietary reporting service (SAS Intr/Net) and dynamically generating

HTML pages of statistical tables; (iv) a spatio temporal wrapper, which constitutes an internal additional mediator layer connecting the application and report servers to the spatio temporal database.

Tier 1. The system-user interaction is centred on a Java applet, which extends the capabilities of a freeware product provided by ESRI to allow dynamic layer generation, and is also enriched by dynamically generated HTML pages.

3 Main Functions and Solved Problems

Illustrated here are the main functions of the system, giving special attention to the implementation of spatio-temporal navigation through aggregate data and to the mechanism of metaqueries. We particularly focus on the main problems of current commercial systems which have been addressed and resolved by SIT-IN.

3.1 Wrapping through Metaqueries

One of the most important objectives of the SIT-IN project was to provide a unified framework for the integration of statistics referring to space and time. The main difficulty is due to the different ways statisticians use to partition territories, which depends on the phenomenon under consideration. Many of them were not known in advance and some may even be introduced in the future. For example, census surveys use the administrative hierarchy, but judicial surveys use a different partition based on the territories under the cognizance of the courts, and environmental surveys use further subdivisions, based on orographic characteristics.

In order to cope with this heterogeneity, spatio-temporal data representing territorial partitions have been wrapped by a mechanism of *metaqueries*. The application servers do not access historical data directly, but rather through a spatio temporal wrapper, which mediates the request to the historical database. However, even the wrapper "ignores" the actual queries used to access territorial data: these are stored parametrically in metadata tables. These metadata not only describe the single levels constituting the hierarchy, but also provide the system with the parametric statements (i) to retrieve the territorial entities of a given level whose names match a specified "pattern" and (ii) to retrieve the "child" entities of a given entity.

For example, suppose the user is browsing some census data (collected in 1991 and referring to the administrative territorial hierarchy) and that he/she wants to perform a drill-down from the level of "region" to the more specific level of "province". Particularly, the query expressed by the user is to display data about the provinces of the Lombardia region. In order to determine the correct list of territorial entities, the application server issues a request to the spatio temporal wrapper.

The wrapper receives as input data the chosen time (year 1991), the territorial hierarchy (the administrative one), the type of query (drill down from level n to level $n+1$) and the constraining context (the code of the Lombardia region).

Then, it executes a query on the metadata repository, determined by the specified territorial hierarchy and type of query, and correspondingly retrieves a string, which is itself a SQL query containing some "placeholders". These placeholders are replaced with the specified year and constraining code(s), thus obtaining the actual query to retrieve the provinces of the Lombardia region in 1991, which is executed on the territorial database. The resulting set is returned to the calling component of the application server. The queries in the metadata repository can be combined and cascaded, thus obtaining more complex results like the "grand-children" (drill-down from level n to level $n+2$) of those entities whose name starts with 'Lo'.

In this way each user can introduce - if necessary - its own custom-made territorial hierarchy and use it in the same unified framework. There is no need to recompile code: the number of distinct hierarchies which can be dealt with by the system depends only on the amount of stored metadata and metaqueries.

3.2 The Spatio-temporal Model

Statistical data are collected by referring to a specific territorial hierarchy, but as already noted above, this hierarchy evolves in time. This can cause serious problems when trying to compare statistical data collected at different times. A territorial entity named X may be re-assigned to a different "parent" entity or may exchange territory with other entities due to administrative laws: it may even be abolished or change its name. So how can the data corresponding to X at time t be compared with similar data at time t', when at time t' there may be no entity named X at all? Commercial OLAP systems do not consider dimensions which slowly evolve over time, as defined in [5]. In SIT-IN this problem was resolved by elaborating and implementing a general spatio-temporal data model. This is based on the concept of territorial object identity and is able to effectively describe the possible mutations in time of the objects of interest, i.e. its birth and destruction, modification of its properties (borders, name, statistics, etc.), and its inclusion in a parent object. Our model is based on the one proposed in [3], which has been extended to represent the (temporal) hierarchy relationships between objects, typical of data warehouse systems,

The basic idea in [3] is to associate each territorial object with a unique identifier and with a time interval representing the range of validity of the object. In our model the properties and the relationships between objects have also been time-stamped, particularly the property of being child/parent of other objects, the name, the boundaries, etc. Finally, a directed stratified graph is defined among territorial objects to represent the transfer of a portion of territory from one object to another.

For example, Fig. 2 schematically represents the evolution of an Italian region (Lombardia) after the creation of two new provinces in 1992: the new-born province of Lodi is constituted of some territory from the province of Milano and the new-born province of Lecco is constituted of territory taken from both Como and Bergamo.

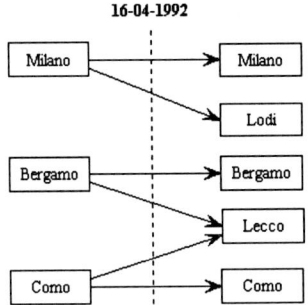

Fig. 2. Temporal evolution of Lombardia provinces

Note that the rectangles have been labeled using names of the provinces only for ease of reading, but the graph is actually defined on the object identifiers. The transfer graph is of fundamental importance when trying to compare data referring to different times, say t and t'. The connected components of the subportion of graph bound by t and t' represent the minimal aggregations of territory for which comparability can be assured. For instance, here an aggregate referring to Milano in 1991 can be correctly compared with an aggregate referring to the provinces of Milano and Lodi together in 1993. This is particularly useful in the case of statistical values obtained by additive aggregation functions (like count and sum), such as in the case of population values, as the aggregate corresponding to a collection of objects can be simply obtained by summing the aggregates of each component object.

From another point of view, this schema is an implementation of a multidimensional model with space acting as a "dynamic dimension" [5].

The choice of time stamp implicitly defines not only the proper set of territorial objects for each administrative level, i.e. the objects which effectively existed at that time, with their corresponding property values (in particular the name), but also the inclusion hierarchies valid at that time. As a consequence, the result of a drill-down from the region to the province level depends on the chosen time stamp. For instance the drill-down of Lombardia to the province level produces a list of nine provinces for 1991, while the same drill-down produces a list of 11 provinces in 1992 (including the new provinces of Lecco and Lodi (see Fig. 2).

3.3 Spatio-temporal Visualization of Data and Territory Evolution

Existing commercial GIS's and DBMS's still do not have enough features to effectively visualize the temporal aspects of spatial data. In fact, GIS's structure data in layers, i.e. sets of spatial objects sharing the same properties, without providing tools to model the temporal evolution of a layer; while DBMS's, although offering specific features for the management of temporal and spatial data, lack primitives and operators for the effective integrated management of the two aspects. In SIT-IN the polygons, as with any entity related to territorial objects, have an associated validity interval and layers are dynamically generated according to the chosen time stamp. As a consequence, data referring to territorial objects in a given time are mapped to the appropriate polygon, thus enabling complex integrations such as the construction of thematic maps based on user's data (see below).

The temporal evolution of the area of interest is dynamically visualized on a set of temporal geographic maps. Here, each map is built using the correct set of spatial objects, which are retrieved on the basis of a spatio-temporal query. For each distinct version of the territorial partition a different layer is generated and the evolution of objects is highlighted by establishing a 1-1 correspondence between objects and colours (see Fig. 3.) The system determines the "relevant" objects to display by starting from the user's selection and then calculating the connected components on the evolution graph. Fig. 3 illustrates the output of the system to represent the evolution of the Lombardia region: note the birth of Lodi from Milano in the lower left of the map.

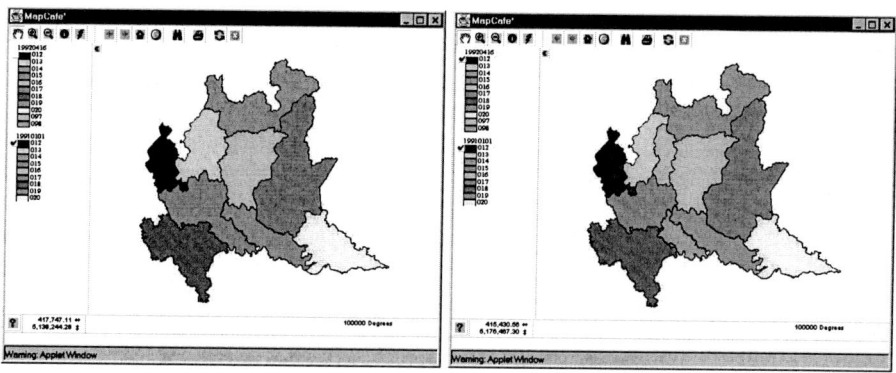

Fig. 3. Visualization of the result of a historical query: maps of the Lombardia region in 1991 and 1992.

3.4 Multidimensional Navigation and Time Series

The spatio-temporal selection is used as the access plane to navigation through aggregate data. Each dynamic report table refers to the chosen time stamp and set of territorial entities.

The SIT-IN system is capable of effective management of dynamic dimensions. It can in fact restrict navigation to the proper dimension instance, i.e. the instance relative to the chosen time stamp. For example, by choosing a certain survey of the year 1991, only those classification variables and hierarchies that were observed in that survey can be selected, rolled-up or drilled down.

Conversely, by first selecting one or more classification variables, only the "facts" that were observed and classified accordingly can be selected. In this way the user always has the maximum degree of freedom compatible with the already performed selections and is led to express a "successful" query, i.e. one corresponding to data actually in existence. A time-slice selection of spatial aggregated data can be "extruded" along the time dimension to produce a time series of spatial data which takes into account the heterogeneity of the space dimension. Particularly, for each year the correct composition of the Lombardia region is considered and by exploiting the historical information made available by the system, the researcher can perform effective comparisons along the time dimension. In the (rather frequent) case that the aggregate function is summable, the aggregates corresponding to the minimal invariant territories are obtained from the connected component of the transfer graph and then by summing the correspondent values.

Finally aggregate data referring to different times can be used to build thematic maps on the correspondent territory. For example Figure 4 shows the dynamic thematic map generation obtained from the population density values of the Lombardia provinces in 1991 and 1994. Note that the values are correctly mapped to distinct polygons in the two years.

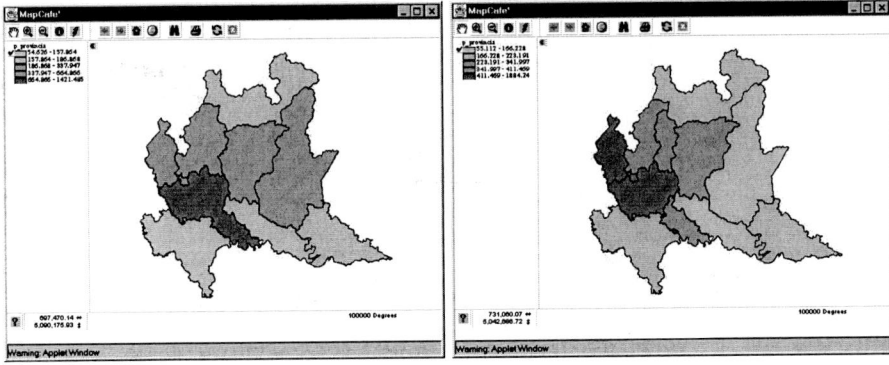

Fig. 4. Thematic maps: population densities of the Lombardia provinces in 1991 and 1994.

References

1. T. Critchlow, Ganesh M., and R. Musick. Metadata based mediator generation. In *Third IFCIS Conference on Cooperative Information Systems*, pages 168–176, 1998.
2. G. Fang, J. Hammer, and D. McLeod. The identification and resolution of semantic heterogeneity in multidatabase systems. In *International Workshop on Interoperability in Multidatabase Systems, Kioto, Japan, April 1991*, 1991.
3. K. Hornsby and M. J. Egenhofer. Identity-based change: A foundation for spatio-temporal knowledge representation. *International Journal of Geographical Information Science*, 14(3):207–224, 2000.

4. R. King, M. Novak, C. Och, and F. Vélez. Sybil: Supporting heterogeneous database interoperability with lightweight alliance. In *NGITS97*, pages 306–320, 1997.
5. A. O. Mendelzon and A. A. Vaisman. Temporal queries in olap. In *International Conf. on Very Large Data Bases (VLDB'00), Cairo, Egypt, September 10-14*, pages 242–253, 2000.
6. F. Naumann, U. Leser, and J. C. Freytag. Quality-driven integration of heterogeneous information systems. Informatik bericht 117, Humboldt University, 1999.
7. S. Navathe and M. Donahoo. Towards intelligent integration of heterogeneous information sources, 1995.
8. F. Neven, J. Van den Bussche, D. Van Gucht, and G. Vossen. Typed query languages for databases containing queries. *Information Systems*, 24(7):569–595, 1999.
9. M. Paolucci, G. Sindoni, S. De Francisci, and L. Tininini. Sit-in on heterogeneous data with java, http and relations. In *Workshop on Java and Databases: persistent Options*, 2000. In conjunction with NetObject.Days conference.
10. N. Pissinou, R. T. Snodgrass, R. Elmasri, I. S. Mumick, M. Tamer Ozsu, B. Pernici, A. Segev, B. Theodoulidis, and U. Dayal. Towards an infrastructure for temporal databases. *SIGMOD RECORD*, 23(1):35–51, March 1994.
11. Amit P. Sheth and James A. Larson. Federated database systems for managing distributed, heterogeneous, and autonomous databases. *ACM Computing Surveys*, 22(3):183–236, 1990.
12. G. Sindoni, L. Tininini, A. Ambrosetti, C. Bedeschi, S. De Francisci, O. Gargano, R. Molinaro, M. Paolucci, P. Patteri, and P. Ticca. Sit-in: a real-life spatio-temporal information system. In *International Conf. on Very Large Data Bases (VLDB'01), Roma, Italy, September 11-14*, pages 711–712, 2001.
13. J. Van den Bussche, D. Van Gucht, and G. Vossen. Reflective programming in the relational algebra. *Journal of Computing and System Sciences*, 52(3):537–549, June 1996.
14. G. Wiederhold. Mediators in the architecture of future information systems. *IEEE Computer*, 25(3):38–49, March 1992.

A Systematic Approach to Selecting Maintenance Policies in a Data Warehouse Environment

Henrik Engström[1], Sharma Chakravarthy[2], and Brian Lings[3]

[1] Department of computer science, University of Skövde, Sweden
henrik@ida.his.se
[2] Computer Science and Engineering Department, University of Texas at Arlington
sharma@cse.uta.edu
[3] Department of Computer Science, University of Exeter, UK
B.J.Lings@exeter.ac.uk

Abstract. Most work on data warehousing addresses aspects related to the internal operation of a data warehouse server, such as selection of views to materialise, maintenance of aggregate views and performance of OLAP queries. Issues related to data warehouse maintenance, i.e. how changes to autonomous sources should be detected and propagated to a warehouse, have been addressed in a fragmented manner. Although data propagation policies, source database capabilities, and user requirements have been addressed individually, their co-dependencies and relationships have not been explored. In this paper, we present a comprehensive framework for evaluating data propagation policies against data warehouse requirements and source capabilities. We formalize data warehouse specification along the dimensions of staleness, response time, storage, and computation cost, and classify source databases according to their data propagation capabilities. A detailed cost-model is presented for a representative set of policies. A prototype tool has been developed to allow an exploration of the various trade-offs.

1 Introduction

The research community is currently addressing a number of issues in response to an increased reliance of organisations on data warehousing. Numerous definitions of data warehousing can be found in the literature (e.g. [5], [12], [23], [32], [34]). From a system perspective, a data warehouse (DW) is a database that collects and stores information from multiple data sources [12]. As such, the contents of the warehouse can be described as a set of materialized views based on distributed, heterogeneous, and autonomous sources [14]. In a widely used warehouse architecture, sources are wrapped to communicate with an integrator which interacts with the warehouse and metadata repository. Reasons for using a DW include: to evaluate complex queries without causing severe impact on the sources; to increase data availability; to decrease response time for OLAP queries; and to provide historical trends for state-oriented data.

In a somewhat simplified way, DW maintenance can be seen as a generalization of view maintenance used in relational databases. A DW maintenance policy determines when and how to refresh the content of a warehouse view to reflect changes to its sources. Various view maintenance policies have been suggested and analysed in the literature [3], [15], [27], [29]. A policy can, for example, be to recompute a view or do incremental maintenance; and maintain the view immediately changes are detected, or when the view is queried.

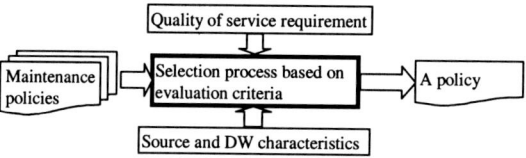

Fig. 1. Components of the data warehouse maintenance problem

1.1 Problem Statement

We define *the data warehouse maintenance problem* as the problem of choosing an appropriate set of data propagation (or view maintenance) policies to match source capabilities and satisfy quality of service attributes for a DW. It has been shown, for homogeneous systems, that the selection of the most appropriate maintenance policy is a complex process affected by several dynamic and static system properties [15], [30], [7]. The autonomy and heterogeneity of sources impose important constraints on the design of a DW system. However, changes to, and optimisation of the DW server can be made independently and under the control of the DW designer. This is an important characteristic which differentiates DW maintenance from distributed view maintenance in general. In this paper we emphasise the early phases of DW maintenance, as we claim these impact on any internal DW maintenance solution. DW maintenance, as we define it, is primarily related to the tasks of the integrator and wrappers . Fig. 1 illustrates how we approach the problem. For any realistic scenario there will be a finite set of policies to choose from. Expected quality of service (QoS) for a DW is derived from user requirements. The goal is to derive a data warehouse maintenance policy (DWMP) with minimal cost in meeting QoS requirements. The DWMP is likely to be a collection of propagation policies, one for each warehouse fragment (or partition). Cost is measured over a number of resources, such as disk I/O, storage, and communication needed for maintaining the DW. Source and warehouse characteristics capture properties that may affect maintenance activity, including capabilities of the sources, the nature of views, and update and query behaviour etc. These all affect and constrain maintenance policies.

In this paper, we review existing literature and synthesise a more comprehensive approach to DW maintenance. User specification is carefully analysed to arrive at a novel definition of view staleness. We highlight and define important properties that have an impact on the warehouse maintenance problem.

Source capabilities are classified to cover a large number of sources. A detailed, cost-based approach is presented that ties all components of Fig. 1 together and forms a basis for generating a DWMP. The solution presented in this paper is restricted to single-source views based on, for example, databases, web pages, and conventional files.

The contributions of this paper are as follows. We develop a framework that allows a DW designer to understand the relationship between a QoS specification and the cost of achieving it; define a number of source capabilities which may affect maintenance; identify meaningful policies taking into account source capabilities; present, as a part of the framework, a detailed cost-model and a user-centric specification framework for QoS; show how user specification and cost-model can be utilised to select a maintenance policy; and present a prototype implementation which enables a high-level relative comparison of policies.

It is important to point out that a fully automated process may not be realistic for the design of a complex warehouse. However, a tool and framework such as the one presented in this paper is intended to help DW designers to understand the complex inter-relationships between source capabilities, warehouse user requirements and maintenance policies. The cost formulas and source properties introduced in this paper are geared towards selecting maintenance policies and are not intended to address optimization issues related to physical data access at the sources or at the warehouse. Current work is focussed on validation through benchmarks, and generalising the results to address a broader class of sources and views.

1.2 Roadmap

The remainder of the paper is organized as follows. In section 2 we give an overview of related work. In section 3 we use previous work to synthesize a framework in terms of the components of the DW maintenance problem. In addition, we present novel definitions of view staleness and source capabilities. In section 4 we present a detailed cost-model for maintenance policies. The applicability of the cost-model is shown in section 5, where we suggest a high level QoS specification and a policy selection algorithm. We moreover present a prototype implementation, which incorporates the cost-model, user specifications, and selection algorithm. The prototype enables its users to compare and evaluate various trade-offs involved in maintenance policy selection. Finally, we draw some conclusions and discuss future work in section 6.

2 Related Work

Materialised views [4], snapshots [1], [22], and data warehouses [33] all relate in that they handle (possibly transformed) copies of source data. The problem of maintenance, i.e., the impact of source updates, has been addressed for a number of different view, snapshot and warehouse scenarios. An extensive overview of incremental maintenance of relational views can be found in [12].

Blakeley et al. [3] suggest screening algorithms and techniques for efficient maintenance of materialised views. These techniques were further developed by Hanson [15] who compares three different maintenance policies in a centralised environment. In a similar study, Srivastava et al. [30] compares maintenance algorithms using a queueing theory based analytical model which, in addition, considers user aspects. Colby et al. [6] address the problem of how to defer maintenance of a view and still avoid what they call the state bug. In subsequent work [7] Colby et al. introduce "view-groups" and discuss issues related to supporting multiple maintenance policies in centralised DBMSs.

In the ADMS prototype [25], [26], [8] materialised views are used to optimise performance and system utilisation in a client-server database. Segev et al. [27], [28], [29] present pioneering work on materialised views for distributed databases which resembles the ideas of data warehousing. Zhou et al. [35] and Hull et al. [17], [18] address DW maintenance as a part of the Squirrel project where the system supports virtual and materialised views as well as their hybrids. Quass et al. [24] introduce algorithms which enable on-line maintenance, i.e., concurrent execution of maintenance and user queries. Vavouras et al. [32] present an object-oriented approach to incremental maintenance of warehouses that can be based on a wide set of sources. DW quality issues have been addressed in a number of studies within the DWQ project [20].

In a warehousing environment, a view may contain data from autonomous and "transaction unaware" sources which may yield inconsistent views if the integration is performed in a straightforward manner. Zhuge et al. [36], [37], [38] identify this problem and define four consistency levels for a warehouse view. Several algorithms have been suggested [2], [38] preserving different levels of consistency. Another possible way to avoid inconsistencies, used by Hull et al. [17], is to maintain a copy of each source.

There are several studies on how to select and efficiently maintain views within a warehouse environment [16], [21], [13], [31]. In this paper we will not consider such views as they can be handled, from a maintenance perspective, as local, homogeneous views. A DWMP only involves maintenance of views that are based on external data.

3 Establishing the Components of DW Maintenance

To address the data warehouse maintenance problem in a comprehensive manner, we need to analyse policies and user specification, as well as source and warehouse characteristics. In this section, we analyse existing work in these areas and present some important extensions. We are especially concerned with how quality of service can be made intuitive and precise from a DW designer's perspective. Furthermore, we identify source capabilities that have a significant impact on maintenance activity, but have been ignored or over-simplified in previous studies.

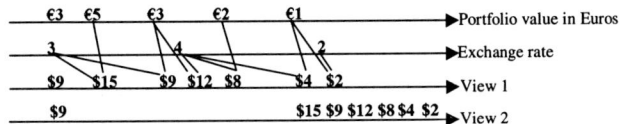

Fig. 2. Two view traces offering the highest consistency level

3.1 User-Oriented Quality of Service Measures

A number of terms related to the user perspective have been introduced in the view and warehouse literature. These include: response time [30], availability [6], [24], consistency [38], [2], [6], staleness [17], freshness [18], and currency [28]. *Response time* is defined as the delay between submission of a query and the return of its result [30]. *Availability* is defined in terms of view-downtime [6] (for example, expressed as a percentage). *Consistency* (convergence, weak, strong, and complete) is defined and discussed thoroughly by Zhuge [38]. *Staleness*, *freshness*, and *currency* are all related but are defined and based on different prerequisites. This section highlights consistency and staleness-related measures as these are found to be the most complex.

Consistency. Despite its extensiveness, Zhuge's work [38] is only concerned with consistency. It moreover focuses on a subset of maintenance policies and source capabilities. From a user's perspective there are several additional important QoS requirements that need to be captured [10]. Fig. 2 illustrates how the highest consistency requirement can be met and still result in poor quality of service. It shows two identical views maintained by different maintenance algorithms. The views represent a user's current European stock portfolio value in Dollars and are based on two sources; one is the portfolio value in Euros and the other is the exchange rate between Euros and Dollars. Both algorithms preserve completeness, which is the highest consistency level in Zhuge's classification. From a user perspective, it is apparent that the difference between these traces can have severe implications. It is easy to observe that view 1 does not lag behind source changes. On the other hand, view 2 lags significantly behind source changes and may not be acceptable for a user even though it guarantees the highest consistency level. Most maintenance algorithms suggested (including Zhuge's) may not behave in the same way as view 2 in most situations, but there is no other *guarantee* than consistency. Consistency specification needs to be complemented with other QoS requirements to be useful as a user requirement.

Staleness, Freshness, Currency and View Age. *Currency* was introduced by Segev et al. [28] as a measure of the time elapsed since a view ceased to reflect the state of its sources. A zero currency value means that a view is up to date. As a working definition of currency, Segev et al. use the difference since last refresh. In other words, it is based on the pessimistic assumption that the source will change immediately after each refresh. A subtle problem with the definition suggested by Segev et al. [28] is that it is defined in terms of the (dynamic) *view state*, whereas a user is only concerned with the quality of the result returned. The implication of this will be different for different policies but Segev et al., who are focusing on a subset of policies, do not acknowledge this. An implication may be, for example, that immediate policies are penalized due to pessimistic estimations. On-demand policies may benefit from not including maintenance delay in the currency measure. Hull et al. [17], [18] introduce definitions of both freshness and staleness. Freshness is defined as a vector of values for each source. Staleness, on the other hand, is defined as the maximum difference in time between when results are returned and the latest time when the view reflected the source. In other words, the internal *state* of the view is considered rather than the *quality* of the result returned.

We believe there is a need to make a clear distinction between quality of service as requested by users and guaranteed by the system, and the dynamic behaviour of view maintenance policies. Neither currency as defined by Segev et al. nor staleness (or freshness) as defined by Hull et al. has a user-oriented definition. We suggest that two distinct measures should be used: *view staleness* and *view age*. View age is a dynamic, system-oriented measure that we do not consider further in this paper.

Assuming that strong consistency is provided (or more precisely that the view will use some valid state from each source) we define the measure of staleness of a view informally as follows:

For a view with guaranteed maximum staleness Z, the result of any query over the view, returned at time t, will reflect all source changes prior to t-Z.

This means that users have an intuitive measure of how recent the information returned by a view can be expected to be. For example, if we query a view that guarantees a maximum staleness of 60 seconds, then we know that all changes performed more than a minute ago will be reflected in the result. This can be vital if the view contains any time-critical information. We formally define staleness below:

A view V is based on sources $S^1, S^2, \ldots, S^M$, where $M \geq 1$. The state transitions of source S^i occur on occasions stored in the vector $\vec{t}^i$. S^i is initialised at t_0^i and the nth state transition of S^i occurs at t_n^i. For all $n \geq 1$ we have: $t_{n-1}^i < t_n^i < t_{n+1}^i$. Our strong consistency assumption implies that each state in the vector is a valid source state. A query over the view returned at t_{ret} will be based on source states entered at $t_{q_1}^1, t_{q_2}^2, \ldots, t_{q_M}^M$, for some positive integers $q_1, q_2, \ldots, q_M$.

Definition: A view guarantees maximum staleness Z *iff* for all query invocations over the view and all sources S^i for which $t_{q_i+1}^i$ exists, the following holds: $t_{q_i+1}^i > t_{ret} - Z$.

In other words, no state transitions may occur in the time interval preceding $t_{ret} - Z$, without being reflected in the result. The different components are illustrated in Fig. 3. On the timeline of S^1, the period from t_1^1 to $t_{ret} - Z$ is marked. This is a critical area in the sense that a state change here will imply

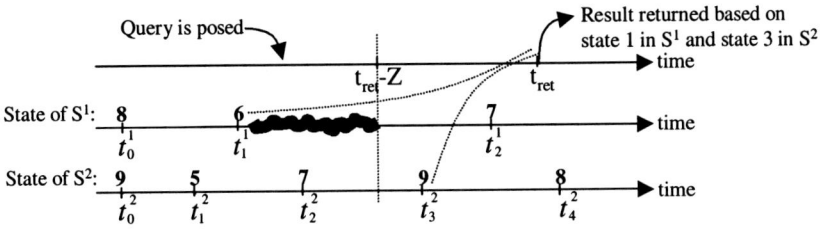

Fig. 3. Example of a view guaranteeing maximal staleness Z

that the staleness requirement is not met (assuming that state 1 of S^1 is used in the query result). On the other hand, state 2 of S^2 may have been used in the result without breaking the staleness requirement.

This definition of staleness[1] has a number of useful properties. *(i)* It applies to *any* maintenance strategy and can be applied to virtual views as well. *(ii)* The definition makes no reference to the view-state or the time of query-invocation, which means it is not biased with respect to on-demand maintenance (or immediate for that matter). *(iii)* Finally, if a view guarantees maximum staleness Z it will also guarantee maximum staleness $Z + d$, where $d \geq 0$.

3.2 DWMP Evaluation Criteria

Evaluation criteria define yardsticks for use in the DWMP selection process. Commonly mentioned criteria (also typical of distributed databases) are processing cost (CPU and I/O) [15], [30], storage requirements [35], and communication [22], [8]. One important characteristic of a DW environment is that there is a distinction between source and warehouse impact [18]. Source impact may be considered more expensive than warehouse impact. One reason for introducing a warehouse is to off-load OLAP queries from sources. For these applications the cost of maintaining a warehouse must not be greater than that of executing the queries directly over the sources.

3.3 Source Capabilities

A limitation with existing work on view and warehouse maintenance (e.g., [15], [30], [29], [35], [38]) is that it assumes that sources are capable of actively participating in maintenance activity. This is not the case for typical DW sources, as most commercial DBMSs have no mechanism for obtaining external notifications when transactions commit. Some authors recognise that sources may lack some capabilities but assume that compensation is possible by wrapping sources. There exist source categorisations [19], [33] that are aimed at exploring the solution space of wrapping, based on the nature of existing data sources.

---
[1] This measure is not intended for use in computing staleness for queries at runtime, though it may be possible to approximate it for a sequence of updates and queries.

Table 1. Classification of change detection capabilities

CHAW	Change aware - the ability to, on request, tell when last change was made
CHAC	Change active - the ability to automatically detect and report that changes have been made
DAW	Delta aware - the ability to deliver delta changes

We, however, claim that the wrapping alternatives should take into account the overall maintenance process and not just source capabilities.

Change Detection Capabilities. We suggest that change detection in a wrapper should be made an explicit part of maintenance, and that source capabilities should be used in the policy selection process. This permits one to determine whether wrapping a source is beneficial based on DW requirements. Zhou et al. [35] classify source change detection capabilities as sufficient, restricted, and no activeness. We claim that this classification is too imprecise to be used in policy selection. Instead, we suggest three change detection capabilities which a source may have, as shown in Table 1, each affecting its ability to participate in view maintenance. These capabilities are orthogonal in the sense that a source can have one, two or three of them in any combination [10]. As an example, a webserver is typically CHAW in that the time of last modification can be derived from the HTTP-header. It is, however, not possible to retrieve changes to a page (DAW) or to get active notification whenever the page is updated (CHAC). The important thing with CHAC is the ability to *actively* notify that changes have occurred. If clients have to query the source to see if it has changed, it is not CHAC.

Localisation of Wrapper. As mentioned previously, the system viewpoint is divided into a (source) server and a (DW) client side. A wrapper process may, depending on the nature of the source, be located on either side. If, for example, a web-source external to the warehouse is to be extended to provide DAW it must be queried from the client side. This will introduce processing and storage costs in the warehouse and additional communication. If, on the other hand, the extraction process is located in the server, there is no additional communication cost but the source will be penalised with storage and processing costs. The localisation of the extraction process is a trade-off between communication, processing and storage. At first glance it may seem obvious that delta extraction should be located in the server whenever possible, but the cost of storage and processing in the sources may be the most critical criteria, in which case client wrapping will be preferable.

View Awareness. In a warehousing scenario sources may be more or less conformant to the view definition language used in the warehouse. As an example, a view may be defined as the median of some attribute in a relation. If the source is a legacy system it may not be possible to retrieve the median value through a single query. Instead, the whole column may have to be retrieved and the value computed by the wrapper. This will obviously have communication and processing implications similar to those discussed above for delta extraction. We will classify a source as *view-aware* (VA) if it has a query interface that returns the desired set of data through a *single* query.

3.4 Maintenance Policies

View maintenance algorithms can be described in terms of *when* and *how* maintenance is to be performed. The *how* part of maintenance may be broken down into a number of choices described in the literature. A view could be: maintained incrementally or recomputed; maintained on-line or off-line; more or less consistency preserving. It is important to note that a large number of variants and combinations of policies are possible. The set of algorithms is not fixed and more variants can be introduced in the future.

Maintenance timing addresses the question of *when* to refresh a view. Maintenance activity may be triggered by different types of event [35] such as updates to base data, reading of a view, explicit requests, or periodic events.

For the purposes of this paper, we consider a limited but still representative set of maintenance strategies. We have chosen immediate, periodic and on-demand timings to trigger either incremental or recompute maintenance. This gives us six different policies. For incremental policies we assume that a view is incrementally self-maintainable. Periodic policies are parameterised on polling frequency p. Table 2 shows the source and view requirements for the six policies.

4 A Cost-Model for Evaluating Maintenance Policies

In the previous section we established the components of DW maintenance. From this we conclude that the problem has a vast solution space and for any non-trivial warehouse scenario, support is needed to make quality decisions on maintenance policy. In this section we present a parameterised cost-model for maintenance policies which captures a wide set of the components discussed in the previous section. The solution presented is restricted to a subset of views,

Table 2. Maintenance policies used in this paper

Policy	Description	Requirements
I_I	On change→find and send changes	Source is CHAC, incremental view
I_R	On change→recompute	Source is CHAC
P_I	Periodically→find and send changes	Incremental view
P_R	Periodically→recompute	None
O_I	When queried→find and send changes	Incremental view
O_R	When queried→recompute	None

policies, sources and user-specifications, but still is powerful enough to demonstrate the applicability of our approach.

4.1 Principles for the Cost-Model

The following principles have guided the development of the cost-model:

- it should be possible to distinguish individual costs for a policy. The balancing between, for example, QoS and system cost may change;
- the cost for a policy should be formulated for each possible combination of source capabilities. No assumptions should be made about systems providing a specific capability;
- it should be possible to distinguish costs which are imposed on the source system from those imposed on the warehouse system. This complicates the model but is important in a DW environment;
- it should be possible to adapt the cost-model for various data-models and source systems. Therefore it should formulate the cost at a high abstraction level which allows tailoring for a specific environment.

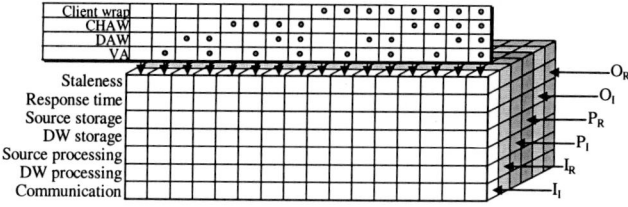

Fig. 4. The cost-model as a 3D matrix where each position has a cost-formula

The cost-model can be seen as a matrix which captures system costs as well as QoS measures for a set of policies for different combinations of source capabilities. Fig. 4 illustrates the dimensions of the cost-model. The cost-model formulates the cost of each policy (z-axis: I_I to O_R) for each combination of source capabilities (x-axis: 16 combinations). There is one cost for each measure (y-axis: staleness to communication) The x-axis represents all different combinations of source capabilities that may affect the cost of a policy. CHAC capability is required for immediate policies but does not affect costs[2]. The remaining four capabilities make the sixteen potential combinations shown. Fortunately, for a specific policy and measure, these combinations can be grouped into sets with identical cost formulas.

---

[2] In contrast to other work in this field, we make a clear distinction between true immediate which receives active notifications from the source, and polled immediate, which we claim is a variation of periodic maintenance.

Table 3. Cost functions used to represent elementary operations

r	The processing delay to recompute a view, which includes loading of the necessary source data, performing necessary computations/comparisons and storing the view
$i(n,m)$	The processing delay of incremental maintenance with m changes on a view of size n; this includes storing changes as they arrive, retrieving necessary parts of existing view, and updating it accordingly
$e(m)$	The processing delay to extract the given amount (m) of data
$s(m)$	The processing delay to store the given amount (m) of data
$a(n,m)$	The processing delay of change detection (to compare two snapshots with size n resulting in a change of size m); this includes retrieving the necessary data and saving the changes as well as maintaining the snapshot
$d(m)$	Communication delay to send the given amount (m) of data

4.2 Parameters of the Cost-Model and Assumptions

There are several properties of the sources and the warehouse that affect the selection of a policy: the source size (N), the view predicate selectivity (f), the size of each update (L), the source update frequency (c), the polling frequency (p), the DW query frequency (q), the wrapper localisation, and whether the source is CHAC, DAW, CHAW, and/or VA. These properties are stored as metadata and are available to the selection process. Costs are formulated using cost functions, shown in Table 3, that represent the cost for elementary operations. These cost-functions will be instantiated for specific DW view scenarios. To simplify expressions (for the formulas shown), we assume that costs are identical in source and warehouse. We further assume that *streaming* is not used, which means that intermediate results have to be stored. Processing and communication formulas are per-time unit cost. To get per-query cost the formulas should be divided by q (query frequency). We furthermore assume that all events are evenly distributed with the same inter-arrival time. An even distribution of events is assumed in order to reduce the complexity of our model. The implications of this assumption, and the applicability of the model to a real environment, depend on the nature of the update and query distributions. Again, different scenarios are possible and the cost-model can be adjusted if this assumption proves to have a significant impact on results[3].

4.3 An Example of Cost Formulation - Immediate Incremental

In this section we present an example of how costs are formulated. Due to space limitations we present costs in a concise format and only for the slice of the matrix in Fig. 4 with policy I_I. For full details of the cost-model we refer the interested reader to [9], where each policy is fully elaborated.

---
[3] Preliminary benchmark experiments indicate that cost-model predictions are applicable even when events are Poisson distributed.

Staleness for immediate maintenance is composed of the processing and communication delay. For most source capability scenarios (i.e. DAW) staleness is caused by the delay to extract the changes, and send them to the warehouse where they are stored and used to incrementally update the view: $e(L) + d(L) + s(L) + i(fN, L)$. An exception to this is if the source is wrapped in the client, is non-DAW, and is not view aware; the communication delay will be to extract and send the whole source, store it at the warehouse and compute changes. The total staleness cost will hence be: $e(N)+d(N)+s(N)+r+a(fN,L)$. The observant reader will object and correctly claim that it should be sufficient to recompute the view and use it as is. However, this would turn the incremental policy into a recompute. This illustrates the consequences of not considering wrapping as an integral part of maintenance. We will comment on this later in the paper. If the source is VA, is wrapped in the client, and non-DAW the cost will instead be: $r + e(fN) + d(fN) + s(fN) + a(fN, L)$. If the source is non-DAW, and is wrapped in the server then the source processing is to recompute the view, perform change detection and extract the changes. The communication is merely to send the changes. At the warehouse the changes are stored and the view is updated incrementally. The cost will hence be: $r + a(fN, L) + e(L) + d(L) + s(L) + i(fN, L)$.

Response time for I_I is always 0. In our formulation, response time does not include query execution time (as defined by Hull et al. [18]), as it is common to all policies. This formulation allows us to differentiate between query processing time that is independent of policies, and the time for data propagation which is based on policies[4]. This implies that I_I, I_R, P_I, and P_R have 0 response time.

Source storage cost is always 0 unless the source is non-DAW and it is wrapped in the server in which case the storage cost is fN. Warehouse storage cost is to store the view, of size fN. As we use the view for change detection no additional storage is required even if the wrapping is done in the client.

If the source is wrapped in the client, is non-DAW and is not view aware then the source processing cost will be a processing cost to extract the whole source (N) each time a change occurs: $c \cdot e(N)$. If the source, in addition, is view aware this cost will be replaced by the cost of recomputing the view and extracting it: $c(r + e(fN))$. A third alternative applies when the source is non-DAW but may be wrapped in the server. For that case, the processing required for each change is to recompute the view, find the changes and extract them: $c(r + a(fN, L) + e(L))$. Finally, the source processing costs for all sources that are DAW (the other formulas all apply to non-DAW sources) is to record and extract changes: $c(s(L) + e(L))$.

Warehouse processing cost is complementary to source processing. When the source is wrapped in the client, and is neither DAW nor VA the cost is: $c(s(N)+r+a(fN,L))$. If it is VA the cost will instead be: $c(s(fN)+a(fN,L))$. For all remaining source scenarios (wrapped in server or DAW) the warehouse

---

[4] To enable a uniform comparison of virtual and materialized data warehouses the total response time needs to be considered. This work, however, does not consider virtual warehouses, which makes it possible to cancel the query execution time.

cost is simply to temporarily store the changes and incrementally update the view: $c(s(L) + i(fN, L))$.

If the source is wrapped in the client, and is neither delta- nor view aware, we have to send the whole source for each update; the communication cost will be: $c \cdot d(N)$. If the source is view aware (and wrapped in the client and non-DAW) the view has to be sent each time: $c \cdot d(fN)$. In all other scenarios, only changes have to be sent: $c \cdot d(L)$.

5 Applications of the Cost-Model

The cost-model presented in the previous section has a significant number of parameters and criteria. It is not trivial to compare policies under different assumptions on warehouse and source characteristics and QoS requirements. In this section we present a QoS specification language and a simple yet powerful selection algorithm which, based on user specification, source capabilities, and cost formulas selects the most appropriate maintenance policy. We moreover present a prototype tool, which allows users to explore the trade-offs involved in the selection process.

Note that, in this paper, we have restricted the solution space by making a choice from a given set of policies, based on a given set of QoS and source characteristics. The selection algorithm presented in this section is complete with respect to these sets. It is possible to extend the solution in any dimension. Extension will imply a change of the selection algorithm and specification language as well. This means we are not trying to make claims for completeness of the specification language or the selection algorithm.

5.1 QoS Specification and Automatic Policy Selection

The purpose of user specifications is twofold: to enable users to specify their requirements and to enable the system to select a strategy to meet these requirements. The first implies that our logical specification needs a clear and intuitive semantics to make it easy for users to communicate their needs.

We introduce three non-numerical specifications for staleness and response time representing three levels of requirements. The lowest level, *ignore*, is specified if the user is not concerned with this criterion. The intermediate level, *consider*, is used to indicate that the user considers the criterion to be as important as other aspects. The highest level, *best possible* (BP), is used to specify that this criterion is most important, and the policy should be optimised to give the best possible performance with respect to this property. Despite the conceptual simplicity of non-numerical specifications, situations may still exist in which a user wants to specify an acceptable departure from the best possible situation. We therefore introduce a way to specify a fixed limit as an offset from the BP-value. It is a relaxation of the BP specification based on user need to reduce overall cost of maintenance. It should be noted that BP and offset could be specified using different statistical measures such as maximum, average, or median. A full specification language would include such details.

User specification can be used to guide the automatic selection of a maintenance policy. We have developed a branch and bound algorithm [9] that, based on user specifications and system characteristics, returns the most appropriate maintenance policy. The idea behind the algorithm is that it should reduce the set of potential policies primarily based on user specification and secondly on system cost. If user requirements are such that no policy meets them, the algorithm should report this as an exception. For each step, the algorithm derives the optimal cost amongst remaining policies and uses it to restrict and prune policies. Parameterised policies are restricted in terms of acceptable parameter values. If a policy has no acceptable parameter value, it is pruned. To be able to combine different criteria, we assume that each cost has an associated weight. These indicate the relative importance of each cost considered in such a way that several costs can be combined into a weighted sum. Weights are typically assigned by system designers to "scale" different measures into comparable units.

5.2 Prototype Tool and Experiences

The cost-model and selection process described in the previous section have been implemented in a prototype tool. Through a number of dialogs the user is asked to specify quality of service requirements, source capabilities and parameters as described above. The prototype can be run from:

http://www.his.se/ida/research/groups/dbtg/demos/dwmp/

It is important to notice that the purpose of the tool is to enable relative comparison of policies and to analyse trends. It is not intended for use in deriving absolute values. The implementation has enabled us to verify our cost formulas for boundary conditions where the choices are intuitive. It has also helped our understanding of the importance of the source capabilities highlighted in section 3. This section presents the tool and observations from its use.

Preliminaries. The prototype tool is based on a specific scenario in which a warehouse view selects a fraction of a single relation. The cost components presented in Table 3 have been derived from assumptions on buffer size, block size, tuple size and block read time. The extraction and insertion formulas $e(m)$ and $s(m)$ are estimated as linear functions of m. The cost of incremental updates is a scan through the view plus an additional cost for each update. Change detection is assumed to be done using sort-merge-join at a cost of $O(n \ln n)$. Recomputation of the view requires a sequential scan through the whole source, a cost for applying the selection predicate to each tuple, and the cost to store the view. It is assumed that no indexes are built for any view. This means that there is no additional cost for recompute. If indexes are used, recompute gets an additional cost compared with incremental maintenance Balancing between different components of the cost-model is done by setting weights. In the prototype staleness and response time are given equal weight. Storage costs are weighted to have low importance while the other system costs are weighted to be very important. Among these, source processing is given the highest weight.

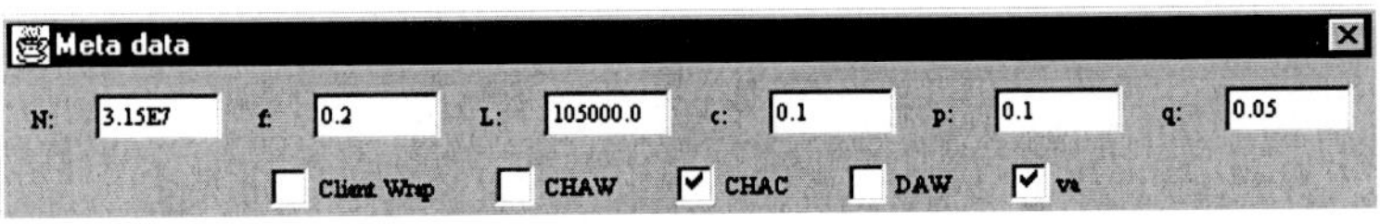

Fig. 5. The dialog for specifying source and warehouse characteristics

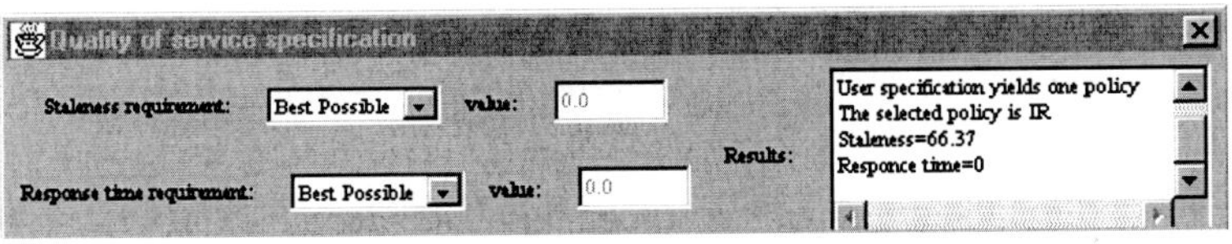

Fig. 6. The dialog for specifying QoS requirements and observing policy selection

Using the Prototype for Analysis. Users of the prototype can specify system characteristics and capabilities in a dialog as shown in Fig. 5. The fields in this dialog correspond to the metadata discussed in section 4.2. Quality of service specification is handled in a separate dialog. A user may, for example, specify that both staleness and response time should be best possible, as shown in Fig. 6. The right side of the dialog presents the result of the selection process, i.e. whether the selection process was successful and, if so, the policy that was selected (in Fig. 6 I_R is selected). The dialog gives a brief indication of how the policy was derived and what values for staleness and response time the selected policy has. This allows one to investigate the impact of changes in specification, in selection process and in the costs associated with each policy. Individual components of the cost-model can be inspected in another dialog shown in Fig. 7. The table presents individual costs for each policy where the rows correspond to the seven evaluation criteria used in the cost-model and the columns correspond to the policies. Any combination of costs can be selected to be weighted together and any number of policies can be selected to be included in the graph to the right in the dialog. The weighted sum is plotted as a function of a selected parameter. In this way the user can observe the behaviour of the cost-function in a neighbourhood of the specified parameter.

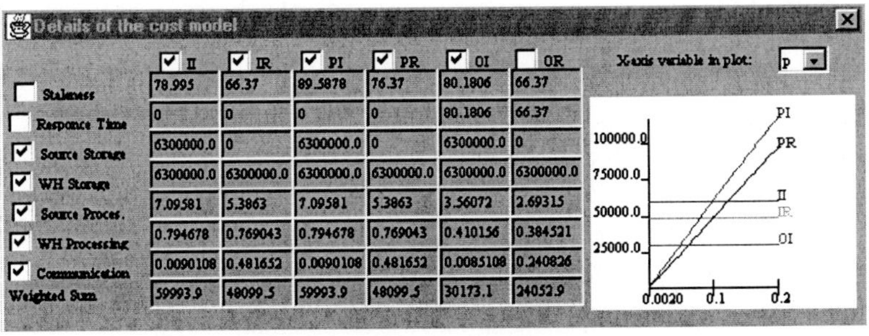

Fig. 7. A dialog presenting the details of the cost-model

5.3 Observations

As mentioned in section 5.2, the prototype has enabled us to explore the cost-model, for example by examining boundary conditions where the choices are intuitive:

- If the view is rarely queried, on-demand gives the lowest processing cost
- If the source is rarely updated, immediate gives the lowest processing cost
- The choice between incremental and recompute policies is dependant on the size of updates. This has been reported in the literature but it is, however, interesting to note that DAW capability is required for this to be true.
- Recompute policies are not affected by the size of the delta.
- Periodic policies are highly dependent on setting appropriate periodicities: too low and we penalise staleness; too high and system costs increase.

By altering the QoS specification as well as other metadata we have made a number of interesting observations that we believe have a strong bearing on the general maintenance case. Specifically, all of the source characteristics presented in section 3 have an impact on the selection of a policy and its cost-function. For example, if communication is not the main cost, the weighted cost of maintenance is higher for incremental policies if the source is non-DAW. Fig. 8 illustrates this for the scenario presented above with the weighted cost (for all criteria) as a function of p. As can be seen from the diagrams the recompute policies have a much higher cost as compared with incremental ones when the source is DAW. Without DAW capability the incremental policies are never better than their recompute counterpart. Another interesting observation made is that if sources are DAW the cost of incremental policies becomes less dependent on the location of the wrapper.

The diagrams of Fig. 8 show the typical shapes of the cost graphs for periodic policies when staleness is combined with other costs. There is a trade-off between staleness and the price of maintenance. It is the task of the optimiser to detect this global minimum.

6 Conclusions and Future Work

We believe that the framework presented in this paper is useful for understanding the effect QoS specification and source capabilities have on the cost incurred

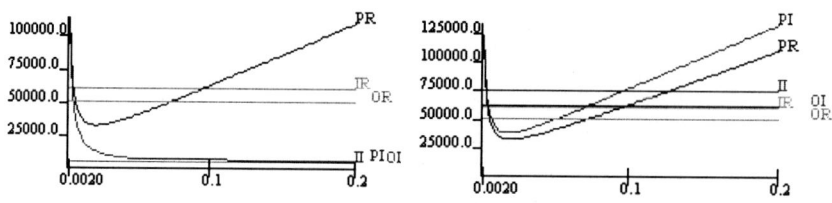

Fig. 8. The total cost as a function of p, with a DAW(left) and non-DAW(right) source

for maintaining a view. The utility of our approach is in its ability to provide a feel for how changes to the specification impact on the choice of propagation policies. Although the cost formulas seem complex, they represent costs that are typically used (such as size of the increments, communication, storage, and processing) when data warehouses are designed in an ad hoc manner. Our framework provides a systematic approach to understanding a complex problem using the same components.

There are many possible extensions and unexplored problems that are currently being considered. One important issue is how well predictions of the cost-model correspond with the performance of a real system. We have developed a benchmark environment which contains most of the components of the cost-model, including policies and source capabilities. The empirical results show a very close correspondence between cost-model predictions and measurements of the real system [11]. We are currently extending the test-bed to cover a wider set of sources.

The user specification and selection algorithm presented in this paper exemplifies the approach, but needs to be extended to include consistency and availability aspects. Other maintenance algorithms could also be brought into the framework. One aspect of this is to explore the use of view age to dynamically modify propagation policies, incorporating some of the ideas from [29]. Most importantly, to make this approach viable we need to analyse how views based on multiple sources can best be handled; optimisation of policies on shared sources is equally important.

To conclude, we believe the approach proposed in this paper has the potential to handle the complexity inherent in warehouse maintenance. The observations reported here indicate that QoS requirements as well as source capabilities have a significant impact on maintenance activity. If an incorrect policy is selected, the consequences for system and users may be very different from those expected, even to the extent that the original goals of data warehousing are invalidated.

References

1. M.E. Adiba, B.G. Lindsay: Database Snapshots. VLDB (1980)
2. D. Agrawal, A.E. Abbadi, A.K. Singh, T. Yurek: Efficient View Maintenance at Data Warehouses. SIGMOD Conf. (1997)
3. J.A. Blakeley, P.Å. Larson, F.W. Tompa: Efficiently Updating Materialized Views. SIGMOD Conf. (1986)
4. P. Buneman, E.K. Clemons: Efficient Monitoring Relational Databases. ACM Transactions on Database Systems 4(3) (1979)
5. C. Chaudhuri, U. Dayal: An Overview of Data Warehousing and OLAP Technology. SIGMOD Record 26(1) (1997)
6. L.S. Colby, T. Griffin, L. Libkin, I.S. Mumick, H. Trickey: Algorithms for Deferred View Maintenance. SIGMOD Conf. (1996)
7. L.S. Colby, A. Kawaguchi, D.F. Lieuwen, I.S. Mumick, K.A. Ross: Supporting Multiple View Maintenance Policies. SIGMOD Conf. (1997)
8. A. Delis, N. Roussopoulos: Management of Updates in the Enhanced Client-Server DBMS. IEEE-ICDCS (1994)

9. H. Engström, S. Chakravarthy, B. Lings: A Holistic Approach to the Evaluation of Data Warehouse Maintenance Policies. Technical report HS-IDA-TR-00-001, University of Skövde, Sweden (2000)
10. H. Engström, S. Chakravarthy, B. Lings: A User-centric View of Data Warehouse Maintenance Issues. BNCOD (2000)
11. H. Engström, G. Gelati, L. Lings: A Benchmark Comparison of Maintenance Policies in a Data Warehouse Environment. Technical Report HS-IDA-TR-01-005, University of Skövde, Sweden (2001)
12. A. Gupta, I.S. Mumick: Maintenance of Materialized Views: Problems, Techniques, and Applications. IEEE Data Engineering Bulletin 18(2) (1995)
13. H. Gupta, I.S. Mumick: Selection of Views to Materialize Under a Maintenance Cost Constraint. International Conf. on Database Theory (1999)
14. J. Hammer, H. Garcia-Molina, J. Widom, W. Labio, Y. Zhuge: The Stanford Data Warehousing Project. IEEE Data Engineering Bulletin 18(2) (1995)
15. E.N. Hanson: A Performance Analysis of View Materialization Strategies. SIGMOD Conf. (1987)
16. V. Harinarayan, A. Rajaraman, J.D. Ullman: Implementing Data Cubes Efficiently. SIGMOD Conf. (1996)
17. R. Hull, G. Zhou: A Framework for Supporting Data Integration Using the Materialized and Virtual Approaches. SIGMOD Conf. (1996)
18. R. Hull, G. Zhou: Towards the Study of Performance Trade-offs Between Materialized and Virtual Integrated Views. VIEWS'96 (1996)
19. A. Koschel, P.C. Lockemann: Distributed events in active database systems: Letting the genie out of the bottle. DKE 25(1-2) (1998)
20. M. Jarke, Y. Vassiliou: Data Warehouse Quality Design: A Review of the DWQ Project. Conf. on Information Quality, Cambridge (1997)
21. M. Lee, J. Hammer: Speeding Up Warehouse Physical Design Using A Randomized Algorithm. DMDW (1999)
22. B. Lindsay, L. Haas, C. Mohan, H. Pirahesh, P. Wilms: A Snapshot Differential Refresh Algorithm. SIGMOD Conf. (1986)
23. D. Lomet (editor), J. Widom (editor): Special Issue on Materialized Views and Data Warehousing. IEEE Data Engineering Bulletin 18(2) (1995)
24. D. Quass, J. Widom: On-Line Warehouse View Maintenance. SIGMOD Conf. (1997)
25. N. Roussopoulos, H. Kang: Principles and Techniques in the Design of ADMS±. IEEE Computer 19(12) (1986)
26. R. Roussopoulos, C.M. Chen, S. Kelley, A. Delis, Y. Papakonstantinou: The ADMS Project: Views "R" Us. IEEE Data Engineering Bulletin 18(2) (1995)
27. A. Segev, J. Park: Updating Distributed Materialized Views. TKDE 1(2) (1989)
28. A. Segev, W. Fang: Currency-Based Updates to Distributed Materialized Views. ICDE (1990)
29. A. Segev, W. Fang: Optimal Update Policies for Distributed Materialized Views. Management Science 37(7) (1991)
30. J. Srivastava, D. Rotem: Analytical Modeling of Materialized View Maintenance. PODS (1988)
31. D. Theodoratos, M. Bouzeghoub: Data Currency Quality Factors in Data Warehouse Design. DMDW (1999)
32. A. Vavouras, S. Gatziu, K.R. Dittrich: The SIRIUS Approach for Refreshing Data Warehouses Incrementally. BTW'99 (1999)
33. J. Widom: Research Problems in Data Warehousing. CIKM (1995)

34. M.C. Wu, A.P. Buchmann: Research Issues in Data Warehousing. BTW'97 (1997)
35. G. Zhou, R. Hull, R. King, J.C. Franchitti: Data Integration and Warehousing Using H2O. IEEE Data Engineering Bulletin 18(2) (1995)
36. Y Zhuge, H. Garcia-Molina, J. Hammer, J. Widom: View Maintenance in a Warehousing Environment. SIGMOD Conf. (1995)
37. Y. Zhuge, H. Garcia-Molina, J.L. Wiener: The Strobe Algorithms for Multi-Source Warehouse Consistency. PDIS (1996)
38. Y. Zhuge: Incremental Maintenance of Consistent Data Warehouses. PhD Thesis, Stanford University (1999)

Efficient OLAP Query Processing in Distributed Data Warehouses

Michael O. Akinde[1], Michael H. Böhlen[1], Theodore Johnson[2],
Laks V.S. Lakshmanan[3], and Divesh Srivastava[2]

[1] Aalborg University
{strategy, boehlen}@cs.auc.dk
[2] AT&T Labs–Research
{johnsont, divesh}@research.att.com
[3] University of British Columbia
laks@cs.ubc.ca

Abstract. The success of Internet applications has led to an explosive growth in the demand for bandwidth from ISPs. Managing an IP network requires collecting and analyzing network data, such as flow-level traffic statistics. Such analyses can typically be expressed as OLAP queries, e.g., correlated aggregate queries and data cubes. Current day OLAP tools for this task assume the availability of the data in a centralized data warehouse. However, the inherently distributed nature of data collection and the huge amount of data extracted at each collection point make it impractical to gather all data at a centralized site. One solution is to maintain a distributed data warehouse, consisting of local data warehouses at each collection point and a coordinator site, with most of the processing being performed at the local sites. In this paper, we consider the problem of efficient evaluation of OLAP queries over a distributed data warehouse. We have developed the Skalla system for this task. Skalla translates OLAP queries, specified as certain algebraic expressions, into distributed evaluation plans which are shipped to individual sites. Salient properties of our approach are that only partial results are shipped – never parts of the detail data. We propose a variety of optimizations to minimize both the synchronization traffic and the local processing done at each site. We finally present an experimental study based on TPC(R) data. Our results demonstrate the scalability of our techniques and quantify the performance benefits of the optimization techniques that have gone into the Skalla system.

1 Introduction

The success of Internet applications has led to an explosive growth in the demand for bandwidth from Internet Service Providers. Managing an IP (Internet Protocol) network involves debugging performance problems, optimizing the configuration of routing protocols, and planning the rollout of new capacity, to name a few tasks, especially in the face of varying traffic on the network. Effective management of a network requires collecting, correlating, and analyzing a variety of network trace data.

Typically, trace data such as packet headers, flow-level traffic statistics, and router statistics are collected using tools like packet sniffers, NetFlow-enabled routers, and SNMP polling of network elements. A wide variety of analyses are then performed to characterize the usage and behavior of the network (see, e.g., [5, 10]). For example, using flow-level traffic statistics data one can answer questions like: *"On an hourly basis, what fraction of the total number of flows is due to Web traffic?"*, or *"On an hourly basis, what fraction of the total traffic flowing into the network is from IP subnets whose total hourly traffic is within 10% of the maximum?"* Currently, such analyses are usually implemented by the networking community in an ad hoc manner using complex algorithms coded in procedural programming languages like Perl. They can actually be expressed as OLAP queries, including SQL grouping/aggregation, data cubes [12], using marginal distributions extracted by the unpivot operator [11], and multi-feature queries [18]. Indeed, leveraging such a well-developed technology can greatly facilitate and speed up network data analysis.

A serious impediment to the use of current-day OLAP tools for analyzing network trace data is that the tools require all the data to be available in a single, centralized data warehouse. The inherently distributed nature of data collection (e.g., flow-level statistics are gathered at network routers, spread throughout the network) and the huge amount of data extracted at each collection point (of the order of several gigabytes per day for large IP networks), make it impractical to gather all this data at a single centralized data warehouse: for example, Feldmann et al. [10] report that use of a single centralized collection server for NetFlow data resulted in a loss of up to 90% of NetFlow tuples during heavy load periods!

The natural solution to this problem is to maintain a *distributed data warehouse*, where data gathered at each collection point (e.g., router) is maintained at a local data warehouse, adjacent to the collection point, to avoid loss of collected trace data. For such a solution to work, we need a technology for *distributed processing of complex OLAP queries* — something that does not yet exist. The goal of this paper is to take the first steps in this important direction.

1.1 Outline and Contributions

The rest of this paper is organized as follows. We first present related work in Sect. 1.2. In Sect. 2, we describe a motivating application and define the GMDJ operator for expressing OLAP queries. Our technical contributions are as follows:

- We present a general strategy for the distributed evaluation of OLAP queries, specified as GMDJ expressions, and present the Skalla system, developed by us for this task (Sect. 3).
- We develop and define optimization strategies for distributed OLAP that can exploit distribution knowledge, if known, as well as strategies that do not assume any such knowledge, to minimize both the synchronization traffic, and the local processing done at each site (Sect. 4).
- We conducted a series of experiments, based on TPC(R) data, to study the performance of the Skalla approach. Our results show the effectiveness of

our strategies for distributed OLAP query processing, and also quantify the performance benefits of our optimizations. This demonstrates the validity of the Skalla approach (Sect. 5).

While we illustrate our techniques using examples drawn from the network management application, our approach and results are more generally applicable to *distributed* data warehouses and OLAP query processing in other application domains as well (e.g., with heterogeneous data marts distributed across an enterprise). To the best of our knowledge, ours is the first paper on this important topic.

1.2 Related Work

The most closely related prior work is that of Shatdal and Naughton [19], who use a similar coordinator/sites model for the parallel evaluation of aggregates, and present various strategies where the aggregate computation is split between the sites and the coordinator, to optimize performance. Aggregates are also considered in a number of parallel database systems, such as in [3,4]. There are two main differences with our work. First, their results are tuned for a parallel computer, where communication is assumed to be very cheap, which is certainly not the case in our distributed data warehouse setting. Second, they deal only with the case of simple SQL aggregates, while we consider significantly more complex OLAP queries.

A variety of OLAP queries have been proposed in the literature, allowing a fine degree of control over both the group definition and the aggregates that are computed using operators such as cube by [12], unpivot [11], and other SQL extensions (e.g., [6]). Recently, Chatziantoniou et al. [7] proposed the MDJ operator for complex OLAP queries, which provides a clean separation between group definition and aggregate computation, allowing considerable flexibility in the expression of OLAP queries. The processing and optimization of these complex OLAP queries has received a great deal of attention in recent years (see, e.g., [1, 2, 7, 8, 12, 17, 18]), but it has all been in the context of a single centralized data warehouse. Our results form the basis for extending these techniques to the distributed case.

A considerable body of research has been performed for processing and optimizing queries over distributed data (see, e.g., [15, 16]). However, this research has focused on distributed join processing rather than distributed aggregate computation. The approach we explore in this paper uses an extended aggregation operator to express complex aggregation queries. Some of the distributed evaluation optimizations that we have developed resemble previously proposed optimizations, e.g. exploiting data distributions [15] or local reduction [20]. However, our architecture for evaluating distributed aggregation queries allows for novel optimizations not exploited by conventional algorithms for distributed processing.

2 Preliminaries

In this section, we give an example of an application area that motivates the use of distributed data warehouse techniques. We then define the GMDJ operator and demonstrate how the GMDJ operator allows us to uniformly express a variety of OLAP queries.

2.1 Motivating Example

Analysis of IP flow data is a compelling application that can tremendously benefit from distributed data warehouse technology. An IP flow is a sequence of packets transferred from a given source to a given destination (identified by an IP address, Port, and Autonomous system), using a given `Protocol`. All packets in a flow pass through a given router, which maintains summary statistics about the flow and which dumps out a tuple for each flow passing through it.

Data warehouses are typically modeled using, e.g., *star schemas* or *snowflake schemas* [14,8]. Our techniques are oblivious to which of these data warehouse models are used for conceptually modeling the data, and our results would hold in either model. For simplicity, in our examples the table `Flow` is a denormalized fact relation, with `NumPackets` and `NumBytes` as the measure attributes and with the following schema:

```
Flow ( RouterId, SourceIP, SourcePort, SourceMask, SourceAS, DestIP,
       DestPort, DestMask, DestAS, StartTime, EndTime, NumPackets,
       NumBytes )
```

We assume that flow tuples generated by a router are stored in a local data warehouse "adjacent" to the router, i.e., `RouterId` is a partition attribute. Each local warehouse is assumed to be fully capable of evaluating any complex OLAP query. We refer to this collection of local data warehouses (or sites), along with a coordinator site that correlates subquery results, as a *distributed data warehouse*.

2.2 GMDJ Expressions

The *GMDJ* operator is an OLAP operator that allows for the algebraic expression of many complex OLAP queries [2].

Let θ be a condition, b be a tuple, and R be a relation. We write $attr(\theta)$ to denote the set of attributes used in θ. $RNG(b, R, \theta) =_{\text{def}} \{r \mid r \in R \wedge \theta(b, r)\}$ denotes the set of tuples in R that satisfies θ, with respect to the tuple b. E.g., $RNG(b, R, b.A = R.B)$ denotes those tuples in R whose B-value matches the A-value of b. We use $\{\{\ldots\}\}$ to denote a multiset.

Definition 1. *Let $B(\mathbf{B})$ and $R(\mathbf{R})$ be relations, θ_i a condition with $attr(\theta_i) \subseteq \mathbf{B} \cup \mathbf{R}$, and l_i be a list of aggregate functions $(f_{i1}, f_{i2}, \ldots, f_{in_i})$ over attributes*

$c_{i1}, c_{i2}, \ldots, c_{in_i}$ in **R**. The GMDJ, $MD(B, R, (l_1, \ldots, l_m), (\theta_1, \ldots, \theta_m))$, is a relation with schema[1]

$$\mathbf{X} = (\mathbf{B}, f_{11}\_R\_c_{11}, \ldots, f_{1n}\_R\_c_{1n_1}, \ldots, f_{m1}\_R\_c_{m1}, \ldots, f_{mn}\_R\_c_{mn_m}),$$

whose instance is determined as follows. Each tuple $b \in B$ contributes to an output tuple **x**, such that:

- $\mathbf{x}[A] = b[A]$, for every attribute $A \in \mathbf{B}$
- $\mathbf{x}[f_{ij}\_R\_c_{ij}] = f_{ij}\{\{t[c_{ij}] \mid t \in RNG(b, R, \theta_i)\}\}$, for every attribute $f_{ij}\_R\_c_{ij}$ of **x**.

We call B the base-values relation and R the detail relation.

Usually, one can determine a subset K of key attributes of the base-values relation B for each θ_i, which uniquely determine a tuple in B (K can be **B**). We make use of key attributes in several of our strategies.

It should be noted that conventional SQL groupwise and hash-based aggregation techniques cannot be directly applied to GMDJ expressions, since the set of tuples in the detail relation R that satisfy condition θ with respect to tuples b_1 and b_2 of the base-values relation, i.e., $RNG(b_1, R, \theta)$ and $RNG(b_2, R, \theta)$, might not be disjoint. However, see [2, 7] for a discussion of how GMDJ expressions can be evaluated efficiently in a centralized system.

A GMDJ operator can be composed with other relational algebra operators (and other GMDJs) to create complex GMDJ expressions. While arbitrary expressions are possible, it is often the case that the result of a GMDJ expression serves as the base-values relation for another GMDJ operator. This is because the result of the GMDJ expression has exactly as many tuples as there are in the base-values relation B. In the rest of this paper, when we refer to (complex) GMDJ expressions, we mean only expressions where the result of an (inner) GMDJ is used as a base-values relation for an (outer) GMDJ.

Example 1. Given our IP Flows application, an interesting OLAP query might be to ask for the total number of flows, and the number of flows whose NumBytes (NB) value exceeds the average value of NumBytes, for each combination of source and destination autonomous system (e.g., to identify special traffic). This query is computed by the complex GMDJ expression given below.

MD(MD($\pi_{\text{SAS,DAS}}$(Flow)→B_0,
          Flow→F_0,
          (($cnt(*)$→$cnt1, sum(NB)$→$sum1$)),
          (F_0.SAS = B_0.SAS & F_0.DAS = B_0.DAS)
)→B_1,
      Flow→F_1,
      (($cnt(*)$→$cnt2$)),
      (F_1.SAS = B_1.SAS & F_1.DAS = B_1.DAS & F_1.NB ≥ sum1/cnt1)
)

---

[1] Attributes are appropriately renamed if there are any duplicate names generated this way. We note that the renaming scheme employed in the examples will use a shorthand form.

The flow data may or may not be clustered on SourceAS or DestAS. If it is not, the distributed evaluation of this query requires correlating aggregate data at multiple sites, and alternating evaluation (in multiple passes) at the sites and at the coordinator. We develop efficient evaluation strategies for both cases.

We call queries such as in Example 1 *correlated aggregate queries* since they involve computing aggregates w.r.t. a specified grouping and then computing further values (which may be aggregates) based on the previously computed aggregates. In general, there may be a chain of dependencies among the various (aggregate or otherwise) attributes computed by such a query. In Example 1, the length of this chain is two. Several examples involving correlated aggregates can be found in previous OLAP literature [7, 6, 11, 18].

It is possible to construct many different kinds of OLAP queries and identifying distributed evaluation strategies for each would be quite tedious. The GMDJ operator provides a clean separation between the definition of the groups and the definition of aggregates in an OLAP query. This allows us to express a significant variety of OLAP queries (enabled by disparate SQL extensions) in a uniform algebraic manner [2, 7]. Thus, it suffices to consider the distributed evaluation of GMDJ expressions, to capture most of the OLAP queries proposed in the literature.

3 Distributed GMDJ Evaluation

In this section, we will describe the distributed GMDJ evaluation algorithm implemented in the Skalla prototype. We defer the presentation of query optimizations of the core Skalla evaluation algorithm until the next section.

3.1 Skalla: An Overview

The Skalla system for distributed data warehousing is based on a coordinator architecture (i.e., strict client-server) as depicted in Fig. 1. It consists of multiple local data warehouses (Skalla sites) adjacent to data collection points, together with the Skalla coordinator (we note that the coordinator can be a single instance as in Fig. 1 or may consist of multiple instances, e.g., each client may have its own coordinator instance). Conceptually, the fact relation of our data warehouse is the *union* of the tuples captured at each data collection point. However, users can pose OLAP queries against the conceptual data model of our distributed data warehouse, without regard to the location of individual tuples at the various sites.

We define a *distributed evaluation plan* (*plan* for short) for our coordinator architecture as a sequence of rounds, where a round consists of: (i) each skalla site performing some computation and communicating the results to the coordinator, and (ii) the coordinator synchronizing the local results into a global result, and (possibly) communicating the global result back to the sites. Thus, the overall cost of a plan (in terms of response time) has many components:

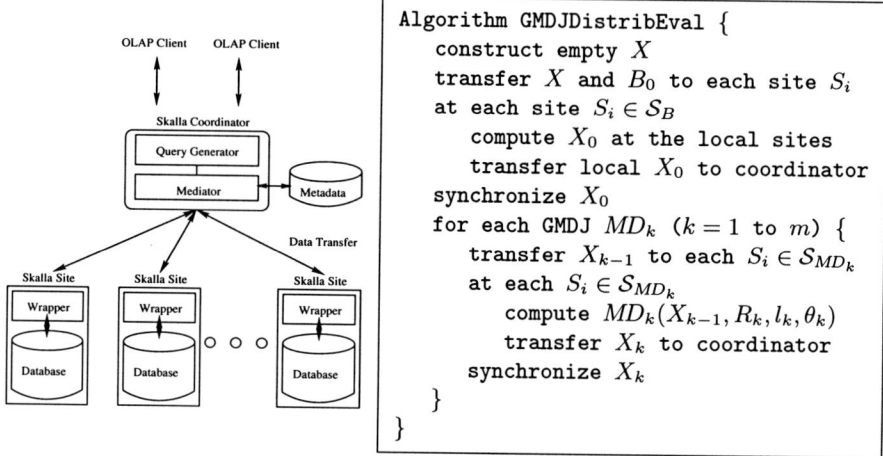

Fig. 1. Skalla architecture (left) and evaluation algorithm (right)

(i) communication (or, synchronization traffic), and (ii) computation (or, the query processing effort at the local sites as well as the coordinator).

The query generator of the Skalla system constructs query plans from the OLAP queries, which are then passed on to and executed by the mediator, using Alg. `GMDJDistribEval`.

3.2 Algorithm Description

We will now describe how Skalla works when receiving an OLAP query, using Example 1 to illustrate the Skalla evaluation.

First, the Skalla query engine uses *Egil*, a GMDJ query optimizer, to translate the OLAP query into GMDJ expressions. These GMDJ expressions are then optimized for distributed computation. We note that even simple GMDJ expressions can involve aggregation and multiple self-joins, which would be hard for a conventional centralized — let alone a distributed — query optimizer to handle. We defer a study of these optimizations to Sect. 4.

Alg. `GMDJDistribEval` gives an overview of the basic query evaluation strategy of Skalla for complex GMDJ expressions. Given the GMDJ query of Example 1, the coordinator will construct the empty *base-result structure* $X(\mathbf{X})$ with the schema:

$$\mathbf{X} = (\texttt{SourceAS}, \texttt{DestAS}, \texttt{count\_md1}, \texttt{sum\_md1\_numbytes}, \texttt{count\_md2})$$

The query $B_0 = \pi_{\texttt{SourceAS},\texttt{DestAS}}(\texttt{Flow})$ is then shipped to each of the sites, executed locally, and the result shipped back to the coordinator. During evaluation, the coordinator maintains the base-result structure by synchronization of the sub-results that it receives.

The term *synchronization* as used in this paper refers to the process of consolidating the results processed at the local sites into the base-results structure

X. We refer to each local-processing-then-synchronization step as a *round* of processing. An evaluation of a GMDJ expression involving m GMDJ operators uses $m + 1$ rounds. The notation X_k in Alg. `GMDJDistribEval` refers to the instance of X after the computation of the kth GMDJ, where we assume there are m rounds in all, m depending on the dependency chain in the original OLAP query. Aggregates of X are computed from the local aggregate values computed at the sites as appropriate. For example, to compute `count_md1`, we would need to compute the sum of the `COUNT(*)`s computed at the local sites. Following Gray et al. [12], we call the aggregates computed at the local sites the *sub-aggregates* and the aggregate computed at the coordinator the *super-aggregate*. S_B is the set of all local sites, while S_{MD_k} is set of local sites which participate in the kth round.[2] We use R_k to denote the detail relation at round k.[3] Again, depending on the query, the detail relation may or may not be the same across all rounds. This shows the considerable class of OLAP queries the basic Skalla evaluation framework is able to handle. In this paper, we give only examples where the detail relation does not change over rounds. Finally, l_k is the list of aggregate functions to be evaluated at round k and θ_k is the corresponding condition (see Definition 1).

The following theorem establishes the basis of the synchronization in Skalla:

Theorem 1. *Let $X = MD(B, R, (l_1, \ldots, l_m), (\theta_1, \ldots, \theta_m))$, where B has key attributes K. Let $R_1, \ldots, R_n$ be a partition of R. Let l'_j and l''_j be the lists of sub-aggregates and super-aggregates, respectively, corresponding to the aggregates in l_j. Let $H_i = MD(B, R_i, (l'_1, \ldots, l'_m), (\theta_1, \ldots, \theta_m))$ for $i = 1, \ldots, n$. Let $H = H_1 \sqcup \cdots \sqcup H_n$, where $\sqcup$ indicates multiset union. Then $X = MD(B, H, (l''_1, \ldots, l''_m), \theta_K)$ where θ_K is a test for equality on the attributes in K.*

In practice, the scheme given by Theorem 1 is executed very efficiently. The base-results structure maintained at the coordinator is indexed on K, which allows us to efficiently determine $RNG(X, t, \theta_K)$ for any tuple t in H and then update the structure accordingly; i.e., the synchronization can be computed in $\mathcal{O}(|H|)$. Since the GMDJ can be horizontally partitioned, the coordinator can synchronize H with those sub-results it has already received while receiving blocks of H from slower sites, rather than having to wait for all of H to be assembled before performing the synchronization. Between each computation at the local sites and synchronization, we ship the base-results structure (or fragments thereof) between the sites and the coordinator.

The following result bounds the maximum amount of data transferred during the evaluation of Alg. `GMDJDistribEval` for distributive aggregate queries.

Theorem 2. *Let the distributed data warehouse contain n sites, and the size of the result of query Q, expressed as a GMDJ expression with m GMDJ operators be $|Q|$. Let s_0 denote the number of sites participating in the computation of the*

---

[2] Typically, $S_{MD_k} = S_B$, but it is possible that $S_{MD_k} \subset S_B$.
[3] Note that every site refers to its local detail relation as R_k at round k. To avoid clutter, we preferred this notation to something like R_k^i.

base values relation and s_i the number of sites participating in the computation of the i'th GMDJ operator. Then the maximum amount of data transferred during the evaluation of Alg. `GMDJDistribEval` on Q is bounded by

$$\left(\sum_{i=1}^{n}(2*s_i*|Q|)\right) + (s_0*|Q|).$$

Recall that Alg. `GMDJDistribEval` only ships the base-result structure X_k. Since $X_k \subseteq Q$, it follows that the maximum size of any X_k is $|Q|$. The significance of Theorem 2 is that it provides a bound on the maximum amount of data transferred as a function of the size of the query result, the size of the query (i.e. number of rounds), and the number of local sites in the distributed data warehouse, which is *independent of the size of the fact relation in the database*. $|Q|$ depends only on the size of the base values relation and the aggregates to be computed, not the detail relation. This is significant in that such a bound does not hold for the distributed processing of traditional SQL join queries (see, for example, [15, 16]), where intermediate results can be arbitrarily larger than the final query result, even when using semijoin-style optimizations.

3.3 Summary

Let B_0 be the base-values relation, $R_1, R_2, \ldots, R_m$ be detail relations, $l_1, \ldots, l_m$ be lists of aggregate functions, and $\theta_1, \ldots, \theta_m$ be lists of conditions.[4] Let B_k denote the result of the GMDJ MD_k. Let $\mathcal{S}_B$ be the set of sites required for the computation of B_0, and let $\mathcal{S}_{MD_i}$ be the set of sites required for the computation of the GMDJ MD_i. Alg. `GMDJDistribEval` is a simple and efficient algorithm for distributed OLAP processing that does not transfer any detailed data between the sites.

Theorem 3. *Given a GMDJ expression* $Q = MD_n(\cdots(MD_1(B_0, R_1, (l_{11}, \ldots, l_{1k}), (\theta_{11}, \ldots, \theta_{1k}))\cdots), R_n, (l_{n1}, \ldots, l_{nm}), (\theta_{n1}, \ldots, \theta_{nm}))$, *the set of sites* $\mathcal{S}_B$ *required for computing* B_0, *and the sets of sites* $\mathcal{S}_{MD_i}, i \leq n$, *required for computing GMDJ* MD_i, *then Alg.* `GMDJDistribEval` *correctly computes the result of* Q.

While Alg. `GMDJDistribEval` is efficient in relation to the size of the detail relations, the amount of data transfer and the computation can still be objectionably large for very large distributed data warehouses and thus these resources need to be optimized substantially. This is the subject of Sect. 4.

4 Distributed Evaluation Optimizations

Clearly, query optimization techniques used for centralized evaluation of GMDJ expressions (e.g., indexing, coalescing), which have been previously studied [2, 7] apply in an orthogonal way to their distributed processing. Classical distributed

---
[4] l_i is a list of aggregates and θ_i is a list of grouping conditions for each of them.

query optimization techniques developed for SQL queries such as row blocking, optimization of multi-casts, horizontal partitioning of data, or semijoin programs [15] apply to the distributed processing of GMDJs. We do not dwell on these any further. In Sect. 4.1 we generalize local reductions to GMDJ expressions. Sections 4.2 and 4.3 describe optimizations specific to distributed GMDJ query processing.

It should be stressed that in each case, we present what are best characterized as optimization schemes. Depending on the specific situation (i.e. the amount of distribution knowledge available), one may be able to come up with specific optimization strategies, which are instances of these optimization schemes. In this sense, our optimization schemes can be used for determining whether a strategy is correct in the sense that it computes the right result. Throughout this section, we give examples which illustrate this point.

4.1 Distribution-Aware Group Reduction

Recall the definition of the function, $RNG(b, R, \theta) = \{r \in R \mid \theta(b, r) \text{ is true}\}$. Given information about the partitioning of tuples in the distributed data warehouse, we may be able reduce the size of the base-results structure transferred between the sites and the coordinator. The following theorem provides the basis for this optimization.

Theorem 4. *Consider the GMDJ expression $Q = MD(B, R, (l_1, \ldots, l_m), (\theta_1, \ldots, \theta_m))$. Let $R_1 \cup \cdots \cup R_n$ be a partitioning of the detail relation R. For each R_i, let ϕ_i be a predicate such that for each $r \in R_i$, $\phi_i(r)$ is true. Let $\psi_i(b)$ be the formula $\forall_r \phi_i(r) \Rightarrow \neg(\theta_1 \vee \ldots \vee \theta_m)(b, r)$. Let RNG_i be $RNG(b, R_i, \theta_1 \vee \ldots \vee \theta_m)$. Then, we have:*

$$\sigma_{|RNG_i|>0}(MD(B, R_i, (l_1, \ldots, l_m), (\theta_1, \ldots, \theta_m))) =$$
$$\sigma_{|RNG_i|>0}(MD(\sigma_{\neg \psi_i}(B), R_i, (l_1, \ldots, l_m), (\theta_1, \ldots, \theta_m)))$$

Using Alg. GMDJDistribEval, a local site will compute $H_i = MD(B, R_i, (l'_1, \ldots, l'_m), (\theta_1, \ldots, \theta_m))$. Let $\overline{B_i} = \{b \in B \mid \psi_i(b)\}$. Theorem 4 states that if we have a-priori knowledge about whether $RNG(b, R_i, \theta)$ is empty for any given b, we need to send to site S_i only $B - \overline{B_i}$. Given knowledge about the data distribution at the individual sites, group reductions can be performed by restricting B using the $\neg \psi_i$ condition.

Example 2. Assume that each of the packets for a specific SourceAS passes through a router with a specific RouterId. For example, site S_1 handles all and only autonomous systems with SourceAS between 1 and 25. The condition θ in the query of Example 1 contains the condition Flow.SourceAS = B.SourceAS. We can deduce that at S_1, $\psi_i(b)$ is true when $b.\text{SourceAS} \notin [1, 25]$. Therefore, $\neg \psi_i(b)$ is the condition $b.\text{SourceAS} \in [1, 25]$.

Example 2 gives a simple example of the kind of optimization possible using distribution-aware group reductions. The analysis is easy to perform if ψ_i and θ are conjunctive and the atoms of the predicates involve tests for equality.

In fact, far more complex constraints can be handled. For example, assume the condition θ in example 2 is revised to be $B.DestAS + B.SourceAS < Flow.SourceAS*2$. Then condition $\neg\psi_i(b)$ becomes $B.DestAS+B.SourceAS < 50$. The significance of Theorem 4 is that we can use it to determine the correctness of the optimizer.

Other uses of Theorem 4 are also possible. For example, SourceAS might not be partitioned among the sites, but any given value of SourceAS might occur in the Flow relation at only a few sites. Even in such cases, we would be able to further reduce the number of groups sent to the sites.

4.2 Distribution-Independent Group Reduction

A significant feature of the GMDJ processing, compared to traditional distributed algorithms, is the possibility of performing distribution-independent group reduction.

We extend Theorem 1 for distribution-independent group reduction:

Proposition 1. *Consider the GMDJ $Q = MD(B, R, (l_1, \ldots, l_m), (\theta_1, \ldots, \theta_m))$ where B has key attributes K. Let $R_1, \ldots, R_n$ be a partition of R. Let l'_i and l''_i be the lists of sub-aggregates and super-aggregates, respectively, corresponding to the aggregates in l_i. Then: $MD(B, R, (l_1, \ldots, l_m), (\theta_1, \ldots, \theta_m)) = MD(B, \sigma_{|RNG|>0} (MD(B, R_1, (l'_1, \ldots, l'_m), (\theta_1, \ldots, \theta_m))) \sqcup \cdots \sqcup \sigma_{|RNG|>0}(MD(B, R_n, (l'_1, \ldots, l'_m), (\theta_1, \ldots, \theta_m))), (l''_1, \ldots, l''_m), \theta_K)$ where $\sqcup$ indicates multiset union, and θ_K is a test for equality on the attributes in K.*

Let $H_1, H_2, \ldots, H_n$ be the results of processing the GMDJ expressions at the local sites. Then Proposition 1 states that the only tuples of H_i required for synchronization of the results are those tuples t such that $|RNG(t, R_i, (\theta_1 \vee \ldots \vee \theta_m))| > 0$, as otherwise the tuple does not contribute any information to the global aggregate. A simple way of detecting $|RNG| > 0$ with respect to tuples in H_i is to compute an additional aggregate $l_{m+1} = \text{COUNT}(*)$ on H_i such that $\theta_{m+1} = (\theta_1 \vee \ldots \vee \theta_m)$. The only overhead to this optimization then becomes the additional computing time for the extra COUNT(*), and to perform the selection COUNT(*)> 0 at the sites.

Example 3. We return to Example 1. The result of a GMDJ computation is transmitted to the coordinator by Alg. GMDJDistribEval. Assuming n sites, and that the size of the GMDJ is $|B|$, we transmit $n * |B|$ data. Assuming that each site, on average, computes aggregates for $1/k$ tuples in B, then distribution-independent group reduction will reduce the amount of data transmitted by each site to $|B|/k$ and the total data transmission to $n/k * |B|$.

An advantage of distribution-independent group reduction is that it improves performance even without semantic information about the distribution of R (which might not be available).

4.3 Synchronization Reduction

Synchronization reduction is concerned with reducing data transfer between the local sites and the coordinator by reducing the rounds of computation. One of the algebraic transformations possible on GMDJ operators is to coalesce two GMDJs into a single GMDJ. More precisely:

$$MD_2(MD_1(B, R, (l_{11}, \ldots, l_{1l}), (\theta_{11}, \ldots, \theta_{1l})), R, (l_{21}, \ldots, l_{2m}), (\theta_{21}, \ldots, \theta_{2m})) =$$
$$MD(B, R, (l_{11}, \ldots, l_{1l}, l_{21}, \ldots, l_{2m}), (\theta_{11}, \ldots, \theta_{1l}, \theta_{21}, \ldots, \theta_{2m}))$$

if the conditions $\theta_{21}, \ldots, \theta_{2m}$ do not refer to attributes generated by MD_1 [7].

However, in many instances the OLAP query may consist of only one or two simple GMDJ expressions. In this case, the advantage of the coalescing is limited, because we may still have to synchronize the base-results structure at the coordinator after its construction. We present two results specific to the distributed query processing of GMDJs, that permit synchronization reduction.

Proposition 2. *Consider the GMDJ $Q = MD(B, R, (l_1, \ldots, l_m), (\theta_1, \ldots, \theta_m))$. Let B be the result of evaluating query $\mathcal{B}$ on R, let $R_1, \ldots, R_n$ be a partition of R, and let B_i be the result of evaluating query $\mathcal{B}$ on R_i. Suppose that $B = \bigsqcup_i B_i$. Let B have key attributes K. If θ_j entails θ_K, the test for equality on the attributes in K, $\forall j | 1 \leq j \leq m$, then:*

$$MD(B, R, (l_1, \ldots, l_m), (\theta_1, \ldots, \theta_m)) = MD(\pi_B H, H, (l''_1, \ldots, l''_m), (\theta_K, \ldots, \theta_K))$$

where $H = \bigsqcup_i H_i$ and $H_i = MD(B_i, R_i, (l'_1, \ldots, l'_m), (\theta_1, \ldots, \theta_m))$.

Proposition 2 states that, if $\mathcal{B}$ is evaluated over the relation R and each condition tests for equality on the key attributes K, then we can omit the synchronization of the base-values relation.

Example 4. Consider again Example 1. Following Proposition 2, we can compute B_0 and the first GMDJ B_1 directly, instead of synchronizing in between the two computations as would otherwise be the case. Thus the number of synchronizations can be cut down from three to two, with a potential 40% reduction in the amount of data transferred.

Theorem 5. *Consider the GMDJ $Q = MD_2(MD_1(B, R, (l_{11}, \ldots, l_{1l}), (\theta_{11}, \ldots, \theta_{1l})), R, (l_{21}, \ldots, l_{2m}), (\theta_{21}, \ldots, \theta_{2m}))$. Let $R_1 \cup \cdots \cup R_n$ be a partitioning of the detail relation R. For each R_i, let ϕ_i be a predicate such that for each $r \in R_i$, $\phi_i(r)$ is true. Let $\psi_i^1(b)$ be the formula $\forall_r \phi_i(r) \Rightarrow \neg(\theta_{11} \vee \ldots \vee \theta_{1l})(b, r)$, and let $\psi_i^2(b)$ be the formula $\forall_r \phi_i(r) \Rightarrow \neg(\theta_{21} \vee \ldots \vee \theta_{2m})(b, r)$. Suppose that $\forall j (j \neq i) \Rightarrow (\psi_j^1(b) \;\&\; \psi_j^2(b))$. Then site i does not need to synchronize tuple b between the evaluation of MD_1 and MD_2.*

Theorem 5 states that it is not necessary to synchronize a tuple $b \in B$ if we know that the only site which updates b's aggregates during MD_1 and MD_2 is site i. If we have strong information about the distribution of R among the sites, we can avoid synchronizing between the evaluation of MD_1 and MD_2 altogether.

Definition 2. *An attribute A is a* partition attribute *iff:* $\forall_{i \neq j} \pi_A(\sigma_{\phi_i}(R)) \cap \pi_A(\sigma_{\phi_j}(R)) = \emptyset$

Corollary 1. *Consider the GMDJ $Q = MD_2(MD_1(B, R, (l_{11}, \ldots, l_{1l}), (\theta_{11}, \ldots, \theta_{1l})), R, (l_{21}, \ldots, l_{2m}), (\theta_{21}, \ldots, \theta_{2m}))$. If $\theta_{11}, \ldots, \theta_{1l}, \theta_{21}, \ldots, \theta_{2m}$ all entail condition $R.A = f(A)$, where $f(A)$ is a bijective function on A, and A is a partition attribute, then MD_2 can be computed after MD_1 without synchronizing between the GMDJs.*

Thus, by performing a simple analysis of ϕ_i and θ, we are able to identify a significant subset of queries where synchronization reduction is possible. We note that more than one attribute can be a partition attribute, e.g., if a partition attribute is functionally determined by another attribute.

Example 5. Consider the query of Example 1. Without any synchronization reduction, the evaluation of this GMDJ expression would require multiple passes over the `Flow` relation, and three synchronizations, one for the base-values relation and one each for the results of the two GMDJs is required.

Let us assume that all packets from any given `SourceAS` only pass through a router with a particular `RouterId`. If this is the case, `SourceAS` is a partition attribute. Using Corollary 1, the second synchronization is avoided. Further, since (`SourceAS`, `DestAS`) form a key, Proposition 2 is applicable as well, and no synchronization of the base-values relation is needed. As a result, the query can be evaluated against the distributed data warehouse with *the entire query being evaluated locally, and with a single synchronization at the coordinator*.

Synchronization reduction is a distinctive feature of distributed GMDJ processing, which is difficult or impossible to duplicate using traditional distributed query optimizations methods. In addition, it is a key factor in keeping the distributed processing of OLAP queries scalable, as we shall show in Sect. 5.

5 Experimental Evaluation

In this section, we describe a set of experiments to study the performance of Skalla. We show the scalability of our strategies and also quantify the performance benefits of our optimizations.

5.1 Setup and Data

We used Daytona [13] as the target DBMS for GMDJ expression evaluation in Skalla, both for the local data warehouse sites and the coordinator site. We derived a test database from the TPC(R) `dbgen` program, creating a denormalized 900 Mbyte data set with 6 million tuples (named TPCR). We partitioned the data set on the `NationKey` attribute (and therefore also on the `CustKey` attribute). The partitions were then distributed among eight sites.

In each of our test queries, we compute a `COUNT` and an `AVG` aggregate on each GMDJ operator. We ran two different experiments with different attributes of the TPCR relation as the grouping attribute. The first set of experiments (high cardinality) use the Customer.Name attribute, which has 100,000 unique values partitioned among eight sites. The second set of experiments (low cardinality) uses attributes with between 2000 to 4000 unique values. For the following experiments, we examine only group reduction, synchronization reduction, and combined reductions.

5.2 Speed-up Experiments

In this section, we divide the TPCR relation equally among eight sites, and vary the number of sites participating in the evaluation of a query. We use this experimental setup to evaluate the impact of the various optimizations.

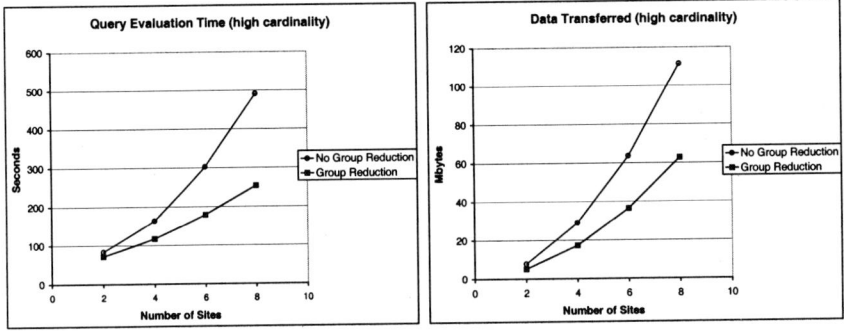

Fig. 2. Group reduction query

Figure 2 depicts graphs showing the query evaluation time (left) and the amount of data transferred for distribution-independent group-reduced and the non group-reduced versions of the group reduction query (right). The set of non group-reduced curves shows a quadratic increase in query evaluation time and in the number of bytes transferred. This behavior is due to a linearly increasing number of groups being sent to a linearly increasing number of sites; thus the communication overhead and synchronization overhead increases quadratically. When group reduction is applied, the curves are still quadratic, but to a lesser degree. The distribution-independent (i.e., site side) group reduction solves half of the inefficiency, as the sites send a linear amount of data to the coordinator, but the coordinator sends a quadratic amount of data to the sites. Distribution-aware (i.e., coordinator side) group reduction would make the curves linear.

To see this, we perform an analysis of the number of bytes transferred. Let the number of groups residing on a single site be g, the number of sites be n, and the fraction of sites' group aggregates updated during the evaluation of a grouping variable be c. In the first round, ng groups are sent from the sites to the coordinator. Without group reduction, n^2g groups are sent from the coordinator to the sites, and n^2g groups are sent back. With group reduction, only cng

groups are returned. Therefore, the proportion of groups transferred with group reduction versus without group reduction is $(ng(2c+1+2n))/(ng(4n+1)) = (2c+2n+1)/(4n+1)$. The number of bytes transferred is roughly proportional to the number of groups transferred, and in fact this formula matches the experimental results to within 5%.

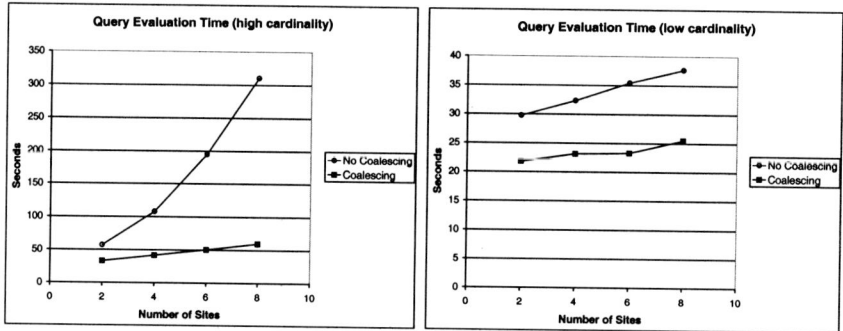

Fig. 3. Coalescing query

Figure 3 shows the evaluation time of the coalesced and non coalesced query for high cardinality (left) and low cardinality (right) queries. The non coalesced curve in the high cardinality query shows a quadratic increase in execution time. The coalesced GMDJ curve is linear. There is only one evaluation round, at the end of which the sites send their results to the coordinator, so the volume of data transferred increases linearly with the number of sites. For the low cardinality query the difference is less dramatic. Even though the amount of data transferred is small, coalescing reduces query evaluation time by 30%, primarily due to a reduction in the site computation time.

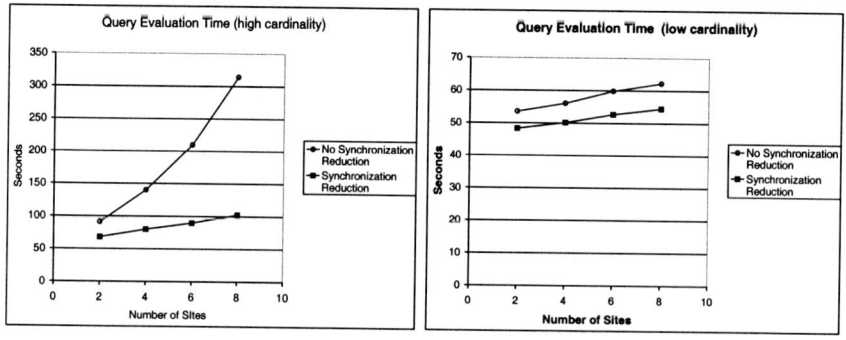

Fig. 4. Synchronization reduction query

Finally, we test the effect of synchronization reduction without coalescing. Figure 4 shows the query evaluation time of the an OLAP query evaluated with and without synchronization reduction for the high cardinality (left) and low cardinality (right) versions of the query. Without synchronization reduction in the high cardinality query, the query evaluation time is quadratic with an increasing number of sites. With synchronization reduction, the query is evaluated in a single round, and shows a linear growth in evaluation time (due to the linearly increasing size of the output). Thus, synchronization reduction removes the inefficiencies (due to attribute partitioning) seen in the previous experiments. For the low cardinality query, synchronization reduction without coalescing reduces the query evaluation time, but not to the same degree achieved with coalescing of GMDJs on the high cardinality query. This is because coalescing improves computation time as well as reducing communication; thus the work performed by the sites is nearly the same, and the difference in query evaluation time only represents the reduction in synchronization overhead.

5.3 Scale-up Experiments

In this section, we fix the number of sites at four, and vary the data set size at each of these sites. We start with the data set used in the speed-up experiments and increase its size by up to a factor of four. We used the combined reductions query, and applied either all of the reductions or none of them.

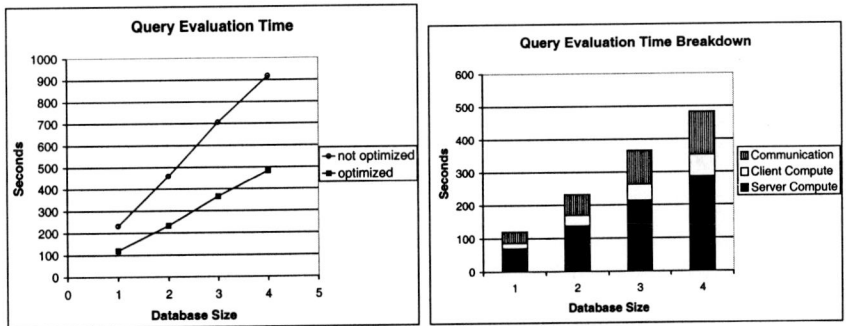

Fig. 5. Combined reductions query

In our first set of experiments, the number of groups increased linearly with the data set size. The graph in Fig. 5 (left) shows the query evaluation time when the optimizations are turned on or off. In both cases there is a linear increase in query evaluation time with increasing database size. Using the optimizations improved the query evaluation time by nearly half. The bar graph of Fig. 5 (right) breaks down the evaluation time of the optimized query into the site computation time, coordinator computation time, and communication overhead, showing linear growth in each component. We ran the same set of experiments using a data set in which the number of groups remains constant with an increasing database size, and obtained comparable results.

5.4 Summary

For many queries (e.g., with a moderate number of groups), distributed OLAP evaluation is effective and scalable (see, e.g., Fig. 3). The optimizations discussed in this paper are effective in reducing query evaluation time by a large fraction (see, e.g., Fig. 5).

Distributed OLAP faces a scalability problem when a partition attribute is used as one of the grouping attributes, leading to a quadratic increase in query evaluation time with a linearly increasing number of sites. Most of the work is wasted as the sites do not have tuples for most of the groups sent to them. Two of the optimizations we have considered in this paper are effective in eliminating this inefficiency. Group reduction (both at the coordinator and at the sites) reduces the data traffic (and thus the query evaluation time) from quadratic to linear. Synchronization reduction further takes advantage of the partition attribute by eliminating much of the data traffic altogether.

6 Conclusions

In this paper, we have developed a framework for evaluating complex OLAP queries on distributed data warehouses. We build efficient query plans using GMDJ expressions, which allow the succinct expression of a large class of complex multi-round OLAP queries. In our distributed OLAP architecture, a coordinator manages, collects and correlates aggregate results from the distributed warehouse sites.

The use of GMDJ expressions allows us to avoid complex distributed join optimization problems. However, query plans involving GMDJ operators also require optimization for best performance. We show a collection of novel GMDJ transformations which allow us to minimize the cost of computation and of communication between the sites and the coordinator.

We built Skalla, a distributed OLAP system which implements the distributed OLAP architecture. Skalla also implements most of the optimizations discussed in this paper. We ran a collection of experiments, and found that the optimizations lead to a scalable distributed OLAP system.

The results we present in this paper are the first steps in the exploration of research issues in the important area of distributed OLAP. Future research topics could include the exploration of alternative architectures (e.g., a multi-tiered coordinator architecture or spanning-tree networks) and additional query optimization strategies.

References

1. S. Agarwal, R. Agrawal, P. M. Deshpande, A. Gupta, J. F. Naughton, R. Ramakrishnan, and S. Sarawagi. On the computation of multidimensional aggregates. In *Proc. of the Int. Conf. on Very Large Databases*, pages 506–521, 1996.
2. M. O. Akinde, and M. H. Böhlen. Generalized MD-joins: Evaluation and reduction to SQL. In *Databases in Telecommunications II*, pages 52–67, Sept. 2001.
3. D. Bitton, H. Boral, D. J. DeWitt, and W. K. Wilkinson. Parallel algorithms for the executions of relational database operations. *ACM TODS* 8(3):324-353, 1983.
4. H. Boral, W. Alexander, L. Clay, G. Copeland, S. Danforth, M. Franklin, B. Hart, M. Smith, and P. Valduriez. Prototyping Bubba, a highly parallel database system. *IEEE TKDE* 2(1), March 1990
5. R. Cáceres, N. Duffield, A. Feldmann, J. Friedmann, A. Greenberg, R. Greer, T. Johnson, C. Kalmanek, B. Krishnamurthy, D. Lavelle, P. Mishra, K. K. Ramakrishnan, J. Rexford, F. True, and J. van der Merwe. Measurement and analysis of IP network usage and behavior. *IEEE Communications Magazine*, May 2000.
6. D. Chatziantoniou. Ad hoc OLAP: Expression and evaluation. In *Proc. of the IEEE Int. Conf. on Data Engineering*, 1999.
7. D. Chatziantoniou, M. O. Akinde, T. Johnson, and S. Kim. The MD-join: An operator for complex OLAP. In *Proc. of the IEEE Int. Conf. on Data Engineering*, 2001.
8. S. Chaudhuri and U. Dayal. An overview of data warehousing and OLAP technology. *SIGMOD Record*, 26(1):65–74, Mar. 1997.
9. R. Elmasri and S. B. Navathe. *Fundamentals of Database Systems*. Benjamin/Cummings Publishers, second edition, 1994.
10. A. Feldmann, A. Greenberg, C. Lund, N. Reingold, J. Rexford, and F. True. Deriving traffic demands for operational IP networks: Methodology and experience. In *Proc. of ACM SIGCOMM*, 2000.
11. G. Graefe, U. Fayyad, and S. Chaudhuri. On the efficient gathering of sufficient statistics for classification from large SQL databases. In *Proc. of Int. Conf. on Knowledge Discovery and Data Mining*, pages 204–208, 1998.
12. J. Gray, S. Chaudhuri, A. Bosworth, A. Layman, D. Reichart, M. Venkatrao, F. Pellow, and H. Pirahesh. Datacube : A relational aggregation operator generalizing group-by, cross-tab, and sub-totals. *Data Mining and Knowledge Discovery*, 1(1):29–53, 1997.
13. R. Greer. Daytona and the fourth-generation language Cymbal. In *Proc. of the ACM SIGMOD Conf. on Management of Data*, pages 525–526, 1999.
14. R. Kimball. *The data warehouse toolkit*. John Wiley, 1996.
15. D. Kossman The state of the art in distributed query processing. *ACM Computing Surveys*, 32(4):422–469, 2000.
16. M. T. Özsu and P. Valduriez. *Principles of Distributed Database Systems*. Prentice Hall, 1991.
17. K. A. Ross and D. Srivastava. Fast computation of sparse datacubes. In *Proc. of the Int. Conf. on Very Large Databases*, pages 116–125, 1997.
18. K. A. Ross, D. Srivastava, and D. Chatziantoniou. Complex aggregation at multiple granularities. In *Proc. of the Int. Conf. on Extending Database Technology*, pages 263–277, 1998.
19. A. Shatdal and J. F. Naughton. Adaptive parallel aggregation algorithms. In *Proc. of the ACM SIGMOD Conf. on Management of Data*, pages 104–114, 1995.
20. C. T. Yu, K. C. Guh, and A. L. P. Chen. An integrated algorithm for distributed query processing. In *Proc. of the IFIP Conf. on Distributed Processing*, 1987.

Incremental Maintenance of Schema-Restructuring Views*

Andreas Koeller and Elke A. Rundensteiner

Department of Computer Science
Worcester Polytechnic Institute
Worcester, MA 01609-2280
{koeller|rundenst}@cs.wpi.edu

Abstract. An important issue in data integration is the integration of semantically equivalent but schematically heterogeneous data sources. Declarative mechanisms supporting powerful source restructuring for such databases have been proposed in the literature, such as the SQL extension *SchemaSQL*. However, the issue of incremental maintenance of views defined in such languages remains an open problem.

We present an incremental view maintenance algorithm for schema-restructuring views. Our algorithm transforms a source update into an incremental view update, by propagating updates through the operators of a *SchemaSQL* algebra tree. We observe that schema-restructuring view maintenance requires transformation of data into schema changes and vice versa. Our maintenance algorithm handles any combination of data updates or schema changes and produces a correct sequence of data updates, schema changes, or both as output. In experiments performed on our prototype implementation, we find that incremental view maintenance in *SchemaSQL* is significantly faster than recomputation in many cases.

1 Introduction

Information sources, especially on the Web, are increasingly independent from each other, being designed, administered and maintained by a multitude of autonomous data providers. Nevertheless, it becomes more and more important to integrate data from such sources [13, 11]. Issues in data integration include the heterogeneity of data and query models across different sources, called model heterogeneity [3] and incompatibilities in schematic representations of different sources even when using the same data model, called schema heterogeneity [13, 11]. Much work on these problems has dealt with the integration of schematically different sources under the assumption that all "data" is stored in tuples and all "schema" is stored in attribute and relation names. We now relax

---

* This work was supported in part by several grants from NSF, namely, the NSF NYI grant #IRI 97-96264, the NSF CISE Instrumentation grant #IRIS 97-29878, and the NSF grant #IIS 99-88776.

this assumption and focus on the integration of heterogeneous sources under the assumption that schema elements may express data and vice versa.

One recent promising approach at overcoming such schematic heterogeneity are *schema-restructuring query languages*, such as *SchemaSQL*, an SQL-extension devised by Lakshmanan et al. [11, 12]. Other proposals include IDL by Krishnamurthy et al. [9] and HiLog [2]. These languages, in particular *Schema-SQL*, support querying schema (such as lists of attribute or relation names) in SQL-like queries and also to use sets of values obtained from *data tuples* as *schema* in the output relation. This extension leads to more powerful query languages, effectively achieving a transformation of semantically equivalent but syntactically different schemas [11] into each other.

Previous work on integration used either SQL-views, if the underlying schema agreed with what was needed in the view schema [14], or translation programs written in a programming language to reorganize source data [3]. We propose to use *views* defined in schema-restructuring languages in a way analogous to SQL-views. This makes it possible to include a larger class of information sources into an information system using a query language as the integration mechanism. This concept is much simpler and more flexible than ad-hoc "wrappers" that would have to be implemented for each data source. It is also possible to use or adapt query optimization techniques for such an architecture.

However, such an integration strategy raises the issue of maintaining schema-restructuring views, which is an open problem. As updates occur frequently in any database system, view maintenance is an important topic [1]. View maintenance in a restructuring view is different from SQL view maintenance, due to the disappearance of the distinction between data and schema, leading to new classes of updates and update transformations. In this paper, we present the first incremental maintenance strategy for a schema-restructuring view language, using *SchemaSQL* as an example.

1.1 Motivating Example

Consider the two relational schemas in Fig. 1 that are able to hold the same information and can be mapped into each other using *SchemaSQL* queries. The view query restructures the input relations on the left side representing airlines into attributes of the output relations on the right side representing destinations. The *arrow*-operator (->) attached to an element in the FROM-clause of a *Schema-SQL*-query allows to query schema elements, giving *SchemaSQL* its meta-data restructuring power. Standing by itself, it refers to "all relation names in that database", while attached to a relation name it means "all attribute names in that relation".

SchemaSQL is also able to transform data into schema. For example, *data* from the attribute Destination in the input schema is transformed into *relation names* in the output schema, and vice versa *attribute names* in the input (Business and Economy) are restructured into *data*.

Now consider an update to one of the base relations in our example. Let a tuple t(Destination $\Rightarrow$ Berlin, Business $\Rightarrow$ 1400, Economy $\Rightarrow$ 610) be added to

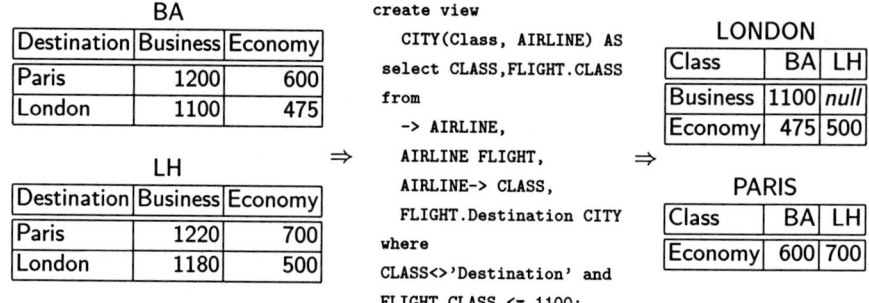

Fig. 1. A Schema-Restructuring Query in *SchemaSQL*.

the base table **LH** (a **data update**). The change to the output would be the addition of a new relation Berlin (a **schema change**) with the same schema as the other two relations. This new relation would contain one tuple t(Type $\Rightarrow$ Economy, BA $\Rightarrow$ null, LH $\Rightarrow$ 610). In this example, a data update is transformed into a schema change, but all other combinations are also possible. The effect of the propagation of an update in such a query depends on numerous factors, such as the input schema, the view definition, the set of unique values in the attribute **Destination** across *all* input relations (city names), and the set of input relations (airline codes). For example, the propagation would also depend on whether other airlines offer a flight to Berlin in the Economy-class, since in that case the desired view relation already exists.

1.2 Contributions

We propose to use schema-restructuring *query* languages to define *views* over relational sources and we solve several new problems that arise, using *SchemaSQL* as an example. We observe that, due to the possible transformation of "schema" into "data" and vice-versa, we must not only consider data updates (DUs) for *SchemaSQL*, but also schema changes (SCs). A consequence is that, as shown in this paper, using the standard approach of generating query expressions that compute some kind of "delta" relation Δ between the old and the new view after an update is not sufficient, since the schema of Δ would not be defined. Our algorithm in fact transforms an incoming (schema or data) update into a sequence of schema changes and/or data updates on the view extent.

The contributions of this work are as follows: (1) we identified the new problem of schema-restructuring view maintenance, (2) we gave an algebra-based solution to the problem, (3) we proved this approach correct, (4) we implemented a prototype and assessed performance experimentally.

This work is different from previous approaches in view maintenance since the problem of view maintenance of schema-restructuring views is fundamentally different from the traditional view maintenance problem, as we argue in Sec. 3.2.

1.3 Outline of Paper

Section 2 reviews some background on *SchemaSQL*, in particular the algebra operators used in *SchemaSQL* evaluation. Section 3 explains our view maintenance strategy and Section 4 gives an outline of a proof for our approach. Finally, Sections 5 and 6 give related work and conclusions, respectively.

2 Background

2.1 *SchemaSQL*

In relational databases it is possible to store equivalent data in different schemas that are incompatible when queried in SQL [13]. However, for information integration purposes it is desirable to combine data from such heterogeneous schemas. *SchemaSQL* is an SQL derivative designed by Lakshmanan et al. [11] which can be used to achieve schema-restructuring transformations of relational databases. In [12], Lakshmanan et al. describe an extended algebra and algebra execution strategies to implement a *SchemaSQL* query evaluation system. It extends the standard SQL algebra which uses operators such as $\sigma(R)$, $\pi(R)$, and $R \bowtie S$ by adding four operators named UNITE, FOLD, UNFOLD, and SPLIT originally introduced by Gyssens et al. [6] as part of their "Tabular Algebra". Lakshmanan et al. show that any *SchemaSQL* query can be translated into this extended algebra.

***SchemaSQL* Algebra Operators.** We will give an overview over the four operators introduced in [12]. Due to space consideration, we will not give precise mathematical definitions but rather refer to our Technical Report [8]. Additionally, Lakshmanan's original definition has a slight ambiguity in the FOLD/UNFOLD-operator pair that we clarified below. The original SchemaSQL proposal can be supported as well, with slight changes in the update propagation scheme.

Examples for the four operators defined in this section can be found in Fig. 2. We will refer to the input relation of each operator as R and to the output relation as Q.

The Unite-Operator is defined on a set of k relations $R^* = \{R_1, \ldots, R_k\}$ with attribute name a_p as an argument. The operator assumes input relations with identical schema and has as output one new relation Q. Q is constructed by taking the union of all input relations and adding a new attribute A_p whose values are the *relation names* of the input relations. In Fig. 2, the UNITE-operator is defined over the set of relations BA, LH and has the attribute name Airline as its argument.

The Fold-Operator works on a relation R in which a set of attributes must have the same domain. We denote the set of names of these attributes as $A^* = \{a_1, \ldots, a_n\}$. The operator takes as arguments the *names* of the pivot and data attributes a_p and a_d in its output relation. Furthermore, we require the attribute set A^* to satisfy a uniqueness constraint in order to avoid ambiguities in the operator (this requirement is not explicit in [12]).

The operator then takes all data values from the set A^* of related attributes, and sorts them into *one* new attribute a_d, introducing another new attribute a_p that holds the former attribute names. To motivate the above uniqueness constraint, note that its violation would require us to introduce multiple tuples in the output relation that differ only in their attribute a_d. The semantics of such tuples are not clear in a real-world application.

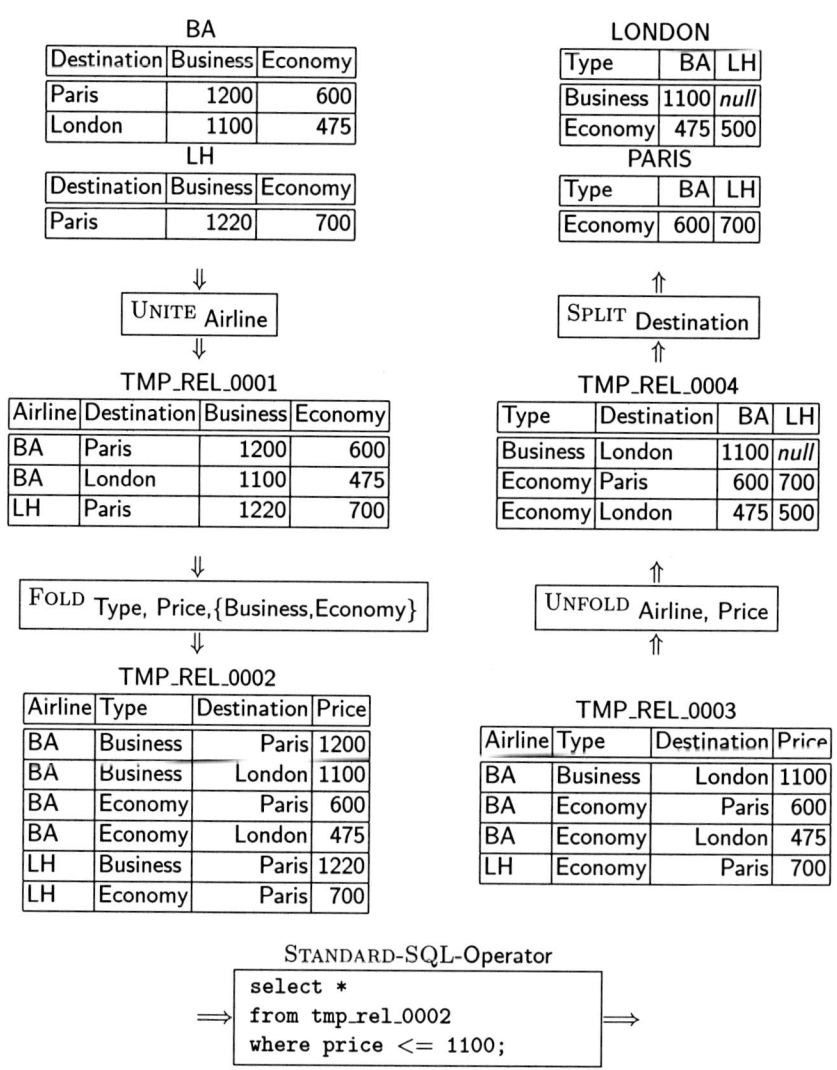

Fig. 2. An Example Using All Four *SchemaSQL* Operators UNITE, FOLD, UNFOLD, SPLIT.

In Fig. 2, the FOLD-operator is defined on relation TMP_REL_0001 and has the arguments $a_p = $ Type, $a_d = $ Price, $A^* = $ {Business, Economy}.

The Unfold-Operator is the inverse of FOLD. It is defined on a relation R and takes two attribute names a_p, a_d from R as arguments. We call A_p the *pivot attribute* and A_d the *data attribute*. We also define A^* as the set of distinct values in A_p.

The schema of Q then consists of all attributes in R except the data and pivot attribute, plus one attribute for each distinct data value in the pivot attribute. Each tuple t' in Q is constructed by taking a tuple t in R and filling each new attribute A_i with the value from attribute A_d in a tuple from R that has the name a_i as value in A_p (assuming an implicit conversion between names and values as required above). The new attributes all have the domain D_d of the old attribute A_d.

In Fig. 2, the UNFOLD-operator is defined over relation TMP_REL_0003 and takes as its arguments $a_p = $ Airline and $a_d = $ Price. The operator produces output by taking tuples from TMP_REL_0003, and filling the attributes representing airlines with values from the data attribute Price in TMP_REL_0003, matching attribute names in the output relation with the values of the pivot attribute Airline in the input relation.

The Split-Operator is the inverse of the UNITE-operator. It takes as its argument the attribute name a_p. We define A^* as the set of unique values in A_p, similar to the UNFOLD-case. SPLIT then transforms a single relation R into a *set* of $k = |A_p|$ relations with the schema of R except for the pivot attribute A_p. We require that A_p does not have NULL-values. SPLIT then breaks relation R into k relations with the same schema, with the new relation names the k distinct values from R's attribute A_p.

In Fig. 2, the SPLIT-operator is defined over relation TMP_REL_0004, takes as its only argument $a_p = $ Destination, and produces 2 tables names LONDON and PARIS.

SchemaSQL **Query Evaluation.** Similar to traditional SQL evaluation, [12] proposes a strategy for *SchemaSQL* query evaluation that first constructs and then processes an algebra query tree, leading to an efficient implementation of *SchemaSQL* query evaluation over an SQL database system. In order to evaluate a *SchemaSQL* query, an algebra expression using standard relational algebra plus the four operators introduced above is constructed. This expression is of the following form [12]:

$$V = \text{SPLIT}_a(\text{UNFOLD}_{b,c}(\pi_{\bar{d}}(\sigma_{cond}(\text{FOLD}_{e_1,f_1,\bar{g}_1}(\text{UNITE}_h(R_1)) \times \ldots \times \quad (1)$$
$$\text{FOLD}_{e_m,f_m,\bar{g}_m}(\text{UNITE}_h(R_m))))))$$

with attribute names a, b, c, e_i, f_i, h_i, the sets of attribute names $\bar{d}$ and $\bar{g}_i$, and selection predicates *cond* determined by the query. Any of the four *SchemaSQL* operators may not be needed for a particular query and would then be omitted from the expression. $R_1 \ldots R_m$ are base relations or, in the case that the expression contains a UNITE-operator, sets of relations with equal schema.

The algebraic expression for our running example (Fig. 1) is:

$$V = \text{SPLIT}_{\text{Destination}}(\text{UNFOLD}_{\text{Airline,Price}}(\sigma_{\text{Price}<1100}(\quad (2)$$
$$\text{FOLD}_{\text{Type, Price, \{Business,Economy\}}}(\text{UNITE}_{\text{Airline}}(\text{BA,LH})))))$$

This algebraic expression is then used to construct an algebra tree whose nodes are any of the four *SchemaSQL* operators or a "Standard-SQL"-operator (including the π, σ, and ×-operators of the algebra expression) with standard relations "traveling" along its edges. The query is then evaluated by traversing the algebra tree and executing a query processing strategy for each operator, analogous to traditional SQL query evaluation.

3 The *SchemaSQL* Update Propagation Strategy

3.1 Classes of Updates and Transformations

The updates that can be propagated through *SchemaSQL* views can be grouped into two categories: *Schema Changes (SC)* and *Data Updates (DU)*. Schema changes are: *add-relation(n, S)*, *delete-relation(n)*, *rename-relation(n, n′)* with relation names n, n' and schema S and *add-attribute(r, a)*, *delete-attribute(r, a)*, *rename-attribute(r, a, a′)* with r the name of the relation R that the attribute named a belongs to, a' the new attribute name in the rename-case, and the notation otherwise as above. Data updates are any changes affecting a tuple (and not the schema of the relation), i.e., *add-tuple(r,t)*, *delete-tuple(r,t)*, *update-tuple(r,t,t′))*, with t and t' tuples in relation R with name r. Note that we consider *update-tuple* as a basic update type, instead of breaking it down into a *delete-tuple* and an *add-tuple*. An *update-tuple* update consists of two tuples, one representing an existing tuple in R and the other representing the values of that tuple after the update. This allows to keep relational integrity constraints valid that would otherwise be violated temporarily.

3.2 *SchemaSQL* Update Propagation vs. Relational View Maintenance

Update propagation in *SchemaSQL*-views, as in any other view environment, consists in recording updates that occur in the input data and translating them into updates to the view extent. In incremental view maintenance for SQL [16, 5], many update propagation mechanisms have been proposed. Their common feature is that the new view extent is obtained by first computing *extent differences* between the old view V and the new view V' and then adding them to or subtracting them from the view, i.e., $V' = (V \setminus \nabla V) \cup \Delta V$, with ∇V denoting some set of tuples computed from the base relations that needs to be deleted from the view and ΔV some set that needs to be added to the view [16].

In *SchemaSQL*, this mechanism leads to difficulties. If *SchemaSQL* views must propagate both schema *and* data updates, the schema of ΔV or ∇V does not necessarily agree with the schema of the output relation V. But even when considering only data updates to the base relations, the new view V' may have a different schema than V. That means the concept of set difference between the tuples of V' and V is not even meaningful. Thus, we must find a way to incorporate the concept of schema changes. For this purpose, we now introduce a data structure ∂ which represents a sequence of n data updates DU and schema changes SC.

Definition 1 (defined update). *Assume two sets DU and SC which represent all possible data updates and schema changes, respectively. A change $c \in DU \cup SC$ is **defined (or valid)** on a given relation R if one of the following conditions holds:*

- *if $c \in DU$, the schema of the tuple added or deleted must be equal to the schema of R.*
- *if $c \in SC$, the object c is applied to (an attribute or relation) must exist (for delete- and update-changes) or must not exist (for add-changes) in R.*

Definition 2 (valid update sequence). *A sequence of updates $(c_1, \ldots, c_n)$ with $c_i \in DU \cup SC$, denoted by ∂R, is called **valid for** R if for all i $(1 < i \leq n)$, c_i is defined on the relation $R^{(i-1)}$ obtained by applying $c_1, \ldots, c_{i-1}$ to R.*

For simplicity, we will also use the notation $\partial \omega$ to refer to a valid update sequence to the output table of an algebra operator ω. Note that these definitions naturally extend to views, since views can also be seen as relational schemas. For an example, consider propagation of update add-tuple('Berlin',1400,610) to LH in Fig. 4 (p. 364). Having the value Berlin in the update tuple will lead to the addition of a new relation BERLIN in the output schema of the view—forming a sequence ∂V which contains both a schema change and a data update:

$$\partial V = (\textit{add-relation}(\text{BERLIN}, (\text{Type,Destination,BA,LH})),$$
$$\textit{add-tuple}(\text{BERLIN}, (\text{'Economy',null,610})))$$

The *add-relation*-update is valid since the relation BERLIN did not exist in the output schema before, and the *add-tuple*-update is valid since its schema agrees with the schema of relation BERLIN defined by the previous update.

3.3 Overall Propagation Strategy

Given an *update sequence* implemented by a List data structure, our update propagation strategy works according to the algorithm in Fig. 3. Each node in the algebra tree has knowledge about the operator it represents. This operator is able to accept *one* input update and will generate a sequence of updates as output. Each (leaf node) operator can also recognize whether it is affected by an update (by comparing the relation(s) on which the update is defined with its own input relation(s)). If it is not affected, it simply returns an empty update sequence.

```
function propagateUpdate(Node n, Update u)
    List r ← ∅, s ← ∅
    if (n is leaf)
        if (n.operator is affected by u)
            r.append(n.operator.operatorPropagate(u))
    else
        for(all children c_i of n)
            /* s will change exactly once, see text */
            s.append(propagateUpdate(c_i, u))
        for(all updates u_i in s)
            r.append(n.operator.operatorPropagate(u_i))
    return r
```

Fig. 3. The *SchemaSQL* View Maintenance Algorithm

After all the updates for the children of a node n are computed and collected in a list (variable s in the algorithm in Fig. 3), they are propagated one-by-one through n. Each output update generated by the operator of n when processing an input update will be placed into one update sequence, all of which are concatenated into the final return sequence r (see Fig. 3, ← is the assignment operator).

The algorithm performs a postorder traversal of the algebra tree. This ensures that each operator processes input updates after all its children have already computed their output[1]. At each node n, an incoming update is translated into an output sequence ∂n of length greater than or equal to 0 which is then propagated to n's parent node. Since the algebra tree is connected and cycle-free (not considering joins of relations with themselves) all nodes will be visited exactly once. Also note that since updates occur only in one leaf at a time, only exactly one child of any node will have a non-empty update sequence to be propagated. That is, the first **for**-loop will find a non-empty addition to s only once per function call. After all nodes have been visited, the output of the algorithm will be an update sequence ∂V to the view V that we will prove to have an effect on V equivalent to recomputation.

3.4 Propagation of Updates through Individual *SchemaSQL* Operators

Since update propagation in our algorithm occurs at each operator in the algebra tree, we have to design a propagation strategy for each type of operator.

Propagation of Schema Changes through SQL Algebra Operators.
The propagation of updates through standard SQL algebra nodes is simple. Deriving the update propagation for data updates is discussed in the literature on view maintenance [16, 5]. It remains to define update propagation for selection, projection, and cross-product operators under schema changes, as these

---
[1] We are not considering concurrent updates in this paper.

are the only operators necessary for the types of queries discussed in this paper. In short, *delete-relation*-updates will make the output invalid, while other *relation*-updates do not affect the output. *Attribute*-updates are propagated by appropriate changes of update parameters or ignored if they do not affect the output. For example, a change *delete-attribute*(r, a) would not be propagated through a projection operator $\pi_{\bar{A}}$ if $a \notin \bar{A}$, and would be propagated as *delete-attribute*(q, a) otherwise, with q the name of the output relation of $\pi_{\bar{A}}$. We refer to our technical report [8] for further details, as they are not important for the comprehension of this paper.

***SchemaSQL* Operators.** In the appendix (Figs. 5–8), we give the update propagation tables for the four *SchemaSQL* operators. In order to avoid repetitions in the notation, the cases for each update type are to be read in an "if-else"-manner, i.e., the first case that matches a given update will be used for the update generation (and no other). Also, NULL-values are like other data values, except where stated otherwise.

Inspection of the update propagation tables shows several properties of our algorithm. For example, the view becomes invalid under some schema changes or data updates, mainly if an attribute or relation that was necessary to determine the output schema of the operator is deleted (e.g., when deleting the pivot or data attribute in UNFOLD). In the case of *rename*-schema changes (e.g., under *rename-relation* in FOLD), some operators change their parameters. Those are simple renames that do not affect operators otherwise. The operator will then produce a zero-element output sequence. In those cases we denote renaming by $\Rightarrow$.

3.5 Update Propagation Example

Continuing our running example, Fig. 4 gives an example for an update that is propagated through the *SchemaSQL*-algebra-tree in Fig. 2. All updates are computed by means of the propagation tables in the appendix.

The operators in Fig. 4 appear in boxes with their output attached below each box (SQL-statements according to our update tables in [8]). The actual tuples added by these SQL-statements are shown in tabular form. The sending of updates to another operator is denoted by double arrows ($\Uparrow$), while single arrows ($\uparrow$) symbolize the transformation of SQL-statements into updates. We are propagating an *add-tuple*-update to base relation LH. Algorithm *propagateUpdate* will perform a postorder tree traversal, i.e., process the deepest node (UNITE) first, and the root node (SPLIT) last. The operators are denoted by ω_1 through ω_5, in order of their processing. First, the UNITE operator propagates the incoming update into a one-element sequence $\partial \omega_1$ of updates which is then used as input to the FOLD-operator. The FOLD-operator propagates its input into a two-element sequence $\partial \omega_2$, sent to the StandardSQL-operator. This operator then propagates each of the two updates separately, creating two sequences $\partial \omega_{3_1}$ and $\partial \omega_{3_2}$, with 1 and 0 elements, respectively. Those sequences can simply

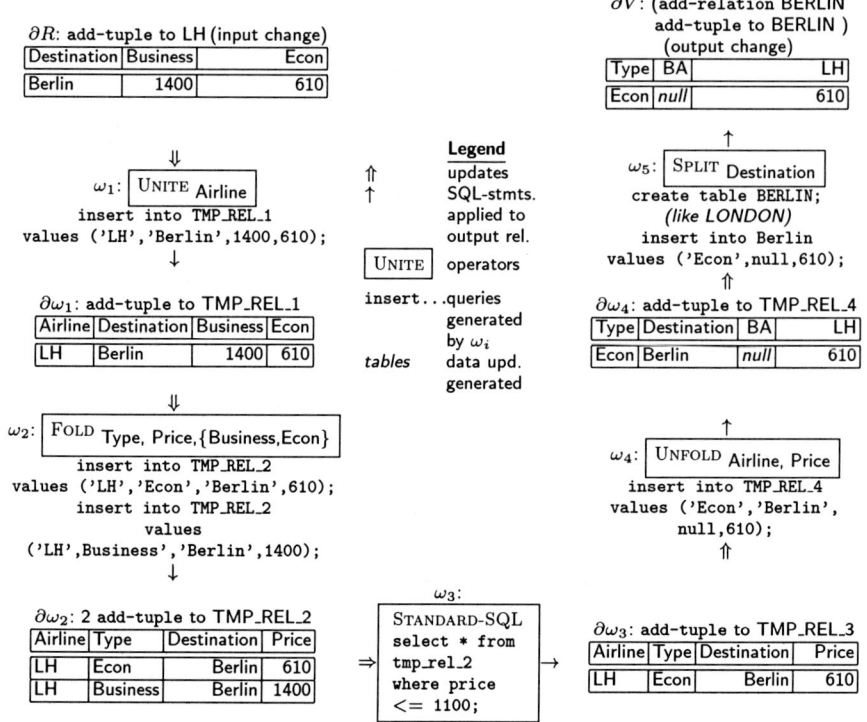

Fig. 4. Update Propagation in the View from Figure 2.

be concatenated before the next operator's propagation is executed (Sec. 3.3), yielding $\partial\omega_3$. Since one update is not propagated due to the WHERE-condition in the StandardSQL-node, we have $\partial\omega_3 = \partial\omega_{3_1}$. UNFOLD now transforms its incoming one-element update sequence $\partial\omega_3$ into another one-element sequence $\partial\omega_4$ which becomes the input for the SPLIT-operator. This operator then creates the two-element final update sequence ∂V, consisting of an *add-relation* schema change followed by an *add-tuple* data update.

4 Correctness

Our update propagation strategy is equivalent to a stepwise evaluation of the algebraic expression constructed for a query. Each operator transforms its input changes into a set of semantically equivalent output changes, eventually leading to a set of changes that must be applied to the view to synchronize it with the base relation change.

The structure of the algebra tree for a view depends only on the query, not on the base data [12]. The only changes to operators under base relation updates are possible changes of parameters (schema element names) inside the operators. An algebra operator cannot disappear or appear as the result of a base update.

However, the entire view query may be rendered invalid, for example under some *delete-relation*-updates.

Theorem 1 (Correctness of *SchemaSQL* View Maintenance). *Let V be a view defined over the set of base relations $R_1, \ldots, R_p$, and $\Delta R_u \in \{DU, SC\}$ an update applied to one relation R_u ($1 \leq u \leq p$). Let R'_u be the relation R_u after the application of ΔR_u and V'_{REC} be the view after recomputation. Furthermore, let the SchemaSQL View Maintenance Algorithm as defined in Section 3.3 produce a change sequence ∂V that transforms view V into view V'_{INC}. Then, $V'_{\text{REC}} = V'_{\text{INC}}$.*

Proof. (Sketch) We only give the proof idea, the full proof can be found in [8]. We prove by first showing that each operator by itself propagates updates correctly, i.e., produces results equivalent to recomputation. We then prove overall correctness by induction over the unique path in the algebra tree from the algebra node (leaf) in which the update occured to the root of the tree. □

5 Related Work

The integration of data stored in heterogeneous schemas has long been an object of intensive studies. The problem of schematic heterogeneity or different source capabilities is repeatedly encountered when attempting to integrate data. Some more recent examples are Garlic [17] and TSIMMIS [3]. Several logic-based languages have been developed to integrate heterogeneous data sources (e.g., SchemaLog [4]). Some SQL-extensions have also been proposed, in particular, *SchemaSQL* [11] (see below).

Those approaches overcome different classes of schematic heterogeneities. However, the important class of schematic heterogeneities in semantically equivalent relational databases is often excluded from integration language proposals, and even if it is covered, the problem of incremental view maintenance in a view over an integrated schema is rarely discussed. Krishnamurthy et al. [9] were the first to recognize the importance of schematic discrepancies and developed a logic-based language called IDL to deal with such problems. Miller et al. [13] show that relational databases may contain equivalent information in different schemas and give a formal model (Schema Intension Graphs) to study such "semantic equivalence" of heterogeneous schemas. An overview over object-oriented approaches can be found in [15]. Pitoura *et al.* also discuss a number of OODBMS implementation that support views. However, none of the projects listed has a comprehensive incremental view maintenance strategy.

An important approach at integrating semantically equivalent schemas has been done by Gyssens et al. [6] and later by Lakshmanan, Sadri, and Subramanian [11, 12]. In [11], the authors present *SchemaSQL*, which is used as the basis for our work. *SchemaSQL* builds upon earlier work in SchemaLog [4]. It is a direct extension of SQL, with the added capability of querying and restructuring not only data, but also schema in relational databases, and transforming data into schema and vice-versa. Thus, using *SchemaSQL* as a query language makes it possible to overcome schematic heterogeneities between relational data sources.

A second foundation of our work is the large body of work on incremental view maintenance. Many algorithms for efficient and correct view maintenance for SQL-type queries have been proposed. One result, taking concurrency into account, is SWEEP [1]. Most of those approaches follow an *algorithmic* approach in that they propose algorithms to compute changes to a view.

Related to our work are also performance studies on incremental view maintenance algorithms. An early paper on measuring the performance of incremental view maintenance strategies is Hanson [7]. More recently, there are performance studies on some OO view maintenance algorithms for example by Kuno et al. [10].

6 Conclusions

In this paper, we have proposed the first incremental view maintenance algorithm for schema-restructuring views. We have shown that the traditional approach at incremental view maintenance—rewriting view queries and executing them against the source data—is not easy to adapt for such views, and that in addition it is necessary to include schema changes into the picture. We have solved this problem by defining an algebra-based update propagation scheme in which updates are propagated from the leaves to the root in the algebra tree corresponding to the query. We have also proved the correctness of the algorithm.

The update propagation strategy described in this paper has been implemented in Java on top of a *SchemaSQL* query evaluation module also written by us [8]. The algebra tree builder was constructed along the lines of [12]. Our experiments showed that for most queries and schemas, incremental maintenance performs significantly better than recomputation. A case in which incremental maintenance does not outperform recomputation occurs when a base update such as **delete-relation** is translated into a long sequence of single-tuple updates by one of the *SchemaSQL*-operators (up to one update per tuple in the deleted base relation). We plan to address this issue by introducing *update batches* as a new class of updates in addition to individual data updates and schema changes.

In summary, we believe our work is a significant step towards supporting the integration of large yet schematically heterogeneous data sources into integrated environments such as data warehouses or information gathering applications, while allowing for incremental propagation of updates. One application that comes to mind is in a larger data integration environment such as EVE [14], in which the *SchemaSQL* wrapper would help to integrate a new class of information sources into a view.

References

[1] D. Agrawal, A. El Abbadi, A. Singh, and T. Yurek. Efficient View Maintenance at Data Warehouses. In *Proceedings of SIGMOD*, pages 417–427, 1997.
[2] W. Chen, M. Kifer, and D. Warren. Hilog as a platform for database languages. *IEEE Data Eng. Bull.*, 12(3):37, September 1989.
[3] H. Garcia Molina, J. Hammer, K. Ireland, et al. Integrating and accessing heterogeneous information sources in TSIMMIS. In *AAAI Spring Symposium on Information Gathering*, 1995.
[4] F. Gingras, L. Lakshmanan, I. N. Subramanian, et al. Languages for multidatabase interoperability. In Joan M. Peckman, editor, *Proceedings of SIGMOD*, pages 536–538, 1997.
[5] T. Griffin and L. Libkin. Incremental Maintenance of Views with Duplicates. In *Proceedings of SIGMOD*, pages 328–339, 1995.
[6] M. Gyssens, L. V. S. Lakshmanan, and I. N. Subramanian. Tables as a paradigm for querying and restructuring (extended abstract). In ACM, editor, *Proceedings of ACM Symposium on Principles of Database Systems*, volume 15, pages 93–103, New York, NY 10036, USA, 1996. ACM Press.
[7] E. N. Hanson. A performance analysis of view materialization strategies. In *Proceedings of SIGMOD*, pages 440–453, 1987.
[8] A. Koeller and E. A. Rundensteiner. Incremental Maintenance of Schema-Restructuring Views in SchemaSQL. Technical Report WPI-CS-TR-00-25, Worcester Polytechnic Institute, Dept. of Computer Science, January 2001. http://www.cs.wpi.edu/Resources/techreports.
[9] R. Krishnamurthy, W. Litwin, and W. Kent. Language features for interoperability of databases with schematic discrepancies. *SIGMOD Record (ACM Special Interest Group on Management of Data)*, 20(2):40–49, June 1991.
[10] H. A. Kuno and E. A. Rundensteiner. Incremental maintenance of materialized object-oriented views in *MultiView*: Strategies and performance evaluation. *IEEE Transaction on Data and Knowledge Engineering*, 10(5):768–792, Sept/Oct. 1998.
[11] L. V. S. Lakshmanan, F. Sadri, and I. N. Subramanian. SchemaSQL — A Language for Interoperability in Relational Multi-database Systems. In T. M. Vijayaraman et al., editors, *International Conference on Very Large Data Bases*, pages 239–250, Mumbai, India, Sept. 1996.
[12] L. V. S. Lakshmanan, F. Sadri, and S. N. Subramanian. On Efficiently Implementing SchemaSQL on an SQL Database System. In *International Conference on Very Large Data Bases*, pages 471–482, 1999.
[13] R. J. Miller, Y. Ioannidis, and R. Ramakrishnan. The use of information capacity in schema integration and translation. In *International Conference on Very Large Data Bases*, pages 120–133, Dublin, Ireland, August 1993.
[14] A. Nica, A. J. Lee, and E. A. Rundensteiner. The CVS Algorithm for View Synchronization in Evolvable Large-Scale Information Systems. In *EDBT'98*, pages 359–373, 1998.
[15] E. Pitoura, O. Bukhres, and A. Elmagarmid. Object orientation in multidatabase systems. *ACM Computing Surveys*, 27(2):141–195, June 1995.
[16] X. Qian and G. Wiederhold. Incremental recomputation of active relational expressions. *IEEE Transactions on Knowledge and Data Engineering (TKDE)*, 3(3):337–341, September 1991.
[17] M. Tork Roth, M. Arya, L. M. Haas, et al. The Garlic project. *SIGMOD Record (ACM Special Interest Group on Management of Data)*, 25(2):557 ff., 1996.

Input Change	Conditions	Propagation
add-tuple (r,t)	$t[a_1,\ldots,a_r,a_p] \in R$	invalid view (key violation)
	$t[a_p] \in A^*$ $t[a_1,\ldots,a_n] \in R$	update Q set $[t[a_p]] = t[a_d]$ where $a_1,\ldots,a_n = t[a_1,\ldots,a_n]$
	$t[a_p] \in A^*$ $t[a_1,\ldots,a_n] \notin R$	insert into Q $(a_1,\ldots,a_n,a_p)$ values $(a_1,\ldots,a_n,a_d)$
	$t[a_p] \notin A^*$ $t[a_1,\ldots,a_n] \in R$	add-attribute$(q,t[a_p])$, update Q set $[t[a_p]] = t[a_d]$ where $a_1,\ldots,a_n = t[a_1,\ldots,a_n]$
	$t[a_p] \notin A^*$ $t[a_1,\ldots,a_n] \notin R$	add-attribute$(q,t[a_p])$, insert into Q $(a_1,\ldots,a_n,a_p)$ values $(a_1,\ldots,a_n,a_d)$
delete-tuple (r,t)	$t[a_p]$ exists in $R[a_p]$ exactly once	delete-attribute$(q,t[a_p])$
	$t[a_p]$ exists in $R[a_p]$ more than once	update Q set $[t[a_p]]$ = NULL where $a_1,\ldots,a_n = t[a_1,\ldots,a_n]$ [2]
update-tuple (r,t,t')	$t[a_1,\ldots,a_r,a_p] = t'[a_1,\ldots,a_n,a_p]$	update Q set $[t[a_p]] = t[a_d]$ where $a_1,\ldots,a_n = t[a_1,\ldots,a_n]$
	$t[a_1,\ldots,a_r,a_p] \neq t'[a_1,\ldots,a_n,a_p]$	break down into (delete-tuple, add-tuple)
add-attribute(r,a)		add-attribute(q,a)
delete-attribute(r,a)	$a \in \{A_d, A_p\}$	invalid view
	$a \notin \{A_d, A_p\}$	delete-attribute(q,a)
rename-attribute(r,a,a')	$a = A_d$	$\text{UNFOLD}_{a_p,a} \Longrightarrow \text{UNFOLD}_{a_p,a'}$
	$a = A_p$	$\text{UNFOLD}_{a,a_d}(R) \Longrightarrow \text{UNFOLD}_{a',a_d}(R)$
	$a \notin \{A_d, A_p\}$	rename-attribute(q,a,a')
delete-relation(r)		delete-relation(q)
rename-relation(n,n')		$\text{UNFOLD}_{a_p,a_d}(N) \Longrightarrow \text{UNFOLD}_{a_p,a_d}(N')$ (renaming the input relation)

[2] if this update leads to a tuple with all NULL-values, the tuple must be deleted.

Fig. 5. Propagation Rules for Q=$\text{UNFOLD}_{a_p,a_d}(R)$

Input Change	Conditions and Variable Binding	Propagation
add-tuple (r,t)	$(A^* = \{a_1^*,\ldots,a_k^*\}, k \leftarrow \lvert A^*\rvert)$	for $i := 1..k$ insert into Q values $(a_1,\ldots,a_n, a_i^*, t[a_i^*])$
delete-tuple (r,t)		delete from Q where $a_1,\ldots,a_n = t[a_1,\ldots,a_n]$
update-tuple (r,t,t')	$A \in A^*$; set $t[a]$ to a value c	update Q set $a_d = c$ where $a_1,\ldots,a_n = t[a_1,\ldots,a_n]$ and $a_p = a$
	$A \notin A^*$; set $t[a]$ from a value b to a value c	update Q set $a = c$ where $a = b$
add-attribute (r,a)	$A \in A^{*3}$	foreach tuple $u \in R$ insert into Q $(a_1,\ldots,a_n, a_p, a_d)$ values $(u[a_1,\ldots,a_n], a,\text{NULL})$
	$A \notin A^*$	add-attribute(q,a)
delete-attribute (r,a)	$A \in A^*$	delete from Q where $a_p = a$
	$A \notin A^*$	delete-attribute(q,a)
rename-attribute (r,a,a')	$A \in A^*$	update Q set $a_p = a'$ where $a_p = a$
	$A \notin A^*$	rename-attribute(q,a,a')
delete-relation (r)		delete-relation(q)
rename-relation (n,n')		$\text{FOLD}_{a_p,a_d}(N) \Longrightarrow \text{FOLD}_{a_p,a_d}(N')$

Fig. 6. Propagation Rules for Q=$\text{FOLD}_{a_p,a_d,A^*}(R)$

[3] Note that the decision whether a *new* attribute should be a member of $a_1,\ldots,a_n$ can only be made by evaluating the view query.

Input Change	Conditions	Propagation
add-tuple (r,t)	$t[a_p] \notin A^*$	add-relation $[t[a_p]]$ with schema $(S_R \setminus R.A_p)$; insert into $[t[a_p]]$ values $(t[a_1,\ldots,a_n])$
	$t[a_p] \in A^*$	insert into $[t[a_p]]$ values $(t[a_1,\ldots,a_n])$
delete-tuple (r,t)	$t[a_p]$ exists in $R[a_p]$ exactly once	delete-relation $[t[a_p]]$
	$t[a_p]$ exists in $R[a_p]$ more than once	delete from $[t[a_p]]$ where $a_1,\ldots,a_n = t[a_1,\ldots,a_n]$
update-tuple (r,t,t')	$t[a_1,\ldots,a_n,a_p] = t'[a_1,\ldots,a_n,a_p]$	update $[t[a_p]]$ set $[a_d] = t[a_d]$ where $a_1,\ldots,a_n = t[a_1,\ldots,a_n]$
	$t[a_1,\ldots,a_n,a_p] \neq t'[a_1,\ldots,a_n,a_p]$	break down into (delete-tuple, add-tuple)
add-attribute (r,a)		$\forall q \in \{q_1 \ldots q_n\} : add\text{-}attribute(q,a)$
delete-attribute (r,a)	$a = A_p$	invalid view
	$a \neq A_p$	$\forall q \in \{q_1 \ldots q_n\} : delete\text{-}attribute(q,a)^4$
rename-attribute (r,a,a')	$a = A_p$	$\text{SPLIT}_a(R) \Rightarrow \text{SPLIT}_{a'}(R)$
	$a \neq A_p$	$\forall q \in \{q_1 \ldots q_n\} : rename\text{-}attribute(q,a,a')$
delete-relation (r)		$\forall q \in \{q_1 \ldots q_n\} : delete\text{-}relation(q)$
rename-relation (n,n')		$\text{SPLIT}_{a_p}(N) \Rightarrow \text{SPLIT}_{a_p}(N')$

Fig. 7. Propagation Rules for $Q = \text{SPLIT}_{a_p}(R)$

[4] If this update leads to a tuple with all NULL-values in an output relation, the tuple must be deleted.

Input Change	Conditions and Variable Bindings	Propagation
add-tuple (r_x, t)		insert into Q $(a_1, \ldots, a_n, a_p)$ values $(t[a_1, \ldots, a_n], r_x)$
delete-tuple (r_x, t)		delete from Q where $a_1, \ldots, a_n = t[a_1, \ldots, a_n]$ and $a_p = r_x$
update-tuple (r_x, t, t')	$A = A_d$; set $t[a]$ to a value c	update Q set $a = c$ where $a_1, \ldots, a_n = t[a_1, \ldots, a_n]$ and $a_p = r_x$
	$A \neq A_d$; set $t[a]$ from a value b to a value c	update Q set $a = c$ where $a = b$ and $a_p = r_x$
add-attribute(r, a)	add simultaneously to all R_i	add-attribute(q, a)
	otherwise	invalid view
delete-attribute(r, a)	delete simultaneously from all R_i	delete-attribute(q, a)
	otherwise	invalid view
rename-attribute(r, a, a')	rename simultaneously in all R_i	rename-attribute(q, a, a')
	otherwise	invalid view
add-relation(r_x, S)		no change (until first add-tuple to R_x)
delete-relation(r_x)		delete from Q where $a_p = r_x$
rename-relation(n, n')		$\text{UNITE}_{a_p}(\{R_1, \ldots, N, \ldots, R_n\}) \Rightarrow$ $\text{UNITE}_{a_p}(\{R_1, \ldots, N', \ldots, R_n\})$ update Q set $a_p = n'$ where $a_p = n$

Fig. 8. Propagation Rules for Q=$\text{UNITE}_{a_p}(R_1, R_2, \ldots, R_n)$[5]

[5]Note that r_x is the name of Relation R_x, which is one of the n relations of equal schema that are united by the UNITE-operator.

Coupling of FDBS and WfMS for Integrating Database and Application Systems: Architecture, Complexity, Performance

Klaudia Hergula[1] and Theo Härder[2]

[1] DaimlerChrysler AG, ITM, Databases and Data Warehouse Systems (TOS/TDW),
Epplestr. 225, HPC 0516, 70546 Stuttgart, Germany,
klaudia.hergula@daimlerchrysler.com
[2] University of Kaiserslautern, Dept. of Computer Science (AG DBIS),
P. O. Box 3049, 67653 Kaiserslautern, Germany,
haerder@informatik.uni-kl.de

Abstract. With the emergence of so-called application systems which encapsulate databases and related application components, pure data integration using, for example, a federated database system is not possible anymore. Instead, access via predefined functions is the only way to get data from an application system. As a result, retrieval of such heterogeneous and encapsulated data sources needs the combination of generic query as well as predefined function access. In this paper, we present a middleware approach supporting such novel and extended kind of integration. In particular, so-called federated functions combining functionality of one or more application system calls (local functions) have to be integrated. Starting with the overall architecture, we explain the functionality and cooperation of its core components: a federated database system and, connected via a wrapper, a workflow management system composing and executing the federated functions. Due to missing wrapper support in commercial products, we also explore the use of user-defined table functions. In addition to our workflow solution, we present several alternative architectures where the federated database system directly controls the execution of the requested local functions. These two different approaches are primarily compared w.r.t. their mapping complexity and their performance.

1 Motivation

Most enterprises have to cope with heterogeneous system environments where different network and operating systems, database systems (DBSs), as well as applications are used to cover the whole life cycle of a product. Solutions primarily focusing on problems of data heterogeneity exist in the form of federated database systems (FDBSs) and multidatabase systems, even if there are still open questions [1, 2]. But the database environment is changing now. While many enterprises had selected 'their' DBS and designed their tailored DB schema in the past, they are now confronted with databases being delivered within packaged software, so-called application systems. One of the most frequently used application systems is, for example, SAP R/3 [3], whose data can be accessed via predefined functions only. The same characteristics can be found in proprietary software solutions implemented by the enterprises. As a consequence, pure data integration is not possible anymore, since 'traditional' DBSs have to be accessed using a generic query language (SQL) whereas application systems only provide data access via predefined functions.

We introduce an example in order to illustrate how users work with application systems today. The sample scenario is located in the purchasing department of an enterprise and can be found in similar forms in any other department. Assume the employee must decide whether he should order a new component delivered by a supplier already known. A purchasing system supports the employee by providing a function DecidePurchase. This function proposes a decision based on a calculated grade of quality and reliability and the number of the considered component. Unfortunately, the employee only knows the component name as well as the supplier number. As a consequence, he has to query some other systems to get the required input for the function DecidePurchase. Fig. 1 illustrates the single steps the employee has to go through, i.e. the functions he must call. He gets the quality as well as the reliability rate for the supplier calling the functions GetQuality of the stock-keeping system and GetReliability of the purchasing system with the supplier number. He then uses these results as input for the calculation of the component's grade by means of the function GetGrade and gets the first required input value for DecidePurchase. Moreover, he calls the function GetCompNo of the product data management system to query the corresponding number for the component name. With these values – the component's number and grade – he finally can call DecidePurchase to make his decision.

During the decision process, the user has to cope with three different application systems and three different user interfaces. Technically spoken, he manually achieves a kind of integration by calling the application systems' functions and copying and pasting result values between them. So the user's interaction represents the glue between the application systems. In addition, we observe that there are steps that are processed in the same order again and again. This fact has led to our idea to support the user by providing so-called federated functions

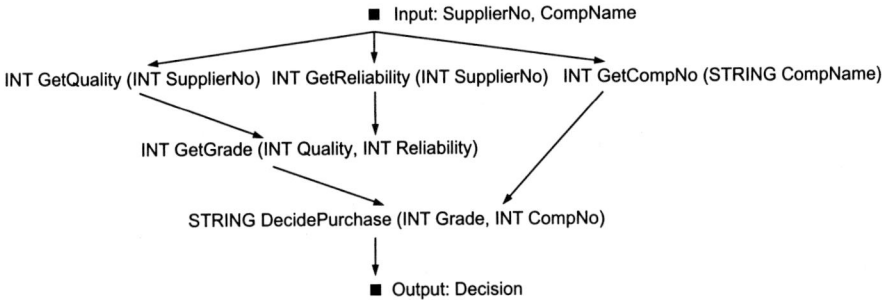

Fig. 1. Workflow process for the federated function BuySuppComp.

that implement single calls of the local functions and that hide these steps from the user. In our example, the user then has to call one federated function – let's denote it BuySuppComp – instead of five local functions.

Thus, an integration of functions or application systems is needed. Since also database systems could be involved in such a user request, a combined approach of data and function access has to be achieved. Such scenarios can be encountered in many practical and/or legacy applications.

We consider an FDBS as an effective integration platform, since it provides a powerful declarative query language. Many user applications are SQL-based to take full advantage of its properties. A query involving both databases and application systems includes SQL predicates as well as some kind of foreign function access.

To implement such an extended kind of integration, we have developed an integration architecture consisting of two key components: an FDBS and a workflow management system (WfMS). Obviously, a WfMS is quite a big engine which seems to be oversized as part of a middleware. Hence, questions crop up, why not directly accessing each of the local functions by a user-defined table function (UDTF for short) instead of using the workflow engine. Therefore, we have implemented both alternatives to be able to examine the differences between them regarding mapping complexity and performance.

In the remainder of this paper, we describe architectures based on UDTFs with and without the workflow system in Sect. 2. In Sect. 3, we point out the mapping complexity these architectures are able to implement. Afterwards, we present the results of our performance tests in Sect. 4, answering the question how much time is consumed by the WfMS. In the remaining sections, we briefly review related work and summarize our ideas.

2 Integration Architectures

The goal of our three-tier integration architecture is to enable the applications to transparently access heterogeneous data sources, no matter if they can be accessed by means of SQL or functions (see Fig. 2). Applications referring to a (homogenized) view to the data comprise the upper tier, and the heterogeneous data sources represent the bottom tier. Due to space limitations, we focus on the middle tier, the so-called integration server, which consists of two key components: an FDBS achieving the data integration and a WfMS which realizes a kind of function integration by invoking and controlling the access to predefined functions. In our terms, function integration means to provide federated functions combining functionality of one or more local functions [4] as introduced in our sample scenario. Considering the federated function BuySuppComp, one can see that the mapping from federated to local functions is guarded by a precedence graph and it typically consists of a sequence of function calls observing the specific dependencies between the local functions.

As a key concept of our approach, we use a WfMS as the engine processing such a graph-based mapping where its activities embody the local function calls

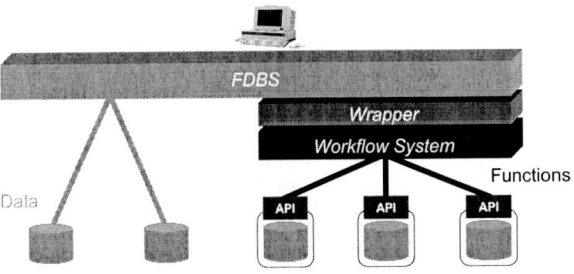

Fig. 2. Integration architecture.

and where the WfMS controls the parameter transfer together with the precedence structure among the local function calls [4]. The workflow to be executed is a production workflow representing a highly automated process [5]. Then, a unified wrapper can be used to isolate the FDBS from the intricacies of the federated function execution and to bridge to the WfMS thereby supplying missing functionality (glue) and making various query optimization options available. In order to be independent of vendor-specific solutions, a standardized wrapper interface according to the draft of SQL/MED (Database Languages – SQL – Part 9: Management of External Data, [6]) is used. As a result, the WfMS provides so-called federated functions used by the FDBS to process queries across multiple external data sources.

We have decided to use the WfMS because we want to use existing technology instead of implementing the engine by ourselves. Moreover, the basic concept of a workflow engine matches our mapping graph and supports very complex mapping scenarios. In addition, the workflow engine enables transparent access to different platforms, hides the interfaces to the application systems to be integrated, and copes with different kinds of error handling. As a result, the WfMS implements distributed programming over heterogeneous applications and, thereby, abstracts the function integration towards the FDBS which then has to deal with only one interface, that is, that of the workflow engine resp. that of the wrapper. Finally, the implemented mapping is much easier to maintain when realized by means of a workflow product.

The applications (users) can access the integration server via an object-relational interface connecting them to the FDBS. The FDBS's query processor evaluates the user queries and those parts requiring foreign function access are handed over to the wrapper which activates the WfMS. The workflow engine performs the function integration by calling the local functions of the referenced application systems as specified in the predefined workflow process. The wrapper returns the result back to the FDBS where it is mapped to an abstract table. The remaining parts of the user query are processed by the FDBS, i.e., the query is divided into the appropriate SQL subqueries for the SQL sources. Eventually, the subquery results are further processed by the query processor, if necessary, and merged to the final result.

At the moment, there is no database vendor supporting the SQL/MED wrappers. As an alternative, we decided to replace the wrapper by user-defined table functions (UDTFs, see Fig. 3). These UDTFs can be referenced in the FROM clause of an SQL query and return their result as a table to the FDBS. They can be implemented in different programming languages accessing any kind of data source. In such an architecture, each federated function is represented by a UDTF. In our example, a UDTF `BuySuppComp` can be referenced in a select statement starting the appropriate workflow process. Unfortunately, UDTFs only support read access, i.e., we are not able to propagate inserts, deletes, and updates. But since we want to get a first impression of the workflow performance, read access is a sufficient first step.

Of course, the use of a workflow engine seems to be oversized to some reader, since, in principle, specialized wrappers or UDTFs could be used to access each of the local functions which are often supplied by different applications systems. These functions are frequently called together in a way where the output data of a function call is the input data of a subsequent function call. The execution of the single functions could be directly controlled by the FDBS. However, such an approach would require substantial extensions of the FDBS components in addition to the writing of the specialized wrappers or UDTFs. Furthermore, the FDBS had to cope with the different application systems and their local functions which could be distributed, heterogeneous, and autonomous.

Despite these potential drawbacks, we discuss possible solutions without a WfMS. In such cases, the integration logic has to be implemented by means of UDTFs only, where each single local function is connected by a UDTF to the FDBS. In the following, we present a spectrum of architectures based on UDTFs.

Simple UDTF Architecture

While providing only a simple connectivity for the local functions, the first approach burdens the application with the integration problem. Each local function is separately accessed by means of a UDTF, which then can be used in SQL queries. Since these UDTFs allow only for a single function access, we will call them *Access UDTFs* or *A-UDTFs* for short (see Fig. 3). The actual integration is not supported by this architecture. Instead, it is achieved by the application[1] by issuing several SQL statements referencing the A-UDTFs and perhaps composing the related result sets even 'manually'. For our sample scenario, we have to implement five A-UDTFs for the corresponding local functions. These A-UDTFs can then be referenced in SQL statements that are embedded in the application programming code. The logic of the federated function `BuySuppComp` is represented by the following select statement. Please note, that the syntax shown in the examples is based on the implementation of IBM's DB2 UDB v7.1 that introduces UDTFs with the key word TABLE and and a mandatory correlation name. UDTFs can be only referenced in the FROM clause which is processed in left-to-right order. This means that there is a precedence structure among the UDTF calls that is determined by the availability of the input parameter values. Since, for instance, UDTF `GetGrade` is dependent on the output values of

---

[1] Or rather by the application programmer.

UDTF `GetQuality` and `GetReliability`, it cannot be executed until the other two UDTFs have been finished. During the processing of the SQL statement, the table functions are called returning the output values. In the SELECT clause, the user can specify which output values to project. Although the statement seems to specify a cross join, we get only single values in the following example:

```
SELECT DP.Answer
FROM TABLE (GetQuality(SupplierNo)) AS GQ,
     TABLE (GetReliability(SupplierNo)) AS GR,
     TABLE (GetGrade(GQ.Qual, GR.Relia)) AS GG,
     TABLE (GetCompNo(CompName)) AS GCN,
     TABLE (DecidePurchase(GG.Grade, GCN.No)) AS DP
```

Obviously, this approach is not satisfactory at all, since the integration logic is hidden within the application code. If the developers have to change the integration scenario by adding or removing application systems and their local functions, they have to understand the current implementation possibly done by developers not present anymore. Usually, its documentation is incomplete or even missing, so they will need much more time to understand and to adjust it. Therefore, we will not further consider this approach.

Enhanced SQL UDTF Architecture

Next, we enhance the simple UDTF approach by pushing down the integration logic from the user code into the FDBS. In order to flexibly compose a federated function using multiple local functions, we introduce so-called *Integration UDTFs* or *I-UDTFs*. These I-UDTFs consist of an SQL statement which includes references to A-UDTFs, thereby implementing the integration logic. Hence, they incorporate our federated functions and lead to our enhanced SQL UDTF architecture (see Fig. 4). Unfortunately, in the product we used, the function body may contain only one single SQL statement, i.e., the logic has to be expressed by one SQL statement. This restriction obviously results in further restrictions regarding the mapping complexity to be implemented. Since we are able to express the mapping logic of our example with one statement, the definition of the I-UDTF `BuySuppComp` looks as follows:

```
CREATE FUNCTION BuySuppComp (SupplierNo INT, CompName VARCHAR)
```

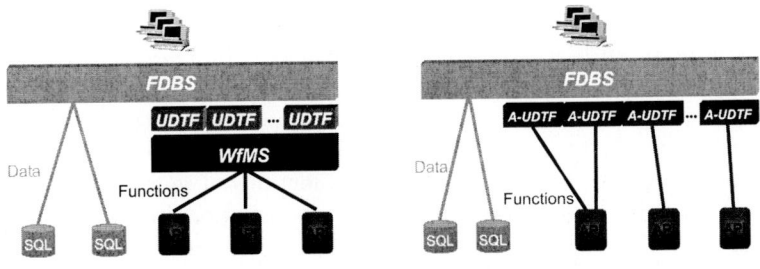

Fig. 3. WfMS approach (on the left) and simple UDTF approach (on the right).

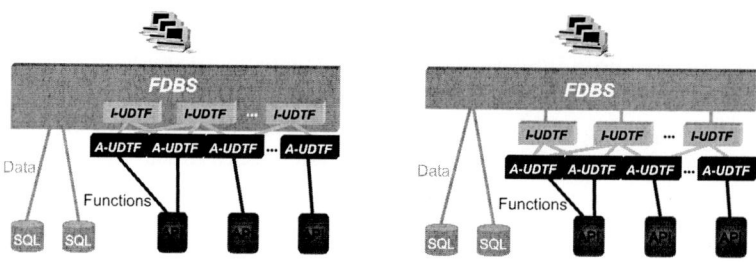

Fig. 4. Enhanced SQL UDTF (on the left) and Java UDTF approach (on the right).

```
RETURNS TABLE (Decision VARCHAR) LANGUAGE SQL RETURN
SELECT DP.Answer
FROM TABLE (GetQuality(BuySuppComp.SupplierNo)) AS GQ,
     TABLE (GetReliability(BuySuppComp.SupplierNo)) AS GR,
     TABLE (GetGrade(GQ.Qual, GR.Relia)) AS GG,
     TABLE (GetCompNo(BuySuppComp.CompName)) AS GCN,
     TABLE (DecidePurchase(GG.Grade, GCN.No)) AS DP
```

In contrast to the simple UDTF architecture, the application code contains a rather simple select statement now:

```
SELECT BSC.Answer
FROM TABLE (BuySuppComp(SupplierNo, CompName)) AS BSC
```

Assessing the enhanced SQL UDTF architecture we can state that it is able to provide the applications with federated functions which can be referenced within SQL statements and, therefore, be combined with references to other federated functions or local and remote tables. Since the federated functions are implemented by means of SQL at the FDBS side, the maintenance of them is much more convenient than for the simple UDTF architecture.

Enhanced Java UDTF Architecture

This architecture is based on the same idea like the enhanced SQL UDTF architecture. The difference is found in the specific implementation of the integration logic to be realized by means of Java (see Fig. 4). So if we consider this architecture from bottom to top, each local function is made accessible to the FDBS via an A-UDTF written in Java. These A-UDTFs can now be used in the FROM clause of an SQL statement. The federated functions that are mapped to the local ones are realized based on Java I-UDTFs which include JDBC calls invoking the A-UDTFs. Proceeding this way, we can avoid the 'one SQL statement' restriction. Instead, the Java I-UDTF can issue as many SQL statements as needed in order to implement federated functions of much more complexity. Moreover, we can make use of all the features a programming language provides like, for instance, control structures. Transferring our sample to this architecture, the Java I-UDTF would contain the same SQL statement like the SQL I-UDTF since the logic can be expressed by one select statement.

The enhanced Java UDTF architecture seems to be the most powerful solution to implement federated functions within the FDBS. However, the maintenance becomes more difficult again, since the integration logic is partially hidden within the programming code. In our view, logic implemented by means of SQL only is easier to understand. Of course, we could use PSM (persistent stored module) stored procedures which support SQL as well as procedural extensions[2], so that we can obtain the same mapping complexity by means of SQL only. However, stored procedures have to be handled as 'procedures', that is, they can only be invoked by a CALL statement. This restriction, in turn, means that a user is not able to reference a stored procedure (which represents a federated function) in a select statement. Hence, such a mechanism cannot be combined with references to other federated functions or tables.

Alternative Architectures
Besides the presented architectures, there is also the possibility to implement an integration based on the WfMS only. In this case, the workflow system represents the top layer of an integration architecture accessing functions as well as data (via an FDBS, for instance). But since we focus on the data we get by means of function calls and its further processing, we believe that a database system provides an engine that is more suitable.

Moreover, there are further solutions possible without using an FDBS and a WfMS at all. For instance, a J2EE compliant application server could represent the integration engine implementing access to database and application systems by means of appropriate J2EE connectors. Enterprise Java Beans have to contain the mapping and integration logic. Another solution could be based on a message broker which is also able to execute a kind of precedence graph to some degree. Or the integration engine is completely implemented by ourselves supporting exactly the functionality needed without introducing a possibly oversized engine like the WfMS.

These hand-made solutions do not seem suitable for several reasons. First, we have to process data, no matter if accessed via SQL or functions, and we believe that a DBMS represents the best solution for processing data in a fast, reliable, and secure way. Second, we want to integrate data and functions providing a flexible and generic interface supporting references to data and functions. Third, it is not desirable at all to implement the integration logic by ourselves, since maintenance as well as further development is quite difficult. Instead, we want to use existing technologies and products that can be adapted or extended if necessary.

In the following sections, we concentrate on the WfMS approach (Fig. 3) and the enhanced SQL UDTF architecture (Fig. 4), since they best meet our requirements described above. Moreover, the workflow architecture is quite a new solution which has to be compared with more 'traditional' solutions regarding mapping complexity and performance.

---

[2] PSM stored procedures are defined by SQL99 and are also supported by DB2.

3 Supported Mapping Complexity

In this section, we compare the enhanced SQL UDTF and the WfMS approach w.r.t. their mapping complexity. This complexity is mainly caused by the heterogeneity gap to be overcome when mapping federated functions to local functions. In the following, we classify the different forms of heterogeneity, listed by increasing complexity:

- **Trivial case**: One federated function is mapped to exactly one local function and their signatures are identical. Only the names of the functions and the parameters may differ.
- **Simple case**: In contrast to the trivial case, the signatures may be different, i.e., the number and data type of parameters do not match.
- **Independent case**: A federated function is mapped to more than one local function. Since the local functions are independent of each other, they can be processed in parallel.
- **Dependent case**: The next step allows dependencies between the local functions including linear, (1:n), (n:1), and cyclic dependencies.
- **General case**: Different forms of dependencies may occur and have to be handled together when more than one federated function has to be mapped to a set of local functions.

In the following, we examine to what extent these cases can be implemented by means of the UDTF and WfMS approach. For this purpose, we introduce suitable examples to illustrate the separate cases. In our sample scenario, three application systems are used. A stock-keeping system provides information about the components in stock, the corresponding supplier as well as their quality. A product management system stores the bill of material, whereas a purchasing system keeps information about the suppliers and their reliability. The data of these systems can be accessed by local functions.

Trivial Case

In the trivial case, a federated function `GibKompNr` represents a German version of an English local function `GetCompNo`. In this case, different function and parameter names have to be resolved by the mapping. Using the UDTF approach, this mapping is achieved by hiding the local function's signature behind that of the federated function.

The same concept is implemented by the WfMS approach where the signature of the connecting UDTF hides the names of the functions and parameters handled by the workflow process.

Simple Case

For the simple case, we demonstrate a type cast by changing the output parameter's data type. In addition, we have to cope with differing numbers of parameters in the function signatures. Assume a federated function `GetNumberSupp1234` that returns the stock-keeping number of a given component number for supplier 1234. It is mapped to the local function `GetNumber` which asks for two input parameter values. Since the federated function provides only one (`CompNo`), we have to specify a constant value for the second input parameter. This constant is defined by the federated function which returns information about supplier 1234. In addition, the resulting data type has to be converted from INT to LONG. As a result, the following federated function may be composed:

```
CREATE FUNCTION GetNumberSupp1234 (CompNo INT)
RETURNS TABLE (Number INT)
LANGUAGE SQL RETURN
SELECT BIGINT(GN.Number)
FROM TABLE (GetNumber(1234, GetNumberSupp1234.CompNo)) AS GN
```

The WfMS approach introduces so-called helper functions which are defined as additional activities in the workflow process and which implement the required type conversions. Comparable to the UDTF approach, the workflow solution can supply a constant value when calling the local function.

Independent Case
A federated function GetSubCompDiscounts returns the sub-components and the related supplier for a given component number which can be purchased with a given discount by calling the local functions GetSubCompNo and GetCompSupp4-Discount. This operation requires the composition of the single result sets of the local functions to a common abstract table:

```
CREATE FUNCTION GetSubCompDiscounts (CompNo INT, Discount INT)
RETURNS TABLE (SubCompNo INT, SupplierNo INT)
LANGUAGE SQL RETURN
SELECT GSCD.SubCompNo, GCS4D.SupplierNo
FROM TABLE (GetSupCompNo(GetSubCompDiscounts.CompNo)) AS GSCD,
     TABLE (GetCompSupp4Discount(GetSubCompDiscounts.Discount)) AS GCS4D
WHERE GSCD.SubCompNo=GCS4D.CompNo
```

The local functions return separate result tables for which the join predicate is used to select the tuples relevant for our query. For instance, result tuples of GetCompSupp4Discount representing component numbers that are not sub-components of the given component are removed.

Using the WfMS approach, the independent case is still a rather simple task to be accomplished. The independent, i. e. parallel execution of functions is implemented by defining parallel activities whose results are combined by a helper function.

Dependent Case
The local functions are dependent on each other resulting in a precedence structure among the function calls, i.e., the output value of one local function is used as the input value of a subsequent local function. We have identified four different cases of dependency: linear, (1:n), (n:1), and cyclic dependency.

Linear dependency: Two local functions have to be composed for a federated function GetSuppQual which returns the quality of a supplier for a given supplier name. Since the local function GetQuality returns the quality for a given supplier number, the local function GetSupplierNo has to be called first to get the corresponding number. Its result is then used as input for GetQuality. This is the point where the UDTF approach encounters limiting factors the first time. Since SQL is a declarative language, there is no way to specify a particular order of function calls within a query. One possible workaround would be to nest the function calls like, for instance, `GetQuality(GetSupplierNo(SupplierName))`. Unfortunately, nesting of functions is not supported. Nevertheless, the DBMS we used for our prototype supports another implementation. In our case, we are able to reference two types of parameters as input of a local function: input parameters of the federated function as well as output parameters of other local function. In this way, we can model a kind of dependency between two functions. In our example, the input parameter of `GetQuality` references the output parameter of `GetSupplierNo` and, therefore, is dependent of `GetSupplierNo` and its result. This, in turn, implies that `GetQuality` cannot be processed before `GetSupplierNo`. We implement this solution by performing a cross product between the result values of our local functions. `GetSupplierNo` gets the input value of the federated function and, therefore, can be executed immediately. In contrast, the input of `GetQuality` is specified as the output value of `GetSupplierNo`. But this value is only available after `GetSupplierNo` has been executed.

```
CREATE FUNCTION GetSuppQual (SupplierName VARCHAR)
RETURNS TABLE (Qual INT)
LANGUAGE SQL RETURN
SELECT GQ.Qual
FROM TABLE (GetSupplierNo(GetSuppQual.SupplierName)) AS GSN,
     TABLE (GetQuality(GSN.SupplierNo)) AS GQ
```

Please note that this solution is supported by the product we used. There is no guarantee that other products also enable such a proceeding. Moreover, one should keep in mind that SQL actually is not intended for such a procedural use[3]. There is no further selection required if the local functions return single values. However, if the result consists of tables, a selection has to be specified in the WHERE clause.

Considering the WFMS approach, a simple sequential order has to be defined by the control flow.

(1:n) dependency: Assume a federated function is mapped to three local functions where one local function is dependent on the other two local functions. This case is a combination of the independent case and the linear dependent case. Consequently, the implementation is comparable, because the dependency of the one local function is realized by using the output values of the other local functions which, in turn, get the input values of the federated function.

With a WfMS, a workflow process is defined in which two function calls are specified as parallel activities. The control flow specifies that the third function has to be processed after the first two functions have finished.

(n:1) dependency: In contrast to the (1:n) dependency, several local functions are dependent on a single local function. This mapping is solved in the same way as in the dependent cases above.

---
[3] Except for the procedural extensions for SQL stored procedures.

The WfMS approach can handle this case by the appropriate forks in the control flow.

cannot be implemented by the UDTF approach, since there are no control structures like a loop which are needed to iterate the cycle. At the moment, such control structures are only supported in PSM stored procedures. But when we use stored procedures representing federated functions, we are not able to combine them with other function or table references. On the other hand, the WfMS approach provides such control structures. The cyclic case is implemented by defining sub-workflows containing activities to be invoked several times. Such a sub-workflow is then activated in a do-until-loop which realizes the cycle.

Finally, we want to return to our sample introduced in Sect. 1 to demonstrate the difference between the UDTF and workflow approaches by a more complex example including several of the introduced heterogeneity cases. The resulting I-UDTF for the enhanced SQL UDTF architecture solution is illustrated once again below:

```
CREATE FUNCTION BuySuppComp (SupplierNo INT, CompName VARCHAR)
RETURNS TABLE (Decision VARCHAR) LANGUAGE SQL RETURN
SELECT DP.Answer
FROM TABLE (GetQuality(BuySuppComp.SupplierNo)) AS GQ,
     TABLE (GetReliability(BuySuppComp.SupplierNo)) AS GR,
     TABLE (GetGrade(GQ.Qual, GR.Relia)) AS GG,
     TABLE (GetCompNo(BuySuppComp.CompName)) AS GCN,
     TABLE (DecidePurchase(GG.Grade, GCN.No)) AS DP
```

Comparing this function definition to the mapping graph resp. workflow process shown in Fig. 1, it is obvious that it is quite difficult to identify the relations and dependencies among the local functions in the `CREATE FUNCTION` statement. In contrast, the workflow solution in Fig. 1 is much clearer. Moreover, we would like to point out again that this solution is supported by the product we used, but cannot be taken for granted in general.

The following table summarizes our results:

Case	UDTF approach	WfMS approach
trivial	hidden behind the federated function's signature	hidden behind the federated function's signature
simple	cast functions, supply of constant parameters	helper functions
independent	join with selection	parallel execution of activities
dependent: linear	join with selection; execution order defined by input parameters[a]	sequential execution of activities
dependent: (1:n) and (n:1)	join with selection; execution order defined by input parameters[a]	parallel and sequential execution of activities
dependent: cyclic	not supported	loop construct with sub-workflow

[a] Not supported in general.

Obviously, the UDTF approach is able to support many of the cases we examined, going a long way towards a restricted but lightweight workflow technology. However, the WfMS supports still more functionality like conditions, that cannot be expressed by SQL. The examples show that it is easier to specify and implement the mappings by means of workflows. Moreover, with an increasing number of local functions involved, the SQL statements become more and more complex and confusing. Nevertheless, the UDTF approach can be beneficial for simple applications that do not need a full-flegded WfMS.

4 Performance

In the following, we will explore the performance of our reference architectures. For this reason, we have implemented the workflow as well as the enhanced SQL UDTF architecture and have built a test and measurement environment for several examples representing the different cases introduced in Sect. 3. The processing time, i.e. the elapsed time, for these examples has been measured for each solution and compared to each other. The implementation is based on IBM's DB2 UDB v7.1 and MQ Series Workflow v3.2.2.

Because of security restrictions in DB2 UDB, we had to modify our architecture slightly by introducing a so-called controller. This controller is needed to connect a UDTF to a database on the same server (which is the case in our test implementation). It ensures that the UDTF process and the connection to the database are two different processes. The same process isolation is implemented in the workflow architecture in order to separate the UDTF process from the process invoking the workflow. In addition, the controller is started only once at the beginning when the whole environment is booted. It calls the WfMS providing the connect information and keeps the WfMS active. If these tasks would not be performed by the controller, each single integration UDTF would have to repeat it each time it calls the WfMS. Hence, we optimize the WfMS access, since the execution time for a federated function is reduced by the time needed for connecting the workflow engine. Since these modifications have the same impact on both solutions, we can likewise compare the alternative implementations.

First of all, we consider the processing time for function calls in three different situations: right after the entire system has been booted, after some other function has been invoked, and after the same function has been processed. Of course, the initial function calls are the slowest, since all underlying processes have to be started and memory as well as caches are empty. As expected, the repeated function call is the fastest. Please note, that the cyclic dependent case is not implemented and, therefore, not measured for the UDTF approach. Moreover, we note that the function GetSuppQualRelia based on parallel activities is processed faster than the function GetSuppQual with a sequential processing order in the workflow architecture. In contrast, the UDTF approach achieves processing times which show a contrary result. Obviously, the workflow approach can process parallel function calls in a more efficient way.

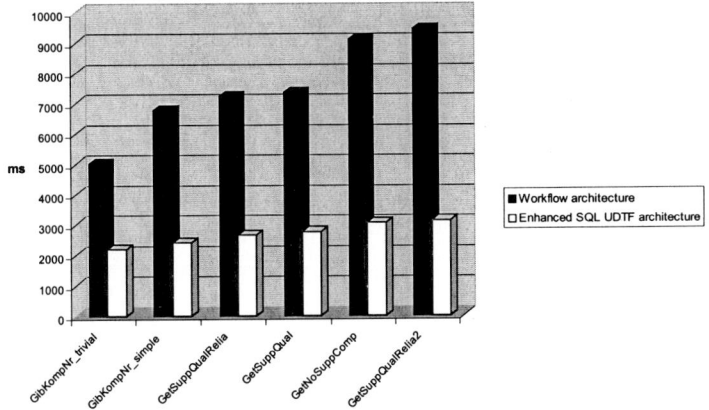

Fig. 5. Comparison of the results for the workflow and the enhanced UDTF approach.

The following measurement results are based on repeated function calls. First, we directly compare the measured processing times to each other. Fig. 5 shows that the WfMS approach is up to three times slower than the UDTF solution. Furthermore, we can observe that the processing times do not rise as intensely for the UDTF approach as for the workflow approach when the number of functions increases. Taking the facts into account that the WfMS approach implies the use of a second, very big engine and that the time scale remains in the expected range, the gap between the processing times measured is acceptable.

Another interesting aspect is the question about the single actions the overall processing time consists of. Fig. 6 shows how much time the single steps consume when running the federated function `GetNoSuppComp`.

Workflow approach	
Step	Time
Start UDTF	9%
Process UDTF	11%
RMI call	3%
Start workflows and Java environment	10%
Process activities	51%
Workflow	9%
Controller	5%
RMI return	0%
Finish UDTF	2%

UDTF approach	
Step	Time
Start I-UDTF	11%
Prepare 3 A-UDTFs	28%
3 RMI calls	24%
3 controller runs	0%
Process activities	6%
Finish 3 A-UDTFs	21%
3 RMI returns	1%
Finish I-UDTF	9%

Fig. 6. Time portions of the overall function calls in the WfMS and UDTF approach.

Considering the workflow architecture we observe that the processing of activities takes the lion share of the time with 51% of the overall processing time. 23% of the time is needed for preparing actions like calling and processing the UDTF and the controller until the workflow system is involved. Another 19% is consumed by the workflow environment and the remaining time is needed for the controller (5%), the result return, and finishing the UDTF (2%). Starting the workflow process instances and the Java environment for the Java API of the WfMS seem to take up a lot of time with 10%. But this share will be smaller when the number of activities is increasing since it will always take the same constant time, irrespective of how many activities have to be executed. The introduction of the controller makes a difference with a total of 8%.

Looking at the UDTF architecture, the time is divided in other proportions. Starting and finishing the integration UDTF requires 20% of the overall time. This relative time portion is comparable to that of the workflow approach[4] with 22% for starting (9%), processing (11%), and finishing (2%) the integration UDTF. The overall processing time of the three access UDTFs consumes about 49% of the time. The processing of the local functions requires only 6%. Hence, the time portion corresponding to the activities in the workflow approach accounts for 55% (49% + 6%) and, thus, represents a bigger part of the overall elapsed time than the activities in the workflow. The controller consumes a rather big percentage of the time with a total of 25%.

Comparing the two time portions, we observe the extreme difference regarding the various process activities. This is mainly due to the start of the Java programs. In the UDTF solution, the activities are processed within the controller which is already running, whereas the workflow architecture requires the start of a new Java program for each single activity including the booting of the Java virtual machine. Moreover, the workflow activities have the additional task of handling the input and output containers.

Assume, we can implement our prototypes without the controller. Then, the total time of the WfMS solution would decrease by 8%, whereas the UDTF solution would decrease by even 25%. As a result, the overall processing time ratio between workflow and UDTF approach would increase from 3 to 3.7.

Moreover, we have used the cyclic dependent case in the workflow solution to get an impression how the number of functions influences the overall processing time. The federated function `AllCompNames` is realized by means of a do-until loop. We have used this loop structure to measure the impact of an increasing number of calls of the same local function within a single federated function. This scenario shows that the overall processing time rises linearly to the number of function calls. Of course, this is only true, if we always call the identical function. Several measurements have shown that it is pretty difficult to define a formula for the overall time based on the number of functions integrated, since the elapsed time to execute a local function can differ immensely. So we can state that, currently, the parallel execution of functions is the only action we can make an assumption about: activities that are defined as parallel activities

---

[4] However, the ratio for the absolute elapsed time is still 1:3.

in a control flow actually are processed in parallel and, therefore, reduce the time consumed. Our examples `GetSuppQualRelia` and `GetSuppQual` show that the UDTF approach is unable to exploit the advantage of parallelism to such an extent since the execution of the parallel case takes more time than that of the sequential case.

In summary, our evaluated scenario indicates that a workflow system in the middleware does not produce such an overhead that the resulting processing times are not acceptable anymore.

5 Related Work

Most approaches dealing with the integration of heterogeneous data sources focus on the capability to combine different data models and heterogeneous systems providing an interface which is not as powerful as SQL. Approaches like Garlic [7], Information Manifold [8], or TSIMMIS [9] embody mediator- or wrapper-based solutions where missing functionality of the data sources is compensated by the integration server. In contrast to our work, these approaches provide general solutions and algorithms for accessing any kind of data source. In our case, all non-SQL sources are integrated by the WfMS (or the use of UDTFs) and the SQL sources are managed by the FDBS. As a consequence, the FDBS has to communicate with a single non-SQL source only: the WfMS. Hence, we can concentrate on a specific solution supporting the interoperability between the FDBS and the workflow system (on the assumption that the access to heterogeneous SQL sources is already provided by the FDBS).

Furthermore, we focus on the integration of a functional interface on the FDBS side. Chaudhuri at al. [10] have discussed this topic very early thereby demonstrating how references to foreign functions can be expressed in a query language. But they did not address the problem of limited access patterns. In such cases, for example, a particular function input must be stated similar to specific selection criteria in the WHERE clause of an SQL statement. Approaches like [11] and [12] propose solutions for this limitation by binding attributes in order to support queries on such data sources.

The approaches mentioned above mainly obtain their solutions by fully-fledged implementations whereas our intention is to use existing technologies and products. Reinwald et al. [13] present a solution based on user-defined table functions to access non-SQL data sources. But these table functions are limited to Windows sources, since they implement them by means of OLE DB.

6 Summary

In this paper, we have introduced an approach for the integration of heterogeneous data sources accessible via a generic query language or predefined functions. We have described the components of our integration architecture introducing the FDBS and the WfMS connected via standardized SQL/MED wrappers. Since there is no product available yet supporting such wrappers, we have decided to implement a first prototype with so-called user-defined table functions. These table functions support read access to any kind of data source returning the result as tables and, therefore, can be referenced in the FROM clause of a select statement. Since the workflow engine may be considered as a component too big for the middleware, we have described several alternative architectures which realize the function integration via direct access to the local functions by means of table functions.

In order to assess the function mapping capabilities, we have compared the workflow architecture and a table function architecture regarding their mapping complexity. The comparison has shown that the workflow approach is able to realize all possible scenarios whereas the table function approach has some limitations. Moreover, we have implemented two prototypes and have measured the performance for each solution. With a workload of increasing mapping complexity, the measurement results revealed a factor of 3 in favor of the UDTF solution. However, when the overall effort for implementing a foreign function integration is considered, the workflow approach represents a solution, easy to implement and to use, which is not as slow as many readers may expect.

Not all questions could be answered concerning the suitability of an architecture for data and function integration where the data sources are autonomous, distributed, and heterogeneous. To the best of our knowledge, empirical studies on their related issues are missing so far. Therefore, an initial study cannot be exhaustive. Further questions to be considered include, for instance, the mapping between the data model and the functional model and how it can be realized absolutely transparently to the application. Moreover, the functionality provided by the wrapper is interesting including the discussion of wrapper-internal operations for requested functionality not natively supported by the WfMS [14]. Further research has to clarify issues of query optimization, scalability, access control, ease of administration and evolution, and so on.

References

1. Härder, T., Sauter, G., Thomas, J.: The Intrinsic Problems of Structural Heterogeneity and an Approach to their Solution. VLDB Journal 8:1 (1999) 25–43
2. Sheth, A.P., Larson, J.A.: Federated Database Systems for Managing Distributed, Heterogeneous, and Autonomous Databases. ACM Computing Surveys 22:3 (1990) 183–236
3. SAP AG: SAP R/3. (2001). www.sap.com/solutions/r3/
4. Hergula, K., Härder, T.: A Middleware Approach for Combining Heterogeneous Data Sources – Integration of Generic Queries and Predefined Function Access. Proc. 1st Int. Conf. on Web Information Systems Engineering, Hongkong (2000) 22–29
5. Leymann, F., Roller, D.: Production Workflow: Concepts and Techniques, Prentice Hall (2000)
6. ISO & ANSI: Database Languages – SQL – Part 9: Management of External Data, Working Draft (2000)

7. M.Tork Roth, P. Schwarz: Don't Scrap It, Wrap It! A Wrapper Architecture for Legacy Data Sources. Proc. 23rd Int. Conf. on Very Large Data Bases, Athens (1997) 266–275
8. Levy, A.Y., Rajaraman, A., Ordille, J.J.: Querying Heterogeneous Information Sources Using Source Descriptions. Proc. 22nd Int. Conf. on Very Large Data Bases, Bombay (1996) 251–262
9. Papakonstantinou, Y., Garcia-Molina, H., Widom, J.: Object Exchange Across Heterogeneous Information Sources. Proc. 11th Int. Conf. on Data Engineering, Taipei (1995) 251–260
10. Chaudhuri, S., Shim, K.: Query Optimization in the Presence of Foreign Functions. Proc. 19th Int. Conf. on Very Large Data Bases, Dublin (1993) 529–542
11. Florescu, D., Levy, A., Manolescu, I., Suciu, D.: Query Optimization in the Presence of Limited Access Patterns. Proc. ACM SIGMOD Int. Conf. on Management of Data, Philadelphia (1999) 311–322
12. Garcia-Molina, H., Labio, W., Yerneni, R.: Capability-Sensitive Query Processing on Internet Sources. Proc. 15th Int. Conf. on Data Engineering, Sidney (1999) 50–59
13. Reinwald, B., Pirahesh, H., Krishnamoorthy, G., Lapis, G., Tran, B., Vora, S.: Heterogeneous Query Processing through SQL Table Functions. Proc. 15th Int. Conf. on Data Engineering, Sidney (1999) 366–373
14. Hergula, K., Härder, T.: How Foreign Function Integration Conquers Heterogeneous Query Processing. Proc. 10th Int. Conf. on Information and Knowledge Management, Atlanta (2001) 215–222

Optimizing Scientific Databases for Client Side Data Processing

Etzard Stolte and Gustavo Alonso

Dept. of Computer Science, Swiss Federal Institute of Technology (ETH)
ETH Zentrum, CH-8092 Zürich, Switzerland

Abstract. Databases are nowadays one more building block in complex multi-tier architectures. In general, however, they are still designed and optimized with little regard for the applications that will run on top of them. This problem is particularly acute in scientific applications where the data is usually processed at the client and, hence, conventional server side optimizations are of limited help. In this paper we present a variety of techniques and a novel client/server architecture designed to optimize the client side processing of scientific data. The main building block in our approach is to store frequently accessed data as relatively small, wavelet encoded segments. These segments can be processed at different qualities and resolutions, thereby enabling efficient processing of very large data volumes. Experimental results demonstrate that our approach significantly reduces overhead (I/O, transfer across network, decoding and analysis), does not require changes to the analysis routines and provides all possible resolution ranges.

1 Introduction

Databases are very often designed and optimized without taking into consideration the applications that will run on top of them [DHK97]. An excellent example of this problem are scientific databases storing continuous observations of natural phenomena. Such systems typically store multiple TBs of data [SKT00,EC00] and will soon reach the PBs range [HMS00]. Given their size, a very important part of the load in these systems comes from scientists sifting through long stretches of noise in search of relevant data sets. This is a *trial-and-error* procedure where a scientist retrieves a data interval, process it, determines whether the result of the analysis is acceptable, repeats the analysis if that is not the case, decides whether the data interval is relevant in view of the analysis, and proceeds with the next data interval. Given the amount of data involved, the response time associated to such a trial-and-error procedure is a critical performance aspect of the system.

Unfortunately, existing scientific databases lack any support for this type of interaction. First, the analyses are difficult to standardize and the wide range of input parameters makes it impossible to precompute anything but the most basic data products. Second, these analyses are often computationally expensive and can quickly create performance problems at the server. Hence, to simplify the design, the expensive part of the trial-and-error search (executing the analysis) is left to the client: support in existing systems is limited to a web interface for selecting and downloading raw-data from the server into the client computer.

In this paper we describe how to provide a more comprehensive and satisfactory solution to this problem. The solution we propose is twofold. First, on the server side, we store an encoded version the original data. This encoding offers lossy to loss-less signal reconstruction and progressive decoding, thereby minimizing the retrieval and transfer overhead. Second, on the client side, we provide a tool, the *StreamCorder*, that uses low-resolution approximations of the data instead of the original data set. Typically, only 5% of the original data volume has to be downloaded, decoded and analyzed to get acceptable results. These performance gains are even more dramatic if the client accesses the server through a low bandwidth connection (e.g., a modem).

We have implemented these ideas in the HESSI Experimental Data Center (*HEDC*), a scientific database that will manage the high-energy solar observations generated by the High Energy Solar Spectroscopic Imager (*HESSI*)[1] satellite and that already houses an extensive collection of radio observations. In what follows, we describe HEDC and the problem of trial-and-error analysis in more detail (section 2), and how the data can be encoded (section 3) to optimize client side processing. In section 4 we empirically validate these ideas. In section 5 the implementation issues are discussed and with 6 we conclude the paper identifying several directions for future work.

2 Motivation and Related Work

2.1 HESSI and HEDC

The HESSI satellite will be used to study solar flares through observations of the sun in hard X rays and gamma rays. The main instrument is an array of detectors that continuously record the energy and time of each detected photon. HESSI is expected to generate about 1.0 GB of *raw-data* per day. The data produced is buffered and forwarded to a ground station at pre-established intervals. This raw-data stream is analyzed for possibly relevant events, segmented along the time axis, packaged into units of roughly 40MB, formatted as FITS files[2] and compressed using gnu-zip. If relevant events are detected, some summary data and a number of *data products* are generated which are then attached to the raw-data unit. This *basic catalogue* of events is meant as a starting point for analysis.

HEDC, the HESSI Experimental Data Center, has been built to optimize the scientific return of the HESSI mission. The goal of HEDC is to facilitate access to the data and the creation of derived data products. Thus, when the raw-data units reach HEDC, they are once more searched for interesting events. This time with algorithms that detect a wider range of events such as solar flares, gamma

---

[1] http://hesperia.gsfc.nasa.gov/hessi/
[2] FITS (Flexible Image Transport System) http://fits.gsfc.nasa.gov/

ray bursts or quiet periods. The result is the *extended catalogue*. The majority of the data products in both catalogues (and the ones later generated by users) is made up of visual images of between 30KB and 2MB in size.

Towards the end of the HESSI mission, the raw-data volume will rise to about 1.2 TB. The encoded version (see below) of this raw-data will amount to several hundred GBs. The extended catalogue and data products generated by users will be an additional 2 TB. Currently, more than 2 GB of simulated HESSI data and around 25 GB of measurements taken by the Phoenix-2 Broadband Spectrometer in Bleien, Switzerland are available at HEDC. The Phoenix catalogue contains spectrograms for around 3000 identified solar events, and will be part of the extended catalogue.

HEDC has been realized with a 3-tier architecture, where the intermediate layer relays data- and processing-requests by clients to an Oracle 8.1.6 RDBMS and a number of analysis servers. HEDC can be accessed through either a Web based client using a conventional browser[3] or a Java-based client, the Stream-Corder[4]. The former is a thin client solution for users who are only interested in browsing existing data or have the necessary access rights to perform data processing at the server. The latter is a fat client solution that we use to optimize client side processing and to cache data on the client side.

2.2 Response Time in Trial-and-Error Analyses

Our goal is to *minimize the response time* between the submission of a request and the presentation of the analysis results to the user. If no optimizations are introduced, the average response time of a single analysis request varies between 14 seconds for fast analyses (e.g., spectrograms) and 20 minutes for more complex analyses (e.g., imaging spectroscopy) (see Figures 7 and 10). A careful study of the performance overhead incurred during such an analysis shows that the execution of the analysis routine is, by far, the most relevant factor. This creates a problem from the point of view of database design since, obviously, speeding up the retrieval and transfer of the data will not yield any significant improvement.

To solve this problem, we optimize data processing at the client side. The basic idea behind these optimizations is to pre-process the raw data stored in HEDC. The pre-processing step consists mainly in a reorganization of the data that facilitates access to meaningful ranges (for example, to certain energy bands and time sections) and encoding the data using a wavelet transformation. The wavelet transformation is done in such a way so as to allow the data processing routines to work on a fraction of the original data. In other words, we stream to the client only a small fraction of the coefficients of the wavelet transformed data. At the client side, these coefficients are used to reconstruct an approximated view of the original data set and this view is fed to the analyses routines. Since the time complexity of the analysis routines is directly related to the size of the input data (linear for short analyses and exponential for complex ones), the time it takes to perform an analysis is significantly improved.

---

[3] On-line at http://www.hedc.ethz.ch/

[4] Available for download from http://www.hedc.ethz.ch/release.html

The baseline for such an optimization is the time it takes for a client to retrieve a data set from HEDC, download it to the client, perform the necessary analysis and display the results to the user who then decides to either discard the data, store the results, or perform the analysis again with different parameters. This baseline ranges on average between 14 seconds for short analyses and 20 minutes for complex analyses. As a measure of the relevance of the results presented, we have been able to reduce the response times to around 4 seconds for short analyses and 3 minutes for the complex ones. In what follows, we explain in more detail the techniques used, their implementation, and how they are being used in practice.

2.3 Related Work

HEDC compares favorably with existing systems of similar scope. Some are larger [SKT00] yet most have a much simpler interface [ZI94,BSG00]. In practice, many are just plain ftp servers [S99]. In contrast, HEDC not only gives access to the raw-data but also allows users to create data products, interactively and as batch jobs, and to store the data products back into the system. There are also several projects for sharing scientific experiments (e.g., [KSD98,WZS95]), although few of these projects automate the detection of overlapping requests and it is the user's responsibility to find out whether a particular type of search or analysis has already been performed. A novel aspect of HEDC is that it automates the entire procedure and even provides users with tools for offline work.

Directly related to the main theme of this paper, many optimizations have been proposed to speed up access to data although most of them are server side optimizations that are not relevant when data processing is involved (for instance, materialized views [AD97,CKP95,CNS99,DG97,LMS95]). In terms of using approximated data, the most important methods are sampling (e.g. [GM98], [HHW97]), histograms [IPO99] and wavelets. In HEDC, we use wavelet transformations to encode the data so that it can be treated at different quality and resolution levels. It has been shown that the quality of wavelet encoded views is generally higher than that of sampling and histograms for a number of range-sum queries over dense [VI98] and sparse data cubes [VW01]. The last point is especially important, as even low-dimensional view structures tend to contain mostly empty cells and unbounded dimensional variables, such as time, force the generation of arrays with billions of cells. Thus, wavelet encoding is not only important for view approximation but also for compressed view storage. Further work has shown that view updates are possible when using wavelets [MVW00]. In [CGR00] this work was generalized to include aggregated and non-aggregated views, and [BRS99] provides similar probability based estimates in the case of count and sum range-queries.

The use of wavelet encoding has already been demonstrated in a number of experimental systems [SH99,BRS99]. Yet, they do not consider all performance factors, such as the decompression costs on the client side. There is also some work on data encoding [AS98,BE93] as a means to find and analyze the data, but only applied to individual data sets. Other work has focused on query processing inside wavelet space [CGR00] or through some density function [SFB99]. However, and to our knowledge, there has been no work done in the area of optimizing client side data processing.

3 Encoding Data for Client Side Processing

3.1 From Raw-Data to Views

During data-loading all *observations* of relevant satellite instruments are identified and extracted. Currently, these include the 18 photon detectors and the two positioning sensors, which together constitute around 70% of the raw-data. The remaining 30% are non-numerical data, rarely accessed or their complex data format does not lend itself well to view construction. Every observation is a time-tagged tuple, $T_i = (t, A_0^i, A_1^i, .., A_l^i)$, where the number of *attributes*, l, tends to be below five. Then these observations are *cleaned* and *pre-processed*, e.g. by tagging missing or error values and shifting all values into the positive number range. Once the observations have been cleaned, they are calibrated. Note that the calibration will change several times during the lifetime of the satellite. Each time the calibration changes, all raw-data will have to be processed again (possibly forcing a recalculation of the most important data products). After the calibration, observations from redundant instruments are merged. In our case, we merge the observations from the 18 photon detectors into a single data set, thereby offering the possibility of performing analyses over a wide energy range (each detector detects photons at a different energy range).

Next, a subset of $d + 1$ attributes is selected for all tuples inside consecutive time ranges. For each time range, d-dimensional arrays are build. The size of each dimension is determined by the maximum sensitivity of the corresponding instrument. For example, the maximum precision of roll-angle measurements is 0.4 arcmin. Since the roll angle varies between 0 and 360 degrees, we need 900 *cells* to store roll-angle measurements. Outside of solar events only a few observations will be made, creating very sparse arrays or pre-computed *views*. To improve performance and facilitate handling, the views are segmented along all their dimensions, resulting into what we call data *segments* (see Figure 1). This process is equivalent to *range partitioning* and, like any data partition, increases the selectivity and improves the I/O efficiency of small range-queries. The optimal size of each segment depends on a multitude of system parameters. Currently, our encoding method limits the segment size to a maximum of 4000 cells. This yields an average encoded segment size of 2.5 MBs for the following attribute ranges: time (4 seconds), frequency ([3k to 20M] eV), and spacecraft roll-angle ([0..360] degrees). In general we have found that this size is appropriate for our application although the issue will need to be revisited once a very large number of segments exist.

The segments so produced tend to be sparse and large. To further optimize their handling, we compress them. Compression takes place by encoding the segments using a wavelet transformation [JS94]. A wavelet transformation was

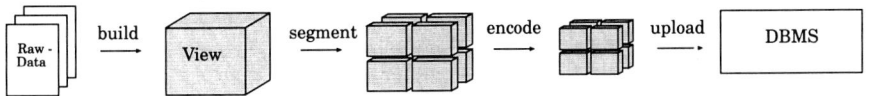

Fig. 1. Views are built as d-dimensional arrays over the attributes of the observations. These views are segmented, wavelet encoded and then loaded into HEDC.

chosen as the best option given our requirements: loss-less compression, high compression ratio, progressive decoding and fast and robust decoding. Using wavelets implies a clear performance trade-off, as other non-progressive codecs, such as gnu-zip are much faster. Yet, the complexity of a wavelet transformation is quasi-linear in the total number of cells on the data array [VI98]. In this trade-off, we follow many others who are currently using wavelet decomposition in signal processing [AS98,BE93], clustering [SH99], query processing ([SFB99], [GTKD00], [CGR00], [RAA01]) or indexing [WW98]. To implement the transformation, we use a commercial package[5].

3.2 Pre-processing Scientific Data

When pre-processing scientific data, care must be taken to avoid artifacts that might later be interpreted as natural phenomena. This was particularly important in HEDC as the wavelet transformed data is used to derived approximated views of the raw-data. Hence, great efforts were made to quantify the effects of using wavelet transformed data and extensive user tests conducted to convince the end users that the approach was sound and would not affect scientific results.

A first part of this evaluation was to show the effects of working with encoded views rather than with the original raw-data. The quality of a view depends on the percentage of coefficients used for decoding. We say that a view has *full-quality* if decoding takes place using as input the entire encoded segment, i.e., all coefficients of the transformed array. Otherwise it is an approximated, *low-quality view*. The *error in a view*, E_v, can be computed as the quadratic norm of the absolute error for a d-dimensional view, where each dimension j has n_j elements:

$$E_v = \frac{1}{d}\sum_{j=1}^{d} \frac{1}{n_j}\sum_{i=1}^{n_j} \|f_i^j - l_i^j\|^2 \quad (1)$$

with f_i^j a full-resolution element and l_i^j the corresponding low-resolution element at position $[i,j]$. E_v measures the error incurred as a function of the fraction of coefficients used for decoding. We define the *view quality*, Q_v, as $Q_v = 1 - E_v$. The quadratic norm of the absolute error is a straightforward method and not as

---

[5] LuraWave, partly developed by the EADS (European Aeronautic Defense and Space Company) http://www.luratech.com

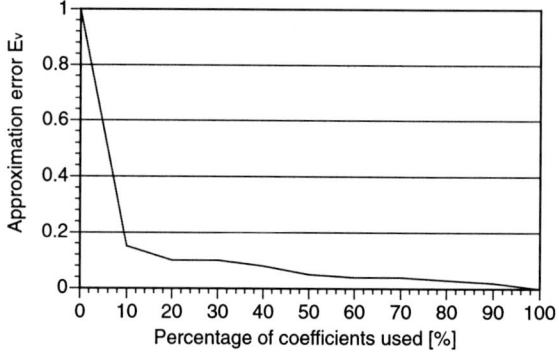

Fig. 2. View approximation error E_v in relation to percentage of coefficients used during decoding for a sample of 55 view segments.

precise as other error measures, such as the *Match and Compare* error measure [IPO99], that includes the actual element values and their distribution inside the view in exchange for a significant computational overhead. Yet, as we needed a measure for E_v only during the integration of new data sources and therefore mostly to calibrate the system (for example, to determine the minimum number of coefficients to transmit) this simpler approach was sufficient.

Figure 2 displays the behavior of E_v in relation to the percentage of coefficients used for decoding in a sample data set from HEDC. As the fraction of coefficients used grows, E_v decreases sharply until 10% of the coefficients have been transferred. With almost 50% of the coefficients, E_v is close to 0.05. These results agree with other studies that have pointed out the adequacy of wavelet based encoders to approximate sparse multi-dimensional arrays [VI98]. The interesting aspect for our purposes is that 10% of the coefficients amounts only to 45KB of data while the original data requires 448KB (one order of magnitude larger). The problem of minimizing the response time of the trial-and-error analysis is how to reduce the time it takes to perform an analysis. Since the time complexity of the analysis routines is directly proportional to the size of the input data, the procedure could be greatly optimize if, instead of the original data, we could use an approximated view.

3.3 Adaptive View Decoding

During trial-and-error analysis encoded data segments are streamed to the client for processing, and data products are uploaded to the server for reuse. The StreamCorder adapts both data-quality and -resolution to speed up processing (see fig. 3). Data-quality depends on the percentage of the segment file used during decoding. Partially downloaded segment files yield approximated views of lossy to loss-less quality and are the basis of low-quality data products. Full-quality views produce genuine, full-quality data products. Download time is thus shortened, while decoding and analysis time remain practically unchanged.

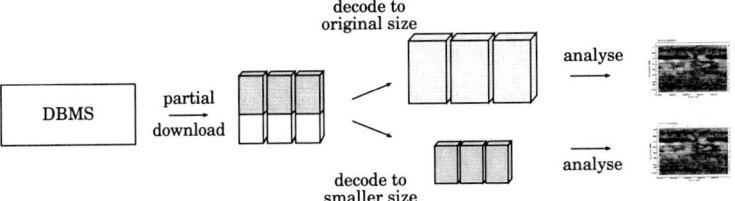

Fig. 3. During adaptive decoding, both data -quality and -resolution is optimized.

Data-quality adaptation requires no changes to the analysis algorithms. *Data-resolution*, on the other hand, depends on the decoded view dimension size. Most HEDC analysis algorithms accept variable size input data, yet some algorithms require *full-resolution* input data. Obviously, data resolution does not affect download time. Decoding time, on the other hand, decreases with the degree of aggregation. As the cost of many important HEDC analyses is proportional to the size of the input data, analysis time is also much reduced. Thus, low-quality analysis are beneficial for slow network connections. Low-resolution analysis greatly accelerate decoding and analysis. The analysis error caused by low-resolution data, compared to the error introduced by low-quality data tends to be different in nature, but similar in degree. The next section will introduce a measure to quantify analysis error.

3.4 Analyses over Approximated Views

Due to the complexity of astrophysical analysis algorithms, it is not possible to provide generic error estimation routines. Therefore, either specific error routines or an interactive quality calibration mechanism is needed for every analysis algorithm. HEDC provides a *data product quality calibration* function. The idea is to decrease the data quality Q_v (section 3.2) until the corresponding *analysis quality* Q_a is outside the acceptable threshold. In other words, the analysis is repeated using a decreasing number of coefficients for decoding the view until the results are no longer acceptable. Since most HEDC analysis routines produce visual images, we use the quadratic norm over the RGB vectors of all n pixels of the data product to calculate the analysis quality:

$$Q_a() = 1 - \frac{1}{n}\sum_{i=1}^{n}\|\overline{f^i} - \overline{l^i}\|^2 \qquad (2)$$

with f^i a full-resolution and l^i the corresponding low-resolution RGB pixel vector. To illustrate the calibration procedure and the effects of Q_a, Figures 4 - 5 show several snapshots of a quality calibration session using the StreamCorder. All figures are based on the same view, analysis routines and input parameters, but differ in the percentage of coefficients used for decoding the view.

In the figures, time extends from the left to the right, energy from top to bottom. Two events can be seen at the start and the end of the time scale in

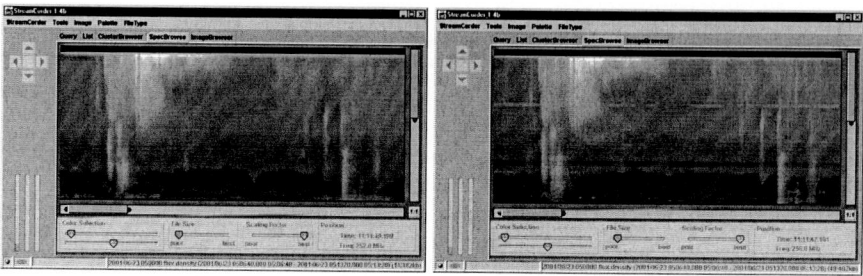

Fig. 4. (left) $Q_a = 0.7$ with 3%, (right) $Q_a = 0.8$ with 10% of coefficients.

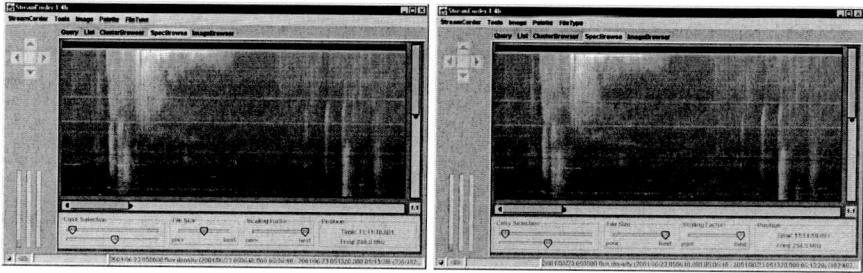

Fig. 5. (left) $Q_a = 1.0$ with 50%, (right) $Q_a = 1.0$ with 100% of coefficients.

the higher energy ranges. Figure 4 (left) displays a spectrogram based on 3% of the encoded view segment. Compared to the full-quality spectrogram in Figure 5 (right) the difference is quite small, and the relevant patterns clearly visible. The effect of increasing Q_a gradually can be seen in Figure 4 (right) for 10% of the coefficients, and in Figure 5 (left) for 50% of the coefficients. Note that Q_a is not linear on the number of coefficients used and reaches 1.0 quickly (implying there is no appreciable difference between the approximated analysis and the full quality analysis). This is an important advantage of working with images. Note that using 3% of the coefficients yields a relatively high error in the view (Figure 2). However, the resulting analysis error is much smaller. Depending on the pattern the scientist is looking for, the calibration procedure indicates which level of approximation to use. For large, easily identifiable patterns, the trial-and-error procedure can be conducted using as low as 3% of the coefficients. In practice, analysis quality is more than acceptable with 10-15% of the coefficients.

4 Performance Evaluation

4.1 Experiments

Most of the experiments have been performed with the StreamCorder running on a Pentium III 450, 256MB RAM, with a 100Mb/s Ethernet network connection to the server. In all experiments, a data set is retrieved at the server, sent to the client, decoded, and the corresponding analysis routine invoked on the decoded view (section 4.2). All experiments were performed on the same 55 selected data sets. The data sets were selected as a representative set to maintain uniformity across all experiments. Their average size is 448KB. While real HESSI data is expected to contain only a small number of relevant events per day, all segments in this set were chosen to contain at least one event and, thus, represent a worst case scenario. In practice, this means that views are sparse but not empty, and data products computed by the analysis routines are scientifically meaningful, i.e., they faithfully represent what a scientific user of HEDC would produce during trial-and-error analysis. For the experiments we use two spectrogram algorithms, one with time complexity linear on the size of the input (section 4.3) and the other exhibiting exponential complexity (section 4.4). To evaluate the impact of the communication network, we have also conducted experiments with Fast Ethernet, ISDN, and modem (section 4.5).

4.2 Measurements

The goal of the experiments is to determine how the use of approximated views affects the overall response time. This response time is the time it takes since a request is made at the StreamCorder until the results of the analysis are displayed. We will refer to this time as the overall *analysis handling time*, T_h, of a data set. This handling time is made up of the following components, which we have measured in each experiment:

- T_r, *retrieval time*, is the time necessary to query the database, retrieve the file(s) and initiate the transfer. T_r is more or less constant, having a slight effect only in those cases where the requested data involves merging many data segments.
- T_n, *network time*, represents the time required to sent the data from the server to the client. T_n varies widely with the bandwidth available and increases linearly with the size of the data to transmit.
- T_d, *decoding time*, is the time needed to decode a view. This time depends on the number of coefficients used and the size of the output.
- T_a, *analysis time*, is the time needed for the analysis routine to create the data product.

Regarding the relative weight of each component, T_r is very small compared with all other components. This is because decoding and analysis are comparatively very large. Also, most solar events (e.g., flares) are relatively short and, thus, very few segments are required in each request. The same happens with T_n when a fast connection is available. In all of our experiments, the retrieval and network time together are one order of magnitude smaller than the decoding time alone (which, in turn, is smaller than the analysis time). Thus, in practice, T_r and T_n play no role in the overall response time except in those cases where the connection is via modem (see section 4.5).

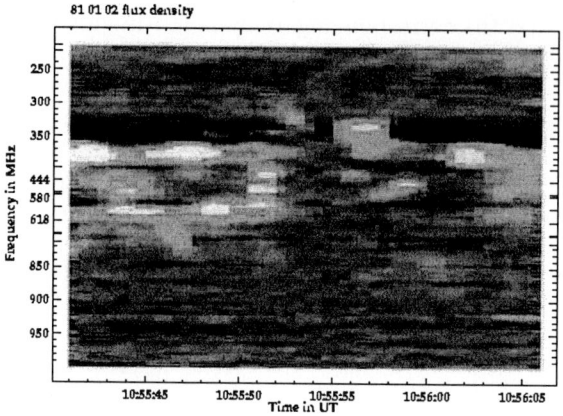

Fig. 6. Example of a full-quality and-resolution spectrogram analysis.

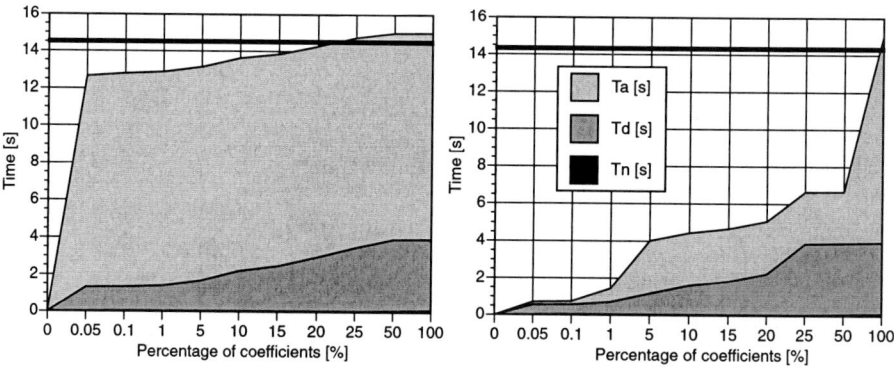

Fig. 7. T_n, T_d and T_a over fixed (left) and varying (right) sizes of the input data for the analysis routine.

4.3 Approximated Data with Fast Analyses

Figure 6 shows the image produced by a standard spectrogram analysis routine on a data set of 334KB in size. This routine is an example of the many routines found in HEDC that exhibit a linear response on the size of the input data. Since the data sets used tend to be small, such routines are computationally inexpensive, hence their grouping under the heading "fast analyses". Fast analysis routines can be further divided into a group accepting or refusing variable input data of varying resolution.

Figure 7 (left) shows the average network, decoding and analysis time for routines that require input of a fixed size as a function of the number of coefficients used for decoding and analysis. The bold line represents the overall response time when the original, gnu-zip compressed data is used. Gnu-zip does not allow progressive decoding, so that these segments have to be downloaded as a whole. As expected, the network time is insignificant compared to the decoding and analysis overhead. For these routines, the advantage of using approximated views is quite small. The problem lies on the dominant role played by the analysis time on the overall response time. Since these routines require the input to be of the same size as that of the original data, they take the same time to execute regardless of whether the original data or an approximated view is used. In fact, if 100 % of the coefficients are used, the resulting time is slightly worse than using the original data due to the decoding cost (decoding wavelet encoded data is more expensive than decompressing gnu-zipped data). Using approximated views in this case makes sense only when the client has a low bandwidth connection and the network time becomes an issue. To give an impression of what analysis results based on approximated views look like, Figure 8 contains the images produced when using 1% and 5% of the original data for the same data set as in Figure 6. Clearly, 5 % of the data suffices to have an image of sufficient quality. The performance advantage then results from the fact that, to produce the image in Figure 6, 334KB need to be transmitted while the image in Figure 8 (right) requires only to transmit 17KB.

Figure 7 (right) shows the same measurements but for analysis routines that accept input of variable resolution. Data resolution is automatically adjusted by the StreamCorder according to the number of coefficients used. The algorithm will reduce resolution in steps of two, e.g. 1/2, 1/4, etc.. Usually, acceptable results are obtained with 3 to 15 % of the coefficients and 1/8 to 1/4th the resolution. For such a degree of approximation, the overall response time is significantly reduced (on average, from over 14 seconds to around 4 seconds). If a low bandwidth connection is involved (a modem) the gain is even more spectacular (from over 4 minutes per image to less than 20 seconds). As above, the reader can compare the results when using the original data (Figure 6) and the results when using 1 % and 5 % of the coefficients and 1/4 the resolution (Figure 9). The effect of lower resolution can be clearly seen as blocky artifacts. User tests have demonstrated that these artifacts are not a problem. Nevertheless, on average, higher quality data is requested to compensate for lower resolution. Overall, for fast analysis, the techniques we propose are a significant improvement over the current state of the art.

4.4 Approximated Data with Slow Analyses

Some HEDC analysis routines exhibit exponential run time on the size of the input data. Currently there are six such analysis routines in the official HESSI software that take from minutes to days to compute when executed on typical data sets. These routines are grouped as "slow analyses". Figure 10 shows the network, decoding and analysis time for such routines as a function of the number of coefficients used. As before, the bold horizontal line represents the response time when using the original gnu-zip compressed data. For these routines, the analysis time is the only component that matters in the overall response time (hundreds of seconds compared with tens of seconds for fast analyses). Here, the advantage of the adaptive processing is obvious. Using 5% to 15% of the

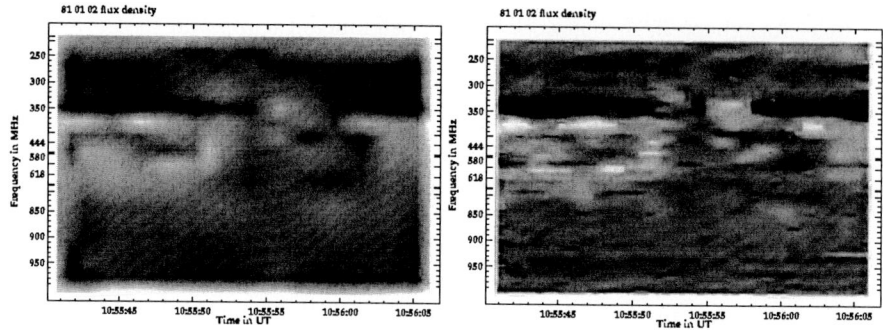

Fig. 8. Low-quality spectrograms based on 1% (3.5KB) and 5% (17KB) of the coefficients and fixed resolution.

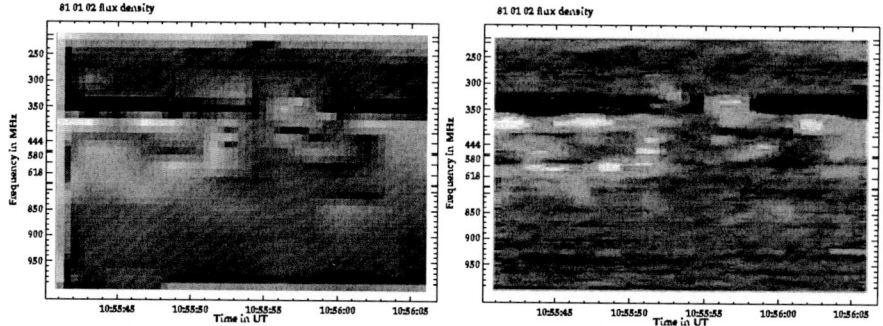

Fig. 9. Low-quality spectrograms based on 1% (3.5KB) and 5% (17KB) of the coefficients and 1/4 the resolution.

coefficients and 1/4 resolution produces results 6 times faster than when using the original data. It must be noted, however, that this routines are still too expensive to be used interactively and, therefore, tend to be executed as batch-jobs. Nevertheless, the use of adaptive processing is a great help when exploring large data ranges with these routines.

4.5 Network Bandwidth

The experiments above were performed over a LAN and, therefore, did not suffer from bandwidth limitations. Yet, we have demonstrated that our techniques significantly improve performance. The gains shown above increase by orders of magnitude when the client uses a low bandwidth connection. Here, the use of approximated data helps in that the data to transmit is much smaller than the original data. Table 1 shows the network required for different data sizes for three different network connections: 100 Mb/s (Fast Ethernet), 0.1 Mb/s (dual ISDN) and 0.056 Mb/s (V90 Modem). The size of the encoded view with respect to the original data is very similar to the percentage of coefficients used. Thus,

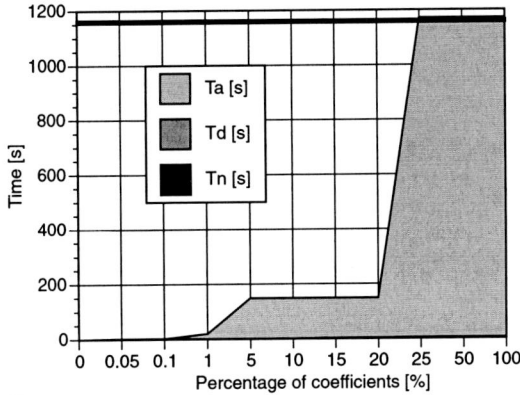

Fig. 10. T_n, T_d and T_a for exponential time routines as a function of the number of coefficients used ($n = 55$).

Table 1. Network time as a function of bandwidth and data transmitted.

View Size[KB]	0.4	8	40	120	400	800
T_n [s] (0.056 Mb/s)	0	3	12	35	117	234
T_n [s] (0.1 Mb/s)	0	1	1	2	7	14
T_n [s] (100 Mb/s)	0	0	0	1	1	2

when using, for instance, approximated views with 10 % of the coefficients, only 10 % of the original (compressed) data needs to be sent. Once the file size is larger than 100KB (as it is in most cases), the gains are obvious. Although we do not really expect many users to connect to HEDC with such low bandwidths, these results show the potential of techniques we propose.

5 Implementation

All the ideas discussed above have been implemented in HEDC and are currently being used to analyze the Phoenix data stored in HEDC. From the point of view of client side processing, however, the most relevant aspect of the system is the StreamCorder. This is where a view is decoded, adapted in size as needed, fed to an analysis routine, and the results displayed to the user. In this section we briefly describe the implementation of the StreamCorder and its basic functionality.

5.1 Architecture of the StreamCorder

The StreamCorder is a fat Java client offering the same functionality as the HEDC web-interface, plus additional features that would have been very difficult to implement using a html/applet approach. Such additions include tools for interactive low-quality/resolution browsing, progressive image display, customizable user interfaces and administrative tools.

Figure 11 shows the basic architecture of the StreamCorder. On top of the data management (DM) layer (the same one as that running on the server), the functionality is divided between the basic services and dynamically loadable modules (or *cordlets*). Core services include job- and resource-management, request queues and interfaces to local analysis programs. To increase performance, some libraries were implemented in C++. Modules are data-type sensitive, in the sense that the StreamCorder offers different modules to the user depending on the context. The context is determined by the data type of the view or analysis in question and kept across all modules. Currently available modules support browsing and download of all data types stored in HEDC, allow local and remote processing and offer administrative tools. Figure 11 (left) is a screenshot of a StreamCorder module displaying a data product.

During trial-and-error analysis, the StreamCorder coordinates the mostly asynchronous download, caching, decoding and analysis of the data. For instance, the StreamCorder will check all analysis requests to see if the analysis has already been performed. The check will take place both at the local cache and at the server. It will also check the local cache for either the raw-data and/or the encoded view, thereby offering considerable performance gains when analyses are repeated or performed over the same data set. In addition, in HEDC, not only raw-data files are wavelet encoded. Many data products (specially images) are also treated in the same way. This allows the StreamCorder to progressively display data products while the download progresses in the background. In addition, when executing low-quality analyses, especially the computationally expensive ones, the StreamCorder can continue downloading the view while the analysis proceeds on a fraction of the coefficients. If the user needs to perform a new analysis with higher resolution, the data is already there and does not need to be obtained from the server. This feature is particularly useful in certain type of analysis where users look at a very broad region and then zoom in for more detail in particular areas. An example of this is the tool provided for browsing large tuple spaces, also incorporated into the StreamCorder.

5.2 Cache Management in the StreamCorder

In a trial-and-error analysis, a data set might be processed many times. Obviously, it does not make sense for the StreamCorder to download the data anew with every analysis. Thus, the StreamCorder caches the data it downloads from the server (in fact, it caches all large data-objects that pass through it: images, encoded views and raw-data files).

Depending on how caching takes place, there are two versions of the StreamCorder. The first and lighter version uses the local file system as cache. Cache allocation is done by the DM in the StreamCorder, which calculates a unique but *static* file path for each object to cache. This path is based on fixed object attributes, such as type and creation date so different instances of the StreamCorder running in different nodes maintain compatible caches. The second, heav-

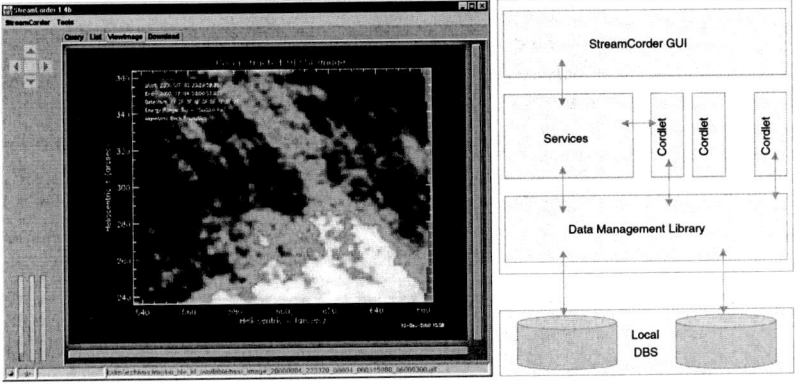

Fig. 11. The StreamCorder is a modular HEDC client written in Java, that includes a copy of the data management and a local RDBMS for offline work.

ier version of the StreamCorder uses a RDBMS[6] for caching purposes (Figure 11). This local database transparently caches query results and manages downloaded files. As the schema used locally is the same as the one on the server, every installation of the StreamCorder is, in fact, a clone of the HEDC server extended with a GUI and extra services. Thus, in combination with semantic caching, global tuple identifiers and synchronization, offline work is possible.

Since this version of the StreamCorder contains a DM and database that are identical to those at the server, it handles requests exactly in the same way as they are handled in the server. That is, when a request arrives, it checks locally for the necessary data, if it is there if responds to the request, otherwise goes to the server to download the data. For instance, if the user browses HEDC events, the StreamCorder does not only download the analysis attributes and dataobjects, but also caches the corresponding event and catalogue tuples following the same schema as in the server. Given sufficient resources (e.g., storage space), the cache will eventually hold a complete replica of all data observations and related data products the user has visited. Eventually, we expect that some of these client sites will become server themselves as they will store specialized selections of HEDC data (for instance, with all gamma ray related events found in the HEDC data). Using the heavier version of the StreamCorder will make this very easy as all the necessary functionality will be present from the start and the schema will be compatible among all systems storing HEDC data.

---

[6] For our standard PC installation, we use Oracle 8i Lite, which can be transparently installed on the client computer without a restart, easily removed and reinstalled after crashes, and which exhibits a reasonable performance. Nevertheless, any JDBC compliant database could be used. Installation of the RDBMS takes place transparently as part of the installation of the StreamCorder.

6 Conclusions and Future Work

HEDC brings together a number of novel techniques that have not been used before in scientific databases. In this paper we have focused on optimizing client side processing and show how the techniques we propose can greatly improve the process of trial-and-error analysis. We believe that these techniques can be applied in a wide range of environments. Given the characteristics of wavelet encoding, the main prerequisite for being able to use the technique is that all attributes must be floating-point numbers. The nature of the algorithms (whether they can work with low-resolution data) is not that relevant as it is always possible to recreate the original data set if necessary. These are not very restrictive requirements and there are several types of data that readily come to mind: financial, stock prices, and any physical signal that evolves as a function of time.

Regarding future work, the introduction of the StreamCorder at the client side opens up several interesting opportunities. First, the introduction of progressively decodable streams for data transfer offers the possibility of implementing Quality-of-Service mechanisms (e.g. deadlines, constraints, trade-offs between processing cost and analysis quality). Second, every StreamCorder is in reality a fully functional server. Currently, property files determine if a query request is executed locally (standalone), remotely (client/server) or simultaneously (caching client). In the future, requests will also be sent to peer StreamCorders to allow *peer to peer* interaction. This would greatly simplify the sharing and dissemination of scientific data.

References

[AD97] S. Abiteboul, O. M. Duschka Complexity of Answering Queries using Materialzied Views Technical report Stanford University, 1997

[AS98] M. J. Aschwanden, B. Kliem, U. Schwarz, J. Kurths, B. R. Dennis, R. A. Schwartz Wavelet Analysis of Solar Flare Hard X-Rays *Astrophysical Journal*, 505, 941–956,1998

[AU98] C. Aurrecoechea, A. Campell, L. Hauw A Survey of QoS architectures *Multimedia Systems*, pp. 138–151, Juni 1998

[BE93] P. Bendjoya, J. M. Petit, F. Spahn Wavelet Analysis of the Voyager Data on Planetary Rings *ICARUS*, Vol 105, pp. 385–299, 1993

[BSG00] T. Barclay, D. R. Slutz, J. Gray TerraServer: A Spatial Data Warehouse *Proc. of the ACM Conference on Management of Data (SIGMOD)*, 2000

[BRS99] F. Buccafurri, D. Rosaci, D. Sacca Compressed Datacubes for Fast OLAP Applications *First International Conference on Data Warehousing and Knowledge Discovery* (DaWaK), pp. 65–77, 1999

[BU99] R. Buyya (Ed.) *High Performance Cluster Computing*, Vol. 1 and 2, Prentice Hall, 1999

[CD97] S. Chaudhuri, U. Dayal An Overview of Data Warehousing and OLAP Technology *ACM SIGMOD Record, 26(1), March 1997*

[CGR00] K. Chakrabarti, M. Garofalakis, R. Rastogi, K. Shim Approximate Query Processing Using Wavelets *Proc. of the VLDB Conference, Cairo, Egypt*, pp. 111–120, 2000

[CKP95] S. Chaudhuri, R. Krishnamurthy, S. Potamianos, K. Shim Optimizing Queries with Materialized Views *ICDE*, pp. 190–200, 1995
[CNS99] S. Cohen, W. Nutt, A. Serenbrenik Algorithms for Rewriting Aggregate Queries Using Views *Proc. of the International Workshop on Design and Management of Data Warehouses (DMDW)*, pp. 9.1–9.12, 1999
[DG97] O. M. Duschka, M. R. Genesereth Answering Recursive Queries using Views *Proc. of the PODS Conference*, pp. 109–116, 1997
[DHK97] Jochen Doppelhammer, Thomas Höppler, Alfons Kemper, Donald Kossmann Database Performance in the Real World - TPC-D and SAP R/3 Proceedings ACM SIGMOD International Conference on Management of Data, May 13-15, 1997, Tucson, Arizona, USA
[EC00] Mining the Digital Skies The Economist http://www.economist.com/, (3.06.2000)
[GM98] P. B. Gibbons, Y. Matias New Sampling-Based Summary Statistics for Improving Approximate Query Answers *Proc. of the Conference on Managment of Data (SIGMOD)*, Seattle, USA, pp. 331-342, June 1998
[GTKD00] D. Gunopulos, V. N. Tsotras, G. Kollios, C. Domeniconi Approximating multi-dimensional aggregate range queries over real attributes *Proc. of the Conference on Management of Data (SIGMOD)*, Dallas, USA, May 2000
[HHW97] J. M. Hellerstein, P. J. Haas, H. J. Wang Online Aggregation *Proc. of the Conference on Management of Data (SIGMOD)*, Tucson, USA, May 1997
[HMS00] W. Hoschek, J. J. Martinez, A. S. Samar, H. Stockinger, K. Stockinger Data Management in an International Data Grid Project *ACM Workshop on Grid Computing (GRID-00)*, Bangalore, India, 17-20 Dec., 2000
[IPO99] Y. E. Ioannidis, V. Poosala Histrogram-Based Approximation of Set-Valued Query Answers *Proc. of the VLDB Conference, Edinburgh, Great Britain*, September 1999
[JS94] B. Jawerth, W. Sweldens An Overview of Wavelet-based Multiresolution Analyses *SIAM Review*, 36(3), pp. 377–412, 1994
[KSD98] G. Kaestle, E. C. Shek, S. K. Dao Sharing Experiences from Scientific Experiments *Proc. of the International Conference on Scientific and Statistical Database Management*, 1998
[LMS95] A. Y. Levy, A. O. Mendelzon, D. Srivastava, Y. Sagiv Answering Queries Using Views *Proc. of the PODS Conference*, 1995
[MVW00] Y. Matias, J. S. Vitter, M. Wang Dynamic Maintenance of Wavelet-Based Histograms *Proc. of the VLDB Conference*, Cairo, Egypt, pp. 101–110, 2000
[OE97] B. Oezden, R. Rastogi, A. Silverschatz Multimedia Support for Databases *Proc. of the PODS Conference*, 1997
[RAA01] M. Riedewald, D. Agrawal, A. E. Abbadi Flexible Data Cubes for Online Aggregation *Proc. of the Int. Conference on Database Theory*, pp. 159-173, 2001
[S99] G. Stoesser et. al. The EMBL Nucleotide Sequence Database *Nuclear Acids Research*, 27(1), 18-24. 1999
[SFB99] J. Shanmugasundaram, U. Fayyad, P. S. Bradley Compressed Data Cubes for OLAP Aggregate Query Approximation on Continuous Dimensions *KDD*, Dan Diego, USA, pp. 223-231, 1999
[SH99] F. Sheikholeslami, S. Chatterjee, A. Zhang WaveCluster: a wavelet-based clustering approach for spatial data in very large Databases *The VLDB Journal*, Vol. 8 No 3-4, pp. 289-304, 2000

[SKT00] A. Szalay, P. Z. Kunszt, A. Thakar, J. Gray, and D. R. Slutz Designing and mining multi-terabyte astronomy archives: The sloan digital sky survey *Proc. of the Conference on Management of Data (SIGMOD)*, Dallas, USA, pp. 451–462, May 16-18, 2000

[VI98] J. S. Vitter, M. Wang, B. Iyer Data Cube Approximation and Histograms via Wavelets *Proc. of the CIKM*, Bethesda, USA, 1998

[VW01] J. S. Vitter, M. Wang Approximate Computation of Multidimensional Aggregates of Sparse Data Using Wavelets *Proc. of the Conference on Management of Data (SIGMOD)*, Philadelphia, USA, June 1999

[WW98] J. Z. Wang, G. Wiederhold, O. Firschein, S. X. Wei Content-based image indexing and searching using Daubechies wavelets *International Jounal on Digital Libraries*, Volume 1, Issue 4, pp. 311–328, 1998

[WZS95] J. T. Wang, K. Zhang , D. Shasha Pattern Matching and Pattern Discovery in Scientific, Program, and Document Databases. *Proc. of the Conference on Management of Data (SIGMOD)*, 1995

[ZI94] M. Zemankova , Y. E. Ioannidis Scientific Databases - State of the Art and Future Directions. *Proc. of the VLDB Conference*, Santiago, Chile, 1994

Supporting Efficient Parametric Search of E-Commerce Data: A Loosely-Coupled Solution

Min Wang, Yuan-Chi Chang, and Sriram Padmanabhan

IBM T. J. Watson Research Center, Hawthorne, NY 10532
{min, yuanchi, srp}@us.ibm.com

Abstract. Electronic commerce is emerging as a major application area for database systems. A large number of e-commerce sites provide electronic product catalogs that allow users to search products of interest.
Due to the constant evolution and the high sparsity of e-commerce data, most commercial e-commerce systems use the so-called vertical schema for data storage. However, query processing for data stored using vertical schema is extremely slow because current RDBMS, especially its cost-based query optimizer, is designed to deal with traditional horizontal schema efficiently.
Most e-commerce systems would like to offer advanced parametric search capabilities to their users. However, most searches are expected to be on-line which means that the query execution should be very fast. RDBMSs require new capabilities and enhancements before they can satisfy the search performance criteria against vertical schema. The tightly-coupled enhancements and additions to a DBMS require considerable amount of work and may take a long time to be accomplished. In this paper, we describe an alternative approach called *SAL*, a Search Assistant Layer that can be implemented outside a database engine to accommodate the urgent need for efficient parametric search on e-commerce data. Our experimental results show that dramatic performance improvement is provided by SAL for search queries.

1 Introduction

Electronic commerce is emerging as a major application area for database systems. A large number of e-commerce sites provide electronic product catalogs that allow buyers, sellers, and brokers to search products of interest.

Imagine we are running a marketplace for a big retail chain such as Sears. The e-catalog of this marketplace may contain tens of thousands of products. Each product has its own set of attributes. For example, a "T-shirt" product in woman's apparel category may be associated with the attribute set {*size, style, color, price*}. Another product "TV set" in the electronics category may have a quite different attribute set {*brand, view_type, signal_type, screen_size, price*}.

A natural technique for storage of the product information in a relational database system is the *horizontal schema*. Each product is represented as a row in a table, and the columns are the union of the attribute sets across all products. However, this natural approach is not practical due to the following reasons [3]:

- The total number of attributes across all the products can be huge, but current commercial DBMSs do not permit a large number of columns in a table (e.g., both DB2 and Oracle permit only up to 1012 columns in a table).
- Even if a DBMS were to allow huge number of columns in a table, we would have a lot of nulls in most of the fields (e.g., any T-shirt product has a null value in *view_type* column). The large number of null values creates a big storage overhead and increases the size of indexes on these columns.
- Due to the large number of columns and null values, query performance would be very poor since the data records are very wide and only a few columns are used in a query.
- In an electronic marketplace, products traded and sold vary from day to day. We would need frequent altering of the table to accommodate new products. Maintenance and processing of altered tables can be quite expensive in RDBMSs.

An alternative is to use *binary schema* [6, 10]. We create one table for each attribute. Each table contains two columns, one is an attribute column and the other is an *OID* column that ties different fields of a tuple across tables. While there are no null values when using a binary schema, the number of join operations is usually large even when processing simple queries. Hence query performance is a big issue for the binary schema solution. An enhancement is to define a table per product set. This becomes unwieldy since the requirement is for dynamically adding and deleting new products.

Many commercial e-commerce systems use the so-called *vertical schema* design for their e-catalogs. Like the horizontal method, only one table is used. However, this table only has three main attributes: *OID*, *Attr* (for attribute name), and *Value* (for attribute value). [1] Each product is represented as a number of tuples in this table, one for each attribute-value combination and multiple attributes of a product are tied together using the same *OID* across multiple tuples in the table.

Table 1 is an example product table in horizontal representation. The table describes products that consist of one or more attributes in the set $\{A_1, A_2, A_3, A_4, A_5\}$. In the table, null values are denoted by empty spaces. The vertical and binary representations of Table 1 are shown in Figure 1.

The vertical schema has the following advantages when compared to the others:

- *High flexibility:* The schema can handle any number of products and attributes.
- *Ease of schema evolution:* When products are added or deleted, alter or create table operations are not needed. We only need to add/delete tuples that correspond to the attributes of the added/deleted products.

---

[1] In reality, the *Value* column needs to be extended to accommodate values of different data types. Figure 4 in Section 4 shows one way of doing it.

Table 1. Horizontal representation

OID	A_1	A_2	A_3	A_4	A_5
1	v_1	v_2	v_3		v_4
2	v_5	v_6	v_7		v_8
3	v_9	v_{10}			v_{11}
4			v_{12}	v_{13}	v_{14}
5			v_{15}		v_{16}
6				v_{17}	v_{18}

– *Low storage overhead:* In contrast to horizontal schema, the vertical table does not contain null values.

Due to the above reasons, many commercial e-commerce systems (e.g., IBM Websphere Commerce Server, Ariba Marketplace, I2 Technology) utilize the vertical schema design for their e-catalogs.

Unfortunately, the vertical schema's flexibility introduces performance challenges for one important activity on e-catalogs, namely, *parametric search queries*. A parametric search query [2] is a lookup of the e-catalog using specific constraints. Since a product usually contains many attributes, a search query in general is likely to impose several constraints that could be combined in a logical expression using AND/OR or even more sophisticated operators. Writing SQL queries against vertical schema could be cumbersome and error-prone. To solve this problem, Agrawal et al. proposed a method of creating a logical horizontal view on top of a vertical schema [3]. They also presented a set of query rewrite algorithms to convert relational algebra operators against the horizontal view to that against the vertical table. However, the performance of the converted query remains an issue. They show that queries against vertical schema performs no better than against binary schemas in most cases. The main reason for poor performance is that the query optimization and planning techniques in traditional RDBMSs are more suitable for horizontal schema containing well defined and meaningful attributes. Section 2 provides the details.

To achieve good query performance within an RDBMS when using vertical schema, several components need to be enhanced and new capabilities need to be added [3]. The tightly-coupled enhancements and additions to a DBMS require considerable amount of work and may take a long time to be accomplished. In this paper, we present a loosely-coupled solution that can be implemented by building a *Search Assistant Layer* (SAL) outside the database engine. We show that the SAL approach is a viable solution for supporting efficient parametric search against vertical data since SAL effectively provides vertical schema specific query planning and execution capability. It intercepts user search queries and determines the constraints using a *workload learner* component. This component identifies important logical attributes of the vertical schema and their relationships. A self-tuning *histogram builder* is employed to generate single

---
[2] See Section 2 for examples.

OID	Attr	Value
1	A_1	v_1
1	A_2	v_2
1	A_3	v_3
1	A_5	v_4
2	A_1	v_5
2	A_2	v_6
2	A_3	v_7
2	A_5	v_8
3	A_1	v_9
3	A_2	v_{10}
3	A_5	v_{11}
4	A_3	v_{12}
4	A_4	v_{13}
4	A_5	v_{14}
5	A_3	v_{15}
5	A_5	v_{16}
6	A_4	v_{17}
6	A_5	v_{18}

(a) Vertical representation

OID	A_1
1	v_1
2	v_5
3	v_9

OID	A_2
1	v_2
2	v_6
3	v_{10}

OID	A_3
1	v_3
2	v_7
4	v_{12}
5	v_{15}

OID	A_4
4	v_{13}
6	v_{17}

OID	A_5
1	v_4
2	v_8
3	v_{11}
4	v_{14}
5	v_{16}
6	v_{18}

(b) Binary representation

Fig. 1. Vertical and binary representations

and multi-dimensional histograms for the most important constraint attributes. SAL's *query planner* consults the histograms before deciding from a number of query execution choices. Finally, a simple *query processor* layer module is used to combine results of sub-queries as well as to perform post processing. We have evaluated SAL for search queries against realistic e-catalogs. Our performance results validate that SAL is required to provide good performance for parametric search queries against vertical schema.

The rest of the paper is organized as follows. In the next section, we analyze the reasons for poor query performance when data are stored using vertical schema. In Section 3, we describe the SAL approach in more detail. We present our experimental results in Section 4 and draw conclusions in Section 5.

2 Why Are Search Queries Against Vertical Schema So Slow?

In e-commerce applications, users usually search for desired products by providing bounds (constraints) on attribute values. For example, a user may be interested in finding all the T-shirts that satisfy the following constraints: $size = \text{'M'}$, $color = \text{'Purple'}$, and $\$45 \leq price \leq \$50$. If we store all T-shirt products in a table T-shirt(*OID, size, style, color, price*), such a query is expressed easily against the horizontal schema as shown below.

Q_1: SELECT *OID*
FROM T-shirt
WHERE *size* = 'M' AND *color* = 'Purple' AND $45 \leq price \leq$ $50

A generic search query against a horizontal schema H has the following format:

SELECT *OID*
FROM H
WHERE (A_{i_1} not null) AND (bound on A_{i_1}) AND
(A_{i_2} not null) AND (bound on A_{i_2}) AND
...
(A_{i_k} not null) AND (bound on A_{i_k})

In this paper, we only consider the above type of queries.

Most RDBMSs transform the logical query plan represented by the query into a *physical query plan* which represents the operations, the method of performing the operations, and the order of processing the different operations [7]. In generating a physical query plan, the RDBMS uses a query optimizer module which considers many different physical plans that are derived from the logical plan, and evaluates or estimates their costs. After this evaluation, also called as *cost-based optimization*, it picks the physical query plan with the least estimated cost and passes that to the query-execution engine. The efficiency of the query execution depends mainly upon the accuracy of the cost estimation.

Usually a query optimizer estimates cost of a query plan based on statistics collected from the base data. The query optimizer builds a *histogram* for each attribute during an offline phase. The histogram contains the statistical information about the distribution of the corresponding attribute and is stored in a database system catalog [16, 13, 15, 11].

Subsequently, when Q_1 (the T-shirt query) is issued, the query optimizer can quickly estimate the (approximate) selectivity [3] of the three predicates in the WHERE clause based on the three histograms in the catalog. For example, if the (estimated) selectivity of the predicate *color* = 'Purple' is 0.01%, and is much lower than those for the other two predicates, it is very likely that the query optimizer will choose an index scan using the index on the *color* column (assuming the existence of such index) before applying the other two predicates.

Suppose all products are stored in a vertical table V. Query Q_1 corresponds to the following query which assumes a single *Value* column. (As mentioned earlier, the *Value* column needs to be extended to accommodate values of different data types. Figure 4 in Section 4 shows one approach.)

Q_2: SELECT *OID*
FROM V

---

[3] The selectivity of a query predicate is the number of rows in the table that satisfy this predicate divided by the table size.

```
WHERE  Attr = 'size' AND Value = 'M'
INTERSECT
SELECT OID
FROM V
WHERE  Attr = 'color' AND Value = 'Purple'
INTERSECT
SELECT OID
FROM V
WHERE  Attr = 'price' AND $45 ≤ Value ≤ $50
```

Note that the three logical constraints in Q_1 are transformed into six constraints in Q_2. Among these six constraints, three of them are selecting specific attribute names (i.e., *size*, *color*, and *price*) while the other three specify values (i.e., 'M', 'Purple', and between 45 and 50). When we use the vertical schema, the *Value* column contains the values for *all attributes across all product categories*. Similarly, the *Attr* column contains the string names of all product attributes. The query optimizer still collects the statistical information about the data distribution on these two columns and constructs histograms. However, the information in the histograms is a poor approximation of the distribution of the all attribute names and values for all products. Since the total number of such logical attributes is huge, the histograms become very misleading when we use it to estimate the selectivity of a constraint (e.g., *color* = 'Purple') on a specific product category (e.g., T-shirt). Additionally, the optimizer must choose methods to combine the results of the individual sets of constraints in order to generate the final result. Usually, predicate selectivities are combined assuming *independence*. However, in parametric search queries, the constraints are usually mutually dependent as is the case in our example above. Thus, the optimizer generates poor cardinality estimates and this translates to poor choices on access methods as well as combining operations. In our study, we found that a traditional RDBMS usually generates a physical plan that involves several poorly chosen access methods and join algorithms on the vertical table for a query that is similar to Q_2. Since the vertical table is large, these query plans result in very long execution time. Essentially, the optimizer is handicapped and can not choose a better plan for search queries against vertical schema.

In an online search environment, any long query execution time is not acceptable. This is the familiar conundrum facing many e-commerce systems today. They would like to provide advanced parametric search capability but are stymied by the inadequate response time for such queries. Users want both the power of advanced search as well as the immediate online response time!

3 SAL: The Search Assistant Layer

We identified the main cause of poor query performance as the inadequacy of the cardinality estimation techniques and statistics of RDBMSs. The cost estimation inside RDBMS is misled by vertical schema due to aggregated statistics of heterogeneous attributes (columns) from different products. There are two possible approaches to solve the performance problem. The first approach is to modify the indexing and query optimization components of the RDBMS to account for vertical schema. This tightly integrated solution requires database kernel change. While it is the likely long term solution, it does not solve the immediate problem at hand. In this paper, we take an alternative approach of building a Search Assistant Layer (SAL) outside the RDBMS. SAL collects the statistics of the vertical table in a more intelligent way and uses it to patrol and remedy the queries that might lead to suboptimal performance. For example, even though the *Value* column is a single column in the vertical table, we should be aware of the fact that this column is actually a combination (union) of many attributes and these attributes should be treated separately. Moreover, if certain attribute names (e.g., *view_type*, *signal_type*) are associated with certain product category (e.g., TV) and are usually queried together, the optimizer should choose to build a multi-dimensional histogram to capture the joint distribution of the multiple attributes. Our loosely integrated solution does not require any change to the database engine and provides a good short-term solution to the vertical schema search problem.

SAL is composed of four components:

- A *workload learner* that learns from the query workload and decides attributes sets on which histograms should be built.
- A *histogram builder* that builds the selected external histograms outside the RDBMS and uses query feedback to refine the histograms in an online manner.
- A *query planner* that estimates the selectivity of the predicates in a query based on the external histograms and choose the most efficient physical plan. The query planner uses a rule-based optimizer approach driven by a deep understanding of the vertical schema parameters.
- A *query processor* that executes the SAL query plan and retrieve the query results from the underlying tables in an RDBMS.

Figure 2 shows SAL's architecture.

Next, we elaborate on the four components of SAL.

3.1 Workload Learner

Query optimizer in an RDBMS has traditionally built single-attribute histograms to compute the selectivity of queries [16, 13, 15]. For queries that involve multiple attributes, most RDBMSs assume *attribute value independence*, which usually leads to significant inaccuracy in selectivity estimation [14]. A better alternative is to construct *multidimensional histogram* over multiple attributes [12, 14, 11]. A lot of work has been reported in the literature on designing different types of histograms [16, 13–15, 12, 11].

In practice, an RDBMS can only allocate very limited amount of space to store the histograms. In our approach, we build histograms in SAL. The storage limitation applies to SAL as well even though it is less strict compared to

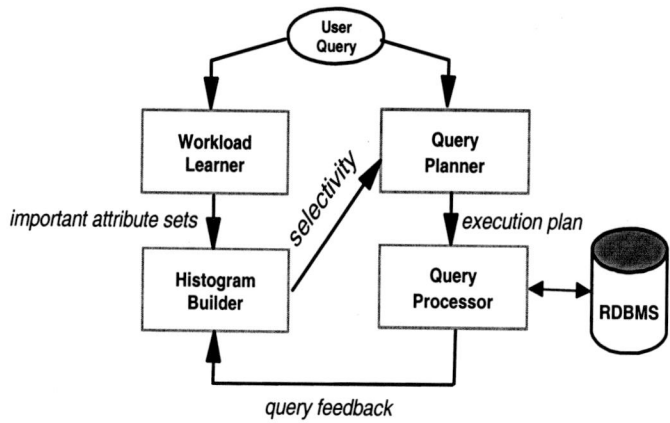

Fig. 2. SAL's architecture

RDBMS histograms. The main reason here is not to conserve memory but rather to conserve query optimization time. The histograms must be small enough to be processed efficiently in a short period of time during query optimization phase.

A typical vertical schema usually contains a large number of logical attribute names and values. Given the vertical schema, we face the problem of *identifying logical attributes that are most important for query processing so that we can effectively use the limited amount of storage*. This requirement can only be addressed by analyzing the search query workload.

Even though this is a fundamental problem in histogram construction and query optimization, there is only very limited amount of past work in this area. Most previous work has focused on identifying the optimal histogram for a *given* attribute or attribute set using fixed amount of storage space. The most relevant work is on global optimization of histograms [9]. In [9], Jadagish et al. presented the idea of global optimization of histograms, i.e., single-attribute histograms for a set of attributes are optimized collectively so as to minimize the overall error in using the histograms. However, the more important problem of choosing the attributes (attribute sets) for constructing histograms remains unsolved.

A naive approach is to build histograms for all possible attribute sets. Since the total number of attributes across all product categories is usual huge, this naive approach is not practical at all. Moreover, a typical search query usually only involves attributes that correspond to a specific product or category. For example, it is very likely that a query contains constraints on attributes *view_type* and *signal_type* at the same time, but it is almost impossible that a query involves both *view_type* (of a TV set) and *style* (of a T-shirt). Hence building histograms for attributes that belong to different product categories becomes a waste of resource. Even for attributes that correspond to the same product category, some attributes are more frequently queried than others. Obviously, building histograms for attributes that frequently appear in queries is more valuable. Also, if a set of attributes is frequently being queried together, we should construct a multidimensional histogram in order to provide better cardinality estimates.

In our method, we propose to build a workload leaner to accomplish the task of identifying the important attribute sets on which histograms should be built. The main features of the workload learner module are:

1. When a query is issued, SAL will parse and record the attributes involved in the query constraints as a *transaction entry* in a *query log*. For example, query Q_1 in Section 2 corresponds to transaction $\{size, color, price\}$ in the query log.
2. When there are more than N (a tunable parameter) transactions in the query log, we process it to discover all the *maximally important attribute sets*.
3. The maximally important attribute sets are passed to the histogram builder.

The critical step is to discover all the important attribute sets. Intuitively, an attribute set is important if and only if it appears in a lot of queries. We use the association rule discovery [2, 4, 17, 8, 19] to guide the important attribute set discovery.

Let Q be the query log and A be a set of attributes. The *support* (or occurrence frequency) of A is the number of transactions in Q that A appears [4] divided by the total number of transactions in Q. An attribute set A is called an *important attribute set* if its support is no less than a predefined *minimum support threshold*. A *maximally important attribute set* is an important attribute set such that none of its supersets is an important attribute set.

Table 2 shows an example query log Q of size 6. For example, the support of attribute set $\{A_1, A_2, A_3\}$ is 1/2 and the support of attribute set $\{A_4, A_5\}$ is 1/3. If the minimum support threshold is 1/2, the important attribute sets are $\{A_1\}$, $\{A_2\}$, $\{A_3\}$, $\{A_4\}$, $\{A_1, A_2\}$, $\{A_1, A_3\}$, $\{A_2, A_3\}$, and $\{A_1, A_2, A_3\}$. Among them, attribute sets $\{A_1, A_2, A_3\}$ and $\{A_4\}$ are maximally important attribute sets.

Table 2. Query Log

QID	Transaction
Q_1	$\{A_1, A_2, A_3, A_4\}$
Q_2	$\{A_1, A_2, A_3\}$
Q_3	$\{A_1, A_2, A_3\}$
Q_4	$\{A_4, A_5, A_6\}$
Q_5	$\{A_4, A_5\}$
Q_6	$\{A_4, A_6\}$

The above definition of (maximally) important attribute set directly corresponds to that of large (frequent) item set in association rule mining studied in the literature [2, 4, 17, 8, 19]. We can hence apply any standard association mining algorithm to the query log to find all the maximally important attribute sets.

---

[4] An attribute set A appears in a transaction t if A is a subset of t (i.e., $A \subseteq t$).

After the important attribute set discovery is done, the query log may keep growing when more queries are issued, and we need to update the important attribute sets to capture the distribution of the changed workload. This can be done in an incremental fashion as suggested in [5, 18].

3.2 Histogram Builder

Suppose we obtain n maximally important attribute sets through the workload learner while the amount of storage allocated for external histograms is M bytes. The histogram builder constructs n (multidimensional) histograms under the storage constraint.

The first question for the histogram builder is *how to allocate the storage amongst the histograms?* In our method, we use a simple heuristic based on two intuitions:

- Even though all the n attribute sets are important, it is possible to rank them based on their support. The ones with higher support should be allocated more space during histogram construction.
- An attribute set containing more attributes should be allocated more space because histograms with higher dimensionality usually need more space to achieve reasonable accuracy.

More precisely, suppose the dimensionality of the ith ($1 \leq i \leq n$) maximally important attribute set is d_i and its support is s_i, we use the following formula to compute the amount of storage that should be allocated to its corresponding histogram:

$$M_i = M \times \frac{\alpha s_i + \beta d_i}{\sum_{1 \leq j \leq n} (\alpha s_j + \beta d_j)},$$

where α and β are both positive constants.

The second set of problems faced by the histogram builder is:

- What type of histograms to construct?
- How to dynamically maintain the histograms as the underlying base data changes (i.e., new products are inserted and old products are deleted) over time?

In our current working prototype, we built multidimensional equi-depth histograms using the self-tuning technique presented in [1]. Even though similar in structure to traditional equi-depth histogram, the self-tuning histogram infers data distribution not by examining the data but by using query feedback from the query execution engine. The feedback is used to progressively refine the histogram. Besides low building cost, the self-tuning histogram also has the nice property of low maintenance cost since it is refined through query feedback when the underlying data distribution changes. For details about self-tuning histogram, please refer to [1].

3.3 Query Planner

The query planner is the crucial module of SAL that is responsible for choosing an efficient processing strategy for the common parametric search queries. Its effectiveness is a result of its intimate knowledge (gained from histograms described previously) of the distribution statistics of the logical attributes and attribute sets in the vertical schema. The query planner generates a higher level logical query processing plan for the original query. Such a logical plan might comprise of one or more logical subqueries that are submitted to the underlying RDBMS and then combined in the SAL query processor module.

By examining and experimenting with a large number of queries and data distributions, we concluded that queries against product categories with hundreds and thousands of products in a large catalog (relative to buffer pool size) can create suboptimal query plans if processed directly by an RDBMS engine. Product category is a natural way to group similar products and conduct parametric searches. Our conclusion is expected since estimation error appears in the statistical deviation on the distribution of subsets of records in the database. These queries need to be intercepted and rewritten following one or more strategies described below. On the other hand, we have also observed that there is no need to alter queries against either very small product categories (tens of products) or extremely large categories (compared to catalog size). The former case is driven by filtering the category and the latter has a smaller estimation error due to its large relative size.

These observations result in three rules for determining a SAL query plan. These options are *Direct Search* (DS), *Nested Invocation* (NI), and *Supervised N-way Join* (SN).

Direct Search. The first option is the Direct Search (DS) approach that leaves the query optimization and execution to the database engine. As mentioned above, SAL will choose this strategy for certain types of queries and certain product categories.

Nested Invocation. The second option is referred as the Nested Invocation (NI) method. An opportunity to apply this method arises when the query planner knows that one or more constraints in the query has very small selectivity that can quickly reduce the number of OIDs in consideration. It is then best to retrieve the much smaller group of OIDs and verify if the other constraints are satisfied by them. For example, in query Q_2, suppose $color = $ 'Purple' is the most selective constraint. SAL can issue a simple query to retrieve OIDs satisfying $Attr = $ 'color' AND $Value = $ 'Purple'. Suppose the resulting OIDs are 1011, 1022, and 1033. The resulting OIDs are then used in an IN clause to drive the following query:

```
SELECT OID
FROM V
WHERE Attr = 'size' AND Value = 'M'
INTERSECT
```

```
SELECT OID
FROM V
WHERE  Attr = 'price' AND $45 ≤ Value ≤ $50
INTERSECT
SELECT OID
FROM V
WHERE  OID IN (1011, 1022, and 1033).
```

Supervised N-way Join. The third option is the Supervised N-way join (SN) method. When the NI method is not applicable, it is often faster to retrieve OIDs satisfying individual constraints and then find their intersection set in memory. For example, to process query Q_2, three separate queries are issued and their OIDs are retrieved to an in-memory data structure. Figure 3 shows the separate queries. The OIDs are joined in-memory inside SAL and a followup query is issued to retrieve other select list items. While the SN method suffers from the cost of reading data from database, the method often delivers surprisingly good performance with fast CPU and large memory in modern computers.

```
SELECT OID              SELECT OID                SELECT OID
FROM V                  FROM V                    FROM V
WHERE Attr = 'size'     WHERE Attr='color'        WHERE Attr='price'
AND Value='M'           AND Value='Purple'        AND 45<=Value <= 50
```

Fig. 3. Independent Subqueries in Supervised N-Way Join

Besides the three options discussed above, there are other ways to improve query performance. The choice is a balance between database execution time and in-memory processing time. In-memory processing time can be significant if a very large number of OIDs are read out of database but are discarded in later steps.

Our loosely-integrated solution relies on additional information to spot "troubled" queries and makes a decision among DS, NI and SN methods. The query planner needs to know the number of products in the queried category, the selectivity of each query constraint, and the expected number of products satisfying all query constraints. A less selective constraint on a large category or large result set is always a concern as estimation error may aggravate search performance.

Since it is expensive to collect the needed information from database, an external histogram becomes the choice of our solution. The histogram builder and its associated workload learner determine the sets of product attributes in a category to be selected for histogram learning. Details are specified in Section 3.1 and Section 3.2

The query planner makes a series of decisions to detect "troubled" queries and remedy potential performance problems. It is observed that in the vertical schema, the cost (query execution time) of the complete database query is highly nonlinear and difficult to characterize analytically. Hence, SAL's query planner is designed to be rule-based. The current implementation follows three simple rules, each of which corresponds to one option:

1. DS: For categories with very small number of products (e.g., a category containing no more than 100 *OID*s), do not change the query and let database execute the complete query.
2. NI: For a query with one or more highly selective constraints (e.g., result is no more than 1000 *OID*s), execute the most selective constraint(s) first and retrieve the qualified *OID*s. Formulate the query with the rest of the constraints and place the retrieved *OID*s in an IN clause to drive the join.
3. SN: For a query with less selective constraints (e.g., each constraint generates more than 1000 *OID*s), break up the query into several queries by applying one logical constraint in each and execute them one by one. The resulting *OID* sets are joined in memory inside SAL.

3.4 Query Processor

With the query plan assigned, SAL's query processor executes the plan and retrieves results requested. Since the query processor may need to find the intersection set of multiple returned results, we implemented the intersection method using the Java utility *hashset*. Hashset is a set class with *hashtable* function associated with the key. Using hashset allows the method to quickly decide whether an *OID* exists in the set or not.

In addition, the query processor is commissioned to retrieve attribute descriptions, values, and other properties associated with an *OID* in the final result.

4 Experimental Results

In this section, we compare the performance of SAL with that of executing parametric searches on vertical schema using a traditional RDBMS directly. We refer the latter as DS method.

All our experiments were run on a 933MHz single processor Intel Pentium machine with 1GB DRAM. The operation system was Windows 2000 and the database system used was DB2 UDB 7.1. The machine had a single 17GB SCSI drive. The buffer pool size was set to 168MB and the prefetch size was set to 256KB.

The schemas used in the experiments are typically seen in electronic catalog datastore. First, a table CATE_PROD is used to store the relationship between product categories (CATEGORY_ID) and product definitions (CATENTRY_ID). Under each product definition (CATENTRY_ID), multiple attributes may be registered in the ATTRIBUTE table. The ATTRIBUTE table maps the attribute name (NAME) and product definition (CATENTRY_ID) to attribute identifier (ATTRIBUTE_ID), which are used in the vertical table. The vertical table ATTRVALUE exhibits the 3-ary form of (OID, ATTRIBUTE_ID, ATTRIBUTE_VALUE). An OID is the reference identifier of a product that can be bought, which must be associated with a product definition through the set of ATTRIBUTE_IDs. The attribute values are represented in the database native format such as VARCHAR, BIGINT, and DOUBLE to facilitate search, and the

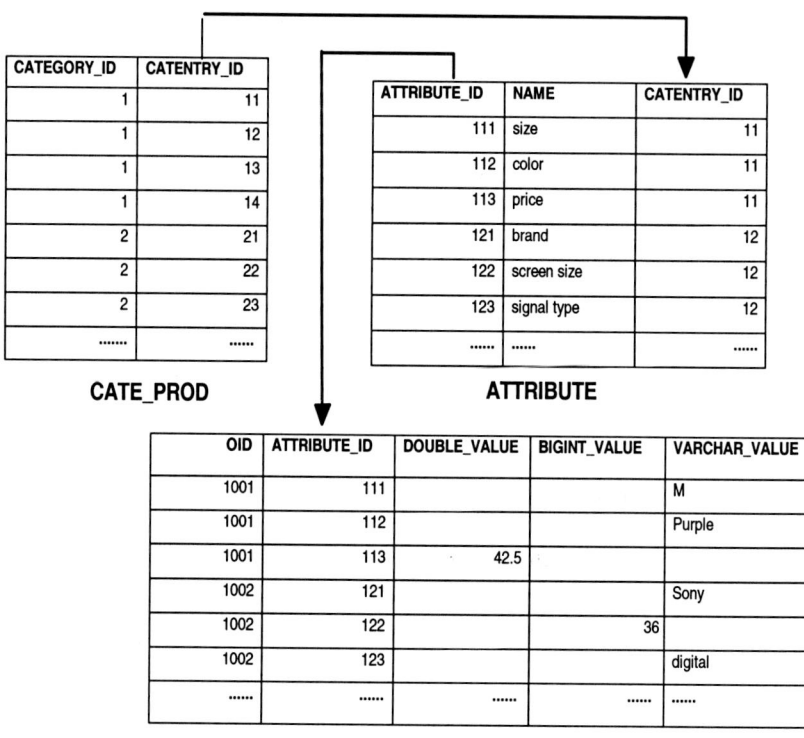

Fig. 4. An example e-catalog

three data types are represented as three columns in the vertical table ATTR-VALUE. The relations among CATE_PROD, ATTRIBUTE, and ATTRVALUE are described using an example shown in Figure 4

We populated 300,000 products and their information were put into the catalog using a Java tool which simulates real data set. The products are evenly divided among 60 product definitions, four of which are associated to the search category. In other words, the category contains 20,000 products. Each product has 10 attributes of VARCHAR, BIGINT, or DOUBLE data types. Attribute values are discrete and were generated randomly and independently. The cardinality of the ATTRVALUE is on the order of 3 million rows. Multi-attribute indices on ATTRVALUE were built on the 3-ary form and detailed distribution statistics was collected by the DBMS before we ran any query. An index on CATE_PROD was also created to link categories and product definitions.

Queries were generated randomly by a Java tool which independently decides value ranges of query constraints. A query consists of 2–6 logical constraints. (Each logical constraint corresponds to two constraints in the query against the vertical schema.) We summarized the main results with benchmark numbers of the following two methods for a set of representative queries only.

- DS: Queries are executed by DBMS directly.
- SAL: Queries are executed using SAL.

We measured the end-to-end execution time for each methods. For SAL, the execution time included execution time within DBMS and in-memory processing time. Queries are issued through JDBC driver offered by the database vendor.

Figure 5 shows the performance of SAL versus that of DS for three typical query sets. Each query set contains 1000 queries with two, three, or four logical constraints. The selectivities of the queries vary from 0% to 20%. We measured the average execution time for queries in different selectivity ranges. We can see from the figures that for any query that contains 2–4 logical constraints, the average query execution time for SAL was always in the range of 0.3 second to 1.5 seconds while that of DS was in the range of 2.2 seconds to 116 seconds.

We also observed that when the number of constraints in the query increases, the gap between the two methods became huge. The execution time for SAL only increased slightly while DS took at lease several minutes to execute any query containing more than three logical constraints. Note that in online e-catalog search applications, any query respond time beyond several seconds usually becomes unacceptable for customers.

5 Conclusions

In this paper, we have proposed and designed a loosely-coupled Search Assistant Layer , SAL, for enabling parametric search queries against electronic catalogs stored using vertical schema. In the past, e-commerce systems did not support ad-hoc parametric search against such catalogs because the response time was usually too long. SAL maintains histogram based distribution statistics for the logical attributes appearing in search constraints. Multidimensional histograms are constructed for logical attributes that appear jointly. SAL's query planner consults these histograms and uses a number of rules to decide on a logical query execution strategy. The query planner could choose Direct Search, Nested Invocation, or Supervised N-way Join methods. We have implemented and evaluated SAL in IBM's Websphere Commerce Suite product. Our results show that SAL produces significant performance improvement for ad-hoc parametric searches and facilitates online searches against e-commerce catalogs greatly.

At present, SAL has several limitations. The query planner could use a more rigorous formula to estimate cost of a query plan. However, this will not be easy even if cost estimation from the database optimizer can be accessed. We have observed that the cost estimates reported are quite often far off the real execution time. Secondly, the current implementation only addresses constraints that are combined using AND operators (conjunction). A general logic expression with hierarchies of ANDs and ORs is more difficult to optimize. Finally, the query planner does not address queries involving both vertical and horizontal schema. This multi-model search problem is our next focus.

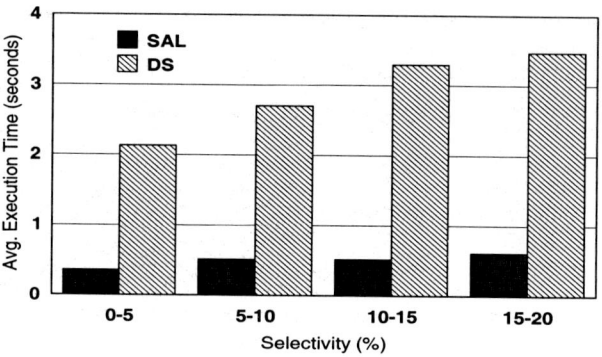

(a) For queries with two logical constraints

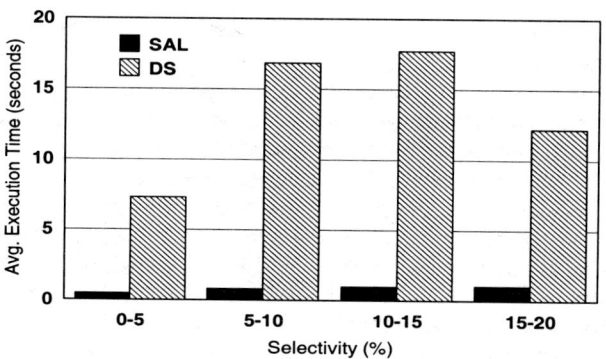

(b) For queries with three logical constraints

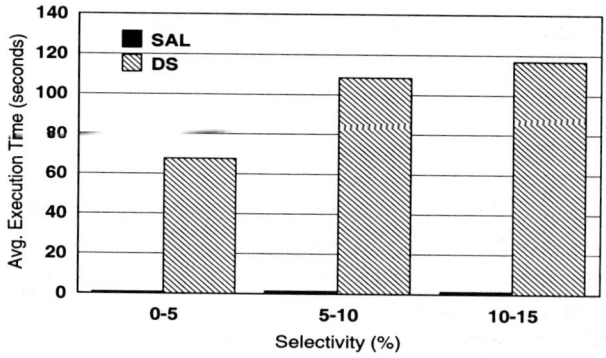

(c) For queries with four logical constraints

Fig. 5. Average query execution time

References

1. A. Aboulnaga and S. Chaudhuri. Self-tuning histograms: Building histograms without looking at data. In A. Delis, C. Faloutsos, and S. Ghandeharizadeh, editors, *SIGMOD 1999, Proceedings ACM SIGMOD International Conference on Management of Data, June 1-3, 1999, Philadephia, Pennsylvania, USA*, pages 181–192. ACM Press, 1999.
2. R. Agrawal, T. Imielinsk, and A. Swami. Mining association rules between sets of items in large databases. In *Proceedings of the 1993 ACM SIGMOD International Conference on Management of Data*, pages 207–216, 1993.
3. R. Agrawal, A. Somani, and Y. Xu. Storage and querying of e-commerce data. In *VLDB'01, Proceedings of 27rd International Conference on Very Large Data Bases, September 11-14, 2001, Roma, Italy*. Morgan Kaufmann, 2001.
4. R. Agrawal and R. Srikant. Fast algorithms for mining association rules. In *Proceedings of the 1994 International Conference on Very Large Databases*, pages 487–499, 1994.
5. D. W.-L. Cheung, J. Han, V. Ng, and C. Y. Wong. Maintenance of discovered association rules in large databases: An incremental updating technique. In S. Y. W. Su, editor, *Proceedings of the Twelfth International Conference on Data Engineering, February 26 - March 1, 1996, New Orleans, Louisiana, USA*, pages 106–114. IEEE Computer Society, 1996.
6. G. P. Copeland and S. Khoshafian. A decomposition storage model. In S. B. Navathe, editor, *Proceedings of the 1985 ACM SIGMOD International Conference on Management of Data, Austin, Texas, May 28-31, 1985*, pages 268–279. ACM Press, 1985.
7. H. Garcia-Molina, J. Ullman, and J. Widom. *Database System Implementation*. Prentice-Hall, 2000.
8. J. Han, J. Pei, and Y. Yin. Mining frequent patterns without candidate generation. In W. Chen, J. F. Naughton, and P. A. Bernstein, editors, *Proceedings of the 2000 ACM SIGMOD International Conference on Management of Data, May 16-18, 2000, Dallas, Texas, USA*, volume 29, pages 1–12. ACM, 2000.
9. H. V. Jagadish, H. Jin, B. C. Ooi, and K.-L. Tan. Global optimization of histograms. In *Proceedings of the 2001 ACM SIGMOD International Conference on Management of Data, May 21-24, 2001, Santa Barbara, CA, USA*, pages 223–234, 2001.
10. S. Khoshafian, G. P. Copeland, T. Jagodis, H. Boral, and P. Valduriez. A query processing strategy for the decomposed storage model. In *Proceedings of the Third International Conference on Data Engineering, February 3-5, 1987, Los Angeles, California, USA*, pages 636–643. IEEE Computer Society, 1987.
11. Y. Matias, J. S. Vitter, and M. Wang. Wavelet-based histograms for selectivity estimation. In *Proceedings of the 1998 ACM SIGMOD International Conference on Management of Data*, pages 448–459, Seattle, WA, June 1998.
12. M. Muralikrishna and D. J. DeWitt. Equi-depth histograms for estimating selectivity factors for multi-dimensional queries. In *Proceedings of the 1988 ACM SIGMOD International Conference on Management of Data*, pages 28–36, 1988.
13. G. Piatetsky-Shapiro and C. Connell. Accurate estimation of the number of tuples satisfying a condition. In *Proceedings of the 1984 ACM SIGMOD International Conference on Management of Data*, pages 256–276, 1984.
14. V. Poosala and Y. E. Ioannidis. Selectivity estimation without the attribute value independence assumption. In *Proceedings of the 1997 International Conference on Very Large Databases*, Athens, Greece, August 1997.

15. V. Poosala, Y. E. Ioannidis, P. J. Haas, and E. Shekita. Improved histograms for selectivity estimation of range predicates. In *Proceedings of the 1996 ACM SIGMOD International Conference on Management of Data*, Montreal, Canada, May 1996.
16. P. G. Selinger, M. M. Astrahan, D. D. Chamberlin, R. A. Lorie, and T. G. Price. Access path selection in a relational database management system. In *Proceedings of the 1979 ACM SIGMOD International Conference on Management of Data*, pages 23–34, 1979.
17. R. Srikant and R. Agrawal. Mining quantitative association rules in large relational tables. In H. V. Jagadish and I. S. Mumick, editors, *Proceedings of the 1996 ACM SIGMOD International Conference on Management of Data, Montreal, Quebec, Canada, June 4-6, 1996*, pages 1–12. ACM Press, 1996.
18. S. Thomas, S. Bodagala, K. Alsabti, and S. Ranka. An efficient algorithm for the incremental updation of association rules in large databases. In *KDD 1997, Proceedings of the Third International Conference on Knowledge Discovery and Data Mining, August 14-17, 1997, Newport Beach, California, USA*, pages 263–266. AAAI Press, 1997.
19. K. Wang, Y. He, and J. Han. Mining frequent itemsets using support constraints. In A. E. Abbadi, M. L. Brodie, S. Chakravarthy, U. Dayal, N. Kamel, G. Schlageter, and K.-Y. Whang, editors, *VLDB 2000, Proceedings of 26th International Conference on Very Large Data Bases, September 10-14, 2000, Cairo, Egypt*, pages 43–52. Morgan Kaufmann, 2000.

Divide-and-Conquer Algorithm for Computing Set Containment Joins

Sergey Melnik* and Hector Garcia-Molina

Stanford University CA 94305, USA

Abstract. A set containment join is a join between set-valued attributes of two relations, whose join condition is specified using the subset ($\subseteq$) operator. Set containment joins are used in a variety of database applications. In this paper, we propose a novel partitioning algorithm called Divide-and-Conquer Set Join (DCJ) for computing set containment joins efficiently. We show that the divide-and-conquer approach outperforms previously suggested algorithms over a wide range of data sets. We present a detailed analysis of DCJ and previously known algorithms and describe their behavior in an implemented testbed.

1 Introduction

Many database applications utilize set containment queries, especially when the underlying database systems support set-valued attributes. For example, consider a database application that recommends to students a list of courses that they are eligible to take. Imagine that the set of courses taken by a student is stored in the set-valued attribute {courseID} of table Attended(studentID, {courseID}). Another table, Prereq(courseID, {reqCourseID}), keeps a set of prerequisite courses. Then, a list of courses that a student may take can be computed using a set containment query SELECT Attended.studentID, Prereq.courseID WHERE Prereq.{reqCourseID} $\subseteq$ Attended.{courseID}. In this query, the tables are joined on their set-valued attributes using the subset operator $\subseteq$ as the join condition. This kind of join is called set containment join.

Set containment joins are used in a variety of other scenarios. If, for instance, our first relation contained sets of parts used in construction projects, and the second one contained sets of parts offered by each equipment vendor, we could determine which construction projects can be supplied by a single vendor using a set containment join. Or, consider a human resource broker that matches the skills of job seekers with the skills required by the employers. In this scenario, a set containment join on the skills attributes can be used to match the qualifying employees and their potential employers. Notice that containment queries can be utilized even in database systems that support only atomic attribute values, as illustrated in [MGM01] (there we give an example of a set containment query expressed using SQL). Additional types of applications for containment joins

---

* On leave from the University of Leipzig, Germany

arise when text or XML documents are viewed as sets of words or XML elements, or when flat relations are folded into a nested representation.

It has been shown in [HM97] and [RPNK00] that naive or standard-SQL approaches to computing set containment queries are very expensive. Each of the papers suggested a more efficient way of computing set containment joins. Unfortunately, the algorithm proposed in [HM97] is a main-memory algorithm and cannot cope with large amounts of data. Furthermore, the partitioning-based algorithm suggested in [RPNK00] has limitations when the cardinalities of the sets are large. Often, however, the sets involved in the join computation are indeed quite large. For instance, biochemical databases contain sets with many thousands elements each. In fact, the fruit fly (drosophila) has around 14000 genes, 70-80% of which are active at any time. A snapshot of active genes can thus be represented as a set of around 10000 elements. The algorithm suggested in [RPNK00] is ineffective for such data sets.

The contributions of this paper are two-fold. First, we suggest a novel partitioning-based algorithm that outperforms the existing approaches for a large variety of data sets. We called this algorithm the Divide-and-Conquer Set Join (DCJ), because it can be viewed conceptually as a series of partitioning steps. Second, we develop a detailed analytical model for comparing different partitioning algorithms. We also analyze the behavior of the algorithms in an implemented testbed and discuss how a best-performing algorithm can be chosen for given input relations. To compare DCJ with the approach of [HM97], we develop a partitioning algorithm called the Lattice Set Join (LSJ), which is in essence a disk-based version of the main-memory algorithm introduced in [HM97]. In this paper, we give only a brief summary of the results obtained for LSJ and show that the divide-and-conquer approach always outperforms LSJ.

This paper is structured as follows. In Section 2 we explain how signatures and partitioning are used for computing set containment joins, and illustrate the algorithm that we developed using a simple example. Section 3 deals with the theoretical analysis of our novel algorithm and the existing partitioning algorithms. After that, in Section 4, we provide a qualitative comparison of the algorithms. In Section 5 we examine the performance of the algorithms in an implemented system. Finally, we discuss related work in Section 6 and conclude the paper in Section 7.

2 Algorithms

We start this section with a brief overview of set containment joins, signatures and partitioning. Then we describe the Partitioning Set Join (PSJ) algorithm [RPNK00], which is to our knowledge the best known method for computing set containment joins for relations that do not fit into main memory. Finally, we explain the Divide-and-Conquer Set Join algorithm that we developed.

2.1 Set Containment Joins, Signatures and Partitioning

A *set containment* join is a join between set-valued attributes of two relations, whose join condition is specified using the subset ($\subseteq$) operator. Consider two sample relations R and S shown in Table 1. Each of the relations contains one column with four sets of integers. For easy reference, the sets of R and S are labeled using letters a, b, c, d and A, B, C, D, respectively. Computing the containment join $R \bowtie_\subseteq S$ amounts to finding all tuples $(s, t) \in R \times S$ such that $s \subseteq t$. In our example, $R \bowtie_\subseteq S = \{(a, A), (b, B), (c, C)\}$.

Table 1. Two sample relations with set-valued attributes

Relation R	Relation S
$a = \{1, 5\}$	$A = \{1, 5, 7\}$
$b = \{10, 13\}$	$B = \{8, 10, 13\}$
$c = \{1, 3\}$	$C = \{1, 3, 13\}$
$d = \{8, 19\}$	$D = \{2, 3, 4\}$

Table 2. 4-bit signatures of sets in R and S

$x \in R$	$sig(x)$	$y \in S$	$sig(y)$
a	0010	A	1010
b	0110	B	0111
c	1010	C	1010
d	1001	D	1101

Obviously, we can always compute $R \bowtie_\subseteq S$ in a straightforward way by testing each tuple in the cross-product $R \times S$ for the subset condition. In our example, such approach would require $|R| \cdot |S| = 4^2 = 16$ set comparisons. For large relations R and S, doing n^2 comparisons becomes very time consuming. The set comparisons are expensive, since each one requires traversing and comparing a substantial portion of the elements of both sets. Moreover, when the relations do not fit into memory, enumerating the cross-product incurs a substantial I/O cost.

For computing set containment joins efficiently, two fundamental techniques have been suggested: signatures [HM97] and partitioning [RPNK00]. The idea behind signatures is to substitute expensive set comparisons by efficient comparisons of signatures. A *signature* of a set is a hash value over the content of the set that has certain order-preserving properties. To illustrate, consider the example in Table 2. In the table, the signature of each set from the sample relations R and S is represented as a vector of 4 bits. Each set element j turns on a bit at the position ($j \mod 4$) in the bit vector. For instance, for set $d = \{8, 19\}$ we set bit 0 (8 mod 4) and bit 3 (19 mod 4), and obtain $sig(\{8, 19\}) = 1001$.

Let $\subseteq^b$ be the bitwise inclusion predicate. Notice that $sig(x) \subseteq^b sig(y)$ holds for any pair of sets x, y with $x \subseteq y$. Thus, we can avoid many set comparisons by just testing the signatures for bitwise inclusion. For instance, since $sig(d) \not\subseteq^b sig(A)$, we know that d cannot be a subset of A. Bitwise inclusion can be verified efficiently by testing the equality $sig(x) \& \neg sig(y) = 0$, where $\&$ and $\neg$ are the bitwise AND and NOT operators. In our example, after 16 signature comparisons we only need to test 7 pairs of sets for containment: $(a, A), (a, B), (a, C), (b, B), (c, A), (c, C)$, and (d, D). Of these remaining pairs, $(a, B), (a, C), (c, A)$ and (d, D) are rejected as false positives.

Using signatures helps to reduce the number of set comparisons significantly, yet still requires n^2 comparisons of signatures. *Partitioning* has been suggested to further improve performance by decomposing the join task $R \bowtie S$ into k smaller subtasks $R_1 \bowtie S_1, \ldots, R_k \bowtie S_k$ such that $R \bowtie S = \bigcup_{i=1}^{k} R_i \bowtie S_i$. The so-called *partitioning function* π assigns each tuple of R to one or multiple partitions $R_1, \ldots, R_k$, and each tuple of S to one or multiple partitions $S_1, \ldots, S_k$. Consider our sample relations R and S from Table 1. Let $\pi(a) = \pi(b) = \pi(A) = \pi(B) = \{1\}$, $\pi(c) = \pi(d) = \pi(C) = \{2\}$, and $\pi(D) = \{1, 2\}$. That is, R is partitioned into $R_1 = \{a, b\}$, $R_2 = \{c, d\}$, and S is partitioned into $S_1 = \{A, B, D\}$, $S_2 = \{C, D\}$. Note that we have constructed π so that tuples in R_1 can only join S_1 tuples, and R_2-tuples can only join S_2-tuples. Thus, finding $R \bowtie_\subseteq S$ amounts to computing $(R_1 \bowtie_\subseteq S_1) \cup (R_2 \bowtie_\subseteq S_2)$. Notice that computing $R_1 \bowtie_\subseteq S_1 = \{a, b\} \bowtie_\subseteq \{A, B, D\}$ and $R_2 \bowtie_\subseteq S_2 = \{c, d\} \bowtie_\subseteq \{C, D\}$ requires only $2 \cdot 3 + 2 \cdot 2 = 10$ signature comparisons. Hence, by using partitioning we reduced the total number of signature comparisons from 16 to 10. We refer to the fraction $\frac{10}{16}$ as a *comparison factor*. The comparison factor ranges between 0 and 1.

Besides reducing the number of required signature comparisons, partitioning helps to deal with large relations R and S that do not fit into main memory by storing the partitions $R_1, \ldots, R_k$ and $S_1, \ldots, S_k$ on disk. To minimize the I/O costs of writing out the partitions to disk and reading them back into memory, the partitions typically contain only the set signatures and the corresponding tuple identifiers. In our example, $|\{a, b\}| + |\{c, d\}| = 4$ signatures from $R_{1,2}$ and $|\{A, B, D\}| + |\{C, D\}| = 5$ signatures from $S_{1,2}$ are stored on disk temporarily. We refer to the ratio between the total number of signatures that are written out to disk and the total number of tuples in R and S as the *replication factor*. In our example, the replication factor is $\frac{4+5}{4+4} = \frac{9}{8}$. Assuming that no partition is permanently kept in main memory, the optimal replication factor that can be achieved in a partition-based join is 1.

A major challenge of effective partitioning is to construct a partitioning function π that minimizes the comparison and replication factors. Obviously, π needs to be correct, i.e., it has to ensure that all joining tuples are found.

2.2 Partitioning Set Join (PSJ)

The Partitioning Set Join (PSJ) is an algorithm proposed by Ramasamy et al [RPNK00]. To illustrate the algorithm, we continue with the example introduced above. Imagine that we want to partition R and S from Table 1 into $k = 8$ partitions. The partition number of each set of R is determined using a single, randomly selected element of the set. Consider the set $a = \{1, 5\} \in R$. Let 5 be a randomly chosen element of a. We assign a to one of the partitions $0, 1, \ldots, 7$ by taking the element value modulo $k = 8$. Thus, a is assigned to partition R_5. Element 10 chosen from $b = \{10, 13\}$ yields partition number $2 = (10 \bmod 8)$. Finally, sets c and d both fall into partition R_3 based on randomly chosen elements $3 \in c$ and $19 \in d$. Now we repeat the same procedure for S, but consider *all* elements of each set for determining the partition numbers. Taking all elements into account ensures that all joining tuples will be found. Thus,

$A = \{1, 5, 7\}$ is assigned to partitions S_1, S_5, and S_7, $B = \{8, 10, 13\}$ goes into partitions S_0, S_2, and S_5, etc. The complete partition assignment for R and S is summarized in Figure 1.

Once both relations are partitioned, i.e. the set signatures and tuple identifiers have been written out to disk, each pair of partitions is read from disk and joined independently. For example, when R_3 and S_3 are joined, the signatures of sets c and d are read from R_3, and are compared with the signatures of sets C and D stored in S_3. Hence, computing $R_3 \bowtie_\subseteq S_3$ results in $2 \cdot 2 = 4$ signature comparisons. The total number of signature comparisons required in our example amounts to $0+0+2+4+0+3+0+0 = 9$, whereas the total of 16 signatures need to be written out to disk. Thus, in this example, we obtain the comparison factor $\frac{9}{16} \approx 0.56$, and replication factor $\frac{16}{4+4} = 2$.

2.3 Divide-and-Conquer Set Join (DCJ)

The Divide-and-Conquer Set Join (DCJ) is a novel partitioning algorithm that we present in this paper. Again, we illustrate the algorithm using our running example of Table 1 and $k = 8$ partitions. We explain DCJ using a series of partitioning steps depicted in Figure 2. In every step, one *boolean hash function* is used to transform an existing partition assignment into a new assignment with twice as many partitions. This transformation, or repartitioning, is done by applying either operator α or operator β to a given pair of partitions $R_i \bowtie S_i$, as indicated by the labels 'α' and 'β' placed on the forks in Figure 2. Although we illustrate DCJ conceptually as a branching tree, the final partition assignment is computed without using any intermediate partitions (see algorithmic specification in [MGM01]).

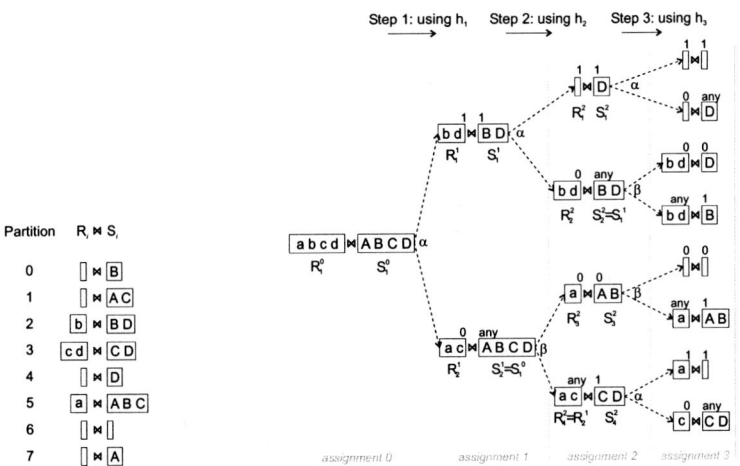

Fig. 1. Partitioning with PSJ: 9 comparisons, 16 replicated

Fig. 2. Divide and conquer: 8 comparisons, 14 replicated

Table 3 defines three boolean hash functions that we will use in our example to partition the relations. Each of the hash functions takes a set of integers as input, and returns 0 or 1 as output. For example, function h_3 returns 1 (i.e. fires) for a given set s if and only if s contains an integer divisible by 5 or by 7. Notice that every of h_1, h_2 and h_3 is *monotone* in the sense that if any of the functions fires for a given set x, then it is guaranteed to fire for each superset of x. The intuition is to make each of the functions fire independently of the other with an approximately equal probability for any randomly selected set of R or S. Each of the functions h_1, h_2, and h_3 are characterized by a set of prime divisors, as shown in Table 3. The boolean values returned by the hash functions for each set of R and S are listed in Table 4. Other types of hash functions can be used by our algorithm. See Section 3 for an additional discussion of hash functions.

Table 3. Definition of three boolean hash functions

Hash fct	Prime divisors	Definition
h_1	$\{2\}$	$h_1(s) = 1 \iff \exists e \in s : (e \mod 2 = 0)$
h_2	$\{3\}$	$h_2(s) = 1 \iff \exists e \in s : (e \mod 3 = 0)$
h_3	$\{5, 7\}$	$h_3(s) = 1 \iff \exists e \in s : (e \mod 5 = 0) \vee (e \mod 7 = 0)$

Table 4. Applying hash functions to elements of R and S

$x \in R$	h_1	h_2	h_3	$y \in S$	h_1	h_2	h_3
a	0	0	1	A	0	0	1
b	1	0	0	B	1	0	1
c	0	1	0	C	0	1	0
d	1	0	0	D	1	1	0

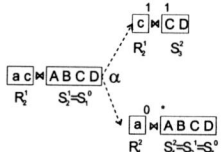

Fig. 3. Why β is needed: applying α when $|R_2^1| < |S_2^1|$ leads to a larger replication factor

Relations $R = \{a, b, c, d\}$ and $S = \{A, B, C, D\}$ form the initial partition assignment $R \bowtie S = R_1^0 \bowtie S_1^0$, where the superscript 0 indicates the step number. In Step 1, we derive a new partition assignment $(R_1^1 \bowtie S_1^1) \cup (R_2^1 \bowtie S_2^1)$ from $R \bowtie S$ using operator α as follows. First, the initial partition R is split into R_1^1 and R_2^1 based on the value of h_1. That is, the sets b and d with $h_1(b) = h_1(d) = 1$ are sent to R_1^1, while the sets a and c with $h_1(a) = h_1(c) = 0$ are assigned to R_2^1. We abbreviate this procedure concisely as $R_1^1 := R/h_1$, $R_2^1 := R/\neg h_1$. The values 1 and 0 taken by h_1 are depicted above the partitions R_1^1 and R_2^1 in Figure 2.

Now imagine that we pick an arbitrary set from S, say set A. Since $h_1(A) = 0$ then, due to monotonicity of h_1, all joining subsets of A are guaranteed to be contained in $R_2^1 := R/\neg h_1$. Therefore, it is sufficient to assign set A to partition S_2^1 only, without losing any joining tuples. The same argument applies for set C. For sets B and D, h_1 takes value 1, meaning that joining subsets of B and those of D may be found both in R_1^1 and in R_2^1. Hence, B and D need to be replicated, i.e., assigned to both partitions S_1^1 and S_2^1. By doing so, S is repartitioned into $S_1^1 := S/h_1$ and $S_2^1 := S$ based on the values taken by h_1 (1 for S_1^1 and 'any' for S_2^1, as shown in the figure). Thus, Step 1 consists of a single application of operator α using hash function h_1, yielding the partition assignment 1, i.e. $(\{b,d\} \bowtie \{B,D\}) \cup (\{a,c\} \bowtie \{A,B,C,D\})$. Notice that instead of $4 \cdot 4 = 16$ signature comparisons required for $R \bowtie S$, only $2 \cdot 2 + 2 \cdot 4 = 12$ signature comparisons would be needed for joining the partitions of assignment 1.

In Step 2, we use function h_2 to derive the partition assignment 2 from assignment 1. Assignment 2 is obtained by first applying operator α to $R_1^1 \bowtie S_1^1$, and then applying a different operator called β, to $R_2^1 \bowtie S_2^1$. Operator β works in the same way as α, except that S_2^1 is split first, and a portion of R_2^1 is replicated. Because β splits partition S_2^1, which contains supersets, we replicate the sets of R_2^1 with $h_2 = 0$ instead of those with $h_2 = 1$. Thus, the 'top' partition of R_2^1 becomes $R_2^1/\neg h_2$, while the 'bottom' partition contains all of R_2. Clearly, operator β performs a correct repartitioning; since h_2 is monotone, all joining supersets of the sets in R_2^1/h_2 are guaranteed to be contained in S_2^1/h_2. Thus, it is sufficient to replicate only those sets from R_2^1 with $h_2 = 0$, i.e. just the set a.

Table 5. Repartitioning of $R \bowtie S$ using operators α and β, and a monotone boolean hash function h

Operator	Ideally, when	Resulting partition assignment
$\alpha(R \bowtie S, h)$	$|R| \geq |S|$	$(R/h \bowtie S/h) \cup (R/\neg h \bowtie S)$
$\beta(R \bowtie S, h)$	$|R| < |S|$	$(R/\neg h \bowtie S/\neg h) \cup (R \bowtie S/h)$

The definition of β, along with that of α, is shown in Table 5. Either operator α and β performs correct repartitioning and can be applied at each fork. The reason for using β in addition to α is to minimize replication. Notice that by using operator β for repartitioning $R_2^1 \bowtie S_2^1$ into $(\{a\} \bowtie \{A,B\}) \cup (\{a,c\} \cup \{C,D\})$, we reduced the number of comparisons from 8 to 6, and increased the number of signatures that need to be stored from 6 to 7. Figure 3 illustrates what would have happened if we used operator α. Although we would have obtained the same reduction in number of comparisons, the number of signatures to be replicated would have grown to 8. Since $|R_2^1| < |S_2^1|$, β causes less replication by splitting the larger partition S_2^1 and replicating the smaller partition R_2^1.

Ideally, we would apply α for repartitioning of any given $R_j \bowtie S_j$ whenever $|R_j| \geq |S_j|$, and use β when $|R_j| < |S_j|$. However, since generating and writing out the intermediate partitions to disk is prohibitive, their exact sizes are not known. Consequently, we use a simple heuristic. To minimize the replication factor, α and β are applied in an alternating fashion as suggested by fork labels in Figure 2. That is, the 'top' pair of partitions produced by applying α in Step i is repartitioned using α in Step $i+1$. In contrast, the 'bottom' pair is repartitioned using β. Thus, we use the pattern $\alpha \to \alpha, \beta$. Similarly, the 'top' and 'bottom' pair of partitions produced by β are repartitioned using β and α, respectively (pattern $\beta \to \beta, \alpha$). The intuition behind this heuristic is to always use β on partitions that were replicated in the previous step. For example, since S_2^1 was obtained by replication in Step 1, we apply β to split it in Step 2.

In Step 3, we arrive at the final partition assignment by applying function h_3 (since we are using 8 partitions, and each repartitioning step doubles the number of partitions, the number of steps is $\log_2 8 = 3$). In the final assignment, the total of $0+0+2+2+0+2+0+2 = 8$ signature comparisons are required, whereas 14 signatures need to be written out to disk. Thus, we obtain a comparison factor of $\frac{8}{16} = 0.5$, and a replication factor of $\frac{14}{4+4} = 1.75$.

3 Analysis of the Algorithms

In this section we present a summary of the theoretical analysis of the partitioning algorithms PSJ, DCJ, and LSJ. For a detailed discussion, which includes the derivation of all formulas, please refer to [MGM01]. As an efficiency measure of the algorithms we utilize the comparison and replication factors. Recall that the comparison factor is the ratio between the actual number of signature comparisons, and $|R| \cdot |S|$. In other words, the comparison factor is the probability that the signatures of two randomly selected sets $r \in R$ and $s \in S$ will be compared during the join computation. The replication factor is the ratio of the number of signatures of R and S stored on disk temporarily, and $|R|+|S|$. The comparison factor approximates the CPU load, whereas the replication factor reflects the I/O overhead of partitioning.

Set containment join $R \bowtie_\subseteq S$ can be characterized by a variety of parameters including the distribution of set cardinalities in relations R and S, the distribution of set element values, the selectivity of the join, or the correlation of element values in sets of both relations. In our analysis, we are making the following simplifying assumptions:

1. The R, S set elements are drawn from an integer domain $\mathcal{D}$ using a uniform probability distribution[1]. The size $|\mathcal{D}|$ of the domain is much larger than the number of partitions k and the set cardinalities of R and S.
2. Each set $r \in R$ contains a fixed number of θ_R elements, while each set $s \in S$ contains θ_S elements, $0 < \theta_R \leq \theta_S$.
3. Joining each pair of partitions R_i and S_i requires $|R_i| \cdot |S_i|$ signature comparisons (for instance, partitions are joined using a nested loop algorithm).

We will relax these assumptions in our experiments in Sections 4 and 5. All other factors relevant to computing the join are considered identical for every of the partitioning algorithms. These factors include the number of bits in the signatures, the size of the available main memory, the buffer management policy of the database system, etc. For estimating the comparison and replication factors, we additionally use a derived parameter $\lambda = \frac{\theta_S}{\theta_R}$ that denotes the ratio of the set cardinalities, and the parameter $\rho = \frac{|S|}{|R|}$ that denotes the ratio of

---
[1] Notice that non-integer domains can be mapped onto integers using hashing.

the relation sizes. The variables that we utilize for analyzing the algorithms are summarized in Table 6. For instance, for our sample relations in Table 1 we obtain $|R| = |S| = 4$, $\rho = \frac{4}{4} = 1$, $\theta_R = 2$, $\theta_S = 3$, and $\lambda = \frac{3}{2} = 1.5$, i.e., the sets in relation S are 50% larger than the sets of R.

Table 6. Variables used for analyzing the algorithms

θ_R, θ_S	Set cardinalities in R and S
λ	Ratio of set cardinalities, $\lambda = \frac{\theta_S}{\theta_R}$
k	Number of partitions
l	Number of boolean hash functions used in LSJ and DCJ ($l = \log_2 k$)
$|R|, |S|$	Relation cardinalities
ρ	Ratio of relation cardinalities, $\rho = \frac{|S|}{|R|}$

The comparison and replication factors derived using the above assumptions are listed in Table 7. The table also shows the results obtained for the Lattice Set Join (LSJ) algorithm (an extension of the algorithm presented in [HM97]), which we analyze in the extended report [MGM01]. LSJ utilizes boolean hash functions like those used in DCJ, and yields the same comparison factor. In LSJ, each set $r \in R$ is assigned to a partition whose index is obtained as a boolean number $h_1(r)h_2(r)\cdots h_l(r)$. Each set $s \in S$ is assigned to partition $h_1(s)h_2(s)\cdots h_l(s)$ and, additionally, to each partition whose index is bitwise included in $h_1(s)h_2(s)\cdots h_l(s)$. Thus, the partitions generated by LSJ logically form a power lattice.

Note that in our model the selectivity of the join $R \bowtie S$ can be varied using the parameters θ_R, θ_S, and $|\mathcal{D}|$. As we show in [MGM01], the expected selectivity is $\frac{\theta_S!(|\mathcal{D}|-\theta_R)!}{(\theta_S-\theta_R)!|\mathcal{D}|!}$. For instance, for $\theta_R = 2$, $\theta_S = 3$, and $|\mathcal{D}| = 10$, we obtain the selectivity of $\frac{3!(10-2)!}{(3-2)!10!} \approx 0.066$. That is, the expected number of joining tuples for relations R and S having 4 tuples each (like those in Table 1) is $0.066 \cdot 4^2 \approx 1$. If $\mathcal{D}$ is large, the selectivity is almost zero. For example, for $|\mathcal{D}| = 1000$, $\theta_R = 10$ and $\theta_S = 20$, the selectivity is below 10^{-18}, i.e., a join between R and S with a billion tuples each is expected to return just one tuple.

Optimal hash functions Recall that DCJ partitions the relations R and S using l monotone boolean hash functions $h_1, \ldots, h_l$ into $k = 2^l$ partitions. In [MGM01] we derive the *optimal* firing probability for these hash functions that minimizes the comparison factor $comp_{\text{DCJ}}$ (and $comp_{\text{LSJ}}$). There are several ways of constructing such optimal functions, i.e., those that fire independently of each other with a fixed optimal probability. One simple approach is the following. Consider that for each given set s of fixed cardinality $|s|$ we compute a bit string[2] of length

---

[2] We use the term bit string instead of signature to avoid ambiguity. Although the bit strings are computed in the same way as signatures, they are not related to the signatures stored in partitions in any way.

Table 7. Summary of replication and comparison factors for PSJ, LSJ, and DCJ

Algorithm	Comparison and replication factors
PSJ	$comp_{PSJ} = 1 - \left(1 - \frac{1}{k}\right)^{\theta_S}$ $repl_{PSJ} = \frac{1}{1+\rho} + \frac{\rho}{1+\rho} k\left(1 - \left(1 - \frac{1}{k}\right)^{\theta_S}\right)$
DCJ	$comp_{DCJ} = \left(1 - \frac{1}{1+\lambda}\left(\frac{\lambda}{1+\lambda}\right)^{\lambda}\right)^{\log_2 k}$ $repl_{DCJ} = (1\ 1) \cdot \left[\frac{1}{1+\rho}\left(\begin{array}{cc}\frac{1}{1+\lambda} & \frac{1}{1+\lambda} \\ \frac{\lambda}{1+\lambda} & \frac{\lambda}{1+\lambda}\end{array}\right)^{\log_2 k} + \frac{\rho}{1+\rho}\left(\begin{array}{cc}1-\left(\frac{\lambda}{1+\lambda}\right)^{\lambda} & 1-\left(\frac{\lambda}{1+\lambda}\right)^{\lambda} \\ 1 & \left(\frac{\lambda}{1+\lambda}\right)^{\lambda}\end{array}\right)^{\log_2 k}\right] \cdot \binom{1}{0}$
LSJ	$comp_{LSJ} = comp_{DCJ}$ $repl_{LSJ} = \frac{1}{1+\rho} + \frac{\rho}{1+\rho} \sum_{t=0}^{\log_2 k} 2^i C_t^{\log_2 k}\left(1 - \left(\frac{\lambda}{1+\lambda}\right)^{\lambda}\right)^t \left(\frac{\lambda}{1+\lambda}\right)^{\lambda(\log_2 k - t)}$

b. For each element $x \in s$, we set a bit in the bit string at position (x mod b). If the set elements are drawn uniformly from a large domain, the probability of each bit to be one is $1 - (1 - \frac{1}{b})^{|s|}$. Let function h_i fire whenever bit i is set in the bit string. Thus, we obtain b functions $h_1, \ldots, h_b$ that fire with equal probability $P(h_i(s)) = 1 - (1 - \frac{1}{b})^{|s|}$. For $b = 1$, we get just one function that fires with the probability of 1. For each larger b, we obtain b functions that fire with smaller probabilities. For example, for $b = 200$ and $|s| = 100$ we obtain 200 functions that fire with a probability of $1 - (1 - \frac{1}{200})^{100} \approx 0.4$.

By varying b, we can approximate any given probability between zero and one. If the domain $\mathcal{D}$ from which the set elements are drawn is much larger than b (e.g. b is less than 5% of $|\mathcal{D}|$), all b functions obtained for a given b fire (roughly) independently from each other. Once the b functions have been obtained, we can select l of them for use in DCJ. Notice that the bit-string approach for computing the boolean hash functions described above gives us a sufficient number of functions to use for partitioning. In [MGM01] we show that the value b that we have to use to obtain the optimal firing probability of the hash functions is $b = \frac{1}{1-(\frac{\lambda}{1+\lambda})^{\frac{1}{\theta_R}}}$. For example, for $\theta_R = 50$, $\theta_S = 100$ we get $b \approx 124$. Thus, we could use up to $l = 124$ hash functions, i.e., up to $k = 2^{124}$ partitions if needed. In [MGM01], we present an algorithmic specification of the approach described above. Also, we investigate an alternative technique based on disjoint sets of prime numbers as illustrated in Table 3.

4 Qualitative Comparison of the Algorithms

In this section we examine what the formulas of Table 7 tell us. We also discuss the accuracy of the predictions of our formulas.

Comparison factor First, we illustrate the reduction of the comparison factor with the growing number of partitions. All comparison factors in Table 7 are determined by the parameters θ_R, θ_S, and k. In Figure 4, we depict $comp_{DCJ}$ and $comp_{PSJ}$ for three containment join problems that correspond to the set cardinalities $\theta_R = \theta_S = 10$, $\theta_R = \theta_S = 100$, and $\theta_R = \theta_S = 1000$. Since $comp_{LSJ}$ is equivalent to $comp_{DCJ}$, we will not consider $comp_{LSJ}$ separately any further. Since DCJ dependends on the ratio λ of set cardinalities only, and $\lambda = 1$ in all three cases, the three curves for DCJ fall into one, depicted as a thick solid line. As can be seen in the figure, both $comp_{DCJ}$ and $comp_{PSJ}$ decrease steadily with growing k. However, the benefit of PSJ diminishes for large set cardinalities. For example, for $k = 128$ and $\theta_R = \theta_S = 1000$, PSJ requires around 7.5 times more comparisons (with $comp_{PSJ} \approx 1$) than DCJ (with $comp_{DCJ} \approx 0.13$). On the other hand, for small sets like $\theta_R = \theta_S = 10$, PSJ outperforms DCJ in the number of comparisons starting with $k \approx 40$. As a matter of fact, as k grows, PSJ eventually catches up with DCJ even for large set cardinalities. For example, for $\theta_R = \theta_S = 1000$ the breakeven point at which $comp_{PSJ} = comp_{DCJ}$ lies at $k \approx 135000$. However, as we explain below, replication overhead increases with k, limiting the maximal number of partitions that we can use effectively for computing the join.

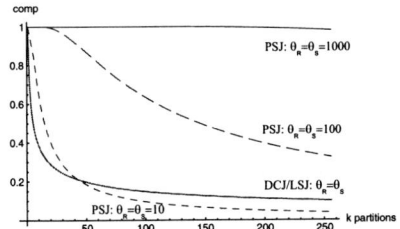

Fig. 4. Comparison factor vs. k **Fig. 5.** Comparison factor vs. θ_S ($k = 128$)

Figure 5 demonstrates how the comparison factor increases with the growing cardinality of sets in relation S. We fix the set cardinalities in R at $\theta_R = 100$ and vary the set cardinalities[3] in S from $\theta_S = 10$ to $\theta_S = 1000$ for a constant number of partitions $k = 128$. Note that varying θ_S corresponds to varying λ from 0.1 to 10. As illustrated in Figure 5, $comp_{DCJ}$ remains below $comp_{PSJ}$ as the cardinality ratio grows (although not shown in the figure, $comp_{DCJ} < comp_{PSJ}$ holds for all $\theta_S > 1000$). Moreover, in all scenarios, even those in which initially $comp_{DCJ} > comp_{PSJ}$, DCJ will eventually catch up and outperform PSJ as θ_S increases[4]. For example, starting with $\theta_R = \theta_S = 10$, and $k = 64$, we obtain

---

[3] When $\theta_S < \theta_R = 100$, then the result of the join is known to be empty.
[4] This fact can be derived from formulas in Table 7.

$0.18 \approx comp_{\text{DCJ}} > comp_{\text{PSJ}} \approx 0.15$. Still, as θ_S grows, DCJ catches up with PSJ at $\theta_S \approx 110$, resulting in a comparison factor of 0.82.

Replication factor We examine the replication factor for the same settings as we utilized in the discussion of the comparison factor. Note that the replication factor depends on the ratio ρ of the relation sizes. Due to space limitations, we focus only on the case where $|R| = |S|$, i.e., $\rho = 1$. Figure 6 shows the growth of the replication factors $repl_{\text{LSJ}}$, $repl_{\text{DCJ}}$, and $repl_{\text{PSJ}}$ with the increasing number of partitions for the cases $\theta_S = \theta_R = 10$, $\theta_S = \theta_R = 100$, and $\theta_S = \theta_R = 1000$. Factors $repl_{\text{LSJ}}$ and $repl_{\text{DCJ}}$ depend only on the ratio of the set cardinalities; thus we obtain just one curve for LSJ and another one for DCJ. Notice that $repl_{\text{DCJ}}$ grows much slower with k than $repl_{\text{LSJ}}$. Moreover, $repl_{\text{DCJ}}$ outperforms $repl_{\text{PSJ}}$ even for $\theta_R = \theta_S = 10$. For large sets, like $\theta_R = \theta_S = 1000$, and $k = 128$, PSJ needs to write out $64.5 \cdot (|R| + |S|)$ signatures as partition data. This is 16.7 times more data to be stored temporarily than that generated by DCJ. Notice, however, that $repl_{\text{PSJ}}$ is bound by $\frac{1}{1+\rho} + \frac{\rho}{1+\rho} \cdot \theta_S$ (to see this, note that $\lim_{k \to \infty} k(1 - (1 - \frac{1}{k})^{\theta_S}) = \theta_S$). In contrast, $repl_{\text{LSJ}}$ and $repl_{\text{DCJ}}$ are unbound with growing k. This observation suggests that for any given θ_R and θ_S, there is a breakeven k, starting from which $repl_{\text{PSJ}}$ becomes smaller than $repl_{\text{DCJ}}$. For large sets, such k may be so enormous that the fact that PSJ is bound and DCJ/LSJ are not is practically irrelevant. For example, for $\theta_R = \theta_S = 1000$, $repl_{\text{DCJ}}$ becomes as large as the maximal value of $repl_{\text{PSJ}}$ ($0.5 + 500 = 500.5$), when $k \approx 2^{36}$.

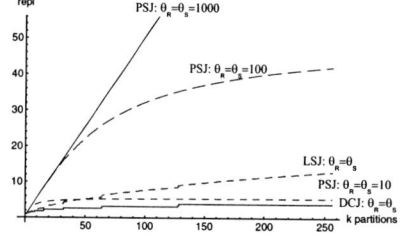

Fig. 6. Replication factor vs. k

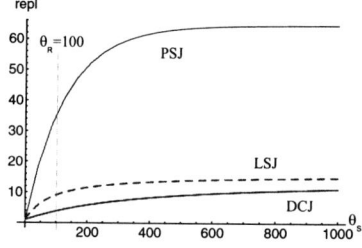

Fig. 7. Replication factor vs θ_S ($k = 128$)

The impact of the set cardinality ratio on the replication factor is demonstrated in Figure 7. Again, we fix $k = 128$, $\theta_R = 100$, and vary θ_S from 10 to 1000. Correspondingly, λ ranges from 0.1 to 10. Notice that $repl_{\text{DCJ}}$ approaches $repl_{\text{LSJ}}$ with increasing λ, but never catches up[4]. Hence, DCJ always outperforms LSJ, and therefore we will focus our subsequent discussion on the superior algorithm DCJ.

The qualitative analysis in this section suggests that for each of the partitioning algorithms the comparison factor (and thus CPU load) decreases with growing k, whereas the replication factor (and thus I/O overhead) increases.

Consequently, there is an *optimal* number of partitions k that minimizes the overall running time for each of the algorithms. Furthermore, our analysis indicates that PSJ is the algorithm of choice for small set cardinalities, while DCJ starts outperforming PSJ when the set cardinalities increase. In Section 5, we present the experimental results that substantiate these observations.

Accuracy of analytical model To study the accuracy of our formulas in realistic scenarios, we used five different distributions of element values, and five distributions of set cardinalities [MGM01]. Using simulations, we examined both the individual impact of varying just the element distribution or just the set cardinality distributions, as well as the combined effect. In summary, we found that for a variety of scenarios, the formulas of Table 7 deliver relatively accurate predictions that lie within 15% of the actual values. Across all experiments we observed that DCJ tends to be more negatively affected by varying the distributions than PSJ.

5 Experiments

We implemented the set containment join operator in Java using the Berkeley DB as the underlying storage manager. In our implementation, each tuple of the input relations R and S consists of a tuple identifier, a set of integers stored as a variable-size ordered list, and a fixed-size payload. The payload represents other attributes of the relations. In the experiments described below we used a payload of 100 bytes. The relations are stored as B-trees with the tuple identifiers serving as keys. To provide a fair evaluation of different partitioning algorithms, we implemented the set containment join operator is such a way that just the actual partitioning algorithm can be exchanged, other conditions remaining equal. In [MGM01] we document the Java implementations of each of the algorithms LSJ, DCJ, and PSJ as deployed in our testbed.

The partitions of both relations are stored in two B-trees[5], one B-tree per relation. We are not storing the partitions in plain files to exploit the buffering mechanisms of the storage manager. Each partition contains a list of pairs (set signature, tuple ID). In an initial implementation, we kept the data of each partition in a single B-tree record. However, we observed that the time required for appending data to the partitions was increasing significantly with growing partition sizes[6]. It proved much more efficient to split each partition into portions of equal sizes, while still keeping the partition in a single B-tree, and to use the combination of the portion number and partition index as the key of the B-tree. In the joining phase, the portions of partitions are read in batches to avoid random I/O. Splitting the partitions has an additional advantage in

---

[5] Since the number of partitions is relatively small, the overhead of maintaining a B-tree is negligible.

[6] Berkeley DB supports appending data to variable-size records incrementally, and does not require reading the records into memory first.

that it allows us to use large partitions that do not fit into the memory available for the join computation. After comparing all signatures in two partition batches, the identifiers of potentially joining tuples of R and S are sorted, and the corresponding tuples are fetched from disk.

Case study The experiments described below were performed on a 600 MHz Pentium III laptop running Linux. A total of 30 MB of memory was available to the Java Virtual Machine. Additionally, 10 MB was used by the Berkeley DB. To minimize the file buffering done by the operating system, we restricted the total available OS memory to 74 MB at boot time.

Figure 8 shows the impact of the partition number k on the execution time of the DCJ join for $|R| = |S| = 10000$, $\theta_R = 50$, and $\theta_S = 100$ (using a uniformly distributed element domain of size 10000 and uniformly distributed set cardinalities $45\ldots55$ in R and $90\ldots110$ in S). Each data point was obtained as an average of five runs using a 'cold' cache. We observe that there is an optimal value of $k = 32$ that yields the best execution time (24 sec). For $k > 32$, the growing partitioning overhead overweighs the reduction of the number of comparisons. Reading the partitions from the disk constitutes a part of the joining phase, therefore we see increasing joining time. Figure 9 illustrates the application of PSJ for the same setting. Notice that increasing the number of partitions does not help PSJ to reduce the execution time. In fact, using PSJ reduces the number of comparisons noticeably only starting from $k \approx 32$ ($comp_{PSJ} = 0.95$). At this point, however, PSJ becomes dominated by the partitioning I/O, and additional reduction of comparisons does not improve the execution time. Thus, in this scenario, PSJ proves ineffective with the best execution time of 48 sec.

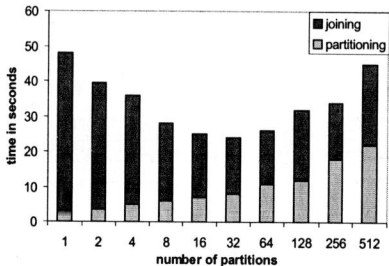 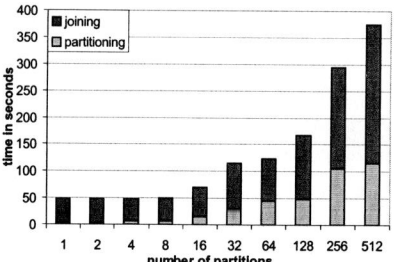

Fig. 8. Optimal partition number for DCJ ($|R| = |S| = 10000$, $\theta_R = 50$, $\theta_S = 100$)

Fig. 9. PSJ is I/O-bound and ineffective ($|R| = |S| = 10000$, $\theta_R = 50$, $\theta_S = 100$)

The above results emphasize that finding an optimal number of partitions is crucial for deploying DCJ and PSJ effectively. In a real system, we cannot afford running the algorithms with different partition numbers to determine the optimal setting. Fortunately, the analytical model that we developed in Section 3 helps us predict the best operational values for the algorithms. Using these values we can estimate the best execution time of each algorithm and choose the best performing one. For predicting the optimal number of partitions and the corresponding best execution time of either algorithm, we use a two-step approach. In the first step, for two given relations R and S, we estimate the comparison and replication factors using the formulas of Table 7. The estimate obtained in this first step depends only on the content of relations R and S, and the partitioning algorithm; it does not depend on hardware or the testbed we are using. In the second step, we predict the execution time knowing the estimated comparison and replication factors. This prediction is clearly system-dependent. However, as we will demonstrate, it can be applied for both partitioning algorithms used on the same system. Finally, for each partitioning algorithm we calculate the optimal number of partitions k that minimizes $time_{\text{DCJ}}$ or $time_{\text{PSJ}}$, and determine which algorithm to use for the given relations R and S.

Predicting execution times We approximate the running time of either algorithm using a function $time(x, y, k)$, where $x = comp \cdot |R| \cdot |S|$ is the total number of comparisons, $y = repl \cdot (|R| + |S|)$ is the total number of signatures to be stored temporarily, and k is the number of partitions. Notice that the join selectivity and the signature size are not included in this function. To choose the parameters for $time$, we build upon the detailed experimental results obtained for PSJ by Ramasamy et al. As reported in [RPNK00], with the growing number of partitions k, fragmentation becomes a significant factor, which we need to take into account. In contrast, the authors demonstrate that the exact choice of the signature size is less critical, as long as the signatures are large enough so that none or very few false positives are produced. Hence, in the experiments below, as well as in Figures 8 and 9, we choose a fixed signature size of 160 bits. To limit the complexity of the study, we are making an additional simplifying assumption that the join selectivity is small, i.e., at most a few tuples are returned as a result. In fact, both algorithms spend a comparable additional amount of time on reading out the result from the relations R and S. This additional time does not need to be considered in the comparison of the algorithms.

In [MGM01] we found that the function $time(x, y, k) = c_1 \cdot x + c_2 \cdot y \cdot k^{c_3}$ results in the smallest average prediction error compared to many other functions. The first part of the equation, $c_1 \cdot x$, represents the CPU time required for signature comparisons. The second part, $c_2 \cdot y \cdot k^{c_3}$, represents the I/O time for writing and reading the partitions, while k^{c_3} reflects the negative fragmentation effect that kicks in with growing k. For a given hardware configuration, the parameters c_1, c_2 and c_3 are obtained by applying the least-squares curve fitting method on data points collected for a variety of synthetic input relations. For each pair of synthetic relations, we run PSJ and DCJ with distinct values of k, and record for each run the overall execution time, the number x of comparisons done, and the number y of signatures stored on disk temporarily. We refer to this step as 'calibration' of hardware. For our testbed implementation and the hardware settings described above, we obtained the equation $time(x, y, k) = 5.12686 \cdot 10^{-7} \cdot x + 8.28197 \cdot 10^{-7} \cdot y \cdot k^{0.691485}$ using 114 data points. The equation returns time in seconds and, applied to the data points that we used, yields an average prediction error of 15.4%.

Choosing the best algorithm Given the time equation, the decision between DCJ and PSJ for two input relations R and S can be made using the following steps:

1. Determine the actual sizes of the relations.
2. Determine the average set cardinalities θ_R and θ_S using sampling or available statistics.
3. Estimate the comparison and replication factors for DCJ and PSJ using the formulas of Table 7 for a number of different values of k, for example for $k = 2^l$, $1 \leq l \leq 13$.
4. Apply the time equation to determine the best execution times of both algorithms for the above values of k using the estimated comparison and replication factors[7].
5. Find the best execution time and pick the algorithm that produced it along with the optimal partition number k.

In addition to using our time equation at run time to select k and the algorithm to run, we can use the equation to understand in what cases DCJ or PSJ perform best. Figure 10 summarizes the experimental analysis of both algorithms. Both graphs in the figure connect breakeven points like the point $\theta_R = 50$, $\theta_S = 100$, $|R| = |S| = 128000$, at which both algorithms yield equal execution times. Each graph divides the first quadrant into two areas, the one where PSJ wins over DCJ (below the graph), and the one in which DCJ outperforms PSJ (above the graph). The solid line corresponds to the cardinality ratio $\lambda = 1$, whereas the dotted line illustrates $\lambda = 2$. Figure 10 allows us to estimate what algorithm to deploy for the given input relations. For example, given $\theta_R = \theta_S = 50$ and $|R| = |S| = 100000$, the figure indicates that DCJ is clearly the algorithm of choice. On the other hand, if $\theta_R = \theta_S = 10$, we should go for PSJ. Please keep in mind that the graphs shown in the figure may have different shapes for other systems.

One final remark is due here; recall that DCJ (and LSJ) can make effective use of k partitions only if k is a power of two. Hence, DCJ is less flexible in choosing the partition number k. However, our experiments suggest that in practice this inflexibility is not critical. For example, in Figure 8 we can see that the execution times of DCJ are roughly similar for $k = 16$, $k = 32$, and $k = 64$. In other words, the inability to choose say $k = 48$ does not cripple the performance of DCJ. Furthermore, as we explain in [MGM01], the limitation in choosing k can be addressed using the modulo approach suggested in [HM97].

6 Related Work

The set containment join and other join operators for sets enjoyed significant attention in the area of data modeling. However, very little work deals with ef-

---

[7] Since the formulas in Table 7 are fairly complex, determining the optimal k analytically is hard. Therefore, we use the probing approach.

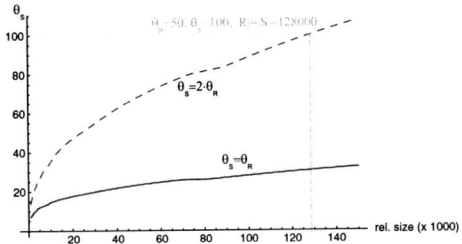

Fig. 10. When use DCJ instead of PSJ? Each graph separates the space of input relations into area where DCJ wins (area above graph) and where PSJ wins (area below graph)

ficient implementations of these operators. Helmer and Moerkotte [HM97] were the first to directly address the implementation of set containment joins. They investigated several main memory algorithms including different flavors of nested-loop joins, and suggested the Signature-Hash Join (SHJ) as a best alternative. Later, Ramasamy et al [RPNK00] developed the Partitioning Set Join (PSJ), which does not require all data to fit into main memory. They showed that PSJ performs significantly better than the SQL-based approaches for computing the containment joins using unnested representation. Prior to [HM97] and [RPNK00], the related work focused on signature files, which had been suggested for efficient text retrieval two decades ago. A detailed study of signature files is provided by Faloutsos and Christodoulakis in [FC84]. Ishikawa et al [IKO93] applied the signature file technique for finding subsets or supersets that match a fixed given query set in object-oriented databases. The inherent theoretical complexity of computing set containment joins was addressed in [CCKN01, HKP97]. Partitioning has been utilized for computing joins over other types of non-atomic data, e.g., for spatial joins [PD96]. Index-based approaches for accessing multi-dimensional data were studied e.g. in [BK00].

In [MGM01] we introduce and study in detail the Lattice Set Join (LSJ), a partitioning algorithm that extends the main-memory algorithm SHJ [HM97] and does not require all data to fit into main memory. We also present an alternative approach to computing the boolean hash function used in LSJ and DCJ, based on disjoint sets of primes.

Many other options for implementing partitioning-based algorithms for atomic attributes have been discussed in the database literature. For example, keeping a fixed number of partitions permanently in main memory improves the execution time when much memory is available. Similarly, separating the joining phase and the verification phase by first writing out potentially joining tuple identifiers of all partitions to disk may improve performance. Due to space limitations, we do not discuss these implementation options. For generating synthetic databases used in our experiments, we deployed the methods described in [GEBW94].

7 Conclusion

In this paper we suggested a novel algorithm called the Divide-and-Conquer Set Join for computing the set containment joins. We compared the performance of DCJ with that of PSJ [RPNK00] and LSJ [MGM01]. We developed a detailed analytical model that allowed us to study the join algorithms qualitatively, and to tune them for different input relations. Furthermore, we explored the behavior of the algorithms experimentally using an implemented testbed. We found that DCJ always outperforms LSJ in terms of the replication factor. In contrast, PSJ and DCJ provide complementary approaches for computing set containment joins. Specifically, when the set cardinalities are large, DCJ introduces a significant performance improvement as compared to PSJ. On the other hand, PSJ wins over DCJ when small sets are used. The work presented in [HM97], [RPNK00], and in this paper raises the question whether even better algorithms for set containment joins exist. Currently, we are trying to develop a hybrid algorithm that combines the strengths of PSJ and DCJ. Developing efficient algorithms for other set join operators, for instance the intersection join, is another challenging and mostly unexplored research direction.

References

[BK00] C. Böhm and H.-P. Kriegel. Dynamically Optimizing High-Dimensional Index Structures. In *Proc. EDBT'00*, 2000.

[CCKN01] J.-Y. Cai, V. T. Chakaravarthy, R. Kaushik, and J.F. Naughton. On the complexity of join predicates. In *Proc. PODS'01*, 2001.

[FC84] C. Faloutsos and S. Christodoulakis. Signature files: An access method for documents and its analytical performance evaluation. *ACM Trans. on Office Information Systems (TOIS)*, 2(4):267–288, 1984.

[GEBW94] J. Gray, S. Englert, K. Baclawski, and P.J. Weinberger. Quickly generating billion-record synthetic databases. In *Proc. SIGMOD'94*, 1994.

[HKP97] J. Hellerstein, E. Koutsoupias, and C. H. Papadimitriou. On the analysis of indexing schemes. In *Proc. PODS'97*, 1997.

[HM97] S. Helmer and G. Moerkotte. Evaluation of main memory join algorithms for joins with set comparison join predicates. In *Proc. VLDB'97*, 1997.

[IKO93] Y. Ishikawa, H. Kitagawa, and N. Ohbo. Evaluation of signature files as set access facilities in OODBS. In *Proc. SIGMOD'93*, 1993.

[MGM01] S. Melnik and H. Garcia-Molina. Divide-and-Conquer Algorithm for Computing Set Containment Joins. Extended Technical Report, http://dbpubs.stanford.edu/pub/2001-32, September 2001.

[PD96] J. M. Patel and D. J. DeWitt. Partition based spatial-merge join. In *Proc. SIGMOD'96*, 1996.

[RPNK00] K. Ramasamy, J. M. Patel, J. F. Naughton, and R. Kaushik. Set Containment Joins: the Good, the Bad and the Ugly. In *Proc. VLDB'00*, 2000.

Universal Quantification in Relational Databases: A Classification of Data and Algorithms

Ralf Rantzau[1], Leonard Shapiro[2], Bernhard Mitschang[1], and Quan Wang[3]

[1] Computer Science Department, University of Stuttgart,
Breitwiesenstr. 20-22, 70565 Stuttgart, Germany
{rantzau, mitsch}@informatik.uni-stuttgart.de

[2] Computer Science Department, Portland State University,
P.O. Box 751, Portland, OR 97201-0751, Oregon, U.S.A.
len@cs.pdx.edu

[3] Oracle Corporation
quan.wang@oracle.com

Abstract. Queries containing universal quantification are used in many applications, including business intelligence applications. Several algorithms have been proposed to implement universal quantification efficiently. These algorithms are presented in an isolated manner in the research literature – typically, no relationships are shown between them. Furthermore, each of these algorithms claims to be superior to others, but in fact each algorithm has optimal performance only for certain types of input data. In this paper, we present a comprehensive survey of the structure and performance of algorithms for universal quantification. We introduce a framework for classifying all possible kinds of input data for universal quantification. Then we go on to identify the most efficient algorithm for each such class. One of the input data classes has not been covered so far. For this class, we propose several new algorithms. For the first time, we are able to identify the optimal algorithm to use for any given input dataset. These two classifications of input data and optimal algorithms are important for query optimization. They allow a query optimizer to make the best selection when optimizing at intermediate steps for the quantification problem.

1 Introduction

Universal quantification is an important operation in the first order predicate calculus. This calculus provides existential and universal quantifiers, represented by $\exists$ and $\forall$, respectively. A universal quantifier that is applied to a variable x of a formula f specifies that the formula is true for all values of x. We say that x is *universally quantified* in the formula f, and we write $\forall x: f(x)$ in calculus.

In relational databases, universal quantification is implemented by the *division* operator (represented by $\div$) of the relational algebra. The division operator is important for databases because it appears often in practice, particularly in business intelligence applications, including online analytic processing (OLAP) and data mining. In this paper, we will focus on the division operator exclusively.

enrollment (dividend) ÷ **course (divisor)** = **result (quotient)**

student_id	course_id
Alice	Compilers
Alice	Theory
Bob	Compilers
Bob	Databases
Bob	Graphics
Bob	Theory
Chris	Compilers
Chris	Graphics
Chris	Theory

course_id
Compilers
Databases
Theory

student_id
Bob

Fig. 1. Division operation representing the query "Which students have taken all courses?"

1.1 Overview of the Division Operator

To illustrate the division operator we will use a simple example throughout the paper, illustrated in Figure 1, representing data from one department at a university [7]. A *course* row represents a course that has been offered by the department and an *enrollment* row indicates that a student has taken a particular course. The following query can be represented by the division operator:

"Which students have taken *all* courses offered by the department?"

As indicated in the table *result*, only Bob has taken all the courses. Bob is enrolled in another course (Graphics) but this does not affect the result. Both Alice and Chris are not enrolled in the Databases course. Therefore, they are not included in the result.

The division operator takes two tables for its input, the *divisor* and the *dividend*, and generates one table, the *quotient*. All the data elements in the divisor must appear in the dividend, paired with any element (such as Bob) that is to appear in the quotient.

In the example of Figure 1, the divisor and quotient have only one attribute each, but in general, they may have an arbitrary number of attributes. In any case, the set of attributes of the dividend is the disjoint union of the attributes of the divisor and the quotient. To simplify our exposition, we assume that the names of the dividend attributes are the same as the corresponding attribute names in the divisor and the quotient.

1.2 Input Data Characteristics

The goal of this paper is to identify optimal algorithms for the division operator, for all possible inputs. Several papers compare new algorithms to previous algorithms and claim superiority for one or more algorithms, but they do not address the issue of which algorithms are optimal for which types of data [2] [3] [7]. In fact, the performance of any algorithm depends on the structure of its input data.

If we know about the structure of input data, we can employ an algorithm that exploits this structure, i.e., the algorithm does not have to restructure the input before it can start generating output data. Of course, there is no guarantee that such an algorithm is always "better" than an algorithm that requires previous restructuring. However, the division operator offers a variety of alternative algorithms that can exploit such a structure for the sake of good performance and low memory consumption.

Suppose we are fortunate and the input data is highly structured. For example, suppose the data has the schema of Figure 1 but is of much larger size, and suppose:

- *enrollment* is sorted by *student_id* and *course_id* and resides on disk, and
- *course* is sorted by *course_id* and resides in memory.

Then the example query can be executed with one scan of the *enrollment* table. This is accomplished by reading the *enrollment* table from disk. As each student appears, the *course_id* values associated with that student are merged with the *course* table. If all courses match, the *student_id* is copied to the result.

The single scan of the *enrollment* table is obviously the most efficient possible algorithm in this case. In the remainder of this paper, we will describe similar types of structure for input datasets, and the optimal algorithms that are associated with them. The notion of "optimality" will be further discussed in the next section.

How could such careful structuring of input data, such as sorting by *student_id* and *course_id*, occur? It could happen by chance, or for two other more commonly encountered reasons:

1. The data might be stored in tables, which were sorted in that order for other purposes, for example, so that it is easy to list enrollments on a roster in ID order, or to find course information when a course ID number is given.
2. The data might have undergone some previous processing, because the division operator query is part of a more complex query. The previous processing might have been a merge-join operator, for example, which requires that its inputs be sorted and produces sorted output data.

1.3 Choice of Algorithms

A query processor of a database system typically provides several algorithms that all realize the same operation. An optimizer has to choose one of these algorithms to process the given data. If the optimizer knows the structure of the input data for an operator, it can pick an algorithm that exploits the structure. Many criteria influence the decision why one algorithm is preferred over others. Some of these criteria of optimality are: the time to deliver the first/last result row, the amount of memory for internal, temporary data structures, the number of scans over the input data, or the ability to be non-blocking, i.e., to return some result rows before the entire input data are consumed.

Which algorithm should we use to process the division operation, given the dividend and divisor tables shown in Figure 1? Several algorithms are applicable but they are not equally efficient. For example, since the dividend and divisor are both sorted on the attribute *course_id* in Figure 1, we could select a division algorithm that exploits this fact by processing the input tuples in a way that is similar to the merge-join algorithm, as we have sketched in the previous section.

What algorithm should we select when the input tables are *not* sorted on *course_id* for each group of *student_id*? One option is to sort both input tables first and then employ the algorithm similar to merge-join. Of course, this incurs an additional computational cost for sorting in addition to the cost of the division algorithm itself. Another option is to employ an algorithm that is insensitive to the ordering of input tuples. One such well-known algorithm is hash-division and is discussed in detail in Section 3.2.4.

We have seen that the decision, which algorithm to select among a set of different division algorithms, depends on the structure of the input data. This situation is true for any class of algorithms, including those that implement database operators like join, aggregation, and sort algorithms.

1.4 Outline of the Paper

The remainder of this paper is organized as follows. In Section 2, we present a classification of input data for algorithms that evaluate division within queries. Section 3 gives an overview of known and new algorithms to solve the universal quantification problem and classifies them according to two general approaches for division. In section 4, we evaluate the algorithms according to both applicability and effectiveness for different kinds of input data, based on a performance analysis. Section 5 gives a brief overview of related work. Section 6 concludes this paper and comments on future work.

2 Classification of Data

This section presents an overview of the input data for division. We identify all possible classes of data based on whether it is grouped on certain attributes. For some of these classes, we will present optimal algorithms in Section 3 that exploit the specific data properties of a class.

2.1 Grouping

Relational database systems have the notion of grouped rows in a table. Let us briefly look at an example that shows why grouping is important for query processing. Suppose we want to find for each course the number of enrolled students in the *enrollment* table of Figure 1. One way to compute the aggregates involves *grouping*: after the table has been grouped on *course_id*, all rows of the table with the same value of *course_id* appear next to each other. The ordering of the group values is not specified, i.e., any group of rows may follow any other group. Group-based aggregation groups the data first, and then it scans the resulting table once and computes the aggregates during the scan.

Instead of grouping, one could use a nested-loops approach to process this query: pick any course ID as the first group value and then search through the whole table to find the rows that match this ID and compute the sum. Then, we pick a second course ID, search for matching rows, compute the second aggregate, pick the third value, etc. If no suitable search data structure (index) is available, this processing may involve multiple scans over the entire dataset.

If the data is grouped, then the grouping algorithm is clearly more efficient. Even if the data is not grouped, the aggregation approach is in general more efficient. For large datasets, the (at most) $n \cdot \log(n)$ cost of grouping and subsequent linear aggregation is typically cheaper than the n^2 cost of nested-loops.

Sorted data appears frequently in query processing. Note that sorting is a special grouping operation. For example, grouping only requires that students enrolled in the same course are stored next to each other (in any order), whereas sorting requires more effort, namely that they be in a particular order (ascending or descending). The overhead of sort-based grouping is reflected by the time complexity $O(n \cdot \log(n))$ as opposed to the nearly linear time complexity for hash-based grouping. Though sort-based grouping algorithms do more than necessary, both hash-based and sort-based grouping perform well for large datasets [6] [7].

2.2 Grouped Input Data for Division

Relational division has two input tables, a dividend and a divisor, and it returns a quotient table. As a consequence of the definition of the division operator, we can partition the attributes of the dividend S into two sets, which we denote D and Q, because they correspond to the attributes of the divisor and the quotient, respectively. The divisor's attributes correspond to D, i.e., for each attribute in the divisor there is a different attribute in D of the same domain. As already mentioned, for simplicity, we assume that the names of attributes in the quotient R are the same as the corresponding attribute names in the dividend S and the divisor T. Thus, we write a division operation as $R(Q) = S(Q \cup D) \div T(D)$. In Figure 1, $Q = \{student\_id\}$ and $D = \{course\_id\}$.

Our classification of division algorithms is based on whether certain attributes are grouped or even sorted. Several reasons justify this decision. Grouped input can reduce the amount of memory needed by an algorithm to temporarily store rows of a table because all rows of a group have a constant group value. Furthermore, grouping appears frequently in query processing. Many database operators require grouped or sorted input data (e.g., merge-join) or produce such output data (e.g., index-scan): If there is an index defined on a base table, a query processor can retrieve the rows in sorted order, specified by the index attribute list. Thus, in some situations, algorithms may exploit for the sake of efficiency the fact that base tables or derived tables are grouped, if the system *knows* about this fact.

In Table 1, we show all possible classes of input data based on whether or not interesting attribute sets are grouped, i.e., grouped on one of Q, D, or the divisor. As we will see later in this paper, some classes have no suitable algorithm that can exploit its specific combination of data properties. The classes that have at least one algorithm exploiting exactly its data properties are shown in italics. In class 0, for example, no table is grouped on an interesting attribute set. Algorithms for this class have to be insensitive to whether the data is grouped or not. Another example scenario is class 10. Here, the dividend is *first* grouped on the quotient attributes Q (denoted by G_1, the major group) and for each group, it is grouped on the divisor D (denoted by G_2, the minor group). The divisor is grouped in the same ordering (G_2) as the dividend.

Table 1. A classification of dividend and divisor. Attributes are either grouped (G) or not grouped (N). We use the same (a different) index of G_i when D and the divisor have the same (a different) ordering of groups in classes 3, 4, 9–12. In addition, when the dividend is grouped on both Q and D in classes 7–12, then G_1 (G_2) denotes the attributes that the table is grouped on first (second).

Class	Dividend Q	Dividend D	Divisor	Description of Grouping
0	N	N	N	
1	N	N	G	
2	N	G	N	
3	N	G_1	G_2	arbitrary ordering of groups in D and divisor
4	N	G_1	G_1	same ordering of groups in D and divisor
5	G	N	N	
6	G	N	G	
7	G_1	G_2	N	Q major, D minor
8	G_2	G_1	N	D major, Q minor
9	G_1	G_2	G_3	Q major, D minor; arbitrary ordering of groups in D and divisor
10	G_1	G_2	G_2	Q major, D minor; same ordering of groups in D and divisor
11	G_2	G_1	G_3	D major, Q minor; arbitrary ordering of groups in D and divisor
12	G_2	G_1	G_1	D major, Q minor; same ordering of groups in D and divisor

Fig. 2. Four important classes of input data, based on the example in Figure 1.

Our classification is based on grouping only. As we have seen, some algorithms may require that the input is even sorted and not merely grouped. We consider this a minor special case of our classification, so we do not reflect this data property in Table 1, but the algorithms in Section 3 will refer to this distinction. We do not consider any data property other than grouping in this paper because our approach is complete and can easily and effectively be exploited by a query optimizer and query processor.

Figure 2 illustrates four classes of input data for division, based on the example data of Figure 1. These classes, which are shown in italics in Table 1, are important for several algorithms that we present in the following section.

If we know that an algorithm can process data of a specific class, it is useful to know which other classes are also covered by the algorithm. This information can be represented, e.g., by a Boolean matrix like the one on the left in Figure 3. One axis indicates a given class C_1 and the other axis shows the other classes C_2 that are also covered by C_1. Alternatively, we can use a directed acyclic graph representing the input data classification, sketched on the right in Figure 3. If a cell of the matrix is marked with "Y" (yes), or equivalently, if there is a path in the graph from class C_1 to C_2, then an algorithm that can process data of class C_1 can also process data of class C_2. The graph clearly shows that the classification is a partial order of classes, not a

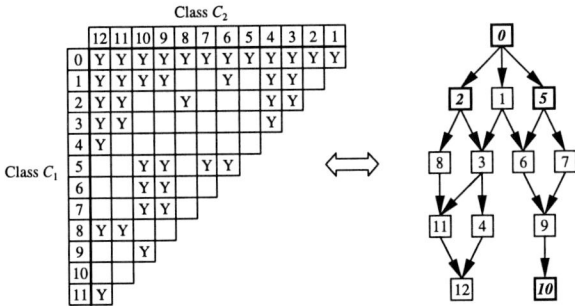

Fig. 3. A matrix and a directed acyclic graph representing the input data classification described in Table 1. All algorithms to be discussed in Section 3 assume data properties of either class 0, 2, 5, or 10.

strict hierarchy. The source node of the graph is class 0, which requires no grouping of D, Q, or divisor. Any algorithm that can process data of class 0 can process data of any other class. For example, an algorithm processing data of class 6 is able to process data of classes 9–12.

For the subsequent discussion of division algorithms, we define two terms to refer to certain row subsets of the dividend. Suppose the dividend S is grouped on Q (D), i.e., suppose the dividend belongs to class 5 (2) and all its descendants in Figure 3. Furthermore, suppose v is one specific value a group in D (Q). Then the set of rows defined by $\sigma_{Q=v}(S)$ ($\sigma_{D=v}(S)$) is called the *quotient group* (*divisor group*) of v. For example, in the *enrollment* table of class 5 in Figure 2, the quotient group of Alice consists of the rows {(Alice, Theory), (Alice, Compilers)}. Similarly, the divisor group of Databases in class 2 in Figure 2 consists of the single row (Bob, Databases).

3 Overview of Algorithms

In this section, we present algorithms for relational division proposed in the database literature together with several new variations of the well-known hash-division algorithm. In Section 4, we will analyze and compare the effectiveness of each algorithm with respect to the data classification of Section 2.

Each division algorithm (analogous to other classes of algorithms, like joins, for example) has performance advantages for certain data characteristics. No algorithm is able to outperform the others for every input data conceivable.

The following algorithms assume that the division's input consists of a dividend table $S(Q \cup D)$ and a divisor table $T(D)$, where Q is a set of quotient attributes and D is the set of divisor attributes, as defined in Section 2.2.

3.1 Algorithm Classification

In this section, we present a classification of algorithms based on what kind of data structures are employed. In addition, we illustrate how universal quantification is expressed in a query language.

There are two fundamental approaches to processing relational division. The first one relies on direct row matches between the dividend's divisor attributes D and the divisor table. We call this class of algorithms *scalar* to contrast them to the second class, called *aggregate* algorithms. Aggregate algorithms use counters to compare the number of rows in a dividend's quotient group to the number of divisor rows. In [2], scalar and aggregate algorithms are called *direct* and *indirect* algorithms, respectively.

Any query involving universal quantification can be replaced by a query that makes use of counting [7]. However, formulating division queries that involve aggregation is non-intuitive and error-prone because one has to take care of duplicates, NULL values, and referential integrity.

3.2 Scalar Algorithms

This section presents division algorithms that use data structures to directly match dividend rows with divisor rows.

3.2.1 Nested-Loops Division

This algorithm is the most naïve way to implement division. However, like nested-loops join, an operator using *nested-loops division* (NLD) has no required data properties on the input tables and thus can always be employed, i.e., NLD can process input data of class 0 and thus any other class of data, according to Figure 3.

We use two set data structures, one to store the set of divisor values of the divisor table, called *seen_divisors*, and another to store the set of quotient candidate values that we have found so far in the dividend table, called *seen_quotients*. We first scan the divisor table to fill *seen_divisors*. After that, we scan the dividend in an outer loop. For each dividend row, we check if its quotient value (Q) is already contained in *seen_quotients*. If not, we scan the dividend iteratively in an inner loop to find all rows that have the same quotient value as the dividend row of the outer loop. For each such row found, we check if its divisor value is in *seen_divisors*. If yes, we mark the divisor value in *seen_divisors*. After the inner scan is complete, we add the current quotient value to the output if all divisors in *seen_divisors* are marked. Before we start processing the next dividend row of the outer loop, we unmark all elements of *seen_divisors* and add the quotient value to *seen_quotients*.

Note that NLD can be very inefficient. For each row in the dividend table, we scan the dividend at least partially to find all the rows that belong to the current quotient candidate. All divisor rows and quotient candidate rows are stored in an in-memory data structure. NLD can be the most efficient algorithm for small ungrouped datasets.

In the illustration in box (1) in Figure 4, we assume hash tables as the data structures used for matching. It shows the divisor/quotient hash tables that represent *seen_divisors* and *seen_quotients*, respectively. The value setting in the hash tables is shown for the time when all dividend rows of Alice and Bob (in this order) have been processed and we have not yet started to process any rows of Chris in the outer loop. We find that Bob is a quotient because all bits in the divisor hash table are equal to 1.

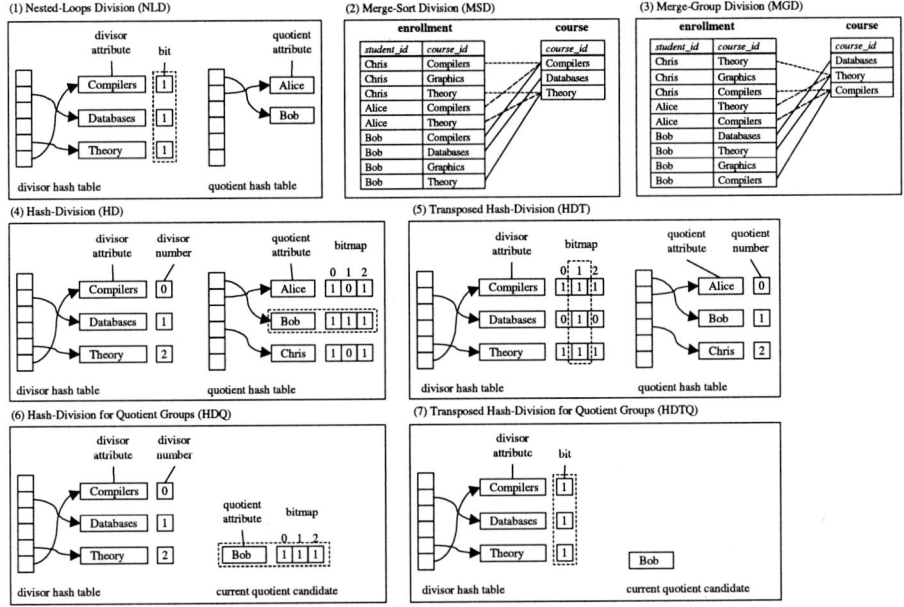

Fig. 4. Overview of the data structures and processing used in scalar algorithms. The value setting is based on the example from Figure 1. Except for boxes (2) and (3), broken lined boxes indicate that a quotient is found.

3.2.2 Merge-Sort Division

The *merge-sort division* (MSD) algorithm assumes that

- the divisor T is sorted, and that
- the dividend S is grouped on Q, and for each group, it is sorted on D in the same order (ascending or descending) as T.

This data characteristic is a special case of class 10, where D and the divisor are sorted and not only grouped.

The algorithm resembles merge-join for processing a single quotient group and is similar to nested-loops join for processing all groups. Due to space restrictions we refer to [12] for details on this algorithm.

Box (2) in Figure 4 illustrates the matches between rows of dividend and divisor. Observe that the data is not sorted but only grouped on *student_id* in an arbitrary order.

3.2.3 Merge-Group Division

We can generalize merge-sort division to an algorithm that we call *merge-group division* (MGD). In contrast to MSD, we assume that (1) both inputs are only grouped and not necessarily sorted on the divisor attributes, but that (2) the order of groups in each quotient group and the order of groups in the divisor are the same.

Note that each group within a quotient group and within the divisor consists of a single row. This ordering can occur (or can be achieved) if, e.g., the same hash function is used for grouping the divisor and each quotient group.

In the MSD algorithm, we can safely skip a quotient candidate if the current value of Q is greater (less) than that of the current divisor row, assuming an ascending (a descending) sort order. Since we do not require a sort order on these attributes in MGD, we cannot skip a group on unequal values, as we do in MSD. Due to space restrictions we refer to [12] for details on this algorithm.

3.2.4 Classic Hash-Division

In this section, we present the classic *hash-division* (HD) algorithm [7]. We call this algorithm "classic" to distinguish it from our variations of this approach in the following sections.

The two central data structures of HD are the divisor and quotient hash tables, sketched in box (4) in Figure 4. The divisor hash table stores divisor rows. Each such row has an integer value, called *divisor number*, stored together with it. The quotient hash table stores quotient candidates and has a bitmap stored together with each candidate, with one bit for each divisor.

In a first phase, hash-division builds the divisor hash table while scanning the divisor. The hash function takes the divisor attributes as an argument and assigns a hash bucket to each divisor row. A divisor row is stored into the hash bucket only if it is not already contained in the bucket, thus eliminating duplicates in the divisor. When a divisor row is stored, we assign a unique divisor number to it by copying the value of a global counter. This counter is incremented for each stored divisor row and is initialized with zero. The divisor number is used as an index for the bitmaps of the quotient hash table.

The second phase of the algorithm constructs the quotient hash table while scanning the dividend. For each dividend row, we first check if its D value is contained in the divisor hash table, using the same hash function as before. If yes, we look up the associated divisor number, otherwise we skip the dividend row. In addition to the look-up, we check if the quotient is already present in the quotient hash table. If yes, we update the bitmap associated with the matching quotient row by setting the bit to 1 whose position is equal to the divisor number we looked up. Otherwise, we insert a new quotient row into the quotient hash table together with a bitmap where all bits are initialized with zeroes and the appropriate bit is set to 1, as described before. Since we insert only quotient candidates that are not already contained in the hash table, we avoid duplicate dividend rows.

The final phase of hash division scans the quotient hash table's buckets and adds all quotient candidates to the output whose bitmaps contain only ones. In box (4) of Figure 4, the contents of the hash tables are shown for the time when all dividend and divisor rows of Figure 1 have been processed. We see that since Bob's bitmap contains no zeroes, Bob is the only quotient, indicated by a broken lined box.

3.2.5 Transposed Hash-Division

This algorithm is a slight variation of classic hash-division. The idea is to switch the roles of the divisor and quotient hash tables. The *transposed hash-division* (HDT) algorithm keeps a bitmap together with each row in the divisor hash table instead of the quotient hash table, as in HD. Furthermore, HDT keeps an integer value with each row in the quotient hash table instead of the divisor hash table, as in the HD algorithm.

Same as the classic hash-division algorithm, HDT first builds the divisor hash table. However, we store a bitmap with each row of the *divisor*. A value of 1 at a certain bit position of a bitmap indicates which quotient candidate has the same values of D as the given divisor row.

In a second phase, also same as HD, the HDT algorithm scans the dividend table and builds a quotient hash table. For each dividend row, the D values are inserted into the divisor hash table as follows. If there is a matching quotient row stored in the quotient hash table, we look up its quotient number. Otherwise, we insert a new quotient row together with a new quotient number. Then, we update the divisor row's bitmap by setting the bit at the position given by the quotient number to 1.

The final phase makes use of a new, separate bitmap. All bits of the bitmap, whose size is the same as the bitmaps in the divisor hash table, are initialized with zero. While scanning the divisor hash table, we apply a bit-wise AND operation between each bitmap contained and the new bitmap. The resulting bit pattern of the new bitmap is used to identify the quotients. The quotient numbers (bit positions) with a value of 1 are then used to look up the quotients using a *quotient vector* data structure that allows a fast mapping of a quotient number to a quotient candidate.

Boxes (4) and (5) of Figure 4 contrast the different structure of hash tables in HD and HDT. The hash table contents is shown for the time when all *enrollment* rows of Figure 1 have been processed. While a quotient in the HD algorithm can be added to the output when the associated bitmap contains no zeroes, the HDT algorithm requires a match of the bit at the same position of all bitmaps in the divisor table and it requires in addition a look-up in the quotient hash table to find the associated quotient row.

The time and memory complexities of HDT are the same as those of classic hash-division.

3.2.6 Hash-Division for Quotient Groups

Both, classic and transposed hash-division can be improved if the dividend is grouped on either D or Q. However, our optimizations based on divisor groups lead to aggregate, not scalar algorithms. Hence, this section presents some optimizations for quotient groups. The optimizations of hash-division for divisor groups are presented in Section 3.3.3.

Let us first focus on classic hash-division. If the dividend is grouped on Q, we do not need a quotient hash table. It suffices to keep a single bitmap to check if the current quotient candidate is actually a quotient. When all dividend rows of a quotient group have been processed and all bits of the bitmap are equal to 1, the quotient row is added to the output. Otherwise, we reset all bits to zero, skip the current quotient row, and continue processing the next quotient candidate. Because of the group-by-group processing of the improved algorithm, we call this approach *hash-division for quotient groups* (HDQ).

The HDQ algorithm is non-blocking because we return a quotient row to the output as soon as a group of (typically few) dividend rows has been processed. In contrast, the HD algorithm has a final output phase: the quotient rows are added to the result table after the entire dividend has been processed because hash-division does not assume a grouping on Q. For example, the "first" and the "last" row of the dividend could belong to the same quotient candidate, hence the HD algorithm has to keep the state of the candidate quotient row as long as at least one bit of the candidate's bitmap is equal to zero. Note that it is possible to enhance HD such that it is not a "fully" blocking algorithm. If bitmaps are checked during the processing of the input, HD could detect some quotients that can be returned to the output before the entire dividend has been scanned. Of course, we would then have to make sure that no duplicate quotients are created, either by preprocessing or by referential integrity enforcements or by keeping the quotient value in the hash table until the end of the processing. In this paper, we do not elaborate on this variation of HD.

We have seen that the HDQ algorithm is a variation of the HD algorithm: if the dividend is grouped on Q, we can do without a quotient hash table. Exactly the same idea can be applied to HDT yielding an algorithm that we call *transposed hash-division for quotient groups* (HDTQ).

For grouped quotient attributes, we can do without the quotient hash table and we do not keep long bitmaps in the divisor hash table but only a single bit per divisor. Before any group is processed, the bit of each divisor attribute is set to zero. For each group, we process the rows like in the HDT algorithm. After a group is processed, we add a quotient to the output if the bit of every divisor row is equal to 1. Then, we reset all bits to zero and resume the dividend scan with the next group.

We sketch the data structures used in the boxes (6) and (7) of Figure 4 for the time when the group of dividend rows containing the quotient candidate Bob have been processed.

3.3 Aggregate Algorithms

This class of algorithms compares the number of rows in each quotient candidate with the number of divisor rows. In case of equality, a quotient candidate becomes a quotient. All algorithms have in common that in a first phase, the divisor table is scanned once to count the number of divisor rows. Each algorithm then uses different data structures to keep track of the number of rows in a quotient candidate. Some algorithms assume that the dividend is grouped on Q or D.

3.3.1 Nested-Loops Counting Division

Similar to scalar nested-loops division, *nested-loops counting division* (NLCD) is the most naïve way in the class of aggregate algorithms. This algorithm scans the dividend multiple times. During each scan, NLCD counts the number of rows belonging to the same quotient candidate.

We have to keep track of which quotient candidates we have already checked, using a quotient hash table as shown in box (1) of Figure 5. A global counter is used to keep track of the number of dividend rows belonging to the same quotient candidate. We fully scan the dividend in an outer loop: We pick the first dividend row, insert its Q value into the quotient hash table, and set the counter to 1. If the counter's value is equal to the divisor count, we add the quotient to the output and continue with the next row of the outer loop. Otherwise, we scan the dividend in an inner loop for rows with the same Q value as the current quotient candidate. For each such row, the counter is checked and in case of equality, the quotient is added to the output. When the end of the dividend is reached in the inner loop, we continue with the next row of the outer loop and check the hash table if this new row is a new quotient candidate.

The time and memory complexities are the same as for nested-loops division.

3.3.2 Merge-Count Division

Assuming that the dividend is grouped on Q, *merge-count division* (MCD) scans the dividend exactly once. After a quotient candidate has been processed and the number of rows is equal to those of the divisor, the quotient is added to the output. Note that the size of a quotient group cannot exceed the number of divisor groups because we have to guarantee referential integrity.

The aggregate algorithm merge-count division is similar to the scalar algorithms MSD and MGD, described in Sections 3.2.2 and 3.2.3. Instead of comparing the elements of quotient groups with the divisor, MCD uses a representative (the row count) of each quotient group to compare it with the divisor's aggregate. Box (2) in Figure 5 illustrates the single scan required to compare the size of the each quotient group with the divisor size.

3.3.3 Hash-Division for Divisor Groups

In Section 3.2.6, we have analyzed optimizations of hash-division that require a dividend that is grouped on Q. We now show some optimizations of hash-division for a dividend that is grouped on D. Unlike the hash-division-like algorithms based on quotient groups, the following two algorithms are blocking.

This algorithm does not need a divisor hash table because after a divisor group of the dividend has been consumed, the divisor value will never reappear. We use a counter instead of a bitmap for each row in the quotient hash table. We call this adaptation of the HD algorithm *hash-division for divisor groups* (HDD). The algorithm maintains a counter to count the number of divisor groups seen so far in the dividend. For each dividend row of a divisor group, we increment the counter of the quotient candidate. If the quotient candidate is not yet contained in the quotient hash table, we insert it together with a counter set to 1. When the entire dividend has been processed, we return those quotient candidates in the quotient hash table whose counter is equal to the global counter.

The last algorithmic adaptation that we present is called *transposed hash-division for divisor groups* (HDTD), based on the HDT algorithm. We can do without a divisor hash table, but we keep an array of counters during the scan of the dividend. The processing is basically the same as the previous algorithm (HDD): We return only those quotient candidates of the quotient hash table whose counter is equal to the value of the global counter. Because all divisor groups have to be processed before we know all quotients, this algorithm is also blocking.

We sketch the data structures used in the boxes (3) and (4) of Figure 5 for the time when the entire dividend has been processed. Note that the dividend contains only three divisor groups (no Graphics rows), because we require that referential integrity between *enrollment* and *course* is preserved, e.g., by applying a semi-join of the two tables before division. Bob is the only student who is contained in all three divisor groups.

3.3.4 Stream-Join Division

The new algorithm *stream-join division* (SJD) [11] is an improvement of hash-division for divisor groups (HDD). As all other algorithms assuming a dividend that is grouped on D as the only or the major set of group attributes, SJD is a blocking algorithm. SJD is hybrid because it counts the number divisor rows, like all other aggregate algorithms, and it maintains several bits to memorize matches between

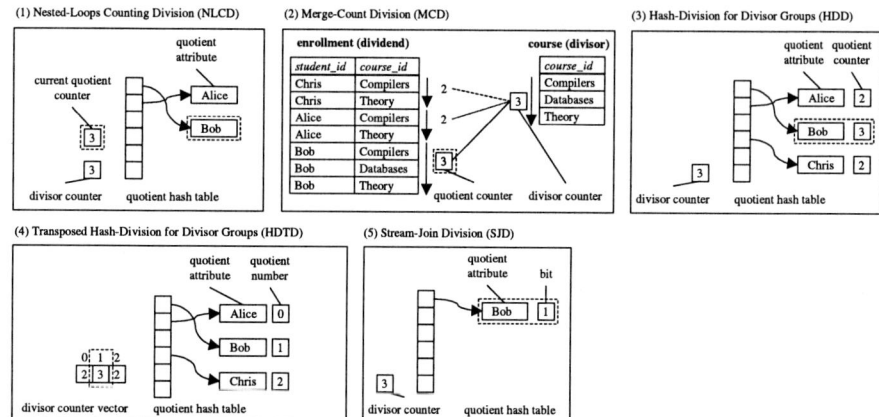

Fig. 5. Overview data structures used in aggregate algorithms. Broken lined boxes indicate that a quotient is found. Only Bob's group has as many dividend rows as the divisor.

dividend and divisor, like all other scalar algorithms. However, in this paper, we consider SJD an aggregate algorithm due to its similarity to HDD.

The major differences between SJD and HDD are:

- SJD stores a bit instead of a counter together with each quotient candidate in the quotient hash table.
- SJD is able to remove quotient candidates from the quotient hash table before the end of the processing.

The SJD algorithm works as follows. As in HDD, we maintain a counter to count the number of divisor groups seen so far in the dividend. First, we insert all quotient candidates, i.e., Q values, of the first group in the dividend together with a bit initialized with zero into the quotient hash table. We thereby eliminate possible duplicates in the dividend. Then, we process each following group as follows. For each dividend row of the current group, we look up the quotient candidate in the quotient hashtable. In case of a match, the corresponding bit is set to 1. Otherwise, i.e., when the Q value of a given dividend row is not present in the quotient hash table, we skip this row. After a group has been processed, we remove all quotient candidates with a bit equal to zero. Then, we reset the bit of each remaining quotient candidate to zero. Finally, when all groups have been processed, we compare the current group counter with the number of rows in the divisor. In case of equality, all quotient candidates in the quotient hash table with a bit equal to 1 are added to the output.

Box (5) of Figure 5 illustrates the use of the quotient hash table in SJD. We assume that the dividend is equal to the *enrollment* table of class 2 in Figure 2 with the exception that the Graphics group {(Bob, Graphics), (Chris, Graphics)} is missing, due to referential integrity.

The advantage of SJD lies in the fact that the amount of memory can decrease but will never increase after the divisors have been stored in the quotient hash table. However, the time and memory complexity is the same as for HDD. Observe that the maximum amount of memory required is proportional to the number of rows of the *first* group in the dividend. It may happen by chance that the first group is the smallest of the entire dividend. In this case, we obtain a very memory-efficient processing.

This algorithm is called stream-join division because it joins all divisor groups of the dividend (called *streams* in [11]) with each other on the attributes Q.

4 Evaluation of Algorithms

In this section, we briefly compare the division algorithms discussed in Section 3 with each other and show which algorithm is optimal, with respect to time and memory complexities, for each class of input data discussed in Section 2.

Table 2 characterizes the algorithms presented so far and shows the time and memory complexities involved. We assigned the algorithms to those data classes that have the least restrictions with respect to grouping. Remember that an algorithm of class C can also process data of classes that are reachable from C in the dependency graph in Figure 3. The overview of division algorithms in Table 2 shows that, despite the detailed classification in Table 1 (comprising 13 classes and enumerating all possible kinds of input data), there are *four* major classes of input data that are covered by dedicated division algorithms:

- class 0, which makes no assumption of grouping,
- class 2, which covers dividends that are grouped only or first on D,
- class 5, which covers dividends that are grouped only or first on Q, and finally
- class 10, which specializes class 5 (and class 0, of course) by requiring that for each quotient group, the rows of D and the divisor appear in the same order. Hence, the dividend is grouped on Q as major and D as minor.

Note that algorithms for class 2, namely HDD, HDTD, and SJD, have not been identified in the literature so far. They represent a new straightforward approach to deal with a dividend that is grouped on D. Together with the other three major classes, a query optimizer can exploit the information on the input data properties to make an optimal choice of a specific division operator.

Suppose we are given input data of a class that is different from the four major classes. Which algorithms are applicable to process our data? According to the graph in Figure 3, all algorithms belonging to major classes, which are direct or indirect parent nodes of the given class, can be used. For example, any algorithm of major classes 0 and 5 can process data of the non-major classes 6, 7, and 9.

Several algorithms belong to each class of input data in Table 2. In class 0, both HD and HDT have a linear time complexity (more precisely, *nearly* linear due to hash collisions). However, they have a higher memory complexity than the other algorithms of this class, NLCD and NLD.

We have designed three aggregate algorithms for class 2. They all have the same linear time and memory complexities.

Class 5 has two scalar and one aggregate algorithm assigned to it, which all have the same time complexity. The constant worst case memory complexity of MCD is the lowest of the three.

The two scalar algorithms HDQ and HDTQ of class 10, which consists of two subgroups (sorted and grouped divisor values) have the same time complexity. The worst case memory complexity of MSD is lower than that of MGD because MSD can exploit the sort order.

Table 2. Overview of division algorithms showing for each algorithm the class of required input data, its algorithm class, and its time and memory complexities. Input data are either not grouped (N), grouped (G), or sorted (S). Class 10 is first grouped on Q, indicated by G_1. For each quotient group, it is grouped (G_2) or sorted (S_2) on D in the same order as the divisor.

Division Algorithm	Abbreviation	Algorithm Class	Data Class	Dividend S Q	Dividend S D	Divisor T	Complexity in O-Notation Time worst	Time avg.	Memory worst	Memory avg.
Nested-Loops Counting Division	NLCD	aggregate	0	N	N	N	$|S|^2 + |T|$	$|S|^2$	1	1
Nested-Loops Division	NLD	scalar	0	N	N	N	$|S|^2 + |T|$	$|S|^2$	$|S| + |T|$	$|S|$
Hash-Division	HD	scalar	0	N	N	N	$|S| + |T|$	$|S|$	$|S| \times |T|$	$|S| \times |T|$
Transposed Hash-Division	HDT	scalar	0	N	N	N	$|S| + |T|$	$|S|$	$|S| \times |T|$	$|S| \times |T|$
Hash-Division for Divisor Groups	HDD	aggregate	2	N	G	N	$|S| + |T|$	$|S|$	$|S|$	$|S|$
Transp. Hash-Div. for Divisor Groups	HDTD	aggregate	2	N	G	N	$|S| + |T|$	$|S|$	$|S|$	$|S|$
Stream-Join Division	SJD	aggregate	2	N	G	N	$|S| + |T|$	$|S|$	$|S|$	$|S|$
Merge-Count Division	MCD	aggregate	5	G	N	N	$|S| + |T|$	$|S|$	1	1
Hash-Division for Quotient Groups	HDQ	scalar	5	G	N	N	$|S| + |T|$	$|S|$	$|T|$	1
Transp. Hash-Div. for Quotient Groups	HDTQ	scalar	5	G	N	N	$|S| + |T|$	$|S|$	$|T|$	1
Merge-Group Division	MGD	scalar	10	G_1	G_2	G_2	$|S| \times |T|$	$|S| \times |T|$	$|T|$	1
Merge-Sort Division	MSD	scalar	10	G_1	S_2	S_2	$|S| + |T|$	$|S|$	1	1

It is important to observe that one should not directly compare complexities of scalar and aggregate algorithms in Table 2 to determine the most efficient algorithm overall. This is because *aggregate* algorithms require duplicate-free input tables, which can incur a very costly preprocessing step. There is one exception of aggregate algorithms: SJD ignores duplicate dividend rows because of the hash table used to store quotient candidates. It does not matter if a quotient occurs more than once inside a divisor group because the bit corresponding to a quotient candidate can be set to 1 any number of times without changing its value (1). However, SJD does not ignore duplicates in the divisor because it counts the number of divisor rows.

In general, *scalar* division algorithms ignore duplicates in the dividend and the divisor. Note that the scan operations of MGD and MSD can be implemented in such a way that they ignore duplicates in both inputs [7].

5 Related Work

Quantifiers in queries can be expressed by relational algebra. Due to the lack of efficient division algorithms in the past, early work has recommended avoiding the relational division operator to express universal quantification in queries [2]. Instead, universal quantification is expressed with the help of the well-known anti-semi-join operator, or *complement-join*, as it is called in that paper.

Other early work suggests approaches other than division to process (universal) quantification [4] [5]. Universal quantification is expressed by new algebra operators and is optimized based on query graphs in a non-relational data model [5]. Due to the lack of a performance analysis, we cannot comment on the efficiency of this approach.

The research literature provides only few surveys of division algorithms [3] [6] [7]. Some of the algorithms reviewed in this paper have been compared both analytically and experimentally [7]. The conclusion is that hash-division outperforms all other approaches. Complementing this work, we have shown that an optimizer has to take the input data characteristics and the set of given algorithms into account to pick the best division algorithm. The classification of four division algorithms in [7] is based on a two-by-two matrix. One axis of the matrix distinguishes between algorithms based on sorting or based on hashing. The other axis separates "direct" algorithms, which allow processing the (larger) dividend table only once, from "indirect" algorithms, which require duplicate removal (by employing semi-join) and aggregation. For example, the merge-sort division algorithm of Section 3.2.2 falls into the category "direct algorithm based on sorting," while the hash-division for divisor groups algorithm of Section 3.3.3 belongs to the combination "indirect algorithm based on hashing." Our classification details these four approaches and focuses on the fact that data properties should be exploited as much as possible by employing "slim" algorithms that are separated from preprocessing algorithms, like grouping and sorting. Our analysis is more sensitive to the properties of input data. For example, if the input data is in class 2 (where the data is grouped on the dividend's divisor attributes), then as shown in Section 3.3.4, the stream-join division algorithm is at least as efficient as the hash-division algorithm of [7] but requires less memory.

Based on a classification of queries that contain universal quantification, several query evaluation techniques have been analyzed [3]. The input data of this algorithm analysis is stored in an object-oriented or object-relational database, where set-valued attributes are available. Hence, the algorithms they examine can presuppose that the input data is grouped on certain attributes. For example, the table *enrollment* in Figure 1 could be represented by a set-valued *enrolled_courses* attribute of a *student* class. The authors conclude that universal quantification based on anti-semi-join is superior to all other approaches, similar to the conclusion of [2]. Note, however, that paper has a broader definition of queries involving universal quantification than the classic definition that involves the division operator. However, the anti-semi-join approach requires a considerable overhead for preprocessing the dividend. An equivalent definition of the division operator using anti-semi-join ($\bar{\ltimes}$) as well as semi-join ($\ltimes$) and left outer join ($⟕$), is: $S \div T = ((S \ltimes T) ⟕ T) \bar{\ltimes} T$.

In this paper, we focused on the universal (for-all) quantifier. *Generalized quantifiers* have been proposed to specify quantifiers like "at least ten" or "exactly as many" in SQL [9]. Such quantifiers can be processed by algorithms that employ multi-dimensional matrix data structures [13]. In that paper, however, the implementation of an operator called *all* is presented that is similar but different form relational division. Unlike division, the result of the *all* operator contains some attributes of the divisor. Hence, we have to employ a projection on the quotient attributes of the *all* operator's result to achieve a valid quotient.

Transformation rules for optimizing queries containing multiple (existential and universal) quantifications are presented in [10]. Our contribution complements this work by offering strategies to choose a single (division) operator, which may be one element of a larger query processing problem.

6 Conclusion and Future Work

Based on a classification of input data properties, we were able to differentiate the major currently known algorithms for relational division. In addition, we could provide new algorithms for previously not supported data properties. Thus, for the first time, an optimizer has a full range of algorithms, separated by their input data properties and efficiency measures, to choose from.

We are aware of the fact that database system vendors are reluctant to implement several alternative algorithms for the same query operator, in our case the division operation. One reason is that the optimizer's rule set has to be extended, which can lead to a larger search space for queries containing division. Another reason is that the optimizer must be able to detect a division in a query. This is a non-trivial task because a division cannot be expressed in SQL:1999 [1]. No keyword similar to "FOR ALL" [8] is available and division has to be expressed indirectly, for example by using two negated "NOT EXISTS" clauses or by using the "division by counting" approach on the query language level. To the best of our knowledge, there is no database system that has an implementation of hash-division (or any of its improvements), although this efficient algorithm has been known for many years [6]. However, we believe that as soon as a dedicated keyword for universal quantification is supported by a standard and its benefit is recognized and exploited by applications, many options and strategies are available today for database system vendors to implement an efficient division operator.

Note that division requires a "constant" divisor. It is also common that queries involve a correlated divisor, e.g. "Which students have taken all courses of their major?" Unfortunately, such queries cannot be translated into a simple division query. However, it may be possible to employ several divisions for such a single query, each division having a single constant divisor. This could be a worthwhile strategy if the number of divisors is low and if they can be easily computed in advance.

Our future work includes the analysis of further data properties that have an influence on optimization of division queries, like the current data distribution or the availability of certain indexes. Furthermore, we will study the potential of parallelizing division algorithms, based on the detailed studies in [7] on parallelizing hash-division and aggregate algorithms. Finally, we plan to investigate the potential of using universal quantification in queries of business intelligence applications.

References

1. ANSI/ISO/IEC 9075-2: Information Technology – Database Language – SQL – Part 2: Foundation (SQL/Foundation). (1999)
2. Bry, F.: Towards an Efficient Evaluation of General Queries: Quantifier and Disjunction Processing Revisited. SIGMOD 1989. 193–204
3. Claußen, J., Kemper, A., Moerkotte, G., Peithner, K: Optimizing Queries with Universal Quantification in Object-Oriented and Object-Relational Databases. VLDB 1997: 286–295
4. Dayal, U.: Processing Queries with Quantifiers: A Horticultural Approach. PODS 1983: 125–136
5. Dayal, U.: Of Nests and Trees: A Unified Approach to Processing Queries that Contain Nested Subqueries, Aggregates, and Quantifiers. VLDB 1987: 197–208
6. Graefe, G.: Query Evaluation Techniques for Large Databases. ACM Computing Surveys 25(2): 73–170 (1993)
7. Graefe, G., Cole, R.: Fast Algorithms for Universal Quantification in Large Databases. ACM Transactions on Database Systems 20(2): 187–236 (1995)
8. Gulutzan, P., Pelzer, T.: SQL-99 Complete, Really: An Example-Based Reference Manual of the New Standard. R&D Books, Lawrence, Kansas, U.S.A., 1999
9. Hsu, P.-Y., Parker, D.: Improving SQL with Generalized Quantifiers. ICDE 1995: 298–305

10. Jarke, M., Koch, J.: Range Nesting: A Fast Method to Evaluate Quantified Queries. SIGMOD 1983: 196–206
11. Nippl, C., Rantzau, R., Mitschang, B.: StreamJoin: A Generic Database Approach to Support the Class of Stream-Oriented Applications. IDEAS 2000: 83–91
12. Rantzau, R., Shapiro, L., Mitschang, B., Wang, Q.: Universal Quantification in Relational Databases: A Classification of Data and Algorithms. Technical Report, Computer Science Department, University of Stuttgart, 2002 (to appear)
13. Rao, S., Badia, A., van Gucht, D.: Providing Better Support for a Class of Decision Support Queries. SIGMOD 1996: 217–227

Efficient Algorithms for Mining Inclusion Dependencies

Fabien De Marchi[1], Stéphane Lopes[2], and Jean-Marc Petit[1]

[1] Laboratoire LIMOS, CNRS FRE 2239
Université Blaise Pascal – Clermont-Ferrand II,
24 avenue des Landais, 63 177 Aubière cedex, France
{demarchi,jmpetit}@math.univ-bpclermont.fr
[2] Laboratoire PRISM, CNRS UMR 8636
45, avenue des Etats-Unis, 78035 Versailles Cedex, France
stephane.lopes@prism.uvsq.fr

Abstract. Foreign keys form one of the most fundamental constraints for relational databases. Since they are not always defined in existing databases, algorithms need to be devised to discover foreign keys. One of the underlying problems is known to be the inclusion dependency (IND) inference problem. In this paper a new data mining algorithm for computing unary INDs is given. From unary INDs, we also propose a levelwise algorithm to discover all remaining INDs, where candidate INDs of size $i+1$ are generated from satisfied INDs of size $i, (i > 0)$.

An implementation of these algorithms has been achieved and tested against synthetic databases. Up to our knowledge, this paper is the first one to address in a comprehensive manner this data mining problem, from algorithms to experimental results.

1 Introduction

Inclusion dependencies (INDs) are one of the most important kind of integrity constraints in relational databases [6, 4, 22]. Together with functional dependencies, they represent an important part of database semantic.

Some recent works were proposed to discover functional dependencies (FDs) holding in a relation [11, 15, 21, 23], but IND discovery in databases has not raised great interest yet. We identify two reasons for that: 1) the difficulty of the problem due to the potential number of candidate INDs (cf [4, 12] for complexity results) and 2) the fact that INDs "lack of popularity". To illustrate this fact, let us compare with FDs: FDs are studied as a basic concept of databases since they are used to define normal forms (e.g. BCNF or 3NF) and to define keys, very popular constraints in practice. We think that what is good for FDs is good for INDs too: they can be used 1) to define other normal forms, such as IDNF (see [17, 13, 14] for details on such normal forms), 2) to avoid update anomalies and to ensure data coherence and integrity, and 3) to define foreign keys (or referential integrity constraints), since recall that a foreign key is the left-hand side of an IND having a right-hand side which is a key.

Moreover, in many existing databases, foreign keys are only partially defined, or not defined at all. As an example, recall that old versions of many DBMS (e.g. Oracle V6) did not support foreign key definition. Thus, even if an old Oracle database has been upgraded to Oracle V7 or V8, analysts would probably not have defined foreign keys during the migration process. So, there is an obvious practical interest for discovering this kind of knowledge.

Another practical application of IND inference is pointed out in the CLIO project [20] devoted to data/schema integration. As a perspective, the authors mention the necessity to discover keys and referential integrity constraints over existing databases. More generally, INDs are known to be a key concept in various applications, such as relational database design and maintenance [17, 3, 13], semantic query optimization [9, 5] or database reverse engineering [19].

Contribution. In this paper, a new data mining algorithm for computing unary INDs is given. A data pre-processing step is performed in such a way that unary IND inference becomes straightforward.

From discovered unary INDs, a levelwise algorithm, fitting in the framework defined in [18], has been devised to discover all remaining INDs in a given database (i.e. INDs between attributes of size greater than 1). We propose an elegant Apriori-like algorithm to generate candidate INDs of size $i + 1$ from satisfied INDs of size $i, (i > 0)$.

Despite the inherent complexity of this inference task, experiments on synthetic databases show the feasibility of this approach, even for medium size databases (up to 500000 tuples).

Paper organization. The layout of the rest of this paper is as follows: Related works is introduced in Section 2. Section 3 recalls some basic concepts of relational databases. Section 4 deals with IND inference: a new approach for unary IND inference is given in Section 4.1, and a levelwise algorithm is proposed to discover all remaining INDs in Section 4.2. Experimental results on synthetic databases are presented in Section 5, and we conclude in Section 6.

2 Related Works

To the best of our knowledge, only a few papers deal with IND inference problem.

For unary IND inference, the domain of attributes, their number of distinct values and the transitivity property can be used to reduce the number of data accesses, as proposed in [12, 2]. Nevertheless, these technics do not provide an efficient pruning, and a large number of tests have to be performed against the database.

The IND discovery is also an instance (among many others) of a general framework for levelwise algorithms defined in [18]. However, unary IND inference is not considered as an important sub-problem, no details are given about a key step of such an algorithm, i.e. the generation of candidate INDs of size $i+1$ from satisfied INDs of size i, and no implementation is achieved.

Only one implementation achieving IND inference was presented in [16]; the principle is to reduce the search space by considering only *duplicated attributes*. Such duplicate attributes are discovered from SQL join statements performed during a period of time over the database server. This approach uses semantic information "to guess" relevant attributes from SQL workloads. However, this work does not provide an exhaustive search of satisfied INDs, i.e. only a subset of INDs satisfied in the database can be discovered. For instance, if an IND between A and B holds in the database, and if there is no join between these attributes in a workload, this IND will never be discovered. Moreover, even if we have $A \subseteq C$ and $B \subseteq D$, the candidate $AB \subseteq CD$ is never considered.

3 Basic Definitions

We briefly introduce some basic relational database concepts used in this paper (see e.g. [17, 13] for details).

Let R be a finite set of *attributes*. For each attribute $A \in R$, the set of all its possible values is called the *domain of A* and denoted by $Dom(A)$. A *tuple* over R is a mapping $t : R \rightarrow \times_{A \in R} Dom(A)$, where $t(A) \in Dom(A), \forall A \in R$. A *relation* is a set of tuples. The cardinality of a set X is denoted by $|X|$. We say that r is a relation *over R* and R is the *relation schema* of r. If $X \subseteq R$ is an attribute set[1] and t is a tuple, we denote by $t[X]$ the restriction of t to X. The projection of a relation r onto X, denoted as $\pi_X(r)$, is defined by $\pi_X(r) = \{t[X] \mid t \in r\}$.

A *database schema* **R** is a finite set of *relation schemas R_i*. A *relational database instance* **d** (or *database*) over **R** corresponds to a set of relations r_i over each R_i of **R**. Given a database **d** over **R**, the set of distinct domains (e.g. int, string ...) is denoted by $Dom(\mathbf{d})$.

An attribute sequence (e.g. $X = \{A, B, C\}$ or simply ABC) is an ordered set of distinct attributes. Given a sequence X, $X[i]$ refers to the ith element of the sequence. When it is clear from context, we do not distinguish a sequence from its underlying set.

Two attributes A and B are said to be *compatible* if $Dom(A) = Dom(B)$. Two distinct attribute sequences X and Y are *compatible* if $|X| = |Y| = m$ and if for $j = [1, m]$, $Dom(X[j]) = Dom(Y[j])$.

Inclusion dependencies and the notion of satisfaction of an inclusion dependency in a database are defined below.

An *inclusion dependency* (IND) over a database schema **R** is a statement of the form $R_i[X] \subseteq R_j[Y]$, where $R_i, R_j \in \mathbf{R}$, $X \subseteq R_i, Y \subseteq R_j$, X and Y are compatible sequences. An inclusion dependency is said to be *trivial* if it is of the form $R[X] \subseteq R[X]$. An IND $R[X] \subseteq R[Y]$ is of size i if $|X| = i$. We call *unary inclusion dependency* an IND of size 1.

Let **d** be a database over a database schema **R**, where $r_i, r_j \in \mathbf{d}$ are relations over $R_i, R_j \in \mathbf{R}$ respectively. An inclusion dependency $R_i[X] \subseteq R_j[Y]$ is satisfied

---

[1] Letters from the beginning of the alphabet introduce single attributes whereas letters from the end introduce attribute sets.

in a database **d** over **R**, denoted by $\mathbf{d} \models R_i[X] \subseteq R_j[Y]$, iff $\forall u \in r_i, \exists v \in r_j$ such that $u[X] = v[Y]$ (or equivalently $\pi_X(r_i) \subseteq \pi_y(r_j)$).

Let $\mathcal{I}_1$ and $\mathcal{I}_2$ be two sets of inclusion dependencies, $\mathcal{I}_1$ is a *cover* of $\mathcal{I}_2$ if $\mathcal{I}_1 \models \mathcal{I}_2$ (this notation means that each dependency in $\mathcal{I}_2$ holds in any database satisfying all the dependencies in $\mathcal{I}_1$) and $\mathcal{I}_2 \models \mathcal{I}_1$.

A sound and complete axiomatization for INDs was given in [4]. Three inference rules form this axiomatization:

1. (reflexivity) $R[A_1, ..., A_n] \subseteq R[A_1, ..., A_n]$
2. (projection and permutation) $if R[A_1, ..., A_n] \subseteq S[B_1, ..., B_n]$ then $R[A_{\sigma 1}, ..., A_{\sigma m}] \subseteq S[B_{\sigma 1}, ..., B_{\sigma m}]$ for each sequence $\sigma 1, ..., \sigma m$ of distinct integers from $\{1, ..., n\}$
3. (transitivity) if $R[A_1, ..., A_n] \subseteq S[B_1, ..., B_n]$ et $S[B_1, ..., B_n] \subseteq T[C_1, ..., C_n]$ then $R[A_1, ..., A_n] \subseteq T[C_1, ..., C_n]$

The satisfaction of an IND can be expressed in relational algebra in the following way [16]:

Let **d** be a database over a database schema **R**, where $r_i, r_j \in \mathbf{d}$ are relations over $R_i, R_j \in \mathbf{R}$ respectively. We have: $\mathbf{d} \models R_i[X] \subseteq R_j[Y]$ iff $|\pi_X(r_i)| = |\pi_X(r_i) \bowtie_{(X=Y)} \pi_Y(r_j)|$. An SQL query can easily be devised from this property, performing two costly operations against the data: a join and a projection.

4 Inclusion Dependency Inference

The IND inference problem can be formulated as follows: "Given a database **d** over a database schema **R**, find a cover of all non trivial inclusion dependencies $R[X] \subseteq S[Y]$, $R, S \in R$, such that $d \models R[X] \subseteq S[Y]$".

In this paper, we propose to re-formulate this problem into two sub-problems: the former is the unary IND inference problem, and the latter is the IND inference problem being understood that unary INDs have been discovered.

Two reasons justify this reformulation: 1) INDs in real-life databases are most of the time of size one, and 2) no efficient pruning method can be applied for unary IND inference. Therefore, specialized algorithms need to be devised to discover unary INDs.

4.1 Unary Inclusion Dependency Inference

We propose a new and efficient technic to discover unary INDs satisfied in a given database. The idea is to associate, for a given domain, each value with every attributes having this value. After this preprocessing step, we get a binary relation from which unary INDs can be computed.

Data pre-processing. Given a database **d** over a database schema **R**, for each data type $t \in dom(\mathbf{d})$, a so-called extraction context $\mathbb{D}_t(\mathbf{d}) = (\mathbb{V}, \mathbb{U}, \mathbb{B})$ is associated, defined as follows:

- $\mathbb{U} = \{R.A \mid dom(A) = t, A \in R, R \in \mathbf{R}\}$. $\mathbb{U}$ is the set of attributes[2] whose domain is t;
- $\mathbb{V} = \{v \in \pi_A(r) \mid R.A \in \mathbb{U}, r \in \mathbf{d}, r \text{ defined over } R\}$. $\mathbb{V}$ is the set of values taken by attributes in their relations;
- $\mathbb{B} \subseteq \mathbb{V} \times \mathbb{U}$ is a binary relation defined by: $(v, R.A) \in \mathbb{B} \iff v \in \pi_A(r)$, where $r \in \mathbf{d}$ and r defined over R.

Example 1. Let us consider the database **d** given in table 1 as a running example.

Table 1. A running example

r

A	B	C	D
1	X	3	11.0
1	X	3	12.0
2	Y	4	11.0
1	X	3	13.0

s

E	F	G	H
1	X	3	11.0
2	Y	4	12.0
4	Z	6	14.0
7	W	9	14.0

t

I	J	K	L
11.0	11.0	1	X
12.0	12.0	2	Y
11.0	14.0	4	Z
11.0	9.0	7	W
13.0	13.0	9	R

Domains of attributes of these relations are of three types: int, real, string. For the type int, $\mathbb{U} = \{A, C, E, G, K\}$ and $\mathbb{V} = \{1, 2, 3, 4, 6, 7, 9\}$. For instance, the value 1 appears in $\pi_A(r), \pi_E(s), \pi_K(t)$, and thus $(1, A), (1, E)$ and $(1, K) \in \mathbb{B}$. Table 2 summarizes the binary relations associated with int, real and string.

Table 2. Extraction contexts associated with the database **d**.

int

V	U
1	A E K
2	A E K
3	C G
4	C E G K
6	G
7	E K
9	G K

real

V	U
9.0	J
11.0	D H I J
12.0	D H I J
13.0	D I J
14.0	H J

string

V	U
R	L
X	B F L
Y	B F L
Z	F L
W	F L

Such extraction contexts can be built from existing databases, for instance with an SQL query (with only one full scan on each relation) or with external programs and cursors computed via ODBC drivers.

A new algorithm for unary IND inference. With this new data organization, unary INDs can be now discovered efficiently. Informally, if all values of

---
[2] When clear from context, we will omit to prefix attributes by their relation schema.

attribute A can be found in values of B, then by construction B will be present in all lines of the binary relation containing A.

Property 1. Given a database **d** and a triple $\mathbb{D}_t(d) = (\mathbb{V}, \mathbb{U}, \mathbb{B}), t \in dom(d)$,

$$d \models A \subseteq B \iff B \in \bigcap_{v \in \mathbb{V}|(v,A) \in \mathbb{B}} \{C \in \mathbb{U} \mid (v, C) \in \mathbb{B}\}$$

where $A, B \in \mathbb{U}$.

Proof. Let $A \in R, B \in S$ such that $d \models R[A] \subseteq S[B]$. $\iff \forall v \in \pi_A(r), \exists u \in s$ such that $u[B] = v \iff \forall v \in \mathbb{V}$ such that $(v, A) \in \mathbb{B}$, we have $(v, B) \in \mathbb{B}$

Thus, the whole task of unary IND inference can be done in only *one pass* of each binary relation. Algorithm 1 finds all unary INDs in a database **d**, between attributes defined on a type $t \in dom(\mathbf{d})$, taking in input the extraction context as described before. For all attribute A, we note $rhs(A)$ (for right-hand side) the set of attributes B such that $A \subseteq B$.

Algorithm 1 Unary IND inference

Input: the triplet $\mathbb{V}, \mathbb{U}, \mathbb{B}$, associated with **d** and t.
Output: $\mathcal{I}_1$ the set of unary INDs verified by **d** between attributes of type t.
1: **for all** $A \in \mathbb{U}$ **do** $rhs(A) = \mathbb{U}$;
2: **for all** $v \in \mathbb{V}$ **do**
3:     **for all** A s.t. $(v, A) \in \mathbb{B}$ **do**
4:         $rhs(A) = rhs(A) \cap \{B \mid (v, B) \in \mathbb{B}\}$;
5: **for all** $A \in \mathbb{U}$ **do**
6:     **for all** $B \in rhs(A)$ **do**
7:         $\mathcal{I}_1 = \mathcal{I}_1 \cup \{A \subseteq B\}$;
8: **return** $\mathcal{I}_1$.

Example 2. Let us consider the type int (cf Table 2) in example 1. The initialization phase (line 1) gives: $rhs(A) = rhs(C) = \ldots = rhs(K) = \{A, C, E, G, K\}$.

Then, we consider the set of attributes in the first line of the binary relation: $l_1 = \{A, E, K\}$. For each attribute in l_1, its rhs set is updated (line 4) as follows: $rhs(A) = \{A, E, K\}, rhs(E) = \{A, E, K\}, rhs(K) = \{A, E, K\}$; $rhs(C)$ and $rhs(G)$ remain unchanged.

These operations are repeated for each value of the binary relation (line 2). Finally, after one pass of the relation, the result is: $rhs(A) = \{A, E, K\}, rhs(C) = \{C, G\}, rhs(E) = \{E, K\}, rhs(G) = \{G\}, rhs(K) = \{K\}$

From these sets, unary INDs between attributes of type int are (lines 5, 6 and 7): $\{A \subseteq E, A \subseteq K, C \subseteq G, E \subseteq K\}$.

The same operation has to be repeated for each context (each data type), and then, thanks to property 1, we deduce the following set of unary inclusion dependencies satisfied by **d**: $\{A \subseteq E, A \subseteq K, E \subseteq K, C \subseteq G, D \subseteq I, D \subseteq J, H \subseteq J, I \subseteq J, B \subseteq F, B \subseteq L, F \subseteq L\}$.

4.2 A Levelwise Algorithm

Once unary INDs are known, the problem we are interested in can be reformulated as follows: "Given a database **d** over a database schema **R** and the set of UINDs verified by **d**, find a cover of all non trivial inclusion dependencies $R[X] \subseteq S[Y]$, $R, S \in \mathbf{R}$, such that $d \models R[X] \subseteq S[Y]$".

We first recall how IND properties justify a levelwise approach to achieve their inference [18]. Then, we give a algorithm, with an natural but not trivial method to generate candidate INDs of size $i+1$ from satisfied INDs of size i [8].

Definition of the search space. Candidate INDs are composed of a left-hand side and a right-hand side. Given a set of attributes, we do not have to consider all the permutations to build a left-hand side or a right-hand side, thanks to the second inference rule presented in section 3.

Example 3. Let $R[AB] \subseteq S[EF]$ and $R[AB] \subseteq T[KL]$ be two satisfied INDs. Then, thanks to the second inference rule of INDs (permutation), $R[BA] \subseteq S[FE]$ and $R[BA] \subseteq T[LK]$ are also satisfied.

Then, we are faced with the following problem: in which order attribute sequences have to be built to avoid considering several permutations of the same IND ? We have chosen to fix an order for the left-hand side. This order is the lexicographic order on attributes.

Reduction of the search space. In this set of candidates, a specialization relation $\prec$ can be defined as follows [18]:
Let $I_1 : R_i[X] \subseteq R_j[Y]$ and $I_2 : R'_i[X'] \subseteq R'_j[Y']$ be two candidate INDs. We define $I_2 \prec I_1$ iff:
- $R_i = R'_i$ and $R_j = R'_j$ and
- $X' = <A_1, ..., A_k>$, $Y' = <B_1, ..., B_k>$, and there exists a set of indices $i_1 < ... < i_h \in \{1, ..., k\}$ with $h \leq k$ such that $X = <A_{i_1}, ..., A_{i_h}>$, $Y = <B_{i_1}, ..., B_{i_h}>$[3].

Note that X, Y, X' and Y' are sequences, and thus the specialization relation respects the order of attributes.

Example 4. We have $(R_i[AC] \subseteq R_j[EG]) \preceq (R_i[ABC] \subseteq R_j[EFG])$, but $(R_i[AC] \subseteq R_j[GE]) \npreceq (R_i[ABC] \subseteq R_j[EFG])$.

We note $I_1 \prec I_2$ if $I_1 \preceq I_2$ and $I_2 \npreceq I_1$.

From the second inference rule of INDs, we can deduce the following property, which justifies a levelwise approach for IND inference.

Property 2. Let I_1, I_2 be 2 candidate INDs such that $I_1 \prec I_2$.
- If $d \models I_2$ then $d \models I_1$ and
- If $d \not\models I_1$ then $d \not\models I_2$.

---
[3] This definition is slightly different from that given in [18]. Here, we impose an order for indices $i_1, ..., i_h$ without any loss of information.

This property extends the Apriori property to our problem; we say that the relation $\prec$ is anti-monotone w.r.t. the satisfiability of INDs [10]. Then, knowing not satisfied INDs at a given level, allows us to prune candidates for the next level. More precisely, only satisfied INDs will be used to generate candidate INDs for the next level. Thus, the search space will be considerably reduced, for levels higher than one.

The algorithm. From now, notations given in Table 3 will be used throughout the paper.

Table 3. Notations

C_i	Set of candidate inclusion dependencies of size i.
$\mathcal{I}_i$	Set of satisfied inclusion dependencies of size i.
$I.lhs$	Left-hand side sequence of the IND I
$I.rhs$	Right-hand side sequence of the IND I
$X.rel$	Relation schema of attributes of the sequence X

Algorithm 2 finds all INDs holding in a given database **d**, taking in input the set of unary INDs satisfied by **d** (cf section 4.1). The first phase consists in computing candidate INDs of size 2, from satisfied INDs of size 1. Then, these candidates are tested against the database. From the satisfied ones, candidate INDs of size 3 are generated and then tested against the database. This process is repeated until no more candidates can be computed.

Algorithm 2 IND inference

Input: d a database, and $\mathcal{I}_1$ the set of UINDs satisfied by **d**.
Output: Inclusion dependencies satisfied by d
1: $C_2 := GenNext(\mathcal{I}_1);$
2: $i := 2;$
3: **while** $C_i \neq \emptyset$ **do**
4:     **forall** $I \in C_i$ **do**
5:         **if** $d \models I$ **then**
6:             $\mathcal{I}_i := \mathcal{I}_i \cup \{I\};$
7:     $C_{i+1} := GenNext(\mathcal{I}_i);$
8:     $i := i + 1;$
9: **end while**
10: **return** $\cup_{j<i} \mathcal{I}_j$

The theoretical complexity of such an algorithm has been well studied in [18]. It is equal to the cost of one test against the database (here the test of an IND), times the number of satisfied INDs plus the number of not satisfied INDs whose all specializations are satisfied, so-called *negative border* of satisfied INDs.

Candidate INDs generation. Generation of candidate inclusion dependencies of size greater or equal than 2 is an important - and not trivial - contribution of the paper. The function *GenNext* extends the principle of candidate generation, whose archetype is the AprioriGen function [1] used for frequent itemset discovery. Algorithm 3 performs this task; it is made of two main parts: a generation phase and a pruning phase, both based on the anti-monotony property of the relation $\prec$ w.r.t. INDs satisfisfability (cf. property 2).

Algorithm 3 $GenNext$: Generation of candidate INDs of size $i+1$

Input: $\mathcal{I}_i$, inclusion dependencies of size i.
Output: $\mathcal{C}_{i+1}$, sequence of candidate inclusion dependencies of size i+1
1: **insert into** $\mathcal{C}_{i+1}$
2: **select** $p.lhs.rel"["p.lhs[1], p.lhs[2], ..., p.lhs[i], q.lhs[i]"]"$ " $\subseteq$ "
         $p.rhs.rel"["p.rhs[1], p.rhs[2], ..., p.rhs[i], q.rhs[i]"]"$
3: **from** $\mathcal{I}_i$ p, $\mathcal{I}_i$ q
4: **where** $p.lhs.rel = q.lhs.rel$ **and** $p.rhs.rel = q.rhs.rel$
5: **and** $p.lhs[1] = q.lhs[1]$ **and** $p.rhs[1] = q.rhs[1]$
6: **and** ...
7: **and** $p.lhs[i-1] = q.lhs[i-1]$ **and** $p.rhs[i-1] = q.rhs[i-1]$
8: **and** $p.lhs[i] < q.lhs[i]$
9: **for all** $I \in \mathcal{C}_{i+1}$ **do**
10:    **for all** $\delta \prec I$ and δ of size i **do**
11:        **if** $\delta \notin \mathcal{I}_i$ **then**
12:            $\mathcal{C}_{i+1} = \mathcal{C}_{i+1} \setminus \{I\}$
13:        **end if**
14:    **end for**
15: **end for**

The generation phase (lines 1 to 8) constructs candidate INDs from satisfied INDs of the previous level. Let $I_1 = (R_i[XA] \subseteq R_j[YC])$ and $I_2 = R_i[XB] \subseteq R_j[YD]$ be two satisfied INDs of level i, with $|X| = |Y| = i - 1$ and $A < B$; Then the candidate: $I_3 = R_i[XAB] \subseteq R_j[YCD]$ is formed.

Example 5. From the running example, table 4 shows satisfied INDs at level 1 ($\mathcal{I}_1$) in the first column, classified by relations. Candidate INDs of size 2 are represented in the second column of the table.

The pruning phase (lines 9 to 14) removes all candidates which are not in agree with the anti-monotony property.

Example 6. To illustrate this pruning phase, suppose that the INDs $R[AB] \subseteq S[EF]$ and $R[AC] \subseteq S[EG]$ are satisfied at level 2. For level 3, the generation phase constructs the candidate IND : $R[ABC] \subseteq S[EFG]$.
   The pruning phase verifies that each IND of size 2 which specializes $R[ABC] \subseteq S[EFG]$ are satisfied at level 2. Since $R[BC] \subseteq S[FG]$ is not satisfied, the candidate is removed from $\mathcal{C}_2$.

Table 4. Generation of level 2 candidates from satisfied level 1 INDs.

	$\mathcal{I}_1$	$\mathcal{C}_2$
R to S	$R[A] \subseteq S[E]$	$R[AB] \subseteq S[EF]$
	$R[B] \subseteq S[F]$	$R[AC] \subseteq S[EG]$
	$R[C] \subseteq S[G]$	$R[BC] \subseteq S[FG]$
R to T	$R[A] \subseteq T[K]$	$R[AB] \subseteq T[KL]$
	$R[B] \subseteq T[L]$	$R[AD] \subseteq T[KI]$
	$R[D] \subseteq T[I]$	$R[AD] \subseteq T[KJ]$
	$R[D] \subseteq T[J]$	$R[BD] \subseteq T[LI]$
		$R[BD] \subseteq T[LJ]$
S to T	$S[E] \subseteq T[K]$	$S[EF] \subseteq T[KL]$
	$S[F] \subseteq T[L]$	$S[EH] \subseteq T[KJ]$
	$S[H] \subseteq T[J]$	$S[FH] \subseteq T[LJ]$
T to T	$S[I] \subseteq T[J]$	

5 Experimental Results

System environment. All our experiments were provided on an Intel Pentium III with a CPU clock rate of 500 Mhz, 400 MB of main memory and running Windows NT 4. Algorithm were implemented using the C++ language and STL (Standard Template Library). Oracle 8 was used to provide tests while DBMS accesses were done via ODBC.

Test databases. Test are providing against a set of 6 synthetic databases, all with the same database schema: 5 relations, 10 attributes by relation schemas, and the same set of satisfied INDs by each of them (10 unary INDs, 15 INDs of size 2, 20 of size 3, 15 of size 4, 6 of size 5 and 1 of size 6). All attributes in these databases are of the same type and have approximately 70% of distinct values. They only differ in the number of rows: 5 000, 15 000, 30 000, 90 000, 200 000 and 500 000 rows by relations.

5.1 Experiments for Unary IND Inference

We propose to compare our data-mining algorithm with the approach consisting in generating candidate unary INDs and then test them against the database [12, 2] referred to as *SQL approach* in the sequel.

In table 5 are reported, for each synthetic database described before, execution times to discover unary INDs with both our data-mining algorithm (including the pre-processing step) and our implementation of the SQL approach. We did not report execution times exceeding 7 hours, and replace them with a "*".

These results show with evidence that our algorithm outperforms the SQL approach since with SQL, each candidate leads to a join performed against base relations. Even if our implementation of SQL method is not really optimized (we

Table 5. Times (seconds) to discover unary INDs, with data-mining and SQL approaches.

$|r|$	Data Mining (s.)	SQL (s.)
5000	28	1750
15000	98	4750
30000	269	10000
90000	871	*
200000	2590	*
500000	4195	*

do not exploit transitivity property of INDs), such a method remains obviously unappropriated w.r.t. the data-mining approach.

Note that we assume the binary representation of the database used for computing unary INDs fits in main memory; for the scalability of our algorithm with very large databases, external memory algorithms can be easily devised.

Moreover, the performances of our algorithm do not depend neither on the number of relations nor on the number of satisfied INDs. The key parameter is the number of distinct values occurring in the database for a given type.

5.2 Experiments for IND Inference

Table 6 gives execution times on test databases for the whole task of IND inference, including times to find unary INDs (context extraction + unary INDs computation).

Despite the inherent complexity of the IND inference problem, execution times never exceed 7 hours.

6 Conclusion

The discovery of inclusion dependencies in relational databases is a (relatively new) data mining problem useful in many database applications such as database

Table 6. Execution times for the whole task of IND inference.

nb of tuples	Time (s)
5000	149
15000	479
30000	1017
90000	2720
200000	7458
500000	20806

maintenance or semantic query optimization. Until this work, up to our knowledge, no algorithm had been proposed to infer all inclusion dependencies in a database.

In this paper we have first address the problem of unary IND inference, since they convey most of the semantic of existing databases. For the sake of completeness, we have proposed to discover all remaining INDs using the framework of levelwise algorithms.

From these results, the discovery of approximate INDs, i.e. INDs which almost hold in a database, can be easily integrated in our propositions. In fact, we do not loose any property justifying our approach; the main goal is to deal with incoherences that can appear among tuples in real-life databases.

We are currently working on a depth-first version of our algorithm, and we plan to conduct further experiments on both synthetic and real-life databases.

This work takes place in an ongoing project devoted to logical database. Its objective is to be able to connect any database (independently of the underlying DBMS) in order to give some insights to DBA/analyst such as the FDs satisfied in a given relation [15], the inclusion dependencies satisfied by the database [16] or small informative examples of a given relation [7].

References

1. Rakesh Agrawal and Ramakrishnan Srikant. Fast algorithms for mining association rules in large databases. In Jorge B. Bocca, Matthias Jarke, and Carlo Zaniolo, editors, *International Conference on Very Large Data Bases, Santiago de Chile, Chile*, pages 487–499. Morgan Kaufmann, 1994.
2. S. Bell and P. Brockhausen. Discovery of constraints and data dependencies in databases (extended abstract). In Nada Lavrac and Stefan Wrobel, editors, *European Conference on Machine Learning, Crete, Greece*, pages 267–270, 1995.
3. G. Vossen C. Fahrner. A survey of database design transformations based on the entity-relationship model. *Data and Knowledge Engineering*, 15(3):213–250, 1995.
4. M. Casanova, R. Fagin, and C. Papadimitriou. Inclusion dependencies and their interaction with functional dependencies. *Journal of Computer and System Sciences*, 24(1):29–59, February 1984.
5. Qi Cheng, Jarek Gryz, Fred Koo, T. Y. Cliff Leung, Linqi Liu, Xiaoyan Qian, and Berni Schiefer. Implementation of two semantic query optimization techniques in DB2 universal database. In Malcolm P. Atkinson, Maria E. Orlowska, Patrick Valduriez, Stanley B. Zdonik, and Michael L. Brodie, editors, *International Conference on Very Large Data Bases, Edinburgh, Scotland, UK*, pages 687–698. Morgan Kaufmann, 1999.
6. C. J. Date. Referential integrity. In *International Conference on Very Large Data Bases, Cannes, France*, pages 2–12. IEEE Computer Society Press, 1981.
7. F. De Marchi, S. Lopes, and J-M. Petit. Informative armstrong relations: Application to database analysis. In *Bases de Données Avancées, Agadir, Maroc*, October 2001.
8. F. De Marchi, M. Rivon, S. Lopes, and J-M. Petit. Mind: Algorithme par niveaux de découverte des dépendances d'inclusion. In *Inforsid 2001 (french information system conference), Martigny, Swiss*, May 2001.

9. Jarek Gryz. Query folding with inclusion dependencies. In *International Conference on Data Engineering, Orlando, Florida, USA*, pages 126–133. IEEE Computer Society, 1998.
10. J. Han and M. Kamber. *Data Mining: Concepts and Techniques*. Morgan Kaufmann, August 2000.
11. Y. Huhtala, J. Karkkainen, P. Porkka, and H. Toivonen. TANE: An efficient algorithm for discovering functional and approximate dependencies. *The Computer Journal*, 42(2):100–111, 1999.
12. M. Kantola, H. Mannila, K. J. Räihä, and H. Siirtola. Discovering functional and inclusion dependencies in relational databases. *International Journal of Intelligent Systems*, 7:591–607, 1992.
13. M. Levene and G. Loizou. *A Guided Tour of Relational Databases and Beyond*. SPRINGER, 1999.
14. M. Levene and M. W. Vincent. Justification for inclusion dependency normal form. *IEEE Transactions on Knowledge and Data Engineering*, 12(2):281–291, 2000.
15. S. Lopes, J.-M. Petit, and L. Lakhal. Efficient discovery of functional dependencies and armstrong relations. In Carlo Zaniolo, Peter C. Lockemann, Marc H. Scholl, and Torsten Grust, editors, *International Conference on Extending Database Technology, Konstanz, Germany*, volume 1777 of *Lecture Notes in Computer Science*, pages 350–364. Springer, 2000.
16. S. Lopes, J-M. Petit, and F. Toumani. Discovering interesting inclusion dependencies: Application to logical database tuning. *Information System*, 17(1):1–19, 2002.
17. H. Mannila and K. J. Räihä. *The Design of Relational Databases*. Addison-Wesley, second edition, 1994.
18. H. Mannila and H. Toivonen. Levelwise Search and Borders of Theories in Knowledge Discovery. *Data Mining and Knowledge Discovery*, 1(1):241–258, 1997.
19. V.M. Markowitz and J.A. Makowsky. Identifying Extended Entity-Relationship Object Structures in Relational Schemas. *IEEE Transactions on Software Engineering*, 16(1):777–790, August 1990.
20. R. J. Miller, M. A. Hernández, L. M. Haas, L. Yan, C. T. H. Ho, R. Fagin, and L. Popa. The clio project: Managing heterogeneity. *SIGMOD Record*, 30(1):78–83, 2001.
21. Noel Novelli and Rosine Cicchetti. Fun: An efficient algorithm for mining functional and embedded dependencies. In Jan Van den Bussche and Victor Vianu, editors, *8th International Conference on Databases Theory, London, UK*, volume 1973 of *Lecture Notes in Computer Science*, pages 189–203. Springer, 2001.
22. E. Pichat and R. Bodin. *Ingénierie des données*. Masson, 1790.
23. C. Wyss, C. Giannella, and E. Robertson. Fastfds: A heuristic-driven depth-first algorithm for mining functional dependencies from relation instances. In Yahiko Kambayashi, Werner Winiwarter, and Masatoshi Arikawa, editors, *Data Warehousing and Knowledge Discovery, Munich, Germany*, volume 2114 of *Lecture Notes in Computer Science*, pages 101–110, 2001.

The Index-Based XXL Search Engine for Querying XML Data with Relevance Ranking

Anja Theobald and Gerhard Weikum

University of the Saarland, Germany
WWW: http://www-dbs.cs.uni-sb.de
{theobald, weikum}@cs.uni-sb.de

Abstract. Query languages for XML such as XPath or XQuery support Boolean retrieval: a query result is a (possibly restructured) subset of XML elements or entire documents that satisfy the search conditions of the query. This search paradigm works for highly schematic XML data collections such as electronic catalogs. However, for searching information in open environments such as the Web or intranets of large corporations, ranked retrieval is more appropriate: a query result is a rank list of XML elements in descending order of (estimated) relevance. Web search engines, which are based on the ranked retrieval paradigm, do, however, not consider the additional information and rich annotations provided by the structure of XML documents and their element names. This paper presents the XXL search engine that supports relevance ranking on XML data. XXL is particularly geared for path queries with wildcards that can span multiple XML collections and contain both exact-match as well as semantic-similarity search conditions. In addition, ontological information and suitable index structures are used to improve the search efficiency and effectiveness. XXL is fully implemented as a suite of Java servlets. Experiments with a variety of structurally diverse XML data demonstrate the efficiency of the XXL search engine and underline its effectiveness for ranked retrieval.

1. Introduction

1.1 Motivation

XML is becoming the standard for integrating and exchanging data over the Internet and within intranets, covering the complete spectrum from largely unstructured, ad hoc documents to highly structured, schematic data [Kos99]. XML data collections can be viewed as a directed, labeled data graph with XML elements as nodes (and their names as node labels) and edges for subelement relationships as well as links both within and across documents [ABS00]. A number of XML query languages have been proposed, such as XPath, XML-QL, or the recently announced W3C standard XQuery. These languages combine SQL-style logical conditions over element names, content, and attributes with regular-expression pattern matching along entire paths of elements. The result of a query is a set of paths or subgraphs from a given data graph that represents an XML document collection; in information retrieval (IR) terminology this is called Boolean Retrieval.

This search paradigm makes sense for queries on largely schematic XML data such as electronic product catalogs or bibliographies. It is of very limited value, however, for searching highly heterogeneous XML document collections where either data comes from many different information sources with no global schema or most documents have an ad hoc schema or DTD with element names and substructures that occur only in a single or a few documents. The latter kind of environment is typical for document management in large intranets, scientific data repositories such as gene expression data collections and catalogs of protein structures, and, of course, also for the Web. For example, a bank has a huge number of truly semistructured documents, probably much larger in total size than the production data held in (object-) relational databases; these include briefing material and the minutes of meetings, customer-related memos, reports from analysts, financial and business news articles, and so on. Here, the variance and resulting inaccuracies in the document structures, vocabulary, and document content dictate ranked retrieval as the only meaningful search paradigm.

So the result of a query should be a list of potentially relevant XML documents, elements, or subgraphs from the XML data graph, in descending order of estimated relevance. This is exactly the rationale of today's Web search engines, which are also widely used for intranet search, but this technology does not at all consider the rich structure and semantic annotations provided by XML data. Rather state-of-the-art IR systems restrict themselves to term-frequency-based relevance estimation [BR99, Ra97] and/or link-based authority ranking [BP98,Kl99,KRR+00]; note that the latter has been fairly successful for improving the precision of very popular mass-user queries but does not help with advanced expert queries where recall is the main problem.

This paper presents a query language, coined XXL (for Flexible XML Search Language), and the prototype implementation of the XXL search engine, as steps towards more powerful XML querying that reconciles the more schematic style of logical search conditions and pattern matching with IR-style relevance ranking.

1.2 Related Work

Related approaches, which combine search over structural and textual information, have already been proposed in the context of hypertext data (see, e.g., [CSM97, BAN+97, FR98, MJK+98]). However, this work predates the introduction of XML and does not have the same expressiveness for querying semistructured data as more recent languages such as XML QL [XMLQL] or XQuery [XQuery]. Extending such XML query languages with text search methods has been suggested by [CK01, FKM00, FG00, HTK00, NDM+00, TW00]. However, [NDM+00] and [FKM00] are limited to pure keyword search for Boolean retrieval and do not support relevance ranking. In contrast, the simultaneously developed languages XIRQL [FG00] and XXL [TW00] (the latter is our own approach) have been designed to support ranked retrieval. A restricted approach along these lines is [HTK00], which assumes advance knowledge of the document structure and provides similarity search only on element contents, not on element names. Extensions of conventional database query languages a la SQL in order to support similarity search have been addressed also in the WHIRL project [Coh98, Coh99], but with focus on structured data with uniform, fixed schema and not in the context of XML. Another text retrieval extension of XML-QL has recently been proposed by [CK01]: XML data is mapped onto relational storage and similarity conditions are translated into subqueries that are evaluated using WHIRL. To our knowledge, none of the above approaches uses ontological information in their similarity metrics.

1.3 Contribution and Outline of the Paper

The contributions of this paper are twofold:

1) At the conceptual level, we show how to reconcile pattern matching along paths of XML elements with similarity conditions and IR-style relevance ranking as well as simple ontological reasoning. In contrast to the prior work on probabilistic query evaluation on structured data, most notably [Coh98, Coh99], our language XXL supports path expressions in the spirit of modern XML query languages. In contrast to IR research, XXL can exploit the structural information and the rich semantic annotations that are immanent in XML documents. In comparison to our own prior work reported in [TW00] the current paper goes a significant step further and integrates ontological relationships as a basis for effective similarity search.

2) At the implementation level, we present techniques for efficiently evaluating a simple but widely useful class of XXL queries using several index structures and a heuristic strategy for decomposing compound search conditions into subqueries. The index structures include an element path index similar to the data guides approach of [MAG+97, MWA+98], a term-occurrence index as commonly used in IR engines for element contents, and an ontological index for the occurrences of element names. None of these structures is fundamentally new, but their combination proves to be a powerful and, to our knowledge, novel backbone for XML query evaluation with relevance ranking. Our prototype implementation of XXL is fully operational as a suite of Java servlets and includes a Java-based GUI for graphically composing XXL queries. We report measurements that demonstrate the effectiveness and efficiency of the XXL search engine.

2. XXL: A Flexible XML Search Language for Ranked Retrieval

2.1 Example Scenario

As an example, consider the following fragments of three XML documents about zoos of the world. The first document is a web portal to XML documents about zoos. The second and the third document contain descriptions of animals in particular zoos.

URL 1: http://www.myzoos.edu/zoos.xml

```
<zoos> Zoos of the World
   <name href="http://www.allzoos.edu/american_zoos.xml"> San Diego Wild Animal Park,CA,USA </name>
   <name href="http://www.animals.edu/european_zoos.xml"> Tierpark Berlin, Germany </name>
   ...
</zoos>
```

URL 2: http://www.allzoos.edu/american_zoos.xml

<animal_park name="San Diego Wild Animal Park" country="USA" city="Escondido">
<animals>
<animal name="Teddy">
<specimen>
<species>brown bear</species>
<range>Europe</range>
<location no="411"/>
<birthplace href="
http://www.animals.edu/european_zoos.xml#
XPointer(id('Tierpark Berlin'))"/> ...
...
</animal_park>

URL 3: http://www.animals.edu/european_zoos.xml

<zoo name="Tierpark Berlin" country="Germany" city="Berlin">
<animals>
<specimen name="Bobby">
<species>snow leopard</species>
<region>Central Asia</region>
<location no="327"/>
<birthplace href="
http://www.parks.edu/asian_zoos.xml#
XPointer(id('Zoo Tokyo'))"/>...
<enclosure no="327">
<size>16m2</size> ...
</zoo>

As an example query consider the search for "zoos that have big cats such as lions which are born in a zoo of their natural geographic area". This query is easily expressible in our language XXL, shown in Fig. 1a, with keywords in boldface. The XXL search engine also has a graphical user interface based on a Java that allows clients to compose queries in an interactive manner. Fig. 1b shows a screenshot with the graphical representation of query Q1.

Q1:
SelectZ
From
http://www.myzoos.edu/zoos.xml
  Where zoos.#.~zoo **As** Z
  And Z.animals.(animal)?.specimen
As A
  And A.species ~ "lion"
  And A.birthplace.#.country **As** B
  And A.~region ~ B.CONTENT

Fig. 1: Query Q1 in **a)** textual form (left) and **b)** represented in the Visual XXL GUI (right)

In this query uppercase characters denote element variables that are bound to a node (i.e., element) and its attributes of a qualifying path (i.e., A, B, Z in our example), # is a wildcard placeholder for arbitrary paths, ? indicates an optional element on a path, and dots stand for path concatenation. ~ is a similarity operator for semantic similarity, which is used as a unary operator when applied to element names and as a binary operator when applied to element content.

XML data can be viewed as a directed, labeled data graph where the vertices are XML elements marked with the element names. Each node consists of a unique object identifier (oid) and a label. A label can be an element name, an attribute name, the content of an element, or the value of an attribute. The edges represent element-attribute, element-subelement, or element-element links within XML documents, as well as element-element relations between elements of different XML documents based on XLink and XPointer. To simplify matters, we will focus on simple XLinks which can be recognized by href attributes as well as simple XPointers which consists of absolute references (root(), id()) and a sequence of relative references such as child() and descendant(). Fig. 2 shows (the relevant part of) the XML data graph for the sample data introduced above. In this graph we distinguish *n-nodes* for element names and attribute names and *c-nodes* for contents/values.

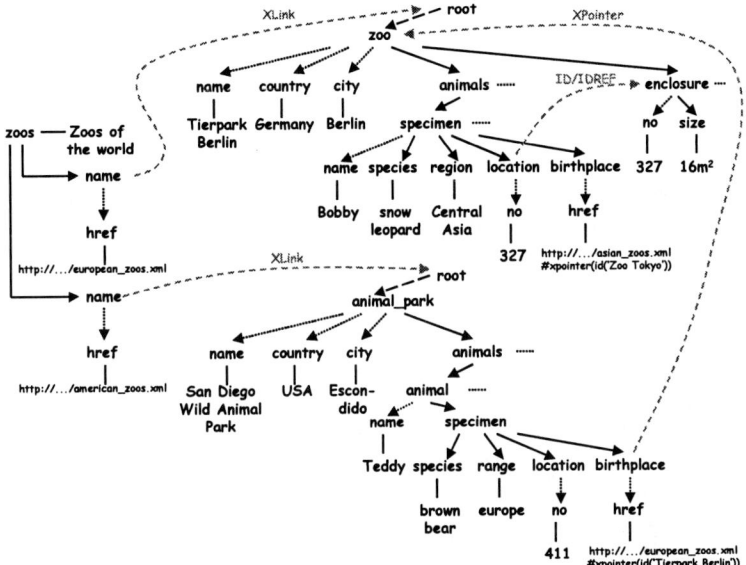

Fig. 2: XML data graph

Queries such as Q1 are evaluated by traversing the XML data graph, possibly using "shortcuts" obtained from index lookups, and comparing the various search conditions against the nodes of the data graph. Exact-match conditions such as "Z.animals.(animal)?.specimen **As** A" return true or false for a given subgraph, and the end node of a matching path is bound to an element variable, A in this case. Similarity conditions such as "A.~region ~ B.CONTENT" assign a similarity score to a candidate element or path.

The similarity scores of different conditions are composed using simple probabilistic reasoning. Complete results, as determined by the element variables that appear in the Select clause, are returned in descending order of similarity to the query (i.e., relevance). With the given sample data, both Bobby, the snow leopard, and Teddy, the brown bear, will be returned as search results, but Bobby will be ranked higher because snow leopards have a closer relationship to lions. Note that Teddy qualifies as an approximate match although he lives in an "animal park" rather than a "zoo" and the geographic distribution of his species is indicated by "range" rather than "region"; that is, element names with sufficient semantic similarity to the ones in the query are considered as relevant, too.

2.2 XXL Syntax and Semantics

The Select clause of an XXL query specifies the output, for example a list of URLs or all bindings of certain element variables. The From clause defines the search space, which can be a set of (seed) URLs or the index structure that is maintained by the XXL search engine. The Where clause of an XXL query specifies the search conditions. We define the Where clause of a query as the logical conjunction of *path expressions*, where a path expression is a regular expression over *elementary conditions* and an elementary condition refers to the name or content of a single element or attribute.

In addition to the standard set of operators on strings and other simple data types ("=", "≤", etc.), the elementary conditions supported by XML include a semantic similarity operator "~", which is used as a unary operator on element names and as a binary operator on element content.

Each path expression can be followed by the keyword "As" and a variable name that binds the end node of a qualifying path (i.e., the last element on the path and its attributes) to the variable. A variable can be used within path expressions, with the meaning that its bound value is substituted in the expression.

The relevance-enabled semantics of a query then is to return a ranked list of approximately matching subgraphs called *result graphs* each with a measure of its relevance (i.e., semantic similarity) to the query. Our relevance measure is defined inductively as follows. We interpret the similarity score for an elementary condition as a relevance probability. Then we need to combine the relevance probabilities for elements with regard to elementary conditions into a relevance measure for a path or subgraph with regard to a composite query condition. In the absence of any better information, we simply postulate probabilistic independence between all elementary conditions, and derive the combined probabilities in the straightforward standard way (i.e., by simply multiplying probabilities for conjunctions and along the elements of a path, etc.)

The result of an XXL query is a subgraph of the XML data graph, where the nodes are annotated with local relevance probabilities for the elementary search conditions given by the query. These relevance values are combined into a global *relevance score* for the entire result graph. Full details of the semantics of XXL and especially the probabilistic computation of similarity scores can be found in [TW00].

2.3 Ontology Based Similarity

The use of ~ as a binary operator, i.e., in the form "element ~ term", requires a two-step computation. The first step of the computation determines similar terms (with relevance score π_1) to the given term based on the ontology. The second step computes the tf*idf-based relevance (π_2) of each term for a given element content (where tf*idf refers to the standard formula of IR-style relevance based on term frequencies (tf) and inverse document frequencies (idf), see, e.g., [BR99]). The element content under consideration then satisfies the search condition with relevance $\pi_1 \cdot \pi_2$.

To define the basic probabilities π_1 and π_2 we now give details on the similarity metric for terms or element names within an ontology. Consider the example shown in Fig. 3 as a part of an ontology about animals. In XXL an ontology is a directed acyclic labeled graph G=(V,E) where V is the set of nodes, the terms (in our case element names, attribute names, and terms in element/attribute contents), and E is the set of edges (see, e.g., [MWK00] for more general variants of ontological graphs). The outgoing edges of a node have integer weights, which are unique among siblings, as shown in Fig. 3, thus leading to a total order among siblings.

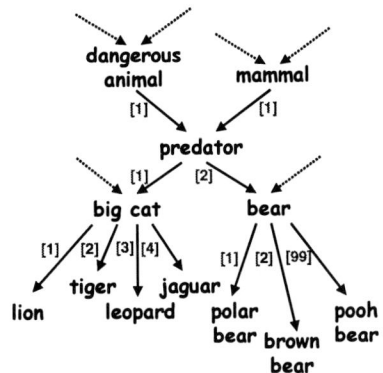

Fig. 3: Part of an ontology

Edges describe relationships between hypernyms (broader terms) and hyponyms (narrower terms), the weights and order of edges express the similarity among sibling nodes. For example, the local similarity of big cats is given as follows: 1 – lion, 2 – tiger, 3 – leopard, 4 – jaguar, and so on. This means that lions are more related to tigers than to leopards.

In order to use an ontology for similarity search we have to define the similarity of two graph nodes (terms) of the ontology. The general rationale for this similarity metric is to use the number of edges on the shortest path between two graph nodes as their "semantic distance", and then derive a normalized similarity metric from this consideration. The notion of distance is actually a bit more sophisticated because we consider also the "semantic distance" between all siblings of a node rather than treating all siblings as equally related to each other. Generally, when we refer to paths in G, we interpret the edges of the DAG as undirected edges.

The similarity between two nodes of the ontology is defined as follows:
a) Let v_1 and v_2 be nodes with v_1 being an ancestor of v_2 or vice versa; then
   $dist(v_1,v_2) = length(v_1,v_2)$.
   Examples: dist(dangerous animal, brown bear)=3; dist(predator, brown bear)=2

b) A node $p \in V$ on the shortest path between two nodes v_1 and v_2 is called the lowest common ancestor (lca) of v_1 and v_2 if there are two paths $p...v_1$ and $p...v_2$ such that $length(p, v_1)$ and $length(p,v_2)$ are both minimal. (If there are multiple shortest paths, we choose one arbitrarily.)
   Example: predator is the lca of lion and brown bear.

c) Let v_1 and v_2 sibling nodes with parent node p; then the sibling distance of v_1 and v_2 is defined as $\quad$ siblingdist$(v_1,v_2) = \dfrac{|\text{weight}(p,v_1) - \text{weight}(p,v_2)|}{\text{maxweight}}$

where maxweight is the maximal weight of all outgoing edges of node p.
Example: siblingdist(lion, leopard) = (|1 – 4|) / 4 = 3/4

d) Let v_1 and v_2 be arbitrary nodes of T, let p be the lca of v_1 and v_2, and let p_1 and p_2 be children of p such that $p\ p_1\ ...\ v_1$ and $p\ p_2\ ...\ v_2$ are paths of T; then the distance of v_1 and v_2 is defined as

$$\text{dist}(v_1,v_2) = \text{length}(p_1,v_1) + \text{length}(p_2,v_2) + \text{siblingdist}(p_1,p_2)$$

Example: dist(lion, brown bear) = 1 + 1 + (|1 – 2|)/2 = 2.5

e) Now we can define the normalized similarity of two nodes v_1 and v_2 of an ontology tree T as sim(v_1,v_2) = 1 / (1 + dist(v_1,v_2))
Example: sim(lion, tiger) = 1 / (1+1/4) = 0.8

With each node of the ontology we can associate a set of synonyms. These are treated as a single semantic concept, with the same predecessors and successors in the graph. For example, the node "big cat" could have a fifth child with the three synonyms "cougar", "puma", "mountain lion".

3. Index Support for XXL Queries

Similarly to Web search engines, the XXL engine builds on precomputed index structures for evaluating the various search conditions in a query. These indexes are constructed and maintained based on a crawler that periodically or incrementally traverses documents that are reachable from specified roots within the intranet or Web fragment of interest. We use three index structures, element path index (EPI), element content index (ECI), and ontology index (OI), which are described in the subsequent subsections.

3.1 Element Path Index (EPI)

The EPI contains the relevant information for evaluating simple path expressions that consist of the concatenation of one ore more element names and path wildcards #. Each element name that occurs at least once in the underlying data is stored exactly once in the index. Associated with each element name is a list of its occurrences in the data: the URL of the document and the oid of the element. Furthermore, short index-internal pointers to the parent and the children of an element are stored with each element occurrence. In addition to this information on parent-child edges of the data graph, outgoing (XLink and XPointer) links such as href attributes can optionally be stored with each element occurrence in the index. Attributes are treated as if they were children of their corresponding elements, along with a flag to indicate the attribute status.

The parent-child information of the EPI is illustrated in Fig. 4a, which refers to the example data graph shown in Fig. 2. For notation we treat the entire index as if it were a nested relation. The subentries of the form "↑..." are short, index-internal pointers.

The optionally maintained information on links is depicted in Fig. 4b, again referring to the example data of Fig. 2.

(element name, (element instance, pointer to the father element), (pointer to a child element))			(element name, (element instance, pointer to linked element)	
zoo			birthplace	
[URL1, 0]	---		[URL2, 12]	↑zoo (...)
	↑name (URL1, 1)		[URL3, 13]	↑zoo (URL2, 1)
	↑name (URL1, 2)		...	
	...		location	
[URL2, 1]	↑... (URL2, ...)		[URL2, 10]	↑enclosure (URL2, 30)
	↑name (URL2, 2)		[URL3, 11]	↑enclosure (URL3, ...)
	↑country (URL2, 3)		...	
	...			
...				

Fig. 4: a) Schema for EPI on parent-child relationships (left side), and **b)** links (right side)

The EPI very much resembles the notion of "data guides" introduced [GW97] and similar structures in other XML query engines (e.g., [FM00]). However, the EPI only stores paths of length 2 explicitly and reconstructs longer paths by combining multiple index entries based on the index-internal pointers. This way the EPI can answer the following kinds of subqueries in a very efficient manner:
- retrieve all URLs and element IDs for a given element name,
- retrieve all children (and link successors) of a given element instance or a given element name,
- retrieve all descendants or ancestors of a given element, up to a specified depth,
- test whether there is a path from element x to element y.

Elements retrieved from the EPI for a given subquery always have a relevance score of 1.

The EPI is implemented as an in-memory red-black tree on element names; index-internal pointers are virtual memory addresses. The entire index is loaded from disk when the XXL search engine starts.

3.2 Element Content Index (ECI)

The element content index (ECI) contains all terms, that is word stems, that occur in the contents of elements and attributes. For stemming we use the Porter algorithm [BR99]. Each term has associated with it its inverse document frequency (the idf value, which is the quotient of the total number of elements that are known to the index and the number of elements that contain the term), its occurrences, and for each occurrence the term frequency (the tf value). So the ECI largely corresponds to a standard text index as used by virtually all Web search engines [BP98, BR99]. The main difference is that our units of indexing and tf*idf computations are elements rather than entire documents. For query evaluation the ECI is used to answer subqueries of the form: find all element instances that contain a given term, along with the corresponding tf*idf values.

Our implementation of the ECI uses the text retrieval engine of Oracle8i, known as interMedia [Ora8i]. We store element contents and attribute values in a database table of the form *data (URL, oid, content)*, similarly to [BR01, FK99], and create an interMedia index for the attribute „content". Thus we are able to exploit Oracle's special Contains predicate for ranked text retrieval using the tf*idf formula for relevance scores.

3.3 Ontology Index (OI)

The quality of similarity search and result ranking on semistructured data can be improved by exploiting ontological information. Motivated by the visionary but still somewhat vague idea of a "Semantic Web" [SemWeb], we consider element (and attribute) names as the semantically most expressive components of XML data. This assumes that many XML documents will be constructed according to standardized, domain-specific ontologies (see, e.g., www.ebxml.org for e-business data, www.fpml.org for financial instruments, or www.geneontology.org for bioinformatics data) with meaningful, carefully chosen element names. Note that this does by no means imply that all data is schematic: ontologies may include a large number of terminological variants, and there is large diversity of ontologies for the same or overlapping application domains anyway.

The ontology index (OI) contains all element names that occur in the indexed XML data, and organizes these names into an ontological graph as explained in Section 2.3. The XXL query processor exploits the OI for query expansion: a path expression of the form "~e" for an element name e is expanded into a disjunctive path expression of the form "e | $term_1$ | ... | $term_k$", with k terms returned by the OI (with relevance scores $\pi_1, ..., \pi_k$) as most similar to the given element name e. This broadened expression will then be evaluated by the EPI. We also use the OI to evaluate similarity conditions on element contents, that is conditions of the form "e ~ t" with e being an element name and t being a term. The XXL query processor first determines similar terms for the given query term t, and then the ECI retrieves relevant element instances for the broadened set of terms. The relevance score of a matching element is the product of the relevance score provided by the OI and the relevance score provided by the ECI.

As an example, consider a query with the search condition ~region ~ "India". The element name "region" will be expanded into "region | country | continent" and the ECI lookups for "India" will consider also related terms such as "Asia", "Bangladesh", "Tamil Nadu", etc., provided the similarity scores returned by the OI are above some threshold.

The OI is constructed and maintained as follows. When the crawler passes an XML document to the indexer, all element names that are not yet in the OI are added to the index. Their positions in the ontology graph are determined by calling WordNet [WordNet], which is a comprehensive thesaurus (or linguistically oriented ontology) put together by cognitive scientists. Specifically, we retrieve the concept description (i.e., the "word sense" in WordNet terminology), all synonyms, and all hypernyms and hyponyms for the given word from WordNet. In our current prototype the OI itself is implemented using the user-defined thesaurus functionality of Oracle8i interMedia [Ora8i]. The information obtained from WordNet is directly mapped onto terms and synonym, hypernym, and hyponym relationships between terms. All this information is dynamically inserted into the thesaurus using the ctx_thes.create_phrase function of interMedia. For query expansion the information is retrieved using the Contains predicate of Oracle's SQL extensions.

4. Query Processing

The evaluation of the search conditions in the Where clause consists of four main steps:
1. The XXL query is decomposed into subqueries, and each subquery is internally represented in the form of a query graph, which is essentially a finite state automaton.
2. The order in which the various subqueries are evaluated is chosen (global evaluation order).
3. For each subquery, the order in which the components of the corresponding path expression are tested is chosen (local evaluation order).
4. For each subquery, subgraphs of the data graph that match the query graph are computed, exploiting the various indexes to the best possible extent.

4.1 Query Decomposition

The Where clause of an XXL query is of the form "Where P_1 AS V_1 And ... And P_n As V_n" where each P_i is a regular path expression over elementary conditions and the V_i are element variables to which the end node of a matching path is bound. As in other XML query languages, variables can occur in the place of an element within a path expression in multiple subqueries; we assume, however, that there is no cyclic use of variables (i.e., there is no cycle in the variable dependency graph with V_i depending on all variables that occur in the path expression of P_i.

The regular path expression of a subquery can be described by an equivalent nondeterministic finite state automaton (NFSA). For subquery $Q_i = P_i$ AS V_i, NFSA(Q_i) is constructed and represented as a *query graph* $QG_i = QG(NFSA(Q_i))$. Fig. 5 shows the query graphs of the subqueries of our example query Q1 from Section 2.1. Nodes with dashed ovals are final states of a regular path.

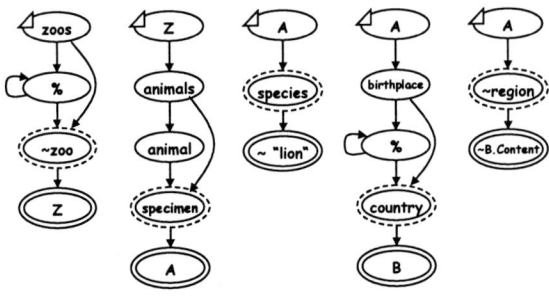

Fig. 5: Query graph representations of subqueries

4.2 Evaluation Order

The global evaluation order specifies the order of executing the query graphs QG_1, ..., QG_n. Ideally, this would take into account selectivity estimates for the various subqueries, but note that the order is constrained by the possible use of element variables in the path expressions. So before evaluating a query graph that uses certain variables in the place of element names, all subqueries whose results are bound to these variables must be evaluated. For simplicity, our current prototype simply evaluates subqueries in the order in which they appear in the original query; we assume that variables are first bound by an As clause before they are used in the path expressions of subsequent subqueries.

The local evaluation order for a subquery specifies the order in which it is attempted to match the query graph's nodes with elements in the data graph. The XXL prototype supports two alternative strategies: in top-down order the matching begins with the start node of the query graph and then proceeds towards the final state(s); in bottom-up order the matching begins with the final state(s) and then proceeds towards the start node. These options are similar to the left-to-right and right-to-left strategies for evaluating path expressions in the object-oriented database query language OQL.

4.3 Index-Based Subquery Evaluation

A *result path* is a path of the XML data graph that satisfies the path expression p of a subquery. The nodes of this path are annotated with local relevance values as described in 2.2. This result for a single subquery (query graph) determines a local variable binding, which is part of a global variable binding. Taking one result path from each subquery yields a *result graph*, which is a subgraph of the underlying XML data graph, by forming the union of the result paths for a given variable binding. The global relevance score for this result graph is computed as outlined in Section 2.2. Here it is important to emphasize that the same variable binding must be used for all subquery results, as the variables link the various subqueries.

For a local variable binding the evaluation of a subquery always produces a single path of the XML data graph annotated with appropriate local relevance scores for each node according to the elementary conditions given by the considered subquery.

As mentioned before we exploit the various index structures in finding matching subgraphs for a given query graph. This is done by identifying subgraphs of the query graph for which the matching subgraphs from the data graph have been precomputed and stored in one of the indexes. This is feasible in many, albeit not in all cases, but we expect that most applications would use a rather simple structure for XXL subqueries, namely, path expressions of the form $\sim e_1.\#.\sim e_2.\#. \ldots .\#.\sim e_n \sim t$ where e_1 through e_n are element names and some or all of the ~ symbols in front of the element names and the path wildcards # may be omitted. This subquery type does not use the full expressiveness of regular expressions (e.g., there is no Kleene star recursion over nested subexpressions) and can therefore be efficiently evaluated. As an example consider the subquery zoos.#.~zoo.animals.species ~ "lion" with the query graph shown in Fig. 6.

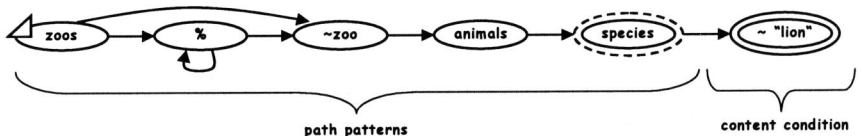

Fig. 6: Example query graph for XXL subquery

A *path pattern* is a path in the query graph from a start node to a final node. Each node of a path pattern is an elementary path condition (see Section 2.2), that is an element name, possibly with lexical wildcards %, or a name prefixed by the unary ~ operator. A *content condition* is an elementary content condition (see Section 2.2) to be met by the content of the end node in a matching path. A *result path* for a query graph is a path of the XML data graph that satisfies both the path pattern and the content condition of the given query graph.

Path patterns are evaluated using the following methods on the element path index (EPI) and the ontology index (OI), and content conditions are evaluated using the element content index (ECI) and the ontology index (OI). Recall from Section 2.2 that n-nodes are nodes of the XML data graph containing element names and c-nodes are nodes of the XML data graph containing the content of an XML element.

1. For a given elementary path condition without the unary ~ operator, e.g., "zoos" or a version with lexical wildcards such as "zoo%", the EPI returns a set of n-nodes of the XML data graph that satisfies this condition with relevance $\pi = 1$.
2. For a given elementary path condition with the unary ~ operator, e.g., "~zoo", the OI returns a set of similar terms with relevance $\pi > 0$, e.g., "animal_park", and then the EPI returns a set of n-nodes of the XML data graph that corresponds to one of these terms.
3. For two concatenated elementary path conditions "$c_1.c_2$" and a given n-node that satisfies condition c_1 with relevance π_1 computed by method 1 or 2, the EPI returns a set of n-nodes of the XML data graph that satisfies the condition c_2 with relevance π_2 using method 1 or 2 such that these are children of the given n-node. Finding parents is analogous.
4. For two given n-nodes the EPI can test the existence of a path between the given nodes, e.g., solving „zoos.#.~zoos".

With the following three methods supported by the ECI and the OI we evaluate content conditions for a given c-node of the XML data graph.

5. For a given content condition without the binary ~ operator, e.g., "= lion", and a given n-node the ECI returns a c-node that satisfies the given search condition with relevance $\pi = 1$ and this c-node is a child of the given n-node.
6. For a given content condition with the binary ~ operator, e.g., "~ lion", and a given n-node the OI returns a set of similar terms with relevance $\pi_1 > 0$, and then the ECI returns a c-node that corresponds to one of these terms with relevance π_2 such that the c-node is a child node to the given n-node. The final relevance is $\pi_1 * \pi_2$.
7. For a given elementary content condition of the form 1 and 2 and no information about the n-node, the ECI returns a set of c-nodes that satisfies the given condition with relevance $\pi > 0$.

4.4 Result Composition

The result paths for the various subqueries of a given XXL query are composed into a global result, which is a subgraph of the underlying data graph, by forming the union of the result paths for a given variable binding. Relevance scores of this result graph are computed as outlined in Section 2.2. Here it is important to emphasize that the same variable binding must be used for all subquery results, as the variables link the various subqueries. The exhaustive search algorithm computes all results for all possible variable bindings according to the global evaluation order for the subqueries and their As clauses.

5. Architecture of the XXL Search Engine

Our prior work [TW00] already described a preliminary and incomplete implementation of XXL based on Oracle. That implementation was fairly limited in that all XML data had to be loaded into an Oracle database upfront and all XXL queries were mapped onto SQL queries with some use of the Oracle interMedia text retrieval engine. The full-fledged prototype that we refer to in the current paper has been completely re-implemented. It now includes the three index structures described in Section 3, relies on Oracle only as a storage manager for index data (but not for the actual XML documents themselves), and has a full-fledged query processor implemented as a set of Java servlets (i.e., running under the control of a Web server such as Apache) and does no longer rely on an underlying SQL engine.

The architecture of the XXL search engine is depicted in Fig. 6. It consists of three types of components:
1. Service components: the crawler, the query processor (both Java servlets), and a Visual XXL GUI (a Java applet)
2. Algorithmic components: parsing, indexing, word stemming, etc.
3. Data components: structures and their methods for storing various kinds of information such as DTD/schema files, the EPI, the ECI, query templates, etc.

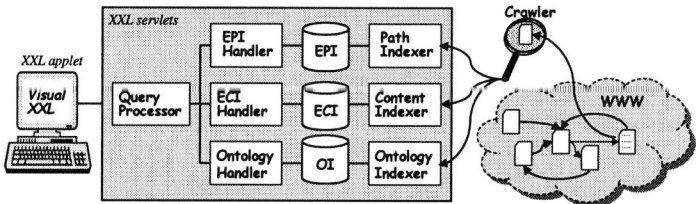

Fig. 7: Architecture of the XXL search engine

The ECI and the OI are stored as Oracle tables. So index lookups to these two structures involve SQL statements. These are very simple statements that can be executed very efficiently, but the query processor may invoke them very frequently. To avoid repeated lookups for the same element name or term and to minimize the number of JDBC calls to Oracle, both ECI and OI entries can be cached in the query processor servlet.

6. Experimental Evaluation

For the experimental setup we crawled four collections of XML documents and constructed the corresponding index structures: a collection of religious books (Bible, Koran, etc.), a collection of Shakespeare plays, bibliographic data about ACM Sigmod Record, and synthetic documents with the structure of bibliographic data. Altogether this data collection contained 45 XML documents, some of which were extremely long and richly structured, with a total number of 208 449 elements (with 62 different element names). Note that the diversity of this data posed a challenge for the search engine that would not be present with a homogeneous XML collection that follows a single DTD or XML schema.

6.1 Ontology-Based Similarity Search for Element Names and Contents

Table 1 shows the results for simple similarity queries with both the unary and binary ~ operator. Note that the large number of results is explained by the fact that the queries retrieved all matching paths, and there were many different matching paths within the same document. The "Select URL ..." option would have condensed this result into a small number of matching documents, but we were especially interested in evaluating XXL's capability to find and rank all semantically relevant pieces of information.

Table 1: Experimental results for XXL similarity search (td=top down, bu=bottom-up)

Where clause of query	# results	Runtime (sec) td	Runtime (sec) bu	Relevance Score	Example results
~headline	2531	0.1	0.09	1.0 0.8 0.8 ... 0.6	headline="DBS" (book.xml) title="The Quran" (quran.xml) title="The New Testament" (nt.xml) ... subhead="The Song" (a_and_c.xml)
~publication. ~headline	1509	0.45	0.2	0.8 0.64 0.64 ... 0.48	publication.heading="..." (publication.xml) book.title="..." (book.xml) article.title="..." (SigmodRecord.xml) ... work.heading="..." (book.xml)
~headline ~ "XML"	36	2.5	2.4	0.208 0.108 0.108 ... 0.082	Heading="XML-QL: ..." (publication.xml) headline="DBS" (book.xml) title="XML and ..." (SigmodRecord.xml) ... heading="Draft...in Java" (book.xml)
~publication. ~headline ~ "XML"	35	0.83	2.5	0.208 0.083 0.083 ... 0.049	publication.heading="XML-QL:..." (publ.xml) article.title="XML and ..." (SigmodRec.xml) article.heading="Adding...XML" (article.xml) ... work.heading="Draft...in Java" (book.xml)

The variants "top-down" and "bottom-up" refer to the two strategies for the local evaluation order, either starting from the start nodes of the query graph (top-down) or from the final nodes (bottom-up). As the run-time figures in the table show, there is no clear preference for one of the two strategies; the discriminating factor is the selectivity of the elementary conditions (i.e., element names to be approximately matched) at the begin and end of the path patterns.

For the third and fourth queries the relevance scores were relatively low as a result of multiplying a relevance score from the OI (for the conditions with the unary ~ operator) and a relevance score from the ECI (for the conditions with the binary ~ operator), which in turn stems from an independence assumption in our probabilistic model. Note, however, that this does not distort the relative ranking of the results; the situation is similar to that of Web search engines, and we could as well have applied their standard trick of re-normalizing the scores in the final result list.

6.2 Queries with Path Expressions

Table 2 shows the results for more sophisticated path expressions in the Where clause of a query. All run-times were in the order of seconds; so the XXL search engine is fairly efficient. Note that even queries whose Where clause starts with a path wildcard # (e.g., the second query and the fifth query in Table 2) could be evaluated with reasonably short response time. This is because the XXL query processor first evaluates the specified element names in the path pattern and only then tests whether the retrieved paths are connected to the roots specified in the From clause.

Table 2: Experimental results for XXL queries with path expressions

Where clause of query	# results	Run-time (sec)	
		top-down	bottom-up
~headline	2531	0.10	0.10
#.~headline	11335	19.80	2.88
~author ~ "King"	10	0.43	1.61
~author AS A AND A ~ "King"	10	0.51	0.51
#.~author AS A AND A ~ "King"	60	16.21	0.83
~headline ~ "XML"	36	2.45	2.45
~headline AS A AND A ~ "XML"	36	2.51	2.51
#.~headline AS A AND A ~ "XML"	165	20.19	6.49
~title ~ "Testament"	2	0.70	1.37
~title AS A AND A ~ "Testament"	2	0.77	0.77
#.~title AS A AND A ~ "Testament"	6	7.72	1.22
~figure ~ "King"	62	3.66	4.21
~figure AS A AND A ~ "King"	62	3.68	3.76
#.~figure AS A AND A ~ "King"	190	18.15	4.42
#.(pgroup)?.~figure ~ "King"	190	20.19	3.09
#.~chapter.(vlline) ~ "Testament"	52	8.71	2.65

In this set of queries the bottom-up evaluation strategy mostly outperformed the top-down strategy. This is because the element names at the end of the path patterns tended to occur less frequently in the underlying data, so the corresponding elementary conditions were more selective. For queries with multiple subqueries either all subqueries were evaluated top-down or all of them were evaluated bottom-up.

For the example queries of Table 2 we measured the number of calls to the various index structures, and for the ECI and OI, which are based on Oracle tables, also the number of DBS calls that resulted from the index methods. The number of DBS calls, which were simple SQL queries with many Fetch calls, incurred significant overhead, simply by having to cross a heavy-weight interface many times, in some queries more than 100 000 times. With caching of index entries enabled in the query processor, the number of DBS calls were drastically reduced from down to the order of a few hundred calls. This optimization resulted in acceptable response times shown in Table 2.

6.3 Complex Queries

Finally we considered two more complex queries:

Query 1: Select * From Index
    Where #.~publication AS A
    And A.~headline ~ "XML"
    And A.author% AS B
    And B.title AS C

Query 2: Select * From Index
    Where #.play AS A
    And A.#.personae AS B
    And B.~figure ~ "King"

Table 3 shows the run-times for these more challenging queries, which were again in the acceptable time range of a few seconds, provided the proper evaluation strategy was chosen. In addition to the top-down and bottom-up strategies for the local evaluation order, we also tested an optimization heuristics, coined *start optimization (so)*, for automatically deciding on the most selective node of the query graph based on statistics about the frequency of the corresponding element name(s) in the indexed data. Once the most selective node is determined the evaluation proceeds both ways, top-down and bottom-up, from this node; with the top-down direction being inspected first, we refer to this strategy as td+so, otherwise we refer to it as bu+so. Furthermore we use a simple heuristic (opt. heur.) algorithm that chooses the evaluation order of the subqueries, i.e., 2,1,3 for query Q1 and 1, 2, 3, 4 for query Q2, and the local evaluation strategy (t=top down or b=bottom-up) for each subquery individually. In Table 3 we give the actual query execution times (exec) and the plans (plan) obtained from the optimization. The optimization time itself was about 0,3 sec for each of the two queries. The heuristics are based on considering the syntax and the selectivity of all start nodes and end nodes of each subquery. For example, as the first subquery of Q1 starts with # and ends with a similarity condition involving the relatively frequent term "publication", it is considered less selective than the second subquery; so our heuristic optimizer decides to evaluate the second subquery first.

Table 3: Experimental results for complex XXL queries
(td = top down, bu = bottom-up, so = start optimization)

	# results	td (sec)	bu (sec)	td + so (sec)	bu + so (sec)	opt. heur. exec (sec)	plan	opt.heur. + so exec (sec)
Q1	131	14,30	694,62	14,20	3,24	2,69	2bu,1bu,3td	2,68
Q2	58	8,56	3,76	8,52	3,69	4,63	1bu,2td,3td,4td	4,64

7. Ongoing and Future Work

Ongoing and future work includes a more advanced kind of ontology index, performance improvements of the query processor algorithms, and the broad and challenging issue of query optimization. More specifically, we plan to extend the OI so as to capture more semantic relationships between concepts. This also requires extending our similarity metric. As for query evaluation performance, we are considering various heuristics for finding some good approximate matches in the result list as quickly as possible with possibly deferred or slowed-down computation of the (nearly) complete result. This way we strive for the best ratio of retrieval effectiveness (i.e., search result quality) and efficiency (i.e., response time). Finally, we plan further studies on query optimization heuristics for both global and local evaluation ordering of subqueries and elementary search conditions based on selectivity estimations.

References

[ABS00] S. Abiteboul, P. Buneman, D. Suciu: Data on the Web – From Relations to Semistructured Data and XML. Morgan Kaufmann Publishers, 2000.

[BAN+97] K. Böhm, K. Aberer, E.J. Neuhold, X. Yang: Structured Document Storage and Refined Declarative and Navigational Access Mechanisms in HyperStorM, VLDB Journal Vol.6 No.4, Springer, 1997.

[BP98] S. Brin, L. Page: The Anatomy of a Large Scale Hypertextual Web Search Engine, 7th WWW Conference, 1998.

[BR99] R. Baeza-Yates, B. Ribeiro-Neto: Modern Information Retrieval, Addison Wesley, 1999.

[BR01] T. Boehme, E. Rahm: XMach-1: A Benchmark for XML Data Management. 9th German Conference on Databases in Office, Engineering, and Scientific Applications (BTW), Oldenburg, Germany, 2001.

[CK01] T. T. Chinenyanga, N. Kushmerick: Expressive and Efficient Ranked Querying of XML Data. 4th International Workshop on the Web and Databases (WebDB), Santa Barbara, California, 2001.

[Coh98] W.W. Cohen: Integration of Heterogeneous Databases Without Common Domains Using Queries Based on Textual Similarity, ACM SIGMOD Conference, Seattle, Washington, 1998.

[Coh99] W. W. Cohen: Recognizing Structure in Web Pages using Similarity Queries. 16. Nat. Conf. on Artif. Intelligence (AAAI) / 11th Conf. on Innovative Appl. Of Artif. Intelligence (IAAI), 1999.

[CSM97] M. Cutler, Y. Shih, W. Meng: Using the Structure of HTML Documents to Improve Retrieval, USENIX Symposium on Internet Technologies and Systems, Monterey, California 1997.

[FG00] N. Fuhr, K. Großjohann: XIRQL: An Extension of XQL for Information Retrieval, ACM SIGIR Workshop on XML and Information Retrieval, Athens, Greece, 2000.

[FK99] D. Florescu, D. Kossmann: Storing and Querying XML Data using RDBMS. In: IEEE Data Eng. Bulletin (Special Issues on XML), 22(3), pp. 27-34, 1999.

[FKM00] D. Florescu, D. Kossmann, I. Manolescu: Integrating Keyword Search into XML Query Processing, 9th WWW Conference, 2000.

[FM00] T. Fiebig, G. Moerkotte: Evaluating Queries on Structure with Extended Access Support Relations. 3rd International Workshop on Web and Databases (WebDB), Dallas, USA, 2000, LNCS 1997, Springer, 2001.

[FR98] N. Fuhr, T. Rölleke: HySpirit – a Probabilistic Inference Engine for Hypermedia Retrieval in Large Databases, 6th International Conference on Extending Database Technology (EDBT), Valencia, Spain, 1998.

[GW97] R. Goldman, J. Widom: DataGuides: Enabling Query Formulation and Optimization in Semistructured Databases, Very Large Data Base (VLDB) Conference, 1997.

[HTK00] Y. Hayashi, J. Tomita, G. Kikui: Searching Text-rich XML Documents with Relevance Ranking. ACM SIGIR 2000 Workshop on XML and Information Retrieval, Greece, 2000.

[Kl99] J.M. Kleinberg: Authoritative Sources in a Hyperlinked Environment, Journal of the ACM Vol. 46, No. 5, 1999.

[Kos99] D. Kossmann (Editor), Special Issue on XML, IEEE Data Engineering Bulletin Vol. 22, No. 3, 1999.

[KRR+00] S.R. Kumar, P. Raghavan, S. Rajagopalan, D. Sivakumar, A. Tomkins, E. Upfal: The Web as a Graph, ACM Symposium on Principles of Database Systems (PODS), Dallas, Texas, 2000.

[MAG+97] J. McHugh, S. Abiteboul, R. Goldman, D. Quass, and J. Widom. Lore: A Database Management System for Semistructured Data. SIGMOD Record, 26(3): 54-66 (1997).

[MJK+98] S.-H. Myaeng, D.-H. Jang, M.-S. Kim, Z.-C. Zhoo: A Flexible Model for Retrieval of SGML Documents, ACM SIGIR Conference on Research and Development in Information Retrieval, Melbourne, Australia, 1998.

[MWA+98] J. McHugh, J. Widom, S. Abiteboul, Q. Luo, A. Rajaraman: Indexing Semistructured Data. Technical Report 01/1998, Computer Science Department, Stanford University, 1998.

[MWK00] P. Mitra, G. Wiederhold, M.L. Kersten: Articulation of Ontology Interdependencies Using a Graph-Oriented Approach, Proceedings of the 7th International Conference on Extending Database Technology (EDBT), Constance, Germany, 2000.

[NDM+00] J. Naughton, D. DeWitt, D. Maier, et al.: The Niagara Internet Query System. http://www.cs.wisc.edu/niagara/Publications.html

[Ora8i] Oracle 8i interMedia: Platform Service for Internet Media and Document Content, http://technet.oracle.com/products/intermedia/

[Ra97] Raghavan, P.: Information Retrieval Algorithms: A Survey, ACM-SIAM Symposium on Discrete Algorithms, 1997.

[SemWeb] World Wide Web Consortium: Semantic Web Activity, http://www.w3.org/2001/sw/

[TW00] A. Theobald, G. Weikum: Adding Relevance to XML, 3rd International Workshop on the Web and Databases, Dallas, Texas, 2000, LNCS 1997, Springer, 2001.

[WordNet] http://www.cogsci.princeton.edu/~wn

[XLink] XML Linking Language (XLink) Version 1.0. W3C Recommendation, 2001. http://www.w3.org/TR/XLink/

[XMLQL] XML-QL: A Query Language for XML, User's Guide, Version 0.9, http://www.research.att.com/~mff/xmlql/doc

[XPointer] XML Pointer Language (XPointer) Version 1.0. W3C Candidate Recommendation, 2001. http://www.w3.org/TR/xptr/

[XQuery] XQuery 1.0: An XML Query Language. W3C Working Draft, 2001. http://www.w3.org/TR/xquery/

Tree Pattern Relaxation

Sihem Amer-Yahia[1], SungRan Cho[2], and Divesh Srivastava[1]

[1] AT&T Labs–Research,
Florham Park, NJ 07932, USA
{sihem,divesh}@research.att.com
[2] Stevens Institute of Technology,
Hoboken, NJ 07030, USA
scho@attila.stevens-tech.edu

Abstract. Tree patterns are fundamental to querying tree-structured data like XML. Because of the heterogeneity of XML data, it is often more appropriate to permit approximate query matching and return ranked answers, in the spirit of Information Retrieval, than to return only exact answers. In this paper, we study the problem of approximate XML query matching, based on tree pattern relaxations, and devise efficient algorithms to evaluate relaxed tree patterns. We consider weighted tree patterns, where exact and relaxed weights, associated with nodes and edges of the tree pattern, are used to compute the scores of query answers. We are interested in the problem of finding answers whose scores are at least as large as a given threshold. We design data pruning algorithms where intermediate query results are filtered dynamically during the evaluation process. We develop an optimization that exploits scores of intermediate results to improve query evaluation efficiency. Finally, we show experimentally that our techniques outperform rewriting-based and post-pruning strategies.

1 Introduction

With the advent of XML, querying tree-structured data has been a subject of interest lately in the database research community, and tree patterns are fundamental to XML query languages (e.g., [2, 6, 11]). Due to the heterogeneous nature of XML data, exact matching of queries is often inadequate. We believe that approximate matching of tree pattern queries and returning a ranked list of results, in the same spirit as Information Retrieval (IR) approaches, is more appropriate. A concrete example is that of querying a bibliographic database, such as DBLP [4]. Users might ask for books that have as subelements an `isbn`, a `url`, a `cdrom` and an electronic edition `ee`. Some of these are optional subelements (as specified in the DBLP schema) and very few books may have values specified for all these subelements. Thus, returning books that have values for some of these elements (say `isbn`, `url` and `ee`), as approximate answers, would be of use. Quite naturally, users would like to see such approximate answers ranked by their similarity to the user query.

Our techniques for approximate XML query matching are based on *tree pattern relaxations*. For example, node types in the query tree pattern can be relaxed using a type hierarchy (e.g., look for any document instead of just books). Similarly, a parent-child edge in the query tree pattern can be relaxed into an ancestor-descendant one (e.g., look for a book that has a descendant isbn subelement instead of a child isbn subelement). Exact matches to such relaxations of the original query are the desired approximate answers.

One possibility for ranking such approximate answers is based on the number of tree pattern relaxations applied in the corresponding relaxed query. To permit additional flexibility in the ranking (e.g., a book with a descendant isbn should be ranked higher than a document with a child isbn, even though each of these answers is based on a single relaxation), we borrow an idea from IR and consider *weighted tree patterns*. By associating exact and relaxed weights with query tree pattern nodes and edges, we allow for a finer degree of control in the scores associated with approximate answers to the query.

A query tree pattern may have a very large number of approximate answers, and returning all approximate answers is clearly not desirable. In this paper, we are interested in the problem of finding answers whose scores are at least as large as a given threshold, and we focus on the design of efficient algorithms for this problem. Our techniques are also applicable for the related problem of finding the top-k answers, i.e., the answers with the k largest scores; we do not discuss this problem further in the paper because of space limitations.

Given a weighted query tree pattern, the key problem is how to evaluate all relaxed versions of the query efficiently and guarantee that only relevant answers (i.e., those whose scores are as large as a given threshold) are returned. One possible way is to rewrite the weighted tree pattern into all its relaxed versions and apply multi-query evaluation techniques exploiting common subexpressions. However, given the exponential number of possible relaxed queries, rewriting-based approaches quickly become impractical. We develop instead (in Section 4) an algebraic representation where all our tree pattern relaxations can be encoded in a *single* evaluation plan that uses binary structural joins [1,19]. A post-pruning evaluation strategy, where all answers are computed first, and only then is pruning done, is clearly sub-optimal. Hence, we develop algorithms that eliminate irrelevant answers "as soon as possible" during query evaluation. More specifically, our technical contributions are as follows:

- We design an efficient data pruning algorithm Thres that takes a weighted query tree pattern and a threshold and computes all approximate answers whose scores are at least as large as the threshold (Section 5).
- We propose an adaptive optimization to Thres, called OptiThres, that uses scores of intermediate results to dynamically "undo" relaxations encoded in the evaluation plan, to ensure better evaluation efficiency, without compromising the set of answers returned (Section 6).
- Finally, we experimentally evaluate the performance of our algorithms, using query evaluation time and intermediate result sizes as metrics. Our results

validate the superiority of our algorithms, and the utility of our optimizations, over post-pruning and rewriting-based approaches (Section 7).

In the sequel, we first present related work in Section 2, and then present preliminary material in Section 3.

2 Related Work

Our work is related to the work done on keyword-based search in Information Retrieval (IR) systems (e.g., see [15]). There has been significant research in IR on indexing and evaluation heuristics that improve the query response time while maintaining a constant level of relevance to the initial query (e.g., see [7, 13, 18]). However, our evaluation and optimization techniques differ significantly from this IR work, because of our emphasis on tree-structured XML documents.

We classify more closely related work into the following three categories.

Language Proposals for Approximate Matching: There exist many language proposals for approximate XML query matching (e.g., see [3, 8, 9, 12, 16, 17]). These proposals can be classified into content-based approaches and approaches based on hierarchical structure. In [16], the author proposes a pattern matching language called approXQL, an extension to XQL [14]. In [8], the authors describe XIRQL, an extension to XQL [14] that integrates IR features. XIRQL's features are weighting and ranking, relevance-oriented search, and datatypes with vague predicates. In [17], the authors develop XXL, a language inspired by XML-QL [6] that extends it for ranked retrieval. This extension consists of *similarity conditions* expressed using a binary operator that expresses the similarity between an XML data value and an element variable given by a query (or a constant). These works can be seen as complementary to ours, since we do not propose any query language extension in this paper.

Specification and Semantics: A query can be relaxed in several ways. In [5], the authors describe querying XML documents in a mediated environment. Their specifications are similar to our tree patterns. The authors are interested in relaxing queries whose result is empty, and they propose three kinds of relaxations: unfolding a node (replicating a node by creating a separate path to one of its children), deleting a node and propagating a condition at a node to its parent node. However, they do not discuss efficient evaluation techniques for their relaxed queries. Another interesting study is the one presented in [16] where the author considers three relaxations of an XQL query: deleting nodes, inserting intermediate nodes and renaming nodes. These relaxations have their roots in the work done in the combinatorial pattern matching community on tree edit distance (e.g., see [20]). A key difference with our work is that these works do not consider query weighting, which is of considerable practical importance.

Recently, Kanza and Sagiv [10] proposed two different semantics, flexible and semiflexible, for evaluating graph queries against a simplified version of the Object Exchange Model (OEM). Intuitively, under these semantics, query paths are mapped to database paths, so long as the database path includes all the labels of the query path; the inclusion need not be contiguous or in the same order; this is quite different from our notion of tree pattern relaxation. They identify cases where query evaluation is polynomial in the size of the query, the database and the result (i.e., combined complexity). However, they do not consider scoring and ranking of query answers.

Approximate Query Matching: There exist two kinds of algorithms for approximate matching in the literature: *post-pruning* and *rewriting-based* algorithms. The complexity of post-pruning strategies depends on the size of query answers and a lot of effort can be spent in evaluating the total set of query answers even if only a small portion of it is relevant. Rewriting-based approaches can generate a large number of rewritten queries. For example, in [16], the rewritten query can be quadratic in the size of the original query. In our work, we experimentally show that our approach outperforms post-pruning and rewriting-based ones.

3 Overview

3.1 Background: Data Model and Query Tree Patterns

We consider a data model where information is represented as a forest of node labeled trees. Each non-leaf node in the tree has a type as its label, where types are organized in a simple inheritance hierarchy. Each leaf node has a string value as its label. A simple database instance is given in Figure 1.

Fundamental to all existing query languages for XML (e.g., [2, 6, 11]) are *tree patterns*, whose nodes are labeled by types or string values, and whose edges correspond to parent-child or ancestor-descendant relationships. These tree patterns are used to match relevant portions of the database. While tree patterns do not capture some aspects of XML query languages, such as ordering and restructuring, they form a key component of these query languages. Figure 1 shows an example query tree pattern (ignore the numeric labels on the nodes and edges for now). A single edge represents a parent-child relationship, and a double edge represents an ancestor-descendant relationship.

3.2 Relaxed Queries and Approximate Answers

The heterogeneity of XML data makes query formulation tedious, and exact matching of query tree patterns often inadequate. The premise of this paper is that *approximate matching of query tree patterns and returning a ranked list of answers, in the same spirit as keyword-based search in Information Retrieval (IR)* is often more appropriate.

Our techniques for approximate XML query matching are based on *tree pattern relaxations*. Intuitively, tree pattern relaxations are of two types: content relaxation and structure relaxation. We consider four specific relaxations, of which the first two are content relaxations, and the last two are structure relaxations.

Node Generalization: This permits the type of a query node to be generalized to a super-type. For example, in the query tree pattern of Figure 1, Book can be generalized to Document, allowing for arbitrary documents (that match the other query conditions) to be returned instead of just books.

Leaf Node Deletion: This permits a query leaf node (and the edge connecting it to its parent node in the query) to be deleted. For example, in the query tree pattern of Figure 1, the Collection node can be deleted, allowing for books that have an editor (with a name and address) to be returned, whether or not they belong to a collection.

Edge Generalization: This permits a parent-child edge in the query to be generalized to an ancestor-descendant edge. For example, in the query tree pattern of Figure 1, the edge (Book, Editor) can be generalized, allowing for books that have a descendant editor (but not a child editor) to be returned.

Subtree Promotion: This permits a query subtree to be promoted so that the subtree is directly connected to its former grandparent by an ancestor-descendant edge. For example, in the query tree pattern of Figure 1, the leaf node Address can be promoted, allowing for books that have a descendant address to be returned, even if the address does not happen to be a descendant of the editor child of the book.

Having identified the individual tree pattern relaxations we consider, we are now in a position to define relaxed queries and approximate answers.

Definition 1 [Relaxed Query, Approximate Answer]. *Given a query tree pattern Q, a relaxed query Q' is a non-empty tree pattern obtained from Q by applying a sequence of zero or more of the four relaxations: node generalization, leaf node deletion, edge generalization and subtree promotion.*

We refer to a node (resp., edge) in a relaxed query that has been affected by a tree pattern relaxation as a relaxed node *(resp.,* relaxed edge*). The nodes and edges that are not affected by a tree pattern relaxation are referred to as* exact nodes *and* exact edges.

An approximate answer *to Q is defined as an exact match to some relaxed query obtained from Q.* □

Note that, by definition, the original query tree pattern is also a relaxed query, and hence exact matches to the original query tree pattern are included in the set of approximate answers to a query.

Note that the tree relaxations we consider have several interesting properties. First, the number of nodes in a relaxed query is no more than in the original query. Second, an answer to the original query continues to be an answer to a relaxed query. Finally, each individual tree pattern relaxation is local, involving either a single node/edge change (in the cases of node generalization and edge generalization), or two changes (in the cases of leaf node deletion and subtree promotion). These properties will serve as the bases for efficient algorithms for the computation of approximate answers.

3.3 Answer Ranking, Weighted Tree Patterns and Answer Scores

Returning approximate answers in ranked order, based on the extent of approximation, is important, as is evident from IR research and web search engines. One possibility for ranking such approximate answers is based on the *number* of tree pattern relaxations present in the corresponding relaxed query, i.e., all answers corresponding to relaxed queries with the same number of relaxations have the same rank. While such a coarse ranking may suffice for some applications, additional flexibility is typically desirable. For this purpose, we consider weighted tree patterns, defined as follows.

Definition 2 [Weighted Tree Pattern]. *A weighted tree pattern is a tree pattern where each node and edge is assigned two non-negative integer weights: an exact weight ew, and a relaxed weight rw, such that $ew \geq rw$.* □

Figure 1 shows an example of a weighted query tree pattern. A detailed discussion of the origin of query weights is outside the scope of this paper. It may be specified by the user, determined by the system (e.g., in a fashion analogous to inverse document frequency, used in IR), or a combination of both. What is important to keep in mind is that once these weights are chosen, our techniques can be used for efficient computation of approximate answers.

Relaxation of a weighted query tree pattern results in a weighted tree pattern as well. The weights on nodes and edges in a relaxed query Q' are used to determine scores of the corresponding matches, by adding up the contributions of the individual nodes and edges in Q', as follows:

- The contribution of an exact node or edge, ne, in Q' to the score of an exact match A' to Q' is its exact weight $ew(ne)$.
- The contribution of a relaxed node or edge, ne, in Q' to the score of an exact match A' to Q' is required to be no less than its relaxed weight $rw(ne)$, and no more than its exact weight $ew(ne)$.

A simple approach, which we use in our examples and our experiments, is to make the relaxed weight $rw(ne)$ be the contribution of the relaxed node or edge ne. More sophisticated alternatives are possible as well. We do not discuss these further for reasons of space.

As an example, the score of exact matches of the weighted query tree pattern in Figure 1 is equal to the sum of the exact weights of its nodes and edges, i.e., 45. If Book is generalized to Document, the score of an approximate answer that is a document (but not a book) is the sum of the relaxed weight of Book and the exact weights of the other nodes and edges in the weighted query, i.e., 39.

In general, an approximate answer can match different relaxed queries, and, depending on how one defines the contributions due to relaxed nodes and edges, may end up with different scores. To deal with such a situation, we define the score of an approximate answer as follows.

Definition 3 [Score of an Approximate Answer]. *The score of an approximate answer is the maximum among all scores computed for it.* □

We are now finally ready to define the problem that we address in this paper.

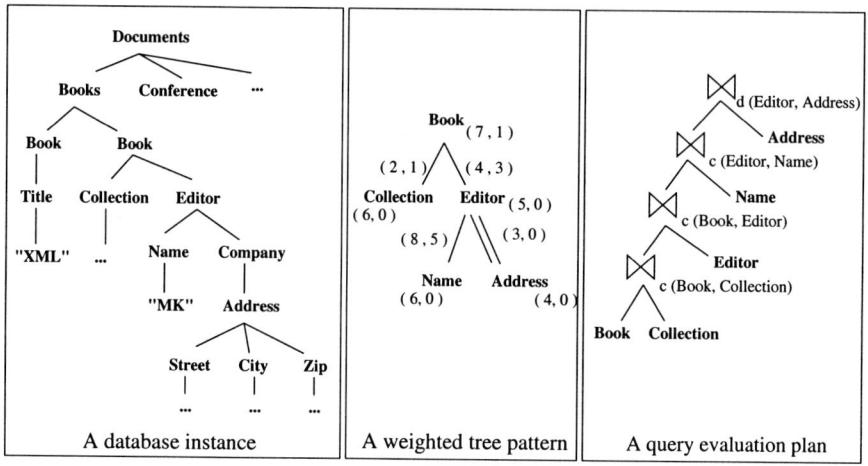

Fig. 1. Example Database Instance, Weighted Tree Pattern, Query Evaluation Plan

3.4 Problem Definition

A query tree pattern may, in general, have a very large number of approximate answers, and returning all approximate answers to the user is clearly not desirable. In this paper, we focus on an approach to limiting the number of approximate answers returned based on a threshold.

Definition 4 [Threshold Problem]. *Given a weighted query tree pattern Q and a threshold t, the* threshold problem *is that of determining all approximate answers of Q whose scores are $\geq t$.* □

4 Encoding Relaxations in a Query Evaluation Plan

4.1 Query Evaluation Plan

Several query evaluation strategies have been proposed for XML (e.g., [11, 19]). They typically rely on a combination of index retrieval and join algorithms using specific structural predicates. For the case of tree patterns, the evaluation plans make use of two binary structural join predicates: $c(n_1, n_2)$ to check for the parent-child relationship, and $d(n_1, n_2)$ to check for the ancestor-descendant one.

The query evaluation techniques we have developed (and will present in subsequent sections), for efficiently computing approximate answers, rely on the use of such join plans to evaluate tree patterns.[1] Figure 1 shows a translation of the (unweighted) query tree pattern of Figure 1 into a left-deep, join evaluation plan with the appropriate structural predicates. According to this evaluation plan, an

---

[1] However, our techniques are not limited to using a particular join algorithm, even though we use the stack-based join algorithms of [1] in our implementation.

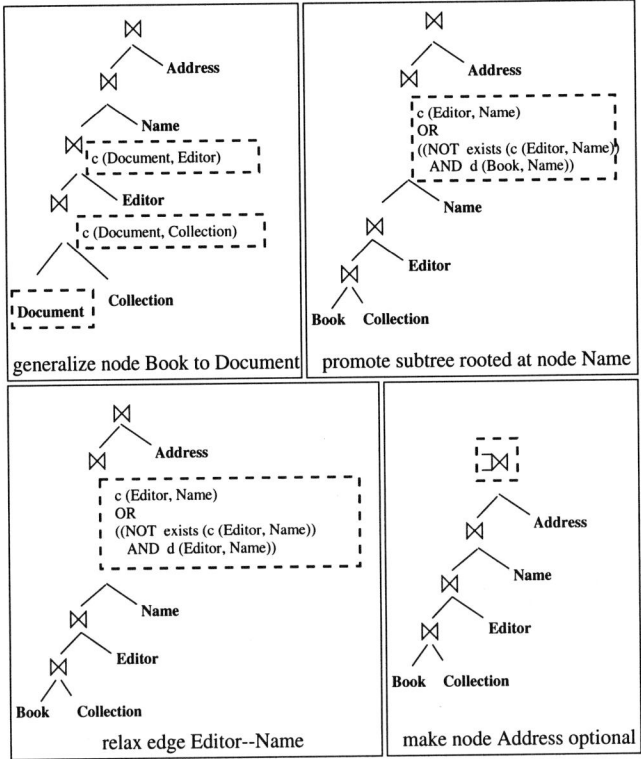

Fig. 2. Encoding Individual Tree Pattern Relaxations

answer to a query is an *n*-tuple containing a node match for every leaf node in the evaluation plan (i.e., for every node in the query tree pattern).

4.2 Encoding Tree Pattern Relaxations

We show how tree pattern relaxations can be encoded in the evaluation plan. Figure 2 presents some example relaxations of the (unweighted) query tree pattern of Figure 1, and specifies how the query evaluation plan of Figure 1 needs to be modified to encode these relaxations. The modifications to the initial evaluation plan are highlighted with bold dashed lines. Predicates irrelevant to our discussion are omitted.

Node Generalization: In order to encode a node generalization in an evaluation plan, each predicate involving the node type is replaced by a predicate on its super-type. For example, Figure 2 depicts how Book can be generalized to Document in the evaluation plan.

Edge Generalization: In order to capture the generalization of a parent-child edge to an ancestor-descendant edge in an evaluation plan, we transform the join predicate $c(\tau_1, \tau_2)$ into the predicate:

$$c(\tau_1, \tau_2) \text{ OR } ((\not\exists\, c(\tau_1, \tau_2)) \text{ AND } d(\tau_1, \tau_2))$$

This new join predicate can be checked by first determining if a parent-child relationship exists between the two nodes, and then, if this relationship doesn't exist, determining if an ancestor-descendant relationship exists between them. For example, Figure 2 depicts how the parent-child edge (Editor, Name) can be generalized to an ancestor-descendant edge in the evaluation plan.

In subsequent figures, this predicate is simplified to $(c(\tau_1, \tau_2) \text{ OR } d(\tau_1, \tau_2))$, where the OR has an ordered interpretation (check $c(\tau_1, \tau_2)$ first, $d(\tau_1, \tau_2)$ next).

Leaf Node Deletion: To allow for the possibility that a given query leaf node may or may not be matched, the join that relates the leaf node to its parent node in the query evaluation plan becomes an outer join. More specifically, it becomes a left outer join for left-deep evaluation plans. For example, Figure 2 illustrates how the evaluation plan is affected by allowing the Address node to be deleted. The left outer join guarantees that even books whose editor does not have an address will be returned as an approximate answer.

Subtree Promotion: This relaxation causes a query subtree to be promoted to become a descendant of its current grandparent. In the query evaluation plan, the join predicate between the parent of the subtree and the root of the subtree, say $jp(\tau_1, \tau_2)$ needs to be modified to:

$$jp(\tau_1, \tau_2) \text{ OR } ((\not\exists\, jp(\tau_1, \tau_2)) \text{ AND } d(\tau_3, \tau_2))$$

where τ_3 is the type of the grandparent. For example, Figure 2 illustrates how the evaluation plan is affected by promoting the subtree rooted at Name.

Again, in subsequent figures, this new join predicate is simplified to $(c(\tau_1, \tau_2)$ OR $d(\tau_3, \tau_2))$, where the OR has an ordered interpretation.

Combining Relaxations: Figure 3(a) shows the evaluation plan obtained by encoding all possible tree pattern relaxations of the query tree pattern of Figure 1. Each node is generalized if a type hierarchy exists (in our example query, only Book becomes Document). All parent-child edges are generalized to ancestor-descendant edges. All nodes, except the tree pattern root, are made optional. Finally, all subtrees are promoted. Note that even non-leaf nodes such as Editor can be deleted once its subtrees are promoted, and it becomes a leaf node.

5 An Efficient Solution to the Threshold Problem

The goal of the threshold approach is to take a weighted query tree pattern and a threshold, and generate a ranked list of approximate answers whose scores are at least as large as the threshold, along with their scores. A simple approach to achieve this goal is to (i) translate the query tree pattern into a join evaluation

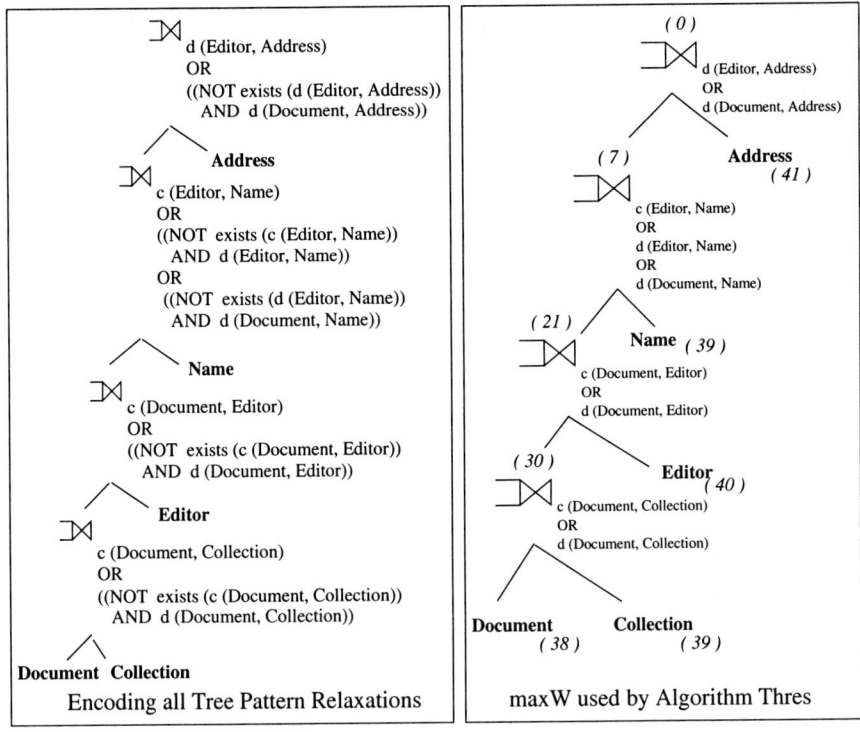

Fig. 3. Encoding All Relaxations, Weights used by Thres

plan, (ii) encode all possible tree pattern relaxations in the plan (as described in Section 4), (iii) evaluate the modified query evaluation plan to compute answers to all relaxed queries (along with their scores), and (iv) finally, return answers whose scores are at least as large as the threshold. We show that this *post-pruning* approach is suboptimal since it is not necessary to first compute all possible approximate answers, and only then prune irrelevant ones.

In order to compute approximate answers more efficiently, we need to detect, as soon as possible during query evaluation, which intermediate answers are guaranteed to not meet the threshold. For this purpose, we took inspiration from evaluation algorithms in IR for keyword-based searches, and designed Algorithm Thres. Thres operates on a join evaluation plan. Before describing this algorithm, we discuss an example to illustrate how approximate answer scores are computed at each step of the join evaluation plan.

5.1 Computing Answer Scores: An Example

The following algebraic expression (a part of the join plan of Figure 3) illustrates the types of results computed during the evaluation of the join plan:

$$\text{Document} \bowtie_{c(\text{Document},\text{Collection})\ \text{OR}\ d(\text{Document},\text{Collection})} \text{Collection}$$

Suppose that the node Document is a generalization of an initial node Book. Evaluating Document (say, using an index on the node type) results in two kinds of answers: (i) answers whose type is the exact node type Book, and (ii) answers whose type is the relaxed node type Document, but not Book. An answer in the first category is assigned the exact weight of this node as its score, i.e., 7. An answer in the second category is assigned the (typically smaller) relaxed weight as its score, i.e., 1.

Let *doc* denote answers of type Document (with score s_1) and *col* denote answers of type Collection (with score s_2). The result of the above algebraic expression includes three types of answers:

- (*doc*, *col*) pairs that satisfy the structural predicate *c*(*doc*, *col*).
- (*doc*, *col*) pairs that do not satisfy *c*(*doc*, *col*), but satisfy the structural predicate *d*(*doc*, *col*).
- *doc*'s that do not join with any *col* via *c*(*doc*, *col*) or *d*(*doc*, *col*).

The score of a (*doc*, *col*) pair is computed as $s_1 + s_2 + s(doc, col)$, where $s(doc, col)$ is the contribution due to the edge between Document and Collection in the query (see Section 3.3 for more details). The score of a *doc* that does not join with any *col* is s_1.

5.2 Algorithm Thres

The basis of Algorithm Thres, which prunes intermediate answers that cannot possibly meet the specified threshold, is to associate with each node in the join evaluation plan, its *maximal weight*, maxW, defined as follows.

Definition 5 [Maximal Weight]. *The maximal weight, maxW, of a node in the evaluation plan is defined as the largest value by which the score of an intermediate answer computed for that node can grow.* □

Consider, for example, the evaluation plan in Figure 3. The maxW of the Document node is 38. This number is obtained by computing the sum of the exact weights of all nodes and edges of the query tree pattern, excluding the Document node itself. Similarly, maxW of the join node with Editor as its right child is 21. This is obtained by computing the sum of the exact weights of all nodes and edges of the query tree pattern, excluding those that have been evaluated as part of the join plan of the subtree rooted at that join node. By definition, maxW of the last join node, the root of the evaluation plan, is 0.

Algorithm Thres is summarized in Figure 4. It needs maxW to have been computed at each node of the evaluation plan. The query evaluation plan is executed in a bottom-up fashion. At each node, intermediate results, along with their scores, are computed. If the sum of the score of an intermediate result and maxW at the node does not meet the threshold, this intermediate result is eliminated. Note that Figure 4 shows a nested loop join algorithm for simplicity of exposition. The algorithms we use for inner joins and left outer joins are based on the structural join algorithms of [1].

```
Algorithm Thres(Node n)
   if (n is leaf) {
      list = evaluateLeaf(n);
      for (r in list)
         if (r->score + n->maxW ≥ threshold)  append r to results;
      return results; }
   list1 = Thres(n->left);
   list2 = Thres(n->right);
   for (r1 in list1) {
      for (r2 in list2) {
         if (checkPredicate(r1,r2,n->predicate))
            s = computeScore(r1,r2,n->predicate);
         if (s + n->maxW ≥ threshold)
            append (r1,r2) to results with score s; }
      if (∄ r2 that joins with r1)
         if (r1->score + n->maxW ≥ threshold)
            append (r1,-) to results with score r1->score;
   }
   return results;
```

Fig. 4. Algorithm Thres

6 An Adaptive Optimization Strategy

6.1 Algorithm OptiThres

The key idea behind OptiThres, an optimized version of Thres, is that we can predict, during evaluation of the join plan, if a subsequent relaxation produces additional matches that will *not* meet the threshold. In this case, we can "undo" this relaxation in the evaluation plan. Undoing this relaxation (e.g., converting a left outer join back to an inner join, or reverting to the original node type) improves efficiency of evaluation since fewer conditions need to be tested and fewer intermediate results are computed during the evaluation.

While Algorithm Thres relies on maxW at each node in the evaluation plan to do early pruning, Algorithm OptiThres additionally uses three weights at each join node of the query evaluation plan:

- The first weight, relaxNode, is defined as the largest value by which the score of an intermediate result *computed for the left child of the join node* can grow if it joins with a relaxed match to the right child of the join node. This is used to decide if the node generalization (if any) of the right child of the join node should be unrelaxed.
- The second weight, relaxJoin, is defined as the largest value by which the score of an intermediate result *computed for the left child of the join node* can grow if it cannot join with any match to the right child of the join node.

```
Algorithm OptiThres(Node n)
   if (n is leaf) {
      // evaluate, prune, and return results as in Algorithm Thres
   }
   list1 = OptiThres(n->left);
   /* maxLeft is set to the maximal score of results in list1 */
   if (maxLeft + relaxNode < threshold) unrelax(n->right);
   list2 = OptiThres(n->right);
   /* maxRight is set to the maximal score of results in list2 */
   if (maxLeft + relaxJoin < threshold) unrelax(n->join);
   if (maxLeft + maxRight + relaxPred < threshold)
      unrelax(n->join->predicate);
   // now, evaluate, prune and return join (and possibly outer join)
   // results as in Algorithm Thres
```

Fig. 5. Algorithm OptiThres

This is used to decide if the join node should remain a left outer join, or should go back to being an inner join.
- The third weight, relaxPred, is defined as the largest value by which the sum of the scores of a pair of intermediate results for the left and right children of the join node can grow if they are joined using a relaxed structural predicate. This is used to decide if the edge generalization and subtree promotion should be unrelaxed.

Algorithm OptiThres is given in Figure 5. Only the parts that are modifications to Algorithm Thres are specified, and we indicate where the code fragments from Algorithm Thres need to be inserted. It is easy to see that OptiThres has very few overheads over Algorithm Thres, since OptiThres makes use of the maximal score of answers at each step of the evaluation process (which can be maintained in limited space while the intermediate answers are being computed), and some precomputed numbers at each node in the evaluation plan.

Finally, note that Algorithm OptiThres makes only *local* decisions about undoing relaxations (not generalizing the right child of the join, turning the outer join to an inner join, or turning the join predicate from descendant to child). A natural question is whether a more global approach could do better. It is not too difficult to see that applying OptiThres locally at each node is at least as good as applying it globally since a global optimization would have to rely on more conservative estimates of possible scores of intermediate results.

6.2 An Illustrative Example

We illustrate Algorithm OptiThres using an example. Consider the weighted query tree pattern in Figure 6. This query looks for all Proceedings that have as children subelements a Publisher and a Month. Exact and relaxed weights

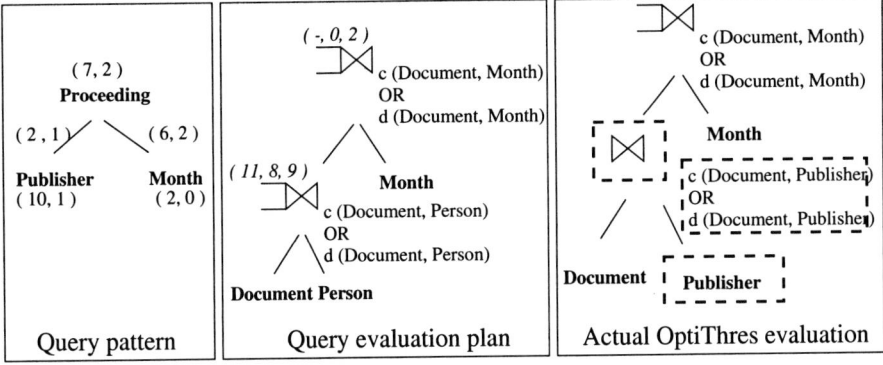

Fig. 6. A Simple OptiThres Example

are associated with each node and edge in the query tree pattern. Proceeding is relaxed to Document, Publisher is relaxed to Person, the parent-child edges are relaxed to ancestor-descendant ones, and nodes Person and Month are made optional. The threshold is set to 14.

First, weights are computed at each evaluation plan node statically. Recall that in our examples, we have chosen to use the relaxed weight as the contribution due to matching a relaxed node or edge. For example, at the first join node in the evaluation plan, relaxNode = 11 (ew(Month) + ew((Proceeding, Month)) + ew((Proceeding, Publisher)) + rw(Publisher)), relaxJoin = 8 (ew(Month) + ew((Proceeding, Month))), and relaxPred = 9 (ew(Month) + ew((Proceeding, Month)) + rw((Proceeding, Publisher))).

Next, Algorithm OptiThres evaluates the annotated query evaluation plan in Figure 6. Document is evaluated first. Assume that the maximal score in the list of answers we get is 2, i.e., there are no Proceeding's in the database. At the next join, relaxNode = 11, relaxJoin = 8, and relaxPred = 9. The sum relaxNode +2 = 13, which is smaller than the threshold. In this case, OptiThres decides to unrelax Person to Publisher, and the plan is modified suitably. Next, Publisher is evaluated, and let the maximal score in the result list be 10 (i.e., exact matches were obtained). The sum relaxJoin +2 = 10, which is also smaller than the threshold, and OptiThres decides to unrelax the left outer join to an inner join, since we cannot "afford to lose Publisher". The algorithm then checks whether to retain the descendant structural predicate. Since the sum relaxPred +2 + 10 = 21, which is larger than the threshold, OptiThres decides to retain the relaxed structural join predicate d(Document, Publisher).

During the evaluation of the first join, join results are pruned using maxW, as in Algorithm Thres. Assume that the maximal score of answers in the first join result is 14 (10+2+2). OptiThres then uses the weights at the second join node to determine whether any other relaxations need to be undone. Note that Month node has not been generalized, and this is reflected in the fact that relaxNode at the second join is not specified. Next, Month is evaluated, and matches have

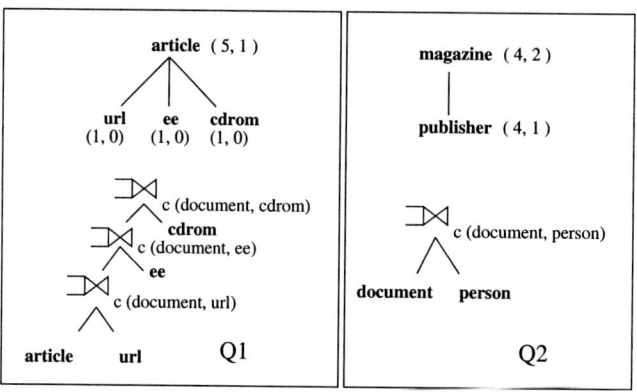

Fig. 7. Queries Used in the Experiments

a score of 2. The sum `relaxJoin` $+14 = 14$, which meets the threshold. So the outer join is not unrelaxed. Similarly, `relaxPred` $+14 + 2 = 18$, which meets the threshold. So the join predicate is not unrelaxed. Finally, the second join is evaluated, and join results are pruned using `maxW`, as in Algorithm `Thres`.

The algebraic expression that we have effectively computed is given in Figure 6, where the dynamically modified portions of the evaluation plan are highlighted.

7 Experiments

7.1 Experimental Setup

We use the DBLP XML dataset which is approximately 85MBytes and contains 2.1M elements. Some information about relevant elements is given in the table below. The DTD of this dataset as well as the data itself can be found at http://dblp.uni-trier.de/db.

Label	No. of elements	Label	No. of elements
article	87,675	url	212,792
cdrom	13,052	ee	55,831
document	213,362	magazine	0
publisher	1,199	person	448,788

In our type hierarchy, `document` is a super-type of `book`, `incollection`, `inproceedings`, `proceedings`, `article`, `phdthesis`, `mastersthesis`, `www` and `magazine`; and `person` is a super-type of `author`, `editor` and `publisher`. We use the queries of Figure 7. Since the DTD does not have long root-to-leaf paths, we do not consider edge generalization and subtree promotion in our experiments.

In order to prune data at each step of the query evaluation, we modified the stack-based structural join algorithm of [1] so that each input (and output) is

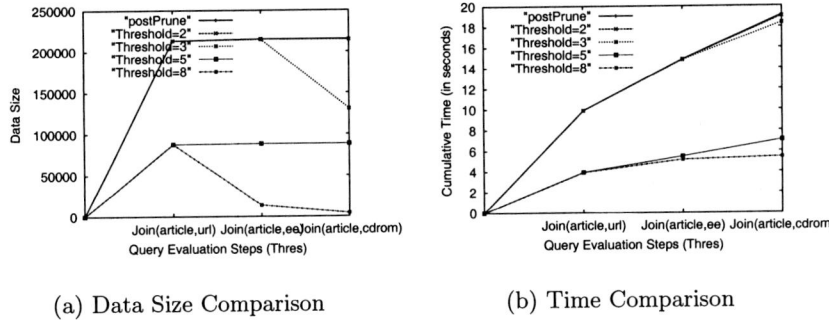

Fig. 8. Comparing `Thres` and `postPrune`

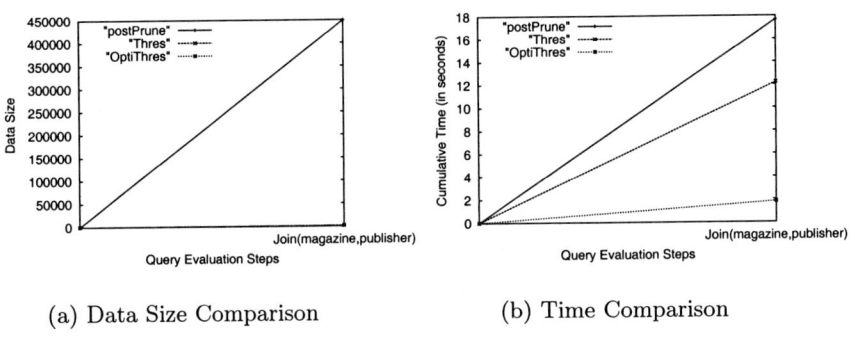

Fig. 9. Comparing `OptiThres`, `Thres` and `postPrune`

materialized in a file. We ran all our experiments on a HP-UX machine with 32MBytes of memory. In all experiments, query evaluation time is reported in seconds and result sizes in the number of answers.

7.2 Studying Algorithm `Thres`

We use **Q1** where `url`, `ee`, and `cdrom` are made optional and `article` is relaxed to `document`. We compare (i) the evaluation times for `Thres` (for multiple thresholds) and `postPrune`, and (ii) the cumulative sizes of the data processed by each algorithm. The results are given in Figure 8 where the X-axis represents each step of **Q1** evaluation. Figure 8(a) shows that the higher the threshold, the earlier is irrelevant data pruned and the smaller is the evaluation time. This is explained by the fact that with a higher threshold, the amount of data that remains in the evaluation process is reduced (as shown in Figure 8(b)). For `postPrune`, data pruning occurs only at the last step of query evaluation.

7.3 Benefit of Algorithm `OptiThres`

We compare `postPrune`, `Thres` and `OptiThres`. We use query **Q2** with a threshold = 5 because we want to illustrate how `OptiThres` decides that `publisher` should not be relaxed to `person`. `magazine` is relaxed to `document`, `publisher` to `person`, and `person` is made optional. Figure 9 shows an intermediate data size and an evaluation time comparison. `OptiThres` detects that `publisher` should not have been relaxed to `person` and should not have been made optional (the outer join is turned back to an inner join). This is because there is no `magazine` in the database, and the only instances that are selected when evaluating `document` are documents that are not magazines. Thus, their scores are 2 and would not meet the threshold if `publisher` is relaxed. The graphs of Figure 9(a) show that both `postPrune` and `Thres` scan all of `person` which results in processing more data than `OptiThres` (which scans only `publisher`). This also results in a higher evaluation time as shown in Figure 9(b). In addition, since `OptiThres` performs an inner join operation (instead of an outer join), there are evaluation time and data size savings at the last step of query evaluation.

Since `OptiThres` prunes data earlier than the other strategies, it manipulates the least amount of data, and thus its evaluation time is the smallest. Due to its ability to undo unnecessary relaxations, `OptiThres` achieves a significant improvement in query evaluation performance.

7.4 Comparison with Rewriting-Based Approaches

We run all our algorithms on query **Q1** with a threshold set to 2 (to select a large number of answers). We compare `postPrune`, `OptiThres`, `MultiQOptim` and `MultiQ`. `MultiQ` and `MultiQOptim` are two rewriting-based approaches. `MultiQ` is the case where we generate all relaxed versions of **Q1** and execute each of them separately. The total evaluation time is obtained by adding each of their evaluation times. `MultiQOptim` is the case where we share common subexpressions.

`postPrune` took 22.384 seconds, `OptiThres` took 18.550, `MultiQOptim` took 30.782 and `MultiQ` took 40.842. Our results show that the execution time of `OptiThres` is considerably faster than rewriting-based approaches. The reason is that `MultiQ` performs 10 joins, `MultiQOptim` performs 8 joins and `OptiThres` performs only 3 joins.

8 Conclusion

In this paper we have developed techniques for relaxing weighted query tree patterns, and efficiently computing approximate answers to weighted tree patterns by encoding the relaxations in join evaluation plans. Our preliminary experimental evaluation has shown the benefits of our techniques over post-pruning and rewriting-based approaches.

There are many interesting directions of future work in this area. What is the analog of the $tf * idf$ score used in Information Retrieval for keyword-based queries? How can one combine our optimizations with traditional cost-based join ordering to identify the cheapest evaluation plan? How does one quickly estimate the number of approximate answers that meet a given threshold? Solutions to these problems will be important for the XML database systems of tomorrow.

References

1. S. Al-Khalifa, H. V. Jagadish, N. Koudas, J. M. Patel, D. Srivastava, and Y. Wu. Structural joins: Efficient matching of XML query patterns. In *Proceedings of ICDE*, 2002.
2. S. Boag, D. Chamberlin, M. Fernandez, D. Florescu, J. Robie, J. Simeon, and M. Stefanescu. XQuery 1.0: An XML query language. http://www.w3.org/TR/xquery.
3. Y. Chiaramella, P. Mulhem, and F. Fourel. A model for multimedia information retrieval. Technical report, FERMI ESPRIT BRA 8134, University of Glasgow. www.dcs.gla.ac.uk/fermi/tech_reports/reports/fermi96-4.ps.gz.
4. DBLP Database. http://www.informatik.uni-trier.de/ ley/db.
5. C. Delobel and M. C. Rousset. A uniform approach for querying large tree-structured data through a mediated schema. In *Proceedings of International Workshop on Foundations of Models for Information Integration (FMII)*, 2001.
6. A. Deutch, M. Fernandez, D. Florescu, A. Levy, and D. Suciu. A query language for XML. In *Proceedings of WWW*, 1999.
7. C. Faloutsos. Access methods for text. *ACM Computing Surveys*, 17(1), 1985.
8. N. Fuhr and K. Grossjohann. XIRQL: An extension of XQL for information retrieval. In *Proceedings of SIGIR*, 2001.
9. Y. Hayashi, J. Tomita, and G. Kikui. Searching text-rich XML documents with relevance ranking. In *Proceedings of SIGIR Workshop on XML and Information Retrieval*, 2000.
10. Y. Kanza and Y. Sagiv. Flexible queries over semistructured data. In *Proceedings of PODS*, 2001.
11. J. McHugh, S Abiteboul, R. Goldman, D. Quass, and J. Widom. Lore: A database management system for semistructured data. SIGMOD Record, 26(3):45-66, 1997.
12. S. Myaeng, D.-H. Jang, M.-S. Kim, and Z.-C. Zhoo. A flexible Model for retrieval of SGML documents. In *Proceedings of SIGIR*, 1998.
13. M. Persin. Document filtering for fast ranking. In *Proceedings of SIGIR*, 1994.
14. J. Robie, J. Lapp, and D. Schach. XML query language (XQL). Available from http://www.w3.org/TandS/QL/QL98/pp/xql.html.
15. G. Salton and M. J. McGill. *Introduction to modern information retrieval*. McGraw-Hill, New York, 1983.
16. T. Schlieder. Similarity search in XML data using cost-based query Transformations. In *Proceedings of SIGMOD WebDB Workshop*, 2001.
17. A. Theobald and G. Weikum. Adding relevance to XML. In *Proceedings of SIGMOD WebDB Workshop*, 2000.
18. H. Turtle and J. Flood. Query evaluation: Strategies and optimization. *Information Processing & Management*, Nov. 1995.
19. C. Zhang, J. Naughton, D. DeWitt, Q. Luo, and G. Lohman. On supporting containment queries in relational database management systems. In *Proceedings of SIGMOD*, 2001.
20. K. Zhang and D. Shasha. Tree pattern matching. *Pattern Matching Algorithms, Apostolico and Galil (Eds.), Oxford University Press*, 1997.

Schema-Driven Evaluation of Approximate Tree-Pattern Queries

Torsten Schlieder*

Institute of Computer Science
Freie Universität Berlin
schlied@inf.fu-berlin.de

Abstract. We present a simple query language for XML, which supports hierarchical, Boolean-connected query patterns. The interpretation of a query is founded on cost-based query transformations: The total cost of a sequence of transformations measures the similarity between the query and the data and is used to rank the results. We introduce two polynomial-time algorithms that efficiently find the best n answers to the query: The first algorithm finds all approximate results, sorts them by increasing cost, and prunes the result list after the nth entry. The second algorithm uses a structural summary –the schema– of the database to estimate the best k transformed queries, which in turn are executed against the database. We compare both approaches and show that the schema-based evaluation outperforms the pruning approach for small values of n. The pruning strategy is the better choice if n is close to the total number of approximate results for the query.

1 Introduction

An XML query engine should retrieve the best results possible: If no exactly matching documents are found, results *similar* to the query should be retrieved and *ranked* according to their similarity.

The problem of similarity between keyword queries and text documents has been investigated for years in information retrieval [3]. Unfortunately, the most models (with some recent exceptions, e.g., [15, 6, 7]) consider unstructured text only and therefore miss the change to yield a more precise search. Furthermore, it is not clear whether retrieval models based on term distribution can be used for *data centric* documents as considered in this paper.

XML query languages, on the other hand, do incorporate the document structure. They are well suited for *applications* that query and transform XML documents [5]. However, they do not well support *user* queries because results that do not fully match the query are not retrieved. Moreover, the user needs substantial knowledge of the data structure to formulate queries.

---

* This research was supported by the German Research Society, Berlin-Brandenburg Graduate School in Distributed Information Systems (DFG grant no. GRK 316).

Consider a catalog with data about sound storage media. A user may be interested in a CD with piano concertos by Rachmaninov. A keyword query retrieves all documents that contain at least one of the terms "piano", "concerto", and "Rachmaninov". However, the user cannot specify that she *prefers* CDs with the title "piano concerto" over CDs having a track title "piano concerto". Similarly, the user cannot express her preference for the composer Rachmaninov over the performer Rachmaninov.

Structured queries yield the contrary result: Only exactly matching documents are retrieved. The XQL [11] query

```
/catalog/cd[composer="Rachmaninov" and title="Piano concerto"]
```

will neither retrieve CDs with a *track* title "Piano concerto" nor CDs of the *category* "Piano concerto" nor concertos *performed* by "Rachmaninov", nor other sound storage media than CDs with the appropriate information. The query will also not retrieve CDs where only one of the specified keywords appears in the title. Of course, the user can pose a query that exactly matches the cases mentioned – but she must know beforehand that such similar results exist and how they are represented. Moreover, since all results of the redefined query are treated equally, the user still cannot express her preferences.

As a first step to bridge the gap between the vagueness of information retrieval and the expressiveness of structured queries with respect to data-centric documents, we introduce the simple pattern-matching language approXQL. The interpretation of approXQL queries is founded on cost-based query transformations. The total cost of a sequence of transformations measures the similarity between a query and the data. The similarity score is used to *rank* the results.

We present two polynomial-time algorithms that find the best n answers to the query: The first algorithm finds all approximate results, sorts them by increasing cost, and prunes the result list after the nth entry. The second algorithm is an extension of the first one. It uses the *schema* of the database to estimate the best k transformed queries, sorts them by cost, and executes them against the database to find the best n results. We discuss the results of experiments, which show that the schema-based query evaluation outperforms the pruning approach if n is smaller than the total number of approximate results.

2 Related Work

The semantics of our query language is related to cost-based distance measures for unordered labeled trees such as the tree-edit distance [14] and the tree-alignment distance [9]. Our approach is different concerning its semantics and concerning its computational complexity.

We believe that different nodes of a tree-shaped query pattern should be treated differently: Leaf nodes specify the *information* the user is looking for. The root node defines the *scope* of the search. The inner nodes determine the *context* in which the information should appear. None of the tree-similarity measures we know has a semantics tailored to XML data.

The problem of finding the minimal edit or alignment distance between unordered trees is MAX SNP-hard [2]. Even the problem of including a query tree into a data tree is NP-complete [10]. In [16] a restricted variant of the edit distance and its adaption to tree-pattern matching has been proposed. All matching subtrees can be found in polynomial time. The proposed algorithm touches every data node, which is inadequate for large databases.

To our knowledge, our work is the first in the context of approximate tree-pattern matching that proposes an *XML-tailored* query interpretation, supports *Boolean operators*, evaluates a query using *indexes* and *list operations*, and takes advantage of a *schema* to find the *best n* answers.

3 The ApproXQL Query Language

ApproXQL [12] is a simple pattern-matching language for XML. The syntactical subset of the language that we will use throughout the paper consists of (1) name selectors, (2) text selectors, (3) the containment operator "[]", and (4) the Boolean operators "and", "or". The following query selects CDs containing piano concertos composed by Rachmaninov:

```
cd[title["piano" and ''concerto"] and composer["rachmaninov"]].
```

Note that the text selectors match both text data and attribute values. A conjunctive query can be interpreted as a labeled, typed tree: Text selectors are mapped to leaf nodes of type *text*; name selectors are represented as nodes of type *struct*. Each "and" expression is mapped to an inner node of the tree. The children of an "and" node are the roots of the paths that are conjunctively connected. Figure 1(a) shows the tree interpretation of the above query.

A query that contains "or"-operators is broken up into a set of conjunctive queries, which is called *separated query representation*. The query

```
cd[title["piano" and ("concerto" or ''sonata")] and
   (composer["rachmaninov"] or performer["ashkenazy"])].
```

consists of two "or"-operators and can be converted into 2^2 conjunctive queries:

```
{ cd[title["piano" and ''concerto"] and composer["rachmaninov"]],
  cd[title["piano" and ''concerto"] and performer["ashkenazy"]],
  cd[title["piano" and ''sonata"] and composer["rachmaninov"]],
  cd[title["piano" and ''sonata"] and performer["ashkenazy"]] }.
```

4 Modeling and Normalization of XML Documents

We model XML documents as labeled trees consisting of two node types: *text* nodes represent element text as well as attribute values; nodes of type *struct* represent elements and attributes. The name of an element is used as node label. Text sequences are splitted into words. For each word, a leaf node of the

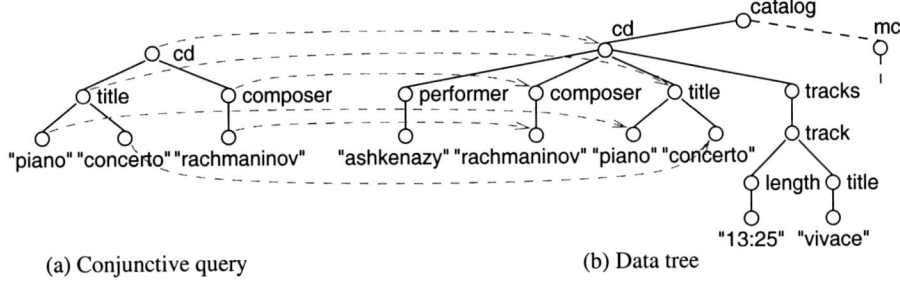

(a) Conjunctive query (b) Data tree

Fig. 1. Embedding of a conjunctive query in a data tree.

document tree is created and labeled with the word. Attributes are mapped to two nodes in parent-child relationship: The attribute name forms the label of the parent, and the attribute value forms the label of the child. We add a new root node with a unique label to the collection of document trees and establish an edge between this node and the roots of the document trees. The resulting tree is called *data tree*. Figure 1(b) shows a part of a data tree.

5 Querying by Approximate Tree Embedding

In this section, we introduce the semantics of approXQL queries. We first define an embedding function that maps a conjunctive query to a data tree. The embedding is *exact* in the sense that all labels of the query occur in the result, and that the parent-child relationships of the query are preserved. Then, we introduce our approach to find *similar* results to a query.

5.1 The Tree-Embedding Formalism

Our definition of tree embedding is inspired by the *unordered path inclusion problem* proposed by Kilpeläinen [10]. We discard the injectivity property of the path inclusion problem in order to get a function that is efficiently computable[1]:

Definition 1 (Embedding). *An embedding of a conjunctive query into a data tree is a function f that maps the query nodes to data nodes such that f is (1) label preserving, (2) type preserving, and (3) parent-child preserving.*

Let u be a node of a conjunctive query. We call the data node $f(u)$ a *match* of u. The match of the query root is the *embedding root* of f; the matched data nodes together with the connecting edges are called *embedding image*; and the data subtree anchored at the embedding root is a *result*. Note, that for a fixed query and a fixed data tree, several results may exist, and several embeddings may

---

[1] The injectivity of the embedding function together with the implicit relaxation of the parent-child-relationship to an ancestor-descendant relationship (Section 5.2) would lead to the *unordered tree inclusion problem*, which is NP-complete [10].

lead to the same result. Figure 1 shows an embedding of a conjunctive query into a data tree. The result of this embedding is the subtree rooted at the left cd node; all nodes with incoming arrows, together with their connecting edges, form the embedding image.

5.2 Basic Query Transformations

The tree-embedding formalism allows exact embeddings only. To find similar results to the query, we use *basic query transformations*. A basic query transformation is a modification of a conjunctive query by inserting a node, deleting a node, or renaming the label of a node. In contrast to the tree-edit distance [14], our model does not allow arbitrary sequences of insert, delete, and rename operations. We restrict the basic transformations in order to generate only queries that have intuitive semantics. For example, it is not allowed to delete *all* leaves of the original query, since every leaf captures information the user is looking for.

Definition 2 (Insertion). *An insertion is the replacement of an edge by a node that has an incoming edge and an outgoing edge.*

Note that this definition does not allow to add a new query root or to append new leaves. A node insertion creates a query that finds matches in a *more specific context*. As an example, consider the insertion of two nodes labeled tracks and track, respectively, between the nodes cd and title in the query shown in Figure 1(a). The insertions create a query that searches for subtree matches in the more specific context of track titles.

Definition 3 (Deletion of inner nodes). *A deletion removes an inner node u (except the root) together with its incoming edge and connects the outgoing edges of u with the parent of u.*

The deletion of inner nodes is based on the observation that the hierarchy of an XML document typically models a containment relationship. The deeper an element resides in the data tree the more specific is the information it describes. Assume that a user searches for CD tracks with the title "concerto". The deletion of the node track creates a query that searches the term "concerto" in CD titles instead of track titles.

Definition 4 (Deletion of leaves). *A deletion removes a leaf u together with its incoming edge iff the parent of u has two or more children (including u) that are leaves of the query.*

The deletion of leaves adopts the concept of "coordination level match" [3], which is a simple querying model that establishes ranking for queries of "and"-connected search terms.

Definition 5 (Renaming). *A renaming changes the label of a node.*

A renaming of a node u changes the search space of the query subtree rooted at u. For example, the renaming of the query root from cd to mc shifts the search space from CDs to MCs.

Each basic transformation has a cost, which is specified, for example, by a domain expert.

Definition 6 (Cost). *The cost of a transformation is a non-negative number.*

There are several variants to assign costs to transformations. In this paper we choose the simplest one: We bind the costs to the labels of the involved nodes.

5.3 The Approximate Query-Matching Problem

In this subsection, we define the approximate query-matching problem. We first define the terms *transformed query* and *embedding cost*:

Definition 7 (Transformed query). *A transformed query is derived from a conjunctive query using a sequence of basic transformations such that all deletions precede all renamings and all renamings precede all insertions.*

Each conjunctive query in the separated representation of an approXQL query is also a transformed query, which is derived by an empty transformation sequence.

Definition 8 (Embedding cost). *The embedding cost of a transformed query is the sum of the costs of all applied basic transformations.*

To evaluate an approXQL query, the *closure* of transformed queries is created from the separated query representation:

Definition 9 (Query closure). *The closure of a query Q is the set of all transformed queries that can be derived from the separated representation of Q.*

Every query in the closure of Q is executed against the data tree. Executing a query means finding a (possibly empty) set of embeddings of the query tree in the data tree according to Definition 1. All embeddings that have the same root are collected in an embedding group:

Definition 10 (Embedding group). *An embedding group is a set of pairs, where each pair consists of an embedding and its cost. All embeddings in a group have the same root.*

As an example, consider the query shown in Figure 1 and assume a further query that has been derived from the depicted query by deleting the node "concerto". Both queries have an embedding in the data subtree rooted at the left cd node. Therefore, both embeddings belong to the same embedding group. To get a single score for each group, we choose the embedding with the lowest embedding cost:

Definition 11 (Approximate query-matching problem). *Given a data tree and the closure of a query, locate all embedding groups and represent each group by a pair (u, c), where u is the root of the embeddings in the group and c is the lowest cost of all embeddings in the group.*

We call the pair (u, c) a *root-cost pair*. Each root-cost pair represents a result of the query. An algorithm solving the approximate query-matching problem must find *all* results of query. Since a user is typically interested in the *best* results only, we define the best-n-pairs problem as follows:

Definition 12 (Best-n-pairs problem). *Create a cost-sorted list of the n root-cost pairs that have the lowest embedding costs among all root-cost pairs for a query and a data tree.*

The following steps summarize the evaluation of an **approXQL** query:

1. Break up the query into its separated representation.
2. Derive the closure of transformed queries from the separated representation.
3. Find all embeddings of any transformed query in the data tree.
4. Divide the embeddings into embedding groups and create the root-cost pairs.
5. Retrieve the best n root-cost pairs.

In an additional step, the results (subtrees of the data tree) belonging to the embedding roots are selected and retrieved to the user. The five steps describe the evaluation of an **approXQL** query from the theoretical point of view. In the following sections we give a more practicable approach to evaluate a query.

6 Direct Query Evaluation

The approximate tree-matching model explicitly creates a (possibly infinite) set of transformed queries from a user-provided query. In this section, we show that the explicit creation of transformed queries is not necessary. Moreover, we show that the images of all approximate embeddings of a query can be found in polynomial time with respect to the number of nodes of the data tree. The evaluation of a query is based on three ideas: First, we encode all allowed renamings and deletions of query nodes in an *expanded representation* of the query. The expanded representation implicitly includes all so-called *semi-transformed* queries. Second, we detect all possible insertions of query nodes using a special numbering of the nodes in the data tree. Third, we simultaneously compute all embedding images of the semi-transformed query using a bottom-up algorithm. In the examples used in this section we assume the following costs:

insertion	cost	deletion	cost	renaming	cost
category	4	composer	7	cd $\to$ dvd	6
cd	2	"concerto"	6	cd $\to$ mc	4
composer	5	"piano"	8	composer $\to$ performer	4
performer	5	title	5	"concerto" $\to$ "sonata"	3
title	3	track	3	title $\to$ category	4

All delete and rename costs not listed in the table are infinite; all remaining insert costs are 1.

6.1 The Expanded Representation of a Query

Many transformed queries in the closure of an **approXQL** query are similar; they often differ in some inserted nodes only. We call a query that is derived from a

Schema-Driven Evaluation of Approximate Tree-Pattern Queries   521

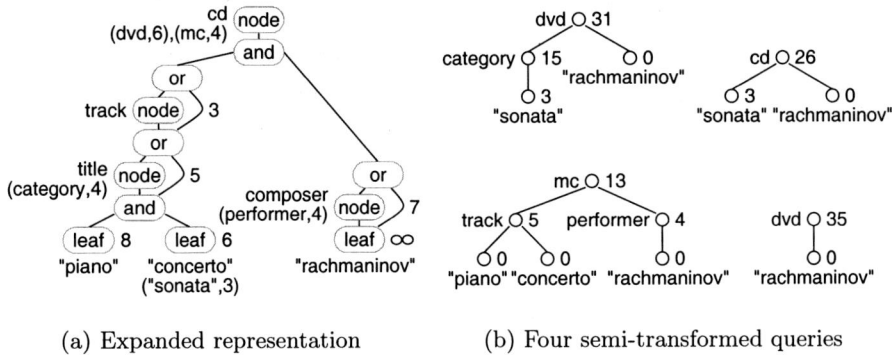

(a) Expanded representation   (b) Four semi-transformed queries

Fig. 2. Expanded representation and semi-transformed queries derived from the query
cd[track[title["piano" and ''concerto"]] and composer["rachmaninov"]].

conjunctive query using a sequence of deletions and renamings (but no insertions) a *semi-transformed query*. The *expanded representation* of a query Q encodes all distinct semi-transformed queries that can be derived from the separated representation of Q. It consists of nodes belonging to four *representation types*:

node: A node of representation type "node" represents all nodes of all semi-transformed queries that are derived from the same inner node of the original query. Consider Figure 2(a). The top-level node represents the cd node of the original query and its renamings dvd and mc that have the costs 6 and 4, respectively.

leaf: A "leaf" represents all leaves of all semi-transformed queries derived from the same leaf of the original query. The middle leaf of the query in Figure 2(a) represents the "concerto" node of the original query. It is labeled with the original term and its single renaming "sonata", which has cost 3. Assigned to the right side of the leaf is the delete cost 6 of the node.

and: Any "and"-node represents an "and"-operator of the original query.

or: Nodes of type "or" have two applications: First, they represent "or"-operators of the original query. Second, for each inner node that may be deleted, an "or" node is inserted in the expanded query representation. The left edge leads to the node that may be deleted. The right edge bridges the node. It is annotated with the delete cost of the bridged node. In our example, every inner node (except the root) may be deleted and has therefore an "or"-parent.

A semi-transformed query can be derived from the expanded representation by following a combination of paths from the root to the leaves. The total cost of the derived query consists of the rename cost of the choosen labels, the costs assigned to the edges and the costs of the deleted leaves. Figure 2(b) depicts four out of 84 semi-transformed queries included in the expanded query representation shown in Figure 2(a). The number assigned to each node represents the *minimal* cost of approximate embeddings of the subtree rooted at the node. Node insertions in the subtree may increase the costs.

We define a number of attributes for each node u of an expanded query representation: $reptype(u)$ is the representation type of u (and, or, node, leaf), $label(u)$ is the label, and $type(u)$ is the node type of u (*struct, text*). For each "node" and "leaf" the set $renamings(u)$ contains all alternative label-cost pairs for u, and $delcost(u)$ is the cost of deleting u. If u is an "or" node then $edgecost(u)$ denotes the cost assigned to the edge leading to the right child of u.

6.2 Encoding of the Data Tree

The embedding of a (transformed) conjunctive query into a data tree is defined as function that preserves labels, types, and parent-child relationships. In order to construct an embeddable query, nodes must be inserted into the query. This "blind" insertion of nodes creates many queries that have no embedding at all. We completely avoid the insertion of nodes into a query. Instead, we use a encoding of the data tree in order to determine the *distance* between the matches of two query nodes. More precisely, we change property (3) of the embedding function (see Definition 1) from "parent-child preserving" to "ancestor-descendant preserving" and define the distance between two nodes u and v as the sum of the insert costs of all nodes along the path from u to v (excluding u and v).

We assign four numbers to each data node u: $pre(u)$ is the preorder number of u; $bound(u)$ is the number of the rightmost leaf of the subtree rooted at u; $inscost(u)$ is the cost of inserting u into a query; and $pathcost(u)$ is the sum of the insert costs of all ancestors of u. Given two nodes u and v we can now test if u is an ancestor of v by ensuring the invariant

$$pre(u) < pre(v) \land bound(u) \geq pre(v).$$

If u is an ancestor of v then the distance between u and v is

$$distance(u,v) = pathcost(v) - pathcost(u) - inscost(u).$$

An example of an encoded data tree is shown in Figure 3(a). The preorder number and the bound value are assigned to left side of each node; the pathcost value and the insert cost are located at the right side. We know that node 15 ("vivace") is a descendant of node 10 (tracks) because $10 < 15 \land 15 \geq 15$ evaluates to true. Using the expression $9 - 3 - 2 = 4$ we can determine the sum of the insert costs of the nodes 11 and 14 and thus, the distance between the nodes 10 and 15.

The indexes I_{struct} and I_{text} provide access to the nodes of the data tree by mapping each label to all nodes that carry the label. The Figures 3(b) and 3(c) show the indexes of the encoded data tree depicted in Figure 3(a).

6.3 Lists and List Entries

The query-evaluation algorithm computes all approximate embeddings using an algebra of lists. A *list* stores information about all nodes of a given label and is

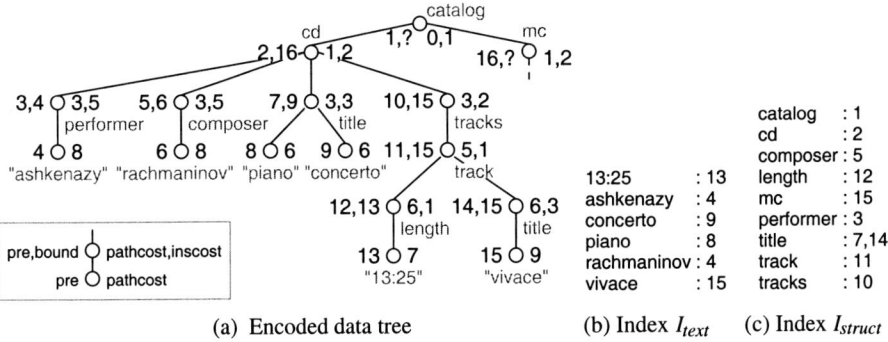

Fig. 3. An encoded data tree with its text index and structural index.

initialized from the corresponding index posting. A list entry e is a tuple

$$e = (pre, bound, pathcost, inscost, embcost),$$

where the first four values are copies of the numbers assigned to the corresponding node u. If u is a *text* node then *bound* and *inscost* are set to zero. All operations on lists are based on these four numbers. In particular, they serve to test the ancestor-descendant relationship and to compute the distance between two nodes. The value *embcost* stores the cost of embedding a query subtree into the data subtree rooted at u. The value is zero if u is the match of a query leaf. For convenience, we use the set notation $e \in L$ to refer to an entry of L.

6.4 Operations on Lists

We now introduce the basic list operations used by our query-evaluation algorithm. List operations are realized as functions that essentially perform standard transformations of lists but additionally calculate the embedding costs during the bottom-up query evaluation. The function join, for example, assumes that the embedding cost of each descendant $e_D \in L_D$ has already been calculated. The embedding cost of an ancestor $e_A \in L_A$ of e_D is therefore $distance(e_A, e_D) + embcost(e_D)$. Because e_A may have several descendants $e_{D_1}, \ldots, e_{D_m}$, we choose the one with the smallest sum of embedding cost and distance:

$$embcost(e_A) = \min\{\, distance(e_A, e_{D_i}) + embcost(e_{D_i}) \mid 1 \leq i \leq m \,\}.$$

The cost is increased by the c_{edge}, which represents the cost of a deleted query node. We use the same principle for the function intersect, which calculates the sums of the embedding costs of corresponding entries in the operand lists, for the function union, which chooses the lowest embedding costs of each pair of entries in the operand lists, and for the function outerjoin, which keeps the minimum of the cheapest matching leaf and the cost of deleting the leaf.

function `fetch`(l, t)
  Fetches the posting belonging to label l from the index I_t ($t \in \{struct, text\}$). Returns a new list L that is initialized from the nodes the posting entries refer to.
function `merge`(L_L, L_R, c_{ren})
  Returns a list L consisting of all entries from the distinct lists L_L and L_R. For each entry copied from L_R (but not L_L) the embedding cost is incremented by c_{ren}.
function `join`(L_A, L_D, c_{edge})
  Returns a new list L that consists of copies of all entries from L_A that have descendants in L_D. Let $e_A \in L_A$ be an ancestor and $[e_{D_1}, \ldots, e_{D_m}]$ be the interval in L_D such that each interval entry is a descendant of e_A. The embedding cost of the copy of e_A is set to $\min\{ distance(e_A, e_{D_i}) + embcost(e_{D_i}) \mid 1 \leq i \leq m \} + c_{edge}$.
function `outerjoin`$(L_A, L_D, c_{edge}, c_{del})$
  Returns a new list L that consists of copies of all entries from L_A. Let $e_A \in L_A$ be an entry. If e_A does not have a descendant in L_D then the embedding cost of the copy of e_A is set to $c_{del} + c_{edge}$. Otherwise, let $[e_{D_1}, \ldots, e_{D_m}]$ be the interval in L_D such that each interval entry is a descendant of e_A. The embedding cost of the copy of e_A is set to $\min(c_{del}, \min\{ distance(e_A, e_{D_i}) + embcost(e_{D_i}) \mid 1 \leq i \leq m \}) + c_{edge}$.
function `intersect`(L_L, L_R, c_{edge})
  Returns a new list L. For each pair $e_L \in L_L$, $e_R \in L_R$ such that $pre(e_L) = pre(e_R)$, appends a copy of e_L to L. The embedding cost of the new entry is set to $embcost(e_L) + embcost(e_R) + c_{edge}$.
function `union`(L_L, L_R, c_{edge})
  Returns a new list L that consists of all entries from the lists L_L and L_R. If a node is represented in one list only (say by $e_L \in L_L$) then the embedding cost of the new entry is set to $embcost(e_L) + c_{edge}$. Otherwise, if there are entries $e_L \in L_L$, $e_R \in L_R$ such that $pre(e_L) = pre(e_R)$, then the embedding cost of the new entry is set to $\min(embcost(e_L), embcost(e_R)) + c_{edge}$.
function `sort`(n, L)
  Sorts L by the embedding cost of its entries. Returns the first n entries of L.

6.5 Finding the Best Root-Cost Pairs

Our general algorithm (see Figure 4) for the approximate query-matching problem makes use of the ideas presented in the previous subsections: It takes the expanded representation of an `approXQL` query as input, uses indexes to access the nodes of the data tree, and performs operations on lists to compute the embedding images recursively.

The algorithm expects as input a node u of an expanded query representation, a cost c_{edge} of the edge leading to u, and a list L_A of ancestors. The indexes I_{struct} and I_{text}, used by function `fetch`, are global parameters. Let u be the root of the expanded representation of a query and [ ] be an empty list. Then

$$\texttt{sort}(n, \texttt{primary}(u, 0, [\,]))$$

returns a cost-sorted list of the best n root-cost pairs.
  The depicted algorithm is simplified. It allows the deletion of *all* query leaves, which is forbidden by Definition 4. To keep at least one leaf, the full version of the algorithm rejects data subtrees that do not contain matches of any query leaf.

```
function primary(u, c_edge, L_A)
  case reptype(u) of
    leaf:  L_D ← fetch(label(u), type(u))
           foreach (l, c_ren) ∈ renamings(u) do
             L_T ← fetch(l, type(u))
             L_D ← merge(L_D, L_T, c_ren)
           return outerjoin(L_A, L_D, c_edge, delcost(u))
    node:  L_D ← fetch(label(u), type(u))
           L_D ← primary(child(u), 0, L_D)
           foreach (l, c_ren) ∈ renamings(u) do
             L_T ← fetch(l, type(u))
             L_T ← primary(child(u), 0, L_T)
             L_D ← merge(L_D, L_T, c_ren)
           if u has no parent then return L_D
           else return join(L_A, L_D, c_edge)
    and:   L_L ← primary(left_child(u), 0, L_A)
           L_R ← primary(right_child(u), 0, L_A)
           return intersect(L_L, L_R, c_edge)
    or:    L_L ← primary(left_child(u), 0, L_A)
           L_R ← primary(right_child(u), edgecost(u), L_A)
           return union(L_L, L_R, c_edge)
```

Fig. 4. Algorithm primary finds the images of all approximate embeddings of a query.

Furthermore, the full version uses dynamic programming to avoid the duplicate evaluation of query subtrees.

Let s be the maximal number of data nodes that have the same label and let l be the maximal number of repetitions of a label along a path in the data tree. The join functions need $O(s \cdot l)$ time; all other functions need $O(s)$ time. If n is the number of query selectors then the expanded representation has $O(n)$ nodes. The algorithm performs $O(n^2)$ node evaluations, each resulting in at most $O(r)$ function calls, where r is the maximal number of renamings per selector. The overall time complexity of algorithm primary is $O(n^2 \cdot r \cdot s \cdot l)$.

7 Schema-Driven Query Evaluation

The main disadvantage of the direct query evaluation is the fact that we must compute *all* approximate results for a query in order to retrieve the *best n*. To find *only* the best n results, we use the *schema* of the data tree to find the best k embedding images, which in turn are used as "second-level" queries to retrieve the results of the query in the data tree. The sorting of the second-level queries guarantees that the results of these queries are sorted by increasing cost as well.

7.1 On the Relationship between a Data Tree and Its Schema

In a data tree constructed from a collection of XML documents, many subtrees have a similar structure. A collection of sound storage media may contain several

CDs that all have a title, a composer, or both. Such data regularities can be captured by a *schema*. A schema is similar to a DataGuide [8].

Definition 13 (Label-type path). *A label-type path* $(l_1, t_1).(l_2, t_2)\ldots(l_n, t_n)$ *in a tree is a sequence of label-type pairs belonging to the nodes along a node-edge path that starts at the tree root.*

Definition 14 (Schema). *The schema of a data tree is a tree that contains every label-type path of the data tree exactly once.*

In practice we use *compacted schemata* where sequences of text nodes are merged into a single node and the labels are not stored in the tree but only in the indexes.

Definition 15 (Node class). *A schema node u is the class of a data node v, denoted by $u = [v]$, iff u and v are reachable by the same label-type path.*

Node v is called an *instance* of u. Every data node v has exactly one class. Node classes preserve the parent-child relationships of their instances. For each triple u, v, w of data nodes holds:

$$v \text{ is a child of } u \Leftrightarrow [v] \text{ is a child of } [u]$$
$$v \text{ and } w \text{ are children of } u \Rightarrow [v] \text{ and } [w] \text{ are children of } [u]$$

Note that the last proposition is an implication: There are node classes that have a common parent in the schema – but no combination of their instances has a common parent in the data tree.

We have seen that the mapping between node instances and their class is a function. A node class preserves the labels, the types, and the parent-child relationships of its instances. The same properties hold for embeddings. We can therefore establish a simple relationship between a data tree, its schema, and their included trees (i. e., subgraphs of trees that fulfill the tree properties):

Definition 16 (Tree class). *Let T be an included tree of a data tree. The image of an embedding of T in the schema is called tree class of T.*

Every included data tree has exactly one tree class, which follows from Definition 14. Embeddings are transitive because all three properties of Definition 1 are transitive. The existence of tree classes and the transitivity of embeddings have an interesting implication: If we have an algorithm that finds the images of all approximate embeddings of a query in the data tree then we can use the same algorithm to find all tree classes of embeddings in the schema of the data tree. We present an adapted version of algorithm `primary` in the following subsection.

Not every included schema tree T is a tree class. It is a tree class only if there are "reverse embeddings" from T into the data tree such that each embedding result contains an instance of T directly. Each result found this way is an approximate result of the query. In Section 7.3, we present an algorithm `secondary` that uses the embedding images found by algorithm `primary` as "second-level" queries to find the results of the original query.

7.2 Finding the Best k Second-Level Queries

The selection of the best k second-level queries using a schema is a straightforward extension of the direct query-evaluation algorithm introduced in Section 6. There, we have tracked the best embedding cost per query subtree and per *data* subtree. Now we track the *images* of the *best k embeddings* (and their costs) per query subtree and per *schema* subtree. We extend the list entries by a value *label* and a set *pointers* yielding the following structure:

$$e = (pre, bound, pathcost, inscost, embcost, label, pointers).$$

The component *label* is initialized by the label of the matching query node; the set *pointers* contains references to descendants of the schema node represented by e. If e represents an embedding root then e and the entries reachable from the pointer set form a second-level query with the embedding cost $embcost(e)$.

To find not only the best second-level query per schema subtree but the best k ones, we use list *segments*. Recall that lists are sorted by the preorder numbers of the list entries. A segment is a sequence of list entries that have the same preorder number but different embedding costs. All entries of a fixed segment represent embedding images of the *same* query subtree in the *same* schema subtree. Segments are sorted by embedding cost in ascending order. The prefix of k entries of a segment represents the best k embeddings of a certain query subtree in a certain schema subtree. To find the best k second-level queries, only four functions of algorithm `primary` must be adapted:

function $\texttt{join}(L_A, L_D, c_{edge}, k)$
  Returns a new list L. Let $e_A \in L_A$ be an entry. The function calculates the embedding cost of e_A with respect to all entries in all segments in L_D that represent descendants of e_A. For each entry e_D among the k descendants with the lowest costs, a copy of e_A is appended to L. The embedding cost of the copy is set to $distance(e_A, e_D) + embcost(e_D) + c_{edge}$ and its pointer set is initialized with e_D.

function $\texttt{outerjoin}(L_A, L_D, c_{edge}, c_{del}, k)$
  Works like the `join` function but additionally calculates the embedding cost $c = c_{edge} + c_{del}$ of each entry $e_A \in L_A$ that does not have a descendant in L_D. If c is among the lowest k embedding costs in the segment generated for e_A then a copy of e_A is appended to L such that the segment for e_A remains sorted. The embedding cost of the new entry is set to c and its pointer set remains empty.

function $\texttt{intersect}(L_L, L_R, c_{edge}, k)$
  Returns a new list L. Let S_L and S_R be segments in L_L and L_R, respectively, that represent the same schema node. The function chooses from both segments the k pairs with the smallest sum of the embedding costs. For each pair (e_L, e_R), a copy of e_L is appended to L. Its embedding cost is set to $embcost(e_L) + embcost(e_R) + c_{edge}$ and its pointer set is initialized with $pointers(e_L) \cup pointers(e_R)$.

function $\texttt{union}(L_L, L_R, c_{edge}, k)$
  Returns a new list L. Let S_L and S_R be segments in L_L and L_R, respectively, that represent the same schema node. The function merges S_L and S_R and copies the prefix of the best k entries to the end of L. If S_L (S_R) does not have a corresponding segment then a copy of S_L (S_R) is appended to L. The embedding cost of each entry appended to L is increased by c_{edge}.

The algorithm `primary` also takes an additional parameter k and passes it to the four modified functions. If u is the root of an expanded query representation and I_{text}, I_{struct} are the indexes of a schema, then

$$\text{sort}(k, \text{primary}(u, 0, [\,], k))$$

returns the best k second-level queries for the original query.

7.3 Finding the Results of a Second-Level Query

The adapted version of algorithm `primary` returns a list of second-level queries sorted by embedding cost. Using an algorithm `secondary`, each second-level query must be executed against the data tree in order to find all approximate results for the original query.

As a slight difference to the theoretical setting in Section 7.1, algorithm `primary` does not return embedding images but "skeletons" of embedding images that do not represent the inserted nodes (because the cost of the nodes to insert has been derived from the encoding of the schema). Fortunately, it is not necessary to know the nodes inserted implicitly between two skeleton nodes u and v since all pairs of instances of u and v have by definition the same distance as u and v (see Section 7.1).

To find all instances of a schema node, we propose *path dependent postings*. A path dependent posting is a sorted list that contains all node instances of a certain schema node, represented as preorder-bound pairs. A *secondary index* I_{sec} maps the nodes of the schema to their postings. A key for I_{sec} is constructed by concatenating the preorder number of a node of a second-level query (which represents a schema node) and the label of the query node: $pre(u)\#label(u)$. Figure 5 shows a simple algorithm that finds all exact embeddings of a second-level query (represented by e_A) in a data tree.

---

function secondary(e_A)
  $L_A \leftarrow I_{sec}(pre(e_A)\#label(e_A))$
  foreach e_D in $pointers(e_A)$ **do**
    $L_D \leftarrow$ secondary(e_D)
    $L_T \leftarrow [\,]$
    foreach data node u in L_A **do**
      if u has a descendant in L_D **then**
        add u to L_T
    $L_A \leftarrow L_T$
  return L_A

Fig. 5. The function finds all exact results for a second-level query.

$L_R \leftarrow [\,]$; $k_{prev} \leftarrow 0$
while $|L_R| < n$ **do**
  $L_P \leftarrow \text{sort}(k, \text{primary}(u, 0, [\,], k))$
  erase the first k_{prev} entries from L_P
  $k_{prev} \leftarrow k$; $k \leftarrow k + \delta$
  foreach $e_P \in L_P$ **do**
    $L_S \leftarrow$ secondary(e_P)
    foreach data node u in L_S **do**
      if $pre(u)$ is not in L_R **then**
        add $(pre(u), embcost(e_P))$ to L_R

Fig. 6. An incremental algorithm for the best-n-pairs problem.

7.4 An Incremental Algorithm for the Best-n-Pairs Problem

So far, we have seen how to find the best k second-level queries and how to find all results for each second-level query. However, we are interested in the *best n results* for a query. Unfortunately, there is no strong correlation between k and n; some second-level queries may retrieve many results, some may not return any result at all. Therefore, a good intial guess of k is cruical and k must be incremented by δ if the first k second-level queries do not retrieve enough results. Fortunately, the increase of k does not invalidate the previous results: The list L_P returned by algorithm `primary` for a certain k is a prefix of the list L'_P returned for a $k' > k$. Our incremental algorithm, depicted in Figure 6, erases at each step the prefix of all second-level queries that have already been evaluated.

Recall from Section 6 that the time complexity of all functions used by algorithm `primary` is bound by $O(s \cdot l)$, where s is the selectivity and l is recursivity of the data tree. In the following, we use the letters s_s to denote the selectivity in the schema and s_d to denote the maximal number of instances of a node class. The time complexity of the functions adapted in Section 7.2 rises by the factor $k^2 \cdot \log k$, which is the time needed to compute sorted segments of size k. Therefore, the time needed to generate k second-level queries is $O(n^2 \cdot r \cdot s_s \cdot l \cdot k^2 \cdot \log k)$. The evaluation time of k second-level queries is $O(s_d \cdot m)$, where m is the number of nodes of a second-level query.

8 Experiments

In this section, we present selected (but typical) results of the experiments we have carried out to evaluate the efficiency of our algorithms.

8.1 Test Settings

In order to have a high level of control over the characteristics of the data used in our experiments, we employed the XML data generator described in [1]. We varied several parameters of the generator (e.g., the number of elements per document, the total number of terms, and the distribution of terms) and tested our algorithms using the data created for those parameters. Here, we exemplarily present the results of a single test series: We use a document collection that consists of 1,000,000 elements, 100,000 terms, and 10,000,000 term occurrences (words). There are 100 different element names so that on average 10,000 elements share the same name. The words follow a Zipfian frequency distribution.

All queries used in our experiments are produced by a simple generator for approXQL queries. The generator expects a query pattern that determines the structure of the query. A query pattern consists of templates and operators. The query generator produces approXQL queries by filling in the templates with names and terms randomly selected from the indexes of the data tree. For each produced query, the generator also creates a file that contains the insert costs, the delete costs, and the renamings of the query selectors. The labels used for renamings are selected randomly from the indexes. From the set of tested query patterns we exemplarily choose three patterns that represent a "simple path query", a "small Boolean query", and a "large Boolean query", respectively:

query pattern 1	name[name[name[term]]]
query pattern 2	name[name[term and (term or term)]]
query pattern 3	name[name[name[term and term and (term or term)] or name[name[term and term]]] and name]

For each query pattern and each collection, we created three sets of queries. The sets differ in the number of renamings $(0, 5, 10)$ per query label. Each set contains 10 queries.

All tests have been carried out on a 450 MHz Pentium III with 256 MB of memory, running Linux. Our system is implemented in C++ on top of the Berkeley DB [4].

8.2 Test Results

Our tests results show that the schema-driven query evaluation is faster than the direct evaluation if n, the number of results, is small. For some queries the schema-based algorithm is faster even if all results are requested ($n = \infty$).

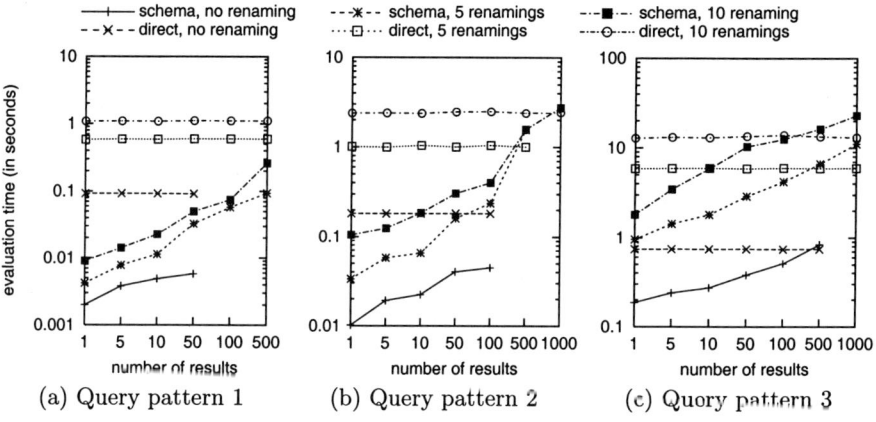

Fig. 7. Evaluation times of the three query patterns.

Each diagram depicted in Figure 7 shows the evaluation time of a query pattern with respect to different numbers of renamings per node and with respect to the schema-based algorithm (labeled "schema") and the direct algorithm ("direct"). Any point in the diagrams is the mean of the evaluation time of 10 queries randomly generated for the same pattern. Note that the y-axis has logarithmic scale. Figure 7(a) shows the evaluation time of the path query. The schema-based query evaluation outperforms the direct evaluation in all cases – even if no renamings are permitted. This is due to the facts that all second-level queries generated by the algorithm primary have at least one embedding in the data tree (each second-level query is a label-type path) and that the postings of the secondary index are much shorter than the postings of I_{struct} and I_{text}. Figure 7(b) displays the evaluation times of the small Boolean query. The diagrams show that the execution time of the schema-based algorithm rises slightly. The reason is that some generated queries may find no results and thus, a larger k must be chosen. However, for small values of n, the schema-based algorithm is always faster than the algorithm for direct evaluation. The larger size of query pattern 3 again increases the average execution times of the algorithms, particularly if 10 renamings per node must be tested (see Figure 7(c)). For small values of n and few renamings, however, the schema-driven algorithm is still fast and outperforms the direct evaluation.

9 Conclusion

In this paper, we introduced an approach to find approximate results for tree-pattern queries using cost-based query transformations. By adjusting the costs of the transformations, our model can be adapted to different types of XML documents. However, the development of domain-specific rules for choosing basic transformation costs is a topic of future research.

We presented and compared two polynomial-time algorithms that retrieve the best n results for a query. We have shown that the schema-driven query-evaluation outperforms the direct evaluation if n is smaller than the total number of results. A further advantage of the schema-based approach is the incremental retrieval: Once the best k second-level queries have been generated, they can be evaluated successively, and the results can be sent immediately to the user.

More details about the schema-driven evaluation of approXQL queries can be found in the extended version [13] of this paper.

References

1. A. Aboulnaga, J.F. Naughton, and C. Zhang. Generating synthetic complex-structured XML data. In *Proceedings of WebDB'01*, 2001.
2. A. Apostolico and Z. Galil, editors. *Pattern Matching Algorithms*, Chapter 14: Approximate Tree Pattern Matching. Oxford University Press, 1997.
3. R. Baeza-Yates and B. Ribeiro-Neto. *Modern Information Retrieval*. Addison Wesley Longman, 1999.
4. The Berkeley DB. Sleepycat Software Inc., 2000. http://www.sleepycat.com.
5. A. Bonifati and S. Ceri. Comparative analysis of five XML query languages. *SIGMOD Record*, 29(1), 2000.
6. T.T. Chinenyanga and N. Kushmerick. Expressive retrieval from XML documents. In *Proceedings of SIGIR*, 2001.
7. N. Fuhr and K. Großjohann. XIRQL: A query language for information retrieval in XML documents. In *Proceedings of SIGIR*, 2001.

8. R. Goldman and J. Widom. DataGuides: Enabling query formulation and optimization in semistructured data. In *Proceedings of VLDB*, 1997.
9. T. Jiang, L. Wang, and K. Zhang. Alignment of trees - an alternative to tree edit. In *Proceedings of Combinatorial Pattern Matching*, 1994.
10. P. Kilpeläinen. *Tree Matching Problems with Applications to Structured Text Databases*. PhD thesis, University of Helsinki, Finland, 1992.
11. J. Robie, J. Lapp, and D. Schach. XML query language (XQL), 1998. http://www.w3.org/TandS/QL/QL98/pp/xql.html.
12. T. Schlieder. ApproXQL: Design and implementation of an approximate pattern matching language for XML. Report B 01-02, Freie Universität Berlin, 2001.
13. T. Schlieder. Schema-driven evaluation of ApproXQL queries. Report B 02-01, Freie Universität Berlin, 2002.
14. K.-C. Tai. The tree-to-tree correction problem. *Journal of the ACM*, 26(3):422–433, 1979.
15. A. Theobald and G. Weikum. Adding relevance to XML. In *Proceedings of WebDB'00*, 2000.
16. K. Zhang. A new editing based distance between unordered labeled trees. In *Proceedings of Combinatorial Pattern Matching*, 1993.

A Robust and Self-tuning Page-Replacement Strategy for Spatial Database Systems

Thomas Brinkhoff

Institute for Applied Photogrammetry and Geoinformatics (IAPG)
Fachhochschule Oldenburg/Ostfriesland/Wilhelmshaven
(University of Applied Sciences)
Ofener Str. 16/19, D-26121 Oldenburg, Germany
tbrinkhoff@acm.org

Abstract. For a spatial database management system, it is an important goal to minimize the I/O-cost of queries and other operations. Several page-replacement strategies have been proposed and compared for standard database systems. In the context of spatial database systems, however, the impact of buffing techniques has not been considered in detail, yet. In this paper, different page-replacement algorithms are compared for performing spatial queries. This study includes well-known techniques like LRU and LRU-K as well as new algorithms observing spatial optimization criteria. Experiments show that *spatial page-replacement algorithms* outperform LRU buffers for many distributions, but not for all investigated query sets. Therefore, a combination of spatial page-replacement strategies with LRU strategies is proposed and experimentally investigated. An algorithm is presented, which is self-tuning and adapts itself to different or changing query distributions. This *adaptable spatial buffer* outperforms LRU in respect to the I/O-cost by performance gains of up to 25%.

1 Introduction

Considering today's computers, it can be observed that the speed of the CPU and the size of the main memory are still dramatically increasing. In addition, spatial applications have become more sophisticated and the amount of spatial data as well as of nonspatial data demanded by them seems to grow with the size of available main memory. However, the time to access a randomly chosen page stored on a hard disk requires still about 10 ms [7]. As a result, the gap between CPU speed and size of main memory on the one hand and I/O-cost on the other hand has increased considerably with the consequence that the access to secondary storage is still a bottleneck for executing spatial queries and other operations. Several techniques are commonly used in order to optimize the I/O-performance of database systems. Among these methods, one technique is of special interest in context of this paper: the buffering of data.

A *buffer manager* caches a disk page, which has been read from secondary storage before. For a further request, such a page can be taken from main memory instead of reading it from disk. Essential for the performance gain of a buffer is to keep pages in main memory that are frequently requested. Pages no longer needed should be dropped out of the buffer as soon as possible. Therefore, the essential question is which page should be removed from the buffer when a new page is read from secondary storage. The most common *replacement strategy* is *LRU* (least recently used): the LRU buffering policy replaces the page that has not been accessed for the longest time. However, the LRU policy has essential drawbacks: for example, it is not able to distinguish between pages that are accessed with a relatively high frequency over a longer period and pages which are requested infrequently over a long time but more frequently over a short period.

For standard database systems, many page-replacement algorithms have been proposed and investigated in literature (e.g. [3], [4], [9], [10]). An overview is given in [6]. In the area of spatial database systems, the effect of other page-replacement strategies than LRU has not been investigated, yet. Leutenegger and Lopez showed in their paper [8] the importance of a buffer for measuring the I/O-cost of R-trees [5]. Based on their buffer model, they especially demonstrated the effect of pinning top levels of an R-tree in the buffer.

In this paper, existing algorithms as well as new replacement strategies are presented and investigated in respect to their performance for different spatial queries and buffer sizes. First, the buffers considered in this paper are variants of the LRU buffer that use the type or the level of pages for improving the replacement. Besides, the *LRU-K page-replacement algorithm* by O'Neil, O'Neil, and Weikum [10] is considered. In addition, a new type of replacement algorithms – *spatial page-replacement algorithms* – is presented. These try to determine hot spots and candidates to be dropped out of the buffer according to the spatial properties of the pages. The experiments in this paper will show that such spatial page-replacement algorithms outperform LRU buffers for many distributions, but not for all investigated query sets. Therefore, a combination of spatial page-replacement strategies with LRU strategies is proposed. This algorithm divides the buffer into two parts managed by different page-replacement algorithms.

One essential objective is to minimize the effort of administration. Therefore, it is important that a buffer is self-tuning and adapts itself to the characteristics of the data stored in the database and to the type and sequence of the processed queries without human intervention. In case of the combination of spatial page-replacement strategies with LRU strategies, the division of the buffer into two parts must be automatically adapted to the current query profile. For this purpose, an algorithm will be proposed that changes the division according to the properties of the pages that are found in a special section of the buffer. This type of buffer will be called *adapting spatial buffer*.

Section 2 presents the basic page-replacement strategies investigated in this paper. Especially, spatial page-replacement algorithms are proposed. A performance evaluation follows in the third section. After presenting the data and query sets of the experiments, the results of the tests using different categories of page-replacement algorithms are presented. Section 4 presents a self-tuning and robust combination of spatial page-replacement strategies with LRU strategies. The experiments show that this combination improves the performance of spatial queries by up to 25% compared to LRU without the drawbacks of pure spatial page-replacement algorithms and without increasing the memory requirements. The paper concludes with a summary of the most important findings and an outlook to future work.

2 Page-Replacement Algorithms

Since the LRU policy has essential drawbacks, different page-replacement algorithms suitable for spatial database systems are presented in this section. The presentation starts with a type-based and a priority-based LRU page-replacement policy. Then, the LRU-K page-replacement algorithm is presented. Finally, spatial page-replacement algorithms are proposed.

2.1 Type-Based and Priority-Based LRU

For an LRU buffer, all (non-fixed) pages have the same type. Therefore, the only selection criterion is the time of the last access. If the buffer knows the type of a page, this information may be used for deciding if it is a suitable candidate to be dropped out of the buffer. For pages stored in a spatial database system, we typically distinguish three categories of pages: directory pages and data pages of the *spatial access method (SAM)* as well as object pages storing the exact representation of spatial objects (see e.g. [2]). Using a *type-based LRU (LRU-T)*, object pages would be dropped immediately from the buffer. Then, data pages would follow. Directory pages would be stored in the buffer as long as possible because it is assumed that they are more often required than data or object pages. For pages of the same category, the LRU strategy is used for determining the page to be removed.

A generalization of this approach is a *priority-based LRU strategy (LRU-P)*. In this case, each page has a priority: the higher the priority of a page, the longer it should stay in the buffer. For example, the object page may have the priority 0 whereas the priority of a page in an index depends on its height in the corresponding tree, if a tree-based spatial access method is used. The root has the highest priority. Such an approach is a generalization of a buffer that pins distinct levels of the SAM [8]. Figure 1 illustrates LRU-T and LRU-P.

2.2 The LRU-K Page-Replacement Algorithm

In order to improve the replacement strategy, several solutions have been suggested in the literature. A typical representative of a replacement algorithm determining the next page to be replaced only by recording and analyzing the access history is the *LRU-K page-replacement algorithm* by O'Neil, O'Neil, and Weikum [10].

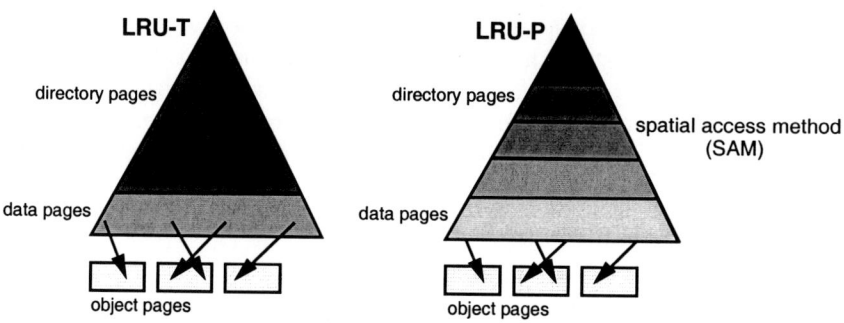

Fig. 1. Categories of pages; the darker a page, the higher its priority

For recording the history, the LRU-K algorithm requires an additional data structure called $HIST$[1]: $HIST(p)$ contains the time stamps of the K most recent references to a page p; $HIST(p, 1)$ denotes the time stamp of the last reference, $HIST(p, 2)$ the time stamp of the last reference before $HIST(p, 1)$, and so on. The authors observed that it is typical that a page is often accessed immediately after it has been accessed before. Therefore, $HIST(p)$ does contain only the last access of a sequence of correlated accesses. In order to decide whether accesses are correlated or not, an additional data structure may be necessary. In the following, two page accesses will be regarded as correlated if they belong to the same query.

A query typically requests several pages from the buffer. If a page p is requested, three cases may occur:

- Page p is in the buffer and the current access and the most recent reference to p are correlated: $HIST(p, 1)$ gets the value of the current time.
- Page p is in the buffer and the current access and the most recent reference to p are not correlated: The value of the current time is added to $HIST(p)$ as new $HIST(p, 1)$.
- Page p is not in the buffer: Among the pages in the buffer whose most recent reference to p is not correlated to the access to p, the page q with the oldest value of $HIST(q,k)$ is determined. The page q is removed from the buffer and the value of the current time is added to $HIST(p)$ as new $HIST(p, 1)$[2].

The usage of $HIST(q,k)$ allows determining which pages are frequently requested over a short period but infrequently used over a long time. For maintaining $HIST$, an LRUK buffer typically requires more memory than a standard LRU buffer. For the case that a page that was dropped out of the buffer before is reloaded into the buffer, the information of $HIST$ collected previously for this page should be available, i.e. the history information $HIST$ must also be stored (in main memory) for pages which have left the buffer. This is an essential disadvantage.

---

[1] The definition given here slightly differs from the definition in the original paper. The functionality, however, is the same.

[2] Some special cases may occur in this situation that are not discussed here.

Therefore, the memory requirements of LRUK buffers are not only determined by the number of pages in the buffer but also by the total number of requested pages. The space requirements of the history information of one page are quite low, but the number of such records can be become rather high. This number corresponds to the number of pages stored in the buffer during its lifetime.

The investigations in the original paper demonstrated for a standard database system that the LRU-K page-replacement strategy is worthwhile for rather small values of K.

2.3 Spatial Page-Replacement Algorithms

The LRU-K page replacement does not have any knowledge about the type or content of the stored pages. The priority-based LRU buffer uses the type of a page or some other structural properties of a page for performing a (pre-) selection. However, in a spatial database it may be reasonable to analyze also the content of pages for selecting the page that should be removed from the buffer. Spatial access methods optimize their structure according to different optimization criteria. Beckmann et al. proposed four criteria for the design of an R*-tree [1]:

(O1) Minimizing the area of a directory rectangle.
(O2) Minimizing the overlap between directory rectangles.
(O3) Minimizing the margin of a directory rectangle.
(O4) Maximizing the storage utilization.

The criteria (O1) to (O3) are spatial criteria, which can be applied for designing a *spatial page-replacement strategy*.

It will be assumed in the following that a page p in a spatial database system contains a set of entries $e_i \in p$. For each of these entries, a *minimum bounding rectangle (MBR)* can be determined. For an object page, the entries may correspond to the spatial objects (or parts of them) stored in the page. For a data or directory page of an R-tree [5], these entries are the rectangles stored in the pages. In a quadtree [13], the quadtree cells match these entries. The same holds for z-values stored in a B-tree [11].

Maximizing the Area of a Page (A)
The optimization goal (O1) was to minimize the area of a (directory) page. The larger its area, the more frequently the page is assumed to be requested. That means that a page having a large area should stay in the buffer as long as possible. In other words, the (non-fixed) page with the smallest area is the first page to be dropped out of the buffer. The area of a page p is defined as the area of the MBR containing all entries of p.

Formally, a spatial page-replacement algorithm requires a function spatialCrit(p) computing the corresponding spatial criterion of a page p. In case of the variant A, this function is defined by the area of the MBR containing all entries of the page:

$$\text{spatialCrit}_A(p) = \text{area}(\text{mbr}(\{e | (e \in p)\}))$$

If a page d_p must be dropped out of the buffer, this page is determined as follows:
1. $C := \{p | p \in \text{buffer} \wedge (q \in \text{buffer} \Rightarrow SpatialCrit(p) \leq SpatialCrit(q))\}$
2. if $|C| > 1$ then : $d_p \in C$ is determined by using the LRU strategy
   else: d_p is the only element of C

Maximizing the Area of the Entries of a Page (EA)

The strategy EA is also based on the optimization goal (O1). Instead of the area of a page, the sum of the areas of its entries is maximized. This sum is not normalized to the number of entries. That means that also optimization goal (O4) is considered by this algorithm. For directory pages of SAMs partitioning the data space completely and without overlap, the algorithms A and EA behave identically. The function spatialCrit$_{\text{EA}}(p)$ is defined as follows:

$$\text{spatialCrit}_{\text{EA}}(p) = \sum_{e \in p} \text{area}(\text{mbr}(e))$$

Maximizing the Margin of a Page (M)

According to optimization goal (O3), the margin of a page is maximized. The larger its margin, the longer a page will stay in the buffer. The margin of a page p will be defined as the margin of the MBR containing all entries of p. The function spatialCrit$_{\text{M}}(p)$ is defined as follows:

$$\text{spatialCrit}_{\text{M}}(p) = \text{margin}(\text{mbr}(\{e | e \in p\}))$$

Maximizing the Margin of the Entries of a Page (EM)

This strategy is similar to the previous algorithm. Instead of the margin of the page, the sum of the margins of its entries is maximized. As for EA, this sum is not normalized to the number of entries. The function spatialCrit$_{\text{EM}}(p)$ is defined as follows:

$$\text{spatialCrit}_{\text{EM}}(p) = \sum_{e \in p} \text{margin}(\text{mbr}(e))$$

Maximizing the Overlap between the Entries of a Page (EO)

The fifth spatial page-replacement algorithm tries to maximize the overlap between the entries of a page. This overlap is the sum of the intersection areas of all pairs of entries whose MBRs overlap. For directory pages of spatial access methods, which partition the data space without overlap, this algorithm should not be applied. The function spatialCrit$_{\text{EO}}(p)$ is defined as follows:

$$\text{spatialCrit}_{\text{EO}}(p) = \sum_{e \in p, f \in p, e \neq f} \frac{\text{area}(\text{mbr}(e) \cap \text{mbr}(f))}{2}$$

The area and the margin of a page or of its entries can be computed causing only a small overhead when a new page is loaded into the buffer. The computation of

A Self-tuning Page-Replacement Strategy for Spatial Database Systems

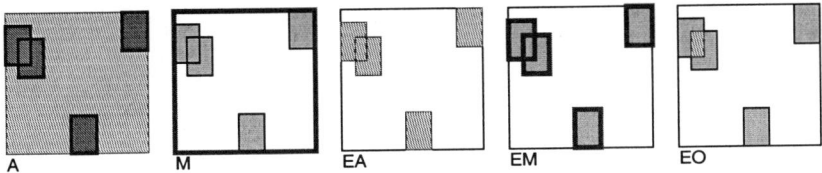

Fig. 2. Illustration of the criteria of the different spatial page-replacement strategies

the overlap of the entries of a page is costlier – storing this information on the page may be worthwhile for this variant of a spatial page-replacement algorithm.

Figure 2 depicts the criteria of the five spatial page-replacement algorithms. The hatched areas and the bold boundaries illustrate the criterion of the respective strategy.

3 Performance Evaluation

The primary spatial database used in the following tests consists of geographical features of the mainland of the USA. These data originate from the USGS Mapping Information System (GNIS) (http://mapping.usgs.gov/www/gnis/) like the data sets of the SEQUOIA 2000 storage benchmark [14]. The data set consists of 1,641,079 points and extended spatial objects. The objects are managed by an R*-tree [1]. The maximum number of entries per directory page and per data page is 51 and 42, respectively. The R*-tree consists of 58,405 pages (thereof 1,660 directory pages = 2.84%) and has height 4. The pages of the spatial objects are stored in separate files and buffers. Only the pages accesses concerning the trees are reported in the following. A second database is used for validating the results of the experiments using database 1. It consists of the line and area features of a world atlas [12]. The data set comprises 244,472 polygons and 328,222 lines. The R*-tree managing these objects consists of 20,884 data pages and 617 directory pages (2.87%). Figure 3 illustrates the databases.

The size of the buffers in the following experiments are determined in respect to the size of the data sets ranging from 0.3% to 4.7%. Because of using relative buffer sizes, the results of the experiments should hold for the case of larger databases and buffers. For assessing the size of a buffer, the reader must also consider that the main memory of a database server is not only used for buffering pages of a single spatial data set.

Before performing a new set of queries, the buffer was cleared in order to increase the comparability of the results. For the same reason, only the relative performance will be reported in this paper. The tables containing the absolute number of disk accesses and other figures can be downloaded from http://www.geodbs.de/buffer.html. The reader will find there also the data sets and the query sets used by the following experiments.

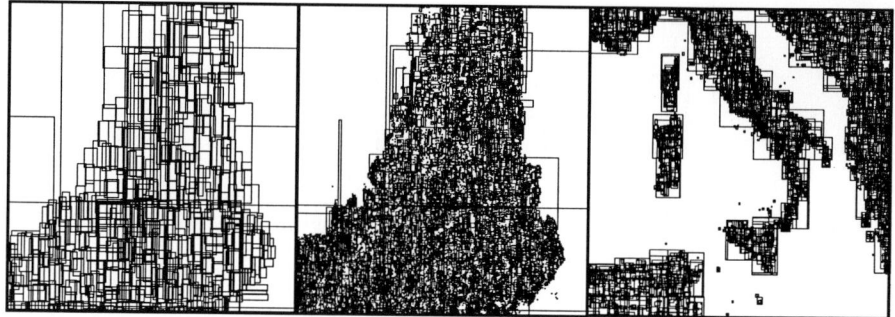

Fig. 3. The MBRs of a part of database 1 (area of Maine), the respective directory regions of the lowest level of the R*-tree, and the MBRs of a part of database 2 (area of Italy)

3.1 The Query Sets

A further ingredient of an experiment is the set of queries. For a systematic investigation of a page-replacement strategy, query sets obeying different data distributions are required. Unfortunately, no benchmark for spatial databases offers a suitable set of queries. The following distributions try to cover a wide range of spatial query profiles.

Uniform Distribution
The query sets *U-P* and *U-W-ex* consist of uniformly distributed query points and windows for performing point queries and window queries, respectively. *ex* denotes the reciprocal value of the extension of the query windows in one dimension; in the set *UW-33*, the x-extension of a query window is 1/33 of the x-extension of the data space. Other values for *ex* in the experiments are 100, 333, and 1000. The query objects cover also the parts of the data space where no objects are stored.

Identical Distribution
The query sets *ID-P* and *ID-W* consist of a random selection of objects stored in the database. For the window queries, the size of the objects is maintained. The distribution of the queries is the same as the distribution of the objects in the database.

Similar Distribution
In the case of similar distributions, there exists a dependency between the distribution of the query objects and the database objects. This typically happens when two layers of a map are combined with some functional dependencies between them. The query sets *S-P* and *S-W-ex* were computed by randomly selecting US cities and towns from a file containing all US places. This file originates also from the USGS Mapping Information System.

Intensified Distribution

For the intensified distribution, the probability of selecting a city from the same file that was already used for the similar distribution is correlated to the square root of the population of the city. These query sets are denoted by *INT-P* and *INT-W-ex*.

Independent Distribution

In this case, the distributions of the database objects and of the query objects are independent from each other. These query sets were constructed using like the sets *S-P* and *S-W-ex* after flipping the x-coordinates of the spatial objects, i.e. an object lying in the west of the map retrieves an area in the east of the database and vice versa. These query sets are denoted by IND-P and IND-W-ex.

The number of queries per query set was set a value, so that the number of disk accesses was about 10 to 20 times higher than the buffer size in the case of the largest buffer investigated. For smaller buffers, this factor increases.

3.2 Type-Based and Priority-Based LRU

A performance comparison between the type-based and the priority-based LRU buffer (LRU-T and LRU-P) has shown no differences between both approaches in the case of larger buffers. Then, all or most of the directory pages are kept in main memory. Using small buffer sizes, LRU-P has beaten LRU-T for all investigated query sets.

The diagrams in Figure 4 show the performance gains using LRU-P. The results for the primary database are shown in the upper diagrams and for the second database in the lower diagrams. The left diagrams depict the results for performing uniformly distributed queries and the right diagrams of queries according to the intensified distribution. The performance gain is given in percent compared to using a standard LRU buffer (defined by |disk accesses of LRU|/|disk accesses of LRU-P| − 1).

The performance impact depends on the buffer size as well as on the size of the query regions. The largest performance gains are achieved for small buffers performing window queries of medium (and sometimes of small) size. In the case of database 1 using large buffers and small query windows (or point queries), the performance has not been improved. Instead, it has been worse compared to using a standard LRU buffer. An explanation of the good performance for small buffers is that it is important to store the upper levels of the R*-tree in the buffer. Is observation corresponds to the results of the work of Leutenegger and Lopez [8]. However, if the buffer becomes larger it will be possible to store the lower levels of the index. Then, the height of a page in the tree becomes less important for indicating its residence time in the buffer.

3.3 LRU-K Buffers

In this subsection, the impact of using LRU-K buffers on the query performance will be investigated. In [10], the usage of LRU-2 showed a significant improvement

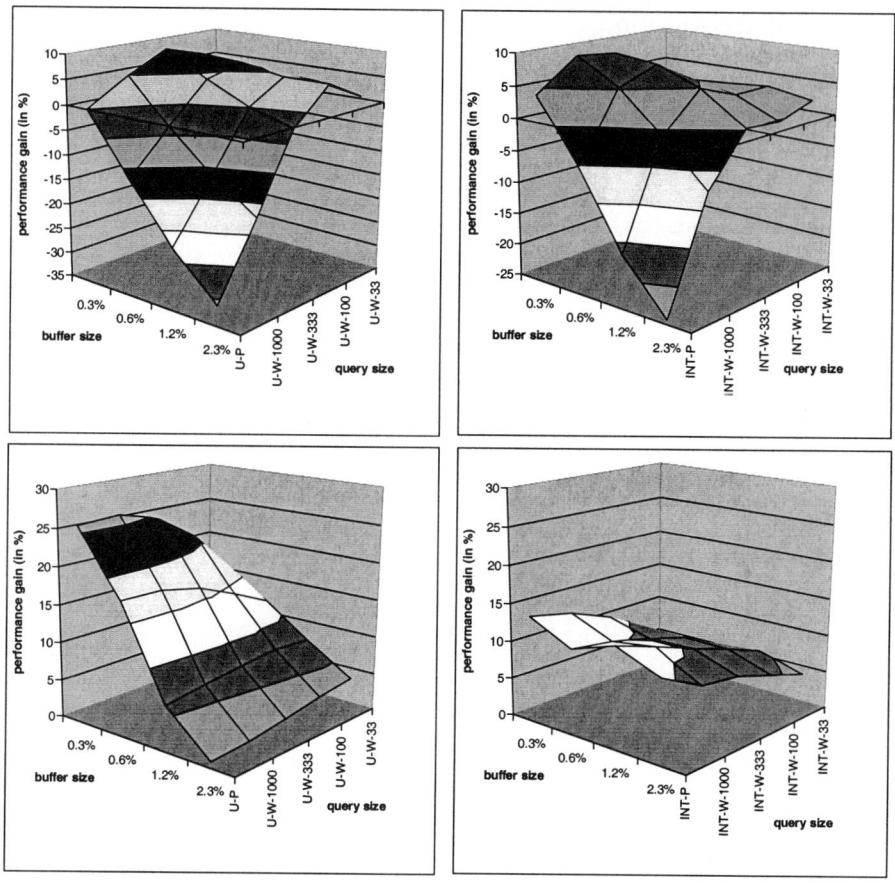

Fig. 4. Performance gain of LRU-P compared to LRU using database 1 (upper diagrams) and database 2 (lower diagrams)

compared to a standard LRU buffer whereas using LRU-3 had almost no impact compared to LRU-2. Figure 5 depicts the performance gains of using LRU-2, LRU-3, and LRU-5 buffers compared to an LRU buffer.

Especially for point queries and small and medium window queries, considerable performance gains are attained. Performance gains of 15% to 25% are achieved by using LRU-2. However, for large window queries, almost no improvement can be observed. In one case (*U-W-33*; 4.7% buffer), the performance is actually decreased. Surprisingly, the performance differences between the different types of query sets are not significant. The LRU-K buffer is not especially suitable – for example – for processing the intensified query sets. Like in [10], no significant difference between the performance of LRU-2, of LRU-3, and of LRU-5 can be observed. Therefore, LRU-2 is used as the representative for the comparison in Section 3.5.

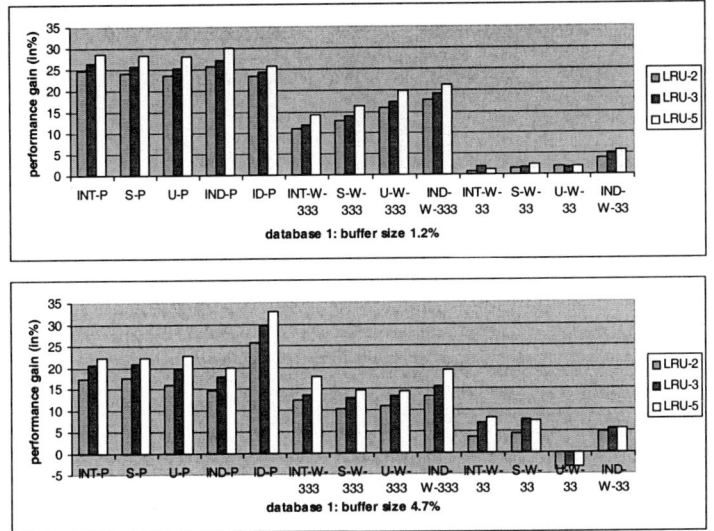

Fig. 5. Performance gain using LRU-K compared to LRU for the primary database

3.4 Spatial Page-Replacement Algorithms

Now, the best spatial page-replacement strategy will be determined. Figure 6 depicts two diagrams representing the relative number of disk accesses. For each query set, the number of disk accesses required by using replacement criterion A is taken as 100%. For the other strategies, the number of accesses in comparison to this base is depicted in percent.

For the test series using a 0.3% buffer, the criterion page area (A) shows the best performance whereas the algorithm that uses the overlap between the entries (EO) has the worst performance. In the experiments using the larger buffer (4.7%), the algorithms A and M have about the same performance and EA, EM and EO lose the competition more clearly.

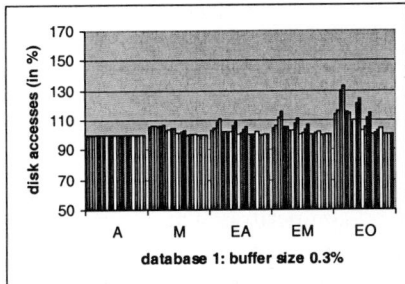 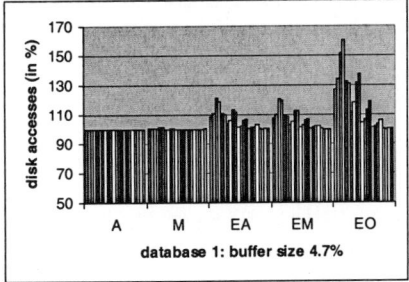

Fig. 6. Comparison of the performance of the different spatial replacement algorithms

Taking these results and the fact that the area of a page can be determined without noticeable overhead, the algorithm maximizing the area of a page (A) is taken in the following comparisons as the representative of the spatial page-replacement strategy.

3.5 Comparison of the Different Types of Page-Replacement Algorithms

In this section, the different types of page-replacement algorithms are investigated. The algorithms LRU-P, A, and LRU-2 are compared to the standard LRU strategy. The results for both databases are presented.

3.5.1 Uniform Distribution

Figure 7 depicts the relative performance gains of the three algorithms using a uniform distribution of queries and a buffer size of 0.6% and of 4.7%. The left diagrams show the results for the primary database and the right diagrams for database 2.

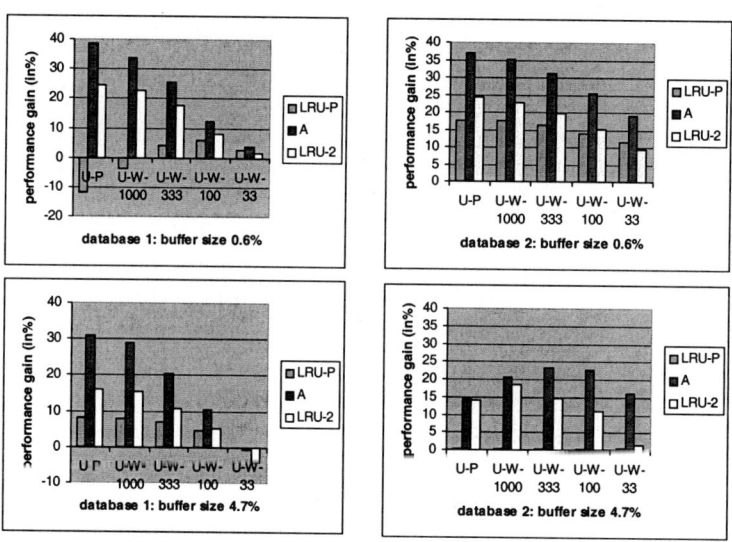

Fig. 7. Performance gain of the algorithms for the uniform distribution

The LRU-P strategy is clearly the worst competitor. The clear winner of these tests is the buffer using the spatial page-replacement strategy. Especially in this case, subtrees of the SAM are often requested that have a large spatial extension. Then, the spatial page-replacement strategy using the area criterion profits most.

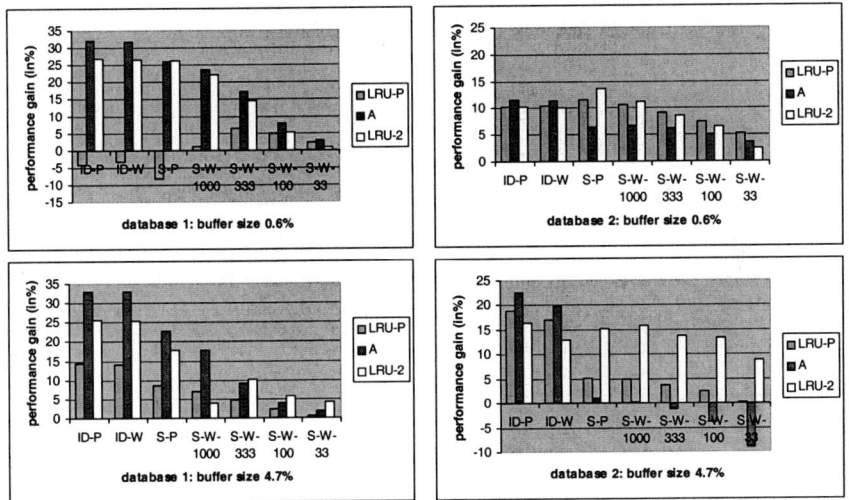

Fig. 8. Performance gain of the algorithms for the identical and similar distribution

3.5.2 Identical and Similar Distributions

The results of the identical and similar distributions are depicted in Figure 8. The left diagrams show the results for database 1 and the right diagrams for the second database. In the most cases, the spatial page-replacement strategy A has the same or a better performance than the LRU-2 buffer. Performance gains of 30% are achieved. However, we can also observe that in some cases – see the lower right diagram – the performance gains collapse. Instead, a loss of performance can occur performing large window queries. An explanation for this behavior corresponds to the explanation given for the intensified distribution in the next subsection.

3.5.3 Independent and Intensified Distributions

The results for the independent and intensified distributions are presented in Figure 9. For test series using the independent query sets *(IND-x)*, there are significant discrepancies between the results of the spatial page-replacement strategy for database 1 and for database 2. For the primary database, this strategy achieves considerable performance gains. For the second database, however, we observe a significant increase of the I/O-cost. The reason is that this query set was constructed by flipping the x-coordinates. In the case of database 1 – the US mainland map – most query points meet again the mainland. Using the world map (i.e. database 2), this observation does not hold. Most query points meet water and can be performed only using the root page of the R*-tree.

For both databases, the performance of the spatial page-replacement strategy is also inferior in the case of query sets obeying the intensified distribution. The reason is that areas of intensified interest are not characterized by large page areas; typically, the opposite case occurs, i.e., in such regions there are often

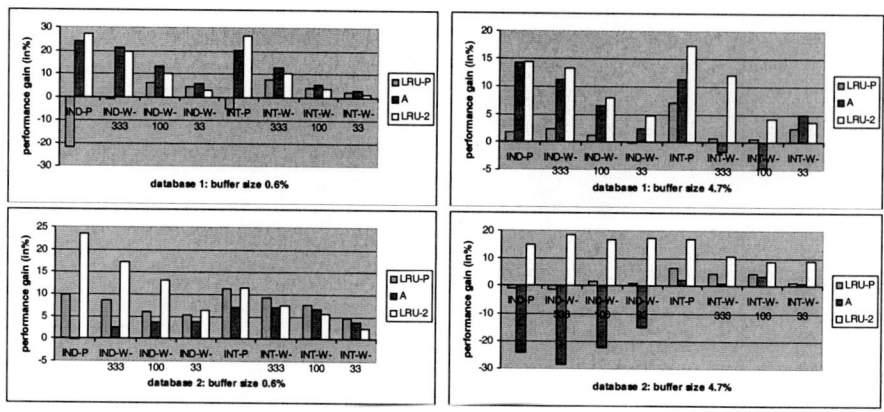

Fig. 9. Performance gain of the algorithms for the independent and the intensified distribution

more objects stored than outside of such region. As consequence, the page area (or other spatial properties of the page or of its entries) tends to be smaller and not larger than the average.

In the other cases, the performance of the spatial page-replacement strategy is comparable to the I/O-cost of the LRU-2 buffer, which is the winner for the independent and intensified distribution.

4 Combining LRU-Based and Spatial Page-Replacement Algorithms

The results of the last experiments have shown that it is not advisable to use pure spatial page-replacement algorithms in the case of some of the investigated query sets. In order to solve this drawback, an adaptable and robust combination of spatial page-replacement strategies with LRU strategies will be proposed and experimentally investigated in this section.

4.1 The Combination

The basic idea for combining LRU-based and spatial page-replacement algorithms is 1.) to compute a set of candidates by using LRU (or another page-replacement algorithm) and 2.) to select the page to be dropped out of the buffer from the candidate set by using a spatial page-replacement algorithm. The larger the candidate set, the larger is the influence of the spatial page-replacement algorithm, and the smaller the candidate set, the larger is the influence of the LRU algorithm. Figure 10 illustrates this effect.

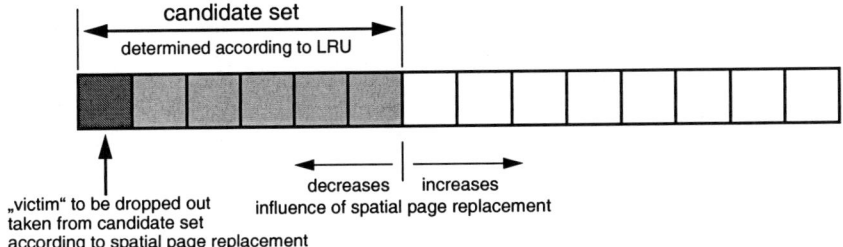

Fig. 10. Combination of LRU-based and spatial page-replacement algorithms

4.2 A Self-tuning Algorithm for Computing the Size of the Candidate Set

An important question concerns the size of the candidate set. For the uniform query distribution, its size should be as large as possible. However, having an intensified distribution, a very small candidate set may be preferable. Therefore, the size of the candidate set should be adapted to the query distribution. For this task, we need a suitable algorithm. According to the introduction in Section 1, this algorithm should be self-tuning in order to minimize the efforts for an efficient database management. The size of the candidate set should be determined without the intervention of the database administrator.

The basic idea of the algorithm is to reserve a part of the buffer for storing pages that have already dropped out of the buffer according to the approach described in Section 4.1. In this part of the buffer, which is called *overflow buffer*, a victim is determined using the first-in first-out technique. If a requested page p is found in the overflow buffer, p is moved to the standard part of the buffer. In this situation, we can distinguish three different cases:

1. The number of pages in the overflow buffer having a better spatial criterion than p is higher than the number of pages having a better LRU criterion than p. Then, the LRU strategy seems to be more suitable than the spatial page-replacement strategy: the size of the candidate set will be decreased.
2. The number of pages in the overflow buffer having a better spatial criterion than p is smaller than the number of pages having a better LRU criterion than p. Then, the spatial page-replacement strategy seems to be more suitable than the LRU strategy: the size of the candidate set will be increased.
3. Both numbers are the same: Then, the size of the candidate set will not be changed.

An illustration of this approach can be found in Figure 11. This type of buffer is called ASB in the following, abbreviating *adaptable spatial buffer*.

4.3 Performance Evaluation

In the following, the results of a performance comparison are presented. Figure 12 compares the performance gains of the spatial page-replacement strategy A

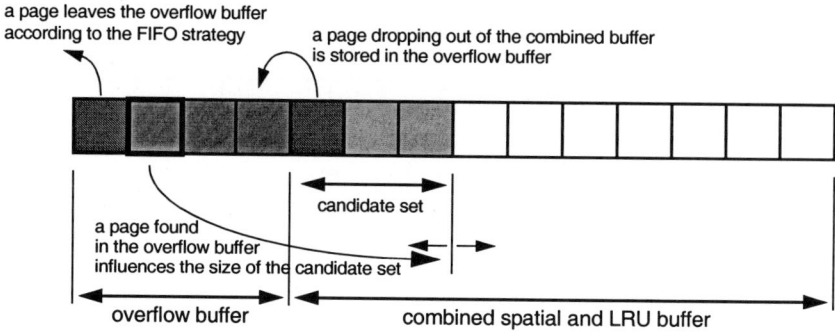

Fig. 11. Illustration of the adapting spatial buffer

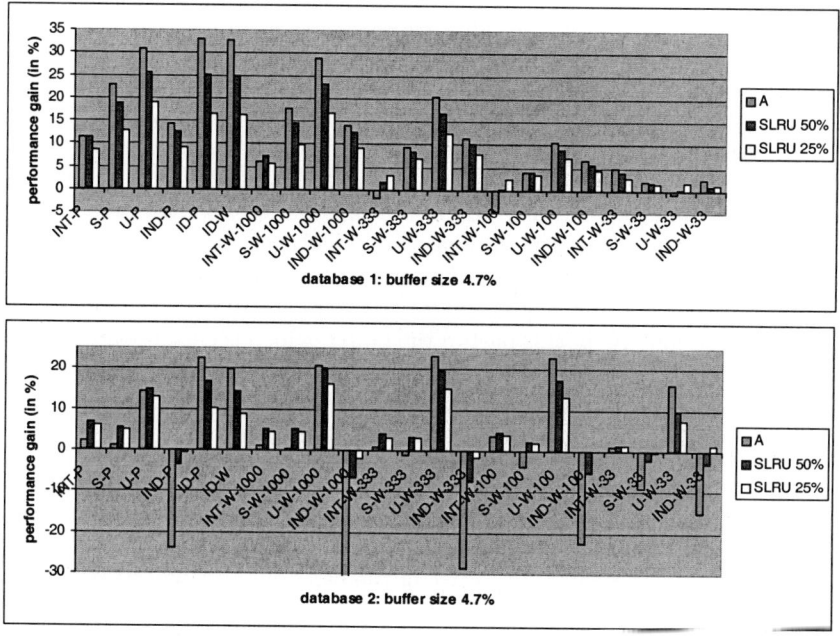

Fig. 12. Performance gains using a candidate set of static size

with the combined approach using a candidate set of static size, i.e. using no overflow buffer. The size of the candidate sets was set to 50% (denoted in the legend of the diagram as SLRU 50%) and to 25% of the buffer (denoted as SLRU 25%).

As expected, we can observe that the performance of the combination of the LRUbased and spatial page-replacement algorithm shifts the behavior of the spatial page-replacement strategy into the direction of the LRU strategy. Consequently, the I/O-cost for query sets performed by algorithm A with large performance gains increases. In the other case, in which A has shown a loss of performance, the I/O-cost is decreased. In the most cases, the performance loss has become a (slight) performance gain. These observations especially hold for the case, in which the candidate set had a size of 25% of the buffer (SLRU 25%).

In the following experiments, an overflow buffer is used for adapting the size of the candidate set. The size of the overflow buffer has been 20% of the complete buffer. The initial size of the candidate set has been 25% of the remaining buffer (i.e. 20% of the complete buffer). The size of the candidate set has been changed in steps of 1% of the remaining buffer. The memory requirements are not increased compared to the other page-replacement strategies.

Figure 13 depicts the performance gains of the spatial page-replacement strategy A, of the combination of LRU and algorithm A using a candidate set having a static size of 25% (denoted in the legend of the diagram as SLRU), of the adapting spatial buffer (denoted as ASB), and of LRU-2 compared to using only LRU.

Like in the experiments before, the behavior of the adapting spatial buffer is a mixture of the performance of an LRU buffer and the spatial page-replacement strategy. In contrast to SLRU, the behavior of ASB is more similar to algorithm A in the cases, in which A shows a very good performance, and more dissimilar to A in the cases, in which A shows a loss of performance. In all cases, a performance gain can be achieved by using ASB.

Comparing the behavior of ASB with LRU-2, we can observe a similar I/O-cost in many cases. However, there are still several cases, in which LRU-2 outperforms ASB. Nevertheless, the reader should be aware about the fact that an LRU-2 buffer requires storing the history information of pages that have already left the buffer. Because this space requirement cannot be predicted (in real life), it is not considered in the experiments. The adapting spatial buffer does not require storing information about pages that have dropped out of the buffer.

For the last experiment, three query sets are concatenated: *INT-W-33*, *U-W-33*, and *SW-33*. Figure 14 shows the size of the candidate set during this test using the adapting spatial buffer with the same parameter settings as in the experiments before.

In the first phase, the queries are distributed according to the intensified distribution. Starting with a size of 684, the size drops to an average value of about 300. During this phase, the influence of the LRU strategy is predominating. Then, the queries are distributed according the uniform distribution. Consequently, the size of the candidate set increases to an average value of about 1620. During this second phase, the buffer primarily applies the spatial page-replacement strategy. During the last phase, the queries obey the similar distribution. Thus, the average size of the candidate set drops to an average of about 650. The influence of the LRU strategy and of the spatial page-replacement strategy is approximately balanced.

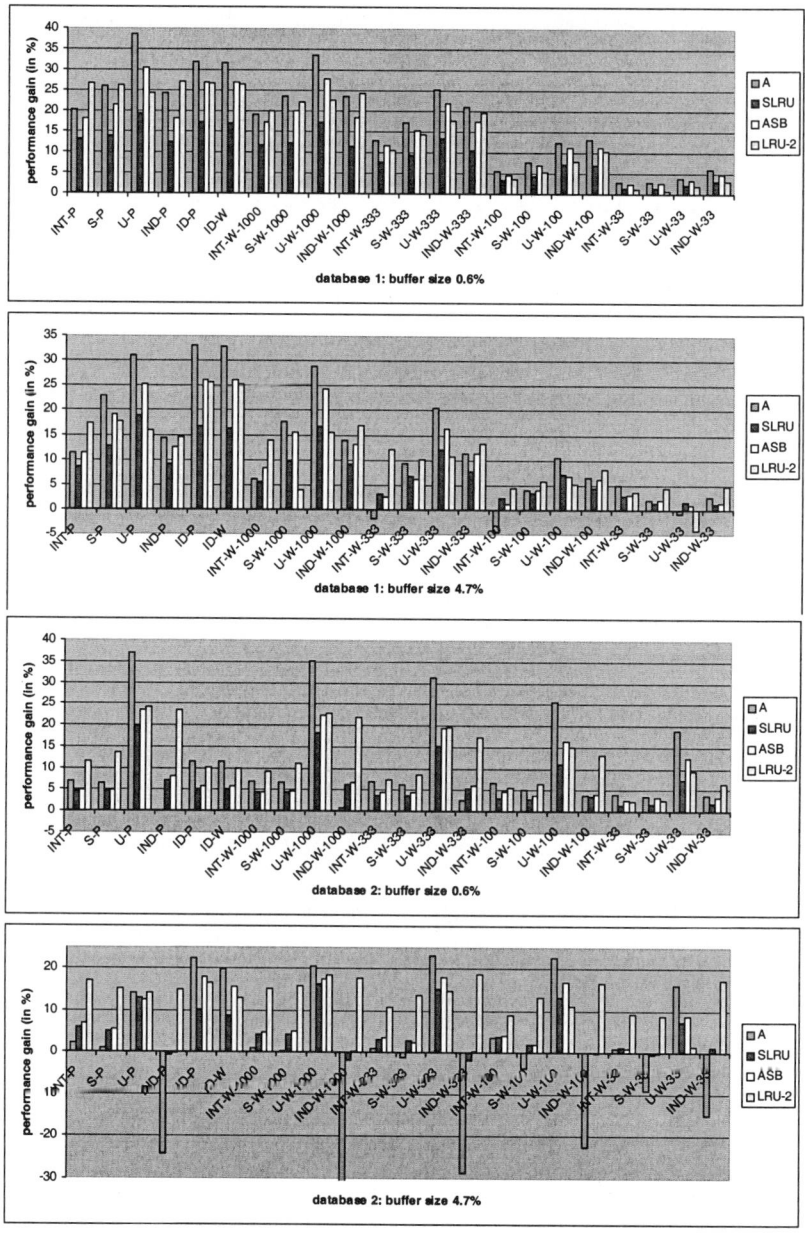

Fig. 13. Performance gains of A, SLRU, ASB, and LRU-2 compared to LRU

5 Conclusions

In order to optimize the I/O-performance of a database system, the buffering of pages in main memory is one of the most important techniques. However, in the

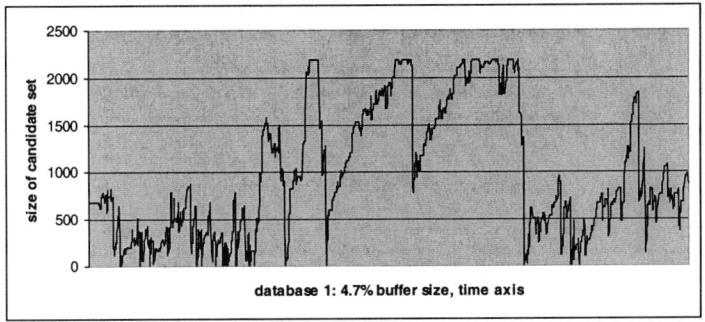

Fig. 14. Size of the candidate set using ASB for a mixed query set

context of spatial database systems, this topic has not been considered in detail. The impact of different page-replacement algorithms on the performance of spatial queries is one of the open questions. Therefore, existing page-replacement strategies have been investigated in this paper in respect to their impact on the performance of spatial queries. Furthermore, new replacement algorithms – so-called *spatial page-replacement algorithms* – have been presented. These algorithms try to determine pages to be dropped out of the buffer according to spatial properties like the area, the margin and the overlap of pages and page entries.

The tests have shown that spatial page-replacement algorithms have a very good performance for many query distributions. However, they are not robust. For some distributions, their performance is worse than the performance of a standard LRU buffer. Therefore, a combination of spatial page-replacement algorithms with other buffer policies like LRU has been proposed. The basic idea of this combination is 1.) to compute a set of candidates by using LRU (or another policy) and 2.) to select the page to be dropped out of the buffer from the candidate set by using a spatial page-replacement algorithm. For a robust and self-tuning algorithm, it is necessary to adapt the size of the candidate set to the requested query profiles. An algorithm for dynamically adjusting the size of the candidate set has been presented. This adapting spatial buffer achieves considerable performance gains. In the cases in which the pure spatial page-replacement algorithms clearly outperforms other policies, the combination achieves performance gains of up to 25% compared to LRU. In contrast to the pure spatial page-replacement, the I/O cost increases for none of the investigated query distributions.

Future work consists of the following tasks: 1. to extend the experiments by investigating the influence of the size of the overflow buffer and by distinguishing random and sequential I/O, 2. to study the influence of the strategies on updates and spatial joins, and 3. to investigate the impact of (spatial) page-replacement algorithms on the management of moving spatial objects in spatiotemporal database systems.

References

1. Beckmann, N., Kriegel, H.-P., Schneider, R., Seeger, B.: The R*-tree: An Efficient and Robust Access Method for Points and Rectangles. In: Proceedings ACM SIGMOD International Conference on Management of Data, Atlantic City, NJ, 1990, 322-331.
2. Brinkhoff, T., Horn, H., Kriegel, H.-P., Schneider, R.: A Storage and Access Architecture for Efficient Query Processing in Spatial Database Systems. In: Proceedings 3rd International Symposium on Large Spatial Databases, Singapore, 1993. Lecture Notes in Computer Science, Vol. 692, Springer, 357-376.
3. Chen, C.M., Roussopoulos, N.: Adaptive Database Buffer Allocation Using Query Feedback. In: Proceedings 19th International Conference on Very Large Data Bases, Dublin, Ireland, 1993, 342-353.
4. Chou, H.T., DeWitt, D.J.: An Evaluation of Buffer Management Strategies for Relational Database Systems. In: Proceedings 11th International Conference on Very Large Data Bases, 1985, Stockholm, Sweden, 127-141.
5. Guttman, A.: R-trees: A Dynamic Index Structure for Spatial Searching. In: Proceedings ACM SIGMOD International Conference on Management of Data, Boston, 1984, 47-57.
6. Härder, T., Rahm, E.: Datenbanksysteme: Konzepte und Techniken der Implementierung. Springer, 1999.
7. IBM: Hard Disk Drives. http://www.storage.ibm.com/hardsoft/diskdrdl.htm
8. Leutenegger, S.T., Lopez, M.A.: The Effect of Buffering on the Performance of R-Trees. In: Proceedings of the 14th International Conf. on Data Engineering, Orlando, 1998, 164-171.
9. Ng, R.T., Faloutsos, C., Sellis, T.K.: Flexible Buffer Allocation Based on Marginal Gains. In: Proceedings ACM SIGMOD International Conference on Management of Data, Denver, CO, 1991, 387-396,
10. O'Neil, E.J., O'Neil, P.E., Weikum, G.: The LRU-K Page Replacement Algorithm for Data Disk Buffering. In: Proceedings ACM SIGMOD International Conference on Management of Data, Washington, DC, 1993, 297-306.
11. Orenstein, J.A., Manola, F.A.: PROBE Spatial Data Modelling and Query Processing in an Image Database Application. IEEE Transactions on Software Engineering, Vol.14, No.5, 1988, 611-629.
12. Rossipaul Medien GmbH: Der große Weltatlas - Unsere Erde multimedial. CD-ROM edition, 1996.
13. Samet, H.: Applications of Spatial Data Structures. Addison-Wesley, 1990.
14. Stonebraker, M., Frew, J., Gardels, K., Meredith, J.: The SEQUOIA 2000 Storage Benchmark. In: Proceedings ACM SIGMOD International Conference on Management of Data, Washington, DC, 1993, 2-11.

Broadcast-Based Data Access in Wireless Environments

Xu Yang and Athman Bouguettaya

Department of Computer Science
Virginia Tech, USA
xuyang@nvc.cs.vt.edu, athman@cs.vt.edu

Abstract. Broadcast is one of the most suitable forms of information dissemination over wireless networks. It is particularly attractive for resource limited mobile clients in *asymmetric* communications. To support faster access to information and conserve battery power of mobile clients, a number of indexing schemes have been proposed in recent years. In this paper, we report on our extensive study of some of the most representative indexing schemes. We present a novel adaptive testbed for evaluating wireless data access methods. A comprehensive analytical study of the sample indexing schemes is also presented. Exhaustive simulations of these indexing schemes have been conducted. As a result, selection criteria for the suitability of the indexing schemes for different applications are proposed.

1 Introduction

Wireless and mobile computing is one of the high growth areas in information technology. Mobile users require information while on the move. This gives great flexibility and convenience for data access. There are increasing number of applications that utilize wireless data access. For example, in *Geographical Information Systems (GIS)*, mobile clients could ask for geographical information to find a restaurant of their choice in the vicinity or the highest peak in the area of interest. Another example is *wireless stock market data delivery*. Stock information from any stock exchange in the world could be broadcast on wireless channels or sent to mobile users upon requests. There are several research issues related to wireless and mobile computing [5]. In this paper, we focus on efficient data access. There are two fundamental modes for providing information for wireless applications: *Broadcast* and *on-demand*. For broadcast mode, information is broadcast over the wireless channel. Clients "listen" to the channel and filter the interested information. This mode is also called *push-based* mode. On-demand mode provides information to the mobile clients by the fixed server only upon a request. Such message delivery method is sometimes referred to as *pull-based* mode.

Two key requirements for data access in wireless environments are conserving power consumption and minimizing client waiting time. In push-based systems, mobile clients must wait until the server broadcasts the required information. Therefore, client waiting time is determined by the overall length of broadcast data, which is usually referred to as *broadcast cycle*. Mobile clients in wireless environments are usually equipped with limited power supply. Research shows that most of power consumption for mobile clients like battery-powered palmtops is on listening to the wireless channel and examining the received packets. For systems working in push-based mode, mobile clients must keep listening to broadcast channel until the arrival of required information. The power consumption by mobile clients in such systems is usually critical, especially when the broadcast cycle is large. In [6], the concept of *selective tuning* is introduced for reducing power consumption for push-based systems. By using selective tuning, mobile clients stay in *doze mode* most of the time and turn into *active mode* only when the requested information is expected to arrive. Indexing techniques are used to implement selective tuning in wireless environments. Indices are broadcast together with data to help mobile clients locate the required information. As a result, clients stay in doze mode most of the time. This considerably reduces power consumption. However, broadcasting indices with data introduces overhead in the broadcast cycle, which results in an increase of client waiting time. In real life, different applications may have different requirements on client waiting time and power consumption. How to balance these two requirements has become one of the key issues in applying indexing techniques to wireless environments.

In recent years, several indexing schemes have been proposed to improve performance of data access by introducing indexing techniques to push-based wireless environments. Most of these indexing schemes are based on three techniques: index tree [6, 1, 2, 9], signature indexing [8], and hashing [7]. Some indexing schemes are proposed using hybrid schemes. For example, [3, 4] presented indexing schemes taking advantages of both index tree and signature indexing techniques. However, little work has been done on evaluating these indexing schemes in *common* environments and providing *uniform* selection criteria for different applications. In this paper, we evaluate and compare three most representative indexing schemes, namely, *distributed indexing*, *signature indexing*, and *hashing*. We present a novel testbed we developed for evaluating these indexing schemes. The criteria we use for evaluating the indexing schemes are *access time* and *tuning time*:

– *Access Time*: The average time that has elapsed from the moment a client requests information up to the point when the required information is downloaded by the client. This factor corresponds to client waiting time.
– *Tuning Time*: The amount of time that has been spent by a client listening to the channel. This is used to determine the power consumed by the client to retrieve the required information.

The paper is organized as follows. In Section 2, an analytical evaluation of the indexing schemes covered in this paper is given. In Section 3, we present the system architecture of our novel testbed. In Section 4, the simulation results of each single indexing scheme are detailed. In Section 5, we present how the performance of these indexing schemes is affected by various other factors. In Section 6, we provide some concluding remarks.

2 Analytical Evaluation of Wireless Indexing Schemes

In disk-based environments, indexing techniques are widely used to make data access more efficient. Indices in these techniques are usually key-address pairs stored in distinct locations on disk. Since the size of an index is usually much smaller than that of a data record, the overall access time can be drastically reduced with the help of such indexing techniques. Similar techniques are applied in wireless-based environments, particularly push-based systems. In this section, we discuss three indexing schemes. For each indexing scheme, we show the data organization of broadcast channel, access protocol, and the expected access time and tuning time. The following symbols are used:

A_t: access time

T_t: tuning time

I_t: time to browse an index bucket

D_t: time to browse a data bucket

F_t: time spent to reach the first complete bucket after tuning into broadcast channel (initial wait)

B_t: time to finish broadcasting the whole broadcast cycle

N_r: number of data records in broadcast cycle

N: total number of buckets in the broadcast cycle

2.1 B+ Tree Indexing

B+ tree indexing is a widely used indexing technique in traditional disk-based environments. It is also one of the first indexing techniques applied to wireless environments. The use of B+ tree indexing in wireless environments is very similar to that of traditional disk based environments. Indices are organized in B+ tree structure to accelerate the search processes. An offset value is stored in each index node pointing at corresponding data item or lower level index node. However, there are some differences that introduce new challenges to wireless environments. For example, in disk based environments, offset value is the location of the data item on disk, whereas in wireless environments, offset value is the arrival time of the bucket containing the data item. Moreover, indices and data in wireless environments are organized in one-dimensional mode in broadcast channel. Missing the bucket containing index of the requested data item may cause the client to wait until the next broadcast cycle to find it again. In [6], two indexing schemes based on B+ tree data structure, *(1,m) indexing* and *distributed indexing*, are presented. We only analyze distributed indexing in this section, because it is derived from *(1,m)* indexing and they have very similar data structure.

Data Organization. In distributed indexing, every broadcast data item is indexed on its primary key attribute. Indices are organized in a B+ tree structure. Figure 1 shows a typical full index tree consisting of 81 data items [6]. Each index node has a number of pointers (in Figure 1, each node has three pointers) pointing at its child nodes. The pointers of the bottom level indices point at the actual data nodes. To find a specific data item, the search follows a top-down manner. The top level index node is searched first to determine which child node contains the data item. Then the same process will be performed on that node. This procedure continues till it finally reaches the data item at the bottom. The sequence of the index nodes traversed is called the *index path* of the data item. For example, the index path of data item 34 in Figure 1 is I, a2, b4, c12.

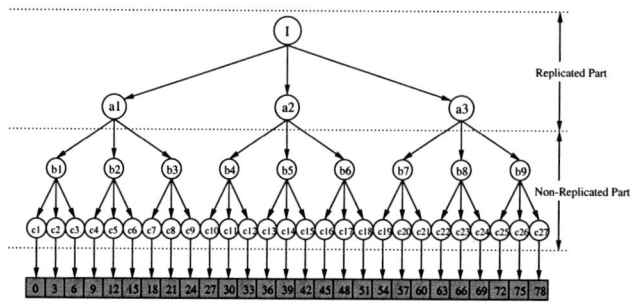

Fig. 1. A sample index tree

What was discussed so far is similar to the traditional disk-based B+ tree indexing technique. The difference arises when the index and data are put in the broadcast channel. A node in the index tree is represented by an index bucket in the broadcast channel. Similarly, a broadcast data item is represented by a data bucket. In the traditional disk-based systems, index and data are usually stored in different locations. The index tree is searched first to obtain the exact location of the requested data item. This process often requires frequent shifts between index nodes or between index and data nodes. As data in a wireless channel is one dimensional, this kind of shift is difficult to achieve. Therefore, in distributed indexing, data and index are interleaved in the broadcast channel. The broadcast data is partitioned into several data segments. The index tree precedes each data segment in the broadcast. Users traverse the index tree first to obtain the time offset of the requested data item. They then switch to doze mode until the data item arrives. Figure 2 illustrates how index and data are organized in the broadcast channel.

In *(1,m)* indexing [6], the whole index tree precedes each data segment in the broadcast. Each index bucket is broadcast a number of times equal to the number of data segments. This increases the broadcast cycle and thus access time. Distributed indexing achieves better access time by broadcasting only part of the index tree preceding each data segment. The whole index tree is partitioned

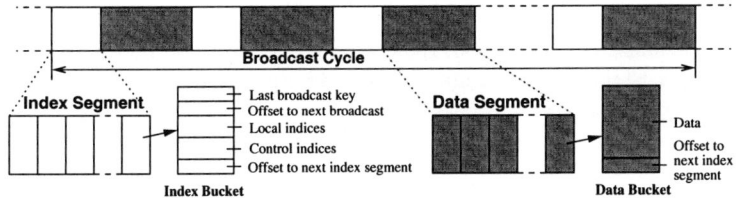

Fig. 2. Index and data organization of distributed indexing

into two part: replicated part and non-replicated part. Every replicated index bucket is broadcast before the first occurrence of each of its child. Thus the number of times it is broadcast is equal to the number of children it has. Every non-replicated index node is broadcast exactly once, preceding the data segment containing the corresponding data records. Using the index tree in Figure 1 as an example, the first and second index segments will consist of index buckets containing nodes I, a1, b1, c1, c2, c3 and a1, b2, c4, c5, c6 respectively.

Each index bucket contains pointers that point to the buckets containing its child nodes. These pointers are referred to as *local index*. Since the broadcast is continuous and users may tune in at any time, the first index segment users come across may not contain the index of the requested data item. In this case, more information is needed to direct users to other index segment containing the required information. *Control index* is introduced for this purpose. The control index consists of pointers that point at the next occurrence of the buckets containing the parent nodes in its index path. Again using the index tree in Figure 1 as an example, index node a2 contains local index pointing at b4, b5, b6 and control index pointing at the third occurrence of index node I. Assume there is a user requesting data item 62 but first tuning in right before the second occurrence of index node a2. The control index in a2 will direct the user to the next occurrence of I, because data item 62 is not within the subtree rooted at a2.

Access Protocol. The following is the access protocol of distributed indexing for a data item with key K:

```
    mobile client requires data item with key K
    tune into the broadcast channel
    keep listening until the first complete bucket arrives
    read the first complete bucket
    go to the next index segment according to the offset value
        in the first bucket
(1) read the index bucket
    if K < Key most recently broadcast
        go to next broadcast
    else if K = Key being broadcast
        read the time offset to the actual data records
        go into doze mode
        tune in again when the requested data bucket comes
        download the data bucket
```

```
else
    read control index and local index in current index bucket
    go to higher level index bucket if needed according to
    the control index
    go to lower level index bucket according to the local index
    go into doze mode between any two successive index probes
    repeat from (1)
```

Analysis. We now derive the formulas for access time and tuning time. First, we define symbols which are specific to B+ tree indexing. Let n be the number of indices contained in an index bucket, let k be the number of levels of the index tree, and let r be the number of replicated levels. It is obvious that $k = \lceil \log_n(N_r) \rceil$. The access time consists of three parts: *initial wait, initial index probe*, and *broadcast wait*.

initial wait (F_t): It is the time spent to reach the first complete bucket. Obviously we have: $F_t = \frac{D_t}{2}$

initial index probe (P_t): This part is the time to reach the first index segment. It can be expressed as the average time to reach the next index segment, which is calculated as the sum of the average length of index segments and data segments. Given the number of replicated levels is r, the number of replicated indices (N_{rp}) is: $1 + n + ... + n^{r-1} = \frac{n^r - 1}{n-1}$. The number of non-replicated index (N_{nr}) is: $n^r + n^{r+1} + ... n^{k-1} = \frac{n^k - n^r}{n-1}$.

As mentioned before, each replicated index is broadcast n times and each non-replicated index is broadcast exactly once. Thus the total number of index buckets can be calculated as $N_{rp} \times n + N_{nr} = n \times \frac{n^r - 1}{n-1} + \frac{n^k - n^r}{n-1} = \frac{n^k + n^{r+1} - n^r - n}{n-1}$. The number of data segments is n^r because the replicated level is r. Thus the average number of index buckets in an index segment is: $\frac{1}{n^r} \times (n \times \frac{n^r - 1}{n-1} + \frac{n^k - n^r}{n-1}) = \frac{n^{k-r} - 1}{n-1} + \frac{n^{r+1} - n}{n^{r+1} - n^r}$. The average number of data buckets in a data segment is $\frac{N_r}{n^r}$. Therefore, the initial index probe is calculated as $P_t = \frac{1}{2} \times (\frac{n^{k-r} - 1}{n-1} + \frac{n^{r+1} - n}{n^{r+1} - n^r} + \frac{N_r}{n^r}) \times D_t$.

broadcast wait (W_t): This is the time from reaching the first indexing segment to finding the requested data item. It is approximately half of the whole broadcast cycle, which is $\frac{N}{2} \times D_t$. Thus, the total access time is:

$$A_t = F_t + P_t + W_t = \frac{1}{2} \times (\frac{n^{k-r} - 1}{n-1} + \frac{n^{r+1} - n}{n^{r+1} - n^r} + \frac{N_r}{n^r} + N + 1) \times D_t$$

The tuning time is much easier to calculate than access time, because during most of the probes clients are in doze mode. The tuning time includes the initial wait ($\frac{D_t}{2}$), reading the first bucket to find the first index segment (D_t), reading the control index to find the segment containing the index information of the requested data item (D_t), traversing the index tree ($k \times D_t$), and downloading the data item (D_t). Thus, the tuning time is:

$$T_t = (k + \frac{3}{2}) \times D_t$$

2.2 Hashing

Hashing is another well-known data access technique for traditional database systems. In this subsection, we introduce a *simple hashing* scheme, which was proposed to suit wireless environments [7].

Data Organization. Simple hashing scheme stores hashing parameters in data buckets without requiring separate index buckets or segments. Each data bucket consists of two parts: *Control part* and *Data part*. The *Data part* contains actual data record and the *Control part* is used to guide clients to the right data bucket.

The control part of each data bucket consists of a *hashing function* and a *shift value*. The hashing function maps the key value of the data in the broadcast data record into a hashing value. Each bucket has a hashing value H assigned to it. In the event of a collision, the colliding record is inserted right after the bucket which has the same hashing value. This will cause the rest of records to shift, resulting in data records being "out-of-place". The shift value in each bucket is used to find the right position of the corresponding data record. It points to the first bucket containing the data record with the right hashing value. Assume the initial allocated number of buckets is N_a. Because of collisions, the resulting length of the broadcast cycle after inserting all the data records will be greater than N_a. The control part of each of the first N_a buckets contains a shift value (offset to the bucket containing the actual data record with the right hashing value), and the control part of each of the remaining data buckets contains an offset to the beginning of the next broadcast.

Access Protocol. Assume the hashing function is H, thus the hashing value of key K will be $H(K)$. The access protocol of hashing for a data item with key K is:

```
    mobile client requires data item with key K
    tune into the broadcast channel
    keep listening until the first complete bucket arrives
(1) read the bucket and get the hashing value h
    if h < H(K)
        go to doze mode
        tune in again when h = H(K) (hashing position)
    else
        go to doze mode
        tune in again at the beginning of the next broadcast
        repeat from (1)
    read shift value at the bucket where h = H(K)
    go to doze mode
    tune in again when the bucket designated by the shift value
    arrives (shift position)
    keep listening to the subsequent buckets, till
        the wanted record is found
            search terminated successfully
        or a bucket with different hashing value arrives
            search failed
```

Analysis. The access time of the hashing scheme consists of an initial wait time (F_t), time to reach the *hashing position* (H_t), time to reach the *shift position* (S_t), time to retrieve colliding buckets (C_t), and time to download the required bucket (D_t). Since there is only one type of bucket used in hashing, the initial wait is $F_t = \frac{D_t}{2}$. Let N_c be the number of colliding buckets, the average number of shifts of each bucket is thus $\frac{N_c}{2}$. Therefore, we have $S_t = \frac{N_c}{2} \times D_t$. Furthermore, the average number of colliding buckets for each hashing value is $\frac{N_c}{N_r}$. Thus, we have $C_t = \frac{N_c}{N_r} \times D_t$. The calculation of H_t is more involved. Assume the number of initially allocated buckets is N_a. The resulting total number of buckets in the broadcast cycle is $N = N_a + N_c$. We have the following three possibilities that result in different values of H_t (assume the position of the first arriving bucket is n).

$$H_{t1} = \frac{N_c}{N} \times (\frac{1}{2} \times (N_c + N_a)) \quad (n > N_a)$$

$$H_{t2} = (\frac{1}{2} \times \frac{N_a}{N}) \times \frac{N_a}{3} \quad (n \le N_a,\ request\_item\_broadcast = False)$$

$$H_{t3} = (\frac{1}{2} \times \frac{N_a}{N}) \times (\frac{N_a}{3} + N_c + \frac{N_a}{3}) \quad (n \le N_a,\ request\_item\_broadcast = True)$$

The *request_item_broadcast* above designates if the requested information has already been broadcast in the current broadcast cycle. The first part of each formula above is the probability the scenario will happen. As a result, we have $H_t = H_{t1} + H_{t2} + H_{t3}$. Based on the above discussion, the access time is:

$$A_t = F_t + H_t + S_t + C_t + D_t = (\frac{1}{2} + \frac{N}{N_a} + N - \frac{1}{2} \times N_a) \times D_t$$

The tuning time consists of an initial wait time (F_t), time to read the first bucket to obtain the hashing position (D_t), time to obtain the shift position (D_t), and time to retrieve the colliding buckets (C_t), and time to download the required bucket (D_t). The probability of collision is $\frac{N_c}{N_r}$. Thus, we have $C_t = \frac{N_c}{N_r} \times D_t$. For those requests that tune in at the time which the requested bucket has already been broadcast, one extra bucket read is needed to start from the beginning of the next broadcast cycle. The probability of this scenario occurrence is $(N_c + \frac{1}{2} \times N_r)/(N_c + N_r)$. As a result, the expected tuning time is:

$$T_t = (\frac{1}{2} + \frac{N_c + \frac{1}{2} \times N_r}{N_c + N_r} + \frac{N_c}{N_r} + 3) \times D_t$$

2.3 Signature Indexing

A signature is essentially an abstraction of the information stored in a record. It is generated by a specific signature function. By examining a record's signature, one can tell if the record possibly has the matching information. Since the size of a signature is much smaller than that of the data record itself, it is considerably more power efficient to examine signatures first instead of simply searching through all data records. Indexing schemes making use of signatures of data records are called signature indexing. In [8], three signature indexing schemes are proposed: simple signature, integrated signature, and multi-level signature. The latter two schemes originate from the simple signature indexing. Since our focus is on comparing different indexing techniques, only the simple signature scheme is covered in this paper.

The signatures are generated based on all attributes of data records. A signature is formed by hashing each field of a record into a random bit string and then superimposing together all the bit strings into a record signature. The number of collisions depends on how perfect the hashing function is and how many attributes a record has. Collisions in signature indexing occur when two or more data records have the same signature. Usually the more attributes each record has, the more likely collisions will occur. Such collisions would translate into false drops. False drops are situations where clients download the wrong data records but with matching signatures.

In signature based indexing schemes, signatures are broadcast together with data records. The broadcast channel consists of index (signature) buckets and data buckets. Each broadcast of a data bucket is preceded by a broadcast of the signature bucket, which contains the signature of the data record. For consistency, signature buckets have equal length. Mobile clients must sift through each broadcast bucket until the required information is found.

Access Protocol. The access protocol for simple signature indexing is as follows (assume K and S are the key and signature of the required record respectively, and $K(i)$ and $S(i)$ are the key and signature of the i-th record):

```
    mobile client requires data item with key K
    tune in to broadcast channel
    keep listening until the first complete signature bucket arrives
(1) read the current signature bucket
    if S(i) = S(k)
        download the data bucket that follows it
        if K(i) = K
            search terminated successfully
        else
            false drop occurs
            continue to read the next signature bucket
            repeat from (1)
    else
        go to doze mode
        tune in again when the next signature bucket comes
        repeat from (1)
```

Analysis. Because clients must scan buckets one by one to find the required information, access time is determined by the broadcast cycle. A signature bucket contains only a signature of the corresponding data record. No extra offset or pointer value is inserted into the signature/index bucket as in other indexing schemes. Since the total length of all data records is a constant, the length of a signature is the only factor that determines the broadcast cycle. Access time, therefore, is determined by the length of the signature. The smaller the signatures are, the better the access time is. As for tuning time, it is determined by two factors: size of signature bucket and number of false drops. It is obvious that smaller signature lengths reduce tuning time. However, smaller signature sizes usually imply more collisions, thus more false drops. In cases of false drops, wrong data records are downloaded by mobile clients, hence increasing tuning time. From this analysis, we derive two tradeoffs: (1) signature length against tuning time, and (2) access time against tuning time.

Signature indexing uses two types of buckets (with varying sizes): signature bucket and data bucket. The initial wait is considered as the time to reach the closest signature bucket: $F_t = \frac{1}{2} \times (D_t + I_t)$.

As discussed above, access time is determined by the broadcast cycle. It consists of two parts: initial wait (F_t) and time to browse the signature and data buckets (SD_t). The average value of SD_t for retrieving a requested bucket is half of the broadcast cycle ($\frac{1}{2} \times (D_t + I_t) \times N_r$). Therefore, the access time is: $A_t = F_t + SD_t = \frac{1}{2} \times (D_t + I_t) + \frac{1}{2} \times (D_t + I_t) \times N_r = \frac{1}{2} \times (D_t + I_t) \times (N_r + 1)$

Tuning time is determined by both the length of index buckets and number of false drops. It consists of four parts: initial wait (F_t), time to browse signature buckets (SB_t), time to scan the false drop data buckets (FD_t), and the time to retrieve the requested data bucket (D_t). The average value of SB_t is half of the total length of signature buckets, which is $\frac{1}{2} \times I_t \times N_r$. Assuming F_d is the number of false drops, the value of FD_t will be $F_d \times D_t$. Hence the resulting tuning time is: $T_t = F_t + SB_t + FD_t + D_t = \frac{1}{2} \times (N_r + 1) \times I_t + (F_d + \frac{1}{2}) \times D_t$

3 Adaptive Testbed

This section presents the testbed we propose for the evaluation of data access methods in wireless environments. The broadcasting of each data item, generation of each user request and processing of the request are all considered to be separate events in this testbed. They are handled independently without interference with each other. The adaptability of the testbed lies in (1) it can be easily extended to implement new data access methods; (2) it is capable of simulating different application environments; (3) new evaluation criteria can be added. The components of the testbed are described as follows:

Simulator: The *Simulator* object acts as the coordinator of the whole simulation process. It reads and processes user input, initializes data source, and starts broadcasting and request generation processes. It also determines which data access method to use according to the user input.

BroadcastServer: It is a process to broadcast data continuously. The *BroadcastServer* constructs broadcast channel at the initialization stage according to the input parameters and then starts the broadcast procedure.

RequestGenerator: *RequestGenerator* is another process initialized and started by the *Simulator*. It generates requests periodically based on certain distribution. In the simulations covered by this paper, the request generation process follows exponential distribution.

Data: Information to be broadcast is represented by a *Data* object. The information is read from files or databases. The *Data* object consists of a number of records.

Record: It is used to represent a broadcast data item. Each record has a primary key and a few attributes.

Bucket: Broadcast data items are reorganized as buckets to put in broadcast channel. A bucket can be either index (signature) or data. The *Bucket* object is used to represent such bucket. Different access methods have different bucket organization.

Channel: The *Channel* object consists of a number of *Buckets*. It is constructed at initialization stage based on which data access method is being used. The *BroadcastServer* process broadcasts information contained in the broadcast *Channel*.

Request: User request is represented by *Request* objects. Each request is considered to be an independent process. Once generated by the *RequestGenerator*, it starts listening to the broadcast channel for the required data item till it is found.

ResultHandler: In our testbed, we use access time and tuning time as criteria to evaluate the performance of the indexing schemes. The *ResultHandler* object extracts and processes the simulation results and output them in the proper format.

AccuracyController: To ensure the accuracy of our simulation, we use an *AccuracyController* object to control the accuracy of the simulation results. Users can specify the accuracy expectation for the simulation. The simulation process will not terminate unless the expected accuracy is achieved.

Figure 3 shows the generic architecture of the testbed. When a particular data access method is used, specific objects are created. For example, if user chooses to use signature indexing, the *BroadcastServer* constructs a *SigChannel*

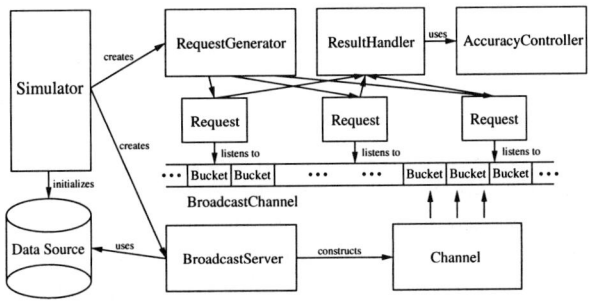

Fig. 3. Testbed Architecture

which would consist of a number of *SigBuckets*. The *RequestGenerator* would periodically generate *SigRequests*. The *Simulator* would create a *SigResultHandler* object to process the signature indexing specific results. The generic objects store only information that is common to all data access methods.

The testbed is implemented as a discrete event driven simulation system. The following procedures explain how the testbed works:

- Initialization stage:
    - Create *Simulator* object
    - *Simulator* initializes the *Data* object, *BroadcastServer* object, *RequestGenerator* object and specific *ResultHandler* object.
    - *Data* object reads the data source and creates all *Record* objects.
    - Depending on which indexing scheme is selected, *BroadcastServer* creates the corresponding *Channel* object.
    - Specific *Channel* object is created. A number of corresponding *Bucket* objects are created based on data records. Buckets are inserted into the broadcast channel according to the data organization of the chosen data access method.
- Start stage:
    - *Simulator* starts *BroadcastServer*.
    - *Simulator* starts *RequestGenerator*.
- Simulation stage:
    - Broadcast channel broadcasts the information continuously.
    - *RequestGenerator* generates *Request* periodically using the exponential distribution.
    - Generated requests listen to the broadcast channel and query the required information.
    - When completed, *Request* objects inform *ResultHandler* object of the results.
    - *Simulator* checks if the results are within the expected confidence and accuracy level to determine whether to terminate or continue the simulation.
- End stage:
    - *Simulator* stops *BroadcastServer*.
    - *Simulator* stops *RequestGenerator*.
    - *ResultHandler* processes the results and outputs them in a proper format.

4 Simulation

This section presents the simulation results obtained from our testbed for each indexing scheme. The simulation results are compared against the analytical results. The simulation results are based on the access protocols. The analytical results are produced from the formulas presented in Section 2. Comparing them can prove/disprove the correctness of our testbed and the predictiveness of the proposed analytical model. We also show the simulation results for broadcasting without using any data access method, i.e., flat or plain broadcast.

4.1 Simulation Settings

The data source our testbed uses is a dictionary database consisting of about 35,000 records. Table 1 shows the common settings for all simulation experiments:

Table 1. Simulation settings

Data type	text
Number of records	7000–34000
Record size	500 bytes
Key size	25 bytes
Number of requests	> 50000
Confidence level [1]	0.99
Confidence accuracy [1]	0.01
Request interval	exponential distribution

The *Confidence level* and *confidence accuracy* shown in Table 1 are used to control the accuracy of the simulation results. Users can specify the values of confidence level and accuracy before starting simulation. The simulation is not complete until the expected confidence level and accuracy are achieved.

The testbed reads the data records from the data source and constructs them into data buckets using specific indexing schemes. The access time and tuning time of each indexing scheme are evaluated in terms of the number of bytes read. Often possible parameters like the number of buckets or actual time elapsed are not used for the following reasons:

1. Bucket sizes may vary depending on the indexing scheme.
2. Some indexing schemes use varied bucket sizes. For example, signature indexing uses two types of buckets, data bucket and signature bucket. Their sizes are different.
3. There are many factors that may affect time measurement during simulation, such as CPU speed, network delay, CPU workload, etc.

Mobile user requests are simulated through a random request generator. During each simulation round, there are 500 requests generated. At the end of the round, the result is checked against the confidence level and confidence accuracy. The simulation continues if the confidence conditions are not satisfied. In most of our simulation experiments, more than 100 simulation rounds are required

---
[1] Given N sample results $Y_1, Y_2, ..., Y_N$, the *confidence accuracy* is defined as H/Y, where H is the *confidence interval half-width* and Y is the sample mean of the results ($Y = (Y_1 + Y_2 + ... + Y_N)/N$). The *confidence level* is defined as the probability that the absolute value of the difference between the Y and μ (the true mean of the sample results) is equal to or less than H. H is defined by $H = t_{\alpha/2; N-1} \times \sigma/\sqrt{N}$ where σ^2 is the sample variance given by $\sigma^2 = \Sigma_i (Y_i - Y)^2/(N-1)$ (thus σ is the standard deviation), and t is the standard t distribution.

to satisfy the confidence conditions we defined in Table 1. The generation of requests follows the exponential distribution. In all simulation experiments discussed in this section, we assume all requested data records are found in the broadcast.

4.2 Simulation Results

Based on the above simulation settings, each indexing scheme is simulated using the testbed. Figure 4 shows the simulation results for flat broadcast, distributed indexing, signature indexing and simple hashing. The lines marked with (S) are simulation results. Those marked with (A) are analytical results. We observe in both figures that the simulation results match the analytical results very well.

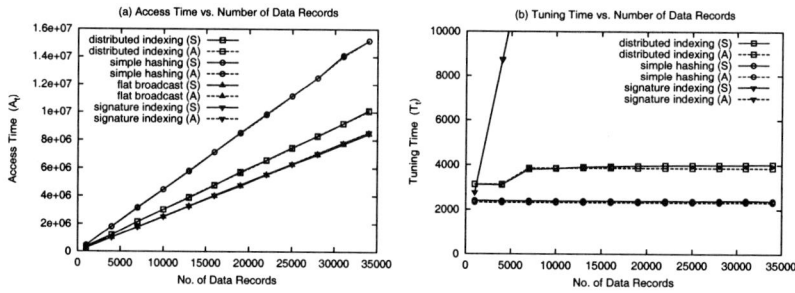

Fig. 4. Comparison for different indexing schemes

Flat broadcast exhibits the best access time but worst tuning time. With the introduction of data access methods, extra information is inserted into broadcast channel to help clients get to the required data item. This also introduces overhead in the broadcast cycle that consequently increases access time. In the flat broadcast, information is broadcast over the wireless communication channel without using any access method. Mobile clients must traverse all buckets to find the requested data. In such a case, mobile clients keep listening to the broadcast channel. This results in the worst tuning time. The expected average access time and tuning time are the same, which is approximately half of the broadcast cycle. Both access time and tuning time increase linearly with number of broadcast data records.

For distributed indexing, we use the optimal value of r as defined in [6]. If we consider the formula presented in Section 2.1 and the fact that D_t is constant, it is obvious that the tuning time of distributed indexing is determined by k, the number of levels in the index tree. The increase in the number of broadcast data records does not necessarily increase the tuning time, unless the bottom level of the index tree is filled and the number of levels in the index tree is, as a result, increased. The simulation result shows the same trend. We can also observe that the tuning time of distributed indexing only increases at one point (somewhere between 5000 and 10000 data records), where the number of levels in index tree is increased. The value of tuning time is much less than that of flat broadcast. With the help of indices, clients selectively listen to the broadcast channel, thus reducing the tuning time drastically.

From Figure 4(a), we see that simple hashing has the worst performance in terms of access time. This is because simple hashing introduces more overheads to the broadcast cycle. However, simple hashing has the best tuning time, as shown in Figure 4(b). According to the analysis in Section 2.2, it takes no more than four probes to reach the first bucket containing the requested hashing value. The tuning time is determined only by the average number of buckets containing the requested hashing value, which is the average overflow. Since we use the same hashing function for varied number of broadcast data records, the overflow rate is a fixed value. That is why we observe a straight horizontal line in the figure. Depending on how good the hashing function is, simple hashing achieves different average tuning times. Generally, it outperforms most of other indexing schemes in terms of tuning time.

As shown in Figure 4(a), signature indexing achieves a much better access time than all other indexing schemes. The only overhead signature indexing scheme introduces in broadcast cycle is the signatures of data records. Signatures are usually very small in size compared to the size of data records. Furthermore, unlike other indexing schemes, there is no extra offset pointers in broadcast buckets (signature buckets or data buckets). The resulting broadcast cycle of signature indexing is smaller than that of other indexing schemes, translating in smaller access time. Like in flat broadcast, signature indexing requires clients to serially browse through the broadcast buckets. The only difference is that signature is read first each time. Clients do not read the successive data buckets unless the signature matches the signature of the requested data record. Therefore, the tuning time of signature indexing is much larger than that of other indexing schemes. We also note that the tuning time increases linearly with the number of broadcast data records. This is because when the signature length is fixed, increasing the number of broadcast data records leads to a larger number of signature buckets and false drops, which in turn result in a larger tuning time.

5 Comparison

In this section, we compare the indexing schemes under different scenarios. We define the following two parameters: (1) *Data availability* which defines the possibility of the requested information to be present in broadcast channel, and (2) *Record/key ratio* which is the proportion of record size to key size.

In real settings, the requested information may not exist at all in the broadcast channel. How data availability affects performance becomes an important issue. In applications with very low data availability, indexing schemes requiring one-at-a-time browsing have usually very poor efficiency because clients scan the whole broadcast channel. In other indexing schemes, such as distributed indexing, however, clients need to scan only the indexing section to determine the presence of requested information.

The record/key ratio is another important factor that may affect the efficiency of different indexing schemes. For B+ tree indexing schemes, such as distributed indexing, higher record/key ratio implies more indices likely to be placed in a single bucket, which in turn would reduce the number of index tree levels. As previously discussed, tuning time is mainly determined by the number of index tree levels in these two indexing schemes. Therefore, record/key ratio has a substantial influence on the performance of B+ tree based indexing schemes. Record/key ratio has also great impact on the efficiency of signature or hashing based indexing schemes. Smaller record/key ratio usually means less overhead being introduced to the broadcast cycle, which results in better access time. However, smaller record/key ratio may also lead to more false drops in signature indexing and higher overflow in hashing, causing worse tuning time. In real world applications, record/key ratios in different wireless applications may vary largely. Therefore, it is important to study how record/key ratio affects the efficiency of indexing schemes.

5.1 Comparing Indexing Schemes Based on Data Availability

We vary data availability from 0% to 100% in our simulation to evaluate the performance of different indexing schemes. Figure 5 shows the result of access time and tuning time against data availability.

Figure 5(a) clearly shows that data availability in hashing has little impact on access time. This is because changing the data availability does not change broadcast cycle and the access sequence of hashing scheme is determined only by the hashing function. We note that when the data availability is high (towards 100%), flat broadcast and signature indexing have the best performance. When the data availability is low (towards 0%), *(1,m)* indexing and distributed indexing outperform all other schemes. The reason is that *(1,m)* indexing and distributed indexing can determine the presence of the requested information by reading only the index segment.

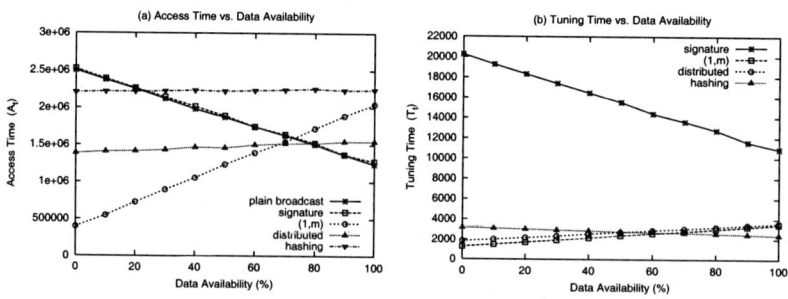

Fig. 5. Comparison for different data availability

As to tuning time, we do not consider it for flat broadcast simply because it is much larger than that of all other schemes. Tuning time of signature indexing decreases with the increased data availability. This is because when data availability increases, there is less probability that clients scan the whole broadcast cycle to find out whether the requested record is in the broadcast. Figure 5(b) shows that *(1,m)* and distributed indexing perform better under low data availability, whereas signature indexing and hashing have better performance when data availability is high. For *(1,m)* and distributed indexing, it takes only a few probes (by reading only a few levels of index tree) to determine whether the requested information is present. Therefore, they have the best performance when there is very low data availability. However, when data availability is high, extra probes are needed to find the actual data buckets in the broadcast. Therefore, the tuning time increases with data availability. For the hashing scheme, all overflow buckets must still be read when the requested information is not in the broadcast. It outperforms *(1,m)* indexing and distributed indexing at high data availability because it may need to read fewer overflow buckets before reaching the required bucket.

5.2 Comparing Indexing Schemes Based on Record/Key Ratio

In this experiment, we assume that data availability is achieved at 100%. We vary the record to index ratio from 5 to 100. This is a reasonable range that record/key ratios of data in most applications fall in. The simulation results are shown in Figure 6.

Figure 6(a) shows that access time changes with the record to key ratio. We see that the ratio has a strong impact only on *(1,m)* indexing and distributed indexing. That is because different record to key ratios may result in different index tree structures. For B+ tree based indexing schemes, the ratio changes the number of buckets in the index tree and thus the index levels. For distributed indexing, the ratio also changes the number of replication levels. Figure 6(a) shows that both *(1,m)* indexing and distributed indexing have very large access times when the record to key ratio is small. This is because the overhead introduced

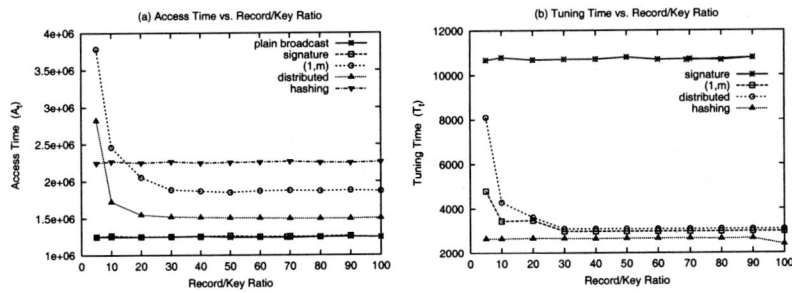

Fig. 6. Comparison for different record/key ratio

by adding the index segment, is prominent when the key size is comparable with the record size. They perform much better when the ratio is large. Both *(1,m)* indexing and distributed indexing outperform hashing as record/key ratio gets larger.

As to tuning time, flat broadcast is ignored because it is not comparable with the other schemes. From our previous discussion, the tuning time of hashing is much better than that of other indexing schemes. Figure 6(b) shows that *(1,m)* indexing and distributed indexing exhibit similar performance to hashing when the record/key ratio is large. The explanation is similar to that of access time. When the key size is large compared to the data record, fewer indices fit into a single bucket. Thus, more buckets are read to traverse the index tree. This results in a larger tuning time. On the other hand, smaller key sizes result in smaller tuning time for *(1,m)* indexing and distributed indexing.

5.3 Summary

Based on the simulation and comparison presented above, we note the following observations: (1) Flat broadcast has the best access time but the worst tuning time. Since the tuning time of flat broadcast is far larger than that of any indexing schemes, it is usually not a preferred method in power limited wireless environments; (2) Signature indexing achieves better access time than most of the other indexing schemes. However, the tuning time of signature indexing is comparatively larger. When energy is of less concern than waiting time, signature indexing is a preferred method; (3) Hashing usually achieves better tuning time. In energy critical applications, hashing scheme (with a good hashing function) is preferred; (4) *(1,m)* indexing and distributed indexing achieve good tuning time and access time under low data availability. Therefore, they are a better choice in applications that exhibit frequent search failures; (5) *(1,m)* indexing and distributed indexing have good overall performance (both access time and tuning time) when the key size of the broadcast data is very small compared to the record size. If access time is of concern, *(1,m)* indexing is preferable, otherwise distributed indexing is preferable.

6 Conclusion

In this paper, we described a framework for evaluating indexing schemes in wireless environments. We proposed a novel testbed for the evaluation of these indexing schemes. We presented an analytical model for each indexing technique. We also conducted exhaustive simulations to gauge the behavior of each indexing technique. We then compared the simulation results with those of the analytical models. The comparison results show that the analytical model has a very high accuracy depicting the behavior of the indexing techniques.

References

1. Y. Chehadeh, A. Hurson, and L. Miller. Energy-efficient indexing on a broadcast channel in a mobile database access system. In *Proceedings of the International Conference on Information Technology: Coding and Computing (ITCC'00)*, Las Vegas, Nevada, March 2000.
2. Ming-Syan Chen, Philip S. Yu, and Kun-Lung Wu. Indexed sequential data broadcasting in wireless mobile computing. In *Proceedings of the 17th International Conference on Distributed Computer Systems*, Baltimore, Maryland, USA, May 1997.
3. Qinglong Hu, Dik Lun Lee, and Wang chien Lee. Indexing techniques for wireless data broadcast under data clustering and scheduling. In *Proceedings of the Eighth ACM International Conference on Information and Knowledge Management (CIKM'99)*, pages 351–358, Kansas City, Missouri, November 1999.
4. Qinglong Hu, Dik Lun Lee, and Wang chien Lee. Power conservative multi-attribute queries on data broadcast. In *Proceedings of 16th IEEE International Conference on Data Engineering (ICDE'2000)*, pages 157–166, San Diego, CA, USA, February 28 - March 3 2000.
5. T. Imielinski and H. F. Korth, editors. *Mobile Computing*. Kluwer Academic Publishers, 1996.
6. Tomasz Imielinski, S. Viswanathan, and B. R. Badrinath. Energy efficient indexing on air. In *Proceedings of the 1994 ACM SIGMOD International Conference on Management of Data*, pages 25–36, Minneapolis, Minnesota, March 24-27 1994.
7. Tomasz Imielinski, S. Viswanathan, and B. R. Badrinath. Power efficient filtering of data an air. In *Proceedings of 4th International Conference on Extending Database Technology (EDBT'94)*, pages 245–258, Cambridge, United Kingdom, March 28-31 1994.
8. W.-C. Lee and D.L. Lee. Using signature techniques for information filtering in wireless and mobile environments. *Special Issue on Databases and Mobile Computing, Journal on Distributed and Parallel Databases*, 4(3):205–227, July 1996.
9. Shou-Chih Lo and Arbee L.P. Chen. An adaptive access method for broadcast data under an error-prone mobile environment. *IEEE Transactions on Knowledge and Data Engineering*, 12(4):609–620, July/August 2000.

Bridging the Gap between Response Time and Energy-Efficiency in Broadcast Schedule Design

Wai Gen Yee, Shamkant B. Navathe,
Edward Omiecinski, and Christopher Jermaine

College of Computing, Georgia Institute of Technology
Atlanta, GA 30332-0280
{waigen,sham,edwardo,jermaine}@cc.gatech.edu

Abstract. In this paper, we propose techniques for scheduling data broadcasts that are favorable in terms of both response and tuning time. In other words, these techniques ensure that a typical data request will be quickly satisfied and its reception will require a low client-side energy expenditure. By generating broadcast schedules based on Acharya et al.'s broadcast disk paradigm, we bridge the gap between these two mutually exclusive bodies of work–response time and energy expenditure. We prove the utility of our approach analytically and via experiments. Our analysis of optimal scheduling is presented under a variety of assumptions about size and popularity of data items, making our results generalizable to a range of applications.

1 Introduction

Data broadcast is a well-known way of scalably answering data requests for a large client population [1, 2]. A single broadcast of a data item can satisfy an unbounded number of outstanding requests for that item. The relevance of scalable data dissemination techniques increases with the number of computer users, especially in light of emerging wireless technologies and applications requiring only asymmetric communications capabilities. Some sample applications include traffic information systems, wireless classrooms, financial data, and news services.

Research in wireless broadcast typically assumes a high-powered server that transmits data to mobile clients over a wide area. The consequences of this architecture relate to *application performance* and *energy conservation* because data rates are low and battery lifetimes are limited.

In order to alleviate the poor performance due to low bandwidth, servers can skew the average amount of bandwidth allocated to each data item so that more popular data are transmitted more frequently [3, 1, 4, 5]. Clients can further improve application performance via client-side caching [6, 7]. In order to conserve energy, on the other hand, servers can reduce the amount of work a client must do to find data by broadcasting data indices [8, 9].

1.1 Shortcomings of the State of the Art

Much of the work on response time and energy expenditure has been mutually exclusive. A typical bandwidth allocation algorithm constructs a schedule bottom-up by deciding at each time interval the priorities of each data item, and broadcasts the one with the highest priority. Although the average time required for an average client to receive a given data item is near-minimal, such schedules preclude the generation of indices, and makes client-side caching more difficult, resulting in poor energy conservation and application performance. The main reason for these poor results is that clients cannot predict the next data item to be broadcast and therefore cannot doze, prefetch or pin data. Our simulations show that even with uniform access to all items in the database, bottom-up schedules result in significant variation in the interarrival time of consecutive instances of a given data item. This variation increases with the number of data items in the database. (See [10] for more details of these experiments.) Moreover, these bandwidth allocation algorithms lack the notion of a beginning and an end of a schedule, making techniques such as consistency control among data items more complicated [11].

In contrast, work focusing on issues such as consistency and energy conservation [12, 9, 11, 13] typically assumes a *flat* schedule – no data item can be broadcast twice before all other data in the database is broadcast once. Flat scheduling has benefits – such schedules are short, and the worst-case wait for any data item is minimal. If there is skew in data access, however, the average time required to receive data with a flat schedule (about one-half the time it takes to transmit the entire database) is far from optimal.

1.2 Goals and Outline of the Paper

The work presented in this paper attempts to bridge the gap between broadcast research that optimizes bandwidth usage and that which designs predictable schedules. To this end, we propose a top-down design based on broadcast disks [6]. Broadcast disks are logical *partitions* of the database. The average frequency that a data item is broadcast is inversely proportional to the size of the partition to which it belongs. We can use this property to skew the amount of bandwidth toward more popular data items. Furthermore, using broadcast disks allows us to generate predictable schedules in a straightforward manner. See Figure 1.

We start by modeling our problem and formalizing our problem statement in Section 2. We then show how broadcast disks can be optimally generated in Section 3. Since the optimal solution is computationally expensive, we also propose a cheap approximation that yields near-optimal results. We then show how our schedule can be applied to handle the case of different-sized data items (Section 3.4) and indexing (Section 3.5). We discuss related work in Section 4, and conclude the paper and describe future work in Section 5.

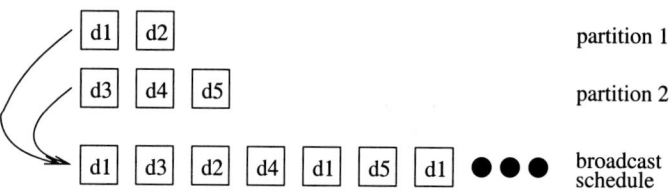

Fig. 1. An Example Broadcast Disk System. Clients listen for data items broadcast from each partition in a round-robin manner. In this example, the database consisting of 5 data items is partitioned into 2 broadcast disks, consisting of 2 and 3 data items, respectively.

2 Model and Problem Statement

In this paper, we assume that a server transmits the contents of a database containing N data items. Time is divided into units called *ticks*, and each unit of data requires a single tick to be transmitted. Clients request single data items. Each data item d_i ($1 \leq i \leq N$) has a probability p_i of being requested. Requests are assumed to be exponentially distributed–the probability that a data item is requested at each time interval is fixed. A broadcast *schedule* is a sequence of L data items, where $L \geq N$–all data items must be transmitted at least once, and some may be transmitted multiple times during a schedule.

Our goal is to generate a broadcast schedule that minimizes the expected delay of a data request subject to the following constraints:

1. There is a fixed interarrival time between all successive transmissions of a given data item in a schedule.
2. There is a notion of a cycle – i.e., the schedule has a beginning and an end.

As in [1], we assume that all interarrival times w_i of a data item d_i that occurs multiple times in a schedule are equal. This assumption stems from a basic result in probability theory which states that fixed interarrival times minimize expected delay given exponentially distributed requests and a known arrival rate. For a given schedule, the average expected delay over all data items is therefore

$$\text{average expected delay} = \frac{1}{2} \sum_{i=1}^{N} p_i w_i. \qquad (1)$$

By minimizing Equation 1 subject to constraints 1 and 2, we satisfy the goal of this paper, which is to bridge the work done in bandwidth allocation with other work done in the area of broadcast.

3 Heuristic

In this section, we describe a top-down technique for generating broadcast schedules. Bottom-up formulations of the broadcast bandwidth allocation problem have typically yielded intractable optimization problems [1]. Although heuristics that are near-optimal in terms of average expected delay (Equation 1) are available [3–5], none satisfies Constraints 1 and 2. (See Section 2.) In contrast, we show how to compute an optimal top-down solution subject to Constraints 1 and 2, and offer an inexpensive but effective approximation.

We borrow the concept of broadcast disks from [6]. A broadcast server picks a broadcast disk in a round-robin manner and transmits the least recently broadcast unit of data from it. Given K broadcast disks, the *beginning* of the broadcast schedule is defined as the transmission of the first data item of the first disk given that it is followed by the first data item of each of the next $K-1$ disks. The *end* is typically defined as the end of the last data item of the last disk, given that it is preceeded by the last data item of each of the previous $K-1$ disks.

Clearly, broadcast disk scheduling satisfies Constraints 1 and 2. Our goal is therefore to generate a set of broadcast disks that minimize average expected delay (Equation 1). Consider an arbitrary partitioning of N data items over K disks. The number of data items in each disk C_i is N_i, $\sum_{i=1}^{K} N_i = N$. We can reframe Equation 1 in terms of broadcast disks:

$$\text{broadcast disk average expected delay} = \frac{K}{2} \left(\sum_{i=1}^{K} N_i \sum_{d_j \in C_i} p_j \right). \quad (2)$$

In minimizing Equation 2, we first try to minimize the summation on the right-hand side. In other words, given K, how do we minimize $\sum_{i=1}^{K} N_i \sum_{d_j \in C_i} p_j$? (We call this subproblem the *partitioning problem*.)

In [10], we show how to optimally solve the partitioning problem using dynamic programming (DP). DP has $O(KN^2)$ computational complexity and consumes $O(KN)$ space to keep track of partial solutions.

3.1 A Cheaper Approximation for Partitioning

Although DP yields an optimal partitioning, its time and space complexity may preclude it from practical use. For example, depending on the application, redesign may occur frequently, or, as in the $DATACYCLE$ case, the size of the problem may be large [14], i.e., data sets may be orders of magnitude larger than those of wireless applications. We therefore offer an alternative, significantly cheaper algorithm.

Assuming that each data item is equally sized, define C_{ij} as the average expected delay of a request for a data item in a partition containing data items i through j [15]:

$$C_{ij} = \left(\frac{j-i+1}{2} \right) \sum_{q=i}^{j} p_q, \quad j \geq i, \quad 1 \leq i,j \leq N. \quad (3)$$

Our partitioning algorithm, called $GREEDY$, finds the *split point* among all the partitions that minimizes cost. Cost change by splitting a partition (i,j)

at point s is computed in constant time by:

$$C_{ij}^s = C_{is} + C_{s+1,j} - C_{ij}, \quad i \leq s < j \qquad (4)$$

The split process performed a total of $K - 1$ times. This algorithm is similar to the ones used in [16, 17], but is differs in its assumptions about the data and applications.

Algorithm 1

GREEDY
input: set of N unit sized data items ordered by popularity, K partitions
begin
  $numPartitions := 1$;
  while $numPartitions < K$
    do for each partition k with data items i through j
      do comment: Find the best point to split in partition k
      for $s := i$ **to** j
        comment: Initialize the best split point for this partition
          as the first data item. If we find a better one
          subsequently, update the best split point.
        do if $s := i \lor localChange > C_{ij}^s$
          do
            $localS = s$; $localChange = C_{ij}^s$;
          od fi od
      comment: Initialize the best solution as the one for the first
        partition. If we find a better one subsequently,
        update the best solution.
      if $k := 1 \lor globalChange > localChange$
        do
          $globalChange := localChange$; $globalS := localS$;
          $bestpart := k$;
        od fi od
      split partition $bestpart$ at point $globalP$
      $numPartitions := numPartitions + 1$;
  od
end

Example 1. Consider the problem of allocating the set of $N = 6$ data items to $K = 3$ partitions. Using the *GREEDY* algorithm, the first split occurs between data items 2 and 3. This is the point at which C_{ij}^s, $(i = 1, j = 6, s = 2)$ is minimized. The second split occurs between data items 1 and 2 for the same reason. These two splits reduce the average expected delay from 3 ticks to 0.95 ticks. See Figure 2.

Theorem 1. *The complexity of GREEDY is $O((N + K) \log K)$.*

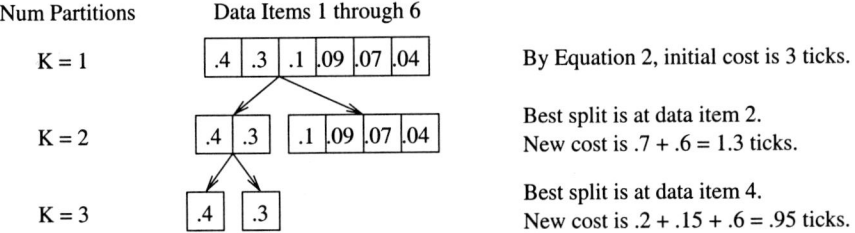

Fig. 2. Example of application of $GREEDY$, to generate $K = 3$ partitions. The numbers in the boxes are the popularities of the data items.

Since sorting the data items generally has $O(N \log N)$ complexity and $N \geq K$, by Theorem 1 the asymptotic complexity of $GREEDY$ is minimal. The implementation details of $GREEDY$ and proof of Theorem 1 can be found in [10]. In that work, we also present experimental results that prove $GREEDY$'s near-optimal performance over a wide range of parameters.

3.2 Generating Broadcast Disk Schedules

In this section, we apply the partitioning results described above to a technique for generating broadcast schedules. We first formalize the means of mapping the broadcast disks onto a broadcast medium first mentioned at the beginning of this section.

Algorithm 2

MAPPING
input: K disks of data, each containing N_i data items
begin
   $x := 0$;
  while $TRUE$
       do
        for $i := 1$ **to** K
          do
            broadcast the $((x \bmod N_i) + 1)^{th}$ unit of data from disk i
        od
        $x := x + 1$;
  od
end

One can see that the average expected delay of a schedule generated by Algorithm 2 is the cost given by Equation 2. Although this algorithm bears resemblance to one given in [6], it does not generate *holes*; all ticks contain data, thereby using bandwidth more efficiently.

Having solved the partitioning problem, our goal now is to find a value of K that minimizes the entire expression of Equation 2. We propose the simple algorithm for optimal **K** (abbreviated as *Safok*). This algorithm solves the partitioning problem for all values of K between 1 and N and returns the solution that is minimal when multiplied by K.

Algorithm 3

SAFOK
input: set of N unit sized data items ordered by popularity
begin
   $initial\_cost := C_{1N}$
   $current\_cost := initial\_cost$
   for $i := 1$ **to** N
      do
      $cost_i = current\_cost;$
      $kCost_i = \frac{k}{2} * cost_i;$
      if $i = 1 \vee kCost_i < bestKCost$
         do
            $bestKCost = kCost_i;$
            $bestK = i;$
      od
      Search all partitions for the best split point, s, between partition boundaries l and r;
      Make a split at s.
      $current\_cost = current\_cost - C^s_{lr}.$
   od
end

Corollary 1. *Safok has $O(N \log N)$ computational complexity and requires $O(N)$ memory.*

Proof: The proof is similar to that of Theorem 1.

3.3 Experimental Results

In this section, we compare the performance of *flat* (mentioned in Section 1) against that of *Safok*. We also report the analytical lower bound[1] (denoted **opt**) derived in [1]:

$$\frac{1}{2}\left(\sum_{i=1}^{N} \sqrt{p_i}\right)^2. \qquad (5)$$

We conduct two sets of experiments. In the first set, we vary the skew of the access probabilities. Assuming a Zipfian distribution, skew varies from low ($\theta = 0$) to high ($\theta = 1$). In the second set, we vary the number of data items in the database from 10 to 1000. The control skew is an 80/20 distribution and the

---
[1] Not achievable in general.

control database size is 500 data items. These values are in the range of those typically used in broadcast studies [18, 11].

As we can see, the performance of *Safok* is at least as good as that of *flat*. When there is no skew ($\theta = 0$), there is no need to transmit any data item more frequently than others, and therefore *Safok* does nothing. When skew increases, the performance difference becomes quite large (Figure 3). Moreover, the benefits of *Safok* over *flat* increase linearly with database size (Figure 4). Note that the average expected delay of the *Safok* schedules are near-optimal.

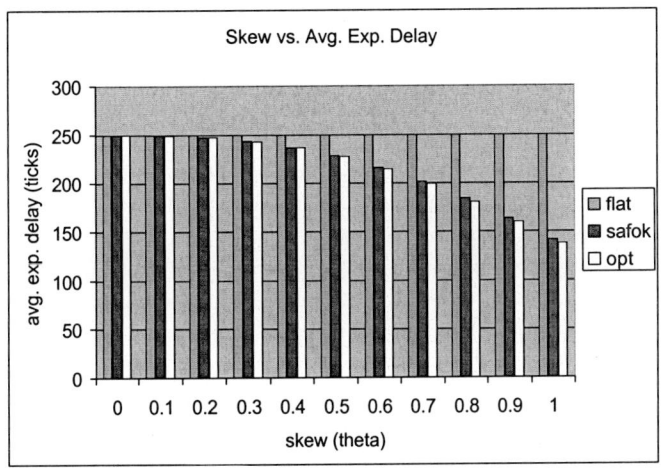

Fig. 3. *Safok* Performance. Varying Skew. Database Size = 500

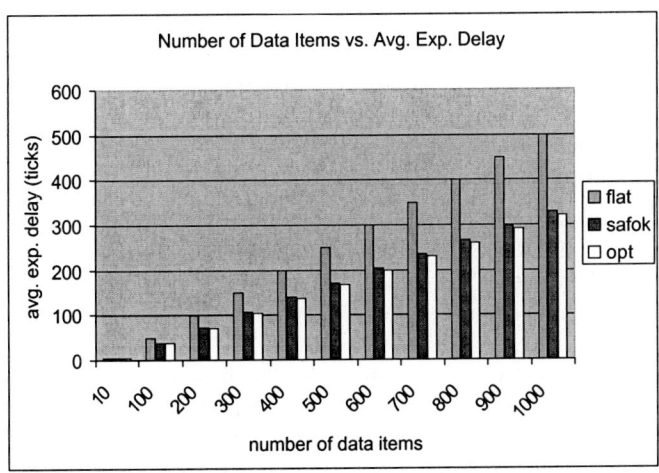

Fig. 4. *Safok* Performance. Varying Number of Data Items. Skew = 80/20

3.4 Different Sized Data Items

In many practical applications, data items span more than a single unit of data. For example, given multimedia content consisting of images and text, the data items can vary substantially in size. In this section, we consider the impact of size on *Safok*.

Given sizes $l_i \in Z^+, 1 \leq i \leq N$, the cost function from Equation 1 becomes

$$\frac{1}{2} \sum_{i=1}^{K} \left[\sum_{d_k \in C_i} l_k \sum_{d_j \in C_i} p_j \right]. \qquad (6)$$

Clearly, the problem of minimizing Equation 6 is a form of the NP-complete minimum sum of squares problem. We can, however, optimally solve Equation 6 exactly as we did in the unit-sized data item case (see Section 3). But again, because of the complexity of the optimal solution, we show how to adapt *GREEDY* to the varying size case.

GREEDY depends on ordering data items so that data that should be broadcast at similar frequencies are adjacent. For example, unit-sized data items are ordered by their access probabilities, $p_i, 1 \leq i \leq N$. To order data items of varying size, we borrow the *square-root rule* from [5]. This rule states that, in an optimal schedule, the number of ticks between consecutive instances of data item d_i is proportional to $\sqrt{\frac{l_i}{p_i}}$. The only modifications we make to Algorithms 2 and 3 are therefore:

- Data items are to be ordered by $\sqrt{\frac{l_i}{p_i}}, 1 \leq i \leq N$.
- Splits may not occur within data items d_i, where $l_i > 1, 1 \leq i \leq N$.
- The amount of data broadcast at each tick becomes $\gcd\{l_1, l_2, ..., l_N\}$ units.

The first modification is a way of clustering data items that should be broadcast at the same frequency. Because data items with similar $\sqrt{\frac{l_i}{p_i}}$ are contiguous, they can exist in the same partition and have similar broadcast frequencies.

The second and third modifications preserve the broadcast disk "semantics." In other words, the idea that multiple disks are simultaneously broadcasting their contents at different rates is preserved because the interarrival times between consecutive data items from a given disk are fixed. One practical implication of this is a simplified search. To find a data item of any size, a client only needs to listen to a single broadcast disk.

Experimental Results We compare the impact of different ways of ordering the data items on the average expected delay. We assume a database of 500 data items, and vary the Zipfian skew (θ) from 0 to 1. The ordering keys are

p_i	Access probability (denoted **p**), as done in previous experiments.
l_i	Size (denoted **l**).
$\frac{p_i}{l_i}$	Normalized access probability (denoted **p/l**).
$\sqrt{\frac{p_i}{l_i}}$	Square root of normalized access probability (denoted **root(p/l)**).

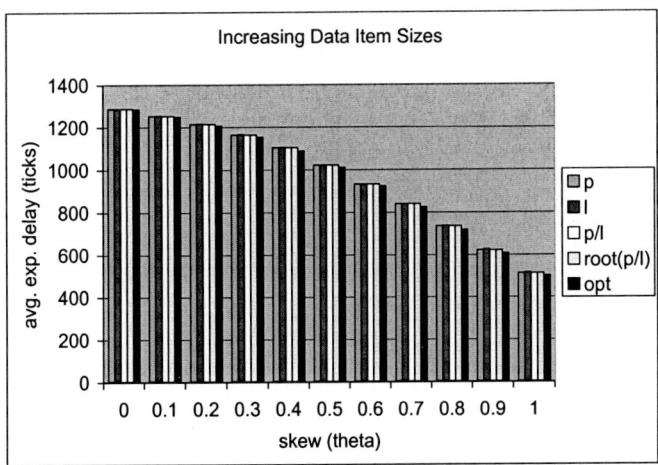

Fig. 5. *Safok* Performance With Varying Sized Data Items. p denotes ordering data by p_i. l denotes ordering data by l_i. p/l denotes ordering data by $\frac{p_i}{l_i}$. $root(p/l)$ denotes ordering data by $\sqrt{\frac{p_i}{l_i}}$. *opt* denotes the analytical lower bound. Number of data items = 500.

In the first set of experiments (Figure 5), we linearly increase the size of the data items with the following formula [5]:

$$l_i = l_{\min} + \text{round}\left(\frac{i \times (l_{\max} - l_{\min})}{N}\right), 1 \leq i \leq N, \qquad (7)$$

where *round* is the round-off function.

In the second set of experiments (Figure 6), we uniformly distribute l_i between $l_{\min}$ and $l_{\max}$. Other experiments using different size-assignment functions yield similar results. As in [5], we set $l_{\min}$ and $l_{\max}$ to 1 and 10, respectively, for all experiments. All results are compared against the analytical lower bound of average expected delay[2] (denoted **opt**)[5]:

$$\frac{1}{2}\left(\sum_{i=1}^{N} \sqrt{p_i l_i}\right)^2. \qquad (8)$$

Ordering by $\frac{p_i}{l_i}$ and $\sqrt{\frac{p_i}{l_i}}$ yielded identical results, which were better than those yielded by ordering by either p_i or l_i and are close to optimal. The performance improvements are only marginal in the increasing-sizes case (Figure 5), but are more noticeable in the random-sizes case (Figure 6). Both $\frac{p_i}{l_i}$ and $\sqrt{\frac{p_i}{l_i}}$ yielded near-optimal results.

In general, however, we expect the results of using $\frac{p_i}{l_i}$ to be worse than those of using $\sqrt{\frac{p_i}{l_i}}$. The key $\frac{p_i}{l_i}$ has been used in data partitioning algorithms for disk

---
[2] Not achievable in general.

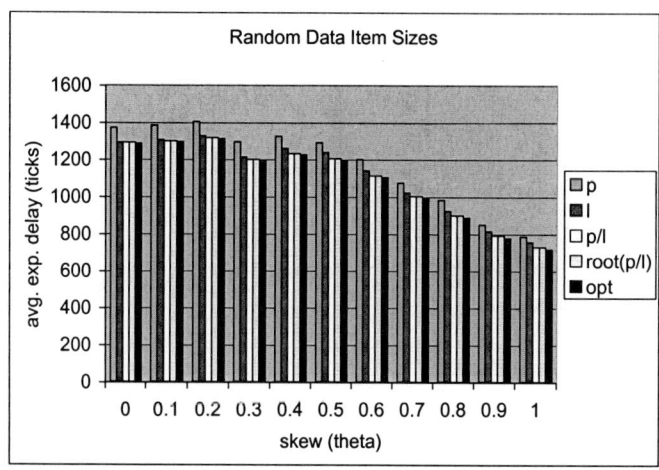

Fig. 6. $Safok$ Performance With Random Sized Data Items.

arrays [19]. However, these disk arrays are assumed to allow simultaneous access to multiple disks. In the broadcast case, in contrast, the transmission of a data item necessarily excludes the transmission of other data. This tradeoff acts as the intuitive justification for using the square-root.

3.5 Indexing

Indexing and careful data organization are important to any broadcast scheme since they allow efficient client battery power management. If a client knows exactly when a desired data item is scheduled to appear, then it need only tune in when that data item is to be broadcast. Otherwise, it can stay in an energy-conserving *doze* mode. When indices are present, the delay in receiving desired data is broken up into *probe wait* – the average time it takes to read the index information – and *broadcast wait* – the average time it takes to read the data item once indexing information is known. Note that when indices are absent, probe wait is zero and broadcast wait is equal to our original formulation of expected delay. Another parameter is *tuning time*, which is the amount of time the client must *actively* listen to the broadcast channel (for data and/or index information). Tuning time is therefore one rough measure of client energy consumption. The goal of indexing is to minimize tuning time with minimum impact on delay.

In this section, we argue that $Safok$ schedules are amenable to existing indexing techniques and demonstrate how a well-known indexing scheme can be applied. We prove the usefulness of $Safok$ by measuring the resulting average expected delay and tuning time.

In general, how might an existing indexing method be incorporated into our framework? We take advantage of the fact that while data items from different partitions may be transmitted at different frequencies in a $Safok$ schedule, within a partition, each data item is broadcast in a flat manner. We can therefore apply existing indexing schemes that assumes flat schedules [12, 8, 9] to each partition, and index and organize them independently. These separate partitions are then interleaved into a single channel.

For example, we consider the simple $(1, m)$ indexing method proposed by Imielinski, et al [9]. In this method, an index for all of the data items is regularly broadcast m times over a flat schedule. Say we compute three partitions, having 1, 4, and 20 data items, respectively. To use the $(1, m)$ scheme in combination with our partitioning, all we need to do is to interleave a $(1, m)$ organization for each partition into our broadcast schedule, as is shown in Figure 7.

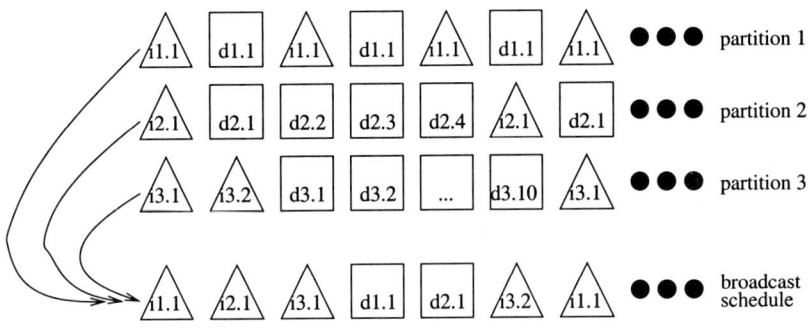

Fig. 7. Applying $(1, m)$ to a *Safok* Broadcast Schedule. Triangles denote units of index information. Squares denote units of data. d$m.n$ and i$m.n$ denote the nth data and index units from partition m, respectively. Each triangle or square requires a single tick to transmit.

The only additional modification we need to make to the $(1, m)$ organization is that each data item contains an offset to the next i$n.1$ unit (that is, for *any* $1 \leq n \leq K$), not just to the next index unit within its own partition.

Using this modified $(1, m)$ scheme, whenever a client wishes to find a data item, it listens to the broadcast channel, encountering a random data item. The client uses offsets contained in the data item to determine when the start of the next index unit will be broadcast. It then sleeps until this index unit comes up, and follows the pointers in the index, looking for the desired data item. It also follows the offsets to index units in other partitions. This process continues until the desired data item (or a pointer to the item) is found.

Note that the searching of the different indices in each partition are done concurrently, since there is no reason to wait until one index has been totally searched before we begin searching the others. Likewise, we may stop searching all indices once a pointer to the desired data item has been found.

An important characteristic of this mapping to our partition-based framework are that many of the desirable performance characteristics of the original algorithm are preserved. In the example application of the $(1, m)$ organization to our partitioned model, the expected delay of a data request from partition i is

$$\overbrace{\frac{K}{2}\left(Index_i + \frac{N_i}{m_i}\right)}^{probe\_wait_i} + \overbrace{\frac{K}{2}\left(m_i \times Index_i + N_i\right)}^{broadcast\_wait_i}. \qquad (9)$$

In this expression, m_i refers to the m value (the number of times a complete set of index information appears in the partition) for partition i, and $Index_i$ is the number of units required to store the index for partition i. We point out how closely this analytical formula mirrors that of the original $(1, m)$ scheme [9].

In general, the tuning time is increased at most by a factor of K from the tuning time required by the original algorithm. However, the tuning time required will be much less than K for a data item from a smaller partition (which by definition will be a more popular data item). Why? If the item requested is from a smaller partition, then we will likely find a pointer to it in some index before we ever need to turn on and search other indices. Formally, for the $(1, m)$ algorithm, the expected tuning time to find an item located in partition i is

$$1 + \sum_{j=1}^{K} index\_lookups(j, probe\_wait_i), \qquad (10)$$

where $index\_lookups(j, t)$ is the number of index units from partition j that we expect to actively listen to over a duration of t ticks. In Equation 10, we limit t to $probe\_wait_i$ because that is the expected amount of time required before finding the final pointer in partition i to the desired data item. The 1 on the left-hand side of Equation 10 comes from the fact we must tune in once after the indices have been searched to actually read the data item.

How might we calculate $index\_lookups$? The expected number of index units for partition j that are broadcast in t ticks is

$$\frac{t}{K}\left(\frac{Index_j}{Index_j + \frac{N_j}{m_j}}\right). \qquad (11)$$

Note that for a tree-based index, we only need to read one index entry at each level in the index. The final formula for $index\_lookups$ for partition j over t ticks is therefore[3]

$$index\_lookups(j, t) = 1 + \left\lceil \log_n\left(\min\left(Index_j, \frac{t}{K}\left(\frac{Index_j}{Index_j + \frac{N_j}{m_j}}\right)\right)\right) \right\rceil, \qquad (12)$$

where the 1 on the left-hand side is roughly the cost of finding an offset to the next index unit to be broadcast and n is the fanout (the number of (key, pointer) pairs an index unit may store) of each index unit.

---
[3] When the argument of the log function is at or below 1, we round the right-hand term.

The construction would be similar if an indexing scheme other than $(1, m)$ were used. For example, the *Distributed Indexing* scheme from [9] could also be used with a similar modification. In general, the tuning time is increased by at most a factor of K, but is significantly less for a more popular data item.

Experimental Results In this section, we describe some experimental results using $(1, m)$ indexing on a database consisting of 500 unit-sized data items. We assume that at each tick, 4K is transmitted. We assume that an index entry consists of a 16-byte (key, pointer) pair. The fanout, n, is therefore $4096/16 = 256$. Because of the tree-structure of each index, the size of the index information for each partition j is

$$Index_j = \sum_{i=1}^{\log_n N_j} \frac{N_j}{n^i}. \tag{13}$$

We also compute m_i^* (the optimal value of m_i, as described in [9]) for partition i as

$$m_i^* = \sqrt{\frac{N_i}{Index_i}}. \tag{14}$$

In the experiments we compare the average expected delay and tuning times of four scheduling algorithms.

flat	A typical flat schedule *without* indexing information.
flat_idx	A flat schedule augmented with $(1, m)$ indexing.
safok_idx	*Safok*, augmented with $(1, m)$ indexing.
opt	The analytically optimal solution *without* indexing information.

As expected, the time *safok_idx* takes to satisfy an average request decreases with increasing skew, but is always significantly worse than the optimal solution. In fact, in terms of average expected delay, *Safok_idx* does not beat *flat_idx* until medium skew ($\theta \approx .4$). The performances of both flat schedules is fixed and are outdone by both *safok_idx* and *opt* at high skew (Figure 8).

The tuning times of both indexed schedules are significantly lower than those of the non-indexed schedules, potentially saving lots of energy at the client. *safok_idx* is slightly worse than *flat_idx* at low skew, but is superior at high skew. At low skew, both algorithms should produce flat schedules, so should have similar index organizations. At high skew, using *safok_idx*, index information for very popular data items is easier to find and is smaller than it is with *flat_idx* (Figure 9).

4 Related Work

Su et al. studied the impact of various scheduling routines on client-side cache performance [7]. He uses some statistical information on client interests to partition data, but then uses a real-time priority-based scheme to pick each data item

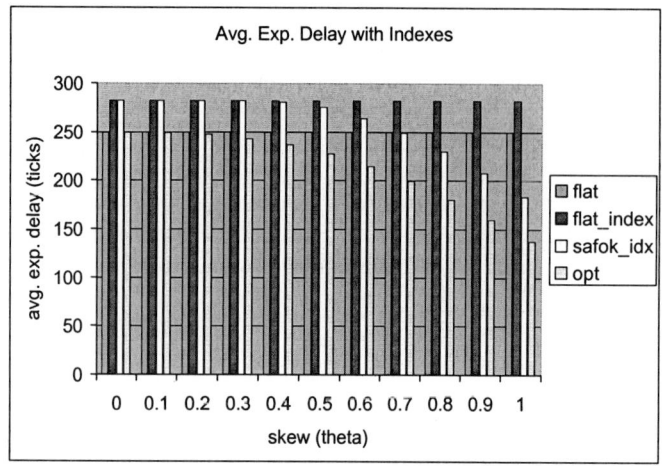

Fig. 8. Effect of Skew on Average Expected Delay using Indexed Schedules. Number of data items = 500.

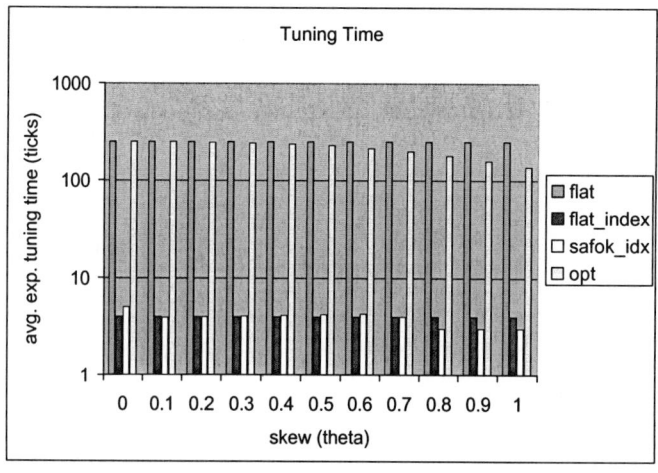

Fig. 9. Effect of Skew on Tuning Time using Indexed Schedules. Number of data items = 500. Note the log scale.

to transmit. So, although the resultant schedule has some fixed organization, it is basically bottom-up.

The partitioning problem from Section 3 is discussed in [16, 15]. However, the algorithm in [15] is unnecessarily complex and has unreliable results over some range of parameters [10]. Furthermore [15] never considers mapping its results to a single channel and does not go into detail about the benefits of a predictible schedule. In [16], the partitioning problem was investigated for a query histogram application using stronger assumptions of the data.

5 Conclusions and Future Work

In this paper, we make improvements on bandwidth allocation algorithms while preserving the property of a predictable schedule. Our proposed algorithm, *Safok*, yields near-optimal average expected delays, and more importantly, *Safok* requires fewer computational resources than typical scheduling algorithms. For example, the scheduling algorithm described in [1] requires $O(L)$ memory to store a schedule of length $L \geq N$, and has $O(N^3)$ computational complexity. The more modern *priority-based* schemes [3–5] require $O(N)$ computations *at each tick*. Furthermore, none of these algorithms, in contrast to the one proposed here, generates predictable fixed-length schedules, excluding them from enhancements such as indexing [9] or consistency control [11]. Our scheme requires $O(N \log N)$ computations and $O(N)$ memory regardless of the length of the schedule and results in near-optimal average expected delay given both unit-sized and varying-sized data items. A complete set of our experimental results is available upon request.

We also generate good tuning time results. Besides having superior average expected delay, the tuning time with *safok_idx* (*Safok* using $(1,m)$ indexing) improves with increasing skew and beats *flat_idx* (flat using $(1,m)$ indexing) under high skew. We have therefore shown that a repetitive schedule can be easy to compute, deliver data in near-optimal time, and incorporate previous work on broadcast requiring flat schedules.

Due to space limitations, we do not discuss some other important results. One important consideration is related to schedule length and worst-case delay. Shorter schedules are desirable, because they allow schedules to change with user interests and workload [20] and consistency control is simpler [11]. Bounded worst-case delay is desirable for real-time applications [21]. Although other schedule-measuring schemes exist, the length of a *Safok* schedule is typically $O(\text{lcm}\{N_i, i = 1, ..., K\}) \leq O(\Pi_{i=1}^{K} N_i)$. There are simple ways to control schedule-length and worst-case delay. See [1, 10] for more details.

Our work is ongoing. We are keenly interested in generating broadcast schedules given requests consisting of *sets* of data items. Clearly, given two requests, or multiple non-overlapping requests, a shortest-job-first algorithm is best. In the general case, however, generating an optimal schedule is a combinatorial problem. Initial investigations of this problem have already been done in [22] with pre-emptible transmissions of long data items, and in [8] with multi-attribute indexing. But reflecting the divide in most of the literature, the former work focuses on bandwidth allocation while the latter focuses on power conservation. Our work would again bridge the gap.

We are also working on mapping our results into the multiple broadcast channel case [10]. The availability of multiple broadcast channels allows improved scalability and adaptability to changing environmental conditions and equipment configurations. Our partitioning results can be directly mapped to multiple channels, but we are also considering various indexing strategies as well. Indexing can have a serious impact as search over multiple channels can be more time and energy consuming than in a single channel case [23].

Acknowledgements

The authors would like to thank Professors Mostafa Ammar and Krithi Ramamritham for their technical comments and Mireille Jacobson for her editorial advice.

References

1. Ammar, M.H., Wong, J.W.: The design of teletext broadcast cycles. Performance Evaluation **5** (1985) 235–242
2. Herman, G., Gopal, G., Lee, K.C., Weinrib, A.: The datacycle architecture for very high throughput database systems. Proceedings of ACM SIGMOD International Conference on Management of Data (1987) 97–103
3. Aksoy, D., Franklin, M.: Scheduling for large-scale on-demand data broadcasting. Joint Conference Of The IEEE Computer and Communications Societies (1998)
4. Su, C.J., Tassiulas, L., Tsortras, V.J.: Broadcast scheduling for information distribution. Wireless Networks **5** (1999) 137–147
5. Vaidya, N.H., Hameed, S.: Scheduling data broadcast in asymmetric communication environments. Wireless Networks **5** (1999) 171–182
6. Acharya, S., Alonso, R., Franklin, M., Zdonik, S.: Broadcast disks: Data management for asymmetric communication environments. Proceedings of ACM SIGMOD International Conference on Management of Data (1995)
7. Su, C.J., Tassiulus, L.: Joint broadcast scheduling and user's cache management for efficient information delivery. Wireless Networks **6** (2000) 279–288
8. Hu, Q., Lee, W.C., Lee, D.L.: Power conservative multi-attribute queries on data broadcast. In: Proceedings of the IEEE International Conference on Data Engineering. (1998)
9. Imielinski, T., Viswanathan, S., Badrinath, B.: Energy efficient indexing on air. Proceedings of ACM SIGMOD International Conference on Management of Data (1994)
10. Yee, W.G., Omiecinski, E., Navathe, S.B.: Efficient data allocation for broadcast disk arrays. Technical report, College of Computing, Georgia Institute of Technology (2001)
11. Shanmugasundaram, J., Nithrakashyap, A., Sivasankaran, R., Ramamritham, K.: Efficient concurrency control for broadcast environments. Proceedings of ACM SIGMOD International Conference on Management of Data (1999) 85–96
12. Datta, A., VanderMeer, D., Celik, A., Kumar, V.: Adaptive broadcast protocols to support efficient and energy conserving retrieval from databases in mobile computing environments. ACM Transactions on Database Systems **24** (1999)
13. Stathatos, K., Roussopoulos, N., Baras, J.S.: Adaptive data broadcast in hybrid networks. Proceedings of the International Conference on Very Large Databases (1997)
14. Bowen, T.F., Gopal, G., Herman, G., Hickey, T., Lee, K.C., Mansfield, W.H., Raitz, J., Weinrib, A.: The datacycle architecture. Communications of the ACM **35** (1992)
15. Peng, W.C., Chen, M.S.: Dynamic generation of data broadcasting programs for broadcast disk array in a mobile computing environment. Conference On Information And Knowledge Management (2000) 38–45

16. Konig, A.C., Weikum, G.: Combining histograms and parametric curve fitting for feedback-driven query result-size estimation. Proceedings of the International Conference on Very Large Databases (1999)
17. Navathe, S.B., Ceri, S., Wiederhold, G., Dou, J.: Vertical partitioning algorithms for database design. ACM Transactions on Database Systems **9** (1984)
18. Acharya, S., Franklin, M., Zdonik, S.: Disseminating updates on broadcast disks. Proceedings of the International Conference on Very Large Databases (1996)
19. Scheuermann, P., Weikum, G., Zabback, P.: Data partitioning and load balancing in parallel disk systems. The VLDB Journal **7** (1998) 48–66
20. Lee, W.C., Hu, Q., Lee, D.L.: A study on channel allocation for data dissemination in mobile computing environments. The Journal of Mobile Networks and Applications **4** (1999) 117–129
21. Fernandez, J., Ramamritham, K.: Adaptive dissemination of data in time-critical asymmetric communication environments. Proceedings of Euromicro Real-Time Systems Symposium (1999) 195–203
22. Acharya, S., Muthukrishnan, S.: Scheduling on-demand broadcasts: New metrics and algorithms. In: Proceedings of the ACM/IEEE International Conference on Mobile Computing and Networking. (1998)
23. Prabhakara, K., Hua, K.A., Oh, J.: Multi-level multi-channel air cache designs for broadcasting in a mobile environment. Proceedings of the IEEE International Conference on Data Engineering (2000)

Estimating Answer Sizes for XML Queries

Yuqing Wu, Jignesh M. Patel, and H.V. Jagadish

Univ. of Michigan, Ann Arbor, MI, USA*
{yuwu,jignesh,jag}@eecs.umich.edu

Abstract. Estimating the sizes of query results, and intermediate results, is crucial to many aspects of query processing. In particular, it is necessary for effective query optimization. Even at the user level, predictions of the total result size can be valuable in "next-step" decisions, such as query refinement. This paper proposes a technique to obtain query result size estimates effectively in an XML database.

Queries in XML frequently specify structural patterns, requiring specific relationships between selected elements. Whereas traditional techniques can estimate the number of nodes (XML elements) that will satisfy a node-specific predicate in the query pattern, such estimates cannot easily be combined to provide estimates for the entire query pattern, since element occurrences are expected to have high correlation.

We propose a solution based on a novel histogram encoding of element occurrence position. With such *position histograms*, we are able to obtain estimates of sizes for complex pattern queries, as well as for simpler intermediate patterns that may be evaluated in alternative query plans, by means of a *position histogram join* (pH-join) algorithm that we introduce. We extend our technique to exploit schema information regarding allowable structure (the *no-overlap* property) through the use of a *coverage histogram*.

We present an extensive experimental evaluation using several XML data sets, both real and synthetic, with a variety of queries. Our results demonstrate that accurate and robust estimates can be achieved, with limited space, and at a miniscule computational cost. These techniques have been implemented in the context of the TIMBER native XML database [22] at the University of Michigan.

1 Introduction

XML data [2] is becoming ubiquitous, and an XML document (or database) is naturally modeled as a (collection of) node-labeled tree(s). In such a tree, each node represents an XML *element*, and each tree edge represents an *element-subelement inclusion relationship*.

A natural way to query such hierarchically organized data is by using small node-labeled trees, referred to as *twigs*, that match portions of the hierarchical

---

* H.V. Jagadish and Yuqing Wu were supported in part by NSF under grant IIS-9986030 and DMI-0075447. Jignesh M. Patel was supported in part by a research gift donation from NCR Corporation.

data. Such queries form an integral component of query languages proposed for XML (for example, [4]), and for LDAP directories [11]. For example, the XQuery expression

FOR $f IN document("personnel.xml")//department/faculty
WHERE count($f/TA) > 0 AND count($f/RA) > 0
RETURN $f

matches all faculty members that has at least one TA and one RA, in the example data set shown in Fig. 1. This query can be represented as a node-labeled tree, with the element tags **department** and **faculty** as labels of non-leaf nodes in the tree, and the element tags **TA** and **RA** as labels of leaf nodes in the tree, as shown in Fig. 2.

A fundamental problem in this context is to accurately and quickly estimate the number of matches of a twig query pattern against the node-labeled data tree.

An obvious use is in the cost-based optimization of such queries: knowing selectivities of various sub-queries can help in identifying cheap query evaluation plans. For example, the query of Fig. 2 can be evaluated by identifying all faculties with RAs, and joining this set with the set of departments, then joining the result of this with the set of all the TAs. An alternative query plan is to join the faculties and RAs first, and then join the result set with TAs, then, departments. Depending on the cardinalities of the intermediate result set, one plan may be substantially better than another. Accurate estimates for the intermediate join result are essential if a query optimizer is to pick the optimal plan. Furthermore, if there are multiple join algorithms, the optimizer will require accurate estimates to enable it to choose the more efficient algorithm. Similar choices must be made whether the underlying implementation is a relational or a native XML database.

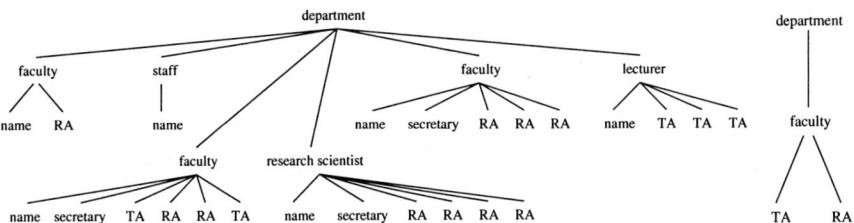

Fig. 1. Example XML document **Fig. 2.** Pattern Tree

Result size estimation has additional uses in an Internet context. For instance, there may be value in providing users with quick feedback about expected result sizes before evaluating the full query result. Even when the query involved is an on-line query where only partial results are requested, it is helpful to provide an estimate of the total number of results to the user along with the first subset of results, to help the user choose whether to request more results of the same query or to refine the query. Similarly, result size estimation can be very useful when space allocation or parallelism are involved.

Histograms are by far the most popular summary data structures used for estimating query result sizes in (relational) databases. When used in the XML context, they could indeed be used to estimate accurately the number of nodes satisfying a specified node predicate. One could build a histogram for the predicate associated with each node in a query pattern, and obtain individual estimates for the number of occurrences of each. However, structural relationship information is not captured in traditional histograms, and it is not obvious how to combine estimates for individual nodes into estimates for the whole query tree pattern.

The central contribution of this paper is the introduction of *position histograms* to capture this structural information. A position histogram is built over "base" predicates, such as "elementtag = faculty". The position histograms on two base predicates, P_1 and P_2, can be used to accurately estimate the selectivity of queries with the pattern $P_1//P_2$, which matches all "P_2" nodes that are descendants of all "P_1" nodes in the data tree. Some special features of predicates, such as no-overlap property, which dramatically affects the selectivity of the pattern matching, are also considered. Even though these histograms are two-dimensional, they behave like one-dimensional histograms for many purposes, including in their storage requirements.

We formally define our problem in Section 2, and summarize our overall solution approach in Section 3. We also establish various properties of this new summary data structure, and show how to use this to obtain query result sizes estimates efficiently in Section 3. Schemata often impose constraints on allowed structural relationships. In Section 4, we show how, at least in some key cases, such schema information can be exploited to obtain better estimates. We experimentally demonstrate the value of our proposal in Section 5, considering not just the quality of the estimate, but also issues such as computation time and storage requirement. And related work is discussed in Section 6. Conclusions and directions for future work are outlined in Section 7.

2 Problem Definition

We are given a large rooted node-labeled tree $T = (V_T, E_T)$, representing the database.

We are given a set of boolean predicates, $\mathcal{P}$: $\{v : v \in T\} \to \{0, 1\}$. For each predicate $\alpha \in \mathcal{P}$, for each node $v \in T$, we have either $\alpha(v)$ is true or $\alpha(v)$ is false. (See Sec 3.4 for a discussion of how to obtain this set $\mathcal{P}$ for a real database).

A query is a smaller, rooted, node-labeled tree $Q = (V_Q, E_Q)$. The goal is to determine the number of "matches" of Q in T. The labels at the nodes of Q are boolean compositions of predicates from $\mathcal{P}$.

A *match* of a pattern query Q in a T is a total mapping $h : \{u : u \in Q\} \to \{x : x \in T\}$ such that:

- For each node $u \in Q$, the predicate node label of u is satisfied by $h(u)$ in T.
- For each edge (u,v) in Q, $h(v)$ is a descendant of $h(u)$ in T.

Fig. 1 shows a very simple XML document. The personnel of a department can be faculty, staff, lecturer or research scientist. Each of them has a name as identification. They may or may not have a secretary. Each faculty may have both TAs and RAs. A lecturer can have more than one TAs, but no RA. A research scientist can have numerous RAs, but no TA. Consider a simple twig pattern with only two nodes, faculty and TA, with parent-child relationship among them. There are three faculty nodes and five TA nodes in the XML document. The schema says that a faculty can have any number of TAs. Without any further schema information, the best we can do in estimating the result size is to compute the product of the cardinality of these two nodes, which yields 15. Consider the fact that faculty nodes are not nested, one TA can only be the child of one faculty node, we can tell that the upper-bound of the result number is the cardinality of TA nodes, which is 5. But as we can see from the figure, the real result size is 2. The question we address in this paper is how to capture the structure information of the XML document to get a better estimation.

Our problem can be stated succinctly as follows:

Define a summary data structure T' corresponding to a node-labeled data tree T, and a set of primitive predicates of interest $\mathcal{P}$, such that the size of T' is a small percentage of the size of T; and for any query Q, defined as a structural pattern of nodes satisfying combinations of predicates from $\mathcal{P}$, correctly estimate the total number of matches of Q in T, using only Q and the summary data structure T'.

3 Our Proposal

3.1 The Basic Idea

We associate a numeric start and end label with each node in the database, defining a corresponding interval between these labels. We require that a descendant node has an interval that is strictly included in its ancestors' intervals.

This numbering scheme is inspired by, and quite similar to, the node numbering based on document position frequently used in information retrieval and adopted for XML database use by Univ. of Wisconsin researchers in the course of the Niagara [18] project.

We obtain these labels as follows. First, we merge all documents in the database into a single mega-tree with a dummy element as the root, and each document as a child subtree. We number nodes in this tree to obtain the desired labels – the start label by a pre-order numbering and the end label of a node is assigned to be at least as large as its own start label and larger than the end label of any of its descendant.

Given a limited set $\mathcal{P}$ of predicates of interest, one should expect that there will be index structures that identify lists of nodes satisfying each predicate in $\mathcal{P}$. For many, even most, predicates, these lists can be very long. While queries may be answered through manipulating such lists, the effort involved is far too great for an answer size estimation task. The standard data structure for maintaining summary data in a database is a histogram. We compress each such list into a two-dimensional histogram summary data structure, as we describe next.

We take the pairs of **start** and **end** pair of values associated with the nodes that satisfy a predicate α, and construct a two-dimensional histogram $Hist_\alpha$ with them. Each grid cell in the histogram represents a range of **start** position values and a range of **end** position values. The histogram $Hist_\alpha$ maintains a count of the number of nodes satisfying α that have **start** and **end** positions within the specified ranges. We call such a data structure a *position histogram*.

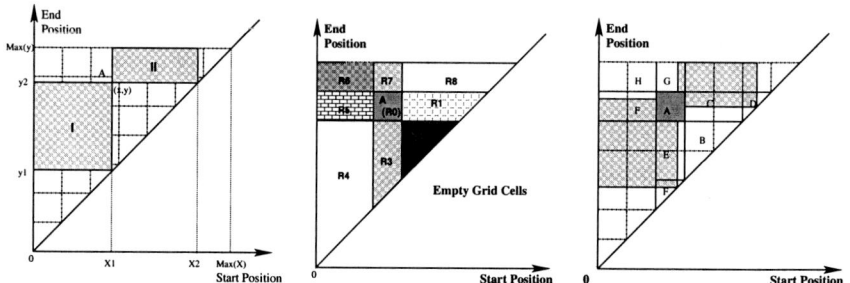

Fig. 3. Forbidden Regions in a Position Histogram due to one node

Fig. 4. Layout of Position Histogram

Fig. 5. Estimating Join Counts with Position Histogram

Position histograms, even though defined over a two-dimensional space, have considerable structure, as shown in Fig. 3.

Since the **start** position and **end** position of a node always satisfies the formula that **start** <= **end**, none of the nodes can fall into the area below the diagonal of the matrix. So, only the grid cells to the upper left of the diagonal can have count of more than zero.

Given a point A with coordinates (x,y), the regions marked I and II are guaranteed to be empty, since the **start** and **end** ranges of any two nodes can either have no overlap, or the range of one node fully contained within the range of the other node. This leads to the following Lemma:

Lemma 1 *In a position histogram for any predicate, a non-zero count in grid cell (i,j) implies a zero count in each grid cell (k,l) with (a) $i < k < j$ and $j < l$, or (b) $i < l < j$ and $k < i$.*

3.2 Primitive Estimation Algorithm

Each document node is mapped to a point in two dimensional space (in each position histogram corresponding to a predicate satisfied at the node). Node u is an ancestor of node v iff the **start** position of u is less than the **start** position of

v and the end position of u is no less than the end position of v. In other words, u is to the left of and above every node v that it is an ancestor of, and vice versa.

Consider the grid cell labeled A in Fig. 4. There are nine regions in the plane to consider, marked A (R_0), R_1 through R_8 in the Figure. All points v in region R_2 are descendants of each point u in the grid cell A. All points v in region R_6 are ancestors of each point u in grid cell A. No point in region R_4 and R_8 is a descendant or ancestor of any point in the grid cell A. Points in region R_1 and R_3 *may* be descendants of points in grid cell A. Similarly, points in region R_5 and R_7 *may* be ancestors of points in grid cell A. To estimate how many, we exclude the forbidden region, and then assume a uniform distribution over the remainder of each grid cell. For this purpose, we overlap Fig. 3 with Fig. 4 to get Fig. 5.

Given predicates P_1 and P_2, both in $\mathcal{P}$, we show how to estimate the number of pairs of nodes u, v in the database such that u satisfies P_1, v satisfies P_2 and u is an ancestor of v, using two position histograms, one for predicate P_1 and one for predicate P_2.

When computing the estimate of a join, we can compute the estimate based on either the ancestor or the descendant. When computing an *ancestor-based* estimate, for each grid cell of the ancestor we estimate the number of descendants that join with the ancestor grid cell. Similarly, for the *descendant-based* estimate, for each grid cell of the descendant we estimate the number of ancestors that join with the grid cell.

The formulae for these two types of estimation are different, and are derived in the next two subsections. But first, we need the following definition:

Definition 1 *A grid cell in a position histogram is said to be* on-diagonal *if the intersection of the start-position interval (X-axis) and end-position interval (Y-axis) is non-empty. Otherwise, the grid cell is said to be* off-diagonal.

Ancestor-Based Join Estimation. If A is off-diagonal, as shown in Fig. 5, all points in the grid cells in region B are descendants of all points in grid cell A. Using the position histogram for predicate P_2, we can simply add up the counts of all grid cells in this region. Now consider region E. Each point in grid cell A introduces two forbidden regions. No points in region E can fall in the forbidden regions of the right-most point in A (as shown in Fig. 5), so all points in region E must be descendants of all points in grid cell A. Similarly, for a given point in grid cell A, part of region F is forbidden; the points that fall in the right triangle of F are descendants of A, and the points in the left triangle are not. Integrating over the points in region F, we estimate that half the points in F, on average, are descendants of any specific point in grid cell A. Similar discussions apply to regions C and D. For the points in the same grid cell (grid cell A) in the histogram for predicate P_2, for each point in grid cell A of the histogram for the predicate P_1, only the points in the bottom-right region can be descendants. Assuming a uniform distribution and performing the necessary integrals in each dimension, we derive on average a quarter chance. Putting all these estimates together, the ancestor-based estimation for each off-diagonal grid cell can be expressed as the first formula in Fig. 6.

When grid cell A is on-diagonal, regions B, C, D, E, F don't exist. Since a diagonal grid cell is a triangle rather than a rectangle, the chance that a descendant point can join with an ancestor point is 1/12.

```
Primitive Estimation: ancestor-based
    For off-diagonal grid cell A:
```
$$Est_{P_{12}}[A] = Hist_{P_1}[A] \times \{\tfrac{1}{4} \times Hist_{P_2}[A] + Hist_{P_2}[B] + Hist_{P_2}[C] + Hist_{P_2}[E]$$
$$+ \tfrac{1}{2} \times (Hist_{P_2}[D] + Hist_{P_2}[F])\}$$
```
    For on-diagonal grid cell A:
```
$$Est_{P_{12}}[A] = \tfrac{1}{12} \times Hist_{P_1}[A] \times Hist_{P_2}[A]$$
```
Primitive Estimation: descendant-based
    For off-diagonal grid cell A:
```
$$Est_{P_{12}}[A] = Hist_{P_2}[A] \times \{Hist_{P_1}[F] + Hist_{P_1}[G] + Hist_{P_1}[H] + \tfrac{1}{4} \times Hist_{P_1}[A]\}$$
```
    For on-diagonal grid cell A:
```
$$Est_{P_{12}}[A] = Hist_{P_2}[A] \times \{Hist_{P_1}[F] + Hist_{P_1}[G] + Hist_{P_1}[H] + \tfrac{1}{12} \times Hist_{P_1}[A]\}$$
```
Notation:
    Hist_P : position histogram for predicate P
    Est_P12 : estimation histogram of a twig pattern, where the ancestor
              satisfies P_1 and the descendant satisfies P_2.
    H[A] : summation of the grid cells in region A in histogram H.
```

Fig. 6. Formulae for Primitive Join Estimation

Descendant-Based Join Estimation. Referring to Fig. 5, no matter whether A is on-diagonal or off-diagonal, all ancestors of a point in the grid cell A will be in the regions A, F, G, or H. Following argument similar to those in the ancestor-based estimation above, all points in region F, G and H are guaranteed to be ancestors of all points in grid cell A. For the points in the same grid cell (grid cell A), the chance is 1/4 for an off-diagonal grid cell, while it is 1/12 for an on-diagonal grid cell.

Fig. 7. Position Histograms   **Fig. 8.** Coverage Histogram for faculty

Let's have a look at the example XML document in Fig. 1 again, with the same query pattern we discussed in section 2. The 2×2 histograms of predicates "element tag = faculty" and "element tag = TA" are shown in Fig. 7. Using the primitive estimation algorithm introduced above, we estimate the result size to be 0.6, much closer to the real result size. Note that the position histograms we used here are 2×2. By refining the histogram to use more buckets, we can get a more accurate estimate.

3.3 Analysis

The primary concern with any estimation technique, of course, is how good the estimates are. We will perform an extensive evaluation in Section 5. However, there are two other metrics of concern: the storage required and the time to compute the estimate. We address these issues next.

Storage Requirement. There can only be $O(g)$ non-zero grid cells in a $g \times g$ grid, unlike the $O(g^2)$ one might expect in general. Therefore the storage requirements are quite modest. We establish this result as a theorem here, and verify experimentally in Section 5.

Theorem 1 *In a $g \times g$ grid, the number of position histogram grid cells with non-zero counts is $O(g)$*

Time Required. Based on the formulae for both ancestor-cased estimation and descendant-based estimation, the procedure to compute the expected size of result for a simple 2-node pattern is to loop through all grid cells for counts of nodes satisfying the outer predicate, and for each grid cell loop through the histogram for the inner predicate, adding up the regions as described in the preceding section, and multiplying by the count of the outer grid cell. The grand summation of all these is the desired result. We have a choice of which of the two nodes in the pattern is the inner loop, and the other is the outer.

The summation work in the inner loop is repeated several times in the simple nested loop algorithm outlined above. A small amount of storage for intermediate results can result in the much more efficient algorithm shown in Fig. 9.

Algorithm *pH-Join* is a three-pass algorithm. In the first pass, column partial summations (as on region E and columns in region B in Fig. 5) are obtained. In the second pass, row partial summations (as in region C), as well as region partial summations (as in region B using column partial summations) are obtained. In the third pass, these partial summations are used, along with the matrix entries themselves, to obtain the necessary multiplicative coefficients derived from the inner matrix operand and these can be multiplied by the corresponding elements of the outer operand matrix and the summation taken.

Algorithm *pH-Join*, as stated, computes coefficients assuming that the inner operand is the descendant node in the pattern. Obvious minor changes are required if the inner operand is the ancestor node.

Observe also that all of Algorithm *pH-Join*, except for the final multiplication, deals with the histogram of only one predicate in the join operation. In consequence, it is possible to run the algorithm on each position histogram matrix in advance, pre-computing the multiplicative coefficients at each grid cell. The additional storage required is approximately equal to that of the original position histogram. So such pre-computation may provide a useful space-time tradeoff in some situations. In any event, the time required for the computation is simply $O(g)$ for a $g \times g$ grid.

```
Algorithm pH_Join (histA, histB)
// Inputs: Two histograms histA and histB,
// Output: Estimation of answer of A join with B .
for (i=0; i<grid_size; i++)
    for (j=i; j<grid_size; j++) {
        pSum[i][j].self = HistB[i][j];
        if (j == i) pSum[i][j].down = 0; // column summation
        else if (j == i+1) pSum[i][j].down = pSum[i][j-1].self;
        else pSum[i][j].down = pSum[i][j-1].self + pSum[i][j-1].down;
    }
for (j=grid_size-1; j>=0; j--)
    for (i=j; i>=0; i--) {
        if (i == j) {
            pSum[i][j].right = 0;
            pSum[i][j].descendant = 0;
        }
        else if (i == j-1) {
            pSum[i][j].right = pSum[i+1][j].self; // row summation
            pSum[i][j].descendant = pSum[i+1][j].down; // region summation
        }
        else{
            pSum[i][j].right = pSum[i+1][j].self + pSum[i+1][j].right;
            pSum[i][j].descendant = pSum[i+1][j].down + pSum[i+1][j].descendant;
        }
    }
for (i=0; i<grid_size; i++)
    for (j=i; j<grid_size; j++){
        if (i==j) rHist[i][j] = HistA[i][j] * pSum[i][j].self / 12;
        else rHist[i][j] = HistA[i][j] * (pSum[i][j].descendant
                         + pSum[i][j].self / 4 + pSum[i][j].down - pSum[i][i].self / 2
                         + pSum[i][j].right - pSum[j][j].self / 2 );
        total+=rHist[i][j]
    }
output(total);
```

Fig. 9. Algorithm *pH-Join* for Computing the Join Estimate

3.4 Predicate Set Selection

Often, the predicats applied at node may not belong to the set of basic predicates $\mathcal{P}$. In such a case, there may be no precomputed position histogram of start and end positions for nodes satisfying the specified predicate. However, if the specified predicate can be expressed as a boolean combination of basic predicates, we can estimate a position histogram assuming independence (between basic predicate components of the compound predicate) *within a grid cell*. To be able to manipulate counts, we need to convert these into the appropriate probabilities. For this purpose, we can compute a position histogram for the predicate "TRUE", including all elements in the database, and simply using their start and end positions to obtain the needed grid cell counts. For each grid cell, this count is the appropriate normalization constant to carry out the conversion.

Compound predicates can arise not only because the query expression has a compound predicate in it, but also because of the choices made in defining the set $\mathcal{P}$ of basic predicates. Predicates in XML queries fall into two general categories:

Element-Tag Predicates. These predicates are defined on the element tags. An example of such predicate is $elementtag = faculty$. Element tag predicates are likely to be common in XML queries, and are a good candidates for building position histograms on. Usually, there are not many element tags defined in an XML document, so it is easy to justify the storage requirement of one histogram for each such predicate and build a histogram on each one of these distinct element tags.

Element-Content Predicates. These predicates specify either an exact or partial match on the contents of element. For example, text nodes with a parent node year are numerical values (integer) within a small range. It is not unreasonable to build histogram for each of these values. In some cases, some part of the content has some general meaning, and tends to be queried extensively. It would be helpful to set a predicate that evaluates to true if the prefix (suffix) of the content of a text element matches to a certain value. We will see some examples of both in Section 5.

It is likely that such predicates far outnumber the element-tag predicates, and position histograms will only be built on element-content predicates that occur frequently. In any event, minimizing error in the estimation of these values is likely to be more important than errors in estimates of less frequent items. The value of this general concept has been amply demonstrated in the context of end-biased histograms [8].

4 Factoring in Schema Information

Up to this point, we assumed that the data was uniformly distributed within any grid cell, and this is indeed a reasonable thing to do if no other information is available. However, we may frequently have information from the schema that can substantially modify our estimate.

For instance, if we know that no node that satisfies predicate P_2 can be a descendant of a node that satisfies P_1, then the estimate for the number of results for a query that asks for P_1 satisfied at a node that is an ancestor of P_2 is simply zero – there is no need to compute histograms. Similarly, if we know that each element with tag author must have a parent element with tag book, then the number of pairs with book as ancestor and author as descendant is exactly equal to the number of author elements.

We recommend that such schema information be brought to bear when possible. Our work here concerns itself with the vast majority of the cases where schema information alone is insufficient.

4.1 No Overlap

We frequently know, for a given predicate, that two nodes satisfying the predicate cannot have any ancestor-descendant relationship. For instance, in Fig. 1, a faculty node cannot contain another faculty node. It follows that there can be no node that is a descendant of two distinct faculty nodes. (For instance, a particular TA node can appear under at most one faculty node). In such situations, the uniformity assumption within a histogram grid cell can lead to erroneous estimates. We present, in this section, an alternative estimation technique appropriate when the ancestor node predicate in a primitive two-node pattern has the no-overlap property. It turns out that there is no impact on the estimation of the descendant node in the pattern having a no-overlap property since multiple descendants could still pair with the same (set of nested) ancestor node(s).

Definition 2 *A predicate P is said to have the* no-overlap *property if for all elements x, y such that $P(x)$ and $P(y)$ are TRUE, we have: $endpos(x) < startpos(y)$ or $endpos(y) < startpos(x)$.*

4.2 Summary Data Structure for Predicates with No-Overlap

For a primitive pattern with a no-overlap ancestor node a, the number of occurrences is upper-bounded by the count of the descendant node d in the pattern. (Since each descendant node may join with at most one ancestor node). The question is how to estimate the fraction of the descendant nodes that participate in the join pattern. Within any one grid cell, the best one can do is to determine what fraction of the total nodes in the cell are descendants of a, and assume that the same fraction applies to d nodes. We call this fraction, the *coverage* of a in that particular cell. Thus, our technique for dealing with the no-overlap situation is to keep additional information, in the form of *coverage*. Formally, we define the *coverage histogram* for predicate P: $Cvg_P[i][j][m][n]$ to be the fraction of nodes in grid cell (i, j) that are descendants of some node that satisfies P and fall in grid cell (m, n).

At first glance, it may appear that the storage requirements here are exorbitant – rather than store counts for each grid cell, we are keeping information for *cell pairs*. However, for a given grid cell r in the position histogram, and consider its coverage in grid cell s, the coverage fraction is guaranteed to be one whenever cell s is both to the right of and below r. And the coverage fraction is obviously zero for cells that cannot include descendants of elements in r. As such, it is only the cells s along the "border" for which one is required explicitly to keep coverage information. In fact, one can establish the following theorem:

Theorem 2 *In a $g \times g$ grid, the number of coverage histogram cell pairs with partial (non-zero and non-one) coverage is $O(g)$. In other words, the coverage histogram requires only $O(g)$ storage.*

The proof relies on the fact that, due to the overlap property, if the grid cell of focus is populated (by a node satisfying the "ancestor" predicate), then there can be no node (satisfying this predicate) in any of the cells in the (black) region with coverage $= 1$.

This, together with the algorithms we established for position histograms in Section 3, estimation formulae for No-Overlap predicates can be derived, as shown in Fig. 10.

Let's go back to the example XML document again, and estimate the result size for the same query pattern. This time, the no-overlap estimation algorithm

Ancestor-based pattern count estimate:
$Est_{AB}[i][j] = Jn\_Fct_{A\_P_1}[i][j] \times \sum_{m=i..j, n=m..j}(Cvg_{A\_P_1}[m][n][i][j] \times Hist_{B\_P_2}[[m][n]]$
$\quad \times Jn\_Fct_{B\_P_2}[m][n])$

Descendant-based pattern count estimate:
$Est_{AB}[i][j] = Hist_{B\_P_2}[i][j] \times Jn\_Fct_{B\_P_2}[i][j] \times \sum_{m=0..i, n=j..max\_y}(Cvg_{A\_P_1}[i][j][m][n]$
$\quad \times Jn\_Fct_{A\_P_1}[m][n])$

Join factor estimate:
$Jn\_Fct_{AB\_P_x}[i][j] = \frac{Est_{AB}[i][j]}{Hist_{AB\_P_x}[i][j]}$ if $Hist_{AB\_P_x}[i][j] > 0$, $= 0$ otherwise

Participation Estimation:
  case1: the node (P_x) that the estimation is based on can overlap
    $Hist_{AB\_P_x} = Est_{AB}$
  case2: P_1 is no-overlap, estimation is ancestor-based
    $N[i][j] = Hist_{A\_P_1}[i][j]$
    $M[i][j] = \sum_{m=i..j, n=m..j} Hist_{B\_P_2}[[m][n]$
    $Hist_{AB\_P_1}[i][j] = N[i][j] \times (1 - (\frac{N[i][j]-1}{N[i][j]})^{M[i][j]})$
  case3: item P_2 is no-overlap, estimation is descendant-based
    $Hist_{AB\_P_2}[i][j] = Hist_{B\_P_2}[i][j] \times \sum_{m=0..i, n=j..max\_y}(notzero(Hist_{A\_P_1}[m][n])$
    $\quad \times Cvg_{A\_P_1}[i][j][m][n])$
  Here, function $notzero(x) = 1$ if $x \neq 0$, $= 0$ otherwise

Coverage Estimation:
  case1: P_1 is no-overlap, the join is ancestor-based
    $Cvg_{AB\_P_1}[i][j][m][n] = Cvg_{A\_P_1}[i][j][m][n] \times \frac{Hist_{AB\_P_1}[m][n]}{Hist_{A\_P_1}[m][n]}$
  case2: P_2 is no-overlap, and the join is descendant-based
    $Cvg_{AB\_P_2}[i][j][m][n] = Cvg_{B\_P_2}[i][j][m][n] \times \frac{Hist_{AB\_P_2}[i][j]}{Hist_{B\_P_2}[i][j]} \times notzero(Hist_{A\_P_1}[m][n])$

* **Notation:**
  Est_{AB}: estimation histogram of the pattern obtained by joining subpattern A, B.
  $Hist_{AB\_P_x}$: number of nodes that satisfy P_x and participate in the join of A and B.
  $Jn\_Fct_{AB\_P_1}$: number of nodes satisfying P_2 that join with each distinct node,
    that satisfy P_1, in the join of subpattern A and B.
  $Cvg_{AB\_P_1}$: the coverage histogram of the distinct nodes that satisfy P_1 and
    participate in the join of subpattern A and B.

Fig. 10. Estimation Formulae for No-Overlap Predicates

is used. The Coverage Histogram of predicate "element tag = faculty" is shown in Fig. 8. The estimate we get is 1.9, almost the same as the real result size.

5 Experimental Evaluation

We tested our estimation techniques extensively on a wide variety of both real and synthetic data sets. First, we report on the accuracy of the estimates obtained. Later, we present results on the storage size and the impact of storage size on the accuracy of the estimate.

5.1 The DBLP Data Set

We ran experiments on several well-known XML data sets, including the XMark Benchmark [15] and the Shakespeare play data set [20]. Results obtained in all cases were substantially similar. In the interests of space, we present results only for the DBLP data set [19] that is probably most familiar to readers of this paper. The DBLP data set is 9M bytes in size and has approximately 0.5M nodes.

For the DBLP data set, we picked a mix of element-tag and element-content predicates and built histograms on exact matching of all the element tags, the content value of years, and the prefix matching of the content of 'cite' (e.g conf, journal, etc.). A few of these predicates, along with the count of the nodes that match each predicate, and the overlap property of the predicate is summarized in Table 1. Note that the predicates 1990's and 1980's are compound predicates, obtained by adding up 10 corresponding primitive histograms for element-content predicate (e.g. 1990, 1991 ...). In all, there are 63 predicates; and the total size of all the corresponding histograms added up to about 6K bytes in all – roughly 0.7% of the data set size. (We used 10×10 histograms in all experiments, except where explicitly stated otherwise.)

Table 1. Characteristics of Some Predicates on the DBLP Data Set

Predicate Name	Predicate	Node Count	Overlap Property
article	element tag = "article"	7,366	no overlap
author	element tag = "author"	41,501	no overlap
book	element tag = "book"	408	no overlap
cdrom	element tag = "cdrom"	1,722	no overlap
cite	element tag = "cite"	33,097	no overlap
title	element tag = "title"	19,921	no overlap
url	element tag = "url"	19,542	no overlap
year	element tag = "year"	19,914	no overlap
conf	text start-with "conf"	13,609	N/A
journal	text start-with "journal"	7,834	N/A
1980's	compound	13,066	N/A
1990's	compound	3,963	N/A

Estimating Simple Query Answer Sizes. We tested the effectiveness of position histograms on a number of queries using a combinations of predicates from Table 1. In the interest of space, we only present results for a few representative queries in Table 2. The first row of this table considers a query pattern where an element with **author** tag appears below an element with **article** tag. Other rows consider similar other simple queries.

Without the position histograms, and without any schema information, a (very) naive estimate for the answer size is the product of the cardinalities of the node counts for the two predicates (*i.e.*, **article** and **author**). The naive estimate is far from the real result, since it does not consider the structural relationship between nodes. With the schema information and no position histogram, if the ancestor node has no-overlap property, the best (upper-bound) estimate of the

Table 2. Result Size Estimation for Simple Queries on DBLP Data Set

Ance	Desc	Naive Estimate	Desc Num	Overlap Estimate	Overlap Est Time	No-Overlap Estimate	No-Overlap Est Time	Real Result
article	author	305,696,366	41,501	2,415,480	0.000344	14,627	0.000263	14,644
article	cdrom	12,684,252	1,722	4,379	0.000290	112	0.000261	130
article	cite	243,792,502	33,097	671,722	0.000229	3,958	0.000261	5,114
book	cdrom	702,576	1,722	179	0.000142	4	0.000259	3

result size is the number of descendants involved in the join. When position and coverage histograms are available, overlap or no-overlap estimation algorithms can be used. When no schema information is available, using position histograms and the primitive *pH-Join* estimation algorithm brings the estimate closer to the real answer size. In some cases, the primitive estimation is better than the upper-bound estimation using only the schema information, while the no-overlap estimation using position histogram and coverage histogram gives almost exactly the right answer size.

Finally, the time spent on estimating the result size of a simple twig query pattern, in all cases, using both the overlap algorithm and the no-overlap algorithm, is only a few tenths of a millisecond, which is very small compared to most database operations.

5.2 Synthetic Data Set

Whereas our tests on real data give us confidence, real data sets like DBLP are limited in size and complexity. We wanted to understand how our techniques would do given a more complex situation, with deeply nested and repeating element tags. For this purpose we used the IBM XML generator[21] to create synthetic data using a realistic DTD involving managers, departments and employees, as shown below:

```
<!ELEMENT manager (name,(manager | department | employee)+)>
<!ELEMENT department (name, email?, employee+, department*)>
<!ELEMENT employee (name+,email?)>
<!ELEMENT name (#PCDATA)>
<!ELEMENT email (#PCDATA)>
```

The predicates that we consider for this DTD are summarized in Table 3.

Table 3. Characteristics of Predicates on the Synthetic Data Set

Predicate Name	Predicate	Node Count	Overlap Property
manager	element tag = "manager"	44	overlap
department	element tag = "department"	270	overlap
employee	element tag = "employee"	473	no overlap
email	element tag = "email"	173	no overlap
name	element tag = "name"	1,002	no overlap

On the synthetic data set, we ran all types of queries we presented above. Here, for lack of space, we present only the results of some representative simple queries in Table 4.

Table 4. Synthetic Data Set: Result Size Estimation for Simple Queries

Ancs	Desc	Naive Est	Overlap Estimate	Overlap Est Time	No-Overlap Estimate	No-Overlap Est Time	Real Result
manager	department	11,880	656	0.000070	N/A	N/A	761
manager	employee	20,812	1,205	0.000054	N/A	N/A	1,395
manager	email	7,612	429	0.000052	N/A	N/A	491
department	employee	127,710	2,914	0.000050	N/A	N/A	1,663
department	email	46,710	1,082	0.000054	N/A	N/A	473
employee	name	473,946	8,070	0.000062	559	0.000082	688
employee	email	81,829	1,391	0.000054	96	0.000080	99

In this data set, some of the nodes have the no-overlap property, some don't. We obtain the estimate with the *pH-Join* algorithm for all the queries, and use no-overlap estimation algorithm whenever possible. From Table 4 we can see that whenever there is no-overlap property, the no-overlap estimation algorithm gives an estimate that is much closer to the real answer size than those obtained by using the primitive *pH-Join* algorithm. For joins where the ancestor node doesn't have the no-overlap property, the primitive *pH-Join* algorithm computes an estimate that is very close to the real answer size. In spite of the deep recursion, the time to compute estimates remains a small fraction of a millisecond.

5.3 Storage Requirements

In this section, we present experimental results for the storage requirements of both position histograms and coverage histograms (recall as per Theorem 2, we expect the storage requirement to be $O(n)$). We also consider the impact of storage space on the accuracy of the estimates.

Fig. 11 shows the effect of increasing grid size on the storage requirement and the accuracy of the estimate, for the **department-email** query on the synthetic data set. Since the predicate **department** does not have the no-overlap property, the department-email pair join does not require any coverage information, therefore, only position histograms are built on predicate **department** and predicate **email**. The storage requirement for the two predicates are all linear to the grid size, with a constant factor close to 2. The result estimate is not very good when the histogram is very small. However, the ratio of the estimate to the real answer size drops rapidly and is close to 1 for grid sizes larger than 10-20.

Article-cdrom join is an example of query with no-overlap property. Here, both predicates (article, cdrom) have the no-overlap property, and consequently, we store both a position histogram and a coverage histogram for each of them. The storage requirement of these two predicates, as well as the accuracy of the

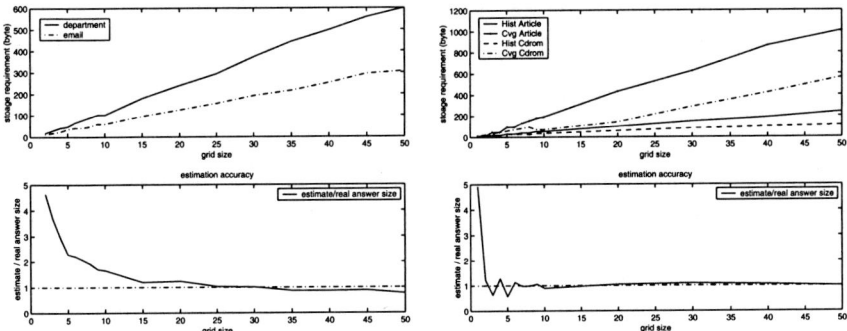

Fig. 11. Storage Requirement and Estimation Accuracy for Overlap Predicates (department-email)

Fig. 12. Storage Requirement and Estimation Accuracy for No-Overlap Predicates (article-cdrom)

estimation is shown in Fig. 12. Note that the storage requirement for both the position histogram and the coverage histogram are linear to the grid size, which results in the total storage requirement grow linearly with a constant factor between 2 and 3. Another observation is that the estimate is not good when the grid size is very small, but it very quickly converges to the correct answer. Starting from the point where the grid size is larger than 5, the ratio of estimate to the real answer size is within 1 ± 0.05, and keeps in this range thereafter. The reason is that more information is caught by the coverage histogram than by only the position histogram.

6 Related Work

In [5], estimation techniques have been suggested for "twig" pattern queries in a hierarchical database, including XML. These techniques generalize the work on pruned suffix trees, presented in [16, 10], and the notion of set hashing [3, 6]. These techniques, while powerful where they apply, suffer from some limitations. For one thing, the techniques only apply to fully specified twig patterns, involving only parent-child links. However, one expects many, perhaps even the majority, of XML queries to involve patterns with ancestor-descendant links. For another thing, the computation techniques only provide the selectivity estimate for the entire query pattern. If estimates are required for sub-patterns, representing intermediate results in a potential query plan, these have to be computed separately. Finally, the entire technique relies on notions of pruning in suffix trees, and on maintaining small hashes for set similarity. These space-saving solutions obviously lose information, and much ingenuity is used to minimize this loss. In contrast, our techniques are insensitive to depth of tree, and require no pruning and do not admit the possibility of a non-local information loss. (However, our techniques are sensitive to the size of "symbol alphabet", and the techniques in the reference are probably more appropriate if a large number of basic node predicates are required).

McHugh and Widom [13] describe Lore's cost-based query optimizer, which maintains statistics about subpaths of length $\leq k$, and uses it to infer selectivity estimates of longer *path queries*. Estimating selectivity of path queries has also been the focus of a recent paper by Aboulnaga et al. [1], in which the authors propose two techniques for estimating the selectivity of path expressions. The first technique called *path trees* are similar to the pruned suffix trees of [5], but are more accurate for estimating the selectivity of certain path expressions. The second technique uses a Markov table to maintain statistics about all paths up to a certain length. The Markov table approach is similar to [13], but can be aggressively summarized, thereby reducing the amount of memory used to maintain statistics. The techniques presented in these two papers do not maintain correlations between paths, and consequently, these techniques do not allow them to accurately estimate the selectivity of tree query patterns, which are very natural in XML query languages.

Histograms of various types, including multi-dimensional histograms, have been used for query estimation in databases [14, 12, 7–9]. However, XML queries often involve an ancestor-descendant or parent-child relationships among nodes. Traditional one dimensional histograms are not enough to catch the position information of each single node, relationship among nodes, as well as other structure information of the XML data. Therefore, a novel histogram is introduced here which can capture the structure information native to XML data and estimate the result size effectively and accurately.

7 Conclusions and Future Work

As XML continues to grow in popularity, large repositories of XML documents are likely to emerge, and users are likely to pose complex queries on these data sets. Efficient evaluation of these complex queries will require accurate estimates. Queries in XML frequently specify structural patterns that specify specific relationships between the selected elements. Obtaining accurate estimates for these is not easy, by traditional means. In this paper we have proposed a novel histogram technique called *position histogram*, and estimation algorithms using the position histograms, that can be used for accurately estimating the answer size for arbitrarily complex pattern queries. While the histograms we develop are two-dimensional, they are sparse and only require storage that grows linearly (rather than quadratically) with grid size. The estimation algorithms are computationally efficient and require only a very small running time.

In many cases, schema information may be available, and frequently can be used to set an estimate to zero or (through uniqueness) equal to some other simpler estimate. We identify one specific schema restriction that occurs frequently in XML, namely the *no-overlap property*. We exploit this property in a modified estimation algorithm, which produces estimates that are more accurate than the estimates produced without factoring in this schema information. An open question is which other schema information can be considered together with the position histogram to further improve the accuracy.

Extensive experimental evaluation using both real and synthetic data sets demonstrates the effectiveness of the proposed techniques, for different type of queries, simple or complex, and on XML documents of different structure, shallow or deep and nested. The summary data structures and estimation techniques developed in this paper are an important piece of the query optimizer in the TIMBER[22] native XML database system under development at the University of Michigan.

Theoretical and experimental studies have also be done on how to exploit the estimation technique, using both position histograms and coverage histogram, to estimate the answer size for query patterns that are arbitrarily complex. Issues on estimation for queries with ordered semantics, with parent-child relationship, and estimation using histogram with non-uniform grid cells are also looked into. Please refer to [17] for detailed information of these techniques, as well as proofs of all the lemmas and theorems in this paper.

References

1. A. Aboulnaga, A.R. Alameldeen and J.F. Naughton. Estimating the Selectivity of XML Path Expressions for Internet Scale Applications. *VLDB*, 2001
2. T. Bray, J. Paoli, and C. M. Sperberg-McQueen. Extensible markup language (XML) 1.0. W3C Recommendation. Available at http://www.w3.org/TR/1998/REC-xml-19980210, Feb. 1998.
3. A. Broder. On the Resemblance and Containment of Documents. *IEEE SEQUENCES '97*, pages 21–29, 1998.
4. D. Chamberlin, J. Clark, D. Florescu, J. Robie, J. Siméon and M. Stefanescu XQuery 1.0: An XML Query Language. *W3C Working Draft*, http://www.w3.org/TR/xquery/, June 7, 2001.
5. Z. Chen, H. V. Jagadish, F. Korn, N. Koudas, S. Muthukrishnan, R.T. Ng, D. Srivastava. Counting Twig Matches in a Tree. *ICDE*, 2001.
6. Z. Chen, F. Korn, N. Koudas, and S. Muthukrishnan. Selectivity estimation for boolean queries. In *Proceedings of the ACM Symposium on Principles of Database Systems*, 2000.
7. Yannis E. Ioannidis. Universality of Serial Histograms. In *VLDB*, pages 256-267, 1993.
8. Y.E. Ioannidis, V. Poosala. Balancing Histogram Optimality and Practicality for Query Result Size Estimation. In *SIGMOD Conference*, pages 233-244, 1995.
9. H. V. Jagadish, N. Koudas, S. Muthukrishnan, V. Poosala, K.C. Sevcik, T. Suel. Optimal Histograms with Quality Guarantees. *VLDB*, pages 275-286, 1998.
10. H. V. Jagadish, O. Kapitskaia, R. T. Ng, and D. Srivastava. One-dimensional and multi-dimensional substring selectivity estimation. In *VLDB Journal*, 9(3), pp.214–230, 2000.
11. H. V. Jagadish, L. V. S. Lakshmanan, T. Milo, D. Srivastava, and D. Vista. Querying network directories. In *Proceedings of the ACM SIGMOD Conference on Management of Data*, Philadelphia, PA, June 1999.
12. R. J. Lipton and J. F. Naughton. Query size estimation by adaptive sampling. In *Proceedings of the ACM SIGACT-SIGMOD-SIGART Symposium on Principles of Database Systems*, March 1990.

13. J. McHugh and J. Widom. Query optimization for XML. In *Proceedings of the International Conference on Very Large Databases*, pages 315–326, 1999.
14. M. Muralikrishna and D.J. DeWitt. Equi-Depth Histograms For Estimating Selectivity Factors For Multi-Dimensional Queries. In *SIGMOD Conference*, pages 28-36, 1988.
15. A.R. Schmidt, F. Waas, M.L. Kersten, D. Florescu, I. Manolescu, M.J. Carey and R. Busse. The XML Benchmark Project. Technical Report INS-R0103, CWI, Amsterdam, The Netherlands, April 2001.
16. M. Wang, J. S. Vitter, and B. Iyer. Selectivity estimation in the presence of alphanumeric correlations. In *Proceedings of the IEEE International Conference on Data Engineering*, pages 169–180, 1997.
17. Yuqing Wu, Jignesh M. Patel, H.V.Jagadish. Histogram-based Result Size Estimation for XML Queries. University of Michigan Tech Report, 2002.
18. C. Zhang, J.F. Naughton, D.J. DeWitt, Q. Luo and G.M. Lohman. On Supporting Containment Queries in Relational Database Management Systems. *SIGMOD*, 2001
19. DBLP data set. Available at http://www.informatik.uni-trier.de/ley/db/index.html.
20. ibiblio Organization. XML dataset for Shakesapeare drama. Available at http://sunsite.unc.edu/pub/sun-info/xml/eg/shakespeare.1.10.xml.zip.
21. IBM. XML generator. Available at http://www.alphaworks.ibm.com/tech/xmlgenerator.
22. TIMBER Group. TIMBER Project at Univ. of Michigan. Available at http://www.eecs.umich.edu/db/timber/.

Selectivity Estimation for Spatial Joins with Geometric Selections[*]

Chengyu Sun, Divyakant Agrawal, and Amr El Abbadi

Department of Computer Science
University of California, Santa Barbara
{cysun,agrawal,amr}@cs.ucsb.edu

Abstract. Spatial join is an expensive operation that is commonly used in spatial database systems. In order to generate efficient query plans for the queries involving spatial join operations, it is crucial to obtain accurate selectivity estimates for these operations. In this paper we introduce a framework for estimating the selectivity of spatial joins constrained by geometric selections. The center piece of the framework is *Euler Histogram*, which decomposes the estimation process into estimations on vertices, edges and faces. Based on the characteristics of different datasets, different probabilistic models can be plugged into the framework to provide better estimation results. To demonstrate the effectiveness of this framework, we implement it by incorporating two existing probabilistic models, and compare the performance with the Geometric Histogram [1] and the algorithm recently proposed by Mamoulis and Papadias [2].

1 Introduction

Many applications such as geographical information systems (GIS) and computer-aided design (CAD) systems require a large amount of spatial objects to be stored, accessed and manipulated efficiently, which gives rise to the area of *spatial databases*. The data stored in spatial databases are *spatial objects* such as locations, road segments, and geographical regions, which can be abstracted as points, polylines and polygons in a 2D or 3D coordinate system.

One of the most important operations in spatial databases is *geometric selection* [3], which in general can be classified as *windowing* and *clipping*. Given a set of spatial objects and a query rectangle, a windowing query retrieves all the objects that intersect the query rectangle. A clipping query can be considered as a windowing query with a post-processing phase: once the objects that intersect the query rectangle are found, a clipping algorithm is applied to the objects to trim off parts of the objects that are outside the query rectangle.

Another important operation in spatial databases is *spatial join*, which retrieves *pairs* of objects from two datasets. An object pair is a valid result of a join if they satisfy certain criteria. Two commonly used criteria are *distance*

---

[*] This work was partially supported by NSF grants EIA-9818320, IIS-98-17432, EIA-9986057 and IIS-99-70700.

and *intersection*, and the spatial joins based on these two criteria are referred to as distance join and intersection join. Distance join is typically used for finding pairs of objects that are within a given distance to each other. For example, the query "find all hotels that are within 10 miles to an airport" can be answered by the distance join of a hotel dataset and an airport dataset. For intersection joins, two objects constitute a result pair if they intersect each other. Intersection join is commonly used in applications such as *map overlays*. For example, answering the query "find all French-speaking administrative regions in Europe" involves the intersection join of an administrative map and a language coverage map. In this paper we only consider intersection joins.

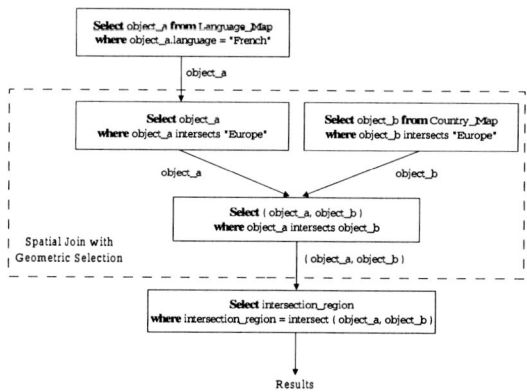

Fig. 1. An Execution Plan for the Query "Find all French-speaking regions in Europe"

It can be observed that the query "find all French-speaking regions in Europe" is not a simple spatial join. In fact, it is a composite query involving several operations. Figure 1 shows a likely execution plan for this query in an SQL-like syntax, assuming the database holds two datasets, one of which is a language coverage dataset of the world and the other is a political/regional dataset of the world. Note that the first step on the dataset *Language_Map* is a simple attribute selection query which is well-studied in relational databases, and the last step applies a computation geometry algorithm which calculates the intersection regions of two sets of objects. What is more interesting from a spatial database perspective are the steps in the middle, which we term as a *spatial join with geometric selections* query, or a SJGS query for short. We are interested in these types of queries for two reasons. First of all, these types of queries are very common in spatial databases, and they are also very expensive in term of execution cost. For example, it is not uncommon in real world datasets that a single polygon consists of *thousands* of vertices. Therefore, optimizing SJGS queries is crucial for the performance of a spatial database management system. Secondly, to optimize queries that consist of SJGS subqueries, it is important to get accurate selectivity estimations of the SJGS subqueries. However, although much work has been done in estimating the selectivity of geometric selection *or* spatial join queries, the efforts so far to combine these two has been unsatisfactory. In this paper, we address this problem by developing a new approach that gives accurate selectivity estimation for SJGS queries. Our contributions are as follows:

- We demonstrate the use of *Euler Histogram* to solve a special case of SJGS queries. Euler histograms are powerful histograms that were previously used in selectivity estimation for spatial *intersection* [4] and *containment* [5] queries.
- We generalize Euler Histogram to serve as a framework for selectivity estimation for common types of SJGS queries. The framework is capable of accommodating different probabilistic models for datasets with different characteristics.
- We incorporate two existing probabilistic models into our framework, and demonstrate the effectiveness of the framework by comparing it to two existing algorithms.

The rest of the paper is organized as follows: in Section 2 we formally define the problem and discusse some related work. In Section 3 we present a solution based on Euler Histogram for a special case of SJGS queries. In Section 4 we generalize Euler Histogram to serve as a selectivity estimation framework, and discuss two probabilistic models that can be used under this framework. An implementation of the generalized Euler Histogram is evaluated in Section 5. Section 6 concludes the paper and discusses some future work.

2 Problem Definition

We formally define the problem of selectivity estimation for spatial join with geometric selection (SJGS) queries as follows:

Definition 1. *Let $A = \{a_1, ..., a_i, ...a_n\}$ and $B = \{b_1, ..., b_j, ..., b_m\}$ be two spatial datasets, and let S_A and S_B be two selection rectangles over A and B, respectively. The selectivity estimation problem for the join of A and B with selections S_A and S_B is to estimate the number of object pairs (a_i, b_j) that satisfy the following three conditions:*

1. *a_i intersects S_A, and*
2. *b_j intersects S_B, and*
3. *a_i intersects b_j.*

Figure 2 shows two datasets A and B, and two selection windows S_A and S_B of a SJGS query. From Definition 1, we can see that the object pairs (a_1, b_1), (a_1, b_3) and (a_2, b_1) are all valid results of the query. On the other hand, (a_1, b_2) is not a valid result because b_2 does not intersect S_B, and similarly, (a_3, b_3) is not a valid result because a_3 does not intersect S_A.

There are several points we would like to clarify about Definition 1 and our system assumptions in general.

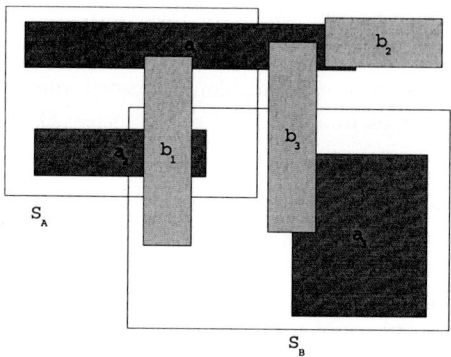

Fig. 2. An Example of a SJGS Query

First of all, the spatial objects considered in this definition and the rest of the paper are rectangles, including the special cases where the rectangles are reduced to vertical/horizontal line segments or points. For simplicity and readability, we assume the objects are in a 2-dimensional space, but our technique can be easily extended to higher dimensions. On the other hand, we do acknowledge that since our technique is based on uniform partitioning, it is subject to the *dimensionality curse*, namely, the number of partitions increases exponentially as the dimensionality increases.

Secondly, a *data space* for a dataset is the bounding rectangle that encloses all the objects in the dataset, and we assume that both datasets A and B have a common data space. For example, a rainfall map of Orange County and a land cover map of Orange County will have the common data space *Orange County*, or the rectangle $(-118.27W, -117.34E, 32.58S, 34.02N)$ in a longitude-latitude coordinate system. Note that this assumption is not restrictive, since if two datasets have different data spaces, we can always take the bounding rectangle of the two data spaces as the common data space.

Finally, in this paper we concentrate on the selectivity estimation problem where the two selection windows select the same region, or $S_A = S_B = S$. The solution developed in this paper can be applied to two common classes of SJGS queries:

– *Spatial Joins with Same Selections*. This class of query is the most common in applications such as map overlays. The sample query in Section 1, "finding all French-speaking administrative regions in Europe", is an example of this class of query. Full dataset joins discussed in previous work [1] can also be considered as a special case of this class of query where the selection windows are the data space.
– *Spatial Joins with Clipping Selections*. Even for SJGS queries with different selection windows, our technique is still applicable if the selections are *clipping* instead of *windowing*. For example, Figure 2 shows that (a_1, b_1) and (a_1, b_3) are valid results under windowing selections. However, note that for

clipping selections, these object pairs are *not* valid results because after clipping, a_1 no longer intersects b_1 or b_3. In fact, for selectivity estimation, a spatial join with different clipping selections S_A and S_B can be considered the same as a spatial join with the same selection window S, where S is the intersecting region of S_A and S_B, or $S = S_A \cap S_B$.

Selectivity estimation for spatial joins has only recently attracted much research attention. In [6], Faloutsos et. al. proposed a parametric approach to estimate distance join selectivity based on the observation that the data distribution of many real world datasets follow a *power law*. For intersection joins, the state of the art are two histogram-based techniques recently proposed in [1] and [2]. The first technique, called Geometric Histogram (GH), is very effective for full dataset joins, and the second one, which we will refer to as the MP algorithm, takes selections into consideration and partially inspired our work.

The technique developed in this paper is based on Euler Histogram, which was first introduced by Beigel and Tanin in [4] for browsing objects in a spatial dataset that intersect a selected region. [5] extends the work to spatial relations including *contains*, *contained* and *overlap*. The mathematical foundation of the Euler Histogram is based on Euler's Formula in graph theory, hence the name *Euler* Histogram.

3 Basic Euler Histogram

In this section we give a brief introduction to the Euler Histogram, and show how it can be used to solve a special case of SJGS query selectivity estimation where the datasets to be queried satisfy certain restrictions.

3.1 Euler Histogram

The conventional approach to build a histogram for region objects is as follows: given a grid of the data space, allocate a set of buckets with each bucket corresponding to a grid cell; and for each object, if it intersects a bucket, then increase the value stored in the bucket by 1. Conventional histograms suffer from a severe drawback which we call the *multiple-count problem*. Unlike point objects which either fall inside a histogram bucket or not, a region object may span several buckets and therefore is counted multiple times. The multiple-count problem is illustrated in Figure 3(a) and (b), where Figure 3(a) shows a dataset with a large object spanning four buckets, and Figure 3(b) shows the conventional histogram for this dataset. Note that for a spatial selection query covering the four buckets, the single object will be counted four times, resulting in a 300% over estimation.

Euler Histograms are designed to address the multiple-count problem. Compared to the conventional histogram, an Euler histogram allocate buckets not only for grid cells, but also for grid cell edges and vertices. For example, the Euler histogram for the dataset in Figure 3(a) is shown in Figure 3(c), and for comparison, another dataset with four small objects and its corresponding Euler

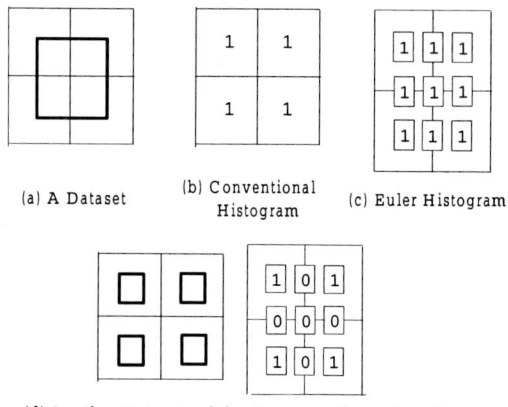

Fig. 3. Comparison between Conventional Histogram and Euler Histogram

histogram is shown in Figure 3(d). Note that with additional buckets for grid cell edges and vertices, it is now possible to distinguish between a large object spanning several cells and several small objects contained in each cell.

In [4], Beigel and Tanin presented an algorithm to estimate the selectivity of geometric selection queries using Euler histograms. The mathematical foundation of the algorithm is based on Euler's Formula in graph theory, therefore we refer to this type of histograms as the *Euler Histograms*. The development of the algorithm is lengthy and was discussed in full detail in [4], so here we only give the algorithm and highlight some important results:

Given a selection window S, the selectivity of S can be calculated with an Euler histogram as follows:

$$Selectivity(S) = \sum_{0 \leq k \leq d} (-1)^k F_k(S) \tag{1}$$

where $F_k(S)$ is a *k-dimensional face* inside S. In particular, a 0-dimensional face is a vertex, a 1-dimensional face is an edge and a 2-dimensional face is a cell.

An example of Beigel-Tannin's algorithm is illustrated in Figure 4. Figure 4(a) shows a dataset with three rectangular objects, and a selection window S at (x_1, x_2, y_1, y_2). Figure 4(b) shows the Euler histogram for this dataset. The one 0-d face, four 1-d faces and four 2-d faces that are *inside* (excluding boundary) Q are highlighted in Figure 4(c). So from Equation 1, the selectivity of S is $(-1)^0 \times 2 + (-1)^1 \times (2+2+2+2) + (-1)^2 \times (2+2+2+3) = 3$.

In [4], Beigel and Tanin established two important properties of Equation 1:

1. If the selection window aligns with the grid, the estimation given by Equation 1 is *without any errors*.
2. Equation 1 holds for any d-dimensional spaces where $d \geq 1$.

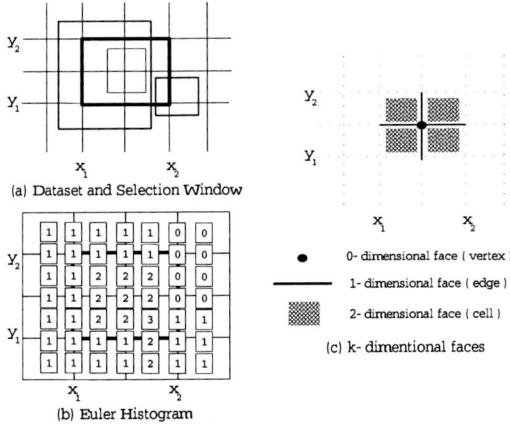

Fig. 4. An Example of Beigel-Tannin's Algorithm

3.2 A Special Case of the SJGS Estimation Problem

In Section 2 we defined the problem of selectivity estimation for SJGS queries, and now we consider a special case of this problem. Namely, given two datasets A and B, and a selection windows S, we require that all objects be "quantized" to align with a given grid. We call this assumption the *Quantization Assumption*, which is illustrated in Figure 5. Notice that objects $(0.2, 1.4, 2.5, 3.5)$ and $(1.6, 2.6, 1.5, 2.7)$ become $(0, 2, 2, 4)$ and $(1, 3, 1, 3)$ after quantization.

The Quantization Assumption is clearly a very strong assumption. Under this assumption, not only the objects are quantized, but selection windows are implicitly quantized, too. Using the two quantized objects in Figure 5(b) as an example, we can see that a selection window at $(0.5, 1.5, 1.5, 2.5)$ (the dotted rectangle in Figure 5(b)) will have the same results as a query window at $(0, 2, 1, 3)$.

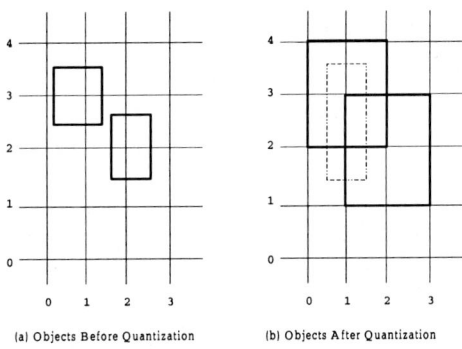

Fig. 5. Two Objects Before and After Quantization

Under the Quantization Assumption, we can now use the Euler Histogram to estimate the selectivity of a SJGS query as follows:

Given two datasets A, B and a grid of the data space, we construct an Euler histogram for each dataset and call them H_A and H_B. Let $h^A_{i,j,k}$ and $h^B_{i,j,k}$ be buckets in H_A and H_B, respectively. The meanings of the subscripts of $h_{i,j,k}$ are the following: i is the row position of h in the histogram, j is the column position, and k means that h corresponds to a k-dimensional face of the grid. For a SJGS query Q with a selection window S, the selectivity of the query can be calculated as

$$Selectivity(Q) = \sum_{i,j,k} (-1)^k [h^A_{i,j,k}(S) \times h^B_{i,j,k}(S)] \qquad (2)$$

where $h^A_{i,j,k}$ and $h^B_{i,j,k}$ are buckets of H_A and H_B, respectively, that are *inside* the selection window S. We further claim that when the Quantization assumption holds, the estimation given by Equation 2 is *without any errors*.

Before we prove the correctness of the algorithm, let's first look at an example. Figure 6(a) shows two datasets A and B. A consists of three objects, and B consists of two objects. The selection window is at (x_1, x_2, y_1, y_2). The Euler histograms for A and B are shown in Figure 6(b). For better readability we removed all buckets except those that are *inside* the selection window. From Equation 2, the selectivity of this SJGS query is

$$(-1)^0 (1 \times 1) + (-1)^1 (2 \times 1 + 1 \times 1 + 1 \times 1 + 1 \times 2) +$$
$$(-1)^2 (2 \times 1 + 2 \times 1 + 1 \times 2 + 2 \times 2)$$
$$= 1 - 6 + 10 = 5$$

Note that the larger object in B intersect all three objects in A, and the smaller object in B intersects two objects in A, so the selectivity of the query is indeed 5.

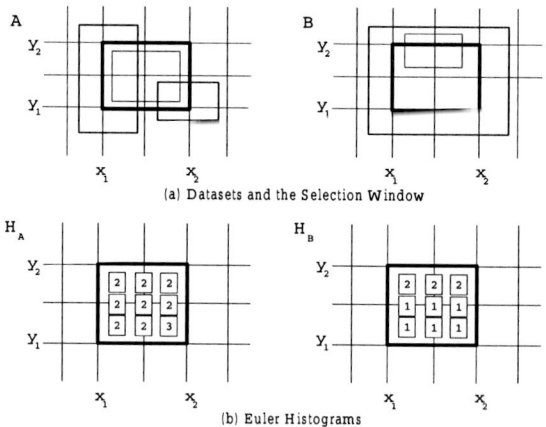

Fig. 6. Selectivity Estimation for the Special Case

We now prove the correctness of the algorithm and justify our claim that under the Quantization Assumption, the estimation is *without any errors*.

Lemma 1. *If two rectangular objects a and b both intersect rectangle S as well as each other, then their intersection region, denoted as ab, also intersects S.*

Lemma 1 is a straight-forward observation and a proof can be found in [7]. Based on this observation, we can prove the correctness of the algorithm as follows:

Theorem 1. *Let Q be an SJGS query with selection window S over datasets A and B. Under the Quantization Assumption, the selectivity estimate of Q produced by Equation 2 is without any errors.*
   Proof.
   Step 1. We first construct a new dataset AB which consists of all the intersecting regions between the objects from A and the objects from B. Formally, $AB = \{ ab \mid ab = a \cap b, a \in A, b \in B \}$.
   Step 2. We construct an Euler histogram H_{AB} for the new dataset AB. Let $h^{AB}_{i,j,k}$ be a bucket in H_{AB}, and $h^{A}_{i,j,k}$ and $h^{B}_{i,j,k}$ be the corresponding buckets in H_A and H_B, respectively. If $h^A_{i,j,k} = x$ and $h^B_{i,j,k} = y$, then by the Quantization Assumption (if two objects intersect the same face they must intersect each other) there are $x \times y$ intersecting regions; and by Lemma 1, these $x \times y$ intersecting regions intersect $h^{AB}_{i,j,k}$ (0-d and 1-d faces can be considered as special cases of S in Lemma 1), so $h^{AB}_{i,j,k} = x \times y = h^A_{i,j,k} \times h^B_{i,j,k}$.
   Step 3. If (a,b) is a valid result of Q with selection window S, then from Lemma 1, ab intersects S; and the reverse is also true (if ab intersects S then (a,b) is clearly a valid result of Q). This means that the selectivity of the SJGS query Q over A and B is the same as the selectivity of the geometric selection query S over AB, or $Selectivity(Q_{A,B}) = Selectivity(S_{AB})$. From Equation 1, we have $Selectivity(S_{AB}) = \sum_{i,j,k} (-1)^k h^{AB}_{i,j,k}$, and it is proved in [4] that when the selection window aligns with the grid (Quantization Assumption), the selectivity estimation is without any errors. Note that from Step 2 we have $h^{AB}_{i,j,k} = x \times y = h^A_{i,j,k} \times h^B_{i,j,k}$, so $Selectivity(Q_{A,B}) = Selectivity(S_{AB}) = \sum_{i,j,k} (-1)^k h^{AB}_{i,j,k} = \sum_{i,j,k} (-1)^k [h^A_{i,j,k} \times h^B_{i,j,k}]$, which is exactly Equation 2. Therefore the selectivity estimate of Q produced by Equation 2 is *without any errors*.

From Theorem 1 and the discussion in Section 2, we can also conclude that under the quantization assumption, Euler Histogram provides *exact* results for SJGS queries with clipping selections, even when the selection windows for the two datasets are different.

4 Generalized Euler Histogram

In this section we generalize the Euler Histogram approach to handle objects and selection windows that do not align with a given grid.

4.1 Euler Histogram Framework

We first revisit Equation 2. In a 2-dimensional space, Equation 2 can be written as follows:

$$Selectivity(Q) = \sum_{i,j,k=0,1,2} (-1)^k [h^A_{i,j,k}(S) \times h^B_{i,j,k}(S)] \qquad (3)$$

where $h^A_{i,j,2}(S) \times h^B_{i,j,2}(S)$, $h^A_{i,j,1}(S) \times h^B_{i,j,1}(S)$ and $h^A_{i,j,0} \times h^B_{i,j,0}(S)$ are the estimated number of intersection regions that intersect a 2-d face (cell), a 1-d face (edge) or a 0-d face (vertex), respectively.

Under the Quantization Assumption, when two objects intersect the same face, they must intersect each other. So if there are h^A objects from dataset A that intersect a face (i, j), and there are h^B objects from dataset B that intersect the same face, then the number of intersection regions that intersect face (i, j) is *exactly* $h^A \times h^B$. However, with objects that do not align with the histogram grid, the number of intersection regions may be less than $h^A \times h^B$. To address this problem, we generalize the Euler Histogram approach by introducing an *intersection factor p*, so in a 2-dimensional space, Equation 2 becomes

$$Selectivity(Q) = \sum_{i,j,k=0,1,2} (-1)^k [h^A_{i,j,k}(S) \times h^B_{i,j,k}(S) \times p_{i,j,k}] \qquad (4)$$

Intuitively, $p_{i,j,k}$ is the *probability* that one set of objects intersect another set of objects *inside* face (i, j, k). For 0-d faces, or vertices, $p_{i,j,0}$ is always 1; for higher dimensional faces, the value of $p_{i,j,k}$ is between 0 and 1, depending on the sizes and spatial distributions of the objects inside the face.

Note that Equation 4 does not specify how $p_{i,j,k}$ should be computed. Instead, Equation 4 serves as a framework where different probabilistic models can be applied. For certain datasets, some probabilistic models may capture the data distribution better than the others, which will result in more accurate selectivity estimation. In the next subsection, we will discuss two existing probabilistic models. Our discussion will focus on the case of 2-d faces, which can be easily generalized to handle 1-d faces.

4.2 Probabilistic Models

Given two sets of objects $A = \{a_1, ..., a_i, ..., a_{n_1}\}$ and $B = \{b_1, ..., b_j, ..., b_{n_2}\}$ that are enclosed in a 1×1 space, our goal is to find the number of object pairs (a_i, b_j) where a_i intersect b_j. Clearly, finding the exact number of intersecting pairs requires keeping track of the shape and the position of each object, which is not efficient for selectivity estimation purposes. So the common approach is to keep a set of parameters which summarize the information about each dataset, and rely on a probabilistic model to provide an estimated result.

In [2], Mamoulis and Papadias proposed keeping three parameter for each dataset: the number of objects n, the average object height $\overline{h}$ and the average object width $\overline{w}$. The, the number of intersecting pairs N is estimated using the following equation:

$$N = n_1 \times n_2 \times min(1, (\overline{h_1} + \overline{h_2})) \times min(1, (\overline{w_1} + \overline{w_2})) \qquad (5)$$

In [1], An et al. proposed another probabilistic model for the Geometric Histogram (GH) algorithm for spatial joins without selections. The GH model keeps four parameters: the total number of corner points C, the sum of the areas of the objects O, the sum of the lengths of the vertical edges V, and the sum of the lengths of the horizontal edges H. Under the GH model, the number of intersecting pairs can be estimated as follows:

$$N = \frac{C_1 \times O_2 + C_2 \times O_1 + V_1 \times H_2 + V_2 \times H_1}{4} \qquad (6)$$

For comparison purpose, we rewrite Equation 6 as follows:

$$N = n_1 \times n_2 \times (\overline{a_1} + \overline{a_2} + \overline{h_1} \times \overline{w_2} + \overline{h_2} \times \overline{w_1}) \qquad (7)$$

where $\overline{a}$ is the average area of the objects. Note that

$$C = 4 \times n$$
$$O = \overline{a} \times n$$
$$V = 2 \times \overline{h} \times n$$
$$H = 2 \times \overline{w} \times n$$

So Equation 6 and 7 are equivalent.

In order to decide which model is more suitable for the generalized Euler Histogram, we compare the accuracy of the GH model and Mamoulis-Papadias's model (MP model) under two conditions:

- $\overline{h_1} + \overline{h_2} >= 1$ and $\overline{w_1} + \overline{w_2} >= 1$
  In this case, Equation 5 reduces to $N = n_1 \times n_2$. Intuitively, the result of the MP model may be an over estimate, since it is possible that some objects from one dataset do not intersect *all* objects in the other dataset. On the other hand, the GH model is likely to perform even worse. For example, assume dataset A has one object $(0.1, 0.9, 0.1, 0.9)$ and dataset B also has one object $(0.1, 0.9, 0.1, 0.9)$. According to Equation 7, the estimated number of intersections is

$$0.8 \times 0.8 + 0.8 \times 0.8 + 0.8 \times 0.8 + 0.8 \times 0.8 = 2.56$$

while the correct answer is 1.

The poor performance of the GH model in this case is because the GH model estimates four types of intersection points *independently*. When $\overline{h_1} + \overline{h_2} >= 1$ and $\overline{w_1} + \overline{w_2} >= 1$, the correlations among different types of intersection points cannot be ignored. For example, if one object falls completely inside another object, then no matter what their edge lengths are, the probability of edge intersection should be 0.

- $\overline{h_1} + \overline{h_2} < 1$ and $\overline{w_1} + \overline{w_2} < 1$.
  In this case, Equation 5 is reduced to

$$N = n_1 \times n_2 \times (\overline{h_1} \times \overline{w1} + \overline{h_2} \times \overline{w_2} + \overline{h_1} \times \overline{w_2} + \overline{h_2} \times \overline{w_1}) \tag{8}$$

Comparing Equation 8 to Equation 7, we can observe that the only difference is the MP model uses $\overline{h_1} \times \overline{w1}$ and $\overline{h_2} \times \overline{w2}$ while the GH model uses $\overline{a_1}$ and $\overline{a_2}$.

Note that $(\overline{h_1} \times \overline{w1} + \overline{h_2} \times \overline{w2})$ and $(\overline{a_1} + \overline{a_2})$ are used to compute the probability of corner points inside objects, so we expect the GH model to perform better than the MP model. We can further predict that the MP model is likely to over estimate since $\overline{h} \times \overline{w} \geq \overline{a}$ holds for all datasets.

4.3 Implementation of Generalized Euler Histogram

We now present an implementation of the generalized Euler Histogram based on the discussion above. In particular, we adaptively use the GH model and the MP model depending on the properties of the objects in a histogram bucket.

Given a dataset and a grid of the data space, a generalized Euler histogram can be constructed as follows:

- allocate a bucket for each vertex, edge and cell of the grid.
- at a vertex, store the tuple $\langle n \rangle$, where n is the number of objects that intersect the vertex.
- at an edge, store the tuple $\langle n, \overline{e} \rangle$, where n is the number of objects intersecting the edge, and $\overline{e}$ is the average projection of the objects on this edge.
- at a cell, store the tuple $\langle n, \overline{h}, \overline{w}, \overline{a} \rangle$, where n is the number of objects intersecting the cell, and $\overline{h}$, $\overline{w}$ and $\overline{a}$ are the average height, width and area of the intersection regions between the objects and the cell.

An example of a generalized Euler histogram is shown in Figure 7.

To estimate the selectivity of a given query, we use Equation 4 combined with a hybrid probabilistic model of GH and MP. For edges, the intersection factor $p_{i,j,1}$ is

$$p_{i,j,1} = min(1, \overline{e_1} + \overline{e_2}) \text{ (MP Model)}$$

and for cells, the intersection factor $p_{i,j,2}$ is

$$p_{i,j,2} = \begin{cases} n1 \times n2 & \text{if } \overline{h_1} + \overline{h_2} \geq 1 \text{ and } \overline{w_1} + \overline{w_2} \geq 1 \text{ (MP model)} \\ \overline{a_1} + \overline{a_2} + \overline{h_1} \times \overline{w_2} + \overline{h_2} \times \overline{w_1} & \text{otherwise (GH Model)} \end{cases}$$

5 Performance Evaluation

To evaluate the effectiveness of the generalized Euler Histogram (EH), we compare it with the Geometric Histogram (GH) algorithm [1] and Mamoulis-Papadias's (MP) algorithm [2]. In this section, we describe our experimental setup and report the performance results.

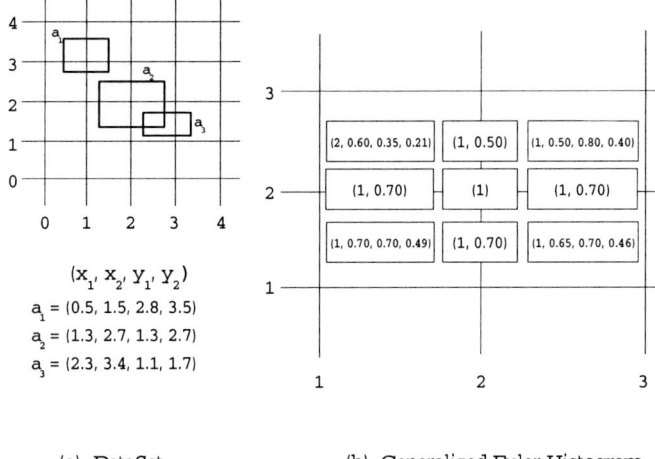

Fig. 7. A Generalized Euler Histogram

5.1 Experimental Setup

Our experiments were conducted on a Pentium III 800MHz PC with five real world datasets and two synthetic datasets, which are listed in Table 1, where N is the number of objects in each dataset.

Table 1. Datasets

Label	N	Description
LANDC [8]	14,731	Land cover (mostly vegetation types) information for the state of Wyoming at 1:100,000 scale.
LANDO [9]	33,860	Land ownership and management information for the state of Wyoming at 1:100,000 scale.
SOIL [10]	29,662	Digital soil maps for the state of Wyoming at 1:100,000 scale.
SQ1 [11]	22,094	Sequoia 2000 Benchmark, Polygon Dataset Level 1.
SQX [11]	36,492	Sequoia 2000 Benchmark, Polygon Dataset Level 2-9.
SZSKEW1,2	100,000	Two synthetic datasets consisting of uniformly distributed rectangles with varied widths and lengths.

In each experiment we run a set of SJGS queries with randomly generated selection windows. The aspect ratios of the selection windows are uniformly distributed between 0.3 and 3. The queries are further divided into groups, with 20 queries in each group. The queries in the same group have the same *area selectivity*, which is the area of the selection window normalized to the area of the data space. The area selectivities used in the experiments are 25%, 10%, 1%, 0.1%, and 0.01%.

For each query group, the estimation accuracy of the algorithm is measure by the *Average Relative Error*, which is defined as follows: If e_i is the estimated answer and r_i is the actual answer for a given query q_i, the average relative error for a query group Q is $(\sum_{q_i \in Q} |r_i - e_i|)/(\sum_{q_i \in Q} r_i)$.

5.2 Implementation Details

A simple example is shown in Figure 8 to illustrate the three types of histograms MP, GH and EH. Figure 8(a) shows a single object inside a 2×1 grid. The coordinates of the object is $(0.25, 0.75, 0.5, 1.4)$, and the MP, GH and EH histogram for this object is shown in Figure 8(b), (c) and (d). Besides the different probabilistic models discussed in Section 4.2 and 4.3, we also note from Figure 8 another important difference between MP histograms and GH/EH histograms: for MP histograms, an object spanning several buckets will only be counted in the bucket where the center of the object lies; for GH and EH histograms, the object will be split into *pieces*, and the pieces of the objects are counted separately.

The original Geometric Histogram was designed for full datasets joins. In our implementation, we made a slight modification so it can handle SJGS queries. Namely, the construction of a geometric histogram is still the same as described in [1], but during estimation, we only estimate the number of intersection points

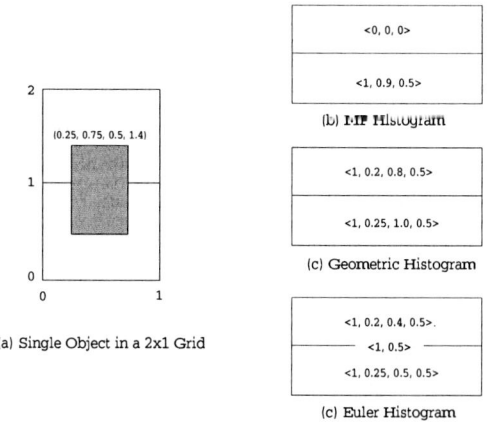

Fig. 8. Three Types of Histograms

inside the selection window. This modification may incur some additional estimation error, because some intersection points may be outside the selection window. The probability of an intersection point falling outside the selection window is given by the following equation:

$$1 - \frac{H \times W}{(H + \overline{h}) \times (W + \overline{w})} \tag{9}$$

where H and W are the height and width of the selection windows, and $\overline{h}$ and $\overline{w}$ are the average height and width of the objects that intersect the selection window. In most test cases, this error is negligible because $H >> \overline{h}$ and $W >> \overline{w}$.

In our experiments, we follow the convention in [1] and use a parameter *Level*, denoted as l, to represent the granularity of the grid. Formally, a Level l grid is an $n \times n$ grid of the data space where $n = 2^l$. For example, a level 0 grid is a 1×1 grid and a level 2 grid is a 4×4 grid.

5.3 Experimental Results

In this section we study the performance of MP, GH and EH with respect to the grid granularity and the sizes of the selection windows.

Impact of Grid Granularity. The estimation accuracy as a function of the grid level is shown in Figure 9. The Y-coordinate of a data point is the average relative estimation error computed from 20 randomly generated selection windows with the same area selectivity 1%. The X-coordinate of a data point is the grid level of the histogram.

From Figure 9, we make the following observations:

Geometric Histogram (GH) is the most stable algorithm among the three algorithms tested. In most cases, the estimation errors of GH consistently decreases as the grid granularity increases. As we discussed in Section 4.2, the probabilistic model of GH relies on the assumption that the heights and widths of the objects are relatively small with respect to the height and width of the selection window. So for datasets with small objects such as SQ1 and SQX, GH performs very well (Figure 9(c)), but for datasets with large objects such as SZSKEW1 and SZSKEW2, GH performs rather poorly (Figure 9(d)).

Mamoulis-Papadias's algorithm (MP) has high errors rates at all grid levels. There are two reasons for the poor performance of MP. First of all, the probabilistic model of MP is less accurate than the GH model except for extreme cases where the sizes of the objects are comparable to the size of the selection window. Secondly, unlike GH or EH, MP does not split objects which span several buckets, therefore benefits less from finer grid granularity. Furthermore, with finer grid granularity, although the centers of the objects are more uniformly distributed, the variance of the heights and the widths of the objects may actually increase, which also has a negative impact on the estimation accuracy of MP.

In all four test cases, Euler Histogram (EH) achieves the lowest estimation error, ranging from 0.3% in Figure 9(b) to about 10% in Figure 9(d). At the lower grid levels, EH uses the same probabilistic model as GH, but in addition to keeping information on grid cells, EH also keeps information on grid edges and vertices. Another important difference between EH and GH is that EH uses the *interiors* of the intersection regions, while GH uses the *corner points* of the intersection regions. From Lemma 1, we know that the interior of an intersection region always intersects the selection windows, but some of the corner points may be outside the selection window. The advantage of the EH approach is more evident in Figure 9(d), where the objects are relatively large. However, note that at the the higher grid levels, the estimation accuracy of EH decreases sharply. The reason for the performance degradation is that as the grid granularity increases, the heights and widths of the objects (or *pieces* of the objects) becomes comparable to the heights and widths of the grid cell. As we discussed in Section 4.2, neither MP model nor GH model handles this case very well.

Impact of Area Selectivity. Based on the results from previous section, we identify the "optimal" grid level of a dataset for each algorithm, and use this grid level to study the impact of different area selectivity on the estimation accuracy. The results of this experiment are shown in Figure 10. The Y-coordinate of a data point is the average relative estimation error computed from 20 randomly generated selection windows, and the X-coordinate is the area selectivity of these selection windows, ranging from 0.01% to 25%.

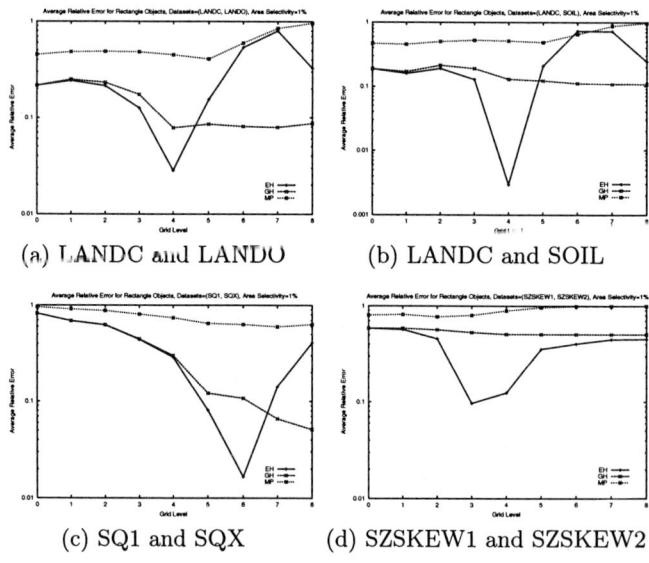

(a) LANDC and LANDO (b) LANDC and SOIL

(c) SQ1 and SQX (d) SZSKEW1 and SZSKEW2

Fig. 9. Average Relative Error for Queries with 1% Area Selectivity

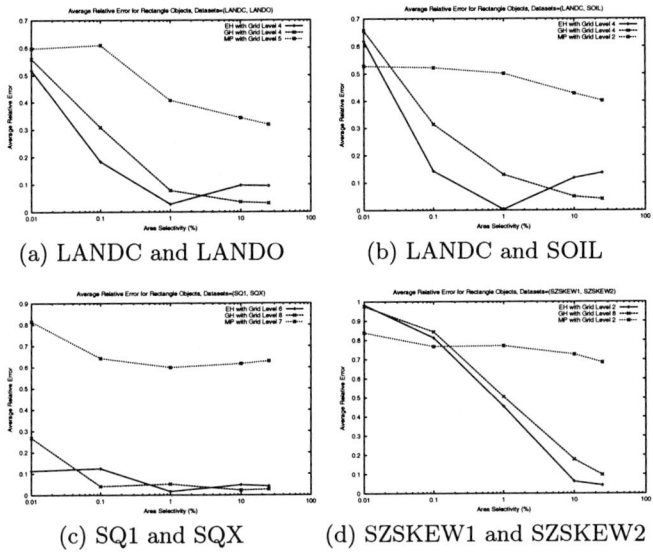

Fig. 10. Average Relative Error for Queries with Different Area Selectivity

The general trend of the graph is that the estimation accuracy improves as the area selectivity increases. This is because with small selection windows, the number of the actual result is small, which leads to large *relative* errors.

In most cases, both EH and GH outperform MP by a large margin. Between EH and GH, EH generally performs better at lower area selectivity. As we discussed in the previous section, EH estimates the number of intersection regions, while GH estimates the number of intersection points. So when the selection window is small, a relatively large number of intersection points may fall outside the selection window, which decreases the estimation accuracy of GH.

6 Conclusion and Future Work

To estimate the selectivity of spatial joins, histogram based techniques must address two important issues: the objects that span multiple buckets and the probabilistic model that provides per-bucket estimations. The problem is further complicated when the spatial joins are constrained by selection windows, which has a significant impact on the design of the histogram as well as the accuracy of the probabilistic model.

In this paper, we propose the generalized Euler Histogram as a framework for estimating the selectivity of SJGS queries. This framework is designed to estimates the number of intersection regions, which ensures that for an SJGS query, the information needed for estimation is *inside* the selection window. More importantly, under this framework, different probabilistic models can be used to better capture the size and spatial distributions of the data objects.

Our current implementation of the generalized Euler histogram has validated the effectiveness of this framework. In the future, we plan to further improve the performance of this implementation by exploring alternative probabilistic models. We are also interested in extending the Euler Histogram approach to polygon datasets, which provides more accurate cost estimation for spatial operations that use aggressive filtering techniques [12, 13].

References

1. Ning An, Zhen-Yu Yang, and Anand Sivasubramaniam. Selectivity estimation for spatial joins. In *ICDE 2001, Proceedings of the 17th International Conference on Data Engineering*, pages 368–375, April 2001.
2. Nikos Mamoulis and Dimitris Papadias. Selectivity estimation of complex spatial queries. In *SSTD'01, Proceedings of the 7th International Symposium on Spatial and Temporal Databases*, July 2001.
3. Philippe Rigaux, Michel Scholl, and Agnès Voisard. *Spatial Databases with Applications to GIS*, chapter 1.3.1, page 14. Morgan Kaufmann Publishers, 2001.
4. R. Beigel and Egemen Tanin. The geometry of browsing. In *Proceedings of the Latin American Symposium on Theoretical Informatics, 1998, Brazil*, pages 331–340, 1998.
5. Chengyu Sun, Divyakant Agrawal, and Amr El Abbadi. Exploring spatial datasets with histograms. In *ICDE 2002, Proceedings of the 18th International Conference on Data Engineering*, Feburary 2002.
6. Christos Faloutsos, Bernhard Seeger, Agma J. M. Traina, and Caetano Traina Jr. Spatial join selectivity using power laws. *SIGMOD Record*, 29(2):177–188, 2000.
7. Chengyu Sun, Divyakant Agrawal, and Amr El Abbadi. Selectivity estimation for spatial joins with geometric selections (extended version). Technical report, Computer Science Department, University of California, Santa Barbara, 2002. http://www.cs.ucsb.edu/research/trcs/docs/2002-01.ps.
8. Wyoming Gap Analysis. Land cover for wyoming. Technical report, University of Wyoming, Spatial Data and Visualization Center, December 1996.
9. Wyoming Gap Analysis. Land ownership and management for wyoming. Technical report, University of Wyoming, Spatial Data and Visualization Center, December 1996.
10. Larry C. Munn and Christopher S. Arneson. Draft 1:100,000-scale digital soils map of wyoming. Technical report, University of Wyoming Agricultural Experiment Station, 1999.
11. Michael Stonebraker, James Frew, Kenn Gardels, and Jeff Meredith. The sequoia 2000 benchmark. In *Proceedings of the 1993 ACM SIGMOD International Conference on Management of Data, Washington, D.C., May 26-28, 1993*, pages 2–11, 1993.
12. Wael M. Badawy and Walid G. Aref. On local heuristics to speed up polygon-polygon intersection tests. In *ACM-GIS '99, Proceedings of the 7th International Symposium on Advances in Geographic Information Systems*, pages 97–102, 1999.
13. Ravi K. Kothuri and Siva Ravada. Efficient processing of large spatial queries using interior approximation. In *Proceedings of the 7th International Symposium on Advances in Spatial and Temporal Databases (SSTD 2001)*, pages 404–421, 2001.

A Framework for the Physical Design Problem for Data Synopses

Arnd Christian König and Gerhard Weikum

Department of Computer Science, University of the Saarland,
P.O. Box 151150, 66041 Saarbrücken, Germany
{koenig,weikum}@cs.uni-sb.de

Abstract. Maintaining statistics on multidimensional data distributions is crucial for predicting the run-time and result size of queries and data analysis tasks with acceptable accuracy. To this end a plethora of techniques have been proposed for maintaining a compact data "synopsis" on a single table, ranging from variants of histograms to methods based on wavelets and other transforms. However, the fundamental question of how to reconcile the synopses for large information sources with many tables has been largely unexplored. This paper develops a general framework for reconciling the synopses on many tables, which may come from different information sources. It shows how to compute the optimal combination of synopses for a given workload and a limited amount of available memory. The practicality of the approach and the accuracy of the proposed heuristics are demonstrated by experiments.

1 Introduction

Maintaining compact and accurate statistics on data distributions is of crucial importance for a number of tasks: (1) traditional query optimization that aims to find a good execution plan for a given query [4, 17], (2) approximate query answering and initial data exploration [9, 1, 14, 3, 8], and (3) prediction of run-times and result sizes of complex data extraction and data analysis tasks on data mining platforms, where absolute predictions with decent accuracy are mandatory for prioritization and scheduling of long-running tasks. This broad importance of statistics management has led to a plethora of approximation techniques, for which [11] have coined the general term *"data synopses"*: advanced forms of histograms [24, 12, 16], spline synopses [18, 19], sampling [5, 13, 10], and parametric curve-fitting techniques [27, 7] all the way to highly sophisticated methods based on kernel estimators [2] or Wavelets and other transforms [22, 21, 3]. However, most of these techniques take the local viewpoint of optimizing the approximation error for a single data distribution such as one database table with pre-selected relevant attributes. The equally important problem which combination of synopses to maintain on the application's various datasets and how to divide the available memory between them has received only little attention [1, 6, 19], putting the burden of selecting and tuning appropriate synopses on the database administrator. This creates a *physical design problem for data synopses*, which can be very difficult in advanced settings such as predicting run-times of data analysis tasks or information wealth of Web sources by a mediator. The state of the art is inadequate for a number of reasons:

- Since the accuracy of all approximation techniques depends on the memory size allotted to them, synopses for different data distributions compete for the available memory. In query optimization, for example, a small sized synopsis that does not improve query plan selection might have impact when given more memory.
- All proposed techniques are limited in the types of queries they support well. Most techniques aim at range-query selectivity estimation only and are thus unsuitable for complex queries with joins or aggregation/grouping unless additional synopses are maintained that are geared for approximations that cannot be inferred from the base representations (e.g., join synopses [1, 19]). These additional synopses compete for the same memory space, and tuning the memory allocation for the various synopses is very difficult.
- Because the choice of an optimal combination of synopses is dependent on the workload (i.e., the query mix for which run-time and result size predictions or approximate answers need to be computed), it needs to be continuously adapted to the evolving workload properties.

1.1 Related Work

The reconciliation of different synopses as well as dedicated synopses for join queries (a uniform random sample over a foreign key join) was initially considered in [1]. Our work adapts these ideas and generalizes them, as their realization in the previous paper is limited to samples as base synopses and a data warehouse environment with a central fact table connected (via foreign keys) with the respective dimension tables. An extension of this approach to incorporate workload information (in the form of access locality) can be found in [8], but it is also limited to the above scenario.

The reconciliation problem for spline synopses was first discussed in [19], where a dynamic programming approach is proposed to minimize the error for a given set of synopses. However, this work offers no solution regarding which set of synopses to construct and does not take into account the characteristics of the workload. A similar approach for histograms was proposed in [15], extending [19] by offering heuristics that reduce the overhead of the dynamic programming problem. [6] considers a limited version of the problem: a set of synopses for query optimization are selected, based on whether or not they make a difference in plan selection. However, the approach is limited in a number of ways. Most importantly, synopsis selection is a series of yes-or-no decisions, with no consideration of the effect that variations of the size of a synopsis may have. This also has the consequence that the overall memory allotted to the selected synopses is utilized in a sub-optimal way. Furthermore, there is no consideration of special, dedicated (join-) synopses which do not constitute a (sub-)set of the attributes of a single relation.

1.2 Contribution and Outline

This paper develops a novel framework for the physical design problem for data synopses. Our framework covers the entire class of SPJ (i.e., select-project-join) queries. Note that projections are important also for predicting result sizes and run-times of grouping/aggregation, but have been almost completely ignored in prior work on data synopses. In contrast to the work in [6], our approach goes beyond the binary decisions on building vs. not building a certain synopsis, but also addresses the fundamentally important issue of how much memory each synopsis should be given. This is especially important when the role of statistics management goes beyond choosing good query execution plans, and synopses also serve to predict absolute run-times and result sizes, which in turn is highly relevant in data mining or Web source mediation environments. We characterize the exact solution for the optimal choice of synopses for a given workload. Taking into account the workload is a major step beyond our own prior work [19].

The remainder of this paper is organized as follows. In Section 2 we define the underlying optimization problem, briefly review the relevant parts from earlier work on spline synopses [19], and introduce our error model. Section 3 then describes how to determine the optimal set of synopses exactly, using two assumptions which (in earlier experiments) have been found to hold for nearly all datasets and which lead to a compact formulation of the necessary computations. In Section 4 we show how to combine the various building blocks of our framework into a unified algorithm. Section 5 contains an empirical validation of our approach in form of several experiments conducted with the *TPC-H* decision support benchmark. Finally, in Section 6 we summarize our work and give an outlook on future research.

2 Framework

We address the following optimization problem: given a number of datasets $\mathcal{R} := \{R_1, \ldots, R_n\}$ and a workload consisting of SPJ (select-project-join) queries $\mathcal{Q} := \{Q_1, \ldots, Q_k\}$, what is the best combination $\mathcal{S}$ of synopses such that the estimation error over all queries is minimized.

We assume that each query Q_i is mapped to exactly one synopsis $S_j \in \mathcal{S}$ which captures all attributes that are relevant for Q_i, i.e., attributes on which filter conditions are defined as well as attributes that appear in the query output. This is no limitation, as we can always decompose a more complex query into subqueries such that the above condition holds for each subquery. In fact, an SPJ query would often be the result of decomposing a complex SQL query (e.g., to produce an intermediate result for a group-by and aggregation decision-support query). The subqueries that matter in our context are those for which we wish to estimate the result or result size. In commercial query engines and in virtually all of the prior work on data synopses, these subqueries were limited to simple range selections. Our approach improves the state of the art in that we consider entire SPJ queries as the building blocks for data synopses.

So for a select-project query on a single dataset R we consider synopses that capture all of the selection's filter attributes and all attributes in the projection list (unless some of these attributes are considered irrelevant for the purpose of result approximation). For join queries that access attributes from multiple datasets $R_1, ..., R_l$ it is conceivable to construct a result approximation or result size estimation from multiple synopses. On the other hand, it is known that this approach may lead to unbounded approximation errors [5]. Therefore, we have adopted the approach of [1] to use special join synopses for this purpose. A join synopsis can be viewed as a regular synopsis that is derived from a virtual dataset that materializes the full result of the join. Such a materialized join view does not really have to be stored, but merely serves to construct the statistical data in the corresponding join synopsis.

2.1 Notation

We consider a set of relations $\mathcal{R} = \{R_1, \ldots, R_n\}$ and a set of queries $\mathcal{Q} := \{Q_1, \ldots, Q_k\}$. Each relation $R_i \in \mathcal{R}$ has at_i attributes $Att(R_i) = \{R_i.A_1, \ldots, R_i.A_{at_i}\}$. Queries can be "approximately answered" by a set of synopses $\mathcal{S} := \{S_1, \ldots, S_l\}$ corresponding to the data distributions $\mathcal{T}_1, \ldots, \mathcal{T}_l$; each S_i is the approximation of a relation R_p over the attributes $Att(S_i) \subseteq Att(R_p)$. Because in our context there is never more than one synopsis for a given set of attributes we also write S_x with x being the set of attributes captured by the synopsis, i.e., $S_{\{R_1.A_2, R_1.A_3\}}$ denotes the synopsis of R_1 over the two attributes A_2 and A_3. Analogously, we use the notation $\mathcal{T}_{\{R_1.A_2, R_1.A_3\}}$ to describe the corresponding joint data distribution in the full data set. The size of a synopsis S_x (in terms of the number of values necessary to store S_x) is denoted by $Size(S_x)$.

A simple (range) selection or projection query can be answered using the data distribution of the queried relation over the attributes involved in the range selection. A join query can be processed by examining the joint data distribution of the joining relations. Thus it is possible to assign to each query Q_i on relation R_p the *minimum* set $Min(Q_i)$ of attributes $\subseteq Att(R_p)$, whose corresponding data distributions must be examined to answer the query. For example consider the query q_1

SELECT $R_1.A_1$ WHERE $R_1.A_2 > 100$

This query can be answered by examining the joint data distribution of relation R_1 over the attributes $R_1.A_1$ and $R_1.A_2$, thus $Min(q_1) = \{R_1.A_1, R_1.A_2\}$.

When only the size of a result is of interest (for example in the context of query optimization), it is sufficient to query the attributes that determine the number of tuples in the result; assuming that no duplicate elimination is performed, in this case the minimum set becomes $Min(q_1) = \{R_1.A_2\}$. Consequently, the set $Min(Q_i)$ contains the information which synopses need to be built in order to answer query q_i while observing all correlations between the relevant attributes.

Concerning data distributions, we adopt the notation used in [24]. The *domain* $\mathcal{D}_{R_i.A_j}$ of a single attribute $R_i.A_j$ is the set of all possible values of $R_i.A_j$, and the value set $\mathcal{V}_{R_i.A_j} \subseteq \mathcal{D}_{R_i.A_j}, \mathcal{V}_{R_i.A_j} = \{v_1, \ldots, v_n\}$, is the set of values for A_j actually present in the underlying relation R_i. The *density* of attribute X in a value range from a to b, $a, b \in \mathcal{D}_{R_i.A_j}$, is the number of unique values $v \in \mathcal{V}_{R_i.A_j}$ with $a \leq v < b$. The *frequency* f_i of v_i is the number of tuples in $\mathcal{R}$ with value v_i in attribute $R_i.A_j$. The *data distribution* of $R_i.A_j$ is the set of pairs $\mathcal{T} = \{(v_1, f_1), (v_2, f_2), \ldots, (v_n, f_n)\}$. Similarly, a joint data distribution over d attributes $R_i.A_{j_1}, \ldots, R_i.A_{j_d}$ is a set of pairs $\mathcal{T} = \{(v_1, f_1), (v_2, f_2), \ldots, (v_n, f_n)\}$, with $v_t \in \mathcal{V}_{R_i.A_{j_1}} \times \cdots \times \mathcal{V}_{R_i.A_{j_d}}$ and f_t being the number of tuples of value v_t.

2.2 Join Synopses

As pointed out in [5] (in the context of sampling), it is usually not feasible to estimate arbitrary join queries from approximations of the joining base relations with acceptable accuracy. For sampling, this phenomenon is discussed extensively in [5], but it does also hold for all other data reduction techniques that estimate join queries from approximations of the base relations.

For histograms, this is due to the fact that even small errors incurred when approximating the density of attribute values lead to drastic changes in the number and position of attribute values that find a join partner. This problem becomes worse in multi-dimensional histograms through the use of the assumption that, if $value_i$ unique attribute values are present in the i-th dimension within a bucket, then all $\prod_{l=1}^{\#dimensions} value_l$ combinations of these values are present [23]. Regarding join estimation via wavelets, consider the following example:

$$\mathcal{T}_1 = \{(v_1, 2), (v_2, 0), (v_3, 7), (v_4, 2)\} \quad \mathcal{T}_2 = \{(v_1, 10), (v_2, 10000), \ldots\}$$

Even if the approximation keeps all coefficients necessary to represent $\mathcal{T}_2$ and drops only a single coefficient of the representation of $\mathcal{T}_1$, the approximation of the join between the two distributions exhibits a large error, for the approximation $\hat{\mathcal{T}}_1 = \{(v_1, 1), (v_2, 1), (v_3, 7), (v_4, 2)\}$ now joins the 1000 $\mathcal{T}_2$ tuples with value v_2. The reason for this phenomenon is the fact that the *thresholding scheme* employed in [3] minimizes the overall mean squared error $\sum_{i=1}^{\mathcal{T}} (f_i - \hat{f}_i)^2$ for each relation, which minimizes the error regarding range selection queries, but disregards accurate join estimation.

As a solution, special synopses dedicated to estimating the data distribution resulting from a *foreign key* join were proposed in [1]. In [19] the issue was examined in the context of spline synopses and general equijoin queries; we proposed an algorithm that examines for each join the result of joining the base relations and adds special join synopses for join results. The trade-off to consider is that additional join synopses leave less memory for the synopses of the base relations.

Experiments showed that for virtually all examined datasets the addition of (even very small) join synopses improved the estimation quality greatly. Thus we adopt the following approach for join synopses: for all queries in $\mathcal{Q}$ involving joins, we add a "virtual relation" R' to $\mathcal{R}$ representing the joint data distribution of the top node in the corresponding join tree (i.e. the complete n-way join if the join tree has n leaves). A query involving a join could thus be modeled by introducing join synopsis over the relevant attributes from the joining relations; consider query q_2:

SELECT $R_1.A_1$ FROM R_1, R_2, R_3 WHERE $R_1.A_2 = R_2.A_3$ AND $R_2.A_4 = R_3.A_5$

Here we introduce $R' := R_1 \stackrel{A_2=A_3}{\bowtie} R_2 \stackrel{A_4=A_5}{\bowtie} R_3$. Then $Min(q_2) = \{R'.A_1\}$.

2.3 Spline Synopses

As the underlying statistics representation, we use *spline synopses*, which are described in detail in [18, 19]. Our results also apply (with some adaptation) to other data reduction techniques (e.g. histograms). Spline synopses have particular properties that are advantageous in our physical design context. The approximation of a distribution $\mathcal{T}$ is again a data distribution $\hat{\mathcal{T}}$ with $|\mathcal{T}| = |\hat{\mathcal{T}}|$, i.e., for every attribute value pair (v_i, f_i) there is an approximate representation $(\hat{v}_i, \hat{f}_i)$. This makes it possible to use spline synopses for query estimation for virtually any query type, including more advanced operators such as top-k proximity search or spatial joins.

Spline synopses use two different approximation techniques for approximating attribute value density and attribute value frequencies. This means that the memory available for a single synopsis S over a distribution $\mathcal{T}$ is divided between the approximations based on each technique - the first one approximating the attribute frequencies, minimizing $\sum_{i=1}^{|\mathcal{T}|}(f_i - \hat{f}_i)^2$; the second technique approximates the value density, in case of a one-dimensional distribution minimizing $\sum_{i=1}^{|\mathcal{T}|}(v_i - \hat{v}_i)^2$. For d-dimensional distributions, a space-filling curve $\phi : [0,1]^d \mapsto [0,1]$ (more specifically, the Sierpiński curve) is employed to map each attribute-value $v_i \in \mathbb{R}^d$ to a value $v_i^l \in [0,1]$. We then approximate the latter values as $\hat{v}_{i,i=1...n}^l$, minimizing $\sum_{i=1}^{|\mathcal{T}|}(v_i^l - \hat{v}_i^l)^2$. In order to use the resulting approximation for query estimation, the $\hat{v}_i^l$ are mapped back via ϕ^{-1} at query processing time. The key feature here is that the Sierpiński mapping preserves proximity, as it can be shown that

$$\forall v_i^l, \hat{v}_i^l \in [0,1] : \|\phi^{-1}(v_i^l) - \phi^{-1}(\hat{v}_i^l)\| \leq 2\sqrt{d+6}\, |v_i^l - \hat{v}_i^l|^{\frac{1}{d}} \quad [26]$$

with $\|\cdot\|$ denoting the L_2 norm (*Euclidian Distance*) between the data-points; i.e. by minimizing $|v_i^l - \hat{v}_i^l|$ we also reduce $\|\phi^{-1}(v_i^l) - \phi^{-1}(\hat{v}_i^l)\|$.

In this sense, the synopsis-construction process can be characterized as minimizing

$$\sum_{i=0}^{|\mathcal{T}|}(f_i - \hat{f}_i)^2 + r \cdot (\|v_i - \hat{v}_i\|)^2 \quad (1)$$

for an appropriately chosen r. Which values to choose for r is discussed in [19].

For both density and frequency, the resulting approximation is stored in buckets, with each bucket storing 3 values each: leftmost value, the start-point and gradient of the frequency approximation (for frequency approximation), or leftmost value, number of distinct values and size of the interval between adjacent approximate values (for density approximation).

The above approach to capturing both value frequency and value density allows us to use a well defined error metric for the tuples contained in the result an arbitrary query (see the next section), whereas this is not easily possible for other techniques. For multi-dimensional distributions, histograms use the assumption, that all combinations of values in a bucket are realized [23], which generally leads to over-estimation of the number of distinct attribute values and under-estimation of their frequencies (see [19]). In wavelet-based approximation, the attribute-value distribution (i.e, density) is approximated only indirectly through the position of the values that have a frequency other than zero. Because the thresholding scheme used in [3] aims to minimize the overall mean square error $\sum_{i=0}^{|T|}(f_i - \hat{f}_i)^2$ only, wavelet-based approximation generally does not result in a particularly accurate representation of the attribute-value density and thus cannot cope well with projection queries or grouping.

2.4 The Error Model

Our goal is to minimize the estimation error over all queries $Q_j \in \mathcal{Q}$. First consider a scenario in which all queries only depend on a single synopsis S_0 over the data distribution $\mathcal{T} = \{(v_1, f_1), (v_2, f_2), \ldots, (v_n, f_n)\}$. We define the error for a given query $Q_j \in \mathcal{Q}$ by characterizing how well the query result $Result(Q_j) \subseteq \mathcal{T}$ is approximated. Then we define the error over all queries in $\mathcal{Q}$ with respect to a data distribution $\mathcal{T}$ as

$$Error(\mathcal{Q}, S_0) := \sum_{Q_j \in \mathcal{Q}} \left(\sum_{i \in \{k | v_k \in Result(Q_j)\}} (f_i - \hat{f}_i)^2 + r \cdot (\|v_i - \hat{v}_i\|)^2 \right) \quad (2)$$

Thus, if we define $w_i := |\{Q' \mid v_i \in Result(Q'), Q' \in \mathcal{Q}\}|$, the sum of the errors for each query posed to synopsis S_0 can be written as:

$$Error(\mathcal{Q}, S_0) := \sum_{i=1}^{|T|} w_i \cdot (f_i - \hat{f}_i)^2 + r \cdot w_i \cdot (\|v_i - \hat{v}_i\|)^2. \quad (3)$$

Except for the weights w_i, this is the error function (equation 1) minimized by spline synopses. Since the weights w_i can be easily incorporated into the spline construction process, minimizing the query error in the case of a single distribution has become a problem of constructing the optimal spline synopsis, which has been solved in [19].

This is a slight simplification as it ignores approximation errors with regard to the boundary conditions of a query: when using a synopsis for answering a query some attribute values $\hat{v}_i$ may be included in the approximate answer even though the corresponding v_i would not be in the query result. Likewise, some attribute values may be erroneously excluded.

In a scenario with multiple synopses $\mathcal{S} := \{S_1, \ldots, S_l\}$, each query Q_j is answered (depending on $Min(Q_j)$) by a synopsis in $\mathcal{S}$. We use a mapping function $map : \bigcup 2^{\{Att(R)|R \in \mathcal{R}\}} \mapsto \{1, \ldots, l\}$ to assign each queried attribute combination to exactly one synopsis. We will describe how to obtain this mapping in Section 3.2. Note that this model assumes that queries over the same attribute combination are always mapped to the same synopsis (otherwise it would be necessary to store additional information on the mapping of specific queries, which would in turn compete for the memory available for synopses). Thus, the error over a set of synopses $\mathcal{S} := \{S_1, \ldots, S_l\}$ is defined as:

$$Error(\mathcal{Q}, \mathcal{S}) = \sum_{i=1}^{l} (Error(\{Q_j \in \mathcal{Q} \mid map(Min(Q_j)) = i\}, S_i)).$$

Since the error of each synopsis S_i is dependent on the memory size $Size(S_i)$ of the synopsis, this is more accurately stated as:

$Error(\mathcal{Q}, \mathcal{S})$

$$= \min_{(Size(S_1), \ldots, Size(S_l)) \in \mathbb{N}^l} \sum_{i=1}^{l} (Error(\{Q_j \in \mathcal{Q} \mid map(Min(Q_j)) = i\}, S_i)) \quad (4)$$

under the constraint that $\sum_{i=1}^{l} Size(S_l)$ is equal to the memory size M available for all synopses together. Thus the problem of optimizing the estimation error for the entirety of queries in the workload can be seen as a problem of selecting the optimal set of synopses and choosing their sizes.

3 Synopsis Selection and Memory Allocation

To illustrate the issues involved in our method consider a workload $\mathcal{Q} = \mathcal{Q}_1 \cup \mathcal{Q}_2$, $\mathcal{Q}_1$ containing no_1 queries Q' (i.e., queries of type Q' whose fraction in the entire workload is proportional to no_1) with $Min(Q') = \{\{R_1.A_1\}\}$ and $\mathcal{Q}_2$ containing no_2 queries Q'' with $Min(Q'') = \{\{R_1.A_2\}\}$. Then these can be answered by either (a) two synopses $S_{\{R_1.A_1\}}$ and $S_{\{R_1.A_2\}}$ over each single attribute, or (b) one synopsis $S_{\{R_1.A_1, R_1.A_2\}}$ over the joint data distribution of $R_1.A_1$ and $R_1.A_2$. Therefore, to compute the optimal error for the overall available memory M we have to evaluate

$$Error(\mathcal{Q}) := \min \left\{ \overbrace{Error(\mathcal{Q}, S_{\{R_1.A_1, R_1.A_2\}})}^{\text{Error for combination (b)}}, \underbrace{\min_{\substack{Size(S_{\{R_1.A_1\}}) \in \mathbb{N} \\ Size(S_{\{R_1.A_2\}}) \in \mathbb{N}}} (Error(\mathcal{Q}_1, S_{\{R_1.A_1\}}) + Error(\mathcal{Q}_2, S_{\{R_1.A_2\}}))}_{\text{Error for combination (a)}} \right\}$$

(with $Size(S_{\{R_1.A_1, R_1.A_2\}}) = M$ and $Size(S_{\{R_1.A_1\}}) + Size(S_{\{R_1.A_2\}}) = M$) and keep track of the resulting synopses and memory partitioning. So we can characterize the problem of computing the optimal set of synopses (and the corresponding memory allocation) as a two-step process:

(1) Computing $Error(Q', S_x)$ for all candidate synopses S_x and all possible combinations of queries $Q' \subseteq Q$ that may be mapped to S_x and the maximum amount of Memory M to be used for S_x. This requires $O(M \cdot |T_x|^2)$ steps (for optimal partitioning, see [19]) for each pair of S_x and Q' and also generates the values of $Error(Q', S_x)$ for all values of $Size(S_x) \leq M$.

(2) Selecting the optimal set of synopses from a set of candidates computing an optimal memory partitioning such that the weighted sum over all synopsis errors (weighted by the number of times each synopsis is queried) becomes minimal for the synopses included in the optimal solution. Since the weights change according to the combinations of synopses in the solution, this is a different and more difficult problem than finding the optimal combination of synopses for different relations (which was solved by dynamic programming in [19]). As we will see in Section 3.2, the problem of synopsis selection and memory partitioning are closely related and thus solved together.

In the following (Sections 3.1 and 3.2), we will show how to solve the above problem for a single dataset $R \in \mathcal{R}$. The sub-solutions for all datasets in $\mathcal{R}$ can then be combined to solve the overall problem (Section 3.3).

3.1 Pruning the Search Space

Note that in the above example we never considered the combinations $\mathcal{S}' = \{S_{\{R_1.A_1\}}, S_{\{R_1.A_1, R_1.A_2\}}\}$ or $\mathcal{S}'' = \{S_{\{R_1.A_2\}}, S_{\{R_1.A_1, R_1.A_2\}}\}$. This is due to a simple property of spline synopses, which also normally holds for both histograms and Wavelet-based approximations:

Observation 1, "Pruning Property": When answering queries over the set of attributes a, a synopsis S_x, over the set of attributes x with $a \subseteq x$ will yield more accurate answers than a synopsis S_y if $x \subset y$ and both synopses are of identical size.

While artificial data distributions can be constructed that do not obey the above observation, we have found the pruning property to hold in all experiments on real-life datasets. The intuition behind it is the fact that by including more attributes in a synopsis, the number of unique attribute-value combinations v_i in the corresponding data distribution increases as well (in this respect, the synopsis selection problem is similar to the one of index selection), making it harder to capture all attribute values/frequencies with acceptable accuracy.

In the above case, it means that $S_{\{R_1.A_1\}}$ answers queries posed to $R_1.A_1$ better than $S_{\{R_1.A_1, R_1.A_2\}}$ (using the same memory). Similarly $S_{\{R_1.A_2\}}$ is an improvement over $S_{\{R_1.A_1, R_1.A_2\}}$ for queries posed to $R_1.A_2$. Thus the combination $\mathcal{S} = \{S_{\{R_1.A_1\}}, S_{\{R_1.A_2\}}\}$ generally outperforms $\mathcal{S}'$ or $\mathcal{S}''$.

Using the above observation, it becomes possible to characterize the set of candidate synopses in a compact manner. Consider a single relation R. Then the sets of attributes of R queried is $Syn(R, Q) := \{Min(Q_i) \mid Q_i \in Q\}$. Now the set of all candidate synopses for R can be defined as:

$$Cand(R, \mathcal{Q}) := \{S_x \mid x = \bigcup z, z \subseteq Syn(R, \mathcal{Q})\}$$

The intuition behind the definition of $Cand(R, \mathcal{Q})$ is the following: if a Synopsis S_y is in $Cand(R, \mathcal{Q})$, it must be considered, for it is the most efficient way to answer a subset of queries of R using only one synopsis (all other synopses capable of answering the same subset would be less efficient, due to the pruning property). Conversely, if $S_y \notin Cand(R, \mathcal{Q})$ then y must be of the form $y = cand \cup nocand$ with $cand \in \{\bigcup z, z \subseteq Syn(R, \mathcal{Q})\}, nocand \subseteq Att(R), \forall x \in nocand : (cand \cup x) \notin \{\bigcup z, z \subseteq Syn(R, \mathcal{Q})\}$. But then S_{cand} answers the same set of queries as S_y and does so more efficiently, since $cand \subset y$. We further utilize a second observation for further pruning of the search space.

Observation 2, "Merge Property": For a set of queries $\mathcal{Q}$ each querying the same combination of attributes A, the error for answering the queries using one synopsis S over A with M memory is smaller than the error using two synopses S_1, S_2 over A, which together use memory M.

The intuition for this property is the following: By joining the synopses S_1 and S_2, the estimation for the (potentially) overlapping regions in S_1 and S_2 is improved, as additional memory is invested in its estimation. It is a trivial consequence that the merge property also holds for combinations of more than two synopses over A. In contrast to the pruning property, it is possible to prove that the merge property always holds (see [20] for the proof).

3.2 Selecting the Synopses for a Single Relation R

In the following we will describe, for a given set $\mathcal{Q}$ of queries over a single relation R, how to compute the optimal combination $\mathcal{S}$ of synopses, their sizes, and the corresponding mapping of queries, such that all queries can be answered and the overall error becomes minimal.

As shown before, the optimal combination of synopses $\mathcal{S}_{opt}$ can consist of synopses over single attribute combinations from $Syn(R, \mathcal{Q})$ that are optimal for a particular query in $\mathcal{Q}$, as well as synopses for the joint attribute combinations of multiple members of $Syn(R, \mathcal{Q})$, which are not optimal for any single query but more efficient than other combinations of synopses (using the same amount of memory) capable of answering the same queries. Now we want to capture this notion algorithmically, giving a method to construct a set of synopses for a given workload/data combination. We first introduce the necessary notation:

$Opt\_Syn_{\mathcal{A},M} :=$ the combination of synopses for answering all queries over the attribute combinations in $\mathcal{A} \subseteq Syn(R, \mathcal{Q})$ using memory M as constructed below.

$Opt\_Err_{\mathcal{A},M} :=$ the overall error resulting from $Opt\_Syn_{\mathcal{A},M}$.

Now consider the problem of computing the optimal combination of synopses $Opt\_Syn_{\mathcal{A},M}$ for given $\mathcal{A}$ and M. $Opt\_Syn_{\mathcal{A},M}$ has one of the following forms:

(a) **Opt_Syn**$_{A,M}$ = $\{S_{\bigcup A}\}$ with $Size(S_{\bigcup A}) = M$ (one synopsis for all queries over the attribute combinations in $\mathcal{A}$).
(b) **Opt_Syn**$_{A,M}$ = **Opt_Syn**$_{\mathcal{A}',m'}$ ∪ **Opt_Syn**$_{\mathcal{A}-\mathcal{A}',M-m'}$ (a combination of the optimal synopses for answering two disjoint subsets of $\mathcal{A}$ with $\mathcal{A}' \neq \emptyset$). Because of the merge property, we consider only decompositions for which $Opt\_Syn_{\mathcal{A}',m'} \cap Opt\_Syn_{\mathcal{A}-\mathcal{A}',M-m'} = \emptyset$.

Which combination is optimal depends on the error resulting from each alternative:

In case (a) $Opt\_Err_{\mathcal{A},M} = Error(\underbrace{\{Q' \mid Min(Q') = \bigcup \mathcal{A}\}}_{\text{The set of queries answered by } S_{\bigcup \mathcal{A}}}, \{S_{\bigcup \mathcal{A}}\})$

with $Size(S_{\bigcup \mathcal{A}}) = M$.

In case (b) $Opt\_Err_{\mathcal{A},M} = \min_{m' \in \{1,\ldots,M-1\}} Opt\_Err_{\mathcal{A}',m'} + Opt\_Err_{\mathcal{A}-\mathcal{A}',M-m'}$

Therefore, we can compute the optimal set of synopses for $\mathcal{A}$ by computing the minimal error for cases (a) and (b) and choosing the memory partitioning that minimizes the corresponding error. Note that by computing the optimal combination of synopses in the above manner, we implicitly also compute a mapping that dictates which attribute combinations from $Syn(R, \mathcal{Q})$ are mapped to which synopses: because of the above decomposition, $\mathcal{S} := Opt\_Err_{\bigcup Syn(R,\mathcal{Q}),M}$ is of the form $\mathcal{S} = \{S_{\bigcup \mathcal{A}_1}, \ldots, S_{\bigcup \mathcal{A}_l}\}$ with each $a \in Syn(R, \mathcal{Q})$ being a member of exactly one $\mathcal{A}_1, \ldots, \mathcal{A}_l$. While more complex models are possible in which queries over the same attribute combination are mapped to different members of $\mathcal{S}$, this would mean that additional information, from which the correct mapping for each single query could be derived at run-time, would have to be stored (creating contention for memory with the actual data synopses).

Using the above definitions, the final set of synopses kept for R using memory M is $Opt\_Syn_{\bigcup Syn(R,\mathcal{Q}),M}$, the corresponding error being $Opt\_Err_{\bigcup Syn(R,\mathcal{Q}),M}$. However, it is still necessary to prove that the optimal solution can indeed be obtained based on the decompositions described above:

Theorem: $Opt\_Syn_{\mathcal{A},M}$ constructed in the above manner is the *optimal* combination of synopses for answering all queries in $\mathcal{Q}$ over the attribute combinations in $\mathcal{A}$, when the *pruning* and *merge* properties hold.

Proof: We show that $\mathcal{S} := Opt\_Syn_{\mathcal{A},M}$ using the above construction implies that $\mathcal{S}$ is the optimal combination of synopses answering all queries over the attribute combinations in $\mathcal{A}$ using memory M. This is proven by induction over $|\mathcal{A}|$:

$|\mathcal{A}| = 1$: Then $Opt\_Syn_{\mathcal{A},M} = \{S_{\mathcal{A}}\}$ (no partitioning involving multiple synopses possible because of the merge property), and because of the pruning property $S_{\mathcal{A}}$ is the best way to answer queries over $\mathcal{A}$.

$|\mathcal{A}| \rightarrow |\mathcal{A}| + 1$: Now we assume that all $Opt\_Syn_{\mathcal{A},M}$ for $|\mathcal{A}| \leq h$ are indeed optimal and try to show the optimality for $Opt\_Syn_{\mathcal{A},M}$ with $|\mathcal{A}| = h+1$. This is shown by contradiction:

Assumption: There exists a solution $\mathcal{S}_{opt} = \{S_{x_1}, \ldots, S_{x_t}\}$ (with $Size(S_{x_i}) = m_i, i = 1, \ldots, t$) such that the resulting overall error Err_{opt} over all queries is indeed smaller than $Opt\_Err_{\mathcal{A},M}$ with $\mathcal{S}_{opt} \neq Opt\_Syn_{\mathcal{A},M}$.

(Case 1) $|\mathcal{S}_{opt}| = 1$: Then $\mathcal{S}_{opt} = \{S_{\mathcal{A}'}\}$, with $Size(S_{\mathcal{A}'}) = M$. Since $\mathcal{S}_{opt}$ has a smaller Error than $Opt\_Err_{\mathcal{A},M}$, $\mathcal{S}_{opt} \neq \{S_{\mathcal{A}}\}$ (as $S_{\mathcal{A}}$ is a possible synopsis combination for $Opt\_Syn_{\mathcal{A},M}$ and thus $Error(\mathcal{Q}, \{S_{\mathcal{A}}\}) \geq Opt\_Err_{\mathcal{A},M} > Err_{opt}$). However, since $\mathcal{S}_{opt}$ must be able to answer all queries over $\mathcal{A}$, $\mathcal{A} \subset \mathcal{A}'$ holds. Then it follows from the pruning property that $Opt\_Syn_{\mathcal{A},M}$ results in better accuracy than $\mathcal{S}_{opt}$, contradicting the previous assumption.

(Case 2) $|\mathcal{S}_{opt}| > 1$: Because of the merge property, we assume that all queries to the same attribute combination $a \in \mathcal{A}$ are mapped to the same synopsis. Should this not be the case, we can replace $\mathcal{S}_{opt}$ by $\mathcal{S}'_{opt}$, for which all synopses over the same attribute have been merged, resulting in a smaller error. If we can now contradict the assumption for $\mathcal{S}'_{opt}$, we thereby contradict it for $\mathcal{S}_{opt}$, too.

Now $\mathcal{S}_{opt}$ can be written as $\mathcal{S}_{opt} = \mathcal{S}_1 \cup \mathcal{S}_2, \mathcal{S}_1 \neq \emptyset, \mathcal{S}_1 \neq \mathcal{S}, \mathcal{S}_2 := \mathcal{S} - \mathcal{S}_1$ with $\mathcal{S}_1 = \{S_{x_1^1}, \ldots, S_{x_p^1}\}, \mathcal{S}_2 = \{S_{x_1^2}, \ldots, S_{x_q^2}\}, p \leq h, q \leq h$. Because all queries over the same attribute combination are mapped to the same synopsis, both $\mathcal{S}_1$ and $\mathcal{S}_2$ each answer queries over the attribute combinations in disjoint subsets $\mathcal{A}_1, \mathcal{A}_2$ of $\mathcal{A}$ with $\mathcal{A}_1 \cup \mathcal{A}_2 = \mathcal{A}$. Then it follows from the induction hypothesis that $Opt\_Syn_{\mathcal{A}_1, \sum_{i=0}^{p} Size(S_{x_i^1})}$ results in a smaller error than $\mathcal{S}_1$ for queries over attribute combinations in $\mathcal{A}_1$, and $Opt\_Syn_{\mathcal{A}_1, \sum_{i=0}^{q} Size(S_{x_i^1})}$ results in a smaller error than $\mathcal{S}_2$ for queries over attribute combinations in $\mathcal{A}_2$. It follows that the error for $Opt_{\mathcal{A},M}$ is less than the one caused by $\mathcal{S}_{opt}$, contradicting the assumption. □

3.3 Selecting the Synopses for All Relations

The error over all relations for total memory size M can now be written as

$$Error(\mathcal{Q}, \mathcal{S}) = \min_{(M_1, \ldots, M_{|\mathcal{R}|}) \in \mathbb{N}^{|\mathcal{R}|}} \sum_{i=1}^{|\mathcal{R}|} Opt\_Err_{\bigcup Syn(R_i, \mathcal{Q}), M_i} \quad (5)$$

under the constraint that $\sum_{i=1}^{|\mathcal{R}|} M_i = M$. Note that this is equivalent to the initial definition in equation 4. Expression 5 can be solved by dynamic programming using $O(M^2 \cdot |\mathcal{R}|)$ operations. By keeping track of the memory partitioning $(M_1, \ldots, M_{|\mathcal{R}|})$, we can then determine the optimal set of synopses

$$\mathcal{S} := \bigcup_{i=1, \ldots, |\mathcal{R}|} Opt\_Syn_{\bigcup Syn(R_i, \mathcal{Q}), M_i}.$$

4 Putting the Pieces Together

Solving the *physical design problem* for data synopses can be characterized as a 4-step process:

1) Collection of workload information: We first need to acquire the necessary information about the access behavior of the workload, which can be done automatically by the data manager that processes the queries.

2) Enumeration of all possible synopsis combinations: As described in Section 3.3 the synopses selection problem can be solved for each relation independently; from the resulting sub-solutions the overall combination can then be obtained by solving equation 5. To obtain the sub-solution for each relation $R_i \in \mathcal{R}$, we first compute all possible synopsis combinations for $Opt\_Syn_{\mathcal{A},M}$ for R_i. This is done by traversing the lattice of the attribute combinations in $Cand(R_i, \mathcal{Q})$ in the order of the sizes $|\mathcal{T}_x|$ of the data distributions at each node. For each node we compute all synopsis combinations possible from its attribute combinations $\mathcal{A}_i$ and all subsets of $\mathcal{A}_i$ corresponding to nodes in the lattice (as well as potential mappings from queries to synopses).

3) Minimization of the error values: As described in Section 3.2, each of the combinations of synopses and mappings corresponds to an Opt_Err expression, which is defined in the form of a minimization problem. In order to determine the best synopsis combination, we have to compute the corresponding values for Opt_Err. This is done by constructing the corresponding synopses and evaluating the error for the resulting data distributions. The minimum Opt_Err expression corresponds to the optimal synopsis combination.

By combining the *enumeration* and *minimization* steps, it is furthermore possible to avoid solving identical minimization-problems more than once. Each time a new (sub-) combination of synopses/mapping is created the corresponding minimization problem is solved immediately. Because each new combination is either created by joining two previously know combinations together, plus at most one additional synopsis, the corresponding minimization problem can be solved using the solutions for the two joining synopses in at most $O(M)$ steps.

4) Construction of the final synopses: The overall optimal solution can now be obtained from the sub-solutions for each relation by minimizing equation 5.

The computational overhead of our techniques is caused by (a) the computation of the candidate synopses, (b) the solving of the resulting minimization problems, and (c) the enumeration of all possible minimization problems. A detailed discussion of the running times for (a) and (b) can be found in [19]. In order to assess the cost of (c), enumerating all minimization problems, we had our algorithm construct all possible synopses for a given set of attributes $\mathcal{A}$ for which all possible subsets were queried (i.e. $2^{|\mathcal{A}|}$ different types of queries and thus the same worst-case number of potential synopses). The running times for this worst-case stress test are shown in Table 1. Obviously, even though the space of all combinations grows exponentially with the size of $\mathcal{A}$, the enumeration is still reasonably efficient for up to 20 attributes, which covers the range of query-relevant attributes in most tables (including join views) in relational

Table 1. Running times for the enumeration on a *SUN UltraSPARC 4000* (168 Mhz)

# Attributes	Running time (sec.)	# Attributes	Running time (sec.)
4	0,009 sec.	12	1,23 sec.
8	0,049 sec.	16	93,93 sec.

databases. We have also developed a number of heuristic algorithms, that alleviate the potential bottlenecks arising from our approach. A detailed description of these can be found in the extended version of this paper [20].

5 Experiments

To validate our approach and to demonstrate both its accuracy and low overhead, we have implemented our techniques and applied them to a scenario based on the *TPC-H* decision support benchmark. We compared the synopses selection techniques introduced in this paper against several simpler heuristics. Because we are not aware of other approaches to the given problem, these heuristics are not intended to represent opponents. Rather, some represent assumptions commonly used in connection with synopses selection in commercial database systems. Others are used to examine how much approximation accuracy is affected by simpler approaches to either synopses selection or memory allocation.

5.1 Base Experiment

We used a subset of the queries of *TPC-H*, chosen to be large enough to make the synopses-selection problem non-trivial yet small enough to facilitate understanding of the resulting physical design. The queries selected were Q_1, Q_6, Q_{13}, Q_{15} and Q_{17}, referring to the LINEITEM, PART, ORDERS, and CUSTOMER tables[1]. Table 2 shows the query-relevant attribute sets, the *minimum sets* $Min(Q_i)$, for the above five queries. We chose these minimum sets according to a result-size approximation scenario, i.e., we only selected those attributes that are necessary to estimate the *number* of tuples in the query results (for queries which have an aggregation as the last operator, we estimate the result-size before the aggregation). This results in five multidimensional data distributions. Three of these are projections of the LINEITEM table, referred to as L onto subsets of its attributes (which all overlap so that there are a number of different, potentially suitable combinations of synopses). The other two data distributions to be approximated are join synopses J_1 = LINEITEM ⋈ ORDERS and J_2 = LINEITEM ⋈ PART. For our experiments, we used a scaled-down version of the *TPC-H* data with scale factor SF= $\frac{1}{100}$) and SF ∗ 500 KBytes memory available for all synopses together).

---
[1] The non-numerical values present in a TPC-H database are coded as numbers. For example, P.BRAND consists of a constant text string and two integers in the range [1, 5]. We only store the 25 possible number combinations.

Table 2. The *Mininmum Sets* for the used queries

Query	Min-Set
Q_1	L.SHIPDATE
Q_6	L.SHIPDATE, L.DISCOUNT, L.QUANTITY
Q_{13}	J_1.EXTENDED_PRICE, J_1.CLERK, J_1.DISCOUNT, J_1.RETURN_FLAG
Q_{15}	L.EXTENDED_PRICE, L.SHIPDATE, L.DISCOUNT
Q_{17}	J_2.CONTAINER, J_2.DISCOUNT, J_2.QUANTITY, J_2.BRAND

We compared the physical design technique presented in this paper against six heuristic competitors that were generated from the following two option sets for synopses selection and memory allocation.

Synopses selection:

Single. A single-dimensional synopsis was allocated for each attribute that appears at least once in the minimum sets of the five queries. While this heuristics cannot be expected to perform comparably to the more sophisticated allocation schema, we included it since most commercial database systems still use one-dimensional synopses/histograms only. So this heuristics gives an idea of the loss in accuracy when ignoring multi-attribute correlation.

Table. One multidimensional synopsis is allocated for each table, and this synopsis covers all attributes of the table that appear in the minimum sets. This heuristic results in a large single synopsis reflecting all correlations between attributes. However, because of the merge-property, the its accuracy may be significantly less than synopses using subsets of attributes.

and **Memory allocation:**

Uniform. Each synopsis is given the same size. Again, this assumption can be found in commercial database systems.

Tuples. The size of a synopsis is proportional to the size of the table that it refers to, measured in the number of tuples that reside in the table (where a join result is viewed as a table, too) multiplied with the number of attributes covered by the synopsis.

Values. The size of a synopsis is proportional to the size of the unique value combinations among the attributes over which the synopsis is built.

The synopsis-selection technique of this paper is referred to as *Opt_Syn*, the corresponding memory reconciliation as *Opt_Size*. To illustrate the importance of memory reconciliation for our overall approach, we also combined our synopsis-selection with the *Uniform*, *Tuples* and *Values*-based memory allocation; i.e., the optimal set of synopses was first generated and the sizes of these synopses were then computed using the above heuristics. For each set of synopses we executed 1000 instances of each query (using different, uniformly distributed, inputs for the query parameters, as specified in the benchmark) and used the available synopses to estimate the result sizes. We measured the average relative error of the result sizes:

$$\mathbf{Relative\_Error} := \frac{1}{n} \sum_{i=1,\ldots,n} \frac{|(exact\_size(i) - estimated\_size(i))|}{exact\_size(i)}$$

with n being the number of instances of all queries together. All queries occur with the same frequency in all experiments. The results of the first experiment are shown in the first three columns of Table 3.

Table 3. Error for the original *TPC-H*, skewed, and locally accessed data

Selection	Memory	Original data	Skewed data	Query locality
SINGLE	UNIFORM	1.98	7.98	10.19
	TUPLES	1.98	7.42	9.72
	VALUES	1.92	7.62	9.34
TABLE	UNIFORM	1.46	3.14	4.96
	TUPLES	1.47	3.17	5.11
	VALUES	1.43	3.47	5.01
Opt_Syn	UNIFORM	1.05	1.14	1.04
Opt_Syn	VALUES	1.04	1.01	1.27
Opt_Syn	TUPLES	1.03	1.08	1.17
Opt_Syn	Opt_Size	1.04	0.83	0.85

In this set of experiments, our technique employed for synopses selection had significant impact on the resulting approximation accuracy, whereas the way memory is allocated only results in negligible changes to the overall error.

5.2 Skewed and Correlated Data

As described earlier, for purposes of approximation it is crucial to preserve the correlation contained in the data. Unfortunately, the original TPC-H data is generated using uniformly random distributions for each attribute, resulting in almost completely uncorrelated data[2], which is not a good benchmark for data approximation techniques. Therefore, we ran a second set of experiments using the same schema, but with skewed and correlated data. This more realistic kind of data was generated the following way:

Skew in attribute-value frequencies. We generated the attribute-value frequencies so that the frequency of the attribute values was Zipf-like distributed;

---
[2] The exceptions being O.TOTALPRICE (correlated with L.TAX, L.DISCOUT, L.EXTENDEDPRICE), L.SHIPDATE (correlated with O.ORDERDATE), L.COMMITDATE (correlated with O.ORDERDATE) and L.RECEIPTDATE (correlated with L.SHIPDATE).

i.e., the frequency of the i-th most frequent value is proportional to $(1/i)^\theta$ where θ is a control parameter for the degree of skew. In this experiment we used $\theta = 1$.

Correlation between attributes. Here we permuted the generated data in order to obtain the desired correlation. After creating the data according to the TPC-H specification, we then performed (randomly chosen) permutations on the values of selected attributes in order to create specific correlations between pairs of attributes. The correlation itself is specified in terms of the linear correlation coefficient r_s [25]. For each of the following pairs of attributes we created data with a linear correlation coefficient $r_s \in [0.725, 0.775]$: (L.SHIPDATE, L.QUANTITY),(J$_2$.BRAND, J$_2$.CONTAINER), (P.PARTKEY, P.BRAND).

The results for this experiment are shown in the fourth column of Table 3. Again, the choice of the synopses-selection technique was most important with regards to the resulting approximation error: our *Opt_Syn* technique developed in this paper reduced the error by a factor of 7 and 3 compared to the Single and Table heuristics, respectively. In addition, with *Opt_Syn* for synopses selection, the use of our memory reconciliation technique *Opt_Size* resulted in noticeable further improvement. So for this more realistic dataset, the combination of *Opt_Syn* and *Opt_Size* outperformed all competitors by a significant margin.

5.3 Query Locality

We repeated the above experiments using a workload that exhibited significant locality, again using the data exhibiting significant skew and correlation. For this experiment, we generated the input parameters for the TPC-H queries using a Zipf-like distribution ($\theta = 0.25$), first executing 1000 queries of each type to obtain the weights w_i (see equation 3) we then used to construct the synopses. Subsequently, we ran another 1000 queries (with different parameters generated by the same probability distribution) for which we measured the error. The results for this experiment are shown in the fifth column of Table 3. The trends from the previous experiment can be observed here as well: the synopses-selection technique clearly outperforms the simpler approaches, with the estimation accuracy further improving when memory reconciliation is used.

6 Conclusions

In this paper we motivated and defined the *physical design problem for data synopses*. We proposed an algorithmic approach to its solution, discussed heuristics to alleviate computational bottlenecks, and provided an experimental evaluation. The experiments showed that the developed method achieves substantial gains over simpler heuristics in terms of the accuracy within the given memory constraint. They also showed that both aspects of our approach, synopses selection and tuning of the memory allocation, are important. Although we have carried out the derivation and implementation of our approach in the context of spline synopsis, our approach is orthogonal to the specific form of synopses and applies equally well to histograms as well as other techniques (with some minor modifications).

References

1. S. Acharya, P. B. Gibbons, V. Poosala, and S. Ramaswamy. Join Synopses for Approximate Query Answering. In *Proceedings of the ACM SIGMOD Conference*, pages 275–286. ACM Press, 1999.
2. B. Blohsfeld, D. Korus, and B. Seeger. A Comparison of Selectivity Estimators for Range Queries on Metric Attributes. In *Proceedings of the ACM SIGMOD Conference*, pages 239–250, 1999.
3. K. Chakrabarti, M. N. Garofalakis, R. Rastogi, and K. Shim. Approximate query processing using wavelets. In Proceedings of 26th International Conference on Very Large Data Bases, Cairo, Egypt, pages 111–122, 2000.
4. S. Chaudhuri. An overview of query optimization in relational systems. In *Proceedings of ACM PODS Conference*, pages 34–43, 1998.
5. S. Chaudhuri, R. Motwani, and V. R. Narasayya. On Random Sampling over Joins. In *Proceedings of the ACM SIGMOD Conference*, pages 263–274, 1999.
6. S. Chaudhuri and V. R. Narasayya. Automating Statistics management for Query Optimizers. *IEEE Conference on Data Engineering*, pages 339–348, 2000.
7. C. M. Chen and N. Roussopoulos. Adaptive Selectivity Estimation Using Query Feedback. In *Proceedings of the ACM SIGMOD Conference*, pages 161–172, 1994.
8. V. Ganti, M.-L. Lee, and R. Ramakrishnan. Icicles: Self-tuning samples for approximate query answering. In *VLDB 2000, Proceedings of 26th International Conference on Very Large Data Bases, Cairo, Egypt*, pages 176–187, 2000.
9. P. B. Gibbons, S. Acharya, Y. Bartal, Y. Matias, S. Muthukrishnan, V. Poosala, S. Ramaswamy, and T. Suel. Aqua: System and techniques for approximate query answering. Technical report, Bell Labs, 1998.
10. P. B. Gibbons and Y. Matias. New Sampling-Based Summary Statistics for Improving Approximate Query Answers. In *Proceedings of the ACM SIGMOD Conference*, 1998.
11. P. B. Gibbons and Y. Matias. Synopsis Data Structures for Massive Data Sets. In *Symposium on Discrete Algorithms*, 1999.
12. P. B. Gibbons, Y. Matias, and V. Poosala. Fast Incremental Maintenance of Approximate Histograms. In *Proceedings of the 23rd International Conference on Very Large Databases*, 1997.
13. P. J. Haas. Selectivity and Cost Estimation for Joins Based on Random Sampling. *Journal of Computer and System Sciences*, pages 550–569, 1996.
14. Y. E. Ioannidis and V. Poosala. Histogram-Based Approximation of Set-Valued Query-Answers. In *Proceedings of 25th International Conference on Very Large Data Bases*, pages 174–185, 1999.
15. H. Jagadish, H. Jin, B. C. Ooi, and K.-L. Tan. Global Optimization of Histograms. In *Proceedings of the ACM SIGMOD Conference*. ACM Press, 2001.
16. H. V. Jagadish, N. Koudas, S. Mutukrishnan, V. Poosala, K. Sevcik, and T. Suel. Optimal Histograms with Quality Guarantees. In *Proceedings 24th International Conference on Very Large Databases*, pages 275–286, 1998.
17. N. Kabra and D. J. DeWitt. Efficient mid-query re-optimization of sub-optimal query execution plans. In *Proceedings of the ACM SIGMOD Conference*, 1998.

18. A. König and G. Weikum. Combining Histograms and Parametric Curve Fitting for Feedback-Driven Query Result-size Estimation. In *25th International Conference on Very Large Databases*, 1999.
19. A. König and G. Weikum. Auto-Tuned Spline Synopses for Database Statistics Management. 10th Int. Conference on the Management of Data, Pune, India, 2000.
20. A. König and G. Weikum. A Framework for the Physical Design Problem for Data Synopses (*extended version*) available at: http://www-dbs.cs.uni-sb.de/.
21. J.-H. Lee, D.-H. Kim, and C.-W. Chung. Multi-dimensional Selectivity Estimation Using Compressed Histogram Information. In *Proceedings of the ACM SIGMOD Conference*, pages 205–214, 1999.
22. Y. Matias, J. S. Vitter, and M. Wang. Wavelet-Based Histograms for Selectivity Estimation. In *Proceedings of the ACM SIGMOD Conference*, pages 448–459, 1998.
23. V. Pooosala and Y. E. Ioannidis. Selectivity Estimation Without the Attribute Value Independence Assumption. In *Proceedings of the ACM SIGMOD Conference*, Athens, Greece, 1997.
24. V. Poosala. *Histogram-based Estimation Techniques in Database Systems*. PhD thesis, University of Wisconsin-Madison, 1997.
25. W. Press, S. Teukolsky, W. Vetterling, and B. Flannery. *Numerical Receipes in C*. Cambridge University Press, 1996.
26. E. Skubalska-Rafajlowicz. The Closed Curve Filling Multidimensional Cube, Technical Report no. 46/94. ICT Technical University of Wroclaw, 1994.
27. W. Sun, Y. Ling, N. Rishe, and Y. Deng. An instant and accurate Size Estimation Method for Joins and Selections in an Retrival-Intensive Environment. In *Proceedings of the ACM SIGMOD Conference*, pages 79–88, 1993.

Temporal Aggregation over Data Streams Using Multiple Granularities

Donghui Zhang[1], Dimitrios Gunopulos[1,*],
Vassilis J. Tsotras[1,**], and Bernhard Seeger[2]

[1] Computer Science Department,
University of California, Riverside, CA 92521
{donghui,dg,tsotras}@cs.ucr.edu
[2] Fachbereich Mathematik & Informatik,
Philipps Universität Marburg, Germany
seeger@Mathematik.Uni-Marburg.de

Abstract. Temporal aggregation is an important but costly operation for applications that maintain time-evolving data (data warehouses, temporal databases, etc.). In this paper we examine the problem of computing temporal aggregates over data streams. Such aggregates are maintained using multiple levels of temporal granularities: older data is aggregated using coarser granularities while more recent data is aggregated with finer detail. We present specialized indexing schemes for dynamically and progressively maintaining temporal aggregates. Moreover, these schemes can be parameterized. The levels of granularity as well as their corresponding index sizes (or validity lengths) can be dynamically adjusted. This provides a useful trade-off between aggregation detail and storage space. Analytical and experimental results show the efficiency of the proposed structures. Moreover, we discuss how the indexing schemes can be extended to solve the more general range temporal and spatio-temporal aggregation problems.

1 Introduction

With the rapid increase of historical data in data warehouses, temporal aggregates have become predominant operators for data analysis. Computing temporal aggregates is a significantly more intricate problem than traditional aggregation. Each database tuple has an attribute value (e.g. the dosage of a prescription) and is accompanied by a time interval during which the attribute value is valid. Consequently, the value of a tuple attribute affects the aggregate computation for all those instants included in the tuple's time interval. An *instantaneous* temporal aggregate is the aggregate value of all tuples whose intervals contain a given time instant. A *cumulative* temporal aggregate is the aggregate value of all

---

* This work was partially supported by NSF CAREER Award 9984729, NSF IIS-9907477, the DoD and AT&T.
** This work was partially supported by NSF grants IIS-9907477, EIA-9983445, and the Department of Defense.

tuples whose intervals intersect a given time interval. For example, "find the total number of phone calls made in 1999". In the rest we concentrate on cumulative aggregates since they are more general; thus the term "temporal aggregation" implies "cumulative temporal aggregation". Furthermore, in this paper we focus on the SUM aggregate but our solutions apply to COUNT and AVG as well.

Many approaches have been recently proposed to address temporal aggregation queries [26, 19, 27, 11, 22, 28, 29]. They are classified into two categories: approaches that compute a temporal aggregate when the aggregate is requested (usually by sweeping through related data) and those that maintain a specialized aggregate index [28, 29]. The latter approaches dynamically precompute aggregates and store them appropriately in the specialized index. This leads to less space (since the aggregation index is typically much smaller than the actual data) as well as much faster query times (an ad-hoc aggregate is computed by simply traversing a path in the index). In particular, [28] proposed the SB-tree, an elegant index used to solve the *scalar* temporal aggregation problem: the aggregation involves all tuples whose intervals intersect the query time interval. [29] introduced the MVSB-tree and solved a more general problem, the *range* temporal aggregation, where the aggregate is taken over all tuples intersecting the query time interval and having keys in a query specified key range.

However, all previous works assume that the temporal aggregation is expressed in a single time granularity. Usually this granularity is the same as the granularity used to store the time attributes. Recently, there has been much research on multiple time granularities [4, 9, 8, 6, 3]. In many data warehousing query languages, e.g. Microsoft's MDX, one query can return results at multiple granularities. Consider a database tracking the phone calls records and let the time granularity be in seconds. Each phone call record is accompanied by an interval [*start, end*) (both in seconds) indicating the time period this call took place. A temporal aggregate example is: "find the total number of phone calls made between 12:30:01 and 15:30:59 today". While aggregating per second may be necessary for queries on the recent enterprise history (say within 10 days), for many applications it is not crucial when querying the remote history (for example, data older than a year ago). In the latter case, the aggregation at a coarser time granularity (e.g., per minute or per day) may be satisfactory enough. The ability to aggregate using coarser granularities for older data is crucial for applications that accumulate large amounts of data. As an example, [18] cites that a major telecommunications company collects 75GB of detailed call data every day or 27TB a year. With this huge amount of source data, even the specialized aggregation index under a single time granularity will soon grow too large.

Saving storage space is especially useful for applications under the stream model, which was formalized recently by [17]. A stream is an ordered sequence of points that are read in increasing order. The performance of an algorithm that operates on streams is measured by the number of passes the algorithm must make over the stream, when constrained by the size of available storage space. The model is very appropriate for example when analyzing network traffic data [15, 10, 12, 13]. The amount of data that is generated in such applications is very large, and certainly can exceed any reasonable amount of available memory quickly. Therefore any analysis technique has to assume that it can make only one pass over the data. Recently proposed techniques include clustering algorithms when the objects arrive as a stream [15], computing decision tree classifies when the classification examples arrive as a stream [10], as well as computing histograms and answering range queries when the values arrive in a stream [12, 13].

It is reasonable to consider two stream models: the *window* model, where we are only interested in data that arrived recently, within a window W, from current time, and the *complete* model, when all data are equally interesting. Both of the models have limitations, since in the first model old data are completely lost, and in the second model accuracy can suffer since the size of available storage remains constant while the amount of data increases continuously.

In this paper we assume that insertions and deletions of tuples come as a stream. Since both the window model and the complete model have disadvantages, we propose a *hybrid* model called the *Hierarchical Temporal Aggregation (HTA) model*. We keep full information of all tuples that arrived during the most recent time, but we aggregate earlier records at coarser granularities. We further separate the HTA model into the *fixed storage model* and the *fixed time window model*. The difference is based on the mechanisms to control the aggregation. The former one is based on the size of the structures, and the latter one is based on the amount of time that passes.

Besides considering the temporal aggregation problem, we also consider the more general range temporal aggregation problem and the spatio-temporal aggregation problem. An range temporal aggregation query may be: "find how many phone calls were made in 1999 from phones in the 626 area (Los Angeles)". A spatio-temporal aggregation query may be: "given an arbitrary spatial region, compute the total precipitation of rain falls in this region in 1999".

The contributions of the paper can be summarized as:

- We provide efficient solutions using specialized aggregation indices for the temporal aggregate problems under multiple granularities. In particular we propose solutions for both the fixed storage model and for the fixed time window model. Analytical and experimental results prove the efficiency of our solutions.
- We show how the proposed solutions can be extended to solve the range temporal aggregation and the spatio-temporal aggregation problems under the fixed time window model.
- Furthermore, the proposed specialized index structures can be parameterized. That is, the levels of granularity as well as the corresponding index sizes or validity lengths can be dynamically adjusted. This provides a useful trade-off between the aggregation detail and the storage space.

The ability to aggregate with fixed storage is reminiscent of the *on-line aggregation* proposed in [16]. There, when an aggregation query is asked, an approximate answer is given very quickly. This answer is progressively refined, while the user is provided with the confidence of the current answer and the percentage of the elapsed computation time out of the total time needed to get the final answer. [20] achieved a similar goal by keeping aggregate information in the internal nodes of index structures. The problem examined in this paper is different since we do not keep all the information as the existing works do, and we always give exact answers to the aggregation queries very fast, with the exact answers for the remote history being aggregated at coarser time granularities.

Aggregating with different granularities also resembles the *roll-up* operation examined in the data warehousing studies. A data warehouse is usually based on a multi-dimensional data model. Along each dimension, a *concept hierarchy* may exist, which defines a sequence of mappings from a set of low-level concepts to high-level, more general concepts. For example, along the *location* dimension, we may have a concept hierarchy $city \in state \in country \in continent$. The roll-up operation performs aggregation by climbing up a concept hierarchy for a dimension. In a sense the HTA model also aims to "roll-up" by climbing up the time hierarchy. However, the problem examined here is different for two reasons: (1) In a data warehouse, the information is stored at the finest granularity, while in the HTA model, information is stored at different time granularity, according to whether the information is old or new; and (2) The roll-up in data warehousing takes place at query time, which allows the user to get the aggregation results at coarser granularity; while in the HTA model, the roll-up takes place automatically and systematically as data accumulates.

A very related work is [25], which presents an effective technique for data reduction that handles the gradual change of the data from new detailed data to older, summarized data in a dimensional data warehouse. Although the time dimension can be considered as an ordinary dimension in the data warehouse, our work differs from their work in the semantics of data over the time dimension. Consider the case when a tuple is valid across all days in a week. In our temporal database environment, the tuple value will be counted once towards any query which intersects the valid week. In the data warehouse environment, however, the tuple value will be counted once for every day of the week. Thus to aggregate by week, the technique of [25] will multiply the tuple value by 7. Clearly, both semantics have practical meanings. However, they apply to different scenarios.

The rest of the paper is organized as follows. Section 2 presents the models of aggregation and identifies four implementation issues. The solution for the temporal aggregation problem under the fixed storage model is presented in section 3, while the solution under the fixed time window model is presented in section 4. The performance results appear in section 5. The solutions are extended to solve the range temporal aggregation problem and the spatio-temporal aggregation problems in section 6. Section 7 discusses related work. Finally, section 8 presents our conclusions.

2 Problem Definition

The time dimension naturally has a hierarchy. A k-level time hierarchy is denoted as $gran_1 \rightarrow \ldots \rightarrow gran_k$, where $gran_1$ is at the coarsest granularity and $gran_k$

is at the finest granularity. Here each granularity has a value range (normally a finite subset of the set of integers). Any time instant corresponds to a full assignment of the k granularities. For example, a 3-level time hierarchy may be: $year \rightarrow month \rightarrow day$. Here at the finest granularity we have days, which are grouped in months, which are further grouped in years. A time instant "Oct 1, 2001" corresponds to the following full assignment of the three granularities: "$year=2001, month=10, day=1$".

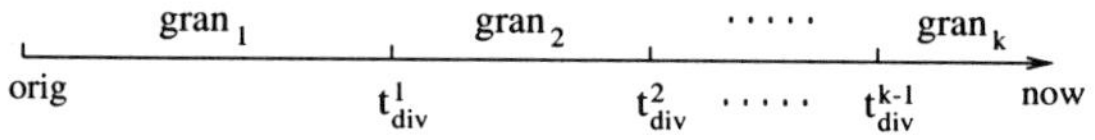

Fig. 1. The HTA model.

Given a k-level time hierarchy, the *Hierarchical Temporal Aggregation (HTA)* model divides the time space [$orig, now$) into k segments and for each segment $i \in \{1, \ldots, k\}$, the aggregates are maintained with granularity $gran_i$ (figure 1). Here $orig$ is a fixed time specifying the creation time of the database and now corresponds to the ever-increasing current time. The *dividing times* between pairs of adjacent segments are denoted as $t_{div}^1, \ldots, t_{div}^{k-1}$.

As now progresses and as new objects are inserted, the initial assignments of the dividing times may become obsolete. Thus, any solution to the temporal aggregation problem under the HTA model should allow the corresponding segments to be dynamically adjusted. Depending on what triggers the dynamic adjustment, we further separate the HTA model into two sub-models:

- **Fixed Storage Model.** The assumption for this model is that the available storage is limited. When the total storage of the aggregate index becomes more than a fixed threshold S, older information is aggregated at a coarser granularity.
- **Fixed Time Window Model.** Here we assume that the lengths of all segments (except the first $segment_1$) are fixed. For example, in $segment_k$ where records are aggregated by $gran_k$ (say by day), we may want to keep information for one year; for $segment_{k-1}$ where records are aggregated by $gran_{k-1}$ (say by month), we may want to keep information for five years, etc. Hence, as now advances, we need to increase the dividing time instants $t_{div}^1, \ldots, t_{div}^{k-1}$.

The two models are geared towards different requirements. For example, in a telephone traffic application we may want to always maintain the aggregate over the most recent day (i.e., the window size of the latest segment, $segment_k$ is set to a day). On the other hand, the fixed storage model guarantees its storage requirements but the length of the aggregation maybe less, equal or more than a day.

To increase a dividing time t_{div}^i in the fixed time window model, both the aggregate indices for $segment_i$ and $segment_{i+1}$ should change. To maintain efficiency the following is needed: (a) We should avoid building the complete index structures for the two segments around t_{div}^i whenever it advances. Rather, some kind of *patching* should be performed. (b) We should avoid frequent dividing time advances. If we actually maintain $length_i$ to be a fixed value, the dividing times should advance every time *now* advances. Instead, we allow $length_i$ to be a value within a certain range $[W_l, W_h)$ and we increase t_{div}^{i-1} whenever $length_i$ reaches W_h.

To design an aggregation index under any of the two models, there are four issues that need to be addressed.

1. **Structure:** We need to maintain an index for each of the k segments and we need to integrate these indices (and possibly some additional information) together as a unified index structure.

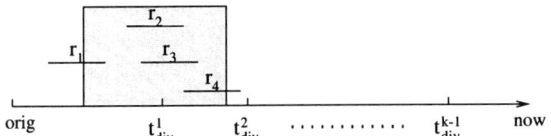

Fig. 2. A record may affect several segments.

2. **Query:** We need an algorithm to evaluate an aggregation query by looking up the unified index structure. One important issue is that for a query which touches several segments, we should avoid counting the same record more than once. In figure 2, the shadowed box illustrates the query, which involves segment 1 and segment 2. The query result is the total weight of records r_1, r_2, r_3, r_4. However, since we maintain the aggregates for each segment individually, record r_2 and r_3 are maintained in both segments. So if the query is divided into two, one per segment and aggregate the two query results, r_2 and r_3 would be counted twice, which should be avoided. Another issue that arise upon query is the query granularity. As figure 2 shows, a query may span more than one segments, where each segment has a different granularity. In this case, we assume the query granularity to be the coarsest one among all these segments.
3. **Update:** We need to incrementally maintain the unified index structure as new objects are inserted/deleted.
4. **Advancing the dividing times:** The two sub-models differ in how the advancement is triggered. However, for both models, we need to advance the dividing times systematically. Moreover, information before the new dividing time should be removed from the index and aggregated at a coarser granularity.

3 Temporal Aggregation with Fixed Storage

[28] proposed two approaches to incrementally maintain temporal aggregates. Both approaches rely on using two *SB-trees* collectively. In this section we first propose a slightly different approach and then we present a technique to extend the approach under the fixed storage model.

3.1 The 2SB-tree

A single SB-tree as proposed in [28] can be used to maintain instantaneous temporal aggregates. One feature about the SB-tree is that a deletion in the base table is treated as an insertion with a negative value. Thus in the rest we focus on the insertion operation. [28] also proposed two approaches to maintain the cumulative temporal aggregate. The first approach is called *Dual SB-tree*. Two SB-trees are kept. One maintains the aggregates of records valid at any given time, while the other maintains the aggregates of records valid strictly before any given time. The latter SB-tree can be implemented via the following technique: whenever a database tuple with interval i is inserted in the base table, an interval is inserted into the SB-tree with start time being $i.end$ and end time being $+\infty$. To compute the aggregation query with query interval i, the approach first computes the aggregate value at $i.end$. It then adds the aggregate value of all records with intervals strictly before $i.end$ and finally subtracts the aggregate value of all records with intervals strictly before $i.start$.

The second approach is called the *JSB-tree*. Logically, two SB-trees are again maintained. One maintains the aggregates of records valid strictly before any given time, while the other maintains the aggregates of records valid strictly after any given time. Physically, the two SB-trees can be combined into one tree, where each record keeps two aggregate values rather than one. To compute an aggregate with query interval i, this approach subtracts from the total value of all maintained intervals (which is a single value and is easily maintained) the aggregate of all records with intervals strictly before $i.start$ and the aggregate of all records with intervals strictly after $i.end$. As [28] points out, the two approaches have tradeoffs and no one of them is obviously better than the other.

We hereby propose a new approach called the *2SB-tree*. The idea is again to maintain two SB-trees. One maintains the aggregates of records whose *start* times are less than any given time, while the other maintains the aggregates of records whose *end* times are less than any given time. To compute a temporal aggregate regarding interval i, we find the total value of records whose *start* times are less than $i.end$ and then subtract the total value of records whose *end* times are less than $i.start$. Note that each such SB-trees takes as input, besides a value, a point instead of an interval. The point implies an interval from it to $+\infty$. Compared with the Dual SB-tree, to answer an aggregation query we need to perform two SB-tree traversals instead of three. Compared with the JSB-tree approach (note that the two trees used in the 2SB-tree approach can also be physically combined into one), there is no need to maintain the total weight of all records, and the two SB-trees have unified point input. In the JSB-tree, we can also let the two SB-trees take point input; however, the input points have different meanings for the two trees. In one tree, it implies an interval from $-\infty$ to the point, while in the other tree, it implies an interval from the point to $+\infty$.

3.2 The 2SB-tree with Fixed Storage

When we have fixed storage space, we extend both SB-trees in the 2SB-tree approach with multiple time granularities under the fixed storage model. Each of the extended SB-trees is called the *SB-tree with fixed storage (SB-tree^{FS})* and the complete index is called the *2SB-tree with fixed storage (2SB-tree^{FS})*. It is enough to discuss the four implementation issues on a single SB-tree^{FS}.

Structure: Similarly with a single SB-tree in the 2SB-tree approach, the SB-tree^{FS} maintains a set of time points and is able to answer the 1-dimensional *dominance-sum query* of the form: "given a time t, find the total value of all points less than t". The extension is that the time dimension is divided into k segments. For each segment, an SB-tree I_i is maintained. The total storage size S can be enforced by requiring that each index I_i occupies no more than S_i disk pages, where $S_1, \ldots, S_k$ can be set by the warehouse manager depending on applications. Furthermore, $\sum_{i=1}^{k} S_i = S$. For simplicity we assume that $S_1 = \ldots = S_k = S/k$. For each dividing time t_{div}^i, a value $Snap_i$ is also kept. This value is the total value of all points inserted before t_{div}^i. Figure 3 illustrates the structure.

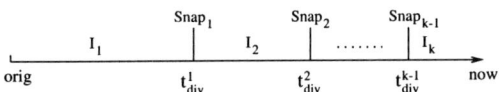

Fig. 3. Structure of the SB-tree^{FS}.

Query: In order for the SB-tree^{FS} to compute a dominance-sum, we first find the segment i which contains t and query index I_i. Then, if $i > 1$, $Snap_{i-1}$ is added to the query result. Note that by reducing the temporal aggregation query into dominance-sum queries, we have automatically avoided the problem illustrated in figure 2. This is because in the reduced problem, each input, as well as query, deals not with an interval, but with a point, which falls into exactly one of the segments.

Update: To insert a point with time t and value v, we find the segment i which contains t and insert the point into I_i. Next, v is added to $Snap_i, \ldots, Snap_{k-1}$. Last, if the size of I_i becomes larger than the threshold S/k, we advance the dividing time t_{div}^{i-1}. This reduces the size of I_i by removing part of the index while the removed information is aggregated at $gran_{i-1}$ and stored in index I_{i-1}.

Advancing the dividing time: Figure 4a depicts an example where I_1 is aggregated by month while I_2 is aggregated by day. Assume I_2 becomes too big and thus t_{div}^1 needs to be advanced. Consider the time intervals of the records in the root page of index I_2 (figure 4b). The lifespan of I_2 is between t_{div}^1 and t_{div}^2. The major ticks represent the months and the minor ticks represent the days. The dividing time t_{div}^1 should occur at a major tick since it is also the end time of the lifespan of index I_1, which is aggregated by month. The rectangles in figure 4b represent the root-level records in SB-tree I_2. The lifespans of these root-level records are contiguous to one another. Since I_2 is aggregated by day, the connection times of these records fall on the minor ticks, but they may not fall on major ticks.

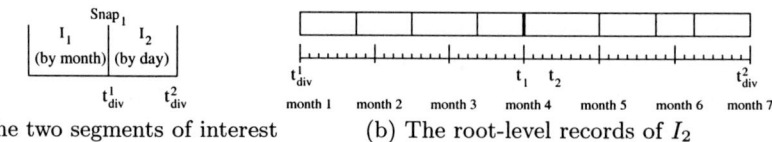

(a) The two segments of interest (b) The root-level records of I_2

Fig. 4. Advancing the dividing time t_{div}^1.

To advance the dividing time t_{div}^1, we need to choose a new dividing time t_{newdiv} and move the information before t_{newdiv} from I_2 to I_1 (aggregated at a coarser granularity). For simplicity let's assume that half of the information is moved over. Straightforwardly, one wishes to go to the root page of I_2 and move the sub-trees pointed to by the left half of the records. For example, in figure 4b, we should move the sub-trees pointed to by the first four root-level records from I_2 to I_1. We first assume that the last root-level record to be moved ends at a major tick (which is the case in the figure, as illustrated by the thick line segment). The case when the record ends somewhere inside a month is discussed afterwards. To remove information from I_2 is easy: we just perform a tree traversal on the sub-trees and deallocate all tree pages met. We thus focus on how to update I_1 and we propose two algorithms.

Algorithm 1. Note that the SB-tree I_2 logically maintains a set of points, each of which corresponds to a month and a day. Since I_1 aggregates by month, we should standardize these points such that they correspond to months only. The algorithm is to find for every month before t_{newdiv}, the total value of points inserted some time during this month. If the value is not zero, we update I_1. For the example of figure 4b, we find the total value of points inserted during months 1, 2 and 3, respectively. To find the value for a given month, say month 2, we perform a dominance-sum query at the first day of month 3 and then subtract from it the dominance-sum at the first day of month 2.

In the above algorithm, the number of queries we perform on I_2 for an advance of dividing time is equal to M, the number of months between t_{div}^1 and t_{newdiv}. Thus the total I/O spent for these queries is $O(M \log_B N)$, where N is the number of leaf records in I_2 and B is the page size in number of records. Although M is normally smaller than N, this is not always true; e.g. when the application generates sparse data where each record spans several months and different records have little overlap. We hereby propose a $O(N \log_B N)$ algorithm. We can choose between the two algorithms at run time when the values of M and N are known.

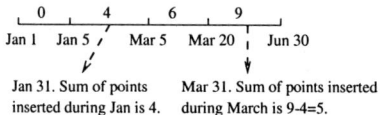

Jan 31. Sum of points inserted during Jan is 4. Mar 31. Sum of points inserted during March is 9-4=5.

Fig. 5. Illustration of algorithm 2.

Algorithm 2. The idea is that we reconstruct the entire aggregates on the part of I_2 that needs to be removed. As shown in [28], this can be performed by a depth-first traversal to reach all leaf nodes. The result is a list of intervals, one connecting to another, each of which is associated with a value (the dominance-sum at all time instants during this interval). An example of such a list is shown in figure 5. We use this example to illustrate how we can identify the months and values to be inserted into I_1 by traversing this list only once. Initially, we meet the first interval [Jan 1, Jan 5). Since it starts and ends in the same month, no change is needed. When we see the second interval [Jan 5, Mar 5), we conclude that in January (the month of the start time of the interval), the sum of all inserted points is 4. This triggers an update of I_1. The next interval [Mar 5, Mar 20) can be ignored again. The last interval [Mar 20, Jun 30) has value 9. The value is the sum of all points inserted in January and in March. To get only the sum of points inserted in March, we subtract 4 from it and we get $9 - 4 = 5$. This triggers the other insertion in I_1.

Now we consider the case when the last root-level record to be moved does not end at a major tick. E.g. in figure 4b, assume that the fourth record ends not at t_1, but at t_2. To handle this situation, we choose t_{newdiv} to be the last major tick before t_2 (which is t_1 in this example). There is a single path in I_2 from root to leaf along which each record contains t_1. These records are all split at t_1; the left copies are aggregated and recorded (along with the sub-tree rooted by the first three root-level records) in I_1, while the right copies are retained in I_2.

After the sub-trees are removed from I_2, index I_1 is updated and the dividing time t_{div}^1 is advanced to t_{newdiv}, there is one more issue to resolve. Suppose the dominance-sum at t_{newdiv} on the previous I_2 is v, we need to add v to $Snap_1$. Furthermore, we need to update I_2 such that a dominance-sum query within the new I_2 is not affected by the part that were removed. This is achieved by inserting into I_2 value $-v$ at time t_{newdiv}.

Theorem 1. *Given a storage limit S, expressed in number of disk pages, the complexities of the 2SB-tree^{FS} with k time granularities are as follows. To compute a temporal aggregate takes $O(\log_B (S/k))$ I/Os, and the amortized insertion cost is $O(k \log_B (S/k))$. Here B is the page capacity in number of records.*

Proof. An SB-tree^{FS} with k time granularities contains k SB-trees, one for each granularity. Thus a 2SB-tree^{FS} with k time granularities contains $2k$ SB-trees. We can allocate $S/2k$ pages for each SB-tree. Thus the max number of leaf records in every SB-tree is $O(SB/k)$. Since the query cost for a single SB-tree is $O(\log_B n)$ [28], where n is the number of leaf records, and to compute a temporal aggregate the 2SB-tree^{FS} performs one query in each of the two SB-trees, the query cost is $O(\log_B (SB/k)) = O(\log_B (S/k))$.

Now we consider the insertion cost. We know that the insertion cost of a single SB-tree is $O(\log_B n)$. By applying similar reasoning as in the previous paragraph, we arrive at the conclusion that the insertion cost of the 2SB-tree^{FS} is $O(\log_B (S/k))$ if no advancing of the dividing time takes place. If an SB-tree I_i occupies more than S/k pages due to an insertion, we need to move half of the tree to I_{i-1}. Assume that we use the second algorithm as discussed earlier in this section. The cost contains three parts: (1) the cost to reconstruct the aggregates for the to-be-removed part of I_i; (2) the cost to remove from I_i; and (3) the cost to insert into I_{i-1}. The cost of part 1 is $O(S/k)$ [28]. The cost to remove from I_i is also $O(S/k)$. The cost to insert into I_{i-1} is $O(\frac{SB}{k} \log_B (S/k))$, since there are $O(SB/k)$ intervals in the reconstructed aggregate list and (in the worst case) for each one of them an insertion takes place in I_{i-1}. In the worst case, the operation of moving half of the tree to another SB-tree (which aggregates at a coarser granularity) is executed recursively for $k-1$ times. So we conclude that the cost of advancing a dividing time is $O(SB \log_B (S/k))$. Now, since after each such advancement, the SB-tree where half of the tree was removed is only half full, to fill it takes another $O(SB/k)$ insertions. Thus the cost of advancing a dividing time can be amortized among the $O(SB/k)$ insertions, or $O(k \log_B (S/k))$ per insertion. To sum up, the amortized insertion cost of the 2SB-tree^{FS} is $O(k \log_B (S/k))$.

4 Temporal Aggregation with Fixed Time Window

For simplicity, we assume that there are two levels in the time hierarchy: $day \to minute$. Our solution in this section can be extended to three or more levels. The time dimension $[orig, now)$ is divided into two segments by the dividing time t_{div}. As discussed before, the difference between now and t_{div} should be within a certain range $[W_l, W_h)$. Without lose of generality, we assume that $W_l = W$ and $W_h = 2W$, i.e. $now \in [t_{div} + W, t_{div} + 2W)$. Similar to the methodology of section 3, we extend each of the SB-trees in the 2SB-tree under the fixed time window model (SB-tree^{FTW}), and we call the collective structure the *2SB-tree with fixed time window (2SB-tree^{FTW})*. We now focus on a single SB-tree^{FTW}.

Structure: Figure 6 shows the structure. Here we use SI to represent *sparse index*, which means to aggregate by day; we use DI to mean *dense index*, which means to aggregate by minute. The dividing time is currently t_1. For points before t_1, we maintain a sparse index SI_{01}. For points after t_1, we maintain two dense indices DI_{12} and DI_{23}, corresponding to the points before and after $t_2 = t_1 + W$. For points belonging to $[t_1, t_2)$ and points belonging to $[t_2, now)$, we also maintain sparse indices SI_{12} and SI_{23}. These indices will be augmented to index SI_{01} later as time advances. Furthermore, at t_1, t_2 and $t_3 = t_2 + W$, we maintain three values $Snap_1$, $Snap_2$ and $Snap_3$ as the total value of the points before t_1, the total value of the points before t_2 and the total value of the points before t_3, respectively.

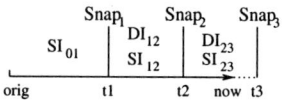

Fig. 6. Structure of the SB-tree^{FTW}.

Query: The algorithm to compute a dominance-sum regarding time t is as follows:

- If $t < t_1$, return the query result on SI_{01};
- otherwise, if $t < t_2$, query SI_{12} or DI_{12}, depending on whether t is the first minute of some day; return the query result plus $Snap_1$;
- otherwise, query DI_{23} or SI_{23}, depending on whether t is the first minute of some day; return the query result plus $Snap_2$;

Update: The algorithm to insert a point with time t and value v is:

- If $t < t_1$, insert into SI_{01}; add v to $Snap_1$, $Snap_2$ and $Snap_3$;
- otherwise, if $t < t_2$, insert into SI_{12} and DI_{12}; add v to $Snap_2$ and $Snap_3$;
- otherwise, insert into SI_{23} and DI_{23}; add v to $Snap_3$.

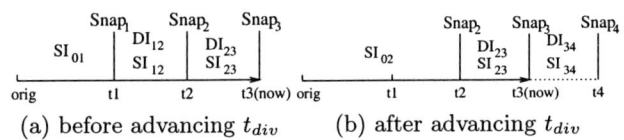

Fig. 7. Advancing the dividing time in the SB-tree^{FTW}.

Advancing the dividing time: When the current time now advances to t_3 (figure 7a), we need to advance the dividing time t_{div} from t_1 to t_2. The algorithm is:

- Integrate SI_{12} into SI_{01}. First, reconstruct the aggregates of SI_{12}. Then, scan through the result list of intervals; for each interval $[start, end)$ with value v, insert $\langle start, v - v' \rangle$ into SI_{01}, where v' is the value of the previous interval (for the first interval, v' is 0).
- Set $Snap_4 = Snap_3$ which stands for the total value of points inserted before $t_4 = t_3 + W$;
- Initialize the dense index DI_{34} and the sparse index SI_{34} to be empty;
- Remove indices DI_{12} and SI_{12}.

After the modifications, the layout of the SB-tree^{FTW} is as shown in figure 7b. We note that the window size W can be adjusted by the warehouse manager. A large W means that the 2SB-tree^{FTW} behaves similar as the 2SB-tree which aggregates only by minute. A small W means that the 2SB-tree^{FTW} behaves similar as the 2SB-tree which aggregates only by day.

5 Performance Results

While the efficiency of the 2SB-tree^{FS} is guaranteed by theorem 1, this is not the case for the 2SB-tree^{FTW}. The difference is that in the latter case, the advancing of dividing times depends not on the index sizes, but on the length of time intervals of the segments. In the worst case, all original data fall on the last partition and thus are kept at the finest granularity. Thus we use performance results to show its efficiency. As baseline cases, we compare with the approaches which involve a single time granularity. Specifically, we assume the time hierarchy has two levels: $day \rightarrow minute$, and we compare our 2SB-tree^{FTW} (denoted as *SB_FTW*) with the 2SB-tree which aggregates only by day (denoted as *SB_day*) and the 2SB-tree which aggregates only by minute (denoted as *SB_min*). We expect that the SB_day uses the least space, since it aggregates at a coarse granularity; however, at the same time it has the least aggregation power in the sense that it does not possess the ability to compute by-minute aggregates. The SB_min is exactly the opposite. We expect that the new approach combines the benefits of both baseline approaches.

The algorithms were implemented in C++ using GNU compilers. The programs ran on a Sun Enterprise 250 Server machine with two 300 MHz UltraSPARC-II processors using Solaris 2.8. We compare the index generation time, the query time and the result index sizes. When generating the indices, the CPU cost is an non-trivial part of the total time. So we report the combined generation time spent in CPU and for I/O. We measure the CPU cost by adding the amounts of time spent in *user* and *system* mode as returned by the *getrusage* system call. We measure the I/O cost by multiplying the number of I/O's by the average disk page read access time (10ms). We used a 8KB page size. For all the algorithms we used the LRU buffering scheme and the buffer size was 100 pages.

Except figure 9b, the data set we used contains 10 million updates. The current time *now* advances gradually by 40 years, which is equal to 14,610 days. The average distance between the dividing time and *now* is a parameter in the performance graphs. We call this distance the *by-minute window size* since the records in this *moving window* are aggregated by minute. The by-minute window size varies from 0.1% to 10% of the 40-year time space. To generate a record, we choose the end time of its interval to be exponentially near to *now*. The length of the record intervals are on average 1000 minutes.

Figure 8a compares the index generation time while varying the by-minute window size. The single-granularity indices SB_day and SB_min are not affected when the by-minute window size varies. As expected, the SB_day takes the shortest time to generate, while the SB_min takes the longest time. The generation time of the SB_FTW is between the other two (11 times less than that of the SB_min for 1% window size). As the by-minute window size becomes larger, the generation time of the SB_FTW tends to be longer, too. The effect of the size of the by-minute window on the generation time is twofold. On the one hand, a larger window size means that the dividing time is increased less often. On the other hand, however, a larger window size means that the sizes of the indices which exist after the dividing time are larger and thus the updates in them takes longer. The combined effect is as shown in figure 8a.

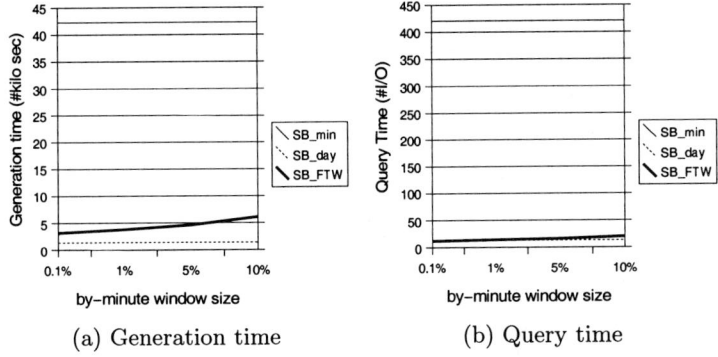

(a) Generation time (b) Query time

Fig. 8. Comparing the generation time and the query time.

For the query performance we measured the execution time in number of I/Os of 100 randomly generated queries. For the SB_day, the aggregates are computed at a by-day granularity. For the SB_min, the aggregates are computed at a by-minute granularity. For the SB_FTW, the *recent* aggregates (if the query interval is later than the dividing time) are computed by-minute and the earlier aggregates are computed by-day. As shown in figure 8b, the SB_FTW and the SB_day have similar query performance which is much better than that of the SB_min. For 1% window size, the SB_FTW is 30 times faster than the SB_min. The SB_FTW is preferred over the SB_day since for the recent history, the SB_FTW has the power to aggregate at a finer granularity.

We now examine the index sizes. As figure 9a shows, the SB_FTW uses a little more space than the SB_day, but much less than the space used by the SB_min. For 1% window size, the SB_FTW uses 23 times less space than the SB_min. In figure 9b we compare the index sizes where the number of objects changes from 1 million to 20 million. Here we fix the by-minute window size to be 1% of the time space. As the number of objects increases, the sizes of all the three indices increase as well. Still, we observe that the size of the SB_FTW is a lot less than that of the SB_min.

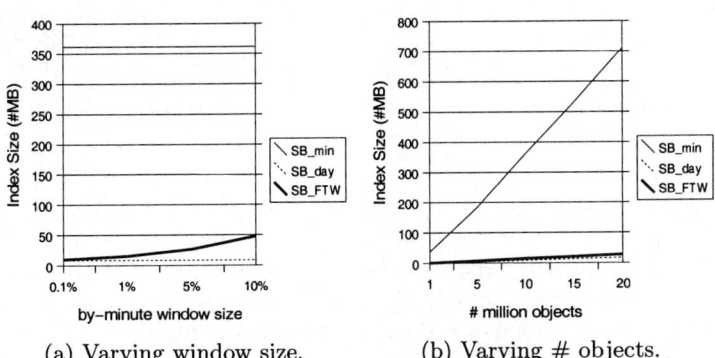

(a) Varying window size. (b) Varying # objects.

Fig. 9. Comparing the index sizes.

6 The Range Temporal and the Spatio-temporal Aggregations

We now provide solutions to these two problems under the HTA model. We first describe the problems in their original form. Then we briefly discuss, based on the solutions to the original problems, how to apply the HTA model.

1. **range temporal aggregation:** *Maintain a set of objects, each of which has a key, a time interval and a value, so as to efficiently compute the total value of objects whose keys are in a given range and whose intervals intersect a given time interval.* This problem was introduced in [29]. Compared with the previously discussed temporal aggregation problem, a query is further limited by a key range. The previous problem is a special case in that the query key range is always the whole key space. An example scenario is to maintain a database of phone call records, each of which has a key as the telephone number, a time interval during which the call occurred and a value 1. A query may be: "find how many phone calls were made in 1999 from phones in the 626 area (Los Angeles)".

2. **spatio-temporal aggregation:** *Maintain a set of objects, each of which has a d-dimensional point, a time interval and a value, so as to efficiently compute the total value of objects whose points are in a given d-dimensional rectangle and whose intervals intersect a given time interval.* An example scenario is to maintain a database of measured rain falls. Each record has a 2-dimensional point as the location of the measuring instrument, a time interval during which a rainfall occurred, and a value as the measured precipitation. A query may be: "given an arbitrary spatial region, compute the total precipitation of rain falls in this region in 1999".

[29] proposed to use two MVSB-trees collectively to solve the range temporal aggregation problem. To extend the solution to the fixed time window model, we use an approach similar to how the 2SB-tree^{FTW} extends the 2SB-tree. The new index still has the structure of figure 6. However, there are a couple of differences. For example, $Snap_1$, $Snap_2$, $Snap_3$ which correspond to t_1, t_2, t_3 are no longer single values, but SB-trees indexing the key dimension. Due to space limitations, the details of the solution are omitted but can be found in the full version of the paper [31].

For the spatio-temporal aggregation problem, there exist both main-memory solutions (the *ECDF-tree* which was proposed by [2]) and external-memory solutions (the *BA-tree* which was proposed by [30]). We can extend the solutions to the fixed time window model similar to how the 2SB-tree^{FTW} extends the 2SB-tree. The details appear in the full version of the paper [31].

7 Related Work

Temporal Aggregation. [26] presented a non-incremental two-step approach where each step requires a full database scan. First the intervals of the aggregate result tuples are found and then each database tuple updates the values of all result tuples that it affects. This approach computes a temporal aggregate in O(mn) time, where m is the number of result tuples (at worst, m is

$O(n)$; but in practice it is usually much less than n). Note that this two-step approach can be used to compute range temporal aggregates, however the full database scans make it inefficient. [19] used the *aggregation-tree*, a main-memory tree (based on the segment tree [23]) to incrementally compute instantaneous temporal aggregates. However the structure can become unbalanced which implies $O(n)$ worst-case time for computing a scalar temporal aggregate. [19] also presented a variant of the aggregation tree, the k-ordered tree, which is based on the k-orderness of the base table; the worst case behavior though remains $O(n)$. [11,27] introduced parallel extensions to the approach presented in [19]. [22] presented an improvement by considering a balanced tree (based on redblack trees). However, this method is still main-memory resident. Finally, [28] and [29] proposed the SB-tree and the MVSB-tree, respectively, which can be used to compute the scalar and range temporal aggregates. Both of them are disk-based, incrementally maintainable and efficient for queries (logarithmic).

Point Aggregation. The solutions proposed in this paper utilizes existing structures to compute dominance-sums. The computational geometry field possesses much research work on the dominance-sum and the more general geometric range searching problem [21,7,1]. Most solutions are based on the *range tree* proposed by [2]. A variation of the range tree which is used to solve the d-dimensional dominance-sum query is called the *ECDF-tree* [2]. The d-dimensional ECDF-tree with n points occupies $O(n \log_2^{d-1} n)$ space, needs $O(n \log_2^{d-1} n)$ preprocessing time and answers a dominance-sum query in $O(\log_2^d n)$ time. Note that the ECDF-tree is a static and internal-memory structure. For the disk-based, dynamic case, [30] proposed two versions of the *ECDF-B-tree*. [30] also presented the *BA-tree* which combines the benefits of the two ECDF-B-trees.

Time Granularity. A glossary of time granularity concepts appears in [4]. [6] deeply investigates the formal characterization of time granularities. [3] shows a novel way to compress temporal databases. The approach is to exploit the semantics of temporal data regarding how the values evolve over time when considered in terms of different time granularities. [8] considers the mathematical characterization of finite and periodical time granularities and identifies a user-friendly symbolic formalism of it. [9] examines the formalization and utilization of semantic assumptions of temporal data which may involve multiple time granularities.

Data Warehousing. The time hierarchy we used is similar to the concept hierarchy in the data warehousing study. [25] proposed a technique to reduce the storage of data cubes by aggregating older data at coarser granularities. [24] states that one difference between the spatio-temporal OLAP and the traditional OLAP is the lack of predefined hierarchies, since the positions and the ranges of spatio-temporal query windows usually do not confine to pre-defined hierarchies and are not known in advance. [24] presented a spatio-temporal data warehousing framework where the spatial and temporal dimensions are modeled as a combined dimension on the data cube. Data structures are also provided which integrate spatio-temporal indexing with pre-aggregation. [14] presented a framework which supports the expiration of unneeded materialized view tuples. The motivation was that data warehouses collect data into materialized views for analysis and as time evolves, the materialized view occupies too much space and some of the data may no longer be of interest.

8 Conclusions

Temporal aggregates have become predominant operators in analyzing time-evolving data. Many applications produce massive temporal data in the form of streams. For such applications the temporal data should be processed (pre-aggregation, etc.) in a single pass. In this paper we examined the problem of computing temporal aggregates over data streams. Furthermore, aggregates are maintained using multiple levels of temporal granularities: older data is aggregated using coarser granularities while more recent data is aggregated with finer detail. We presented two models of operation. In the fixed storage model it is assumed that the available storage is limited. The fixed time window model guarantees the length of every aggregation granularity. For both models we presented specialized indexing schemes for dynamically and progressively maintaining temporal aggregates. An advantage of our approach is that the levels of granularity as well as their corresponding index sizes and validity lengths can be dynamically adjusted. This provides a useful trade-off between aggregation detail and storage space. Analytical and experimental results showed the efficiency of the proposed structures. Moreover, we discussed how our solutions can be extended to solve the more general range temporal and spatio-temporal aggregation problems under the fixed time window model. As future work, we plan to extend our solutions to the multiple data stream environment.

References

1. P. Agarwal and J. Erickson, "Geometric Range Searching and Its Relatives", *Advances in Discrete and Computational Geometry*, B. Chazelle, E. Goodman and R. Pollack (ed.), American Mathematical Society, Providence, 1998.
2. J. L. Bentley, "Multidimensional Divide-and-Conquer", *Communications of the ACM* 23(4), 1980.
3. C. Bettini, "Semantic Compression of Temporal Data", *Proc. of WAIM*, 2001.
4. C. Bettini, C. E. Dyreson, W. S. Evans, R. T. Snodgrass, and X. S. Wang, "A Glossary of Time Granularity Concepts", O. Etzion, S. Jajodia and S. M. Sripada (eds.), *Temporal Databases: Research and Practice*, LNCS 1399, 1998.
5. B. Becker, S. Gschwind, T. Ohler, B. Seeger and P. Widmayer, "An Asymptotically Optimal Multiversion B-Tree", *VLDB Journal* 5(4), 1996.
6. C. Bettini, S. Jajodia and X. S. Wang, *Time Granularities in Databases, Data Mining, and Temporal Reasoning*, Springer, 2000.
7. M. de Berg, M. van Kreveld, M. Overmars and O. Schwarzkopf, *Computational Geometry: Algorithms and Applications*, Springer-Verlag Berlin Heidelberg, Germany, ISBN 3-540-61270-X, 1997.
8. C. Bettini and R. De Sibi, "Symbolic Representation of User-Defined Time Granularities", *Proc. of TIME*, 1999.

9. C. Bettini, X. S. Wang and S. Jajodia, "Temporal Semantic Assumptions and Their Use in Databases", *IEEE TKDE* 10(2), 1998.
10. P. Domingos and G. Hulten, "Mining high-speed data streams", *Proc. of SIGKDD*, 2000.
11. J. Gendrano, B. Huang, J. Rodrigue, B. Moon and R. Snodgrass, "Parallel Algorithms for Computing Temporal Aggregates", *Proc. of ICDE*, 1999.
12. J. Gehrke, F. Korn and D. Srivastava, "On Computing Correlated Aggregates over Continual Data Streams", *Proc. of SIGMOD*, 2001.
13. S. Guha, N. Koudas and K. Shim, "Data-Streams and Histograms", *Proc. of STOC*, 2001.
14. H. Garcia-Molina, W. Labio and J. Yang, "Expiring Data in a Warehouse", *Proc. of VLDB*, 1998.
15. S. Guha, N. Mishra, R. Motwani and L. O'Callaghan, "Clustering Data Streams", *Proc. of FOCS*, 2000.
16. J. Hellerstein, P. Haas and H. Wang, "Online Aggregation", *Proc. of SIGMOD*, 1997.
17. M. R. Henziger, P. Raghavan and S. Rajagopalan, "Computing on Data Streams", *TechReport 1998-011, DEC*, May 1998.
18. H. V. Jagadish, I. S. Mumick and A. Silberschatz, "View maintenance issues for the chronicle data model", *Proc. of PODS*, 1995.
19. N. Kline and R. Snodgrass, "Computing Temporal Aggregates", *Proc. of ICDE*, 1995.
20. I. Lazaridis and S. Mehrotra, "Progressive Approximate Aggregate Queries with a Multi-Resolution Tree Structure", *Proc. of SIGMOD*, 2001.
21. J. Matoušek, "Geometric Range Searching", *Computing Surveys* 26(4), 1994.
22. B. Moon, I. Lopez and V. Immanuel, "Scalable Algorithms for Large Temporal Aggregation", *Proc. of ICDE*, 2000.
23. F. Preparata and M. Shamos, *Computational Geometry: An Introduction*, Springer-Verlag, Berlin/Heidelberg, Germany, 1985.
24. D. Papadias, Y. Tao, P. Kalnis and J. Zhang, "Indexing Spatio-Temporal Data Warehouses", *Proc. of ICDE*, 2002.
25. J. Skyt, C. S. Jensen and T. B. Pedersen, "Specification-Based Data Reduction in Dimensional Data Warehouses", *TimeCenter TechReport* TR-61, 2001.
26. P. Tuma, "Implementing Historical Aggregates in TempIS", *Master's thesis*, Wayne State University, Michigan, 1992.
27. X. Ye and J. Keane, "Processing temporal aggregates in parallel", *Proc. of Int. Conf. on Systems, Man, and Cybernetics*, 1997.
28. J. Yang and J. Widom, "Incremental Computation and Maintenance of Temporal Aggregates", *Proc. of ICDE*, 2001.
29. D. Zhang, A. Markowetz, V. J. Tsotras, D. Gunopulos and B. Seeger, "Efficient Computation of Temporal Aggregates with Range Predicates", *Proc. of PODS*, 2001.
30. D. Zhang, V. J. Tsotras, D. Gunopulos and A. Markowetz, "Efficient Aggregation over Objects with Extent", *TechReport UCR_CS_01_01, CS Dept., UC Riverside*, 2001. http://www.cs.ucr.edu/~donghui/publications/boxaggr.ps
31. D. Zhang, D. Gunopulos, V. J. Tsotras, and B. Seeger, "Temporal Aggregation over Data Streams using Multiple Granularities" (full version), http://www.cs.ucr.edu/~donghui/publications/hta_full.ps

ProPolyne: A Fast Wavelet-Based Algorithm for Progressive Evaluation of Polynomial Range-Sum Queries*

Rolfe R. Schmidt and Cyrus Shahabi

University of Southern California,
Los Angeles CA 90089-0781, USA,
{rrs,shahabi}@usc.edu, http://infolab.usc.edu/

Abstract. Many range aggregate queries can be efficiently derived from a class of fundamental queries: the *polynomial range-sums*. After demonstrating how any range-sum can be evaluated exactly in the wavelet domain, we introduce a novel pre-aggregation method called ProPolyne to evaluate arbitrary polynomial range-sums progressively. At each step of the computation, ProPolyne makes the best possible wavelet approximation of the submitted query. The result is a data-independent approximate query answering technique which uses data structures that can be maintained efficiently. ProPolyne's performance as an exact algorithm is comparable to the best known MOLAP techniques. Our experimental results show that this approach of approximating queries rather than compressing data produces consistent and superior approximate results when compared to typical wavelet-based data compression techniques.

1 Introduction

Range aggregate queries are a fundamental part of modern data analysis applications. Many recently proposed techniques can be used to evaluate a variety of aggregation operators from simple COUNT and SUM queries to statistics such as VARIANCE and COVARIANCE. Most of these methods attempt to provide efficient query answering at a reasonable update cost for a single aggregation operation. An interesting exception is [21], which points out that all second order statistical aggregation functions (including hypothesis testing, principle component analysis, and ANOVA) can be derived from SUM queries of second order polynomials in the measure attributes. Higher order statistics can similarly be reduced to sums of higher order polynomials. The power of these observations leads us to introduce the class of *polynomial range-sum* aggregates in Section 3.

There is a generic way to support polynomial range-sums of any degree using existing OLAP techniques- simply treat each independent monomial up to the

---

* This research has been funded in part by NSF grants EEC-9529152 (IMSC ERC) and IIS-0082826, NIH-NLM grant nr. R01-LM07061, DARPA and USAF under agreement nr. F30602-99-1-0524, and unrestricted cash/equipment gifts from Okawa Foundation, Microsoft, NCR and SUN

required degree as a separate measure and build a new datacube for each of these. This requires the measure attributes to be specified when the database is populated, and has unwieldy storage and maintenance cost for higher order polynomials.

We propose a novel MOLAP technique that can support any polynomial range-sum query (up to a degree specified when the database is populated) using a single set of precomputed aggregates. This extra power comes with little extra cost: the query, update, and storage costs are comparable to the best known MOLAP techniques (see Table 1). We achieve this by observing that polynomial range-sums can be translated and evaluated in the wavelet domain. When the wavelet filiter is chosen to satisfy an appropriate *moment condition*, most of the query wavelet coefficients vanish making the query evaluation faster. We make this observation practical by introducing the *lazy wavelet transform*, an algorithm that translates polynomial range-sums to the wavelet domain in poly-logarithmic time (Section 6).

Wavelets are often thought of as a data approximation tool, and have been used this way for approximate range query answering [7, 22]. The efficacy of this approach is highly data dependent; it only works when the data have a concise wavelet approximation. Furthermore the wavelet approximation is difficult to maintain. To avoid these problems, we use wavelets to approximate incoming queries rather than the underlying data. By using our exact polynomial range-sum technique, but using the largest query wavelet coefficients first we are able to obtain accurate, data-independent query approximations after a small number of I/Os. This approach naturally leads to a progressive algorithm.

We bring these ideas together by introducing ProPolyne (Progressive Polynomial Range-Sum Evaluator, Section 7), a polynomial range-sum evaluation method which

1. Treats all dimensions, including measure dimensions, symmetrically and supports range-sum queries where the summand is *any* polynomial in the data dimensions. All computationa are performed entirely in the wavelet domain (see Section 5).
2. Uses the lazy wavelet transform to achieve query and update cost comparable to the best known exact techniques (see Table 1 and Section 6).
3. By using the most important query wavelet coefficients first, provides excellent approximate results and guaranteed error bounds with very little I/O and computational overhead, reaching low relative error far more quickly than analogous data compression methods (see Section 7).

Table 1. Query/update/storage tradeoff for several exact SUM algorithms

Algorithm	Query Cost	Update Cost	Storage Cost
ProPolyne-FM	$(2\log N)^d$	$\log^d N$	$\min\{|I|\log^d N, N^d\}$
SDDC [16]	$(2\log N)^d$	$\log^d N$	N^d
Prefix-Sum [11]	2^d	N^d	N^d
Relative Prefix-Sum [6]	2^{2d}	$N^{d/2+1}$	N^d

Our experimental results on several empirical datasets show that the approximate results produced by ProPolyne are very accurate long before the exact query evaluation is complete (Section 8). These experiments also show that the performance of wavelet based data approximation methods varies wildly with the dataset, while *query approximation* based ProPolyne delivers consistent, and consistently better, results.

2 Related Work

Extensive research has been done to find efficient ways to evaluate range aggregate queries. The prefix-sum method [11] publicized the fact that careful pre-aggregation can be used to evaluate range aggregate queries in time independent of the range size. This led to a number of new techniques that provide similar benefits with different query/update cost tradeoffs [6, 5, 16, 3]. Iterative Data Cubes [17] generalize all of these techniques, and allow different methods to be used on each dimension. It is pointed out in [21] that statistical analysis of summary data can lead to significant errors in applications such as regression rule mining. In order to provide efficient OLAP-style range statistics, Multivariate Aggregate Views are proposed. These provide a ROLAP technique to support polynomial range-sums of degree 2. ProPolyne takes a MOLAP approach to this problem, and is able to use one set of precomputed aggregates to support all polynomial range-sums up to an arbitrary degree.

Approximate query answering can be used to deliver fast query results. Use of synopsis data structures such as histograms has been analyzed thoroughly [13, 7]. References [20, 9, 19] create synopses that estimate the data frequency distribution. The flexible measures supported by this approach inspire its use in this paper. Online aggregation, or progressive query answering, has also been proposed [10, 15, 24, 12]. These methods, whether based on sampling, R-trees, or multiresolution analysis, share a common strategy: answer queries quickly using a low resolution view of the data, and progressively refine the answer while building a sharper view. ProPolyne is fundamentally different. It makes optimal progressive estimates of the query, not the data. Furthermore, the progressive evaluation comes for free since ProPolyne is an excellent exact algorithm

Recently wavelets have emerged as a powerful tool for approximate answering of aggregate [7, 22, 24] and relational algebra [2] queries. Streaming algorithms for approximate population of a wavelet database are also available [8]. Most of the wavelet query evaluation work has focused on using wavelets to compress the underlying data, reducing the size of the problem. ProPolyne can use compressed data, but is designed to work as an exact algorithm with uncompressed data. ProPolyne produces approximate query results by compressing queries, not data.

3 Range Queries

In this section we introduce the class of *polynomial range-sum* queries, and show how we use the *data frequency distribution* to recast these queries as *vector* queries. Throughout this paper we work with a finite instance I of a schema F (the 'fact table'). We assume that each attribute of F is numeric with domain of size $N = 2^j$, and that F has d attributes. We study the following:

Definition 1. *Given a range $R \subset \text{Dom}(F)$ along with a measure function $f : \text{Dom}(F) \to \mathbb{R}$, the range-sum query $Q(R, f)|_I$ is equal to $Q(R, f)|_I = \sum_{\bar{x} \in I \cap R} f(\bar{x})$ The sum counts multiplicities in the multiset I. If f is a polynomial of degree δ we call this a* polynomial range-sum *of degree δ.*

Example 1. Consider a table of employee ages and salaries, taken from the example in [20], with entries [age, salary]: { [25, 50K], [28, 55K], [30, 58K], [50, 100K], [55, 130K], [57, 120K]} . Choose the range R to be the set of all points where $25 \leq$ age ≤ 40 and $55000 \leq$ salary ≤ 150000.

By choosing $f(\bar{x}) \equiv \mathbf{1}(\bar{x}) = 1$ the range-sum query returns the COUNT of the tuples that lie in R:

$$Q(R, \mathbf{1}, I) = \sum_{\bar{x} \in R \cap I} \mathbf{1}(\bar{x}) = \mathbf{1}(28, 55K) + \mathbf{1}(30, 58K) = 2$$

Choosing $f(\bar{x}) \equiv \text{salary}(\bar{x})$ the range-sum query computes the SUM of salary for tuples in the set R:

$$Q(R, \text{salary}, I) = \sum_{\bar{x} \in R \cap I} \text{salary}(\bar{x}) = 113K$$

An AVERAGE query for a measure function given a range is the ratio of the SUM query with the COUNT query for that range. Finally, taking $f(\bar{x}) \equiv \text{salary}(\bar{x}) \times \text{age}(\bar{x})$ the range-sum query computes the total product of salary and age for tuples in the set R:

$$Q(R, \text{salary} \times \text{age}, I) = \sum_{\bar{x} \in R \cap I} \text{salary}(\bar{x}) \times \text{age}(\bar{x}) = 3280M$$

This is an important component for the computation of covariance in the range R. In particular

$$\text{Cov}(\text{age}, \text{salary}) = \frac{Q(R, \text{salary} \times \text{age}, I)}{Q(R, \mathbf{1}, I)} - \frac{Q(R, \text{age}, I) Q(R, \text{salary}, I)}{(Q(R, \mathbf{1}, I))^2}$$

The variance, kurtosis, or any other statistics in a range can be computed similarly.

Definition 2. *The* **data frequency distribution** *of I is the function $\Delta_I : \text{Dom}(F) \to \mathbb{Z}$ that maps a point $\bar{x}$ to the number of times it occurs in I. To emphasize the fact that a query is an operator on the data frequency distribution, we write $Q(R, f)|_I = Q(R, f, \Delta_I)$. When I is clear from context we omit subscripts and simply write Δ.*

Example 2. For the table of Example 1, we have $\Delta(25, 50K) = \Delta(28, 55K) = \ldots = \Delta(57, 120K) = 1$ and $\Delta(\bar{x}) = 0$ otherwise.

Now we can rewrite the basic definition of the range-sum as.

$$Q(R, f, \Delta_I) = \sum_{\bar{x} \in \text{Dom}(F)} f(\bar{x}) \chi_R(\bar{x}) \Delta_I(\bar{x}) \qquad (1)$$

where χ_R is the characteristic function of the set R: $\chi_R(\bar{x}) = 1$ when $\bar{x} \in R$ and is zero otherwise. Equation 1 can be thought of as a vector dot product, where any function $g : \text{Dom}(F) \to \mathbb{R}$ is a vector and for any $\bar{x} \in \text{Dom}(F)$, $g(\bar{x})$ is the $\bar{x}$-coordinate of g. We denote this scalar product by $\langle g, h \rangle = \sum_{\bar{x} \in \text{Dom}(F)} g(\bar{x}) h(\bar{x})$. Allowing us to write

$$Q(R, f, \Delta_I) = \langle f\chi_R, \Delta_I \rangle \qquad (2)$$

defining a range-sum query as a *vector query*: the scalar product of a function completely defined by the database instance (Δ_I) and another completely defined by the query ($f\chi_R$). We refer to the function $f\chi_R$ as the *query function*.

4 Wavelets

Before proceeding, we need some basic results about the fast wavelet transform. We refer the reader to [23] for a treatment similar to the one presented here. Readers familiar with Haar wavelets will see that the wavelet construction used in this paper is a generalization of the Haar transform which maintains many of the essential properties of the transform while providing more room for wavelet design.

We use wavelets arising from pairs of orthogonal convolution-decimation operators. One of these operators, H, computes a local average of an array at every other point to produce an array of *summary coefficients*. The other operator, G, measures how much values in the array vary inside each of the summarized blocks to compute an array of *detail coefficients*. Specifically we have filters h and g such that for an array $\mathbf{a}$ of length $2q$

$$H\mathbf{a}[i] = \sum_{j=0}^{2q-1} h[(2i-j) \mod 2q] \, \mathbf{a}[j] \text{ and } G\mathbf{a}[i] = \sum_{j=0}^{2q-1} g[(2i-j) \mod 2q] \, \mathbf{a}[j]$$

In order to ensure that H and G act as "summary" and "detail" filters, we also require that $\sum h[j] = \sqrt{2}$, $\sum g = 0$, $\sum h^2 = \sum g^2 = 1$, and $g[j] = (-1)^j h[1-j]$. These conditions imply that splitting an array into summaries and details preserves scalar products:

$$\sum_{j=0}^{2q-1} \mathbf{a}[j]\mathbf{b}[j] = \sum_{i=0}^{q-1} H\mathbf{a}[i] H\mathbf{b}[i] + \sum_{i=0}^{q-1} G\mathbf{a}[i] G\mathbf{b}[i] \qquad (3)$$

Example 3. The Haar wavelet summary filter h is defined by $h[0] = h[1] = 1/\sqrt{2}$, and $h[i] = 0$ otherwise. The Haar wavelet detail filter has $g[0] = 1/\sqrt{2}$, $g[1] = -1/\sqrt{2}$, and $g[i] = 0$ otherwise. The convolution-decimation operators H and G corresponding to these filters are orthogonal.

To obtain the discrete wavelet transform, we continue this process recursively, at each step splitting the summary array from the previous step into a summary of summaries array and details of summaries array. In time $\Theta(N)$ we have computed the discrete wavelet transform.

Definition 3. *Given orthogonal convolution-decimation operators H and G, and an array $\mathbf{a}$ of length 2^j, the discrete wavelet transform [DWT] of $\mathbf{a}$ is the array $\hat{\mathbf{a}}$ where*

$$\hat{\mathbf{a}}[2^{j-j_*} + k] = GH^{j_*}\mathbf{a}[k]$$

for $1 \leq j_* \leq j$ and $0 \leq k < 2^{j-j_*}$. Define $\hat{\mathbf{a}}[0] = H^j\mathbf{a}[0]$. We often refer to the elements of $\hat{\mathbf{a}}$ as the wavelet coefficients *of $\mathbf{a}$. We refer to the arrays $H^{j_*}\mathbf{a}$ and $GH^{j_*-1}\mathbf{a}$ respectively as the* summary coefficients *and* detail coefficients *at level j_*.*

The following consequence of Equation 3 is of fundamental importance

Lemma 1. *If $\hat{\mathbf{a}}$ is the DWT of $\mathbf{a}$ and $\hat{\mathbf{b}}$ is the DWT of $\mathbf{b}$ then $\sum \hat{\mathbf{a}}[\eta]\hat{\mathbf{b}}[\eta] = \sum \mathbf{a}[i]\mathbf{b}[i]$.*

To define wavelet transformations on multidimensional arrays we use the tensor product construction, which has appeared recently in the database literature as the foundation of Iterative Data Cubes [17]. The idea of this construction is simple: given a library of one dimensional transforms, we can build multidimensional transforms by applying one dimensional transforms in each dimension separately.

Specifically, we note that since the one dimensional DWT is linear, it is represented by a matrix $[W_{\eta,i}]$ such that for any array $\mathbf{a}$ of length N: $\hat{\mathbf{a}}[\eta] = \sum_{i=0}^{N-1} W_{\eta,i}\mathbf{A}[i]$ Given a multidimensional array $\mathbf{a}[i_0,\ldots,i_{d-1}]$, performing this transform in each dimension yields the *multivariate DWT* of $\mathbf{a}$

$$\hat{\mathbf{a}}[\eta_0,\ldots,\eta_{d-1}] = \sum_{i_0,\ldots,i_{d-1}=0}^{N-1} W_{\eta_0,i_0} W_{\eta_1,i_1} \cdots W_{\eta_{d-1},i_{d-1}} \mathbf{a}[i_0,\ldots,i_{d-1}]$$

Using the fast wavelet transform for each of these one dimensional matrix multiplications allows us to compute this sum in $\Theta(\ell N^d)$ for d-dimensional data. Repeated application of Lemma 1 yields

$$\sum_{\eta_0,\ldots,\eta_{d-1}} \hat{\mathbf{a}}[\eta_0,\ldots,\eta_{d-1}]\hat{\mathbf{b}}[\eta_0,\ldots,\eta_{d-1}] = \sum_{i_0,\ldots,i_{d-1}} \mathbf{a}[i_0,\ldots,i_{d-1}]\mathbf{b}[i_0,\ldots,i_{d-1}] \quad (4)$$

5 Naive Polynomial Range-Sum Evaluation Using Wavelets

Now we show how any range-sum query can be evaluated in the wavelet domain. This discussion allows us to see how data can be preprocessed using the wavelet transform, stored, and accessed for query evaluation. We also see that this method imposes no storage cost for dense data, and increases the storage requirements by a factor of $O(\log^d N)$ in the worst case. We fix orthogonal wavelet filters h and g of length ℓ.

Combining Equations 2 and 4, and interpreting functions on $\text{Dom}(F)$ as d-dimensional arrays, we obtain a new formula for range-sums

$$Q(R, f, \Delta) = \langle \widehat{f\chi_R}, \hat{\Delta} \rangle = \sum_{\eta_0,\ldots,\eta_{d-1}=0}^{N-1} \widehat{f\chi_R}(\eta_0,\ldots,\eta_{d-1}) \hat{\Delta}(\eta_0,\ldots,\eta_{d-1}) \quad (5)$$

Giving a technique for evaluation of range-sums with arbitrary measures entirely in the wavelet domain: given a dataset with data frequency distribution Δ we preprocess it as follows

WAVELET PREPROCESSING

1. Prepare a [sparse] array representation of Δ. This requires time proportional to $|I|$, the size of the dataset.
2. Use the multidimensional fast wavelet transform to compute the [sparse] array representation of $\hat{\Delta}$. For sparse data, this requires time $O(|I|\ell^d \log^d N)$. If the data are dense, this requires time $N^d = O(|I|)$.
3. Store the array representation of $\hat{\Delta}$. If the data are sparse, use a hash-index. If the data are dense, use array-based storage. In either case we have essentially constant time access to any particular transform value.

For dense data, this preprocessing step introduces no storage overhead. The worst possible storage overhead arises when the dataset has only one record. $O(\ell^d \log^d N)$ nonzero wavelet transform values need to be stored in this case.

With our storage and access methods established, we now discuss query evaluation. In order to use Equation 5 to evaluate a general range-sum with query function $f\chi_R$ using the stored wavelet transform data, we proceed as follows

NAIVE WAVELET QUERY EVALUATION

1. Compute the wavelet transformation $\widehat{f\chi_R}$. Using the fast wavelet transform requires time $O(\ell \log^d N)$. Initialize sum $\leftarrow 0$.
2. For each entry $\bar{\eta} = (\eta_0, \ldots, \eta_{d-1})$ in the array representation of $\widehat{f\chi_R}$, retrieve $\hat{\Delta}(\bar{\eta})$ from storage and set sum $\leftarrow$ sum $+ \widehat{f\chi_R}(\bar{\eta})\hat{\Delta}(\bar{\eta})$. For general query functions, there are $O(N^d)$ items retrieved from storage. When complete, sum is the query result.

This is a *correct* method for evaluating range-sum in the wavelet domain, but it is not an *efficient* method. In Section 6 we show that for polynomial range-sums it is possible to improve both the query transformation cost and the I/O cost dramatically.

6 Fast Range-Sum Evaluation Using Wavelets

With this background established, we present a first version of ProPolyne. For polynomial range-sums of degree less than δ in each attribute, this algorithm has time complexity $O((2\ell \log N)^d)$ where $\ell = 2\delta + 1$. The data structure used for storage can be updated in time $O((\ell \log N)^d)$. To our knowledge there are no existing COUNT or SUM evaluation algorithms that provide faster query evaluation without having slower update cost. The algorithm requires preprocessing the data as described in Section 5. If the storage cost is prohibitive, it is possible to store a wavelet synopsis of the data and use this algorithm to evaluate approximate query results [22] or use this technique for dense clusters [11]. In Section 7 we show how ProPolyne can be refined to deliver good progressive estimates of the final query result by retrieving data in an optimal order.

At the heart of our query evaluation technique is a fast algorithm for computing wavelet transforms of query functions, and an observation that these transforms are very sparse. This allows us to evaluate queries using Equation 5 quickly.

Intuition. We can see why query functions can be transformed quickly and have sparse transforms by looking at a very simple example: consider the problem of transforming the indicator function χ_R of the interval $R = [5, 12]$ on the domain of integers from 0 to 15. We use the Haar filters defined in Example 3. Before computing the first recursive step of the wavelet transformation we already can say that

1. The detail coefficients are all zero unless the detail filter overlaps the boundary of R: $G\chi_R(i) = \chi_R(2i+1) - \chi_R(2i) = 0$ if $i \notin \{2, 6\}$
2. The summary coefficients are all zero except when the summary filter overlaps R: $H\chi_R(i) = 0$ when $i \notin [2, 6]$
3. The summary coefficients are constant when the summary filter is contained in R: $H\chi_R(i) = \sqrt{2}$ when $2 < i < 6$.

Without applying the operators H and G we are able to determine most of the values of $H\chi_R$ and $G\chi_R$ in constant time. The only interesting points, $2 = \lfloor \frac{5}{2} \rfloor$ and $6 = \lfloor \frac{12}{2} \rfloor$, arise from the boundaries of R. We can compute these values in constant time and see that $G\chi_R(2) = 1/\sqrt{2}, G\chi_R(6) = -1/\sqrt{2}$ and $H\chi_R(2) = H\chi_R(6) = 1/\sqrt{2}$. In constant time, we can build a data structure containing all of the information needed to evaluate any summary or detail coefficient. It turns out that we can always do this: at any recursive step in the Haar transform of a constant function the summary coefficients are constant on an interval, zero outside, and "interesting" on at most two boundary points. Also, there are at most two non-zero detail coefficients. Each of the $\log N = j$ steps can be carried out in constant time, allowing us to perform the entire transform in time and space $\Theta(\log N)$. Using the standard DWT algorithm would require time and space $\Theta(N)$. Because there are at most two nonzero detail coefficients per step, the resulting transform has less than $2 \log N$ nonzero terms. Carrying our example through to the end we see that

$$\chi_R = \{0,0,0,0,0,1,1,1,1,1,1,1,1,0,0,0\}$$
$$\widehat{\chi_R} = \{2, \frac{1}{2}, \frac{3}{2\sqrt{2}}, -\frac{3}{2\sqrt{2}}, 0, \frac{1}{2}, 0, -\frac{1}{2}, 0, 0, \frac{1}{\sqrt{2}}, 0, 0, 0, -\frac{1}{\sqrt{2}}, 0\} \quad (6)$$

Now if we have stored the wavelet coefficients for a data density function Δ on $[0, 15]$ and want to use Equation 5 to evaluate $Q(R, f, \Delta)$ we only retrieve the values of $\hat{\Delta}$ where $\widehat{\chi_R} \neq 0$. Because there are at most $2 \log N$ of these coefficients, we can evaluate the query in time $O(\log N)$.

The Lazy Wavelet Transform. We now formalize these arguments and extend them to deal with general one dimensional polynomial range-sums. The important features of the Haar transformation noted above are (1) the recursive step of the DWT can be made in constant time and (2) the number of nonzero wavelet coefficients of the query function is $O(\log N)$. Now we show that with appropriate restrictions and choices of wavelet filters, we can obtain both of these features for general polynomial range-sums. We call this algorithm the *lazy wavelet transform* since it only evaluates convolution results when they are needed at the next recursive step. To make this work, we must use wavelets that satisfy a *moment condition*:

Definition 4. *G is said to satisfy condition $M(\delta)$ if $Gx^k = 0$ for $0 \leq k \leq \delta$. In other words, $\sum g[i]i^k = 0$ where g is the filter corresponding to the detail operator G.*

Example 4. The Db4 wavelet summary filter h_4 is defined by $h_4(0) = (1+\sqrt{3})/(4\sqrt{2})$, $h_4(1) = (3+\sqrt{3})/(4\sqrt{2})$, $h_4(2) = (3-\sqrt{3})/(4\sqrt{2})$, $h_4(3) = (1-\sqrt{3})/(4\sqrt{2})$, and $h_4(i) = 0$ otherwise. The Db4 wavelet detail filter has $g_4(i) = (-1)^i h_4(1-i)$. The convolution-decimation operators corresponding to this pair of filters are orthogonal and satisfy $M(1)$. The Haar filters satisfy $M(0)$. For higher moment conditions, we can use higher order Daubechies filters [23, 14, 4].

Now we can state the result that lies at the core of our technique, and is proved in the extended version of this paper [18].

Theorem 1 (Lazy Wavelet Transform). *Assume that $f\chi_R$ is a query function for a polynomial range-sum with $\deg f = \delta$ on a domain of size N, and that h and g are filters of length ℓ generating orthogonal convolution-decimation operators that satisfy $M(\delta)$. Then the sparse representation of the wavelet transform of $f\chi_R$ with filters h and g can be computed in time $\Theta(\ell \log N)$ and the resulting transform has at most $2(\ell-1)\log N$ nonzero values.*

Note that we can use Daubechies' construction of compactly supported orthogonal wavelets to produce wavelets satisfying $M(\delta)$ that have filter length $\ell = 2\delta + 2$. Using these filters it is possible to transform polynomial query functions of degree less than δ in time $\Theta(\delta \log N)$ and the result has less than $(4\delta + 2)\log N$ nonzero coefficients.

Polynomial Range-Sum Evaluation. In Section 5 we discussed how wavelet data can be preprocessed, stored, and accessed. Now we show how using the lazy wavelet transform can dramatically speed up query evaluation in the wavelet domain. First we define a special type of polynomial range query that is particularly easy to work with.

Definition 5. *A polynomial range-sum with measure function* $f : \text{Dom}(F) \to \mathbb{R}$ *is said to satisfy condition* $S(\delta)$ *if* $f(x_0, \ldots, x_{d-1}) = \prod_{i=0}^{d-1} p_i(x_i)$ *and each* p_i *has degree less than or equal to* δ, *and* R *is a hyper-rectangle.*

All of the queries in Example 1 satisfy this condition: COUNT satisfies $S(0)$, SUM, AVERAGE, and COVARIANCE are computed with range-sums satisfying $S(1)$, and VARIANCE is computed with range-sums satisfying $S(2)$. As Example 1 makes clear, the class of polynomial range-sums is rich, even restricted to satisfy condition $S(\delta)$.

Consider a range-sum with query function $f\chi_R = \prod_{j=0}^{d-1} p_j(i_j) \chi_{R_j}(i_j)$. By Equation 4, $\widehat{f\chi_R} = \widehat{\prod p_j \chi_{R_j}} = \prod \widehat{p_j \chi_{R_j}}$. If $f\chi_R$ satisfies $S(\delta)$, then we can use Daubechies' filters of length $2\delta + 2$ to compute (a data structure representing) $\widehat{f\chi_R}$ in time $\Theta(d\delta \log N)$, and $\widehat{f\chi_R}$ has $O((4\delta + 2)^d \log^d N)$ nonzero coefficients. Thus we have the following query evaluation technique, which we present for queries satisfying $S(\delta)$. General multivariate polynomials of degree δ can always be split into a sum of polynomials satisfying $S(\delta)$, each of which is transformed separately.

FAST WAVELET QUERY EVALUATION

1. Use the lazy wavelet transform to compute the d one-dimensional wavelet transforms $\widehat{p_j \chi_{R_j}}$. Initialize sum $\leftarrow 0$.
2. Iterate over the Cartesian product of the nonzero coefficients of the $\widehat{p_j \chi_{R_j}}$.
   For each $\bar{\eta} = (\eta_0, \ldots, \eta_{d-1})$ in this set, retrieve $\hat{\Delta}(\bar{\eta})$ from storage and set sum $\leftarrow$ sum $+ \hat{\Delta}(\bar{\eta}) \prod \widehat{p_j \chi_{R_j}}(\eta_j)$. When complete, sum is the query result.

Notice that this algorithm is dominated by the I/O phase (step 2) for $d > 1$. The online preprocessing phase (step 1) takes time and space $\Theta(d\delta \log N)$.

The lazy wavelet transform also gives us a way to perform fast updates of the database. To insert a record $\bar{i} = (i_0, \ldots, i_{d-1})$, let $\chi_{\bar{i}}$ denote the function equal to 1 at $\bar{i}$ and zero elsewhere. Then the updated data frequency distribution is $\Delta_{\text{new}} = \Delta + \chi_{\bar{i}}$. By the linearity of the wavelet transform, we have $\hat{\Delta}_{\text{new}} = \hat{\Delta} + \hat{\chi}\bar{i}$. Thus to perform an update, we simply compute $\hat{\chi}\bar{i}$ and add the results to storage.

Furthermore, $\chi_{\bar{i}}$ can be thought of as a query function satisfying $S(0)$, so we can transform it just as we transform other query functions. A careful look reveals that in this case the "interesting intervals" overlap completely, and $\hat{\chi}\bar{i}$ can be computed in time $\Theta((2\delta + 1)^d \log^d N)$.

WAVELET UPDATE

1. To insert $\bar{i} = (i_0, \ldots, i_{d-1})$ use the lazy wavelet transform to compute $\hat{\chi}_{\bar{i}_j}$ for $0 \leq j < d$.
2. For each $\bar{\eta} = (\eta_0, \ldots, \eta_{d-1})$ in the Cartesian product of the nonzero entries of $\hat{\chi}_{\bar{i}_j}$, set $\hat{\Delta}(\bar{\eta}) \leftarrow \hat{\Delta}(\bar{\eta}) \prod \hat{\chi}_{\bar{i}_j}(\eta_j)$. For hash table access, this may require an insertion.

Theorem 2. *Using Daubechies' wavelets with filter length $2\delta+2$, the WAVELET PREPROCESSING strategy to store data, WAVELET UPDATE to insert new records, and FAST WAVELET QUERY EVALUATION to evaluate queries it is possible to evaluate any polynomial range-sum satisfying $S(\delta)$ in time $O((4\delta+2)^d \log^d N)$. It is possible to insert one record in time $O((2\delta+1)^d \log^d N)$.*

7 Progressive Polynomial Range-Sum Evaluation

Note that in Equation 6 some of these coefficients are larger than others. For larger ranges and higher dimensions, this phenomenon becomes dramatic: most of the information is contained in a handful of coefficients. Intuitively, if we use the largest coefficients first we should obtain an accurate estimate of the query result before the computation is complete. This is the basic idea behind ProPolyne, but before proceeding we pause to ask precisely why we think that evaluating queries using the 'big' coefficients first gives better approximate answers. Once we can state precisely how this evaluation order is better, we prove that ProPolyne uses the best possible evaluation order.

Definition 6. *A progressive evaluation plan for a sum $S = \sum_{0 \leq i < N} \mathbf{a}[i]$ is a permutation σ of the integers 0 to $N-1$. The estimate of S at the jth progressive step of this plan is $\sum_{0 \leq i < j} \mathbf{a}[\sigma(i)]$.*

Query Best-B ProPolyne. How do we determine whether one progressive evaluation plan produces better results than another? When evaluating range aggregate queries using Equation 5, we must choose a data independent progressive evaluation plan for a sum of the form $\sum \hat{f \chi_R}(i) \hat{\Delta}(i)$. We cannot look at $\hat{\Delta}$ until executing our plan, but we want to minimize the average square error observed at each progressive step when operating on a random dataset.

Definition 7. *Let $\tilde{Q}_1(\Delta)$ and $\tilde{Q}_2(\Delta)$ be approximations of the query $Q(R, f, \Delta)$. We say $\tilde{Q}_1$ dominates $\tilde{Q}_2$ if*

$$E_\Delta[(\tilde{Q}_1(\Delta) - Q(R, f, \Delta))^2] \leq E_\Delta[(\tilde{Q}_2(\Delta) - Q(R, f, \Delta))^2]$$

where Δ is randomly selected from the set $\{\Delta \mid \sum \Delta^2(i) = 1\}$. We say that one progressive query plan dominates another if the estimate of the first plan dominates the estimate of the second at every progressive step.

We want to find a progressive evaluation plan that dominates all others. It is not obvious that this is possible, but the following result shows that the 'biggest coefficient' plan suggested at the beginning of the section is in fact the best.

Theorem 3. *Let y be a vector randomly selected from the set $\{y \mid \sum_{i=0}^{N-1} y_i^2 = 1\} = S^{N-1}$ with uniform distribution, let $I \subset [0, N-1]$ be a set of size B, and for a vector x let $\tilde{x}_I$ denote x with all coordinates except those in I set to zero. Denote the set of the B biggest (largest magnitude) coordinates of x by I^*. Then for any choice of I we have*

$$E_y[\langle x - \tilde{x}_{I^*}, y \rangle^2] \leq E_y[\langle x - \tilde{x}_I, y \rangle^2]$$

In other words, approximating x with its biggest B terms gives us the best B term approximation of $\langle x, y \rangle$- an approximation that dominates all others.

Corollary 1 *The progressive query plan obtained by using the largest query coefficients first dominates all other plans.*

This evaluation plan is the foundation for our progressive algorithm, Pro-Polyne. Because after B progressive steps ProPolyne provides the best-B wavelet approximation of a query, we refer to this technique as *query best-B ProPolyne*. We implement this progressive query plan by first evaluating the query function transformation using Theorem 1, then building a heap from the resulting set of nonzero wavelet coefficients. Compute the sum repeatedly extracting the top element from this heap- the partial sums provide accurate progressive query estimates. As described in the extended version of this paper, this analytical framework also provides efficiently computable guaranteed error bounds at each progressive step.

Data Best-B ProPolyne. Previous uses of wavelets for approximate query evaluation have focused on *data approximation*, using wavelets to produce a precomputed synopsis data structure. The reader may note that the rôle of the data and the query in the results of Section 7 were entirely symmetric. If we can say "the biggest-B approximation of a query is the best-B approximation for random data", we can just as easily say "the biggest-B approximation of the data is the best-B approximation for random queries". Hence we can obtain a different sort of progressive query evaluation by sorting the data wavelet coefficients offline, then retrieving them in decreasing order of magnitude. This is the spirit of the approximate query evaluation algorithms of [22], where it is shown that this gives reasonable estimates quickly. The technique presented here has the extra benefit of treating measure dimensions symmetrically, supporting general polynomial range-sums. We call this technique *data best-B ProPolyne*.

Unfortunately, query workloads are very far from being randomly distributed on the unit sphere. In practice, the best ordering would be weighted by the expected query workload. In any case, this technique only works well if the data are well approximated by the chosen wavelets. This stands in contrast to query best-B ProPolyne, where the query functions are always well approximated by wavelets. In Section 8 we see that the performance of data best-B ProPolyne varies dramatically with the dataset, and is consistently less accurate than query best-B ProPolyne.

Evaluation of Fixed-Measure SUM Queries. In practice, there are situations where the measures and aggregate functions are known at the time the database is built. When this is the case, ProPolyne can be optimized. In particular, it can be adapted to operate on the wavelet transform of the measure function rather than the frequency distribution. We call this adaptation *fixed measure* ProPolyne, or ProPolyne-FM. One notable optimization that ProPolyne-FM allows is the use of Haar wavelets in all dimensions. The fact that one-dimensional Haar wavelets do not overlap brings query evaluation cost down to $(2j)^{d-1}$ and update cost to j^{d-1} for a table with $d-1$ j-bit attribute and one measure attribute. We note that this cost is identical to that of the Space-efficient Dynamic Data Cube [16]. ProPolyne-FM serves another useful rôle : it solves the same problem as other pre-aggregation methods, so it is directly comparable.

The process of turning ProPolyne-FM into a data or query best-B progressive algorithm is identical to the process for unrestricted ProPolyne. It happens that when using Haar wavelets, the data best-B version of ProPolyne-FM is simply a progressive implementation of the *compact data cube* presented in [22]. The query best-B version of ProPolyne-FM is novel, and we see in Section 8 that approximate results it produces are significantly more accurate than those produced by the compact data cube. For the remainder of the paper we use ProPolyne-FM to mean this query best-B version.

8 Experimental Results

In this section we present results from our experiments with ProPolyne and related algorithms in order to provide the reader with an overview of how these techniques perform on real-world data. ProPolyne-FM's worst-case performance as an exact algorithm (which is very similar to the performance of ProPolyne) is compared with related exact pre-aggregation methods in Table 1. Our focus in this section is on the accuracy of ProPolyne's progressive estimates. Our experiments show that wavelet-based query approximation delivers consistently accurate results, even on datasets that are poorly approximated by wavelets. Not only is the performance consistent, it is consistently better than data approximation. By directly comparing our methods with the wavelet-based data compression method proposed by Vitter and Wang [22] we see that query approximation based ProPolyne delivers significantly more accurate results after retrieving the same number of values from persistent storage.

Experimental Setup. We report results from experiments on three datasets. PETROL is a set of petroleum sales volume data with 56504 tuples, sparseness of 0.16%, and five dimensions: location, product, year, month, and volume (thousands of gallons). PETROL is our example of a dataset for which traditional data approximation works well [1].

GPS[1] is a set of sensor readings from a group of GPS ground stations located throughout California. We use a projection of the available data to produce a dataset with 3358 tuples, sparseness of 0.01%, and four dimensions: latitude, longitude, time, and height velocity. The presence of a tuple (lat, long, t, v) means that a sensor observed that the ground at coordinates (lat, long) was moving upward with a velocity of v at time t. GPS is our example of a dataset for which traditional data approximation works poorly.

TEMPERATURE is a dataset holding the temperatures at points all over the globe and at 20 different altitudes on March 1, 2001. It has 207360 tuples, sparseness of 1.24%, and four dimensions: latitude, longitude, altitude, and temperature. The TEMPERATURE dataset is considerably larger than the GPS and PETROL datasets, and we use it to emphasize the fact that as datasets get larger, the benefit of using ProPolyne increases.

For all tests, 250 range queries were generated randomly from the set of all possible ranges with the uniform distribution. If a generated range selects fewer than 100 tuples from the dataset, it is discarded and a new range is generated.

All graphs display the progressive accuracy improvement of various approximation techniques for queries on a single dataset. The horizontal axis always displays the number of values retrieved by an algorithm on a logarithmic scale. The vertical axis of each graph displays the median relative error for a set of generated queries. Relative error is used so that queries returning large results do not dominate the statistics. Median error is used rather than mean error in order to avoid the noise caused by the one-sided fat tail of observed relative error. The results using mean error are qualitatively similar, but are not as smooth.

Performance for Fixed Measure Range-Sums. Figure 1 compares the performance of ProPolyne-FM with a progressive version of the *compact data cube* (CDC) [22] on the PETROL and GPS datasets. Other techniques, including [9], have been compared favorably to the CDC. We do not directly compare ProPolyne to these because they have no progressive analog. We see that CDC works very well on the PETROL dataset, producing a median relative error under 10% after using less than 100 wavelet coefficients. Still, ProPolyne-FM works better than CDC from the beginning, and this difference only grows as evaluation progresses. The difference between the performance of the two techniques on the GPS dataset is striking: CDC must use more than five times as many wavelet coefficients as there were tuples in the original table before providing a median relative error of 10%. ProPolyne-FM reaches this level of accuracy after retrieving less than 300 wavelet coefficients.

Performance for General Range-Sums. Figure 2 compares the performance of data best-B ProPolyne and query best-B ProPolyne on the PETROL and GPS datasets. Unlike the previous section, the queries for these tests slice in all dimensions, including the measure dimension. Data best-B ProPolyne can be thought

---
[1] We would like to thank our colleagues at JPL, Brian Wilson and George Hajj, for providing us with the GPS and TEMPERATURE datasets.

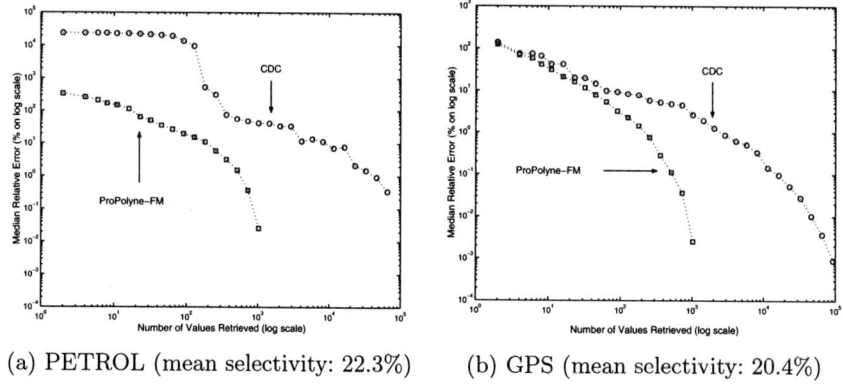

(a) PETROL (mean selectivity: 22.3%) (b) GPS (mean selectivity: 20.4%)

Fig. 1. Progressive accuracy for Compact Data Cube (CDC) [22] and ProPolyne-FM.

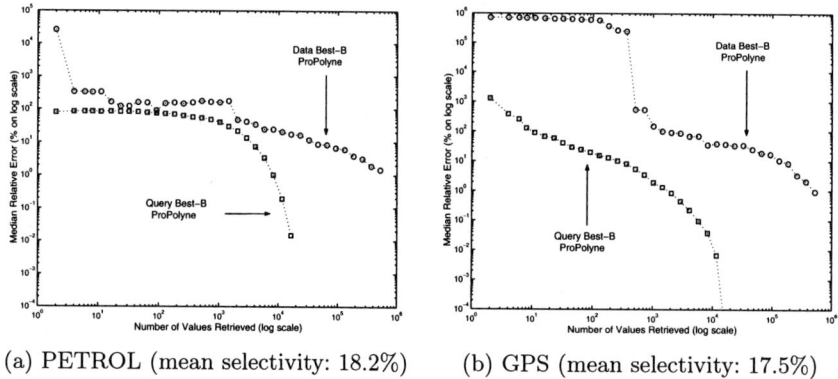

(a) PETROL (mean selectivity: 18.2%) (b) GPS (mean selectivity: 17.5%)

Fig. 2. Progressive query accuracy for data best-B and query best-B ProPolyne.

of as an extension of CDC that supports this richer query set. As in the previous section, the method based on query approximation consistently and significantly outperforms the analogous data compression method. By the time query best-B ProPolyne has achieved a median error of 10%, data best-B ProPolyne still has a median error of near 100% for the PETROL dataset. The data best-B ProPolyne error for the GPS dataset at this point is enormous. Notice also that the data best-B results exhibit accuracy "cliffs" where the progression reaches a set of coefficients that are particularly important for the given query workload. This hints that query workload information is critical to improving the ordering of data best-B coefficients.

Finally, Figure 3 illustrates the progressive accuracy of query best-B ProPolyne On the TEMPERATURE dataset. Figure 3(a) displays relative error for AVERAGE queries on randomly generated ranges of different sizes. We define the size of a range to be the product of the lengths of its sides. Larger ranges have better approximate results, suggesting that a basis other than wavelets may provide better approximation of query workloads with small ranges.

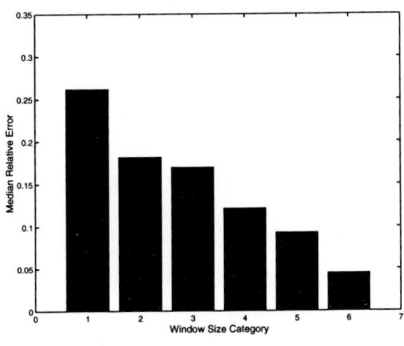 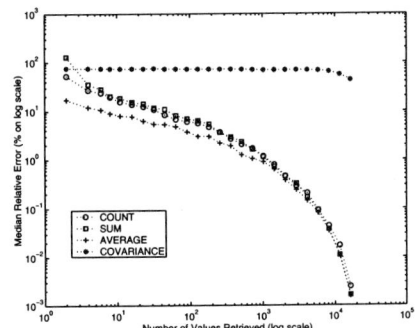

(a) Relative error vs. range size after retrieving 500 values

(b) Second order statistics (mean selectivity 16.5%)

Fig. 3. Query Best-B ProPolyne on the TEMPERATURE dataset. For (a), range size categories are as follows. category 1: size < 5000, category 2: $5000 \leq$ size < 10000, category 3: $10000 \leq$ size < 20000, category 4: $20000 \leq$ size < 40000, category 5: $40000 \leq$ size < 80000, category 6: $80000 \leq$ size.

Figure 3(b) displays progressive relative error for COUNT, SUM, AVERAGE, and COVARIANCE queries on the TEMPERATURE dataset. Here we note that COUNT, SUM, and AVERAGE all obtain excellent accuracy after retrieving a very small number of wavelet coefficients. AVERAGE is significantly more accurate early in the computation, obtaining a median relative error below 10% using just 16 data wavelet coefficients. COUNT and SUM both achieve this level of accuracy using close to 100 data wavelet coefficients. COVARIANCE stands out by not having significantly improving accuracy until near the end of the computation. We emphasize that we obtain exact results for COVARIANCE just as quickly as for other query types. This slow convergence largely due to the fact that we compute the covariance by subtracting two large approximate numbers to obtain a relatively small number.

9 Conclusions and Future Plans

In this paper we present ProPolyne, a novel MOLAP pre-aggregation strategy which can be used to support conventional queries such as COUNT and SUM alongside more complicated *polynomial range-sums*. ProPolyne is the first pre-aggregation strategy that does not require measures to be specified at the time of database population. Instead, measures are treated as functions of the attributes which can be specified at query time. This approach leads naturally to a new *data independent* progressive and approximate query answering technique which delivers excellent results when compared to other proposed data compression methods. ProPolyne delivers all of these features with provably poly-logarithmic worst-case query and update cost, and with storage cost comparable to or better than other pre-aggregation methods.

We intend to extend this work in several ways. Preliminary experiments indicate that using synopsis information about query workloads or data distributions can dramatically improve sort orders for both query best-B and data best-B techniques. Dimensionality reduction techniques can improve I/O complexity at the expense of some accuracy in the final results. As presented here, ProPolyne requires random access to stored data; we will explore clustering strategies which take advantage of ProPolyne's unique access patterns. Finally we wish to explore the limits of linear algebraic query approximation for approximate query answering. This includes finding complexity lower bounds, investigating more complex queries (e.g., OLAP drill-down, relational algebra), and making an efficient adaptive choice of the best basis for evaluating incoming queries.

References

1. J. L. Ambite, C. Shahabi, R. R. Schmidt, and A. Philpot. Fast approximate evaluation of OLAP queries for integrated statistical data. In *Nat'l Conf. for Digital Government Research, Los Angeles*, May 2001.
2. K. Chakrabarti, M. N. Garofalakis, R. Rastogi, and K. Shim. Approximate query processing using wavelets. In *Proc. VLDB*, pages 111–122, 2000.
3. C.-Y. Chan and Y. E. Ionnidis. Hierarchical cubes for range-sum queries. In *Proc. VLDB*, pages 675–686, 1999.
4. I. Daubechies. Orthonormal bases of compactly supported wavelets. *Comm. Pure and Appl. Math.*, 41:909–996, 1988.
5. S. Geffner, D. Agrawal, and A. E. Abbadi. The dynamic data cube. In *Proc. EDBT*, pages 237–253, 2000.
6. S. Geffner, D. Agrawal, A. E. Abbadi, and T. Smith. Relative prefix sums: An efficient approach for querying dynamic OLAP data cubes. In *Proc. ICDE*, pages 328–335, 1999.
7. A. C. Gilbert, Y. Kotidis, S. Muthukrishnan, and M. J. Strauss. Optimal and approximate computation of summary statistics for range aggregates. In *Proc. ACM PODS*, pages 228–237, 2001.
8. A. C. Gilbert, Y. Kotidis, S. Muthukrishnan, and M. J. Strauss. Surfing wavelets on streams: One-pass summaries for approximate aggregate queries. In *Proc. VLDB*, 2001.
9. D. Gunopulos, G. Kollios, V. J. Tsotras, and C. Domeniconi. Approximating multidimensional aggregate range queries over real attributes. In *Proc. ACM SIGMOD*, pages 463–474, 2000.
10. J. M. Hellerstein, P. J. Haas, and H. Wang. Online aggregation. In *Proc. ACM SIGMOD*, pages 171–182, 1997.
11. C. Ho, R. Agrawal, N. Megiddo, and R. Srikant. Range queries in OLAP data cubes. In *Proc. ACM SIGMOD*, pages 73–88, 1997.
12. I. Lazaridis and S. Mehrotra. Progressive approximate aggregate queries with a multi-resolution tree structure. In *Proc. ACM SIGMOD*, pages 401–412, 2001.
13. V. Poosala and V. Ganti. Fast approximate answers to aggregate queries on a data cube. In *Proc. SSDBM*, pages 24–33, 1999.
14. W. Press, S. Teukolsky, W. Vetterling, and B. Flannery. *Numerical Recipes in C*. Cambridge Univ. Press, 1992.
15. M. Riedewald, D. Agrawal, and A. E. Abbadi. pCube: Update-efficient online aggregation with progressive feedback. In *Proc. SSDBM*, pages 95–108, 2000.

16. M. Riedewald, D. Agrawal, and A. E. Abbadi. Space-efficient datacubes for dynamic environments. In *Proc. of Conf. on Data Warehousing and Knowledge Discovery (DaWaK)*, pages 24–33, 2000.
17. M. Riedewald, D. Agrawal, and A. E. Abbadi. Flexible data cubes for online aggregation. In *Proc. ICDT*, pages 159–173, 2001.
18. R. R. Schmidt and C. Shahabi. Propolyne: A fast wavelet-based technique for progressive evaluation of polynomial range-sum queries, 2001. USC Tech. Report, available at http://infolab.usc.edu/publication.html.
19. R. R. Schmidt and C. Shahabi. Wavelet based density estimators for modeling OLAP data sets. In *SIAM Workshop on Mining Scientific Datasets*, Chicago, April 2001. Available at http://infolab.usc.edu/publication.html.
20. J. Shanmugasundaram, U. Fayyad, and P. Bradley. Compressed data cubes for OLAP aggregate query approximation on continuous dimensions. In *Proc. SIGKDD*, August 1999.
21. S.-C. Shao. Multivariate and multidimensional OLAP. In *Proc. EDBT*, pages 120–134, 1998.
22. J. S. Vitter and M. Wang. Approximate computation of multidimensional aggregates of sparse data using wavelets. In *Proc. ACM SIGMOD*, pages 193–204, 1999.
23. M. V. Wickerhauser. *Adapted Wavelet Analysis: From Theory to Software*. IEEE Press, 1994.
24. Y.-L. Wu, D. Agrawal, and A. E. Abbadi. Using wavelet decomposition to support progressive and approximate range-sum queries over data cubes. In *Proc. CIKM*, pages 414–421, 2000.

Aggregate Processing of Planar Points

Yufei Tao, Dimitris Papadias, and Jun Zhang

Department of Computer Science
Hong Kong University of Science and Technology
Clear Water Bay, Hong Kong
{taoyf, dimitris, zhangjun@cs.ust.hk}

Abstract. Aggregate window queries return summarized information about objects that fall inside a query rectangle (e.g., the number of objects instead of their concrete ids). Traditional approaches for processing such queries usually retrieve considerable extra information, thus compromising the processing cost. The paper addresses this problem for planar points from both theoretical and practical points of view. We show that, an aggregate window query can be answered in logarithmic worst-case time by an indexing structure called the aP-tree. Next we study the practical behavior of the aP-tree and propose efficient cost models that predict the structure size and actual query cost. Extensive experiments show that the aP-tree, while involving more space consumption, accelerates query processing by up to an order of magnitude compared to a specialized method based on R-trees. Furthermore, our cost models are accurate and can be employed for the selection of the most appropriate method, balancing the space and query time tradeoff.

1. Introduction

Window queries retrieve the objects that fall inside (or intersect) a multi-dimensional window. Such queries are important for numerous domains and have been studied extensively in the database literature. Recently a related type, called the *window aggregate* query (WA for short), is gaining increasing attention in the context of OLAP applications. A WA query returns summarized information about objects that fall inside the query window, for example the number of cars in a road segment, the average number of mobile phone users per city block etc. An obvious approach to answer such queries is to first retrieve the actual objects by performing traditional window queries, and then compute the aggregate function. This, however, entails a lot of unnecessary effort, compromising performance. A solution for the problem is to store aggregate information in the nodes of specialized index structures. Such aggregate trees have already been employed in the context of temporal databases for computing aggregates over temporal data [KS95, KKK99, YW01, ZMT+01].

In order to improve the performance of WA queries in OLAP applications involving multi-dimensional ranges, Jurgens and Lenz [JL98] proposed the storage of summarized data in the nodes of the R-tree [BKS+90] used to index the fact table. The same concept was applied in [PKZ+01] for spatial data warehouses. Each entry of the resulting *aggregate R-tree* (*aR-tree*), in addition to the minimum bounding rectangle (MBR), stores summarized data about objects under the corresponding subtree. As a result, nodes totally contained by the query window do not have to be accessed during the processing of WA queries. aR-trees and other aggregate multi-dimensional indexes were employed by [LM01] in order to compute fast approximate answers of OLAP queries. By traversing the index, a rough approximation is obtained from the values at the higher levels, which is progressively refined as the search continues towards the leaves. Papadias et al [PTK+02] proposed combinations of aggregate R- and B-trees for indexing spatio-temporal data warehouses.

Although aR-trees (and other aggregate trees based on the straightforward adaptation of multi-dimensional structures) improve performance of WA queries considerably compared to regular R-trees, their processing cost can still be very high, especially for queries with large ranges common in OLAP applications. In this paper, we focus on aggregate processing of planar points and show that any WA query can be answered with $O(\log_b n)$ page accesses by a specialized indexing structure, the *aggregate Point-tree* (*aP-tree*), which consumes $O(n/b \log_b n)$ space, where n is the number of data points and b the disk page size. The intuition behind aP-trees, is that two-dimensional points can be viewed as intervals in the key-time plane and indexed by temporal access methods.

In addition to asymptotic performance, we analyze the practical behavior of aP-trees, and propose cost models for their sizes and query costs. Extensive experimentation shows that the aP-tree is more than just theoretical contribution, since it answers WA queries significantly faster than the aR-tree while consuming some more space. Besides their applicability in traditional OLAP applications, aP-trees are important for spatial [PT01] and spatio-temporal [PTK+02] data warehouses.

The rest of the paper is organized as follows. Section 2 surveys the aR-tree and proposes cost models for query performance. It also introduces the multi-version B-tree, which provides the main motivation for the aP-tree. Section 3 discusses the aP-tree in detail and proves its asymptotical performance. Section 4 contains cost models that accurately predict the structure size and query cost of aP-trees. Section 5 presents an extensive experimental evaluation with synthetic and real datasets, and Section 6 concludes the paper with directions for future work.

2. Related Work

Existing work on aggregate trees has been based mostly on the R-tree due to its popularity as a multi-dimensional access method. In this section, we describe the aR-tree and analyze its expected performance on WA queries. Next we overview the multi-version B-tree and its related algorithms.

2.1 The Aggregate R-Tree (aR-Tree) and Analysis

The aggregate R-tree improves the original R-tree towards aggregate processing by storing, in each intermediate entry, summarized data about objects residing in the subtree. In case of the COUNT function, for example, each entry stores the number of objects in its subtree (the extension to any non-holistic functions is straightforward). Figure 1a shows a simple example where 8 points are clustered into 3 leaf nodes R_1, R_2, R_3, which are further grouped into a root node R. The solid rectangles refer to the MBR of the nodes. The corresponding R-tree with intermediate aggregate numbers is shown in Figure 1b. Entry e_1:2, for instance, means that 2 points are in the subtree of e_1 (i.e., node R_1). Notice that each point is counted only once, e.g., the point which lies inside the MBRs of both R_1 and R_2 is added to the aggregate result of the node where it belongs (e_1). The WA query represented by the bold rectangle in Figure 1a is processed in the following manner. First the root R is retrieved and each entry inside is compared with the query rectangle q. One of the 3 following conditions holds: (i) the (MBR of the) entry does not intersect q (e.g., entry e_1) and its sub-tree is not explored further; (ii) the entry partially intersects q (e.g., entry e_2) and we retrieve its child node to continue the search; (iii) the entry is contained in q (e.g., entry e_3), in which case, it suffices to add the aggregate number of the entry (e.g., 3 stored with e_3) without accessing its subtree. As a result, only two node visits (R and R_2) are necessary. Notice that conventional R-trees would require 3 node visits.

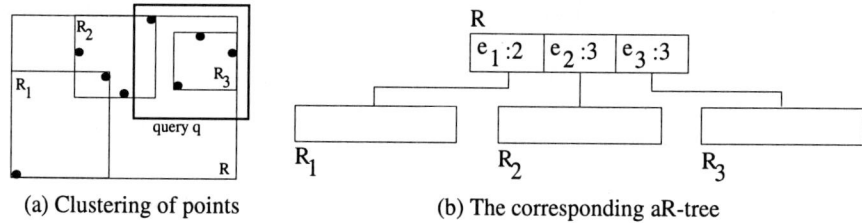

(a) Clustering of points (b) The corresponding aR-tree

Fig. 1. An aR-tree example

In summary, the improvement of the aR-tree over the conventional R-tree is that we do not need to visit the nodes (whose MBRs are) inside the query window, but only those nodes that intersect the edges of the window. To answer the query in Figure 2a (where the nodes correspond to the clustering on uniform points as in [TS96]), for example, the aR-tree only needs to retrieve the white nodes, while the R-tree must also access the gray ones. The cost savings obviously increase with the size of the query window, an important fact because OLAP queries often involve large ranges. Notice, however, that despite the improvement of the aR-tree, query performance is still sensitive to the window size since, the larger the window, the higher the number of node MBRs that are expected to intersect its sides.

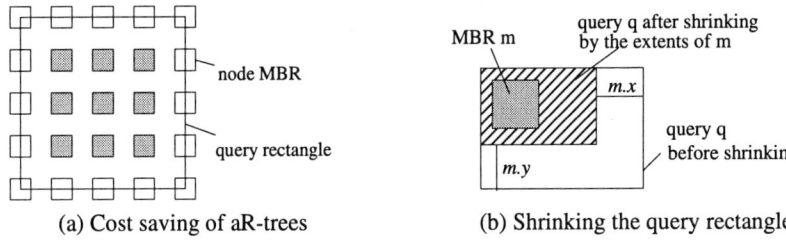

Fig. 2. Cost analysis of aR-trees

This sensitivity of aR-trees to window area, is confirmed by the following analysis. For a query q and a node MBR m, let $PR_{intr}(q,m)$, $PR_{part}(q,m)$, and $PR_{cont}(q,m)$ refer to the probabilities that q intersects, partially intersects, and contains m respectively:

$$PR_{intr}(q,m) = PR_{part}(q,m) + PR_{cont}(q,m)$$

The estimation of $PR_{intr}(q, m)$ was previously studied in [KF93]. Assuming a unit universe and uniform distribution of points, $PR_{intr}(q, m)$ can be represented as

$$PR_{intr}(q,m) = (q.x + m.x) \cdot (q.y + m.y)$$

where $q.x$ and $q.y$ refer to the lengths of the horizontal and vertical extents of q respectively (and similarly for $m.x$ and $m.y$). On the other hand, observe that query q contains m if and only if, after shrinking q from the lower-right corner point by the corresponding extents of m along each dimension, the resulting rectangle still contains the upper-left corner point of m, as illustrated in Figure 2b. Hence, the probability that the query window contains m is:

$$PR_{cont}(q,m) = (q.x - m.x) \cdot (q.y - m.y)$$

So the probability of partial intersection is:

$$PR_{part}(q,m) = PR_{intr}(q,m) - PR_{cont}(q,m) = 2(m.x \cdot q.y + m.y \cdot q.x)$$

$PR_{part}(q, m)$ corresponds to the probability that a node with MBR m is visited in answering the WA query q using the aR-tree. Let h be the height of the aR-tree, N_i the number of nodes at level i, and s_i the average MBR of nodes at level i; then, the expected number of node accesses in answering q is:

$$NA(q) = \sum_{i=0}^{h-1} [N_i \cdot PR_{part}(q, s_i)]$$

The estimation for h, N_i, and s_i was studied in [TS96], where the following results were obtained (f_R is the average fanout):

$$h = \lfloor \log_{f_R} n \rfloor, \; N_i = n / f_R^{i+1}, \text{ and } s_{i1} = s_{i2} = \sqrt{D_{i+1} \frac{f_R^{i+1}}{n}} \quad (0 \bullet i \bullet h - 1)$$

where $D_{i+1} = \left[1 + \frac{\sqrt{D_i} - 1}{\sqrt{f_R}}\right]^2$ and $D_0 = 0$

Therefore the cost of processing a WA query q with aR-trees is:

$$NA(q) = \sum_{i=0}^{\lfloor \log_{f_R} n \rfloor - 1} [2\sqrt{\frac{D_{i+1} \cdot n}{f_R^{i+1}}} (q.x + q.y)] \quad (2.1)$$

It is clear that the cost increases with the lengths of the query's extents and can be prohibitive for large query windows. This is a serious problem because aR-trees were motivated by the need to efficiently process queries with large windows in the first place. aP-trees overcome this problem (i.e., the cost is independent of the query extent) by transforming points to intervals in the key-time plane and adapting specialized interval indexing methods such as the multi-version B-tree introduced next.

2.2 The Multi-version B-Tree (MVB-Tree)

The multi-version B-tree [BGO+96] is an extension of the B-tree for indexing the evolution of one-dimensional data in *transaction time temporal databases* [ST97], which are best described as intervals in the key-time plane. In the example of Figure 3, intervals a_1, a_2, a_3, and b correspond to the bank balances of two accounts a and b. The key axis represents the amount of the balance. Both accounts are created at time t_0 and cancelled at t_3. There are two changes to account a: one withdrawal at t_1 and one deposit at t_2, while account b remains constant during the period $[t_0, t_3)$. In the sequel, we represent an interval (e.g., a_1) in the form *lifespan: key* (e.g., $[t_0, t_1):a_1$).

Intervals are inserted into a MVB-tree in a plane-sweep manner. To be specific, at the beginning a vertical sweeping line is placed at the starting point of the left-most interval before it starts moving right. An interval is inserted when its starting point is reached by the sweeping line. For example, at t_0, a_1 and b are inserted as $[t_0, *):a_1$ and $[t_0, *):b$ respectively, where * means that the ending point of the interval is not determined yet, but progresses with the sweeping line (such intervals are said to be *alive*). When the ending point of an interval is encountered, its lifespan is finalized, and the interval *dies* (it is *logically deleted*). For instance, when the sweeping line reaches t_1, interval a_1 is modified to $[t_0, t_1): a_1$.

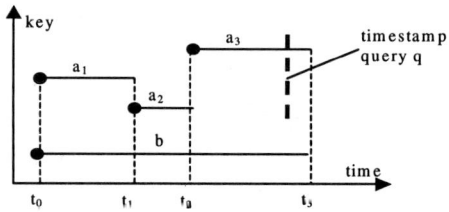

Fig. 3. Representation of temporal data

The MVB-tree is optimized for the so-called *timestamp query*, which, as shown in Figure 3, is a vertical line segment q that retrieves the horizontal line segments intersecting q. Figure 4 illustrates a simple MVB-tree when the sweeping line is at time 3. Each entry has the form <*key*, t_{start}, t_{end}, *pointer*>. For leaf entries, the *pointer* points to the actual record with the corresponding *key* value, while, for intermediate entries, it points to a next level node. The temporal attributes t_{start} and t_{end} denote the time that the record was inserted and (logically) deleted in the tree respectively.

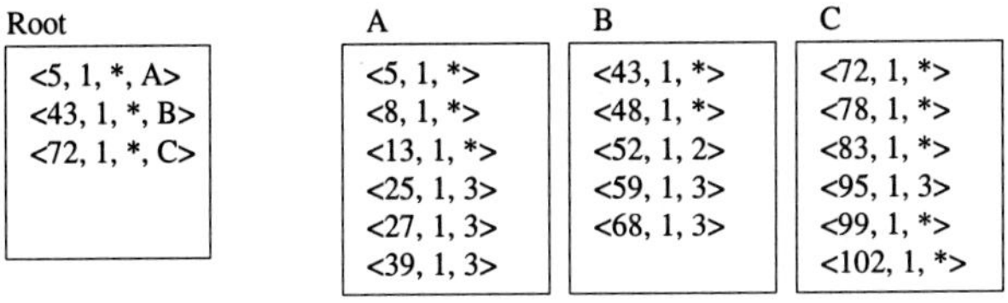

Root	A	B	C
<5, 1, *, A>	<5, 1, *>	<43, 1, *>	<72, 1, *>
<43, 1, *, B>	<8, 1, *>	<48, 1, *>	<78, 1, *>
<72, 1, *, C>	<13, 1, *>	<52, 1, 2>	<83, 1, *>
	<25, 1, 3>	<59, 1, 3>	<95, 1, 3>
	<27, 1, 3>	<68, 1, 3>	<99, 1, *>
	<39, 1, 3>		<102, 1, *>

Fig. 4. Example of MVB-tree

There can be multiple logical B-trees in a MVB-tree, and each root of a logical tree has a *jurisdiction interval,* which is the minimum bounding interval of the lifespans of all the entries in the logical tree. Processing of a timestamp query starts by retrieving the corresponding root whose jurisdiction interval contains the queried timestamp, after which the search is guided by *key,* t_{start}, and t_{end}. For each timestamp t and each node except the roots, it is required that either none, or at least $b \cdot P_{version}$ entries are alive at t, where $P_{version}$ is a tree parameter (for the following examples $P_{version}=1/3$ and $b=6$). This *weak version condition* ensures that entries alive at the same timestamps are mostly grouped together in order to facilitate timestamp query processing. Violations of this condition generate *weak version underflows,* which occur as a result of deletions.

Insertions and deletions are carried out in a way similar to B-trees except that overflows and underflows are handled differently. *Block overflow* occurs when an entry is inserted into a full node, in which case a *version split* is performed. To be specific, all the live entries of the node are copied to a new node, with their t_{start} modified to the insertion time. The t_{end} of these entries in the original node is changed from * to the insertion time (in practice this step can be avoided since the deletion time is implied by the entry in the parent node). In Figure 5, the insertion of <28,4,*> at timestamp 4 (in the tree of Figure 4) causes node *A* to overflow. A new node *D* is created to store the live entries of *A*, and *A* "dies" (notice that all * are replaced by 4) meaning that it will not be modified in the future.

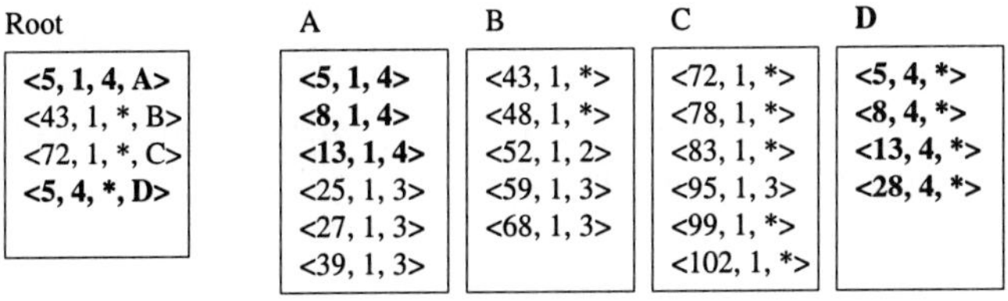

Root	A	B	C	D
<5, 1, 4, A>	<5, 1, 4>	<43, 1, *>	<72, 1, *>	<5, 4, *>
<43, 1, *, B>	<8, 1, 4>	<48, 1, *>	<78, 1, *>	<8, 4, *>
<72, 1, *, C>	<13, 1, 4>	<52, 1, 2>	<83, 1, *>	<13, 4, *>
<5, 4, *, D>	<25, 1, 3>	<59, 1, 3>	<95, 1, 3>	<28, 4, *>
	<27, 1, 3>	<68, 1, 3>	<99, 1, *>	
	<39, 1, 3>		<102, 1, *>	

Fig. 5. Example of block overflow and version split

In some cases, the new node may be almost full so that a small number of insertions would cause it to overflow again. On the other hand, if it contains too few entries, a small number of deletions will cause it to underflow. To avoid these problems, it is required that the number of entries in the new node must be in the range $[b \cdot P_{svu}, b \cdot P_{svo}]$ where P_{svo} and P_{svu} are tree parameters (for the following examples, $P_{svu}=1/3$, $P_{svo}=5/6$). A *strong version overflow (underflow)* occurs when the number of entries exceeds

$b \cdot P_{svo}$ (becomes lower than $b \cdot P_{svu}$). A strong version overflow is handled by a *key split*, a version-independent split according to the key values of the entries in the block. Notice that the strong version condition is only checked after a version split, i.e., it is possible that the live entries of a node are above $b \cdot P_{svo}$ before the node block-overflows.

Strong version underflow is similar to weak version underflow, the only difference being that the former happens after a version split, while the latter occurs when the weak version condition is violated. In both cases a merge is attempted with the copy of a sibling node using only its live entries. If the merged node strong version overflows, a key split is performed. Assume that at timestamp 4 we want to delete entry <48,1,*> from the tree in Figure 4. Node B weak version-underflows since it contains only one live entry <43,1,*>. A sibling, let node C, is chosen and its live entries are copied to a new node, let C'. The insertion of <43,4,*> into C' causes strong version overflow, leading to a key split and finally nodes D and E are created (Figure 6).

Root	A	B	C	D	E
<5, 1, *, A>	<5, 1, *>	<43, 1, 4>	<72, 1, 4>	<43, 4, *>	<83, 4 *>
<43, 1, 4, B>	<8, 1, *>	<48, 1, 4>	<78, 1, 4>	<72, 4, *>	<99, 4, *>
<72, 1, 4, C>	<13, 1, *>	<52, 1, 2>	<83, 1, 4>	<78, 4, *>	<102, 4, *>
<43, 4, *, D>	<25, 1, 3>	<59, 1, 3>	<95, 1, 3>		
<83, 4, *, E>	<27, 1, 3>	<68, 1, 3>	<99, 1, 4>		
	<39, 1, 3>		<102, 1, 4>		

Fig. 6. Example of weak version underflow

As shown in [BGO⁺96], MVB-trees require $O(n/b)$ space, where n is the number of updates ever made to the database and b is the block capacity. Answering a timestamp query requires $O(\log_b m + r/b)$ node accesses, where m is the number of live intervals at the queried timestamp, and r is the number of output intervals. Both the space requirements and query performance are asymptotically optimal. A variation of MVB-trees, which reduces the tree size by a constant factor can be found in [VV97]. Several algorithms for processing interval queries and temporal joins with MVB-trees, are proposed in [BS96] and [ZTS02], respectively. The multi-version framework has also been applied to R-trees to obtain various bi-temporal and spatio-temporal access methods [KTF98, TP01, KGT]. General cost models for multi-version structures can be found in [TPZ02].

3. The Aggregate Point-Tree (aP-Tree)

A WA query can be formally defined as follows: given a set of points in the 2D universe $[0, M_x]:[0, M_y]$, retrieve the number $WA(q)$ of points contained in a rectangle $[x_0, x_1]:[y_0, y_1]$. In order to optimally solve the problem we start with the observation that a two-dimensional point can be transformed to an open-ended interval (in the key-time plane as described in section 2.2) as follows: the y-coordinate of the point can be thought of as a key value, while the x-coordinate represents the starting time of the interval. The ending time of all intervals is the current time (lying on the right boundary of the time axis). Figure 7a shows the points used in the example of Figure 1a, and Figure 7b illustrates the resulting intervals.

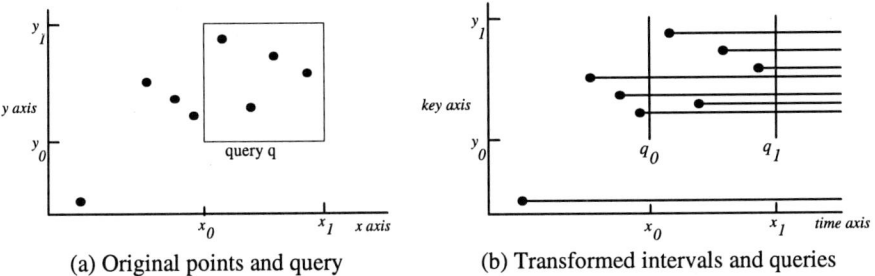

(a) Original points and query (b) Transformed intervals and queries

Fig. 7. Transformation of the problem

The original query is also transformed since the goal of query processing now is to retrieve the number of intervals that intersect the vertical line segment q_1 but not q_0. Query q_1 is represented as $x_1:[y_0, y_1]$, while q_0 as $\rightarrow x_0:[y_0, y_1]$. The symbol "$\rightarrow$" indicates that the x-coordinate of q_0 infinitely approaches (but does not equal) x_0 from the left. In the sequel, we refer to q_1 and q_0 as *vertical range aggregate* (VRA) queries. In words, a VRA query $x_1:[y_0, y_1]$ will retrieve the number $VRA(q_1)$ of intervals that start before or at timestamp x_1, and their keys are in the range $[y_0, y_1]$. Similarly, $\rightarrow x_0:[y_0, y_1]$ will retrieve the number $VRA(q_0)$ of intervals that start before (but not at) timestamp x_0 (this is needed in order to retrieve points at the left boundary of the query window). The result of $WA(q)$ is the (arithmetic) difference $VRA(q_1)$- $VRA(q_0)$.

Thus, WA query processing can be reduced to the vertical line segment intersection problem optimally solved by the MVB-tree, except that here we are interested in the aggregate number, instead of the concrete ids, of the qualifying objects. This fact differentiates query processing since we can avoid the retrieval of the actual objects intersecting q_1 and q_0 and the expensive computation of their set difference. In the sequel, we present the aP-tree, which modifies MVB-trees to support VRA queries.

3.1 Insertion and Overflow Handling

The aP-tree is similar to the MVB-tree, consisting of several logical B-trees each responsible for a jurisdiction interval, which is the minimum bounding interval of all the lifespans of its entries. An entry of the aP-tree has the form <y, [x_{start}, x_{end}), agg, $pointer$>, where $pointer$ is the same as in MVB-trees, while y and [x_{start}, x_{end}) correspond to *key* and [t_{start}, t_{end}) as defined in section 2.2 respectively. The additional field agg denotes the aggregate number over the entries alive during [x_{start}, x_{end}) in the child node. Without ambiguity, in the sequel we refer to the y-field and [x_{start}, x_{end}) of each entry as the *key* and *lifespan* of the entry respectively. The minimum bounding interval of all the lifespans in a node is called the *lifespan of the node*. Figure 8a illustrates a simple example. The agg fields in leaf entries are omitted since they are all equal to

1 for the COUNT function. The leaf entry <5,[1,*)> in node A, for example, refers to the horizontal interval [1, M_x]:5, transformed from point (1, 5). The intermediate entry <5,[1,*),6,A> implies that there are 6 entries in node A such that (i) the key of each interval is equal to or greater than 5; (ii) the lifespan of each entry is contained in [1, M_x]. Figure 8b shows the equivalent tree where all leaf entries are represented in (p_x, p_y) format.

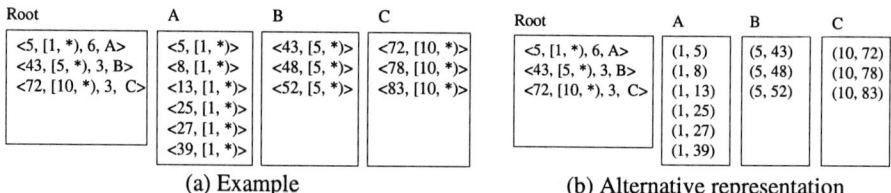

(a) Example   (b) Alternative representation

Fig. 8. An aP-tree

A preprocessing step is required to sort the original points in ascending order of their x-coordinates because, as with MVB-trees, the transformed intervals must be inserted in this order. Furthermore, since all the intervals have their right end-points on the right boundary of the universe, no logical deletion is necessary. As a result, the number of live entries in any node will never decrease until the node dies, so weak and strong version underflows never happen. Therefore, the aP-tree has only a single parameter P_{svo} (no parameters $P_{version}$ and P_{svu}), which denotes the strong version overflow threshold.

Insertion is performed as in MVB-trees except that it may be necessary to duplicate intermediate entries on the path. As an example, assume that an interval <55,[15,*)> (or equivalently point (15,55)) is inserted into the tree in Figure 8. Following the intermediate entry <45,[5,*),3,B>, the leaf node B that accommodates the new entry is first identified. As shown in Figure 9, the following changes are applied to the root node: (i) entry <45,[5,*),3,B> dies, having its x_{end} modified to 15; (ii) a new live entry, pointing to the same child node, is created with its x_{start} set to 15. The aggregate number of the new entry is incremented to accommodate the insertion. Such entry duplication is required by the aP-tree (but not the MVB-tree) to ensure that the *agg* field correctly reflects the aggregate result during the entry's lifespan [x_{start}, x_{end}]. In general, duplication is necessary when the x_{start} of the intermediate entry is smaller than the x_{start} of the interval being inserted.

Root	A	B	C
<5, [1, *), 6, A>	<5, [1, *)>	<43, [5, *)>	<72, [10, *)>
<43, [5, 15), 3, B>	<8, [1, *)>	<48, [5, *)>	<78, [10, *)>
<43, [15, *), 4, B>	<13, [1, *)>	<52, [5, *)>	<83, [10, *)>
<72, [10, *), 3, C>	<25, [1, *)>	<55, [15, *)>	
	<27, [1, *)>		
	<39, [1, *)>		

Fig. 9. Duplicating intermediate entry

Since no logical deletion is performed, all the entries in a leaf node must be alive when the node overflows. Therefore, a strong version overflow will always occur after version copies at the leaf level. Figure 10 illustrates a leaf overflow caused by the insertion of <40,[15,*)> (in the tree of Figure 9). Node A overflows and is version copied to node D, which generates a strong version overflow, and is finally split into itself and node E. Corresponding parent entries are added into the root node to reflect the changes. Notice that, due to the absence of logical deletions, the x_{end} fields of leaf entries are never modified. As an optimization method, they are not stored on the disk and this knowledge is inferred.

	Root	A	D	E	B	C
a	<5, [1, 15), 6, A>	<5, [1, *)>	<5, [15, *)>	<25, [15, *)>	<43, [5, *)>	<72, [10, *)>
b	<5, [15, *), 3, D>	<8, [1, *)>	<8, [15, *)>	<27, [15, *)>	<48, [5, *)>	<78, [10, *)>
c	<25, [15, *), 4, E>	<13, [1, *)>	<13, [15, *)>	<39, [15, *)>	<52, [5, *)>	<83, [10, *)>
d	<43, [5, 15), 3, B>	<25, [1, *)>		<40, [15, *)>	<55, [15, *)>	
e	<43, [15, *), 4, B>	<27, [1, *)>				
f	<72, [10, *), 3, C>	<39, [1, *)>				

Fig. 10. Overflow of leaf node

3.2 Vertical Range Aggregate (VRA) Query Processing

As discussed before, a WA query in aP-trees is reduced to two VRA queries q_1 and q_0. The processing of a VRA query $x:[y_0, y_1]$ starts by locating the corresponding root for x, after which search is guided by the keys and lifespans of intermediate entries. For example, in Figure 10, to answer the VRA query 15:[25, 75] we only consider those entries whose lifespans include 15; thus, entries a and d are eliminated immediately. Next, we purge the ones whose y-ranges do not intersect with [25, 75] (e.g., entry b). Among the remaining entries, some are totally inside the range [25, 75] (i.e., c and e), and for these entries, it suffices to simply add their aggregate numbers (i.e., 4 and 4). Only if the y-range of an entry *partially intersects* [25, 75], we have to access its child node. Continuing the example, only one leaf node C is visited (from entry f), in which one object <72,10,*> is counted. Therefore, the final answer to the query is 4 + 4 + 1 = 9.

The processing of query $\rightarrow x:[y_0, y_1]$ is the same, except that intervals starting at x should be excluded. As an example, consider the query $\rightarrow$15:[25, 75]. After retrieving the corresponding root node, we eliminate those entries whose intervals start at or after 15. So entries b, c, and e are discarded from further consideration. Then the processing proceeds as in the previous case by examining the y-ranges of the entries. Finally the result 8 is returned by visiting leaf nodes A and C.

An important observation is that, in the worst case, processing a VRA query only needs to visit two paths from the root to the leaf level of a B-tree. This is because, at each non-leaf level, the y-ranges of the entries alive at any x-coordinate (e.g., x=15 in the query example above) are continuous and disjoint. As a result, there can be at most two y-ranges partially intersecting the y-range of the query (at the start, or the end point). The y-ranges of the other entries are either contained by (in which cases their *agg* fields are simply added) or disjoint with the query *y*-range. Therefore, *the query cost (number of node accesses) of a WA query is at most four times the height of the B-tree* (two times for each q_1 and q_0). Since we only care about the aggregate number, it suffices to return the arithmetic difference of the two VRA queries VRA(q_1)-VRA(q_0), without computing the set difference of their results (which would require cost up to $n\log n$, where *n* is the number of intervals).

3.3 Asymptotical Performance

We first analyze the asymptotical space consumption of the aP-tree. Recall that a node is created from a version split, and dies by generating another version split, which spawns a new node. When a node is created, it is ensured that it contains fewer than $P_{svo} \cdot b$ entries; otherwise, a strong version overflow is generated and a key split is performed. It follows that a node will generate the next version split by receiving at least $(b-P_{svo} \cdot b)$ insertions after its creation. Let N_0 be the number of leaf nodes. Since each insertion will create only one entry in a leaf node, we have:

$$N_0 \cdot (b - P_{svo} \cdot b) \le n \Rightarrow N_0 \le \frac{n}{(1-P_{svo})b} = O(\frac{n}{b})$$

where *n* is the total number of insertions (i.e., points). For a node at higher levels, the number of new entries incurred from an insertion is at most 2. This corresponds to the 2 parent entries for new nodes created at the next level (through strong version overflows). Hence, a non-leaf node dies after at least $(b-P_{svo} \cdot b)/2$ insertions. Assuming that the number of nodes at level *i* is N_i, we have:

$$N_i \cdot (b - P_{svo} \cdot b)/2 \le n \Rightarrow N_i \le \frac{2n}{(1-P_{SVO})b} = O(\frac{n}{b})$$

Since every node contains at least $P_{svo} \cdot b/2 = O(b)$ entries at each point during its lifespan, the height of any B-tree is $O(\log_b n)$. Therefore, the space complexity of the aP-tree is $O(n/b \log_b n)$ nodes in the worst case[1]. Furthermore, since, as with conventional B-trees, each insertion incurs at most $2\log_b n$ node accesses, the aP-tree can be constructed with $O(n\log_b n)$ node accesses, which also dominates the cost of the preprocessing sorting step.

Answering a VRA query involves visiting at most 2 paths from the root of a B-tree to the leaf level, i.e., $2\log_b n$ node accesses in the worst case. Since there are at most $O(n)$ logical B-trees (as shown later the number is very small in practice because each B-tree includes many data points), the corresponding B-tree can be located in $\log_b n$ node accesses as well, for example, by looking up a separate B-tree built on the root table. Therefore, a VRA query takes at most $O(\log_b n)$ node accesses. Given that, a WA query is transformed into 2 VRA queries, a WA query can be answered in $O(\log_b n)$ node accesses in the worst case. The following theorem summarizes the discussion above.

---

[1] The space consumption of aP-trees is higher than that of MVB-trees ($O(n/b)$) due to the entry duplication that occurs in the aP-tree when the x_{start} of an intermediate entry is smaller than the x_{start} of the interval being inserted.

Theorem 3.1: A WA query for spatial points can be answered in $O(\log_b n)$ node accesses by building an aP-tree that consumes $O(n/b \log_b n)$ nodes and can be constructed with $O(n\log_b n)$ node accesses. •

4. Cost Models for aP-trees

In the last section, we have shown theoretically that any WA query can be answered in logarithmic worst case time by introducing the aP-tree. In this section, we analyze the practical performance of the structure. This is motivated by the following facts: (i) asymptotical performance gives only limited indication towards the actual performance in practice; and (ii) the crucial factors that a database administrator needs to consider usually include the tradeoff between the size of the structure and the query response time provided. Therefore, it is important to derive accurate cost models that estimate the number of disk pages occupied by a structure, and the number of page accesses in answering a WA query.

We start by estimating the size of the aP-tree, considering, for simplicity, the case that all points have different x-coordinates. Let the *live fanout* f_l of a leaf node be the average number of entries in the node alive at an x-coordinate during the node's lifespan. Similarly f_{nl} represents the *live fanout* of a non-leaf node. For example, in node B of Figure 10, there are 3 entries alive at $x=5$, and 4 at $x=15$. So the live fanouts of node B are 3 and 4 respectively at these two x-coordinates. Note that leaf and non-leaf nodes are distinguished because their structural changes are different.

The live nodes at some x- coordinate increase due to key splits. Recall that when an overflow occurs at the leaf level, the new leaf node will always be key split, while, for non-leaf levels, key splits will happen only when the number of entries in the new node exceeds the strong version overflow threshold. To distinguish this, we define *split points* as follows. The *split point* SP_l of a leaf node denotes the number of entries in a leaf node before it is key split. Similarly SP_{nl} corresponds to the *split point* of a non-leaf node. Let b_l and b_{nl} represent the block capacities of leaf and non-leaf nodes respectively. Then we have:

$$SP_l = b_l \text{ and } SP_{nl} = b_{nl} \cdot P_{svo} \qquad (4.1)$$

As shown in [Yao78], the fanout of a B-tree is $ln2$ times the split point of a node. Hence in our case, the relation between live fanouts and split points is as follows:

$$f_l = SP_l \cdot ln2 \text{ and } f_{nl} = SP_{nl} \cdot ln2 \qquad (4.2)$$

An aP-tree consists of multiple logical B-trees, where more recent trees have larger heights as more insertions are performed. The height h of the last logical B-tree is:

$$h = 2 + \left\lceil \log_{f_{nl}} \frac{n/f_l}{SP_{nl}} \right\rceil \qquad (4.3)$$

If N_i is the total number of nodes at level i, the size of an aP-tree is:

$$size(aP) = \sum_{i=0}^{h-1} N_i \qquad (4.4)$$

The estimation for N_0, the total number of leaf nodes, is relatively straightforward, observing that the only type of structural change at the leaf level is a version split followed by a key split. Therefore, each version split (i) increases the total number of nodes by 2, and (ii) the number of live nodes by 1. Notice that after all the insertions are complete, the number of live nodes is n/f_l; thus, the total number of leaf-level version splits is $V_l = n/f_l - 1$. Hence we have:

$$N_0 = 2V_l + 1 = 2n/f_l - 1 \tag{4.5}$$

A similar analysis, however, does not apply to the estimation for N_i of non-leaf levels because key splits do not always happen after version splits. Furthermore, note that higher levels will appear only after a sufficient number of insertions. In the sequel, we say that the *level-up point* (LuP) for level i is L_i, if this level appears after L_i insertions. Since a new level appears when the previous root at the lower level strong version overflows, the estimation for L_i ($i \geq 1$) is as follows.

$$L_1 = SP_l$$
$$L_i = f_l \cdot f_{nl}^{i-2} \cdot SP_{nl} \quad (1 < i \leq h-1) \tag{4.6}$$

where SP_l, SP_{nl} and f_l, f_{nl} are split points and live fanouts for leaf and non-leaf nodes respectively as defined earlier. Next we focus on N_1 before generalizing to higher levels. Since no two points have the same x-coordinate, an entry will be duplicated in every intermediate node along the insertion path. Therefore, the total number of entry insertions at each level is also n. Notice, however, that this estimation excludes strong version overflows because: (i) the number of strong version overflows is considerably lower than n; so omitting it will not bias the results significantly, and (ii) although capturing strong version overflows is straightforward, it would lead to excessively complicated equations.

Recall that a node already contains a number of entries (version copied from the previous node) when it is created. Another observation is that this number equals the number of live entries in the previous node. Since the average live fanout of non-leaf nodes is f_{nl}, it follows that a node contains f_{nl} initial entries on average. Therefore, a node will, on the average, take $(b_{nl} - f_{nl})$ entries before it dies. Note that, however, the live fanout applies only to nodes other than roots of logical trees (i.e., for N_1, it applies after level 2 has appeared). Hence the number of level 1 nodes created after the LuP L_2 can be estimated as $(n - L_2)/(b_{nl} - f_{nl})$.

At any time between LuPs L_1 and L_2, there is only one live node at level 1, which is the root of the logical tree. The live entries in the root increase gradually from 2 (when level 1 appears) to SP_{nl} (when level 2 appears). It follows that on the average $(L_2 - L_1)/(SP_{nl} - 2)$ insertions are performed before the live entries in the root increase. For each value of j, by the same analysis as above, the number of newly created nodes is $\dfrac{(L_2 - L_1)/(SP_{nl} - 2)}{(b_{nl} - j)}$; thus, we have the following estimation for N_1:

$$N_1 = \left[\sum_{j=2}^{SP_{nl}} \frac{(L_2 - L_1)/(SP_{nl} - 2)}{(b_{nl} - j)} \right] + \frac{n - L_2}{b_{nl} - f_{nl}} \tag{4.7}$$

Similar analysis also applies to higher levels except level $h-1$. In general we have:

$$N_i = \left[\sum_{j=2}^{SP_{nl}} \frac{(L_{i+1} - L_i)/(SP_{nl} - 2)}{(b_{nl} - j)} \right] + \frac{n - L_{i+1}}{b_{nl} - f_{nl}} \quad (1 \leq i \leq h-2) \tag{4.8}$$

Now it remains to clarify the estimation of N_{h-1}, which is different from the other non-leaf levels on two aspects: (i) there is no LuP for the higher level; (ii) the number of live entries in the root node increases up to $\lceil n/(f_l \cdot f_{nl}^{h-2}) \rceil$. Following the analysis of N_i, we have:

$$N_{h-1} = \sum_{j=2}^{\lceil n/(f_l \cdot f_{nl}^{h-2}) \rceil} \frac{(n - L_{h-1}) / (\lceil n/(f_l \cdot f_{nl}^{h-2}) \rceil - 2)}{(b_{nl} - j)} \quad (4.9)$$

Replacing variables in equation (4.4) correspondingly with results in equations (4.1 to 4.9), we obtain the cost model that predicts the structure size of the aP-tree. Note that this estimation does not include the size of the root table, which stores one entry for each root node. As will be shown in the experimental section, however, the size of the root table is negligible. Furthermore in this paper we assume that each disk page corresponds to one structure node; hence the model also gives the number of disk pages required by an aP-tree. It is straightforward to extend the equation to the general case where a node corresponds to multiple disk pages.

The estimation for query costs is relatively simple. As discussed in the previous section, processing a VRA query involves visiting at most 2 paths from the root to the leaf level of a B-tree. Since the 2 paths start from the root node of the same logical B-tree, the number of node accesses in answering a VRA query is at most:

$$NA(VRA) = 2h - 1 = 3 + 2 \left\lceil \log_{f_{nl}} \frac{n/f_l}{SP_{nl}} \right\rceil \quad (4.10)$$

Thus the cost of answering a WA query, which involves two VRA queries, is given by equation 4.11. Notice that the query costs involve a very low constant value irrespective of the sizes and positions of the queries.

$$NA(WA) = 2NA(VRA) = 6 + 4 \left\lceil \log_{f_{nl}} \frac{n/f_l}{SP_{nl}} \right\rceil \quad (4.11)$$

5. Experiments

In this section, we evaluate the sizes and query performance of aP- and aR-trees with synthetic and real datasets. All queries are quadratic, i.e., both sides of each query window have the same length, which is represented as a percentage of the unit axis. In our implementation, we optimize the performance of both structures by storing only necessary information in leaf and non-leaf entries. For example, for aR-trees, points are stored in leaf entries while MBRs are stored in non-leaf entries. For aP-trees, on the other hand, the x_{end} field of each entry does not need to be stored (see section 3.1). The page size is set to 4,096 bytes, for which the leaf and non-leaf node capacities of aP-trees are 255 and 204 respectively, while the corresponding figures for aR-trees are 255 and 170 (more information is needed in an intermediate aR-entry to store its MBR). The P_{svo} parameter of the aP-tree is set to 0.5 in all cases.

5.1 Uniform Datasets

In the first set of experiments, datasets are generated uniformly in a unit square universe, ensuring that no two points have the same *x*-coordinate. Query performance is measured by the average number of node accesses in answering a workload consisting of 500 queries. Each query in the same workload has the same side length, ranging from 10% to 60% of the universe axis, resulting in query areas from 1% to 36%. The position of a query is randomly generated in the universe. Figure 11a demonstrates the number of node accesses as a function of the query side for the aP- and aR-tree indexing a uniform dataset with 150K points. It is clear that the aR-tree is comparable to the aP-tree only for very small query windows, and its performance keeps increasing linearly with the query side. On the other hand, the performance of the aP-tree stabilizes around 10 accesses irrespective of the query side, which makes it considerably more efficient than its competitor. Further, since the height of the aP-tree is 3, the cost (10 accesses) is exactly our estimation given by equation (4.11).

Figure 11b demonstrates the query cost (using the workload with side length 50%) as a function of the cardinality for uniform datasets with 50K, 100K, 150K, 200K, and 250K points. The performance of the aR-tree deteriorates quickly when the cardinality increases, while that of the aP-tree remains constant (at 10 node accesses), as there is no change in the height. Notice that our estimation (by equation 2.1) of the aR-tree performance is very accurate in all cases, producing error less than 5%.

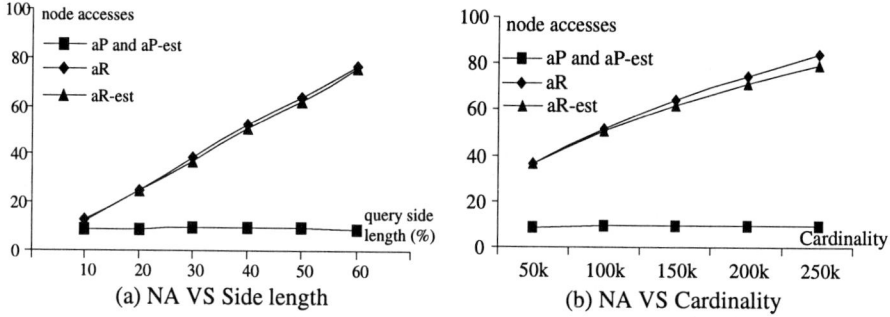

Fig. 11. Query costs of WA queries

As discussed in the analysis, the excellent performance of aP-trees comes at the expense of extra space consumption. Figure 12 shows the sizes of aP- and aR-trees as a function of the data cardinality. aP-trees consume more space than the corresponding aR-trees, because each insertion must create a new entry in each node on the insertion path, while, for aR-trees, new non-leaf entries are needed only when new nodes at the lower level are spawned. Furthermore, despite the fact that the size complexity of the aP-tree is $O(n/b \log_b n)$, its growth is quite linear with the cardinality. This is expected because the factor $\log_b n$ in the complexity actually corresponds to the height of the tree. Therefore, the size of the aP-tree grows linearly as long as its height remains unchanged, which is true for the 5 cardinality values in the figure. Note that the estimated values (by equation 4.4) capture the actual behavior of the aP-tree very well, producing error below 5% in all cases. It is worth mentioning that the sizes of the root tables of the aP-trees are about 0.1% of the total tree sizes.

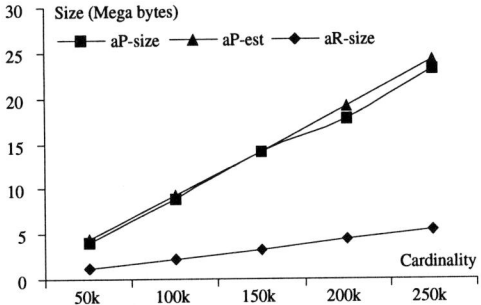

Fig. 12. Size comparison of aP- and aR-trees

5.2 Non-uniform Datasets

In this section we compare the two structures using 6 non-uniform datasets described as follows: (i) *gauss* contains 100K points distributed following the gaussian distribution; (ii) *skewed* has the same cardinality but the distribution is skewed (*gauss* and *skewed* were generated using the GSTD utility [TSN99]); (iii) *CFD1* (52K points) and *CFD* (200K points) are vertex data from various Computation Fluid Dynamic models measured for a cross section of a Boeing 737 wing with flaps out in landing configuration [Web1]; (iv) *SCG* contains 62K points representing gravity data for South California [Web2]; (v) *SCP* contains 46K points describing places in South California [Web3]. The datasets are shown in Figure 13.

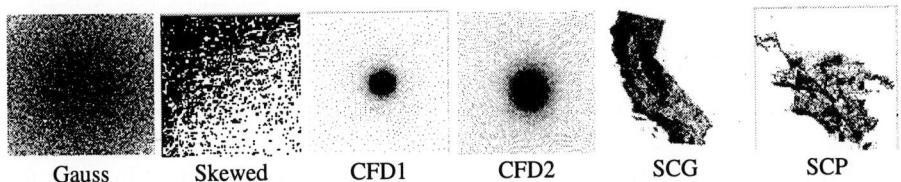

Fig. 13. Visualization of non-uniform datasets

To study query performance, we generated workloads specifically for each dataset such that the queries in a workload distribute similarly to the corresponding dataset in order to avoid queries falling into empty areas. Figure 14 illustrates, for each dataset, the number of node accesses as a function of the query length. It is clear that aP-trees outperform aR-trees in all cases, and the difference is up to an order of magnitude. An interesting observation is that, when data is skewed, the processing cost of aR-trees usually drops when the query length exceeds a threshold. This happens because skewed data lead to skewed MBRs of the nodes. Hence when the query rectangle is large enough, many MBRs tend to assemble inside the query window, so fewer

MBRs intersect the window sides. Note that this phenomenon does not exist for uniform datasets, where the MBRs of nodes are also uniformly distributed.

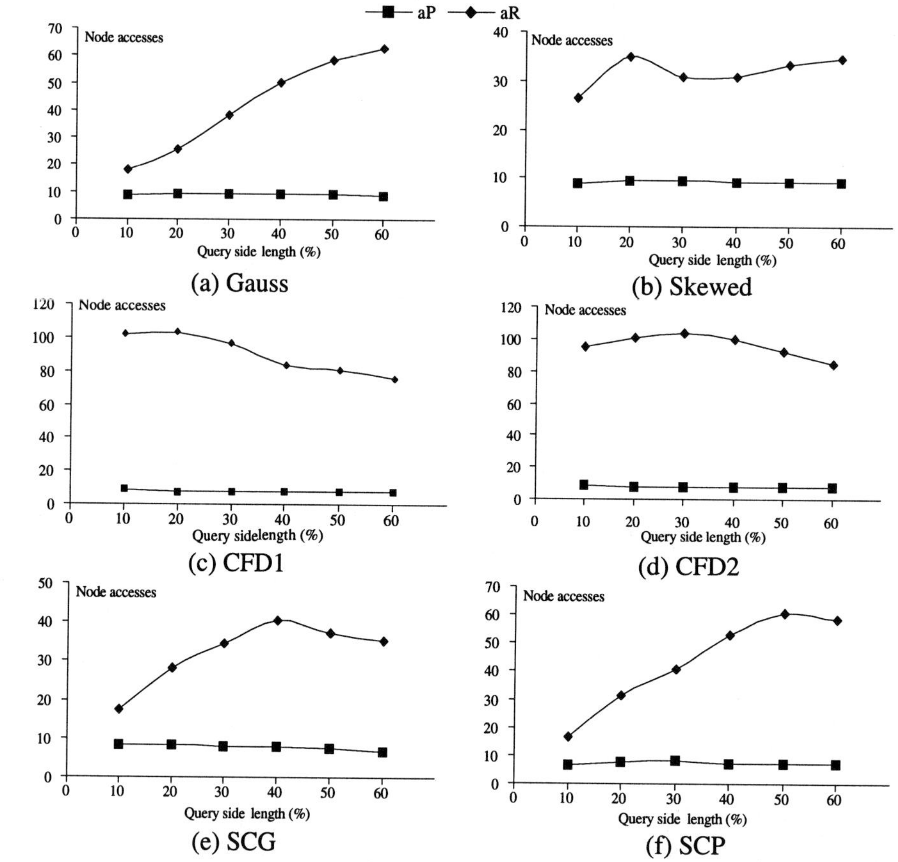

Fig. 14. Query performance for non-uniform datasets

Finally, Figure 15 demonstrates the sizes of corresponding aP- and aR-trees for the datasets above, as well as the estimated values from our model (equation 4.4). The difference between the two structures is similar to that of the uniform case, and our cost models again predict the performance very accurately.

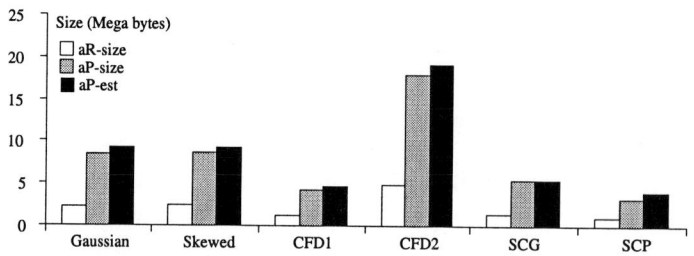

Fig. 15. Sizes of both structures for non-uniform datasets

6. Conclusions and Future Work

This paper addresses the problem of processing WA queries on planar points, proposing a new indexing structure, the aP-tree, that answers any WA query in logarithmic worst case time. Extensive experiments have shown that the aP-tree outperforms its most significant competitor, the aR-tree, by up to an order of magnitude. Its main advantage compared to any R-tree based method, is that the query cost is independent of the window size. We believe that, given the significant performance benefits and the dropping cost of secondary memory, the extra space requirements of the aP-tree do not constitute a serious shortcoming, especially for applications that require fast, real-time query processing. In addition, we present efficient cost models (with less than 5% error) that predict the structure size of the aP-tree and, consequently query performance.

An interesting direction for future work is to investigate whether it is possible to improve the space requirements of the aP-tree, or to prove a theoretical bound for any indexing structure that answers WA queries in logarithmic worst case time. A challenging extension is to apply the same approach to support more general spatial objects (such as rectangles, spheres, etc), possibly in multiple dimensions.

Acknowledgments

This work was supported by grants HKUST 6081/01E and HKUST 6070/00E from Hong Kong RGC.

References

[BGO+96] Becker, B., Gschwind, S., Ohler, T., Seeger, B., Widmayer, P. An Asymptotically Optimal Multiversion B-Tree. *VLDB Journal*, Vol. 5(4), pp. 264-275, 1996.

[BKS+90] Beckmann, B., Kriegel, H.P., Schneider, R, Seeger, B. The R*-tree: An Efficient and Robust Access Method. *ACM SIGMOD*, 1990.

[BS96] Bercken van den, J., Seeger, B. Query Processing Techniques for Multiversion Access Methods. *VLDB*, 1996.

[JL98] Jurgens, M., Lenz, H. The Ra*-tree: An Improved R-tree with Materialized Data for Supporting Range Queries on OLAP-Data. *DEXA Workshop*, 1998.

[KF93] Kamel, I., Faloutsos, C. On Packing R-trees. *CIKM*, 1993.

[KGT+] Kollios, G., Gunopulos, D., Tsotras, V., Dellis, A., Hadjieleftheriou, M. Indexing Animated Objects Using Spatiotemporal Access Methods. To appear in *IEEE TKDE*.

[KKK99] Kim, J., Kang, S., Kim, M. Effective Temporal Aggregation using Point-based Trees. *DEXA*, 1999.

[KS95]   Kline, N., Snodgrass, R. Computing Temporal Aggregates. *IEEE ICDE*, 1995.
[KTF98] Kumar, A, Tsotras, V., Faloutsos, C. Design Access Methods for Bitemporal Databases. *IEEE TKDE* 10(1): 1-20, 1998.
[LM01]   Lazaridis, I., Mehrotra, S. Progressive Approximate Aggregate Queries with a Multi-Resolution Tree Structure. *ACM SIGMOD*, 2001.
[PKZ+01] Papadias, D., Kalnis, P., Zhang, J., Tao, Y. Efficient OLAP Operations in Spatial Data Warehouses. *SSTD*, 2001.
[PT01]   Pedersen, T., Tryfona, N. Pre-aggregation in Spatial Data Warehouses. *SSTD*, 2001.
[PTK+02] Papadias, D., Tao, Y., Kalnis, P., Zhang, J. Indexing Spatio-temporal Data Warehouses. *IEEE ICDE*, 2002.
[ST97]   Salzberg, B., Tsotras, V. A Comparison of Access Methods for Temporal Data. *ACM Computing Surveys*, 31(2): 158-221, 1997.
[TP01]   Tao, Y., Papadias, D. The MV3R-tree: A Spatio-Temporal Access Method for Timestamp and Interval Queries. *VLDB*, 2001.
[TPZ02] Tao, Y., Papadias, D., Zhang, J. Efficient Cost Models for Overlapping and Multi-Version Structures. *IEEE ICDE*, 2002.
[TS96]   Theodoridis, Y., Sellis, T. A Model for the Prediction of R-tree Performance. *ACM PODS*, 1996.
[TSN99] Theodoridis, Y., Silva, J. Nascimento, M. On the Generation of Spatiotemporal Datasets. *SSD*, 1999.
[VV97]   Varman, P., Verma, R. An Efficient Multiversion Access Structure. *IEEE TKDE*, Vol. 9, No. 3, pp. 391-409, 1997.
[Web1]   http://www.cs.du.edu/~leut/MultiDimData.html
[Web2]   http://www.gps.caltech.edu/~clay/gravity/gravity.html
[Web3]   http://dias.cti.gr/~ytheod/research/datasets/spatial.html
[Yao78] Yao, A. Random 2-3 Trees. *Acta Informatica*, Vol. 2(9), 159-179, 1978.
[YW01]   Yang, J., Widom, J. Incremental Computation and Maintenance of Temporal Aggregates. *IEEE ICDE*, 2001.
[ZMT+01] Zhang, D., Markowetz, A., Tsotras, V., Gunopulos, D., Seeger, B. Efficient Computation of Temporal Aggregates with Range Predicates. *ACM PODS*, 2001.
[ZTS02] Zhang, D., Tsotras, V., Seeger, B. Efficient Temporal Join Processing Using Indices. *IEEE ICDE*, 2002.

TDB: A Database System for Digital Rights Management

Radek Vingralek, Umesh Maheshwari, and William Shapiro

STAR Lab, InterTrust Technologies Corporation
4750 Patrick Henry Drive, Santa Clara, CA 95054
radek.vingralek@oracle.com,umesh@zambeel.com,bill_shapiro@yahoo.com

Abstract. In this paper we describe the architecture and implementation of an embedded database system for Digital Rights Management (DRM), TDB. We concentrate on the aspects of TDB's design, which were affected by the requirements of DRM applications. We show that, although it provides additional functionality for DRM applications, TDB performs better then Berkeley DB and has a code footprint comparable to other embedded database systems.

1 Introduction

Some emerging applications pose new challenges to the design of database systems. One example is Digital Rights Management (DRM). DRM systems ensure that digital goods such as music and books are consumed (i.e., viewed or played) according to the contracts associated with them. A contract may be simple, such as pay-per-view, subscription, or one-time-fee, or it may be more complex, such as "free after first ten paid views", "free, if usage data can be collected" or "$10 one-time-fee or free for every 1000th customer".

Enforcement of some contracts requires storing persistent state associated with the contract, such as usage meters, pre-paid account balances, audit records, discount-club membership, or access keys. The state is often stored locally in the consumer's device to provide better performance and privacy and to enable disconnected content consumption. Since some of the state has monetary value, it requires the same protection against accidental corruption as provided by most database systems: transactional semantics for updates, backups, type-safety, and automatic index maintenance. However, DRM systems also have characteristics that require a departure from traditional database design:

Protection against malicious corruption. DRM database systems must protect the data not only against accidental, but also malicious corruption. A consumer who could successfully tamper with the database, for example, by resetting a usage count or debit balance, might be able to obtain content for free. The consumer has full control over the device, which makes protection against tampering more difficult.

Protection against unauthorized reading. DRM database systems must protect the data against unauthorized reading. Consumers may find secrets such as content decryption keys or access codes by analyzing the database and use them to circumvent the DRM system. Protection against malicious corruption and unauthorized reading is further complicated by the fact that most persistent storage systems can be analyzed and modified off-line.

Single-user workload. DRM database systems are not typically used as shared servers that are accessed by many concurrent users. Instead, they are embedded in devices that are used by a single user at a time, such as MP3 players, set-top boxes, e-book readers, and desktop PCs. Consequently, DRM database systems should be optimized for response time rather than throughput.

Small database size. DRM systems typically create relatively small databases. Therefore, DRM database systems can often cache the working set and physical clustering of data is less important.

Small code footprint. DRM systems need to run on many platforms ranging from high-end desktop PC's to handheld devices with limited resources. Therefore, the code footprint is an important constraint.

In this paper we report on our design of a DRM database system, TDB. We concentrate on those aspects of TDB's design where we depart from the common database design principles to accommodate DRM applications. We compare the basic design decisions against their alternatives. Finally, we show that although TDB implements more functionality than most embedded database systems, it has a comparable code footprint and provides better performance than Berkeley DB, a widely used embedded database system. The rest of this paper is organized as follows. In Section 2 we describe the layered architecture of TDB. In Sections 3—4, we discuss the design of the two topmost layers. In Section 5 we compare the size of TDB's code footprint against other embedded database systems. In Section 6 we compare the performance of TDB against Berkeley DB.

2 TDB Architecture

We assume that the platform provides a small *secret store,* which can be read only by the database system, and a *one-way persistent counter,* which cannot be decremented. We also assume that the platform provides a *trusted processing environment,* which executes only trusted programs and protects the run-time state of an executing program from being read or modified by untrusted programs. The secret store can be implemented in a ROM, which most devices use to store firmware and which is not accessible to most applications. The one-way counter may be implemented using special-purpose hardware [12]. The trusted processing environment can be implemented using a secure co-processor. On platforms without special-purpose hardware, the secret store, one-way counter and trusted processing environment can be implemented using various techniques for software protection [1, 2]. For more details on the platform security model see [9]. We assume that the platform also provides an *untrusted store* for storing the database and an *archival store* for maintaining backups of the database. We assume that the untrusted store and the archival store can be arbitrarily read or modified by an attacker.

The architecture of TDB consists of four layers: the *chunk store,* the *backup store,* the *object store* and the *collection store.*

The *chunk store,* the bottom layer, securely stores a set of variable-sized sequences of bytes, which we term *chunks.* It guarantees that chunks can be read only by authorized programs (programs linked with the DRM database system) and detects tampering by unauthorized programs. Applications can update a number of chunks atomically with respect to system crashes. Unlike other database systems, the chunk store implements a *log-structured* storage model.

The *backup store* creates and securely restores database backups, which can be either full or incremental. The backup store validates backups before restoring them. In addition, it restores incremental backups in the same sequence as they were created. Backups are created using copy-on-write snapshots provided by the chunk store.

The *object store* provides type-safe access to a set of named C++ objects. The object store maps objects into chunks. It implements full transactional semantics, including concurrency control. The object store maintains a cache of frequently accessed or dirty objects.

The *collection store,* the top layer, allows applications to create indexed collections of objects. The indexes, which are *functional,* are automatically maintained while the objects in a collection are updated. The applications can access objects in collections using scan, exact-match and range queries.

More details on design of the chunk and backup stores can be found in [9]. In this paper, we concentrate on describing the design of object and collection stores.

3 The Object Store

The object store extends the functionality of the chunk store by storing typed objects and providing full transactional semantics (as opposed to atomic updates). It is designed to balance ease of use and type safety against implementation complexity.

For simplicity, we wanted to provide direct storage for application-defined C++ objects instead of objects in a separate database language with a separate type system. We leveraged existing C++ language and its runtime features to provide this functionality. We did not want to invest the effort and incur the implementation complexity of providing transparent persistence. Transparent persistence includes automatic swizzling of persistent ids into memory pointers, automatic locking for concurrency control, and in some cases garbage collection based on reachability. These features usually require a tool to parse, compile, or instrument object representations. We settled for requiring explicit application calls to lock, swizzle, and reclaim objects[1]. Nonetheless, we were able to design the object store interface such that locking omissions and type-unsafe swizzling

---

[1] While explicit reclamation is in line with regular C++ usage, explicit locking and swizzling make the representation and use of persistent objects different from regular, volatile C++ objects.

by the application are caught using a combination of static and dynamic checks. The purpose of these mechanisms is to catch common programming mistakes, not provide an unyielding type-safe environment, which is also in line with regular C++ usage.

3.1 Specification

Objects are instances of C++ classes defined by the application. The application may insert, read, write, or remove objects in the object store. When an object is inserted into the object store, it is given a persistent id. The application can use this id to "open" the object in read-only or read-write mode. It may store this id in other persistent objects and retrieve it later, possibly after a system restart. The application can group a sequence of object accesses into a transaction. It can run multiple transactions concurrently, possibly in different threads.

When the application opens an object in read-only or read-write mode, it receives a "smart pointer" for accessing the object. A read-only smart pointer provides access to a `const` object; i.e., public data members are accessible as if they were declared `const`, and only `const` public methods can be invoked. A smart pointer is valid only until the transaction it was created in is committed or aborted; any attempt to use it further results in a checked runtime error.

A persistent object must be an instance of an application-defined subclass of class `Object`. Subclasses of `Object` must implement a method to pickle an object into a sequence of bytes, and a constructor to unpickle an object from a sequence of bytes. The application may choose to pickle objects in an architecture-independent format so that the stored database can be moved from one platform to another. It may also compress the object state so that the unpickled state is optimized for fast access and the pickled state is optimized for small storage. While the pickling and unpickling operations are provided by the application, the application does not have to invoke them explicitly; they are invoked by the object store as needed. TDB provides implementations of pickling and unpickling operations for basic types. We illustrate the interface and its use with an example in Figure 1.

3.2 Implementation

The object store is implemented on top of the chunk store. Committed states of persistent objects are stored in chunks. Recently used objects and dirty (i.e., modified but uncommitted) objects are cached in memory. Transactional isolation is provided using strict two-phase locking; the object store locks objects when they are opened for reading or writing. Below we describe the implementation.

Object Storage. A chunk could store one or more objects. There is a tradeoff between storing single or multiple objects per chunk. Using single-object chunks has the following advantages:

```
class Meter: public Object {
    int _viewCount;
};
class Profile: public Object { // Contains information on all goods used by a consumer.
    vector<ObjectId> _meters;
};

// Add a new Meter to the Profile registered as root object.
Transaction t;
ObjectId meterId = t.insert(new Meter());
ObjectId profileId = getRoot();
WritableRef<Profile> profile = t.openWritable(profileId);
profile->_meters.push_back(meterId);
t.commit();
```

Fig. 1. Sample usage of the object store interface.

- Single-object chunks use log space efficiently because only modified objects are written to the log.
- Single-object chunks reduce access latency by reducing the amount of data that must be processed (e.g., copied, hashed, and encrypted or decrypted) when reading and writing a single object.
- Multi-object chunks complicate the implementation of the object cache in the presence of concurrent transactions. Different objects in a chunk could be modified by different transactions. Committing an object would require re-composing the container chunk with the unmodified versions of other objects in the chunk.

Using multi-object chunks has the following advantages:

- Log-structuring destroys inter-chunk clustering as chunks are updated. Multi-object chunks retain physical clustering between objects in a chunk, and thus benefit from spatial locality.
- Multi-object chunks result in fewer chunks and therefore lower space overhead from metadata such as the location map and the chunk headers in the log.

We chose to use single-object chunks in the current implementation because the stated disadvantages are not severe for DRM systems. DRM databases are relatively small and their working sets are often cacheable. Therefore, clustering is not as important as in traditional database systems. Also, our per-chunk space overhead is about 20 bytes without crypto overhead and 38 bytes with crypto overhead, and DRM records are often a few hundred bytes, so the space overhead is tolerable.

Object Cache. The object store maintains an in-memory cache of objects indexed by object ids. We chose to cache objects in the object store (compared to, say, caching chunks in the chunk store) because objects are ready for direct access by the application: they are decrypted, validated, unpickled, and type checked. If the database system provided a cache of unprocessed data, there would be incentive for the application to keep a separate cache of processed data, resulting in double caching and additional complexity. Furthermore, because the indexes in the collection store are implemented using objects in the object store, the object cache provides caching of indexes as well.

4 Collection Store

The collection store extends the functionality of the object store by organizing objects into *collections* and indexing them using one or more *indexes*. Collections contain objects, which can be accessed using smart pointers. Applications can create one or more indexes on a collection, which are maintained automatically during updates of objects in the collection. The indexes can be created and removed dynamically. Objects in a collection can be accessed using exact match, range or scan queries.

The collection store is designed to achieve maximal flexibility by supporting multiple indexes per collection, dynamic index creation and removal, automatic index maintenance in presence of key updates, type-checked object insertion and querying. However, we considered the overhead of requiring applications to use a separate database language that would be compiled by TDB to be unreasonable for most DRM applications and an unnecessary increase in the complexity of the collection store implementation. Instead, we achieve flexibility through a combination of C++ templatized classes, C++ RTTI and use of *functional indexes* [8] (indexes on derived values).

4.1 Specification

A *collection* is a set of objects that share one or more indexes. All objects in a collection must inherit from a common superclass, the *collection schema class*, which is associated with the collection. The database schema can be evolved by subclassing the collection schema class. However, the collection store can only index the data members that are defined in the collection schema class. An *index* maps keys to their corresponding objects.

The collection store implements functional indexes. Keys in functional indexes are generated by applying an *extractor function* to objects in a collection. The extractor function must be pure, that is, its output should depend solely on its input. One of the main benefits of using functional indexes in TDB is the compact key representation using a C++ function.

Applications can create new collections, create and remove indexes from existing collections, insert and delete objects from collections and enumerate collection objects using iterators, which implement scan, exact-match and range queries. The iterators can be dereferenced in either read-only or writable modes to obtain smart pointers to the objects.

In Figure 2 we illustrate the interface of collection store using a simple example based on the classes defined in Figure 1.

```
// Create a new collection called profile that contains meters.
Int idEx( Meter& m ) { return m._viewCount; }  // extractor function
Transaction t;
Indexer<Meter,Int,idEx> indexer(nonUnique, B-tree);
WritableRef<Collection> profile = t->createCollection("profile", &indexer );

profile->insert(&t, new Meter());  // Insert a new Meter object to the profile collection.

// Reset view counts of all Meter objects in the profile collection with view count > 100
Iterator* i = profile->query(&t,&indexer,100,plusInfinity);
for( ; !i->end(); i->next() ){
    WritableRef<Meter> m = i->openWritable(); m->_viewCount = 0;
}
t.commit();
```

Fig. 2. Sample usage of the collection store interface.

4.2 Implementation

The collection store is implemented on top of the object store. Collections, indexers and index nodes are represented as objects and are updated in transactions. This means that even the index nodes are locked according to the strict two-phase policy, which is a reasonable tradeoff for simplicity in DRM database systems that do not need to support many concurrent users. Below we provide some details of the implementation.

Iterator Sensitivity to Updates A common problem in implementing iterators is their sensitivity to updates performed by the same transaction while the iterator is open. A special case of this problem is the Halloween syndrome [7], where an application updates an index key that is used as an access path for the iterator, which may lead to indefinite iteration. The collection store implements insensitive iterators, i.e., applications do not see the effects of their updates while the iterator remains open. Compared to database systems that themselves compile queries and updates, the collection store has no control over which index is used to query a collection. Consequently, the collection store cannot avoid the Halloween syndrome by selecting an appropriate index.

The collection store enforces several constraints that together guarantee iterator insensitivity:

1. No other iterators on the same collection can be open when an iterator is dereferenced in writable mode.
2. Iterators can only be advanced in a single direction.
3. Index maintenance is deferred until iterator close.

The first constraint isolates the state of each iterator from updates performed in other iterators that were opened by the same transaction. The second and third constraints protect the state of each iterator from the effects of its own updates. In particular, the third constraint prevents the Halloween syndrome.

Index Maintenance. The collection store updates all indexes on a collection when an iterator is closed to guarantee iterator insensitivity. For each iterator, the collection store maintains a list of ids of objects that were dereferenced in writable mode using the iterator. The list is used to redo all index updates when the corresponding iterator is closed. Index updates are complicated by the fact that the collection store cannot statically determine which of the indexes will require an update. The application can call any public method on objects that it dereferenced in writable mode, which in turn may affect any of the indexed keys.

For each object dereferenced in writable mode, the collection store determines which of the indexes needs to be updated by comparing snapshots of all indexed keys before and after each object is updated. The post-update key snapshot can be easily obtained during an iterator close by calling all extractor functions on the object version in the object store cache. The pre-update key snapshot is stored along with the ids of updated objects prior to returning a writable reference to an application.

5 Code Footprint

TDB is designed as an embedded database system for DRM applications. Consequently, its code footprint is an important design constraint. In Figure 3 we compare the code footprint of TDB against other embedded database systems. The comparison is based on the size of the .text segment on the x86 platform using Visual C++ 6.0 compiler. The .text segment typically represents the bulk of static memory space requirement of the system. As shown in Figure 3, TDB's footprint is comparable to other embedded database systems, although it delivers more functionality. TDB can also trade off functionality for performance: Its minimal configuration, requires only 142 KB space of static memory space.

6 Performance

We compared the performance of TDB with Berkeley DB 3.0.55 [11] using the TPC-B benchmark [6]. We chose Berkeley DB as a yardstick because it is widely

db name	.text size (KB)	TDB module name	.text size (KB)
Berkeley DB [11]	186	collection store	45
C-ISAM [5]	344	object store	41
Faircom [4]	211	backup store	22
RDB [3]	284	chunk store	115
TDB - all modules	250	support utilities	27

Fig. 3. Code footprint size.

used in many applications. We chose TPC-B, which is a dated benchmark, because the Berkeley DB distribution includes an implementation of a TPC-B driver, which we assume is efficient. Therefore, we avoided optimizing a system we do not understand.

6.1 Platform

All experiments were run on a 733 MHZ Pentium 3 with 256 MB of RAM, running Windows NT 4.0. Both database systems used files created on a NTFS on an EIDE disk with 8.9 ms (read) and 10.9 ms (write) seek time, 7200 rpm (4.2 ms average rotational latency), and a 2MB disk controller cache. The one-way counter was emulated as a file on the same NTFS partition. In all experiments we configured both database systems to use 4MB of cache, which is the default for BerkleyDB implementation of TPC-B.

6.2 Setup

We conducted two experiments to compare performance of the two database systems. In the first experiment we compared the average response time for a transaction of Berkeley DB to TDB with security (TDB-S) and without security (TDB). We configured the security parameters of TDB-S to use SHA-1 for hashing and 3DES for encryption. In this experiment we configured the maximum database utilization (i.e., the maximal fraction of the database files that contain live chunks) at 60%, which is the default for TDB. In the second experiment we studied the impact of database utilization level on performance and space efficiency of TDB (without security) because the database utilization has been shown to greatly effect the performance of log-structured systems [10].

6.3 Results

The results from the first experiment can be found in Figure 4. The average response time per transaction for TDB was approximately 56% of that of Berkeley

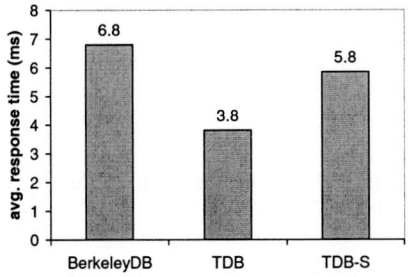

Fig. 4. Performance of Berkeley DB, TDB and TDB-S.

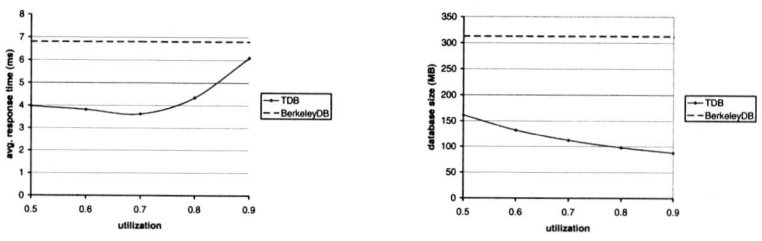

Fig. 5. Performance and database size vs. utilization.

DB. Surprisingly, even the average response time for TDB-S was only about 85% of that of BerkeleyDB. The large difference in response time is largely because Berkeley DB writes approximately twice as much data per transaction as TDB (1100 bytes vs. 523 bytes, on average).

The results for the second experiment can be found in Figure 5. The initial response time decrease is caused by an improvement of file-system cache efficiency with each block containing more useful data. Even at a utilization levels approaching 90%, TDB performed comparably to Berkeley DB. Figure 5 also shows the rate at which the resulting database size decreases as utilization increases. The size for Berkeley DB remains constant because it did not checkpoint the log during the benchmark.

References

1. D. Aucsmith. Tamper resistant software: an implementation. In *Proc. International Workshop on Information Hiding,* 1996. Cambridge, UK.
2. C. Collberg, C. Thomborson, and D. Low. Manufacturing cheap, resilient, and stealthy opaque constructs. In *Proceedings of the ACM Conference on Principles of Programming Languages,* 1998. San Diego, CA.
3. Centura Software Corp. RDM (database manager). available at www.centurasoft.com/products/databases/rdm, November 2000.
4. Faircom Corp. C-Tree Plus. available at www.faircom.com/product_tech/ctree/c-tree.html, 2000.
5. Informix Corp. C-ISAM. available at www.informix.com/informix/techbriefs/cisam/cisam.htm, 2000.
6. J. Gray. *The Benchmark Handbook For Databse and Transaction Processing Systems.* Morgan Kaufmann, 1991.
7. J. Gray and A. Reuter. *Transaction Processing: Concepts and Techniques.* Morgan Kaufmann, 1993.
8. A. Kemper, C. Kilger, and G. Moerkotte. Function materialization in object bases. In *Proceedings of the ACM SIGMOD International Conference on Management of Data,* 1991.
9. U. Maheshwari, R. Vingralek, and W. Shapiro. How to build a trusted database system on untrusted storage. In *Proceedings of the 4th Symposium on Operating Systems Design and Implementation,* 2000. San Diego, CA.

10. M. Rosenblum and J. Ousterhout. The design and implementation of a log-structured file system. In *Proceedings of the 13th ACM Symposium on Operating Systems Principles,* 1991. Pacific Grove, CA.
11. M. Seltzer and M. Olson. Challenges in embedded database system administration. In *Proceeding of the Embedded System Workshop,* 1999. Cambridge, MA (software available at www.sleepycat.com).
12. Infineon Technologies. Eurochip II – SLE 5536. available at www.infineon.com/cgi/ecrm.dll/ecrm/scripts/prod_ov.jsp?/oid=14702&/cat_oid=-8233, November 2000.

Content Schema Evolution in the CoreMedia® Content Application Platform CAP

Axel Wienberg[1,2], Matthias Ernst[1], Andreas Gawecki[1],
Olaf Kummer[1], Frank Wienberg[1], and Joachim W. Schmidt[2]

[1] CoreMedia AG,
Erste Brunnenstr. 1, Hamburg, Germany
axel.wienberg@coremedia.com, http://www.coremedia.com
[2] Software Systems Institute (AB 4.02),
Harburger Schloßstr. 20, TUHH Hamburg
sts-office@tu-harburg.de, http://www.sts.tu-harburg.de

Abstract. Based on experience gathered with several releases of the CoreMedia Content Application Platform (CAP), we argue that a modern, generalized Content Management System should, as database systems do, support explicit *content schemata*. To control the inevitable *evolution* of the content schema, the schema should be subject to *configuration management* together with the actual content. We propose a two-layered approach to content schema evolution consisting of
- a system level responsible for bookkeeping and integrity issue detection, and
- a semi-automatic application level responsible for resolving schema-related issues.

A prototype using the proposed approach has been successfully implemented at CoreMedia.

1 Introduction and Motivation

Simply put, a Web Content Management System (WCMS) addresses the desire to produce larger and better web sites more quickly. A WCMS does this by combining the following partial solutions:

Multi user access. Large web sites are developed collaboratively by several users whose access has to be coordinated and controlled [1]. WCMSs usually do this by offering exclusive locks on individual documents (check in / check out), by verifying proper authorization, and by versioning, i.e., immutably recording versions and thereby tracking changes to the content.

Separation of content and layout. Users have specialized roles and responsibilities with respect to the web site, e.g., text editor, designer, programmer, and administrator. A WCMS therefore tries to structure the information so that different roles can work as independently as possible, e.g., allowing a text editor to focus on producing text without bothering with layout.

The actual web site is generated from a content base using templates which select and combine the content. For example, navigation bars are computed from the current position in the navigation hierarchy, a center pane receives article full text, and a side bar features related content.

Quality assurance. Material published on a web site immediately goes public. To exploit the web's potential for up-to-date information, publication should be as fast as possible. On the other hand, published material should adhere to certain quality standards, at minimum contain no spelling mistakes, dangling links, or broken HTML. WCMSs solve this in three ways: firstly, by offering tools for consistency checking (e.g., spell checking and link management); secondly, by offering staging: Two copies of the entire site are maintained, a production copy for editing and preview, and a live copy that is updated only by publicizing content from the production copy;[1] and thirdly, by defining editorial workflows, requiring at least one other person to counter-check each change before it is publicized.

Around these core features there are important classes of applications whose requirements shape the WCMS. Sometimes these applications are also considered part of the WCMS itself.

Content syndication. The production of high-quality content covering diverse areas is complex and expensive. Many web sites therefore reuse existing content bought from third parties, while selling their specialized content contributions. A WCMS typically supports this by offering import and export of content in a neutral format, allowing content to be integrated into a customer's site using the customer's own layout.

Personalization. Adapting the content presented on a web site to the current customer increases attractivity and accessibility of the site. WCMS therefore often interface to user management, session tracking and profiling components. The responsibility of the WCMS in this application is to structure the content in sufficient detail to allow the automatic selection of content items, and to dynamically create coherent web pages presenting the selected items.

How can research and development in computer science help to find generalized solutions to these problems, turning a WCMS into a Content Application Platform? The problem of coordinating multi-user authoring of sets of files has been covered in science and practice under the topic of configuration management[2, 3]. The management of links suggests ingredients from the area of hypertext research; taken together, this results in versioned hypertext [4, 5].

However, the content is not just meant for access by human users but is also the data on which import, export and integrity checking tools as well as the personalization service operate. This warrants an analysis of a web site's content needs using database and software engineering methods and notations such as the UML [6]. Using an explicit schema brings us close to object-oriented databases, especially versioned databases, and presents the problem of schema evolution [7–9].

---

[1] Staging also serves security purposes: By physically separating production and live system on different machines, the production area can be protected from the Wild Wild Web behind firewalls.

We begin by examining the notion of a Content Schema in section 2, and present our meta-model for schema and content in section 3. In section 4, we turn to the topic of Content Configuration Management, putting it in relation to schema evolution. On this basis, our two-layered approach to content schema evolution is described in section 5. Section 6 concludes the paper with a summary.

2 Content Schema

In our approach, a content schema is explicitly defined, stored in, and understood by the Content Management System. Content objects are classified by their structure, and their properties and associations are defined.

Some Content Management Systems come with a predefined schema tailored to the specific target domain of that system. In contrast, CoreMedia CAP aims to be an application *platform*, providing the basic services and frameworks upon which various applications can be built. Therefore, the schema needs to be a variable, with a concrete schema developed and adapted on a per project basis. The schema and structure for a web site is usually created by starting from a "best practice" sample solution and modifying it until it fits the site's requirements.[2]

Many of the general arguments [6] for using a modelling language can be directly applied to content modelling. However, developing a good schema takes time and expertise. We believe that this up-front investment is amortized as soon as the aggregated content reaches a volume that can only be managed using automated tools, or even earlier when sophisticated export and import transformations are applied to the content for presentation and syndication.

A schema is almost impossible to get right on the first attempt; due to initial lack of understanding, and also due to changing application requirements, the schema continues to change even when the web site is already in production.[3] We therefore state that content schema evolution should be possible and nondisruptive even when a considerable volume of content has already accumulated.

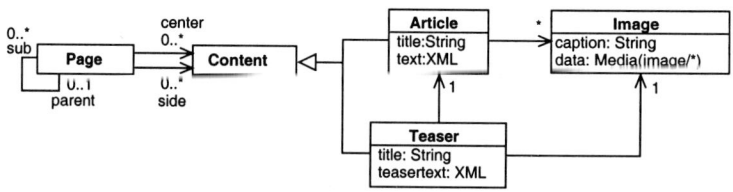

Fig. 1. A simple Content Schema, represented as UML

---

[2] The AutoWeb [10] and Araneus [11] systems also follow a schema-driven approach; Their approach is complementary in that these systems focus on specifying and modelling presentation and navigation, while we focus on content management, and consider schema evolution and configuration management.

[3] This was also frequently observed for relational and object-oriented databases.[8]

In OODBs, schema evolution is mostly concerned with always presenting the database in the shape of a current schema, either by emulating the new schema through views, or by automatically migrating instances. However, humans are generally flexible enough to handle content that deviates from the schema. Humans are also slow enough that large-scale modifications involving human interaction lead to extended periods of inconsistency. And, schema changes are generally complex enough to require human intervention. Therefore, inconsistent intermediate states will need to be managed persistently by the system. Obviously, the automated parts of the system will not be fully functional during these inconsistent periods, but the core components need to be sufficiently operational that inconsistencies can be resolved.

There are systems that claim to do Content Management, but do not model the actual content at all. Instead, these systems just store binary objects in application specific formats, mixing content and layout. We would rather describe those systems as document management systems. A document management system is only concerned with internal structure of the stored files as far as needed for retrieval (extracting some meta data, or words for full text search). Documents rarely link to other documents; relations are only established by categorization and similarity of extracted meta information. Transformation and presentation of documents into hypertext (e.g., WWW) format is difficult, and is often not done at all: Instead, the system presents an HTML front end for navigating the document space. This must not be confused with Content Management, which involves the detailed construction of web pages (and other output formats) integrating fragments of different content objects, and therefore requires a much more fine-grained understanding of content by the system.

3 The CoreMedia Meta-model

In this section, we describe our meta-model, i.e., our language for expressing a schema and for expressing content. As shown in Fig. 2, the model chosen is basically object-oriented, implementing a subset of UML. Objects are the semantic unit for reference, locking, and versioning. Objects are classified in a single-inheritance type hierarchy, which prescribes the expected object properties.

A number of constraints relate the schema to the instances. These rules have been formalized for our prototype. We only give natural language examples here:

- An object only binds properties declared in its declared type or a supertype thereof.
- If a property p is declared as *non-nullable*, then it must be bound in all instances of p's declared type, and all instances of transitive subtypes thereof.
- For all targets t in a binding of a link property p, the declared type of t is a transitive subtype of or equal to the target type of p.
- The number of targets in a binding of a link property p is not less than p's minimum cardinality and is not larger than p's maximum cardinality.

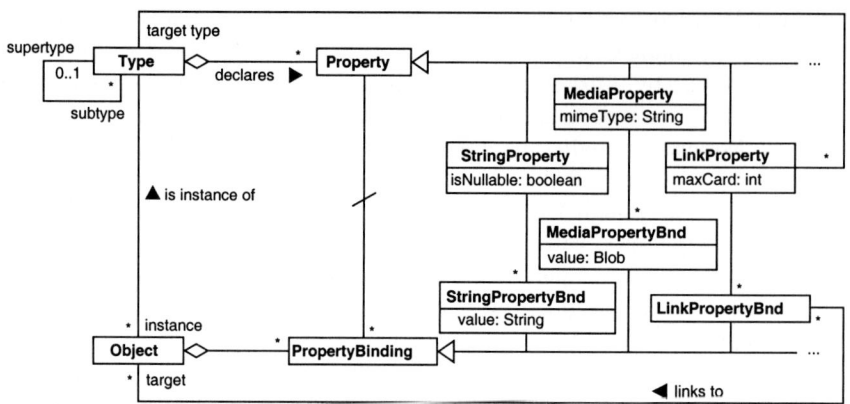

Fig. 2. UML class diagram for the meta-model (simplified)

We decided not to use an XML approach, because as a producer of enterprise level software, CoreMedia has to apply proven storage technology, i.e., relational databases. Objects can store XML in media properties, however structural and partial access to XML is not directly supported by the system.

4 Content Configuration Management

The requirements for quality control and multi-user access put forth in section 1 fit well into the general context of Software Configuration Management (SCM), from where additional concepts can be borrowed and applied back to Content Management Systems. We call this Content Configuration Management (CCM).

Among other things, configuration management is concerned with the reproducible construction of versions of a product, and its controlled evolution into new versions. Controlled evolution requires change management, status accounting, audit and review, some form of workflow support, and team work [2].

An SCM concept applicable to CCM is that of the *workspace* (also known as *long-term transaction*), where a user or a group of users work together on advancing the web site in some direction. Changes can be applied to all objects making up the product, but remain local to the workspace until explicitly transferred to another workspace. This allows to review changes in context, detecting subtle side-effects. Conversely, it allows to temporarily ignore changes applied in other workspaces. Since development happens in parallel, there is a potential for incompatible changes. These conflicts have to be resolved, generally involving user interaction, but also involving tool support for visualizing the changes and proposing merges.

An important difference between CCM and SCM is that CCM deals with explict links between the versioned objects, firstly because of the web's hypertext links, and secondly because of structured content modelling.

Storing links to fixed versions could lead to a proliferation of versions in the referring or aggregating objects, because for every new version of the link target, the link source would have to be updated as well. Instead, the version of the target object to use is resolved depending on context (in our case, the current workspace).[4]

4.1 Using Workspaces in Content Management

With the background of Configuration Management, we see that the WCMS notion of *staging* mentioned in section 1 is just a special case of applying workspaces. The production copy of the web site becomes a production workspace, and the live copy is another workspace that is only accessed by merging updates from the production workspace.

As soon as developments begin to interfere, the creation of additional workspaces becomes worthwhile. If the site layout is represented as content, then we do not want broken intermediate layout versions to appear on the web site, nor do we want broken layout to block the authoring of content. As shown in Fig. 3, this is solved by introducing an additional layout *development* workspace, with only stable layout states being merged into the content *production* workspace, and from there to the *live* site.

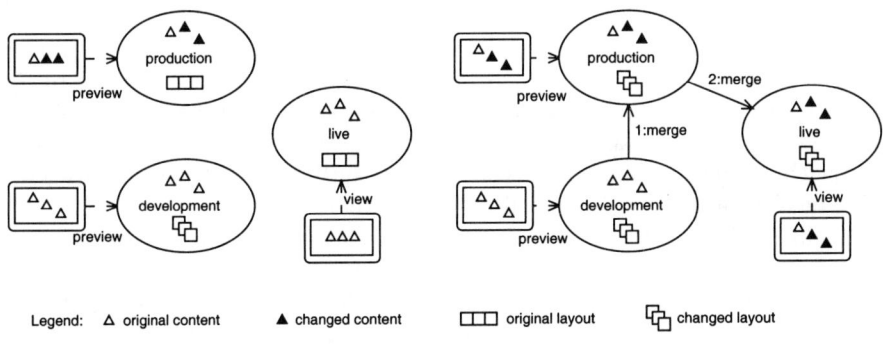

Fig. 3. Concurrent evolution of content and layout

Refinements include the introduction of an additional quality assurance staging level, and the introduction of an additional level of layout or editorial workspaces responsible for specific independent areas of the web site, increasing parallelism and protecting from unwanted interference, but decreasing awareness and provoking later merging problems. [14].

---

[4] In the terminology of versioned object-oriented databases, the version resolution context is also called a *database version*[12, 13].

4.2 Versioning the Schema

As stated in section 2, a Content Application Platform needs to support an explicitly stored, evolving schema. This problem has been thoroughly researched within the object-oriented database community [7, 8]; however, in concert with merging, and due to the more fuzzy nature of content compared with computational objects, our focus is different again.

When updating a workspace with changes from another workspace, we naturally expect schema changes to be applied as well. This configuration management functionality requires recording multiple versions of and changes to the schema.

The schema is in fact an aggregation of several meta objects, namely types and property declarations, interconnected by inheritance and association. So the first question is, at what granularity do we record schema versions? We might version only the complete schema [15], closed under the mentioned relationships, with the advantage that types can be seen in context. However, this approach cannot be maintained when independent modifications to the schema are to be merged – for example, when two new types are independently added to the schema. A merge tool should recognize the modifications as affecting disjoint meta objects, and therefore potentially being compatible.

We therefore version each meta object separately, and consider a schema version to be an aggregation of individual versions. Associations between meta objects are treated just like links between content objects: The version of the target object to use is determined by the workspace, not by the link.

This, however, may violate of meta-level integrity constraints when seemingly independent changes are applied. For example, when combining changes to the inheritance hierarchy, a merge may produce cycles. In order to allow manual resolution of integrity violations of this type, the system will not only have to cope with objects not matching their schema, but even with the schema itself being inconsistent during extended periods of time.

Realizing that, just like content, the schema is actively developed even when a project is already in production, and realizing that schema and content are developed together and mutually influence each other, we directly apply the mechanisms that have proven successful for collaborative work on content to work on the schema, relaxing the distinction between schema and content—for us, the schema *is* content.

5 A Two-Layered Approach to Content Schema Evolution

Our approach to content schema evolution divides the problem into two layers: A system level responsible for storage, bookkeeping and integrity issue detection, and a semi-automatic application level responsible for resolving schema-related issues.

5.1 System Layer

The system layer has the following responsibilites: keeping up its *storage* functionality independent of the user-defined schema, *bookkeeping* concerning the changes applied to content and schema, and detecting the *integrity issues* caused by a change.

Storage. The store is concerned with the schema only as far as the schema affects the format of the data to be made persistent. In this way, the store implements an "emergency power semantics": It continues to function if the stored content and the user-defined schema deviate, and even if the user-defined schema itself is inconsistent; therefore the application layer can always escape from any inconsistency, and move the content base back into a consistent state.

Any integrity constraint that involves mutable properties of at least two objects may be violated by an unfortunate merge or during an intermediate evolution state, and therefore must not be guaranteed by the store. The inheritance relation between types, the set of properties declared by a type, and the attributes of property declarations shown in Fig. 2 are all mutable and versioned (compare section 4.2). All constraints involving this information apply at least to the instance object and the meta object, and therefore have to be ignored on the storage level. This means that the store cannot use the set of properties inherited by a type to determine the shape of the type's instances. The set of properties bound by an object has to be stored individually for each object. The store only depends on the constant *class* of property declarations, which determines the format of the values bound by that property. The user-defined schema may still be used as a hint for optimization, offering sufficient performance without sacrificing flexibility.

Bookkeeping. The user-defined schema is stored as objects, instances of predefined, immutable meta-types. It is therefore subject to check-in/check-out access control and versioning just like regular content objects: all changes are recorded, when merging them between workspaces at the latest. Recorded states of individual objects and aggregates can be retrieved and compared later on the application level.

If possible, the store allows the interpretation of previously stored data according to an evolved schema, by delivering default values for absent properties, implementing a simple view. In this way, the creation of additional versions is avoided, which simplifies (or avoids) merging. This is necessary especially when a schema update is merged into a busy production workspace; in this case, editorial work is disturbed as little as possible.

Integrity Issues. The part of the system level closest to the application level is the integrity issue detection. To detect integrity issues, the system interprets the rules expressed in the user-defined schema (if possible), applies them to the content base, and reports any violations. Checks are performed incrementally for efficiency reasons.

Since all intra-schema integrity constraints can be expressed using an immutable meta-schema, integrity issues in the user-defined schema are reported like any other integrity issue. To avoid reporting aftereffects, integrity issues in instances of a type are suppressed if the type itself has issues.

It is possible to preclude integrity issues in certain workspaces, most importantly in live workspaces accessible by a public audience. Any merge attempt that would cause an integrity issue in such a workspace gives an error message to the user, who must resolve the issue in the production workspace.

5.2 Application Layer

The application layer is responsible for reacting to schema problems by

- analyzing the change history, and evaluating problems in context,
- determining a course of action, probably by proposing different solutions to the user, and
- implementing the resolution of schema issues by migrating content or merging incompatible schema changes.

Automated support for analyzing schema changes is feasible, even for changes involving multiple types and their relation to each other, as demonstrated in the TESS system [9]. Still, a human operator has to verify the proposed transformer before it is applied to the contents.

Human interaction is also required when the modified schema demands additional information not computable from the current state of the content objects, for example because the changes relate to "fuzzy" data like natural language text properties. In this case, editorial work is unavoidable.

6 Summary and Concluding Remarks

In this paper we claim that a Content Application Platform should maintain content schemata but be able to handle long-term content schema violations. Even if schema evolution within a workspace might be possible using consistency-maintaining atomic operations, schema-related cross-workspace operations such as the following require user interaction:

- instance migration after schema evolution induced by a merge from another workspace (because the exact sequence of schema operations may not be available and may not be definitely reconstructible);
- conflict resolution between the local schema and a schema merged from another workspace (because even if the exact sequence of operations in the source workspace is known, the operations may not be compatible with local modifications).

In our approach this is achieved by allowing each object in an integration workspace to have an individual shape, independent of the type it aims to conform to eventually. When all issues are resolved, the integrated result is transferred to a public (non-integration) workspace, implementing a strict schema interpretation. In this way we hope to have found a balance between the semistructured world of content, where ultimately only human users can decide how to proceed, and the structured world of databases with its potential for automation and efficiency.

References

1. Goland, Y., Whitehead, E., Faizi, A., Carter, S., Jensen, D.: HTTP Extensions for Distributed Authoring – WebDAV. IETF RFC 2518, Standards Track, Proposed Standard (1999)
2. Dart, S.: Concepts in configuration management systems. In: Proc. 3rd int'l workshop on Software Configuration Management, ACM Press, New York (1991) 1–18
3. Conradi, R., Westfechtel, B.: Version models for software configuration management. Technical Report AIB 96-10, RWTH Aachen (1996)
4. Halasz, F.: Reflections on NoteCards: seven issues for the next generation of hypermedia systems. Communications of the ACM **31** (1988) 836–852
5. Haake, A., Hicks, D.: Verse: Towards hypertext versioning styles. In: Proc. 7th ACM Conf. on Hypertext, ACM Press, New York (1996) 224–234
6. OMG: Unified Modeling Language (UML), version 1.4 (2001) http://www.omg.org/technology/documents/formal/uml.htm.
7. Kim, W., Chou, H.T.: Versions of Schema for Object-Oriented Databases. In: Proc. 14th Intl. Conf. on Very Large Data Bases (VLDB), Los Angeles, USA, ACM SIGMOD (1988) 148–159
8. Roddick, J.F.: A survey of schema versioning issues for database systems. Information and Software Technology **37** (1995) 383–393
9. Lerner, B.S.: TESS: Automated support for the evolution of persistent types. In: Proc. 12th Automated Software Engineering Conf., Lake Tahoe, Nevada (1997)
10. Fraternali, P., Paolini, P.: Model-driven development of web applications: the AutoWeb system. ACM TOIS **18** (2000) 323–382
11. Mecca, G., Atzeni, P., Masci, A., Merialdo, P., Sindoni, G.: The araneus web-base management system. In: Proc. SIGMOD'98, Exhibits Program. (1998) 554–546
12. Cellary, W., Jomier, G.: Consistency of versions in object-oriented databases. In McLeod, D., Sacks-Davis, R., Schek, H.J., eds.: Proc. 16th Int'l Conf. on Very Large Data Bases, Morgan Kaufmann (1990) 432–441
13. Bellosta, M.J., Wrembel, R., Jomier, G.: Management of schema versions and versions of schema instance in a multiversion database. Technical Report Verso Report number 99, INRIA Rocquencourt, France (1996)
14. Appleton, B., Berczuk, S.P., Cabrera, R., Orenstein, R.: Streamed lines: Branching patterns for parallel software development. In: Proceedings of PLoP '98, published as TR #WUCS-98-25, Washington Univ., Dept. of Computer Science (1998)
15. Odberg, E.: A Global Perspective of Schema Modification Management for Object-Oriented Databases. In: Proc. 6th Int'l Workshop on Persistent Object Systems (POS), Tarascon, Provence, France (1994) 479–502

Gene Expression Data Management: A Case Study

Victor M. Markowitz, I-Min A. Chen, and Anthony Kosky

Gene Logic Inc., Data Management Systems
2001 Center Street, Berkeley, CA 94704, U.S.A.
{victor, ichen, anthony}@genelogic.com

Abstract. One of the major challenges facing scientists dealing with gene expression data is how to integrate, explore and analyze vast quantities of related data, often residing in multiple heterogeneous data repositories. In this paper we describe the problems involved in managing gene expression data and discuss how these problems have been addressed in the context of Gene Logic's GeneExpress system. The GeneExpress system provides support for the integration of gene expression, gene annotation and sample (clinical) data with various degrees of heterogeneity, and for effective exploration of these data.

1. Introduction

DNA microarray technologies allow measurement of mRNA expression levels, that is the degree to which a gene is expressed within a cell or tissue sample, for tens of thousands of genes in parallel [7]. In order to associate biological meaning with these data, it is necessary to associate them with sample data and gene annotations. In this paper we discuss the management of gene expression, sample and gene annotation data in the context of Gene Logic's GeneExpress data management system [4]. The GeneExpress system contains quantitative gene expression information on normal and diseased tissues, and on experimental animal model and cellular tissues, subject to a variety of treated and untreated conditions. Most of Gene Logic's expression data are generated using the Affymetrix GeneChip technology [6] in a high throughput production environment. The system also contains comprehensive information on samples, clinical profiles and rich gene annotations.

This paper focuses on the data integration problems encountered with GeneExpress. Data integration for molecular biology applications has gained a great deal of attention (see, for example, the papers published in [9]), and many of the problems described in this paper apply to such applications. Solutions traditionally discussed in the literature for molecular biology data integration applications involve various degrees of resolution for semantic data heterogeneity, and different types of data access mechanisms (see, for example [3] for a description of a system that supports distributed querying across heterogeneous molecular biology data sources).

Initially the GeneExpress system was developed with the goal of supporting effective exploration and analysis of gene expression data generated at Gene Logic using the Affymetrix GeneChip platform. Achieving this goal required (1) resolution of problems related to the semantic heterogeneity of gene expression, sample and gene annotation data, and (2) development of a high performance data exploration mechanism with centralized access to the integrated data.

A subsequent goal set for the GeneExpress system was to provide support for gene expression data generated outside of Gene Logic, possibly using different technologies. Addressing this additional goal required resolution of further semantic heterogeneity problems related to the integration of gene expression data (often generated under different experimental conditions), sample data, and gene annotations, while using the same centralized data exploration mechanism for the integrated data. Both of these goals have been addressed using a data warehousing methodology [2] adapted to the special traits of the gene expression domain [8]. GeneExpress also involves a data acquisition component designed to support data content collection for gene expression, sample, and gene annotation data.

The remainder of this paper is organized as follows. In section 2 we describe the key characteristics of the data involved in a gene expression application. In section 3 we describe the GeneExpress data management system developed at Gene Logic, and the data integration tasks performed in order to build a GeneExpress product containing native Gene Logic data. In section 4 we discuss the problems of integrating gene expression data from sources outside Gene Logic into GeneExpress and describe the mechanisms that address these problems. We conclude with a brief discussion and summary in section 5.

2. The Gene Expression Application

Gene expression applications involve exploring biological sample, gene annotation and gene expression data, each of which is sufficiently complex to warrant modeling it as a separate data space [8].

Biological samples may be collected from a variety of sources, such as hospitals or laboratories. The main object in the sample data space is the *sample* representing a biological material that is involved in an experiment. A sample can be of tissue, cell or processed RNA type, and originates from a donor of a given species (e.g., human, mouse, rat). Attributes associated with samples describe their structural and morphological characteristics (e.g., organ site, diagnosis, disease, stage of disease), and their donor data (e.g., demographic and clinical record for human donors, or strain, genetic modification and treatment information for animal donors). Samples may also be grouped into *studies* which may be further subdivided, based on their time/treatment parameters, in order to form *study groups*. The core of the sample data structure is illustrated in Figure 1.

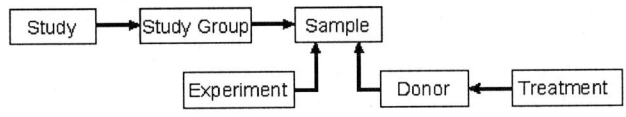

Fig. 1. Sample Data Structure

Gene expression data may be generated using a variety of technologies such as different microarray platforms, and employing different algorithms for interpreting these data. For microarray data, the main object in the gene expression data space is the estimated *expression value* for a given gene or EST fragment and sample, generated using a specific microarray experiment. Data generated from microarray experiments range from raw data, such as images generated by scanners, to analyzed data, such as quantitative gene expression measurements derived using various analysis methods.

For example, each Affymetrix GeneChip probe array contains a number of *probes* designed to bind to a particular sequence occurring within a known target mRNA fragment, which, in turn, is representative of a gene or EST of interest. Affymetrix' analysis software derives intensities for each probe by averaging the values for pixels corresponding to an individual probe in the scanned image, and then applies *analysis methods* to derive summary data for each target gene or EST fragment. The summary data generated includes expression present/absent (P/A) calls and quantitative gene expression measurements. Different analysis methods may also be applied in order to find alternative expression measurements.

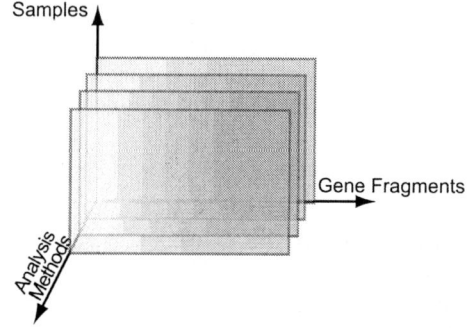

Fig. 2. Gene Expression multi-dimensional array

The gene expression data may be represented by a three-dimensional matrix, with two axes representing gene fragments (identified by their target sequence and the microarray type) and samples, and a third axis representing different analysis methods (see Figure 2).

Gene annotations are collected from various public and proprietary genomic resources. The main object in the gene annotation data space is the *gene fragment*, representing an entity for which the expression level is being determined as described above. For microarray technologies, gene fragments are associated with a specific microarray type, such as a GeneChip human probe array (e.g. HG_U95A). The annotations associated with a gene fragment describe its biological context, including its associated primary EST sequence entry in Genbank, membership in a gene-oriented sequence cluster, association with a known gene (i.e., a gene that is recorded in an official nomenclature catalogue, such as the Human Gene Nomenclature Database [5]), functional characterization, and known metabolic pathways. The core of the gene annotation data structure is illustrated in Figure 3.

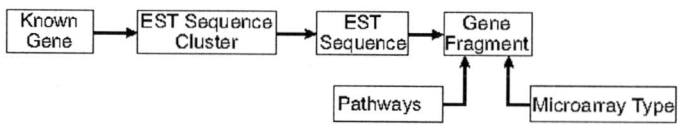

Fig. 3. Gene Annotation Data Structure

3. Primary Gene Expression Data Integration

Gene Logic's expression data are generated mainly using the Affymetrix GeneChip platform in a high throughput production environment, and are managed using the GeneExpress system. This system includes a data acquisition system for sample, gene annotation and gene expression data, a data warehouse providing support for data exploration, and data transfer and integration mechanisms for migrating data from the data acquisition system into the data warehouse (see Figure 4).

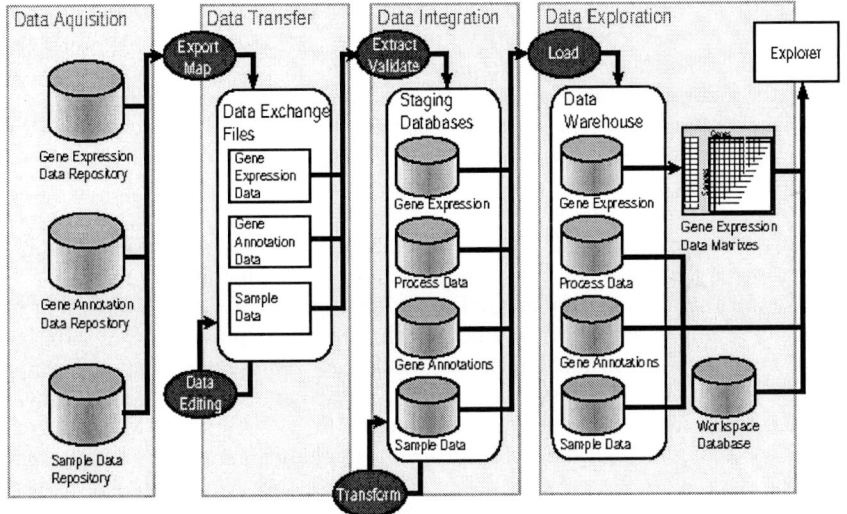

Fig. 4. The main components of the GeneExpress Data Management System

The GeneExpress Data Acquisition System (GXDAS) consists of operational databases and laboratory information management system (LIMS) applications employed for data acquisition. Data management tools are used for ensuring data consistency, including checking the correct execution of the data migration and integration processes, and domain specific rules validating the sample, expression and gene annotation data.

Samples are collected from a variety of sources, such as hospitals and research centers, with sample information structured and encoded in heterogeneous formats. Format differences range from the type of data being captured to different controlled vocabularies used in order to represent anatomy, diagnoses, and medication. The *sample* component of GXDAS provides support for various sample data collection and quality control protocols, via data entry and reporting tools. This system uses domain specific vocabularies and taxonomies, such as SNOMED [11], to ensure consistency during data collection.

The *gene expression* component of GXDAS provides support for GeneChip-based production. Gene expression experiment data are recorded in GeneChip specific files containing: (i) the binary image of a scanned probe array; (ii) average intensities for the probes on the probe array; and (iii) expression values of gene fragments tested in the probe array. The GeneChip LIMS provides support for loading the data in these files into a relational database based on Affymetrix AADM representation [1], which is the main source for gene expression data.

The gene annotation component of GXDAS provides support for assembling consistent annotations for the gene fragments underlying gene expression experiments, by acquiring, integrating, and curating data from various, mainly public, data sources. Acquiring gene annotations from public data sources involves identifying important and reliable data sources, regularly querying these sources, parsing and interpreting the results, and establishing associations between related entities such as the correlation of gene fragments and known genes. Gene fragments are organized in non-redundant classes based on UniGene, which provides a partitioning of GenBank nucleotide sequences in gene-oriented non-redundant clusters[1], and are associated with known genes recorded in LocusLink, which provides curated sequence and descriptive information, such as official nomenclature, on genes[2]. Gene fragments are further associated with gene products (e.g., from SwissProt, a curated protein sequence database that includes the description of the function of a protein, etc.[3]), enzymes, pathways (e.g., metabolic, signaling pathways), chromosome maps, genomic contigs and cross-species gene homologies.

The GeneExpress Data Warehouse (GXDW) consists of integrated component databases containing sample, gene annotation and gene expression data, and information on the analysis methods employed for generating these data.

The gene expression data in GXDW is exported to a Gene Expression Array (GXA) that implements the multi-dimensional array shown in Figure 2, as a collection of two-dimensional matrices, with axes representing samples and gene fragments. Each matrix is associated with a particular GeneChip probe array type (e.g. HG_U95), and a particular analysis method (e.g. Affymetrix MAS4 analysis). The GXA provides the basis for efficient implementation of various analysis methods.

GXDW data is explored using the *GeneExpress Explorer* application, which provides support for constructing gene and sample sets, for analyzing gene expression data in the context of gene and sample sets, and for managing individual or group analysis workspaces. The results of gene expression exploration can be further examined in the context of gene annotations, such as metabolic pathways and chromosome cytogenetic maps. The results of gene data exploration can also be exported to third-party tools for visualization or further analysis.

The GeneExpress system also contains mechanisms for migrating sample, gene annotation and gene expression data from GXDAS to GXDW (see Figure 4). These mechanism employ staging databases, and support mapping, validation, integration and loading of sample, gene annotation and gene expression data into GXDW.

4. Secondary Gene Expression Data Integration

GeneExpress is generally provided to customers with gene expression data generated at Gene Logic based on samples acquired by Gene Logic. Some Gene Logic

---

[1] See http://www.ncbi.nlm.nih.gov/UniGene/
[2] See http://www.ncbi.nlm.nih.gov/LocusLink/index.html
[3] See http://www.expasy.ch/sprot/

customers also have their own internal efforts to generate gene expression data. Incorporating these data into GeneExpress allows Gene Logic and customer data to be analyzed together using the same tools.

The process of incorporating customer and other external data into GeneExpress requires data migration mechanisms similar to those described in section 3 for Gene Logic's internal data sources. However, data migration from external sources needs to deal with degrees of heterogeneity that are not known ahead of time and therefore are hard to predict and support using generic tools. We describe below mechanisms that allow data from external data sources to be incorporated into the GeneExpress Data Warehouse (GXDW).

4.1 Data Export and Mapping

In order to allow data from multiple data sources to be integrated into GXDW, data exchange formats have been defined for each data space involved in the application. Data exchange formats for sample, gene expression, and gene annotation data follow the general structure described in section 3:

1. The Sample Data Exchange Format involves object classes representing samples, donors, treatments, experiments, studies and study groups (see Figure 1).
2. The Gene Expression Data Exchange Format involves object classes representing gene expression values, analysis methods, and associations of individual gene expression values with samples and gene fragments (see Figure 2), as well as related experimental parameters.
3. The Gene Annotation Data Exchange Format involves object classes representing gene fragments, known genes, EST sequences, EST sequence clusters, pathways and microarray types (see Figure 3).

All data exchange formats contain a *"catch-all"* class which can accommodate any data, represented as tagged-value pairs, that does not otherwise fit the formats.

The most significant problems in importing data into GeneExpress are involved in mapping source data to the data exchange formats. Gene expression data have, in general, well-defined semantics and usually benefit from being represented in a standard (often platform specific) format, such as AADM [1]. Gene annotations also have well understood semantics, although there are ambiguities with regard to the classification of some of these annotations (see [10] for a discussion of problems associated with gene nomenclature and identification). The mapping for sample data is usually the most difficult since there is no widely accepted standard for representing clinical data (see [12], presentations at the working group on ontologies). We describe below some of the problems of exporting sample data into data exchange formats. Note that similar problems arise with gene annotation or expression data as well.

In order to map individual sample data values to the Sample Data Exchange Format it is first necessary to resolve differences of nomenclature, units and formatting. Differences in nomenclature are the most difficult to deal with, and often there is no single, optimal resolution for such differences. Various attributes in the data exchange formats are represented using controlled vocabularies. In particular, in the Sample Data Exchange Format, sample organ types, pathologies and disease diagnoses are represented using subsets of the SNOMED vocabulary [11]. Independent sample data repositories often use their own vocabularies for such concepts, and, even with a given standard such as SNOMED, different pathologists or other experts may not agree on which term should be used for a certain disease or organ type. Sample data may also differ in the choice of units: for example drug treatments can use units such as µMol or ng/ml, while age can be provided in days, weeks or years. A conversion table is required to map any units to comparable units in the Sample Data Exchange Format.

Formatting of individual items also needs to be resolved. For example the Sample Data Exchange Format may use the terms *Male* and *Female* to represent the sex of a donor, while a customer database may use *male* and *female*, or just *M* and *F*. Further, data may contain typographic errors, such as misspelling the name of a supplier. In some cases, when vocabularies are small, or for controlled vocabularies, it may be possible to spot and correct such errors manually, but in general, these errors are hard to spot and may go undetected.

Data from individual data sources may be supplied in a flattened or un-normalized form, such as Excel spreadsheets, so that determining their structure, and how best to map them to the various data exchange formats, is a complex task. First it is necessary to determine the identifiers and correlations between individual data objects, which are either provided during the data export process, or need to be determined by analyzing data patterns. In either case, it is necessary to confirm that the correlations found in the data fit the intended semantics of the data.

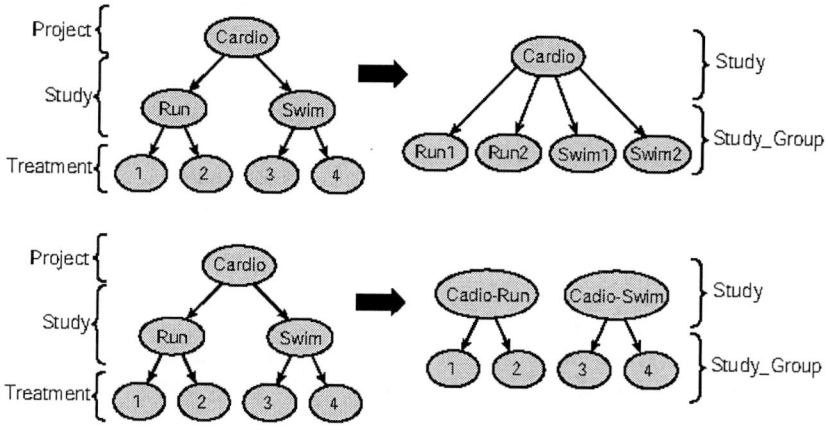

Fig. 5. Alternatives for flattening data from three levels into two

Object identifiers and correlations can be used to form an object model for the source data, and to define a mapping from this model to the data exchange formats. Defining such a mapping requires resolving structural conflicts between the models, and, in some cases, it may be necessary to choose between several possible solutions. For example, the GeneExpress Sample Data Exchange Format classifies samples in a two-level hierarchy, with the levels represented by classes *Study* and *Study-Group*. Sample data exported from an external data source may employ a three level hierarchy, such as *Project*, *Study* and *Treatment*. This difference in structure can be resolved in two ways: either combining the exported *Study* and *Treatment* classes into the Sample Data Exchange Format *Study-Group* class and mapping the exported

Project class to Sample Data Exchange Format *Study* class, or by mapping the exported *Project* and *Study* classes to Sample Data Exchange Format *Study* class, and the *Treatment* class to the *Study-Group* class. These two alternatives are illustrated in Figure 5. Note that the choice is neither obvious nor unique.

In addition to the problems described above, it is also necessary to deal with the evolution of databases and formats over time. Both the external data sources and the GeneExpress Data Warehouse may change either their structure or their controlled vocabularies or data formats, in order to reflect changes in requirements. These changes require updates to the mappings and integration tools.

4.2 Data Editing, Transformation and Loading

Once data from external data sources have been mapped to the data exchange formats, additional editing may be required before integrating and loading them into the warehouse.

First it is necessary to detect invalid data, such as missing or inconsistent data. In general the integration tools handle such cases by skipping the data effected by errors, and issuing warning messages in a log file. Data editing can be used in order to correct problems that have not been resolved during the mapping process, such as missing clinical data associated with samples and inconsistent associations of sample and gene expression data.

Next, it is necessary to resolve differences between identifiers of external objects and objects already in the warehouse in order to maintain database consistency. Transformations of this type are carried out using *staging databases*, before loading data into the warehouse.

Finally *derived data*, such as quality control data (e.g., measures of saturation for the scanners) are also computed during the transformation stage.

4.3 Data Integration Applications

Data from external data sources have been incorporated into GeneExpress as part of several integration projects. The complexity of an integration project is determined by a number of factors, including whether customer data is structured using a standard format (e.g. AADM) or using a loosely defined format (e.g. a spreadsheet); whether the data involves standard commercial probe arrays or custom probe arrays (which may involve specially designed sets of gene fragments); the richness of the sample data; and the frequency of updates required for the system.

All GeneExpress integration projects have involved exporting data from external sources into data exchange formats for sample, gene annotation and gene expression data. For most of these projects, the source of gene expression data was the GeneChip LIMS, and consequently AADM was used as the gene expression data exchange format, with straightforward data export and mapping. In one project, gene expression data was stored in a custom format, and consequently the expression data was loaded directly into GXA data files, bypassing the stage of loading it into the expression database component of GXDW. Data export and mapping for gene annotations have been limited to proprietary gene annotations and, in most cases, have involved straightforward mappings to the Gene Annotation Data Exchange

Format. The most difficult problem has been presented by the sample data as discussed in section 4.1.

An additional challenge of incorporating data from external sources into GeneExpress is presented by the need to asynchronously update the Gene Logic data and data from external sources. Gene Logic provides customers with periodic updates to the GeneExpress content, on a monthly, bi-monthly, or quarterly schedule. For a standard GeneExpress installation, these updates are carried out by replacing the GXDW and GXA instances with new versions. However, if customer data is incorporated into GXDW, it is necessary to preserve these data while updating the Gene Logic data. In some cases, this problem is addressed by partitioning the GXDW databases and GXA data files into Gene Logic data and customer specific parts. The partitions are organized in such a way that the Gene Logic data can be replaced while leaving the customer data intact. The GeneExpress Explorer then accesses the union of these partitions, which are created using database or GXA union tools.

For certain databases, such as the Gene Annotations Database, the complexity of the dependencies between the data, and the overlap between the Gene Logic and the customer data, means that partitioning does not provide an adequate solution for the database update problems. It is not uncommon that customer and Gene Logic data share some controlled vocabularies, or that customer proprietary annotations refer to public genomic information such as UniGene clusters. Since controlled vocabularies, UniGene clusters and so on may change (e.g., a sequence cluster may be merged into another cluster), it is essential to re-examine customer data, and to re-establish correlations with public or Gene Logic data. For such databases it is necessary to keep track of customer data, and to re-load these data into GXDW after each periodic update, so that the consistency between public, Gene Logic and customer proprietary data is maintained.

5. Summary and Future Work

We described the challenges involved in managing and integrating gene expression data in the context of Gene Logic's GeneExpress system. The GeneExpress Warehouse is hosted on an Oracle 8i database server back-end and is supplied with a continuous stream of data from the GeneExpress Data Acquisition System. Data exploration and analysis is carried out using the GeneExpress Explorer in a three-tier (database server - analysis engine and query processor - user interface client) architecture.

Through the end of 2001, the GeneExpress system had been deployed at over twenty biotech and pharmaceutical companies, as well as at several academic institutions. At the same time, Gene Logic has completed two GeneExpress data integration projects, with the integrated systems deployed at customer sites, and has started several new integration projects. One of the completed integrated systems included support for custom Affymetrix GeneChip probe arrays, for proprietary gene annotations, and for daily incremental updates of customer data into the GXDW. All the projects have included support for integration of sample (clinical) data based on proprietary data formats, as well as gene expression data.

Based on the experience gained in developing tools for incorporating customer data into GeneExpress, we have recently developed tools that provide support for interactive extraction, transformation and loading of gene expression data generated using the Affymetrix GeneChip LIMS into GXDW.

Acknowledgements

We want to thank our colleagues at Gene Logic who have been involved in the development of the GeneExpress system for their outstanding work. Special thanks to Mike Cariaso and Krishna Palaniappan for their contributions to this paper.

References

[1] Affymterix, *"Affymetrix Analysis Data Model"*, http://www.affymetrix.com/support/aadm/aadm.html.
[2] Chaudhuri, S., and Dayal, U., *An Overview of Data Warehousing and OLAP Technology*, SIGMOD Record, 1999.
[3] Eckman, B.A., Kosky, A.S., and Laroco, L.A., *Extending Traditional Query-Based Integration Approaches for Functional Characterization of Post-Geomic Data*, Journal of Bioinformatics, 17:587-601, 2001.
[4] *Gene Logic Products.* http://www.genelogic.com/products/ge.htm
[5] *Human Gene Nomenclature Database*, http://www.gene.ucl.ac.uk/nomenclature/.
[6] Lockhart D.J., Dong, H., Byrne, M.C., Follettie, M.T., Gallo, M.V., Chee, M.S., Mittmann, M., Wang C., Kobayashi, M., Horton, H. and Brown, E.L., *Expression Monitoring by Hybridization to High-Density Oligonucleotide Arrays*, Nature Biotechnology, 14:1675-1680, 1996.
[7] Lockhart D.J., and Winzeler, A.E., *Genomics, Gene Expression, and DNA Arrays*, Nature, 405:827-836, 2000.
[8] Markowitz V.M., and Topaloglou, T., *Applying Data Warehousing Concepts to Gene Expression Data Management*. Proceedings of the 2nd IEEE International Symposium on Bioinformatics and Bioengineering, November 2001.
[9] Markowitz V.M. (ed), *Special Section on Heterogeneous Molecular Biology Databases*, Journal of Computational Biology, Vol 2, No. 4, 1995.
[10] Pearson, H., *Biology's name game*, Nature, 417, pp. 631-632, 2001.
[11] *SNOMED, Systematized Nomenclature for Medicine.* http://www.snomed.org/
[12] *Third International Meeting on Microarray Data Standards, Annotations, Ontologies, and Databases.* Presentations. http://www.mged.org/presentations/index.html.

With HEART Towards Response Time Guarantees for Message-Based e-Services

Achim Kraiss[2,*], Frank Schoen[1], Gerhard Weikum[3], and Uwe Deppisch[1]

[1] Dresdner Bank, Software-Technology and -Architecture, IT Research and Innovations
{frank.schoen, uwe.deppisch}@dresdner-bank.com
[2] SAP AG, Customer Relationship Management
achim.kraiss@sap.com
[3] University of the Saarland, Computer Science Department
weikum@cs.uni-sb.de

Abstract. The HEART tool (Help for Ensuring Acceptable Response Times) has been developed by the IT Research and Innovations department of Dresdner Bank for the computation of viable message prioritization in message-based e-services, such as stock brokerage services where service requests of different customer classes with class-specific performance goals have to be served by a server. HEART determines viable message prioritizations in the sense that they satisfy the specified performance goals of customer classes. In this paper, we describe the practical problem setting we address with HEART and outline the functionality of HEART. The demo will show HEART's underlying concepts, its architecture and an example scenario.

1 Motivation

Quality-of-Service (QoS) is a hot topic for existing Internet-based e-commerce applications and it will become "hotter" as enterprises make more and more Web Services accessible to a wider range of customers via Internet, using UDDI registries and SOAP-based messaging. Guaranteeing good performance is highly critical to the acceptance and business success of e-services [1], such as online stock brokerage where minimum response times are required by customers for their trading transactions such as buying and selling of stocks. In this setting, it is not sufficient to the customer to get "best-effort" promises about the e-service performance, but to get specific performance guarantees which may even be cast into a formal service level agreement (SLA). These performance guarantees have not only to focus on mean response times averaged over long time periods like weeks or months. Rather they have to consider mean values, standard deviations as well as the tail of response time distributions taken in short-term intervals in order to guarantee acceptable response times even in peak load situations where the number of response time outliers may be most critical to business success. Consequently, future e-service servers have to guarantee customer-class-specific performance goals. Typically, e-services are embedded in a component-based architecture where requests (e.g. in form of a SOAP message or

---

[*] This work was performed while the author was at Dresdner Bank.

as a message within some message-oriented middleware (MOM)) are sent to the e-service server where the request is processed and the answer is sent back to the service requestor. If the server serves all the incoming requests in first-come-first-served (FCFS) order, it is not possible to guarantee customer-class-specific response times. A commonly provided base mechanism to guarantee some form of class-specific response times is to assign different priorities to requests of different customer classes and to serve incoming requests based on their priorities. Many MOM products, such as IBM's MQSeries and Microsoft's MSMQ, as well as messaging interfaces such as Java Message Service (JMS) provide message priorities and priority-based message scheduling as basis for influencing message-class specific response times. However, in practice it is completely unclear how to set message priorities in order to satisfy given response time goals, and this is why we have developed the HEART tool (Help for Ensuring Acceptable Response Times).

2 Example Problem Setting

Figure 1 illustrates the problem setting we address with HEART. A server provides stock brokerage services, such as for the buying of stocks (BuyStocks), and for querying the current portfolio of the customer (QueryPortfolio). These services are accessed by three different customer classes: (1) first-class customers who pay for their brokerage services (e.g. stock brokers), (2) second-class customers who can use the brokerage for free (e.g. a service for students), and (3) inhouse applications (e.g. for recording written customer orders). The first-class and second-class customer applications may send SOAP messages with their service requests over the Internet to a web server of the bank where the service requests are transferred into the request queue of the brokerage server using message-oriented middleware. The inhouse applications may directly send MOM messages to the request queue. Each customer class has specific performance goals for their service requests. The first-class customers require

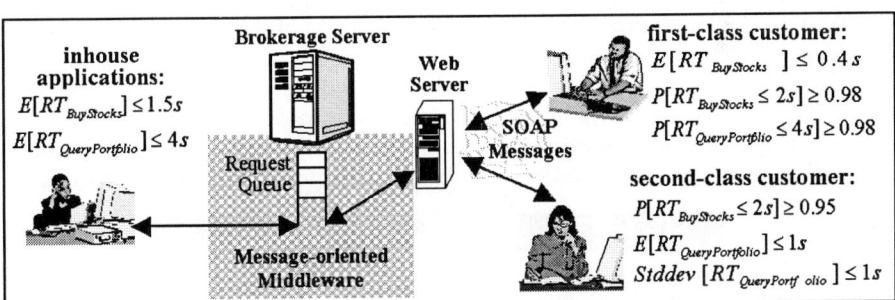

Fig. 1. Example scenario for message-based e-services

that the mean response time of a BuyStocks request does not exceed 0.4 seconds. Furthermore, the probability that the response time of a BuyStocks request does not exceed 2 seconds has to be at least 0.98, that is, the response time of at least 98 percent of all BuyStocks requests must not exceed 2 seconds. Similarly, it is required that the response time of at least 98 percent of all QueryPortfolio requests must not exceed 4 seconds. For second-class customers, at least 95 percent of BuyStocks requests must not exceed a response time of 2 seconds, and the mean response time and the standard deviation of QueryPortfolio requests must not exceed 1 second. The inhouse applications have relaxed performance goals as they have specified only upper bounds on mean response times and do not give restrictions on response time variability. The brokerage server has to serve requests for two different services requested by three different customer classes, leading to a multi-class workload of six different request classes. The challenge is to serve the requests in an order so that all specific performance goals are met. Most messaging products provide a priority-based service of requests where the requests of the six request classes can get different priorities leading to class-specific response times. However, it is unclear if (a) there exists a prioritization satisfying all performance goals, (b) if such a prioritization exists, how it looks like, and (c) if no such prioritization exists, which performance goals are "hardest" in the sense that they contribute most to the elimination of prioritizations and should be reviewed. To answer these questions, we have developed the HEART tool. Based on given request arrival rates and mean service times of the six request classes, the answer given by HEART for our example setting is the following: The only possible prioritization satisfying all given performance goals is to give highest priority *1* to FirstClass_BuyStocks requests, next highest priority *2* to SecondClass_BuyStocks, priority *3* both to FirstClass_QueryPortfolio and SecondClass_QueryPortfolio, priority *4* to Inhouse_BuyStocks, and lowest priority *5* to Inhouse_QueryPortfolio requests. The solution is not obvious at all as it is difficult to compare the "hardness" of the given performance goals.

3 The HEART Tool & Demo

The HEART tool is a web-based system for computing request prioritizations that meet specified performance goals based on given workload parameters for a server. Figure 2 shows a screenshot of the Web interface of HEART for an example user "Frank" who models the "Brokerage Server" shown in figure 1. For each request class the administrator has to provide a (statistical) description of the expected or measured workload and the response time goals for the class. For this purpose, we have extended the GET function used to dequeue the next message from the server message queue. Our extension determines the required workload parameters for HEART automatically based on timestamp information provided by the messaging product. The performance goals are specified by entering the required mean response time, the

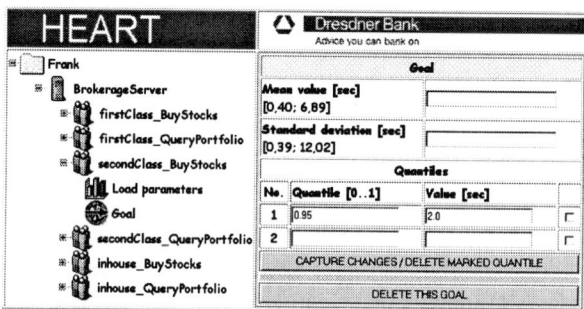

Fig. 2. HEART Screenshot

required standard deviation, and percentiles (which have to be entered in our tool as quantile values. After the administrator *(Frank)* has specified all workload parameters and goals, he initiates the automatic identification of prioritizations satisfying the response time goals. Conceptually, the tool enumerates all possible priority assignments for the given classes, and assesses the performance of each such prioritizations to identify the ones that satisfy all performance goals. The number of possible prioritizations is quite large. For example, with six request classes in our case and *10* different priorities supported by MQSeries the total number of possible prioritizations is *4683* which is much too large to be identified by "trial and error" in a practical setting. The HEART tool identifies the prioritizations that satisfy all performance goals by evaluating each possible prioritization based on analytical results of stochastic queueing models and partially using simulations [2, 3].

The demo shows the architecture and basic principles of the HEART tool as well as an interactive elaboration on an example setting where it is shown that (a) an intuitive prioritization of requests is very difficult and in most cases impossible, and that (b) HEART is able to give the user a "feel" for the interdependencies between prioritizations and the feasibility of response time goals.

References

1. N. Bhatti, A. Bouch, A. Kuchinsky: *Integrating User-Perceived Quality into Web Server Design*, 9th WWW Conference (www9.org), October 2000
2. A. Kraiss, F. Schoen, G. Weikum, U. Deppisch: *Middleware-based Response Time Guarantees for e-Services (in German)*, 9th German Database Conference (BTW), Oldenburg, Germany, March 2001
3. A. Kraiss, F. Schoen, G. Weikum, U. Deppisch: *Towards Response Time Guarantees for e-Service Middleware*, IEEE Data Engineering Bulletin 24(1), March 2001

Cobra: A Content-Based Video Retrieval System

Milan Petković and Willem Jonker

Computer Science Department, University of Twente,
PO BOX 217, 7500 AE, Enschede, The Netherlands
{milan,jonker}@cs.utwente.nl

1 Introduction

An increasing number of large publicly available video libraries results in a demand for techniques that can manipulate the video data based on content. In this paper, we present a content-based video retrieval system called Cobra. The system supports automatic extraction and retrieval of high-level concepts (such as video objects and events) from raw video data. It benefits from using domain knowledge, but at the same time, provides a general framework that can be used in different domains.

The contribution of this work is twofold. Firstly, we demonstrate how different knowledge-based techniques can be used together within a single video database management system to interpret low-level video features into semantic content. The system uses spatio-temporal rules, Hidden Markov Models (HMMs), and Dynamic Bayesian Networks (DBNs) to model and recognize video objects and events. Secondly, we show how these techniques can be effectively used for different application domains. In particular, we validate our approach in the domain of tennis and Formula 1 videos.

2 System Description

The Cobra DBMS is easily extensible, supporting the use of different knowledge-based techniques for identifying the video contents. The content abstractions, which are stored as metadata, are used to organize, index and retrieve the video source (Fig. 1). The meta data is populated off-line most of the time, but can also be extracted on-line in the case of dynamic feature/semantic extractions in the query time.

At the logical level, the system uses the Moa object algebra [1], enriched with a video data model and several extensions. The algebra accepts all base types of the underlying physical storage system and allows their orthogonal combination using the structure primitives: set, tuple, and object. At the physical level, we use Monet [1] - an extensible parallel database kernel that supports a binary relational model, main memory query execution, extensibility with new abstract data types and index structures, as well as parallelism.

In order to achieve content independence and provide a framework for automatic extraction of semantic content from raw video data, we propose the

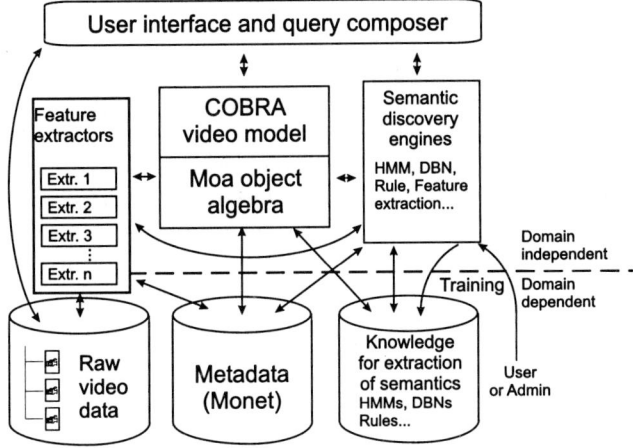

Fig. 1. The architecture of the Cobra system

COntent-Based RetrievAl (COBRA) video data model (a detailed description can be found in [2]). The model is in line with the latest development in MPEG-7, distinguishing four distinct layers within video content: the raw data, the feature, the object and the event layer. The object and event layers are concept layers consisting of entities characterized by prominent spatial and temporal dimensions, respectively. By using this model, we achieved insulation between applications and feature/semantic extraction techniques on one hand, and data on the other hand.

The techniques, which are used to inference high-level semantics from raw video data, are integrated within the system as Moa/Monet extensions. In the current implementation we have three extensions: (1) Video processing and feature extraction, (2) HMM, and (3) rule-based extension.

The video-processing and feature-extraction extension encapsulates operations used for video segmentation, processing and feature extraction. Operations are implemented using Matlab and its image processing toolbox and as such used through a Matlab server directly by the system.

The other two extensions are tightly coupled with the system. The rule-based extension is implemented within the query engine. It is aimed at formalizing descriptions of high-level concepts, as well as their extraction based on features and spatio-temporal reasoning. The HMM extension implements two basic HMM operations: training and evaluation. Here, we exploit the parallelism of our database kernel and implement the parallel evaluation of different HMMs at the physical level. For a more detailed description of these two extensions see [2].

By extending the system at all levels, several knowledge-based techniques have been efficiently integrated within our VDBMS. This is an important advantage over approaches that implement a video extension at the application level, which results in a much slower system.

3 Content-Based Retrieval

Having described our system and the model, this section explains how high-level concepts are extracted from raw video data. We start with segmenting a video into different shots using differences in the color histograms of neighboring frames. Then, shots are classified in different categories. Note that from that step, domain knowledge starts to play a very important role, since the shot classification and event recognition are domain dependent. We continue the process by extracting visual features characterizing color, shape, texture and motion, as well as audio features. In our system we use general, but also domain specific features, such as skeleton features in the tennis domain [2]. Having the features extracted we use domain knowledge coupled with the aforementioned techniques to map them to high-level concepts.

In our experiments, we applied spatio-temporal formalization of video objects and events using rules. In that way, we were able to describe, for example, a tennis player as a video object, and playing close to the net or rallies as video events. Consequently, we were able to interactively query the database for video segments with these semantic concepts. However, this rule-based approach is essentially restricted to the extent of recognizable events, since it might become difficult to formalize complex actions of non-rigid objects using rules. In order to solve this problem, we have exploited the automatic learning capability of HMMs. In our tennis case study, they have been used to recognize different tennis strokes. The results of large experiments we run showed that we were able to recognize six different tennis strokes, namely, forehand, backhand, service, smash, forehand volley and backhand volley, with the accuracy of 88%. The stroke recognition provides our system with the ability to answer even more detailed queries such as: retrieve all video sequences with Sampras approaching the net with the backhand stroke.

On the other hand, to demonstrate the generality of our approach, we have also done some experiments in the domain of Formula 1 videos [3]. Here, we employed dynamic Bayesian networks to find the highlights of Formula 1 programs. We extracted different multi-modal cues (namely text, audio and visual cues) and found that DBNs are very useful for fusing them. The accuracy of about 80% was obtained compared to the human annotation. To the best of our knowledge this is the first time that dynamic Bayesian networks are used for indexing and characterization of TV broadcasting programs.

References

1. P. Boncz, A.N. Wilschut, M.L. Kersten. Flattering an object algebra to provide performance. In *Proc. IEEE Intl. Conf. on Data Engineering*, pages 568-577, 1998.
2. M. Petković, W. Jonker. Content-Based Video Retrieval by Integrating Spatio-Temporal and Stochastic Recognition of Events. In *Proc. IEEE International Workshop on Detection and Recognition of Events in Video*, pages 75-82, 2001.
3. V. Mihajlović, M.Petković. *Automatic Annotation of Formula 1 Races for Content-Based Video Retrieval*, CTIT Technical Report, TR-CTIT-01-41, 2001.

Navigating Virtual Information Sources with Know-ME

Xufei Qian[1], Bertram Ludäscher[1],
Maryann E. Martone[2], and Amarnath Gupta[1]

[1] San Diego Supercomputer Center,
University of California San Diego, USA
{xqian,gupta,ludaesch}@sdsc.edu
[2] Department of Neuroscience,
University of California San Diego, USA
mmartone@ucsd.edu

In many application domains such as biological sciences, information integration faces a challenge usually not observed in simpler applications. Here, the to-be-integrated information sources come from very different sub-specialties (e.g., anatomy and behavioral neuroscience) and have widely diverse schema, often with little or no overlap in attributes. Yet, they can be *conceptually* integrated because they refer to different aspects of the same physical objects or phenomena. We have proposed **model-based mediation** (MBM) as an information integration paradigm where information sources with hard-to-correlate schemas may be integrated using *auxiliary expert knowledge* to hold together widely different data schemas. The expert knowledge is captured in a graph structure called the ***Knowledge Map***. In MBM, we extend the global-as-view architecture by lifting exported source data to conceptual models (CMs) that represent more source specific knowledge than a logical schema. The mediator's IVDs are defined in terms of source CMs and make use of a semantically richer model involving class hierarchies, complex object structure, and rule-defined semantic integrity constraints. Additionally, sources specify *object contexts*, i.e., formulas that relate a source's conceptual schema with the global domain knowledge maintained at the mediator. In this paper, we introduce a tool called Knowledge Map Explorer (Know-ME) for a user to explore both the domain knowledge, and all data sources that have been integrated using it.

Knowledge Map. A Knowledge map consists of four components:

A *domain map* (DM) is an edge-labeled directed graph whose nodes C are called concepts, and whose edge labels R are called relationships. For example, a DM may contain the labeled edge $map\ kinase \xrightarrow{isa} enzyme$ specifying that *map kinase* is a subconcept of *enzyme*. Note that isa is a special relationship and defines the concept hierarchy. Other relationships may define a "has a" hierarchy, spatial relationships such as "inside", and domain-specific relationships such as "projects to". Concepts C and relationships R can be constant symbols or ground atomic formulas.

A *process map* (PM) is an edge-labeled directed graph whose nodes S are called states, and whose edge labels P are called processes or events. Like relationships

R of a domain map, labels P can be ground atomic formulas. For example, a PM may contain the labeled edge $s_i \xrightarrow{activates(map\_kinase, protein\_kinase\_A)} s_j$ specifying a transition from state s_i to s_j under a parameterized process called $activates(map\_kinase, protein\_kinase\_A)$. Such a transition can change the truth value of fluent predicates. For example, a temporal logic axiom like "*IF [S] not active(Y), activates(X,Y) THEN [S+1] active(Y)*" asserts that when the above transition is considered, the fluent $active(protein\_kinase\_A)$ will be true in s_j.

Links between Conceptual and Procedural Knowledge. The knowledge represented in DMs and in PMs can be linked by using processes as concepts, i.e., allowing that process labels P and concepts C come from a common namespace $N = C \cap P$. This means that the PM contains the procedural knowledge about concepts in N, while a DM describes how a process in N relates to other processes. For example, L-LTP (late long-term potentiation) is a process $state_i \xrightarrow{E\_LTP} state_j \xrightarrow{L\_LTP} state_k$ comprising two intermediate steps early and late phase LTP. From the DM, we may know that $L\_LTP \xrightarrow{occurs\_in} hippocampus$ i.e., this process occurs in the hippocampus.

Links from Knowledge Maps to Data. Nodes in DMs and edges in PMs are linked to actual data via *context edges*. For example, a source Src_1 that has immuno-labeling images that may serve as "evidence" of the process $activates(...)$ can declare this fact using a *context edge* of the form $Src_1 \xrightarrow{has_e vidence(immuno\_image)} activates(...)$ linking source data to a process. The declarative semantics of knowledge maps is given via a logic program.

The Demonstration System

System Description. The Knowledge Map database stores the graph structure of domain and process maps. It includes the UMLS ontology from the National Library of Medicine and the Gene Ontology from the Gene Ontology Consortium In the demo system, the wrappers connect to web-accessible Neuroscience information sources. The logic engine is FLORA, an F-Logic preprocessor on top of XSB Prolog. The rules specifying the semantics of Knowledge Maps are implemented in F-Logic. The query engine uses a graph processor and a logic engine as required. The KNOW-ME tool is a query formulation front-end that drives the query engine by sending it relativized and possibly parameterized queries.

The KNOW-ME Tool. The KNOW-ME tool presents to the user a two-window interface showing a DM and a PM, respectively. In either window, the user needs to create an initial graph from which she starts exploration. In the default case, the system presents the user with a preset initial DM and PM – the user starts expanding the graph by querying on their neighboring nodes and edges. In a more involved case, the user selects from a number of concepts, relationships and processes, and asks the system to compute a connected subgraph that contains the chosen nodes and edges. For this request, the graph processor *constructs* the initial graph, and the user may select a node, edge or subgraph to

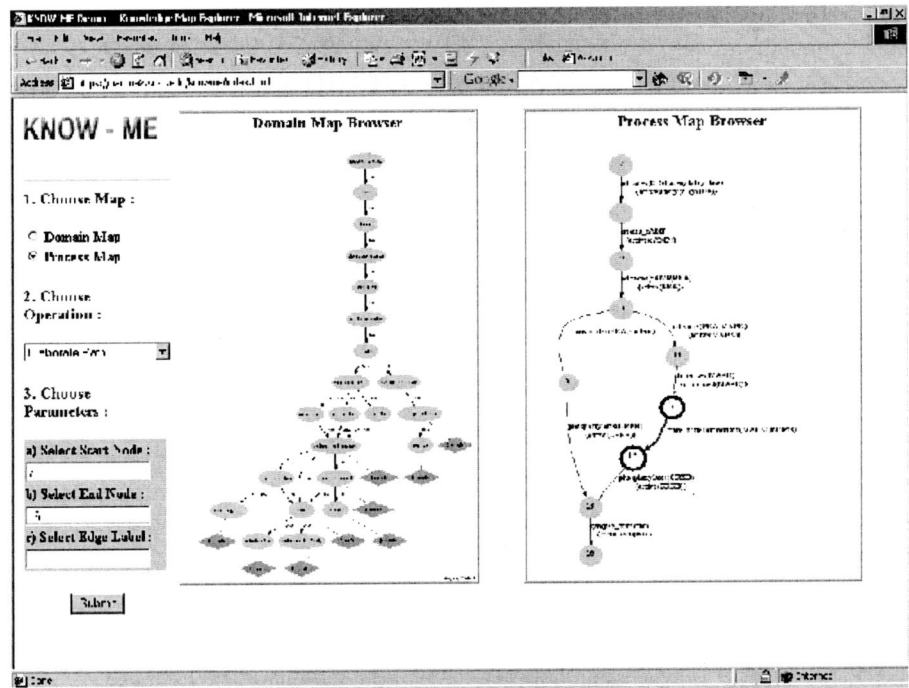

Fig. 1. The prototype Know-ME interface

launch the next "relativized query", applied only to the active subgraph. The KNOW-ME tool internally maintains a list of all visible, active and response subgraphs. A visible subgraph is a fragment of a Knowledge Map that appears on the screen at the time of the next operation; an active subgraph is one that has been highlighted by the user as the "argument" of the next operation; and a response subgraph is returned as the answer to a query. These are represented with different shapes (for nodes) and colors (for edges) on the interface. The user may manually deactivate an active subgraph or set a preference to automatically deselect the active subgraph after a query has been evaluated and make the response subgraph active. After selecting the active subgraph the user can right-click to open a query menu and perform either a basic operation or a predefined parameterized query. An active subgraph of the PM can be seen (in bold) in Figure 1, while the diamonds in the DM shows evidence edges leading to data.

Operations. The basic operations for programming graph queries for the KNOW-ME tool are expressed as generalized path expressions. Two important operations are *elaboration* and *abstraction*. The first substitutes the edge e with a path $\langle e_1, e_2, \ldots e_k \rangle$ that has been logically defined as a more elaborate description of the process denoted by e. The second is the reverse of above operation. The user can formulate more complex queries by selecting the "create new query" option in the query menu. Once created a query can be saved for future use. The demo will exhibit a number of pre-defined complex queries.

XQuery by the Book:
The IPSI XQuery Demonstrator

Peter Fankhauser[1], Tobias Groh[2], and Sven Overhage[2]

[1] Fraunhofer Institute for Integrated Publication and Information Systems (IPSI)
fankhaus@ipsi.fhg.de
[2] Technical University of Darmstadt, Germany
groh@rbg.informatik.tu-darmstadt.de; overhage@bwl.tu-darmstadt.de

Abstract. The IPSI XQuery Demonstrator (IPSI-XQ) implements the XQuery surface syntax, its mapping to the XQuery Core Language, and the static and dynamic semantics of XQuery Core "by the book", following the formal specification as faithfully as possible. Its main purpose is to provide a framework for testing various language design options, and for experimenting with techniques to use type information for efficiently storing and querying XML.

1 Introduction

XQuery is being developed by the W3C XML Query working group as a standard query language for XML. It is a fully compositional, strongly typed functional language to flexibly select, recombine, and restructure XML documents and fragments.

The XQuery specification comprises several documents: XQuery 1.0 [1] specifies the user level syntax. The language consists of four main constituents: (1) for-let-where-return (FLWR) expressions, reminiscent of SQL, bind document fragments to variables and express join conditions on them. (2) XPath [2] expressions select document fragments. (3) XML-expressions construct new elements and attributes from the selected fragments. (4) Optional type declarations specify the input and the output type of queries and of user defined functions.

XQuery 1.0 Formal Semantics [3] maps the user level syntax to XQuery Core, a syntactic subset of XQuery that consists of a small, but fully expressive set of operators together with their static and dynamic semantics. Finally, the query data model [4] formalizes the underlying datamodel for XML, and the functions and operators document [6] enumerates all functions and operators for the simple types of XML Schema [7].

The main goal of IPSI-XQ is to serve as a reality check for XQuery and its formal semantics, and as a framework to experiment with different design alternatives in the course of the specification. To this end, it implements the mapping of the XQuery surface syntax to XQuery Core, and the static and dynamic semantics of XQuery Core "by the book", i.e., the implementation follows the formal specification as faithfully as possible. Furthermore, it implements the

XQuery datamodel as an extension to the W3C-DOM (Document Object Model) [8], the standard API for accessing and manipulating XML- documents, rather than deploying a proprietary data model. Another goal of IPSI-XQ is to provide a basis for experimenting with techniques that use type knowledge to map XML to well tuned storage models and to optimize queries. To this end, IPSI-XQ puts particular emphasis on a clean implementation of XQuery's type system.

2 Architecture

The IPSI-XQ processor gets three kinds of inputs (see Figure 1): A query expression, optional input/output types, and one or more input documents. Processing a query involves two major phases. Query Analysis (Columns 1 and 2) and Query Evaluation (Column 3).

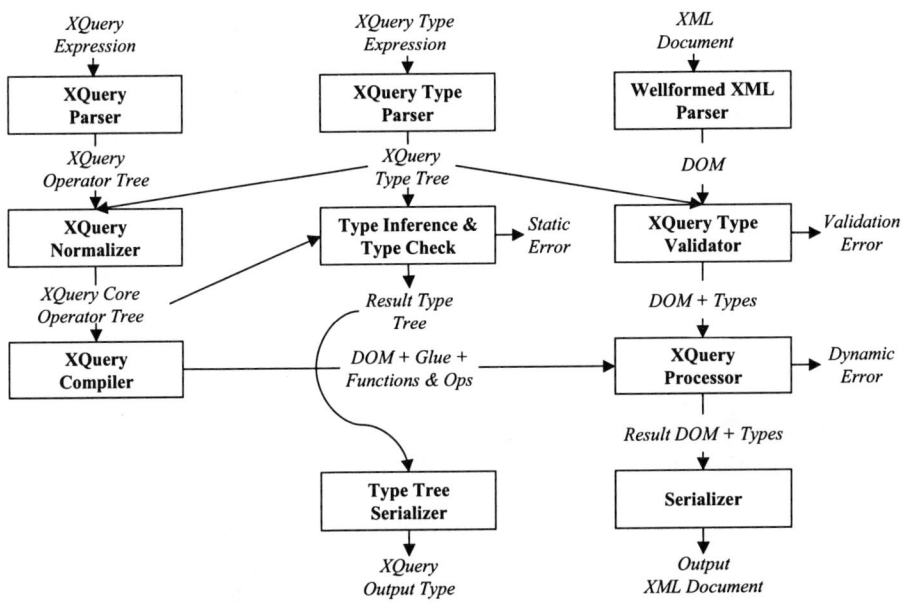

Fig. 1. Architecture

During **Query Analysis**, first the *XQuery Expression* and the (optional) *Input* and *Output Type Expressions* are parsed to produce an *XQuery OperatorTree* and *XQuery Type Trees*. To this end, we use a JavaCC 2.1 parser generated from the grammar in [1]. Then the **XQuery Normalizer** expands the operator tree into an *XQuery Core Operator Tree* using the rules for "mapping-to-core" specified in [3]. Guided by the "type-inference-rules" [3], the **Type Inference** component walks down the core operator tree until it encounters nodes with a declared input type to produce the *Result Type Tree* of the query. When an output type is explicitly declared, the **Type Check** component checks whether the inferred result type is subsumed by the declared output type. If not, a *Static Error* is raised. Otherwise, the **XQuery Compiler** prepares the core operator tree for evaluation by generating a queryplan consisting of *DOM method calls* [8] and basic *Functions & Operators* [6]. This translation is guided by the "dynamic semantics" in [3].

As a first step during **Query Evaluation** the input *XML documents* are processed using Xerces 1.4.3 to instantiate a *DOM*. Then the **XQuery Type Validator** validates the DOM tree against the declared input types, and adorns the *DOM* nodes with *Types*, which are represented by means of the extension mechanisms of Xerces 1.4.3. If validation fails, a *Validation Error* is raised. Otherwise, the **XQuery Processor** evaluates the queryplan to produce the *Result DOM* tree. Explicitly declared and built-in runtime type checks can lead to a *Dynamic Error*.

Finally, the **Serializer** produces the *XML Output Document*, and the **Type Tree Serializer** produces the *XQuery Result Type*.

3 Demonstrator

IPSI-XQ can be tried out on the web [5]. The user interface is realized as a web interface to load and view queries, schemas, and documents. Users can evaluate queries, generate the corresponding query expression in XQuery Core, infer the result type, and statically check it against a given output schema. By applying different input schemas to an input document, users can explore the role of types for detecting type errors and for simplifying queries.

References

1. Chamberlin, D., Florescu, D., Robie, J., Siméon, J., Stefanescu, M. (eds): XQuery 1.0: An XML Query Language. W3C Working Draft 2001. URL: www.w3.org/TR/xquery/
2. Clark, J., DeRose, S. (eds): XML Path Language (XPath) Version 1.0. W3C Recommendation 1999. URL: www.w3.org/TR/xpath/
3. Fankhauser, P., Fernandez M., Siméon J., Malhotra, A., Rys, M., Wadler, P. (eds): XQuery 1.0 Formal Semantics. URL: www.w3.org/TR/query-semantics/
4. Fernandez, M., Marsh, J.: XQuery 1.0 and XPath 2.0 Data Model. W3C Working Draft 2001. URL: www.w3.org/TR/query-datamodel/
5. IPSI-XQ: The IPSI XQuery Demonstrator. URL: xml.ipsi.fhg.de/xquerydemo
6. Malhotra, A., Marsh, J., Melton, J., Robie, J. (eds): XQuery 1.0 and XPath 2.0 Functions and Operators Version 1.0. W3C Working Draft 2001. URL: www.w3.org/TR/xquery-operators/
7. Biron, P.V., Malhotra, A.: XML Schema Part 2: Datatypes. W3C Recommendation 2001. URL: www.w3.org/TR/xmlschema-2/
8. Hors, A. et al. (eds): Document Object Model (DOM) Level 2 Core Specification. W3C Recommendation 2000. URL: www.w3.org/TR/DOM-Level-2-Core/
9. Chamberlin, D., Fankhauser, P., Marchiori, M., Robie, J. (eds): XML Query Use Cases. W3C Working Draft 2001. URL: www.w3.org/TR/xmlquery-use-cases

The ORDB-Based SFB-501-Reuse-Repository[1]

Wolfgang Mahnke and Norbert Ritter

University of Kaiserslautern
P.O.Box 3049, 67653 Kaiserslautern, Germany
{mahnke|ritter}@informatik.uni-kl.de

Abstract. Comprehensive reuse and systematic evolution of reuse artifacts as proposed by the Quality Improvement Paradigm (QIP) require an integrated management of (potentially reusable) experience data as well as project-related data. This demonstration presents an approach exploiting object-relational database technology to implement a QIP-driven reuse repository. Our SFB-501-Reuse-Repository is designed to support all phases of a reuse process and the accompanying improvement cycle by providing adequate functionality. Its implementation is based on object-relational database technology along with an infrastructure well suited for these purposes.

1 Experience Data Management

Learning from experience gained in past projects is seen as a promising way to improve software quality in upcoming projects. As a result, (anti-)patterns, frameworks, and code fragments are being developed to capture the gained experience of software already developed. But experience is not only represented in the form of (directly) reusable software artifacts. To allow comprehensive reuse [2] a large variety of different reusable elements, e. g., process descriptions or lessons learned [3], are to be managed. Consequently, every kind of (software engineering) experience, independent of its type of documentation, is to be regarded as an *experience element*.

However, the benefits that can be achieved by reusing such experience elements strongly depend on their quality. Thus, they always have to represent the latest state of the art. Hence, checking and continuously improving their quality becomes a crucial issue. The Quality Improvement Paradigm (QIP) [1] suggested by Basili et. al. deals with this problem by integrating systematic evolution and comprehensive reuse of experience elements into an improvement cycle. A QIP cycle consists of several steps, mainly dealing with the planning and executing of an experiment (project), analysing its results, and packaging the gained experience for later reuse. To comprehensively support the overall QIP cycle we conceptually extended the notion of an Experience Base (EB) as introduced in [1]. Our resulting repository structure consists of two logically disjunct sections called Organization-Wide Section (OWS) and Experiment-Specific Section (ESS), where the OWS is an instantiation of Basili's

---

[1] This work has been supported by the Deutsche Forschungsgemeinschaft (DFG) as part of the Sonderforschungsbereich (SFB) 501 "Development of Large Systems with Generic Methods".

EB and the ESS holds the experiment documentations. To evaluate the usefulness of the conceptual extension, we implemented a web-based prototype of the reuse repository [4]. Thus, we also concentrate on the technological advancements for such QIP-driven reuse repositories. Besides discussing the organizational repository structure and the interface functions required to provide comprehensive support, we demonstrate that the infrastructure provided by new Object-Relational Database Management Systems (ORDBMSs) [6] can effectively be used for realization purposes. As far as we know, our approach is the first one evaluating *object-relational* database technology in the field of reuse repositories.

2 Our Approach: SFB-501-Reuse-Repository

Representations of *experience elements* (EE) are given in many different data formats. To easily handle the different formats (and to be open for new formats), EE representations should only be saved using a plain data type in the repository without respect to special data formats. ORDBMSs offer a special kind of data type for this purpose, called BLOB (binary, large object). A representation can be composed of several parts. For example, an HTML document (e. g., a framed HTML page) can consist of many files. Therefore, each representation is stored in a set of BLOBs. Also, several alternative representations of the same EE can occur.

For retrieval purposes, each EE needs to be associated with a so-called *characterization vector* (CV) containing describing data, e. g., relevant for (similarity-based) search of potentially reusable design artifacts. For performance reasons, EEs (containing large objects) and corresponding CVs (comparably small amount of data) are stored separately. Whereas all EEs are stored using the same data structure, the CVs are classified into semantically different data structures. CV attributes depend on the section (OWS, ESS) that the corresponding EE belongs to. More precisely, the sections are divided into logical areas, and the areas determine the CV attributes. The object-oriented capabilities of object-relational database technology allowed us to effectively map the mentioned data structures to a database schema.

At its user interface, the SFB-501-Reuse-Repository provides functions specifically supporting the different QIP phases, especially for planning and executing a project as well as analysing project data and packaging results. Several user roles (from *repository manager* to *project team member*) are distinguished. At the beginning of user sessions an authorization component checks security. A user's role, the QIP phase of the experiment (s)he is working for as well as personal access rights determine the functions dynamically provided (to the specific user) at the system interface, the visibility of experience elements (for this specific user) as well as the possible effects of data manipulations (issued by this specific user).

As realization platform, we have exploited the ORDBMS Informix Internet Foundation.2000 [5] including Informix WebBlade as web infrastructure. The database stores EEs, CVs, pre-defined HTML pages as well as extensions (special tables, user-defined functions (UDFs)) needed to dynamically generate HTML pages and answer user requests. In order to answer special user requests, HTML templates including SQL statements can be stored. A user request that has been specified at the browser and passed to the DB Server may address such an HTML template. The UDF *webexplode* (offered by the WebBlade) evaluates the SQL statements contained in the template, incorporates the results into the template and sends it back to the browser. We also exploited the possibility of adapting or even generating the SQL statement(s) to be evaluated in order to create the resulting HTML page dynamically.

3 Focus of Demonstration

To gain experience with the new object-relational technology we have chosen the, as we call it, *extreme extending* (X^2) approach. i. e., almost everything has been implemented by using the extensibility infrastructure of the ORDBMS. Thus, X^2 means that not only the entire application logic runs within the DB Server, but also major parts of the presentation layer (GUI) reside within the DB Server, because HTML pages used for user interaction are dynamically generated within the DBS. To point out our approach, we focus on similarity-based search primarily used to prepare new experiments by identifying potentially reusable artefacts. First of all, the user specifies a comparison instance by providing comparison values for some CV attributes reflecting aspects which are important w. r. t. the goals of the new experiment. Fig. outlines how the components of the SFB-501-Reuse-Repository collaborate to evaluate such a query (follow steps a to e) and to deliver a ranked list of EEs, potentially useful for the requesting user.

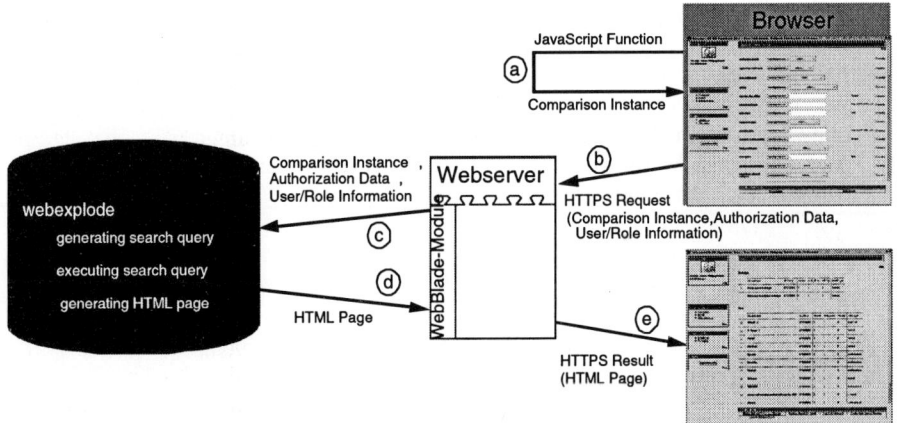

Fig. 1. Process of the Similarity-based Search

This software demonstration of the SFB-501-Reuse-Repository has been designed to: first, point up the capabilities of the system in supporting comprehensive reuse, and, second, to illustrate the (DB-server-)internal processing. For these purposes a simplified software development process is played through and the internal steps of performing similarity search are presented by a visualization component especially implemented for demonstration purposes.

This, on one hand, clarifies that extensibility, which is the key feature of ORDBMSs, can help to effectively implement advanced applications like a reuse repository, but, on the other hand, also poses the question about the reasonable degree of exploiting extensibility, since we feel that counting exclusively on extensibility for the implementation of advanced applications may become counterproductive with a certain threshold of complexity.

Thus, although we want to demonstrate that choosing the X^2 approach has been adequate for implementing our reuse repository, it is not our goal to propagate it unconditionally. Our work also aims at finding rules for a kind of restrained usage of ORDBMS's extensibility features, because at some level of complexity the X^2 approach will definitely lead to a whole bunch of problems, e. g., concerning system performance and robustness as well as ease of development.

References

[1] V. R. Basili, G. Caldiera, H. D. Rombach. Experience Factory. In J. J. Marciniak (ed), *Encyclopedia of Software Engineering, Volume 1*, John Wiley & Sons, 1994, 469–476.

[2] V. R. Basili, H. D. Rombach. Support for comprehensive reuse. In *IEE Software Engineering Journal,* 6(5):303–316, September 1991.

[3] A. Birk, C. Tautz. Knowledge Management of Software Engineering Lessons Learned. In *Proc. of the 10th Int. Conference on Software Engineering and Knowledge Engineering (SEKE'98)*, San Francisco, CA, June 1998.

[4] R.L. Feldmann, B. Geppert, W. Mahnke, N. Ritter, F. Rößler. An ORDBMS-based Reuse Repository Supporting the Quality Improvement Paradigm - Exemplified by the SDL-Pattern Approach, in: TOOLS USA 2000, July 2000, pp. 125-136.

[5] Informix Internet Foundation.2000 Documentation, http://www.informix.com/answers/english/iif2000.htm, 2001.

[6] M. Stonebraker, M. Brown. Object-Relational DBMSs - Traking the Next Great Wave. Morgan Kaufman, 1999.

Building Dynamic Market Places Using HyperQueries*

Christian Wiesner, Peter Winklhofer, and Alfons Kemper

Universität Passau, Fakultät für Mathematik und Informatik
D-94030 Passau, Germany
⟨wiesner|winklhof|kemper⟩@db.fmi.uni-passau.de
http://www.db.fmi.uni-passau.de/

1 Motivation and Introduction

Electronic market places and virtual enterprises have become important applications for query processing [2]. Building a scalable virtual B2B market place with hundreds or thousands participants requires highly flexible, distributed query processing capabilities. Architecting an electronic market place as a data warehouse by integrating *all* the data from *all* participating enterprises in one centralized data repository incurs severe problems:

- *Security and privacy violations:* The participants of the market place have to relinquish the control over their data and entrust sensitive information to the market place host.
- *Coherence problems:* The coherence of highly dynamic data, such as availability and shipping information, may be violated due to outdated materialized data in the market place's data warehouse.
- *Schema integration problems:* Using the warehouse approach all relevant data from all participants have to be converted à priori into the same format. Often, it would be easier to leave the data inside the participant's information systems, e.g., legacy systems, within the local sites, and apply particular local wrapper operations. This way, data is only converted *on demand* and the most recent coherent state of the data is returned.
- *Fixed query operators:* In a data warehouse-like electronic market place, all information is converted into materialized data. This is often not desirable in such complex applications like electronic procurement/bidding.

We propose a reference architecture for building scalable and dynamic market places and a framework for evaluating so-called *HyperQueries* in such an environment. HyperQueries are essentially query evaluation sub-plans "sitting behind" hyperlinks. This way the electronic market place can be built as an intermediary between the client and the providers executing their sub-queries referenced via hyperlinks. The hyperlinks are embedded as attribute values within data objects of the intermediary's database (Figure 1(a)). Retrieving such a virtual

---
* This work was supported by the German National Research Council (DFG) under Contract Ke 401/7-1

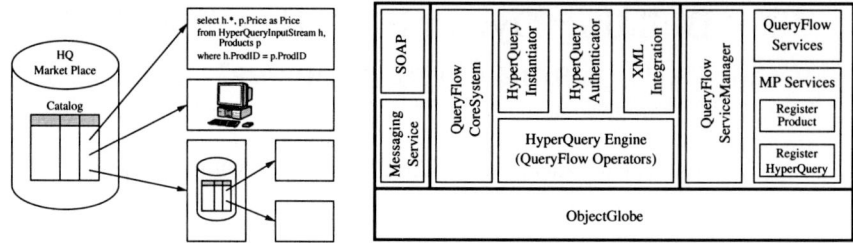

Fig. 1. Overview of the QueryFlow System

object automatically initiates the execution of the referenced HyperQuery in order to materialize the entire object.

2 Architecture of the QueryFlow System

We propose a reference architecture for building scalable electronic market places. During the implementation of our prototypical system, we payed special attention to rely on standardized (or proposed) protocols such as XML, XML Schema, XML Signature, X.509 certificates, HTTP and SOAP. Figure 1(b) depicts the basic components of the system, that can be described as follows:

- The query processing capabilities of the QueryFlow system are based on the *ObjectGlobe* system [1], which is a distributed and open query processor for data sources on the Internet.
- The communication between multiple hosts is implemented via a proprietary *Messaging Service*. Additionally, *SOAP* provides an open interface both to integrate other systems and to be integrated by other systems.
- The *HyperQuery Engine* combines all operators that are specific for Hyper-Query processing, i.e., for resolving the hyperlinks to HyperQueries and operators for optimization of HyperQuery execution.
- The *QueryFlow CoreSystem* manages the instantiated HyperQueries and the distribution of the execution to multiple physical hosts. Furthermore all additional data structures such as caches and administrative data of the executed HyperQueries are managed within this component.
- The *HyperQuery Instantiator* manages the instantiation of HyperQueries at the remote sites. The HyperQueries are stored in a hierarchical repository.
- The certificate-based *HyperQuery Authenticator* is used for signing and verifying requests and queries when communicating with other sites.
- The *XML Integration* component collects all functionality to access XML data sources and to handle semi-structured data.
- The extensible *ServiceManager* for executing Java-based e-services is required for administrative issues of the market place. The services can be accessed via the SOAP interface of the QueryFlow system.

A full description of these components can be found in [4].

3 Processing HyperQueries in the QueryFlow System

We demonstrate the HyperQuery technique with a scenario of the car manufacturing industry. We assume a hierarchical supply chain of suppliers and subcontractors. A typical process of e-procurement to cover unscheduled demands of the production is to query a market place for these products and to select the incoming offers by price, terms of delivery, etc. The price of the needed products can vary by customer/supplier-specific sales discounts, duties, etc.

In traditional distributed query processing systems such a query can only be executed if a global schema exists or all local databases are replicated at the market place. Considering an environment, where hundreds of suppliers participate in a market place, one global query which integrates the sub-queries for all participants would be too complex and error-prone.

Following our approach the suppliers have to register their products at the market place and specify by hyperlinks the sub-plans to compute the price information at *their* sites. These hyperlinks to sub-plans are embedded as virtual attributes into the tables of the market place. When evaluating these hyperlinks, our QueryFlow system distinguishes between two modes: In hierarchical mode the initiator of a HyperQuery is in the charge of collecting the processed data. Under broadcast mode data objects are routed directly to the query initiator. The decision, which processing mode is used, relies – with some restrictions – only to the initiator of a HyperQuery. Thus, the initiator determines, if the results should be sent directly to the client, or if the initiator is in charge of collecting the objects processed by the HyperQueries. Both processing modes can be mixed and nested to obtain arbitrary complex scenarios and involve subcontractors, too. A detailed description including security, optimization issues, and implementation details can be found in [3, 4].

4 The Demo

Our techniques are applicable in many different scenarios. In this demo we show the benefits of our approach with an example B2B market place of the car manufacturing industry. This demo shows that the QueryFlow system enables

1. a company to join an existing market place with very little effort. This is done by registering the products with URIs at the market place and providing HyperQueries at the company. Furthermore the company can determine which operators can be used for the evaluation of requests.
2. a client to simply state queries to the market place that evaluates them by executing HyperQueries at the participating companies.

References

1. R. Braumandl, M. Keidl, A. Kemper, D. Kossmann, A. Kreutz, S. Seltzsam, and K. Stocker. ObjectGlobe: Ubiquitous query processing on the Internet. *The VLDB Journal: Special Issue on E-Services*, 10(3):48–71, August 2001.

2. A. Jhingran. Moving up the food chain: Supporting E-Commerce Applications on Databases. *ACM SIGMOD Record*, 29(4):50–54, December 2000.
3. A. Kemper and C. Wiesner. HyperQueries: Dynamic Distributed Query Processing on the Internet. In *Proc. of the Conf. on Very Large Data Bases (VLDB)*, pages 551–560, Rome, Italy, September 2001.
4. A. Kemper and C. Wiesner. HyperQueries: Dynamic Distributed Query Processing on the Internet. Technical report, Universität Passau, Fakultät für Mathematik und Informatik, October 2001. Available at http://www.db.fmi.uni-passau.de/publications/papers/HyperQueries.pdf.

The APPROXML Tool Demonstration

Ernesto Damiani[1], Nico Lavarini[2], Stefania Marrara[2], Barbara Oliboni[2], Daniele Pasini[1], Letizia Tanca[2], and Giuseppe Viviani[1]

[1] Università di Milano, Dipartimento di Tecnologie dell'Informazione,
Via Bramante 65, 26013 Crema, Italy
edamiani@crema.unimi.it

[2] Politecnico di Milano, Dipartimento di Elettronica e Informazione,
Via Ponzio 1, 20100 Milano, Italy
{oliboni,tanca}@elet.polimi.it

1 Statement of the Problem

XML information items collected from heterogeneous sources often carry similar semantics but turn out to be structured in different ways. Variations in structure make effective search of information across multiple datasources hard to achieve.

Our approach is aimed at a flexible search and processing technique, capable to extract relevant information from a possibly huge set of XML documents. APPROXML is a software tool supporting approximate pattern-based querying, able to locate and extract XML information dealing flexibly with differences in structure and tag vocabulary.

Our method relies on representing XML documents as graphs, through a variant of the DOM model. The relevant information is selected as follows [Dam00a]: first, a *XML pattern*, i.e. a partially specified subtree, is provided by the user. Then, the XML documents of the target dataset are scanned; XML fragments are located and sorted according to their similarity to the pattern.

The edges of documents are weighted, to express their importance: note that this process can be performed once for all, for instance at document design time. We use a content-insensitive *automatic* weighting technique taking into account various characteristics of each edge, generating a separate weight according to each characteristic, and then aggregating these values in a single arc-weight. At this point, a weighted transitive closure of the graph is computed. The closure may be performed either on the oriented graph or on its non-oriented version (*oriented* or *bidirectional closure*), thus allowing more or less recall. The weight of each closure arc, spanning a path of the original graph, is computed by aggregating the weights of the arcs composing the path of the original graph. As we shall see, the choice of the aggregation function impacts the precision/recall balance and is currently left to the user. Then, a thresholded pruning of unimportant edges is performed, allowing us to retain only the most useful information, and thus improving search performance.

APPROXML scans the pruned graph searching for subgraphs matching a user-supplied search pattern, uses weights to compute the match value for each hit, and returns a ranked list of results, sorted according to their match value.

The matching algorithm is *fuzzy*, since it relies on the extended graph-structure. Indeed, the problem of matching a pattern to the extended XML tree structure was described in [Dam00a] as a *fuzzy sub-graph matching* problem.

2 Tool and Demo Overview

The APPROXML query engine is accessed via a graphical user interface, allowing for complex query jobs; we will first deal with the query engine.

Our system receives as input an XML information base whose mark-up structure is in general variable, while hopefully retaining some commonalities in tag repertoire and vocabulary. Input is also provided by the user by writing a *search pattern*. Patterns comply to a graph-based syntax (straightforwardly expressed in XML) which is both easy to understand and suitable for visual representation. The system output is a (set of) well-formed XML fragments, whose content is taken from the information base and is as close as possible to the user-specified pattern.

The system's software architecture is composed of two main modules, the `Pattern Locator` and the `Smusher`, corresponding to operations at two different levels of granularity. The `Pattern Locator` module is the core of our design. First, it parses and pre-processes the target document tree. Then, it uses a `Match` function to look for fragments of the target document having a *topological similarity* with the user pattern. The `Smusher` is a service module, which is called by the `Match` function of the Locator to perform XML *node smushing*[1] i.e. to estimate similarity between elementary granules of information (such as XML nodes with their content and attributes) and create result nodes more suitable for user output. The final result is a list of smushed XML fragments, ordered according to their similarity with the pattern; this list is sent to a final `Post-Processor` module that organizes it in a catalog suitable for user consultation or further processing. Figure 1 depicts our architectural design, showing the flow of information.

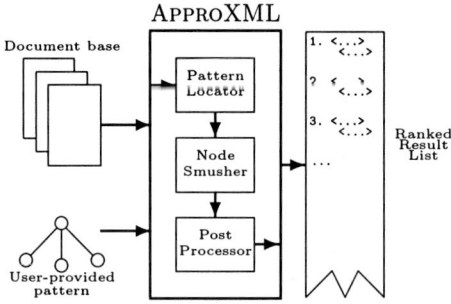

Fig. 1. APPROXML Data Architecture

---

[1] For the original definition of the *smushing* problem by Dan Brinkley, see http://lists.w3.org/Archives/Public/www-rdf-interest/2000Dec/0191.html

All versions of APPROXML have been implemented with Java, in sight of a simple Web-browser integration.

Running the application, a user can choose *where* to search. Any document can be opened and viewed. If it has been processed before (by weighting and computing the transitive closure), its data can be retrieved from a local cache. Otherwise the user can semi-automatically process it (user feedback is required in fine-tuning the recall/precision balance).

The user can then compose a query (or load a previously saved one), and submit it to the system. The results are presented as a ranked list of XML fragments.

Our prototype development considered with care every performance-related aspect. Performance is crucial since a graph matching is itself a delicate task, and is combined with other processes potentially very demanding from the computational point of view. Results are very encouraging, even though we have not yet adopted performance-driven data structures. Anyway, our method works well for documents with less than 3000 nodes, and does not handle well documents with more than 6000-7000 nodes. We are currently optimizing algorithms to deal efficiently with XML documents of 10000 nodes and more. We have thoroughly tested our architecture on the MONDIAL Database [May99], a wide XML World Geographical Atlas, which is recognized as a valid benchmark for performance-sensitive querying techniques.

References

[Dam00a] E. Damiani, L. Tanca. "Blind Queries to XML Data". Proceedings of DEXA 2000, London, UK, September 4-8, 2000. *Lecture Notes in Computer Science*, Vol. 1873, Springer, 2000, Pages: 345-356.

[Dam00b] E. Damiani, L. Tanca, F. Arcelli Fontana. "Fuzzy XML Queries via Context-based Choice of Aggregations". Kybernetika n.16 vol.4, 2000.

[Dam00c] E. Damiani, B. Oliboni, L. Tanca. "Fuzzy Techniques for XML Data Smushing". Proceedings of 7th *Fuzzy Days*, Dortmund, Germany, October 1-3, 2001.

[May99] W. May. "Information extraction and integration with FLORID: The MONDIAL case study". Technical Report 131, Universität Freiburg, Institut für Informatik, 1999. Available from
http://www.informatik.uni-freiburg.de/~may/Mondial/

A Database-Supported Workbench for Information Fusion: INFUSE*

Oliver Dunemann, Ingolf Geist, Roland Jesse,
Kai-Uwe Sattler, and Andreas Stephanik

Department of Computer Science, University of Magdeburg,
P.O. Box 4120, D-39016 Magdeburg, Germany
fusion@cs.uni-magdeburg.de

1 Introduction

Information Fusion is the process of integration and interpretation of heterogeneous data in order to gain new information of higher quality [3]. A successful support for this task requires a tight coupling of different integration and analysis tools: accessing heterogeneous data sources, their integration, preparation and transformation, analysis of syntactic, semantic and temporal structures as well as their visualisation. The INFUSE framework relies on database techniques with the goal to meet these requirements.

The proposed demonstration studies *Comparative Genomics* as one Information Fusion scenario. Gene information from different, heterogeneous sequence databases are used by several operators to analyse the function of unknown gene sequences within the demonstration.

2 The INFUSE System

The INFUSE system is designed as a database centered and component based middleware system to efficiently support the Information Fusion requirements described above. As shown in Figure 1(a) the global architecture of INFUSE consists of three main tiers: the *fusion engine* for process and meta data management, the FRAQL *query processor* for data management of heterogeneous sources and a *front end* for interactive graphical data analysis and exploration.

The *fusion engine* represents the central part of the system and is responsible for different tasks. Because a fusion process consists of several dependent steps, the fusion engine manages the definition and persistence of processes and controls their execution. Process definitions as well as the states of running processes are stored in a meta data repository. Special information gathering operators, which can be thought of as a kind of stored procedures, like data mining or machine learning algorithms, are implemented in the workbench. Besides these main features, the *fusion engine* provides additional basic services and a CORBA based API to connect to different front ends.

---

* This work is supported by DFG (German Research Council) grant FOR 345.

A Database-Supported Workbench for Information Fusion: INFUSE

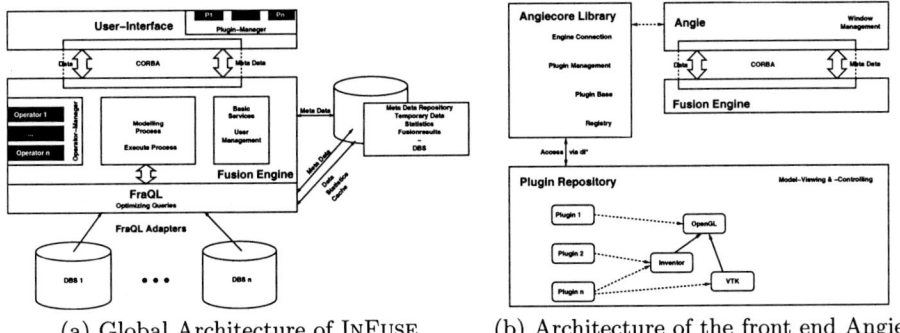

(a) Global Architecture of INFUSE (b) Architecture of the front end Angie

Fig. 1. The Architecture of the workbench

Supporting the data analysis techniques on heterogeneous data sources, the *fusion engine* relies on the features of the query processor FRAQL. A global object-relational view on heterogeneous data is offered by the query processor's adapter architecture. Several extensions in the query language provide integration and data preparation mechanisms [4].

A set of plugins is used by the front end *Angie* to support different means of visual information representation. As part of the system's visualisation network these form individual pipelines. In a visualisation pipeline, data of not necessarily geometric structure is mapped onto available display variables. These variables include but are not limited to colour, shape, and transparency. The set of mapping functions spans from glyph construction and volume rendering via splatting to the use of motion as an individual display dimension [2] for the purpose of representing temporal data behaviour.

3 The Scenario to Be Demonstrated

Comparative Genomics is a technique that compares gene sequences from different organisms or cells in order to determine or isolate specific domains of sequences (subsequences) using known information about other sequences. The analysis results of these comparisons are used to derive information about functions of the analyzed sequences. The process of Comparative Genomics is executed in an iterative and interactive manner.

Figure 2 illustrates a scenario of Comparative Genomics, where a set of unknown sequences A is analyzed for sequences coding photosynthesis. The sources B and D have to be compared with the input sequences using the *blast* operator [1]. The operators *Intersection* and *Difference* determine a set of common or excluded subsequences.

In the proposed demonstration following points are intended to be shown in order to support Comparative Genomics:

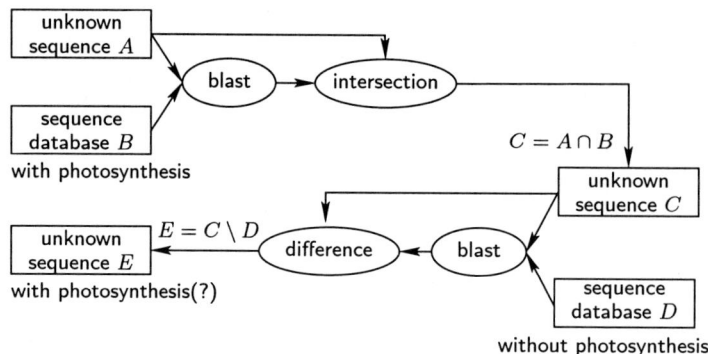

Fig. 2. Example scenario

Transformation and Preparation: Several data sources needed by gene analysis have to be accessed and prepared for different operators. Thus, the schemas and the data have to be transformed into the required structure.
Database Techniques: Several operators are implemented in a database-centric manner. These operators utilise the proposed query language support for data preparation and analysis.
Interaction support: The front end *Angie* provides techniques for guiding users through selection of analysis and visualisation methods. Thereby, the system ensures control of method combination as well as fast reply to query results. For this purpose, access to supported meta data management is provided.
Visualisation: The mapping of not inherent geometric data onto glyphs is shown as well as the appliance of motion for representing temporal behaviour.

References

1. S.F. Altschul, W. Gish, W. Miller, E.W. Myers, and D.J. Lipman. Basic local aligment search tool. *J. Mol. Biol.*, 215:403–410, 1990.
2. Roland Jesse and Thomas Strothotte. Motion Enhanced Visualization in Support of Information Fusion. In Hamid R. Arabnia, editor, *Proceedings of International Conference on Imaging Science, Systems, and Technology (CISST'2001)*, pages 492–497. CSREA Press, June 2001.
3. K. Sattler and G. Saake. Supporting Information Fusion with Federated Database Technologies. In S. Conrad, W. Hasselbring, and G. Saake, editors, *Proc. 2nd Int. Workshop on Engineering Federated Information Systems, EFIS'99, Kühlungsborn, Germany, May 5–7, 1999*, pages 179–184. infix-Verlag, Sankt Augustin, 1999.
4. K.-U. Sattler, S. Conrad, and G. Saake. Adding Conflict Resolution Features to a Query Language for Database Federations. *Australian Journal of Information Systems*, 8(1):116–125, 2000.

ST_YX: Connecting the XML Web to the World of Semantics

Irini Fundulaki[1], Bernd Amann[1], Catriel Beeri[2],
Michel Scholl[1], and Anne-Marie Vercoustre[3]

[1] Cedric-CNAM Paris, INRIA Rocquencourt
irini.fundulaki@inria.fr, amann@cnam.fr, scholl@cnam.fr
[2] Hebrew University, Israel
beeri@cs.huji.ac.il
[3] INRIA-Rocquencourt; currently on leave
at CSIRO Mathematical and Information Sciences, Melbourne, Australia
Anne-Marie.Vercoustre@cmis.csiro.au

1 Introduction

The ST_YX prototype illustrates a new way to publish and query XML resources on the Web. It has been developed as part of the C-Web (Community Web) project[1] whose main objective is to support the sharing, integration and retrieval of information in *Web communities* concerning a *specific domain of interest*.

ST_YX is based on a simple but nevertheless powerful model for publishing and querying XML resources [1]. It implements a set of *Web-based* tools for creating and exploiting *semantic portals* to XML Web resources. The main functions of such a portal can be summarized as follows: (i) XML resources can be *published/unpublished* on the fly; (ii) *structured queries* can be formulated by taking into consideration the conceptual representation of a specific domain in form of an *ontology*; (iii) query results can be customized for display and further exploitation.

The backbone of a ST_YX portal is a *domain specific ontology* comprised of *concepts* and *roles* describing the basic notions in the domain. Our approach [1] takes advantage of the presence of XML Document Type Definitions (DTDs) that capture the structure of XML documents. An XML source is published in a ST_YX portal by a set of *mapping rules* that map XML *document fragments*[2] specified by XPath[3] location paths to *ontology paths*. The user queries the set of the sources by formulating simple queries in terms of ontology paths. The objective is to be able to forward user queries to diverse XML repositories while hiding their structural heterogeneity to the end-user.

As mentioned previously a source is published by *mapping rules* that associate XPath location paths to ontology paths. Consider for example the XML resource *http://www.art.com* which stores XML documents about painters and

---
[1] http://cweb.inria.fr
[2] XML Fragment Interchange: http://www.w3c.org/TR/xml-fragment.html
[3] XML Path language (XPath): http://www.w3c.org/TR/xpath.html

their paintings. The first two rules illustrated below associate PAINTER elements and their NAME attribute to instances of concept Person and role has_name. The other two rules map PAINTING sub-elements and their TITLE attribute to instances of concept Artifact reached by the role produced and role has_title respectively.

R_1: http://www.art.com//Painter as u_1 ← Person
R_2: u_1/@Name ← has_name
R_3: u_1/Painting as u_2 ← produced
R_4: u_2/@Title ← has_title

A user query, formulated in terms of ontology paths, will be rewritten into a set of XML queries that will be send to the XML resources for evaluation. For example, the simple user query Q illustrated below which requests the *"names of persons and the title of their artifacts"*, will be rewritten to the XQuery[4] Q' using the mapping rules and the latter will be send to the XML resources for evaluation (the rewriting algorithm is presented in detail in [1]). The results obtained by each source are then unioned at the mediator site before they are returned to the user.

Q: select b, d
    from Person a,
               a.has_name b,
               a.produced c,
               c.has_title d

Q': **FOR** $a IN document("http://www.art.com//Painter")
      $b **IN** $a/@Name,
      $c **IN** $a/Painting
      $d **IN** $c/@Title
   RETURN $b , $d

2 ST_YX Portal Architecture

The architecture of the system is presented in Figure 1. XML Web resources can be published on the fly by creating/modifying/deleting mapping rules between resource fragments and the ontology using the **Source Publication Interface**. The ontology can be consulted through the **Schema Manager** which is also responsible for its loading in a ST_YX portal. The established mapping rules are first validated by the **Rules Manager** which is also responsible for their storage. The publication of a resource also consists in providing an XSL Stylesheet[5] that can be used for formatting source data in the query result.

    Query Processing is done in several steps: first *user queries* can be formulated using a standard Web browser. They are either created by a generic **Query Interface**, an HTML form or simply be stored in form of a hypertext link (URL). The **Query Interface** communicates with the **Schema Manager** allowing the user to browse the ontology for the formulation of a query. Second, the **Query Interface** forwards the query to the **Query Parser** which performs a syntactical analysis of the query and does some type-checking w.r.t. the ontology. It produces a language neutral intermediate representation of the query,

---
[4] XQuery: An XML Query Language (http://www.w3.org/TR/xquery/).
[5] XSL Transformations (XSLT: http://www.w3c.org/TR/xslt).

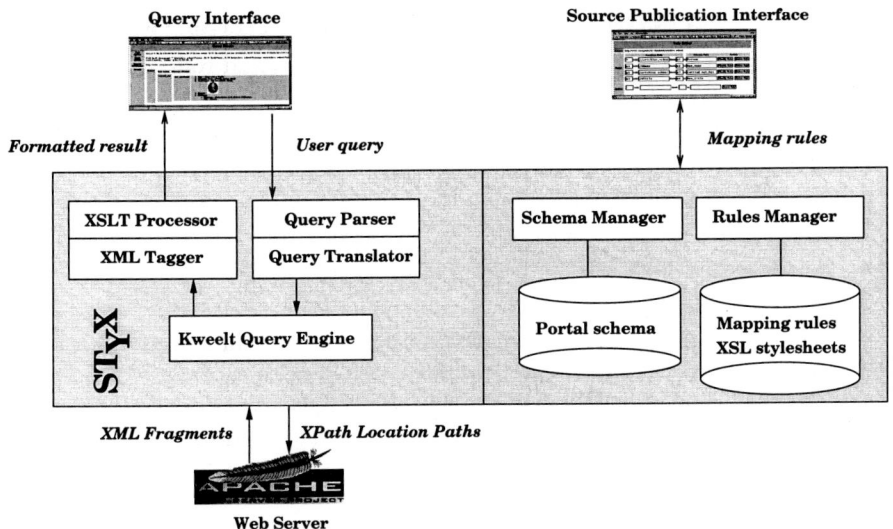

Fig. 1. ST_YX Portal Architecture

which is then forwarded to the **Query Translator**. Third, based on the mapping rules and the ontology, the **Query Translator** generates for the query a *set* of *XML queries*. Last, XML queries are then evaluated using the **Kweelt query engine**[6]. Finally the results obtained by the source are reformatted before returned to the user: the **XML Tagger** inserts schema specific tags using the mapping rules and then the **XSLT Processor** (Cocoon[7]) finally transforms the result into an HTML document which is displayed to the browser of the user.

One of our objectives in the development of ST_YX was to follow and to exploit as much as possible standard XML technologies and recommendations such as XQuery, XPath and XSLT. It shows once more that XML is not only a flexible format for data exchange but has become a mature technology for building Web portals.

Demonstration Summary: During the system demonstration we will illustrate (i) the publication of cultural XML Web resources using the Source Publication Interface, (ii) the formulation of user queries through the Query Interface and (iii) the evaluation of user queries over the published XML resources.

References

1. B. Amann, C. Beeri, I. Fundulaki, M. Scholl, and A-M. Vercoustre. Mapping XML Fragments to Community Web Ontologies. Presented at the Fourth International Workshop on Web and Databases WebDB, Santa Barbara California, May 2001. http://cedric.cnam.fr/PUBLIS/RC255.pdf.

---

[6] Kweelt Query Engine: http://db.cis.upenn.edu/Kweelt/
[7] http://xml.apache.org/cocoon

UMiner: A Data Mining System Handling Uncertainty and Quality

Christos Amanatidis, Maria Halkidi, and Michalis Vazirgiannis

Dept of Informatics, Athens Univ. of Economics and Business
{krisaman, mhalk, mvazirg}@aueb.gr

Abstract. In this paper we present UMiner, a new data mining system, which improves the quality of the data analysis results, handles uncertainty in the clustering & classification process and improves reasoning and decision-making.

1 Introduction

The explosive growth of data collections in the science and business applications and the need to analyse and extract useful knowledge from this data leads to a new generation of tools and techniques grouped under the term data mining [3]. Their objective is to deal with volumes of data and automate the data mining and knowledge discovery from large data repositories. Most data mining systems produce a particular enumeration of patterns over data sets accomplishing a limited set of tasks, such as clustering, classification and rules extraction [1, 2]. However, there are some aspects that are under-addressed by the current approaches in database and data mining applications. These aspects are: i) *the reveal and handling of uncertainty* in context of data mining tasks. ii) *the evaluation of data mining results* based on well established quality criteria. In this paper we present a data mining framework to evaluate the data analysis results, to handle efficiently the uncertainty in the context of classification process and exploit the classification belief in the process of reasoning and decision-making. Then, we present UMiner, a client/server system that we have developed based on this framework while we describe their architecture and its main services.

2 UMiner Development Approach

The importance of the requirements discussed above in the data mining process, that is the usage and reveal of uncertainty and the evaluation of data mining results, led us to the development of UMiner. Fig. 1 depicts the overall framework on which UMiner's architecture is based. The major tasks of the system can be summarised as follows:

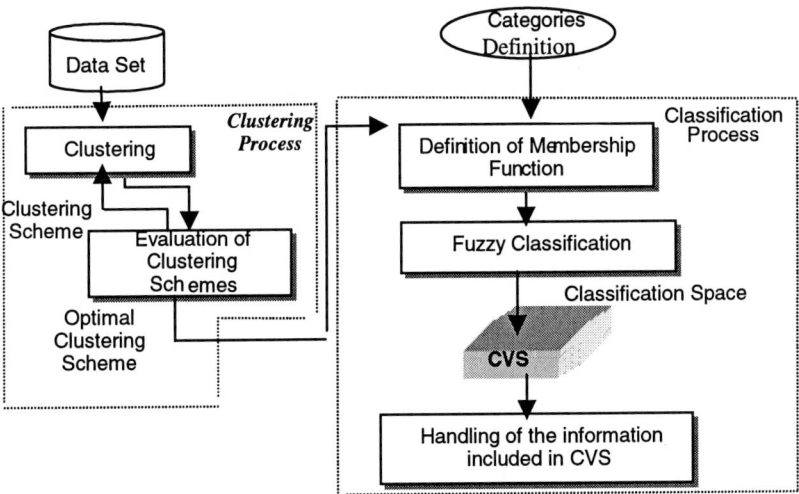

Fig. 1. UMiner Framework

- *Clustering.* In this step we define/extract clusters that correspond to the initial categories for a particular data set. We can use any of the well-established clustering methods that are available in literature.
- *Evaluation of the clustering scheme.* The clustering methods can find a partitioning of our data set, based on certain assumptions. Thus, an algorithm may result in different clustering schemes for a data set assuming different parameter values. UMiner evaluates the results of clustering algorithms based on a well-defined quality index [6] and selects the clustering scheme that best fits the considered data. The definition of this index is based on the two fundamental criteria of clustering quality, which are compactness and well separation.
- *Definition of membership functions.* Most of the clustering methods do not handle uncertainty i.e., all values in a cluster belong totally to it. We introduce a new approach so as to transform crisp clustering schemes into fuzzy ones. This is achieved by defining a scheme for assignment of the appropriate membership functions to the clusters. In the current system the implementation of membership function is based on the *Hypertrapezoidal Fuzzy Membership Functions*[4]. Moreover, a number of some other well-known membership functions are supported such as triangular, linear decreasing or linear increasing functions.
- *Fuzzy Classification.* The values of the non-categorical attributes (A_i) of a data set are classified into categories according to a set of categories L={l_i} (where l_i a category) and a set of classification functions defined in preceding clustering process.
- *Classification Value Space (CVS) Construction.* According to the classification framework proposed in [7] we transform the data set into classification beliefs and store them into a structure called CVS. It is represented by a cube, the cells of which store the degrees of belief for the classification of the attributes' values.

- *Handling of the information included in the CVS.* The CVS includes significant knowledge for our data set. We can exploit this knowledge for decision-making, based on well-established information measures that we define in [7].

3 System Architecture - Demonstration

UMiner is a data mining client-server system based on the framework described in Sect. 2. The server provides the major services of system: i) access to data, ii) implementation of clustering algorithms, iii) CVS construction. The connection to the declared databases is performed through the JDBC application interface. The client is a Java application that retrieves data and requests data mining tasks from the system server. Using the appropriate plug in it could run through a Web Browser. The major client functions are: i) authentication and connection to the server, ii) clustering and cluster validity, iii) CVS construction process, iv) visualization of data and data mining results.

We will demonstrate UMiner emphasizing its advantages. We focus on clustering quality assessment, uncertainty handling and visualization of data mining results. Following are some highlights of the system demonstration.

- **Server Connection:** After logging into the UMiner server, a list of available databases is presented to the user who may select one of them to work with. Once the user has opened a database connection, then a list of all available tables, and CVSs is presented.
- **Visualization:** Selecting a table user may view the data, using one of the available visualization techniques that our system supports. These techniques are: i) 3D, ii) matrix scatterplot, iii) glyph, iv) parallel coordinators, v) table.
- **Clustering:** The user may select one of the available clustering algorithms (i.e., K-means, DBSCAN, CURE) in order to define a partitioning for the data set. Depending on the clustering algorithm, the user defines the values of its input parameters. Then, the algorithm partition the dataset to a specific set of clusters and the defined clusters can be presented to the end user, using one of the available visualization techniques. Each cluster is rendered with a different colour.
- **Cluster Validity:** Selecting the validation task the system searches for the optimal parameters' values for a specific clustering algorithm so as to result in a clustering scheme that best fits our data. The user selects the clustering algorithm and the input parameter based on which the validation task will be performed. Also, the range of input parameters values is defined. Then, the system presents the graph of the quality index versus the number of clusters, based on which we find the number of clusters that best fits the data set.
- **Cube Construction – Classification:** The cube construction choice gives the chance to the user to select a data set and transforms it into a CVS. The system asks the user to define the appropriate parameters, which are the attribute-categories, value domains and transformation functions. For defining categories of the data set the user has the following choices: i) to use the results of clustering produced in the previous step in order to define these parameters, ii) to give

his/her own values, iii) to use the default values proposed by the system. Using the above information a set of tables is created which represents CVS. It maintains the overall classification information of the data set (i.e., the classification belief for each value in the data set).
- **CVS Information Measures:** The user may select an already constructed CVS and ask for energy metrics related to it. The system computes the category energy metric and the overall energy of each attribute and presents the results to the user. Based on these results, the users can extract useful knowledge related to the data sets such as i. relative importance of classes in a data set (i.e., "young vs. old customers"), ii. relative importance of classes across data sets, iii. the quality of a classification model i.e., how well it fits a data set.

4 Conclusion

UMiner aims at supporting data mining tasks while it enhances validity and handling of uncertainty. At the current stage of development we present UMiner as a clustering and classification system that is suitably extended to support uncertainty. It is a client-server corba-based data mining system and uses the JDBC application interface to connect to a data set.

Our further work will be concentrated on the development of new modules for our system such as rules extraction, reasoning with information measures based on user queries.

References

1. M.Berry, G. Linoff. Data Mining Techniques For marketing, Sales and Customer Support. John Willey & Sons, Inc, 1996.
2. U. Fayyad, G. Piatesky-Shapiro, P. Smuth and Ramasamy Uthurusamy. Advances in Knowledge Discovery and Data Mining. AAAI Press 1996
3. U. Fayyad, R. Uthurusamy. "Data Mining and Knowledge Discovery in Databases", *Communications of the ACM.* Vol.39, No11, November 1996.
4. W. Kelly, J. Painter. "Hypertrapezoidal Fuzzy Membership Functions. 5th *IEEE Int. Conf. on Fuzzy Systems*, New Orleans, Sept. 8, pp1279-1284, 1996.
5. S. Theodoridis, K. Koutroubas. *Pattern recognition,* Academic Press, 1999
6. M. Halkidi, M. Vazirgiannis, Y. Batistakis. "Quality scheme assessment in the clustering process", *In Proceedings of PKDD*, Lyon, France, 2000.
7. M. Vazirgiannis, M. Halkidi. "Uncertainty handling in the datamining process with fuzzy logic", in the proceedings of *the IEEE-FUZZY Conf*, Texas, May, 2000.

Managing Web Sites with OntoWebber

Yuhui Jin, Sichun Xu, Stefan Decker, and Gio Wiederhold

InfoLab, Stanford University, Stanford, CA 94305, USA
{yhjin,xusch,stefan,gio}@db.stanford.edu

Abstract. OntoWebber is a system for creating and managing data-intensive Web sites. It aims at reducing the efforts for publishing data as static and dynamic Web pages, personalizing user experience for browsing and navigating the data, and maintaining the Web site as well as the underlying data. Based on a domain ontology and a site modeling ontology, site views on the underlying data are constructed as site models. Instantiation of these models will create the browsable Web site. Rule-based manipulation of site models provides a declarative way to personalize and maintain the Web site. In this paper we present the architecture and demonstrate the major components of the system.

1 Introduction

The rapid growth of data in different disciplines has urged the development of a wide range of Internet technologies, helping to manage these data on the Web. However, there are a number of notable limitations conventional technologies are confronted with. First, building Web sites to publish large amount of data have been primarily focusing on the relational database and server side technologies. This results in limited reusability of software components, as most of the design is hard-coded in Web pages, scripts, active server pages etc.. Second, the only user interface for accessing the data is through static or dynamic Web pages, which are usually not personalized according to individual users preferences. Existing personalization features are mostly site-specific and not reusable either. Lastly, the maintenance of Web sites is a high-effort task, due to the lack of a formalism to process the underlying data. OntoWebber is a system to manage data on the Web using RDF(Resource Description Framework) [5]. It adopts an ontology-based approach for explicitly specifying the semantics of the data, designed to overcome the aforementioned limitations for harnessing Web data. The ontologies serve as the basis for the declarative management of all types of data, so that rule-based mechanisms can reason over these data as instances of ontologies.

2 Architecture

The architecture of OntoWebber system comprises three layers, namely, integration, composition, and generation services (see Figure. 1). Each layer has a

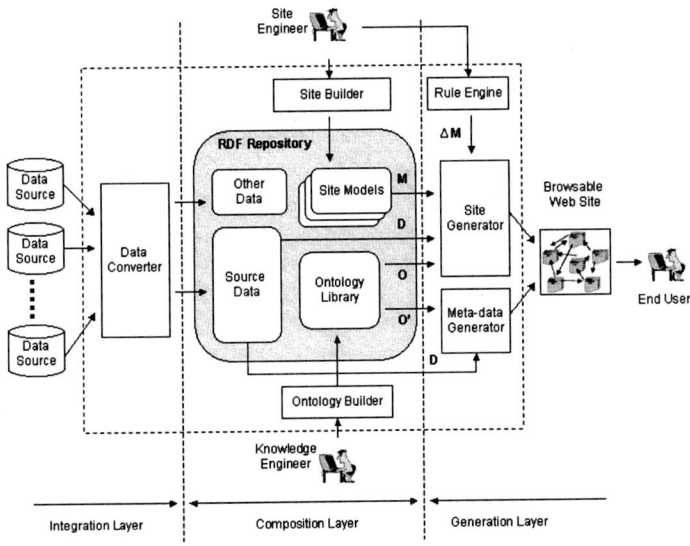

Fig. 1. The OntoWebber Architecture

number of components handling specific tasks in data management. In the integration layer, data from various sources on the Web is retrieved into the local cache and converted into RDF-annotated format, based on the domain ontology. In the composition layer, ontologies are constructed and site views are created on the underlying data as site models. Finally, the browsable Web site is generated by instantiating site models with source data in the generation layer. Personalization as well as the verification of integrity constraints are also performed in the generation layer. The system components that comprise the composition and generation layers will be demonstrated.

3 Demonstration

We demonstrate how to use the set of software tools in the OntoWebber system to construct a portal in the Semantic Web Research Community. The portal integrates information from various participants in a research project, and presents a centralized view tailored for individual users. We will demonstrate the following major components:

1. *Ontology Builder.* We will show how the knowledge engineer can use the ontology builder to create a domain ontology and a site modeling ontology. The domain ontology for the demonstration is specifically designed for the research community domain, whereas the site-modeling ontology is the same for any domain of interest.

2. *Site Builder.* We will demonstrate how to publish source data on the Web by creating site views using the site builder. Specifically, we will show: (a) how, through a user-friendly interface, the site engineer can create a default site view (graph), which is then exported into three site models; (b) example rules will be defined by the site engineer using the site builder, and the execution of these rules against the site models will demonstrate the constraint verification functionality;
3. *Site Generator.* After validation of the site view, the site generator will instantiate the site view while the user is interacting with the Web site. A cache is used for materializing the Web pages to reduce the response time.
4. *Personalization Manager.* We will show how to use the personalization manager to define model-rewriting rules, so that the site view can be modified by these rules to present personalized information access for end users. Two types of personalization will be demonstrated: (a) the user-initiated personalization allows the end user to tweak their site views through a form-based interface; (b) the system initiated personalization will update the site view according to pre-defined model-rewriting rules, so as to help end users browse the final Web site and navigate the information space.

4 Conclusion

The OntoWebber system demonstrates an ontology-based approach to site management, which was inspired by research from different areas such as database, hypermedia methodology and knowledge management[1][2][3][4][6]. It provides a set of software tools to facilitate the design, creation, generation and maintenance of Web sites. By encoding data using RDF data model as instances of a domain ontology, we are able to construct different site views as site models based on the pre-defined modeling ontology. Thus, site views may be tailored for individual users by re-writing the models. Maintenance of the Web site is also automated through rule-based constraint verification against the site models.

References

1. Stefano Ceri, Piero Fraternali, Stefano Paraboschi: Data-Driven, One-To-One Web Site Generation for Data-Intensive Applications. VLDB 1999: 615-620
2. Mary F. Fernandez, Daniela Florescu, Alon Y. Levy, Dan Suciu: Declarative Specification of Web Sites with Strudel. VLDB Journal 9(1): 38–55, 2000
3. Piero Fraternali, Paolo Paolini: A Conceptual Model and a Tool Environment for Developing More Scalable, Dynamic, and Customizable Web Applications. EDBT 1998: 421–435
4. G. Mecca, P. Merialdo, P. Atzeni, V. Crescenzi: The (Short) Araneus Guide to Web-Site Development – Second Intern. Workshop on the Web and Databases (WebDB'99) in conjunction with SIGMOD'99, May 1999
5. Resource Description Framework (RDF). http://www.w3.org/RDF
6. A. Mädche, S. Staab, N. Stojanovic, R. Studer, Y. Sure: SEAL – A Framework for Developing SEmantic portALs. In: BNCOD 2001 – 18th British National Conference on Databases. Oxford, UK, 9th – 11th July 2001, LNCS, Springer Verlag, 2001

Management of Dynamic Location Information in DOMINO

O. Wolfson[1,2,*], H. Cao[1], H. Lin[1],
G. Trajcevski[1], F. Zhang[1], and N. Rishe[3]

[1] Department of Computer Science, University of Illinois,
Chicago, IL 60607
[2] Mobitrac, Inc.,
Chicago, Il 60610, {wolfson,hcao,hlin,gtrajcev,fzhang}@cs.uic.edu
[3] Florida International Univ., School of CS,
University Park, Miami, FL 33199

1 Background

Consider a database that represents information about moving objects and their location. For example, for a database representing the location of taxi-cabs a typical query may be: *retrieve the free cabs that are currently within 1 mile of 33 N. Michigan Ave., Chicago* (to pick-up a customer); or for a trucking company database a typical query may be: *retrieve the trucks that are currently within 1 mile of truck ABT312* (which needs assistance); or for a database representing the current location of objects in a battlefield a typical query may be: *retrieve the friendly helicopters that are in a given region*, or, *retrieve the friendly helicopters that are expected to enter the region within the next 10 minutes*. The queries may originate from the moving objects, or from stationary users. We will refer to applications with the above characteristics as moving-objects-database (MOD) applications, and to queries as the ones mentioned above as MOD queries. In the military MOD applications arise in the context of the digital battlefield (c.f [1]), and in the civilian industry they arise in transportation systems. For example, Omnitracs developed by Qualcomm (see [3]) is a commercial system used by the transportation industry, which enables MOD functionality. It provides location management by connecting vehicles (e.g. trucks), via satellites, to company databases. The vehicles are equipped with a Global Positioning System (GPS), and they automatically and periodically report their location.

Tracking using a moving-objects-database also enables futuristic applications such as augmented reality, where various images, charts, and other voluminous data (that cannot be stored in a portable/wearable computer for a large geographic area) is delivered "just-in-time" to the mobile computer. The delivered information pertains only to the geographic location in the immediate vicinity of the mobile computer, which continuously changes. In electronic commerce, tracking enables delivery of location-dependent dynamic travel information (e.g. local traffic conditions, local sales of interest) to a mobile subscriber.

---

* Research supported by ARL Grant DAAL01-96-2-0003, NSF Grants ITR – 0086144, CCR – 9816633, CCR – 9803974, IRI – 9712967, EIA – 000516, INT – 9812935

2 The Demonstration

Our DOMINO prototype is intended to serve as a platform, or a toolkit for developing MOD type of applications. The system is the third in a three-layer architecture. The first layer is an Object Relational DBMS. The database stores the information about each moving object, including its plan of motion. The second layer is a GIS that adds capabilities and user interface primitives for storing, querying, and manipulating geographic information. The third layer, DOMINO, adds temporal capabilities, capabilities of managing the uncertainty that is inherent in future motion plans, capabilities for location prediction, and a simulation testbed. Currently, DOMINO runs on both Unix and MS/Windows. On both platforms DOMINO uses the Arc-View GIS. It uses the Informix DBMS on Unix, and Oracle on MS/Windows.

We will demonstrate the following features of DOMINO.

2.1 Location Modeling

The database may have various levels of information about the location of a moving object. It may know the current exact point-location, or it may know a general area in which the object is located but not the exact location, or it may know an approximate motion plan (e.g. traveling north on I95, at 60 miles per hour), or it may know the complete motion plan. The motion plan of a moving object is a sequence of way time points, (p1,t1), (p2,t2),... (pn,tn), indicating that the unit will be at geographic point p1 at time t1, at geographic point p2 (closer to the destination than p1) at time t2 (later than t1), etc. DOMINO supports all these levels of location information. In order to do so efficiently, it employs the concept of a dynamic attribute, i.e. an attribute whose value changes continuously as time progresses, without being explicitly updated. So, the location of a moving object is given by its dynamic attribute, which is is instantiated by the motion plan of the object.

In DOMINO a motion plan is specified interactively by the user on a GIS on a map. DOMINO is currently using maps from GDT Corp. ([2]); the map contains the length of each city block, the coordinates of its endpoints, and the average traffic speed along each city block. The speed information in the GDT maps is static, but we update it using real-time traffic information collected periodically from a web site (http://www.ai.eecs.uic.edu/GCM/CongestionMap.html). Based on this information the current location of the object is computed at any point in time. This motion plan may be automatically updated by GPS information transmitted from the moving object.

In DOMINO a moving object can use one of several policies to update the locations database. One of the policies uses a cost based approach approach to quantify the tradcoff between uncertainty and communication cost. Specifically, a moving object updates the database whenever the deviation from the database location exceeds a prespecified bound b given in terms of distance or time [5]. The update includes a revised plan and possibly a new bound on the deviation. The bound b is computed using on a cost based approach that takes into consideration the cost of update messages (in terms of wireless bandwidth consumption and processing power) and the cost of the deviation.

We collected updates by driving several trajectories, about 40 miles each, in the Chicago metropolitan area.

2.2 Spatio-temporal Capabilities

Maintaining motion plan information enables the system to answer queries pertaining to the current, future or past locations of the moving object, for example: $Q1 = $ Retrieve the moving objects that are expected to intersect a region R sometime during a given time interval I. (I may be a time interval that lies entirely in the future, i.e. after the time when $Q1$ is entered).

We will demonstrate the spatial and temporal primitives of the query language and its answer-display screen. The primitives are given in graphical format, and they can be combined with textual SQL in a natural and intuitive way. For example, in the query Q1 above the region R may be drawn with a mouse on a real GIS map, and the time interval I may be specified on a graphical timeline. Information about the moving objects that satisfy the query is displayed in textual form, and the location of each such moving object is displayed as a point on the map. The spatio-temporal functions constitute a data-blade in an ORDBMS.

2.3 Uncertainty

We will demonstrate the capabilities of the query language and its answer-display screen in dealing with uncertainty. These include POSSIBLY and DEFINITELY semantics for queries. In other words, the query $Q1$ above can be specified with POSSIBLY or DEFINITELY semantics [4]. Under the DEFINITELY semantics, an object will be retrieved if all of its possible trajectories intersect the region R during the interval I. Under the POSSIBLY semantics, an object will be retrieved if some of its possible trajectories intersect the region R during the interval I.

References

1. S. Chamberlain. Model-based battle command: A paradigm whose time has come. In *Symposium on C2 Research and Technology*, 1995.
2. Geographic Data Technology Co. *GDT Maps*, 2000. http://www.geographic.com.
3. Qualcomm. *OmniTRACS, Communicating Without Limits*. http://www.qualcomm.com.
4. G. Trajcevski, O. Wolfson, F. Zhang, and S. Chamberlain. The geometry of uncertainty in moving objects databases. In *EDBT*, 2002. (to appear).
5. O. Wolfson, A. P. Sistla, S. Chamberlain, and Y. Yesha. Updating and querying databases that track mobile units. *Distributed and Parallel Databases*, 7, 1999.
6. O. Wolfson, B. Xu, S. Chamberlain, L. Jiang. Moving Objects Databases: Issues and Solutions. In *SSDB*, 1999.

Situation Aware Mobile Access to Digital Libraries

Peter Haase

[1] Database Research Group, Department of Computer Science
University of Rostock, 18051 Rostock, Germany
in cooperation with
Fraunhofer Institute for Computer Graphics, 18059 Rostock, Germany
[2] current affiliation
IBM Silicon Valley Labs, 555 Bailey Ave, CA 95141 San Jose, USA
phaase@us.ibm.com

Abstract. A conference and exhibition guide has been implemented to demonstrate how context information can be exploited to proactively provide situation relevant information in mobile environments. Different mobile devices, a wireless LAN and sensor technology provide the infrastructure for the situation aware mobile access to the Digital Library. Ontology based knowledge representation and reasoning are used to model the content of the Digital Library and user context and to determine situation relevant content.

Introduction

Using state of the art mobile computing technology – ultraportable devices and wireless networks – it is possible to access any information at almost any place and any time. But considering the rapidly growing amounts of digital content, the following question gains importance: How do I find the *right* information at the *right* place and the *right* time. Specifically in mobile environments, lengthy interaction sequences to find the right information are not acceptable. Exploiting context information, i.e. information about the situation of the user and its surroundings, human computer interaction can be enriched by proactively providing situation relevant information. In the scientific context, often Digital Libraries are used for managing digital content such as conference proceedings, technical reports, lecture notes, etc.

In the scope of a master's thesis a system architecture for "Situation Aware Mobile Access to Digital Libraries" has been developed [Haa01]. In the demonstration an intelligent conference and exhibition guide based on this architecture will be presented. A notebook and a PocketPC as well as sensor and wireless technology are used to demonstrate how contextual information can be exploited for the access to a Digital Library. The work is situated in the context of the Digital Library project BlueView [HMTP00] and a framework for Situation Aware Mobile Assistance, SaMOA [KCI98].

MoBible

MoBible, the prototype of a conference and exhibition guide, is able to provide situation relevent content. For example, it suggests events to attend based on the interests and background of the user. On entering a conference room, lecture notes are displayed instantly. When approaching exponats of particular interest to the user, information is provided as well. All documents are presented in a format that matches the capabilities of the device in use.

The system architecture consists of a stationary server and mobile devices to access the content of the Digital Library. To ensure an efficient, fault tolerant access, the architecture makes use of the following concepts:

- *Distributed data management:* Using caching and replication techniques, the client holds a local copy of relevant data. Depending on network availability, information will be queried and retrieved transparently from either the server or the local copy on the mobile device. Different versions of IBM's DB2 are used for data management: DB2 Everyplace on the mobile devices, DB2 UDB on the server side.
- *Level of Detail:* This concept allows to provide only as much information as currently required. When relevant documents are suggested, initially only very condensed information, e.g. the title of a document, will be shown. On demand, more detailed information including an abstract will be presented. Finally, if requested, the full content, e.g. a PDF document or a Powerpoint presentation, will be displayed.

The system has been implemented entirely in Java, therefore ensuring platform independence. For the demonstration, a PocketPC and a notebook are used as mobile devices. A wireless LAN is utilized for client-server communication.

Context Awareness

To proactively provide relevant information it is necessary to discover and take advantage of contextual information. The MoBible system uses the following types of contextual information:

- *Physical environment:* Obviously, location is one important aspect of the physical context. Objects in the proximity of the user are another aspect.
- *User tasks:* Knowing the current activities of the user, it is possible to provide task relevant information. Typical tasks at conferences and exhibitions are for example attending events, scheduling meetings and obtaining information about exponats.
- *User profiles:* These include for example interests and expertise of the user.
- *Device in use:* The capabilities of mobile devices span a wide range. Obviously, information is valuable only if the device in use is able to display it.

To discover certain contextual information, sensor technology can be utilized. For example, to determine the current position and objects in the proximity the system uses infrared technology. IrDA-Beacons^{TM} [Ide00], developed by the Fraunhofer Institute for Computer Graphics, identify objects and locations.

Ontology-Based Knowledge Representation and Reasoning

For the modelling of the user situation and the content of the Digital Library, techniques from ontology-based knowledge representation have been used. This allows to enrich the available information with machine-processable semantics.

The ontology has been expressed in DAML [vHa01], an evolving standard of the Semantic Web community based on the W3C standards RDF and XML. DAML offers rich modelling capabilities, allows for interoperability on a semantic level, and provides reasoning support.

The facts of the knowledge base can be used in an inference engine to automatically reason about situation relevant information. In the implemented system an inference engine based on Frame-Logic – a rule-based, deductive query and inference language [DBSA] – has been used.

Summary

The MoBible system demonstrates that with today's technology it is possible to develop mobile intelligent assistants that allow situation aware access to content in Digital Libraries. The conference and exhibition guide is only one example where contextual information can be used to proactively relevant content. In contrast to existing solutions, this system supports a wide range of mobile devices. Moreover, it does not require a permanent network connection, since relevant information is replicated and processed locally on the mobile device.

References

[DBSA]   Stefan Decker, Dan Brickley, Janne Saarela, and Jürgen Angele. A Query and Inference Service for RDF. http://www.w3.org/TandS/QL/QL98/pp/queryservice.html

[Haa01] Peter Haase. Situationsgesteuerter mobiler Zugriff auf Digitale Bibliotheken. Master's thesis, University of Rostock, Germany, 2001

[HMTP00] Andreas Heuer, Holger Meyer, Patrick Titzler, and Beate Porst. BlueView: Virtual Document Servers for Digital Libraries. In *Proceedings of the IEEE Conference on Advances in Digital Libraries*, 2000. http://wwwdb.informatik.uni-rostock.de/blueview/paper/adl00.pdf

[Ide00] Rüdiger Ide. IrDA Beacon (TM) Transmitter, 2000. http://www.rostock.igd.fhg.de/fhg_igd/abteilungen/a3/projects/irda/

[KCI98] Thomas Kirste, Esteban Chavez, and Rüdiger Ide. SAMoA: An experimental platform for Situation-Aware Mobile Assistance. In *Proceedings of the Workshop IMC 98*, pages 29–36, 1998. http://www.rostock.igd.fhg.de/fhg_igd/abteilungen/a3/files/pdf/imc98-samoa.pdf

[vHa01] Frank van Harmelen, Peter F. Patel-Schneider, and Ian Horrocks. Reference description of the DAML+OIL (March 2001) ontology markup language, 2001. http://www.daml.org/2001/03/reference.html

Author Index

Abbadi, Amr El 609
Agrawal, Divyakant 609
Ahola, Jari 14
Akinde, Michael O. 336
Alonso, Gustavo 390
Amanatidis, Christos 762
Amann, Bernd 759
Amer-Yahia, Sihem 496
Arkoumanis, Dinos 179

Beeri, Catriel 759
Böhlen, Michael H. 336
Bouguettaya, Athman 553
Bressan, Stéphane 215
Brinkhoff, Thomas 533

Cao, Hu 769
Casati, Fabio 287
Chakrabarti, Kaushik 15
Chakravarthy, Sharma 317
Chamberlain, Sam 233
Chang, Yuan-Chi 409
Chen, I-Min A. 722
Chien, Shu-Yao 161
Cho, SungRan 496
Chomicki, Jan 34

Damiani, Ernesto 753
Decker, Stefan 766
Deppisch, Uwe 732
Diop, Cheikh Talibouya 106
Dunemann, Oliver 756

Engström, Henrik 317
Ernst, Matthias 712

Faloutsos, Christos 197
Fankhauser, Peter 742
Francisci, Stefano De 307
Fundulaki, Irini 759

Garcia-Molina, Hector 427
Gardarin, Georges 297
Gawecki, Andreas 712
Geist, Ingolf 756
Giacometti, Arnaud 106

Groh, Tobias 742
Gunopulos, Dimitrios 251, 646
Gupta, Amarnath 739

Haase, Peter 772
Hadjieleftheriou, Marios 251
Härder, Theo 372
Halkidi, Maria 762
Han, Jiawei 70
Hergula, Klaudia 372
Horrocks, Ian 2

Jagadish, H.V. 590
Jermaine, Christopher 572
Jesse, Roland 756
Jin, Yuhui 766
Johnson, Theodore 336
Jonker, Willem 736

Kang, Myoung-Ah 197
Kemper, Alfons 749
Koeller, Andreas 354
König, Arnd Christian 627
Kollios, George 251
Kosky, Anthony 722
Kraiss, Achim 732
Kummer, Olaf 712

Lakshmanan, Laks V.S. 142, 336
Laurent, Dominique 106
Laurini, Robert 197
Lavarini, Nico 753
Lazaridis, Iosif 269
Lee, Mong Li 124
Lings, Brian 317
Ling, Tok Wang 124
Lin, Hai 769
Liu, Guimei 88
Lopes, Stéphane 464
Lou, Wenwu 88
Low, Wai Lup 124
Ludäscher, Bertram 739
Lu, Hongjun 88

Maher, Michael 52
Maheshwari, Umesh 701

Mahnke, Wolfgang 745
Marchi, Fabien De 464
Markowitz, Victor M. 722
Marrara, Stefania 753
Martone, Maryann E. 739
Mehrotra, Sharad 15, 269
Melnik, Sergey 427
Mensch, Antoine 297
Mitschang, Bernhard 445

Navathe, Shamkant B. 572

Oliboni, Barbara 753
Omiecinski, Edward 572
Ortega-Binderberger, Michael 15
Overhage, Sven 742

Padmanabhan, Sriram 409
Paolucci, Mario 307
Papadias, Dimitris 179, 682
Parthasarathy, Sailaja 142
Pasini, Daniele 753
Patel, Jignesh M. 590
Petit, Jean-Marc 464
Petković, Milan 736
Porkaew, Kriengkrai 269

Qian, Xufei 739

Rantzau, Ralf 445
Rishe, N. 769
Ritter, Norbert 745
Rundensteiner, Elke A. 354

Sattler, Kai-Uwe 756
Schek, Hans-Jörg 1
Schlieder, Torsten 514
Schmidt, Joachim W. 712
Schmidt, Rolfe R. 664
Schoen, Frank 732
Scholl, Michel 759
Seeger, Bernhard 646
Servigne, Sylvie 197
Shahabi, Cyrus 664
Shan, Ming-Chien 287
Shapiro, Leonard 445
Shapiro, William 701

Sindoni, Giuseppe 307
Spyratos, Nicolas 106
Srivastava, Divesh 336, 496
Stephanik, Andreas 756
Stolte, Etzard 390
Sun, Chengyu 609

Tanca, Letizia 753
Tao, Yufei 682
Theobald, Anja 477
Tininini, Leonardo 307
Tok, Wee Hyong 215
Tomasic, Anthony 297
Topor, Rodney 52
Trajcevski, Goce 233, 769
Tsotras, Vassilis J. 161, 251, 646

Vazirgiannis, Michalis 762
Vercoustre, Anne-Marie 759
Vingralek, Radek 701
Viviani, Giuseppe 753

Wang, Junhu 52
Wang, Ke 70
Wang, Min 409
Wang, Quan 445
Weikum, Gerhard 477, 627, 732
Wiederhold, Gio 766
Wienberg, Axel 712
Wienberg, Frank 712
Wiesner, Christian 749
Winklhofer, Peter 749
Wolfson, Ouri 233, 769
Wu, Yuqing 590

Xu, Sichun 766

Yang, Qiang 88
Yang, Xu 553
Yee, Wai Gen 572

Zaniolo, Carlo 161
Zhang, Donghui 161, 646
Zhang, Fengli 233, 769
Zhang, Jun 682
Zhou, Senqiang 70

Lecture Notes in Computer Science

For information about Vols. 1–2205
please contact your bookseller or Springer-Verlag

Vol. 2206: B. Reusch (Ed.), Computational Intelligence. Proceedings, 2001. XVII, 1003 pages. 2001.

Vol. 2207: I.W. Marshall, S. Nettles, N. Wakamiya (Eds.), Active Networks. Proceedings, 2001. IX, 165 pages. 2001.

Vol. 2208: W.J. Niessen, M.A. Viergever (Eds.), Medical Image Computing and Computer-Assisted Intervention – MICCAI 2001. Proceedings, 2001. XXXV, 1446 pages. 2001.

Vol. 2209: W. Jonker (Ed.), Databases in Telecommunications II. Proceedings, 2001. VII, 179 pages. 2001.

Vol. 2210: Y. Liu, K. Tanaka, M. Iwata, T. Higuchi, M. Yasunaga (Eds.), Evolvable Systems: From Biology to Hardware. Proceedings, 2001. XI, 341 pages. 2001.

Vol. 2211: T.A. Henzinger, C.M. Kirsch (Eds.), Embedded Software. Proceedings, 2001. IX, 504 pages. 2001.

Vol. 2212: W. Lee, L. Mé, A. Wespi (Eds.), Recent Advances in Intrusion Detection. Proceedings, 2001. X, 205 pages. 2001.

Vol. 2213: M.J. van Sinderen, L.J.M. Nieuwenhuis (Eds.), Protocols for Multimedia Systems. Proceedings, 2001. XII, 239 pages. 2001.

Vol. 2214: O. Boldt, H. Jürgensen (Eds.), Automata Implementation. Proceedings, 1999. VIII, 183 pages. 2001.

Vol. 2215: N. Kobayashi, B.C. Pierce (Eds.), Theoretical Aspects of Computer Software. Proceedings, 2001. XV, 561 pages. 2001.

Vol. 2216: E.S. Al-Shaer, G. Pacifici (Eds.), Management of Multimedia on the Internet. Proceedings, 2001. XIV, 373 pages. 2001.

Vol. 2217: T. Gomi (Ed.), Evolutionary Robotics. Proceedings, 2001. XI, 139 pages. 2001.

Vol. 2218: R. Guerraoui (Ed.), Middleware 2001. Proceedings, 2001. XIII, 395 pages. 2001.

Vol. 2219: S.T. Taft, R.A. Duff, R.L. Brukardt, E. Ploedereder (Eds.), Consolidated Ada Reference Manual. XXV, 560 pages. 2001.

Vol. 2220: C. Johnson (Ed.), Interactive Systems. Proceedings, 2001. XII, 219 pages. 2001.

Vol. 2221: D.G. Feitelson, L. Rudolph (Eds.), Job Scheduling Strategies for Parallel Processing. Proceedings, 2001. VII, 207 pages. 2001.

Vol. 2222: M.J. Wooldridge, G. Weiß, P. Ciancarini (Eds.) Agent-Oriented Software Engineering II. Proceedings, 2001. X, 319 pages. 2002.

Vol. 2223: P. Eades, T. Takaoka (Eds.), Algorithms and Computation. Proceedings, 2001. XIV, 780 pages. 2001.

Vol. 2224: H.S. Kunii, S. Jajodia, A. Sølvberg (Eds.), Conceptual Modeling – ER 2001. Proceedings, 2001. XIX, 614 pages. 2001.

Vol. 2225: N. Abe, R. Khardon, T. Zeugmann (Eds.), Algorithmic Learning Theory. Proceedings, 2001. XI, 379 pages. 2001. (Subseries LNAI).

Vol. 2226: K.P. Jantke, A. Shinohara (Eds.), Discovery Science. Proceedings, 2001. XII, 494 pages. 2001. (Subseries LNAI).

Vol. 2227: S. Boztaş, I.E. Shparlinski (Eds.), Applied Algebra, Algebraic Algorithms and Error-Correcting Codes. Proceedings, 2001. XII, 398 pages. 2001.

Vol. 2228: B. Monien, V.K. Prasanna, S. Vajapeyam (Eds.), High Performance Computing – HiPC 2001. Proceedings, 2001. XVIII, 438 pages. 2001.

Vol. 2229: S. Qing, T. Okamoto, J. Zhou (Eds.), Information and Communications Security. Proceedings, 2001. XIV, 504 pages. 2001.

Vol. 2230: T. Katila, I.E. Magnin, P. Clarysse, J. Montagnat, J. Nenonen (Eds.), Functional Imaging and Modeling of the Heart. Proceedings, 2001. XI, 158 pages. 2001.

Vol. 2231: A. Pasetti, Software Frameworks and Embedded Control Systems. XIV, 293 pages. 2002.

Vol. 2232: L. Fiege, G. Mühl, U. Wilhelm (Eds.), Electronic Commerce. Proceedings, 2001. X, 233 pages. 2001.

Vol. 2233: J. Crowcroft, M. Hofmann (Eds.), Networked Group Communication. Proceedings, 2001. X, 205 pages. 2001.

Vol. 2234: L. Pacholski, P. Ružička (Eds.), SOFSEM 2001: Theory and Practice of Informatics. Proceedings, 2001. XI, 347 pages. 2001.

Vol. 2235: C.S. Calude, G. Păun, G. Rozenberg, A. Salomaa (Eds.), Multiset Processing. VIII, 359 pages. 2001.

Vol. 2236: K. Drira, A. Martelli, T. Villemur (Eds.), Cooperative Environments for Distributed Systems Engineering. IX, 281 pages. 2001.

Vol. 2237: P. Codognet (Ed.), Logic Programming. Proceedings, 2001. XI, 365 pages. 2001.

Vol. 2239: T. Walsh (Ed.), Principles and Practice of Constraint Programming – CP 2001. Proceedings, 2001. XIV, 788 pages. 2001.

Vol. 2240: G.P. Picco (Ed.), Mobile Agents. Proceedings, 2001. XIII, 277 pages. 2001.

Vol. 2241: M. Jünger, D. Naddef (Eds.), Computational Combinatorial Optimization. IX, 305 pages. 2001.

Vol. 2242: C.A. Lee (Ed.), Grid Computing – GRID 2001. Proceedings, 2001. XII, 185 pages. 2001.

Vol. 2243: G. Bertrand, A. Imiya, R. Klette (Eds.), Digital and Image Geometry. VII, 455 pages. 2001.

Vol. 2244: D. Bjørner, M. Broy, A.V. Zamulin (Eds.), Perspectives of System Informatics. Proceedings, 2001. XIII, 548 pages. 2001.

Vol. 2245: R. Hariharan, M. Mukund, V. Vinay (Eds.), FST TCS 2001: Foundations of Software Technology and Theoretical Computer Science. Proceedings, 2001. XI, 347 pages. 2001.

Vol. 2246: R. Falcone, M. Singh, Y.-H. Tan (Eds.), Trust in Cyber-societies. VIII, 195 pages. 2001. (Subseries LNAI).

Vol. 2247: C. P. Rangan, C. Ding (Eds.), Progress in Cryptology – INDOCRYPT 2001. Proceedings, 2001. XIII, 351 pages. 2001.

Vol. 2248: C. Boyd (Ed.), Advances in Cryptology – ASIACRYPT 2001. Proceedings, 2001. XI, 603 pages. 2001.

Vol. 2249: K. Nagi, Transactional Agents. XVI, 205 pages. 2001.

Vol. 2250: R. Nieuwenhuis, A. Voronkov (Eds.), Logic for Programming, Artificial Intelligence, and Reasoning. Proceedings, 2001. XV, 738 pages. 2001. (Subseries LNAI).

Vol. 2251: Y.Y. Tang, V. Wickerhauser, P.C. Yuen, C.Li (Eds.), Wavelet Analysis and Its Applications. Proceedings, 2001. XIII, 450 pages. 2001.

Vol. 2252: J. Liu, P.C. Yuen, C. Li, J. Ng, T. Ishida (Eds.), Active Media Technology. Proceedings, 2001. XII, 402 pages. 2001.

Vol. 2253: T. Terano, T. Nishida, A. Namatame, S. Tsumoto, Y. Ohsawa, T. Washio (Eds.), New Frontiers in Artificial Intelligence. Proceedings, 2001. XXVII, 553 pages. 2001. (Subseries LNAI).

Vol. 2254: M.R. Little, L. Nigay (Eds.), Engineering for Human-Computer Interaction. Proceedings, 2001. XI, 359 pages. 2001.

Vol. 2255: J. Dean, A. Gravel (Eds.), COTS-Based Software Systems. Proceedings, 2002. XIV, 257 pages. 2002.

Vol. 2256: M. Stumptner, D. Corbett, M. Brooks (Eds.), AI 2001: Advances in Artificial Intelligence. Proceedings, 2001. XII, 666 pages. 2001. (Subseries LNAI).

Vol. 2257: S. Krishnamurthi, C.R. Ramakrishnan (Eds.), Practical Aspects of Declarative Languages. Proceedings, 2002. VIII, 351 pages. 2002.

Vol. 2258: P. Brazdil, A. Jorge (Eds.), Progress in Artificial Intelligence. Proceedings, 2001. XII, 418 pages. 2001. (Subseries LNAI).

Vol. 2259: S. Vaudenay, A.M. Youssef (Eds.), Selected Areas in Cryptography. Proceedings, 2001. XI, 359 pages. 2001.

Vol. 2260: B. Honary (Ed.), Cryptography and Coding. Proceedings, 2001. IX, 416 pages. 2001.

Vol. 2261: F. Naumann, Quality-Driven Query Answering for Integrated Information Systems. X, 166 pages. 2002.

Vol. 2262: P. Müller, Modular Specification and Verification of Object-Oriented Programs. XIV, 292 pages. 2002.

Vol. 2263: T. Clark, J. Warmer (Eds.), Object Modeling with the OCL. VIII, 281 pages. 2002.

Vol. 2264: K. Steinhöfel (Ed.), Stochastic Algorithms: Foundations and Applications. Proceedings, 2001. VIII, 203 pages. 2001.

Vol. 2265: P. Mutzel, M. Jünger, S. Leipert (Eds.), Graph Drawing. Proceedings, 2001. XV, 524 pages. 2002.

Vol. 2266: S. Reich, M.T. Tzagarakis, P.M.E. De Bra (Eds.), Hypermedia: Openness, Structural Awareness, and Adaptivity. Proceedings, 2001. X, 335 pages. 2002.

Vol. 2267: M. Cerioli, G. Reggio (Eds.), Recent Trends in Algebraic Development Techniques. Proceedings, 2001. X, 345 pages. 2001.

Vol. 2268: E.F. Deprettere, J. Teich, S. Vassiliadis (Eds.), The Design of Complex Embedded Systems. VIII, 327 pages. 2002.

Vol. 2270: M. Pflanz, On-line Error Detection and Fast Recover Techniques for Dependable Embedded Processors. XII, 126 pages. 2002.

Vol. 2271: B. Preneel (Ed.), Topics in Cryptology – CT-RSA 2002. Proceedings, 2002. X, 311 pages. 2002.

Vol. 2272: D. Bert, J.P. Bowen, M.C. Henson, K. Robinson (Eds.), ZB 2002: Formal Specification and Development in Z and B. Proceedings, 2002. XII, 535 pages. 2002.

Vol. 2273: A.R. Coden, E.W. Brown, S. Srinivasan (Eds.), Information Retrieval Techniques for Speech Applications. XI, 109 pages. 2002.

Vol. 2274: D. Naccache, P. Paillier (Eds.), Public Key Cryptography. Proceedings, 2002. XI, 385 pages. 2002.

Vol. 2275: N.R. Pal, M. Sugeno (Eds.), Advances in Soft Computing – AFSS 2002. Proceedings, 2002. XVI, 536 pages. 2002. (Subseries LNAI).

Vol. 2276: A. Gelbukh (Ed.), Computational Linguistics and Intelligent Text Processing. Proceedings, 2002. XIII, 444 pages. 2002.

Vol. 2277: P. Callaghan, Z. Luo, J. McKinna, R. Pollack (Eds.), Types for Proofs and Programs. Proceedings, 2000. VIII, 243 pages. 2002.

Vol. 2282: D. Ursino, Extraction and Exploitation of Intensional Knowledge from Heterogeneous Information Systems. XXVI, 289 pages. 2002.

Vol. 2284: T. Eiter, K.-D. Schewe (Eds.), Foundations of Information and Knowledge Systems. Proceedings, 2002. X, 289 pages. 2002.

Vol. 2285: H. Alt, A. Ferreira (Eds.), STACS 2002. Proceedings, 2002. XIV, 660 pages. 2002.

Vol. 2287: C.S. Jensen, K.G. Jeffery, J. Pokorny, Saltenis, E. Bertino, K. Böhm, M. Jarke (Eds.), Advances in Database Technology – EDBT 2002. Proceedings, 2002. XVI, 776 pages. 2002.

Vol. 2288: K. Kim (Ed.), Information Security and Cryptology – ICISC 2001. Proceedings, 2001. XIII, 457 pages. 2002.

Vol. 2289: C.J. Tomlin, M.R. Greenstreet (Eds.), Hybrid Systems: Computation and Control. Proceedings, 2002. XIII, 480 pages. 2002.

Vol. 2291: F. Crestani, M. Girolami, C.J. van Rijsbergen (Eds.), Advances in Information Retrieval. Proceedings, 2002. XIII, 363 pages. 2002.

Vol. 2292: G.B. Khosrovshahi, A. Shokoufandeh, A. Shokrollahi (Eds.), Theoretical Aspects of Computer Science. IX, 221 pages. 2002.

Vol. 2300: W. Brauer, H. Ehrig, J. Karhumäki, A. Salomaa (Eds.), Formal and Natural Computing. XXXVI, 431 pages. 2002.